CORPORATE GOVERNANCE

OVERVIEW, CASE STUDIES, AND REFORMS

■ ■ ■

William O. Fisher

Professor of Law
University of Richmond School of Law

AMERICAN CASEBOOK SERIES®

WEST
ACADEMIC
PUBLISHING

American Casebook Series is a trademark registered in the U.S. Patent and Trademark Office.

© 2017 LEG, Inc. d/b/a West Academic
    444 Cedar Street, Suite 700
    St. Paul, MN 55101
    1-877-888-1330

West, West Academic Publishing, and West Academic are trademarks of West Publishing Corporation, used under license.

Printed in the United States of America

ISBN: 978-1-68328-162-7

PREFACE

This book provides a unique, integrated approach to the study of governance at public companies. It combines my text and analysis, primary materials, secondary sources, finance and economics studies, and questions.

The book begins with two overview chapters. These should be particularly helpful in courses for which students are writing papers. Having a sense for the breadth of issues that law and regulation already address will help students select paper topics that will advance, rather than duplicate, work that has already been done.

As it progresses, the book provides an in-depth look at WorldCom and Enron, with (in later chapters) very significant information about Lehman Brothers, a good deal on AIG, and enough about Bear Stearns to appreciate its frighteningly swift demise. The text explains concepts needed to understand the events at these companies, including accounting issues covered in the WorldCom and Enron readings, and the credit crisis central to the events at Lehman Brothers, Bear Stearns, and AIG. The book thereby addresses the core problem that most law school students—even those selecting a large number of business courses—do not know what corporate governance is, have not been a corporate director, have never witnessed a board meeting, may not have a significant accounting background, and may not have been studying business developments during the credit crisis.

After describing the events at WorldCom and Enron, the book sets out the resulting reforms. In the course of examining governance at Lehman, Bear Stearns, and AIG, the book describes reforms put in place during the credit crisis and then describes post-crisis compensation reform in the financial sector. Along the way, the book addresses reforms to strengthen shareholder voting. And the book analyzes the role of sovereign wealth funds, activist hedge funds, and proxy advisers. An entire chapter addresses in detail CEO compensation—its components, whether the amounts paid are too high, whether those amounts results from a competitive market, and whether various forms of equity compensation encourage false financial reporting or excessive risk-taking. The book ends with chapters asking how we might evaluate the reforms, discussing the meaning and possible governance implications of corporate social responsibility, and setting out the role that lawyers play in governing a public company.

In designing a course using this book, a faculty member can chose to focus on one or two of the corporate failures listed above instead of teaching them all. In the same way, the book is friendly to professors who want to concentrate on particular governance actors—boards of directors, outside auditors, activist shareholders, and proxy advisers. Similarly, the chapters and table of contents permit faculty members to teach all of the reforms I include, or select a set that the professor finds most interesting or provocative.

I have tried hard to include not only descriptions of laws, regulations, and listing standards, but also the key text within them. I believe that this book is complete in itself and can be fully effective without any statutory supplement.

Two formatting choices deserve your attention before you plunge into the pages. First, where I include footnotes from a source that I quote, I have retained the footnote numbers used in the source and placed them in brackets. The numbers for the footnotes that I prepared have no brackets around them.

Second, I have retained the formatting and organizational scheme in long excerpts. This includes internal section headings, with letters or numbers. The long quotations are indented and therefore easy to distinguish from my text.

As a last user note, the book contains a large number of images. These include not only helpful charts and graphs but also documents that the boards of WorldCom and Enron saw. I located these images in a variety of sources, including reports of congressional hearings.

To improve readability, 3Crown Creative enhanced many of the images. In some cases, the enhancement consisted of sharpening the image. In others, some text was retyped, keeping the formatting of the original document intact. The table that follows identifies the enhanced images and, for each one, describes the enhancement.

Chapter	Title/Description of Image	Enhancement
3	WorldCom Closing Stock Prices, 1994– June 2002 graph	Image was sharpened and converted to grayscale.
4	Arthur Andersen WorldCom 2001 Audit Plan	Retyped text was substituted for poor quality text items.
4	Arthur Andersen WorldCom 2001 Audit Report	Retyped text was substituted for poor quality text items.

Chapter	Title/Description of Image	Enhancement
5	WorldCom, AT&T, and Sprint Stock Prices During Period of Ebbers' Sale of WorldCom Stock graph	Image was sharpened, black background eliminated, and converted to grayscale.
5	Ebbers Loan Disbursements and WorldCom Stock Price graph	Image was sharpened.
7	FAS 140 transaction diagram	Image was sharpened.
7	Chewco transaction diagram	Image was sharpened and straightened.
8	LJM2 structure diagram	Image was sharpened and straightened.
8	Raptor I structure diagram	Image was sharpened and straightened.
8	Raptor III structure diagram	Image was sharpened and straightened.
9	Selected Observations, 1998 Financial Reporting Senate subcommittee hearing exhibit 2a	Retyped text was substituted for poor quality text items.
9	Selected Observations, 1998 Financial Reporting, with handwriting Senate subcommittee hearing exhibit 3	Retyped text was substituted for poor quality text items.
9	Transcription of Note by David Duncan Senate subcommittee hearing exhibit 4	Image was sharpened.

Chapter	Title/Description of Image	Enhancement
9	2000 Audit Update, Selected Observations, Financial Reporting Senate subcommittee hearing exhibit 8a	Retyped text was substituted for poor quality text items; black marks on original scan were removed.
9	Project Raptor Hedging Program for Enron Assets Senate subcommittee hearing exhibit 28b	Retyped text was substituted for poor quality text items; black marks on original scan were removed.
16	Prevalence of Equity Compensation Design for S&P 500 CEOs graph	Image was sharpened and converted to grayscale.
16	Median Salary Multiples for Equity Ownership Guidelines graph	Image was sharpened and converted to grayscale.
16	Average Cash and Total Remuneration for CEOs in S&P 500 Firms, 1970–2002 graph	Image was sharpened and converted to grayscale.
18	Stock price and stock index graphs 2006–2008 for S&P 500, S&P 500 Financial Sector, Bear Stearns, Lehman Brothers, and AIG (4 total)	Images were converted to grayscale.
20	Passing Percentage of U.S. Companies Say-on-Pay Votes, 2013–2015 graph	Image was sharpened and converted to grayscale.

ACKNOWLEDGMENTS

This book would not have been possible without the wonderful help of many others.

Alison Britton edited chapters and served as pre-production guru. Joshua Ellis and William Miller not only performed checks themselves, but each acted at different times as the foreperson for an effort involving team members in Virginia, Colorado, Washington State, and California. Vitalee Giammalvo added her essential editorial skills. Adam Cain, Colby Ferguson, and Shalayne Davis contributed long hours checking citations, ellipses, grammar, and quotations. They—as well as Alison and Vitalee—drove the manuscript toward a consistency to which my own efforts often proved a threat. Kimberly Fricker performed research which, though at the time directed to another effort, appears now in this book.

I have been fortunate to have the help of experts. Kevin Gold and his colleagues at Analysis Group's Los Angeles office provided analytical assistance. Among other contributions, they improved my summaries of research articles published in finance and economics journals. Ellen Gazlay read and commented on portions of the manuscript that address accounting and auditing. Mark Borges of Compensia read and commented on portions that address executive compensation. Equilar, Inc. provided customized sets of executive compensation numbers and permission to quote from and include graphics from Equilar publications. Audit Analytics agreed that I could use the aggregated counts of financial restatements and provided disaggregated counts as well.

Unlike most law school texts, this book contains many images. Working closely with Alison Britton, Tom Collicott of 3Crown Creative enhanced and sharpened the great majority of those images. Tom and Alison created the cover design as well.

The book is filled with quotations. Kenneth Crews guided me with a skilled hand through the intellectual property issues created by my use of these passages. Sheila Colthorpe tirelessly kept a record of correspondence and permissions.

In that regard, I thank the many authors and publishers who gave me permission to reprint portions of their works. Credits to them appear where I quote their writings.

I thank as well those who supported my use of documents now in the public domain. I am particularly grateful for confirmation that I could use the examiner reports in the Enron, WorldCom, and Lehman bankruptcies, and the reports of the special committees of the Enron and WorldCom boards.

Neither the help they gave me, nor their acknowledgment here or in credits to particular works, should suggest that those who assisted me or who provided permission to quote from their works agree with my prose or any implication that might be derived from it. And, of course, all errors are mine.

SUMMARY OF CONTENTS

TABLE OF CONTENTS

TABLE OF CASES

CORPORATE GOVERNANCE

OVERVIEW, CASE STUDIES, AND REFORMS

CHAPTER 1

THE PARTICIPANTS IN CORPORATE GOVERNANCE AND THE GENERAL SHAPE OF THE REFORMS

■ ■ ■

The principal participants in corporate governance are (i) shareholders; (ii) the board of directors; (iii) officers; and (iv) outside professionals—including particularly auditors, investment bankers, and lawyers.[1] Corporate governance, roughly stated, is the manner in which these different participants interact in ways that cause the corporation to take certain actions and refrain from taking other actions.

This book concerns the governance of public corporations—companies that are organized as corporations and whose stock you or I could buy through a broker because the stock trades on a stock exchange such as the New York Stock Exchange or NASDAQ.

For our purposes, the governance "reforms" are those adopted in the wake of the Enron and WorldCom scandals from mid-2002 forward, and those adopted as a result of the more recent credit crisis. To be sure, before Enron and WorldCom there were a goodly number of scandals and considerable study of possible regulatory changes, some of which were put in place. And long-standing law from a variety of sources forms the essential legal background for the reforms. But Enron and WorldCom prompted an explosion of governance reforms with the credit crisis prompting more. This book concentrates on those.

This Chapter One looks at each of the four principal participants in corporate governance and provides an overview of the reforms' effect on each.

A. SHAREHOLDERS

Shareholder goals. The shareholders own the stock of a corporation and hence own the corporation. Most shareholders buy stock in a corporation in order to make money. Money comes to shareholders in one or both of two ways: (i) the corporation may pay dividends to the

---

[1]   While most commentary does not recognize that lenders also play an important role in corporate governance, lenders can do so. Chapter Two briefly considers the lenders' role.

shareholders[2] or (ii) the shareholders may sell their stock at a higher price than they paid for it.[3]

In addition to a monetary return, most shareholders also want accurate financial reports from the corporation and, in particular, want the corporation to avoid fraudulent reports that cause the shareholders to buy or hold the company's stock. Shareholders also wish to ensure that a company's management does not take advantage of the corporation by, for example, extracting too much money in compensation or engaging in transactions with the corporation in which management receives above-market economic benefits.

Shareholders typically also want control rights, such as the right to vote on certain matters. In addition, shareholders—to a greater or lesser extent—want the corporation to take or avoid particular actions that those shareholders believe to be socially useful or socially harmful.

The relationship of shareholder goals to recent reforms. A few of the reforms seek to increase shareholder influence. These include majority voting rules in director elections, increased shareholder participation in the nomination of director candidates, and required shareholder votes on the overall pay to top officers. These reforms advance the shareholders' goal of controlling the companies whose stock they buy.

Many of the scandals in recent years involved false accounting by corporations that defrauded shareholders and caused them to lose money. Many of the reforms attempt to reduce such losses, and to avoid the false financial reporting that caused them. To the extent the reforms achieve these results, the reforms advance the shareholders' goals to receive accurate financial information and avoid losses caused by revelations that companies have reported false figures.

But shareholders want not only to avoid *losing* money on their investments in stocks. They want to *make* money on those investments. They will use that money to buy houses, pay tuition and other educational expenses for children, and finance retirements. Most shareholders would rather retire to the comfortable house on the beach or in the mountains with the money that they made by investing in companies with "poor governance" than retire to the doublewide in the trailer park with substantially less money that they made by investing in companies that

---

[2]   When the shareholder owns common stock, the board of the corporation has discretion to pay dividends. The board may decide—at any given time—that the company will pay no dividend, that the company will pay a higher dividend than it paid in the past, or that the company will pay a lower dividend than it paid in the past.

[3]   Obviously, the shareholder can make money in this way only if the shareholder can find—through an organized market or otherwise—a buyer who will pay the shareholder more for the stock than the shareholder paid for it.

won awards for "good governance."[4] Whether the reforms further the shareholders' goal to *make* money on stock investments is, as we will see, difficult to answer in any categorical way.

Shareholder primacy as one theory for the shareholder role in corporate governance. Why should we be concerned whether the reforms achieve shareholder goals? What makes the shareholders so special?

In theory at least, the shareholders own a corporation by owning its stock, and control the corporation through the power that stock ownership provides to them. Accordingly, one view is that the corporation should be run for the benefit of the shareholders.

A Chapter Two details, shareholders control corporations only in some gross sense, with most decisions actually made by the board of directors. But the shareholders elect the directors and, the directors are in a very rough economic sense the agents of the shareholders.[5] The board appoints the officers, who run the company on a day-to-day basis. The board monitors the performance of the officers, to check that the officers take actions that benefit the owners—the shareholders—and do not simply use the corporation for their own advantage. As the American Law Institute's *Principles of Corporate Governance* (1994) puts it, a corporation should, as

---

[4]   I do not mean to suggest by this statement that companies that are poorly governed (by standards for good governance prevalent today) provide a greater return to their shareholders than corporations that are well governed. I mean to say only that most investors, given the choice and assuming that neither company is engaged in some truly dreadful activity such as working children to death in order to create a product, would rather invest in corporation A, issuing a stock that will yield a higher return, than in corporation B, issuing a stock yielding a lower return— even if B scores higher than A on a corporate governance rating scale. We will examine the evidence on the relationship between return and governance later.

[5]   The directors are not the agents of the shareholders in a legal sense:

Although a corporation's shareholders elect its directors and may have the right to remove directors once elected, the directors are neither the shareholders' nor the corporation's agents as defined in this section, given the treatment of directors within contemporarycorporation law in the United States. Directors' powers originate as the legal consequence of their election and are not conferred or delegated by shareholders. Although corporation statutes require shareholder approval for specific fundamental transactions, corporation law generally invests managerial authority over corporate affairs in a board of directors, not in shareholders, providing that management shall occur by or under the board of directors. Thus, shareholders ordinarily do not have a right to control directors by giving binding instructions to them. If the statute under which a corporation has been incorporated so permits, shareholders may be allocated power to give binding instructions to directors through a provision in the corporation's articles or through a validly adopted shareholder agreement. The fact that a corporation statute may refer to directors as the corporation's "agents" for a particular purpose does not place directors in an agency relationship with shareholders for purposes of the common law of agency.

American Law Institute, Restatement (Third) of Agency § 1.01 cmt.f(2) (2006). Copyright in the Restatement is held by the American Law Institute, which has granted permission through agreement with West Academic for reprinting in this book.

a general matter, "have as its objective the conduct of business activities with a view to enhancing corporate profit and shareholder gain."[6]

Stakeholder theory as an alternative view of the shareholder role. Some criticize the shareholder primacy view as too simple. They argue that a corporation affects not just its shareholders, but many others as well. Therefore, the corporation should conduct its operations with a view to the welfare of <u>all those stakeholders</u>—including the shareholders, but not limited to them.

Martin Lipton, a famous contemporary corporate attorney, wrote the following in the context of opposing proposals to permit shareholders to nominate director candidates who would be identified in a company's proxy statement and who would challenge the candidates that the sitting board nominated:

> The arguments advanced in support of the proposed election contest rules contain a number of unspoken and flawed assumptions. They rest primarily on a model of the shareholder as "owner" of the corporation, in the manner that an individual might own a car or a building. This model posits that directors and managers should simply be conduits to implement the will of the

---

[6]   AMERICAN LAW INSTITUTE, PRINCIPLES OF CORPORATE GOVERNANCE § 2.01(a) (1994). The *Principles* recognize that a corporation may rightly take actions that do not enhance profit or shareholder wealth in order to comply with law, to advance "ethical considerations that are reasonably regarded as appropriate to the responsible conduct of business," and to "devote a reasonable amount of resources to public welfare, humanitarian, educational, and philanthropic purposes." *Id.* § 2.01(b).

The *Principles* also recognize that corporations can take actions that do not immediately contribute to shareholder wealth but which will do so at a later time:

> In very general terms, Subsection (a) may be thought of as a broad injunction to enhance economic returns, while Subsection (b) makes clear that certain kinds of conduct must or may be pursued whether or not they enhance such returns (that is, even if the conduct either yields no economic return or entails a net economic loss). In most cases, however, the kinds of conduct described in Subsection (b) could be pursued even under the principle embodied in Subsection (a). Such conduct will usually be consistent with economic self-interest, because the principle embodied in Subsection (a)—that the objective of the corporation is to conduct business activities with a view to enhancing corporate profit and shareholder gain—does not mean that the objective of the corporation must be to realize corporate profit and shareholder gain in the short run. Indeed, the contrary is true: long-run profitability and shareholder gain are at the core of the economic objective. Activity that entails a short-run cost to achieve an appropriately greater long-run profit is therefore not a departure from the economic objective. An orientation toward lawful, ethical, and public-spirited activity will normally fall within this description. The modern corporation by its nature creates interdependencies with a variety of groups with whom the corporation has a legitimate concern, such as employees, customers, suppliers, and members of the communities, in which the corporation operates. The long-term profitability of the corporation generally depends on meeting the fair expectations of such groups. Short-term profits may properly be subordinated to recognize that responsible maintenance of these interdependencies is likely to contribute to long-term corporate profit and shareholder gain. The corporation's business may be conducted accordingly.

Id. § 2.01 cmt.f. Copyright in the Principles of Corporate Governance is held by the American Law Institute, which has granted permission through agreement with West Academic for reprinting in this book.

shareholders, just as a building manager is hired to serve the will of the building owner. To the extent that directors or managers of public companies do not implement the will of the shareholders, the argument continues, the corporate governance system is broken and needs to be fixed. The solution, therefore, is to facilitate the nomination of new directors by the shareholders—directors who presumably will do the shareholders' bidding.

The model of the corporation as a piece of personal or real property, however, is far too simplistic. The complex set of legal and contractual relationships that define the modern public corporation goes far beyond the model of a single owner of a single piece of property. Although shareholders may be the residual risk takers in a public company, many other groups, including lenders, suppliers, employees, and communities, also make significant investments in the company. Moreover, "the shareholders" are not a single monolithic body. Far from the single owner of a building, the shareholders are a diverse and ever-shifting group of people and institutions, with differing interests and, in the case of institutional investors, differing obligations to their own diverse constituencies. In addition, unlike a single piece of property, the modern public corporation is the growth engine of our economy, giving the general public its own interest in the operation, governance and success of public companies.[7]

In considering this position, bear in mind that Mr. Lipton has made a very good living over the years defending corporate boards that took actions that critics sometimes maintained were not in the interests of the shareholders who elected the boards.[8] We will consider later whether, in practice, a stakeholder theory of corporate governance is likely to empower such constituencies as labor and the communities in which a company does its business, or whether such a theory is likely to simply provide directors with increased opportunity to implement their own views through the resources of the companies they control.[9]

---

[7] Martin Lipton & Steven A. Rosenblum, *Election Contests in the Company's Proxy: An Idea Whose Time Has Not Come*, 59 BUS. LAW. 67, 68 (2003). Quotation reprinted with permission from the American Bar Association. All rights reserved. This quotation or any portion thereof may not be copied or disseminated in any form or by any means or stored in an electronic database or retrieval system without the express written consent of the American Bar Association. Election Contests in the Company's Proxy: An Idea Whose Time Has Not Come, Business Lawyer volume 59 © 2003 by the American Bar Association.

[8] It is interesting to find a practitioner of what might be called "board supremacy" employing the rhetoric of stakeholder theory.

[9] Note that some state corporate statutes—many enacted to give directors greater freedom to defend against takeovers—expressly permit boards to take into account the effect of corporate actions on "constituencies" other than shareholders. For example, Pennsylvania Business Code section 1715 provides, in pertinent part:

QUESTIONS ON SHAREHOLDERS AND THE PURPOSE OF PUBLIC CORPORATIONS

Which view of public corporations do you find most attractive—the one holding that the purpose of those corporations is to advance the economic interests of the shareholders or the one holding that the purpose of those corporations is to advance the interests of a variety of corporate stakeholders of which the shareholders comprise one group, but which also includes groups of employees, suppliers, customers, communities in which the corporations do business, and the national and world economies?

If you subscribe to the stakeholder view, how would you determine whether a given corporate action, which helps some stakeholders but harms others, is on balance a good one?

Shareholders are not the focus of reforms. Although shareholders own a public corporation and although the purpose of the corporation—at least as seen by most—is to benefit the shareholders, only a few reforms attempt to increase shareholder power. The reforms concentrate on boards of directors, officers, and outside professionals (particularly outside auditors).

Three major reform efforts, however, constitute exceptions worthy of mention now. The directors at most large corporations nominate themselves each year to run for an additional term on the board. The company distributes a proxy statement to the shareholders with the names of the nominees (again, usually current directors) and brief information about each one. The shareholders then vote, with votes usually cast either "for" a particular nominee or "withheld" from that nominee, which is roughly equivalent to voting against a nominee. The board's nominees ordinarily run unopposed—with the number of nominees equaling the number of directors to be elected.

(a)   General rule. In discharging the duties of their respective positions, the board of directors, committees of the board and individual directors of a business corporation may, in considering the best interests of the corporation, consider to the extent they deem appropriate:

    (1)   The effects of any action upon any or all groups affected by such action, including shareholders, employees, suppliers, customers and creditors of the corporation, and upon communities in which offices or other establishments of the corporation are located.

    . . . .

(b)   Consideration of interests and factors. The board of directors, committees of the board and individual directors shall not be required, in considering the best interests of the corporation or the effects of any action, to regard any corporate interest or the interests of any particular group affected by such action as a dominant or controlling interest or factor.

15 PA. CON. STAT. ANN. § 1715.

If a company employs plurality voting for directors, then, if shareholders are electing seven directors, the seven candidates receiving the most votes are elected—regardless of how many votes each of those seven garners. Thus, if a nominee holds even one share of stock and votes for himself or herself, the nominee wins even if all the other shares that voted are "withheld" from that nominee. Assuming that a "withhold" vote indicates displeasure with the nominee, the nominee can win under plurality voting even if the owners of a majority of shares oppose the nominee's election.

In recent years a large number of major public corporations have shifted away from plurality voting to some sort of majority voting system, which aims to ensure that a nominee will take a seat as a director only if the nominee garners an affirmative vote by the holders of a majority of the shares voting.

A second reform effort focuses on the nomination of director candidates. At present, at the great majority of public companies, only the candidates nominated by the current board appear in the company proxy statement and on the proxy card that the company distributes to shareholders.[10] As noted above, the current board usually just renominates itself. Shareholders who want to run alternate candidates face large costs to contact other shareholders, inform them of the alternate candidates, and solicit proxies to vote for those candidates. Since shareholders do not want to pay these charges, they do not generally nominate opposition candidates. And this means that the shareholders, when they vote, do not have a choice of candidates. The absence of any choice weakens shareholder control. A reform effort to provide shareholders with the opportunity to put nominees on the company's proxy statement—which would greatly reduce the cost of running alternate candidates—has provoked a great deal of controversy.

In 2010, the SEC adopted regulations requiring each public company to include—in its proxy statements and on its proxy forms—candidates nominated by a shareholder, or a group of shareholders, for up to 25% of the board seats, provided that the shareholder or the group held at least 3% of the total voting power at the coming election, had held securities with that minimum voting power for three years, and stated its intention to hold such securities through the election in which its nominees participated.[11] The regulations required that the company also include in its proxy statement distributed to all stockholders the sponsoring shareholders'

---

[10]   Most shareholders do not physically attend the meetings at which companies hold director elections. If the absent shareholders vote at all, they do so by proxy. Usually, the company is the only party that distributes a proxy statement and proxy card. The proxy statement describes only those director candidates that the current board has nominated, and the proxy card allows the shareholders to vote only for those candidates or to withhold votes for those candidates.

[11]   Facilitating Shareholder Director Nominations, 75 Fed. Reg. 56,668 (Sept. 16, 2010).

statement, of up to 500 words, in support of each shareholder nominee.[12] The D.C. Circuit vacated that regulation in 2011 on the ground that the SEC had not adequately considered and explained the costs and benefits.[13] Companies can, however, adopt such "proxy access" protocols voluntarily.

A third set of reforms seeks to increase the shareholder role in compensation. Shareholders have the right to vote on equity compensation plans, which pay officers with stock and stock derivatives (such as stock options). More significantly, the Dodd-Frank Wall Street Reform Act requires that the shareholders of each public company have an opportunity to express by vote whether they approve or do not approve of compensation, overall, to top executives at the company.[14]

What role we ascribe to shareholders helps us evaluate the reforms. Although this reader refers to the governance changes following Enron, WorldCom, and the credit crisis as "the reforms," I do not suggest that these changes were, given the costs, beneficial. We will discuss in later chapters whether you think particular changes, and the changes overall, were on balance a good idea.

Evaluating the reforms requires some frame of reference. If we adhere to the shareholder primacy theory, we will evaluate the reforms by trying to determine whether they further the shareholder goals of investment return, fair financial reporting, and shareholder control over the corporation. Such an evaluation may prove difficult, and we will discuss that difficulty.

If we adhere to the stakeholder theory, we will have to find some other way to evaluate the reforms. In particular, for an overall judgment we will need to measure the net benefit or cost to each constituency, then consider those net benefits or costs together, using some formula or other analysis that permits us to weigh the effect on each constituency against the effect on the others.

QUESTIONS ON EVALUATING THE REFORMS

If you subscribe to the shareholder primacy school of thought, how would you determine whether the recent corporate reforms have been helpful?

If you subscribe to the stakeholder theory, how would you determine whether the recent reforms have been helpful?

---

[12]   *Id.* at 56,785 (setting out 17 C.F.R. § 240.14a-11(c)).

[13]   *Bus. Roundtable v. SEC*, 647 F.3d 1144 (D.C. Cir. 2011).

[14]   Pub. L. No. 111-203, § 951; Shareholder Approval of Executive Compensation and Golden Parachute Compensation, 76 Fed. Reg. 6010, 6045–46 (Feb. 2, 2011) (codified at 17 C.F.R. § 240.14a-21) (implementing SEC regulation).

B. BOARDS OF DIRECTORS

The Delaware General Corporation Law provides that "[t]he business and affairs of every corporation organized under this [law] shall be managed by or under the direction of a board of directors. . . ."[15] Reformers have probably spent more time studying and changing boards of directors than studying and changing any other governance participant, with the possible exception of outside auditors.[16]

The definition of a board's job has changed dramatically in the last 40 years.

Pre-reform boards: passive, inactive, without defined tasks, and dominated by the top executive. During 1969–1971,[17] a professor at the Harvard Business School "conducted about seventy-five in-depth interviews and held several hundred shorter discussions with top business executives."[18] Here are some excerpts from the article summarizing his research:

> In most companies, boards of directors serve as a source of *advice and counsel*, offer some sort of *discipline value*, and act in *crisis situations*—if the president dies suddenly or is asked to resign because of unsatisfactory management performance. . . .
>
> *Advise & counsel*
>
> I found that most presidents and outside board members[19] agree that the role of directors is largely advisory and not of a decision-making nature. Management manages the company, and board members serve as sources of advice and counsel to the management. . . .

---

[15]   Del. Code Ann. tit. 8 § 141(a). When discussing state law, this book generally focuses on Delaware corporate law.

[16]   One prominent academic contends that "director primacy" rather than shareholder primacy best characterizes public corporations today. Stephen M. Bainbridge, *Director Primacy: The Means and Ends of Corporate Governance*, 97 NW. U. L. REV. 547, 550 (2003). The reformers' concentration on the board therefore makes some sense.

[17]   Although it is dated, the Mace article captures the experience of many boards up to the time of what we will call the "reforms."

[18]   Myles L. Mace, *The President and the Board of Directors*, 50 HARV. BUS. REV. 37, 38 (1972) [Mace, *President and Board*]. When Mace authored his piece, the top officer at most major U.S. corporations was called the "president." Today, the top officer is usually called the "chief executive officer" or "CEO." Quotations from this article reprinted with permission from Harvard Business Publishing.

[19]   The term "outside" director refers to a director who is not, at the time of the characterization, an officer or employee of the corporation on whose board he or she sits. The term "independent" director has a broader meaning and refers to a director who is independent of top officers not only because the director is not currently employed by the corporation but also because the director is free of other ties to top officers (e.g., the director is not dependent on top officers for consulting or legal or investment banking fees in a way that makes the director beholden to top officers).

Here [is a] typical response[ ] of [a] president[ ] interviewed: "I think of a board as a sort of cabinet, a group of generalists, not specialists, who can advise me on all kinds of problems, new ideas, new services, improvements on what we are doing, and criticisms of what we are doing. A cabinet is an assemblage of sources of advice—the cabinet name is a good one for a board."

Perhaps the strongest but not typical statement was provided by one president who said:

> "We get a little advice from the outside board members, but the management runs the company. The board rubber-stamps the action of management, and the board members are there to mollify the outside stockholders."

Since typically directors do not devote substantial amounts of time to the affairs of the companies they serve, their advice cannot be of the sort which requires lengthy and penetrating analysis. [But] . . . directors, within the time constraints, can provide useful inputs to presidents willing to listen.

Outside directors are especially helpful in the advisory role where their general or specialized backgrounds and experiences can be applied to the specific management problems of the company served. For example, if new loans are to be negotiated or if new financing is to be arranged, these are the kinds of problems commonly faced by those on the board, and their judgments on interest rates or terms are useful to the president. Or if the question of a company's pension plan is under review, the experience of other top executives [on the board] is another bit of useful evidence for the president working for a solution. And if a new plant location, domestic or abroad, is involved in a request for a capital appropriation, members of the board with similar recent experience can often suggest useful and sometimes new factors bearing on the decision to commit large amounts of capital to a specific location.

Sometimes, but not too frequently, the advice and counsel of a board member leads to a reconsideration or modification of a management's commitment or decision. Occasionally, but only very rarely, the advice and counsel of a board member leads to a reversal of a management commitment or decision.

Provide discipline value

A second role performed by board of directors is serving as some sort of discipline for the president and his [or her] subordinate management. The president and his subordinates know that periodically they must appear before a board made up largely of their peers.

I have found that even in those situations where top managements know from previous experience that members of the board will not ask penetrating, discerning, and challenging questions, considerable care is taken in preparing figures and reports for board meetings. Something in the way of discipline results simply from the fact that regular board meetings are held.

Act in crisis situations

There are two critical states of corporate affairs in which the role of the board of directors is more than advisory.

First, if the president dies suddenly or becomes incapacitated, the board has the decision-making responsibility to select his [or her] successor. In some cases, the selection process is largely controlled by the deceased president who has discussed with board members what he [or she] wanted them to do "if I am hit by a truck some day." In other instances, board members and presidents have neglected to consider the problem of succession. Only when confronted with the unexpected death of the president have they been propelled into a decision-making function. But the board is there—and it is legally constituted to pick a successor and to ensure the continuity of an entity organized to operate in perpetuity.

Second, if the leadership and performance of the president are so unsatisfactory that a change must be made, the board of directors performs a decision-making role: here, the president is asked to resign—an important decision; and then the board must decide on his [or her] successor—an equally important decision.

I have concluded that generally boards of directors do not do an effective job of evaluating or measuring the performance of the president. Rarely are standards or criteria established and agreed upon by which the president can be measured other than by the usual general test of corporate profitability; and it is surprising how slow some directors are to respond to years of steadily declining profitability.

Since directors are selected by the president, and group and individual loyalties have been developed through working together, directors are reluctant to measure the executive performance of the president carefully against specific standards. Directors base their appraisals largely on data and reports provided by the president himself [or herself]. Also, top executives serving as outside directors, and being exceedingly busy men [and women], typically do not devote time to pursue through further inquiry any concerns they may deduce from the data presented to them as directors, even when the concern might extend to the performance of the president.

Ask the president to resign

Most boards of directors and most individual directors are intensely reluctant to face the unpleasant conclusion that the president of the company must be replaced. While sometimes the unpleasantness is avoided by hiring outside consultants [to review a president's performance and, if desirable, recommend a change] or by [the director's] resigning from the board, there are some situations in which board members who have procrastinated in taking any action find themselves obligated to face the task of asking the president to resign. These situations are relatively rare.

What directors do not do

The business literature describing the classic functions of boards of directors typically includes three important roles: (a) establishing basic objectives, corporate strategies, and broad policies; (b) asking discerning questions; and (c) selecting the president. . . .

Establish objectives

Boards of directors of most large- and medium-sized companies *do not* establish objectives, strategies, and policies, however defined. These roles are performed by company management. Presidents and outside directors generally are agreed that only management can, and should[,] have . . . these responsibilities.

The typical outside director does not have time to make the kinds of studies needed to establish company objectives and strategies. At most, he [or she] can approve positions taken by management—and this approval is based on scanty facts, not on time-consuming analysis.

In a few instances, boards of directors do establish objectives, strategies, and major policies, but these are exceptions. Here, the president wants the involvement of the directors, and he [or she] not only allows for, but insists on, full discussion, exploration of the issues, agreement, and decisions by the board along with himself [or herself].

Ask discerning questions

A second classic role ascribed to boards of directors is that of asking discerning questions—inside and outside the board meetings. Again, I found that directors *do not* in fact do this. Board meetings are not regarded as proper forums for discussions arising out of questions asked by board members; the president and directors alike feel that such meetings are not intended as debating societies.

In one situation, for example, an outside director, who was concerned about steadily declining earnings and who perceived no apparent management program to reverse the trend, asked the chairman and the president what was being done to correct the situation. The other outside directors also expressed their concern, and the president, obviously embarrassed, responded with unpersuasive and unimpressive replies.

After the meeting, the chairman asked the initial questioner to stop by his office before leaving, and there he explained:

> "It is just plain bad manners to ask those kinds of questions in a board meeting. You must remember that you are challenging the president in the presence of his subordinates, some of who[m] are insiders on the board. If you have questions about what is being done to reverse the trend, the proper way is to make a date to confer with the president privately."

Many board members cited their lack of understanding of the problems and the implications of topics that are presented to the board by the president; thus, to avoid "looking like idiots," they refrain from questioning or commenting.

Presidents generally do not want to be challenged by the questions of directors, especially if subordinates of the president are on the board or in attendance at the meeting. Despite the fact that most presidents profess that they want questions to be asked by interested members of the board, I have concluded that, while they may say this, and may even go to some trouble to make directors feel that they are free to question, actually the presidents do not want discerning questions or comments. The unsophisticated director may learn from experiencing rebuffs that the president does not want penetrating and issue-provoking questions, but only those which are gentle and supportive and an affirmation that the board approves of him [or her].

Many presidents stated that board members should manifest by their queries, if any, that they approve of the management. If a director feels that he [or she] has any basis for doubt and disapproval, most of the presidents interviewed believe that he [or she] should resign.

My research disclosed few exceptions to this routine. In a handful of instances, presidents said that they do in fact want discerning, challenging questions and active discussions of important issues at their board meetings. They think of their boards as accountable and responsible to the company's owners. There are also a few directors who do in fact ask discerning questions, the desires of the president notwithstanding.

Typical garden-variety outside directors, selected by the president and generally members of a peer group, do not ask questions inside or outside board meetings. However, directors who serve on corporate boards of companies because they own or represent the ownership of substantial share of stock generally do in fact ask discerning questions. Their willingness to query presidents is, in part, a manifestation of the split in the de facto powers of control of those companies. The large stockholder-directors are not usually on the board because the president wants them there, but because through cumulative voting procedures they can force their way onto the board.

Directors, as described in the literature, represent the stockholders. Yet, typically, they are actually selected by the president and not by the stockholders.[20] Accordingly, the directors are on the board because the president wants them there. Implicitly, and frequently explicitly, the directors in point of fact represent the president.

Select the president

A third classic role usually regarded as a responsibility of the board of directors is the selection of the president. Yet I found that in most companies directors do not in fact select the president, except under the two crisis situations cited earlier.

One company vice chairman, in commenting on this function of the board stated:

> "The old concept that the stockholders elect the board, and the board selects the management, is fiction. It just doesn't apply to today's large corporations. The board does not select the management; the management selects the board."

In some situations, formal or informal committees of outside members of boards are charged with the responsibility of

---

20   Mace does not mean that presidents simply appointed the directors but that the presidents controlled who was nominated for director positions. The shareholders voted on the nominees but the nominees typically ran unopposed. Since they were elected by a plurality standard explained in the text, the unopposed nominees always won. Accordingly, since the president controlled the nominations and since the nominees always won, the president controlled the board membership.

evaluating candidates inside the management for the presidency. But, generally, these committees have no more control over the naming of the president than do similar committees charged with identifying and recommending the names of candidates for board membership. In both committee situations, the president with de facto powers of control essentially makes the decisions. The administrative use by the president of board committees to evaluate candidates for his successor in the presidency gives the selection process an appearance of careful evaluation and objectivity. But in most cases the decision as to who should succeed the president is made by the president himself [or herself].

Boards of directors, I found, do serve in an advisory role in the selection of a new president—in their capacity as a sort of corporate conscience. The process of electing a new president requires a vote by the board, and the president generally observes the amenities of corporate good manners by discussing his [or her] choice with individual members prior to the meeting. Rarely does a board of directors reject a candidate for the presidency who is recommended by the president.

Powers of control

[In] the large, widely held corporation in which typically the president and members of the board own little stock . . . the de jure powers of control are dispersed among thousands of stockholders who are generally both unorganized as owners and essentially unorganizable. With this absence of control or influence by the corporate owners, the president typically does have the de facto powers to control the enterprise, and with these powers of control it is the president who . . . determines in large part what the board of directors does or does not do.

Ownership influences

My research findings show that many directors who own, or who represent the ownership of, substantial numbers of shares of stock take a deep interest in the operations of the company, spend considerable time in learning the business, and insist on being involved in major company decisions. The degree of the president's de facto powers of control in these cases is affected by the involvement of company stock owners.

Some directors who own, or who represent ownership of, large numbers of shares are passive, compliant, and not involved in major company problems; thus the president's complete powers of control are not diminished or influenced. My analysis of the situations where substantial stockholdings are represented on the board has produced no factors which make possible any reliable prediction of whether the stockholder-director will take an active and involved question-asking role.

Choice of new members

The president, with powers of control, generally selects and invites directors to serve on the board. In some instances, a nominating committee of the board is created to identify, screen, and recommend candidates for board membership. Even with the presumed objectivity of a committee of outside directors, though, the president makes the decision as to new members.

Again, it should be noted that if one or more existing directors own or represent the ownership of substantial stock, the president's de facto power to select new directors may be challenged. . . .

The stockholders, of course, unless their holdings are substantial enough to assure representation on the board through the provisions of cumulative voting or to result in an invitation by the president to serve, play no part in the selection of directors to fill vacancies or in the nomination of directors' names to be included in the annual proxy statement.

Candidates are usually chosen who are (a) in positions equal to those of the other board members or (b) in companies of prestige equivalent to that of the company being served. If existing board members are chairmen and presidents of companies or senior partners of leading financial or legal firms, potential board members with lesser titles are rarely considered.

Here is one company president's comment on the prestige of his board members:

> "We have a standing rule that no one can be an outside director in our company who is not the top person in his organization. If he isn't, he can't be on our board. I don't care how able he is; our board as now constituted has top men as outsiders, so any replacements over the years have got to be their peers. You can't downgrade the prestige of our board membership by inviting, say, a promising vice president to serve as a board member."

In addition to the qualifications of prestige titles in prestige institutions—both business and academic—outside directors are selected because they are noncontroversial, friendly, sympathetic, congenial, and because they understand the system. Boat-rockers and wave-makers generally are not the choice of presidents with de facto powers of control and with freedom of choice as to who should serve on their boards.[21]

The directors that Mace described (except for directors owning or representing large blocks of stock) did not create or critically consider company strategy, did not aggressively monitor top executive performance, asked few probing questions about anything, and ceded to the current top executive control over both board membership and (with some exceptions, such as when the president died unexpectedly and without identifying a preferred replacement) top executive succession. The directors were not independent of top management but controlled by top management.

The reform ideal: active boards, independent of the top executive, with multiple assigned tasks. We will study board reforms in detail as the book progresses. It is useful now, however, to take an overall view. The American Bar Association's sixth edition of its *Corporate Director's Guidebook* (2011) ("*Director's Guidebook*") is representative of the current view, which is that directors should be much more active and independent:

> State corporate statutes emphasize the board's responsibility to make major decisions on behalf of the corporation and to oversee the management of the corporation. Although these statutes do not specifically define board responsibilities, they generally include the following tasks for the board and its committees:
>
> - monitoring the corporation's performance in light of its operating, financial, and other significant corporate plans, strategies, and objectives, and approving major changes in plans and strategies;
>
> - selecting the CEO, setting the goals for the CEO and other senior executives, reviewing their performance, evaluating and establishing their compensation, and making changes when appropriate;
>
> - understanding the corporation's risk profile and reviewing and overseeing the corporation's management of risks;
>
> - developing, approving, and implementing succession plans for the CEO and top senior executives;
>
> - understanding the corporation's financial statements[22] and other financial disclosures and monitoring the adequacy of its

---

[21] Mace, *President and Board, supra* note 18, at 38–46 (emphasis in original).

[22] The "financial statements" include (i) a balance sheet showing the company's assets (e.g., the cash that that the corporation has on hand) and liabilities (e.g., the amounts that the company owes to creditors) at the end of the quarter or year covered by the balance sheet; (ii) an "income statement" showing the revenue that the company received during the quarter or year covered by financial statements, the expenses during that period, and the resulting income; and (iii) a "statement of cash flows" showing the cash that came into the company and the cash that went

financial and other internal controls, as well as its disclosure controls and procedures;

- evaluating and approving major transactions such as mergers, acquisitions, significant expenditures, and the disposition of major assets; and

- establishing and monitoring effective systems for receiving and reporting information about the corporation's compliance with its legal and ethical obligations.[23]

Relying largely on standards imposed by stock markets on companies listing their stocks on those trading platforms, the *Director's Guidebook* states that a majority of directors should be independent and recites a number of conditions that preclude independence[24] (e.g., receipt by a director of more than a specified amount of money paid for consulting or other services besides work on the board).[25] Again relying mostly on current federal law and listing requirements, the *Director's Guidebook* discusses the standing committees and even the qualifications of the directors who serve on the committees.

The *Director's Guidebook* lists 21 required duties for a standing audit committee (including selecting the outside auditor and approving its fees), with eight additional tasks that "many audit committees undertake as matters of good corporate practice."[26] All members of the audit committee

---

out of the company during the quarter or year as well as the increase or decrease in cash held during the period.

[23] American Bar Association, *Director's Guidebook* 12–13 (6th ed. 2011). Like the *Principles, supra* note 6, and taking into account statutes such as the one set out in note 9, the *Director's Guidebook* states that

[a] number of state corporation statutes expressly allow the board to consider the interests of employees, suppliers, and customers, as well as the communities in which the corporation operates and the environment. Of course, the board remains accountable primarily to shareholders for the performance of the corporation. Thus, non-shareholder constituency considerations are best understood not as independent corporate objectives but as factors to be considered in pursuing the best interests of the corporation. Indeed, being responsive to stakeholder interests and concerns can help to contribute positively to a corporation's values, its workplace culture and its reputation for integrity and ethical behavior.

Id. at 14. Quotations from the Director's Guidebook reprinted with permission from the American Bar Association. All rights reserved. These quotations or any portion thereof may not be copied or disseminated in any form or by any means or stored in an electronic database or retrieval system without the express written consent of the American Bar Association. Director's Guidebook © 2011 by the American Bar Association.

[24] Independence is a relative term. It has no meaning absent specifying the person(s) or organization(s) from whom or from which the director must be independent. Generally, corporate governance assesses the independence of a director from the top officers of the corporation. Thus, a current but not top officer of the company would not, as a board member, be "independent" of the top officer because the top officer would be the subordinate's boss. The subordinate officer would be unlikely, as a board member, to vote against his or her boss.

[25] *Director's Guidebook* at 44–46.

[26] *Id.* at 67–70.

must meet the detailed standards for independence established by listing standards and federal securities law, "should also have a sufficient understanding of financial reporting and internal control principles to provide oversight for both," and should consider "[c]ontinuing education" to "stay current in their knowledge of . . . financial issues and accounting practices."[27]

The *Director's Guidebook* lists 10 "principal functions" for a standing compensation committee (including "review[ing] and approv[ing] corporate goals and objectives relevant to CEO and senior executive compensation and annually evaluat[ing] executive performance in light of those goals and objectives").[28] All members of this committee, too, must be independent directors.[29]

The *Director's Guidebook* identifies a nominating/corporate governance committee, which is charged with "recruiting and maintaining board members with appropriate skills and independence for quality decision-making"[30]—a job that entails "establish[ing], or recommend[ing] to the board, criteria for identifying appropriate director candidates."[31] Other typical tasks for this committee include recommending to the full board those directors who should chair the board's other committees[32] and the amount and form of director compensation.[33] The *Director's Guidebook* lists 11 other typical functions for the nominating/governance committee.[34] This committee too should consist only of directors who are independent according to a detailed definition.[35]

As a comparison of the Mace article and the *Director's Guidebook* reflects, and as we will see in detail again, the model of board regulation has changed over time from (i) a model giving each corporation wide latitude in defining the organization and operation of its board to (ii) specific identification of committees that a board must create, qualifications for board and committee membership, and tasks that the committees must perform. Culturally, the reforms have attempted to convert the relatively passive boards that Mace found into active boards today.[36]

---

27   *Id.* at 65–66.

28   *Id.* at 82–83.

29   *Id.* at 81.

30   *Id.* at 97.

31   *Id.* at 98.

32   *Id.* at 102.

33   *Id.* at 105–07.

34   *Id.* at 104–05.

35   *Id.* at 97.

36   Though not as much as the level of activity and skepticism of boards, the number of directors that a board should contain has also received some attention. The *Director's Guidebook* says:

QUESTION ON THE NATURE OF BOARDS

Every board can be placed along a number of continua. For example, there is a continuum from extremely passive boards, such as those Mace describes, to, at the other extreme, boards comprised of directors who, in the words of an SEC chair, constantly "ask [the] tough questions of management,"[37] the "simple—but sometimes unsettling—questions,"[38] the "inconvenient" questions,[39] "the damnedest questions."[40]

What are the advantages of a board of the second type? What are the disadvantages?

> Board size varies substantially among public corporations, with some corporations, like those in the financial services industry, typically having larger boards. Except perhaps for the very largest and most complex corporations, smaller boards (seven to eleven members) generally function more effectively than larger ones, because directors have greater opportunities to participate actively in board deliberations and otherwise contribute. Individuals serving on large boards may feel that their active engagement is less critical to the functioning of the group. Larger boards can overcome this perception and encourage individual director participation by relying more heavily on board committees in which individual directors actively participate.

Id. at 42–43.

A study of 82 public manufacturing corporations continually in business from 1935 through 2000 found that board size varied over time:

> Median board size increases from 11 in 1935 to a peak of 15 in 1960, and declines rather steadily thereafter to a low of 11 in the most recent year, 2000. Mean board size reveals a similar pattern peaking at 14.48 in 1960 and with its minimum value of 11.16 in 2000. Mean board size is substantially lower in 2000 than it is at the beginning of the sample period in 1935 when it takes the value of 12.43.

Kenneth Lehn, et al., *Determinants of the Size and Structure of Corporate Boards: 1935–2000*, 38 FIN. MGMT. 747, 753 (2009), with the sample described at 752–53 and tabular information at 755 (tbl.1, Panel B). The authors also found that the variation in board size within their sample declined over the years, with the standard deviation of the mean size declining rather steadily from 5.545 in 1935 to 2.682 in 2000. *Id.* at 755 (tbl.1, Panel B). *See also* EQUILAR, BOARD COMPOSITION & RECRUITING TRENDS 5 (2014) ("The size of boards has remained consistent across the indices since 2009. In 2013, the average board size of the S&P 500 was 10.8 members, increasing minimally over the years. . . . Mid-cap and small-cap companies have slightly lower average board sizes at 9.2 and 8.3 members, respectively.").

[37]   Arthur Levitt, U.S. Securities and Exchange Commission Chairman, *The "Numbers Game,"* Remarks at NYU Center for Law and Business (Sept. 28, 1998), http://www.sec.gov/news/speech/speecharchive/1998/spch220.txt.

[38]   Arthur Levitt, U.S. Securities and Exchange Commission Chairman, *Corporate Governance: Integrity in the Information Age*, Remarks at Tulane University (Mar. 12, 1998), http://www.sec.gov/news/speech/speecharchive/1998/spch206.txt.

[39]   *Id.*

[40]   Arthur Levitt, U.S. Securities and Exchange Commission Chairman, *Remarks at Directors' College Stanford Law School* (Mar. 22, 1999) (internal quotation marks omitted), http://www.sec.gov/news/speech/speecharchive/1999/spch261.txt.

C. OFFICERS

A public company creates its own financial statements. The company publishes financial statements each quarter (every three months). Those for the first three quarters in the company's fiscal year[41] need not be audited. But the numbers in the financial statements for the full year, which include the numbers for the company's fourth quarter, must be audited by an outside accounting firm.

The chief executive officer ("CEO"), who is typically the top executive at a company and the chief financial officer ("CFO"), who is typically in charge of the company staff preparing financial statements, were generally thought of as controlling the process by which their companies created financial statements.

Reformers concluded that these two officers should take greater responsibility for financial numbers that their companies published and for the systems that their companies set up to collect and process both those numbers and the other information that public companies must disclose under the federal securities laws. The reforms accordingly require the CEO and CFO to sign certifications each quarter. The certifications state that, to the officer's knowledge, the financial information in the statements and accompanying disclosures fairly presents, in all material respects, the company's financial condition and results. The certifications also state that each of these officers recognizes his or her responsibility to create systems inside the company to collect and process information in a manner permitting the company to make accurate disclosures.

In addition, the reforms following on the Enron and WorldCom meltdowns included a provision that CEOs and CFOs repay their companies for incentive compensation if the company's financial statements turn out to be materially wrong as a result of misconduct. The Dodd-Frank Act following the credit crisis added a broader and stronger provision of a similar sort.

As the result of yet further reforms, public companies now adopt codes of conduct for their officers. The codes address conflicts of interest when officers participate directly or indirectly in transactions with their companies and more generally require compliance with laws.

Finally, some reformers placed a part of the blame for the credit crisis on executive compensation that the reformers believed to have encouraged officers to take actions that provided short-term gains to the officers but that created excessive risk for their companies. The SEC adopted

---

[41] Most domestic companies operate on a fiscal year that is the same as the calendar year so that the first quarter (or Q1) runs from January through March, the second quarter (or Q2) from April through June, the third quarter (or Q3) from July through September, and the fourth quarter (or Q4) from October through December. But some companies operate on fiscal years that are different from the calendar year.

regulations requiring every public company to disclose the relationship between risk and compensation policies. The Dodd-Frank law then required regulators "to prescribe guidelines or regulations"—applicable to certain financial institutions—to

> prohibit any types of incentive-based payment arrangement, or any feature of any such arrangement, that the regulators determine encourages inappropriate risks by covered financial institutions—
>
> (1) by providing an executive officer, employee, director, or principal shareholder of the covered financial institution with excessive compensation, fees, or benefits; or
>
> (2) that could lead to material financial loss to the covered financial institution.[42]

D. OUTSIDE PROFESSIONALS

The term "outside professionals," as used in this book, includes outside auditors, outside law firms, compensation consultants, investment bankers, and search firms that help companies find directors and top officers. These different professionals have different relationships with the public company. Thus, while a lawyer for the company is, by ethical rule, required to serve the interest of the company, the auditor is an outside accounting firm that must be independent of the company and skeptically check its financial statements.

Outside professionals as gatekeepers. One view of the WorldCom and Enron scandals focused on the failure of outside professionals to prevent the wrongdoing. Critics labeled those outside professionals "gatekeepers." Here is an excellent summary of that term and its significance in the context most important to us:

> Although the term "gatekeeper" is commonly used, here it requires special definition. Inherently, gatekeepers are reputational intermediaries who provide verification and certification services to investors. These services can consist of verifying a company's financial statements (as the independent auditor does), evaluating the creditworthiness of the company (as the debt rating agency does), assessing the company's business and financial prospects vis-à-vis its rivals (as the securities analyst does), or appraising the fairness of a specific transaction (as the investment banker does in delivering a fairness opinion). Lawyers can also be gatekeepers when they lend their professional reputations to a transaction, but, as later discussed,

---

[42]   Pub. L. No. 111-203, § 956 (2010). Chapter Nineteen describes the resulting regulatory action in detail.

the more typical role of lawyers serving public corporations is that of the transaction engineer, rather than the reputational intermediary.

Characteristically, the professional gatekeeper essentially assesses or vouches for the corporate client's own statements about itself or a specific transaction. This duplication is necessary because the market recognizes that the gatekeeper has a lesser incentive to lie than does its client and thus regards the gatekeeper's assurance or evaluation as more credible. To be sure, the gatekeeper as watchdog is typically paid by the party that it is to watch, but its relative credibility stems from the fact that it is in effect pledging a reputational capital that it has built up over many years of performing similar services for numerous clients. In theory, such reputational capital would not be sacrificed for a single client and a modest fee. Here, as elsewhere, however, logic and experience can conflict. Despite the clear logic of the gatekeeper rationale, experience over the 1990s suggests that professional gatekeepers do acquiesce in managerial fraud, even though the apparent reputational losses seem to dwarf the gains to be made from the individual client.

Why has there been an apparent failure in the market for gatekeeping services? This brief Comment offers some explanations, but also acknowledges that rival explanations lead to very different prescriptions. Thus, the starting point for responding to the Enron debacle begins with asking the right question. That question is not: Why did some managements engage in fraud? But is rather: Why did the gatekeepers let them?[43]

Auditors. Of all the outside professionals participating in corporate governance, the auditors have received the most attention. Every publicly traded company must file with the Securities and Exchange Commission financial numbers covering a 12-month period, with comparable numbers from earlier years. Each such company must retain an outside accounting firm to audit those numbers. We will discuss later what an audit compromises and what the auditor's opinion means. For now, we need only note that an audit does not usually test separately the numbers generated by each and every economic event during the audit year and that the auditor only provides an opinion—based on selective testing—as to whether or not the company's numbers are materially correct, in light of accounting principles.

---

[43]   John C. Coffee, Jr., *Understanding Enron: "It's About the Gatekeepers, Stupid,"* 57 BUS. LAW. 1403, 1405 (2002) (citations omitted). Quotation reprinted with permission from Professor Coffee.

In forming its opinion, an auditor is supposed to be skeptical. The audit is supposed to critically test the company's financial numbers. To perform an adequate audit, therefore, an accounting firm must be independent from the company whose figures the firm tests. A goodly number of the reforms are designed to increase the independence of auditors from their clients.

The major outside accounting firms used to offer to their audit clients not only auditing services but also consulting services addressing a raft of non-audit problems. The reforms dramatically curtail those non-audit services on the theory that an accounting firm providing or seeking to provide non-audit services to an audit client might pull its punches on the audit and approve the company's numbers—even if they were not right—in order to get non-audit business from the company.

The reforms seek to increase the independence of auditors from their clients in other ways: (i) by restricting the circumstances in which members of an accounting firm can join the financial staffs of audit clients, (ii) by prohibiting accounting firms from compensating partners heading audit engagements for selling—to audit clients—the non-audit services that accounting firms can still offer audit clients, and (iii) by requiring that the head of audit engagements rotate after a certain number of years.

Acting on the belief that accounting failures occurred in part because audit committees of boards of directors were too passive, the reforms require audit committees to perform a long list of tasks. The reforms also require specified communications between each audit committee and the company's outside auditor. The effect may be to increase the support that an audit committee provides to the outside auditor during the interaction between the auditor and company management that produces each public company's audited financial statements.

The reforms also create an entirely new system for regulating auditors of public companies.

Lawyers. Lawyers are supposed to work aggressively to advance the interests of their clients. But there has for many years been (i) sentiment that a lawyer for a corporation may also have some sort of direct or indirect duty to the public, particularly to those who own or are about to buy the corporation's stock, and (ii) concern that lawyers for corporations may work so closely with individual officers that the lawyers may not fully differentiate the interests of those officers from the interests of the corporation as an entity.

One reform targets lawyers. The SEC promulgated rules for lawyer conduct. The rules state that, when a corporation retains an attorney, the attorney owes his or her professional and ethical duties to the corporation rather than to an officer or director. Most importantly, the rules require an attorney—who is practicing before the Commission and who comes across credible evidence of (i) a material violation of federal or state securities law,

(ii) a material breach of fiduciary duty created by federal or state law, or (iii) "a similar material violation of any . . . federal or state law"—to report that evidence to the top legal officer at the corporation or to that officer and the CEO.[44] Thereafter, if the reporting attorney does not receive an "appropriate response" to the report within a reasonable time, the attorney must report the evidence to the board of directors. The rules also state that, under certain circumstances, the attorney can reveal to the SEC—without the client corporation's consent—confidential information that the attorney reasonably believes necessary to prevent the company from committing a material violation likely to cause substantial financial damage to investors, or necessary to rectify the consequences of such a violation where the attorney's services were used in furtherance of the violation. The rules are complex and appear in Chapter Twenty-Two.

Keep in mind two points as we consider the role of attorneys. First, a corporation might ask an attorney to advise what actions the corporation or its board or officers *must* take in order to comply with laws and rules. Second, a corporation might ask, or an attorney might volunteer, what actions the attorney believes the corporation *should* take even if they are not required. Attorneys may advise on both.

Second, pay attention to the role that lawyers played in the various corporate meltdowns that we study. Consider the practical ability of lawyers to intervene when similar circumstances arise in other companies. Consider as well whether attorneys are likely to play a useful role, taking into account such factors as the degree of expertise attorneys are likely to have in matters like accounting and firm-specific and systemic risk.

INITIAL QUESTIONS ON THE ROLE OF LAWYERS

If you

1. are advising a corporate client, and

2. the board or the top executive asks you what the company must do to comply with a law or other rule of corporate governance, and

3. you not only know the answer to that question but also have a strongly held view of what additional steps the company should take in order that it comply with good governance practice;

should you, as general practice, provide your view on good governance practice in addition to advising on the law or other rule?

Thinking about it generally, what are the advantages of a lawyer who represents the corporation contributing to a conversation between a

---

[44]   17 C.F.R. §§ 230.2(i), 230.3(b).

corporation and its outside auditor on the manner in which to resolve an accounting disagreement between the company and the auditor? What are the disadvantages?

What are the advantages of a lawyer contributing his or her ideas on executive compensation (beyond the legal issues that pay raises) to a compensation committee of a board of directors that is in the process of constructing the next year's pay package for the CEO? What are the disadvantages?

Other outside professionals. Boards of directors interact with outside professionals other than auditors and attorneys. Board compensation committees often employ compensation consultants. We will consider their role in some detail in Chapter Thirteen. For now, note that such consultants often tell the compensation committee of corporation A, which is considering the compensation to pay to A's CEO next year, the amount and composition of compensation being paid to CEOs at companies comparable to A. The reforms require the disclosure of compensation consultants and their role in setting compensation. Reformers have displayed some concern that such consultants may not be independent if, in addition to recommending or evaluating compensation for top executives, the consulting firms provide other services to a company— services for which they are hired by the very top executives on whose compensation the consulting firms advise. SEC regulations adopted in 2009 require, under some circumstances, disclosure of the amount of money paid to a compensation consultant for help on executive pay and the amount paid to the consultant for all other work it performs for the company.

Boards also seek advice from investment bankers. An investment banker is different from a commercial banker. A commercial banker sets up bank accounts for a company and performs other tasks such as arranging money transfers. An investment banker, among other things, helps a company raise money by selling stocks and bonds. An investment banker also helps companies that are trying to sell themselves in whole or in part, or seeking to buy all or part of another company, by placing a value on the company (or part of a company) to be sold or bought. An investment banker may also help market a company that is selling itself, in whole or in part, or, for a company trying to buy business, find a company (or part of a company) to buy.

Investment banking can be very lucrative. For example, if an investment bank is the lead or "managing" underwriter for a stock offering by corporation A, the investment bank will form a syndicate of other investment bankers, and the syndicate members typically will buy the stock from the A, then resell the stock to investors directly or to dealers, who will then resell to investors. The bankers make money by keeping the underwriting profit, which is the difference or "spread" between the price that the investment banks pay the corporation for the stock and the price at which the banks sell the stock to the public. The median "spread" for initial public offerings[45] in each year during the 1990s and 2000 was 7%, and the annual median spread for seasoned stock offerings varied between 5% and 5.489%.[46] Therefore, if a corporation going public sold $50 million in stock, the spread was $3.5 million.

Many investment banking firms employ stock analysts, who make recommendations to institutional investors and retail investors to buy, sell, or hold certain stocks. In the 1990s, the analysts at these firms became involved in helping the firms win lucrative investment banking business, such as winning the role of managing underwriter for the sale of stock.[47] A major set of reforms sought to break the connection between analysts and investment bankers so that the objectivity of the analysts' buy, sell, and hold recommendations would not be compromised by efforts to win investment banking business—in particular, so that an analyst would not explicitly or implicitly agree to recommend that investors buy the stock of company A in order that A direct investment banking business to the analyst's firm.[48]

Assisting on mergers and acquisitions is also very lucrative. The investment bankers advising on such transactions often receive in fees some percentage of the total deal price, with the percentage smaller on very large deals but the absolute amount quite high.[49] This work, too, presents potential conflicts of interest. Since the amount that investment bankers make on offerings and acquisitions is dependent on the offerings and acquisitions closing, the investment bankers may have incentives that bias them towards recommending that deals go forward to conclusion even if some other path might be better for the company they are advising.

---

[45] A company that has been privately held sells its stock to the public—and at the same time starts trading on an exchange—in an "initial public offering."

[46] Dongcheol Kim, et al., *Are Initial Returns and Underwriting Spreads in Equity Issues Complements or Substitutes?*, 39 FIN. MGMT. 1403, 1409 tbl.I. (2010), with the study examining 4,348 seasoned offerings and 4,875 initial public offerings during the period 1980 through 2000 (at 1406, 1409).

[47] The managing role is particularly desirable because it gives a firm a particularly large piece of the spread. *See* 1 LOUIS LOSS, ET AL., FUNDAMENTALS OF SECURITIES REGULATION 107–08 (6th ed. 2011).

[48] *See* William O. Fisher, *Does the Efficient Market Theory Help Us Do Justice in a Time of Madness?*, 54 EMORY L.J. 843, 934–66 (2005).

[49] *See* Anita Raghavan, *Big Deals, Not Such Rich Fees for Bankers*, N.Y. TIMES (Aug. 20, 2014), http://dealbook.nytimes.com/2014/08/20/big-deals-not-such-rich-fees-for-bankers/?_r=1: (reporting that bankers on the $70.6 billion Comcast/Time Warner Cable merger received approximately $139.5 million in fees, reflecting 0.19% of the deal, but that Thomson Reuters said that the average percentage on deals between $1 billion and $5 billion was 0.96% and that deals below $500 million paid bankers 1.2% to 2.5%).

CHAPTER 2

THE PRINCIPAL SOURCES OF CORPORATE GOVERNANCE RULES

■ ■ ■

This chapter discusses the sources of corporate governance rules. It focuses on rules imposed from outside the company rather than rules that the corporation makes for itself (e.g., through its articles of incorporation [or certificate of incorporation as Delaware denominates this document] and its bylaws). These outside sources principally include: (i) corporate law in the state in which the company is incorporated; (ii) federal statutes and related rules, principally federal securities laws and rules adopted by the Securities and Exchange Commission; and (iii) listing standards of the exchange on which the stock of a public corporation trades. After discussing these sources, the chapter briefly considers debt covenants as a constraint on corporate governance and special rules from yet other sources that apply to lawyers and auditors. The chapter ends by considering the relative desirability of state versus national governance regulation.

Where the book addresses a matter in greater detail later, the discussion in this chapter is short and of a summary sort, with the exception of examples to illustrate the depth into which the laws and rules reach. The discussion is longer where the chapter addresses matters that the book does not revisit in detail at some later point. This summary of existing corporate law does not focus on the reforms, but provides a wider view including long-standing law.

A. STATE CORPORATIONS LAW

The internal affairs doctrine. A corporation may incorporate in any state. The law of the state the company chooses governs the company's internal affairs. "Every State in this country has enacted laws regulating corporate governance. . . . [A] corporation—except in the rarest situations—is organized under, and governed by, the law of a single jurisdiction, traditionally the corporate law of the State of its incorporation."[1]

---

[1]   *CTS Corp. v. Dynamics Corp. of Am.*, 481 U.S. 69, 89–90 (1987).

We will study Delaware law.[2] This book summarizes mandatory and default provisions of Delaware law. Except in a few instances, the book will not stop to describe when or how a corporation can vary a default rule. The summary here is selective. Delaware corporate law encompasses a vast caselaw that the book does not purport to summarize.

State corporations law and shareholders. Stockholders of Delaware corporations elect the board of directors at annual shareholders meetings.[3] Stockholders can, by vote, remove directors with or without cause.[4] With some exceptions, shareholders vote on mergers, but only after the board agrees to the merger.[5] Shareholders also vote on transactions in which the company sells "all or substantially all of its property and assets," but the statute contemplates that the board of directors will determine that the sale is "expedient and for the best interest of the corporation" before the shareholder vote.[6] The shareholders vote on increases in the number of shares of stock that the corporation is authorized to issue, by amending the certificate of incorporation; but the shareholder vote comes after the board approves the amendment.[7] Dissolution of the corporation requires a shareholder vote, but again that vote comes only after board action.[8]

Stockholders have the right, subject to some limitations, to inspect the corporation's books and records.[9] Stockholders can sue officers and directors for breach of officer and director duties owed to the corporation, but since such a claim belongs to the corporation and the board manages the company, a shareholder bringing such a suit as a derivative action must either make a demand on the board that the company bring the suit itself, or allege specific facts showing that making such a demand would be futile.[10]

---

[2]   The laws of different states differ. Thus, more than 30 states have adopted all or substantially all of the Model Business Corporation Act ("MBCA"). COMMITTEE LAWS COMMITTEE OF THE BUSINESS LAW SECTION, AMERICAN BAR ASSOCIATION, MODEL BUSINESS CORPORATION ACT ANNOTATED xii (4th ed. rev. 2013). The MBCA differs from the Delaware General Corporation Law ("Del.") on some of the very matters discussed in the text.

[3]   Del. § 211(b).

[4]   Del. § 141(k).

[5]   Del. § 251.

[6]   Del. § 271(a).

[7]   Del. § 242(a)(3), (b)(1)–(2). Once the shares are authorized, the shareholders play no direct role, under Delaware law, in the issuance of the shares, as the board of directors—without shareholder action—can issue shares up to the full number that are authorized but unissued. Del. § 161. It is the board that determines that the value paid for the stock is satisfactory. Del. §§ 152, 153(a).

[8]   Del. § 275(a), (b).

[9]   Del. § 220(b).

[10]   The demand requirement is located in subpart (a) of Delaware Court of Chancery Rule 23.1, which provides:

> In a derivative action brought by one or more shareholders or members to enforce a right of a corporation or of an unincorporated association, the corporation or association having failed to enforce a right which may properly be asserted by it, the complaint shall allege

As you can see from these examples, and stating it very generally, shareholders become directly involved when a corporate action will work a fundamental change in the company or shareholders sue in a derivative action. But when there is a fundamental change, the board initiates and the shareholders vote later. And a shareholder can sue derivatively only if the board either will not initiate the suit, or is so unlikely to do so that no request to the board need precede a shareholder action.

An important exception to shareholder deference to the board is that the shareholders elect the board and do so without the board first making a determination that such an election should occur.

Delaware law leans towards shareholder primacy in the sense that the corporation should be run for the benefit of the shareholders (though not, as we have just seen, in the sense that the shareholders control corporate actions in detail). In this course, we will not study the details of law setting out board fiduciary duties during mergers and acquisitions. But a few snippets from cases in that setting provide insight into the Delaware view on the competition between shareholder primacy and stakeholder theory.

In *Unocal Corp. v. Mesa Petroleum Co.*,[11] the Delaware Supreme Court set out the test by which it evaluates board actions to defend against unwanted takeover attempts. The decision included this passage, stating that a board might justify a defense in part on the basis that it would benefit corporate constituencies other than shareholders:

> If a defensive measure is to come within the ambit of the business judgment rule, it must be reasonable in relation to the threat posed. This entails an analysis by the directors of the nature of

---

that the plaintiff was a shareholder or member at the time of the transaction of which the plaintiff complains or that the plaintiff's share or membership thereafter devolved on the plaintiff by operation of law. The complaint shall also allege with particularity the efforts, if any, made by the plaintiff to obtain the action the plaintiff desires from the directors or comparable authority and the reasons for the plaintiff's failure to obtain the action or for not making the effort.

But the demand requirement is substantive law:

In derivative litigation, the demand requirement is a recognition of the fundamental statutory precept that section 141(a) vests boards of directors with the power to manage the business and affairs of corporations. [FN18. *Aronson v. Lewis*, 473 A.2d 805, 812 (Del. 1984); *see also* DEL. CODE ANN. tit. 8, § 141(a) ("the business and affairs of every corporation organized under this chapter shall be managed by or under the direction of a board of directors").] The demand requirement of Rule 23.1 is a "substantive right designed to give a corporation the opportunity to rectify an alleged wrong without litigation, and to control any litigation which does arise." [FN19. *Aronson v. Lewis*, 473 A.2d at 809. *See also Brehm v. Eisner*, 746 A.2d 244, 254–55 (Del. 2000); *Grimes v. Donald*, 673 A.2d 1207, 1216–17 (Del. 1996).] Under Delaware law, a derivative plaintiff must give the board of directors the opportunity to exercise that substantive right or demonstrate that the board is incapable of evaluating the demand in a disinterested and independent manner, *i.e.*, because that demand would be futile, it is excused.

Braddock v. Zimmerman, 906 A.2d 776, 784 (Del. 2006).

[11]   493 A.2d 946 (Del. 1985).

the takeover bid and its effect on the corporate enterprise. Examples of such concerns may include: inadequacy of the price offered, nature and timing of the offer, questions of illegality, the impact on "constituencies" other than shareholders (*i.e.*, creditors, customers, employees, and perhaps even the community generally), the risk of nonconsummation, and the quality of securities being offered in the exchange. *See* Lipton and Brownstein, *Takeover Responses and Directors' Responsibilities: An Update*, p. 7, ABA National Institute on the Dynamics of Corporate Control (December 8, 1983). While not a controlling factor, it also seems to us that a board may reasonably consider the basic stockholder interests at stake. . . .[12]

In a later decision, the court backtracked, stating that (i) even in evaluating a takeover defense, other stakeholder interests can be considered only to the extent that furthering those interests benefits the shareholders; and (ii) in the context of simply selling the company, a board must concentrate solely on securing the best price for the stockholders:

The Revlon board argued that it acted in good faith in protecting the noteholders because *Unocal* permits consideration of other corporate constituencies. Although such considerations may be permissible, there are fundamental limitations upon that prerogative. A board may have regard for various constituencies in discharging its responsibilities, provided there are rationally related benefits accruing to the stockholders. *Unocal*, 493 A.2d at 955. However, such concern for non-stockholder interests is inappropriate when an auction among active bidders is in progress, and the object no longer is to protect or maintain the corporate enterprise but to sell it to the highest bidder.[13]

One other decision deserves quotation. In this opinion, the Delaware court held that when a board is faced with alternatives, it can choose one that does not produce the highest immediate return to shareholders. A board can, for example, reject a bid for the company at a high premium over the current trading price for the company's stock on the basis that an alternative course accords with a business strategy that, in the board's view, will yield greater long-term benefits. In the case producing the passage below, the board of Time Incorporated fought off an all-cash offer from Paramount Communications, Inc., at a near 59% premium over the market price of Time stock in order to pursue a merger with Warner Communications, Inc. Here is part of what the Delaware Supreme Court

---

[12]   *Id.* at 955–56. It is interesting that the court cites Mr. Lipton as its one source, not any academic.

[13]   *Revlon, Inc. v. MacAndrews & Forbes Holdings, Inc.*, 506 A.2d 173, 182 (Del. 1986).

wrote in affirming a trial court decision that the Time Board did not violate its fiduciary duties:

> [A]bsent a limited set of circumstances as defined under *Revlon* [as when a board has put a company up for immediate sale], a board of directors, while always required to act in an informed manner, is not under any *per se* duty to maximize shareholder value in the short term, even in the context of a takeover.[14]

* * *

> One concern was that Time shareholders might elect to tender into Paramount's cash offer in ignorance or a mistaken belief of the strategic benefit which a business combination with Warner might produce.[15]

* * *

> Paramount argues that, assuming its tender offer posed a threat, Time's response was unreasonable in precluding Time's shareholders from accepting the tender offer or receiving a control premium in the immediately foreseeable future. Once again, the contention stems, we believe, from a fundamental misunderstanding of where the power of corporate governance lies. Delaware law confers the management of the corporate enterprise to the stockholders' duly elected board representatives. 8 Del.C. § 141(a). The fiduciary duty to manage a corporate enterprise includes the selection of a time frame for achievement of corporate goals. That duty may not be delegated to the stockholders. [*Smith v. Van Gorkom*, 488 A.2d 858, 873 (Del. 1985)]. Directors are not obliged to abandon a deliberately conceived corporate plan for a short-term shareholder profit unless there is clearly no basis to sustain the corporate strategy. *See, e.g., Revlon*, 506 A.2d 173.[16]

Taken together, these passages suggest a Delaware view that corporations should be run for the economic benefit of the shareholders but that the shareholders might not know what is really in their best economic interest. So the board can make decisions that deprive the shareholders of the greatest immediate profit and take into account other stakeholder interests; provided that in the end, the board is trying to produce the best long-term shareholder return. That view fits in well with the many statutory sections giving shareholders power in making fundamental changes only after the board has made an initial decision.

---

[14]   *Paramount Communications, Inc. v. Time, Inc.*, 571 A.2d 1140, 1150 (Del. 1989) (footnote omitted).

[15]   *Id.* at 1153.

[16]   *Id.* at 1154.

If the shareholders do not like what the directors are doing as the directors exercise the kind of benign dictatorial power that Delaware law confers upon them, the shareholders can vote the directors out.

QUESTION ON THE SHAREHOLDER ROLE

If the corporation exists for the economic benefit of the shareholders, why give the board of directors the freedom to take actions that the shareholders do not want?

State corporations law and boards: overview. Delaware gives corporations near total freedom in organizing boards of directors, and gives boards near total freedom in how they operate. Delaware imposes fiduciary duties on directors, but includes a variety of mechanisms that effectively shield directors from having to pay personally for making poor business decisions that turn out to be unprofitable.

Boards of directors: organization and operation left to each corporation. The Delaware statute says very little about the composition and operation of the board. It provides that "[t]he business and affairs of every corporation organized under this chapter shall be managed by or under the direction of a board of directors."[17] A board must have "1 or more members, each of whom shall be a natural person," but the Delaware statute does not otherwise establish qualifications for board members and expressly states that "[d]irectors need not be stockholders."[18] Delaware also states, however, that "[t]he certificate of incorporation or bylaws may prescribe other qualifications for directors."[19]

The statute expressly reserves certain tasks for the board, such as (i) initiating (a) mergers, (b) changes in the certificate of incorporation, and (c) the sale of all or substantially all of the corporation's assets; and (ii) issuance of stock. Caselaw also makes clear that the board has the power to determine in its discretion whether to declare dividends and, if so, in what amount.[20]

The statute provides that a board "may designate 1 or more committees, each committee to consist of 1 or more of the directors of the corporation" and that "[a]ny such committee . . . shall have and may exercise all the powers and authority of the board of directors in the

---

[17]   Del. § 141(a).
[18]   Del. § 141(b).
[19]   *Id.*
[20]   *See, e.g., Gabelli & Co., Inc. v. Liggett Group, Inc.,* 479 A.2d 276, 280 (Del. 1984).

management of the business and affairs of the corporation" as shall be set out "in the resolution of the board of directors, or in the bylaws of the corporation."[21] But the statute does not require a board to establish any standing committees. The statute also does not set the number of times a board must meet during a year or prescribe the agenda for board meetings or assign tasks to any board committee.

QUESTIONS ON THE FREE-FORM BOARD PROVISIONS OF THE DELAWARE LAW

What are the advantages offered by the freedom that Delaware law provides to companies in organizing and operating their boards?

What are the disadvantages of such freedom?

Procedures for board meetings, including telephone participation in meetings and unanimous consent without meetings. The Delaware statute provides that "[a] majority of the total number of directors shall constitute a quorum" and that "[t]he vote of a majority of the directors present at a meeting at which a quorum is present shall be the act of the board of directors."[22]

Two other statutorily permitted protocols will interest us. First, "any action required or permitted to be taken at any meeting of the board of directors or of any committee thereof may be taken without a meeting if all members of the board or committee, as the case may be, consent thereto in writing, or by electronic transmission and the writing or writings or electronic transmission or transmissions are filed with the minutes of proceedings of the board, or committee."[23] This is action by unanimous written consent. Second, "members of the board of directors of any corporation, or any committee designated by the board, may participate in a meeting of such board, or committee by means of conference telephone or other communications equipment by means of which all persons participating in the meeting can hear each other, and participation in a meeting pursuant to this subsection shall constitute presence in person at the meeting."[24]

---

[21]   Del. § 141(c)(2).

[22]   Del. § 141(b).

[23]   Del. § 141(f).

[24]   Del. § 141(i).

QUESTIONS ON UNANIMOUS CONSENT AND TELEPHONE BOARD MEETINGS

What are the disadvantages of board action by unanimous written consent? What are the disadvantages of director participation in board meetings via telephone?

How should boards decide what actions to take by unanimous consent?

Should boards have rules to determine which matters can be discussed and decided in telephone conference calls, and which matters cannot?

The two fiduciary duties that directors owe to their corporation: care and loyalty. By court decisions rather than by statute, boards of companies incorporated in Delaware owe two general duties to their corporations: the duty of care and the duty of loyalty.[25] In broad brush, "[t]he duty of care requires that directors 'use that amount of care which ordinarily careful and prudent men [and women] would use in similar circumstances.' "[26] As we will see, when the duty of care is viewed in conjunction with the business judgment rule, the directors for all practical purposes satisfy the duty by the *process* that they follow—gathering and considering information—with the *substance* of their decisions largely beyond the reach of judicial review.

"The duty of loyalty 'in essence, mandates that the best interest of the corporation and its shareholders take[ ] precedence over any interest possessed by a director, officer or controlling shareholder and not shared by the stockholders generally.' "[27] It "embodies not only an affirmative duty to protect the interests of the corporation, but also an obligation to refrain from conduct that would injure the corporation and its stockholders or deprive them of profit or advantage."[28] This is the duty that, among other things, (i) requires that directors deal with the corporation fairly, and charge or pay a fair price, when they conduct business with the corporation for their own account; (ii) prevents directors from taking corporate opportunities for their own benefit, absent approval by the company; (iii) demands that the directors disclose all material facts to shareholders when

---

[25]   Again, we will mostly concern ourselves with these duties outside the context of mergers and acquisitions. In that context, the rules—otherwise mostly simple—become quite complex, and the two duties interact.

[26]   EDWARD P. WELCH, ET AL., FOLK ON THE DELAWARE GENERAL CORPORATION LAW (FUNDAMENTALS) § 141.02[A][1] at GCL-136 (quoting *In re Walt Disney Co. Derivative Litig.*, 907 A.2d 693, 749 (Del. Ch. 2005), *aff'd*, 906 A.2d 27 (Del. 2006)) (2016 ed.) [WELCH, FOLK FUNDAMENTALS].

[27]   *Id.* § 141.02[A][2] at GCL-137 (quoting *In re Walt Disney Co. Derivative Litig.*, 907 A.2d 693, 751 (Del. Ch. 2005), *aff'd*, 906 A.2d 27 (Del. 2006) (in turn quoting *Cede & Co. v. Technicolor, Inc.* 634 A.2d 345, 361 (Del. 1993) (second set of internal quotation marks omitted)).

[28]   *Id.* § 141.02[A][2] at GCL-137.

they urge shareholders to vote as the directors recommend and otherwise to be truthful in communicating with shareholders;[29] and (iv) requires that directors (a) make at least some effort to determine that management has in place systems to provide information as to whether their company is complying with law and accounting rules and (b) pursue inquiries when the directors are aware of "red flags" suggesting that the company may not be complying.[30] This last is sometimes called the duty to monitor or referred

---

[29] "The directors of a Delaware corporation are required to disclose fully and fairly all material information within the board's control when it seeks shareholder action," "balanced against [the board's] concomitant duty to protect the corporate enterprise, in particular, by keeping certain financial information confidential." *Malone v. Brincat*, 722 A.2d 5, 12 (Del. 1998) (citations omitted).

> When the board communicates with shareholders in any context—whether seeking shareholder action or not—the board cannot lie. "When the directors are not seeking shareholder action, but are deliberately misinforming shareholders about the business of the corporation, either directly or by a public statement, there is a violation of fiduciary duty." *Id.* at 14.

> Delaware directors disseminate information in at least three contexts: public statements made to the market, including shareholders; statements informing shareholders about the affairs of the corporation without a request for shareholder action; and, statements to shareholders in conjunction with a request for shareholder action. Inaccurate information in these contexts may be the result of a violation of the fiduciary duties of care [or] loyalty. . . .

Id. at 11; *but see Jackson Nat'l Life Ins. Co. v. Kennedy*, 741 A.2d 377, 388–90 (Del. Ch. 1999) (characterizing the duty to be truthful as a part of the duty of loyalty).

Neither Delaware statutes nor Delaware decisions require the elaborate and specific disclosures demanded of public companies by the federal securities laws and regulations, which are discussed below.

[30] The Delaware Supreme Court has held that a board's obligation to see that management establishes information systems to assure directors that the corporation is complying with law falls under the duty of loyalty rather than the duty of care (*Stone v. Ritter*, 911 A.2d 362, 369–70 (2006)), but sets a low bar for satisfying this obligation:

> We hold that . . . the necessary conditions predicate for director oversight liability [are]: (a) the directors utterly failed to implement any reporting or information system or controls; *or* (b) having implemented such a system or controls, consciously failed to monitor or oversee its operations thus disabling themselves from being informed of risks or problems requiring their attention. In either case, imposition of liability requires a showing that the directors knew that they were not discharging their fiduciary obligations. Where directors fail to act in the face of a known duty to act, thereby demonstrating a conscious disregard for their responsibilities, they breach their duty of loyalty by failing to discharge that fiduciary obligation in good faith.

Id. at 370 (footnotes omitted) (affirming dismissal of derivative complaint against directors of bank holding company based on bank failure to file Suspicious Activity Reports required by the federal law; noting trial court determination that "plaintiffs did not plead the existence of 'red flags'— 'facts showing that the board ever was aware that AmSouth's internal controls were inadequate, that these inadequacies would result in illegal activity, and that the board chose to do nothing about problems it allegedly knew existed.' " (*id.*)).

Rich v. Yu Kwai Chong, 66 A.3d 963 (Del. Ch. 2013) provides an example of conduct violating this undemanding standard:

> An analysis of the dates of Fuqi's disclosures demonstrates that it is reasonable, based on the facts pled, to infer that the directors knew that the internal controls were inadequate and failed to act in the face of a known duty. Fuqi announced to stockholders that it was restating its 2009 financial statements and investigating possible "material weaknesses" in its controls in March 2010. [The plaintiff] sent the Demand Letter in July 2010, and the board appointed the Special Committee in October 2010. In March 2011, Fuqi announced that the cash transfer transactions [that were inadequately documented] had occurred between September 2009 and November 2010. These dates indicate that (1)

to as the board's oversight responsibility. This duty imposes a very loose control on governance, with directors protected against liability for violating oversight obligations by the business judgment rule.[31]

Delaware law shields directors, in a number of ways, from having to pay personally for breach of the duty of care.

Protections for boards against suits alleging breach of the duty of care: reports from board committees, management, and experts. "A member of the board of directors, or a member of any committee designated by the board of directors, shall, in the performance of such member's duties, be fully protected in relying in good faith upon the records of the corporation and upon such information, opinions, reports or statements presented to the corporation by any of the corporation's officers or employees, or committees of the board of directors, or by any other person as to matters the member reasonably believes are within such other person's professional or expert competence and who has been selected with reasonable care by or on behalf of the corporation."[32] It is hard to overstate the protection that this language supplies when the board acts on a report that management provides or when a board—faced with a potentially controversial decision—retains an outside "expert."

Fuqi's directors knew that there were material weaknesses in Fuqi's internal controls at the latest in March of 2010; (2) [the plaintiff's] stockholder demand in July 2010 (as well as the myriad securities litigation suits filed) put the directors on notice that the stockholders would carefully scrutinize what was going on at Fuqi; (3) Fuqi had purportedly already begun to "act" on [the plaintiff's] demand by November 2010; and (4) despite their knowledge of the weaknesses in Fuqi's internal controls, the directors allowed $130 million in cash to be transferred out of the company, some as late as November 2010. . . . [T]hese facts [derive] directly from Fuqi's public disclosures. Facially, these disclosures are enough to allow me to reasonably infer scienter on the part of the Defendants.

That these cash transfers were not discovered until March of 2011, when Fuqi's auditor discovered them, reinforces the inference that the internal controls were (and possibly still are) grossly inadequate. That Chong was able to transfer $130 million out of the company's coffers, without the directors knowing about it for over a year, strains credulity. Either the directors knew about the cash transfers and were complicit, or they had zero controls in place and did not know about them. If the directors had even the barest framework of appropriate controls in place, they would have prevented the cash transfers.

When faced with knowledge that the company controls are inadequate, the directors must act, i.e., they must prevent further wrongdoing from occurring. A conscious failure to act, in the face of a known duty, is a breach of the duty of loyalty. At the very least, it is inferable that even if the Defendants were not complicit in these money transfers, they were aware of the pervasive, fundamental weaknesses in Fuqi's controls and knowingly failed to stop further problems from occurring. This knowing failure, as alleged by the Plaintiff, states a claim for breach of the duty of good faith. . . .

Id. at 984–85.

[31]   See the *Citigroup* decision, *infra* note 36.

[32]   Del. § 141(e).

QUESTIONS ON THE PROTECTION PROVIDED BY
MANAGEMENT REPORTS AND OUTSIDE EXPERTS

Under what circumstances should reports by management or an expert provide no protection to directors?

Should the protection be conditioned on the board's intelligent use of management or experts to provide information and advice—e.g., by asking the right questions?

———————

Protections for boards against suits alleging breach of the duty of care: the business judgment rule. Here is an oft-quoted summary of the business judgment rule, as embodied in Delaware law:

> The business judgment rule is an acknowledgment of the managerial prerogatives of Delaware directors under Section 141(a). It is a presumption that in making a business decision the directors of a corporation acted on an informed basis, in good faith and in the honest belief that the action taken was in the best interests of the company. Absent an abuse of discretion, that judgment will be respected by the courts. The burden is on the party challenging the decision to establish facts rebutting the presumption. . . .

> First, its protections can only be claimed by disinterested directors whose conduct otherwise meets the tests of business judgment. From the standpoint of interest, this means that directors can neither appear on both sides of a transaction nor expect to derive any personal financial benefit from it in the sense of self-dealing, as opposed to a benefit which devolves upon the corporation or all stockholders generally. Thus, if such director interest is present, and the transaction is not approved by a majority consisting of the disinterested directors, then the business judgment rule has no application. . . .

> Second, to invoke the rule's protection directors have a duty to inform themselves, prior to making a business decision, of all material information reasonably available to them. Having become so informed, they must then act with requisite care in the discharge of their duties. While the Delaware cases use a variety of terms to describe the applicable standard of care, our analysis satisfies us that under the business judgment rule director liability is predicated upon concepts of gross negligence.

> However, it should be noted that the business judgment rule operates only in the context of director action. Technically speaking, it has no role where directors have either abdicated

their functions, or absent a conscious decision, failed to act. But it also follows that under applicable principles, a conscious decision to refrain from acting may nonetheless be a valid exercise of business judgment and enjoy the protections of the rule.[33]

If the board is grossly negligent in assembling the information it considers before making a decision or in failing to devote sufficient time to considering the information, a court will find that directors have violated their duty of care by the decision. For example, in *Smith v. Van Gorkom*,[34] the court found that a board violated its duty of care when it agreed to the sale of the entire company for $55/share at a two-hour meeting—(i) without having before it (a) any study of the value of the corporation or (b) any document supporting the price; (ii) without any pre-meeting notification to most of the directors that the board would be considering such a sale; and (iii) without any explanation of how the $55/share figure was reached.

Van Gorkom is one of the rare examples of a court holding that directors violated their duty of care, taking account of the business judgment rule. Provided that a board adheres to a reasonable process in reaching its decisions (particularly by gathering and considering information), acts in good faith, and is disinterested, the business judgment rule protects the board from a claim that it breached its duty of care:

> What should be understood, but may not widely be understood by courts or commentators who are not often required to face such questions, is that compliance with a director's duty of care can never appropriately be judicially determined by reference to *the content of the board decision* that leads to a corporate loss, apart from consideration of the good faith *or* rationality of the process employed. That is, whether a judge or jury considering the matter after the fact, believes a decision substantively wrong, or degrees of wrong extending through "stupid" to "egregious" or "irrational", provides no ground for director liability, so long as the court determines that the *process* employed was either rational or employed in *a good faith* effort to advance corporate interests. To employ a different rule—one that permitted an "objective" evaluation of the decision—would expose directors to substantive second guessing by ill-equipped judges or juries, which would, in the long-run, be injurious to investor interests. Thus, the business

---

[33]   *Aronson v. Lewis*, 473 A.2d 805, 812–13 (Del. 1984) (citations and footnotes omitted), *overruled on other grounds by Brehm v. Eisner*, 746 A.2d 244, 253–54 (Del. 2000).

[34]   488 A.2d 858 (Del. 1985), *overruled on a matter unrelated to the text by Gantler v. Stephens*, 965 A.2d 695, 713 n.54 (Del. 2009).

judgment rule is *process oriented* and informed by a deep respect for all *good faith* board decisions.[35]

Assuming that a board has assembled and considered relevant information, a Delaware court will find a breach of the duty of care only in the rare instance in which the court cannot attribute the board's decision to *any* rational business purpose whatsoever.[36]

Protections for boards against suits alleging breach of the duty of care: 102(b)(7) provisions in certificates of incorporation. Delaware law permits, but does not require, a corporation to include in its certificate of incorporation "[a] provision eliminating or limiting the personal liability of a director to the corporation or its stockholders for monetary damages for breach of fiduciary duty as a director, provided that such provision shall not eliminate or limit the liability of a director: (i) for any breach of the

---

[35]   *In re Caremark Intern. Inc. Derivative Litig.*, 698 A.2d 959, 967–68 (Del. Ch. 1996) (some emphasis added).

[36]   *See, e.g., Binks v. DSL.net, Inc.*, C.A. No. 2823-VCN, 2010 WL 1713629, at *5 (Del. Ch. Apr. 29, 2010).

As an example of the Delaware deference to director work, consider *In re Citigroup Inc. Shareholder Derivative Litig.*, 964 A.2d 106 (Del. Ch. 2009). Citi shareholders brought the suit, contending among other things, that Citi's Board had violated its oversight duty to monitor and respond to "red flags" and that Citi was overexposed to risks by its direct and indirect ownership of subprime-mortgage-related assets. *Id.* at 112–14, 126–28. Although Delaware doctrinally categorizes oversight responsibilities as part of the duty of loyalty, *supra* note 30, the court turned to the business judgment rule, *Citi* at 126. In holding that the plaintiffs had failed to plead facts excusing a demand on the board, *supra* note 10, on the basis that the majority of directors faced a substantial likelihood of personal liability on the claim, *Citi* at 127, the court wrote:

> To recognize such claims under a theory of director oversight liability would undermine the long established protections of the business judgment rule. It is well established that the mere fact that a company takes on business risk and suffers losses—even catastrophic losses—does not evidence misconduct, and without more, is not a basis for personal director liability. That there were signs in the market that reflected worsening conditions and suggested that conditions may deteriorate even further is not an invitation for this Court to disregard the presumptions of the business judgment rule and conclude that the directors are liable because they did not properly evaluate business risk. What plaintiffs are asking the Court to conclude from the presence of these "red flags" is that the directors failed to see the extent of Citigroup's business risk and therefore made a "wrong" business decision by allowing Citigroup to be exposed to the subprime mortgage market.

Id. at 130 (footnote omitted).

> Citigroup was in the business of taking on and managing investment and other business risks. To impose oversight liability on directors for failure to monitor "excessive" risk would involve courts in conducting hindsight evaluations of decisions at the heart of the business judgment of directors. Oversight duties under Delaware law are not designed to subject directors, even expert directors, to *personal liability* for failure to predict the future and to properly evaluate business risk.

Id. at 131 (footnote omitted; emphasis in original).

See also In re the Goldman Sachs Group, Inc. Shareholder Litig., Civil Action No. 5215-VCG, 2011 WL 4826104 (Del. Ch. Oct. 12, 2011) (dismissing derivative claim against directors for allegedly approving a compensation structure that encouraged excessive risk-taking; "this Court has not definitively stated whether a board's *Caremark* duties include a duty to monitor business risk" (at *21); "If an actionable duty to monitor business risk exists, it cannot encompass any substantive evaluation by a court of a board's determination of the appropriate amount of risk. Such decisions plainly involve business judgment" (at *22)).

director's duty of loyalty to the corporation or its stockholders; (ii) for acts or omissions not in good faith or which involve intentional misconduct or a knowing violation of law; (iii) under § 174 of this title [having to do with unlawful payment of dividends or unlawful stock repurchases or redemptions]; or (iv) for any transaction from which the director derived an improper personal benefit."[37]

Protections for boards against suits alleging breach of the duty of care: indemnification and insurance. Section 145(c) of the Delaware General Corporation Law, cross-referencing 145(a), requires corporations to indemnify present and former directors who are "successful on the merits or otherwise in defense of any action" brought or threatened against them "by reason of the fact that the person is or was a director," with the indemnity payments covering "expenses (including attorneys' fees) . . . actually and reasonably incurred by such person. . . ." This mandatory indemnification extends both to actions brought by those outside the corporation (including administrative and criminal cases) and by suits brought by or on behalf of the corporation itself.

Section 145(a) also permits, but does not require, a corporation to indemnify a director against defense costs, judgments, settlements, and fines in suits resulting from director service—other than suits brought by or on behalf of the corporation—even if the director loses, provided that the director "acted in good faith and in a manner the person reasonably believed to be in or not opposed to the best interests of the corporation, and, with respect to any criminal action or proceeding, had no reasonable cause to believe [that] the . . . conduct was unlawful." Section 145(b) permits, but does not require, a corporation to indemnify a current or former director against defense costs of and settlements of claims made by or on behalf of the corporation, provided that the director "acted in good faith and in a manner [he or she] reasonably believed to be in or not opposed to the best interests of the corporation."[38] Indemnification may include payment of defense fees and costs for current directors "in advance of the final disposition of such action, suit or proceeding upon receipt of an undertaking by or on behalf of such director or officer to repay such amount if it shall ultimately be determined that such person is not entitled to be

---

[37]   Del. § 102(b)(7).

[38]   In the case of an action brought by or on behalf of the corporation,

no indemnification shall be made in respect of any claim, issue or matter as to which such person shall have been adjudged to be liable to the corporation unless and only to the extent that the Court of Chancery or the court in which such action or suit was brought shall determine upon application that, despite the adjudication of liability but in view of all the circumstances of the case, such person is fairly and reasonably entitled to indemnity for such expenses which the Court of Chancery or such other court shall deem proper.

Del. § 145(b).

indemnified by the corporation as authorized in this section."[39] For former directors, fees and costs "may be paid [in advance of final disposition] upon such terms and conditions, if any, as the corporation deems appropriate."[40]

A corporation is permitted, but not required, to "purchase and maintain insurance on behalf of any person who is or was a director . . . against any liability asserted against such person and incurred by such person in any such capacity, or arising out of such person's status as such, whether or not the corporation would have the power to indemnify such person against such liability under" section 145.[41] Virtually all public corporations purchase insurance for their directors, with the insurance effectively covering both defense costs and settlement costs.

Protections for boards are effective. Taken together, the various protections radically reduce the probability that an outside director—i.e., one who was not also an officer of the corporation at the time of the alleged wrongdoing—will have to pay out of his or her pocket in a private lawsuit charging a breach of fiduciary duty or a securities law violation, unless the director is found to have personally profited from the breach or violation.

QUESTIONS ON DIRECTOR PROTECTIONS OVERALL

What valid purposes do the many protections for directors serve?

How could the protections hurt director performance?

How could we tell whether the protections are on balance helpful or harmful?

State corporations law and officers: overview. Delaware law gives each corporation a relatively free hand in determining what officers it will have and their duties. The corporate law imposes fiduciary duties on officers, as on directors. The protections that officers have from personally paying for making bad business decisions are not as robust as for directors.

Officers: number, titles, and duties left to each corporation. Delaware law does not require any particular set of officers except for such matters as signing stock certificates, providing in Section 142(a) that "[e]very corporation organized under this chapter shall have such officers with such

---

[39]   Del. § 145(e). Advancement of fees and costs is often critical, as the expense of defending against a breach of fiduciary duty suit, or a securities suit, can easily run into the hundreds of thousands of dollars. Without the advancement of fees by the corporation pursuant to an indemnity obligation, or payment of the fees by an insurance carrier, the defendant may have no realistic option but to settle.

[40]   *Id.*

[41]   Del. § 145(g).

titles and duties as shall be stated in the bylaws or in a resolution of the board of directors which is not inconsistent with the bylaws. . . ."[42] The corporate statute does not define the duties of the officers, with the exception that "[o]ne of the officers shall have the duty to record the proceedings of the meetings of the stockholders and directors in a book to be kept for that purpose."[43]

Officers' duties of care and loyalty. "[O]fficers of Delaware corporations, like directors, owe fiduciary duties of care and loyalty" to the company.[44]

Protections for officers. It is unclear whether, in Delaware, the business judgment rule protects officers as well as directors.[45]

Section 102(b)(7), which permits but does not require corporations to include in certificates of incorporation provisions relieving *directors* of monetary liability for breaches of the duty of care taken in good faith, does not authorize such provisions applying to officers.

The mandatory subpart and the other permissive subparts of Section 145—regarding indemnification and insurance—apply to officers to the same extent as directors.

State corporations law and outside professionals. Delaware corporate law does not specifically regulate advisers such as attorneys, accountants auditing a corporation's financial statements, and investment bankers,

---

[42]   The statute goes on to require that each corporation have officers sufficient to permit the company to comply with: (i) section 103(a)(2), which governs documents that a corporation files with the Secretary of State and permits the filing of a document signed by "any authorized officer" or, if there are no such officers, by "a majority of the directors or by such directors as may be designated by the board"; and (ii) section 158, which governs stock certificates and permits a stockholder to insist on a certificate signed by (a) the board chair, board vice-chair, president or vice president and (b) the "treasurer or an assistant treasurer, or the secretary or an assistant secretary."

[43]   Del. § 142(a).

[44]   WELCH, FOLK FUNDAMENTALS § 142.06 at GCL-412, *supra* note 26 (quoting *Gantler v. Stephens*, 965 A.2d 695, 708–09 (Del. 2009) (internal quotation marks omitted).

[45]   *Compare* Lyman P. Q. Johnson, *Corporate Officers and the Business Judgment Rule*, 60 BUS. LAW. 439 (2005) (arguing that the law is unclear as to whether the rule applies to officers and that the rule should not apply to officers; discussing Delaware law treatises and cases at 441–47), *with* Lawrence A. Hamermesh & Gilchrist Sparks III, *Corporate Officers and the Business Judgment Rule: A Reply to Professor Johnson*, 60 BUS. LAW. 865 (2005) (arguing that the rule does, and should, apply to officers but "acknowledg[ing] . . . that the Delaware Supreme Court has not definitely weighed in on the debate" (at 870)). A Delaware Vice Chancellor and a Delaware Superior Court judge in 2008 and 2009, respectively, stated that the protection extended to officers. *Freibott v. Miller*, C.A. No. S08C-11-025-RFS, 2009 WL 1526912, at *2 (Del. Super. Ct. June 2, 2009) ("the business judgment rule applies to officers, as well as directors"); *Underbrink v. Warrior Energy Services Corp.*, Civil Action No. 2982-VCP, 2008 WL 2262316, at *10 (Del. Ch. May 30, 2008) ("Officers and directors are protected by the business judgment rule"). But another Vice Chancellor appeared to treat the issue as open in 2010—referring to the two articles cited in this note. *Hampshire Group, Ltd. v. Kuttner*, C.A. No. 3607-VCS, 2010 WL 2739995, at *11 n.77 (Del. Ch. July 12, 2010). So did an even more recent lower court decision. *Chen v. Howard-Anderson*, 87 A.3d 648, 666 n.2 (Del. Ch. 2014).

although some decisions address the actions of such professionals in particular settings.[46]

B.   FEDERAL LAW, PRINCIPALLY SECURITIES LAW

Even before the passage of the Sarbanes-Oxley Act of 2002 ("SOX"),[47] the federal securities statutes contained corporate governance prescriptions. Since SOX, federal law—including particularly federal securities law—contains even more corporate governance rules. As with Delaware law, the summary below sets out selectively federal securities laws—and some other federal law—that affect corporate governance. We will study some of them—especially those in SOX—more extensively later in the book.

Two federal securities laws will concern us most: the Securities Act of 1933 (the "Securities Act" or the "33 Act") and the Securities Exchange Act of 1934 (the "Exchange Act" or the "34 Act").[48] The Securities Exchange Commission (the "SEC" or "Commission") issues regulations under each of these statues.[49]

As you read the statutes and SEC rules, bear in mind that the public company issuing stock is often called "the registrant" (because its stock is registered under the 34 Act) or "the issuer" (because it issued the stock).

---

[46]   *See, e.g., In re Rural Metro Corp. Stockholders Litig.*, 88 A.3d 54, 96–109 (Del. Ch. 2014) (investment bankers aided and abetted breach of fiduciary duty by directors in sale of corporation).

[47]   The Sarbanes-Oxley Act of 2002, Pub. L. No. 107-204, 116 Stat. 745 (2002).

[48]   These acts are codified in a strange way. The first section of the 33 Act appears at 15 U.S.C. § 77a. The "a" in the citation has no parentheses around it. The second section of the 33 Act is at 15 U.S.C. § 77b. It has subparts that are designated by letters that do have parentheses around them, like § 77b(a).

The 34 Act is codified in a similar way. The first section of the 34 Act appears at 15 U.S.C. § 78a. The second section lies at § 78b.

Practitioners generally will refer to a section in one of these acts by the section number in the act itself, instead of by the codified section number. That means that we have to translate the section number from the act into the code section in order to find it in the code.

[49]   The

Securities and Exchange Commission [is] composed of five commissioners to be appointed by the President by and with the advice and consent of the Senate. Not more than three of such commissioners shall be members of the same political party, and in making appointments members of different political parties shall be appointed alternately as nearly as may be practicable. No commissioner shall engage in any other business, vocation, or employment than that of serving as commissioner, nor shall any commissioner participate, directly or indirectly, in any stock-market operations or transactions of a character subject to regulation by the Commission pursuant to this chapter. Each commissioner shall hold office for a term of five years and until his [or her] successor is appointed and has qualified, except that he [or she] shall not so continue to serve beyond the expiration of the next session of Congress subsequent to the expiration of said fixed term of office. . . .

15 U.S.C. § 78d(a).

Federal law and shareholders: overview. Federal securities laws affect shareholder participation in corporate governance in at least three ways. First, federal securities law requires specific and detailed disclosures to shareholders before they vote, including extensive disclosures before director elections. Second, federal securities law gives shareholders certain procedural rights by, for example, requiring that they receive proxy cards permitting them to withhold votes from all director candidates nominated by the sitting board, or any one of those candidates, and giving shareholders limited rights to use the company's proxy materials to solicit support for shareholder resolutions presented at annual meetings. Third, the disclosures required before shareholder votes, and ongoing disclosures that the federal securities laws require, provide investors with a continual flow of information that is not only helpful to them as they exercise their right to vote but also helpful as they decide to buy and sell securities. Those purchases and sales, in turn, drive share prices up and down and in that way reward or punish officers and directors for their decisions, and their governance. The information-driven purchases and sales therefore indirectly affect those decisions and governance.

Federally required disclosure before shareholder votes. For our purposes, publicly traded companies are those issuing shares traded on national stock exchanges. Federal law effectively requires shares traded on the exchanges to be registered under the Exchange Act.[50] The federal proxy rules issued by the Commission apply to solicitation of proxies to vote shares so registered.[51]

Since most stockholders do not physically attend shareholder meetings and vote by giving their proxy, the solicitation of proxies is critical to shareholder votes. Normally, a proxy solicitation approved by the board of directors and distributed by the issuer at its expense is the only one that the shareholders receive. When another party also solicits proxies, there is a proxy fight. In that case, shareholders receive a proxy solicitation from both the company and the issuer.

The federal proxy rules mandate that shareholders who are asked for proxies receive a wealth of information. Today, the rules permit companies to provide the proxy solicitation materials and annual reports described below via electronic access, subject to certain restrictions.

No proxy solicitation may be sent to shareholders unless accompanied by or preceded by a proxy statement that has been filed with the SEC and contains the information set out in SEC Schedule 14A.[52] Among other things, Schedule 14A generally requires identification of the participants

---

[50]   The Exchange Act does so by prohibiting brokers or dealers from effecting, on a national exchange, a transaction in a stock unless the stock is registered under the act. 15 U.S.C. § 78*l*(a).

[51]   15 U.S.C. § 78n(a).

[52]   17 C.F.R. § 240.14a-3(a).

in the solicitation which, if not the company issuing the stock and its board, include all those who are financing the solicitation or loaning money to a participant for the purpose of buying, selling, holding, or voting the company's stock.[53]

When the issuer asks shareholders to vote for directors at an annual shareholder meeting, the federal proxy rules require that

> shareholders receive with or before the company's proxy statement an annual report[54] that includes, among other things,
>
> > "audited balance sheets as of the end of each of the two most recent fiscal years and audited financial statements of income and cash flows for each of the three most recent fiscal years prepared in accordance with Regulation S-X";[55]
> >
> > "selected financial data required by Item 301 of Regulation S-K";[56]
> >
> > "management's discussion and analysis of financial condition and results of operation required by Item 303 of Regulation S-K";[57]

---

[53]   17 C.F.R. § 240.14a-101 [Schedule 14A]. Schedule 14A, Item 4(2) & Instruction 3(a)(iv) & (v).

[54]   17 C.F.R. § 240.14a-3(b).

[55]   17 C.F.R. § 240.14a-3(b)(1).

The federal securities rules feature an integrated disclosure system. See generally the history set out in LOUIS LOSS, ET AL., FUNDAMENTALS OF SECURITIES REGULATION 222–29 (6th ed. 2011) [LOSS, SECURITIES FUNDAMENTALS]. Under that system, Regulation S-X (17 C.F.R. §§ 210.1-01 to 210.12-29) contains rules governing financial statements, and Regulation S-K (17 C.F.R. §§ 229.10–229.1208) contains rules governing other disclosures. Many of the SEC Forms and Schedules call for disclosures by referring to Items within Reg. S-K. The number of an "Item" in Reg. S-K generally corresponds to the first three digits after the decimal in 17 C.F.R. § 229.___. Thus, Item 302 of Reg. S-K appears at 17 C.F.R. § 229.302.

Reg. S-X requires, among other things, that the annual balance sheets and statements of income and cash flows be audited. 17 C.F.R. §§ 210.3-01(a); 210.3-02(a).

[56]   17 C.F.R. § 240.14a-3(b)(5)(i). That data must present, in columns to allow for easy comparison and cover each of the company's last five fiscal years, "net sales or operating revenues; income (loss) from continuing operations; income (loss) from continuing operations per common share; total assets; long-term obligations . . . ; and cash dividends declared per common share." 17 C.F.R. § 229.301(a) & Instruction 2.

[57]   17 C.F.R. § 240.14a-3(b)(5)(ii). Practitioners often refer to management's discussion and analysis of financial conditions and results of operations as "MD&A." Item 303 includes a number of very specific matters that MD&A must address. As you read the following rule, and all the SEC rules issued under the 34 Act, remember that the "registrant" is the company that has issued the stock that is registered under the Act. Here are portions of Item 303:

(1) *Liquidity*. Identify any known trends or any known demands, commitments, events or uncertainties that will result in or that are reasonably likely to result in the registrant's liquidity [*i.e.*, its ability to pay in cash obligations as they come due] increasing or decreasing in any material way. If a material deficiency is identified, indicate the course of action that the registrant has taken or proposes to take to remedy the deficiency. Also identify and separately describe internal and external sources of liquidity, and briefly discuss any material unused sources of liquid assets.

"supplementary financial information required by Item 302 of Regulation S-K";[58]

"a brief description of the business done by the [company] . . . during the most recent fiscal year";[59] and

the identity of the directors and officers.[60]

The proxy statement itself must contain, among other things,

very elaborate disclosures of compensation paid to top executives and directors;[61]

---

(2) *Capital resources.*

(i) Describe the registrant's material commitments for capital expenditures as of the end of the latest fiscal period, and indicate the general purpose of such commitments and the anticipated source of funds needed to fulfill such commitments. . . .

(3) *Results of operations.*

(i) Describe any unusual or infrequent events or transactions or any significant economic changes that materially affected the amount of reported income from continuing operations and, in each case, indicate the extent to which income was so affected. In addition, describe any other significant components of revenues or expenses that, in the registrant's judgment, should be described in order to understand the registrant's results of operations.

(ii) Describe any known trends or uncertainties that have had or that the registrant reasonably expects will have a material favorable or unfavorable impact on net sales or revenues or income from continuing operations. If the registrant knows of events that will cause a material change in the relationship between costs and revenues (such as known future increases in costs of labor or materials or price increases or inventory adjustments), the change in the relationship shall be disclosed.

(iii) To the extent that the financial statements disclose material increases in net sales or revenues, provide a narrative discussion of the extent to which such increases are attributable to increases in prices or to increases in the volume or amount of goods or services being sold or to the introduction of new products or services.

17 C.F.R. § 229.303(a)(1), (2)(i), (3)(i)–(iii). MD&A must also, in a specially captioned section, discuss "off-balance sheet arrangements that have or are reasonably likely to have a current or future effect on the registrant's financial condition, changes in financial condition, revenues or expenses, results of operations, liquidity, capital expenditures or capital resources that is material to investors," and, in a special table, set out certain contractual obligations such as long-term debt, together with amounts due in less than 1 year, in 1–3 years, in 3–5 years, and in more than 5 years. 17 C.F.R. § 229.303(a)(4) & (5).

Beyond all this, however, the SEC hopes that MD&A will not be formulaic but a creative discussion that not only attends to the specifics in Item 303 subparts but also "give[s] the investor an opportunity to look at the company through the eyes of management by providing both a short and long-term analysis of the business of the company . . . [as] management . . . discuss[es] the dynamics of the business and . . . analyze[s] the financials." Concept Release on Management's Discussion and Analysis of Financial Condition and Operations, 52 Fed. Reg. 13,715, 13,717 (Apr. 24, 1987).

[58] 17 C.F.R. § 240.14a-3(b)(3). Among other things, Item 302 requires companies to include "income (loss) before extraordinary items and cumulative effect of a change in accounting, [and] per share data based upon such income (loss), and net income (loss)." 17 C.F.R. § 229.302(a)(1).

[59] 17 C.F.R. § 240.14a-3(b)(6).

[60] 17 C.F.R. § 240.14a-3(b)(8). Practitioners usually refer to this rule simply as Rule 14a-3. The SEC proxy rules generally begin with the number and letter "14a." They are found at 17 C.F.R. §§ 240.14a-1 to 14-16.

[61] Schedule 14A, Item 8 (cross-referencing Reg. S-K Item 402).

amounts paid by the company to its outside auditor over the last two fiscal years, with the amounts broken down into audit fees, audit-related fees, tax fees, and all other fees;[62]

descriptions of all transactions during the last fiscal year, and any currently proposed, in which (i) the company was or is to be a participant, (ii) any executive officer, director, or director nominee was or is to be a participant, (iii) the amount involved exceeded $120,000, and (iv) the executive officer, director, or director nominee had or will have a direct or indirect material interest;[63]

a description of the company's "policies and procedures for the review, approval, or ratification" of such transactions;[64] and

very elaborate disclosures concerning board composition, attendance of directors at board meetings, and the composition and operation of board committees.[65]

---

[62]   Schedule 14A, Item 9(e).

[63]   Schedule 14A, Item 7(b) (cross-referencing Reg. S-K Item 404(a)).

[64]   Schedule 14A, Item 7(b) (cross-referencing Reg. S-K Item 404(b)).

[65]   Schedule 14A, Item 7(c) & (d) (cross-referencing portions of Reg. S-K Item 407, which is titled "Corporate Governance").

We will study these disclosures later. But here are two of them, one regarding the board overall and the other regarding the compensation committee, which I quote now so that you appreciate the detail that these disclosures must provide:

(a)   *Director independence.* Identify each director and, when the disclosure called for by this paragraph is being presented in a proxy or information statement relating to the election of directors, each nominee for director, that is independent under the independence standards applicable to the registrant under paragraph (a)(1) of this Item. In addition, if such independence standards contain independence requirements for committees of the board of directors, identify each director that is a member of the compensation, nominating or audit committee that is not independent under such committee independence standards. . . .

(1) In determining whether or not the director or nominee for director is independent for the purposes of paragraph (a) of this Item, the registrant shall use the applicable definition of independence, as follows:

(i) If the registrant is a listed issuer whose securities are listed on a national securities exchange or in an inter-dealer quotation system which has requirements that a majority of the board of directors be independent, the registrant's definition of independence that it uses for determining if a majority of the board of directors is independent in compliance with the listing standards applicable to the registrant. . . .

. . . .

(e)   *Compensation committee.*

(1) If the registrant does not have a standing compensation committee or committee performing similar functions, state the basis for the view of the board of directors that it is appropriate for the registrant not to have such a committee and identify each director who participates in the consideration of executive officer and director compensation.

(2) State whether or not the compensation committee has a charter. If the compensation committee has a charter, provide the disclosure required by Instruction 2 to this Item regarding the compensation committee charter.

The federal proxy regulations require other specific disclosures when solicitations seek proxies for votes in favor of mergers[66] or equity compensation plans.[67]

An SEC rule prohibits, in proxy statements, either false statements or ones that mislead by omitting material facts.[68]

These disclosure rules constitute a critical element of corporate governance because they ensure that shareholders of public companies receive ample information before exercising their right to vote. Without adequate information, that right would be worth little or nothing.

Federally required procedural rights for shareholder voting. In some instances, federal regulations governing proxies go beyond disclosure. They require that the form of proxy give the shareholder the option to withhold authority to vote for any or all of the director nominees or, if permitted by

---

(3) Provide a narrative description of the registrant's processes and procedures for the consideration and determination of executive and director compensation, including:

> (i)(A)   The scope of authority of the compensation committee (or persons performing the equivalent functions); and

>> (B) The extent to which the compensation committee (or persons performing the equivalent functions) may delegate any authority described in paragraph (e)(3)(i)(A) of this Item to other persons, specifying what authority may be so delegated and to whom;

> (ii) Any role of executive officers in determining or recommending the amount or form of executive and director compensation; and

> (iii) Any role of compensation consultants in determining or recommending the amount or form of executive and director compensation (other than any role limited to consulting on any broad-based plan that does not discriminate in scope, terms, or operation, in favor of executive officers or directors of the registrant, and that is available generally to all salaried employees; or providing information that either is not customized for a particular registrant or that is customized based on parameters that are not developed by the compensation consultant, and about which the compensation consultant does not provide advice) during the registrant's last completed fiscal year, identifying such consultants, stating whether such consultants are engaged directly by the compensation committee (or persons performing the equivalent functions) or any other person, describing the nature and scope of their assignment, and the material elements of the instructions or directions given to the consultants with respect to the performance of their duties under the engagement.

17 C.F.R. § 229.407(a) (partial quotation); (e)(1), (2) & (3).

[66]   *See* Schedule 14A, Items 3 (requiring an outline of any rights, available to shareholders who object to the proposed transaction, to obtain cash for their shares equal to fair value as determined in a state court proceeding) and 14 (cross-referencing not only Regs. S-X and S-K but a special set of disclosure regulations for mergers and acquisitions in Reg. M-A, 17 C.F.R. §§ 229.1000–229.1016) (requiring, among other things, disclosure of the consideration offered to securities holders, the reasons for the transaction, the vote required for its approval, the accounting treatment of the transaction, and the income tax consequences of the deal (Schedule 14A, Item 14(b)(4), cross-referencing Reg. M-A, Item 1004(a)(2)).

[67]   *See, e.g.*, Schedule 14A, Item 10(b)(2)(i)(A), requiring disclosure of the "title and amount of securities underlying [the] options, warrants or rights" that may be exercised under such a plan.

[68]   17 C.F.R. § 240.14a-9.

state law, vote against candidates.[69] As we will see in Chapter Fourteen, the "withhold" or against vote has become a potent means by which shareholders can express opposition to directors and the policies they pursue. Federal regulations also provide a shareholder's right, subject to some important limitations, to include shareholder proposals in the company's proxy statement and set out arguments in the company's proxy statement in favor of those proposals.[70]

---

[69]   17 C.F.R. § 240.14a-4(b)(2) & Instruction 2.

[70]   17 C.F.R. § 240.14a-8. Shareholders exercise this right to advocate all kinds of proposals. For example, DuPont's proxy statement for its April 30, 2008 meeting of shareholders—E. I. du Pont de Nemours & Co., Definitive Proxy Statement, Schedule 14A (filed Mar. 20, 2008)—included these resolutions:

1.   by the International Brotherhood of DuPont Workers that the board consider creating a "committee, with members drawn from the employee work force of DuPont, the union leadership of DuPont, the management of DuPont, and any necessary independent consultants, to report to the Board of Directors regarding (1) the impact to communities as a result of DuPont's action in laying off mass numbers of employees, selling its plants to other employers, and closing its plants and (2) alternatives that can be developed to help mitigate the impact of such actions in the future" (at 49);

2.   by an individual owning 60 shares that the board "analyze and report in an open and timely manner to the shareholders of the Company on the advisability of amending the Company by-laws to require that the Chairman of the Board of Directors shall not serve concurrently as Chief Executive Officer, and that whenever possible an independent Director shall serve as Chairman of the Board of Directors" (at 50);

3.   by the Free Enterprise Action Fund that the board "prepare by October 2008, at reasonable expense and omitting proprietary information, a Global Warming Report. The report may describe and discuss how action taken to date by DuPont to reduce its impact on global climate change has affected global climate in terms of any changes in mean global temperature and any undesirable climatic and weather-related events and disasters avoided" (at 52);

4.   by the Sisters of Charity of Saint Elizabeth and others that the board "review and amend the DuPont Human Rights Policy, to include respect for and adherence to seed saving rights of traditional agricultural communities" (at 54–55); and

5.   by The Great Neck Capital Appreciation LTD Partnership that the board "adopt a policy to give shareholders the opportunity at each annual shareholder meeting to vote on an advisory resolution, proposed by management, to ratify the compensation of the named executive officers (NEOs) set forth in the proxy statement's Summary Compensation Table (SCT) and the accompanying narrative disclosure of material factors provided to understand the SCT (but not the Compensation Discussion and Analysis). The proposal submitted to shareholders should make clear that the vote is non-binding and would not affect any compensation paid or awarded to any NEO" (at 56).

The DuPont Board recommended in the proxy statement that shareholders vote against all of these proposals. All of them failed. E. I. du Pont de Nemours & Co., Quarterly Report, Form 10-Q (filed July 28, 2008) at 34–35, although the votes were fairly close on 2 and 5. As we will see, federal law now effectively imposes the change advocated in the fifth proposal.

QUESTIONS ON FEDERAL LAW REQUIRING THAT SHAREHOLDERS RECEIVE SPECIFIC AND DETAILED INFORMATION BEFORE SHAREHOLDER VOTES ON DIRECTORS, MERGERS, AND COMPENSATION PLANS

Why doesn't Delaware law dictate, in prescriptive detail, the information that shareholders must receive before voting on such matters as directors and mergers?

What is the advantage to shareholders of requiring the same disclosures before director votes at all public companies?

Why would we think that SEC commissioners and staffers (basically attorneys and accountants, with some economists too) are the best judges of what information shareholders need before they vote?

Is it appropriate for the federal government to tell a corporation that it must provide access to its proxy statement for shareholder proposals on everything from plant closures to the impact of company operations on "seed saving rights of traditional agricultural communities" (see note 70)?

Required federal disclosures during stock sales. With important exceptions, the Securities Act requires public companies selling stock to file a registration statement with the SEC, with no sales to occur until and unless the SEC declares the registration statement effective.[71] While there are a number of different SEC forms for registration statements that can be used in different situations,[72] a company making an initial public offering (the "registrant") will use Form S-1.[73] S-1 and the other forms select disclosure requirements set out in Reg. S-X (governing financial statements) and Reg. S-K (governing most everything else).[74] The forms include lists of S-X and S-K disclosures that an offering company must include in its prospectus, which is included in the registration statement and which is the document specifically prepared for review by investors who consider buying the stock.[75] A company selling stock through a registration statement on Form S-1 must include in the prospectus, among many other things,

---

[71]   15 U.S.C. § 77e(a).

[72]   *See* 15 U.S.C. § 77g (authorizing the SEC to set out the information that registration statements must contain).

[73]   17 C.F.R. § 239.11. SEC Form S-1, http://www.sec.gov/about/forms/forms-1.pdf.

[74]   See *supra* note 55.

[75]   I refer here to prospectuses such as the Rule 430 preliminary prospectus, the Rule 430A prospectus, and the final Section 10(a) statutory prospectus filed under Rule 424(b)(1)—not free writing prospectuses. The SEC issues rules under the 33 Act that can be found in Title 17 of the Code of Federal Regulations, with the rule number preceded by "230."—so, for these prospectuses, 17 C.F.R. §§ 230.430, 230.430A, 230.424.

a description of the company's business;[76]

"audited balance sheets as of the end of each of the two most recent fiscal years," provided that "[i]f the registrant has been in existence for less than one fiscal year, there shall be filed an audited balance sheet as of a date within 135 days of the date of filing the registration statement" and "audited statements of income and cash flows for each of the three fiscal years preceding the date of the most recent audited balance sheet being filed or such shorter period as the registrant (including predecessors) has been in existence";[77]

"the principal purposes for which the net proceeds to the [company] from the securities to be offered are intended to be used and the approximate amount intended to be used for each such purpose," provided that, if the company "has no current specific plan for the proceeds, or a significant portion thereof, the registrant shall so state and discuss the principal reasons for the offering";[78] and

much of the same information that public companies must include in their proxy statements for annual meetings at which directors

---

[76]   Form S-1, Item 11(a), cross-referencing 17 C.F.R. § 229.101, which requires disclosure of, among other things: (1) "the year in which the [company] was organized and its form of organization"; (2) its "plan of operation for the remainder of the fiscal year" or, if the registration statement is filed after the end of the company's second fiscal quarter, for the rest of the current fiscal year and half of the next one; (3) for each "segment" of its business, the revenues, profit (or losses) and total assets attributable to that segment; and (4) a narrative description of the "business done and intended to be done by the [company]," including where material (i) the "principal products produced and services rendered" by the company; (ii) the "sources and availability of raw materials"; (iii) the "importance to the [business] and the duration and effect of all patents, trademarks, licenses, franchises and concessions held"; (iv) the "dependence . . . upon a single customer, or a few customers, the loss of any one or more of which would have a material adverse effect on the [business]," together with the names of any customer accounting for 10% or more of total revenues; (v) the "dollar amount of backlog orders believed to be firm, as of a recent date and as of a comparable date in the preceding fiscal year, together with an indication of the portion thereof not reasonably expected to be filled within the current fiscal year, and seasonal or other material aspects of the backlog"; (vi) "[c]ompetitive conditions in the business involved including, where material, the identity of the particular markets in which the registrant competes, an estimate of the number of competitors and the registrant's competitive position"; (vii) the "estimated amount spent during each of the last three fiscal years on company-sponsored research and development activities"; and (viii) the "effects that compliance with Federal, State and local provisions which have been enacted or adopted regulating the discharge of materials into the environment, or otherwise relating to the protection of the environment, may have upon the capital expenditures, earnings and competitive position of the [company]." 17 C.F.R. § 229.101(a)(1), (a)(2), (b), (c)(1)(i), (iii), (iv), (vii), (viii), (x), (xi), & (xii).

[77]   Form S-1, Item 11(e), cross-referencing Reg. S-X, which includes 17 C.F.R. §§ 210.3-01(a) and 210.3-02(a), containing the words quoted in the text.

[78]   Form S-1, Item 4, cross-referencing 17 C.F.R. § 229.504, which contains the quoted language.

will be elected, including the Reg S-K Item 303 disclosures (with MD&A)[79] and information about:

compensation paid to top executives and directors;[80]

pending, material legal proceedings;[81] and

certain transactions that involve the company and in which top officers or directors had or will have a material interest.[82]

Further required federal disclosures by periodic filings and disclosures between periodic filings. Stocks that are traded on the national exchanges are registered under the Exchange Act.[83] The companies issuing such stocks must, after the end of each fiscal year, file a Form 10-K with the SEC and must file a Form 10-Q with the Commission after the end of each of the first three quarters of their fiscal years.[84] These forms, like the 33 Act registration forms, consist largely of cross-references to parts of Regulations S-X and S-K, which set out specific disclosure requirements. Many of these are the same as the cross-references in Form S-1. Thus, a 10-K must, for example, include a description of the company's business;[85] audited balance sheets for the just concluded fiscal year and for the year before, together with audited statements of income and cash flow for the just concluded fiscal year and the two immediately preceding years;[86] a description of material, non-routine, pending litigation involving the company;[87] and Item 303 disclosures (with MD&A).[88] A 10-K also includes a "performance graph," which shows the performance of the company's stock on a graph comparing that performance with that of a broad market index and with the performance of stocks issued by comparable companies (for example, as shown by an industry or line-of-business index).[89]

---

[79] Form S-1, Item 11(h), cross-referencing 17 C.F.R. § 229.303, as discussed in note 57 *supra.*

[80] Form S-1, Item 11(*l*), cross-referencing 17 C.F.R. § 229.402.

[81] Form S-1, Item 11(c), cross-referencing 17 C.F.R. § 229.103.

[82] Form S-1, Item 11(n), cross-referencing 17 C.F.R. § 229.404.

[83] See *supra* note 50 and accompanying text.

[84] 15 U.S.C. § 78m(a)–(b); 17 C.F.R. § 240.13a-1 (requiring publicly traded companies to file annual reports); Form 10-K, General Instruction A(1), http://www.sec.gov/about/forms/form10-k.pdf; 17 C.F.R. § 240.13a-13(a); Form 10-Q, General Instruction A(1), http://www.sec.gov/about/forms/form10-q.pdf.

[85] Form 10-K, Item 1, cross-referencing Item 101 of Reg. S-K, discussed in *supra* note 76.

[86] Form 10-K, Item 8(a), cross-referencing Reg. S-X, which includes these requirements at 17 C.F.R. §§ 210.3-01(a), 210.3-02(a).

[87] Form 10-K, Item 3, cross-referencing 17 C.F.R. § 229.103.

[88] Form 10-K, Item 7, cross-referencing 17 C.F.R. § 229.303.

[89] Form 10-K, Item 5(a), cross-referencing 17 C.F.R. § 229.201, subpart (e) of which requires a performance graph. This graph, like a good deal of other data required in a Form 10-K, may be incorporated by reference from the annual report to shareholders that precedes or accompanies the company's proxy solicitation for that meeting. *See* Form 10-K, General Instruction G2. Since the information required in the annual report to shareholders overlaps to a great extent with the information required in the 10-K, many companies simply put a fancy cover

A 10-Q contains an unaudited balance sheet for the end of the just completed fiscal quarter and a balance sheet for the end of the last fiscal year, as well as an income statement covering the last fiscal quarter and the fiscal year to date and for comparable periods of the preceding fiscal year.[90] A 10-Q also includes Item 303 disclosures with MD&A, although in an abbreviated form.[91]

Companies with stocks registered under the 34 Act must also file Form 8-Ks shortly after the occurrence of certain events that are considered to be so important to investors that their disclosure cannot await the filing of the next 10-Q or 10-K.[92] The events that companies must disclose— generally within four business days of their occurrence[93]—include, among other things,

- entry into a material definitive agreement other than in the ordinary course of business;[94]

- termination of such an agreement;[95]

- completion of acquisition or disposition of a significant amount of assets other than in the ordinary course of business;[96]

- creation of a material financial obligation on the part of the company;[97]

---

around their 10-K, add a few pages for such things as a CEO letter to shareholders, and distribute that document as the annual report.

[90]   Form 10-Q, Item 1, cross-referencing 17 C.F.R. § 210.10-01, subpart (a)(1) of which states that the financial information need not be audited and subparts (c)(1) & (2) of which set out the periods covered by the financial information.

[91]   Form 10-Q, Item 2, cross-referencing 17 C.F.R. § 229.303, subpart (b) of which discusses MD&A in 10-Qs. The quarterly MD&A should discuss material changes in the subjects addressed in the full-year MD&A, such as liquidity and capital resources (see *supra* note 57), and also material changes in the company's financial condition and results of operations—with the regulation making specific reference to comparisons (i) between the balance sheet at the end of the most recent quarter compared with the balance sheets (a) at the end of the last fiscal year and (b) at the end of the comparable quarter in the preceding year, and (ii) between the year-to-date income statement ending with the most recent quarter and the year-to-date income statement for the same period of the preceding year.

[92]   15 U.S.C. § 78m(a)(1) & (*l*) (the latter requiring public companies to "disclose to the public on a rapid and current basis such additional information concerning material changes in the financial condition or operations of the issuer, in plain English, which may include trend and qualitative information and graphic presentations, as the Commission determines, by rule, is necessary or useful for the protection of investors and in the public interest."); Form 8-K, http://www.sec.gov/about/forms/form8-k.pdf.

[93]   Form 8-K, General Instruction B.1.

[94]   Form 8-K, Item 1.01.

[95]   Form 8-K, Item 1.02.

[96]   Form 8-K, Item 2.01.

[97]   Form 8-K, Item 2.03.

- any event that triggers the increase or acceleration of the company's debt, with consequences that are material to the company;[98]

- sale of unregistered stock by the company;[99]

- a determination by the board or an authorized officer that previously issued financial statements should no longer be relied upon because of material error in those statements;[100] or

- resignation of a director, or refusal by a director to run for re-election because of disagreement with the company, and a description of that disagreement.[101]

The importance of federal securities law disclosure requirements to shareholder participation in corporate governance by buying and selling stock. In addition to the specifically required information preceding the solicitation of proxies for shareholder votes, the further information that a public company distributes through 10-Qs, 10-Ks, and 8-Ks is also available to shareholders for their use in deciding how to vote. Moreover, all this information—from the publicly available proxy statements to the publicly available 10-Ks, 10-Qs, and 8-Ks—helps investors decide whether to buy or sell the company's stock. One of the time-honored ways for investors to display dissatisfaction with management, the directors, or company governance is to simply sell their shares, and one of the ways in which the market can express confidence in management, the directors, and company governance is by buying stock.

QUESTIONS ON SHAREHOLDER BUY/SELL DECISIONS AS A GOVERNANCE MECHANISM

What are the advantages to the shareholder of expressing dissatisfaction with a corporate board's decision by selling stock rather than by voting against the board in a director election?

What are the disadvantages to the shareholder?

Which method of expressing dissatisfaction is likely to put the most pressure on the board to change the company's strategy?

---

98 Form 8-K, Item 2.04.
99 Form 8-K, Item 3.02.
100 Form 8-K, Item 4.02.
101 Form 8-K, Item 5.02(a).

None of the extensive disclosure requirements would be effective without enforcement. The federal securities laws provide for both public and private enforcement.

Enforcement of the federal disclosure requirements. The information in all of the disclosure documents required by the federal securities laws is mostly compiled by the officers of public companies and their subordinates. The directors also sign some of the disclosure documents.[102] There is an elaborate system of private civil liabilities and SEC and criminal enforcement penalties that enforce these requirements and punish officers and directors for false or incomplete disclosures.[103]

---

[102] Instruction 1 to the Signatures section of Form S-1 states that the principal executive officer (usually the CEO), the principal financial officer (usually the CFO), its controller or principal accounting officer, and at least a majority of the board of directors must sign. General Instruction D(2)(a) to Form 10-K identifies the same set of required signatories, but adds the principal accounting officer as well. General Instruction G to Form 10-Q states that it must be signed by "a duly authorized officer . . . and by the principal financial or chief accounting officer." Neither Form 8-K nor Schedule 14A specifies which officers must sign.

[103]   As examples

- If a registration statement omits required information or contains false information or omits information necessary to avoid misleading by what the statement says, all those who sign the statement as well as all non-signing directors are civilly liable to those who buy stock in an offering covered by the registration statement unless the signatories or other directors can establish a due diligence defense, which essentially requires the officers and directors to show that they were not negligent. 15 U.S.C. § 77k(a) & (b).

- When a registration statement, 10-K, 10-Q, Schedule 14A, or 8-K is false or misleading, all those who knew the information was false or misleading (or were severely reckless) and who either signed the document or otherwise had ultimate control over its content may be liable to any shareholder who bought or sold the company's stock in reliance on the false or misleading information and who can prove that that information caused them economic harm due to their purchase or sale. 17 C.F.R. § 240.10b-5; *Dura Pharmaceuticals, Inc. v. Broudo*, 544 U.S. 336, 341–42 (2005) (setting out elements of a Rule 10b-5 private civil claim); *Ernst & Ernst v. Hochfelder*, 425 U.S. 185, 193 n.12, 197–214 (1976) (requiring scienter in 10b-5 cases and defining that to be a "a mental state embracing intent to deceive, manipulate, or defraud"); 8 LOUIS LOSS, ET AL., SECURITIES REGULATION 150–56 & n.544 (4th ed. 2012) (all circuits recognize that some form of severe recklessness also suffices for scienter); *Janus Capital Grp., Inc. v. First Derivative Traders*, 131 S. Ct. 2296, 2302–03 (2011) (a party "makes" a statement for purposes of Rule 10b-5 only if that party has "ultimate control over the content of a statement"—i.e., has "authority over the content of the statement and whether and how to communicate it.").

- The SEC can sue *in federal district court* for an *injunction* against any person who is engaged, or is about to engage, in any violation of the 33 Act or 34 Act, or any of the rules or regulations issued under them. 15 U.S.C. §§ 77t(b), 78u(d)(1).

- The SEC can sue *in federal district court* for *civil monetary penalties* against persons who have violated either of those laws or the rules or regulations issued under them. 15 U.S.C. §§ 77t(d), 78u(d)(3). The penalties are tiered:

  Tier 1: for each violation, an amount not exceeding the greater of (1) $8,908 for a natural person, $89,078 for an entity or (2) the gross amount of pecuniary gain to the defendant for the violation;

  Tier 2: for each violation that involved fraud, deceit, manipulation, or deliberate or reckless disregard of a regulatory requirement, an amount not exceeding the greater of: (1) $89,078 for a natural person, $445,390 for an entity or (2) the gross amount of pecuniary gain to the defendant for the violation; and

Federal law and boards: overview. Federal law affects boards of directors in two ways. First, the securities laws require public companies to disclose facts about boards and board committees, and some of the disclosure requirements discourage behavior that the companies would be embarrassed to report. Second, federal law—either directly or through a

---

Tier 3: for each violation that (i) involved fraud, deceit, manipulation, or deliberate or reckless disregard of a regulatory requirement and (ii) directly or indirectly resulted in substantial losses or created a significant risk of substantial losses to other persons, an amount not exceeding the greater of: (1) $178,156 for a natural person, $890,780 for an entity or (2) the gross amount of pecuniary gain to the defendant for the violation.

15 U.S.C. §§ 77t(d)(2), 78u(d)(3)(b), and Adjustments to Civil Monetary Penalty Amounts, 81 Fed. Reg 43,042, 43,044 (July 1, 2016).

- The SEC can seek, in an *injunction* action *in federal district court, orders barring defendants* who have violated the 33 Act or 34 Act, or rules or regulations issued under those acts, *from serving as officers or directors of public companies.* 15 U.S.C. §§ 77t(e), 78u(d)(2). The SEC can also seek other equitable relief such as disgorgement of bonuses and other remuneration derived from the violations. J. WILLIAM HICKS, CIVIL LIABILITIES: ENFORCEMENT AND LITIGATION UNDER THE 1933 ACT §§ 2:43–44 (2015) (33 Act); 15 U.S.C. § 78u(d)(5) (34 Act) (authority for general equitable relief); *see also SEC v. Cavanagh*, 445 F.3d 105, 120 (2d Cir. 2006) (district courts have equitable power under the Judiciary Act to order disgorgement).

- The SEC can pursue not only primary violators *in federal district court* but
  - o   any aider and abettor who "knowingly or recklessly provides substantial assistance to another person" violating the 33 Act or the 34 Act or any rule or regulation issued under either of them (15 U.S.C. §§ 77o(b), 78t(e)), and
  - o   anyone who is a control person for another who commits a violation of the 34 Act. 15 U.S.C. § 78t(a).

- The SEC can seek a *cease-and-desist order in an administrative enforcement action* brought before an Administrative Law Judge against any person who has engaged, is violating, has violated, or is about to violate any provision of the 33 Act or 34 Act, or any rules or regulations under either of them. 15 U.S.C. §§ 77h-1(a), 78u-3(a).

- The SEC can seek *civil monetary penalties in such an administrative proceeding* against anyone who is violating or has violated any provision of either act or rules or regulations under either, with the civil monetary penalties tiered in the same way as in the penalties that the SEC can seek in federal district court. 15 U.S.C. §§ 77h-1(g), 78u-2(a)(2) & (b); with original statutory amounts adjusted per Adjustments to Civil Monetary Penalty Amounts, 81 Fed. Reg. 43,042, 43,044 (July 1, 2016).

- The SEC can also seek *disgorgement in such an administrative proceeding.* 15 U.S.C. §§ 77h-1(e), 78u-3(e). And the SEC can seek *orders barring defendants from serving as officers or directors of public companies.* 15 U.S.C. §§ 77h-1(f), 78u-3(f).

- As is true in federal district court actions, the SEC can—*in administrative proceedings*—pursue not only primary violators but secondary ones. In particular, the SEC can bring such a proceeding *against anyone who "causes" a violation of the 33 or 34 Acts,* or any rule or regulation under either act, "due to an act or omission the person knew or should have known would contribute to such violation." 15 U.S.C. §§ 77h-1(a), 78u-3(a). The "should have known" language in this statute imports a negligence standard. *KPMG, LLP v. SEC*, 289 F.3d 109, 120 (D.C. Cir. 2002). The SEC frequently employs this authority to pursue officers or employees who cause their companies to commit a violation that only an issuer can commit.

- The Department of Justice can bring a criminal action in federal district court against anyone who "willfully" violates the 33 Act or 34 Act or the rules and regulations implementing them. 15 U.S.C. §§ 77x, 78ff(a). A willful violation in this context requires that the defendant know that the action constituting the crime was wrong, even if the defendant did not know that it was illegal. *U.S. v. Tarallo*, 380 F.3d 1174, 1188 (9th Cir. 2004), *amended by* 413 F.3d 928 (9th Cir. 2005).

requirement that stock exchanges adopt certain listing standards—requires many specific actions by board committees, particularly the audit committee. What follows are some examples.

Required federal disclosures about the board as a whole that encourage independence and hard work. Federal disclosure requirements encourage board compliance with listing standards and other norms that the federal government would like board governance to reflect. Thus, each public company must identify each director who is independent according to the definition of independence in the listing standards of the exchange on which the company lists its stock, if those standards require that a majority of board members be independent (as do both the NYSE and NASDAQ).[104] Since companies will not want to report that they are violating listing standards requiring director independence, this requirement adds to the already considerable reasons why companies will police themselves to ensure that they comply with exchange-imposed rules. This disclosure also helps shareholders police compliance with listing standards and determine whether a company has more independent directors than required. Each public company must also disclose "whether or not the . . . board of directors provides a process for security holders to send communications to the board of directors and, if the [company] does not have such a process . . . , state the basis for the view of the board of directors that it is appropriate for the [company] not to have such a process."[105] For most companies, it would be quite awkward to state publicly that it had no system for shareholders to communicate with the board, so the effect of this disclosure requirement is to force companies to put such a system in place.[106]

Federal regulations also require a company to disclose the number of board meetings in the last year; whether the board has standing audit, compensation, and nominating committees; the numbers of meetings of each committee and the names of directors who failed to attend at least 75% of the total of (i) full board meetings and (ii) meetings of those

---

[104]   17 C.F.R. § 229.407(a)(1)(i); citations to NYSE and NASDAQ requirement for a majority of independent directors at note 210 *infra*.

[105]   17 C.F.R. § 229.407(f)(1).

[106]   Since the disclosures are quite detailed, they effectively force companies to develop detailed processes. Thus, the SEC regulations require that, if the company does say it has a process, it must

(i)   describe the manner in which security holders can send communications to the board and, if applicable, to specified individual directors; and

(ii)   if all security holder communications are not sent directly to board members, describe the registrant's process for determining which communications will be relayed to board members.

17 C.F.R. § 229.407(f)(2). The disclosures about the process for shareholders to communicate with the board must appear in the company's proxy statement regarding election of directors per Item 7(d) of Schedule 14A.

committees on which the directors served.[107] These disclosures are clearly aimed at encouraging boards, committees, and individual directors to work hard.[108]

Federal regulation of the composition and operation of audit committees. Federal law indirectly regulates the composition of public company audit committees. Thus, SOX section 301 required the SEC to adopt a regulation that, in turn, would require the national exchanges to each promulgate a listing standard mandating that "[e]ach member of the audit committee . . . shall . . . be independent," with independence defined, among other ways, to exclude any director who received "any consulting, advisory, or other compensatory fee from the [company]," "other than in his or her capacity of a member of the audit committee, the board of directors, or any other board committee."[109]

Federal law similarly regulates the operation of public company audit committees; for example, by effectively requiring such committees to establish procedures for "the receipt, retention, and treatment of complaints received by the issuer regarding accounting, internal accounting controls, or auditing matters" and "the confidential, anonymous submission by employees of the issuer of concerns regarding questionable accounting or auditing matters."[110]

Federal law also requires that each public company audit committee "shall have authority to engage independent counsel and other advisers, as it deems necessary to carry out its duties" and requires that the audit

---

[107]   17 C.F.R. § 229.407(b)(1); disclosure required in company proxy solicitation regarding election of directors per Item 7(d) of Schedule 14A.

[108]   The ABA's *Corporate Director's Guidebook* (6th ed. 2011) states:

Boards should hold regularly scheduled meetings at least quarterly, but many schedule six to eight regular meetings a year and hold additional special meetings as needed.

At 51.

[An] audit committee should meet at least four times a year. It is common for public company audit committees to have an in-person or telephonic meeting with the company's CEO, CFO, other senior financial managers, and external auditor in advance of each quarterly or annual earnings release. As a result, almost all audit committees schedule at least four, and some as many as five to eight, meetings per year.

At 77. Quotations from the Director's Guidebook reprinted with permission from the American Bar Association. All rights reserved. These quotations or any portion thereof may not be copied or disseminated in any form or by any means or stored in an electronic database or retrieval system without the express written consent of the American Bar Association. Director's Guidebook © 2011 by the American Bar Association.

[109]   15 U.S.C. § 78j-1(m)(3), with the SEC rule at 17 C.F.R. § 240.10A-3(b)(1)(i) & (ii).

[110]   SOX § 301; 15 U.S.C. § 78j-1(m)(4). Again, the law imposed this requirement in a roundabout way, commanding the SEC to issue a regulation charging the exchanges with issuing rules requiring that a company's audit committee have such procedures in order that the company's securities be listed for trading. That regulation is 17 C.F.R § 240.10A-3(b)(3).

committee will determine the "appropriate funding" for the outside auditor and for any advisers that the audit committee retains.[111]

Federal regulation of the interaction between auditors and audit committees. Federal securities laws, in addition to auditing rules adopted by the Public Company Accounting Oversight Board, govern the interaction between outside auditors and the audit committee. While Chapter Twelve takes up this interaction in more detail, one example is that the federal law effectively requires each audit committee to be

> directly responsible for the appointment, compensation, and oversight of the work of any registered public accounting firm employed by that issuer . . . for the purpose of preparing or issuing an audit report or related work, and each such registered public accounting firm shall report directly to the audit committee.[112]

Federal law also requires the outside accounting firm performing the audit to report to the audit committee all "material written communications between [that accounting firm] and the management of the [company]."[113] And federal law imposes tasks on the audit committee beyond selection and compensation of the outside auditor. For example, the committee is charged with "resolution of disagreements between management and the auditor regarding financial reporting."[114]

Federal regulations requiring disclosures about audit committees that encourage those committees to take desirable actions. A company must not only state whether its audit committee has a written charter (which it must under listing standards that the book will soon discuss) but must also either post that charter on its website or include the charter as an appendix to the company's proxy statement every three years.[115] And some required disclosures are obviously designed to push companies into certain actions. For example, the company must disclose whether its audit committee has reviewed and discussed the audited financial statements with management and received certain information from the outside auditor and had certain discussions with the auditor and whether the committee—based on these steps—has "recommended to the board of directors that the audited financial statements be included in the company's . . . Form 10-

---

[111]   SOX § 301; 15 U.S.C. § 78j-1(m)(5) & (6), with the SEC regulation requiring that national exchanges include these requirements in their listing standards at 17 C.F.R. § 240.10A-3(b)(4) & (5).

[112]   SOX § 301; 15 U.S.C. § 78j-1(m)(2); with the statutes tasking the SEC with issuing a regulation mandating that exchanges include this requirement in their listing standards, and the SEC rule discharging this task appearing at 17 C.F.R. § 240.10A-3(b)(2).

[113]   SOX § 204; 15 U.S.C. § 78j-1(k)(3); 17 C.F.R. § 210.2-07(a)(3).

[114]   SOX § 301; 15 U.S.C. § 78j-1(m)(2), with the SEC regulation requiring national exchanges to put this requirement for audit committees into their listing standards at 17 C.F.R. § 240.10A-3(b)(2).

[115]   17 C.F.R. § 229.407(d)(1) & Instruction 2 to Item 407.

K."[116] Clearly, a public company would be embarrassed if it could not report that the audit committee made such a recommendation.

Required federal disclosures about other board committees. Federal securities rules require disclosures about the compensation and nominating committees of the boards at public companies. For example, SEC regulations require that companies disclose whether they have written charters for those committees and that, if so, the companies either post those charters on websites or include them every three years as appendices to proxy statements distributed for director elections.[117] The rules require other committee disclosures as well. Just as examples,

- if the company "pays a fee to any third party or parties to identify or evaluate or assist in identifying or evaluating potential [director] nominees" for the nominating committee, then it must "disclose the function performed by each such third party";

- the company must include—in a "narrative description of the [company's] processes and procedures for the consideration and determination of executive and director compensation"— "[a]ny role of compensation consultants in determining or recommending the amount or form of executive and director compensation . . . ";[118] and

- if the compensation committee uses a compensation consultant, "and the compensation consultant or its affiliates also provided additional services to the [company] or its affiliates in an amount in excess of $120,000 during the [company's] last completed fiscal year, then [the company must] disclose" the fees for the compensation consulting and the fees for "additional services" as well as any role that management played in hiring the consultant for executive compensation advice and whether the compensation committee approved the retention of the consultant for the "additional services."[119]

---

[116]   17 C.F.R. § 229.407(d)(3)(i). Item 7(d) of Schedule 14A requires all these disclosures in a proxy statement sent out by a public company regarding the election of directors.

[117]   17 C.F.R. § 229.407(c)(2)(i), (e)(2) & Instruction 2 to Item 407; Schedule 14A, Item 7(d).

[118]   17 C.F.R. § 229.407(c)(2)(viii) and (e)(3)(ii)–(iii), both disclosures to be included in company proxy statements regarding director elections per Item 7(d) of Schedule 14A.

[119]   17 C.F.R. § 229.407(e)(3)(iii)(A). If the compensation committee uses a consultant, that committee must "be directly responsible for the appointment, compensation, and oversight of the work of [that] compensation consultant." 15 U.S.C. § 78j-3(c)(1)(B).

QUESTIONS ABOUT THE FOCUS OF FEDERAL SECURITIES LAW ON BOARD COMMITTEES

Is it a good idea for the federal government to get inside the boards of public companies and prescribe membership qualifications and operation of board committees? To require disclosure of such details as whether the company has a specific process by which shareholders can contact the board and what role a compensation consultant to a compensation committee plays in that committee's consideration of the pay packages for top executives?

———————

Federal law and officers: overview. Federal securities laws and rules include provisions that directly affect the manner in which officers assemble the information that the securities laws require the company to report. The federal securities laws also dictate some of the compensation relationships between public companies and their officers, and prohibit certain actions by officers as they interact with the accounting firm auditing the company's financial statements. The following discussion is illustrative, not exhaustive.

Federal requirements affecting how officers assemble the information that the federal securities laws require their companies to report. As set out above, the federal securities laws require that public companies provide a tremendous volume of information to investors. The officers in each company must collect that information and put together the many securities filings the companies make. Federal law regulates how the officers perform that task.

Public companies must "make and keep books, records and accounts, which, in reasonable detail, accurately and fairly reflect the transactions and dispositions of the assets of the issuer."[120] They must also "devise and maintain a system of internal accounting controls sufficient to provide reasonable assurances that [among other things]—transactions are recorded as necessary . . . to permit preparation of financial statements in conformity with generally accepted accounting principles."[121] These are sometimes referred to as the "books and records" requirements, and securities regulations prohibit "directly or indirectly, falsify[ing] or caus[ing] to be falsified" any federally required books and records.[122]

Public companies must also "maintain . . . internal control over financial reporting," which effectively means creating and maintaining "a process designed by, or under the supervision of, the [company's] principal executive and principal financial officers . . . , and effected by the

———————

[120]   15 U.S.C. § 78m(b)(2)(A).

[121]   15 U.S.C. § 78m(b)(2)(B).

[122]   17 C.F.R. § 240.13b2-1.

[company's] board of directors, management and other personnel, to provide reasonable assurance regarding the reliability of financial reporting and the preparation of financial statements for external purposes in accordance with generally accepted accounting principles."[123] This rule is similar to the statutory requirement to "devise and maintain a system of internal accounting controls."[124]

The law and related regulations further require public companies to create and maintain "disclosure controls and procedures," which are

> controls and other procedures of an issuer that are designed to ensure that information required to be disclosed by the issuer in the reports that it files or submits under the [Exchange] Act . . . is recorded, processed, summarized and reported, within the time periods specified in the Commission's rules and forms. Disclosure controls and procedures include, without limitation, controls and procedures designed to ensure that information required to be disclosed by an issuer in the reports that it files or submits under the Act is accumulated and communicated to the issuer's management, including its principal executive and principal financial officers, or persons performing similar functions, as appropriate to allow timely decisions regarding required disclosure.[125]

The securities laws and rules require management to evaluate internal controls over financial reporting and disclosure controls periodically and report on their evaluations.[126] Chapter Ten discusses these evaluations and reports in detail, but note here that, in an effort to emphasize the personal responsibility of top executives for the processes producing the financial numbers and other disclosures in SEC filings, the federal securities laws require the CEO and CFO to execute certifications attached to 10-Qs and 10-Ks that, among other things, acknowledge the responsibility of these officers to create, or supervise the creation of, effective internal control over financial reporting and effective disclosure controls.[127]

---

[123]   17 C.F.R. §§ 240.13a-15(a) & (f); 240.15d-15(a) & (f).

[124]   Compare 17 C.F.R. §§ 240.13a-15(f), 240.15d-15(f) with the language of 15 U.S.C. § 78m(b)(2)(B).

[125]   17 C.F.R. §§ 240.13a-15(e); 240.15d-15(e).

[126]   SOX § 404; 15 U.S.C. § 7262; 17 C.F.R. § 240.13a-15(b), (c) & (d); 17 C.F.R. § 240.15d-15(b), (c) & (d); 17 C.F.R. § 229.307; 17 C.F.R. § 229.308(a) & (c); Form 10-K, Item 9A; Form 10-Q, Item 4.

[127]   SOX §§ 302, 906; 15 U.S.C. § 7242; 18 U.S.C. § 1350; 17 C.F.R § 229.601(b)(31); 17 C.F.R. §§ 240.13a-14(a), 240.15d-14(a); Form10-K, Item 15(c); Form10-Q, Item 6.

QUESTIONS ON FEDERAL REGULATION OF THE MANNER IN WHICH OFFICERS ASSEMBLE INFORMATION FOR REPORTS THAT THE SECURITIES LAWS REQUIRE

Federal securities laws require that companies report certain information and prescribe penalties for failure to do so and for inaccurate reports. With this "tailpipe test" regulation in place, why should the federal government also get inside corporate operations (the engine, if you will) to regulate the manner in which the information is assembled for the reports?

As an alternative to regulations on internal operations, would you favor changing the criteria for and severity of the sanctions on individual officers when their companies fail to report required information or report falsely— e.g., by using a strict liability standard for civil sanctions, increasing the amounts of civil monetary penalties, lowering the standard for criminal conviction for negligence, increasing sentences, or some combination of these steps? Or increasing enforcement budgets?

Federal law regulating the compensation that public companies pay their officers. Federal laws regulate quite specifically certain aspects of compensation that public companies pay their officers. For example, with some exceptions, federal law prohibits public companies from making personal loans to executive officers or directors.[128] As another example, the federal law includes this clawback provision:

> If an issuer is required to prepare an accounting restatement[129] due to the material noncompliance of the issuer, as a result of misconduct, with any financial reporting requirement under the securities laws, the chief executive officer and chief financial officer of the issuer shall reimburse the issuer for—
>
> > (1) any bonus or other incentive-based or equity-based compensation received by that person from the issuer during the 12-month period following the first public issuance or

---

[128]   SOX § 402, 15 U.S.C. § 78m(k). Though the statute does not define the "executive officers" to which the prohibition applies, one leading practice treatise advises that "[i]n determining who is an executive officer [for purposes of the loan prohibition], [companies] should apply Exchange Act Rule 3b-7. . . ." 2 ROBERT E. BUCKHOLZ, JR., ET AL., PUBLIC COMPANY DESKBOOK § 5N:4.4 (3d ed. 2016) [BUCKHOLZ, DESKBOOK]. That definition provides that "executive officer" "means [the company's] president, any vice president of the [company] in charge of a principal business unit, division or function (such as sales, administration or finance), any other officer who performs a policy making function or any other person who performs similar policy making functions for the [company]." 17 C.F.R. § 240.3b-7.

[129]   When a company discovers that a previously published set of financial numbers was materially wrong, the company issues a new set of corrected numbers called a "restatement." A restatement may result from an innocent mistake, but may also result from misconduct such as fraud. The announcement that a company will restate financial numbers may cause the price of a company's stock to drop.

filing with the Commission (whichever first occurs) of the financial document embodying such financial reporting requirement; and

(2) any profits realized from the sale of securities of the issuer during that 12-month period.[130]

As we will see, this clawback has been little used for a technical, legal reason. But the Dodd-Frank law includes what should become a more effective clawback requirement. The larger point is this: the clawback provisions in the law constitute, in a way, an indirect addition to the compensation contracts between public companies and their top officers.

QUESTIONS ON THE CLAWBACK IN FEDERAL LAW

Is it better to include a clawback provision in federal law or leave clawbacks to the employment contracts that companies negotiate with their executives? What about loans from a company to its officers?

Federal law regulating the relationship between officers and the public company's auditor. The securities laws regulate the interaction between a public company's officers and the outside auditor. SEC rules prohibit directors and officers, directly or indirectly, from making, or causing to be made, false statements to outside accountants performing an audit.[131] The rules also provide that "[n]o officer or director of an issuer, or any other person acting under the direction thereof, shall directly or indirectly take any action to coerce, manipulate, mislead, or fraudulently influence any independent public or certified public accountant engaged in the performance of an audit or review of the financial statements of that issuer that are required to be filed with the Commission . . . if that person knew or should have known that such action, if successful, could result in rendering the issuer's financial statements materially misleading."[132]

Federal law and outside professionals: overview. Federal laws and regulations extensively regulate the accounting firms that audit public company annual financial statements. To a lesser degree, those laws and regulations also regulate attorneys who represent public companies on securities matters.

---

[130]   SOX § 304(a), 15 U.S.C. § 7243(a).

[131]   17 C.F.R. § 240.13b2-2(a)(1).

[132]   17 C.F.R. § 240.13b2-2(b)(1) (SEC rule); *see also* SOX § 303(a) (which required the SEC to issue the rule), 15 U.S.C. § 7242(a) (codification of that requirement).

Federal regulation of auditors by the requirement that they be "independent." Federal securities law and rules require that the financial statements public companies include in their 10-Ks[133] and annual reports[134] be "audited" and that the financial statements included in their 10-Qs be "reviewed."[135] Only an "independent accountant" can perform an "audit" or "review" that satisfies the SEC filing requirements.[136]

Congress and the SEC have placed manifold restrictions on accounting firms for public companies by providing that accountants, unless they abide by the restrictions, are not "independent." Such restrictions are effectively mandated by this method as only auditors that are "independent" under SEC rules can create the audit opinions and review reports that public companies must have in order to produce the 10-Ks, annual reports, and 10-Qs that the securities laws and regulations require. Some of the "independence" requirements are no surprise—e.g., an accounting firm is not independent if any member of the team working on an audit owns stock in the company being audited.[137] Similarly, an accounting firm is not "independent" if it works for a contingent fee (such as a fee contingent on finding that the company's financial statements pass accounting tests).[138] Nor is it "independent" if a current partner is on the audited company's board.[139]

But other requirements for accountant "independence" reach into the accounting firm to an initially surprising degree and affect such matters as the services it can offer, the manner in which it can compensate its partners, and the employment opportunities of those partners when they leave the firm. For example, an accounting firm is not "independent" unless, with some exceptions, it does *not* provide to an audit client any of 10 different kinds of non-audit services.[140] An accounting firm is not

---

[133]   Form 10-K, Item 8(a), cross-referencing Reg. S-X, which provides in 17 C.F.R. §§ 210.3-01(a) and 210.3-02(a) that the balance sheets, income statements, and statements of cash flows must be "audited."

[134]   17 C.F.R. § 240.14a-3(b)(1), requiring that the annual report provided with or before the company's proxy statement for a meeting at which directors will be elected include "audited" balance sheets and "audited" statements of income and cash flows.

[135]   Form 10-Q, Item 1, cross-referencing the portion of Reg. S-X concerning "interim financial statements," 17 C.F.R. § 210.10-01, which provides (in subpart (d)) that such statements must be "reviewed by an independent public accountant" before being included in a 10-Q.

While an audit and a review are very different, it suffices for our purposes to note only that both an "audit" and a "review" are performed by an outside accounting firm and that the accounting firm does considerably more checking when performing an audit than when performing a review. Note that the outside accounting firm does not, at the conclusion of either an audit or review, guarantee the accuracy of financial statements.

[136]   17 C.F.R. §§ 210.1-02(d), 210.10-01(d).

[137]   17 C.F.R. § 210.2-01(c)(1)(i)(A), (f)(7)(i), (f)(8), (f)(11).

[138]   17 C.F.R. § 210.2-01(c)(5).

[139]   17 C.F.R. § 210.2-01(c)(2)(i).

[140]   SOX § 211, 15 U.S.C. § 78j-1(g), 17 C.F.R. § 210.2-01(c)(4). The cited statutes say that it is "unlawful" for an auditor to provide the services to an audit client, and the cited SEC rule then

"independent" unless the lead audit partner rotates out of that role after five years.[141] Nor is a firm "independent" if "at any point during the audit and professional engagement period, any audit partner earns or receives compensation based on the audit partner procuring engagements with [the] audit client to provide any products or services other than audit, review or attest services."[142] Nor is a firm "independent" if one of its former partners—except one who has been off the audit team for at least one year—is "in a financial reporting oversight role" at the audited company, which is defined to include employment as a member of the board of directors or "chief executive officer, president, chief financial officer, chief operating officer, general counsel, chief accounting officer, controller, director of internal audit, director of financial reporting, treasurer, or any equivalent position."[143] A firm cannot be "independent" if it hires a "former officer, director, or employee of an audit client . . . , unless the individual does not participate in, and is not in a position to influence, the audit of the financial statements of the audit client covering any period during which he or she was employed by or associated with that audit client."[144]

QUESTIONS ON FEDERAL REGULATION OF THE SERVICES AUDITORS PROVIDE TO CLIENTS, INTERNAL COMPENSATION ARRANGEMENTS IN ACCOUNTING FIRMS, AND MOVEMENT OF ACCOUNTANTS BETWEEN AUDITORS AND THEIR CLIENTS

Why should the federal government regulate the services that auditors provide to clients, whether the accounting firm can compensate an audit partner for cross-selling non-audit services to an audit client, and the ability of accountants to move between a public company and the accounting firm that audits that company without worrying about stripping the accounting firm of its ability to conduct the audit?

Why not rely solely on disclosure—with companies disclosing what non-audit services they provide to a public company that is an audit client, with the accounting firm disclosing whether it compensated an audit partner for cross-selling non-audit services to such a company, and with the company

---

puts additional bite into the prohibition by including it in the definition of independence. While committing an "unlawful" act could greatly harm an accounting firm, a public company would also suffer considerable reputational harm, and its stock price might well suffer, if its annual financials were not "audited" because its auditor was not "independent."

[141] SOX § 203, 15 U.S.C. § 78j-1(j), 17 C.F.R. § 210.2-01(c)(6)(i)(A)(1). Aside from embedding the rotation requirement in the definition of auditor "independence," it is simply "unlawful" under the cited statutes for an accounting firm to audit a public company if the lead partner has occupied that position in the audit for each of the previous five years.

[142] 17 C.F.R. § 210.2-01(c)(8).

[143] 17 C.F.R. § 210.2-01(c)(2)(iii)(B), (f)(3)(ii).

[144] 17 C.F.R. § 210.2-01(c)(2)(iv); *see also* SOX § 206, 15 U.S.C. § 78j-1(l).

disclosing whether it has hired into a financial oversight position someone who immediately before worked for the auditor?

———————

Federal regulation of the relationship between auditors and audit committees. Federal law directly affects the relationship between auditors and their clients' audit committees. As we have seen already, federal law requires that the audit committees select and determine the compensation of auditors. The law also requires that audit committees pre-approve, with a *de minimis* exception, all of the work—both audit and non-audit—that the outside accounting firm providing auditing services renders to the company.[145] Federal law requires, as well, a host of reports by the outside accounting firm performing the audit to the audit committee, including as we have seen all "material written communications" between the management of the company and the accounting firm about the audit.[146]

Federal creation of a new auditor regulator. As a result of SOX, audits of a public company must be performed not only by an accounting firm that is "independent" under the SEC's definition, but one that is "a registered public accounting firm,"[147] which means a firm that is registered with the Public Company Accounting Oversight Board ("PCAOB" or "Board").[148] SOX created the PCAOB,[149] which is a nonprofit corporation headed by five members who are selected by the SEC.[150] The PCAOB is charged with establishing "such auditing and related attestation standards, such quality control standards, such ethics standards, and such independence standards to be used by registered public accounting firms in the preparation and issuance of audit reports, as required by [SOX] or the rules of the Commission, or as may be necessary or appropriate in the public

———————

[145]   SOX § 202, 15 U.S.C. § 78j-1(i), with this requirement also included in the definition of an "independent" accountant at 17 C.F.R. § 210.2-01(c)(7)(i).

[146]   SOX § 204, 15 U.S.C. § 78j-1(k), repeated in SEC regulations at 17 C.F.R. § 210.2-07(a)(3). Not all of the required communication was newly minted by SOX.

[147]   SOX § 102(a), 15 U.S.C. § 7212(a).

[148]   SOX § 102(a), 15 U.S.C. § 7212(a). Technically, the law says only that it is unlawful for any but a "registered public accounting firm" to "prepare or issue, or to participate in the preparation or issuance of, any audit report" for a public company, but since an "audit report" is the "document or other record" that is "prepared following an audit performed for the purposes of compliance with the requirements of the securities laws," SOX § 2(a)(4), 15 U.S.C. § 7201(4)(A), the prohibition effectively limits auditors of public companies to registered firms.

[149]   SOX § 101; 15 U.S.C. § 7211(a).

[150]   15 U.S.C. § 7211 (a), (e)(1) & (4). The SEC has "oversight and enforcement authority over the [PCAOB]," SOX § 107(a), 15 U.S.C. § 7217(a), a general power that is supplemented by many specific powers, including the powers to "relieve the [PCAOB] of any responsibility to enforce compliance with any provision of [SOX], the securities laws, the rules of the [PCAOB], or professional standards," to "censure or impose limitations upon the activities, functions, and operations of the [PCAOB]," and to "remove from office or censure any . . . member of the [PCAOB]." SOX § 107(d); 15 U.S.C. § 7217(d), with removal at will under *Free Enterprise Fund v. Public Co. Accounting Oversight Bd.*, 561 U.S. 477, 508–09 (2010).

interest or for the protection of investors."[151] No proposed PCAOB rule becomes effective without the Commission's approval, and the SEC has the power to abrogate, delete, or add to Board rules.[152]

The PCAOB must inspect registered firms[153] in order, among other things, to "identify any act or practice or omission to act by the registered public accounting firm, or by any associated person thereof[154] . . . that may be in violation of [SOX], the rules of the [PCAOB], the rules of the Commission, the firm's own quality control policies, or professional standards."[155] Subject to certain significant limitations, the PCAOB shall "[make a written report containing the PCAOB's findings for each inspection] available in appropriate detail to the public . . . , except that no portions of the inspection report that deal with criticisms of or potential defects in the quality control systems of the firm under inspection shall be made public if those criticisms or defects are addressed by the firm, to the

---

[151]   SOX § 103(a)(1); 15 U.S.C. § 7213(a)(1). SOX required the Board to adopt existing audit standards until it developed its own (SOX § 103(a)(3)(B); 15 U.S.C. § 7213(a)(3)(B)), and the PCAOB did so by adopting, generally, through the Board's Rule 3200T, the audit standards of the American Institute of Certified Public Accountants in effect on April 16, 2003. PCAOB Release No. 2003-006 (Apr. 18, 2003). In 2015, the PCAOB reorganized its rules. PCAOB Release No. 2015-002 (Mar. 31, 2015). In doing so, it observed that it had "issued 18 auditing standards (AS Nos. 1–18), which have superseded 12 interim auditing standards and amended the majority of the remaining interim auditing standards to varying degrees." *Id.* at 2. The Board at the same time rescinded some of the interim standards (at 8) and, effective December 3, 2016, converted Rule 3200 from a temporary to a permanent rule (at 14). Rule 3200 continues to provide that accountants auditing public companies "shall comply with all applicable auditing standards adopted by the Board and approved by the SEC, including, to the extent not superseded or amended by the Board, AICPA Statements on Auditing Standards as in existence on April 16, 2003." *Id.* at 21, A4-1.

One Board standard—initially PCAOB Auditing Standard No. 2, now superseded by PCAOB Auditing Standard No. 5—required an *audit* each year of each public company's internal control over financial reporting; that is, an audit of internal financial control systems in addition to an audit of the numbers in the financial statements. As we will see in Chapter Ten, that additional audit—required by the PCAOB—proved costly and engendered efforts to reduce the burden the new audit imposed on public companies, particularly smaller public companies.

The auditing standards govern how accounting firms check the financial numbers that public companies place in their financial statements. But the standards governing calculation of the numbers and how they are categorized—e.g., what can be counted as revenue—are not *auditing standards* but *accounting principles*. The SEC has the right "to recognize, as 'generally accepted' for purposes of the securities laws, any accounting principles established by a standard setting body" defined in such a way that the reference is to the Financial Accounting Standards Board ("FASB"), which is an independent private-sector organization. SOX § 108, 15 U.S.C. § 77s(b); *see also* HAROLD S. BLOOMENTHAL, SARBANES-OXLEY ACT IN PERSPECTIVE § 8:21 (2016 ed.). The SEC has formally recognized the FASB as the private standard setter. Commission Statement of Policy Reaffirming the Status of the FASB as a Designated Private-Sector Standard Setter, Sec. Act Release No. 33-8221 (Apr. 25, 2003).

[152]   SOX § 107(b)(2) & (5); 15 U.S.C. § 7217(b)(2) & (5).

[153]   SOX § 104, 15 U.S.C. § 7214(a)(1). As a condition to registration, accounting firms must agree to provide documents and testimony to the Board. SOX § 102(b)(3)(A), 15 U.S.C. § 7212(b)(3)(A).

[154]   An "associated person" is "any individual proprietor, partner, shareholder, principal, accountant, or other professional employee" who "shares in the profits of, or receives compensation in any other form" from the firm or "participates as agent or otherwise on behalf of such accounting firm in any activity of the firm." SOX § 2(a)(9); 15 U.S.C. § 7201(9)(A).

[155]   SOX § 104(c)(1); 15 U.S.C. § 7214(c)(1).

satisfaction of the Board, not later than 12 months after the date of the inspection report."[156] Obviously, the proviso gives registered firms a tremendous incentive to correct quality control system defects within the 12 months.

In addition to inspections, the PCAOB may investigate registered firms, and the accountants working at them, for possible violation of "any provision of [SOX], the rules of the Board, the provisions of the securities laws relating to the preparation and issuance of audit reports and the obligations and liabilities of accountants with respect thereto."[157]

After conducting disciplinary proceedings in accordance with its rules and as set forth in SOX, the PCAOB may impose a wide variety of sanctions on registered accounting firms or any "associated persons," including (i) temporary or permanent revocation of the firm's registration, (ii) temporary or permanent prohibition of a person from associating with a registered firm, (iii) civil monetary penalties of up to $131,185 for an individual and $2,623,700 for a firm per violation of PCAOB rules, or relevant securities law statutes or rules, or professional standards (with those amounts raised to $983,888 and $19,677,750 if the individual's or firm's violation(s) was (were) either intentional, knowing, or reckless, or consisted of repeated instances of negligent conduct).[158] The SEC "may enhance, modify, cancel, reduce, or require the remission of a sanction imposed by the Board."[159]

Federally imposed auditor duty to report violations of law to a public company's board and, under certain circumstances, to the SEC. Federal law requires each audit to include "procedures designed to provide reasonable assurance of detecting illegal acts that would have a direct and material effect on the determination of financial statement amounts."[160] If the auditor during an audit "becomes aware of information indicating that an illegal act . . . has or may have occurred," the auditor must, "in accordance with generally accepted auditing standards . . . [(i)] determine whether it is likely that an illegal act has occurred" and (ii) "if so, [a] determine and consider the possible effect of the illegal act on the financial statements of the issuer . . . " and [b] "unless the illegal act is clearly inconsequential," "inform the appropriate level of the management of the issuer and assure

---

[156]   SOX § 104(g)(2), 15 U.S.C. § 7214(g)(2).

[157]   SOX § 105(b)(1), 15 U.S.C. § 7215(b)(1). The PCAOB may discover such a violation during an inspection and open an investigation as a result. SOX § 104(c)(3); 15 U.S.C. § 7214(c)(3). But it has jurisdiction to undertake an investigation "regardless of how the [violation] is brought to [its] attention." 15 U.S.C. § 7215(b)(1).

[158]   SOX § 105(c)(4), 15 U.S.C. § 7215(c)(4) &(5); and Adjustments to Civil Monetary Penalty Amounts, 81 Fed. Reg. 43,042, 43,047 (July 1, 2016).

[159]   SOX § 107(c)(3), 15 U.S.C. § 7217(c)(3).

[160]   15 U.S.C. § 78j-1(a)(1). This law dates back to 1995.

that the audit committee of the issuer . . . is adequately informed."[161] For our purposes, we will call this the "first 10A report." If, after making this first 10A report, the auditor concludes that (i) "the illegal act has a material effect on the financial statements of the issuer"; (ii) "the senior management has not taken, and the board of directors has not caused senior management to take timely and appropriate remedial actions"; and (iii) the failure to take such actions "is reasonably expected to warrant departure from a standard report of the auditor, when made, or warrant resignation from the audit engagement"—then the auditor must report those conclusions to the company's board.[162] We will call this the "second 10A report." A public company receiving this second 10A report from its auditor must "inform the [SEC] by notice not later than 1 business day after the receipt of such report" and provide the auditor with a copy of the notice.[163] If the company does not provide the notice to the auditor, then the auditor must do so, even if it resigns.[164]

Auditor liability in government enforcement actions and private lawsuits based on violations of the federal securities laws. The SEC can bring civil enforcement actions against accounting firms or individual accountants who themselves violate, or assist their clients in violating, the federal securities disclosure rules—both civil lawsuits in federal court and administrative actions.[165] For example, the SEC sued KPMG and named partners in federal district court alleging that—in conducting audits of Xerox and providing audit opinions for Xerox financial statements—the partners had violated Rule 10b-5, section 17(a) of the 33 Act, and aided and abetted Xerox in violating federal law and rules requiring public companies to keep accurate books and records and maintain internal controls to produce financial statements complying with accounting rules.[166] In addition to filing the federal lawsuit, the Commission filed an administrative proceeding against KPMG.[167] KPMG and the four partners that the Commission pursued individually all settled, without admitting or denying the SEC's allegations. KPMG paid $22.475 million in disgorgement, interest, and a civil penalty; it also agreed to a cease-and-desist order being entered against it and to make a number of internal

---

[161]   15 U.S.C. § 78j-1(b)(1).

[162]   15 U.S.C. § 78j-1(b)(2).

[163]   15 U.S.C. § 78j-1(b)(3).

[164]   15 U.S.C. § 78j-1(b)(3)–(4).

[165]   15 U.S.C. §§ 77t, 78u.

[166]   First Amended Complaint [for] Securities Fraud, *SEC v. KPMG LLP, et al.,* C.A. No. 03 CV 0671 (DLC) (S.D.N.Y. Oct. 3, 2003), http://www.sec.gov/litigation/complaints/comp18389.htm.

[167]   Order Instituting Public Administrative and Cease-and-Desist Proceedings Pursuant to Section 8A of the Securities Act of 1933, Section 21C of the Securities Exchange Act of 1934 and Rule 102(e) of the Rules of Practice, Making Findings, and Imposing Remedial Sanctions and a Cease-and-Desist Order, *In re KPMG LLP,* SEC Admin. Proceeding, File No. 3-11905 (Apr. 19, 2005).

reforms.[168] The individual partners that the Commission pursued agreed to a variety of sanctions including, in particular cases, suspension from practice before the Commission subject to a right to apply for reinstatement, injunctions against further violations, civil penalties (of $150,000 in two cases and $100,000 in another), and censure.[169]

Private investors can also recover against auditors under the federal securities laws. For example, investors who purchase stock in a public offering pursuant to a registration statement containing false audited figures can sue the auditor under section 11 of the 33 Act, and the auditor will be liable unless it can show that its audit was not negligent.[170] As another example, private investors who can show that they bought or sold stock on the basis of false audited financial statements can recover against auditors if they can show that the auditors were at least severely reckless in the audit with respect to the false numbers and that the false audit caused the investors economic loss.[171] But today, accountants are seldom sued in private securities class actions. Auditors were defendants in only 1% of the securities class actions filed in 2015.[172]

SEC power to deny auditors the opportunity to practice before the Commission. The SEC can temporarily or permanently bar an accountant from practicing before the Commission,[173] which effectively forbids the accountant from auditing public companies. One of the grounds for such a bar is that the accountant engaged in "unethical or improper professional conduct," with "improper professional conduct" for accountants meaning

(A) Intentional or knowing conduct, including reckless conduct, that results in a violation of applicable professional standards; or

(B) Either of the following two types of negligent conduct:

(1) A single instance of highly unreasonable conduct that results in a violation of applicable professional standards in circumstances in which an accountant knows, or should know, that heightened scrutiny is warranted.

---

[168]   SEC Litig. Release No. 19191 (Apr. 19, 2005), http://www.sec.gov/litigation/litreleases/lr19191.htm.

[169]   Order Instituting Public Administrative Proceedings, Making Findings and Imposing Remedial Sanctions Pursuant to Rule 102(e) of the Commission's Rules of Practice, *In re Joseph T. Boyle, CPA,* SEC Admin. Proceeding, File No. 3-12120 (Dec. 2, 2005), http://www.sec.gov/litigation/admin/34-52878.pdf; SEC Litig. Release No. 19573 (Feb. 22, 2006), http://www.sec.gov/litigation/litreleases/lr19573.htm.

[170]   15 U.S.C. § 77k(a)–(b).

[171]   *See, e.g., In re Suprema Specialties, Inc. Sec. Litig.,* 438 F.3d 256, 279–81 (3d Cir. 2006) (reversing district court dismissal of Rule 10b-5 claims against accountant).

[172]   Cornerstone Research, *Securities Class Action Case Filings, 2015 Year in Review* 8 (2016).

[173]   17 C.F.R. § 201.102(e).

(2) Repeated instances of unreasonable conduct, each resulting in a violation of applicable professional standards, that indicate a lack of competence to practice before the Commission.[174]

The SEC can similarly bar an accountant who (i) has "willfully violated, or willfully aided and abetted the violation of any provision of the Federal securities laws or the rules and regulations thereunder"; (ii) lacks "the requisite qualifications to represent others"; or (iii) is "lacking in character or integrity."[175]

QUESTIONS ON NATIONAL ACCOUNTING AND AUDITING STANDARDS

Why might it be helpful to have national auditing standards?

Should a federally established non-profit develop those standards? If so, should the SEC have the ability to change them?

The federal securities laws regulate attorneys in at least three ways.

Attorney liability in government enforcement actions and private lawsuits based on violations of the federal securities laws. The SEC can pursue in civil enforcement actions an attorney who violates the federal securities laws or who aids and abets a client in violating the disclosure requirements of those laws.[176] The SEC can also bring an enforcement action against an attorney who himself or herself creates false or misleading offering materials either knowingly or, under some circumstances, negligently.[177]

---

[174]   17 C.F.R. § 201.102(e)(1)(ii) & (iv).

[175]   17 C.F.R. § 201.102(e)(1)(i), (ii) & (iii).

[176]   15 U.S.C. §§ 78u, 78t(e); *see, e.g., SEC v. Fehn*, 97 F.3d 1276 (9th Cir. 1996).

[177]   A defendant must have scienter with respect to the misleading nature of a disclosure in order to be liable under Rule 10b-5 or section 17(a)(1) (i.e., know that the document misleads or be severely reckless in not knowing). 17 C.F.R. § 240.10b-5; 15 U.S.C. § 77q(a)(1); *Aaron v. SEC*, 446 U.S. 680, 691, 695–96 (1980). However, a defendant can be liable for violating section 17(a)(2) or (a)(3) by mere negligence. 15 U.S.C. § 77q(a)(2)–(3); *Aaron*, 446 U.S. at 695–97; *SEC v. Morgan Keegan & Co., Inc.*, 678 F.3d 1233, 1244 (11th Cir. 2012); *SEC v. Smart*, 678 F.3d 850, 857 (10th Cir. 2012); *SEC v. Ficken*, 546 F.3d 45, 47 (1st Cir. 2008).

For examples of an action against an attorney, *see* Complaint, *SEC v. Biopure Corp., et al.*, No. 05-CA-11853 WGY (D. Mass. Sept. 14, 2005), http://sec.gov/litigation/complaints/comp19376.pdf (alleging 10b-5 violations against, among others, the general counsel of a biotechnology company on the ground that she "substantially participated in drafting, reviewing and/or approving" misleading offering documents, other SEC filings, and press releases), SEC Litig. Release No. 19825 (Sept. 12, 2006), http://www.sec.gov/litigation/litreleases/2006/lr19825.htm (Biopure general counsel settled the action by agreeing, without admitting or denying the alleged facts, to an injunction prohibiting her from aiding and abetting future violations of the SEC "books

While shareholders in the past could, in some circuits, sue attorneys under Rule 10b-5 who knowingly prepared deceptive disclosure documents on which the shareholders relied in buying stock,[178] shareholders cannot do so today, except for statements in the documents that are attributed to the attorneys under conditions that permit the attorneys to prevent the attribution.[179]

SEC power to deny attorneys the opportunity to practice before the Commission. Second, the SEC can temporarily or permanently deny an attorney the privilege of practicing before it if the Commission finds that the attorney does not possess the "requisite qualifications[,]" lacks "character or integrity[,]" has engaged in "unethical or improper professional conduct," or has willfully violated or aided and abetted the violation of federal securities laws.[180] The rule gives the Commission the right to discipline an attorney in this way even if he or she has not committed a securities violation, or aided or abetted such an offense— simply, for example, because the attorney does "not possess the requisite qualifications to represent others" or because the attorney "lack[s] . . . character or integrity" or because the attorney "has engaged in unethical or improper professional conduct."[181] While Rule 102(e) does not itself "establish professional standards," it "enables the [SEC] to discipline professionals who have engaged in improper professional conduct by failing

---

and records" statute and related rules, with the SEC agreeing to dismiss the 10b-5 count); *and see Weiss v. SEC*, 468 F.3d 849, 855–56 (D.C. Cir. 2006) (denying petition for review by attorney found by the SEC to have violated 33 Act section 17 by negligently representing that the interest on certain municipal debt would be free from federal income taxation).

[178]   15 U.S.C. §§ 78j(b), 78u-4; 17 C.F.R. § 240.10b-5. *See, e.g., In re Enron Corp. Sec., Derivative & ERISA Litig.*, 235 F. Supp. 2d 549, 705, n.129 (S.D. Tex. 2002) (denying law firm motion to dismiss 10b-5 claim because the law firm "chose not once, but frequently, to make statements to the public about Enron's business and financial situation" by allegedly "drafting and approving over years a great many of Enron's 'disclosures' for public SEC filings, press releases, and shareholder reports, which [the firm] knew or had reason to expect potential investors to have access to and rely upon in deciding to invest in Enron securities").

[179]   *See, e.g., Ziemba v. Cascade Int'l, Inc.*, 256 F.3d 1194, 1205–07 (11th Cir. 2001) (affirming dismissal of law firm; attorneys' "role in drafting, creating, reviewing or editing allegedly fraudulent . . . press releases" could not support 10(b) claim where no misrepresentations were publicly attributed to firm). The Supreme Court has endorsed this approach, holding that a party "makes" a statement for purposes of Rule 10b-5(b) only if that party has "ultimate control over the content of the statement"—i.e., has "authority over the content of the statement and whether and how to communicate it." *Janus Capital Grp., Inc. v. First Derivative Traders*, 131 S. Ct. 2296, 2302–03 (2011). The Court embraced the "attribution" analysis, saying that "in the ordinary case, attribution within a statement or implicit from surrounding circumstances is strong evidence that a statement was made by—and only by—the party to whom it is attributed." *Id.* at 2302. One federal court of appeals has held that this limitation on Rule 10b-5 liability does not apply to criminal cases brought under the rule. *Prousalis v. Moore*, 751 F.3d 272 (4th Cir. 2014), *cert. denied*, 135 S. Ct. 990 (2015).

[180]   17 C.F.R. § 201.102(e)(1).

[181]   17 C.F.R. § 201.102(e)(1)(i)–(ii). *See Marrie v. SEC*, 374 F.3d 1196, 1205 (D.C. Cir. 2004) (saying in the context of a Commission proceeding against an accountant: "The Commission's authority to discipline professionals has long been distinguished from the execution of its substantive enforcement functions.").

to satisfy the rules, regulations or standards to which they are already subject, including state ethic[s] rules governing attorney conduct."[182] Accordingly, the SEC could use Rule 102(e) to discipline an attorney who violates state ethical rules in practicing before the Commission, or who violates the new SEC "up the ladder" reporting requirement discussed later in this chapter and more extensively in Chapter Twenty-Two.

Even when the Commission does not impose discipline in a Rule 102(e) proceeding, it can provide guidance to securities lawyers through its words. In *Carter and Johnson*,[183] a company that leased telephone equipment systems to commercial customers sent letters to shareholders, issued press releases, and sent a quarterly report to stockholders without disclosing the need for additional financing in order to continue operations at existing levels. The company also announced an amended credit agreement, but did not set out the limitations on company operations that a related document included. The company filed an 8-K that did not attach that related document nor adequately describe the severe restrictions on company operations that a specified amount of additional borrowing or failure to meet a liquidity test would trigger.[184] The company went bankrupt. The outside counsel who were respondents in a Rule 2(e)[185] proceeding had urged the company to provide more disclosure, but the company had not followed that advice. The SEC determined that the attorneys' "periodic exhortations . . . to improve the quality of [the client's] disclosure, leads us to believe that [the attorneys] did not intend to assist the violations by their inaction or silence. Rather, they seemed to be at a loss for how to deal with a difficult client."[186]

Since the attorneys gave their client solid substantive advice, the question was what the lawyers should have done when the client did not follow that advice and, in particular, whether the attorneys had acted in an unprofessional way by not taking additional steps, such as resigning. The Commission did not find unethical or improper professional conduct, reasoning that it had never defined such conduct in this context.

For guidance in future cases, and speaking specifically to the "unethical or improper professional conduct" standard in what is now Rule 102(e), the Commission said this:

> When a lawyer with significant responsibilities in the effectuation
> of a company's compliance with the disclosure requirements of the

---

[182]   Implementation of Standards of Professional Conduct for Attorneys, 67 Fed. Reg. 71,670, 71,671, n.13 (Dec. 2, 2002).

[183]   *In re William R. Carter and Charles A. Johnson, Jr.*, SEC Admin. Proceeding, File No. 3-5464, 1981 WL 384414 (Feb. 28, 1981).

[184]   *Id.* at *15–16.

[185]   The SEC redesignated Rule 2(e) as Rule 102(e) in 1995.

[186]   *In re William R. Carter and Charles A. Johnson, Jr.*, at *27.

federal securities laws becomes aware that his [or her] client is engaged in a substantial and continuing failure to satisfy those disclosure requirements, his [or her] continued participation violates professional standards unless he [or she] takes prompt steps to end the client's noncompliance. . . .[187]

We recognize [ ] that the "best result" is not always obtainable, and that there may occur situations where the lawyer must conclude that the misconduct is so extreme or irretrievable, or the involvement of his [or her] client's management and board of directors in the misconduct is so thoroughgoing and pervasive that any action short of resignation would be futile. We would anticipate that cases where a lawyer has no choice but to resign would be rare and of an egregious nature.[188]

SEC rules requiring attorneys to report to public company boards violations of securities laws or breaches of fiduciary duty by corporate officers and employees. Third, SOX section 305 included a provision requiring the SEC to issue rules "for attorneys appearing and practicing before the Commission in any way in the representation of issuers"

(1) requiring an attorney to report evidence of a material violation of securities law or breach of fiduciary duty or similar violation by the company or any agent thereof, to the chief legal counsel or the chief executive officer of the company (or the equivalent thereof); and

(2) if the counsel or officer does not appropriately respond to the evidence (adopting, as necessary, appropriate remedial measures or sanctions with respect to the violation), requiring the attorney to report the evidence to the audit committee of the board of directors of the issuer or to another committee of the board of directors comprised solely of directors not employed directly or indirectly by the issuer, or to the board of directors.[189]

The SEC complied by adopting the rules set out at 17 C.F.R. §§ 205.1–205.7. Because these rules require attorneys, under certain circumstances, to report evidence of wrongdoing to the board of directors—which occupies the top rung in the corporate hierarchy ladder—these rules are sometimes

---

[187] These steps, today, would involve reporting "up the ladder" in connection with the rules that the Commission adopted pursuant to SOX section 307.

[188] *In re William R. Carter and Charles A. Johnson, Jr.*, at *30–31 (footnotes omitted). With minor changes, I have taken my summary of *Carter and Johnson* from a chapter that I contribute to a treatise. The summary was originally published in Section 5F, "SEC Rule 102(e)" of Chapter 36, "Obligations and Potential Liabilities of Attorneys in Public and Private Offerings" by William O. Fisher, in the treatise, VENTURE CAPITAL & PUBLIC OFFERING NEGOTIATION, Michael J. Halloran, et al., Editors, © CCH Incorporated, 1994 and Supplemented 2015. Reprinted with the permission of CCH Incorporated. To order a complete copy of this work, please contact the publishers at https://lrus.wolterskluwer.com/.

[189] 15 U.S.C. § 7245.

called the "up the ladder" rules. We will study these rules in detail in Chapter Twenty-Two.

QUESTION ON SEC RULES FOR LAWYERS

Why should the federal government adopt rules governing the relationship between attorneys and public companies, at the level of detail that prescribes a report by an attorney to particular officers or the board of directors under certain circumstances?

C. LISTING STANDARDS

As used in this book, a "public company" is one that lists its stock on a national stock exchange. Each national stock exchange is a "self-regulated organization," or SRO, registered under the 34 Act.[190] Each exchange must submit proposed rules to the SEC and, with some exceptions, no proposed rule change can take effect without the approval of the SEC.[191]

By its rules, each exchange imposes requirements on the companies that list their stock. We will call these rules "listing standards." We will study only the requirements of the New York Stock Exchange ("NYSE") and NASDAQ. The NYSE listing standards are part of its Listed Company Manual ("NYSE Manual"), which you can find at http://nysemanual.nyse.com/lcm/. The NASDAQ listing standards are part of the NASDAQ Stock Market Rules ("NASDAQ Rules"), which you can find at http://nasdaq.cchwallstreet.com/.

Each of these exchanges restricts listing to companies that meet certain numerical criteria for number of shareholders, and financial criteria such as pretax earnings[192] or number and market value of publicly held shares.[193]

But the exchanges also impose listing requirements that go directly to corporate governance.[194]

---

[190]   15 U.S.C. § 78s(a).

[191]   15 U.S.C. § 78s(b)(1).

[192]   NYSE MANUAL § 102.01C (I)(1). Quotations from the New York Stock Exchange Listed Company Manual reprinted with permission from the New York Stock Exchange.

[193]   NASDAQ Rule 5315(e) & (f). Quotations from the NASDAQ Stock Market Rules reprinted with permission from Nasdaq, Inc. Copyright © 2016 by Nasdaq, Inc. All rights reserved.

[194]   The chief executive officer of each NYSE issuer must annually certify that "he or she is not aware of any violation by the listed company of the NYSE corporate governance listing standards, qualifying the certification to the extent necessary" and "must promptly notify the NYSE in writing after any executive officer of the listed company becomes aware of any non-compliance with any applicable provisions of this Section 303A," the section that contains the

Shareholders. Some listing standards protect shareholders. For example, the NYSE requires that

- "[i]mmediate publicity . . . be given to the calling of a shareholders' meeting where any matter affecting the rights or privileges of shareholders or any other matter not of routine nature is to be considered";[195]

- "[a]ctively operating companies . . . solicit proxies for all meetings of shareholders . . . [in order] to afford shareholders a convenient method of voting";[196]

- listed companies hold annual stockholders meetings;[197]

- shareholders approve equity compensation plans, and issuance of stock in connection with a merger or asset acquisition where the shares issued would either equal or exceed—in number of shares or voting power—20% of the number or voting power of the shares before the issuance;[198] and

- "[w]here shareholder approval is a prerequisite to the listing of any additional or new securities of a listed company, or where any matter requires shareholder approval, [the shareholders must approve by a] minimum vote[,] . . . defined

---

corporate governance standards. NYSE MANUAL § 303A.12(a) & (b). In addition, each listed company must annually provide the exchange with a Written Affirmation that states that the company is complying with the listing standards or identifies in what ways it is not and provide an interim Written Affirmation whenever the company makes a change in its board or a board committee subject to the corporate governance listing standards. NYSE MANUAL § 303A.12(c), with the affirmations at 2 BUCKHOLZ, DESKBOOK, *supra* note 128, at §§ 5B:2.4, 5D:2.4. If a company is not in compliance with a corporate governance requirement, the NYSE may issue a public reprimand letter. NYSE MANUAL § 303A.13. If a company repeatedly or flagrantly violates listing standards, the NYSE may delist the company (*id.* Commentary), but delisting only occurs after notice to the company and an opportunity for a review by a committee of the board of directors of the exchange. NYSE MANUAL § 804.00.

NASDAQ requires each listed company to promptly notify the exchange "after an Executive Officer of the [company] becomes aware of any non-compliance . . . with the requirements of [the] Rule 5600 series," which contains that exchange's corporate governance requirements. NASDAQ Rule 5625. NASDAQ has an elaborate process for delisting companies that violate listing standards, with a formal written notice of non-compliance from NASDAQ and an opportunity to demand a hearing. *See* NASDAQ Stock Market Rules in the 5800 series.

A public company must file a Form 8-K if (i) the company receives a notice from an exchange that the company's stock does not qualify for continued listing or receives a notice that an exchange has taken all steps necessary to delist the stock; (ii) the company informs an exchange that it is materially out of compliance with listing standards; or (iii) the company receives a public reprimand from an exchange indicating that the company has violated a standard for continued listing. Form 8-K, Item 3.01. Most companies work hard to maintain compliance with listing standards, in part because they do not want the publicity that could be generated by such an 8-K filing.

[195]   NYSE MANUAL § 401.01.
[196]   NYSE MANUAL § 402.04.
[197]   NYSE MANUAL § 302.00.
[198]   NYSE MANUAL § 312.03(a) & (c).

as approval by a majority of votes cast on a proposal in a proxy bearing on the particular matter."[199]

NASDAQ listing standards impose somewhat similar requirements. For example, NASDAQ requires listed companies to: hold annual stockholders meetings;[200] solicit proxies and provide proxy statements for all shareholder meetings;[201] obtain shareholder approval for equity compensation plans,[202] and for issuance of stock for a merger or asset purchase that would increase either the number or voting power of shares by 20% or more;[203] and obtain, at a minimum, when shareholder approval is required by NASDAQ rule, "a majority of the total votes cast on the proposal."[204]

The listing standards also seek to ensure that shareholders receive information from listed companies. The NYSE requires, independently of the federal securities laws and rules, that listed companies make annual reports available to shareholders on the companies' websites[205] and that they release to the press "an interim [i.e., quarterly] earnings release as soon as its interim financial statements are available."[206] Again, NASDAQ has similar requirements: for example, that each listed company "shall make prompt disclosure to the public . . . of any material information that would reasonably be expected to affect the value of its securities or influence investors' decisions."[207]

Board of directors. The listing standards include elaborate definitions of "independent directors."[208] The detail in these definitions is so fine that a director of a NYSE-listed company is not independent if his or her daughter-in-law is a current executive officer of a company that received, in any of the last three years, the greater of either $1 million or 2% of its gross revenues from the NYSE-listed company.[209]

---

[199]   NYSE MANUAL § 312.07.

[200]   NASDAQ Rule 5620 (a).

[201]   NASDAQ Rule 5620 (b).

[202]   NASDAQ Rule 5635 (c).

[203]   NASDAQ Rule 5635 (a)(1).

[204]   NASDAQ Rule 5635 (e)(4).

[205]   NYSE MANUAL § 203.01.

[206]   NYSE MANUAL § 203.02.

[207]   NASDAQ Rule 5250(b)(1).

[208]   NYSE MANUAL § 303A.02; NASDAQ Rule 5605(a)(2).

[209]   NYSE MANUAL § 303A.02(b)(v) & General Commentary to 303A.02(b); *see* the similar NASDAQ Rule 5605(a)(2)(D) (with the limits set so that the director is not independent if the daughter-in-law is an executive officer of an organization receiving, in any of the last three years, the greater of $200,000 or 5% of its gross revenues from the listed company; IM-5605 states that this applies even if the recipient organization is a charity).

The listing standards then provide that a majority of each listed company's board must consist of independent directors.[210]

The listing standards also directly regulate the operation of boards of directors. They require, for example, that the non-management directors regularly meet in executive session, with no management present.[211] The NYSE rules require boards to "adopt and disclose corporate governance guidelines."[212] The commentary to that requirement states that the guidelines "must" address all of the following:

- **Director qualification standards.** These standards should, at minimum, reflect the independence requirements set forth in Sections 303A.01 and 303A.02. Companies may also address other substantive qualification requirements, including policies limiting the number of boards on which a director may sit, and director tenure, retirement and succession.

- **Director responsibilities.** These responsibilities should clearly articulate what is expected from a director, including basic duties and responsibilities with respect to attendance at board meetings and advance review of meeting materials.

- **Director access to management and, as necessary and appropriate, independent advisors.**

- **Director compensation.** Director compensation guidelines should include general principles for determining the form and amount of director compensation (and for reviewing those principles, as appropriate). The board should be aware that questions as to director's independence may be raised when director's fees and emoluments exceed what is customary. Similar concerns may be raised when the listed company makes substantial charitable contributions to organizations in which a director is affiliated, or enters into consulting contracts with (or provides other indirect forms of compensation to) a director. The board should critically evaluate each of these matters when determining the form and amount of director compensation, and the independence of a director.

- **Director orientation and continuing education.**

- **Management succession.** Succession planning should include policies and principles for CEO selection and

---

[210]   NYSE MANUAL § 303A.01; NASDAQ Rule 5605(b)(1).

[211]   NYSE MANUAL § 303.A03; NASDAQ Rule 5605(b)(2) (limiting the executive sessions to independent directors).

[212]   NYSE MANUAL § 303A.09.

performance review, as well as policies regarding succession in the event of an emergency or the retirement of the CEO.

- **Annual performance evaluation of the board.** The board should conduct a self-evaluation at least annually to determine whether it and its committees are functioning effectively.[213]

The NYSE requires that boards have compensation committees, audit committees, and nominating committees populated exclusively by directors who are independent by the listing standards' definitions.[214] NASDAQ requires that each listed company have an audit committee and that all its members, with a limited exception for a maximum of one member, be independent by the NASDAQ standard.[215] NASDAQ requires a compensation committee composed entirely of directors independent under that standard (with a limited exception for a single committee member) and that either a nominations committee consisting only of independent directors (again with a limited exception for one committee member), or all of the independent directors on the board (acting together), select nominees for board seats or recommend nominees to the full board.[216]

The listing standards also directly address the operation of board committees. For example, the NYSE standards require audit, compensation, and nominating committees to have written charters.[217] The NYSE rules also include lists of duties for committees.[218]

---

[213]   *Id.*, Commentary.

[214]   NYSE MANUAL §§ 303A.04(a), 303A.05(a), 303A.07(a). In addition, the board must consider special factors relevant to determining the independence of compensation committee members, and the audit committee members must satisfy statutory standards for independence. NYSE MANUAL §§ 303A.02(a)(ii), 303A.06.

[215]   NASDAQ Rule 5605(c)(2). As does the NYSE, NASDAQ requires that audit committee members satisfy statutory standards for independence. NASDAQ Rule 5605(c)(2)(A)(ii).

[216]   NASDAQ Rule 5605(d) & (e).

[217]   NYSE MANUAL §§ 303A.04(b), 303A.05(b), 303A.07(b); *and see* NASDAQ Rule 5605(c)(1), (d)(1) (requiring charters for audit and compensation committees, but by (e)(2) requiring a "formal written charter or board resolution . . . addressing the nominations process . . .").

[218]   The list for the audit committee is longest, setting out the "duties and responsibilities" of the committee to include all of the duties and responsibilities set out in SEC rules "as well as to:"

(A)   at least annually, obtain and review a report by the independent auditor describing: the firm's internal quality-control procedures; any material issues raised by the most recent internal quality-control review, or peer review, of the firm, or by any inquiry or investigation by governmental or professional authorities, within the preceding five years, respecting one or more independent audits carried out by the firm, and any steps taken to deal with any such issues; and (to assess the auditor's independence) all relationships between the independent auditor and the listed company;

(B)   meet to review and discuss the listed company's annual audited financial statements and quarterly financial statements with management and the independent auditor, including reviewing the listed company's specific disclosures under "Management's Discussion and Analysis of Financial Condition and Results of Operations";

Both sets of standards specify that audit committee members must have or attain accounting knowledge. NYSE: "Each member of the audit committee must be financially literate . . . [and] at least one member of the audit committee must have accounting or related financial management expertise, as the listed company's board interprets such qualification in its business judgment."[219] NASDAQ: Each audit committee member must "be able to read and understand fundamental financial statements" and each committee must include "at least one member of the audit committee who has past employment experience in finance or accounting, requisite professional certification in accounting, or any other comparable experience or background which results in the individual's financial sophistication. . . ."[220]

Officers. The listing standards concentrate on boards of directors and contain few provisions that aim directly at officers. But each set of standards does demand the adoption of codes of ethics, with the codes for each NYSE and NASDAQ company to apply to all "directors, officers and employees."[221]

Outside professionals. The listing standards do not regulate auditors and lawyers directly, although the provisions concerning audit committees affect the interactions between auditors and those committees.[222]

D. DEBT COVENANTS AS A CONSTRAINT ON GOVERNANCE

Every time a corporation enters into a contract, it constrains the future choices of its board and officers. The corporation must either perform its contractual commitments or face possible liability for failing to do so. But when a company enters into a large long-term debt obligation, the

---

(C) discuss the listed company's earnings press releases, as well as financial information and earnings guidance provided to analysts and rating agencies;

(D) discuss policies with respect to risk assessment and risk management;

(E) meet separately, periodically, with management, with internal auditors (or other personnel responsible for the internal audit function) and with independent auditors;

(F) review with the independent auditor any audit problems or difficulties and management's response;

(G) set clear hiring policies for employees or former employees of the independent auditors; and

(H) report regularly to the board of directors.

NYSE MANUAL § 303A.07(b)(iii). The reference to "earnings press releases" reflects public companies' practice of releasing quarterly earnings to the press before filing a 10-Q (after the end of each of the first three quarters) or a 10-K (after the end of the fourth quarter).

[219] NYSE MANUAL § 303A.07(a) Commentary.

[220] NASDAQ Rule 5605(c)(2)(A).

[221] NYSE MANUAL § 303A.10; NASDAQ Rule 5610.

[222] See note 218 *supra.*

creditor(s) may include covenants in the documents that restrict a corporation in ways that touch pretty directly on governance.

Suppose that a company obtains a long-term loan from a syndicate of banks, and the loan documents contain a covenant that the company will not pay a dividend to shareholders until the company pays off the debt. By entering into that agreement, the board, which in the typical state scheme of governance has almost complete discretion to declare dividends or not, cedes that discretion. The same is true, though to a lesser degree, if the covenant provides that the corporation cannot increase dividend payments until the company pays off the debt.

The documents for a large, long-term loan might require that the borrowing company maintain certain financial ratios, such as a debt/equity ratio of no more than 2:1. The loan documents might also provide that the entire debt will become due on an accelerated basis if the company violates the covenant. If the company, after the loan, has a debt/equity ratio close to 2:1, the loan document may effectively prohibit the board from making a new capital investment financed by further debt—something that the board would otherwise be free to do.[223] We do not often think of debt

---

[223]   As a practical matter and assuming that the corporation in the example was otherwise financially sound, the company might negotiate with the lender(s) for a modification or waiver of the covenant, with the possible result that the company would pay the lender(s) for that modification or waiver. But the prospect of such a payment might, at least in a close case, deter a board from authorizing the new debt-financed capital expenditure. And, even if the company succeeds in obtaining a modification or waiver, the sequence of events will have given the creditors a voice in the capital expenditure decision that would otherwise simply be made by the board.

A lender might, as a condition of waiving a default, even require a change of management. The possibility that the lender might do so is arguably useful to corporate governance. *See, e.g.,* Douglas G. Baird & Robert K. Rasmussen, *The Prime Directive,* 75 U. CIN. L. REV. 921 (2007) (contending that (i) the principal job of a board of directors is to put the right person in the top executive position and to replace that individual when it is in the interest of the company to do so (at 933); (ii) boards are not good at replacing top executives because (a) they may be friends with the CEO and therefore too likely to "give the CEO the benefit of the doubt" (at 929); (b) the board picked the CEO and therefore may "overweight information that suggests that their decision was correct and underweight information that calls that decision into question" (at 936); and (c) the board receives its information largely from the CEO, who may give "[s]uccessful and promising projects . . . top billing [while] those that go awry receive scant mention" (at 935); bank lenders, however, "have better information than do directors" (at 938) and "may be better able than directors to guard against bias" in favor of the CEO (at 938); accordingly, it may be beneficial if "the price of the lender's agreeing not to call the loan [after an event constituting a default] can be the dismissal of the CEO" (at 938)).

Two academics provide further detail on how provisions in loan agreements affect governance:

The presence of . . . an institutional lender fundamentally alters corporate governance. The lending agreement contains many affirmative and negative covenants that give the lender de facto control over every aspect of the business. Moreover, the complete control the lender has over the debtor's cash flow gives the lender veto power over every course of action, whether internal to the corporation or outside it. Decisions normally reserved for directors and stockholders—such as whether to sell a division, change the business plan, or replace the managers—require the lender's explicit blessing. Trip wires are tied to the performance of the business and its discrete units, and a general provision gives the lender the ability to call the loan in the event of any material adverse change. The purpose of these trip wires is not to force repayment of the loan, but rather to ensure that

covenants as a part of corporate governance. But perhaps we should, when the covenants effectively transfer governance powers—particularly powers normally reserved to the board—to lenders.

E. SPECIAL RULES THAT GOVERN OUTSIDE PROFESSIONALS

Auditors. The purpose of an audit is to determine whether, in the opinion of the outside accounting firm performing the audit, the audited company's financial statements fairly present, in all material respects, the company's financial condition and results of operations in conformity with generally accepted accounting principles ("GAAP"). As set out in footnote 151, although the SEC has legal authority to establish the accounting principles for public companies, it uses the principles adopted by a private standard-setting body, the Financial Accounting Standards Board.

Similarly, although the PCAOB has legal authority to establish standards for audits of public companies, it has not yet adopted a full suite of standards, and relies for the rest on standards adopted by the American Institute of Certified Public Accountants. Again, see footnote 151.

Attorneys. Attorneys must abide by the standards of professional conduct of the jurisdiction in which they are admitted to the bar. The standards differ from state to state. Many states have adopted—often with important modifications—the Model Rules of Professional Conduct promulgated by the American Bar Association. Those rules include some that directly affect attorneys who represent corporations in instances in which officers or employees or directors are violating the law or are considering action that would constitute a violation. Three such rules are particularly important to us.

Rule 1.2(d) provides that a lawyer "shall not counsel a client to engage, or assist a client, in conduct that the lawyer knows is criminal or fraudulent. . . ."

Rule 1.6 generally requires lawyers to maintain the confidentiality of "information relating to the representation," but provides a number of exceptions. Included among those exceptions is one permitting a lawyer "to the extent the lawyer reasonably believes necessary" to reveal such information

(2) to prevent the client from committing a crime or fraud that is reasonably certain to result in substantial injury to the financial

---

lenders have control over major decisions and the ability to insist on changes in management when the business encounter reverses.

Douglas G. Baird & Robert K. Rasmussen, *Private Debt and the Missing Lever of Corporate Governance*, 154 U. PA. L. REV. 1209, 1227–28 (2006) (footnote omitted).

interests or property of another and in furtherance of which the client has used or is using the lawyer's services; [or]

(3) to prevent, mitigate or rectify substantial injury to the financial interests or property of another that is reasonably certain to result or has resulted from the client's commission of a crime or fraud in furtherance of which the client has used the lawyer's services. . . .[224]

Finally, Rule 1.13 governs a lawyer's representation of an organization such as a corporation. This is a long rule, and we will consider only parts.

Rule 1.13 provides that a lawyer representing a corporation represents the company, not the individual officers or directors.[225] If the

lawyer for an organization knows that an officer, employee or other person associated with the organization is engaged in action, intends to act or refuses to act in a matter related to the representation that is a violation of a legal obligation to the organization, or a violation of law that reasonably might be imputed to the organization, and that is likely to result in substantial injury to the organization, then the lawyer shall proceed as is reasonably necessary in the best interest of the organization.[226]

The presumptive best course of action is for the lawyer to "refer the matter to higher authority in the organization, including, if warranted by the circumstances to the highest authority that can act on behalf of the organization as determined by applicable law," which would be the board of directors if the client is a corporation.[227] If the board "insists upon or fails to address in a timely and appropriate manner an action, or a refusal to act, that is clearly a violation of law" and the lawyer "reasonably believes that the violation is reasonably certain to result in substantial injury to the organization, then the lawyer may reveal information relating to the representation whether or not Rule 1.6 permits such disclosure, but only if and to the extent the lawyer reasonably believes necessary to prevent substantial injury to the organization."[228]

Together, Rules 1.6 and 1.13 set out the circumstances in which attorneys could, for example, report their clients to the SEC.[229]

---

[224]   MODEL CODE OF PROF'L CONDUCT R. 1.6(b)(2)–(3).

[225]   *Id.* at R. 1.13(a); *see also* R. 1.7 cmt.34.

[226]   *Id.* at R. 1.13(b).

[227]   *Id.*

[228]   *Id.* at R. 1.13(c).

[229]   In practice, it is essential that you consult your own state's rules. For example, California has enacted a statute that flatly prohibits attorneys from revealing client confidences, except "to the extent that the attorney reasonably believes the disclosure is necessary to prevent a criminal

State law outside corporations codes touches accountants and attorneys. For example, both an accounting firm performing an audit for a public company and a law firm engaged to provide legal advice to that company owe the company a duty of care which, if violated, will give rise to a negligence claim.

F. THE FEDERALIZATION OF CORPORATE GOVERNANCE

At the state level, Delaware holds only a loose rein on corporations. At the federal level, Congress, the SEC, and the exchanges (through rules that the SEC approves, some of which Congress has required) impose detailed rules in large numbers. Is this displacement of state corporate law with federal corporate law a good idea?

Here is one provocative view:

[I]n the recent literature on the comparative advantages of state versus federal regulation of corporate governance, it seems to us that a significant point in favor of the states has been overlooked. It is a point that stresses differences in institutional design and approach between federal and state regulators, differences that give the states a considerable advantage in both flexibility and responsiveness as new problems arise. It is the unique ability of states to engage in what we will refer to as "thaumatrope analytics."

A thaumatrope is a device, popularized in the early nineteenth century, that generates an optical illusion through the spinning of a disc with a different image on each side—a horse and a man, for example, or a bird and a cage. When the viewer spins the thaumatrope, these images blend together to produce what appears to be a composite whole—the man atop the horse or the bird in the cage. In a previous article, one of us used the metaphor of the thaumatrope to describe the doctrinal evolution of "good faith" in corporate law. In this article, we use the phrase more broadly to describe the ability of state corporate law, especially in Delaware, to alternate between lax and stringent regulation, shifting between hard-edged rules and fuzzy standards and between strong and weak interpretations of fiduciary constraints. We argue that this back-and-forth between the vague and the concrete, the stringent and the lax, enables the states to generate

---

act that the attorney reasonably believes is likely to result in death of, or substantial bodily harm to, an individual." CAL. BUS. & PROF. CODE § 6068(e)(2). This rule forbids attorneys from disclosing a client confidence revealing a financial fraud.

a more subtle and effective form of regulation than the federal pattern of enacting governance mandates.[230]

* * *

The most commonly cited difference between regulators and courts, of course, is that regulators act prospectively while courts can only react. In Delaware, however, this difference is muted by the tendency of its judges to make pronouncements from the bench that, although unnecessary to reach the holding in the case at hand, announce the viewpoint of the particular judge on a particular issue and therefore indicate the likely approach of the court with respect to that issue. Although these statements are not binding on the court, they are, like regulatory guidelines, widely relied upon by parties in shaping their conduct and structuring their transactions. Through the concise and limited use of dicta, state courts can act prospectively in much the same way as regulators.

Indeed, the greatest difference between state corporate law courts and a regulatory agency is the ability of the judiciary, in Delaware especially, both to make and apply the law. In contrast to the typically rigid framework that would guide a regulatory agency, Delaware courts decide cases under the general principles of fiduciary duty. Fiduciary duty adjudication is, of course, accretive—like cases can be expected to be decided in a like manner—but it is also highly fact-specific, proceeding on a case-by-case basis. Because of the high degree of fact-specificity inherent in fiduciary-duty adjudication, corporate law judges are less bound by principles of *res judicata* and *stare decisis* than judges in other areas of law. This doctrinal flexibility distinguishes the Delaware judiciary not only from rule-bound regulatory agencies but also from the doctrinal confinement of other courts, including federal courts interpreting and applying federal statutes. Thus, not only are corporate law courts not constrained by a highly-specified legislative framework, but they are also largely unconstrained by their own prior pronouncements. In other words, the corporate law judiciary both makes and applies the law, doing so on a largely *ad hoc* basis.

---

[230]   Sean J. Griffith & Myron T. Steele, *On Corporate Law Federalism: Threatening the Thaumatrope*, 61 BUS. LAW. 1, 2 (2005) (footnotes omitted). Quotations from this article reprinted with permission from the American Bar Association. All rights reserved. These quotations or any portion thereof may not be copied or disseminated in any form or by any means or stored in an electronic database or retrieval system without the express written consent of the American Bar Association. On Corporate Law Federalism: Threatening the Thaumatrope, Business Law volume 61 number 1 ©2005 by the American Bar Association.

The freedom and flexibility of state courts to decide each corporate law matter anew, according to its own unique characteristics, has not been unanimously celebrated. Instead, state corporate law, especially in Delaware, has often been criticized as indeterminate. The critics argue that indeterminacy imposes costs on corporations.[231]

* * *

It is our view that much of this criticism is overstated. First of all, while focusing on the costs of indeterminacy, many of these accounts overlook the benefits. Yes, reduced predictability may complicate transaction planning, but it may also be the case that some degree of uncertainty actually facilitates bargaining by encouraging the parties to write more explicit contracts, coming to precise agreements on those points about which the law appears uncertain. Second, just as predictable rules are a mixed blessing for their tendency to be either over-inclusive (and therefore to discourage efficient transactions) or under-inclusive (and therefore avoidable), certainty itself may be only a qualified good since it enhances the potential of well-counseled corporations to evade the rationale behind the rule. Some degree of uncertainty, in other words, may increase the efficiency of law.[232]

* * *

Because state corporate law is built on a system of *ad hoc* interpretations of fiduciary duty, the state courts can not only act quickly in creating tailored decisions on a case-by-case basis, but equally importantly, Delaware's interventions, because they are highly context-specific, are not permanent. If a solution does not work, it can be quickly discarded in subsequent cases and thereby relegated to the dust-bin of corporate law history. The federal government, by contrast, merely lengthens the list of mandates that it imposes on all public companies, governing the best corporations according to the conduct of the worst and pushing marginal companies out of the public market.[233]

Aside from whether fewer specific legislative rules, supplemented by a common-law "facts and circumstances" elaboration by courts, are better than a long list of detailed requirements in statutes, regulations, and listing standards, another part of the federal versus state debate revolves around a long-running controversy. One side in that controversy argues that states—competing for whatever revenues incorporation in them will provide—will cater to the managements and boards who make the

---

[231] *Id.* at 10–11 (footnotes omitted).
[232] *Id.* at 12–13 (footnotes omitted).
[233] *Id.* at 22 (footnote omitted).

incorporation decisions. This side claims that such incentives produce a "race to the bottom," as states write their corporate law in ways that disadvantage shareholders and advantage the management that will select the jurisdiction in which the company is incorporated.

The other side argues that shareholders will pay more for corporations whose laws add shareholder value, and that accordingly, any competition between self-interested states for incorporations, will drive a "race to the top." Here is one summary of the debate, and where it stands, from Renee M. Jones, *Rethinking Corporate Federalism in the Era of Corporate Reform*, 29 J. CORP. L. 625, 629–32 (2004):

A.   The Modern Debate

For almost thirty years, academics have debated about whether competition among states for corporate charters has precipitated a race to the top or a race to the bottom in corporate law. The debate is central to corporate legal scholarship, for at its essence it is a debate about the proper substance of corporate law rules. In our federal system of corporate law, state governments set the rules governing the relationships among the primary participants in the corporate enterprise: directors, officers and investors. Each state has its own corporate statute and a corporation may incorporate under the laws of any state, regardless of whether it owns assets or conducts operations in that state. Under the "internal affairs doctrine," it is the law of the selected state that governs all disputes regarding a corporation's internal affairs, regardless of the forum in which such disputes are litigated. Although the federal securities laws and other federal laws impose significant limitations on corporate operations, the U.S. has no federal corporate statute.

Because corporations pay franchise taxes and other fees to the states in which they incorporate, many commentators have argued that states compete for corporate charters and the tax revenues they generate. That more than half of all publicly-traded corporations incorporate in Delaware leads most to conclude that Delaware has "won" this competition. The "race" debate thus centers on determining why Delaware has won the race for corporate charters and, more importantly, whether the legal rules generated as a result of this race are the appropriate ones.

Race-to-the-bottom theorists argue that regulatory competition has had a negative impact on the development of corporate law. William Cary most forcefully articulated this view. Cary argued that Delaware, in its zeal to maintain its primacy as the favored state of incorporation, adopted legal rules that favor managers at the expense of shareholders. He asserted that because corporate managers enjoy exclusive power to select or change the state of incorporation, Delaware had declared it to be the "public policy of the State" to adopt legal rules that managers desired. Implicit in Cary's argument is the premise that government regulation is necessary to prevent corporate managers from exploiting shareholders who exercise little meaningful control over the modern corporate enterprise. Having concluded that the federal system discourages such active regulation, Cary urged Congressional legislation as the only means to effect the regulatory regime he viewed as essential to maintain the proper balance of power among managers, shareholders and other corporate constituents. He thus proposed the establishment of federal minimum standards of corporate conduct that would apply to large American corporations.

Defenders of the corporate federal system (referred to here as corporate federalists) argue that the very interstate competition that Cary so excoriated, has led instead to a "race-to-the-top" in corporate law. These theorists, led by Ralph Winter, agree with Cary that the federal system discourages active regulation of corporations, but they embrace this deregulatory bias as the legitimate result of the corporate law race. Race-to-the-top theorists maintain that market forces are sufficient to prevent excessive managerial self-dealing and opportunism. They take the market-based defense of the federal system a step further by arguing that not only do conventional market forces rein in management excess, but that a competitive market for corporate law works to ensure that states will adopt legal rules that appeal to managers and shareholders alike.

Thus, Winter argued, if Delaware law permitted managers to profit at the expense of shareholders, earnings of Delaware corporations would lag behind those of similar corporations chartered in other states. This would result in lower stock prices for Delaware corporations, increasing their capital costs and weakening their position in the product market, ultimately driving stock prices still lower and making such corporations attractive takeover targets. Race-to-the-top theorists thus conclude that market forces require corporate managers to seek out legal rules that are attractive to investors, which in turn encourages states to adopt legal rules that "optimize the shareholder-corporation relationship." Thus, in the view of race-to-the-top scholars, Delaware's laissez faire approach to corporate governance is superior to the interventionist model preferred by race-to-the-bottom theorists, simply because this laissez faire approach has "won" a vigorous competition among all states to attract the most corporate charters.

B.   The Reality

Despite the longevity of the race debate, recent empirical studies demonstrate the fallacy of the fundamental assumption upon which the great debate rests—that states actively compete for corporate charters. In separate studies, Lucian Bebchuk and Assaf Hamdani, and Marcel Kahan and Ehud Kamar have asserted that the interstate competition which has been credited with fueling the corporate law race is largely illusory. These commentators show that not only is Delaware the clear leader in chartering publicly-traded corporations, but that no other state serves as a credible rival to Delaware in attracting charters from out-of-state corporations.

It is common knowledge that Delaware is the state of incorporation for more than half of all publicly-traded companies. Yet, the true extent of Delaware's dominance in the market for corporate charters becomes apparent only when the field is defined as the market for "out-of-state" incorporations. With the market so defined Delaware's market share increases to 85%. In addition, several factors protect Delaware from being displaced from its dominant position by other states. Much of the value that Delaware's legal system offers corporations stems from the large number of other firms that choose to incorporate there. For example, Delaware's extensive body of corporate law decisions developed only because of the volume and diversity of cases presented to its courts. In addition, Delaware's institutional infrastructure, including its specialized court system, expert judiciary, and specialized bar would be difficult for other states to readily duplicate. These advantages work together to protect Delaware's dominant position. As a result, Delaware has no meaningful competition in the market for out-of-state incorporations.

In addition to Bebchuk's and Hamdani's insights, Professors Kahan and Kamar argue that contrary to the central assumption in the corporate race debate, other states are not making serious efforts to compete with Delaware for corporate charters. Kahan and Kamar analyzed the corporate franchise tax and fee structures of all states, and concluded that states other than Delaware stand to gain little economically from attracting additional incorporations. For example, Nevada, the so-called "Delaware of the West," earns marginal annual revenues of only

$26,200 from the eighteen companies that went public as Nevada corporations between 1996 and 2000.

By persuasively demonstrating the absence of interstate competition in the development of corporate law, these recent studies detract from the standard arguments of corporate federalists who advance and defend the free-market approach to corporate law embodied in the states' enabling corporate law codes. Because there is no meaningful interstate competition for corporate charters, competition could not have affected the development of corporate law in the way that corporate federalists posit. Thus, corporate federalists' defense of the states' enabling corporate codes must rest on other grounds.[234]

QUESTIONS ON FEDERAL REGULATION OF PUBLIC COMPANY GOVERNANCE

Are there some advantages to uniform governance rules for public companies? What are they?

How do large additions to federal governance rules, such as those in and mandated by SOX, come into being? Is the dynamic that produces them likely to lead to "good" rules?

To the extent that we rely on specific rules, are we destined to simply add to an already long list whenever new scandals come along? Or are we likely to stop the cycle of scandals at some point when the rules reach some optimum state?

---

[234] Renee M. Jones, *Rethinking Corporate Federalism in the Era of Corporate Reform*, 29 J. CORP. L. 625, 629–32 (2004) (footnotes omitted). Quotation reprinted with permission from Professor Jones and from The Journal of Corporation Law. *See also* Oren Bar-Gill, et al., *The Market for Corporate Law*, 162 J. INST. THEOR. ECON. 134, 136 (2006) (arguing, with a model expressed in equations: "When a corporate issue does not have a significant effect on managers' private benefits of control, state competition will push states to adopt rules that would best serve shareholders. However, with respect to rules that have a substantial effect on managers' private benefits of control, such as rules governing corporate takeovers or managerial conflicts of interests, states might adopt rules that make shareholders worse off."); Lucian A. Bebchuk, *Federal Corporate Law: Lessons from History*, 106 COLUM. L. REV. 1793 (2006) (arguing that "Delaware is influenced by both the threat of federal intervention and the desire to compete with other states over incorporations" (at 1824) and that "but for federal intervention, the regime of investor protection might have been worse than what you would get by simply excluding existing federal arrangements" (at 1827)).

CHAPTER 3

WORLDCOM PART I: THE ACCOUNTING ISSUES, BERNIE EBBERS, AND THE BOARD

■ ■ ■

The accounting scandals at Enron and WorldCom precipitated the passage of SOX.[1] This Chapter Three begins our WorldCom study. It starts with a basic WorldCom chronology, followed by a short briefing on the WorldCom accounting fraud that will concern us, followed by background facts about Bernie Ebbers, the CEO. The chapter then turns to the WorldCom board of directors—its composition, the relationships of the directors to Mr. Ebbers, why the board did not prevent the accounting fraud, and how well the board responded once the improper accounting was brought to its attention.

---

[1]   For brief summaries *see* 3 JOHN T. BOSTELMAN, ET AL., THE PUBLIC COMPANY DESKBOOK, Appx. A (2d ed. 2014); HAROLD S. BLOOMENTHAL, SARBANES-OXLEY ACT IN PERSPECTIVE, §§ 1:1–1:10 (2016 ed.).

WORLDCOM BEGINNING FACTS

June 25, 2002	WorldCom announces that it improperly transferred from line costs to capital accounts $3.055 billion in 2001 and $797 million in the first quarter of 2002—all in violation of generally accepted accounting principles (GAAP). WorldCom states that without these improper transfers the company would have shown a loss instead of a profit for these periods and that the company will restate its financials for the 2001 year and Q1 of 2002.
July 21, 2002	WorldCom and subsidiaries file voluntary petitions for Chapter 11 relief. It is the biggest bankruptcy in history to this time.
August 8, 2002	WorldCom says that it has discovered additional improper accounting stretching back to 1999 and that the company will restate financials for the year 2000, as well as for 2001 and the first quarter of 2002. The combined effect of these errors and the errors reported in June 2002 means that WorldCom overstated its earnings before interest, taxes, depreciation, and amortization (EBITDA) by $7.1 billion over the period 1999 through Q1 2002.
March 13, 2003	WorldCom states that it is writing down $79.8 billion in goodwill and other assets.

These events generated civil shareholder actions against WorldCom and its leaders, an SEC case against the company, SEC actions against a number of individuals, and criminal prosecutions. Multiple WorldCom accounting personnel pled guilty to criminal charges, including the CFO, Scott Sullivan. Bernie Ebbers, the CEO, was convicted on criminal counts. The court sentenced Ebbers to 25 years in prison and sentenced Sullivan, who had cooperated with the government and testified against Ebbers, to 5 years.

A.   THE WORLDCOM ACCOUNTING ISSUE WE WILL STUDY

According to a report by a special committee of its board, WorldCom employed three improper accounting techniques. We will focus on one.

WorldCom offered telecommunications services. "Line costs" constituted one of WorldCom's largest expenses. When WorldCom connected a telephone call—say from Chicago to Paris—WorldCom owned only some of the lines through which the call travelled. WorldCom rented from other companies the right to use the rest of the needed lines. The cost of renting those lines comprised "line costs."

Since line costs were an expense, WorldCom could decrease expenses and increase profits in any given accounting period by reducing line costs. Since line costs were operating expenses, WorldCom was supposed to charge those costs in the accounting period in which they were incurred. WorldCom improperly reduced line costs charged in current periods by "capitalizing" those costs, which improperly charged the line costs off over time. By this means, WorldCom deferred a part of the operating expenses incurred in a current period until later periods, thus improperly decreasing operating expenses in the current period and increasing profits in the current period.

Here is a simplified example showing how capitalizing costs defers costs and increases profit in a current accounting period. Suppose that a company receives $10 in revenue this year. Suppose that it has $8 in operating costs. If the company properly records that $8 as a cost this year, its profit is $10 − $8 = $2. Now suppose the company improperly records that $8 payment not as operating costs but as the cost of purchasing a capital asset with a useful life of four years. The company then "capitalizes" the $8 and charges it off over those four years—charging off $2 a year. Now, it reports a profit *this* year of $10 − $2 = $8. Of course, it will be charging $2 in each of the next three years and that will hurt its profits then. But for now—and now is very important when a company is trying to meet Wall Street profit predictions—it reports inflated profits.[2]

B. BERNIE EBBERS

Bernard Ebbers was WorldCom's chief executive officer ("CEO") during its accounting failure. While he did not perform the company's accounting himself, most agree that he personally had a great impact on the company.

He was a main force in the company's growth by acquisition.

---

[2]   In addition to making recommendations to buy, sell, or hold stock (as described in the Chapter One reading), analysts predict the earnings (and often other financial numbers such as revenue) of the companies that the analysts cover. Thus, analysts covering General Electric will predict the number of dollars that GE will earn in each of the next four quarters, or even further out. Dividing those earnings numbers by the number of outstanding GE shares, the analysts will also predict GE's earnings per share (or "eps") in each of those quarters. Financial information companies collect the predictions from various analysts and publish a consensus estimate of earnings (and other numbers). When a company then announces its earnings for a quarter, investors will compare the actual earnings with the predicted earnings. If the actual earnings are less than the consensus estimate, the price of the company's stock may immediately fall.

He allegedly instilled a culture that made meeting Wall Street expectations (and thereby keeping the stock price high) an unhealthy priority.

Here are some additional facts:

During the three-year period from January 1, 1999, through December 31, 2001, Mr. Ebbers received more than $77 million in total compensation or an average of $25.7 million per year. These amounts include $20.5 million (or an average of $6.8 million per year) in cash compensation in the form of salary and bonuses. When Mr. Ebbers left WorldCom . . . the Company approved [ ] a severance package that included a cash payment of $1.5 million per year for life, lifetime medical and life insurance, lifetime use of a corporate jet and conversion of approximately $408 million in demand notes into 5-year callable term notes with a significant interest rate subsidy.[3]

Mr. Ebbers had substantial business interests outside WorldCom, which he financed by using his WorldCom stock as collateral for loans:

Ebbers, in addition to his full-time job as [CEO] of WorldCom, was actively involved in buying, building, and running several businesses unrelated to WorldCom.

Prior to 1998, he already had a number of businesses, including hotels and interests in real estate ventures. Between 1998 and 2000, Ebbers and the companies he controlled significantly expanded their holdings by purchasing, among other things, the largest working cattle ranch in Canada (approximately 500,000 acres), and approximately 540,000 acres of timberland in four Southern U.S. states. The total scope of Ebbers' non-WorldCom businesses . . . included a Louisiana rice farm, a luxury yacht building company, a minor league hockey team, an operating marina, and a building in downtown Chicago.

The method Ebbers chose to finance many of his acquisitions involved substantial financial risk. Ebbers and companies he controlled took out loans from commercial banks. Many of these commercial loans were margin loans secured by shares of Ebbers' WorldCom stock. Although the terms varied among the various margin loans, each required that the value of Ebbers' stock remain greater than or equal to some multiple of the amount of the loan.

---

[3]   First Interim Report of Dick Thornburgh, Bankruptcy Court Examiner, dated November 4, 2002 and filed in the WorldCom bankruptcy, *In re WorldCom, Inc.*, Case No. 02-15533 (AJG), U.S. Bankruptcy Court, Southern District of New York at 64–65, http://www.klgates.com/files/upload/WorldCom_Examiner_Report_firstinterim.pdf [First Interim WorldCom Examiner Report].

These margin loans totaled hundreds of millions of dollars—perhaps more at various times. This massive indebtedness left Ebbers exposed to declines in the price of WorldCom stock, which began to occur in late 1999.[4]

While the specifics of Ebbers' loans differed from loan to loan, what follows illustrates the concept. The debtor borrows $4. The terms, for the sake of this simplified example, require that the debtor give the bank a security interest in stock worth at least twice that amount. Suppose that the debtor therefore pledges stock that is worth $10 at the time he or she takes out the loan. For simplification, suppose that the debtor uses the money to finance a business but does not pledge that business as collateral for the loan, leaving the stock as the only security for the debt. Suppose that the market price of the stock then falls so that all of the stock that the debtor pledged to the bank is now worth only $6. At this point, the bank does not hold a security interest in collateral worth at least twice the $4 loan but only collateral worth 1.5 times the $4 loan. So, the bank advises the debtor that he or she must, according to the terms of the loan, either (1) pay down $1 on the loan (thereby reducing the loan to $3 so that the collateral the bank holds [now worth $6] is twice the value of the loan amount); or (2) pledge more stock worth, at the current market price, at least an additional $2 so that the amount loaned remains at $4 but the bank still has twice that amount in collateral (a total of $8, with $6 from the current value of the stock the debtor pledged before and $2 from the additional stock the debtor pledges now).

As the price of WorldCom stock went down, the value of the stock Ebbers had pledged as collateral fell. Effectively, this forced Ebbers to either pay down part of his loans or pledge additional collateral.

With that background, read the following May 1, 2002 story from the New York Times, written when Ebbers left WorldCom but before the company filed for bankruptcy. The story provides you with Ebbers' business background and describes the phenomenal growth that WorldCom experienced during part of his tenure.

Bernard J. Ebbers, who spent 19 years building WorldCom into one of the biggest long-distance companies and Internet carriers in the world, has resigned as chief executive, president and director, the company said yesterday.

If any executive represented the entrepreneurial epoch that was supposed to make telecommunications cheaper and the choices abundant in an era of deregulation, it was Mr. Ebbers. It was he who exploited the deregulation of the telecommunications

---

[4]   Report of Investigation by the Special Investigative Committee of the Board of Directors of WorldCom, Inc. (Mar. 31, 2003) at 294–96 (footnote omitted), http://www.sec.gov/Archives/edgar/data/723527/000093176303001862/dex991.htm [WorldCom Special Committee Report].

industry more than anyone else during the last two decades. With ruthless cost-cutting and fervent deal-making, he showed for years that it was possible to undercut AT&T in the long-distance market and still make a lot of money.

But Mr. Ebbers was brought down by wounds that, to some measure, were self-inflicted. He personally owes the company more than $366 million for loans and loan guarantees to cover his potential losses on his WorldCom stock as the share price plummeted. And the company, under his watch, became the subject of a wide-ranging and continuing investigation by the Securities and Exchange Commission, which is scrutinizing WorldCom's accounting practices and financial relations with Mr. Ebbers.

Yet Mr. Ebbers was also undone by industry and economic forces beyond any one executive's or company's control.

While consumers enjoyed the long-distance price wars, the service eventually became a commodity from which few carriers could squeeze a profit, especially as e-mail and cellphones siphoned off traffic. And the glut of network capacity that was built by start-up companies fueled by easy financing during the stock market boom only further depressed network pricing.

Finally, as the bursting of the stock market bubble in 2000 made it harder for telecommunications companies to raise money and make deals like WorldCom's acquisition of MCI for $30 billion in 1998, the company's growth-by-acquisition engine ran out of gas.

Mr. Ebbers's departure, which was decided over the weekend, was reported on Tuesday by The Wall Street Journal.

"This is the collapse of the single-most-successful telecom growth company ever," said Scott Cleland, chief executive of the Precursor Group, a telecommunications and media consulting firm in Washington. "It was a momentum story that ran out of momentum. Bernie was a genius at acquiring customers and cutting costs. His genius was not in operating the companies he bought."

WorldCom says that it has enough cash to continue operating indefinitely, despite being staggered by $30 billion in debt and limping along with a share price of about $2.50—down 82 percent so far this year. Its bonds are trading at prices normally reserved for companies on the brink of bankruptcy.

With dozens of other telecommunications upstarts now bankrupt, WorldCom's mounting problems make it increasingly likely that the dominant players in the telecommunications industry may be the remaining offspring of that old antediluvian Bell System: the local telephone giants like BellSouth, SBC Communications and Verizon.

WorldCom's tribulations may have little direct or lasting impact on consumers and business customers because there are many other providers of long-distance and Internet services. But the strong possibility that the Bell companies may step into the breach—even now, the Bells are slowly being allowed into the long-distance business—may reveal the limits of the two-decade-old vision that deregulation would give communications customers a broad range of choices among providers.

And yet, analysts note that the two decades of competitive ferment that Mr. Ebbers helped symbolize have radically changed the communications landscape. With affordable long-distance calls, Internet e-mail, wireless communications, and cable television systems that can also carry telephone calls, consumer communications options now vastly exceed the possibilities of the old Bell System days—when choice mainly meant picking the color of a phone.

"I think that the Bells are dominant, but in a world that is far more volatile and far more competitive than it was before," said Blair Levin, a former chief of staff at the Federal Communications Commission who is now an analyst for the investment firm Legg Mason.

Mr. Levin cited an historical analogy: "In the mid-1800's, the country went berserk building railroads and a lot of investors lost a lot of money. But those railroads created the economic engine that fueled the country's growth through the next century. WorldCom and MCI largely inspired the same thing."

Mr. Ebbers, who was not available for comment yesterday, did not set out to make WorldCom an inspiration. At its inception it was, instead, little more than a gamble.

In 1983, just months before the old American Telephone and Telegraph Company broke up its Bell System to settle a federal antitrust suit, four men gathered in a Hattiesburg, Miss., coffee shop. They knew that the breakup of Ma Bell would open the door for widespread competition in the long-distance telephone market and they met to sketch out plans for a cut-rate telephone company that they called LDDS. They could hardly have expected that their company, renamed WorldCom, would show more than $35 billion in revenue by 2001.

One of those at the coffee shop was Mr. Ebbers, a former junior high school basketball coach from Edmonton, Alberta, who was then running a string of Mississippi motels.

LDDS stood for Long-Distance Discount Service, so naturally, the company's business plan was to undercut AT&T. In the early 1980's, AT&T and even some long-distance upstarts were starting to sell wholesale time on their networks to other companies, time that the smaller companies could resell on the retail market at a profit.

Because of all of the required regulatory approvals and the search for customers, LDDS did not actually get into business until January 1985. Just a few months later, Mr. Ebbers became the company's president.

"The only experience Bernie had before operating a long-distance company was he used the phone," Carl J. Aycock, an original LDDS investor and WorldCom board member, recalled in 1997.

But Mr. Ebbers produced results. From the beginning, the company was distinguished by its aggressive salesmanship, its ruthless cost-cutting and its passion for corporate acquisitions.

Mr. Ebbers's focus on costs earned him garlands from Wall Street, but also prompted whispered concerns that the company might have been too aggressive in its accounting. That may be one issue that the S.E.C. is looking into as it conducts its investigation. Some analysts say the company may have improperly masked operating losses as one-time charges, enhancing its financial operating results.

But despite its revenue growth and cost controls, WorldCom has been built mostly through dozens of acquisitions. In the 1980's, Mr. Ebbers snapped up rafts of other small long-distance companies, companies that appeared much like LDDS itself. After the company became publicly traded in 1989, the deal-making rose to a new level.

In one of its early breakthrough deals, in 1992, LDDS mounted a $720 million acquisition of the Advanced Telecommunications Corporation. As would be Mr. Ebbers's habit, his company used its own stock as a currency in the transaction, which made LDDS the nation's fourth-biggest telecommunications company, after AT&T, MCI and Sprint.

Perhaps as important, however, that deal brought Mr. Ebbers into contact with Scott D. Sullivan, a young finance executive at Advanced Telecommunications. Mr. Sullivan, now 40, became WorldCom's chief financial officer in 1994 and was hailed by Wall

Street analysts and happy WorldCom investors for much of the 1990's as one of the industry's financial wunderkinds.

In yesterday's announcement, WorldCom said that Mr. Sullivan would continue as chief financial officer and would also be promoted to executive vice president. He will report to John Sidgmore, the former vice chairman, who became president and chief executive on Sunday.

As a team, Mr. Sullivan and Mr. Ebbers blazed through the 1990's with a series of bigger and bigger acquisitions. When WorldCom acquired MFS Communications, an up-and-coming local communications provider, the deal brought along Mr. Sidgmore, who had recently persuaded MFS to buy his Internet company, UUNet.

WorldCom's acquisition binge culminated in the $30 billion acquisition of MCI in 1998. MCI's longtime leader, William McGowan—the man who had helped force the breakup of AT&T—had died, and the company was adrift, ripe for Mr. Ebbers's acquisitive taste. At the time of the deal, MCI was more than three times WorldCom's size.

But Mr. Ebbers's deal-making would find its limit in 2000, when antitrust authorities in Europe and the United States shot down WorldCom's proposed acquisition of Sprint for $129 billion. After that, the acquisitions were less bold, like last year's deal to acquire Intermedia Communications and its Digex Web services subsidiary for $4.1 billion.

During the height of his wheeling and dealing, though, Mr. Ebbers made no secret of the fact that his intentions were purely financial, and that he was less concerned about the fundamentals of his business.

"Our goal is not to capture market share or be global," he was famously quoted as saying by Business Week in 1997. "Our goal is to be the No. 1 stock on Wall Street."

For many years, that focus made Mr. Ebbers a cult figure on Wall Street. And for good reason. A $100 investment in WorldCom stock at the beginning of 1990 would have been worth about $8,700 when the company's stock hit its peak of $64.50 in 1999. By yesterday, that investment would have been worth about $335.

For a time, even as Mr. Ebbers focused more on his company's stock rather than on his company's operations, investors were happy to go along for the ride.

"I attended many, many of his prayer meetings with the New York Society of Securities Analysts and they just said, 'Anything you want, Bernie, you got it,' " said Howard Anderson, founder of the Yankee Group, a consulting firm in Boston. "They did not examine his finances and his books with anything resembling due diligence."

Mr. Ebbers, to be sure, was not cut from the same cloth as Gary Winnick, the chairman of the telecommunications upstart Global Crossing, who sold over $700 million of his company's stock before the shares collapsed and the company filed for bankruptcy protection.

In fact, Mr. Ebbers appears to be in dire personal financial straits precisely because instead of selling WorldCom shares, he kept buying, sometimes pledging the value of shares he already owned to buy still more. As WorldCom's shares fell over the last 18 months and as the margin calls came in, WorldCom extended those big loans to Mr. Ebbers.

"Bernie was not Bill McGowan," Mr. Anderson said, referring to the late MCI leader.

"McGowan understood the delicate balance between customers, network capacity, publicity and raising money," Mr. Anderson said. "Bernie viewed this as a series of financial-engineering maneuvers and never truly understood the business that he was in. In the end, that probably skewered him."[5]

Before considering an initial set of questions about Bernie Ebbers, look at a graph of WorldCom's stock price:[6]

---

[5]   Seth Schiesel, *WorldCom Leader Departs Company in Turbulent Time*, N.Y. TIMES, May 1, 2002, at A1 (picture and graphics omitted). From The New York Times, May 1, 2002 © 2002 The New York Times. All rights reserved. Used by permission and protected by the Copyright Laws of the United States. The printing, copying, redistribution, or retransmission of this Content without express written permission is prohibited.

[6]   This graph is taken from WorldCom Special Committee Report, *supra* note 4, at 53.

WorldCom Closing Stock Prices, Jan. 1994 - June 2002

QUESTIONS ON EBBERS

It is important for directors—and for counsel who advise a company—to decide how comfortable they are with the top management. The more comfortable directors feel about management, the less urgently directors feel the need to check what management says and the less likely directors are to challenge management's judgment. The same is true of counsel.

Overwhelmingly, the reforms that we will study concern the process by which corporations make their decisions. We must not forget, however, that individuals make those decisions. Whether a corporation makes good business decisions or bad ones, and whether it cheats its shareholders or not, will depend in significant part on the quality of its leader. Of course, one of the important jobs of a board of directors is to choose a company's leader.

How comfortable do you feel about Ebbers considering only what you have just read?

What role should a director's (or a lawyer's) visceral feeling play in evaluating the possibility that top management may be too risk-seeking? May be less than completely honest? May be a bit careless with the facts?

Can a director's (or a lawyer's) intuitive reactions to top management be colored by prejudices (e.g., against executives paid millions of dollars each year, against Southerners, against persons displaying certain mannerisms, against persons taking out large loans)?

If so, how can directors or lawyers control for those prejudices? Should they trust their visceral reactions at all?

What are objective indicators that directors and lawyers can use to help them decide whether an individual CEO is likely to be careful and honest in his or her dealings with the board and counsel?

What about Ebbers' background—from junior high school basketball coach and operator of Mississippi motels to the head of one of the largest companies in the world, with more than $35 billion in reported revenue? Is this the American dream come true? Or a train wreck waiting to happen?

C. FIRST LOOK AT THE WORLDCOM BOARD

To meet the WorldCom Board, read now an excerpt from a WorldCom proxy statement, containing some of the directors' business credentials:

JAMES C. ALLEN, 55, a nominee, has been a director of WorldCom since March 1998. Mr. Allen is currently an investment director and member of the general partner of Meritage Private Equity Fund, a venture capital fund specializing in the telecommunications industry. Mr. Allen is the former Vice Chairman and Chief Executive Officer of Brooks Fiber Properties where he served in such capacities from 1993 until its merger with WorldCom in January 1998. Mr. Allen served as President and Chief Operating Officer of Brooks Telecommunications Corporation, a founder of Brooks Fiber Properties, from April 1993 until it was merged with Brooks Fiber Properties in January 1996. Mr. Allen serves as a director of Completel LLC, Xspedius, Inc., Masergy, Inc., David Lipscomb University and Family Dynamics Institute.

JUDITH AREEN, 57, a nominee, has been a director of WorldCom since September 1998. Ms. Areen has been Executive Vice President for Law Center Affairs and Dean of the Law Center, Georgetown University, since 1989. She has been a Professor of Law, Georgetown University, since 1976.

CARL J. AYCOCK, 53, a nominee, has been a director of WorldCom since 1983. Mr. Aycock served as Secretary of WorldCom from 1987 to 1995 and was the Secretary and Chief Financial Officer of Master Corporation, a motel management and ownership company, from 1989 until 1992. Subsequent to 1992, Mr. Aycock has been self employed as a financial administrator.

RONALD R. BEAUMONT, 53, who is an executive officer, but not a nominee, has been Chief Operating Officer of the WorldCom group since December 2000. From 1998 to December 2000 Mr.

Beaumont served as the President and Chief Executive Officer of WorldCom's Operations and Technology unit. From December 1996 to 1998, Mr. Beaumont was President of WorldCom Network Services, a subsidiary of WorldCom. Mr. Beaumont is a director of Digex, Incorporated, or Digex.

MAX E. BOBBITT, 57, a nominee, has been a director of WorldCom since 1992. Mr. Bobbitt is currently a director of Verso Technologies, Inc., and Metromedia China Corporation. From July 1998 to the present, Mr. Bobbitt has been a telecommunications consultant. From March 1997 until July 1998, Mr. Bobbitt served as President and Chief Executive Officer of Metromedia China Corporation. From January 1996 until March 1997, Mr. Bobbitt was President and Chief Executive Officer of Asian American Telecommunications Corporation, which was acquired by Metromedia China Corporation in February 1997.

BERNARD J. EBBERS, 60, a nominee, has been President and Chief Executive Officer of WorldCom since April 1985. Mr. Ebbers has served as a director of WorldCom since 1983. Mr. Ebbers is a director of Digex.

FRANCESCO GALESI, 71, a nominee, has been a director of WorldCom since 1992. Mr. Galesi is the Chairman and Chief Executive Officer of the Galesi Group, which includes companies engaged in real estate, telecommunications and oil and gas exploration and production. Mr. Galesi serves as a director of Keystone Property Trust.

STILES A. KELLETT, JR., 58, a nominee, has served as a director of WorldCom since 1981. Mr. Kellett has been Chairman of Kellett Investment Corp., since 1995. Mr. Kellett serves as a director of Netzee, Inc., Air2web and Virtual Bank.

GORDON S. MACKLIN, 73, a nominee, has been a director of WorldCom since September 1998. Mr. Macklin has been a corporate financial advisor since 1992. From 1987 through 1992, he was Chairman of the Hambrecht and Quist Group, an investment banking and venture capital firm. Previously, Mr. Macklin was President of the National Association of Securities Dealers, Inc. from 1970 through 1987. He also served as Chairman of the National Clearing Corporation (1970–1975) and as a partner and member of the Executive Committee of McDonald & Company Securities Inc., where he was employed from 1950 through 1970. Mr. Macklin serves on the boards of Martek Biosciences Corporation, MedImmune, Inc., Overstock.com, Spacehab, Inc., White Mountains Insurance Group, Ltd., and director, trustee or managing general partner, as the case may be, of 48 of the investment companies in the Franklin Templeton Group of Funds.

BERT C. ROBERTS, JR., 59, a nominee, has been the Chairman of the Board and a director of WorldCom since September 1998. From 1992 until September 1998, Mr. Roberts served as Chairman of the Board of MCI Communications Corporation, or MCI. Mr. Roberts was Chief Executive Officer of MCI from December 1991 to November 1996. He was President and Chief Operating Officer of MCI from October 1985 to June 1992 and President of MCI Telecommunications Corporation, a subsidiary of MCI, from May 1983 to June 1992. Mr. Roberts is a director of The News Corporation Limited, Valence Technology, Inc., CAPCure and Digex and is on the Board of Trustees at Johns Hopkins University.

JOHN W. SIDGMORE, 51, a nominee, has been the Vice Chairman of the Board and a director of WorldCom since December 1996. From December 1996 until September 1998, Mr. Sidgmore served as Chief Operations Officer of WorldCom. Mr. Sidgmore was President and Chief Operating Officer of MFS Communications Company, Inc. from August 1996 until December 1996. He was Chief Executive Officer of UUNET Technologies, Inc. from June 1994 until October 1998, and President of UUNET from June 1994 to August 1996 and from January 1997 to September 1997. Mr. Sidgmore is a director of Microstrategy Incorporated.

SCOTT D. SULLIVAN, 40, a nominee, has been a director of WorldCom since 1996. Mr. Sullivan has served as Chief Financial Officer, Treasurer and Secretary of WorldCom since December 1994. Mr. Sullivan is a director of Digex.

Effective November 1, 2000, Lawrence C. Tucker, 59, became an advisory director of WorldCom. Mr. Tucker served as a director of WorldCom from May 1995 until November 1, 2000, and previously served as a director of WorldCom from May 28, 1992 until December 1992. Mr. Tucker's compensation as an advisory director is the same as that of a director. Mr. Tucker has been a general partner of Brown Brothers Harriman & Co., a private banking firm, since 1979 and currently serves as a member of the Steering Committee of the firm's partnership. He is also a director of Riverwood Holding, Inc., National Healthcare Corporation,

VAALCO Energy Inc., US Unwired, Inc., Network Telephone, Xspedius, Inc., Z-Tel Technologies, Inc. and Digex.[7]

QUESTIONS AFTER YOUR FIRST LOOK AT THE BOARD

Well, what do you think of this board?

Two are in their 70s. Most are in their 50s. Any too old? Or are the older directors just seasoned veterans?

There are twelve directors plus one advisory director. Too few? Too many?

All seem to have business experience, including six who at least appear on paper to have had some experience in the communications industry outside WorldCom (Allen, Bobbitt, Galesi, Roberts, Sidgmore, and Tucker [the advisory member]). The board also appears to have financial sector experience (Macklin, Tucker), real estate experience (Galesi), and experience with other companies dependent on technology (Bobbitt, Kellett, Macklin, Sidgmore, Tucker). Many directors have sat on boards of companies that appear to be independent of WorldCom (Allen, Galesi, Kellett, Macklin, Roberts, Tucker). One (Macklin) was even a former president of the NASD. Is this a good distribution of talents? Anything glaringly missing?

What about the law dean/law professor? A good choice for a telecommunications board?

How about Aycock (former CFO of the motel management and ownership company and now a self-employed "financial administrator")?

D. SECOND LOOK AT THE WORLDCOM BOARD

Consider, next, an October 13, 2002 *BusinessWeek* article describing the relationship between Ebbers and the board.

> For two years, WorldCom Inc. director Max E. Bobbitt looked on while his $300 million stake in the company vaporized. But last April, the former Alltel Corp. president was fed up. In a boardroom maneuver not reported until now, he began plotting to oust friend and WorldCom founder Bernard J. Ebbers and to take his place as CEO. According to current and former executives and two other directors, Bobbitt offered Chief Operating Officer Ronald R. Beaumont, Vice-Chairman John W. Sidgmore, and Chief Financial Officer Scott D. Sullivan retention packages of about $1 million annually for life if they backed him as CEO.

---

[7]   WorldCom, Inc., Definitive Proxy Statement, Schedule 14A (filed Apr. 22, 2002) at 3–4.

The plot blew up. Word of Bobbitt's maneuvers leaked to Chairman Bert C. Roberts Jr., who rallied others on WorldCom's then-11-member board to thwart Bobbitt, say WorldCom insiders. When the board ousted Ebbers on Apr. 30, his replacement was Sidgmore, who continued in his new role to battle with Bobbitt. Sidgmore and Roberts declined comment on the continuing power struggles. Beaumont and Sullivan could not be reached for comment.

Bobbitt's attempted coup was a shocking turn of events for a board that had for years backed Ebbers unquestioningly—to stockholders' detriment. The 57-year-old Arkansas native had been one of four longtime directors who were Ebbers loyalists, according to about a dozen current and former WorldCom directors and executives who mapped out the inner workings of the board for BusinessWeek. Together with three insiders, this foursome operated as a millionaires club. They collected plenty of perks—from use of a corporate jet to financial support from Ebbers' in their pet projects. And they piled up loads of WorldCom stock. Spearheaded by this group, the board O.K.'d mega-loans to Ebbers. They backed him through the stupendous expansion of WorldCom—to the brink of its collapse. They so trusted Ebbers' that they held on to most of their WorldCom shares while they gradually became worthless.

Corporate-governance experts say this boardroom saga illustrates the pitfalls of a big company operating without truly independent directors. "It seems that directors were so beholden to the CEO that no one came forward to say: 'Hey, we're in serious trouble here, and what are we doing to do about it?'" says Charles M. Elson, a governance professor at the University of Delaware.

Like Ebbers himself, the CEO'S four sidekicks on the board had jumped into telecom when Ma Bell was dismantled in the 1980s. As president of Alltel, Bobbitt helped turn it into the largest phone company serving small-town America and invested in WorldCom. Francesco Galesi, a real estate magnate from Upstate New York, and Stiles A. Kellett Jr., an Atlanta investor who had made a fortune in nursing homes during the 1970s, ran telecom startups. The two came on the board when their companies were bought by Ebbers as part of a string of 70-plus acquisitions that turned fledgling Long Distance Discount Service Inc. (LDDS) into the $35 billion WorldCom. The fourth confederate, Carl J. Aycock, worked with Ebbers at a hotel-management company and then became one of the founders of LDDS. The four directors, and Ebbers, declined to comment on board actions.

Now, the entire board could be purged, say creditors and former executives. Court-appointed monitor Richard C. Breeden is investigating directors' roles in the company's collapse, and the Justice Dept. is asking if they knew about accounting irregularities. Says a creditor: "Directors are feeling intense pressure to leave."

That's quite a switch. For a decade, Ebbers and the board had the wind at their backs. In 1989, Ebbers bought Atlanta long-distance carrier Advanced Telecommunications Corp., in which Galesi held a 25% stake. Galesi joined the WorldCom board. Ebbers repeated this pattern over and over, typically inviting executives of the acquired companies to take a turn on the board. Through the '90s, the then-nine-member board was composed of insiders and execs from acquired companies.

At the heart of the group were "Bernie's Boys"—a nickname WorldCom execs gave his four pals. Like other directors, they collected as many as 10,000 stock options per year—on top of the shares they received when their companies were acquired. Their stakes swelled to hundreds of millions of dollars on paper as WorldCom's stock soared to a high of $60.50 in July of 1999. Ebbers frowned on unloading WorldCom stock, say former directors, so there was little selling by directors.

While the stock climbed, few complained. Ebbers stroked their egos. They took turns holding the chairman title, with Roberts, a former MCI president, getting the honorary post after Ebbers bought MCI. As CEO, Ebbers ran the board and doled out special treats to his inner circle. Kellett was permitted to rent company aircraft for $1 a month, plus a $400-an-hour usage fee. The arrangement saved him more than $1 million in a year, according to a bankruptcy court memo written by monitor Breeden. In the memo, Breeden, who would not comment, called for Kellett's removal because he wasn't paying what it cost to operate the aircraft. A source close to Kellett counters that he "did not keep the lease of the aircraft as a secret nor did he consider it a gift."

A week before Ebbers' ouster, Aycock asked for a $600,000 personal loan from the company. Ebbers informally O.K.'d the financing, according to a director and creditors' representatives. The loan was never granted.

When it came to board members, Ebbers could be insensitive to apparent conflicts of interest. He didn't object when Galesi invested $15 million in a suburban-Chicago long-distance carrier, Telesphere Communications Inc., that was trying to grab share in a market WorldCom wanted to dominate. "Ebbers looked the other way as long as Galesi supported him without question," says a former WorldCom executive who competed against Telesphere.

Ebbers wielded the stick as well as the carrot. He publicly belittled any director who dared question him, according to current and former board members. That included his close confidant, ex-CFO and director Sullivan, who was indicted in August on fraud charges. Two years ago, Sullivan queried Ebbers' cutback in a capital-spending project, say two ex-directors. After the meeting, Ebbers gathered info that undermined Sullivan's position, then revealed it at the next board meeting. That shut him up. "Ebbers treated you like a prince—as long as you never forgot who was king," says a former director.

The board took him at his word, say directors, when Ebbers told them in 2001 that the sudden collapse of the telecom industry was a passing squall. At meetings, no one urged Ebbers to reduce the company's $41 billion in debt, say directors. And they did not spot accounting tricks that resulted in $7 billion in bogus revenues.

Even after the directors finally ousted a stunned Ebbers, Bernie's Boys battled on. Bobbitt, say creditors and directors, rallied Kellett, Galesi, and Aycock to resist Sidgmore—opposing his plans to spin off parts of the company and, ultimately, seek protection from creditors in federal court.

Again, Bobbitt played a losing hand. Just before WorldCom filed for bankruptcy protection on July 21, he enlisted directors Kellett and Galesi to write Verizon Communications CEO Ivan G. Seidenberg, offering him WorldCom for about $1 a share, according to a board member. Seidenberg wasn't interested, say sources close to Verizon. WorldCom executives were outraged. "They never sold their shares during the collapse and were desperate to recoup at least a pittance—the interests of the company be damned," says a director.

With WorldCom in bankruptcy, the directors have little say over what happens next. The creditors' committee is essentially running the company, and the WorldCom that reemerges will likely have a new board. Their stock is worthless. So, like Ebbers and everybody else who went down with him, the once-pampered directors are now members of a fraternity with no exclusivity whatsoever—the losers' club.[8]

---

8   Charles Haddad, *How Ebbers Kept the Board in His Pocket: WorldCom's CEO Showered Directors with Perks and Won Their Devotion*, BUSINESSWEEK, Oct. 13, 2002, http://www.bloomberg.com/news/articles/2002-10-13/how-ebbers-kept-the-board-in-his-pocket. Article used with permission of Bloomberg L.P. Copyright © 2016. All rights reserved.

QUESTIONS AFTER YOUR SECOND LOOK AT THE BOARD

So, what do you think now?

Does the fact that Bobbitt tried to oust Ebbers give you comfort? Does it show that at least one director had some gumption?

This is our first brush with the concept of "independent" directors. Lawyers used to think of directors as "inside" directors (who were currently officers or employees of the company on whose board they sat) or "outside" directors (who did not currently work for the company). Outside directors were thought to be independent. Many of the WorldCom directors were independent in this sense. The majority were not officers or employees of WorldCom.

But this article seems to talk about independence in a different way. It says that some directors headed companies that WorldCom bought and implies that Ebbers was the force behind those acquisitions. Is it a good idea for directors to have derived significant financial gain from deals in which they and the CEO were prominent players? Or, so long as those deals are in the past, are they unlikely to affect the directors' inclination to carefully monitor the CEO and subject his proposals to appropriate scrutiny?

What about their pay—the thousands of stock options the directors collected each year? Did this contaminate their judgment in some way? Or did it simply align their interests with those of other stockholders?

Consider the rotating chairman position. Is this Ebbers "strok[ing the directors'] egos" or is it just good governance—making sure that no one has the position for too long a time?

Consider Aycock asking Ebbers for a loan from the company. How could such a request, the response to the request, and the loan itself (not made here, but suppose that it were) affect the ability of a director to do his or her job on the board?

What issues did Galesi's investment in a competitor raise as far as his WorldCom Board service is concerned?

What issues did the airplane lease to Kellett raise?

E. THIRD LOOK AT THE WORLDCOM BOARD

After the scandal broke, WorldCom's Board appointed some of its new members (who had not been on the board when the company was publishing financial numbers that it later restated) as a Special Investigative Committee ("WorldCom Special Committee"). That committee hired its own lawyers and its own accounting advisers. The committee produced a 340-page report. Here is an excerpt from pages 264–

68, which provides the report's overview of the WorldCom Board at the time that WorldCom engaged in improper accounting. Here and elsewhere, this book retains the organizational scheme of excerpted material.

A. WorldCom's Board of Directors and Its Committees

1. The Membership and Functioning of the Board

From 2000 to June 2002, the Board of Directors of WorldCom consisted almost entirely of individuals who had been owners, officers, or directors of companies that WorldCom had acquired over the preceding decade. As a result, some had enjoyed very great financial benefits from Ebbers' deals.

The Directors during this period were the following: Clifford Alexander, Jr., James Allen, Judith Areen, Carl Aycock, Max Bobbitt, Bernard Ebbers, Francesco Galesi, Stiles Kellett, Jr., Gordon Macklin, John Porter, Bert Roberts, Jr., John Sidgmore, Scott Sullivan, Lawrence Tucker, and Juan Villalonga. All of these Directors granted interviews to the Special Committee, with the exception of Ebbers and Sullivan. Membership remained relatively constant during the period addressed in this Report, with most Directors serving for the entire period. None of these individuals remains on the Board of Directors today.

The longest-standing members were Aycock and Ebbers, who had both invested in LDDS and joined the LDDS Board in 1983. Beginning a few years after graduating from college and until 1992, Aycock was employed by LDDS and then another company, Master Corporation, controlled by Ebbers. Porter came to LDDS when it acquired a company he owned in 1988. Kellett joined the LDDS Board in 1989 when a company he served as the Chairman of the Board was acquired by LDDS. Bobbitt, Galesi and Sullivan all came to LDDS by virtue of its merger with Advanced Telecommunications Company ("ATC") in 1992. Galesi owned 25% of ATC, and Bobbitt was President and Chief Operating Officer of a subsidiary of ATC. Both of them joined the LDDS Board after the ATC merger. Sullivan had been part of ATC's financial leadership and became LDDS's Chief Financial Officer in 1994. He joined the Board two years later. Sidgmore and Allen were both senior executive officers at companies WorldCom acquired—MFS (1996) and Brooks Fiber (1998), respectively. Roberts, Alexander, Areen and Macklin were members of the MCI Board of Directors (Roberts was also the Chief Executive Officer) and joined the WorldCom Board after the MCI merger in 1998. Villalonga joined the Board when the company of which he was Chief Executive Officer, Telefonica, entered into a strategic alliance with WorldCom in 1998; he left the Board in mid-2000, after that alliance had terminated. Tucker, an officer of a major investor in LDDS, served on the Board officially during 1992 and from 1995 until late 2000; after that, he served in an unofficial advisory capacity on the Board because of possible competition-law issues raised by his other directorships.

The position of Chairman of the Board was largely an honorary title at WorldCom. WorldCom's bylaws provided that either the Chairman or the Chief Executive Officer could preside at Board meetings, "if requested to do so." These ambiguous provisions in the bylaws did not clarify who would make the request, and, in practice, the Chief Executive Officer—Ebbers—presided at Board meetings and determined their agenda. Roberts held the position of Chairman from 1998 until his resignation in 2002.

Directors received compensation consisting of both cash and stock options, with overall compensation heavily weighted toward the latter. Directors received an annual retainer of $35,000 plus $1,000 for each Board meeting they attended. Committee members received $750 for each meeting attended on the same day as a Board meeting and $1,000 for each meeting attended on a day when a Board meeting did not also occur. Committee chairpersons received an additional $3,000 per year. Directors could elect to receive in stock all or a portion of their annual retainer for services as a Director and chairperson of a committee.

Directors also received options to buy shares of Company stock. In 1999, non-employee Directors were granted options to purchase 15,000 shares. In 2000 and 2001, non-employee Directors were granted options to purchase 10,000 shares. Officer Directors were granted options during those years to purchase amounts ranging from 240,000 to 1.2 million shares.

Because many of WorldCom's Directors had held substantial stakes in companies acquired by WorldCom, they owned a significant amount of WorldCom stock. At some point between 1999 and 2002, eight of the fifteen Directors each owned over a million shares of WorldCom stock. None owned more than one percent of WorldCom's outstanding stock.

The Board held regular meetings between four and six times per year and held special meetings as needed. Approximately one week before each regular meeting, the Directors received packets of materials including an agenda, financial information from the previous quarter, draft minutes of the previous meeting, information from the Investor Relations department such as analyst call summaries, and resolutions to consider for the upcoming meeting. There was little interaction between the outside Directors and WorldCom management and employees outside of Board meetings, which more than one Director stated was not the case with other Boards (including MCI's) on which they served.

Ebbers dominated the Board meetings, which followed a consistent format. Each meeting opened with a prayer. A series of presentations—generally done fairly quickly—followed. Typically, the Chairmen of the Audit Committee and Compensation and Stock Option Committee, Bobbitt and Kellett, respectively, each reported to the Board. Michael Salsbury, General Counsel, reported on legal and regulatory issues.

The Board heard presentations by Sullivan and, on occasion, Ron Beaumont (Chief Operating Officer, WorldCom Group). Financial discussions at Board meetings were "high level" and, while not extremely detailed, presented a degree of detail consistent with what we believe most boards received during that period. Sullivan's presentations typically lasted about 30 minutes. We were told the Board's members—like most of the outside world—considered Sullivan an outstanding Chief Financial Officer and believed his presentations were forthright, professional, polished, and showed intimate knowledge of the Company's business and its financial information. We were told that he gave clear and detailed responses to questions. Board members did not extensively question him—something they credited to his thoroughness and credibility. Sullivan never referred to notes, yet he was always able to answer questions in detail.

Beaumont made presentations to the Board about the Company's operations. In general, they lasted about fifteen minutes and Directors did not question him extensively about the information he presented to them. His presentations also sometimes addressed capital expenditures. These discussions focused on the operational aspects of the Company's capital expenditures, and not on the accounting treatment of those expenditures. In addition, Wayne Huyard (Chief Operating Officer, MCI Consumer Services) sometimes reported on MCI-related issues.

The Board met in Executive Session as a part of regular meetings. These sessions usually excluded all non-Director employees and generally involved reports on topics such as upcoming deals, industry trends, development of individuals at the Company and regulatory issues. The sessions, which Ebbers conducted, were informal and generally no one took official notes at them. The outside Directors never held a separate meeting before April 2002, when they met to discuss the events leading up to Ebbers' resignation.[9]

QUESTIONS AFTER YOUR THIRD LOOK AT THE BOARD

Does the law professor/law dean look better now that you know she served on the MCI board before WorldCom merged with MCI?

Through the WorldCom shares that many of the directors received when their old companies were bought by WorldCom, many directors owned a great deal of company stock. Consider whether the effect of stock ownership on director decisions depended in part on what proportion of a director's total wealth was tied up in WorldCom stock. Would a director with most of his or her net worth in company stock perhaps be too conservative, not wanting to take the kinds of business risks that a company should take? Would the tendency to conservatism depend upon the personality of the director (since some people just seem to be more willing to take risks than others)?

Would the effect of stock ownership on director decisions depend in part on the personal circumstances of the director? Would a director with a large part of his or her wealth in WorldCom stock perhaps be too eager to take risks—and hope that WorldCom could hit the jackpot on some deal, sending the price of the stock through the roof—if he or she had an immediate need for a lot of money; for example, to pay a very large loan that was coming due?

Would a director with a large percentage of net worth in WorldCom stock be reluctant to reveal an accounting fraud that would send the share price tumbling downward?

How do you balance all of these considerations with the notion that it may be a good thing for directors to own stock in the companies on whose boards they sit so that their personal interests are aligned with those of other stockholders?

How can a board avoid a CEO "dominat[ing]" the board meetings (116)? What does "dominating" mean in this context?

Can a board—particularly a full board (remember that we are not yet talking about committees)—of a huge company like WorldCom be reasonably expected to regularly receive financial information at anything other than a "high level" (*id.*)? Was the board reasonable in according respect and imputing reliability to Sullivan because his presentations appeared to be "forthright, professional, polished, and showed intimate knowledge of the Company's business and its financial information" and because, when they asked questions "he gave clear and detailed responses" (*id.*)? Should the fact that *CFO Magazine* called Sullivan a "whiz kid" in 1998 and gave him a CFO

---

[9]   WorldCom Special Committee Report, *supra* note 4, at 264–68.

Excellence Award (Special Committee Report at 21, not included in the chapter) have influenced the board's view of Sullivan's reliability?[10]

Was it a good idea for the CEO to always attend the "executive sessions" that the Board held (*id.*)? How can a board have executive sessions that the CEO does not attend, without by that very circumstance implying that the directors who do attend are discussing something that could reflect poorly on the chief executive officer?

Do four to six regular board meetings a year (115) seem enough for an enormous company like WorldCom? Does the pre-meeting board packet described on page *id.* appear to contain the materials that the board needed to prepare for its sessions? Can you quickly think of additional documents that the board might need?

The Special Investigative Committee criticized the fact that "[t]here was little interaction between the outside Directors and WorldCom management and employees outside of Board meetings" (115–116)? What kind of interaction would have been useful? Do you think that interaction between directors and employees could prevent financial fraud, such as the wrongful capitalization of line costs?

F. THE BOARD AND THE ACCOUNTING FRAUD

Read now the following excerpts from pages 29–30 and 277–82 of the WorldCom Special Committee's report. These discuss why the Board was not aware of the fraud. As elsewhere in the book, these excerpts sometimes include footnotes original to the quotation. In those instances, brackets appear around the footnote numbers, and the footnotes retain their numbers from the original source. Where the book then returns to footnotes that I have authored, no brackets appear around the footnote numbers, and the numbering is consecutive to previous footnotes that I prepared.

1.   Board's Lack of Awareness of Accounting Fraud

We found no evidence that members of the Board of Directors, other than Ebbers and Sullivan, were aware of the improper accounting practices at the time they occurred. We have reviewed materials (including slide presentations) the Board received and have not found information that should reasonably have led it to detect the practices or to believe that further specific inquiry into the accounting practices at issue was necessary.

The Board received regular financial and operational presentations that included a level of detail consistent with what we believe most properly run Boards received during that period. The reduced levels of line costs that resulted from release of

---

[10]   As we will see, Sullivan was the individual most immediately responsible for capitalizing line costs.

accruals and improper capitalization did not appear unusual, in part because the entire purpose of the improper accounting exercise was to hold line costs at a level consistent with earlier periods. It is possible, however, that a Board more closely familiar with what was happening operationally in the Company might have questioned financial trends and comparisons with competitors, including the level of reported capital expenditures: the Board received reports that capital expenditures were declining—as the Board had directed—but in fact capital spending was being slashed much more heavily. There was a disparity between the large cuts that were actually taking place and the reported numbers, which were being pushed back up by the improperly added capitalized line costs.[11]

* * *

B.   The Role of the Board and the Audit Committee

We have carefully examined the available information pertinent to the Board's activities from 1999 until 2002, to answer two basic questions: Did the Board or the Audit Committee know of the improper accounting? If not, should they have detected it? We have found no evidence that the Board or Audit Committee in fact knew of the accounting improprieties. Nor have we found any glaring red flags that should have led the Board or Audit Committee to become aware of it. The Board and the Audit Committee were given information that was both false and plausible.

However, we believe the Board—and in particular the Audit Committee—played so limited a role in the oversight of WorldCom that it is unlikely that any but the most flagrant and open financial fraud *could* have come to their attention. Until April 2002, the Board and the Audit Committee did not exert independent leadership.

1.   Awareness of Improper Accounting

We have found nothing in the materials or presentations received by the Board or the Audit Committee, or in our interviews, that would indicate that either group was aware of the improper accounting entries discussed earlier in this Report.[92] We found no evidence that the improper releases of accruals, the capitalization of line costs, the improper revenue items or the

---

[11]   WorldCom Special Committee Report, *supra* note 4, at 29–30.

[92]   In fact, one member of the Audit Committee purchased a substantial amount of Company stock the day after Ebbers officially resigned as Chief Executive Officer. Additionally, a member of the Compensation Committee purchased numerous shares of WorldCom stock in the weeks after Ebbers resigned.

miscellaneous items described in the preceding Sections of this Report were brought to the attention of the Board or the Audit Committee, either by employees or by Andersen.

We also reviewed the materials presented to the Board or the Audit Committee for any red flags that should have put the Board or the Audit Committee on notice of irregularities in these areas, and found none that we believe would have prompted a reasonable Board or Committee member to suspect the existence of the irregularities.[93] Sullivan was, of course, present at the Board meetings, and there is no indication that he disclosed the improprieties in which he was involved. To the contrary, on at least one occasion he took steps to prevent others from providing information to the Board that might have provoked questions.[94] Additionally, after the Enron story broke, Sullivan told the Board that WorldCom's accounting practices were conservative and that WorldCom was not like Enron.

A more general question we have considered is whether, by the sheer size of the capitalization of line costs, the capitalization should have been detectable by the Board. That is, should it have been obvious to the Board that line costs were artificially low and remained fairly constant as a percentage of revenue, or that capital expenditures were billions of dollars lower than the figures actually reported to the Board? Our conclusion is that these facts were not obvious, but that the reported trend in capital expenditures, as well as other trends and comparisons with competitors did warrant questions to management.

---

[93]   There was a presentation by Ron Beaumont to the Board on June 7, 2001, that contained, on the 20th and 21st slides, references to the "Close the Gap" process discussed in Section V.C above. The first of these showed that WorldCom's operations were, to date, producing revenue growth in the quarter of only $48 million, compared to a projected $230 million; this would represent revenue growth from the previous quarter of only about two percent, compared to over 13% projected. The second slide listed some of the "revenue opportunities" for the second quarter of 2001 discussed above in Section V.D, several of them ultimately inconsistent with GAAP. We have not been able to confirm that either of these slides was in fact shown at the meeting. Moreover, it is unlikely a Director would have detected anything improper in this information, since the items listed were primarily operational rather than accounting items, provided no explanation of the substance of the listed items, and purported to reflect activities underway during (and not after the close of) the quarter. However, at a minimum the slides suggested that the "run rate"—that is, WorldCom's ordinary operations—was falling short of the growth rates that had been expected in that quarter. This could conceivably have prompted inquiry into the means by which the Company was achieving on-target earnings despite its well-below-target run rate.

[94]   Ron Beaumont prepared a presentation to give to the Board at its May 23, 2002 meeting that showed approximately $2.3 billion of capital expenditures that were labeled "Corporate," as opposed to operationally-generated capital expenditures. This could have provoked questioning about the Corporate capital expenditures—which in fact reflected the improperly capitalized line costs. Beaumont revised the charts to eliminate this breakdown at Sullivan's request and on Sullivan's assurance that he would take the issue up with the Chief Executive Officer, John Sidgmore.

Line Costs. The information the Board received concerning line costs during 2001 and early 2002 would not likely have excited suspicion. The Board received line cost figures both in the materials distributed prior to meetings and in the PowerPoint presentations made by Sullivan at Board meetings. Specifically, one page of the financial section (which ranged from about 15 to 35 pages in length) of the Board packets was usually a Statement of Operations that contained line costs as one of about ten line items. Also, Board packets often contained a "Quarterly Comparatives" table that compared line costs between quarters. It was in this table that line costs as a percentage of revenue ratios were displayed.

Sullivan's PowerPoint presentations varied in length, but averaged about 35 slides. They usually included a slide comparing actual to budget figures for the previous quarter in which line costs were a line item. The "Quarterly Comparatives" table described above was also often included as a slide in Sullivan's presentations.

Total line costs as presented to the Board were gradually increasing through the first quarter of 2001, declined by about nine percent in the second quarter, then remained stable in the third quarter and declined by five percent in the fourth quarter and three percent in the first quarter of 2002. These declines may well have appeared to reflect effective management, while in fact they reflected improper capitalization. The most suspicious information was that WorldCom's ratio of line cost expense to revenues stayed at 42% through that period—a striking coincidence in a fluctuating business environment. The Board materials included within them tables reporting this ratio, though they were not prominent in the materials. However, even Andersen apparently found comfort in the lack of variance rather than seeing it as a warning of financial manipulation.

Capital Expenditures. The Board might have noticed anomalies with respect to capital expenditures had it been more familiar with what was occurring operationally, although this is quite speculative. Operating personnel were vigorously cutting capital expenditures. But this was not flowing through to the reported numbers, because the improper capitalization of line costs was driving those numbers back up. (See Section IV.C above.) In the second half of 2000, the Board focused more on cuts in capital expenditures after presentations by management and after the industry-wide downturn indicated continued financial pressure on the Company. By the third quarter of 2000, analysts had begun to question the Company's ability to continue its rate of revenue growth, given the state of the industry and WorldCom's size; and certainly after the November 1, 2000 earnings warning, Directors understood that capital expenditures had to be reduced. Internally, the Company was drastically reducing capital expenditures during 2001, but reductions were not showing up in the reported numbers.

Typically, at least one slide within Sullivan's presentation was a breakdown of capital spending into local, data/long haul, Internet and international spending. This slide also showed total capital spending for the quarter and compared it to the same quarter in the previous year. After the tracker stocks were issued, Sullivan's presentations included capital spending slides for each of the WorldCom Group, the MCI Group and WorldCom Consolidated. Every quarter, Sullivan also showed at least one but often three slides describing the projects that made up the bulk of the Company's capital expenditures.

The false numbers shown to the Board in Sullivan's PowerPoint presentations at Board meetings in 2000, 2001 and 2002 are summarized in the chart below. For comparison purposes, the amounts of actual capital spending in 2001 and 2002 that were not shown to the Board and were in fact drastically lower than the reported numbers, are included as well:

Capital Expenditures
(millions of dollars)

	3Q00	4Q00	1Q01	2Q01	3Q01	4Q01	1Q02
As reported to the Board	2,648	2,418	2,235	2,033	1,786	1,785	1,250[95]
As actually spent (i.e., excluding improper line-cost capitalization), beginning in 1Q01, which were not shown to the Board			1,691	1,473	1,044	944	462

These reported numbers reflected a steady decrease in capital spending, beginning in the third quarter of 2000. In fact, however, true capital spending was being slashed much more heavily. The reported numbers were being inflated by the capitalization of hundreds of millions of dollars of line costs each quarter beginning

[95]   Capital expenditures were presented to the Board in chart format at the May 23, 2002 meeting that focused on the first quarter of 2002 performance, rather than as an exact figure as in previous quarters. The chart shows capital expenditures as about midpoint between $1 billion and $1.5 billion.

in the first quarter of 2001. (See Section IV.C above.) A Board more familiar with the operating activities of the Company would have had a greater chance of detecting this disparity between the activities taken to cut capital expenditures and the numbers presented to the Board. However, in fairness, we note that even some operating personnel who had greater reason to be aware of this disparity apparently did not connect it with wrongdoing at the time.[12]

When WorldCom went into bankruptcy, the Bankruptcy Court appointed an Examiner. Like the WorldCom Special Committee, the Examiner tried to figure out what went wrong. The Examiner issued a series of reports. The following excerpt—from pages 25–29 of the First Interim Report of Dick Thornburgh, Bankruptcy Court Examiner, dated November 4, 2002 and filed in the WorldCom bankruptcy, *In re WorldCom, Inc.*, Case No. 02-15533 (AJG), U.S. Bankruptcy Court, Southern District of New York—recounts the discovery of the line cost accounting irregularity and what steps the board took as a result. In keeping the players straight as you read, keep in mind that WorldCom replaced Arthur Andersen with KPMG as WorldCom's outside auditor after the government indicted Andersen for actions it took during its work for Enron. When the improper accounting was discovered at WorldCom, Andersen was that company's former auditor and KPMG its current auditor.

The Internal Audit Department's investigation of the capitalization of line costs is a story that has already been publicly reported. We will briefly summarize the significant events here. In May 2002, the Company's Internal Audit Department began an investigation concerning the capitalization of line costs. On May 21, 2002, an internal auditor received from another WorldCom employee, a featured article from the May 16 edition of Fort Worth Weekly Online, entitled "Accounting for Anguish." The employee indicated that the issues raised in the article might warrant investigation by the Internal Audit Department at WorldCom. "Accounting for Anguish" is based upon interviews with Kim Emigh, a former WorldCom employee who allegedly was fired for whistle blowing, and details a number of alleged accounting improprieties at the Company, although none related to the capitalization of line costs.

Members of the Internal Audit Department continued their investigation over the next few weeks, attempting to gather relevant documents and information. On or about June 12, 2002, the Internal Audit team contacted Max Bobbitt, the Chairman of the Audit Committee of the Board of Directors, and informed him

---

[12]   *Id.* at 277–82.

of its discoveries regarding the timing and amounts of certain journal entries. The Internal Audit Department told Mr. Bobbitt that these journal entries included entries amounting to $743 million for the third quarter of 2001, entries amounting to $941 million for the fourth quarter of 2001, and entries amounting to $818 million for the first quarter of 2002, for a total of $2.5 billion in line costs that had been capitalized. Mr. Bobbitt then requested that these issues be discussed with KPMG prior to a meeting of the Audit Committee on June 14, 2002. This discussion occurred on June 12.

Between June 12 and June 20, the Internal Audit team continued its investigation. On June 20, the Audit Committee of the Board of Directors met to discuss the issue. In the course of the meeting, representatives from KPMG summarized the circumstances underlying the capitalization of line costs from the second quarter of 2001 through the first quarter of 2002. KPMG representatives told those present at the meeting that, in their view, the capitalization of line costs did not comply with GAAP and that no documentation supporting such capitalization appeared to exist. KPMG was asked if the Company needed to restate its financial statements at that time and KPMG said that it had not reached conclusions with respect to any issue raised. Mr. Sullivan attempted to explain to those attending the Audit Committee meeting his reasoning behind the capitalization of line costs and he requested additional time to support and document the transfers of line costs from the Company's income statement (where they appeared as expenses) to its balance sheet (where they appeared as assets, generally subject to depreciation).

Between June 21 and June 24, the Board of Directors engaged various attorneys and other professionals to review this matter. On June 24, the crisis surrounding the Company's capitalization of line costs reached its peak following a series of events.

Another meeting of the Audit Committee was scheduled for June 24, 2002. In preparation for that meeting, Mr. Sullivan submitted what has come to be known as the "White Paper," setting forth his rationale for the line cost capitalizations in light of the economic conditions prevailing at the time at which the line cost capitalizations occurred. In the White Paper, Mr. Sullivan stated that, following WorldCom's merger with MCI in September of 1998, WorldCom had sold MCI's SHL Systemhouse business for $1.4 billion and announced that it would use the entire proceeds of the sale to expand WorldCom's network. Through the end of 2000, Mr. Sullivan's White Paper continued, WorldCom had engaged in an extended capital investment campaign to increase the size of the Company's Internet backbone, expand local and data networks, and construct a "Pan European network." Mr. Sullivan observed that, at this time, the telecommunications industry was rapidly developing, WorldCom was facing "increased" and "intense" competition, and it was important that the Company have the ability to enter the market quickly and provide the "best network" to its customers with "little provisioning time." Mr. Sullivan noted that WorldCom's decision to increase capital investment significantly was based upon the prevailing belief that Internet use and data demand would continue at the rate of eight times the annual growth that the telecommunications industry was experiencing.

According to Mr. Sullivan's White Paper, it was during this period that WorldCom entered into long-term, fixed-rate line leases to connect its network with the networks of incumbent local exchange carriers. Mr. Sullivan noted that WorldCom also entered into various network leases to complement its data, Internet, and local services, in order to obtain access to large amounts of line capacity "under the theory that revenue would follow and fully absorb these costs and expedite 'time to market.'" Mr. Sullivan also stated that WorldCom was willing to absorb the line lease costs prior to recognizing the revenue to match them, because "it believed that future revenue would be matched up with these costs." The White Paper referenced Staff Accounting Bulletin No.101 ("SAB 101") and Financial Accounting Standards Board No. 91 ("FASB 91") to support Mr. Sullivan's conclusion that the lease costs thereby incurred should not be expensed until WorldCom had recognized matching revenue. Mr. Sullivan reasoned that "the cost deferrals for the unutilized portion" of line leases were "an appropriate inventory of this capacity" that ultimately would be amortized before the expiration of the contractual commitment. To support this reasoning, Mr. Sullivan quoted the definition of an asset as "'probable future economic benefits obtained or controlled by a particular entity as a result of past transactions or events,'" together with a description of the essential characteristics of an asset, as set forth in Statement of Financial Accounting Concepts No. 6.

In the White Paper, Mr. Sullivan went on to observe that the second quarter of 2002 marked the first time in the Company's history that WorldCom had experienced quarterly revenue decreases for two consecutive quarters and that these decreases were the result of challenges posed by a weak economy and the consequent network downsizing of customers, customer bankruptcies, foreign exchange losses, and "product migrations."

According to Mr. Sullivan, these events, together with the resignations of WorldCom's President and CEO, the junk-status of the Company's debt rating, and its liquidity concerns, all contributed to a determination by WorldCom, in the second quarter of 2002, that the "future economic benefits of the deferred costs" of the Company's line leases could not ultimately be realized, necessitating a write-off of the previously capitalized costs. In concluding the White Paper, Mr. Sullivan observed that the preparation of the financial statements of WorldCom "requires the Company to make estimates and assumptions that affect the reported amount of assets and liabilities as well as the reported amount of expenses, including line costs" and that "[s]ignifcant [sic] management judgments and estimates must be made and used in connection with establishing these amounts."

At the Audit Committee meeting on June 24, representatives from Arthur Andersen informed WorldCom that, in light of the line cost transfers that occurred in 2001 and 2002, the opinion of Arthur Andersen concerning the Company's 2001 financial statements no longer could be relied upon. The Arthur Andersen representatives stated that they did not know about the line cost transfers, but they would not answer questions as to why their audit had failed to uncover them. They indicated that they had not seen Mr. Sullivan's White Paper, but that it had been read to them and that they could not accept it as compliant with GAAP. Representatives of KPMG agreed with Arthur Andersen that the capitalization of line costs could not be supported under GAAP. The Audit Committee rejected Mr. Sullivan's reasoning in the White Paper and determined that it would report to the Company's Board of Directors that a full restatement of the financial statements of WorldCom for 2001 and the first quarter of 2002 would be necessary. The Audit Committee advised Messrs. Sullivan and Myers that if they did not resign before the Board of Directors meeting scheduled for the following day, their employment would be terminated.

The full Board of Directors met on June 25, 2002. At that meeting, the Board determined that WorldCom would restate its financial statements for 2001 and the first quarter of 2002. The Board also determined that KPMG would re-audit the Company's financial statements for 2001 and it decided to terminate Mr. Sullivan without severance and to accept the resignation of Mr. Myers without severance. The Board also decided that it would immediately inform the SEC of the Board's decisions and that after representatives of WorldCom had informed the SEC regarding these matters, the Company would inform the public of the Board's conclusions.

c.   June 25 Public Announcement of Restatement of Earnings

Following the Board of Directors meeting, WorldCom representatives met with the SEC staff. WorldCom then issued a press release on June 25, 2002 regarding its intention to restate its financial statements for 2001 and the first quarter of 2002.

The Company's June 25 press release announced that the restatement would cause an aggregate reduction of $3.8 billion in its earnings before interest, taxes, depreciation and amortization ("EBITDA") for 2001 and the first quarter of 2002. The announcement further explained that Arthur Andersen had advised the Company that, in light of the inappropriate transfers of line costs, Arthur Andersen's audit report on the Company's financial statements for 2001, as well as its review of the Company's financial statements for the first quarter of 2002, could not be relied upon.[13]

QUESTIONS ON THE WORLDCOM BOARD'S PERFORMANCE

Isn't it interesting that the Special Committee—which hired Wilmer, Cutler & Pickering and PricewaterhouseCoopers, and reviewed nearly two million pages of documents, imaged the hard drives of about 50% of WorldCom employees, collected 1.2 million e-mails (with over 400,000 attachments), reviewed voice mails that WorldCom had recovered, and interviewed 13 former directors and 122 current and former employees—found nothing to indicate either that the board knew of the accounting fraud or that the board should have taken anything that it saw as a red flag that should have prompted an investigation that would have uncovered the fraud?

The Special Committee's criticism is that the board "played so limited a role in the oversight of WorldCom that it is unlikely that any but the most flagrant and open financial fraud *could* have come to their attention" (119); (emphasis in original). But does this come down to saying: "Gee, the board didn't work very hard and a big fraud occurred"?

Remember that the outside auditor did not discover the fraud. Is it reasonable to believe that the board *would* have found the fraud if it had worked harder? If management is committing a fraud and successfully concealing it from the outside auditors, is it likely that the board will uncover the wrongdoing? Will it depend on the nature of the accounting fraud?

---

[13]   First Interim WorldCom Examiner Report, *supra* note 3, at 25–29.

How will the board make such a discovery? Will directors personally look at accounting records? Or are the board's chances dependent on how well it uses the resources available to it, such as the internal auditors? Keep your thoughts on this last question in mind when we examine the audit committee in the next chapter.

Turning to the events in June 2002, how do you think the board performed once it learned that line costs had been capitalized? If you think it performed well, *why* did it so?

G. WHETHER COMPARATIVE RATIOS WERE A RED FLAG

In the private securities lawsuits arising out of WorldCom's collapse, Bert Roberts, the former WorldCom Board chair (who had run MCI before WorldCom bought MCI) moved for summary judgment on claims against him under (i) section 11 of the Securities Act of 1933, (ii) the control person provision of the Securities Act (section 15), and (iii) the control person provision of the Securities Exchange Act of 1934 (section 20(a)). Crudely stated, the questions on the motion were whether there was a triable issue of fact that Roberts had been negligent with respect to the financial statements that WorldCom had published and whether there was a triable issue of fact that he had failed to act in good faith. The court denied Roberts' motion, holding that there were such triable issues. Here are two quotations from the opinion:

> The Lead Plaintiff has pointed to information, most notably the decline in WorldCom's line costs as a percentage of revenue, that a jury may find should have raised a red flag for Roberts and caused him to question his reliance on the audited financial statements. This is particularly true given Roberts' history within and expertise in the telecommunications industry. While Roberts has an explanation for why he accepted management's explanation regarding WorldCom's singular success in this regard, that explanation serves to highlight that this is a disputed issue of fact for trial. If the line cost data was a red flag, then Roberts had an obligation to inquire until satisfied as to the integrity of the line cost data.[14]

> * * *

> Given Roberts' extensive experience in the telecommunications industry, coupled with what the Lead Plaintiff characterizes as the "great divergence" between the line cost ratios that were

---

[14]   *In re WorldCom Sec. Litig.*, No. 02 Civ. 3288DLC, 2005 WL 638268, at *11 (footnote omitted).

reported by WorldCom, by MCI prior to its merger with WorldCom, and by WorldCom's chief competitors, a reasonable jury could find that Roberts had a reasonable ground to believe that financial improprieties were afoot.[15]

In another WorldCom decision, the court reported computations by the plaintiff apparently showing that, for 1999, WorldCom's reported expenses (which had been artificially reduced by the capitalization of line costs) were 43% of revenue, whereas AT&T's were 46.8% and Sprint's were 53.2%.[16] The former president of AT&T's Business Services testified in the WorldCom litigation, describing his "amazement at WorldCom's [expense/revenue] ratio as reported in its quarterly and annual financial statements, and the concerted efforts he and his team made over a period of months to try to understand why WorldCom's reported performance of such a critical indicator was so superior to AT&T's comparable ratio."[17]

QUESTIONS ON DIRECTOR RESPONSE TO MANAGEMENT'S REPORT THAT THE COMPANY PERFORMED BETTER THAN COMPETITORS

I have been unable to find Roberts' statement of how the WorldCom management explained the company's line-cost-to-revenue ratio. But he apparently got an explanation and was satisfied with it. If so, what else should he have done?

Suppose that, at some company other than WorldCom, the CEO or CFO tells the board that the company's performance—as measured by some financial ratio—is significantly better than the performance of the company's competitors. Should the board congratulate management? Or should the board institute an investigation to determine whether the reported superior performance is the result of management fraud?

---

[15]   *Id.* at *17 (footnote omitted).

[16]   *In re WorldCom Sec. Litig.*, 346 F. Supp. 2d 628, 678 n.47 (S.D.N.Y. 2004) (ruling on summary judgment motions relating to underwriter liability).

[17]   *In re WorldCom Sec. Litig.*, 388 F. Supp. 2d 319, 330–31 (S.D.N.Y. 2005) (approving settlements).

CHAPTER 4

WORLDCOM PART II: THE AUDIT COMMITTEE

■ ■ ■

Before looking at the WorldCom Audit Committee, this Chapter Four provides basic information about accounting in modern corporations. The chapter then reprints some of the criticism of the WorldCom Audit Committee, followed by reproductions of (i) an audit plan and (ii) audit results that WorldCom's auditor gave to the committee for one of the years in which (unbeknownst to the auditor at the time) WorldCom financials included false numbers. Looking at that plan and the results as reported by the auditor, you can consider for yourself what the committee should have done after receiving these documents.

A. A BRIEF DESCRIPTION OF ACCOUNTING AND AUDITING

Each large corporation has its own accounting staff. These accountants are on the company's payroll. Among their duties, they process and record transactions in the company's books and records and create the company's financial statements. They usually report up the organizational chart to the chief financial officer ("CFO").

Every public reporting company has an independent outside auditor. The outside auditor is often a large accounting firm. Today, there are four very large such firms. There are many smaller firms that audit public companies. The auditors do not create a corporation's accounting records or prepare its financial statements. The company's own accountants perform those tasks. Instead, the auditor's job is to check—in the limited way, and for the limited purpose described below—the financial statements that the company's accountants have already created. Except in special circumstances, the outside accounting firm performs that check—the audit—after the end of the company's accounting year. So, the audit is performed once a year.

The auditor usually does *not* check every single accounting entry made in every single transaction. That would be too expensive and time-consuming. Instead, the auditor performs a variety of tests to give the auditor evidence sufficient to form an opinion—which the auditor provides to the company at the end of the audit—as to whether the company's final financial statements (balance sheet, income statement, and cash flow statement) fairly present, in all material respects, the financial position, results of operations, and cash flows of the company, in conformity with generally accepted accounting principles. Even if the auditor's opinion expresses that conclusion, the audit provides only reasonable assurance, rather than any guarantee, that the financial statements are correct.

Auditors perform different types of "tests" as they audit a company's financial statements. What follows illustrates—in a vastly oversimplified way—three types of such tests and then describes how auditors test financial numbers that are forecasts. For the purpose of these illustrations, suppose that an auditor is checking the revenue recorded by a company that manufactures and sells propeller aircraft for general aviation. The company sells most of its planes to three distributors and sells a smaller number of aircraft—usually highly customized—directly to individuals or companies who will use the planes for pleasure or business.

Auditors test (or "assess") the processes ("internal controls") that generate a particular type of number at the audited company.

To help them focus audit efforts where they are most likely to find significant errors (and for other reasons), auditors test the systems in the company that generate the numbers appearing in the financial statements. In our example, the auditor might test the internal controls by which the company records its airplane sales. In doing so, the auditor might find that the company's employees always enter a sale in computers linked to the company's full accounting system, that the price for a sale is entered electronically when sales personnel scan a bar code on the airplane sold, that the accounting system then deducts the airplane from the number of finished planes shown in the accounting system (with figures separately recorded for different models of airplanes), that the numbers of finished planes (by models) in the inventory figures shown in the accounting system are also updated by adding new planes that the company has manufactured and finished, that the inventory figures are periodically checked by physical count to make sure that the numbers and models of finished airplanes still at the company match the numbers and models of finished airplanes in the accounting system, that the transaction documents for each airplane sale are scanned, and that the images of those documents are electronically linked to the accounting entries recording each sale. If the auditor found this state of affairs, the auditor might conclude that the effective controls reduce the evidence that the auditor needs from other testing.

On the other hand, the auditor might find that each sale is entered into the accounting system without scanning any bar code on the airplane sold or otherwise physically verifying that a particular airplane was sold, that the transaction documents for each sale are kept in paper form only, that some of the transaction documents for the year being audited are missing, and that nobody regularly checks the numbers of finished and unsold airplanes at the company against the numbers of finished airplanes that the company's accounting system shows to be in the company's possession. If the auditor found this state of affairs, the auditor might conclude that the controls the company has in place are not effective to support proper recording of airplane sales, and that therefore the auditor needed to perform more extensive substantive testing of the sales numbers.

Auditors employ substantive "analytical" procedures.

Auditors analyze financial numbers to spot those that might need special attention. In our example, the auditor might look at the company's growth in airplane sales on a monthly basis over some number of years preceding the year being audited, compare that growth with sales growth at other manufacturers of general aviation aircraft and with industry trends, and develop an expectation for the growth in airplane sales at the company in the audit year. If, on the basis of this analysis, the auditor expected 3% sales growth in the audit year, and the company's financial records showed a 3% increase, that correlation would provide some evidence that the company's sale numbers were reliable. On the other hand, if the company's numbers showed a 10% increase, then the auditor would perform additional work to understand the difference.

Auditors conduct substantive tests of details.

Auditors test some transactions in detail. In our example, the auditor might seek confirmation of sales from a sample of customers that the company's records show to have purchased one or more airplanes during the audited year.

A company may have engaged in so many different transactions—not just for sales but purchases as well—that it is impractical to substantively test the details of each one. The auditor might then test a sample. The auditor might determine the type and extent of the tests it would perform based on, among other things, its assessment of the company's internal controls and the results of the auditor's analytical procedures.

Sometimes, auditors select particularly large transactions for substantive testing in detail because those transactions have a large impact on the company's overall financial results. In our example, the auditor might seek sales confirmations from the three distributors to which the company sells most of its airplanes.

Auditors may also test transactions recorded close to a year's end because (i) management might stretch to reach bonus goals by counting as end-of-year transactions sales that were not completed in time to properly record them in the year and (ii) a company might simply make a mistake in determining the year in which a sale should be recorded. In our example, the auditor might seek confirmations from customers on sales that the company recorded as occurring in the last two weeks in the audited year.

An auditor might also use statistical sampling techniques to select transactions for detailed testing. The auditor in our example might use such a technique to select a sample of the individual and company customers (who buy directly from the company) and seek sales confirmations from the customers in that sample.

<u>Auditors test key estimates.</u>

Some accounting figures are estimates, and auditors may test such estimates. As an example, the airplane manufacturer might have a reserve to account for the circumstance that customers can return airplanes that do not meet specifications, and might have based that reserve on the company's forecast of the number of customers who would return planes for that reason. The auditor might review the process by which management made the estimate. The auditor might develop an independent expectation and compare it to the company's estimate.[1]

Public companies also have "internal auditors." Like the company's regular accounting staff, these accountants are on the company payroll. However, they are different from the regular accounting staff. The regular accounting staff makes all the accounting entries. The "internal auditors" often assess the functioning of a company's controls, processes, and procedures, focusing on those that directly affect financial reporting. In most companies, the internal auditors do not check every accounting entry in the company. They distribute their attention in different ways at different companies. Their work may enable them to find important accounting errors that others in the company are making, or accounting fraud that others are committing.

Internal auditors may also perform "operational" audits that do not involve checking the accounting system. For example, they might study the way that a company performs a particular task in order to determine whether the company can reduce the cost of that task.

The audit committee is a committee of board members. For example, a 10-person board might have an audit committee of three directors. While we will study the operations of audit committees in detail later, it suffices now to say that an audit committee oversees the preparation and audit of financial statements that the company publishes and that this is arguably the committee's most important responsibility. Typically, an audit

---

[1]   The outside accounting firm that audits the public company's annual financial statements also "reviews" the company's "interim" financial statements, which, for our purposes, simply means the financial statements that the company publishes for each of the first three financial quarters. A review has a substantially smaller scope than an audit and consists principally of performing analytical procedures and making inquiries of persons at the company who are responsible for financial and accounting matters.

committee does not have any staff of its own, and it does not itself prepare or audit financial statements. But it meets with members of management involved with financial reporting (e.g., the CFO), with the outside auditor, and with the internal auditors. Among other things, the audit committee discusses the auditors' plans, and receives reports on the audits that are conducted.

B. THE WORLDCOM AUDIT COMMITTEE

With that brief background, here is what the WorldCom Special Investigative Committee ("WorldCom Special Committee") said in comments that criticize the WorldCom Board overall as well as the Audit Committee specifically. What follows are excerpts from pages 274–75 and 282–92 of the WorldCom Special Committee's report.

3. The Audit Committee

From November 1999 through July 2002, the Audit Committee consisted of Bobbitt (Chairman), Allen, Areen and Galesi. They met between three and five times per year between 1999 and 2001. Meetings lasted about one hour except that the February 2002 meeting, likely in response to heightened awareness growing out of the Enron scandal, lasted closer to two hours. The Audit Committee held no special meetings until June 2002 when it became aware of the accounting irregularities.

All members received a packet of materials several days prior to each meeting that contained an agenda; minutes of previous meetings; and various documents pertaining to the planned discussion, including such materials as lists of proposed, in progress and completed internal audits, key internal audit issues and recommendations, and Andersen audit plans.

WorldCom's Audit Committee was responsible for overseeing three functions: the Internal Audit department, the external auditors, and management's financial reporting. More specifically, the Committee was charged with reviewing the Company's annual financial statements with management and the external auditor; reviewing Internal Audit's reports to management and management's responses to those reports; recommending selection of the external auditors to the Board; discussing the Company's accounting, financial reporting and internal controls with Internal Audit and the external auditors outside the presence of management; and reviewing and concurring with management's selection or termination of the head of Internal Audit.

The Internal Audit department, headed by Cynthia Cooper (Vice President of Internal Audit), monitored the operational systems and internal controls of the Company. The Audit Committee retained Arthur Andersen as WorldCom's external auditor until April 2002.

Representatives of Andersen and Internal Audit attended every Audit Committee meeting. While the Chairman of the Audit Committee has stated that a representative from Internal Audit always attended Andersen presentations, the minutes from the meetings where such presentations were given do not indicate that a representative from Internal Audit was present.[2]

* * *

2.   The Quality of Board and Committee Oversight

The Board and the Audit Committee did not function in a way that made it likely that red flags would come to their attention. Boards are indisputably reliant on information they receive from others. However, they must create the environment and the opportunities that give them the best chance of learning of issues requiring their attention. The WorldCom Board Audit and Compensation Committees were distant and detached from the workings of the Company. Ebbers controlled the Board's agenda, its discussions, and its decisions. The Board did not function as a check on Ebbers and he created a corporate environment in which the pressure to meet the numbers was high, the departments that served as controls within the Company were weak, and the word of senior management was final and not to be challenged.

The Directors had a number of tools available to increase the chances of detecting acts of corporate wrongdoing that may be filtered by top management. Among them were the following: maintaining enough involvement in the Company's business to enable the Board to exert some control over the agenda; ensuring the presence of strong "control" functions within the Company; communicating throughout the Company the value of high ethical standards; having some familiarity and direct contact with people throughout the Company (as well as suppliers and customers); and keeping a close and open relationship with the outside auditors. The WorldCom Board and its Committees were simply out of touch with the Company below the level of Ebbers and Sullivan. Indeed, to the extent they sent signals to employees, those signals were counterproductive.

---

[2]   Report of Investigation by the Special Investigative Committee of the Board of Directors of WorldCom, Inc. (Mar. 31, 2003) at 274–75, http://www.sec.gov/Archives/edgar/data/723527/0000 93176303001862/dex991.htm.

Involvement in the Company's Business and Control of the Agenda. It is easiest for management to deceive or mislead the Board when management is in complete control of the agenda: a Board that is deeply familiar with the Company's business and competitive environment, and focusing on the issues confronting the Company, is less likely to be misled or deceived by management. At WorldCom, however, management had full rein over the agenda. Management almost never consulted with Directors outside of Board meetings, and Ebbers was unchallenged at the Board meetings.

We were told that the members of the Board (other than Ebbers, Sullivan and, for a time, Sidgmore) had little or no involvement in the Company's business other than through attendance at Board meetings. With the exception of Bobbitt and Kellett, Chairmen of the two active Committees, none of the outside Directors had regular communications even with Ebbers or Sullivan—much less with operating personnel—between meetings. And even Bobbitt and Kellett did not often speak with Ebbers or Sullivan outside of Board or Committee meetings.

Although a number of Directors asked questions from time to time, we are aware of no occasions on which a Board member, other than Sidgmore, seriously challenged management until April 2002—when, we must note, the Board acted vigorously in demanding Ebbers' resignation.[96] Nearly all of the Directors were legacies of companies that WorldCom, under Ebbers' leadership, had acquired. They had ceded leadership to Ebbers when their companies were acquired, and in some cases viewed their role as diminished. Moreover, there was no cohesiveness and only limited respect—which later deteriorated into outright hostility—among many of the Directors who came from the different acquisitions.

Bert Roberts was particularly well suited to provide independent judgment, but did not do so. He was the former Chief Executive Officer of MCI, had extensive experience and stature in the industry, had the title of Chairman of the Board of Directors of WorldCom, and was paid more than $1 million a year. Yet he was generally passive at Board meetings and exerted little influence.

Even when Directors had doubts, they deferred. One example is the Board meeting at which the plan to create tracker stocks was presented, on September 7, 2000. Ebbers and Sullivan delivered a

---

[96]   Areen threatened to resign in January 2002 because she felt Ebbers was the wrong person to lead the Company. She acceded to Ebbers' request that she remain on the Board until after the 2002 annual meeting, scheduled for June 2002.

presentation at the Executive Session following the quarterly Board meeting, in which they discussed options for restructuring the Company and emphasized the desirability of issuing a tracker stock for the low-growth businesses. Borghardt's notes from that session indicate that Allen commented that Ebbers' plan was the equivalent of trying to hide "manure in the closet," where it would "still smell." Alexander has told us that he also opposed the tracker plan and preferred a spin-off. Notwithstanding these objections, the Board unanimously approved Ebbers' restructuring plan as of October 31, 2000.[97]

Bobbitt and Kellett did on occasion express opinions about possible business combinations, although both avoided confrontation with Ebbers[98] and neither of them pressed his views with the Board when doing so would involve a challenge to Ebbers. The only Board member (other than Sullivan) who appears to have engaged vigorously concerning the direction of the Company was John Sidgmore. Sidgmore had a number of active battles with Ebbers and Sullivan over corporate strategy and potential transactions, but then largely withdrew from his active role within the Company when he was overruled. From this point on, Sidgmore—though knowledgeable and in a position to make a significant contribution—became a largely passive observer. The result of all of this was a Company in which the Board was far too disengaged from the Company's activities and its oversight. This increased the Board's reliance on senior management.

The need for an understanding of the Company is particularly important to the effective functioning of the Audit Committee. However, its members do not appear to have been sufficiently familiar and involved with the Company's internal financial workings, with weaknesses in the Company's internal control structure, or with its culture. WorldCom was a complicated Company in a fast-evolving industry. It had expanded quickly, through a series of large acquisitions, each of which raised both accounting and internal control and systems concerns that deserved Audit Committee knowledge and attention. These acquisitions had not been integrated, posing serious challenges for

---

[97] Formal action by the Board occurred later, but was treated as having been accomplished on October 31, and minutes reporting that the Board had acted at an October 31 meeting were approved by the Board.

[98] When confronted with what Kellett and Bobbitt viewed as an outright lie by Ebbers at a Board meeting regarding who proposed the loans from the Company, Kellett did not challenge Ebbers about the lie because he did not think it was in the best interests of the Company to confront him in front of other Directors. Bobbitt actually supported Ebbers' statement at the Board meeting (even though he later said it was a lie) because he did not wish to embarrass Ebbers. Also, Kellett chose to express his opposition to the Intermedia deal in a telephone call to Ebbers rather than discuss it at a Board meeting.

the Company and the Audit Committee. WorldCom had accounting-related operations scattered in a variety of locations around the country. To gain the knowledge necessary to function effectively as an Audit Committee would have required a very substantial amount of energy, expertise by at least some of its members, and time—certainly more than the three to five hours a year the Audit Committee met.

The Presence of Strong Control Departments. WorldCom's legal departments and its Internal Audit department were not structured in ways that would make them effective as a control of management wrongdoing. As noted above, the Company's lawyers were in fragmented groups, they were not located geographically near senior management or involved in its inner workings, there was no coherent reporting structure or hierarchy, and they had limited support from senior management. Even at the Board level, it was not until weeks after the Compensation Committee caused the Company to lend tens of millions of dollars to Ebbers that any lawyer at the Company was informed of it. In such an environment, it is not surprising that employees distressed by the accounting irregularities did not think of the legal departments as logical avenues of recourse. The Board did not create these conditions, but it should have been aware of them and concerned about them.

Internal Audit, of course, ultimately did succeed in revealing the financial fraud that had been occurring for several years. The Chairman of the Audit Committee, Max Bobbitt, supported Internal Audit when it began having conflicts with Sullivan in early 2002, and as it was pursuing the investigation that brought to light the capitalization of line costs. This was the right way to interact.

Internal Audit accomplished this despite a structure that we believe had four serious weaknesses. *First*, it reported to the Chief Financial Officer for many purposes. This made it more difficult for Internal Audit to challenge the Chief Financial Officer, and may have deterred employees from going to Internal Audit with their concerns about the accounting entries.

Second, it had (until early 2002) limited its efforts to operational audits, and left financial issues to the outside auditor. This meant that an important internal control over the accounting process was absent, there was no year-round review, and the input of employees with their own perspective and information sources was eliminated from the control process. It is striking that when Internal Audit began looking at financial issues in late 2001 and early 2002, two of its first audits (Wireless bad debt reserves and capital expenditures) found serious problems. (See Section IV.D.4 above.)

Third, the Audit Committee's role in Internal Audit's activities was very limited. It reviewed the list of audits scheduled for each year, and was provided general updates and summaries of information that Internal Audit thought important. However, the Audit Committee did not play a substantial role in setting priorities or in the follow-up on problems found in the course of its audits.

Fourth, WorldCom's Internal Audit department was understaffed and underbudgeted when compared to peers in the industry. According to a 2002 Institute of Internal Audit Benchmarking Study comparing the Internal Audit department at WorldCom to those at other telecommunication companies that was shown to the Committee in May 2002, WorldCom had more employees and higher revenues per auditor than its competitors by a huge margin—nearly twice as many employees per auditor, and more than three times the revenues per auditor.[99] Even allowing for some difference because Internal Audit performed only operational audits, this disparity reflected a serious underallocation of resources.

Communication of the Value Placed on High Ethical Standards. A Board can communicate the value it places on high ethical standards—most convincingly through its own conduct (discussed in Sections that follow), but also through other means. While focusing on ethical conduct is important in every company, it is particularly important in a company that has gone through major acquisitions, because "[e]xperience shows that unless high-level attention is given, the combined company's ethical values find the *lowest* common denominator."[100] The means for a Board to do this includes making ethical conduct a clear part of the compensation process (it was not at WorldCom[101]), seeking opportunities to

---

[99]   WorldCom had 3,111 employees per auditor and $1.3 billion in revenues per auditor. In comparison, according to one study, other telecommunications companies had 1,639 employees per auditor and $408 million in revenues per auditor.

[100]   PRICEWATERHOUSECOOPERS, CORPORATE GOVERNANCE AND THE BOARD—WHAT WORKS BEST 25 (2000).

[101]   WorldCom's new Chief Executive Officer, Michael Capellas, and the Corporate Monitor developed an employment contract for Mr. Capellas that includes several provisions intended to promote healthy governance practices. These include tying all incentive payments to performance standards, use of restricted stock grants rather than stock options to provide equity incentives, and the use of an "Ethics Pledge" as part of the agreement. The Pledge requires the Company under his leadership to make full and candid disclosures concerning all areas of its business, extending beyond SEC requirements. The Pledge calls for investment in a strong and robust compliance system, and making integrity and ethics an integral part of how the Company does

highlight corporate and individual actions exemplifying ethical conduct, and—most commonly employed—adopting and emphasizing a corporate code of ethical conduct.[102]

WorldCom had no code of ethical conduct during the relevant period. The only mention of ethics in its Employee Handbook was contained in a two-page section that simply stated that fraud and dishonesty would not be tolerated and advised employees to report to their managers and/or the Human Resources department any unlawful or unethical behavior. MCI, in contrast, had a 24-page Code of Ethical Conduct at the time of its merger with WorldCom.

WorldCom only began drafting a Code of Ethics in early 2000. A draft was prepared by a senior attorney in the Law and Public Policy Department in Washington. The draft was not acted upon for nearly a year, until the drafting process resumed in May 2001. Between May 2001 and January 2002, counsel distributed drafts to a number of high-level managers and received approval from Sullivan and other senior executives to finalize a Code. However, Ebbers, when presented with a draft, reportedly called a Code of Ethics a "colossal waste of time." The Company formally adopted a Code of Business Ethics in the Fall of 2002—after the fraud was discovered—and posted it to WorldCom's internal website in early October 2002.

Direct Contact with People Throughout the Company. The outside Directors had virtually no interaction with Company operational or financial employees other than during the presentations they heard at meetings. They were not themselves visible to employees. While in these respects the Directors were far from unique among directors of large corporations, this lack of contact meant that they had little sense of the culture within the Company, or whether the tone they believed was being set by themselves and senior management was being received at other levels of the Company. Moreover, there were no systems in place that could have encouraged employees to risk contacting the outside Directors with concerns they had about the accounting entries or operational matters.

A Close and Open Relationship with the Outside Auditors. The Audit Committee met regularly with Andersen, heard and relied upon comforting reports, and received no indication that there were matters that should be of concern to it. We have not seen any evidence that the Committee placed pressure on Andersen to

---

business. This Ethics Pledge has subsequently been signed by the Company's most senior managers as well.

[102] Report of the National Commission on Fraudulent Financial Reporting (1987) ("Treadway Report"). Compliance is generally monitored by the Audit Committee.

perform fewer tests than required in Andersen's professional judgment, or that it failed to support Andersen in any respect.

In its auditors' reports accompanying the financial statements in the annual report, Andersen stated that the Company's financial statements were fairly presented and in accordance with GAAP. In its 2001 audit report provided to the Audit Committee, Andersen reported on whether the Company's processes were "effective," "ineffective" or "effective but need work." These three categories were represented in the report as green, red or yellow, respectively. The 2001 report was awash in green, without even a single yellow or red mark. Committee members believed that this was a perfect report that showed that the Company had excellent controls and was financially healthy.

Nevertheless, there was a serious failure of communication between Andersen and the Audit Committee. Part of it was clearly Andersen's fault. As we described in Section VII above, we have seen no evidence that Andersen informed the Audit Committee of either the concerns that led it to rate WorldCom a maximum risk client or that it was being denied access to WorldCom's General Ledger by management. The Audit Committee was entitled to know these things.

The Audit Committee members, for their part, apparently did not understand—though the evidence indicates that Andersen disclosed—the non-traditional audit approach Andersen employed. As described in our discussion of Andersen, this approach emphasized determining specific business risks, reviewing controls in place to monitor those risks, and only testing those areas where residual risk was perceived. In contrast, a traditional audit places greater emphasis on "verif[ying] . . . information maintained in accounting records and financial statements." Whether Andersen's non-traditional approach was wise or not, it should have been a matter for greater scrutiny by the Audit Committee and discussion with Andersen.

Counterproductive Signals. Board members convey their receptiveness to comments critical of management principally through their actions. The Board's principal role is oversight of management, and its decisions send a message about its independence and objectivity. While we discuss our views of the loans and guaranties to Ebbers and certain other arrangements below, we note here that one of the serious adverse consequences was the message these arrangements conveyed. Employees will not believe that the Board can be approached with concerns about the Chief Executive Officer or his top management when they see the Board using shareholder funds to bail the Chief Executive Officer out of his financial distress, or when they become aware of transactions such as the undisclosed lease of a corporate airplane to a Director on favorable terms. Related party transactions in general, and these in particular, damage employee confidence in the Board's willingness to stand up to senior management.

In sum, the Board served as passive observers in a Company thoroughly controlled by Ebbers. We cannot know whether an active Board would have prevented or even more quickly detected the accounting fraud that occurred here. But this Board did not give itself enough of a chance.[3]

FIRST QUESTIONS ON CRITICISM OF THE AUDIT COMMITTEE

Sure the Audit Committee was not itself checking the books, but three to five meetings *a year* for about one hour each (135)? Doesn't that seem too little? But how much time is enough?

The report says that the Audit Committee was apparently not "sufficiently familiar with and involved with the Company's internal financial workings, with weaknesses in the Company's internal control structure, or with its culture" (138).[4] How were committee members supposed to acquire such familiarity? Through commercially offered seminars on accounting issues? By asking the executives (who were masterminding the fraud) to give them tutorials on WorldCom control systems?

What about company culture? Were directors on the Audit Committee supposed to drop in unannounced when the company was closing the books at the end of the quarter and have coffee with lower-level WorldCom accountants who might tell the directors the truth? Would that really elicit candid comments?

Is there one "culture" for a huge company like WorldCom? Is the culture that is important the culture in the top executive suite? In the sales department? In the lower-level accounting cubicles?

Was one key the relationship between the Audit Committee and the two possibly independent sources of detective power with which that committee communicated—the outside auditor and the internal auditors?

Should the Audit Committee have insisted that Internal Audit not report to the CFO? What is the disadvantage of Internal Audit reporting to the CFO?

---

[3]   *Id.* at 282–92.

[4]   This reflects a more general concern that "the members of the Board (other than the directors who were also officers) had little or no involvement in the Company's business other than through attendance at Board meetings. With the exception of Bobbitt and Kellett, Chairmen of the two active Committees, none of the outside Directors had regular communications even with Ebbers or Sullivan—much less with operating personnel—between meetings" (137).

If Internal Audit is not to report to the CFO, then to whom or to what? To the CEO? To the Audit Committee directly?

Should the Audit Committee have insisted that Internal Audit devote all its time to checking accounting and none to operational audits? What if management said that it really needed an operational audit and that it believed that such an audit could save the company hundreds of millions of dollars—all to the benefit of the shareholders?

How should a board evaluate the staffing level in Internal Audit? Do you see any downside to reliance on industry standards such as "revenues per auditor" (140)? How can such statistics be useful?

The Special Investigative Committee criticized the Audit Committee for not understanding that the outside auditor was relying on risk assessments and not doing enough substantive testing. Is it fair to criticize the Committee for failing to prevent the auditor from using this method? Before answering, consider that the report says elsewhere that "[i]n the accounting industry, this approach became known as the 'controls-based' or 'risk-based' audit. This approach is not unique to Andersen—many accounting firms have adopted similar audit plans." (Not included in the text here, but at 227 of the WorldCom Special Committee Report.)

How should a board decide how much money to spend on an audit? If the outside accounting firm conducting the audit says that it can perform an adequate audit for $X, should an audit committee insist on a change in plan that requires more expensive substantive testing so that the price of the audit is substantially more than $X?

Think about the relationship between the Audit Committee and the outside auditors. The report says that Andersen did not tell the Committee that Andersen considered WorldCom to be a "maximum risk" client (142). Why would the auditor not tell the Committee why the company was a "maximum risk" client? If the "maximum risk" determination rested primarily on the size of the client, would the risk evaluation and reason for it help the Audit Committee? What if the risk judgment rested on the nature of the particular industry in which the company participated?

The report says that Andersen failed to tell the Committee that management was not giving Andersen access to the company's general ledger (*id.*). The general ledger is a primary accounting document that forms the basis for the company's financial statements. Why would an auditor not tell the Committee that the auditor was denied access to the general ledger?

What can an audit committee do to encourage an auditor to be more forthcoming on such matters as the auditor's overall risk assessment for the company and what access the auditor has to company accounting records?

When WorldCom went into bankruptcy, the Bankruptcy Court appointed an Examiner. Like the WorldCom Special Committee, the

Examiner tried to figure out what went wrong. The Examiner issued a series of reports.

Here are excerpts from pages 180–84, 194, and 196–97 of the Second Interim Report of Dick Thornburgh, Bankruptcy Court Examiner, dated June 9, 2003 and filed in the WorldCom bankruptcy, *In re WorldCom, Inc.*, Case No. 02-15533 (AJG), U.S. Bankruptcy Court, Southern District of New York. In these excerpts, the Examiner discusses the WorldCom Audit Committee.

[T]he Audit Committee appears to have missed a meaningful opportunity in its communications with Arthur Andersen when it did not require the preparation and presentation by Arthur Andersen of annual Management comment letters to the Committee. The management comment letter is a reporting tool by which the external auditors identify and report to the Company's Audit Committee issues of concern encountered in the course of their annual audits, together with recommendations for corrective action. Normally, Management is provided with a copy of the Management comment letter and given the opportunity to prepare responses to the issues raised by the external auditors. Those Management responses are also provided to the Audit Committee.

Through at least the 1996 audit, Arthur Andersen prepared and presented to the Audit Committee Management comment letters identifying its concerns and recommendations for corrective action. For example, in a 1997 draft Management comment letter prepared by Arthur Andersen in connection with its audit for the year ended December 31, 1996, Arthur Andersen advised the Audit Committee, among other things, of the need for strengthening the Company's internal controls as the Company was growing through acquisitions, bolstering the Internal Audit Department, and instituting fraud training for the Company's senior Management.[116]

However, this is the last such letter that the Examiner has been able to obtain. There is no evidence that any such letters were prepared and presented to the Audit Committee from 1998 through 2001, nor did the Audit Committee appear to have received a deficiency letter sent by a foreign subsidiary of Arthur Andersen to the Company's Management in the United Kingdom. No one could explain why this commonly accepted practice of providing to the Audit Committee Management comment letters

---

[116] The Examiner has not been able to obtain Management's responses to those recommendations to date or any information as to what steps, if any, were taken by the Company to address the concerns raised by Arthur Andersen.

ceased, and it does not appear that any member of the Audit Committee even remarked about not getting such reports. The Examiner also has not been able to identify any reporting mechanism to the Audit Committee that was substituted in its place. Accordingly, there does not appear to have been any meaningful reporting mechanism used by Arthur Andersen to report to the Committee on internal control weaknesses or deficiencies beyond the quarterly "canned" presentations it made to the members of the Audit Committee, and the pre-earnings discussions held between Arthur Andersen, the Chairman of the Audit Committee and the CFO.[5]

* * *

[T]he Examiner is also troubled by certain practices by the Audit Committee from a corporate governance standpoint. While none of these practices have any bearing on the fraud, they speak to the informality associated with the operations of the Audit Committee, which failed to address the needs of a public company of the size and complexity of WorldCom. For most of the relevant period, the Audit Committee did not conduct its business with the benefit of any advice of counsel, including in-house counsel, except for particular limited projects, such as in connection with the drafting and revisions of its Charter. Until the spring of 2002, in-house counsel did not participate in any of the meetings, including any executive sessions, and played no role in the drafting of the Minutes for the Committee. It was not until after the disclosure of the problems at Enron, and the related criminal indictment of Arthur Andersen, that any suggestion was made by members of the Committee to retain outside counsel.[6]

* * *

[T]here were serious deficiencies in the drafting and maintenance of Minutes memorializing the deliberations of the Audit Committee. Prior to February 2002, the Minutes provided only brief, boiler-plate summaries of the Committee's deliberations with a number of discrepancies and omissions on such important matters as: (i) whether and how often the Committee met in separate executive sessions with the external auditors and with the Director of Internal Audit; (ii) the substance of any discussions by Arthur Andersen or Internal Audit regarding the specific results of their audits; and (iii) whether the retention of Arthur

---

[5]   Second Interim Report of Dick Thornburgh, Bankruptcy Court Examiner, dated June 9, 2003 and filed in the WorldCom bankruptcy, *In re WorldCom, Inc.*, Case No. 02-15533 (AJG), U.S. Bankruptcy Court, Southern District of New York at 180–82, http://news.findlaw.com/wsj/docs/worldcom/bkexmnr60903rpt2d.pdf.

[6]   *Id.* at 182–83.

Andersen as the Company's independent auditors was formally approved by the Committee annually. There are no Minutes for any of the executive sessions and no person we interviewed had any specific memory of issues discussed during those sessions. The Director of Internal Audit was tasked with preparing the Committee's Minutes after each meeting, but that task was often delegated to personnel within the Internal Audit Department who may or may not have attended the meetings, and who, on at least one occasion, solicited feedback about what happened in the meeting from Arthur Andersen personnel who had attended. The final Minutes appear to have been circulated, but few, if any, members of the Committee actually reviewed them, other than the Chairman who signed them. Thus, the reliability of the Minutes of meetings of the Audit Committee is highly suspect.[7]

* * *

Of concern is the lack of any effective participation by the Audit Committee in reviewing the adequacy of the annual internal audit plan, with the Audit Committee appearing to have approved the final plan as a formality. Based upon requests of Management, other audits, not part of the Audit Committee-approved plan, were added while some audits originally scheduled were not completed. At most, the Audit Committee was advised of such changes after the fact. Under such circumstances, senior Management could influence the focus of the Internal Audit Department away from sensitive areas without the oversight that the Audit Committee would normally be expected to provide.[8]

* * *

[T]here appears to be unwarranted influence by Management in the preparation of final reports and recommendations by Internal Audit. Internal Audit appears to have conducted its audits in ways that sought to reach agreements with Management about particular recommendations prior to the issuance of a final report. Accordingly, preliminary drafts of the Internal Audit reports were generally distributed to affected Management as well as to Mr. Sullivan and, at times, to Mr. Ebbers. The Audit Committee did not obtain preliminary drafts. All persons on the distribution list could provide to Internal Audit their comments and/or objections to the conclusions and recommendations made in the reports. It is unknown at this time whether Mr. Sullivan and Mr. Ebbers weighed in with any substantive changes to the reports at their preliminary stage. However, we are aware that the language of

---

[7]   *Id.* at 183–84.

[8]   *Id.* at 194.

the final audit reports was the product of many negotiations between the internal auditors, Ms. Cooper and the affected Management.[9]

SECOND QUESTIONS ON CRITICISM OF THE AUDIT COMMITTEE

If the Examiner is correct, Andersen had not provided a management letter to the Audit Committee in some years (145–146). Such letters were common and the level of experience on the Board suggests that the WorldCom directors should have known this. Shouldn't the absence of such letters have prompted questions from the Audit Committee to Andersen?

The Examiner criticized the Audit Committee for not having enough advice from lawyers and not keeping the minutes properly (146–147)? Were lawyers likely to have found the line cost capitalization? Would good minutes have mattered? Are these just throwaway points or should you take them seriously?

What do you think the Audit Committee could have added if it had been more involved in "reviewing the adequacy of the annual internal auditing plan" (147)?

Do you agree with the suggestion that the Audit Committee should have seen the "preliminary drafts" of Internal Audit reports, given that affected management saw them (147–148)? Pros? Cons?

Bearing in mind that Andersen was one of the major accounting firms at the time, do you see any reason why WorldCom should not have hired Andersen to audit WorldCom's financial statements? Any reason why the Audit Committee should not have relied on Andersen's work?

C. THE AUDIT PLAN FOR WORLDCOM'S 2001 YEAR

Now let's leave the Monday morning quarterbacking for a moment and see what the Audit Committee really faced. Here is the audit plan from Andersen for the 2001 audit. The audit plan is publicly available at pages 250–67 of the U.S. House of Representatives Committee on Financial Services, Hearing on July 8, 2002, titled *Wrong Numbers: The Accounting Problems at WorldCom*. The next several pages provide you an image of this document. This and other images in the book were enhanced for readability as detailed in a table in the preface.

---

[9]   *Id.* at 196–97.

ANDERSEN

WORLDCOM

2001 Audit Plan and Proposed Fee Arrangements

June 6, 2001

E-2

1WCOM/COFS:00345

Members of the Audit Committee:

On the next few pages we have synopsized our proposed 2001 audit plan and proposed fee arrangements for WorldCom, WorldCom Group and MCI Group. In forming the plan and developing the fee proposal we have discussed with executive and senior operating management the significant business risks facing the Company, considered the results of recent audits and used our own judgment to assess the significance and likelihood of financial statement misstatement. We believe our audit plan responds to the traditional risk areas faced by the Company while emphasizing emerging risk areas such as new lines of business and unique transactions. We value the Committee's input to the audit plan and proposed fees and welcome the opportunity to address your questions or concerns.

We have enclosed an overview of our audit process to assist the Committee in understanding the context in which the plan and fee were developed and the method of its execution. We look forward to presenting the plan to the Committee at the June 6th meeting.

If you have any questions before the meeting we would welcome the opportunity to address those individually.

Very truly yours,

ARTHUR ANDERSEN LLP

Mel D. ch

Melvin Dick

E-2

1WCOM/COFS:00346

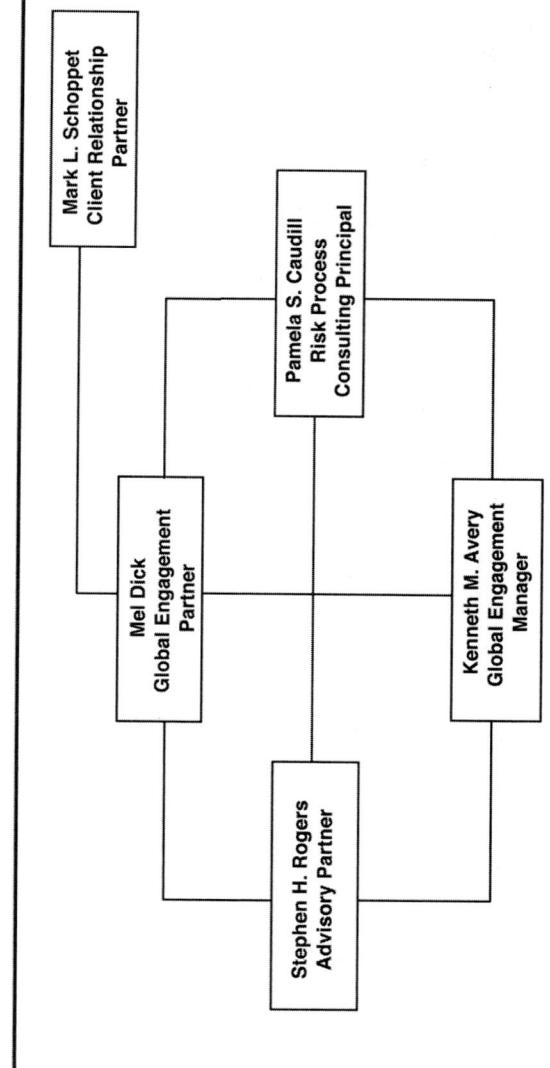

WorldCom Client Service Team

E-2

IWCOM/COFS:0034

Client Service Team, *continued*

Melvin A. Dick
Global Engagement Partner

Mel is an experienced partner who is responsible for Andersen's Global Technology, Media and Communications (TMC) audit, tax and consulting services. Mel has previously served as Andersen's global wireless communications leader. Mel has spent the majority of his career working with diverse telecommunications companies. Mel was the lead engagement partner for US West from 1987 through 1996, and Level 3 Communications from 1998 through 2000. Mel has also served as engagement partner for MediaOne Group, US West New Vector and Teletech.

Stephen H. Rogers
Advisory Partner

Steve is the managing partner of the Atlanta office, as well as the managing partner of Southeast region of which Jackson is a part. He is one of the four principal partners for operations of Andersen in the United States and one of the 12 partners responsible for operations of Andersen worldwide. Steve has served clients for more than 29 years in various industries, including manufacturing, technology, and telecommunications.

Mark L. Schoppet
Client Relationship Partner

Mark has 20 years of experience in the telecommunications profession and served as the engagement partner for WorldCom from 1994 through 2000. He is a member of our Firmwide Telecommunications Industry Team and has dedicated his career to the telecommunications industry.

E-2

Client Service Team, *continued*

Pamela S. Caudill
Risk Process Consulting
Principal

Pam leads the Mid-South Technology Risk Consulting practice and has more than 26 years of experience with Andersen. She has assisted with the development and execution of the technology related audit plan for the past 7 years at WorldCom. Throughout her career she has provided assistance to many multinational clients including Fedex and International Paper among others.

Kenneth M. Avery
Global Audit Manager

Kenny is a senior audit manager in the Jackson office and has been with the firm 11 years. He has served as the audit engagement manager for WorldCom for the past 3 years and has extensive experience in serving global companies.

E-2

IWCOM/COFS:00349

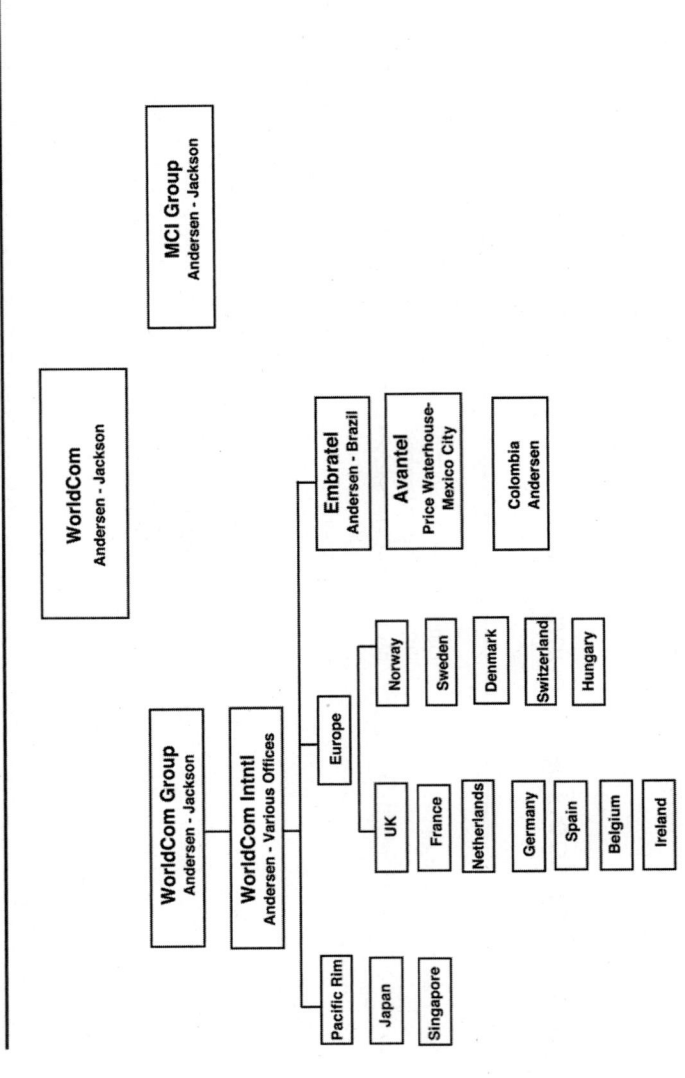

Coordination of Consolidated WorldCom Audit

E-2

1WCOM/COFS:00350

Summary of Audit Process

- The results of our assessment of the Company's control processes allow us to determine the extent of any remaining risks.

- Where residual audit risk exists, detective procedures are designed and executed to reduce the risk to an acceptable level. Detective procedures consist mainly of:

  — Inspection and vouching of business data to source documents

  — Reperformance of computations

  — Corroboration of business data with 3rd parties

  — Performance of analytical procedures to assess reasonableness of business outputs

E-2

1WCOM/COFS:00351

Audit Materiality Used

- Based on our discussions with management and understanding of the business, we identified the significant risks related to the Company's key accounting principles and practices, judgments and estimates and transaction processes.

- In identifying "significant" risks, we consider their potential materiality to the Company's and related group's financial statements.

  – In general, materiality is defined as an amount equal to approximately 5% of anticipated pre-tax income, or approximately $285 million in the case of WorldCom.

  – In order to identify misstatements that could aggregate to a material amount, we will design our work to detect misstatements of $14.0 million (pre-tax) on a consolidated basis (Approximates $9.0 million for the WorldCom group and $5.0 milllion for the MCI group).

E-2

1WCOM/COFS:00352

Process Effectiveness Assessment - Key judgment and Estimate Processes

- We will review the process for formulating each key judgment and estimate in order to assess its effectiveness in preventing a material misstatement in the financial statements.

- In forming our assessment of each process, we will consider the following:

  – is management using the proper data to formulate the particular judgment or estimate (e.g., historical bad debt rates, historical data, trends, etc.)?

  – does the Company have controls in place to ensure that the data utilized has integrity?

  – is management using the data in the proper way (i.e., rendering an appropriate conclusion)?

- In assessing the effectiveness of each process in preventing a material misstatement in the financial statements, we will utilize the following scale:

  – ● Process is effective

  – ○ Process is effective, however certain process improvement opportunities were identified

  – ● Process is ineffective

E-2

Process Effectiveness Assessment - Transaction Processes

- We will review key transaction processes in order to assess their effectiveness in preventing a material misstatement in the financial statements.

- In forming our assessment of each process, we will determine whether management has adequate controls to prevent a material error in financial statements as a result of a failure to properly:
  - capture transactions
  - process data
  - record data in the general ledger

- In assessing the effectiveness of each process in preventing a material misstatement in the financial statements, we will utilize the following scale:

  ● – Process is effective

  ○ – Process is effective, however certain process improvement opportunities were identified

  ● – Process is ineffective

E-2

1WCOM/COFS:00354

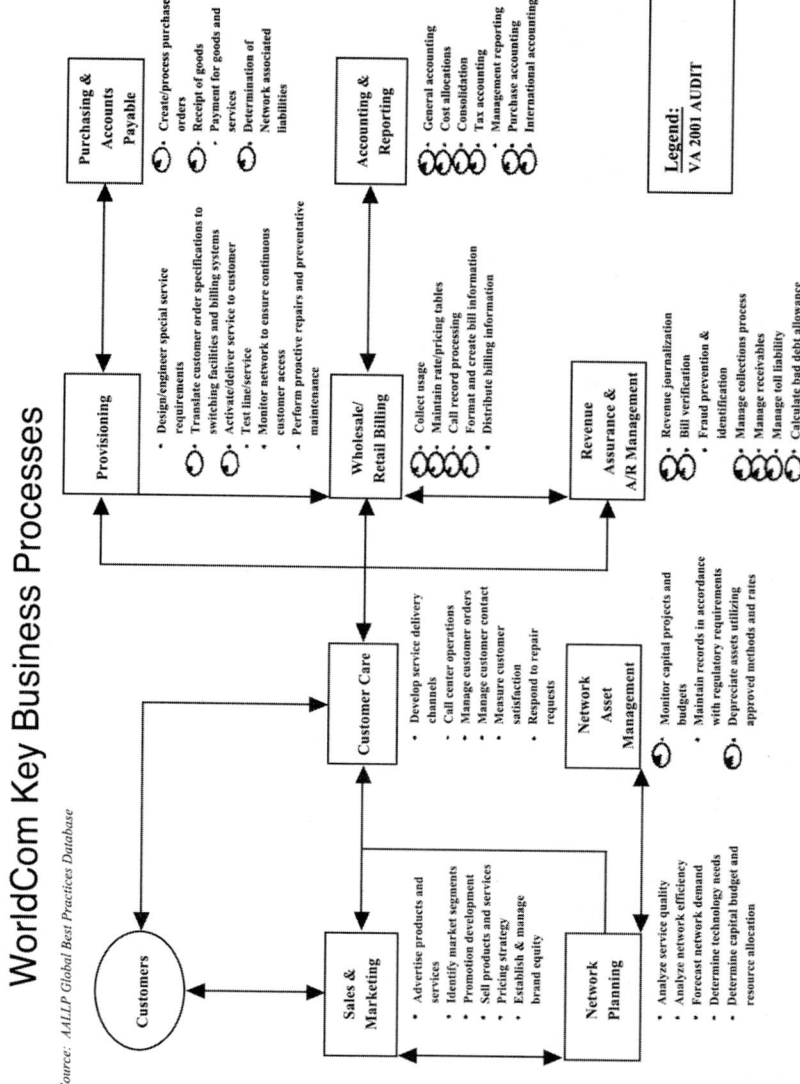

WorldCom Key Business Processes

Source: AALLP Global Best Practices Database

Customers

Sales & Marketing
- Advertise products and services
- Identify market segments
- Promotion development
- Sell products and services
- Pricing strategy
- Establish & manage brand equity

Network Planning
- Analyze service quality
- Analyze network efficiency
- Forecast network demand
- Determine technology needs
- Determine capital budget and resource allocation

Customer Care
- Develop service delivery channels
- Call center operations
- Manage customer orders
- Manage customer contact
- Measure customer satisfaction
- Respond to repair requests

Network Asset Management
- Monitor capital projects and budgets
- Maintain records in accordance with regulatory requirements
- Depreciate assets utilizing approved methods and rates

Provisioning
- Design/engineer special service requirements
- Translate customer order specifications to switching facilities and billing systems
- Activate/deliver service to customer
- Test line/service
- Monitor network to ensure continuous customer access
- Perform proactive repairs and preventative maintenance

Wholesale/ Retail Billing
- Collect usage
- Maintain rate/pricing tables
- Call record processing
- Format and create bill information
- Distribute billing information

Revenue Assurance & A/R Management
- Revenue journalization
- Bill verification
- Fraud prevention & identification
- Manage collections process
- Manage receivables
- Manage toll liability
- Calculate bad debt allowance

Purchasing & Accounts Payable
- Create/process purchase orders
- Receipt of goods
- Payment for goods and services
- Determination of Network associated liabilities

Accounting & Reporting
- General accounting
- Cost allocations
- Consolidation
- Tax accounting
- Management reporting
- Purchase accounting
- International accounting

Legend:
VA 2001 AUDIT

1WCOM/COFS:00355

Overall Business Reality of WorldCom

- Access, info system integrity, Infrastructure & Relevance
- Change Readiness
- Communications
- Competitor
- Compliance
- Customer Satisfaction
- Efficiency
- Human Resources
- Organizational Structure
- Performance Gap
- Performance Incentives
- Performance Measurements
- Pricing
- Product Development
- Service Order Fulfillment
- Service Failure

E-2

IWCOM/COFS:00356

WorldCom Key - Accounting Principles and Practices

- Accrued Liabilities - Line Costs
- Affiliated Transactions
- Capitalization of Internal Use Software
- Income Taxes
- PP&E - Proper Capitalization of Assets
- Long-Term Asset Valuation
- Revenue Recognition

- Earnings Per Share
- Special Charges
- Allowance for Doubtful Accounts
- Other Current Liabilities
- Comprehensive Income
- Consolidation
- Segment Disclosures
- Valuation of Assets - Foreign
- Currency Translation

E-2

1WCOM/COFS:00357

WorldCom Key - Judgments and Estimates

- Income Tax Reserves
- Legal Reserves and Contingent Liabilities
- Asset Depreciable Lives
- Accrued Line Costs
- Impairment of Long-Lived Assets
- Annual Effective Tax Rate in Interim Reporting
- Related Party Transactions

- Settlements - Unbilled Amounts
- Unrecorded Liabilities
- Unbilled Revenue
- Allowance for Doubtful Accounts
- Cost versus Equity method accounting for Investments

E-2

1WCOM/COFS:00358

WorldCom Key - Critical Processes

- Process Accounts Payable
- Bill the Customer
- Journalization of Revenue
- Collection of Accounts Receivable
- PP&E - Capital Expenditures - Initiation of Work Order
- PP&E - Retirements, Inactive, Dispositions
- Network Development and Maintenance
- Customer Care and Retention
- Process Payroll

- Deliver Services to the Customer
- Strategic Planning
- Perform Account Reconciliations
- Revenue Cycle
- Expenditure Cycle
- Property Cycle
- Accounting and Financial Reporting

E-2

1WCOM/COFS:00359

WorldCom Key - Financial Reporting Processes

- Consolidation
- Post-Closing Adjustments and Reclassifications
- Preparation of Financial Statements
- Process Finance and Accounting Transactions
- General Ledger
- Management Reports
- SEC Filings
- Conversion of Data to Accounting and Management Information

E-2

IWCOM/COFS:00360

2001 Proposed Fees and Expenses

We understand your need to control administrative costs of all types, including professional fees. We are committed to delivering the best possible service of the highest quality at a reasonable fee, both now and in the future. We plan to conduct the audit with experienced resources. Our engagement team will ensure that the appropriate focus and analytical skills are brought to bear on the 2001 audit. We also believe your investment in the right level of expertise is crucial to the success of WorldCom.

	2001 Proposed	2000	1999
Audit of WorldCom, WorldCom Group and MCI Group	$ 2,000,000	$ 2,000,000	$ 1,825,000

The above fee proposal does not include out-of-pocket expenses that will be incurred during the course of the audit work. We anticipate that out-of-pocket expenses will not exceed $120,000.

E-2

1WCOM/COFS:00361

2001 Proposed Fees and Expenses, *continued*

We understand that during the course of the next year you will need assistance in certain accounting-related matters. Our billing for such assistance will be based on hours incurred, based on the following rates, plus out-of-pocket expenses:

Partner	$ 305
Senior Manager	240
Manager	185
Experienced Senior	160
Senior	150
Staff	95

E-2

QUESTIONS ON THE AUDIT PLAN
FOR WORLDCOM'S 2001 YEAR

Assume you were a member of the WorldCom Audit Committee and that this rendition of the audit plan constituted the entire written description you received before the audit began. The plan as presented here is only 18 pages long—counting the cover, three pages describing the "client service team," and two pages on fees. Where, in the remaining pages, are the tough matters of substance into which the Audit Committee could sink its teeth?

What should the Committee have done when faced with such a document? Asked for more details? If so, what details?

What should the Committee have done to follow up on the audit plan after approving it?

Suppose that this description of the audit plan met professional requirements for briefing audit committees at the time and reflected the practice of the most respected accounting firms. Would this change your answers to the questions asked above? More generally, what role should accepted practices (and existing law and rules) play in our evaluation of auditor and audit committee performance in a given year?

D. THE AUDITOR'S REPORT ON ITS AUDIT OF WORLDCOM'S 2001 YEAR

Now read the report that Andersen provided to the Audit Committee after Andersen completed the 2001 audit. This report is available at pages 268–84 of the U.S. House of Representatives Committee on Financial Services, Hearing on July 8, 2002, titled *Wrong Numbers: The Accounting Problems at WorldCom.*

ANDERSEN

Report to the Audit Committee
Year Ended December 31, 2001

WORLDCOM

February 6, 2002

1WCOM/COFS:00188

Note: This presentation is intended solely for the information and use of management and the Audit Committee of the Board of Directors of WorldCom, Inc. and is not intended to be used by anyone other than those specified parties.

February 4, 2002

Audit Committee of the Board of Directors WorldCom, Inc.

Clinton, Mississippi

Members of the Audit Commitee:

Over the next few days we will be completing our audit procedures on WorldCom, Inc.'s consolidated results of operations and financial position, as well as, WorldCom Group and MCI Group as of and for the year ended December 31, 2001. At the February 6th meeting we will be prepared to discuss with the committee the results of our audit procedures and respond to any questions. In addition, we will discuss with the Committee certain matters, including our independence as external auditors of the Company, which is required by professional standards and the Securities and Exchange Commission.

We will be prepared to respond to questions from the Committee and management about the enclosed materials on February 6th. Of course, we will be pleased to address any questions you have prior to that time. We look forward to meeting with you next week.

Very truly yours,

ARTHUR ANDERSEN LLP

Melvin Dick

1

IWCOM/COFS:00189

Purpose of Our Report

- Summarize our audit approach and audit results for the year ended December 31, 2001

- Discuss our views regarding WorldCom's key accounting principles and practices, transaction processes and judgments and estimates used in the preparation of the WorldCom, Inc., WorldCom Group and MCI Group financial statements

- Communicate matters required by professional standards

- Provide an opportunity for the Audit Committee to ask questions of us as part of discharging their due diligence responsibility

2

Overall Summary of Results

- WorldCom, Inc. and WorldCom Group and MCI Group balance sheets and income statements are fairly presented in accordance with accounting principles generally accepted in the United States.

- Work is in progress on review of financial statement disclosures and other information to be included in the WorldCom, Inc. Annual Report and SEC filings.

3

Required Communications to the Audit Committee – Quality of the Company's Financial Reporting

Significant Accounting Policies

- There were no significant changes in accounting policies in the current year.

- We noted no significant or unusual transactions, or material transactions in controversial or emerging areas for which there is a lack of authoritative guidance or consensus.

Management Judgments and Accounting Estimates

- Accounting estimates are an intregal part of the financial statements prepared by management and are based upon management's current judgments. Certain accounting estimates are particularly sensitive because of their significance to the financial statements and because of the possibility that future events affecting them may differ markedly from management's current judgments.

- We are satisfied as to the reasonableness of management's current judgments regarding such estimates in the context of the financial statements taken as a whole, based on our knowledge of management's process for making such judgments, inquiries of management and others regarding such matters, and other audit procedures applied during our engagement.

- Those items representing particularly sensitive accounting estimates are discussed in the following slides.

WorldCom Key - Accounting Principles and Practices

- Revenue Recognition
- Affiliated Transactions
- Capitalization of Internal Use Software
- Income Taxes
- PP&E - Proper Capitalization of Assets
- Pensions
- Long-Term Asset Valuation
- Securitization of Receivables

- Earnings Per Share
- Comprehensive Income
- Segment Disclosure
- Valuation of Assets - Foriegn Currency Translation
- New Accounting Standards
- Business Combinations
- Stock Options

WorldCom Key - Accounting Principles and Practices

Area	Assessment
Revenue Recognition	
Affiliated Transactions	
Capitalization of Internal Use Software	
Income Taxes	
PP & E - Proper Capitalization of Assets	
Pensions	
Long-Term Asset Valuation	
Securitization of Receivables	
Earnings Per Share	
Comprehensive Income	
Segment Disclosure	
Valuation of Assets - Foreign Currency Translation	
New Accounting Standards	
Business Combinations	
Stock Options	

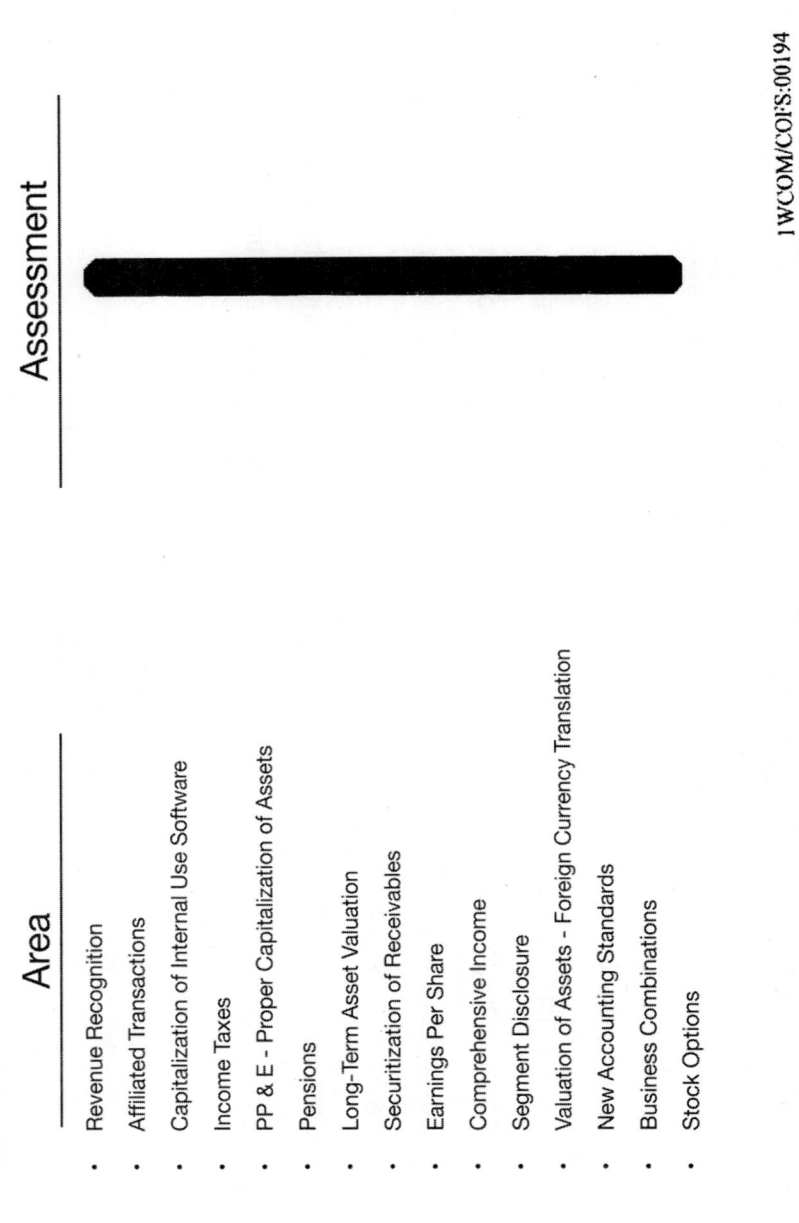

1WCOM/COFS:00194

Process Effectiveness Assessment - Transaction Processes

- We have held updated discussions with members of management and performed testing related to key transaction processes in order to assess their effectiveness in preventing a material misstatement in the financial statements and to determine whether or not any significant changes have occurred.

- In forming our assessment of each process, we determined whether management has adequate controls to prevent a material error in the financial statements as a result of a failure to properly:

  - capture transactions
  - process data
  - record data in the general ledger

- In assessing the effectiveness of each process in preventing a material misstatement in the financial statements, we have utilized the following scale:

  - Process is effective
  - Process is effective, however certain process improvement opportunities were identified
  - Process is ineffective

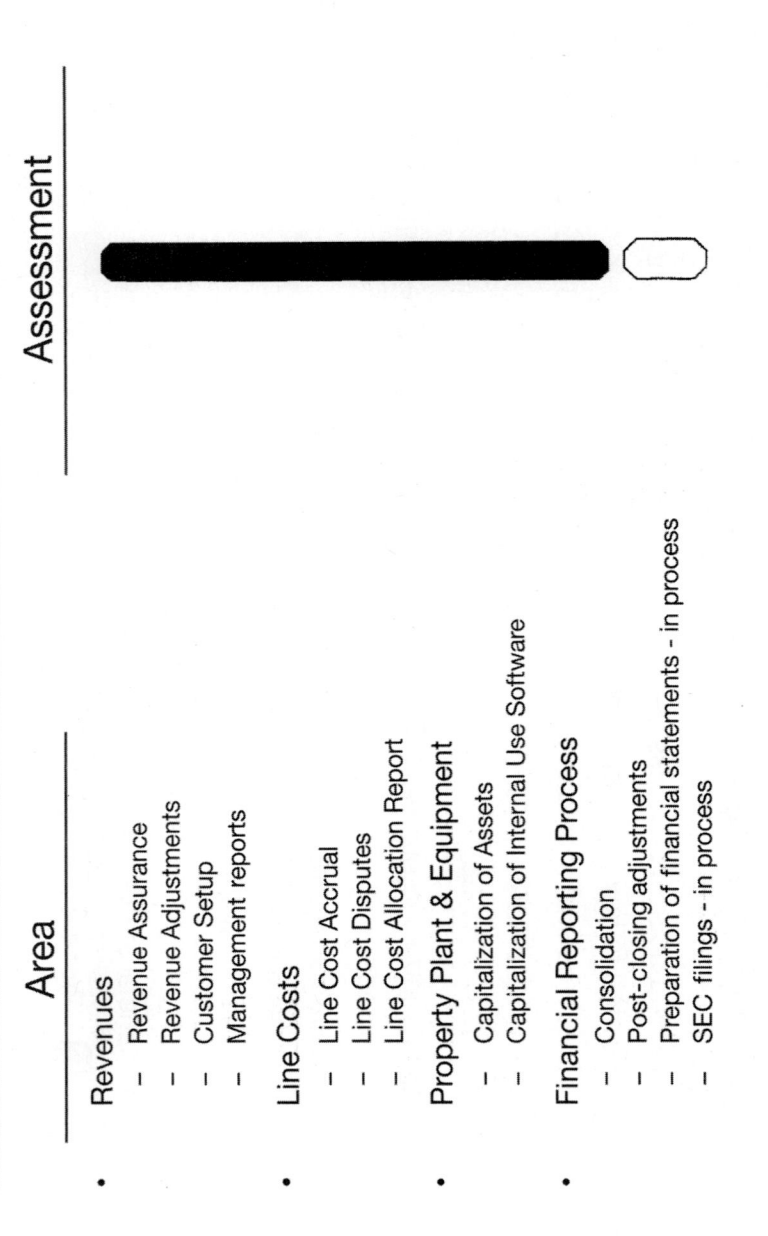

WorldCom Key - Transaction Processing Areas

Area

Assessment

- Revenues
  - Revenue Assurance
  - Revenue Adjustments
  - Customer Setup
  - Management reports

- Line Costs
  - Line Cost Accrual
  - Line Cost Disputes
  - Line Cost Allocation Report

- Property Plant & Equipment
  - Capitalization of Assets
  - Capitalization of Internal Use Software

- Financial Reporting Process
  - Consolidation
  - Post-closing adjustments
  - Preparation of financial statements - in process
  - SEC filings - in process

Process Effectiveness Assessment –
Key Judgment and Estimate Processes

- We have reviewed management's process for formulating each key judgment and estimate in order to assess its effectiveness in preventing a material misstatement in the financial statements. We have updated these procedures on a quarterly basis through discussion and analytical reviews and through our preliminary and final testing.

- In forming our assessment of each process, we consider the following:

  – is management using the proper data to formulate the particular judgment or estimate (e.g., historical bad debt rates, historical data, trends, etc.)?

  – does the Company have controls in place to ensure that the data utilized has integrity?

  – is management using the data in the proper way (i.e., rendering an appropriate conclusion)?

- In assessing the effectiveness of each process in preventing a material misstatement in the financial statements, we will utilize the following scale:

  – Process is effective

  – Process is effective, however certain process improvement opportunities were identified

  – Process is ineffective

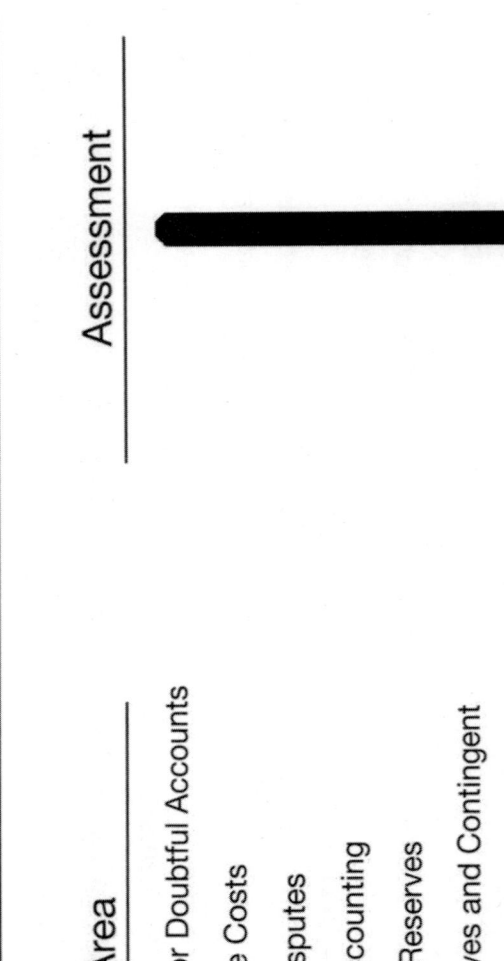

WorldCom Judgment or Estimate Processes

Judgment or Estimate	Description	Process Changes	Discussion and Other	Assessment	Residual Audit Risk
Allowance for Doubtful Accounts	The company maintains reserves designed to cover amounts in accounts receivable which will not be colllected.	None	Initial reserves are provided based upon a historical average of net write-offs in relation to billings; additional amounts are provided for conservatism or alternatively via specific reserves. Various analytical measures are employed to assess the adequacy of the reserve. The Company performs a "look-back" test which compares reserves to subsequent net write-offs to determine the accuracy of the reserve estimation process.	●	None Noted

1WCOM/COFS:00199

WorldCom Judgment or Estimate Processes

Judgment or Estimate	Description	Process Changes	Discussion and Other	Assessment	Residual Audit Risk
Line Cost Accrual	Line costs represent charges from LECs for leased lines or traffic termination. Line costs as a percentage of revenues have remained flat at 41.9% on a YTD basis. Line costs are allocated between the WorldCom Group and the MCI Group based on minutes of use and revenues.	None	Accruals are based on metered traffic as determined by WorldCom. Disputed amounts are reserved for separately see discussion below.	●	None
Line Cost Disputes	Generally, WorldCom accrues 100% of LEC billed amounts prior to dispute resolution.	None	LEC under billing dispute amounts are maintained for a period of 12 months and are reversed on a monthly basis.	●	None

12

WorldCom Judgment or Estimate Processes

Judgment or Estimate	Description	Process Changes	Discussion and Other	Assessment	Residual Audit Risk
Purchase Accounting	In conjunction with the Company's numerous purchase transactions the Company has recorded goodwill and intangible balances on approximately $46 billion. This amount, included in intangibles, represents the largest single asset on the balance sheet and represents excess of purchase price over net assets acquired coupled with unfavorable commitments pursuant to APB 16. Goodwill is divided between the tracked entities based on the respective fair values at date of acquisition. The Company is conducting impairment reviews of all intangible assets and expects to complete this assessment in accordance with the provisions of SFAS No. 142.	None	In the current year, the Company recorded approximately $5 billion of goodwill additions related primarily to the Intermedia transaction. We worked with the Company to ensure that these additions were recorded properly with respect to authoritative accounting literature. Consistent with the provisions of SFAS No. 142, the Company anticipates disclosing an impairment charge range in conjunction with the 2001 Form 10-K.	●	None

13

WorldCom Judgment or Estimate Processes

Judgment or Estimate	Description	Process Changes	Discussion and Other	Assessment	Residual Audit Risk
Income Tax Reserves	Reserves are established as necessary for any tax audit exposures.	None	The Company evaluates the need for reserves related to any tax exposures for U.S. federal, foreign, state and local, property, excise, and sales and uses taxes.	⬤	None
Legal Reserve and Contingent Liabilities	Reserves are established as necessary for legal and regulatory matters.	None	The Company monitors the statues of pending and threatened legal and regulatory matters and provides reserves and/or disclosures based on the expected outcome.	⬤	None
Asset Depreciable Lives and Impairment	The Company's largest tangible assts relate to the network. Changes in technology over the past years requires management to periodically analyze assigned depreciable lives to determine their appropriateness.	None	We completed a benchmark study with industry standards and found that the Company's lives compared favorably with that of the industry averages.	⬤	None

1WCOM/COFS:00202

14

Required Communications to the Audit Committee

Audit Adjustments

- We will provide a list of all audit adjustments and discuss both recorded and passed adjustments at the Committee meeting.

Disagreements with Management

- There were no disagreements with management on financial, accounting and reporting matters which, if not satisfactorily resolved, would have been material to the financial statements or which might cause a modification of our auditors' report.

Irregularities or Illegal Acts

- We are not aware of irregularities or illegal acts committed by the Company or its employees.

Consultation by Management with Other Accountants

- We are not aware of any consultations by management with other independent public accountants during the year about auditing or accounting matters.

Difficulties Encountered in Reporting the Audit

- We encountered no significant difficulties in performing our audit procedures to date.

Major Issues Discussed with Management Prior to Appointment

- No major issues were discussed with management in connection with our appointment as auditors, including the application of generally accepted accounting principles or generally accepted auditing standards.

Required Communications to the Audit Committee

Communications Regarding Internal Controls

- Our review of internal controls was made for the purpose of determining the required scope of our audit procedures, not to render a separate opinion regarding the Company's internal control structure.

- There were no material weaknesses in internal controls noted in our testing and evaluation.

Auditor's Responsibility for Other Information in Documents Containing Audited Financial Statements

- We will review the non-financial information included in the Form 10-K (including management's discussion and analysis of financial condition and results of operations) for consistency with information contained in the audited financial statements.

Communications Regarding Auditor Independence

- We are not aware of any issues related to Arthur Andersen's independence that occurred during the Company's fiscal year through the date of this meeting other than those disclosed in the attached letter, which also describes the scope of our services provided during fiscal 2001.

QUESTIONS ON THE AUDIT REPORT
FOR WORLDCOM'S 2001 YEAR

Anything alarming here?

There are a couple of references to line costs (180). The auditors reported that the "Residual Audit Risk" for both line cost "Accrual" and "Disputes" was "None." What was the Committee supposed to do? How could it have effectively questioned this conclusion?

Suppose that the Committee had questioned vigorously on line costs but that Andersen answered all such questions in a reassuring way and events then played out just as they did. Would that have strengthened the directors' position in later litigation? Can you make the argument on both sides—that such questioning would show that a committee was diligent and, on the other hand, that such questioning would show that a committee suspected something was wrong and so should have looked more deeply? What does this suggest about trying to conduct board meetings in a way that might prove helpful if the directors are sued down the line?

Andersen reported that it encountered "no significant difficulties in performing our audit procedures to date" and that it was "not aware of any irregularities or illegal acts committed by the Company or its employees" (183). In the face of those assurances, should we fault the Committee for not asking flat out whether the auditor had access to the general ledger?

Note the reference on *id.* to "audit adjustments" that were "recorded" and "passed." It is not uncommon, in an audit of a company as large as WorldCom, for the auditors to find some accounting numbers with which they disagree. When that happens, the auditors suggest that the company correct the misstatements. These are the "audit adjustments."[10] Where the company agrees to make changes, the adjustments will be "recorded." But a company may argue that it should not have to make particular adjustments. For example, the company might contend that the effect of changing a number would be "immaterial" to the financial statements taken as a whole. The auditor will also evaluate the effect of the change on the financial statements taken as a whole and may conclude that it can still give the company a "clean opinion" (i.e., one that says that the final figures fairly present the company's financial position and operations in all material respects), even though the company does not make the change. In that event, the company will not make the change and that audit adjustment will be "passed."

---

[10] These are sometimes called "audit differences." Accountants, courts, and lawmakers sometimes refer to the schedule of audit differences—the list of them—as the "SAD." When a company does not make an adjustment that the auditors have recommended, accountants may refer to that adjustment as an "unadjusted difference," and accumulate it and other such adjustments on a schedule of unadjusted differences. The unadjusted differences may also be called "uncorrected misstatements."

Why is it useful for an audit committee to review "audit adjustments"? What should the committee be looking for when conducting that review?

Can you think of questions that the WorldCom Audit Committee might reasonably have asked that would have had some chance of uncovering the wrongful line cost capitalization before Internal Audit discovered that accounting impropriety? Try to think of questions that would have been reasonable for directors to have asked given what the Audit Committee knew at the time the audit of the 2001 year came to an end, not just questions that you can construct after reading criticisms of the committee made with the benefit of hindsight and multi-year study by a small army of lawyers.

E. MORE ON THE AUDIT COMMITTEE, FROM THE WORLDCOM LITIGATION

Plaintiffs in the private WorldCom securities litigation sued all of the directors for certain securities violations that do not require fraudulent intent or severe recklessness with regard to the truth. But the private plaintiffs sued the members of the WorldCom Audit Committee under Rule 10b-5, which applies only where the defendant intends to commit a fraud or is so severely reckless with regard to false and misleading statements that the recklessness is very close to intentional fraud. The federal district court granted the Audit Committee members' motion to dismiss the Rule 10b-5 claim. Here is one part of the court's reasoning:

> The Lead Plaintiff places particular emphasis on the allegations that the Audit Committee Defendants failed to communicate effectively with Internal Audit in the Fall of 2001, when the defendants could have learned of a $2.3 billion capital expenditures discrepancy and thereby uncovered the fraud before they each signed WorldCom's 2001 Form 10-K in March 2002. The Amended Complaint asserts, however, that Internal Audit personnel accepted the explanations provided by WorldCom employees for the discrepancy in the accruals they were investigating. Therefore, even if the Lead Plaintiff had sufficiently alleged a breach of a well-defined duty to communicate, it has not alleged that Internal Audit would have reported to the Audit Committee in the Fall of 2001 that it had uncovered information indicative of fraud or wrongdoing, or even information requiring further investigation.[11]

---

[11]   *In re WorldCom Sec. Litig.*, No. 02 Civ. 3288DLC, 2003 WL 23174761, at *5 (S.D.N.Y. Dec. 3, 2003).

QUESTIONS ON THE AUDIT COMMITTEE'S VALUE

If its principal sources of fraud information do not find and report fraud, or at least suspicions or suspicious facts, how can an audit committee hope to catch fraud?

On the other hand, if every audit committee is automatically off the hook just because the outside and internal auditors do not find a fraud, what is the incentive for the committee to use its resources to uncover accounting wrongdoing?

How can an audit committee help, or direct, the outside or internal auditors in ways that will increase the probability of catching or preventing fraud? And if we are unsure what such a committee can do in that regard, of what use is the committee?

CHAPTER 5

WORLDCOM PART III: THE COMPENSATION COMMITTEE

■ ■ ■

This Chapter Five begins with a rudimentary description of executive compensation and a description of the role that compensation committees play in setting such compensation. The chapter then describes the WorldCom Compensation Committee's actions on loans that WorldCom made to its CEO and loan guarantees that the company provided for the CEO. The chapter concludes with a detailed description of the committee's participation in setting pay for officers and employees at different levels in the company and a discussion of retention bonuses at WorldCom.

A. EXECUTIVE COMPENSATION AND COMPENSATION COMMITTEES

A compensation committee is a committee of the board of directors. Its members are directors. The compensation committee plays a large role in setting the pay package for the CEO and other top officers—typically by setting top executive compensation itself or recommending top executive compensation to the full board. It often plays some less detailed role in setting the compensation for executives lower down. The compensation committee participates in creating or approving equity compensation plans, retention plans, and special compensation programs (particularly for the upper-level executives).

Top executive compensation has generally included a number of different components. As a simplified example, a CEO may receive (1) a base salary paid in cash, (2) a cash bonus that is often linked to the achievement of some goal (which could be a certain level of company-wide revenue or profit or a specific assignment—e.g., a goal for the CEO of finding and hiring a new CFO), and (3) equity in the form of stock or stock options.[1]

Compensation committees typically employ no staff. The company may hire an outside consultant to help the committee, often by presenting figures showing what other executives are being paid at similarly sized companies in the same industry. Committees may gather such information

---

[1]   We will look at a more expanded list of compensation components in Chapter Sixteen.

in other ways. Committees usually listen to what the CEO believes the other top officers should be paid.

B. THE WORLDCOM COMPENSATION COMMITTEE AND LOANS TO, AND LOAN GUARANTEES FOR, THE CEO

In the passages that follow, the WorldCom Special Investigative Committee describes the WorldCom Compensation Committee and then focuses on loans that the company made to Ebbers as well as guarantees that the company provided for loans that others made to Ebbers. The following excerpts are from pages 269–74 and 292–313 of the WorldCom Special Committee's report.

2.   The Compensation Committee

Throughout the relevant period, the members of the Compensation Committee were Kellett (Chairman), Bobbitt, and Macklin. Tucker was a member until late 2000, and an honorary member thereafter. The Compensation Committee met regularly, between seven and seventeen times per year between 1999 and 2001. Many of the meetings were by telephone and related solely to the loans to Ebbers (after those loans had gained public attention and as the Committee began running into difficulties). The Committee relied heavily on compensation data collected by Tucker and on Tucker's experience from serving on many other boards of directors. Ebbers sometimes attended meetings.

Formal Authority. The Compensation Committee had ambiguous authority and a lack of formal procedures. Its authority was set forth in a vague 1993 charter that stated that the Committee's power was to supervise the compensation of officers, directors and other employees, administer all stock option plans, and make recommendations to the Board regarding such compensation. The Company's proxy statements characterize the Committee's authority more broadly, however, and appear to give the Committee more authority with regard to the setting of salaries and bonuses, stating that the Committee was charged with determining the salaries, bonuses and other benefits of executive officers. This lack of clarity was highlighted when the Compensation Committee approved substantial loans to Ebbers without Board approval, only later asking for Board ratification after the borrowed funds had been disbursed to Ebbers. (These loans are discussed more fully in Section VIII.C below.)

Compensation Levels. The Compensation Committee was responsible for setting the salary and bonuses of the top executive officers at WorldCom. It was also responsible for administering WorldCom's stock option plan. We were told the Committee consulted materials such as peer group comparisons, charts and data from consulting firms to determine compensation. The comparisons and reports were generally provided by Tucker, who had access to them through his other work in the industry.

The Compensation Committee set the salary and bonus of Ebbers, Sullivan and Roberts. In 1999, it also set the compensation of John Sidgmore (then Chief Operations Officer) and one other senior executive, and in 2001 it set the compensation of Beaumont. Ebbers' recommendation was of paramount importance in setting executive base salaries: for example, it was at his urging that Roberts' salary was maintained at $1,050,000 after the MCI merger (though Roberts no longer received a bonus). Ebbers maintained Roberts' salary even though Roberts' role in the Company had become modest and Roberts' employment agreement had expired on December 31, 1999. Several Directors, including one member of the Compensation Committee, told us they were doubtful about this decision and even though this was a matter committed to the Committee's judgment, the members deferred to Ebbers' preference.

The Compensation Committee reported that Ebbers' and Sullivan's compensation was usually in the median to high range in the industry. In fact, Ebbers was ranked among the highest paid Chief Executive Officers in the nation several years in a row, and Sullivan was ranked among the highest paid (and, according to one commentator, most overpaid) Chief Financial Officers in new economy businesses (indeed, he was among the highest paid in *any* business).[86] From 1998 through 2001 Ebbers received approximately $1 million per year in base salary plus options for well over one million shares of stock per year. For the same time period, Sullivan received annual compensation between $600,000 and $700,000 in base salary plus options for 600,000 to 900,000 shares of stock per year. Ebbers and Sullivan also each received a $10 million retention bonus in 2000.

Despite the very high level of his compensation, Ebbers put a great deal of his resources into business unrelated to WorldCom. (See Section VIII.C below.) A member of the Compensation Committee told us he was not aware of Ebbers' other business

---

[86]   Printouts of Forbes Lists from the Forbes website indicate that Ebbers was one of the highest paid CEOs from 1999–2001; A 2000 Compensation Survey by Towers Perrin and CFO Magazine, dated June 1, 2000, and an article by Steven Taub, *The Most Overpaid CFOs?*, December 6, 2002, *available at* CFO.com, which covered the period from December 1998– December 2001, name Sullivan as one of the highest paid CFOs.

activities before learning of Ebbers' personal financial crisis in September 2000. When the members of the Compensation Committee learned of these activities, they did not object or insist that Ebbers, in return for the substantial compensation packages he received, divest himself of the large investments that could have distracted him from his WorldCom duties.[87]

The Compensation Committee's hands-off approach to commitments that could be inconsistent with the demands on the Chief Executive Officer continued even after Ebbers' departure. John Sidgmore succeeded Ebbers as Chief Executive Officer in April 2002. He was also the Chief Executive Officer and Chairman of another company (eCommerce Industries, Inc. or "ECI²"), and in addition served on several other corporate boards. The Compensation Committee does not appear to have raised any concerns about these other obligations. (After serving as WorldCom's Chief Executive Officer for a few weeks, Sidgmore decided to step down from his position as Chief Executive Officer at ECI².) Nor did the Chairman of the Compensation Committee, when approached for approval, raise concerns about an irregular arrangement Sidgmore requested under which his compensation would be split between himself and two employees he brought over from ECI² when he became Chief Executive Officer. Other Board members did object, and the arrangement was eventually terminated.[88]

Bonus Programs and Stock Option Plan. The Compensation Committee administered two bonus programs during the relevant period. The Company's Performance Bonus Plan, which began in 1997, required, among other things,[89] that an executive officer achieve a ten percent increase in revenue for his or her unit over

---

[87]   We also note that after the early 1990s, Ebbers did not have an employment agreement with WorldCom, which was unusual for large public companies.

[88]   After he was named Chief Executive Officer in April 2002, Sidgmore requested that his salary of $1,000,000 be allocated among himself and two ECI² executives, Paula Jagemann (who would receive $220,000) and Martina Knee (who would receive $110,000). Both had been employees of UUNet, and Knee had served as a lawyer at WorldCom (and did so again after April 2002). Kellett told Borghardt that the Compensation Committee's role was to approve Sidgmore's compensation, and that it was up to Sidgmore how he wished to allocate that compensation. However, other members of the Board, led by Judith Areen, objected to the arrangement. It appears that for a short period of time at the beginning of June 2002, Jagemann's and Knee's salaries were deducted from Sidgmore's salary; however, that arrangement was terminated and Sidgmore's salary was returned to the initial $1,000,000, and Jagemann and Knee were paid through normal payroll procedures. Jagemann left the Company in late 2002 and Knee left in January 2003.

[89]   The 2001 Proxy Statement states that the 2000 performance goal "was based on the attainment of a specified percentage increase in consolidated gross revenues. . . ." The proxy also states that the amount awarded under the Performance Plan is based on changes in the common stock price; Ebbers' recommendations; an officer's individual performance; changes in an officer's level of responsibility and the current salary of the officer.

the same time period the previous year. This focus on revenues is noteworthy: it created an incentive to sustain even unprofitable operations that provided revenue and it created great pressure to report double-digit revenue growth. This latter incentive may have played a role in motivating the improper entries that inflated revenues to that level during portions of 2000 and 2001. As it happened, however, the Compensation Committee ultimately elected not to award Performance Plan bonuses in 2000 because of the Company's deteriorating stock price, and awarded a bonus only to Beaumont in 2001.

Under a second bonus program, the Compensation Committee awarded retention bonuses in 2000 and 2001. With the decline in WorldCom's stock price and the failed merger with Sprint, the Board was concerned about low morale at the Company, so it instituted a retention bonus program intended to keep key employees in place. The plan required an employee to commit to staying at WorldCom through July 2002. In 2000, 558 employees were awarded up-front[90] bonuses totaling nearly $238 million cash, plus roughly 10 million options. In addition, Ebbers and Sullivan each received a $10 million retention bonus. Employees other than Sullivan and Ebbers were given bonuses in a mix of cash and options, while Sullivan and Ebbers received cash only. (The size of the bonuses awarded is in striking contrast to the retention bonus program approved by the Corporate Monitor after WorldCom's bankruptcy, in which $25 million was shared by 325 employees.) It does not appear that anyone challenged the necessity for such substantial payments under the 2000 program, which were made ostensibly to prevent people from leaving, particularly in light of the locations of WorldCom's principal operations.

The Compensation Committee was also responsible for administering WorldCom's stock option plan. It determined the number of options to be awarded to Ebbers. The Company's proxy statement indicates that the Committee granted options to executive officers based on the same subjective factors it considered in awarding base salaries. Although not clear, it appears from meeting minutes that the Committee approved

---

[90] The Company awarded bonuses up front because, we were told, it would be viewed as a show of good faith of some sort. This followed a model used at MFS, and no Director disagreed with it. It should be noted that the current overwhelming market practice (excluding companies contemplating bankruptcy) is to pay retention awards in arrears. There is good reason for this practice, as demonstrated by the litigation WorldCom had to pursue to recover bonuses paid to employees who left before July 2002.

grants to other WorldCom officers or employees as recommended by Ebbers.[2]

* * *

C. Ebbers Loans

Beginning in September 2000, the Compensation Committee extended to Ebbers a series of loans and guaranties that, by April 29, 2002, reached approximately $408 million (including interest). These loans and guaranties enabled Ebbers to avoid selling most of his WorldCom stock in response to the demands of those banks from which he had borrowed substantial sums of money. The loans from WorldCom provided Ebbers the funds with which to conduct his personal business affairs at advantageous interest rates. In making these loans and guaranties, WorldCom assumed risks that no financial institution was willing to assume. The Company did not have a perfected security interest in any collateral for the loans for most of the time period during which they were outstanding.

We have examined the facts and circumstances of these loans and guaranties, including the justifications given for them. Such loans—though lawful at the time—have now been prohibited by federal legislation, in part as a reaction to the perceived abuses at WorldCom. We believe these loans and guaranties were contrary to the interests of WorldCom and its shareholders. Indeed, we do not understand how the Compensation Committee or the Board could have concluded that these loans were in the best interests of the Company or an acceptable use of more than $400 million of the shareholders' money. These decisions reflected an uncritical solicitude for Ebbers' financial interests, and an insufficient focus on the shareholders' interests.

1. 1994 Loans

The loans from 2000 to 2002 were not the first occasion on which Ebbers had borrowed money from the Company to meet margin calls. In 1994, he borrowed approximately $14 million from LDDS in two loans. In the months preceding these loans, the price of LDDS stock fell by almost half[103] and Ebbers faced margin calls from banks from which he previously had borrowed money to purchase Company stock.

---

[2]   Report of Investigation by the Special Investigative Committee of the Board of Directors of WorldCom, Inc. (Mar. 31, 2003) at 269–74, http://www.sec.gov/Archives/edgar/data/723527/0000 93176303001862/dex991.htm.

[103]   The closing price for LDDS stock was $9.29 on February 2, 1994, $5.37 on May 16, 1994, and $4.89 on June 22, 1994.

According to Company records, Ebbers borrowed $9 million from LDDS on May 16, 1994. It does not appear that this loan was approved in advance by the Board or by the Compensation Committee; and it is shocking that a Chief Executive Officer could or would simply take $9 million out of a public company without serious consequences.[104] However, the Board did ratify the loan after the fact, on a motion made by Board Vice Chairman John Porter.

As LDDS stock continued to decline, Ebbers received further margin calls. Around the same time, Porter also received margin calls on his own stock loans. Ebbers therefore took a second loan from LDDS, in the amount of $4,992,496, a portion for himself and, apparently, a portion for Porter. Of the total loan amount, $474,000 was wired directly from LDDS's account to an account that LDDS's documents label as Porter's, and the balance to Ebbers. Like the first loan, the second was approved by the Board, after the fact, on a motion made by Porter. The minutes of the Board meeting do not indicate that the Board was informed that Porter had received part of the Company's loan, or that he had become indebted to Ebbers. The loans to Ebbers were publicly disclosed in LDDS filings, but the disbursement to Porter was not.[105]

LDDS's filings indicate that Ebbers repaid the 1994 loans within four to five months. Porter has told us that he repaid his loan from Ebbers in a timely fashion.

We have found no evidence that anyone on the Board chastised Ebbers for taking money from the Company without advance Board knowledge or consent, or evidence that anyone considered procedures to prevent such conduct in the future. Kellett, who had been on the Compensation Committee, told us in an interview that he had said nothing to Ebbers because he thought Ebbers was a grown up and could manage his own affairs. So far as we can determine, nobody else on the Board cautioned Ebbers about exposing himself financially to the extent that Company assistance was required to bail him out. There is no indication that anyone on the Board expressed concern to Ebbers or to the

---

[104] The minutes of the Board and the Compensation Committee do not reflect advance approval, and Stiles Kellett, who then served on the Committee, recalls that there was no advance approval. The Board minutes reflect after-the-fact approval.

[105] The disbursement to Porter reflected Ebbers' tendency to offer financial assistance to Company officers and directors, a tendency he acted upon more than once after 1994. In 2000 and 2002, Ebbers loaned Chief Operating Officer Ron Beaumont a total of $650,000. In 2002, he offered to loan director Carl Aycock $600,000, though Aycock declined the offer. See Section VIII.C.8.

Board that Ebbers' appetite for risk, supported by his holdings of Company stock, presented an issue of concern to the Company.

2.   Financing Ebbers' Non-WorldCom Businesses

Ebbers, in addition to his full-time job as Chief Executive Officer of WorldCom, was actively involved in buying, building, and running several businesses unrelated to WorldCom.

Prior to 1998, he already had a number of businesses, including hotels and interests in real estate ventures. Between 1998 and 2000, Ebbers and the companies he controlled significantly expanded their holdings by purchasing, among other things, the largest working cattle ranch in Canada (approximately 500,000 acres), and approximately 540,000 acres of timberland in four Southern U.S. states. The total scope of Ebbers' non-WorldCom businesses was summarized in a 2002 report by WorldCom's internal auditors: they included a Louisiana rice farm, a luxury yacht building company, a lumber mill, a country club, a trucking company, a minor league hockey team, an operating marina, and a building in downtown Chicago.

Nothing we have reviewed indicates that the Compensation Committee or the Board imposed any limits on Ebbers' conduct of non-WorldCom businesses. It does not appear that any Board members seriously pursued, prior to 2002, the question whether Ebbers could devote sufficient attention to managing WorldCom amid his outside business obligations, although Kellett tells us he raised the issue once in connection with the original $50 million loan.

The method Ebbers chose to finance many of his acquisitions involved substantial financial risk. Ebbers and companies he controlled took out loans from commercial banks. Many of these commercial loans were margin loans secured by shares of Ebbers' WorldCom stock. Although the terms varied among the various margin loans, each required that the value of Ebbers' stock remain greater than or equal to some multiple of the amount of the loan.

These margin loans totaled hundreds of millions of dollars— perhaps more at various times.[106] This massive indebtedness left Ebbers exposed to declines in the price of WorldCom stock, which began to occur in late 1999. The stock price went from a high of $62.00[107] a share on June 21, 1999 to $36.52 on Friday, April 14,

---

[106]   In December 2002, The Wall Street Journal reported that over a period of seven years, Ebbers took out loans totaling about $929 million from various non-WorldCom lenders. The Financial Times reported that Ebbers had taken personal and non-WorldCom business loans totaling at least $680 million.

[107]   Unless otherwise noted, all stock prices have been adjusted for splits and dividends.

2000. The following Monday, Bank of America made a margin call to Ebbers, noting that he was in default and calling for him either to pledge additional collateral or to reduce his outstanding loan amount.

3.   The Initial $50 Million Loan to Ebbers

The price of WorldCom stock continued to decline during 2000, and Ebbers continued to face margin calls from his lenders. By September 6, 2000, the day of a scheduled meeting of the Compensation Committee, the stock price was down to $30.27 a share. Shortly before the meeting, Ebbers told Stiles Kellett, the Committee's chairman, about the margin calls he was facing and they discussed the possibility that the Company would give him a loan. There is conflicting evidence whether it was Ebbers who first suggested the loan.[108] Kellett agreed to take the matter to the Committee. At the meeting that followed, the Committee directed the Company to give Ebbers a $50 million loan and—as part of the retention bonus program then being applied to many WorldCom employees—pay him a $10 million bonus.

We have heard a variety of accounts of the reasoning behind making this loan. The minutes of the meeting report that the Committee believed the loan was in the best interests of WorldCom's shareholders in light of "the likely adverse impact on the Company's already depressed stock price of a sale of Mr. Ebbers' stock. . . ." These minutes are not entitled to the weight that formal minutes would normally be given because they were prepared weeks later, by a lawyer who had not attended the portion of the meeting when the loans were discussed, and only subsequent to a sale of stock by Ebbers that had been followed by a price decline in WorldCom stock. Some Committee members said that they expected the loan to be for only a short time, and another said he had hoped that a loan would allow Ebbers to focus on running the Company. One Committee member also told us that, in his view, Ebbers had promoted a strong culture of employee stock ownership that would be undercut by his sale.

The loan was made without the formality one would expect in a commercial transaction of this magnitude. The Committee did not address terms such as an interest rate, a maturity date for repayment, or how or whether the loan would be secured with any of Ebbers' assets. The loan documents, including the promissory note, were not even drafted until about two months after the $50

---

[108]   Kellett told us with certainty that Ebbers sought the loan from the Committee. However, the minutes of the Board meeting at which the loan was first disclosed to the full Board report that Bobbitt supported Ebbers' account that the Committee approached Ebbers.

million had been paid to Ebbers (in September), and the terms were still in flux in early November. For example, on November 1, Sullivan told Borghardt, the in-house lawyer working on the loan documents, that the loan should be repaid in 90 days and Ebbers would be charged 8% interest. However, on November 8, Kellett instructed Borghardt to make the notes payable on demand, and on November 10, Sullivan instructed Borghardt to use the rates from a WorldCom credit facility, as had been done with the 1994 loans.

There is evidence that some members of the Compensation Committee took steps that kept the existence of the loan from becoming known within the Company beyond a small number of employees, at least for a period of time, although these members have said that this was not their intention. For example, Borghardt was excluded from the portion of the September 6 meeting during which the subject of the loan was introduced. Borghardt says he was not informed of the loan until late September, when Ebbers contacted him because Ebbers had reached the $50 million maximum loan amount that had been authorized and was considering selling stock to meet additional margin calls.[109] The Committee did not reveal the existence of the loan to the Board at the two Board meetings following the loan's approval. Rather, the Board was informed of the loans only in mid-November, after they were publicly disclosed (and had been increased in amount), and when there was little the Board could realistically do about the initial loan. Also, according to notes taken by Borghardt on November 3, 2000, Kellett and Bobbitt instructed Borghardt to "tell Stephanie [Scott] if they hear of discussion with anyone other than Scott [Sullivan] or me [about the loans] it is [the] basis for termination." Bobbitt and Kellett told us they were not aware of, and did not give, any such instruction.

4. Ebbers' Sale of Stock

By late September 2000, Ebbers had exhausted the initial $50 million loan from WorldCom, and was receiving additional margin calls. WorldCom's stock price had continued to decline and was $25.11 on September 25. On September 26, Ebbers called Borghardt and told him about the margin calls and the loans. Ebbers explored with Borghardt several ways he could raise the money to meet the margin calls, including letting the banks seize

---

[109] In his interviews, Bobbitt recalled that Borghardt attended the entire Committee Meeting. However, Borghardt says that he did not attend this portion of the meeting, and his extensive notes make no reference to the loan. According to Borghardt, he did not learn of the loans until September 27.

the WorldCom stock he had put up as collateral, selling some of his stock, or taking a loan from the Company. Borghardt also spoke with Kellett, who said that the Compensation Committee could not do more to assist Ebbers with his financial problems.

On September 28, 2000, Ebbers sold three million shares (representing over 10% of his holdings) of his WorldCom stock in a forward sale transaction. This sale was disclosed after the market closed on October 4, 2000. The price of WorldCom stock dropped on October 5 by $2.25 to $25.93. Kellett, the Committee's Chairman, has cited this decline as a rationale for the later Company loans to Ebbers. However, as the following chart shows, it is not clear to what extent the sale caused the decline, because the stocks of other telecommunication companies were also falling.

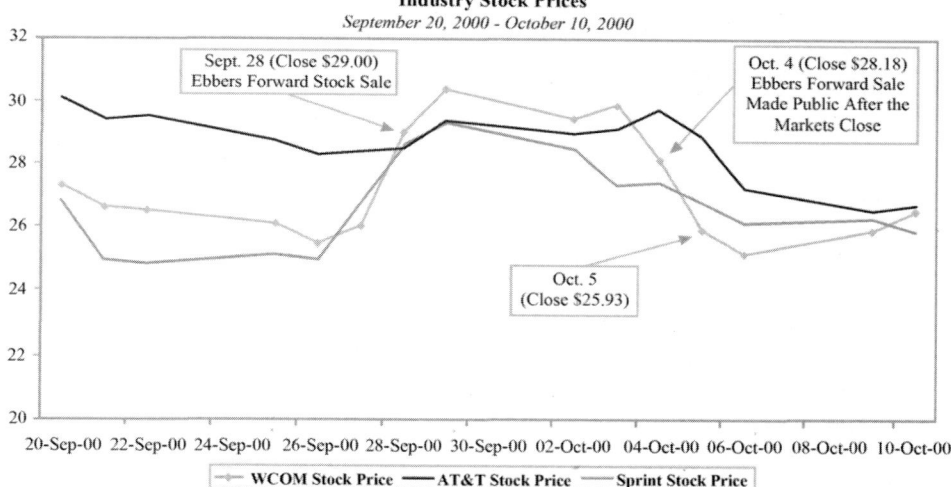

Industry Stock Prices
September 20, 2000 - October 10, 2000

5.   Disclosures to the Board and the Public

Although the Compensation Committee approved Ebbers' $50 million initial loan on September 6, 2000, the Committee did not disclose any loans to the Board at the following two Board meetings.[110] The only explanation for this delay is Kellett's statement that the loan did not require Board approval. Yet when the loans were finally disclosed to the full Board, no one on the Board protested either the process or the substance of the Compensation Committee's action.

---

[110] The Board held a quarterly meeting on September 7, 2000—the day after the Compensation Committee first approved the loan—and a special Board meeting on October 31, 2000.

A number of members of the Compensation Committee and the Board have expressed the view that the Compensation Committee had the power to grant the loans without the Board's approval. It does not appear that Borghardt, in-house counsel to the Committee, was asked for an opinion on this issue[111] and we believe the Committee's authority was unclear, at best.

On November 14, 2000, the Company disclosed the loans to Ebbers to the public for the first time when it filed its quarterly report for the quarter ended September 30, 2000.

Two days after public disclosure of the loans and guaranties, the Compensation Committee reported them to the Board in a presentation by Kellett. According to the minutes, he cited pressure on the Company's stock price "and other reasons" as justifications for the loans. Ebbers' finances were discussed at the meeting and Board members were told that the loans were secured by Ebbers' stock, and that the Company was protected as long as the stock price did not drop below some price. The Board ratified and approved the Compensation Committee's actions.

None of the members of the Board spoke out against the loans at the meeting or questioned the Committee's actions. In interviews, Board members gave various reasons for not opposing the initial loans and guaranties: deference to the Compensation Committee; a sale by Ebbers would be especially damaging to the stock price, and thus to shareholders, because he was such a visible Chief Executive Officer; the fear that Ebbers would have to liquidate all of his stock because his other financial obligations were so great; confidence about Ebbers' ability to repay the loans; the belief the loans were not going to be long term; and confidence that WorldCom's stock price would soon recover, and that there was little else the Board could do as the loans had already been made. At bottom, the rationale had more to do with managing the Company's stock price than managing its business.

As the Compensation Committee subsequently granted additional loans and guaranties to Ebbers, Kellett reported its actions after the fact to the full Board. According to the minutes of the Board, its members ratified and approved Ebbers' loans and guaranties at the March 1, 2001 Board meeting and discussed the loans and guaranties in Executive Session at the November 15, 2001 and March 7, 2002 Board meetings. At no point do minutes of the

---

[111] Stiles Kellett, the Chairman of the Compensation Committee, has indicated that his belief that the Committee had this authority was based upon the Committee's written authority and general legal advice he had been previously given by the Committee's legal counsel. He cannot recall specifically asking Borghardt if Board approval was required, and Borghardt has no recollection of such a question.

Board meetings indicate that the Board members suggested that the Compensation Committee seek Board approval before making additional loans to Ebbers. The Company made further public disclosures about the loans in a registration statement filed December 28, 2000, its 2000 annual report filed in March 2001 (and amended on April 29, 2001), a registration statement filed April 26, 2001, its quarterly report for the quarter ended September 30, 2001 filed on November 14, 2001, a tender offer statement and a periodic report filed on February 7, 2002, its annual report for the year ended December 31, 2001 filed in March 2002, its 2002 Proxy Statement filed in April 2002, its quarterly report for the quarter ended September 30, 2002 filed in May 2002, and a periodic report filed in May 2002.

In addition to receiving information about the loans from the Compensation Committee, the Board was presented with information from a group of three Directors who had been designated by the Board on March 1, 2001 to examine allegations made in a shareholder derivative lawsuit by Harbor Finance Partners challenging the loans. The complaint alleged that the loans and guaranties to Ebbers were inappropriate and a waste of WorldCom's assets. Furthermore, the complaint alleged that Ebbers' motivation in seeking the loans was to postpone the forced sale of his stock until another company could acquire WorldCom for a substantial premium. At the Board meeting on March 1, the Board asked Directors James Allen, Carl Aycock and Francesco Galesi to "review and investigate the demand for action and related matters with the assistance of outside counsel and to report back to the Board."[112]

Allen, Aycock and Galesi met four or five times, usually by phone. It does not appear that any of them took the opportunity to have the Board reconsider the wisdom of lending such large amounts to Ebbers, or to implement limitations on such loans in the future.[113] Instead, the three Directors focused narrowly on the merits of the complaint. At the November 15, 2001, Board meeting, they reported that in their opinion Ebbers never usurped a corporate opportunity by accepting loans from the Company and decided that no further action was necessary in light of the progress that had been made in reaching a settlement with the plaintiffs.

---

[112]   Lawyers from Simpson Thacher & Bartlett assisted the three Directors.

[113]   Some limitations on loans were contained in the proposed settlement of the Harbor Finance Litigation, but the Board did not implement these limitations in the absence of a final settlement. The settlement documents were not yet submitted to the court when WorldCom filed for bankruptcy.

6.   Subsequent Assistance and Loans

From the time of Ebbers' sale of WorldCom stock in late
September 2000 until Ebbers' forced resignation in April 2002, the
Compensation Committee took various steps—including
extending further loans and guaranties—to enable Ebbers to
avoid selling additional WorldCom stock. Ebbers' personal
financial situation became a focus of Compensation Committee
attention, particularly in early 2002. From October 18, 2000 until
April 1, 2002, the Compensation Committee met and discussed
the Company's financial arrangements with Ebbers 26 times, and
for 13 of these meetings, Ebbers' financial situation is the only
topic specifically identified in the minutes.

A striking indication of how far the Compensation Committee
became involved with Ebbers' personal financial exposure is the
fact that Tucker and Bobbitt, both on the Compensation
Committee, accompanied Ebbers in mid-October 2000 to meet
with Ken Lewis, then President of Bank of America. The meeting
was to discuss Ebbers' personal financial situation and to urge
that the bank accept Ebbers' illiquid assets as collateral. Tucker
told us that a reason for the in-person meeting was to show Bank
of America how important Ebbers was to WorldCom. Bank of
America was a major lender to WorldCom. Ebbers later gave Bank
of America explicit authorization to talk to Committee members
about his bank loans. However, Bank of America declined to give
Ebbers relief that would have avoided the margin calls on his
stock.

Unable to persuade Ebbers' lenders to relax their demands or
accept other collateral from Ebbers, the Committee proceeded to
approve numerous additional loans and guaranties for Ebbers,
eventually totaling (including interest) $408 million. The timing
of these loans and guaranties, and their relationship to
WorldCom's stock price, is illustrated in the accompanying chart.

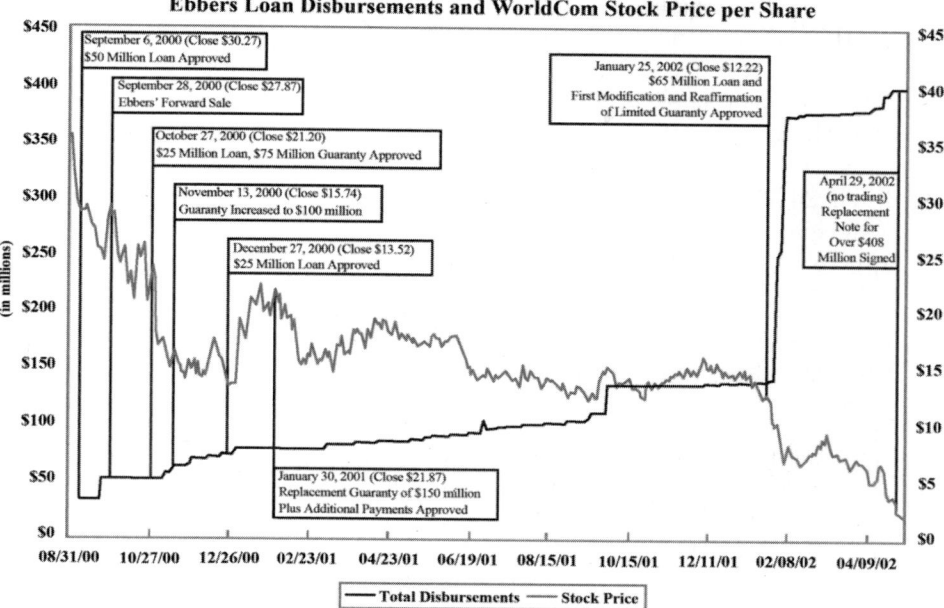

Ebbers Loan Disbursements and WorldCom Stock Price per Share

September 6, 2000 (Close $30.27)
$50 Million Loan Approved

September 28, 2000 (Close $27.87)
Ebbers' Forward Sale

October 27, 2000 (Close $21.20)
$25 Million Loan, $75 Million Guaranty Approved

November 13, 2000 (Close $15.74)
Guaranty Increased to $100 million

December 27, 2000 (Close $13.52)
$25 Million Loan Approved

January 25, 2002 (Close $12.22)
$65 Million Loan and
First Modification and Reaffirmation
of Limited Guaranty Approved

April 29, 2002
(no trading)
Replacement
Note for
Over $408
Million Signed

January 30, 2001 (Close $21.87)
Replacement Guaranty of $150 million
Plus Additional Payments Approved

Total Disbursements — Stock Price

Before being consolidated into a single promissory note dated
April 29, 2002 for approximately $408 million, WorldCom
provided Ebbers with credit in the form of direct loans and in the
form of guaranties, including the collateralization of a letter of
credit.

Direct loans were granted to Ebbers on four separate occasions,
eventually totaling $165 million.[114] Ebbers was not required to
make regular payments; rather, payments were required only on
the Company's demand, and no payments were demanded. The
promissory notes provided that the interest charged to Ebbers
would be equal to the fluctuating rate of interest charged under a
WorldCom credit facility, almost always the lowest rate available
to WorldCom at the time, and a rate of interest lower than that of
Ebbers' other outside loans. Moreover, this rate was lower than
the average rate WorldCom paid on its other debt.

The Company issued guaranties on the debt and other credit
accommodations made by Bank of America to Ebbers and his
companies. The first such guaranty was issued on October 27,
2000 with a limit of $75 million. Two superseding guaranties and

---

[114]   The loans are evidenced by the following promissory notes: a $50 million promissory note
dated September 8, 2000; a $25 million promissory note dated November 1, 2000; another $25
million promissory note dated December 29, 2000; and a $65 million promissory note dated
January 30, 2002.

a modification were issued,[115] eventually increasing the limit to $150 million plus "Additional Payments."[116] In practice, the biggest difference between the direct loans and guaranties was that most of the payments under the guaranties were wired directly to Bank of America, while disbursements under the direct loans were made to Ebbers' accounts or to his other lenders. By April 24, 2002, the day of WorldCom's last payment to Bank of America, total payments under the guaranties amounted to approximately $235 million.

The Company also deposited approximately $36.5 million with Bank of America in connection with a charitable donation by Ebbers to his alma mater, Mississippi College. Ebbers previously had entered into a complicated arrangement with Mississippi College in connection with bonds it had issued. Bank of America issued a letter of credit to support the bonds, and, in turn, Ebbers pledged shares of WorldCom stock to Bank of America as collateral. By operation of the guaranties, WorldCom became obligated to deposit cash into an account with Bank of America as collateral for Ebbers.

All amounts under the loans and guaranties from WorldCom to Ebbers were consolidated into a single promissory note dated April 29, 2002, which then totaled over $408 million. Under the terms of the new promissory note, Ebbers is obligated to repay the loan in five annual payments beginning in April 2003.[117]

7.   Securing WorldCom's Loans to Ebbers

WorldCom did not have a perfected security interest in any of Ebbers' assets, including his WorldCom stock as collateral for the Company's loans and guaranties to him before the first quarter of 2002. This is despite an agreement with Ebbers dated November 1, 2000 (but actually signed later, in mid-November) granting a security interest to the Company in his WorldCom stock. The power of this pledge, however, was limited because it was effective

---

[115]   The guaranty agreements included: A "Limited Guaranty" dated November 14, 2000, another "Limited Guaranty" dated February 12, 2001, and a "First Modification and Reaffirmation of Limited Guaranty" dated January 25, 2002.

[116]   The "Additional Payments" included: (1) $36 million due on June 30, 2001; (2) $25 million due on September 30, 2001; (3) a margin call with respect to certain margin debt; (4) additional amounts depending on the price at which WorldCom Common stock closed; and (5) certain margin debt of Ebbers and Master Hospitality in the event WorldCom's stock closes at less than $10 per share.

[117]   The five annual payments are: $25 million on April 29, 2003; $25 million on April 29, 2004; $75 million on April 29, 2005; $100 million on April 29, 2006; and all of the remaining principal on April 29, 2007. The interest on the loan is calculated at a fluctuating rate equal to that paid by the Company under certain of its revolving credit facilities, and the outstanding balance of the interest is payable on each date of the repayment of principal set forth above.

only "[t]o the extent not prohibited by any covenant or agreement by [Ebbers] in favor of" other lenders, and, until sometime in 2002, all of Ebbers' stock was pledged to other lenders which prohibited Ebbers from permitting any other liens or security interests on the stock. In April 2002, after the loans from WorldCom had been used to repay much of Ebbers' margin debt, WorldCom began to perfect its security interest in some of Ebbers' WorldCom stock.[118]

The Compensation Committee initially believed the value of Ebbers' stock in excess of his margin loans was sufficient to cover his debt to WorldCom. However, Ebbers used the WorldCom loans and guaranties to meet his margin calls resulting from WorldCom's declining stock price, and the value of Ebbers' stock in excess of his margin loans became insufficient to collateralize the funds WorldCom had expended on Ebbers' behalf. Although we have not been able to calculate the precise date when that occurred, it certainly occurred well before the Company began to perfect its security interests in 2002.

It was not until April 2, 2002, however, that the Company obtained a written agreement with Ebbers for him to grant it a security interest in some of his non-stock assets (*i.e.*, his interests in the timberlands, the yacht company, real estate, and his ranch in Canada). Commercial lenders would not (and in fact did not) tolerate such a delay in obtaining satisfactory collateral from Ebbers. Without a perfected security interest in any of Ebbers' assets, the Company would have lost its preferred position with respect to other lenders in the event of Ebbers' bankruptcy.

8.   Use of the Proceeds

According to a November 1, 2000, agreement, the "amounts loaned or to be loaned" to Ebbers were "for payment of certain of [Ebbers'] obligations to institutional lenders which are secured by shares of Company Stock held by" Ebbers. A similar statement was made in WorldCom's quarterly report for the quarter ending September 30, 2000 filed on November 14, 2000 regarding the loans and guaranties: "Mr. Ebbers has used, or plans to use, the proceeds of the loans from the Company and the loan guaranteed by the Company to repay certain indebtedness under margin loans from institutional lenders. . . ."[119]

---

[118]   As of May 20, 2002, the Company had a perfected security interest in approximately 9 million shares of WorldCom Group stock and in 575,149 shares of MCI stock. The Company did not have a security interest in Ebbers' remaining holdings which at that time were approximately 5 million shares of WorldCom Group stock.

[119]   The identical statement was made by the Company in a registration statement filed on December 29, 2000.

Despite the November 1, 2000 agreement and the Company's public statements, Ebbers in fact used at least some of the money for working capital for his luxury boat building business and his rice farms. Because Ebbers has declined our requests to interview him, it is difficult to determine the precise amount of WorldCom's loans used for these purposes. Nevertheless, documents we have reviewed indicate that the figure probably is between approximately $12 million and $33 million.

At some point, in-house counsel to the Compensation Committee discovered that Ebbers was withdrawing money from the direct loans for use in connection with his other companies' operating expenses. When confronted with this fact, Ebbers justified the use of the money for these other businesses as necessary in order to avoid impairing the value of these assets. Instead of objecting and demanding that Ebbers use the loans only for their intended purpose, however, the Committee accepted this rationale, concluding it was in the Company's interest that these assets remain unimpaired so that Ebbers could sell them, if necessary, and repay WorldCom. After discovering Ebbers' other uses of the loan proceeds, the Company characterized the purpose of the loans more neutrally in its filings with the SEC: "We have been advised that Mr. Ebbers has used, or plans to use, the proceeds of the loans from WorldCom principally to repay certain indebtedness under loans secured by shares of our stock owned by him and that the proceeds of such secured loans were used for private business purposes."

While Ebbers was borrowing money from the Company, he continued to be financially generous to himself and others (as opposed to economizing in order to pay down the loans). For example, it appears that he made payments of more than $1.5 million for his new house, and wrote a $2 million check to his ex-wife. In addition, Ebbers made personal loans of $250,000 and $400,000 to Beaumont in October 2000 and February 2002, respectively, and offered to make a personal loan of $600,000 to Aycock, a Board member, in 2002. Aycock did not accept this loan.

9.   Decision to Seek Ebbers' Resignation

By April 2002, the Compensation Committee had encountered problems trying to get Ebbers to agree to the collateralization of the loans, a matter the Committee members were by that time taking seriously. The Compensation Committee had requested that Ebbers provide information relating to the value of his assets in the hope that some of those assets could be pledged as collateral. When Ebbers refused to comply with the request, the

Compensation Committee requested an appraisal of all of Ebbers' assets. Additionally, on April 16, Kellett and Bobbitt initiated a conference call among the non-officer Directors to discuss Ebbers' failure to sign required documentation. Kellett and Bobbitt informed Ebbers that he had to sign the documents immediately. On April 17, Borghardt informed the Compensation Committee that Ebbers' pledge of additional collateral was in place.

On April 26, the non-officer Directors and their counsel met in person in Washington, D.C. to discuss terminating Ebbers. This was the first time this group had ever met on its own in person.[120] Bobbitt and Kellett called this meeting. The Directors were angry that Ebbers had stalled the process of getting his loans collateralized with assets besides his Company stock. While this may have crystallized the decision to ask for Ebbers' resignation, the outside Directors have told us there were several reasons they believed Ebbers should resign. They believed Wall Street had lost confidence in WorldCom and Ebbers. They were also concerned that Ebbers lacked a business strategy for the Company following the failed Sprint merger some two years earlier. After that failure, Ebbers had focused almost entirely on cutting costs and, because he could not control line costs, he spent much effort trying to reduce general and administrative costs, sometimes through petty and demoralizing directives. Bobbitt had recently attended a large WorldCom event at which major customers were present, and had perceived that Ebbers was not only ignoring the customers but interfering with the ability of other managers to interact with them. Some of the outside Directors also felt that Ebbers should resign given difficulties they perceived he had developed in his relationships with Sullivan and Beaumont.

After a unanimous vote of the outside Directors in attendance, Ebbers was informed of the Directors' decision. He signed a Separation Agreement three days later on April 29, 2002.

Rather than demand repayment of the loans at the time Ebbers left the Board, the Board agreed to accept a new promissory note from Ebbers and converted what had been demand notes into notes with a term of five years, with the first payment due in April 2003. Ebbers was allowed to work out of WorldCom office space in Jackson, Mississippi with the assistance of his WorldCom secretary. He also received a promise from the Company to pay him $1.5 million per year for the rest of his life.

---

[120]   The first time the outside Directors met was telephonically during a conference call on April 16, 2002 to discuss Ebbers.

Since then, the Corporate Monitor and WorldCom's management have cancelled the $1.5 million payment and have taken control of some of Ebbers' assets. In late 2002, WorldCom took over Ebbers' yacht company, and subsequently sold the shipyard and recovered the proceeds from the sales of several yachts. In January 2003, the Company obtained control of Ebbers' ranch in Canada, after learning that, beginning in September 2002, the ranch had paid Ebbers $20,000 per month for "consulting services," which, according to Ebbers' contract with the ranch, required that he "discuss with [ranch] management no less than once a month review (sic) of financial statements and review plan of operations." WorldCom currently is trying to sell the ranch. The Company has hired advisers to help determine the best disposition for Ebbers' timberland assets.

10. Conclusions

We believe that the extension of these loans and guaranties was a 19-month sequence of terrible decisions—badly conceived, antithetical to shareholder interests—and a major failure of corporate governance.

Ebbers had overextended himself financially—for the second time in the experience of two members of the Compensation Committee—in a way the Directors believed threatened harm to the Company's shareholders. Commercial lenders, even those favorably disposed to WorldCom because of their business relationships, were unwilling or unable to bear the risk of these loans. If ever there was an occasion for a direct and tough conversation between directors and a chief executive officer, this was it. Yet the members of the Compensation Committee and the Board were not prepared to step up to this task, even though they had ample opportunity to do so over the course of some 19 months. This reluctance included the period when the Board formed a special committee for the specific purpose of examining the loan.

Instead, the Compensation Committee unilaterally permitted the Company to assume the risk associated with the loans—in effect, to become Ebbers' backstop. Even if it had the legal authority, a decision to cause the Company to lend $50 million to Ebbers demanded full and extensive *advance* discussion among all of the outside members of the Board.

These loans did not serve shareholder interests. Temporarily propping up the stock price, at shareholder expense, is not an adequate justification. The loans and guaranties certainly appeared to serve Ebbers' interests at the time: had the situation worked out better—had WorldCom's stock price increased, or had

Ebbers sold assets profitably—it would have been Ebbers, and not WorldCom, who profited. WorldCom nevertheless accepted the risk of loss.

The Compensation Committee did not put into place an approval process for how Ebbers used the proceeds, and it delayed obtaining perfected security interests in Ebbers' assets until very late in the process. The Compensation Committee and Board appear to have had no concrete exit strategy other than the hope that WorldCom stock would increase in price. When the Directors learned that Ebbers had diverted a portion of the proceeds into his outside businesses, a significant red flag, they acceded. There was no firm agreement or timetable for Ebbers to sell assets to pay down the loans in a timely way. And, while the Directors may well have hoped the stock's price would rebound, the events of the preceding several months had demonstrated that it could also decline further. As events proceeded, and the stock price did continue to deteriorate over the next year and a half, the response of the Compensation Committee and the Board was not to re-evaluate their decisions or halt the process. Rather, until April 2002, they extended further credit to Ebbers, following the hydraulic effect the early loans had created, and added to the Company's risk.

The most serious risk the Committee and the Board overlooked was the risk that Ebbers' personal financial stress posed to his corporate decision-making. As a substantial long-term stockholder, Ebbers' interests had been aligned with those of the Company. Beginning in 2000, however, once he was subject to the daily pressure of margin calls and thus in financial jeopardy based on any short-term decline in the price of WorldCom stock, Ebbers' interests were no longer fully aligned with those of the Company. He had strong incentives to pursue whatever short-term action might be necessary to push up the stock price. We do not have a basis either to attribute or not to attribute the financial fraud at WorldCom to Ebbers' personal financial condition as a factual matter, and we do not believe that the Compensation Committee or the Board could reasonably have foreseen it. Nevertheless, the fact that Ebbers was so far overextended financially should have prompted much closer Board attention to the way he was running the Company, and he should not have been allowed to use the Company as his personal bank.[3]

---

[3]   Report of Investigation by the Special Investigative Committee of the Board of Directors of WorldCom, Inc. (Mar. 31, 2003) at 292–313, http://www.sec.gov/Archives/edgar/data/723527/000093176303001862/dex991.htm.

QUESTIONS AFTER YOUR FIRST LOOK AT
THE COMPENSATION COMMITTEE

This Committee was really working! It met between 7 and 17 times a year (190). Can a compensation committee meet too often? Why might that happen?

The report describes efforts to compare the WorldCom compensation with compensation at other companies in the industry (191)? Why is it reasonable to consider such comparisons? What are the pitfalls?

The Special Committee report criticizes the Compensation Committee because no one "challenged the necessity for [the] substantial payments" under the 2000 retention program (193). A retention program is one that pays current executives, and in many cases other employees, for remaining with the company. Companies put such programs in place when they think they are in danger of losing executives and other employees whom they want to keep.

How can a compensation committee test whether a retention program is needed when management says that it is?

The company loans to Ebbers raise many issues.

Do you think that the Board should have been concerned about all the other businesses in which Ebbers was involved and for which he took out margin loans? (196–197) Should boards generally be concerned about such outside activities by the CEO? Why?

How can a board keep track of a CEO's outside business interests? How can it keep track of his or her commitments to charitable work? Is there any privacy limit, or should there be, to the amount of information a board can demand or the degree to which it can investigate to see if the CEO is telling the full story?

Apparently, Compensation Committee members were inclined to provide loans or guarantees in part to forestall Ebbers' sale of WorldCom stock. Ebbers had pledged his very considerable WorldCom stock holdings for loans he had already taken out with banks. Ebbers was getting the "margin calls" described in Chapter Three (98–99, 104, 197), and he was thinking of selling possibly large numbers of his WorldCom shares in order to raise money to reduce those loans. Was the concern that Ebbers would dump a huge amount of WorldCom stock on the market and hurt the stock price a legitimate one for the Compensation Committee to entertain? How much was it worth to the company to prevent that? What if the Compensation Committee had prepared a formal analysis concluding that a stock drop of a certain amount was likely to occur if Ebbers sold a certain amount or percentage of his WorldCom stock and that it was worth making a certain dollar amount of loans to him (at the interest rate that the company charged), or guaranteeing his loans, in order to avoid that drop? Would such a study have made the loans a good idea? Would it have effectively shielded the committee from after-the-fact criticism, or reduced committee members' legal exposure?

Put aside the question of a company loan to a CEO. Put aside legal restrictions on insider trading and assume that companies' legal staffs are preventing such trading. Consider only the possible negative effect on stock price if a CEO sells shares. Should compensation committees try to stay up-to-date on a CEO's plans to sell company shares in order to prevent or moderate such stock price drops? Should compensation committees discourage such sales? Should they require board approval for sales over a given quantity within some designated time period? How far should boards go into what is arguably a private matter—what a CEO does with the shares he or she owns?

Even more generally, should a company try to stay up-to-date on a CEO's overall private financial position? Is there a danger that a CEO with large debts will take ill-advised business risks in the hope that the risks will pay off big in an improved stock price at which the executive can sell his or her stock and pay off the debts? Is there a danger that such an executive will participate in or turn a blind eye to cooking the books? (209) If that is a concern at a particular company, should the company's compensation committee address it or should the audit committee address it? If a company does try to stay current on a CEO's own finances, will the committee wrongly invade the executive's privacy?

Should a board try to stay up-to-date on whether an outside business venture of a CEO is doing well, perhaps to see whether the CEO is losing his or her "touch"? Again, do you see privacy concerns?

Aren't there other privacy concerns specifically involved with loans from the company to Ebbers—like investigating a CEO's entire financial condition to be sure that he or she can repay the loan? Like making sure that the loan is used for the purposes it is intended? Does any of that make you uncomfortable? Or do you think that, since banks demand this kind of information when making and administering loans, a company should as well—in part so that the company can ensure that it is not treating the executive better than the executive would be treated in an arm's-length transaction, or if the company is treating the executive better, that the company knows just how much more generous it is being?

What issues does the interest rate raise?

How could the Compensation Committee have prevented the more technical failures, like not creating the loan documents and obtaining the CEO's signature before Ebbers got the money, and not perfecting security interests (197–198, 204–205)? Think nuts and bolts here.

Consider the relationship between the Compensation Committee and the Board. The Special Investigative Committee criticized the Compensation Committee for approving the loans without first going to the full board (198, 208). Should the Compensation Committee have brought the loans to the full Board before approving them? Why? Should the Compensation Committee have sought full Board approval for the loans or simply let the Board know in advance of approval by the committee? Note that these questions raise both policy issues and technical issues about delegation of power.

More generally, many of the new reforms are designed to boost the effective power of board committees. But how can a *full board* be sure that it keeps *some* control, or more pointedly, *appropriate* control (whatever that is) over matters in which its committees take the lead?

C. WORLDCOM'S PROCESS FOR SETTING PAY AND RETENTION BONUSES

For more on the WorldCom Compensation Committee, read now excerpts from pages 151–52, 154–63, and 166–71 of the Second Interim Report of Dick Thornburgh, Bankruptcy Court Examiner, dated June 9, 2003 and filed in the WorldCom bankruptcy, *In re WorldCom, Inc.*, Case No. 02-15533 (AJG), U.S. Bankruptcy Court, Southern District of New York. These passages describe in some considerable detail WorldCom's compensation structure and the role that the compensation committee played in determining that structure. The excerpts also discuss retention bonuses at WorldCom.

B. Overview of the Compensation Process at WorldCom

The compensation of certain Management-level employees took three basic forms: salary, bonus, and stock options.[90] As the following sections demonstrate, however, the process by which the Company determined each element of compensation varied significantly depending on an employee's grade, or level, within the Company. More important, the "theory" of compensation decision-making at the Company did not always correspond to its reality. While the Compensation Committee was supposed to either make or monitor compensation decisions, its members abdicated their responsibilities and Mr. Ebbers effectively made the decisions.

1. Senior Executives

In <u>theory</u>, the Compensation Committee determined the salary, performance bonus, and stock option grants for each of the Company's Senior Executives, including, among others, the Chief Executive Officer (Mr. Ebbers), the Chief Financial Officer (Mr. Sullivan), and the Chief Operating Officer (as of January 1, 2001, Mr. Beaumont). In <u>practice</u>, Mr. Ebbers had substantial discretion

---

[90]   As discussed in more detail below, employees in the sales divisions received quarterly commission bonuses, while other WorldCom Management employees received yearly performance bonuses.

to determine compensation for every Senior Executive other than himself.

2. The "Restricted Group"

Immediately below the Company's Senior Executives was a level of Management extending down to Senior Vice-Presidents and comprising 30 to 40 individuals. This set of Executives, sometimes referred to as the "Restricted Group," consisted primarily of employees who reported directly either to Mr. Ebbers himself or to another Executive who reported directly to Mr. Ebbers.

In <u>theory</u>, the Compensation Committee was supposed to monitor the compensation process for these Executives by "reviewing and taking action concerning" issues relating to their salary, bonuses, and stock options grants.[91] In <u>practice</u>, however, the Compensation Committee did not monitor this process. Rather, Mr. Ebbers completely controlled it and he did so in the absence of any written policies or procedures for determining Restricted Group compensation.

3. Remaining Non-Sales Employees

For all non-sales management employees below the level of Senior Vice-President, the Company established guidelines, or limits, both on employee salaries at each "grade," and on raises, bonuses, and stock option grants at each grade. In <u>theory</u>, the Human Resources Department was supposed to issue written policies that dictated both the amount, or range of each type of compensation and the manner in which the Company determined it, and the Compensation Committee was supposed to monitor this process.

In <u>practice</u>, however, the Compensation Committee had essentially nothing to do with the compensation or process for these lower-level management employees. Mr. Ebbers retained both the ultimate authority to approve the guidelines and the ability to change compensation decisions for this group of employees.[4]

* * *

---

[91]   With respect to Restricted Group compensation, the Company's proxy statements stated that the Compensation Committee was "to review and take actions, including submission of recommendations to the Board of Directors, concerning compensation, stock plans and other benefits for the Company's directors, officers and employees."

4   Second Interim Report of Dick Thornburgh, Bankruptcy Court Examiner, dated June 9, 2003 and filed in the WorldCom bankruptcy, *In re WorldCom, Inc.*, Case No. 02-15533 (AJG), U.S. Bankruptcy Court, Southern District of New York at 151–52.

2. The Mechanics of Senior Executive Compensation

There were three general elements of compensation for Senior Executives: salary, annual incentive compensation (executive performance bonus), and long-term incentive compensation (stock option grants). Between January 1999 and December 2001, compensation for these individuals was quite substantial. Mr. Ebbers, for example, received a total of $20.5 million in cash and over 4 million stock options, valued at approximately $55 million during this time period.

a. Salary

During the relevant time period, salary played a relatively small role in total Senior Executive compensation and did not vary much year-to-year. In fact, Compensation Committee-approved salaries for these Executives remained relatively consistent for the period 1999–2002:

- The salaries for Mr. Ebbers ($1 million) and Bert C. Roberts ($1.05 million) did not change at all.

- Mr. Sullivan saw his salary increase from $600,000 in 1999 to $700,000 in 2000, where it remained through the time of his dismissal in 2002.[94]

- Mr. Sidgmore saw an identical jump from $600,000 to $700,000 in 2000, his last year in this group.

- Mr. Beaumont's salary was established at $675,000 for both of his two years in this group (2001 and 2002).

The Company's proxy statements reported that when setting Senior Executive salary ranges, the Compensation Committee looked at two factors: (1) the level and scope of the responsibility attached to a particular position; and (2) the salaries of similarly-positioned officers in comparable companies.[95] With regard to actual salaries within the established ranges, the Compensation Committee was to evaluate the following factors:

- Company performance, as evidenced by changes in the price of the Company's common stock compared to that of industry competitors;

- the CEO's recommendations with regard to other Senior Executives;

---

[94]   Although the Company's 2000 Proxy Statements lists Mr. Sullivan's salary for 1999 as $600,000, internal Company data shows a salary of only $500,000.

[95]   To date, the Examiner has not found any evidence that the Compensation Committee established salary ranges. Rather, Mr. Ebbers provided the Committee with his "recommendations."

- each officer's individual performance;

- any significant changes in the officer's responsibilities; and

- each officer's then-current salary.

The proxy statements also stated that among these five factors, the Compensation Committee found Mr. Ebbers' recommendations to be of "paramount importance." Although the Examiner has uncovered no evidence to refute the notion that the Compensation Committee actually considered these factors when establishing Senior Executive compensation, several aspects of the process cast doubt on the Compensation Committee's ability to check independently Mr. Ebbers' influence in this area. First, it was Mr. Ebbers who approached the Compensation Committee with compensation recommendations for the Senior Executives, not vice versa. As noted above, the Compensation Committee viewed these recommendations as being of "paramount importance" in their deliberations. Second, Mr. Ebbers was the sole source of much of the information on which the Compensation Committee ostensibly relied when reviewing those recommendations, including (a) an assessment of the senior Executive's level of responsibility; (b) an appraisal of the senior Executive's performance; and (c) the actual salary recommendation. Third, the only evidence the Examiner has identified relating to external salary surveys consists of some charts, created in 1999, that tabulate executive compensation information from the proxy statements of other public corporations that the Compensation Committee determined were "comparable" to WorldCom. Although one former Compensation Committee member indicated that he had prepared similar charts in other years, the Examiner has been unable to locate them and none has been produced. Fourth, none of the former Compensation Committee members interviewed could recall, or cite to, a single instance where the Compensation Committee changed any of Mr. Ebbers' salary recommendations. Fifth, the Examiner has learned of at least one instance where the Compensation Committee was interested in reducing the salary of a Senior Executive and Mr. Ebbers forbade it.

In sum, based on information currently known by the Examiner, Mr. Ebbers, and not the Compensation Committee, played the most significant role in determining Senior Executive salaries at the Company.

b. Senior Executive Performance Bonuses

Near the beginning of each year, the Compensation Committee established a performance bonus plan for the Senior Executives within its direct purview. The plan included a threshold trigger that would permit payment of performance bonuses if the Company met a specified goal for revenue growth. The plan also set forth dollar value limits on the bonuses as the greater of $1 million or 150 percent of the previous year's bonus. Toward the end of the year, the Compensation Committee would then determine whether the performance criterion had been satisfied and, thus, whether to award bonuses.

In 1999, the Compensation Committee determined that the criterion had been met and, accordingly, awarded bonuses to the Senior Executives totaling $18.9 million. Of this amount, Mr. Ebbers was awarded $11.5 million and Mr. Sullivan was awarded $2.76 million.[96] Although the Compensation Committee made the same determination in 2000, it awarded no performance bonuses in light of the Company's falling stock price.[97]

The situation in 2001 is somewhat murkier. Minutes of the meetings of the Compensation Committee indicate that a decision was made not to award any "performance bonuses" to the three eligible Senior Executives: Messrs. Ebbers, Sullivan, and Beaumont. Nonetheless, the Minutes then reflect that the Compensation Committee awarded Mr. Beaumont a $2 million bonus, "based on individual performance and other circumstances." The Compensation Committee did not identify these "other circumstances."[98]

Perhaps equally curious is the "phantom bonus" awarded to Mr. Sullivan in 2001. According to two former Compensation Committee members, the Committee awarded Mr. Sullivan a $2 million "performance bonus" at the same time it awarded Mr. Beaumont his "special circumstances" bonus. Oddly, the meeting minutes of the Compensation Committee do not reflect this action, but the awarding of Mr. Sullivan's performance bonus is identified in the handwritten notes of Mr. Borghardt taken contemporaneously at the meeting. These former Compensation Committee members believe that Mr. Ebbers ultimately denied Mr. Sullivan this Compensation Committee-approved bonus out of jealousy or anger, because the Compensation Committee did

---

[96] Once again, the amount of the bonus awards stated in the Compensation Committee Meeting Minutes is different from what the Company reported in the proxy statements. According to the 2002 Proxy Statement, the Compensation Committee awarded Mr. Ebbers a performance bonus of $11.5 million," but Mr. Ebbers accepted only $7,500,000 of such an award."

[97] Despite the lack of performance bonuses, however, Senior Executives did receive substantial "retention bonuses" in 2000. We address the retention bonus issue later in this Report.

[98] While the minutes of the pertinent meetings of the Compensation Committee and the Company's proxy statements disclosed the $2 million figure, the Company provided the Examiner with data showing that Mr. Beaumont actually received a bonus of $2.45 million in 2001.

not award a bonus to Mr. Ebbers that year, and that he then had the Minutes "sanitized" to eliminate any reference to a bonus award to Mr. Sullivan.

c.   Senior Executive Stock Option Program

i.   Mr. Ebbers' Authority Over Option Grants

Although the Compensation Committee had explicit authority to award stock options to all of the Company's Senior Executives, it deferred entirely to Mr. Ebbers in this regard.[99] Indeed, the Compensation Committee did nothing more than allocate a specific number of options to Mr. Ebbers each year, then approve stock option awards for other Senior Executives "as recommended by Mr. Ebbers." The Compensation Committee even granted Mr. Ebbers the authority to determine the vesting of those stock options. By giving Mr. Ebbers the authority to determine option recipients, the amount of each option award, and the vesting schedule, the Compensation Committee effectively ceded to Mr. Ebbers all authority to determine option grants to Senior Executives of the Company.

This abdication of responsibility is significant because options were supposed to be the largest portion of Senior Executive Compensation. Indeed, one former Compensation Committee member described the Committee's devotion to stock options as a "religion" at the Company. Assuming this was the case, Mr. Ebbers' unquestioned control over this compensation tool becomes even more significant.

ii.   Mr. Ebbers' Influence Over Option and Stock Sales

For his part, Mr. Ebbers took full advantage of his preeminence in the realm of stock option grants by using stock options as a substitute for higher salaries, then trying to dissuade employees from selling their stock. For example, Mr. Ebbers apparently received a daily list of all employees who exercised options and sold the underlying stock. Mr. Ebbers would on occasion call employees to inquire about the stock sales. Mr. Ebbers discouraged all levels of employees, including senior Management, against stock sales. Thus, when Mr. Beaumont needed money to pay contractors who were working on a ranch he owned, Mr. Ebbers discouraged him from selling his stock and steered him to a bank where Mr. Beaumont obtained a line of credit and used his Company shares as collateral.

---

[99]   Former Compensation Committee members and other Company employees told the Examiner that Mr. Ebbers had exclusive authority to determine option grants.

When WorldCom stock began to decline in value, however, Mr. Beaumont found himself in need of funds to cover the collateral requirements. Knowing Mr. Ebbers' policy against employees selling Company stock, Mr. Beaumont sought a loan from the Company in or about October 2000. Both at this time, and in early 2002 when Mr. Beaumont had to make certain tax payments relating to his ranch, Mr. Ebbers told Mr. Beaumont that he could not borrow the money from the Company and, instead, personally lent Mr. Beaumont a total of $650,000.[100] Mr. Beaumont still owes Mr. Ebbers this money.

Mr. Sullivan was not quite so observant of Mr. Ebbers' "no stock sale" policy. Between 1997 and August 2000, Mr. Sullivan made approximately $29 million from exercising vested options and selling approximately $44 million of the underlying WorldCom stock.[101]

3. Conclusions Regarding Senior Executive Compensation

In sum, the evidence shows that Mr. Ebbers was dominant in matters of Senior Executive compensation. For example:

- In setting Senior Executive salaries, the Compensation Committee considered Mr. Ebbers' recommendations to be of "paramount importance," despite the Committee's sole authority to determine such salaries.

- In awarding Senior Executive performance bonuses, the Compensation Committee deferred completely to Mr. Ebbers' recommendations, or at least acquiesced.

- In setting Senior Executive stock option grants, the Compensation Committee simply deferred to Mr. Ebbers entirely, at least as to Senior Executives other than Mr. Ebbers himself.

The Examiner recognizes that there is not necessarily anything wrong with a compensation committee giving some measure of deference to the wishes of a CEO. In WorldCom's case, however, the Company led the public to believe that the Compensation Committee served as an independent check on Mr. Ebbers' authority, when, in fact, it appears that Mr. Ebbers ultimately controlled all matters related to Senior Executive compensation.

---

[100] Ironically, at the time Mr. Ebbers told Mr. Beaumont that he could not borrow money from the Company, Mr. Ebbers had just borrowed $50 million from WorldCom.

[101] Some former Compensation Committee members said that they were displeased about Mr. Sullivan's extensive sales of stock, but that they never spoke to him about it.

D. Compensation of "Restricted Group" Executives at the Company

1. Mr. Ebbers' Absolute Discretion

As noted above, the "Restricted Group" of Executives generally included individuals at the level of Senior Vice President and above, all of whom reported directly to Mr. Ebbers or to one of Mr. Ebbers' direct reports. The name "Restricted Group" arose from the fact that only Mr. Ebbers had routine access to the actual compensation of these Group members. In fact, even the head of the Human Resources Department was for a time precluded from viewing compensation information for the Restricted Group.

Like "Senior Executives," the Restricted Group received a combination of salary, bonus and stock option grants. Unlike the Senior Executives, however, the Restricted Group was outside the purview of the Compensation Committee. Instead, Mr. Ebbers determined salary, bonus and option grants for this group, either entirely on his own or in response to recommendations from one of his direct reports who supervised the group member at issue. The Examiner's review of evidence to date suggests that Mr. Ebbers used no formal criteria or procedures for setting Restricted Group compensation or for evaluating those compensation recommendations that his direct reports made to him.[102] Indeed, the executive who interacted most closely with Mr. Ebbers on compensation issues stated that, to the best of his knowledge, no one ever questioned the process Mr. Ebbers employed, or the decisions he reached, on Restricted Group compensation. In short, compensation for the Restricted Group apparently was wholly discretionary with Mr. Ebbers.

2. Restricted Group Compensation: Preliminary Findings

The Examiner's investigation into actual Restricted Group compensation is still in its early stages because the process of collecting this information from the Company and verifying it against existing Company records is logistically complicated and time-consuming. Moreover, due to the Company's complex, ever-changing and, in certain respects, unreliable data system, the Examiner repeatedly has received inconsistent compensation data from the Company. At this point, the Examiner can make

---

[102] At least one member of the Restricted Group told the Examiner that he had never received a formal evaluation from Mr. Ebbers, had never discussed his compensation with Mr. Ebbers, and had learned that his compensation had been changed only when he saw a different number on his paycheck. Other members of this Group have confirmed that Mr. Ebbers never told them how he had calculated their compensation.

only general observations about absolute (as opposed to relative) compensation values for certain "Restricted Group" employees.

Specifically, our preliminary analysis of data for certain direct reports to Mr. Sullivan shows notably high compensation awards, including: (a) annual merit salary increases of up to 21 percent (as compared to policy guidelines of between zero and 9.5 percent for employees below the Restricted Group level); plus (b) yearly performance bonuses comprising 30 to 50+ percent of annual salary; plus (c) stock option grants exceeding 300,000 per employee for the years 1999 through 2001. The Examiner is continuing to investigate any relationship between these compensation numbers and the employees' participation in, or knowledge of, accounting fraud or other misconduct at the Company.

E. Compensation of the Remaining WorldCom Employees

1. Compensation of Non-Sales Employees[103]

a. Overview of the Players and the Policy

In contrast to the discretionary compensation process for Executives, the Company had detailed written guidelines for determining the compensation of most other non-sales employees, which the Human Resources Department largely developed and implemented. As a baseline for establishing compensation levels, the Human Resources Department established a three-part indicator, known as a "job grade." Every Company employee had a job grade, and each job grade corresponded to a specific salary range, merit increase range, bonus range and grant of stock options. In other words, one needed only to look at an HR-generated table (or matrix) to determine a given employee's permissible salary, maximum merit salary increase, maximum bonus, and maximum options grant for a given year.

The Human Resources Department did not generate these tables in a vacuum. Although Mr. Ebbers exercised much less control over the compensation of these lower-level employees than he did over the compensation of Senior Executives, he did review, approve, and occasionally change, the policies of the Human Resources Department prior to implementation.

Mr. Ebbers was not supposed to exercise this power unimpeded, however. According to the Company's proxy statements, the

---

[103] Throughout this section of the Report, we refer to the policies and procedures in place during the relevant time period of our inquiry in the past tense. The Examiner understands, however, that many of these policies are still in place today.

Compensation Committee had the designated power to review and to take action "concerning compensation, stock plans and other benefits for the Company's directors, officers and employees." Compensation Committee Meeting Minutes reflect that the Committee paid little or no attention to this task, however, a fact that the Examiner has confirmed through interviews with former Compensation Committee members. Indeed, despite claims in the Company's proxy statements that the Compensation Committee independently monitored compensation decisions at the Company, three former Compensation Committee members denied that such "monitoring" was ever part of the Committee's duties.[5]

* * *

F.   The May 2000 Retention Bonus Program

In May 2000, the Company awarded 558 WorldCom executives some $240 million in cash retention bonuses, along with 10.4 million shares of stock options.[107] The May 2000 Retention Bonus Program serves as a graphic illustration of the weak oversight and excessive deference to Mr. Ebbers that is detailed above.

1.   The Concept of the Program

In the late 1990s, mid-level managers approached Senior Management to complain that they were having difficulty keeping their business units operating efficiently because so many employees were leaving for the "greener pastures" of high-tech, and start-up companies. Senior Management at the Company, including Mr. Ebbers, his Senior Executives and managers in the Human Resources Department, took these complaints to heart and, between late 1999 and early 2000, met to discuss the problem and to evaluate possible responses.

Ultimately, Mr. Ebbers decided to offer certain employees retention bonuses in exchange for their promise to remain at the Company for at least of [sic] two years, beginning in July 2000. As with all other compensation-related decisions at the Company, the final contours of the Retention Bonus Program remained firmly in Mr. Ebbers' hands.

In terms of the amount of the retention bonus, Mr. Ebbers decided to apply a "multiplier" to the total annual compensation of each

---

[5]   Second Interim Report of Dick Thornburgh, Bankruptcy Court Examiner, dated June 9, 2003 and filed in the WorldCom bankruptcy, *In re WorldCom, Inc.*, Case No. 02-15533 (AJG), U.S. Bankruptcy Court, Southern District of New York at 154–63.

[107]   This amount does not include the $10 million bonuses paid to both Mr. Ebbers and Mr. Sullivan.

eligible employee, based on the employee's level of responsibility within the Company. Thus, Senior Vice Presidents would receive a bonus of up to 3 to 3.5 times their annual compensation; Vice Presidents would get up to 2 to 2.5 times their annual compensation; and Senior Directors would receive up to two times their annual compensation.

All of these figures were presumptive, in that each employee's supervisor could propose a smaller retention bonus. Of course, Mr. Ebbers eventually reviewed every retention bonus recommendation and even changed certain awards before announcing them to the affected employees. According to some Company employees, Mr. Ebbers reviewed retention bonus recommendations to make sure that managers were not discriminating against employees who had not come from the same "legacy" company as the manager.

2.   Analysis and Approval of the Program

The evidence that the Examiner has reviewed to date suggests that Mr. Ebbers generated these bonus multipliers without performing or reviewing any market survey of retention compensation at peer companies,[108] without any internal or external professional review of his analysis, and without any meaningful consultation with the Board of Directors.

The Compensation Committee apparently approved the Retention Bonus Program during a meeting on April 7, 2000. Neither the Meeting Minutes nor interviews with former Compensation Committee members, however, suggest that prior to approving the Program, the Compensation Committee received any information about the terms of the Program or about how Management intended to administer the Program. Despite these informational deficiencies, the Compensation Committee approved a Program that: (a) granted stock options to unspecified employees "as recommended by Mr. Ebbers;" (b) allowed vesting "in two equal installments on July 1, 2001 and July 1, 2002, or as otherwise determined by Mr. Ebbers;" and (c) provided "special cash bonuses" to unspecified employees, with the "individual amounts and recipients of such cash bonuses" to be "determined by Mr. Ebbers."

---

[108]   One former member of the Compensation Committee said that Mr. Ebbers did present the Committee with information regarding retention bonuses at comparable companies. No other members of the Committee recalled this, nor has the Examiner identified any documentary support for it.

3. The Execution of the Program

Armed with this vast discretion, Mr. Ebbers proceeded to dispense some $240 million in Company cash upfront and without a written commitment from the recipients. First, despite the fact that several Executives involved in planning the Program had urged Mr. Ebbers to spread out bonus payments over the two-year retention period—July 2000 through July 2002—Mr. Ebbers insisted that the Company pay all bonuses up front.[109]

Second, over the strong objections of many executives—and of the Company's Legal Department—Mr. Ebbers did not require any bonus recipient to sign a contract requiring the recipient to repay the bonus if he or she left the Company's employ before the end of the 2-year period.[110] Instead, Mr. Ebbers merely presented each bonus recipient with a letter explaining the purpose of the bonus and requesting a personal commitment to abide by its conditions. Many of these amounts were extremely generous, including 17 individual awards of $1 million or more to individual employees, other than Messrs. Ebbers and Sullivan.

Perhaps not surprisingly, the Company has been forced to sue several bonus recipients who quit WorldCom before July 2002. It has chosen, however, not to seek recovery from certain employees who were either fired or laid off due to a "reduction in force."

4. Corporate Governance Issues in the Retention Bonus Program

The structure and implementation of the May 2000 Retention Bonus Program points to a number of serious weaknesses in the Company's compensation decision-making process. First, the Program's promoters failed to collect or to review any objective information about the need for such a program or about the type of program that would best ensure the retention of truly key employees.

Second, the Compensation Committee appears to have ignored its publicly-stated role in monitoring such compensation by effectively rubber-stamping a program of enormous financial

---

[109] Mr. Ebbers had observed this same procedure several years earlier in connection with a retention bonus program that followed one of the Company's significant acquisitions. At the time, however, Mr. Ebbers personally knew every bonus recipient, and there were well under 100 of them. In contrast, some 558 employees received bonuses under the May 2000 Bonus Program and Mr. Ebbers did not know them all personally.

[110] At least one Senior Executive tried to convince Mr. Ebbers that the retention bonuses should take the form of a forgivable loan, with accompanying loan documentation, such that any employee who departed before the end of two years would have to repay the "loan."

scope without obtaining sufficient detail to pass any rational judgment on that program.

Third, Mr. Ebbers enjoyed unfettered discretion to dictate the scope and terms of the Program, and he rejected advice from those who had qualms about the implications of its structure, including up-front payments and no written repayment commitment.

5.   May 2000 Senior Executive Retention Bonuses

a.   The Compensation Committee Process

Not only did Mr. Ebbers dispense $240 million in cash retention bonuses in mid-2000, he and Mr. Sullivan also received $10 million bonuses that same year. At the same time that the May 2000 Retention Bonus Program was underway, the Compensation Committee authorized retention bonuses for Messrs. Ebbers and Sullivan, conditioned on their agreement to stay with the Company for a period of two years. No specific plan or grant of authority governed the disbursement of these retention bonuses, and there is a dispute among Compensation Committee members as to how these bonuses even came about.

According to one former Compensation Committee member, the desire to retain Mr. Sullivan drove the Committee's actions. As this former member recalls, the Compensation Committee had two reasons for making this extraordinary grant to Mr. Sullivan. First, the Compensation Committee believed that Mr. Sullivan was an able CFO who provided tremendous value to the Company. Second, the Compensation Committee believed that Messrs. Sullivan and Ebbers had a strained relationship and that Mr. Sullivan needed additional incentives to remain at the Company.

The bonus for Mr. Ebbers, on the other hand, was not motivated by any perceived need to retain Mr. Ebbers. Rather, the Compensation Committee simply concluded that it would not be politically palatable to award a retention bonus to Mr. Sullivan and not to Mr. Ebbers.[111]

No matter how the bonus originated, former Compensation Committee members agree that the Committee offered Messrs. Ebbers and Sullivan several alternatives for the retention bonus, including cash, a stock option grant or some form of future

---

[111]   According to a former Compensation Committee member, Mr. Ebbers was so invested in the Company that the Committee believed "he probably wasn't going anywhere." Nonetheless, the Compensation Committee felt that it would not be politically possible to give Mr. Sullivan a retention bonus without also giving one to Mr. Ebbers. If this was in fact the Compensation Committee's rationale, it was prescient indeed. In 2001, when the Compensation Committee awarded Mr. Sullivan a performance bonus, Mr. Ebbers refused to pay it, because he himself had not received one from the Committee.

retirement package, all with the same nominal value of $10 million. When the Compensation Committee presented these options to Mr. Ebbers, he told the Compensation Committee that he would consult with Mr. Sullivan and get back to them.

Months later, Mr. Ebbers reported back to the Committee that both he and Mr. Sullivan would prefer the $10 million in cash. The Compensation Committee apparently acceded to this request without any further discussion, despite that every other retention bonus recipient had received a combination of cash and options and that the Compensation Committee's theory of executive compensation was to align the interests of the Executives with the interests of the shareholders by awarding stock options as a substantial portion of compensation. Moreover, as noted above, Mr. Ebbers received the $10 million cash bonus at the same time that he received his first loan from the Company in the amount of $50 million.

The Compensation Committee authorized these $10 million cash payments only one year after giving retention bonuses of $7.5 million and $1.85 million to Mr. Ebbers and Mr. Sullivan, respectively. The Examiner is not aware of any evidence that Mr. Ebbers needed a retention bonus to keep him at the very Company that he built or that there was a significant risk that Mr. Sullivan would leave WorldCom.

b.   Mr. Sullivan's Payments to Others

After Mr. Sullivan received his $10 million cash bonus, he shared a portion of this bonus with some of his subordinates, many of whom already had received sizeable retention bonuses themselves (as much as $795,000). Preliminary information suggests that at least seven of Mr. Sullivan's closest subordinates received personal checks in the amount of $10,000 from Mr. Sullivan. Mr. Sullivan also wrote $10,000 personal checks to the spouses of certain of these seven subordinates. Although the Examiner has not identified any evidence linking these payments to illegal conduct, four of the individuals who received these payments pled guilty to accounting fraud.[6]

---

[6]   Second Interim Report of Dick Thornburgh, Bankruptcy Court Examiner, dated June 9, 2003 and filed in the WorldCom bankruptcy, *In re WorldCom, Inc.,* Case No. 02-15533 (AJG), U.S. Bankruptcy Court, Southern District of New York at 166–71.

QUESTIONS AFTER YOUR SECOND LOOK AT
THE COMPENSATION COMMITTEE

From the viewpoint of fraud prevention, what is the danger of attributing "paramount importance" to a CEO's recommendations for other executives' salaries (218)?

As a practical matter, won't CEO recommendations on the compensation for other top executives always influence a compensation committee in a fairly profound way?

Did the WorldCom Compensation Committee make the right decision in 2000 when it declined—because of the falling stock price—to award performance bonuses to executives who met their bonus criteria (216)? Should a corporation award big cash bonuses to executives in years when the stock price of a company goes south or other bad things happen to the shareholders (such as a cut in or discontinuation of a dividend)? Should a corporation award such bonuses if such a year is a bad one for the industry as a whole and the company's financial results have fallen, but by percentages less than industry averages?

Was the Compensation Committee wise in simply approving the number of stock options for senior executives (other than Ebbers) in amounts "as recommended by Mr. Ebbers" (217)? Was it appropriate to give his recommendations great weight? What other information should the Committee have gathered?

Should the committee have left the vesting schedule to Ebbers (*id.*)?

How far down the ladder should compensation committee attention extend? What role do you think the WorldCom Committee should have played in setting the compensation for the Restricted Group, and for the remaining non-sales employees?

What are the nuts-and-bolts steps that the Compensation Committee could have taken to prevent what appears to have been the basic mistake of paying retention bonuses up front without requiring that recipients sign contracts obligating them to either work to the end of the retention period or else repay the bonuses (223)?

Should WorldCom have paid Sullivan a retention bonus because the Compensation Committee believed he needed an additional incentive to stay with the company and then paid a $10 million bonus to Ebbers, not because the bonus was needed to keep him at the company but because "it would not be politically palatable to award a retention bonus to Mr. Sullivan and not to Mr. Ebbers" (224)?

What concerns come to mind as you think about Sullivan giving part of his bonus to others in the company (225)?

CHAPTER 6

WORLDCOM PART IV: STRATEGIC PLANNING AND ACQUISITIONS

■ ■ ■

Up to this point, everything we have discussed has had to do with wrongdoing, preventing wrongdoing, sloppy internal procedures, and preventing sloppiness. But what about helping the shareholders in some way other than by reducing the probability of fraudulent accounting and reducing the probability of overreaching executive compensation?[1] Most investors put money into stocks in order to make money on their investments by receiving dividends and/or selling the stocks for higher prices than those at which the investors bought them.

The Bankruptcy Examiner faulted the WorldCom Board on a matter that *did* have to do with running that company in order to make a profit rather than to reduce fraud: the manner in which the Board approved acquisitions—a matter important because acquiring other companies was a large part of WorldCom's business. This Chapter Six includes the Examiner's criticism, folded into a discussion of the extent to which strategic planning guided acquisitions and fine-grained descriptions of the Board's role in specific deals.

A. WORLDCOM'S BOARD AND ACQUISITIONS

What follows are excerpts from pages 24–27, 31–43, 45–50, and 52–64 of the Second Interim Report of Dick Thornburgh, Bankruptcy Court Examiner, dated June 9, 2003 and filed in the WorldCom bankruptcy, *In re WorldCom, Inc.*, Case No. 02-15533 (AJG), U.S. Bankruptcy Court, Southern District of New York.

1. Introduction

The Examiner's analysis of WorldCom's acquisitions from 1997 through mid-2002 involves three intertwined inquiries: (1) the degree to which the WorldCom Board and Management engaged in strategic planning; (2) whether the WorldCom Board and

---

[1] Those Sarbanes-Oxley-related reforms designed to increase the power of boards vis-à-vis top management may have aimed in part at restraining out-of-control executives (particularly so-called "imperial CEOs"), who run companies for their own benefit rather than for the benefit of shareholders. To that extent, it is fair to characterize the reforms as motivated by the desire to improve shareholder returns.

Management fulfilled their fiduciary duty to the Company's shareholders to become adequately informed before making significant business decisions; and (3) how well the various acquisitions were integrated so that contemplated synergies and cost savings could be achieved.

WorldCom grew to become a telecommunications giant mainly as a result of its numerous acquisitions during the 1990s. In light of those many acquisitions, the Examiner would have expected WorldCom to have had a focused strategic plan for, and approach to, acquisitions that took into account the complexity of a proposed transaction, how it would better position WorldCom, and how to achieve synergies and cost savings. The Examiner's investigation has shown no such reasonable planning or detailed consideration regarding these matters.

a.   Management's Control of Strategic Planning and the Acquisitions Process

To the extent that strategic planning occurred in the 1997–2002 time period, the impetus came from Management, particularly Messrs. Ebbers and Sullivan and to a lesser extent Mr. Sidgmore. The Board seemed content to delegate this important function to Management.[12] The Board formed no strategic planning committee. Within Management, a de facto Management group consisting mainly of Messrs. Ebbers, Sullivan and Sidgmore considered strategy matters.

Similarly, Management, to the exclusion of the Board, exercised virtually total control of WorldCom's acquisition processes. Management decided whether and when an acquisition would be brought to the Board for approval. The Board's role in the Company's acquisition processes appears to have been completely passive. For example, the Board established no guidelines (such as dollar thresholds or degree of complexity) for when WorldCom would retain an investment adviser or obtain a fairness opinion[13] in connection with a transaction. Indeed, Management made all decisions as to when to retain investment bankers, and which investment bankers to retain, in connection with transactions. One Director stated that he would have liked to have had a fairness opinion on any transaction in the $2 billion range or

---

[12]   One Director disagreed and said that "strategy was an ongoing discussion," "was front and center in our minds" and that the Board understood that strategic planning was one of its most important functions. Other Directors and members of Management did not support this assertion.

[13]   A fairness opinion is an opinion issued by an outside financial adviser to the effect that the price being paid by the acquiring company as received by the acquisition target was fair. Companies frequently seek fairness opinions as part of the process by which management and the board of directors become informed of all relevant facts.

higher, but this clearly was not WorldCom's policy. In fact, among the six multi-billion dollar transactions that closed in the 1997–2001 period, a fairness opinion was obtained only with respect to the MCI transaction.

Similarly, the WorldCom Board often did not inquire into the amount of due diligence that Management or outside advisers conducted in connection with even quite large acquisitions. For instance, as discussed in greater detail below, on the Intermedia transaction, no Director made any inquiry of Management at the September 1, 2000 or March 1, 2001 Board meetings about the extent of due diligence performed in connection with the initial merger agreement or the subsequent amendment to that agreement. This lack of inquiry by the Board is all the more surprising given that Management apparently never provided the Board with a single document pertaining to this $6 billion transaction.

b.   Ad Hoc Strategic Planning, But Some Reasonable Due Diligence

To the extent that Management pursued strategic planning, it was mostly *ad hoc* and opportunistic, with the Board, once again, playing a passive role. Although certain documents, denominated "strategic plans," were created by Management in 1997 and 1999, these documents do not appear to be actual strategic plans. Rather, they appear to be financial analyses of WorldCom over a period of years, making projections of how WorldCom would grow if it pursued no further acquisitions. The Examiner has identified no evidence that the Board was shown, or that the Board or Management adopted, either plan.[14] Similarly, each filing by WorldCom on Form 10-K during the relevant period had a section entitled "strategy." However, these descriptions of WorldCom's "strategy" did not reflect any deliberations of the WorldCom Board or any planning group within Management.

Although WorldCom did not pursue "mega" deals, such as the MCI Communications Corporation ("MCI") and Sprint Corporation ("Sprint") acquisitions, as part of a carefully considered strategic plan formulated with input from the Board, our investigation

---

[14]   One Director believes that the Board may have seen a summary of the 1997–2002 plan. The Examiner has been unable to confirm whether this was the case. Further, Mr. Sidgmore believes that Management did have a strategic plan—although this plan was not as formalized as the strategic plans of other companies—and that the plan concerned WorldCom's business focus from 1997 onward on the data, Internet, wireless and international areas. The Examiner does not doubt Mr. Sidgmore's belief that Management had such a plan (at least from 1997 through 1999) and that Messrs. Ebbers and Sullivan generally supported it. However, as discussed . . . , the facts and circumstances surrounding many of the transactions pursued by the Company, undercut the notion that WorldCom Management pursued a focused acquisitions strategy.

suggests that the Company approached these deals in a reasonably systematic manner. WorldCom Management engaged outside financial and legal advisers, and the Board received detailed presentations from investment bankers and law firms about the transactions, supported by documentary data. Moreover, WorldCom Management appears for the most part to have implemented adequate due diligence procedures with respect to acquisition targets. In the case of the "mega" transactions, WorldCom's investment bankers and outside legal counsel mainly were responsible for the due diligence process. On smaller transactions, such as the CompuServe/AOL/ANS, Electronic Data Systems, Inc. ("EDS") and SkyTel transactions, for which WorldCom engaged no outside financial advisers, the WorldCom Corporate Development Department, supported by personnel from other departments, would carry out due diligence. Based upon review of the available evidence, the Examiner believes that, with the exception of the Intermedia transaction, WorldCom Management and/or outside advisers conducted a reasonable amount of due diligence on both "mega" and smaller transactions, prior to asking the Board to approve a transaction. The Board's approach to due diligence procedures, however, was as passive as its approach to strategic planning. The Board established no guidelines for the performance of due diligence, how due diligence was to be memorialized or whether the Board was to be presented with due diligence data or summaries of such data.[2]

* * *

2.   Strategic Planning and Fiduciary Obligations in the Context of Specific Acquisitions

The foregoing general observations can best be illustrated by a review of the actual strategic planning in which WorldCom engaged, and the actual due diligence and approval processes that Management and the Board followed, with respect to particular transactions. This review proceeds chronologically, beginning with some small transactions in May 1997 and continuing through the Intermedia transaction, which closed on July 1, 2001 and which was WorldCom's last large transaction.

---

[2]   Second Interim Report of Dick Thornburgh, Bankruptcy Court Examiner, dated June 9, 2003 and filed in the WorldCom bankruptcy, *In re WorldCom, Inc.*, Case No. 02-15533 (AJG), U.S. Bankruptcy Court, Southern District of New York at 24–27.

a. Strategic Planning and Acquisition Processes for Increasingly Complex Transactions: January 1997 through September 1998

At the end of 1996, WorldCom closed its acquisition of MFS—the largest transaction to date for WorldCom. The purchase price of MFS was approximately $12.5 billion, and MFS brought to WorldCom a diverse set of assets, including an Internet division (UUNET), significant local network facilities, and an international network. One Director believes that, in the wake of this transaction, Mr. Ebbers became "too successful" and "lost focus" due to WorldCom's growth in size.

Between January 1997 and early September 1997, Management and the Board appear to have undertaken little joint strategic planning. This apparent lack of strategic planning may be understandable, given the need to attempt to integrate MFS into WorldCom's existing business. At the Board level, strategic discussions, including those concerning potential acquisitions, were typically conducted during executive sessions held at the end of Board meetings. We can find no indication in the Board meeting minutes and other data that any executive sessions were held between January 1, 1997 and September 11, 1997. This suggests that, at the Board level, there were no extensive discussions of any strategic plan extending one or more years into the future.

b. The May 22, 1997 Acquisitions

At the May 22, 1997 WorldCom Board meeting, Management asked the Board to approve a series of modest divestitures, investments and acquisitions. A week prior to the meeting, Management sent each Board member a Board package that contained, among other things, a short description of each transaction, including its structure and rationale. The transactions had a total estimated value of $221 million.

The Examiner believes that the process Management followed to prepare the Board for the May 22, 1997 meeting was in accord with proper corporate practices. Management did its homework on the transactions and provided meaningful data to the Board in advance of the Board meeting so that Board members would be prepared to raise questions concerning the transactions at the meeting.

c. CompuServe/AOL/ANS[15]

During the period from January 1997 through September 1997, individual members of Management focused on some matters of

---

[15]   Additional data about this transaction is contained in Appendix 1.

strategic importance. Mr. Sidgmore and others worked during this period on a complicated transaction involving CompuServe Corporation ("CompuServe"), AOL and ANS Communications, Inc. ("ANS") (the "AOL Transaction").[16] WorldCom Management and the Board, moreover, appear to have analyzed this transaction in a reasonable manner and to have informed themselves adequately about it.

On September 4, 1997, WorldCom's Board met for a telephonic special Board meeting to consider and vote on the AOL Transaction. The AOL Transaction had the following components: WorldCom acquired CompuServe from H & R Block for $1.3 billion; WorldCom transferred CompuServe's interactive services division and another CompuServe subsidiary to AOL, with WorldCom paying $175 million to AOL; AOL sold ANS to WorldCom for $500 million; and WorldCom entered into a five year outsourcing agreement to provide network capacity and services to AOL. Thus, the entire transaction, not including the outsourcing component, cost WorldCom $1.975 billion.

Management, led by Mr. Sidgmore and Mr. Cannada, did a significant amount of due diligence on this complex transaction. On September 2, 1997, Management sent each Director a Board package that contained a reasonably detailed description of the AOL Transaction and the rationale behind it. The Board then met telephonically on September 4th, and Management (chiefly Mr. Sidgmore and Mr. Cannada) reviewed the information distributed to the Board in the Board package and answered the Board's questions. The Board then approved the AOL Transaction, which closed in January 1998.

WorldCom did not engage a financial adviser on the AOL Transaction. This is somewhat surprising, given the significant dollar amount involved and the deal's complexity. No Board member is reported to have questioned Management's decision not to retain a financial adviser.

The AOL Transaction, however, seems to have made good strategic sense. In acquiring ANS, for example, WorldCom acquired assets similar to those that it had acquired with UUNET, and the acquisition thus enhanced WorldCom's Internet capabilities. Further, the five-year outsourcing agreement with AOL brought to WorldCom a billion-dollar-a-year customer.

---

[16] This AOL Transaction is to be distinguished from reciprocal agreements that WorldCom and AOL entered into in June 2001 under which WorldCom agreed to purchase advertising from AOL and AOL agreed to pay WorldCom more favorable rates for Internet-related services than it had in the past.

Although Management did not retain a financial adviser in connection with the AOL Transaction, the Examiner believes that this transaction provides another example of Management properly doing its job, in part through giving the Board data sufficient to permit the Board to inform itself about relevant facts and circumstances. The time between the September 2nd notice and the September 4th Board meeting was short, to be sure. Time was of the essence after some very intense negotiations, however, and although Management requested that the Board make a quick decision, it also provided the Board with sufficient information before and at the September 4th meeting on which to base that decision. Management's failure to use a financial adviser is somewhat problematic, but Management performed due diligence on this transaction over so long a period (more than eight months) that the WorldCom team probably became very familiar with its intricacies.

d. Brooks Fiber

WorldCom's acquisition of Brooks Fiber exemplifies the opportunistic nature of the Company's strategic planning from January 1997 through September 1998. Brooks Fiber was a competitive local exchange carrier ("CLEC") in secondary markets not previously served by WorldCom. WorldCom had acquired CLEC assets in major markets for the first time in the 1996 MFS transaction. The possibility of acquiring Brooks Fiber appears to have come to WorldCom's attention by chance, some time in July 1997. WorldCom moved rapidly and approved this $2.4 billion acquisition on September 29, 1997. There is no evidence that WorldCom's acquisition of Brooks Fiber was part of any long-term strategy to become a leading player in the CLEC market. However, its strategic rationale seems to have been to add non-overlapping CLEC assets to those previously acquired, thus enhancing the existing WorldCom CLEC network. It was described as a "like kind deal."

The WorldCom Board first learned of this potential transaction on September 11, 1997, during an executive session held after the regular Board meeting. Management told the Board that extensive due diligence had been performed and that more was yet to be completed. It does not appear that Management provided any documents concerning Brooks Fiber to the Board at that time, and notes of the Board's discussion of this possible transaction run for only eight lines, suggesting that Management provided the Board with only a very brief "heads up." Board members appear to have asked no questions on September 11, 1997 about the possible transaction.

On September 25, 1997, Management provided the Directors with a single-page memorandum informing them of a special Board meeting on September 29, 1997. This notice was not accompanied by any agenda or documents. The Board then met on September 29th to consider the Brooks Fiber transaction, as well as the MCI transaction discussed below. It appears that the Brooks Fiber discussion, led by Mr. Cannada, was brief (probably no more than 30–35 minutes) and that the Board was provided only with the proposed merger agreement.

The Examiner has identified a document, entitled "Project Black September 29, 1997," which appears to have been prepared by the WorldCom Corporate Development Department. The document is 13 pages in length and explains in considerable detail the reasons for the proposed Brooks Fiber transaction. This is the sort of document that the Examiner would have expected Management to provide to the Board prior to the September 29th Board meeting. The Examiner has preliminarily concluded that the Project Black document was used by Mr. Cannada as the basis for his Board presentation but that it was never actually provided to the Board. The Board minutes for the September 29th meeting specifically note that the Brooks Fiber merger agreement was provided to the Board. It appears to the Examiner that if the Project Black document had been provided, it would have been referenced as well.[17] Since the Project Black document appears not to have been provided to the Board in advance of the meeting, the Examiner finds it difficult to understand how the Board could have become fully informed about the transaction in merely a 30–35 minute oral presentation.[18] At a minimum, the Examiner observes that it was not a good practice to prepare a detailed explanatory document and then fail to give it to the Board.

WorldCom did not use a financial adviser on the Brooks Fiber transaction, although it had a $2.4 billion value. WorldCom's rationale in not retaining a financial adviser appears to have been that Brooks Fiber was a CLEC company and that WorldCom was

---

[17]   The minutes for the September 29, 1997 Board meeting further reference various MCI-related documents provided to the Board at that meeting, reinforcing the view that the Project Black document probably was not provided to the Board.

[18]   A former member of Management acknowledged that 30–35 minutes was probably too short a time, without provision of prior documentation, for the Board to have become fully informed about the Brooks Fiber transaction. He sought to justify the brevity of the discussion, however, by the fact that the much larger and more complicated MCI transaction was to be considered at the same meeting and that Brooks Fiber was just a "gnat" in comparison. The Examiner cannot agree. The Brooks Fiber transaction was, in and of itself, a significant transaction and the Board had an obligation not to move forward on it absent becoming fully informed. The Examiner has substantial doubt as to whether the Board in this instance fulfilled its responsibilities.

already in the CLEC business and thus felt comfortable in performing its own valuation.

The Examiner has no basis at this time to conclude that Brooks Fiber was a misguided transaction that would have been rejected if the Board had taken more time to consider it. To the contrary, it appears that Management had carefully assessed the transaction and believed, with a reasonable written rationale, that it was in WorldCom's best interests. However, this might have been the first instance in which the Board approved a transaction without requiring Management to provide persuasive written data to justify the transaction. It would not be the last.

e.   MCI[19]

WorldCom's merger with MCI further exemplifies the opportunistic nature of WorldCom's strategic planning during the January 1997 through September 1998 period. In late August or early September 1997, Mr. Sullivan appears to have conceived of the possibility of a mega-transaction in which WorldCom would acquire MCI. Although the size of this transaction was calculated to give WorldCom new credibility in the telecommunications market, WorldCom's merger with MCI was not the fruit of a long-term Company strategy to obtain the operations or assets of the type held by MCI. Rather, the opportunity to acquire MCI suddenly emerged when British Telecom ("BT") renegotiated its prior MCI merger agreement and WorldCom Management then immediately pursued the opportunity.[20]

It appears that WorldCom's Management and Board adequately informed themselves about the MCI merger before approving and proceeding with the transaction. At WorldCom's September 11, 1997 Board meeting, in executive session, Management first advised the Board that a hostile takeover bid for MCI might be possible and told the Board that Mr. Sullivan had already spoken with Salomon and outside lawyers about such a possibility.

The Board then initially considered and approved WorldCom's hostile takeover bid for MCI at a special Board meeting held on September 29, 1997. At the September 29th Board meeting, and again at a Board meeting held on November 9, 1997, at which the Board considered a revised MCI offer, Management and WorldCom's investment advisers and outside counsel made extensive presentations to the Board and provided the Board with

---

[19]   Additional data about the MCI transaction is contained in Appendix 2.

[20]   It appears that a Salomon investment banker advised Mr. Sullivan that the BT/MCI renegotiation presented WorldCom with an opportunity, which Mr. Sullivan then pursued.

many supporting documents.[21] The Directors were also reminded of their fiduciary duties in connection with the transaction. A special Board subcommittee on the MCI transaction was established and met on several occasions to consider details of the transaction.

Thus, instead of being the product of a careful strategic process, the MCI merger a sudden opportunity [*sic*] for a $40 billion merger that could not be passed up. One Director commented that Mr. Ebbers' ego would not let such a deal go by and, accordingly, WorldCom's "strategy," as such, adjusted to the circumstances. This is not to state that the addition of MCI's extensive international network was not strategically important. It appears that WorldCom Management, after the MFS acquisition, had targeted international telecommunications as a growth area, and MCI brought significant international assets to WorldCom. The addition of MCI's large consumer business, however, had not been part of any WorldCom strategy. Further, as discussed in Chapter IV.C.5, below, the success of the MCI merger was impaired by Management's inability to integrate MCI and WorldCom successfully, a factor that Management and the Board may not have extensively considered prior to the closing of the merger. Therefore, the Examiner has preliminarily concluded that Management and its advisers appear to have conducted thorough due diligence and to have apprised the Board in detail about this transaction.

f.   Conclusions

The Examiner has reviewed Board meeting minutes and other data from the period September 11, 1997 through September 14, 1998 to seek to identify any Board sessions devoted to strategic planning. No such planning is apparent, and, in interviews with personnel from WorldCom's Corporate Development Department and with Board members, we have not identified any significant attention to strategic planning. This may not be surprising, however, at a time when Management was devoting a great deal of effort to obtaining regulatory approval of the MCI transaction. At this time, the Examiner does not conclude that Management's and the Board's inattention to strategic planning reflects any error in judgment. The telecommunications industry and WorldCom in particular appeared to be achieving excellent results during this period and the opportunistic approach to expansion that Management and the Board followed appeared to be serving WorldCom well. Based on our current analysis of transactions

---

[21]   Written data about the potential MCI transaction were not provided to the Board prior to September 29th because this was a hostile acquisition, and thus confidentiality was essential.

that WorldCom entered into between January 1997 and September 1998, the Examiner further concludes that, with the exception of the Brooks Fiber transaction, Management provided adequate information to the Board, and that the Board appears to have informed itself adequately, about WorldCom's acquisitions.

3. Strategic Planning and Acquisition Processes in the Wake of MCI: October 1998 Through Early 2000

From September 1998 until early 2000, WorldCom's Management and Board appear to have engaged in more strategic planning than previously. Although Management's and the Board's strategic planning processes may not have been ideal, they were more deliberate during this period. However, the disturbing trend of Management providing scant data to the Board regarding proposed acquisitions continued and, in fact, appears to have accelerated during this period, with no apparent reaction or inquiry from the WorldCom Board.

a. Initial Strategic Planning

At the November 19, 1998 WorldCom Board meeting (the first after the September 14, 1998 closing of the MCI transaction), Management presented a "Strategic Planning and Development Report" as a scheduled part of the meeting. Although this report on strategic objectives could be faulted for its failure to include advance written information for the Board to consider, Management did lay out for the Board three strategic objectives for WorldCom to pursue over the next one to two years: (1) rationalizing some of MCI's assets (in particular, its MCI SystemHouse Corp. ("SHL") subsidiary), an objective that included entering into outsourcing arrangements, possibly with EDS; (2) pursuing broadband opportunities; and (3) expanding into wireless lines of business.

Such sessions devoted to strategic discussions appear to have continued at later Board meetings. The March 3–4, 1999 Board meeting, for example, included an executive session discussion about the pursuit of potential acquisitions in the wireless area (of which Nextel and SkyTel became examples), consistent with the November 1998 objective that WorldCom should consider expanding into wireless services and infrastructure. Further, in later meetings in 1999, the Board, consistent with the strategic report provided in November 1998, considered the acquisitions of SkyTel and Sprint, both of which had wireless assets.

The extent to which WorldCom's Management and Board fulfilled their fiduciary duties to the Company's shareholders to become adequately informed regarding significant transactions may be assessed in the context of the following specific acquisitions.

b.   EDS[22]

The processes followed by Management and the Board in considering and approving the EDS transaction are troubling. Management failed to provide the Board with any written materials on this complex transaction, and the Board considered it for only 20 minutes prior to giving Management permission to proceed.

As noted in the discussion regarding strategic planning, Mr. Sidgmore advised the Board at the November 19, 1998 Board meeting of the possibility that WorldCom would sell SHL and seek to enter into outsourcing agreements with other entities, possibly including EDS. During late 1998 and early 1999, WorldCom and EDS personnel negotiated a series of tentative agreements that rivaled those of the AOL Transaction in their complexity. The contemplated agreements (collectively, the "EDS Transaction") were as follows: an agreement to sell SHL to EDS for $1.65 billion; a 10-year agreement under which WorldCom would outsource major portions of its information technology services to EDS at an estimated cost of $5–7 billion; a 10-year outsourcing agreement under which EDS would outsource its voice and data services to WorldCom under an agreement with an estimated value of $6.5 to $8 billion; and a joint marketing agreement.

On February 10, 1999, WorldCom Management convened a telephonic "informational" meeting of the Board to discuss the proposed EDS Transaction. It is unclear how much notice Board members received of this meeting. Of the 16 WorldCom Board members, three were unable to participate, and two joined the telephonic meeting late. The total duration of the telephone meeting was 20 minutes.

During the meeting, Mr. Sidgmore reviewed the proposed transactions, working from a draft memorandum that he had prepared for, but had not sent to, the Board. The participating Board members received no documents concerning the transaction in advance of the meeting. The Board did not vote on the EDS Transaction during this call. Notes taken by Bruce Borghardt, General Counsel for WorldCom's Corporate Development Department, regarding this informational Board

---

[22]   Additional data about the EDS transaction is contained in Appendix 3.

meeting, however, reflect that a number of Directors favored the EDS Transaction.[23]

At the conclusion of the meeting, an unidentified member of WorldCom's Management is reported to have stated that Management appreciated the Board's participation and that Management "will proceed." WorldCom Management announced the EDS Transaction the next day, February 11, 1999.[24] It was not until three weeks later, at the March 3–4, 1999 Board meeting, that the Board officially approved the EDS Transaction. It does not appear that Management provided the Board with any new information on the EDS Transaction, or that the Board engaged in any material discussion regarding the EDS Transaction, prior to such approval on March 3, 1999.

The Examiner has serious corporate governance concerns about the EDS Transaction. First, both Mr. Sidgmore and outside counsel on the EDS transaction had prepared detailed memoranda addressed to the WorldCom Board explaining the EDS Transaction and its rationale. Neither memorandum was provided to the Board. Second, the EDS Transaction appears to have been complex and it involved billions of dollars. Given that fact, it is surprising that Management did not retain an investment adviser. One Director commented that it would have been wise to have an adviser, but that he thought Mr. Ebbers was trying to save money. Third, the Examiner doubts that the Board could have been adequately informed about this highly complex, multi-billion dollar transaction in a 20-minute informational call, particularly given that Management did not provide the Board with any documents in advance. Indeed, it appears that the WorldCom Board never received a single document from Management providing details of, or a rationale for, the transaction. Finally, the Examiner cannot discern any need for Management to have obtained Board approval on February 10, 1999. From a corporate governance standpoint, it would have been preferable for Management to wait for a sufficient time so that it could follow more orderly procedures.

---

[23]   Mr. Borghardt acted as secretary to the WorldCom Board at many Board meetings, especially from November 1998 onward. Mr. Borghardt took copious notes, which have been made available to the Examiner and which have been a significant source of data about what occurred at various Board meetings. References to Mr. Borghardt's notes should not be construed as a waiver of any applicable privilege by the Company.

[24]   While WorldCom February 11, 1999 Press Release did not specifically state that the WorldCom Board had approved the EDS Transaction, it clearly suggested that all necessary corporate approvals had been obtained.

The Examiner is not suggesting that the EDS Transaction did not make business sense as of early 1999. To the contrary, the Examiner is satisfied that WorldCom Management reasonably determined that the various components of the EDS Transaction, including the outsourcing, made sense.[25] The Examiner is troubled, however, by Management's disregard for the need to inform the Board fully of the details of the EDS Transaction, and the Board's apparent willingness to approve, without adequate data or opportunity for reflection, whatever Management proposed. The Examiner also is troubled by the fact that counsel does not appear to have provided any advice to Management or the Board about its fiduciary duties and the process that the Board should follow to ensure that it fulfilled all of its fiduciary duties.[3]

* * *

d.   SkyTel[28]

On May 28, 1999, WorldCom announced that it had reached an agreement to merge with SkyTel, a Jackson, Mississippi-based company in the wireless messaging business. The value of the transaction was about $2 billion. The Examiner has concerns about the extent to which the WorldCom Board became fully informed about this transaction, including its strategic rationale.

The possibility of a SkyTel transaction was first mentioned to the WorldCom Board at the March 3–4, 1999 Board meeting, during the executive session. The mention of SkyTel was apparently quite brief, with Management suggesting that a SkyTel transaction might make strategic sense in the context of a broader WorldCom entry into the wireless business, which would include the acquisition of Nextel.

Before and after March 4, 1999, a significant amount of SkyTel due diligence was undertaken by WorldCom's Corporate Development Department.[29] Then, on April 15, 1999, WorldCom put the SkyTel transaction on hold, apparently because it wanted

---

[25]   The Examiner is aware that substantial disputes subsequently arose between WorldCom and EDS regarding EDS's failure to fulfill certain outsourcing obligations, and that some accounting irregularities may have arisen from the EDS Transaction as well.

[3]   Second Interim Report of Dick Thornburgh, Bankruptcy Court Examiner, dated June 9, 2003 and filed in the WorldCom bankruptcy, *In re WorldCom, Inc.*, Case No. 02-15533 (AJG), U.S. Bankruptcy Court, Southern District of New York at 31–43.

[28]   Additional data about the SkyTel transaction is contained in Appendix 5.

[29]   WorldCom used no investment banker for, and obtained no fairness opinion on, the SkyTel transaction. It was viewed as a relatively small and straightforward transaction, and a number of Directors and one member of the Corporate Development Department were quite familiar with the paging business. One Director, however, assumed that a fairness opinion had been obtained.

to determine whether the Nextel transaction would proceed. WorldCom had preliminarily determined that an acquisition of SkyTel would make strategic sense only if the Nextel transaction went forward. As noted previously, on or about May 6, 1999, WorldCom terminated consideration of the Nextel deal. Notwithstanding that decision, WorldCom then informed SkyTel on that day that it might still be interested in acquiring SkyTel.

On May 20, 1999, the WorldCom Board held a regular quarterly meeting, followed by an executive session. The Board package for that meeting contained nothing about SkyTel, although the Corporate Development Department had compiled a great deal of information on SkyTel by that time. This is troubling, because it evidences Management's continued pattern of failing to provide the Board, in advance of Board meetings, with sufficient data concerning transactions to enable the Board to consider them thoroughly.

With regard to the May 20 executive session, Mr. Cannada made a presentation regarding the SkyTel transaction that appears to have lasted about 15 minutes and the discussion was described by one Director as "minimal." It does not appear that any documents were provided or presented to the Board on May 20, 1999. The failure of Management to provide documents to the Board is troubling, because the Examiner has determined that, as was the case with the Brooks Fiber and EDS transactions, the Corporate Development Department had developed a document that could have been provided to the Board. This document, developed by no later than May 19th, described SkyTel and briefly discussed some of the potential benefits and risks of the transaction. It is possible that this document was used by Mr. Cannada during his oral presentation to the Directors, but it appears that it was never given to the Board.

The information compiled by the Examiner suggests not only that the executive session presentation was brief, but also incomplete. The presentation did not include certain data from Corporate Development, including the Corporate Development Department's conclusion that a SkyTel acquisition would not be strategic unless combined with other wireless acquisitions or that SkyTel had had "[l]ackluster results" in the last quarter of 1998 and the first quarter of 1999. Further, there is no evidence that Mr. Cannada or others in Management communicated their belief that this was a "mediocre" transaction, which, in fact, was their view. Directors do not recall hearing any such comment.

The Examiner is troubled over the extreme passivity of the Board in its consideration of the SkyTel transaction. The Examiner is not prepared to conclude that a properly informed Board would have rejected this transaction. It appears, however, that if all relevant data had been provided to the Board, it would have been, as of May 1999, a close decision whether this transaction was in WorldCom's best interests.

The Examiner further is troubled by the fact that a number of persons whom we interviewed appeared to consider the SkyTel transaction not to be substantial enough to merit much Board consideration. The Examiner disagrees. The transaction involved a total cost of about $2 billion, including assumption of long term debt that appears to have been in excess of $315 million. Acquiring such a company, with recent losses, should have been undertaken only after careful deliberation and thoughtful consideration. The apparent attitude of WorldCom's Board, and possibly its Management, that such a transaction was too small to worry about is not acceptable, even in light of the Company's circumstances in 1999.

e. Sprint

The Examiner is generally satisfied with the procedures that Management and the Board followed in pursuing and acting upon the "mega" Sprint transaction, although the transaction ultimately failed due to opposition by European regulators and the United States Department of Justice. From June through August 1999, WorldCom Management conducted extensive due diligence and had preliminary discussions with Sprint. Then, on September 9, 1999, Management provided the Board in executive session with a "heads up" about the potential transaction. Management also distributed to the Board materials from SSB in advance of an October 4, 1999, special Board meeting and distributed additional materials at the meeting. The minutes of the Board meeting and the Acting Secretary's notes from this meeting reflect extensive consideration of the proposed merger, as well as advice from counsel regarding the Board's fiduciary duties. WorldCom's attempt to merge with Sprint clearly fit with the Company's strategic goal of becoming a player in the wireless area, although it is not clear how Sprint's remaining assets fit within WorldCom's strategy.

4. Strategic Planning and Acquisition Processes from Early 2000 Onward

The Examiner has even more concerns about the Board's and Management's attention to acquisition strategy in the context of a coherent strategic plan from early 2000 onward. By early 2000, WorldCom's stock price had been falling for six months and the Company's revenue growth had been modest since completion of the MCI transaction. As a consequence, the Examiner believes that, by early 2000, and certainly by the time the Sprint merger was abandoned in July 2000, Management and the Board were obligated to examine seriously WorldCom's future direction. Based upon available information, however, the Examiner believes that the Board and Management engaged in strategic planning practices at this time that were seriously deficient.

As of early 2000, it was apparent that there were significant differences among WorldCom Management as to the strategic direction that the Company should take. During the executive session of the March 2, 2000 Board meeting, Mr. Sidgmore gave a lengthy presentation in which he made clear that he disagreed with the strategic direction that the Company was taking and that he thought that WorldCom should effect a transition from being a telephone company to being a high-technology data company. He voiced his views and responded to Board reactions for over an hour. Such a presentation might be viewed as positive and strategic, except for Mr. Ebbers' introduction: "These are John's views, management has not agreed to [them]." Indeed, Mr. Ebbers disagreed with most of Mr. Sidgmore's views as of March 2000. There is no indication in the Acting Secretary's notes from this executive session or from our interviews that Management or the Board made any decision as to the strategic direction that the Company should take at this time.

The lack of coherent strategic planning in early 2000 may be explained, at least in part, by the fact that the Sprint merger was then pending and members of the Board and Management appear to have believed, at least until approximately June 2000, that WorldCom's proposed merger with Sprint would eventually surmount regulatory hurdles. After these regulatory obstacles caused WorldCom and Sprint to abandon the merger in mid-July 2000, however, Management and the Board apparently recognized that these obstacles would preclude any large acquisitions in the future and that the Company would have to pursue a different strategic direction in order to grow. At this point, the need for careful strategic planning should have been clear.

The Examiner preliminarily concludes that WorldCom's strategic planning efforts and its acquisition activities in 2000 and 2001 reflect significant problems, which probably caused substantial damage to WorldCom. We cover three particular matters in detail:

WorldCom's entry into the managed Web hosting business and the related Intermedia acquisition; the creation of the Tracker stocks; and the failure to pursue WorldCom's potential acquisition by Verizon. These matters point to the continued passivity of the WorldCom Board, even in the light of manifest disregard by Management for proper corporate governance procedures. In short, at a time when the Board should have been more assertive, it instead became increasingly passive and submissive.[4]

B. THE INTERMEDIA ACQUISITION AS A SPECIAL CASE

b.   Intermedia[30]

On September 5, 2000, WorldCom and Intermedia announced that they had entered into a merger agreement, approved on September 1, 2000, by each of their Boards. At that time, Intermedia was engaged primarily in the competitive local exchange carrier business ("CLEC"), but also owned a controlling interest in Digex. WorldCom's primary interest in acquiring Intermedia was to enter the managed Web hosting business through control of Digex. As of September 5, 2000, the transaction was estimated to cost about $6 billion ($3 billion in equity and $3 billion in debt assumption).

The Examiner preliminarily concludes that WorldCom's Board and Management failed to satisfy their fiduciary duties to become fully informed about the Intermedia/Digex transaction, both at the outset on September 1, 2000, and subsequently in early 2001, when WorldCom agreed to amend its merger agreement with Intermedia. The Examiner further concludes preliminarily that if the Board and Management had complied with their fiduciary obligations, this transaction might not have been approved on September 1, 2000, and it almost certainly would have been abandoned in early 2001. Finally, the Examiner preliminarily concludes that by continuing with the transaction, WorldCom wasted Company assets amounting to at least several billion dollars. The exact amount is subject to future calculation.

i.   WorldCom's Interest in Digex

In August 2000, WorldCom was investigating a possible combination with Global Center. Global Center personnel were scheduled to visit WorldCom's headquarters in Jackson,

---

[4]   Second Interim Report of Dick Thornburgh, Bankruptcy Court Examiner, dated June 9, 2003 and filed in the WorldCom bankruptcy, *In re WorldCom, Inc.,* Case No. 02-15533 (AJG), U.S. Bankruptcy Court, Southern District of New York at 45–50.

[30]   Additional data pertaining to the Intermedia transaction is contained in Appendix 6.

Mississippi, on Thursday, August 31, 2000. On August 30th, Global Center informed WorldCom that it understood that the meeting was a week later. This caused Mr. Ebbers to become suspicious and, after several phone calls, Management discovered that Global Center was pursuing the acquisition of Digex. Mr. Ebbers is reported to have been greatly upset with what he viewed as questionable conduct by Global Center, and Mr. Ebbers that day decided that WorldCom would seek to acquire Digex.

At approximately 1:30 p.m. on Thursday, August 31st, a team from WorldCom arrived in New York at the offices of Intermedia's attorneys. They met first with Intermedia lawyers and principals and later with Digex principals. At this time, WorldCom's intent was to pursue an acquisition of Digex, which was expected to cost in the range of $8 billion. Later in the afternoon, the focus changed to an acquisition of Intermedia, at a lesser price, which would also give WorldCom control of Digex. By evening, WorldCom had made a $6 billion offer for Intermedia. It appears that WorldCom's due diligence was minimal. One member of Management, who was part of the WorldCom team in New York, estimated that actual due diligence meetings on August 31 lasted between 60 and 90 minutes.

Intermedia informed WorldCom that a deal had to be concluded by 5:00 p.m. on Friday, September 1, 2000, or Intermedia and/or Digex would likely complete a deal with some other entity. Late in the afternoon of August 31st, WorldCom engaged Chase Securities as its financial adviser on the transaction.[31]

As noted, WorldCom's only interest in seeking to acquire Intermedia was to gain control of Digex. WorldCom was not interested in its CLEC assets and instead planned to sell these non-Digex assets in order to reduce the overall cost of the transaction. WorldCom was concerned, however, about Section 203 of the Delaware Corporate Law, which would have prohibited a combination of Digex and WorldCom for three years. WorldCom was eager to have the flexibility to combine WorldCom and Digex sooner than that and thus insisted on obtaining a Section 203 waiver.

Late in the morning of September 1st, Chase Securities sent Mr. Sullivan certain valuation analyses of Intermedia and Digex, which Chase apparently had prepared during the preceding 18 hours. The Chase data did not contain a specific estimated value of Intermedia's non-Digex assets, although one graph suggested a

---

[31] SSB had been advising WorldCom on Intermedia and Digex, but resigned on the afternoon of August 31, 2000 due to a conflict of interest.

value of between $3.1 and $3.5 billion. On September 1, 2000, Mr. Sullivan also received much lower estimate of $1.457 billion from the WorldCom Corporate Development Department

ii. The September 1, 2000 WorldCom Board Meeting

WorldCom Management convened a telephonic Board meeting at 3:30 p.m. Eastern time on September 1, 2000. It is unclear how much notice Management gave the Board of this meeting. One Director recalled getting 90 minutes notice and participating in the meeting by cell phone. Besides the Directors, the meeting was attended by the WorldCom team that was in New York, by Messrs. Ebbers and Sullivan who were in Mississippi, by WorldCom General Counsel Michael Salsbury, who served as Acting Secretary from Washington, D.C., and by representatives from Chase Securities and an outside law firm. The meeting lasted 35 minutes.

Mr. Ebbers described the background to the transaction, including the fact that the WorldCom team had not arrived in New York until the day before the meeting and that Chase Securities had not been engaged until late that day. He also explained that WorldCom had no real interest in Intermedia, a CLEC entity with a network that overlapped with the WorldCom network in eight of 14 cities. Mr. Ebbers advised the Board that WorldCom's intent would be to sell the non-Digex assets. Mr. Ebbers also explained that WorldCom would pay $39 per share for Intermedia common stock, which was currently trading at $22 per share. Mr. Ebbers emphasized that the acquisition of control of Digex would make WorldCom an important player in the managed Web hosting market much faster than the contemplated Jaguar joint venture.

Next, the WorldCom team briefly described its August 31st meetings with Intermedia and Digex personnel and presented their general views on the transaction. Mr. Sullivan then informed the Board that, if WorldCom proceeded with the transaction, it would issue approximately $3 billion in stock and assume $3 billion in debt. He also stated that WorldCom could likely sell Intermedia's non-Digex assets for close to $3 billion. The Chase Securities representative made a brief presentation about the estimated value of Intermedia, suggesting that Intermedia's non-Digex assets could be worth as much as $3–3.5 billion, but provided no fairness opinion, and no one asked about its absence or even questioned the basis for the estimate.

Mr. Ebbers stated that WorldCom, in effect, was in an auction, an apparent reference to the competing bid that Intermedia and/or

Digex allegedly planned to accept if a WorldCom deal were not struck by 5:00 p.m. After brief further discussion, the Board approved the deal unanimously. No Director voiced any objection to the transaction.[32] No one advised the Board of its fiduciary responsibility to become informed about all relevant facts.[33]

This approval process troubles the Examiner. The Examiner understands that in mergers and acquisitions it is sometimes necessary to act with considerable speed. However, the speed of the $6 billion Intermedia transaction seems quite extraordinary—described as "warp speed" by one member of Management—and it is difficult to conceive how the WorldCom Board could have become adequately informed in the course of a 35-minute "presentation" and without having reviewed any supporting documentation. As one Director stated when asked whether the Board was adequately informed regarding the proposed acquisition of Intermedia on September 1, 2000, "God himself could not have made the decision in one day." Indeed, this appears to be an instance in which the Board simply proceeded based upon Management's word and nothing else.[34]

At the time of the September 1, 2000 Board meeting, WorldCom's financial performance, like that of other telecommunications companies, was declining, and the Board should, as a consequence, have been exercising extra care in evaluating the Company's proposed acquisitions. Instead, it appears to the Examiner that the Board brought virtually no scrutiny to bear on this transaction. One Director stated that the Intermedia transaction was the worst ever completed by WorldCom. Another Director said that "Intermedia was the worst transaction we did" and that "[w]e paid $6 billion and got nothing in return." This same Director also stated that Mr. Sullivan at some point described the Intermedia acquisition as an "ego deal for Bernie,"

[32]   One Director, who had been very involved in the Jaguar joint venture effort, recalled hearing about the meeting from Mr. Ebbers at about 2:00 p.m. on September 1 and telling Mr. Ebbers that he did not think that a $6 billion Intermedia acquisition made sense when compared to the much less expensive Jaguar joint venture. This Director did not repeat these views at the September 1st Board meeting and voted for the transaction to make the vote unanimous. Other Directors had doubts as well but did not express them.

[33]   The Acting Secretary to the Board informed the Examiner that he took detailed notes of the Board meeting because he knew that they would likely be important to a Hart-Scott-Rodino filing. The notes reflect no person advising the Board of its fiduciary responsibilities. Others recollect no such advice.

[34]   Several persons whom we interviewed suggested that the Board might have been sufficiently informed about the Intermedia transaction because the Board had heard about managed Web hosting on two prior occasions—the March 2 and June 1, 2000 presentations by Mr. Sidgmore. The Examiner disagrees. Those discussions concerned managed Web hosting in general and the Jaguar joint venture specifically. There was never any discussion of a transaction such as the Intermedia acquisition, which cost approximately $6 billion and was premised in part on WorldCom's unsubstantiated ability to sell Intermedia's non-Digex assets for $3–3.5 billion.

because Mr. Ebbers did not want Global Center to get Digex. Another Director commented that, with respect to the Intermedia transaction, the Board received "no information" and that the deal should not have been approved on September 1, 2000. He said that the Board had been pressured by Mr. Ebbers to approve the deal. Still another Director stated during an interview when the discussion turned to the Intermedia transaction, "pardon me while I throw up."

iii. The Amendment to the Merger Agreement

As troubling as the September 1, 2000 Intermedia approval process appears, the Examiner is even more troubled by subsequent events. The Intermedia transaction underwent significant changes, which gave WorldCom the right to abandon the acquisition. Instead, Management, with no prior Board approval, decided to renegotiate the transaction and to amend the merger agreement. When this ultimately came to the Board's attention, Board members did not object. The Examiner believes that this process reflects a severe failure on the part of both Management and the Board.

During the fall of 2000, several events occurred that affected the WorldCom/Intermedia merger in material respects. First, shortly after the announcement of the merger, Digex minority shareholders commenced litigation against Intermedia, WorldCom and others, claiming (among other things) that the Section 203 waiver was improper and that minority shareholders were getting insufficient value for their interests in Digex. This litigation was reported to the WorldCom Board at its meetings on September 7 and November 16, 2000. On December 13, 2000, the Delaware Chancery Court issued a decision in which it refused to enjoin the merger, but suggested that WorldCom, if it went through with the merger, could be exposed to significant damages—reportedly as high as $2.5 billion. WorldCom's Directors were at least generally familiar with this decision.

Second, during the fall of 2000 and thereafter, the market for CLEC assets fell sharply, and efforts by Chase Securities to market the Intermedia assets were unsuccessful. Several persons at WorldCom who were involved in the Intermedia transaction stated that, if the decline in the value of CLEC assets could have been predicted, the Intermedia deal clearly would not have made sense from the outset. At a minimum, Management should have been aware that the sharp decline in CLEC values necessitated reconsideration of the Intermedia deal, because the Board previously had been advised that the Intermedia assets could bring $3–3.5 billion and pay down all the Intermedia debt. On November 16, 200[*sic*], Management informed the Board that it had been unable to find a purchaser for Intermedia's assets, and Directors have confirmed that they were generally aware of the decline in the value of the Intermedia assets.

As a result of these developments, WorldCom took the position in early 2001 that it was free not to continue with the Intermedia merger. Indeed, Mr. Salsbury recalls a detailed conversation around Christmas 2000 with Mr. Ebbers in which he advised Mr. Ebbers that WorldCom could terminate the transaction. Outside counsel had similar conversations with Mr. Salsbury, Mr. Ebbers and Mr. Sullivan.

Nevertheless, WorldCom decided not to walk away from the deal. Instead, Management negotiated and executed, with no prior Board approval, the following agreements:

- A settlement of the Digex litigation, requiring WorldCom to pay $15 million and to issue $165 million of WorldCom stock to a settlement fund for Digex minority shareholders;

- An agreement with Digex requiring WorldCom to enter into a series of commercial arrangements, as well as an agreement after the completion of the Intermedia merger to fund Digex's business plans for 2001 and 2002, at a projected cost of as much as $900 million; and

- An amendment to the WorldCom/Intermedia merger agreement, reducing the exchange ratio to one share of WorldCom stock for each share of Intermedia stock and changing other terms so that it would be much more difficult for WorldCom to abandon the transaction if Intermedia's financial fortunes were to worsen further, as they subsequently did.

The cost to WorldCom of the overall transaction, not including the funding of Digex in 2001–02, and not including the $15 million in cash and $165 million in stock paid in the Digex settlement, was estimated in a related registration statement filed on Form S-4 to be $4.974 billion as of February 13, 2001.[35]

---

[35]   Separately, a member of WorldCom's Investor Relations Department estimated the cost of the merger as of February 15, 2001 as follows:

Value of WorldCom Equity to be issued	$1,257,510,000
Intermedia Debt to be assumed	2,462,000,000
Intermedia Preferred Stock to be acquired	656,000,000
Digex Settlement Fund	165,000,000
Digex Litigation Expenses	15,000,000
Estimated Intermedia Cash	(340,000,000)
	$4,215,510,000

The merger amendment was executed on behalf of WorldCom by Mr. Salsbury on February 14 or 15, 2001. Mr. Salsbury advised the Examiner that he believed that Board approval had previously been obtained and that he was informed by Mr. Sullivan or Mr. Ebbers that he could sign the amendment on WorldCom's behalf. The Examiner's investigation has revealed that no prior Board approval had been obtained and to date, the Examiner has found no evidence that Management had polled the Directors for their views before executing the amended agreement.[36]

The Examiner is continuing to investigate the circumstances under which WorldCom's Management executed a material amendment to the Intermedia merger agreement with no prior Board approval. At present, the facts appear to be as follows.

- During the first two weeks of February 2001, there were intensive negotiations to settle the Digex litigation, which negotiations apparently tied any such settlement to an amendment to the WorldCom/Intermedia merger agreement.

- At a meeting on February 7, 2001, WorldCom reached a tentative agreement with Intermedia as to certain revised terms of the merger agreement, subject to Board approval.

- On February 12, 2001, with most or all of the terms of the amended merger agreement apparently negotiated, outside corporate counsel to WorldCom sent an e-mail to Mr. Borghardt, inside counsel for WorldCom, attaching a proposed Written Consent by which the WorldCom Board would approve the merger agreement amendment, the Digex settlement, and the Digex commercial agreements. This e-mail and its attachment reflect the apparent understanding among legal counsel that WorldCom Board approval was required.

---

[36]   One former Director advised the Examiner that he could not recall being polled before the Intermedia merger amendment was executed but that he was confident that Mr. Ebbers had done so. The Examiner has two observations in response. First, there is no evidence that any such polling took place. We talked with many Directors and asked all or virtually all about possible polling. Not one had a specific recollection that it occurred and a number stated that they were sure it did not occur.

Second, while polling would alleviate some of the Examiner's concerns, polling would not eliminate the most significant concerns. The Intermedia merger amendment, with the Digex settlement as part of it, was a complex revision to the original transaction, which would be difficult to summarize adequately in a brief polling telephone call. Further, for polling to have been complete and adequate, Directors would have needed information regarding the status of the Intermedia asset sale efforts and how the lack of sales would likely affect the economics of the transaction. There is no evidence of any such disclosures. In sum, even if there had been polling, the Examiner preliminarily concludes that it is still likely that both Management and the Board failed to fulfill their fiduciary duties.

- On February 13, 2001, at 1:10 p.m., Mr. Borghardt sent Mr. Salsbury and outside counsel a revised draft of the Written Consent that incorporated Mr. Borghardt's suggested revisions. The cover e-mail stated that once Mr. Salsbury approved the draft, Mr. Borghardt would obtain Mr. Ebbers' approval and then "route it to other Directors." This communication appears to reflect counsels' understanding that no Board approval had been obtained as of the afternoon of February 13, 2001.

- According to a February 14, 2001 e-mail to Mr. Sullivan from his secretary, Mr. Salsbury was pressured by Intermedia's investment bankers to have WorldCom execute the merger amendment, which Mr. Salsbury reportedly had said must be signed on February 14.

- On February 14, 2001, Mr. Salsbury received from another in-house counsel a Chase update on efforts to sell Intermedia's assets, stating that the best, hoped-for bid for all of the assets was between $800 million and $1.8 billion—far less than the estimates given to the Directors on September 1, 2000. There is no evidence that the new estimate was presented to WorldCom's Board.[37]

- On February 14, 2001, or possibly February 15, 2001, Mr. Salsbury executed the first amendment to the merger agreement, apparently after being authorized to do so by Mr. Ebbers or Mr. Sullivan. Mr. Salsbury informed the Examiner that Mr. Ebbers told him that the Board already had approved the amended merger agreement.

- On February 15, 2001, WorldCom issued a press release announcing the Digex settlement and the amended merger agreement. The release stated falsely that WorldCom's Board had approved the Digex settlement. Similarly, a subsequent SEC filing by WorldCom on Form S-4 stated falsely that "[t]he WorldCom board of directors approved the merger as contemplated in the amended merger agreement on February 14, 2001."

- In fact, the WorldCom Board did not actually approve the Digex settlement and the amended merger agreement until it met on March 1, 2001.

---

[37] Scott Hamilton, former head of the Investor Relations Department at WorldCom, informed the Examiner that he believed it was "common knowledge" by February 2001 that the Intermedia assets were worth less than $1.4 billion.

On March 1, 2001, a written consent resolution was circulated at the quarterly Board meeting, where Mr. Salsbury briefly (10 minutes or less) described the terms of the Digex settlement. There is no indication that any Director at the meeting spoke up or questioned the actions of Management.[38] Rather, the Board was asked to and did rubber-stamp Management's actions, receiving no substantive data as to why the amended merger agreement made sense. There is no indication that any Director asked for or received an estimate of the value of the Intermedia assets as of March 1, 2001. Instead, it appears that Mr. Salsbury merely reported that sale efforts were continuing, but that he made no estimate of the possible proceeds from any eventual sale of Intermedia's assets. If the Intermedia assets were believed to be worth as little as $800 million as of mid-February 2001, then the estimated $4.974 billion price of the transaction suggested that the associated costs to WorldCom would be substantially higher than the Board assumed when it approved the initial deal.

As of September 1, 2000, the Intermedia merger was expected to cost about $6 billion, with $3 billion of WorldCom equity issued and $3 billion of debt assumed. The $6 billion cost was then to be reduced to $2.5–3 billion, through sale of the Intermedia assets for $3–3.5 billion. As of February 2001, the Intermedia transaction was expected to cost $4.974 billion, plus up to $900 million for Digex operating costs and $180 million of cash and stock for the Digex settlement, for a total cost of as much as $6.054 billion. The prospect of reducing that price by even $1 billion through the sale of Intermedia assets was remote. Accordingly, by February 15, 2001, the "price" of this transaction had risen greatly since September 1, 2000.

iv. Preliminary Intermedia Conclusions

Although the Examiner's investigation is continuing, we have sufficient information to set forth some preliminary conclusions related to the Intermedia transaction.

First, the WorldCom Board never received any documents relating to this transaction. The Examiner finds it disturbing, and almost certainly contrary to its fiduciary responsibilities, for the WorldCom Board to have approved such a material transaction

---

[38]   One Director advised the Examiner that he spoke to Mr. Ebbers in private and expressed his view that proceeding with the Intermedia merger was a grave mistake. The same Director spoke in private with Mr. Sullivan, who agreed that the acquisition of Intermedia was inadvisable, but who told him that Mr. Ebbers was determined to acquire control of Digex. Another Director said the Board had the opportunity to call off the deal, but failed to do so. Certain Directors also suggested that they might not have been aware that Management had already executed the merger amendment. This does not seem credible. Board members have acknowledged reading The Wall Street Journal, which, on February 16, 2001, reported on the amended merger agreement.

without demanding more information. The Board's conduct with respect to the Intermedia transaction is similar to the violative conduct of the Board in the Smith v. Van Gorkom case discussed previously.

Second, the Examiner's investigation has revealed that certain Directors had doubts about this transaction from the outset and great doubts as of March 1, 2001. They also had doubts about Mr. Ebbers' leadership after the Company's loans to him were revealed in November 2000.[39] The Examiner cannot discern why the outside Directors, at a minimum, would not, by March 1, 2001, have recognized their responsibility to consider carefully possible actions to take, including whether Mr. Ebbers should continue as WorldCom's Chief Executive Officer. This is particularly so because, at that March 1, 2001 Board meeting, a special executive session was convened without Mr. Ebbers, to enable the Board to discuss threatened litigation regarding the Company's loans to Mr. Ebbers. Given the fact that the Board was then aware that Management had committed WorldCom to the Intermedia deal without Board approval, the Examiner believes that the Board should have used the occasion to discuss Mr. Ebbers' leadership, as well as possibly the roles of others. Nevertheless, to the Examiner's knowledge, nothing of the sort occurred.

Third, the Examiner preliminarily concludes that if the WorldCom Board had fulfilled its fiduciary responsibilities, it likely would have rejected the Intermedia merger as of the February 2001 amended agreement. A properly informed Board would have learned that the prospects for any large proceeds from an Intermedia asset sale were slim. A properly informed Board also would have learned that Digex's operating results were not overly robust and that it might cost WorldCom as much as $900 million to fund Digex's business plan over the next two years. Further, a properly informed Board would have learned that hoped-for synergies between Digex and WorldCom would be difficult to achieve. . . . At a minimum, the decision whether to approve the amended merger agreement, particularly at a time when WorldCom's results were quite disappointing, should have been a very difficult one for the Board, engendering considerable debate.[5]

---

[39] One Director informed the Examiner that, at least for this Director, confidence in Mr. Ebbers was "totally eroded" when the loans were revealed to the full Board.

[5] Second Interim Report of Dick Thornburgh, Bankruptcy Court Examiner, dated June 9, 2003 and filed in the WorldCom bankruptcy, *In re WorldCom, Inc.*, Case No. 02-15533 (AJG), U.S. Bankruptcy Court, Southern District of New York at 52–64.

QUESTIONS ON THE WORLDCOM BOARD
AND STRATEGIC PLANNING

To a considerable extent, the Examiner's criticism is the stuff of pre-Enron duty of care decisions—real old-time religion. *Smith v. Van Gorkom,* 488 A.2d 858 (Del. 1985) is one of the classic decisions on duty of care. It concluded that a board was grossly negligent because—among other facts too complicated to summarize here—the board approved a proposal to sell the entire company largely on a 20-minute oral presentation by the CEO, without any documentation before the board to support the adequacy of the price and without having before it a written summary of the other terms of the deal. The Examiner's point about the brief consideration that the WorldCom Board gave to some of the acquisitions is in the same vein. Indeed, the Examiner cites and quotes from *Van Gorkom* on pages preceding the excerpt you just read.[6]

Consider first whether a board of directors should ensure that a company has a strategic plan.

The Examiner criticizes the WorldCom Board in part because the Board did not participate in developing a strategic plan that guided the acquisitions, and indeed at times let acquisitions proceed even though management did not have any real strategic plan (227–229). But the Examiner is somewhat ambivalent. He says that the lack of planning was fine in 1997 and 1998 because the "telecommunications industry and WorldCom in particular appeared to be achieving excellent results during this period and the opportunistic approach that Management and the Board followed appeared to be serving WorldCom well" (236). But "[b]y early 2000, WorldCom's stock price had been falling for six months and the Company's revenue growth had been modest since the completion of the MCI transaction. As a consequence, the Examiner believes that, by early 2000, and certainly by the time the Sprint merger was abandoned in July 2000, Management and the Board were obligated to examine seriously WorldCom's future direction. . . . [T]he Examiner believes that the Board and Management engaged in strategic planning practices at this time that were seriously deficient" (243). The Examiner seems to imply that a huge publicly traded company may usefully go without a plan as long as the company is on a roll. Couldn't one just as easily argue that the deleterious effects of a strategically flawed acquisition can take a year or two to develop, and that therefore a sound plan during the fat years might avoid lean times that would otherwise ensue? Should a board wait to assert control until mistakes create problems or the industry in which the company participates suffers a decline?

Suppose that at another company—not WorldCom—

- the board invites a consultant to talk to the board about whether to create a strategic plan;

---

6   *Id.* at 18, 23; not included in this book.

- the consultant advises that the company's industry is too dynamic for any "plan" and that a "plan" will hurt the company by making it slow afoot—unable to take advantage of targets of opportunity;

- management says the same thing;

- the consultant and management provide the board with written analyses to the same effect;

- the board discusses the matter for four hours over two meetings and concludes that the company should not have a "plan"; and

- the minutes extensively document all of these steps.

Would there be any question, under the duty of care standard, that the board had made a protected business judgment that the company should have no plan? Assuming that the absence of a plan created no legal exposure, would the board be making a wise choice by deciding not to adopt a plan under these circumstances? Putting it another way, is there a difference between board conduct that satisfies minimum legal standards and board conduct that constitutes good governance?

Does the circumstance that a company is constantly buying other companies make it more or less desirable to have a plan?

How detailed should such a plan be? Are "strategic objectives" at the level of generality set out on page 237 enough—"(1) rationalizing some of MCI's assets (in particular, its MCI SystemHouse Corp. . . . . subsidiary), an objective that included entering into outsourcing arrangements, possibly with EDS; (2) pursuing broadband opportunities; and (3) expanding into wireless lines of business"? If not, how much detail should a board demand in a strategic plan?

The Examiner seems to think that the Board should have obtained "fairness opinions" for more of WorldCom's acquisitions, or at least should have established some reasonable guideline to determine when a fairness opinion should be obtained (228, with "fairness opinion" defined in n.13 on that page; and see the remark on 232 that WorldCom had no "financial adviser" for the AOL transaction and similar remarks on page 234 about the Brooks Fiber transaction and on page 239 about the EDS transaction). What do you think?

Fairness opinions are undoubtedly useful in litigation if a board is ever challenged on an acquisition. And fairness opinions may be worth the money just for the protection they can provide in any later lawsuit.

But how helpful are fairness opinions to board decision making? Suppose that, before the crucial board meeting, the top officers whisper to the investment bankers (who will most likely be the "financial adviser" to which note 13 refers) that the officers believe the acquisition is a terrific one and that, while the price is high, the synergies should be large. Suppose that the company has made multiple acquisitions in the past with the help of the investment banking firm advising on the transaction here and that the company will likely make more acquisitions in the future. Suppose that management has had a key role in selecting the financial adviser for acquisitions and that the investment banking firm knows that to be the case. Will the investment bankers be tempted to adjust some of the assumptions to their valuation models so that the price the board considers falls within what the investment bankers will say is the reasonable range—and is therefore "fair"?

How can a board work with a financial adviser to obtain the adviser's genuine opinion—not just the opinion that the adviser believes management wants to hear?

The Examiner seems to think that management should have presented to the Board staff conclusions that the SkyTel acquisition would not be strategic unless combined with other wireless acquisitions, and that recent SkyTel results were lackluster (241). The Examiner seems to think that one of the executives who spoke to the Board should have told directors that his personal opinion, and the opinion of some other executives, was that the transaction was mediocre (*id.*). The Examiner notes that Sidgmore made a lengthy presentation to the Board at one point in which he disagreed with the strategic direction of the company (243).

Should different points of view on an acquisition or a strategy be presented to a board? How would such presentations affect the relationship between the CEO and the board? How would they affect the group dynamics of the board itself?

The Examiner appears to believe that it is helpful to have counsel or someone else say—at meetings when the Board is going to vote on acquisitions—that the board should be careful to discharge its fiduciary duties (done for the MCI deal (236) but not for the EDS (240) or Intermedia (247) transactions). Is that likely to make a difference? Or are we just talking about making a record for a defense in any possible lawsuit down the road?

What about the Board and due diligence on acquisitions? Should the Board have told management how to perform due diligence or established "guidelines" for due diligence (230)?

The Examiner says that WorldCom announced the original EDS deal before the Board officially approved it (239), and that management then (i) negotiated amendments to the Intermedia acquisition (at a time when WorldCom might have been able to walk away from the deal), (ii) signed the amendments, and (iii) announced agreement to the amendments before a Board vote (249–252). What should a board do when something like that happens?

Is it possible that Ebbers just got "deal happy" and therefore pursued more acquisitions than were good for WorldCom? Why can that happen to upper management? What can a board do to work against any such tendency?

CHAPTER 7

ENRON PART I: ACCOUNTING BACKGROUND, BROADBAND, AND CHEWCO

■ ■ ■

We now commence our study of the case to which we most frequently trace modern corporate governance. Enron is most famous for opaque structured finance transactions. Those transactions were engineered to create accounting results. Enron's accounting was so complex that we do not have time to study it all. We will study Enron's accounting selectively.

This Chapter Seven begins with concepts we need for that study. It then turns to Enron's broadband transactions, to see the complexity of Enron deals and to consider the effect of complexity on board review of transactions. The chapter concludes with the Chewco transactions, to see how easy it can be for a board to miss a key transaction detail and to provide a first taste of the difficulties created by the circumstance that some Enron insiders made a great deal of money, personally, from their involvement in Enron's deals.

A. CONCEPTS IMPORTANT TO OUR ENRON STUDY

Before we get into any of Enron's transactions, we must review four important concepts.

The first concept is "marking to market." Accounting rules prescribe that companies record many assets on its books at cost—what the company paid to get them. Companies record some such assets at cost minus depreciation or amortization. For example, a building might be purchased for $30 million and depreciated over 30 years, with the company recording $1 million in depreciation cost each year, and its financial statements reflecting a decline in the recorded value of this asset by that amount each year.

Of course, the price that a company paid for an asset may not reflect its current value. So some assets are "marked to market," which means that their value on the balance sheet is adjusted at the end of each reporting period to their then-current fair value. As the value of such assets changes from one quarter to another, the increase or decrease is recorded in the income statement.

The second concept is a "special purpose entity," or SPE. An SPE is a legal entity (such as a partnership) created for a specific purpose. Under the accounting rules in effect at the time Enron was organizing SPEs (now significantly changed), a company did not have to consolidate an SPE's financials with the company's financials if (1) an *owner independent of the company* made a genuine equity investment in the SPE constituting at least *3% of the SPE's total capitalization, with that equity remaining at risk* throughout the SPE's transaction with the company and (2) the *independent owner exercised control* over the SPE. If an SPE met these tests, Enron could treat the SPE as an independent entity. Enron could sell assets to the SPE and record revenue and profit from those sales. And to the extent the SPE incurred debt, Enron would not have to include that debt in its own financial statements. Part of Enron's problems involved setting up SPEs that did not meet the tests in the accounting rules and therefore could not be considered independent entities.

The third concept is a "hedge." A hedge is a way to reduce risk. Here is a short example to illustrate the economic meaning of a hedge. Assume that (i) Company A owns stock in Company X, (ii) the X stock is today worth $1,000,000, but (iii) Company A is worried that the price of the X stock might fall. Company A might want to hedge against that possibility and protect itself against a large loss from an X stock price drop. To do so, Company A might contract with Company B and pay B $50,000, in exchange for B's promise that if A's investment in X falls below $900,000 by January 1 of next year, B will pay A on that date the difference between $900,000 and the January 1 market value of A's X stock. By the contract, Company A would have hedged against a loss in excess of $100,000 in the value of the X stock that A owns.

Of course, it is critically important that Company B have the economic ability to make such a payment. Otherwise, the hedge has no value.[1] Similarly, A does not want to be in a position where A itself has guaranteed the economic ability of B to pay on the hedge. Otherwise, A has not truly hedged its loss. Some of Enron's problems arose from the questionable economic viability of its hedges.

Putting to one side this simple economic explanation, accounting rules include highly technical and complex provisions relating to hedging.

At Enron, hedging was related to marking to market. If a marked-to-market asset lost value in a quarter, that loss hit the Enron income statement *unless* Enron had hedged against the loss and accounting rules permitted the hedge to reduce the mark-to-market loss. To the extent the

---

[1]   The risk that B will be unable to pay on the hedge is called "counterparty risk."

loss was hedged sufficiently for accounting rules, Enron did not need to record it.

The fourth concept is a "related-party transaction." A company's "related parties" include its officers and directors. A transaction to which a company is a party and in which an officer or director has a material interest is a "related-party transaction" and must be reported under the securities law if the transaction exceeds a specified amount, which was $60,000 at the time of the critical events at Enron.

In addition to federal securities laws, generally accepted accounting principles require that related-party transactions be disclosed.

Such a transaction presents the possibility that its form will not accurately reflect its substance and that the price that the company pays or receives will differ—to the disadvantage of the company—from the price the company would have paid or received had the related party not been personally interested in the deal. Companies accordingly use a variety of methods to identify, approve, and monitor related-party transactions. A company might have a code of conduct that prohibits related-party transactions absent a specific approval by the company's board of directors. The company might have in place a protocol requiring that no officer or director at the company who has a material interest in a transaction can negotiate in that transaction on behalf of the company, and that the negotiator for the company must not report to the interested officer or director. The company might employ a system to check whether the price that it pays or receives in any related-party transaction is fair and does not deviate materially from the price that the company would pay or receive if no related party had a personal and material interest in the transaction.

Enron ran into trouble, in part, because some transactions with SPEs were related-party transactions. Many were related-party transactions because of the personal financial interest that Andrew Fastow—Enron's CFO—had in those SPEs. The controls that were set up to ensure that the SPEs did not take advantage of Enron were not effectively implemented, and the disclosure in securities filings about those related-party transactions did not provide sufficient detail for readers to understand the economic importance of those transactions to Fastow.

Fastow's role in some of the SPEs also raised questions about the independence of those SPEs for purposes of determining whether Enron had to consolidate the SPEs' financial numbers into the Enron financial statements.

With that preliminary briefing finished, only one information note remains before we get into the Enron facts: As was true at WorldCom, the Enron board undertook an investigation after the company came undone, and the special board committee conducting that inquiry prepared an extensive report. And, as was true at WorldCom, the bankruptcy court in which Enron filed for protection appointed an examiner who gathered information and produced a long explanation of what had gone wrong. The remainder of this chapter, and the next chapter, quote liberally from the Enron special board committee's report and reports by the Enron bankruptcy examiner.

B. FINANCIAL RESULTS FROM BROADBAND TRANSACTIONS

In the following pages, you will see first an explanation of an "FAS 140" transaction. The explanation includes a diagram. The "Trust" shown in the diagram is an SPE. Then you will find a description of a deal that Enron used to create accounting earnings from a broadband operation that was not yet up and running. The excerpts come from pages 109–10 and 29–32 of the Second Interim Report of Neal Batson, Court-Appointed Examiner, dated January 21, 2003 and filed in the Enron bankruptcy, *In re Enron Corp.* Case No. 01-16034 (AJG), U.S. Bankruptcy Court, Southern District of New York.

B. Background of FAS 140 Transactions

When Enron monetized an asset in a FAS 140 Transaction, the "Sponsor" (generally a subsidiary or unconsolidated equity affiliate of Enron) that transferred the asset received a payment equal to the amount financed through the structure, and Enron recognized as income on its financial statements all, or its share of, the difference between those cash proceeds and the carrying value of the asset. Despite the "sale" of these assets, Enron continued to treat them as part of its own holdings. Then, through a Total Return Swap, Enron: (i) agreed to make payments to its counterparty (usually an SPE created for the transaction or the lenders to the SPE) equal to the scheduled payments (and interest thereon) on the amounts borrowed by the SPE under a credit facility (a "Credit Facility"), which was roughly equal to the purchase price of the transferred asset; and (ii) remained entitled to all amounts produced by the transferred asset (whether by sale of the asset or otherwise), except, in some transactions, for amounts used to satisfy the small portion of the purchase price that the SPE funded through the sale of equity rather than borrowings (typically at least 3% of the purchase price of the asset) and a capped return thereon. In those transactions where there was an equity investor, the Total Return Swap typically provided that the proceeds of the underlying asset were distributed first to the Enron party to the swap in an amount equal to the related debt financing, then to the equity holder up to a capped return and, finally, all remaining amounts to that Enron party.

The following is a simplified diagram of a typical FAS 140 Transaction:

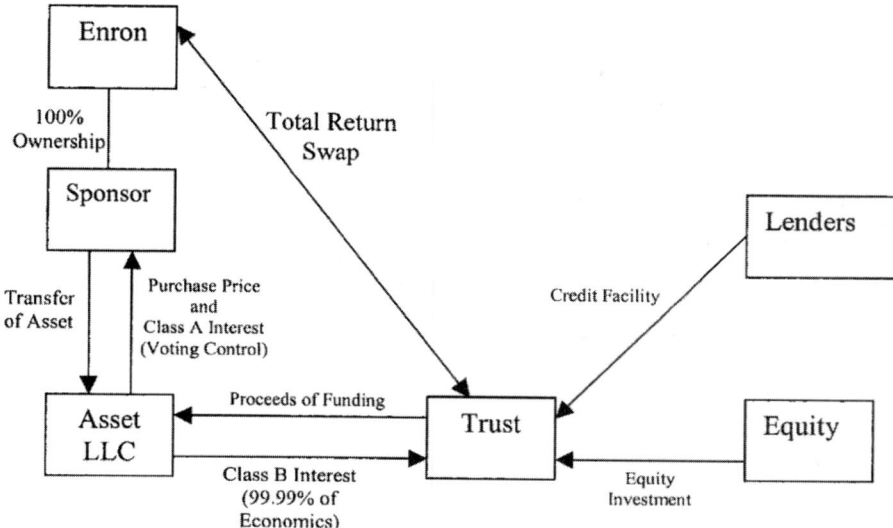

The Total Return Swaps were marked-to-market by Enron. As a result, Enron reported the effects of subsequent decreases or increases in the value of the financed asset on its balance sheet and in its income statement. The Total Return Swaps made Enron's FAS 140 Transactions more closely resemble loans to Enron rather than sales of an asset.[2]

* * *

The Blockbuster Transaction. On July 19, 2000, Enron announced that it had entered into "a 20-year, exclusive agreement to deliver a Blockbuster entertainment service, initially featuring movies-on-demand, via the Enron Intelligent Network."[78] This agreement reflected nothing more than an aspiration. Enron did not have the technology to deliver VOD on a commercially viable basis and Blockbuster did not have rights to movies to be delivered. Nevertheless, Enron contributed this contract to a

---

[2]   Second Interim Report of Neal Batson, Court-Appointed Examiner, dated January 21, 2003 and filed in the Enron bankruptcy, *In re Enron Corp.*, Case No. 01-16034 (AJG), U.S. Bankruptcy Court, Southern District of New York at 109–10, http://www.ragm.com/enron/elib/examinerreport2.pdf.

[78]   Enron Press Release, "Enron and Blockbuster to Launch Entertainment On-Demand Service Via the Enron Intelligent Network," July 19, 2000, at AB025203626 [AB025203626–AB025203629].

subsidiary, EBS Content Systems, LLC ("EBS"), and then sold a 45% interest in EBS to the Hawaii FAS 140 securitization structure[79] for $57 million, recognizing a $53 million gain and $57 million in funds flow from operations.

In order to recognize this gain, applicable GAAP required that it be practical to measure the fair value of the asset.[80] Andersen appraised the value of this contractual arrangement at between $120 million and $150 million, even though the anticipated business did not have the technology to deliver its product or any rights to the product it proposed to deliver. In arriving at this valuation, Andersen made the following assumptions:

- The LLC would begin commercial operations of its VOD business in 10 metro areas, each with a population of 1.6 million, within the next 12 months;

- The LLC would add eight additional metro areas per year until 2010 and these metro areas would grow at 1% per year;

- Digital subscriber lines (DSLs) would run to 5% of the households in these metro areas in 2001 growing to 32% by 2010 (this based on a Morgan Stanley report);

- The number of these DSL lines that would have sufficient speed to carry VOD would be 5% in 2001 growing to 80% in 2010;

- The percentage of eligible DSL subscribers using VOD would be 5% in 2001 and grow to 70% by 2010; and

- EBS would garner 50% of this market (this based on "research" performed by EBS and McKinsey & Co.).[81]

Using these assumptions, Andersen projected future cash flows and discounted the cash flows to present value using discount rates ranging from 31% to 34%. While a venture capitalist might find the analysis informative in assessing whether to make a seed investment in a speculative start-up situation, given the underlying facts, the Examiner questions whether it was appropriate for a public company to transfer this contract to a

---

[79] The Hawaii FAS 140 transaction was discussed in detail in the September Report and is discussed in Appendix M (FAS 140 Transactions).

[80] FAS 125, *Accounting for Transfers and Servicing of Financial Assets and Extinguishments of Liabilities* ("FAS 125") ¶ 45.

[81] Andersen Memorandum to Roger Willard, Andersen, from Warren White, Andersen, and Brent Dickey, Andersen, regarding FMV of EBS Content Systems LLC, Jan. 19, 2000 [PSI00028563–PSA00028575]; Andersen Memorandum to Roger Willard, Andersen, from Warren White, Andersen, and Brent Dickey, Andersen, regarding FMV of EBS Content Systems LLC, Mar. 15, 2001 [PSI00020764–PSA00020777].

structured finance vehicle, assign it a speculative value and recognize that amount currently as income and cash flow from operating activities. Of the $63 million of revenue that Enron reported as earned by its Broadband Services business segment in the fourth quarter of 2000,[82] $53 million was attributable to this monetization transaction, code-named "Braveheart."

On March 9, 2001, Enron announced that it had terminated its exclusive relationship with Blockbuster.[83] The press release stated that:

> Enron intends to initiate discussions with various content providers for delivering their content over the Enron platform. In addition to streaming movies to the television, Enron is working on agreements to deliver games, television programming and music via the Enron Intelligent Network.[84]

Apparently, Enron's intention "to initiate discussions" was even more valuable than its "exclusive relationship with Blockbuster," because in the first quarter of 2001, after this announcement, Enron marked to market the Total Return Swap (as defined below) it used in the fourth quarter Blockbuster monetization and monetized the Total Return Swap within the Hawaii structure, writing up the value by approximately $58 million. As a result, Enron recognized approximately $58 million of revenue and funds flow. To date, the Examiner has not located any executed contracts for EBS to deliver games, television programming or music.

By late summer 2001, Enron recognized that EBS, earlier valued at $115 million, did not have a viable business. It considered several options, and ultimately elected to shut EBS down. Thus, within a span of about one year this investment, which resulted in Enron reporting $111 million of gain and $115 million of funds flow from operations in the fourth quarter of 2000 and first quarter of 2001, proved to be worthless. One of the components of the "non-recurring charge" of $1.01 billion that Enron announced in its October 16, 2001 earnings release was a $180 million charge for "restructuring" its Broadband Services business, the business that Enron had described so effusively in its 2000 Annual Report.[3]

---

[82] Enron Press Release, "Enron Reports Recurring Annual Earnings of $1.47 per Diluted Share in 2000 and Fourth Quarter Earnings of $0.41," Jan. 22, 2001, at AB025203633 [AB025203630–AB025203634].

[83] Enron Press Release, "Enron Expanding Entertainment On-Demand Service: Terminates Exclusive Relationship With Blockbuster Inc.," Mar. 9, 2001 [AB025203639].

[84] *Id.*

[3] *Id.* at 29–32.

QUESTIONS ON BROADBAND

Even at this highly distilled level, does the transaction seem complicated to you?

Assume that a similar transaction accounted for a large percentage of one or more figures in a company's financial results and that the transaction came before the board for approval.

Do you think directors would understand the deal?

Would the multifaceted nature of the transaction create the possibility that only a part of it might be included in a summary for a board or only part of it understood by the board?

As near as you can understand the transaction, does anything about it make you wary of reporting funds flow and gain from this deal?

What concerns should a board have about securities law disclosure of such a transaction?

What do you think about Andersen's role in the description of broadband doings at Enron? Would your view be different if Andersen had not been the outside accounting firm that would audit Enron's financial statements?

C. CHEWCO, JEDI, AND SPES

Turn now to Chewco. Chewco was an SPE. Chewco was a participant, with Enron, in a joint venture investment partnership called JEDI. Eventually, Enron and Andersen concluded that Chewco did not meet the requirements for non-consolidation. And since Chewco's satisfaction of those requirements was necessary in order that Enron not consolidate JEDI's financial numbers into Enron numbers, Enron had to restate its financials to include the JEDI numbers. The restated financials increased Enron's debt and decreased Enron's profits.

The following description of the Chewco transaction excerpts from pages 42, 43–54 and 60–67 in the Report of Investigation by the Special Investigative Committee of the Enron Board of Directors.

A. Formation of Chewco

In 1993, Enron and the California Public Employees' Retirement System ("CalPERS") entered into a joint venture investment partnership called Joint Energy Development Investment Limited Partnership ("JEDI"). Enron was the general partner and contributed $250 million in Enron stock. CalPERS was the limited partner and contributed $250 million in cash. Because Enron and

CalPERS had joint control, Enron did not consolidate JEDI into its consolidated financial statements.

In 1997, Enron considered forming a $1 billion partnership with CalPERS called "JEDI II." Enron believed that CalPERS would not invest simultaneously in both JEDI and JEDI II, so Enron suggested it buy out CalPERS' interest in JEDI. Enron and CalPERS attempted to value CalPERS' interest (CalPERS retained an investment bank) and discussed an appropriate buyout price.

In order to maintain JEDI as an unconsolidated entity, Enron needed to identify a new limited partner. Fastow initially proposed that he act as the manager of, and an investor in, a new entity called "Chewco Investments"—named after the Star Wars character "Chewbacca." Although other Enron employees would be permitted to participate in Chewco, Fastow proposed to solicit the bulk of Chewco's equity capital from third-party investors. He suggested that Chewco investors would want a manager who, like him, knew the underlying assets in JEDI and could help manage them effectively. Fastow told Enron employees that Jeffrey Skilling, then Enron's President and Chief Operating Officer ("COO") had approved his participation in Chewco as long as it would not have to be disclosed in Enron's proxy statement.[7]

Both Enron's in-house counsel and its longstanding outside counsel, Vinson & Elkins, subsequently advised Fastow that his participation in Chewco would require (1) disclosure in Enron's proxy statement, and (2) approval from the Chairman and CEO under Enron's Code of Conduct of Business Affairs ("Code of Conduct").[8] As a result, Kopper, an Enron employee who reported to Fastow, was substituted as the proposed manager of Chewco. Unlike Fastow, Kopper was not a senior officer of Enron, so his role in Chewco would not require proxy statement disclosure (but would require approval under Enron's Code of Conduct).

Enron ultimately reached agreement with CalPERS to redeem its JEDI limited partnership interest for $383 million. In order to close that transaction promptly, Chewco was formed as a

---

[7]   Skilling told us that he recalled Fastow's proposing that the Chewco outside investors be members of Fastow's wife's family, and that Skilling told Fastow he did not think that was a good idea.

[8]   Enron's Code of Conduct provided that no full-time officer or employee should "[o]wn an interest in or participate, directly or indirectly, in the profits of any other entity which does business with or is a competitor of the Company, unless such ownership or participation has been previously disclosed in writing to the Chairman of the Board and Chief Executive Officer of Enron Corp. and such officer has determined that such interest or participation does not adversely affect the best interests of the Company."

Delaware limited liability company on very short notice in early November 1997. As initially formed, Kopper (through intermediary entities) was the sole member of both the managing member and regular member of Chewco. Enron's counsel, Vinson & Elkins, prepared the legal documentation for these entities in a period of approximately 48 hours. Enron also put together a bridge financing arrangement, under which Chewco and its members would borrow $383 million from two banks on an unsecured basis to buy CalPERS' interest from JEDI. The loans were to be guaranteed by Enron.

Enron employees involved in the transaction understood that the Chewco structure did not comply with SPE consolidation rules. Kopper, an Enron employee, controlled Chewco, and there was no third-party equity in Chewco. There was only debt. The intention was, by year end, to replace the bridge financing with another structure that would qualify Chewco as an SPE with sufficient outside equity. Ben F. Glisan, Jr., the Enron "transaction support" employee with principal responsibility for accounting matters in the Chewco transaction, believed that such a transaction would preserve JEDI's unconsolidated status if closed by year end.

While Chewco was being formed, Enron and Chewco were negotiating the economic terms (primarily the profit distribution "waterfall") of their JEDI partnership. Kopper was the business negotiator for Chewco. During the negotiations, Fastow contacted Enron's business negotiator (who reported to him) and suggested that he was pushing too hard for Enron and that the deal needed to be closed. Enron's negotiator explained to Fastow the status of the discussions with Kopper, that he believed it was his job to obtain the best economic terms for Enron, and that accepting Kopper's current position would (based on Enron's economic modeling) result in greater benefits to Chewco than would be required if the negotiations continued. We were told that Fastow indicated he was comfortable closing the transaction on the terms then proposed by Kopper. Enron's negotiator told us he was uncomfortable with this discussion and Fastow's intervention, and believes that Enron could have improved its position if he had been permitted to continue the negotiations.

B. Limited Board Approval

The Chewco transaction was presented to the Board's Executive Committee on November 5, 1997, at a meeting held by telephone conference call. The minutes of the meeting reflect that Skilling presented the background of JEDI, and that Fastow explained that Chewco would purchase CalPERS' interest in JEDI. Fastow described Chewco as an SPE not affiliated with either Enron or CalPERS. According to the minutes, he "reviewed the economics of the project, the financing arrangements, and the corporate structure of the acquiring company." He also presented a diagram of the proposed permanent financing arrangement, which involved (1) a $250 million subordinated loan to Chewco from a bank (Enron would guarantee the loan); (2) a $132 million advance to Chewco from JEDI under a revolving credit agreement; and (3) $11 million in "equity" contributed by Chewco. Neither the diagram nor the minutes contains any indication of the source of this equity contribution. The Committee voted to approve Enron's guaranty of the bridge loan and the subsequent subordinated loan. The minutes of the meeting of the full Board on December 9 show that these approvals were briefly reported by the Committee to the Board at that meeting.

Enron's Code of Conduct required Kopper to obtain approval for his participation in Chewco from the Chairman and CEO. Lay, who held both positions at this time, said he does not know Kopper and is confident that he was neither informed of Kopper's participation nor asked to approve it under the Code.[9] Skilling, who was President and COO, said that Fastow made him aware that Kopper would manage Chewco. Skilling told us that, based on Fastow's recommendation, he approved Kopper's role in Chewco. Skilling's approval, however, did not satisfy the requirements of the Code of Conduct. Skilling also said he believes he discussed Kopper's role in Chewco with the Board at some point.

We have located no written record of the approval Skilling described or any disclosure to the Board concerning Kopper's role. Although the minutes show that Kopper was on the Executive Committee's November 5 conference call when the Chewco loan guaranty was discussed and approved, the minutes do not reflect any mention of Kopper's personal participation in the Chewco transaction. Other than Skilling, none of the Directors we interviewed (including Lay and John Duncan, Chairman of the Executive Committee) recalls being informed of, or approving, Kopper's role in Chewco.

C. SPE Non-Consolidation "Control" Requirement

If Enron controlled Chewco, the accounting rules for SPEs required that Chewco be consolidated into Enron's consolidated financial statements. This principle raised two relevant issues: (1)

---

[9] The minutes of the November 5 Executive Committee meeting reflect that Lay joined the meeting "during" Fastow's presentation concerning Chewco.

did Kopper control Chewco, and (2) did Kopper, by virtue of his position at Enron, provide Enron with control over Chewco? With respect to the first question, as formed in November, Kopper controlled Chewco. Kopper was the sole member of Chewco's managing member, and had complete authority over Chewco's actions.

In December 1997, Enron and Kopper made two changes to the Chewco structure that were apparently designed to address the control element. First, Chewco was converted to a limited partnership, with Kopper as the manager of Chewco's general partner. The new Chewco partnership agreement provided some modest limits on the general partner's ability to manage the partnership's affairs. Second, an entity called "Big River Funding LLC" became the limited partner of Chewco. The sole member of Big River was an entity called "Little River Funding LLC." Those entities had been part of the bridge financing structure and, at the time, Kopper had controlled them both. But by an assignment dated December 18, Kopper transferred his ownership interest in Big River and Little River to William D. Dodson.[10] This transfer left Kopper with no formal interest in Chewco's limited partner.

The assessment of control under applicable accounting literature was, and continues to be, subjective. In general, there is a rebuttable presumption that a general partner exercises control over a partnership. The presumption can be overcome if the substance of the partnership arrangement provides that the general partner is not in control of major operating and financial policies. The changes to the Chewco structure and limitations on the general partner's ability to manage the partnership's affairs may have been sufficient to overcome that presumption, but the issue is not free from doubt. In addition, even if Kopper did control Chewco, it is not clear whether Enron would be deemed to control Chewco. Although Kopper may have been able to influence Enron's actions concerning Chewco, he was not a senior officer of Enron and may not have had sufficient authority within the company for his actions to be considered those of Enron for these purposes.

D. SPE Non-Consolidation "Equity" Requirement

In order to qualify for non-consolidation, Chewco also had to have a minimum of 3% outside equity at risk. As formed in early November, however, Chewco had no equity. There had been

---

[10]   It is presently common knowledge among Enron Finance employees that Kopper and Dodson are domestic partners. We do not have information concerning their relationship in December 1997 or what, if anything, Enron Finance employees knew about it at that time.

efforts to obtain outside equity—including preparing a private placement memorandum and making contact with potential investors—but those efforts were unsuccessful.

In November and December of 1997, Enron and Kopper created a new capital structure for Chewco, which had three elements:

- $240 million unsecured subordinated loan to Chewco from Barclays Bank PLC, which Enron would guarantee;

- $132 million advance from JEDI to Chewco under a revolving credit agreement; and

- $11.5 million in equity (representing approximately 3% of total capital) from Chewco's general and limited partners.

Kopper invested approximately $115,000 in Chewco's general partner, and approximately $10,000 in its limited partner before transferring his limited partnership interest to Dodson. But no third-party investors were identified to provide outside equity. Instead, to obtain the remaining $11.4 million, Enron and Kopper reached agreement with Barclays Bank to obtain what were described as "equity loans" to Big River (Chewco's limited partner) and Little River (Big River's sole member).

The Barclays loans to Big River and Little River were reflected in documents that resembled promissory notes and loan agreements, but were labeled "certificates" and "funding agreements." Instead of requiring Big River and Little River to pay interest to Barclays, the documents required them to pay "yield" at a specified percentage rate. The documentation was intended to allow Barclays to characterize the advances as loans (for business and regulatory reasons), while allowing Enron and Chewco simultaneously to characterize them as equity contributions (for accounting reasons). During this time period, that was not an unusual practice for SPE financing.

In order to secure its right to repayment, Barclays required Big River and Little River to establish cash "reserve accounts." The parties initially made an effort to maintain the "equity" appearance of the transaction—by providing that the reserve accounts would be funded only with the last 3% of any cash distributions from JEDI to Chewco, and that Barclays could not utilize those funds if it would bring Chewco's "equity" below 3%. But Barclays ultimately required that the reserve accounts be funded with $6.6 million in cash *at closing*, and that the reserve accounts be fully pledged to secure repayment of the $11.4 million.

In order to fund the reserve accounts, JEDI made a special $16.6 million distribution to Chewco. In late November, JEDI had sold one of its assets—an interest in Coda Energy, Inc., and its subsidiary Taurus Energy Corp.[11] Chewco's share of the proceeds of that sale was $16.6 million. In a letter agreement dated December 30, 1997, Enron and Chewco agreed that Chewco could utilize part of the $16.6 million to "fund . . . reserve accounts in an aggregate amount equal to $6,580,000: (a) the Little River Base Reserve Account . . . in an amount equal to $197,400 and (b) the Big River Base Reserve Account . . . in an amount equal to $6,382,600." The letter agreement was prepared by Vinson & Elkins and was signed by an officer of Enron and by Kopper. Pursuant to the agreement, at closing on December 30, JEDI wired $6.6 million to Barclays to fund the reserve accounts.

A diagram of the Chewco transaction is set forth below:

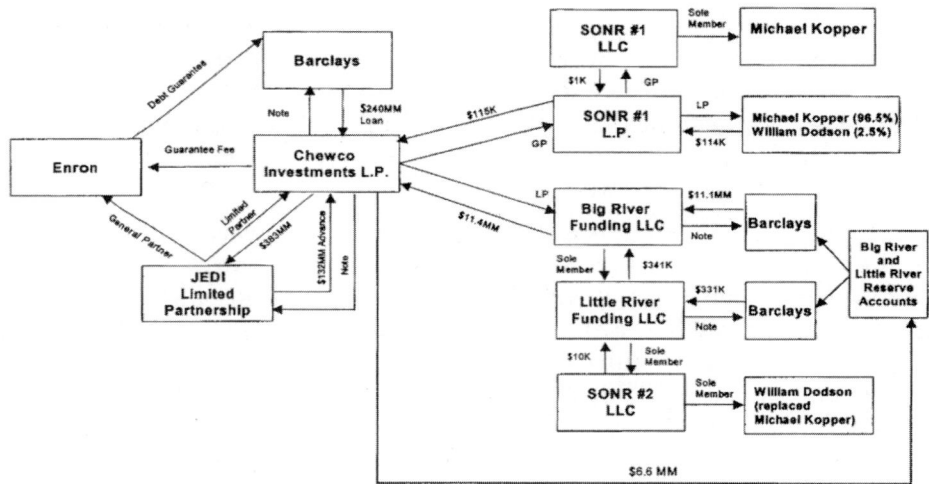

The existence of this cash collateral for the Barclays funding was fatal to Chewco's compliance with the 3% equity requirement. Even assuming that the Barclays funding could properly have been considered "equity" for purposes of the 3% requirement, the equity was *not* at risk for the portion that was secured by $6.6 million in cash collateral. At a minimum, Chewco fell short of the required equity at risk by that amount and did not qualify as an adequately capitalized SPE.[12] As a result, Chewco should have

---

[11]   Enron employees told us that JEDI's decision to sell Coda was not related to Chewco's purchase of CalPERS' interest in JEDI.

[12]   Even if the Barclays loans did qualify as outside equity at risk, there is a question whether Chewco met the 3% requirement because a small portion of the required 3%—Kopper's $125,000—came from a person affiliated with Enron. If Kopper's contribution is not counted, even with the Barclays funding Chewco had slightly less than 3% outside equity.

been consolidated into Enron's consolidated financial statements from the outset and, because JEDI's non-consolidation depended upon Chewco's non-consolidation status, JEDI also should have been consolidated beginning in November 1997.

Many of the people involved in this transaction for Enron profess no recollection of the Barclays funding, the reserve accounts, or the $6.6 million in cash collateral. This group includes the Enron officer who signed the December 30 letter agreement and the authorization for the $6.6 million wire transfer to Barclays at closing. By contrast, others told us that those matters were known and openly discussed. Their recollection is supported by a substantial amount of contemporaneous evidence.

There is little doubt that Kopper (who signed all of the agreements with Barclays and the December 30 letter) was aware of the relevant facts. The evidence also indicates that Glisan, who had principal responsibility for Enron's accounting for the transaction, attended meetings at which the details of the reserve accounts and the cash collateral were discussed. If Glisan knew about the cash collateral in the reserve accounts at closing, it is implausible that he (or any other knowledgeable accountant) would have concluded that Chewco met the 3% standard.[13]

Although Andersen reviewed the transaction at the time it occurred, we do not know what information the firm received or what advice it provided. Enron's records show that Andersen billed Enron $80,000 in connection with its 1997 review of the Chewco transaction. The CEO of Andersen testified in a Congressional hearing on December 12, 2001 that the firm had performed unspecified "audit procedures" on the transaction in 1997, was aware at the time that $11.4 million had come from "a large international financial institution" (presumably Barclays), and concluded that it met the test for 3% residual equity. He also testified, however, that Andersen was unaware that cash collateral had been placed in the reserve accounts at closing.

The Andersen workpapers we were permitted to review indicate that Andersen was aware of the $16.6 million distribution to Chewco in 1997, and that it had traced the cash disbursements to JEDI's records. We do not know what Andersen did to trace those disbursements, or whether its review did or should have identified

---

[13]   Documents from 1997 indicate that Glisan was actively monitoring the accounting literature and guidance on the substantive outside equity requirements for non-consolidated SPEs. We located a handwritten note apparently made by Glisan that identifies one of the "unique characteristics" of the Chewco transaction as "minimization of 3rd party capital." We do not know what Glisan meant by this reference because he declined to be interviewed by us (other than a brief interview on another subject).

facts relating to funding the reserve accounts. We have been otherwise unable to confirm or disprove Andersen's public statements about the transaction.

Largely because Kopper, Glisan, and Andersen declined to speak with us on this subject, we have been unable to determine why the parties utilized a financing structure for Chewco that plainly did not satisfy the SPE non-consolidation requirements. Enron had every incentive to ensure that Chewco was properly capitalized. It is reasonable to assume that Enron employees, if motivated to protect only Enron's interests, would have taken the necessary steps to ensure that Chewco had sufficient outside equity. We do not know whether Chewco's failure to qualify resulted from bad judgment or carelessness on the part of Enron employees or Andersen, or whether it was caused by Kopper or other Enron employees putting their own interests ahead of their obligations to Enron.[4]

* * *

G. Enron's Repurchase of Chewco's Limited Partnership Interest

In March 2001, Enron repurchased Chewco's limited partnership interest in JEDI and consolidated JEDI into its consolidated financial statements. Fastow was personally involved in the negotiations and decision-making on this repurchase. As described below, the repurchase resulted in an enormous financial windfall to Kopper and Dodson (who collectively had invested only $125,000). Much of the payout to these individuals is difficult to justify or understand from Enron's perspective, and at least $2.6 million of the payout appears inappropriate on its face. Moreover, Kopper received most of these benefits—by coincidence or design—shortly before he purchased Fastow's interests in the LJM partnerships (described below in Section III). Because Fastow and Kopper declined to be interviewed by us concerning the Chewco repurchase, we do not have the benefit of their responses to the serious issues addressed in this section.

1. Negotiations

During the first quarter of 2000, senior personnel in Enron's Finance area came to the conclusion that JEDI was essentially in a liquidation mode, and had become an expensive off-balance sheet financing vehicle. They approached Fastow, who agreed

---

4   Report of Investigation by the Special Investigative Committee of the Board of Directors of Enron Corp. (February 1, 2002) at 43–54, http://picker.uchicago.edu/Enron/PowersReport(2-2-02).pdf.

with their conclusion. The next step was to determine an appropriate buyout price for Chewco's interest in JEDI.

The discussions concerning the buyout terms involved, among others, Fastow, Kopper, and Jeffrey McMahon (then Senior Vice President, Finance and Treasurer of Enron).[17] Because JEDI's assets had increased in value since 1997, on paper Chewco's limited partnership interest had become valuable. On the other hand, Kopper and Dodson had invested only $125,000 in Chewco.

McMahon told us that, in light of the circumstances, he proposed to Fastow that the buyout be structured to provide a $1 million return to the Chewco investors.[18] According to a document McMahon identified as the written buyout analysis he provided to Fastow, this would give the investors a 152% internal rate of return on their investment and a return on capital multiple of 7.99. McMahon said that Fastow received the proposal, said he would discuss it with Kopper, and later reported back to McMahon that he had negotiated a payment of $10 million. McMahon also said that Fastow told him that Skilling had approved the $10 million payment. McMahon's recollection of events is consistent with a handwritten memorandum addressed to "Andy" (in what we are told is Kopper's handwriting) that analyzes McMahon's written proposal and refers to Enron's purchasing Chewco's interest for $10.5 million. McMahon said he told Fastow that $10 million would be inappropriate and, if that was the agreement, it would be better for Enron to continue with the current JEDI structure and not buy out Chewco's interest.

By mid-2000, Enron had decided to purchase Chewco's interest on terms that would provide a $10.5 million return to the Chewco investors. Chewco had already received $7.5 million in cash (net) from JEDI, so Chewco would receive an additional cash payment at closing of $3 million.[19] By this point, McMahon had left the

---

[17] During a brief interview, Fastow told us that he had *not* participated in these negotiations because, in light of Kopper's having become his partner in the general partner of LJM2, he believed it would have been inappropriate. Fastow's statement is contrary to information we obtained from interviews of several people familiar with the negotiations, all of whom said he was personally involved. Moreover, Fastow's statement is inconsistent with the handwritten memorandum, addressed to "Andy," that is discussed in the text below. We showed a copy of the memorandum to Fastow during the brief interview, but he declined to respond to any questions about it.

[18] McMahon also said he believed at the time that Dodson was the outside equity investor in Chewco, and that Kopper was representing Dodson in the buyout discussions.

[19] The $7.5 million consisted of several elements: (1) distributions from JEDI that funded the Big River and Little River reserve accounts and interest on those amounts; (2) distributions from JEDI and advances under the revolving credit agreement that funded Chewco's working capital reserve and interest on those amounts; (3) the $400,000 fee paid in December 1998; and (4) other net cash distributions from JEDI, some of which had been used to repay the subordinated

Treasurer's position and the Finance group. We were unable to locate any direct evidence about who made the ultimate decision on the buyout amount. Skilling told us that he had no involvement in the buyout transaction, including being advised of or approving the payment amount.

2. Buyout Transaction

The buyout was completed in March 2001, when Enron and Chewco entered into a Purchase Agreement (dated March 26, 2001) for repurchasing Chewco's interest. (It is not clear why the transaction did not close until the first quarter of 2001.) The contract price for the purchase was $35 million, which was determined by taking:

- The $3 million cash payment that had been agreed to in 2000; plus

- $5.7 million to cover the remaining "required payments" due to Enron under the JEDI partnership agreement (as discussed above in Section II(F)(2));[20] plus

- $26.3 million to cover all but $15 million of Chewco's outstanding $41.3 million obligation under the revolving credit agreement with JEDI.

At closing, pursuant to a letter agreement with Chewco, Enron kept the $5.7 million and wired $29.3 million to Chewco; Chewco then paid down $26.3 million on the revolving credit agreement and retained the remaining $3 million.

Chewco was not required to pay off the entire $41.3 million balance on the revolving credit agreement. Instead, it paid only $26.3 million, and the remaining $15 million was converted to a term loan due in January 2003. The $15 million was left outstanding because, in December 1999, Chewco had paid $15 million to *LJM1* to purchase certificates in Osprey Trust.[21] Although not disclosed in either the Purchase Agreement or the term loan agreement, Enron and Chewco agreed (1) to make the terms of the loan agreement (maturity date, interest rates) match those of the Osprey Trust certificates, and (2) that Chewco would

---

loan and equity loans from Barclays and part of the outstanding balance on the revolving credit agreement.

[20] The $5.7 million payment is referred to in the Purchase Agreement as being for unspecified "breakage costs." There is some evidence that this generic description was used because it was less likely to draw attention from Andersen during their review of the transaction. Because Andersen did not permit us to review workpapers from 2001 or interview their personnel on this matter, we do not know what review Andersen conducted. Enron's records show that it paid $25,000 in fees to Andersen in connection with the Chewco buyout.

[21] Osprey Trust is a limited partner, along with Enron, in Whitewing Associates.

be required to use the principal paid from the Osprey Trust certificates to repay the $15 million term loan, and would retain any yield paid on the certificates (which it could use to pay interest on the term loan). Enron did not, however, require that the Osprey Trust certificates serve as collateral for the $15 million loan. The loan is unsecured and non-recourse to Kopper and Dodson.[22]

3.   Returns to Kopper/Dodson

As a result of the buyout, Kopper and Dodson received an enormous return on their $125,000 investment in Chewco. In total, they received approximately $7.5 million (net) cash during the term of the investment, plus an additional $3 million cash payment at closing. Even assuming Chewco incurred some modest expenses that were not reimbursed at the time by Enron or drawn down on the revolving credit line, this represents an internal rate of return of more than 360%.

This rate of return does not take into account the $1.6 million in management fees received by Kopper. It also does not reflect the fact that the buyout was tax-free to Chewco, as described below.

4.   Tax Indemnity Payment

One of the most serious issues that we identified in connection with the Chewco buyout is a $2.6 million payment made by Enron to Chewco in mid-September 2001. Chewco first requested the payment after the buyout was consummated—under a Tax Indemnity Agreement between Enron and Chewco that was part of the original 1997 transaction. There is credible evidence that Fastow authorized the payment to Chewco even though Enron's in-house counsel advised him unequivocally that there was no basis in the Agreement for the payment, and that Enron had no legal obligation to make it.

When Chewco purchased the JEDI limited partnership interest in 1997, Enron and Chewco executed a Tax Indemnity Agreement. Agreements of this sort are not unusual in transactions where anticipated cash flows to the limited partner may be insufficient to satisfy the partner's current tax obligations. On its face, the Agreement compensates Chewco for the difference between Chewco's current tax obligations and its cash receipts during the partnership. Chewco subsequently requested payments, and Enron made payments, for that purpose prior to 2001.

---

[22]   In effect, if Chewco does not repay the unsecured loan when it comes due in 2003, it will amount to a forgiveness by Enron of $15 million in advances under the revolving credit agreement (which funded, among other things, the payment of management fees to Kopper). We understand that Chewco made the first semi-annual interest payment under the term loan in a timely manner in August 2001.

After the closing of Enron's buyout of Chewco in March 2001, Kopper requested an additional payment under the Tax Indemnity Agreement. Kopper claimed that Chewco was due a payment to cover any tax liabilities resulting from the negotiated buyout of Chewco's partnership interest. Enron's in-house legal counsel (who had been involved in the 1997 negotiations) consulted with Vinson & Elkins (who also had been involved in the negotiations) concerning Chewco's claim. Both concluded that the Agreement was not intended to cover, and did not cover, a purchase of Chewco's partnership interest. In-house counsel communicated this conclusion to Kopper.

The amount of the indemnity payment in dispute was $2.6 million. After further inconclusive discussions, Kopper told Enron's in-house counsel that he would consult with Fastow. Fastow then called the counsel, who says he told Fastow unequivocally that the Agreement did not require Enron to make any payment to Chewco. In a subsequent conversation, Fastow told Enron's counsel that he had spoken with Skilling and that Skilling (who Fastow said was familiar with the Agreement and the buyout transaction) had decided that the payment should be made. As a result, in September 2001, Enron paid Chewco an additional $2.6 million to cover its tax liabilities in connection with the buyout. Skilling told us he does not recall any communications with Fastow concerning the payment. Fastow declined to respond to questions on this subject.

H. Decision to Restate

In late October 2001, the Enron Board (responding to media reports) requested a briefing by Management on Chewco. Glisan was responsible for presenting the briefing at a Board meeting on short notice. Following the briefing, Enron accounting and legal personnel (as well as Vinson & Elkins) undertook to review documents relating to Chewco. This review identified the documents relating to the funding of the Big River and Little River reserve accounts in December 1997 through the $16.6 million distribution from JEDI.

Enron brought those documents to the attention of Andersen, and consulted with Andersen concerning the accounting implications of the funded reserve accounts. *After* being shown the documents by Enron and discussing the accounting issues with Enron personnel, Andersen provided the notice of "possible illegal acts" that Andersen's CEO highlighted in his Congressional testimony on December 12, 2001.

Enron's accounting personnel and Andersen both concluded that, in light of the funded reserve accounts, Chewco lacked sufficient outside equity at risk and should have been consolidated in November 1997.[23] In addition, because JEDI's non-consolidation depended on Chewco's status, Enron and Andersen concluded that JEDI also should have been consolidated in November 1997. In a Current Report on Form 8-K filed on November 8, 2001, Enron announced that it would restate its prior period financials to reflect the consolidation of those entities as of November 1997.[5]

* * *

The retroactive consolidation of Chewco—and the investment partnership [JEDI] in which Chewco was a limited partner—had a huge impact. It decreased Enron's reported net income by $28 million (out of $105 million total) in 1997, by $133 million (out of $703 million total) in 1998, by $153 million (out of $893 million total) in 1999, and by $91 million (out of $979 million total) in 2000. It also increased Enron's reported debt by $711 million in 1997, by $561 million in 1998, by $685 million in 1999, and by $628 million in 2000.[6]

QUESTIONS ON CHEWCO AND JEDI

Isn't this all pretty complicated?

Think about the Executive Committee's approval of Chewco in a telephone conference call (266–267). Most of the money to satisfy Chewco's 3% independent equity came from Barclays through Big River and Little River, which in turn established "reserve accounts" funded by Chewco itself to partially protect Barclay's right to repayment. All of this meant that the portion of the 3% funded by the portion of the Barclays money that was protected by the reserve accounts was not "at risk" and could not be counted toward the 3% total needed to avoid consolidation (269–271).

Note that the presentation to the Executive Committee in the telephone meeting did not identify the source of the 3% equity funding (267). What were the odds that the Committee was going to dig down to the existence of the reserve accounts, discover how they were funded, learn how they protected Barclays, and put this information together to spot the "cash collateral for the Barclays funding [that] was fatal to Chewco's compliance with the 3% equity requirement" (270)?

---

[23] When presented in late October 2001 with evidence of the $6.6 million cash collateral in the reserve accounts, Glisan apparently agreed that the collateral precluded any reasonable argument that Chewco satisfied the 3% requirement, but claimed that he had been unaware of it at the time of the transaction.

5   *Id.* at 60–67.

6   *Id.* at 42.

As transactions become more complicated and some considerable distillation is necessary for presentation to a board, do you see how management may, either inadvertently or by design, present at a level of generality that leaves the board in the dark as to important details?

As a practical matter, how does a board guard against that?

Now, let's turn to the related-party aspects of Chewco.

Michael Kopper was an Enron employee who reported to Enron's CFO, Andrew Fastow. When counsel advised Fastow that he could not run Chewco unless Enron disclosed that fact in its proxy statement, Kopper took Fastow's place (265). Chewco was a limited liability company. Kopper (through intermediary entities) became the sole member of Chewco's managing member (265–266). Later, Chewco was converted to a limited partnership, and Kopper became the manager of Chewco's general partner (268).

Kopper negotiated on Chewco's behalf with Enron over how to split a JEDI profit distribution between Chewco and Enron. The Special Committee recounts evidence (266) suggesting that Fastow leaned on the Enron negotiator to close the deal on Kopper's proposed terms. When Enron decided to liquidate JEDI, Enron negotiated to purchase Chewco's JEDI interest. Although the Enron senior vice president for finance, who was also the treasurer, suggested a price that would have given the Chewco investors (Kopper and his friend Dodson) a $1 million return, Fastow may have engineered a result by which they received ten times that much (273). In addition, Chewco received $2.6 million to cover tax liabilities resulting from Enron's purchase of Chewco's interest in JEDI, even though Fastow was advised by counsel that Enron was *not* obligated to make that tax indemnity payment (276).

The Enron Code of Conduct required that Kopper's participation be disclosed in writing to the Enron CEO and chairman of the Board, and that that officer determine that Kopper's participation did not adversely affect Enron's best interests. Apparently this was not done (265, 267).

How does all this strike you? Would the CEO/chairman have denied the required determination, if consulted? Does this form of control seem adequate? Does it even address the conflicts here—that materialized because Fastow, not Kopper, leaned on Enron to make concessions to Chewco? How would you protect against that with a Code of Conduct?

What about the very large return to Kopper (275)? How can a board be sure that it even knows about such things? What kinds of controls should a company have in place? For example, should it limit returns by officers and employees on investments in entities doing business with the company to some set percentage? Would you feel differently about the large return to Kopper if Kopper had risked more of his own wealth? If Kopper's business with Enron had resulted from some innovative idea that Kopper had come up with by himself?

CHAPTER 8

ENRON PART II: HEDGING AND RAPTORS

■ ■ ■

We turn now to hedging and the infamous Raptor transactions. This Chapter Eight begins with a description of the Raptor vehicles and Enron's arrangements with them. An entity called LJM2 was deeply involved in the Raptor transactions. Enron's CFO was deeply involved in LJM2. Since this made the Raptor deals related-party transactions, the chapter then details Enron's efforts to approve and monitor related-party transactions

A. HISTORY OF THE RAPTORS

Here is the description of LJM2 and the Raptors in pages 70–76 and 99–133 of the Report of Investigation by the Special Investigative Committee of the Board of Directors of Enron Corp. (Feb. 1, 2002).

__LJM2__. In October 1999, Fastow proposed to the Finance Committee of the Board the creation of a second partnership, LJM2 Co-Investment, L.P. ("LJM2"). Again, he would serve as general partner through intermediaries. LJM2 was intended to be a much larger private equity fund than LJM1. Fastow said he would raise $200 million or more of institutional private equity to create an investment partnership that could readily purchase assets Enron wanted to syndicate.

This proposal was taken up at a Finance Committee meeting on October 11, 1999. The meeting was attended by other Directors and officers, including Lay and Skilling. According to the minutes, Fastow reported on various benefits Enron received from transactions with LJM1. He described the need for Enron to syndicate its capital investments in order to grow. He said that investments could be syndicated more quickly and at less cost through a private equity fund that he would establish. This fund would provide Enron's business units an additional potential buyer of any assets they wanted to sell.

The minutes and our interviews reflect that the Finance Committee discussed this proposal, including the conflict of interest presented by Fastow's dual roles as CFO of Enron and general partner of LJM2. Fastow proposed as a control that all transactions between Enron and LJM2 be subject to the approval of both Causey, Enron's Chief Accounting Officer, and Buy, Enron's Chief Risk Officer. In addition, the Audit and Compliance Committee would annually review all transactions completed in the prior year. Based on this discussion, the Committee voted to recommend to the Board that the Board find that Fastow's participation in LJM2 would not adversely affect the best interests of Enron.

Later that day the Chairman of the Finance Committee, Herbert S. Winokur, Jr., presented the Committee's recommendation to the full Board. According to the minutes, he described the controls that had been discussed in the Finance Committee and noted that Enron and LJM2 would not be obligated to engage in transactions with each other. The Board unanimously adopted a resolution "adopt[ing] and ratify[ing]" the determination of the Office of the Chairman necessary to permit Fastow to form LJM2 under Enron's Code of Conduct.

LJM2 was formed in October 1999. Its general partner was LJM2 Capital Management, L.P. With the assistance of a placement agent, LJM2 solicited prospective investors as limited partners using a confidential Private Placement Memorandum ("PPM") detailing, among other things, the "unusually attractive investment opportunity" resulting from the partnership's connection to Enron. The PPM emphasized Fastow's position as Enron's CFO, and that LJM2's day-to-day activities would be managed by Fastow, Kopper, and Glisan. (We did not see any evidence that the Board was informed of the participation of Kopper or Glisan; Glisan later claimed his inclusion in the PPM was a mistake.) It explained that "[t]he Partnership expects that Enron will be the Partnership's primary source of investment opportunities" and that it "expects to benefit from having the opportunity to invest in Enron-generated investment opportunities that would not be available otherwise to outside investors." The PPM specifically noted that Fastow's "access to Enron's information pertaining to potential investments will contribute to superior returns." The drafts of the PPM were reviewed by Enron in-house lawyers and Vinson & Elkins. Both groups focused on ensuring that the solicitation did not appear to come from Enron or any of its subsidiaries.

We understand that LJM2 ultimately had approximately 50 limited partners, including American Home Assurance Co., Arkansas Teachers Retirement System, the MacArthur Foundation, and entities affiliated with Merrill Lynch, J.P. Morgan, Citicorp, First Union, Deutsche Bank, G.E. Capital, and Dresdner Kleinwort Benson. We are not certain of this because

LJM2 declined to provide any information to us. We further understand that the investors, including the general partner, made aggregate capital commitments of $394 million. The general partner, LJM2 Capital Management, L.P., itself had a general partner and two limited partners. The general partner was LJM2 Capital Management, LLC, of which Fastow was the managing member. The limited partners were Fastow and, at some point after the creation of LJM2, an entity named Big Doe LLC. Kopper was the managing member of Big Doe.[25] (In July 2001, Kopper resigned from Enron and purchased Fastow's interest in LJM2.) The following is a diagram of the LJM2 structure:

---

[25]   In his capacity as an Enron employee, Kopper reported to Fastow throughout the existence of LJM2 until his resignation in July 2001. We have seen no evidence that Kopper obtained the required consent to his participation in LJM2 under Enron's Code of Conduct. Kopper certified his compliance with the Code in writing, most recently in September 2000.

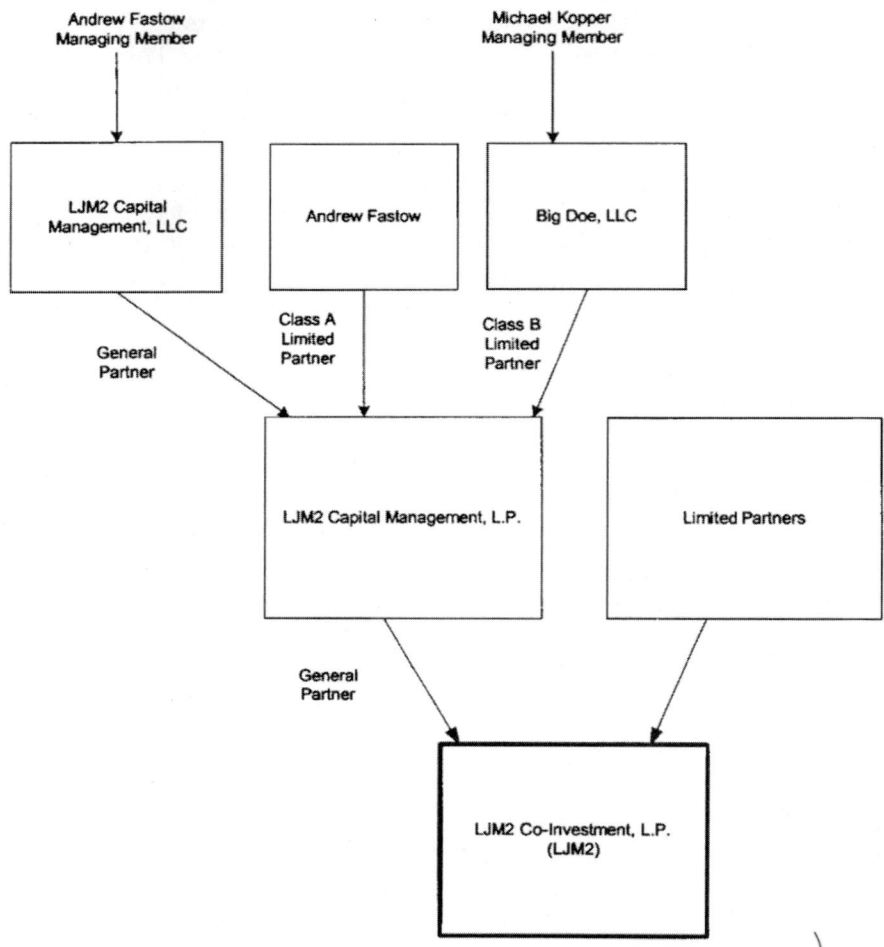

In April 2000, Enron and LJM Management L.P. entered into a "Services Agreement" under which Enron agreed to have its staff perform certain tasks (for a fee), including opening and closing accounts, executing wire transfers, and "Investment Execution & Administration." The Services Agreement described these activities as purely ministerial," and contemplated that LJM would pay market rates. That same month, Causey and Fastow signed an agreement regarding the use of Enron employees by LJM1 and LJM2. The employees would continue to be "regular, full-time" Enron employees for benefits purposes, but the LJM partnerships would pay the bonuses, and in some cases the base salary. LJM would also pay the costs. The memorandum describing this agreement says that "[i]t is understood that some activities conducted by LJM2 employees will also be for the benefit of Enron," and that in such cases Causey and Fastow would "reasonably agree upon allocation of costs to Enron and LJM2." This understanding was memorialized in a second Services Agreement dated July 17, 2000. We were unable to determine what LJM2 actually paid for any services under these agreements.

The LJM partnerships entered into more than 20 distinct transactions with Enron. A substantial number of these transactions raise issues of significant concern, and are described further in Sections IV, V, and VI of this Report.

B. LJM Governance Issues

The structures of LJM1 and LJM2—in which Fastow controlled the general partner of each partnership—raise questions about non-consolidation by Enron of the LJM partnerships and certain entities (described in more detail below) in which one of the LJM partnerships was an investor. In each case, Enron could avoid consolidation under relevant accounting rules only if the entity was controlled by an *independent* third party with substantive equity and risks and rewards of ownership. The first question, then, is whether Fastow controlled LJM1 and LJM2. If so, Enron arguably would control LJM1 and LJM2, and Enron would be required to consolidate them on its financial statements.

As described above, the criteria for determining control with respect to general partners are subjective. Nevertheless, the accounting rules indicate that a sole general partner should *not* be viewed as controlling a limited partnership if the partnership agreement provides for the removal of the general partner by a reasonable vote of the limited partners, without cause, and without a significant penalty. Similarly, other limits on the authority of the general partner, such as requiring approval for the acquisition or sale of principal assets, could be viewed as giving the limited partners sufficient control for non-consolidation.

Both LJM1 and LJM2 present substantial questions about whether Fastow was in effective control. Fastow was the effective general partner of both partnerships, and had management authority over them. On the other hand, both partnership agreements limited the general partner's investment authority, and required approval of certain investment decisions by the limited partners. Moreover, the LJM2 partnership agreement provided for removal of the general partner, without cause, by a recommendation of an Advisory Committee and a vote of the limited partners (initially limited partners with 75% in interest, later reduced to two-thirds). Given the role of the limited partners (which were somewhat different for LJM1 and LJM2, and in the case of LJM2 changed over time), arguments could be made both for and against consolidation based on Fastow's control of the partnerships. Andersen's workpapers include a discussion of the limited partner oversight in LJM2 and changes in June 2000 to strengthen the rights of limited partners to remove the general partner and members of the Advisory Committee.

We have reviewed these issues in detail, and have concluded that there are no clear answers under relevant accounting standards. Fastow declined to speak with us about these issues. As we have noted, the limited partners of both LJM1 and LJM2, citing confidentiality provisions in the partnership agreements, declined to cooperate with our investigation by providing documents or interviews.[1]

* * *

The Raptors made an extremely significant contribution to Enron's reported financial results over the last five quarters before Enron sought bankruptcy protection—*i.e.*, from the third quarter of 2000 through the third quarter of 2001. Transactions with the Raptors during that period allowed Enron to avoid reflecting on its income statement almost $1 billion in losses on its merchant investments. Not including the $710 million pre-tax charge Enron recorded in the third quarter of 2001 related to the termination of the Raptors, Enron's reported pre-tax earnings during that five-quarter period were $1.5 billion. We cannot be certain what Enron might have done to mitigate losses in its merchant investment portfolio had it not constructed the Raptors to hedge certain of the investments. Nonetheless, if one were to subtract from Enron's earnings the $1.1 billion in income (including interest income) recognized from its transactions with the Raptors, Enron's pre-tax earnings for that period would have been $429 million, a decline of 72%.

The following description of the Raptors simplifies an extremely complicated set of transactions involving a complex structured finance vehicle through which Enron entered into sophisticated hedges and derivatives transactions. Although we describe these transactions in some depth, even the detail here is only a summary.

---

[1]   Report of Investigation by the Special Investigative Committee of the Board of Directors of Enron Corp. (February 1, 2002) at 70–76, http://www.sec.gov/Archives/edgar/data/1024401/000090951802000089/big.txt.

A. Raptor I

1. Formation and Structure

In late 1999, at Skilling's urging, a group of Enron commercial and accounting professionals began to devise a mechanism that would allow Enron to hedge a portion of its merchant investment portfolio. These investments were "marked to market," with changes recorded in income every quarter for financial statement purposes. They had increased in value dramatically. Skilling said he wanted to protect the value of these investments and avoid excessive quarter-to-quarter volatility. Due to the size and illiquidity of many of these investments, they could not practicably be hedged through traditional transactions with third parties.

With the logic and seeming success (at that time) of the Rhythms hedge fresh in mind, Ben Glisan, who became Enron's Treasurer in May 2000, led the effort. Accountants from Andersen were closely involved in structuring the Raptors.[45] Attorneys from Vinson & Elkins also were consulted frequently, particularly on securities law issues, and also prepared the transaction documents.

The first Raptor (Raptor I), created effective April 18, 2000, was an SPE called Talon LLC ("Talon"). Talon was created solely to engage in hedging transactions with Enron. LJM2 invested $30 million in cash and received a membership interest. Through a wholly-owned subsidiary named Harrier, Enron contributed $1,000 cash, a $50 million promissory note, and Enron stock and Enron stock contracts with a fair market value of approximately $537 million.[46] Because Talon was restricted from selling, pledging or hedging the Enron shares for three years, the shares were valued at about a 35% discount to their market value. This valuation was supported by a fairness opinion provided by PwC. In return for its contribution, Enron received a membership interest in Talon and a revolving promissory note from Talon, with an initial principal amount of $400 million. Through a series of agreements, LJM2 was the effective manager of Talon.

A very simplified diagram of Raptor I appears below:

---

[45]   Enron's records show that Andersen billed Enron approximately $335,000 in connection with its work on the creation of the Raptors in the first several months of 2000.

[46]   The stock in Raptor I came from shares of Enron stock received from restructuring forward contracts Enron had with an investment bank, which released shares of Enron stock. (This was the same source as the Enron stock used in the Rhythms transaction.) The Enron "stock contract" in Raptor I consisted of a contingent forward contract held by a wholly-owned Enron subsidiary, Peregrine, under which it had a contingent right to receive Enron stock on March 1, 2003 from another entity, Whitewing, if the price of Enron stock exceeded a certain level.

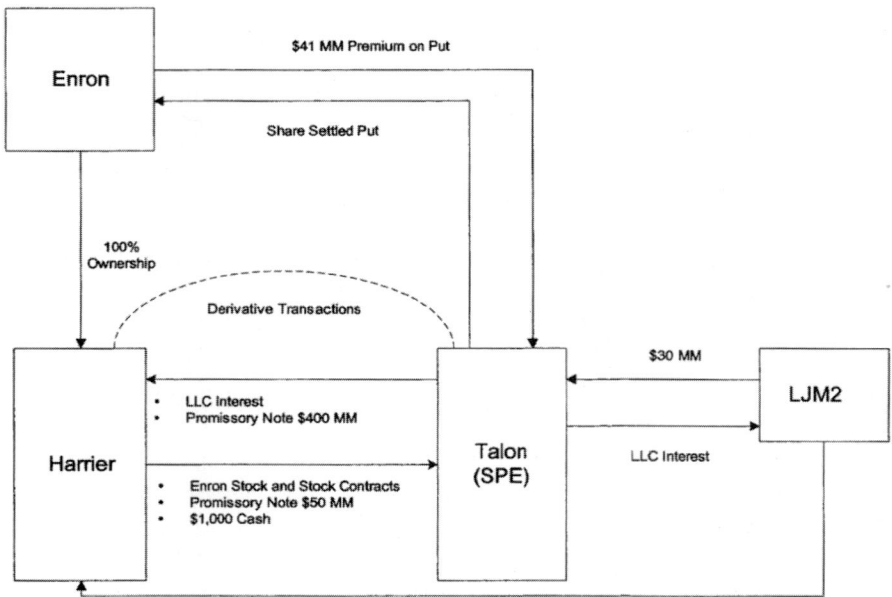

Once Talon received the contributions from Enron and LJM2, it had $30 million of "outside" equity to meet the 3% outside equity requirement for SPE treatment as an unconsolidated entity. Enron calculated that Talon theoretically could enter into derivatives with Enron up to approximately $500 million in notional value. By Enron's calculation, it also had what appeared to be a capacity to absorb losses on derivative contracts up to almost $217 million. This credit capacity consisted of LJM2's $30 million investment plus the $187 million value of the 35% discount on the Enron stock and stock contracts. Enron concluded that Talon could sell the Enron stock at its unrestricted value to meet Talon's obligations.

There was an additional important requirement before Talon could enter into hedging transactions with Enron. It was understood by those who structured Talon—although it is not reflected in the Talon documents or Board presentations—that Talon would not write any derivatives until LJM2 received an initial return of $41 million or a 30% annualized rate of return, whichever was greater, from income earned by Talon. Put another way, before hedging could begin, LJM2 had to have received back the entire amount of its investment plus a substantial return. This allowed LJM2 effectively to receive a return of its capital but, from an accounting perspective, leave $30 million of capital "at risk" to meet the 3% outside equity requirement for non-consolidation. If LJM2 did not receive its specified return in six months, it could require Enron to purchase its interest in Talon at a value based on the *unrestricted* price of Talon's Enron stock and stock contracts. These terms were remarkably favorable to LJM2, and served no apparent business purpose for Enron. Moreover, because Talon's Enron stock and stock contracts would have to decline in value by $187 million before Talon incurred any loss, LJM2 did not bear first-dollar risk of loss, as typically required for SPE non-consolidation. After LJM2 received its specified return, Enron then was entitled to 100% of any further distributions of Talon's earnings.[47] Thus, by the time any hedging began, LJM2 would have received a return that substantially exceeded its initial investment while retaining only a limited economic stake in the ongoing venture—principally the return of its original investment upon Talon's liquidation. In fact, Fastow told his limited partners in LJM2 that the Raptors were "divested investments" after LJM2 received its specified $41 million return.

To create the required $41 million of income for distribution to LJM2, Enron purchased from Talon a put option on Enron stock for a premium of $41 million. The put option gave Enron the right to require Talon to purchase approximately 7.2 million shares of Enron common stock on October 18, 2000, six months after the effective date of the transaction, at a strike price of $57.50 per share. The closing price of Enron stock was $68 per share when Enron purchased the put. As long as Enron's share price remained above $57.50, the put option would expire worthless to Enron, and Talon would be entitled to record the $41 million premium as income. It could then distribute $41 million to LJM2, but continue to treat Talon as an adequately capitalized, unconsolidated SPE.[48]

Enron's purchase of the put option for $41 million was unusual for two reasons. First, from an economic perspective—rather than merely a means to pay LJM2—the put option was a bet by Enron that its own stock price would decline substantially. Second, the price of the put was calculated by a method appropriate only if the transaction were between two fully creditworthy parties. In fact, Talon was not sufficiently creditworthy. Other than the Enron

---

[47]   During Talon's existence, this changed slightly. After LJM2 received its initial $41 million return, it made an additional equity investment of $6 million and was entitled to receive a 12.5% return on that additional contribution, to the extent Talon had sufficient earnings.

[48]   Economically, this $41 million distribution reflected a return of and on LJM2's initial investment, but for accounting purposes the distribution was a return *on* the original investment. Thus, LJM2 technically still had $30 million equity in Talon. Nevertheless, Fastow told his LJM2 investors in April 2001 that after settlement of the Enron puts, "LJM2 had already received its return of and on capital."

stock and stock contracts, it had only $71 million of assets—the $30 million LJM2 investment and the $41 million premium—to meet its obligations on the put, but it had written a put on more than 7 million shares of Enron stock. If the Enron stock price declined below approximately $47 per share (about $10 per share below the strike price), Talon would owe Enron the entire $71 million, and Talon would be unable to meet its remaining obligations. Thus, the put provided only about $10 per share of price protection to Enron, and for that reason was worth substantially less than $41 million. The transaction makes little apparent commercial sense, other than to enable Enron to transfer money to LJM2 in exchange for its participation in vehicles that would allow Enron to engage in hedging transactions.

As it turned out, Enron did not have to wait six months for the put to expire and for hedging transactions to begin. At Fastow's suggestion, Causey, on behalf of Enron, and Fastow, on behalf of Talon and LJM2, settled the option early, as of August 3, 2000. Since Enron stock had increased in value and the period remaining on the put option had dwindled, the option was worth much less. Talon returned $4 million of the $41 million option premium to Enron, but nevertheless paid LJM2 $41 million. That left LJM2 with little further financial interest in what happened to Talon. This distribution resulted in an annualized rate of return that LJM2 calculated in a report to its investors at 193%. Enron also paid LJM2's legal and accounting fees, and a management fee of $250,000 per year. With LJM2 having received a $41 million payment, Talon was now available to begin entering into hedging transactions with Enron.

2.   Enron's Approval of Raptor I

Although the deal-closing documents were dated April 18, 2000, the transaction did not receive formal approval from Enron's Management or Board until several weeks later.

The approval of Raptor I by Enron's Management is reflected in two documents, an "LJM2 Approval Sheet" and an Enron Deal Summary. Both were executed between May 22 and June 12, 2000, long after the transaction closed. The LJM2 Approval Sheet very briefly describes the transaction and the distribution "waterfall" of Talon's earnings (including the initial $41 million payment to LJM2), and reports that Kopper—a Managing Director of Enron—negotiated on behalf of LJM2. The Approval Sheet was signed by Glisan, Causey and Buy, but the signature line for Skilling was blank.[49] The LJM2 Approval Sheet refers to an "attached" DASH. A Deal Summary is attached, which is largely identical to the Approval Sheet, but added: "It is expected that Talon will have earnings and cash sufficient to distribute $41 million to LJM2 within six months, yielding an annualized return on investment to LJM2 of 76.8%." This document was signed only by Glisan and Scott Sefton, the General Counsel of Enron Global Finance, Fastow's group.

Glisan and Causey presented Raptor I to the Finance Committee of the Board on May 1, 2000, with Lay, Skilling, and Fastow in attendance. According to the minutes, Glisan described Raptor as "a risk management program to enable the Company to hedge the profit and loss volatility of the Company's investments." He explained that Enron and LJM2 would establish "a non-affiliated vehicle . . . as a hedge counter-party to selected investments," explained how Talon would be funded, and explained "the level of hedging protection Talon could initially provide."

Although the minutes do not contain any detail regarding what Glisan told the Committee, it appears that his remarks were guided by a three-page written presentation provided to the Committee entitled "Project Raptor: Hedging Program for Enron Assets." The materials stated that Talon would be capitalized with $400 million in "excess [Enron] stock." It also stated that, "[i]nitially, [the] vehicle can provide approximately $200 million of P&L [profit and loss] protection to ENE. As ENE stock price increases, the vehicle's P&L protection capacity increases as well." The materials also disclosed LJM2's investment and expected return: "LJM2 will provide non-ENE equity and will be entitled to 30% annualized return plus fees," with Enron entitled to all upside after LJM2 received its return. The materials did not disclose that LJM2's contractually specified return was the *greater* of a 30% annualized return *or* $41 million.

The Finance Committee was also given information strongly suggesting, if not making perfectly clear, that the Raptor vehicle was not a true economic hedge. Notes on the presentation materials, apparently taken at the meeting by Enron's Corporate Secretary to assist her in preparing the minutes, state: "Does not transfer economic risk but transfers P&L volatility."[50]

---

[49]   We discuss Skilling's role in the management and oversight of transactions with the LJM partnerships in Section VII, below.

[50]   This thought was repeated in a May 2000 presentation describing the Raptor hedging program prepared by Enron Global Finance for Enron Broadband Services. It stated that a "substantial decline in the price of [Enron] stock will cause the program to terminate early and

According to the minutes, Causey informed the Finance Committee that Andersen "had spent considerable time analyzing the Talon structure and the governance structure of LJM2 and was comfortable with the proposed transaction." Glisan apparently presented a chart identifying three principal "risks" of Raptor: (1) "accounting scrutiny"; (2) a substantial decline in Enron stock price; and (3) counter-party credit. For each of them, the chart also identified corresponding "[m]itigants:" (1) the transaction had been reviewed by Causey and Andersen; (2) Enron could negotiate an early termination of Talon with LJM2; and (3) the assets of Talon were subject to a "master netting agreement."

The Finance Committee voted to recommend Project Raptor to the full Board. The Board approved the transaction the following day, May 2, 2000.

3.   Early Activity in Raptor I

The unwritten understanding was that Talon could not engage in hedging transactions with Enron until LJM2 received its initial $41 million return. After LJM2 received its $41 million, Talon then began to execute derivative transactions with Enron. With one exception, these transactions took the form of "total return swaps" on interests in Enron merchant investments—that is, derivatives under which Talon would receive the amount of any future gains in the value of those investments, but also would have to pay Enron the amount of any future losses. The total notional value of the derivatives was approximately $734 million.

All of the documentation for the derivative transactions between Enron and Talon was signed by Causey for Enron and by Fastow for Talon. They all were dated "as of" August 3, 2000. Contemporaneous documents, however, demonstrate that many, if not all, of the transactions were not finally agreed upon until sometime in mid-September, and were back-dated to be effective "as of" August 3, 2000. The purpose of dating the derivative transactions on the same day appears to have been administrative: Andersen required Enron to recalculate whether LJM2's equity investment constituted at least 3% of the Raptor's total assets each time the Raptor entered into a transaction with Enron. Treating each of the Raptor I transactions as if they all occurred on one day allowed Enron to make this calculation only once.

---

may return credit risk to Enron," and thus the Raptor program was "[n]ot an economic hedge; . . . credit risk retained with Enron Corp."

We have found no direct evidence explaining why August 3 was selected as the single date. We note, however, that August 3 was the date on which the stock of Avici Systems, a public company in which Enron held a very large stake, traded at its all-time high ($162.50 per share). By entering into a total return swap with Talon on Avici stock on that date, Enron was able to lock in the maximum possible gains. By September 30, 2000, the quarter end, the stock had declined to $95 per share. By dating the swap "as of" August 3, Enron was able to offset losses of nearly $75 million on its quarterly financial statements. If Enron had treated the swap on Avici as effective on September 15, 2000—approximately when the agreement between Enron and LJM2 actually occurred and when Avici was trading at $95.50 per share—Enron would not have been able to offset any significant losses on Avici in Enron's third quarter financial statements. Because LJM2 had already received back from Talon its $30 million investment along with another $11 million, it had little economic incentive to resist dating or structuring transactions that would benefit Enron for income statement purposes at Talon's expense.

There is some evidence of a concern within Enron North America ("ENA"), which held almost all of the assets that were subject to Raptor derivative transactions, that ENA selected only assets that were expected to decline substantially in value. On September 1, 2000, an ENA attorney, Stuart Zisman, wrote (emphasis added):

> Our original understanding of this transaction was that all types of assets/securities would be introduced into this structure (including both those that are viewed favorably and those that are viewed as being poor investments). *As it turns out, we have discovered that a majority of the investments being introduced into the Raptor Structure are bad ones.* This is disconcerting [because] . . . it might lead one to believe that the financial books at Enron are being "cooked" in order to eliminate a drag on earnings that would otherwise occur under fair value accounting. . . .

ENA's two most senior attorneys received this memorandum, as did several senior ENA business people. Zisman met with the senior ENA attorneys. He told them that, contrary to what the memorandum implied, he did not know whether only "bad" assets had in fact been selected for Raptor, but that he was concerned Raptor could be misused in that way. The senior ENA attorneys and the senior ENA business people who received Zisman's memorandum—for varying reasons and with varying levels of direct knowledge—believed the assertion in Zisman's memo to be untrue, so they did not take any further action.

4.   Credit Capacity Concerns in the Fall of 2000

As the value of Enron's merchant investments declined in the fall of 2000, the amounts Talon owed Enron increased. This became a matter of significant concern at Enron. If Talon's total liabilities (including the amount owed to Enron) exceeded its total assets (which consisted almost entirely of the unrestricted value of Enron stock and stock contracts), Enron would have to record a charge to income based on Talon's credit deficiency. Consequently, Enron's accounting department kept track of Talon's credit capacity on a daily basis.

To protect Talon against a possible decline in Enron stock price—which would decrease the value of Talon's principal asset, and thereby decrease its credit capacity—on October 30, 2000, Enron entered into a "costless collar" on the approximately 7.6 million Enron shares and stock contracts in Talon.[51] The "collar" provided that, if Enron stock fell below $81, Enron would pay Talon the amount of any loss. If Enron stock increased above $116 per share, Talon would pay Enron the amount of any gain. If the stock price was between the floor and ceiling, neither party was obligated to the other. This protected Talon's credit capacity against possible future declines in Enron stock.

This collar was inconsistent with certain fundamental elements of the original transaction. Enron had originally transferred $537 million of its own stock and stock contracts to Talon. It discounted the value of that stock by approximately 35% because it was restricted from being sold, pledged or hedged for a three-year period. These restrictions reduced the value of the stock, and were a key basis for PwC's fairness opinion. By agreeing to the collar, Enron had to lift, in part, the restriction that had justified the 35% discount on the stock ($187 million). Causey signed the document waiving the restriction.

Thus, on October 30, 2000, the value of Talon's principal asset, the Enron stock and stock contracts, was protected from future declines. Even so, the value of Enron's merchant investments was rapidly declining, so Talon's credit capacity was still in jeopardy.

B.   Raptors II and IV

Enron and LJM2 established two more Raptors—known as Raptor II and Raptor IV—that were not materially different from

---

[51]   The collar was "costless" because Enron and LJM2 owed each other equal premiums for the transaction. Because the collar was indexed to Enron's own stock and met certain accounting criteria, Enron was not required to mark it to market. Instead, it was considered an equity transaction.

Raptor I. (A fourth vehicle, Raptor III, is discussed in the next section.) Both Raptors II and IV received only contingent contracts to obtain a specified number of Enron shares.[52] Raptor II was authorized by the Executive Committee of the Board at its meeting on June 22, 2000. The minutes state that Fastow told the Committee that a second Raptor was needed because "there had been tremendous utilization by the business units of Raptor I." In fact, at that point there had been no derivative transactions between Talon and Enron. A presentation distributed to the Executive Committee stated: "Initially, the vehicle can provide approximately $200 million of P&L protection to ENE [Enron]. As ENE stock price increases, the vehicle's P&L protection capacity increases as well." The closing documents for Raptor II were dated June 29, 2000.

Raptor IV was presented to the Finance Committee at its meeting on August 7, 2000.[53] With Skilling, Fastow, Buy and Causey in attendance, Glisan first discussed Raptors I and II. He "noted that Raptor I was almost completely utilized and that Raptor II would not be available for utilization until later in the year." (There is no indication that Glisan explained why Raptor II would not be available—under the unwritten agreement, Raptor II would not write derivatives with Enron until LJM2 received its specified $41 million or 30% return.) Glisan then informed the Committee that "the Company was proposing an additional Raptor structure . . . to increase available capacity." After a discussion that is not described in the minutes, the Finance Committee voted to recommend Raptor IV to the Board. Later that day, Skilling informed the Board that the Executive Committee had approved Raptor II at its June meeting, and that Raptor IV would "provide additional mechanisms to hedge the profit and loss volatility of

---

[52]   As noted above in Section V.A.I., Enron contributed to Raptor I a contingent forward contract held by a wholly-owned Enron subsidiary, Peregrine, under which Peregrine had a right to receive Enron stock on March 1, 2003 from Whitewing. Enron contributed similar contingent stock-delivery contracts to Raptors II and IV. In all, Enron sold the rights to 18 million contingent Enron shares, to be delivered in 2003, to Raptor I (3.9 million shares), Raptor II (7.8 million shares) and Raptor IV (6.3 million shares). The contingency was based on Enron stock price on March 1, 2003. If on that date the price of Enron stock was above $53 per share, Raptor I would receive all of its shares; if it was above $63 per share, Raptor II would receive all of its shares; and if it was above $76 per share, Raptor IV would receive all of its shares. If, on the other hand, the price of Enron stock on that date was below $63 per share, Raptor IV would receive no shares; if it was below $53 per share, Raptor II would receive no shares; and if it was below $50 per share, Raptor I would receive no shares.

[53]   The Finance Committee and Board minutes refer to this vehicle as "Raptor III," not "Raptor IV." However, as we explain below, another Raptor vehicle was activated after Raptor II and before what the Board referred to as "Raptor III." This Raptor vehicle, which is widely referred to as Raptor III by Enron employees involved in the transactions, was not brought to the Board for approval. In order to be consistent with the terms used by the parties at the time (and reflected in contemporaneous documents), we refer to what the Board called Raptor III as Raptor IV.

the Company's investments." The Board then approved Raptor IV. The closing documents for Raptor IV were dated September 11, 2000.[54]

Just as it had done with Talon in Raptor I, Enron paid Raptor II's SPE, "Timberwolf," and Raptor IV's SPE, "Bobcat," $41 million each for share-settled put options. As in Raptor I, the put options were settled early, and each of the entities then distributed approximately $41 million to LJM2.[55] Although these distributions meant that both Timberwolf and Bobcat were available to engage in derivative transactions with Enron, Enron engaged in derivative transactions only with Timberwolf. These transactions, entered into as of September 22, 2000 and December 28, 2000, had a total notional value of $513 million. Enron did not make use of Bobcat because, as we explain below, concerns regarding the declining credit capacity of Raptors I and III led Enron to use Bobcat's available credit capacity to prop them up.

As in Raptor I, Enron entered into costless collars on the Enron stock contracts in Timberwolf and Bobcat to provide credit capacity support to the Raptors. Causey approved the collars. The Timberwolf shares were collared on November 27, 2000, at a floor of $79 and a ceiling of $112. The Bobcat shares were collared on January 24, 2001, at a floor of $83 and a ceiling of $112. As in the case of Raptor I, this collaring was inconsistent with the premise on which the stock contracts had been discounted when they were originally transferred to Timberwolf and Bobcat. The shares were restricted for three years, and their value was thus discounted from market value. The collars, however, effectively lifted the restriction.

C. Raptor III

Raptor III was a variation of the other Raptor transactions, but with an important difference. It was intended to hedge a single, large Enron investment in The New Power Company ("TNPC").[56] Instead of holding Enron stock, Raptor III held the stock of the very company whose stock it was intended to hedge—TNPC. (Technically, Raptor III held warrants to purchase approximately

---

[54]   Skilling signed the LJM2 Approval Sheet for Raptor IV—the only such sheet he signed for the Raptors, and one of the few sheets he signed at all. Notably, the Approval Sheet was not signed by Skilling, Buy and Causey until March 2001, some six months after the deal had closed and the Board had approved the transaction.

[55]   LJM2 made an additional equity investment of $1.1 million in Raptor II at the time the initial put terminated. LJM2 had a potential 15% return on that additional investment.

[56]   When TNPC went public, its name changed to New Power Holdings, Inc., but Enron personnel continued to refer to the company as TNPC. In order to be consistent with the terms used by the parties at the time and contemporaneous documents, we refer to New Power Holdings as TNPC.

24 million shares of TNPC stock for a nominal price. These warrants were thus the economic equivalent of stock.) If the value of TNPC stock decreased, the vehicle's obligation to Enron on the hedge would increase in direct proportion. At the same time, its ability to pay Enron would decrease. Raptor III was thus the derivatives equivalent of doubling-down on a bet on TNPC. This extraordinarily fragile structure came under pressure almost immediately, as the stock of TNPC decreased sharply after its public offering.

1.   The New Power Company

TNPC was a residential and commercial power delivery company Enron created as a separate entity. Enron owned a 75% interest. It was not publicly traded in early 2000. Enron sold a portion of its holdings to an SPE, known as Hawaii 125-0 ("Hawaii"), that Enron formed with an outside institutional investor. Enron's basis in the warrants was zero. Enron recorded large gains in connection with the sales, and then entered into total return swaps under which Enron retained most of the economic risks and rewards of the holdings it had sold. As a result, Enron bore the economic risks and rewards of TNPC, and would have to reflect any gains or losses on its income statement on a mark-to-market basis. In July 2000, Enron also sold warrants for TNPC to other investors (including LJM2) for the equivalent of $10.75 per share.

Enron contemplated an initial public offering of TNPC stock occurring in the Fall of 2000. Anticipating that the stock price would fluctuate—causing volatility in Enron's income statement—Enron wanted to hedge the risk it had taken on through its total return swaps with Hawaii. To "hedge" its accounting exposure, Enron once again used the Raptor structure.

2.   The Creation of Raptor III

As in the creation of the other Raptors, internal Enron accountants worked closely with Andersen in designing Raptor III. Andersen's billings for work on Raptor III were approximately $55,000. Attorneys from Vinson & Elkins were also consulted and prepared the transaction documents. The structure of Raptor III, however, was different from the other Raptors because Enron did not have ready access to shares of its stock to contribute to the vehicle. Rather than seeking Board authorization for new Enron shares, which would have resulted in dilution of earnings per share, Enron Management chose to contribute some of Enron's TNPC holdings to Raptor III's SPE, "Porcupine."

A very simplified diagram of Raptor III appears below:

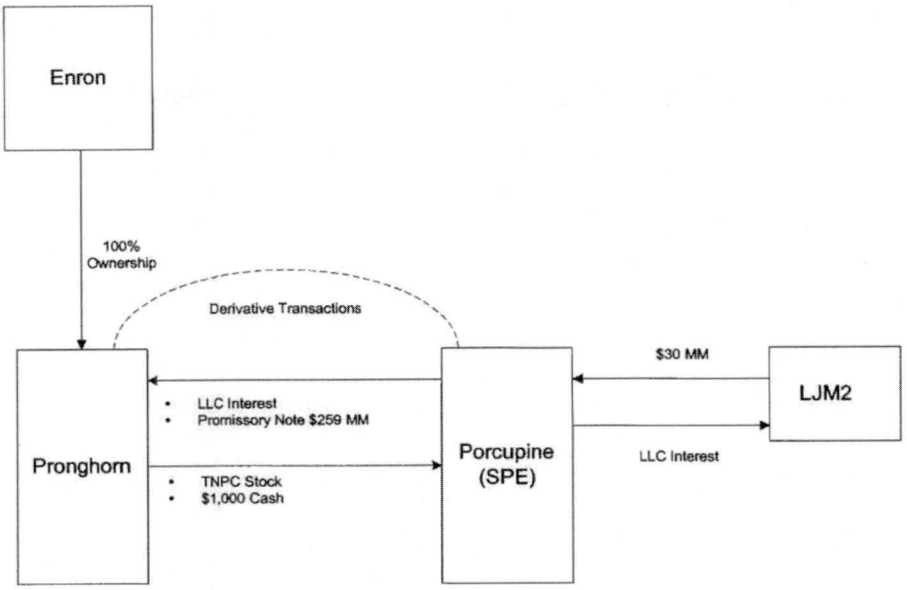

Enron and LJM2 created Raptor III effective September 27, 2000. Unlike the other Raptor transactions, Raptor III was not presented to the Board or to any of its Committees, possibly because no Enron stock was involved. We have seen no evidence that the members of the Board, other than Skilling, were aware of the transaction. Nor have we seen any evidence that an LJM2 Approval Sheet, Enron Investment Summary, or DASH was prepared for this transaction.

As with the other Raptors, LJM2 contributed $30 million to Porcupine. It was understood that LJM2 would receive its substantial return before Porcupine would enter into derivative transactions with Enron. In Raptor III, LJM2's specified return was set at $39.5 million or a 30% annualized rate of return, whichever was greater. It received a return of $39.5 million in only one week.

On September 27 Enron delivered approximately 24 million shares of TNPC stock to Porcupine at $10.75 per share. Enron received a note from Porcupine for $259 million, which Enron recorded at zero because it had essentially no basis in the TNPC stock sold to Porcupine. Enron did not obtain a fairness opinion with respect to the transaction. We are told that Enron, after consulting with Andersen, reasoned that its private sale of TNPC interests several months earlier at $10.75 per share was adequate support for the price of its transfer to Porcupine. The "road show" for the TNPC initial public offering was already underway, and there is evidence that Enron personnel were aware that the offering was likely to be completed at a much higher price. Indeed, on September 22, 2000—five days before the transaction with Porcupine at $10.75 per share—Enron distributed a letter to certain of its employees offering them an opportunity to purchase shares of TNPC in the offering and noting that "the current estimated price range [for the shares] is $18.00 to $20.00 per share." Nonetheless, Enron, with Andersen's knowledge and agreement, concluded that the last actual transaction was the best indicator of the appropriate price in valuing the warrants sold by Enron to Porcupine. On October 5, *one week* after Enron contributed the warrants to Porcupine at a price equivalent to $10.75 per share, TNPC's initial public offering went forward at $21 per share.

On the day of the initial public offering, the TNPC shares (for which Porcupine had paid $10.75 five days earlier) closed at $27 per share. That same day, Porcupine declared a distribution to LJM2 of $39.5 million, giving LJM2 its specified return and permitting Porcupine to enter into a hedging transaction with Enron. LJM2 calculated its internal rate of return on this distribution as 2500%.

Enron and Porcupine immediately executed a total return swap on 18 million shares of TNPC at $21 per share. As a result, Enron locked in an accounting gain related to the Hawaii transactions of approximately $370 million. This gain, however, depended on Porcupine remaining a creditworthy counter-party, which in turn depended on the price of TNPC stock holding steady or increasing in value.

3.   Decline in Raptor III's Credit Capacity

Although the initial public offering of TNPC was a success, the stock's value immediately began to deteriorate. After a week of trading, the share price had dropped below the offering price. By mid-November, TNPC stock was trading below $10 per share. This had a double-whammy effect on Porcupine: Its obligation to Enron on its hedge grew, but at the same time its TNPC stock—the principal, and essentially only, asset with which it could pay Enron—fell in value. In essence, Porcupine had two long positions on TNPC stock. Consequently, Enron's transaction with Porcupine was not a true economic hedge.

D.   Raptor Restructuring

By November 2000, Enron had entered into derivative transactions with Raptors I, II and III with a notional value of over $1.5 billion. Enron's accounting department prepared a daily tracking report on the performance of the Raptors. In its December 29, 2000 report, Enron calculated its net gain (and the Raptors' corresponding net loss) on these transactions to be slightly over $500 million. Enron could recognize these gains—offsetting corresponding losses on the investments in its merchant portfolio only if the Raptors had the capacity to make good on their debt to Enron. If they did not, Enron would be required to record a "credit reserve," reflecting a charge on its income statement. Such a loss would defeat the very purpose of the Raptors, which was to shield Enron's financial statements from reflecting the change in value of its merchant investments.

1.   Fourth Quarter 2000 Temporary Fix

Raptor I and Raptor III developed significant credit capacity problems near the end of 2000. For Raptor I, the problem was that many of the derivative transactions with Enron resulted in losses to Talon, but the price of Enron stock had not appreciated significantly. The collar that Enron applied to the shares in Raptor I in October provided some credit support to Talon as Enron's share price dipped below $81 per share, but by mid-December the derivative losses surpassed the value of Talon's assets, creating a negative credit capacity.

Raptor III was faring no better. The price of TNPC stock had fallen dramatically from its initial public offering price, and was trading below $10 a share. Raptor III's assets had therefore declined substantially in value, and its obligation to Enron had increased. As a result, Raptor III also had negative credit capacity.

In an effort to avoid having to record a loss for Raptors I and III on its 2000 financial statements, Enron's accountants, working with Andersen, decided to use the "excess" credit capacity in Raptors II and IV to shore up the credit capacity in Raptors I and III. A 45-day cross-guarantee agreement, dated December 22, 2000, essentially merged the credit capacity of all four Raptors. The effect was that Enron would not, for year end, record a credit reserve loss unless there was negative credit capacity on a combined basis. Enron paid LJM2 $50,000 to enter into this agreement, even though the cross-guarantee had no effect on LJM2's economic interests. We have seen no evidence that Enron's Board was informed of either the credit capacity problem or the solution selected to resolve that problem. Enron did not record a reserve for the year ending December 31, 2000.[57]

2.   First Quarter 2001 Restructuring

In the first quarter of 2001, the credit capacity of the Raptors continued to decline. By late March, it appeared that Enron would have to take a pre-tax charge against earnings of more than $500 million to reflect the shortfall in credit capacity of Raptors I and III. Enron did not take this charge, and the Board was not informed of the situation. Instead, Enron Management restructured the Raptors. The Board was not informed about that, either.

a.   The Search for a Solution

The December cross-guarantee agreement was intended as a temporary remedy. In early January, a team of Enron accountants worked to find a more permanent solution. The need for a solution increased during the first quarter of 2001 because the values of both Enron and TNPC stock fell, and the Raptors' losses on their derivative transactions with Enron increased. The daily tracking reports that were circulated within the Global Finance, RAC, and Accounting Departments showed that the Raptors' credit shortfall grew to $504 million by the end of the quarter.

Senior Enron employees told us that Skilling, who became Enron's CEO during the first quarter of 2001, was aware of this problem and was intensely interested in its resolution. We were told that, during the first quarter of 2001, Skilling said that fixing the Raptors' credit capacity problem was one of the Company's highest priorities. When the Raptors' restructuring was accomplished, Skilling called one of the accountants who worked on the project to thank him personally. Skilling disputes these accounts. He told us that he recalls being informed in only general terms that there was a credit capacity issue with the hedges in the Raptors due to the falling price of Enron stock and the assets being hedged, and that the problem could be solved. He told us he understood the matter to be an accounting issue, and that he recalls having no significant involvement in, or understanding of, the problem. Skilling also told us that, in his view, if it had been

---

[57] At the time, Andersen agreed with Enron's view that the 45-day cross-guarantee among the Raptors to avoid a credit reserve loss was permissible from an accounting perspective. The workpapers that Andersen made available included a memorandum dated December 28, 2000, by Andersen's local audit team, which states that it consulted two partners in Andersen's Chicago office on the 45-day cross-guarantee. The workpapers also include an amended version of the December 28, 2000 memorandum, dated October 12, 2001, stating that the partners in the Chicago office advised that the 45-day cross-guarantee was *not* a permissible means to avoid a credit reserve loss.

necessary to take a loss in the first quarter, Enron could have done so without undue harm to its stock price because many other companies at that time were reporting losses in high-tech investments.

We found no evidence that Lay, who stepped aside as CEO midway through the first quarter, was aware of these events. It is significant, however, that Skilling claims to have had only a passing involvement in the restructuring. The potential impact of the problem, and the chosen solution, were of considerable consequence to the Company in Skilling's first quarter as CEO. Either Skilling was not nearly as involved in Enron's business as his reputation—and his own description of his approach to his job—would suggest, or he was deliberately kept in the dark by those involved in the restructuring. Whichever is the case, Skilling now says that he has no recollection of the details of the restructuring transaction.

b.   The Restructuring Transaction

The restructuring transaction, which was made effective as of March 26, 2001, consisted of two principal parts: a cross-collateralization of the Raptors and an additional infusion of Enron stock contracts.[58] By Enron's calculations, the restructuring allowed Enron to record only a $36.6 million credit reserve loss for the first quarter of 2001, rather than the $504 million loss Enron would have recorded if the Raptors had not been restructured.

In the first part of the restructuring, Enron assigned its right to receive any distribution upon the termination of any Raptor to any other Raptor that lacked sufficient assets to pay its obligation to Enron. Thus, Enron agreed that if, for example, it were to receive a distribution from Timberwolf upon the termination of Raptor II, but Talon (Raptor I) lacked sufficient assets to back its obligation to Enron, Enron would allow Talon to use the distribution that otherwise would have gone from Timberwolf to Enron to satisfy Talon's obligations. This had the effect of shoring up the credit capacity of the vehicles with credit deficits, but only to the extent of the excess capacity in other Raptors.

But the credit deficiencies in Raptors I and III were too great for the other two Raptors to absorb. This problem was magnified by a risk that most of the Enron stock from the stock contracts

---

[58]   Each of the transaction documents is dated April 13, 2001—after the close of the first quarter—but say they are "effective as of March 26, 2001." A letter agreement was executed on March 30, 2001, which stated an intention to enter into an agreement, and set forth the agreement's material terms and conditions.

included in the Raptors' capital could become unavailable. The source of shares for the stock contracts that Enron had originally transferred to Raptors I, II and IV was a contract that conditioned the availability of the shares on their stock trading at or above $50 per share on March 1, 2003. By March 22, 2001, however, Enron stock was trading at $55, so there was a concern that the shares would not be available to the Raptors. This would further erode their credit capacity.

To make up for this potential shortfall, Enron entered into an extremely complex transaction with Raptors II and IV. The essence of the transaction was that Enron agreed to deliver up to 18 million additional Enron shares, if necessary, to Raptors II and IV to make up any Enron stock shortfall from the original stock contracts. In return, Raptors II and IV increased their notes payable to Enron by a total of approximately $260 million.

In addition, to add credit capacity to Raptors II and IV (which in turn supported Raptors I and III), Enron sold them 12 million shares of Enron stock, to be delivered on March 1, 2005, at $47 per share. In exchange, Raptors II and IV increased their notes payable to Enron by a total of $568 million. The $47 per share price for the Enron stock contracts represented a 23% discount to the current market price of $61 per share. The basis for this discount was that the shares could not be sold, pledged or hedged for a four-year period. This had the effect of increasing the credit capacity of the Raptors by approximately $170 million.

At the same time, however, Enron entered into an agreement with the Raptors to hedge those shares that the restriction agreement had prevented the Raptors from hedging. It did so through additional costless collar derivative transactions. This was inconsistent with having discounted the price of the shares by 23%. Enron did not obtain a fairness opinion on this transaction.[59] Enron based the 23% discount on an analysis done by its internal Research Group. However, the Research Group was not made aware of the collaring arrangement when it performed its analysis. When the group's head, Kaminski, learned several months later that the discounted shares had been simultaneously collared, he informed Andersen and the Enron accountants who had worked on the restructuring that this could not be reconciled with the discount.

Restructuring the Raptors allowed Enron to avoid reflecting the $504 million credit reserve loss in its first quarter financial

---

[59] There is evidence that Enron accountants contacted outside investment banks seeking a fairness opinion and were unable to obtain what they regarded to be a suitable opinion.

statements. Instead, it recorded only a $36.6 million credit reserve loss.

E. Unwind of the Raptors

The complicated restructuring of the Raptors "solved" the problem only temporarily. By late summer of 2001, the continuing decline in Enron and TNPC stock caused a new credit deficiency of hundreds of millions of dollars. The collaring arrangements Enron had with the Raptors aggravated the situation, because Enron now faced the prospect of having to deliver so many shares of its stock to the Raptors that its reported earnings per share would be diluted significantly.

At the same time, an unrelated, but extraordinarily serious, Raptor accounting problem emerged. In August 2001, Andersen and Enron accountants realized that the accounting treatment for the Enron stock and stock contracts contributed to Raptors I, II and IV was wrong. Enron had accounted for the Enron shares sold in April 2000 to Talon (Raptor I), in exchange for a $172 million promissory note, as an increase to "notes receivable" and to "shareholders' equity." This increased shareholders' equity by $172 million in Enron's second, third and fourth quarter 2000 financial reports. Enron made similar entries when it sold Enron stock contracts in March 2001 to Timberwolf and Bobcat (Raptors II and IV) for notes totaling $828 million. This accounting treatment increased shareholders' equity by a total of $1 billion in Enron's first and second quarter 2001 financial reports. Enron accountants told us that Andersen was aware of, and approved, the accounting treatment for the Enron stock contracts sold to the Raptors in the first quarter of 2001. Andersen did not permit us to interview any of the Andersen personnel involved.

In September 2001, Andersen and Enron concluded that the prior accounting entries were wrong, and the proper accounting for these transactions would have been to show the notes receivable as a reduction to shareholders' equity. This would have had no net effect on Enron's equity balance. Enron decided to correct these mistaken entries in its third quarter 2001 financial statements. At the time, Enron accounting personnel and Andersen concluded (using a qualitative analysis) that the error was not material and a restatement was not necessary. But when Enron announced on November 8, 2001 that it would restate its prior financials (for other reasons), it included the reduction of shareholders' equity. The correction of the error in Enron's third quarter financial statements resulted in a reduction of $1 billion ($172 million plus $828 million) to its previously overstated equity balance.[60]

In mid-September, with the quarter-end approaching, Causey met with Lay (who had just recently reassumed the position of CEO because of Skilling's resignation) and Greg Whalley (Enron's COO) to discuss problems with the Raptors. Causey presented a series of options, including leaving the vehicles in place as they were, transactions to ameliorate the situation, and terminating the Raptors. Lay and Whalley directed Causey to terminate the Raptors.

Enron did so on September 28, 2001, paying LJM2 approximately $35 million. This purchase price apparently was the result of a private negotiation between Fastow (who had sold his interest in LJM2 to Kopper in July), on behalf of Enron, and Kopper, on behalf of LJM2. This figure apparently reflected a calculation that LJM2's residual interest in the Raptors was $61 million.

Enron accounted for the buy-out of the Raptors under typical business combination accounting, in which the assets and liabilities of the acquired entity are recorded at their fair value, and any excess cost typically is recorded as goodwill. However, Andersen told Enron to record the excess as a charge to income. As of September 28, 2001, Enron calculated that the Raptors' combined assets were approximately $2.5 billion,[61] and their combined liabilities were approximately $3.2 billion. The difference between the Raptors' assets and liabilities, plus the $35 million payment to LJM2, resulted in a charge of approximately $710 million ($544 million after taxes) reflected in Enron's third quarter 2001 financial statements.

It is unclear whether the accounting treatment of the termination was correct. Enron's transactions with the Raptors had resulted in the recognition of earnings of $532 million during 2000, and $545 million during the first nine months of 2001, for a total of

---

[60] Enron recorded a $1.2 billion reduction to shareholders' equity in its third quarter 2001 financial statement. One billion dollars of this reduction was due to correcting the overstatement of shareholders' equity that had been discovered in August. The additional approximately $200 million resulted from the fact that the notes receivable that Enron held for the stock and stock contracts sold to the Raptors were valued at a total of $1.9 billion, while the Enron stock and stock contracts held by the Raptors, which Enron took back when the Raptors were terminated, was valued at $2.1 billion. The $200 million difference was recorded as a reduction to shareholders' equity, and added to the $1 billion reduction that was recorded to correct the accounting error. Together, these two items accounted for the $1.2 billion reduction in shareholders' equity.

[61] This valued the Enron stock and stock contracts, including the collars, in the Raptors at a restricted value of $2.1 billion. Unrestricted, the Enron stock would have been worth approximately $350 million more, but Andersen insisted that Enron calculate the value of the stock at its restricted value. While Enron's stock price at the termination had decreased significantly to $27 per share, the collars provided a floor on all of the stock and stock contracts at prices ranging from $61 to $83 per share.

almost $1.1 billion. After taking the unwind charge of $710 million, Enron had still recognized pre-tax earnings from its transactions with the Raptors of $367 million. Thus, it may have been more appropriate for Enron to have reversed the full $1.1 billion of previously recorded pre-tax earnings when it bought back the Raptors.

F.   Conclusions on the Raptors

The Raptors were an effort to use gains in Enron's stock price and restriction discounts to avoid reflecting losses on Enron's income statement. Were this permissible, a company with access to its outstanding stock could place itself on an ascending spiral: an increasing stock price would enable it to keep losses in its investments from public view; which, in turn, would spur further increases in its stock price; which, in turn, would increase its capacity to keep losses in its investments from public view.

Moreover, LJM2 invested $30 million in each of the Raptors, but promptly received back the amount of its original investment and much more. Fastow, a fiduciary to Enron and its shareholders, reported to the LJM2 investors in October 2000 that their internal rates of return on the four Raptors were 193%, 278%, 2500%, and a projected 125%, respectively. These extremely large returns were far in excess of the 30% annualized rate of return described in the May 1, 2000 presentation to the Finance Committee. They were the result of very substantial and very rapid transfers of cash—about $41 million per Raptor, in less than six months each time—from the Raptors to LJM2. LJM2 was largely assured of a windfall from the inception of the transaction. Although LJM2 technically still had a $30 million investment in each of the Raptors, its original investment effectively had been returned.

The returns to LJM2 appear *not* to have been for a risk taken, but rather for a service provided: LJM2 lent its name to a vehicle by which Enron could circumvent accounting convention. The losses Enron incurred on its merchant investments were not hedged in any accepted sense of that term. The losses were merely moved from Enron's income statement to the equity section of its balance sheet. As a practical matter, Enron was hedging with itself. There was no interested counter-party in these transactions once LJM2 had been paid its initial return.

Proper financial accounting does not permit this result. To reach it, the accountants at Enron and Andersen—including the local engagement team and, apparently, Andersen's national office experts in Chicago—had to surmount numerous obstacles presented by pertinent accounting rules. Although they apparently believed that they had succeeded, a careful review of the transactions shows that they appear to violate or raise serious issues under several accounting rules:

1. Accounting principles generally forbid a company from recognizing an increase in the value of its capital stock in its income statement except under limited circumstances not present here. The substance of the Raptors effectively allowed Enron to report gains on its income statement that were backed almost entirely by Enron stock, and contracts to receive Enron stock, held by the Raptors.

2. After the distribution of LJM2's specified initial return, LJM2 appears not to have had sufficient equity at risk in the Raptor transactions to satisfy the 3% requirement for unconsolidated SPEs. Fastow himself made this point in a private communication with LJM2 investors in April 2001 (emphasis added):

> After the settlement of the [Enron] puts, Enron and the Raptor vehicles began entering into derivative transactions designed to hedge the volatility of a number of equity investments held by Enron. *LJM2's return on these investments was not at risk to the performance of derivatives in the vehicles, given that LJM2 had already received its return of and on capital.*

This is particularly true for Raptor III, where the impending initial public offering makes any argument that the vehicle was at risk especially difficult to sustain. Indeed, for high-risk derivative transactions, such as the hedges involved here, it is not clear that 3%, which is the *minimum* acceptable third-party investment, would suffice even if it were at risk.

3. In light of Enron's influence over the Raptors, it is not clear that it was entitled to use the cost method of accounting, instead of the equity method. Had Enron used the equity method, any gains in the Raptor hedges would have been required to be eliminated and thus would not have provided Enron with the desired offset to its merchant investment losses.

4. It is not clear that the discount on the value of Enron stock and stock contracts created by the restriction on sale, assignment, transfer, or hedging should have been taken into account in calculating the credit capacity of the Raptors. This is especially true after Enron subsequently collared the shares, effectively removing the justification for at least a portion of the original discount.

5. In the case of Raptor III, Enron did not record a note receivable on its balance sheet reflecting the amount owed it by the Raptor (Porcupine), and did not reduce Porcupine's net assets by the amount of that note ($259 million) in calculating Porcupine's credit capacity. By ignoring Porcupine's legal obligation to repay this note for purposes of calculating its credit capacity, Enron effectively overstated Porcupine's credit capacity by $259 million.

6. By issuing collars simultaneously with providing the Enron stock contracts in the Raptor restructuring, Enron effectively provided the vehicles a fixed return representing the difference between the sales price and the collar floor. It appears that this could have been treated for accounting purposes as a dividend paid to a stockholder, by reducing income available to shareholders in calculating earnings per share.

7. Even if the Raptor restructuring had been valid in other respects, it may not have permitted Enron to avoid reporting the $504 million impairment of the Raptor notes receivable in the first quarter of 2001. Proper accounting for this transaction should have given only prospective effect to the restructuring.

The creation, and especially the subsequent restructuring, of the Raptors was perceived by many within Enron as a triumph of accounting ingenuity by a group of innovative accountants. We believe that perception was mistaken. Especially after the restructuring, the Raptors were little more than a highly complex accounting construct that was destined to collapse.

It is particularly surprising that the accountants at Andersen, who should have brought a measure of objectivity and perspective to these transactions, did not do so. Based on the recollections of those involved in the transactions and a large collection of documentary evidence, there is no question that Andersen accountants were in a position to understand all the critical features of the Raptors and offer advice on the appropriate accounting treatment. Andersen's total bill for Raptor-related work came to approximately $1.3 million. Indeed, there is abundant evidence that Andersen in fact offered Enron advice at every step, from inception through restructuring and ultimately to terminating the Raptors. Enron followed that advice. The Andersen workpapers we were permitted to review do not reflect consideration of a number of the important accounting issues that we believe exist.

As we note above, Enron's use of the Raptors allowed Enron to avoid reflecting almost $1 billion in losses on its merchant investments over a period spanning just a little more than one year. Without the Raptors, and excluding the $710 million pre-tax charge Enron took in the third quarter of 2001, Enron's pre-tax earnings from the third quarter of 2000 through the third quarter of 2001 would have been $429 million, rather than the $1.5 billion that Enron reported. Quarter by quarter, the Raptors' contribution to Enron's pre-tax earnings (in millions) is shown below [table reformatted to some extent]:

Quarter	Reported Earnings	Earnings Without Raptors	Raptors' Contribution to Earnings
3Q 2000	$364	$295	$69
4Q 2000	$286	($176)	$462
1Q 2001	$536	$281	$255
2Q 2001	$530	$490	$40
3Q 2001*	($210)	($461)	$251
TOTAL	$1506	$429	$1,077

*   Third quarter 2001 figures exclude the $710 million pre-tax charge to earnings related to the termination of the Raptors.[2]

QUESTIONS ON THE RAPTORS

Are these confusing enough—even after being simplified by lawyers and accountants for the Special Committee's report? Should the complexity of a transaction itself signal to a board that there might be something fishy about it? Think carefully before you form an answer. Aren't a lot of perfectly legitimate transactions complex?

How can a board evaluate whether the complexity of a transaction signals a possible problem or not? How can a board even be sure that it understands a complex transaction? Should a board have an independent staff to advise it on the adequacy of management's description of such transactions?

Turning to the particulars here, Fastow was the managing member of LJM2 Capital Management, LLC (281). That company was in turn the general partner of LJM2 Capital Management, L.P., which had as its limited partners Fastow individually and Big Doe LLC, whose managing member was Michael Kopper (id.). LJM2 Capital Management, L.P. was, in turn, the general partner of "LJM2" (280), the abbreviation for LJM2 Co-Investment, L.P. (279). LJM2 ended up with about 50 limited partners (280). LJM2 controlled SPEs

---

[2]   Report of Investigation by the Special Investigative Committee of the Board of Directors of Enron Corp. (February 1, 2002) at 99–133, http://www.sec.gov/Archives/edgar/data/1024401/00 0090951802000089/big.txt.

called Talon ((285) and see the "very simplified diagram of Raptor I" on 286), Timberwolf (292–294), and Porcupine (see the "very simplified diagram of Raptor III" on 296), each of which entered into hedging transactions with Enron.

The Special Investigative Committee couldn't seem to make up its mind about whether Fastow's deep involvement in LJM2 deprived that partnership of the independence needed to keep LJM2 financials off the Enron books. The Committee concluded that "arguments could be made both for and against consolidation based on Fastow's control" (284); observed that "there are no clear answers under relevant accounting standards" (*id.*); and noted that LJM2 had, "citing confidentiality provisions in the partnership agreement[ ], declined to cooperate with our investigation by providing documents or interviews" (*id.*). Should Enron have entered into the Raptor deals if there was any doubt that LJM2 would be sufficiently independent so that the transactions could produce the accounting benefits for which Enron hoped? Or is there never any sure thing in life, so that a board ultimately should rely on the accounting experts available to it, even when (or perhaps most of all when) a close question arises?

Now consider the substance of the hedges. Cutting through almost all of the detail, can you see the problem in entering into hedging agreements with entities whose ability to make good on the hedges was dependent on the price of Enron stock?

What about the "costless collars" (292, 294) in which Enron essentially hedged the hedger—promising that if the Enron stock the SPEs held (which were the key to whether they could make good on the hedges) declined in value below a certain price, Enron would make up the amount of the loss caused by that part of the stock price drop?

And what about Raptor III (294–297)? How could Enron effectively hedge against a decline in the value of The New Power Company (TNPC) by entering into a hedge with a company which held TNPC equity as its principal asset?

Do these transactions look like gizmos rather than transactions with economic substance? Particularly when (a) LJM2's outside equity had to effectively be repaid with a profit before the SPEs in which LJM2 invested could enter into the hedge transactions that were the reason for the entire structure, and (b) the money for that repayment and profit came from deals with Enron itself (286–288, 296)?

Then we see the emergency cross-guarantees to avoid losses on the 2000 Enron financials (298–299) followed by the promise of yet more Enron stock to shore up the Raptor credit capacity (300–301). Wasn't Enron in a sense providing a hedge to itself?

Now, what about the Board?

If the directors were really told that Raptor I "[d]oes not transfer economic risk but transfers P&L volatility" (289) and if they approved it nonetheless, what do we have? Is it a corporate governance issue that can be solved by structural change? Or is it simply a question of weak-minded or weak-willed Board members?

Assuming that the Board was told that the deal would not transfer economic risk but would protect Enron's financials from volatility, should this have raised a disclosure issue? But if Enron had disclosed that the transactions did not transfer risk, would that have deprived the company of the benefit of balance sheet and income statement protection it sought by the hedges? Should a board ever approve a transaction that will provide a desired financial statement effect that the market would discount if the market knew the true economics of the deal?

What do you think of Andersen's involvement (285, 290, 295, 299 n. 57)? How do you feel about having the outside auditor consulted about these deals as they were being formed? What are the pluses? What are the minuses?

B. CONFLICT OF INTEREST CONTROLS

Now consider the various checks that Enron had in place to control the conflicts of interest that were inherent in Fastow having such a large hand in LJM2. Here is the description from pages 151–72 in the Report of Investigation by the Special Investigative Committee of the Board of Directors of Enron Corp. (Feb. 1, 2002).

> **LJM2.** In the case of LJM2, the proposal presented to the Board contemplated creation of an entity with which Enron would conduct a number of transactions. The principal stated advantage of Fastow's involvement in LJM2 was that it could then purchase assets that Enron wanted to sell more quickly and with lower transaction costs. This was a legitimate potential advantage of LJM2, and it was proper for the Board to consider it.[68]
>
> Nevertheless, there were very substantial risks arising from Fastow's acknowledged conflict of interest. First, given Fastow's position as Enron's CFO, LJM2 would create a poor public appearance, even if the transactions had been immaculate and there had been sound controls. The minutes do not reflect discussion of this issue, but our interviews indicate that it was raised. During the rising stock market, analysts and investors generally ignored Fastow's dual roles and his conflict of interest, but when doubts were cast on Enron's transactions with LJM1 and LJM2 in connection with Enron's earnings announcement on October 16, 2001, this appearance became a serious problem.

---

[68] The Board was apparently not informed of the involvement of other Enron employees in LJM2, including Kopper's financial stake and the extent of the role played by other Enron employees under the Services Agreement between Enron and LJM2.

Second, Fastow's position at Enron and his financial incentives and duties arising out of LJM1 and LJM2 could cause transactions to occur on terms unfair to Enron or overly generous to LJM1 and LJM2.[69] The Board discussed this issue at length and concluded that the risk could be adequately mitigated. The Directors viewed the prospective LJM2 relationship as providing an additional potential buyer for assets in Enron business units. If LJM2 offered a better price than other buyers on asset purchases or other transactions, Enron would sell to LJM2. This could occur because Fastow's familiarity with the assets might improve his assessment of the risk, or might lower his transaction costs for due diligence. In our interviews, several Directors cited these benefits of permitting Fastow to manage LJM2. If a better price was available elsewhere, Enron could sell to the higher bidder. Based on Fastow's presentation, the Directors envisioned a model in which Enron business units controlled the assets to be sold to LJM2 (or alternative potential buyers) and would be negotiating on behalf of Enron. Because each business unit's financial results were at stake, the Board assumed they had an incentive to insist that the transactions were on the most favorable terms available in the market. This was a plausible assumption, but in practice this incentive proved ineffective in ensuring arm's-length dealings.

Moreover, several Directors stated that they believed Andersen would review the transactions to provide a safeguard. The minutes of the Finance Committee meeting on October 11, 1999 (apparently not attended by representatives of Andersen) identify "the review by Arthur Andersen LLP" as a factor in the Committee's consideration of LJM2. Andersen did in fact (1) provide substantial services with respect to structuring and accounting for many of the transactions, (2) review Enron's financial statement disclosures with respect to the related-party transactions (including representations that "the terms of the transactions were reasonable and no less favorable than the terms of similar arrangements with unrelated third parties"), and (3) confirm Andersen's involvement in representations to the Audit and Compliance Committee at its annual reviews of the LJM transactions. The Board was entitled to rely on Andersen's

---

[69]   The presentation to the Board on LJM1 discussed the structure by which Fastow would be compensated, and therefore provided the Board with a basis for forming an expectation about the level of his compensation. The presentation to the Board on LJM2 did not. It provided only that "LJM2 has typical private equity fund fees and promote [sic]," targeted at "$200 + million institutional private equity." When LJM2 was initially approved, it does not appear that there was discussion at the Board level about a much larger fund and the levels of compensation Fastow would receive, although it was discussed later.

involvement in these respects. In addition, one would reasonably expect auditors to raise questions to their client—the Audit and Compliance Committee—if confronted with transactions whose economic substance was in doubt, or if controls required by the Board of Directors were not followed, as was the case here.[70]

Further, the Board adopted, or was informed that Management had adopted, a number of controls to protect Enron's interests. When the LJM2 proposal was brought to the Finance Committee and the Board in October 1999, two specific controls were recommended and adopted:

- Enron's Chief Accounting Officer, Rick Causey, and Chief Risk Officer, Rick Buy, would review and approve all transactions between Enron and LJM2.

- The Audit and Compliance Committee of the Board would annually review all transactions from the last year "and make any recommendations they deemed appropriate."

In addition, the Board noted that Enron had no "obligation" to engage in transactions with LJM. The Board also was told that disclosures of individual related-party asset sales was [sic] "probably" required in periodic SEC filings and proxy solicitation materials, which would mean involving Enron's internal lawyers, outside counsel at Vinson & Elkins, and Andersen to review the disclosures.

Additional controls were added, or described as having been added, at later meetings. A year later, on October 6 and 7, 2000, respectively, the Finance Committee and the full Board considered a proposal with respect to a new entity, LJM3.[71] Fastow informed the Directors, in a meeting at which Skilling, Causey and Buy were present, that additional controls over transactions between Enron and LJM1 and LJM2 had been put in place. These included:

- Fastow expressly agreed that he still owed his fiduciary responsibility to Enron.

---

[70] We are unable to determine why Andersen did not detect the various control failures described below. At its meeting with the Audit and Compliance Committee on May 1, 2000, an Andersen representative identified related-party transactions as an area to be given "high priorit[y] due to the inherent risks that were present." Moreover, in the engagement letter between Andersen and Enron dated May 2, 2000, the engagement partner wrote that Andersen's work would "consist of an examination of management's assertion that the system of internal control of Enron as of December 31, 2000, was adequate to provide reasonable assurance as to the reliability of financial statements. . . ." Because Andersen declined to permit its representatives to be interviewed, we do not know what, if any, steps Andersen took in light of these observations.

[71] LJM3 was never created.

- The Board or the Office of the Chairman could ask Fastow to resign from LJM at any time.

- Skilling, in addition to Buy and Causey, approved all transactions between Enron and the LJM partnerships.

- The Legal Department was responsible for maintaining audit trails and files on all transactions.

- A review of Fastow's economic interest in Enron and LJM was presented to Skilling.

One Director also proposed that the Finance Committee review the LJM transactions on a quarterly basis. Another Director proposed that the Compensation and Management Development Committee review the compensation received by Fastow from the LJM partnerships and Enron. Both proposals were adopted by the Finance Committee.

Finally, the Finance Committee (in addition to the Audit and Compliance Committee) was informed on February 12, 2001, of still more procedures and controls:

- The use within Enron of an "LJM Deal Approval Sheet"—in addition to the normal DASH—for every transaction with LJM, describing the transaction and its economics, and requiring approval by senior level commercial, technical, and commercial support professionals. (This procedure had, in fact, been adopted by early 2000.)

- The use of an "LJM Approval Process Checklist" that included matters such as alternative sales options and counter-parties; a determination that the transaction was conducted at arm's length, and any evidence to the contrary; disclosure obligations; and review not only by Causey and Buy but also by Skilling.

- LJM senior professionals do not ever negotiate on behalf of Enron.

- People negotiating on behalf of Enron "report to senior Enron professionals apart from Andrew Fastow."

- Global Finance Commercial, Legal and Accounting Departments monitor compliance with procedures and controls, and regularly update Causey and Buy.

- Internal and outside counsel are regularly consulted regarding disclosure obligations and review any such disclosures.

These controls were a genuine effort by the Board to satisfy itself that Enron's interests would be protected.

At bottom, however, the need for such an extensive set of controls said something fundamental about the wisdom of permitting the CFO to take on this conflict of interest. The two members of the Special Committee participating in this review of the Board's actions believe that a conflict of this significance that could be managed only through so many controls and procedures should not have been approved in the first place.

3.   Creation of the Raptor Vehicles

The Board authorized Raptor I in May of 2000. The Board was entitled to rely on assurances it received that Enron's internal accountants and Andersen had fully evaluated and approved the accounting treatment of the transaction, but there was nevertheless an opportunity for the members of the Board to identify flaws and pursue open questions.[72]

Raptor I was presented to the Finance Committee on May 1, 2000. It was presented to the Board the following day. The Committee and Board were not given all of the details, but they were given a substantial amount of information. They understood this transaction to be another version of the Rhythms transaction, which they had approved the previous year and believed to have performed successfully. They were informed that the hedging capacity of Raptor I came from the value of Enron's own stock, with which Enron would "seed" the vehicle. They were informed that Enron would purchase a share-settled put on approximately seven million shares of its own stock. Handwritten notes apparently taken by the corporate secretary suggest that the Committee was informed that the structure "[d]oes not transfer economic risk but transfers P&L volatility." At least some members of the Committee understood that this was an accounting-related transaction, not an economic hedge. On a list the Committee (and, it appears, the Board) was shown about the risks posed by the Raptor vehicle, the first risk was of "[a]ccounting scrutiny." The list said that this risk was mitigated

---

[72]   The Board cannot be faulted for lack of oversight over the most troubling Raptor transactions: Raptor III and the Raptor restructuring. With the possible exception of Skilling, who says he recalls being vaguely aware of these particular events, the members of the Board do not appear to have been informed about these transactions. Neither the minutes nor the witnesses we interviewed indicate that Raptor III was ever brought to the Board or its Committees. This may have been because no Enron stock was issued. Raptor III also does not appear to have been disclosed at the February 2001 meetings of the Audit and Compliance Committee or the Finance Committee. The list presented at the February 2001 meetings refers generally to "Raptors I, II, III, IV," but the Finance Committee had reason to believe the transactions referred to as Raptors III and IV were substantially identical to Raptor I. Raptor III, as described earlier in this Report, was not presented to or authorized by the Board.

by the fact that the "[t]ransaction [was] reviewed by CAO [Causey] and Arthur Anderson [sic]."

We believe that each of these elements should have been the subject of detailed questioning that might have led the Finance Committee or the Board to discover the fundamental flaws in the design and purpose of the transaction. The discussion, if accurately described by the handwritten notes, suggested an absence of economic substance: a hedge that does not transfer economic risk is not a real hedge. While it is often the case that *sales* to SPEs transfer only limited economic risk, a *hedge* that does not transfer economic risk is not a meaningful concept. Enron's purchasing a "put" on its own stock from Talon (Raptor I)—a bet against the value of that stock—had no apparent business purpose. The statement that the first risk to be considered was that of "[a]ccounting scrutiny" was a red flag that should have led to the Board's referring the proposal to the Audit and Compliance Committee for careful assessment of any controversial accounting issues, and should have led that Committee to conduct a probing discussion with Andersen.

The involvement of Enron's internal accountants, and the reported (and actual) involvement of Andersen, gave the Finance Committee and the Board reason to presume that the transaction was proper. Raptor was an extremely complex transaction, presented to the Committee by advocates who conveyed confidence and assurance that the proposal was in Enron's best interests, and that it was in compliance with legal and accounting rules. Nevertheless, this was a proposal that deserved closer and more critical examination.

4. Board Oversight of the Ongoing Relationship with LJM

Two control procedures adopted by the Board (and indeed sound corporate governance) called for specific oversight by Committees of the Board. These were periodic reviews of the transactions and of Fastow's compensation from LJM.[73]

Committee Review. In addition to the meetings at which LJMI and LJM2 were approved, the Audit and Compliance Committee and the Finance Committee reviewed certain aspects of the LJM transactions. The Audit and Compliance Committee did so by means of annual reviews in February 2000 and February 2001.

---

[73]   Enron's Board of Directors met five times each year in regular meetings, and from time to time in special meetings. The regular meetings typically involved committee meetings as well. The Finance Committee and the Audit and Compliance Committee each generally met for one to two hours the afternoon before the Board meeting.

The Finance Committee did so by means of a report from Fastow on May 1, 2000 and an annual review in February 2001.

The Committee reviews did not effectively supplement Management's oversight (such as it was). Though part of this may be attributed to the Committees, part may not. The Committees were severely hampered by the fact that significant information about the LJM relationship was withheld from them, in at least five respects:

First, in each of the two years in which the February annual review occurred, Causey presented to the Committees a list of transactions with LJM1 and LJM2 in the preceding year. The lists were incomplete (though Causey says he did not know this, and in any event a more complete presentation may not have affected the Committee's review): the 1999 list identified eight transactions, when in fact there were ten, and the 2000 list of transactions omitted the "buyback" transactions described earlier. Knowledge of these "buyback" transactions would have raised substantial questions about the nature and purpose of the earlier sales.

Second, Fastow represented to the Finance Committee on May 1, 2000, that LJM2 had a projected internal rate of return on its investments of 17.95%, which was consistent with the returns the Committee members said they anticipated for a "bridge" investor such as LJM2. In contrast, at the annual meeting of LJM2 limited partners on October 26, 2000, Fastow presented written materials showing that their projected internal rate of return on these investments was 51%. While some of this dramatic increase may have been attributable to transactions after May 1—in particular the Raptor transactions—there is no indication that Fastow ever corrected the misimpression he gave the Finance Committee about the anticipated profitability of LJM2.

Third, it appears that, at the meeting for the February 2001 review, the Committees were not provided with important information. The presentation included a discussion of the Raptor vehicles that had been created the preceding year. Apparently, however, the Committees were not told that two of the vehicles then owed Enron approximately $175 million more than they had the capacity to pay. This information was contained in a report that was provided daily to Causey and Buy, but it appears that neither of them brought it to either Committee's attention.

Fourth, it does not appear that the Board was informed either that, by March of 2001, this deficit had grown to about $500 million, or that this would have led to a charge against Enron's earnings in that quarter if not addressed prior to March 31. Nor does it appear that the Board was informed about restructuring the Raptor vehicles on March 26, 2001, or the transfer of approximately $800 million of Enron stock contracts that was part of that transaction. The restructuring was directed at avoiding a charge to earnings. While these transactions may or may not have required Board action as a technical matter, it is difficult to understand why matters of such significance and sensitivity at Enron would not have been brought to the attention of the Board. Causey and Buy, among others, were aware of the deficit and restructuring. Skilling recalls being only vaguely aware of these events, but other witnesses have told us that Skilling, then in his first quarter as CEO, was aware of and intensely interested in the restructuring.

Fifth, recent public disclosures show that Andersen held an internal meeting on February 5, 2001, to address serious concerns about Enron's accounting for and oversight of the LJM relationship. The people attending that meeting reportedly decided to suggest that Enron establish a special committee of the Board of Directors to review the fairness of LJM transactions or to provide for other procedures or controls, such as competitive bidding. Enron's Audit and Compliance Committee held a meeting one week later, on February 12, 2001, which was attended by David B. Duncan and Thomas H. Bauer, two of the Andersen partners who (according to the public disclosures) had also been in attendance at the Andersen meeting on February 5. We are told (although the minutes do not reflect) that the Committee also conducted an executive session with the Andersen representatives, in the absence of Enron's management, to inquire if Andersen had any concerns it wished to express. There is no evidence that Andersen raised concerns about LJM.

There is no evidence of any discussion by either Andersen representative about the problems or concerns they apparently had discussed internally just one week earlier. None of the Committee members we interviewed recalls that such concerns were raised, and the minutes make no mention of any discussion of the subject. Rather, according to the minutes and to written presentation materials, Duncan reported that "no material weaknesses had been identified" in Andersen's audit and that Andersen's "[o]pinion regarding internal control . . . [w]ill be unqualified."[74] While we have not had access to either Duncan or

---

[74]   The written materials included "Selected Observations" on financial reporting. "Related party transactions" were one of five areas singled out in this section. Andersen's comments were that "Relationship issues add scrutiny risk to: [j]udgmental structuring and valuation issues [and] [u]nderstanding of transaction completeness" and "Required disclosures reviewed for adequacy."

Bauer, the minutes do not indicate that the Andersen representatives made any comments to the Committee about controls while Causey was reviewing them, or recommended forming a special committee to review the fairness of the LJM transactions, or recommended any other procedures or review.

The Board cannot be faulted for failing to act on information that was withheld, but it can be faulted for the limited scrutiny it gave to the transactions between Enron and the LJM partnerships. The Board had agreed to permit Enron to take on the risks of doing business with its CFO, but had done so on the condition that the Audit and Compliance Committee (and later also the Finance Committee) review Enron's transactions with the LJM partnerships. These reviews were a significant part of the control structure, and should have been more than just another brief item on the agenda.

In fact, the reviews were brief, reportedly lasting ten to fifteen minutes. More to the point, the specific economic terms, and the benefits to LJM1 or LJM2 (or to Fastow), were not discussed. There does not appear to have been much, if any, probing with respect to the underlying basis for Causey's representation that the transactions were at arm's-length and that "the process was working effectively." The reviews did provide the Committees with what they believed was an assurance that Causey had in fact looked at the transactions—an entirely appropriate objective for a Board Committee-level review of ordinary transactions with outside parties.[75] But these were not normal transactions. There was little point in relying on Audit and Compliance Committee review as a control over these transactions if that review did not have more depth or substance.[76]

Review of Fastow's Compensation. Committee-mandated procedures required reviewing Fastow's compensation from LJM1 and LJM2. This should have been an important control. As much as any other procedure, it might have provided a warning if the

---

[75]   Or. St. § 60.357(2) (1999) ("a director is entitled to rely on information, opinions, reports or statements including financial statements and other financial data, if prepared or presented by: . . . [o]ne or more officers or employees of the corporation whom the director reasonably believes to be reliable and competent in the matters presented [and] legal counsel, public accountants or other persons as to matters the director reasonably believes are within the person's professional or expert competence. . . .").

[76]   The need for careful scrutiny became even greater in May 2000, when Fastow asserted to the Finance Committee that transactions between Enron and the two LJM entities had provided earnings to Enron during 1999 of $229.5 million. Enron's total net income for the two quarters of 1999 in which the LJM partnerships had been [in] existence was $549 million. The following year, Enron's 2000 Form 10-K disclosed that it had generated some $500 million of revenues in 2000 (virtually all of it going directly to the bottom line) from the Raptor transactions alone, thereby offsetting losses on Enron merchant investments that would otherwise have reduced earnings. These were very substantial contributors to Enron's earnings for each of those periods.

transactions were on terms too generous to LJM1 or LJM2. It might have indicated whether the representation that Fastow would not profit from increases in the price of Enron stock was accurate. It might have revealed whether Fastow's gains were inconsistent with the understanding reported by a number of Board members that he would be receiving only modest compensation from LJM, commensurate with the approximately three hours per week he told the Finance Committee in May 2000 he was spending on LJM matters.

We have seen only very limited information concerning Fastow's compensation from the LJM partnerships. As discussed above in Section IV, we have seen documents indicating that Fastow's family foundation received $4.5 million in May 2000 from the Southampton investment. We also have reviewed some 1999 and 2000 Schedules K-1 for the partnerships that Fastow provided. At a minimum, the K-1s indicate that Fastow's partnership capital increased by $15 million in 1999 and $16 million in 2000, for a total of over $31 million, and that he received distributions of $18.7 million in 2000.

The Board's review apparently never occurred until October 2001, after newspaper reports focused attention on Fastow's involvement in LJM1 and LJM2. (The information Fastow provided orally to members of the Board in October 2001 is generally consistent with the figures discussed above.) The only references we have found to procedures for checking whether Fastow's compensation was modest, as the Board had expected, are in the minutes of the October 6, 2000 meeting of the Finance Committee. There, Fastow told the Committee (in Skilling's presence) that Skilling received "a review of [Fastow's] economic interest in [Enron] and the LJM funds," and the Committee then unanimously agreed that the Compensation Committee should review Fastow's compensation from LJM1 and LJM2. Although a number of members of the Compensation Committee were present at this Finance Committee meeting, it does not appear that the Compensation Committee thereafter performed a review. Moreover, Skilling said he did not review the *actual* amount of Fastow's LJM1 or LJM2 compensation. He said that, instead, he received a handwritten document (from Fastow) showing only that Fastow's economic stake in Enron was substantially larger than his economic stake in LJM1 and LJM2.[77]

---

[77]   Skilling reasoned that Fastow's comparatively larger economic stake in Enron relative to his interest in the LJM partnerships would create an incentive for Fastow to place Enron's interests ahead of those of LJM1 and LJM2. This was the objective of the exercise, as Skilling saw

Some witnesses expressed the view that direct inquiry into Fastow's compensation would have been inappropriate or intrusive, or might have compromised the independence of LJM. We do not understand this reticence, and we disagree. First, the Board apparently *did* require inquiry into Fastow's compensation, but it either was not done or was done ineffectively. Second, we do not believe that requiring Fastow to provide a copy of his tax return from the partnerships, or similar information, would have been inappropriate. The independence of LJM was not predicated on Fastow's independence from Enron; rather, it was predicated on the existence of a structure within LJM that created limited partner control because Fastow *was* technically viewed as being controlled by Enron. Thus Enron's scrutinizing Fastow's compensation was not inconsistent with the independence of LJM.

B. Oversight by Management

Management had the primary responsibility for implementing the Board's resolutions and controls. Management failed to do this in several respects. No one accepted primary responsibility for oversight, the controls were not executed properly, and there were apparent structural defects in the controls that no one undertook to remedy or to bring to the Board's attention. In short, no one was minding the store.

The most fundamental management control flaw was the lack of separation between LJM and Enron personnel, and the failure to recognize that the inherent conflict was persistent and unmanageable. Fastow, as CFO, knew what assets Enron's business units wanted to sell, how badly and how soon they wanted to sell them, and whether they had alternative buyers. He was in a position to exert great pressure and influence, directly or indirectly, on Enron personnel who were negotiating with LJM. We have been told of instances in which he used that pressure to try to obtain better terms for LJM, and where people reporting to him instructed business units that LJM would be the buyer of the asset they wished to sell. Pursuant to the Services Agreement between Enron and LJM, Enron employees worked for LJM while still sitting in their Enron offices, side by side with people who were acting on behalf of Enron. Simply put, there was little of the separation and independence required to enable Enron employees to negotiate effectively against LJM2.

---

it. While we understand this explanation, we do not believe that the reasoning is valid. Even if Fastow's economic interest in Enron were far greater than his interest in LJM1 and LJM2, his potential benefits from even one transaction that favored LJM1 or LJM2—in which he had a direct and substantial stake—might far outweigh any detriment to him as a holder of stock or options in Enron, on which the transaction could be expected to have minimal financial impact.

In many cases, the safeguard requiring that a transaction could be negotiated on behalf of Enron only by employees who did not report to Fastow was ignored. We have identified at least 13 transactions between Enron and LJM2 in which the individuals negotiating on behalf of Enron reported directly or indirectly to Fastow.

This situation led one Fastow subordinate, then-Treasurer Jeff McMahon, to complain to Skilling in March 2000. While McMahon's and Skilling's recollections of their conversation differ, McMahon's contemporaneous handwritten discussion points, which he says he followed in the meeting, include these notations:

- "LJM situation where AF [Andy Fastow] wears 2 hats and upside comp is so great creates a conflict I am right in the middle of."

- "I find myself negotiating with Andy [to whom he then reported] on Enron matters and am pressured to do a deal that I do not believe is in the best interests of the shareholders."

- "Bonuses do get affected—MK [Michael Kopper], JM [Jeff McMahon]"[78]

McMahon's notes also indicate he raised the concern that Fastow was pressuring investment banks that did business with Enron to invest in LJM2.

Skilling has said he recalls the conversation focusing only on McMahon's compensation. Even if that is true, it still may have suggested that Fastow's conflict was placing pressure on an Enron employee. The conversation presented an issue that required remedial action: a solution by Management, a report to the Board that its controls were not working properly, or both. Skilling took no action of which we are aware, and shortly thereafter McMahon accepted a transfer within Enron that removed him from contact with LJM. Neither Skilling nor McMahon raised the issue with Lay or the Board.

Conflicts continued. Indeed, the Raptor transactions, which provided the most lucrative returns to LJM2 of any of its transactions with Enron, followed soon after McMahon's meeting with Skilling. The Raptor I transaction was designed by Ben Glisan—McMahon's successor as Treasurer—who reported to

---

[78] McMahon says this was a reference to his perception that Kopper, who had worked closely with Fastow, had received a very large bonus, while McMahon felt he had been penalized for his resistance with respect to LJM.

Fastow, and by others in Fastow's Global Finance Group. Another Enron employee responsible for later Raptors was Trushar Patel. He was in the Global Finance Group and married to Anne Yaeger Patel, an Enron employee who assisted Fastow at LJM2. Both Yaeger Patel and Glisan also shared in the Southampton Place partnership windfall, during the same period the Raptor transactions were in progress.

The Board's first and most-relied-on control was review of transactions by the Chief Accounting Officer, Causey, and the Chief Risk Officer, Buy. Neither ignored his responsibility completely, but neither appears to have given the transactions anywhere near the level of scrutiny the Board understood they were giving. Neither imposed a procedure for identifying all LJM1 or LJM2 transactions and for assuring that they went through the required procedures. It appears that some of the transactions, including the "buybacks" of assets previously sold to LJM1 or LJM2, did not even come to Causey or Buy for review. Although Buy has said he was aware that changes were made to the Raptors during the first quarter of 2001, he also said he was not involved in reviewing those changes. He should have reviewed this transaction, like all other transactions with LJM2.

Even with respect to the transactions that he did review, Causey said he viewed his role as being primarily determining that the appropriate business unit personnel had signed off. Buy said he viewed his role as being primarily to evaluate Enron's risk.[79] It does not appear that Causey or Buy had the necessary time, or spent the necessary time, to provide an effective check, even though the Board was led to believe they had done so.

Skilling appears to have been almost entirely uninvolved in overseeing the LJM transactions, even though in October 2000 the Finance Committee was told by Fastow—apparently in Skilling's presence—that Skilling had undertaken substantial duties.[80] Fastow told the Committee that there could be no transactions with the LJM entities without Skilling's approval, and that Skilling was reviewing Fastow's compensation. Skilling described himself to us as having little or no role with respect to the

---

[79]　Buy and a subordinate who assisted him on certain of the transactions have said that in cases where Enron was selling to LJM2 an interest in an asset that Enron had acquired, they checked to see that the sale price was consistent with the acquisition price. This appears to be the one point in the review process at which there was an appropriate examination of the substance of the transactions; in fact, the price of the assets sold by Enron to LJM2 does not appear to have been where the problems arose.

[80]　The minutes of the October 6, 2000 meeting of the Finance Committee report Fastow saying that "Buy, Causey and Skilling review all transactions between the Company and the LJM funds." The minutes state that Skilling, along with Buy and Causey, "attended the meeting." Skilling told us that he may not have been present for Fastow's remarks.

individual LJM transactions, and said he had no detailed understanding of the Raptor transactions (apart from their general purpose). His signature is absent from many LJM Deal Approval Sheets, even though the Finance Committee was told that his approval was required. Skilling said he would sign off on transactions if Causey and Buy had signed off, suggesting he made no independent assessment of the transactions' fairness. This was not sufficient in light of the representations to the Board.

It does not appear that Lay had, or was intended to have, any managerial role in connection with LJM once the entities became operational. His involvement was principally on the same basis as other Directors. By the accounts of both Lay and Skilling, the division of labor between them was that Skilling, as President and COO (later CEO) had full responsibility for domestic operational activities such as these. Skilling said he would keep Lay apprised of major issues, but does not recall discussing LJM matters with him. Likewise, the Enron employees we interviewed did not recall discussing LJM matters with Lay after the entities were created other than at Board and Board Committee meetings, except in two instances after he resumed the position of CEO in August and September of 2001 (the Watkins letter, discussed in Section VII.C, and the termination of the Raptors, discussed in Section V.E.). Still, during the period while Lay was CEO, he bore ultimate management responsibility.

Still other controls were not properly implemented. The LJM Deal Approval Sheet process was not well-designed, and it was not consistently followed. We have been unable to locate Approval Sheets for some transactions. Other Approval Sheets do not have all the required signatures. The Approval Sheet form contained pre-printed check marks in boxes signifying compliance with a number of controls and disclosure concerns, with the intention that a signature would be added to certify the accuracy of the pre-printed check-marks. Some transactions closed before the Approval Sheets were completed. The Approval Sheets did not require any documentation of efforts to find third party, unrelated buyers for Enron assets other than LJM1 or LJM2, and it does not appear that such efforts were systematically pursued. Some of the questions on the Approval Sheets were framed with boilerplate conclusions ("Was this transaction done strictly on an arm's-length basis?"), and others were worded in a fashion that set unreasonably low standards or were worded in the negative ("Was Enron advised by any third party that this transaction was not fair, from a financial perspective, to Enron?"). In practice, it appears the LJM Deal Approval Sheets were a formality that provided little control.

Apart from these failures of execution, perhaps the most basic reason the controls failed was structural. Most of the controls were based on a model in which Enron's business units were in full command of transactions and had the time *and* motivation to find the highest price for assets they were selling. In some cases, transactions were consistent with this model, but in many of the transactions the assumptions underlying this model did not apply. The Raptor transactions had little economic substance. In effect, they were transfers of economic risk from one Enron pocket to another, apparently to create income that would offset mark-to-market losses on merchant investments on Enron's income statement. The Chief Accounting Officer was not the most effective guardian against transactions of this sort, because the Accounting Department was at or near the root of the transactions. Other transactions were temporary transfers of assets Enron wanted off its balance sheet. It is unclear in some of the cases whether economic risk ever passed from Enron to LJM1 or LJM2. The fundamental flaw in these transactions was not that the price was too low. Instead, as a matter of economic substance, it is not clear that anything was really being bought or sold. Controls that were directed at assuring a fair price to Enron were ineffective to address this problem.

In sum, the controls that were in place were not effectively implemented by Management, and the conflict was so fundamental and pervasive that it overwhelmed the controls as the relationship progressed. The failure of any of Enron's Senior Management to oversee the process, and the failure of Skilling to address the problem of Fastow's influence over the Enron side of transactions on the one occasion when, by McMahon's account, it did come to his attention, permitted the problem to continue unabated until late 2001.[3]

QUESTIONS ON THE CONTROL MECHANISMS
FOR RELATED-PARTY TRANSACTIONS

What about the board's reliance on Arthur Andersen (310)? The Special Investigative Committee concluded that the Enron Board was "entitled to rely" on Andersen to "(1) provide substantial services with respect to structuring

------

[3]   Report of Investigation by the Special Investigative Committee of the Board of Directors of Enron Corp. (February 1, 2002) at 151–72, http://www.sec.gov/Archives/edgar/data/1024401/000090951802000089/big.txt.

and accounting for many of the transactions, [and] (2) review Enron's financial statement disclosures with respect to the related-party transactions (including representations that 'the terms of the transactions were reasonable and no less favorable than the terms of similar arrangements with unrelated third parties')." (*id.*). Assume that relying on an expert satisfies the legal duty of care in this instance. To what extent should a board or committee rely on an expert, as a matter of good governance, under circumstances such as the Raptor transactions presented? Put another way, do you see any difference between satisfying the legal standard and governing a corporation well?

Look again at all the controls outlined on 311–312. Do they look sufficiently comprehensive, especially if you put yourself in the directors' position before all the problems came out?

See how easily board review can be frustrated if management fails to provide the board with information and the outside auditor fails to raise its concerns with the board (315–317)? How can a board ensure that it will get the input it needs on related-party transactions? Is there a point at which the board must trust management? Does a board need its own staff? Should a board use the company's internal auditors to gather information on related-party transactions, including whether the intended controls over such transactions are being implemented? Does your answer depend on what other tasks might usefully be assigned to the internal auditors?

What were the probing questions that the Enron Board committees were supposed to be asking (317)? Is it likely that management would have provided answers that revealed problems?

If you had been a Board member, what steps would you have taken to ensure that the chief accounting officer and the chief risk officer performed the kind of substantive review of LJM2 transactions that you wanted (321)? Consider the same question for the review by Skilling (321–322). And ask yourself what steps you would have taken for just making sure that (i) the control paperwork required more than confirmation of boilerplate conclusions, and (ii) the paperwork was actually completed (322).

Was this an instance in which good controls were in place but simply not followed? Or were the transactions so rife with conflict that no set of controls was likely to be effective? Or, as the Special Investigative Committee concluded, were the controls aimed at the wrong target—whether the prices in the transactions were fair to Enron, rather than whether the transactions made economic sense in the first place? See 323.

———————————

CHAPTER 9

ENRON PART III: THE BOARD

■ ■ ■

This Chapter Nine completes our Enron study with a close look at the Enron Board, based largely on a report prepared by the Permanent Subcommittee on Investigations of the Senate Committee on Governmental Affairs and the hearings preceding that report. The chapter starts with documents showing repeated statements to the Enron Board that the company was engaged in accounting practices that created risk. The chapter then turns to the board's handling of compensation. It concludes by studying the composition of the board and, in particular, whether the directors were sufficiently independent to evaluate management proposals.

A. ACCOUNTING RISK AND THE BOARD

What follows are pages from the subcommittee hearings. First, look at an Arthur Andersen presentation to the Enron Audit Committee (326),[1] as well as another document related to the same presentation and annotated by David Duncan (327),[2] who headed the Arthur Andersen engagement team for the Enron account. See also a typewritten transcription of a part of Duncan's annotation (328).[3] Then examine a portion of another Andersen document prepared for the Enron Audit Committee (329–330)[4] with a handwritten note that the Enron corporate secretary made during the course of the related Andersen presentation. I have added my transcription of that note. Review next a document that the Finance Committee received before approving Raptor I (331–335).[5] I apologize for the difficulty you will have reading the handwriting. But focus particularly on the last page (335). Finally, read selected passages of testimony by Robert Jaedicke (336–338),[6] who was the chair of the Enron Audit Committee. Jaedicke was a professor emeritus of accounting at the Stanford Business School, had been on the Stanford faculty since 1961, and had served as a director not only of Enron,

---

[1]   *The Role of the Board of Directors in Enron's Collapse: Hearing Before the Permanent Subcomm. on Investigations of the Comm. on Governmental Affairs, U.S. Senate*, 107th Cong. 204 Exh. 2a (May 7, 2002).

[2]   *Id.* at 208 Exh. 3.

[3]   *Id.* at 209 Exh. 4.

[4]   *Id.* at 218–19 Exh. 8a.

[5]   *Id.* at 306–10 Exh. 28b.

[6]   *Id.* at 29–32.

but also of Boise Cascade, California Water Service Company, and GenCorp.

Selected Observations
1998 Financial Reporting

ENRON   **ARTHUR ANDERSEN**

Category	Risk Profile — Accounting Judgements	Risk Profile — Disclosure Judgements	Risk Profile — Rate Changes	Comment
Highly Structured Transactions				
Energy Asset Securitizations	(H)	(H)	(H)	• Judgement Relates To General Applicability of Model And Any Retained Control Features • Significance of Earnings Heightens Need for Disclosure • Ongoing Rulemaking Activity Could Drastically Limit Model
Other Income Related	(H)	M	M	• Judgement Usually Relates To Extent of Any Continued Involvement And/Or Contingency Exposures
Commodity and Equity Portfolio				
Commodities (MTM) and Merchant Investments (Fair Value)	(H)	(H)	M	• Inherent Judgement Around Methodologies • Significance of Merchant Earnings Heightens Need For Disclosure
Prudency	(H)	(H)	L	• Assessment and Documentation Procedures Recently Enhanced • Relationship to SEC Hot Areas
Purchase Accounting	(H)	M	L	• Judgement Relates To Original Valuations and Accounting for Subsequent Activity
Balance Sheet Issues				
Equity Investments	(H)	(H)	M	• Judgement Relates To Control And Required Economic Parameters • Continue Appropriate Commitment/Guarentee/Contingency Disclosures
Portfolio Monetizations	(H)	M	(H)	• Judgement Relates To Extent of Any Continued Involvement • Ongoing Rulemaking Activity (Could Be Positive)
Other				

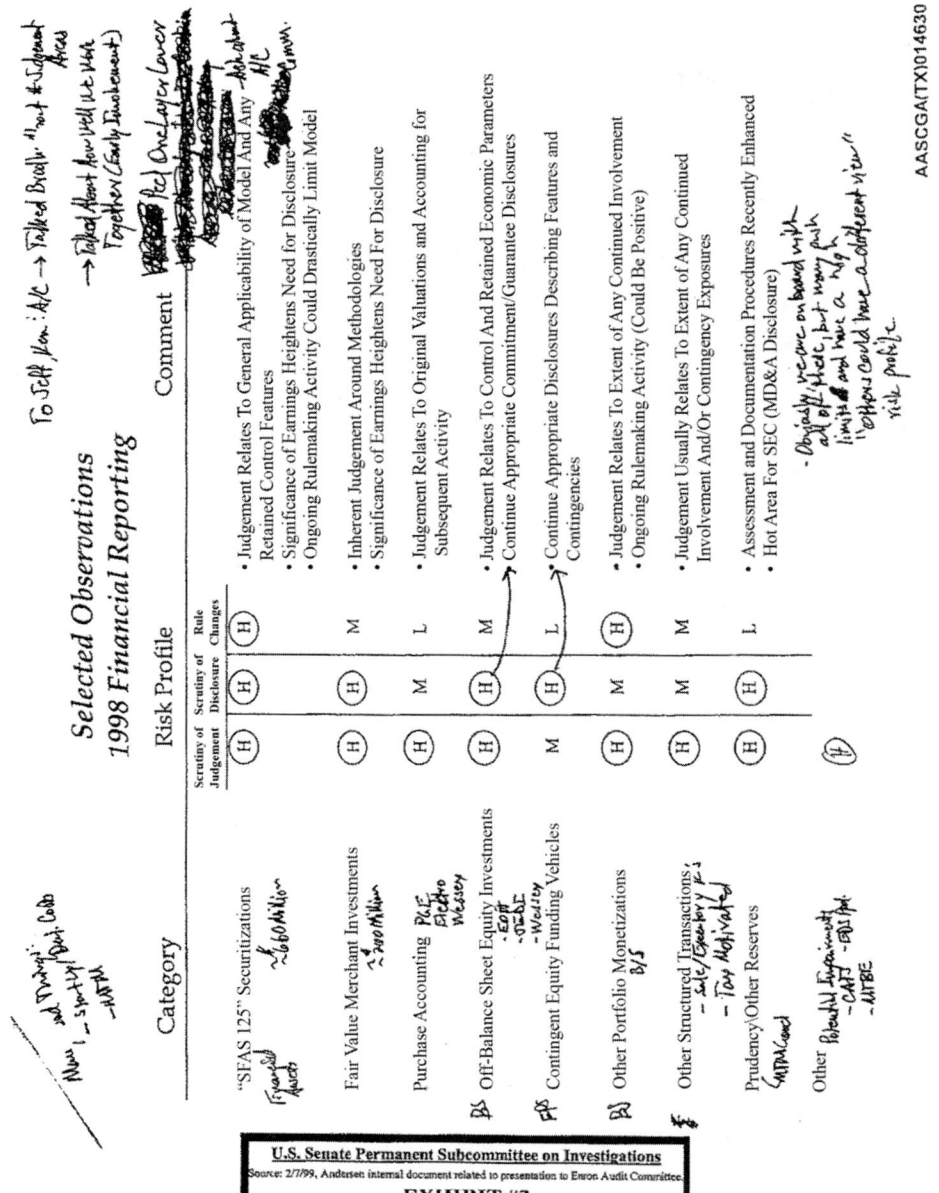

Selected Observations
1998 Financial Reporting

Category	Risk Profile			Comment
	Scrutiny of Judgement	Scrutiny of Disclosure	Rule Changes	
"SFAS 125" Securitizations	H	H	H	• Judgement Relates To General Applicability of Model And Any Retained Control Features • Significance of Earnings Heightens Need for Disclosure • Ongoing Rulemaking Activity Could Drastically Limit Model
Fair Value Merchant Investments	H	H	M	• Inherent Judgement Around Methodologies • Significance of Earnings Heightens Need For Disclosure
Purchase Accounting	H	M	L	• Judgement Relates To Original Valuations and Accounting for Subsequent Activity
Off-Balance Sheet Equity Investments	H	H	M	• Judgement Relates To Control And Retained Economic Parameters • Continue Appropriate Commitment/Guarantee Disclosures
Contingent Equity Funding Vehicles	M	H	L	• Continue Appropriate Disclosures Describing Features and Contingencies
Other Portfolio Monetizations	H	M	H	• Judgement Relates To Extent of Any Continued Involvement • Ongoing Rulemaking Activity (Could Be Positive)
Other Structured Transactions	H	M	M	• Judgement Usually Relates To Extent of Any Continued Involvement And/Or Contingency Exposures
Prudency\Other Reserves	H	H	L	• Assessment and Documentation Procedures Recently Enhanced • Hot Area For SEC (MD&A Disclosure)
Other				

AASCGA(TX)014630

David Duncan of Andersen
to Enron Audit Committee
(Feb. 7, 1999)

"Obviously, we are on board with all of
these, but many push limits and have a high
'others could have a different view' risk profile."

–SFAS 125 Securitizations

–Fair Value Merchant Investments

–Purchase Accounting

–Off-Balance Sheet Equity Investments

–Contingent Equity Funding Vehicles

–Other Portfolio Monetizations

–Other Structured Transactions

–Prudency/Other Reserves

U.S. Senate Permanent Subcommittee on Investigations

EXHIBIT #4

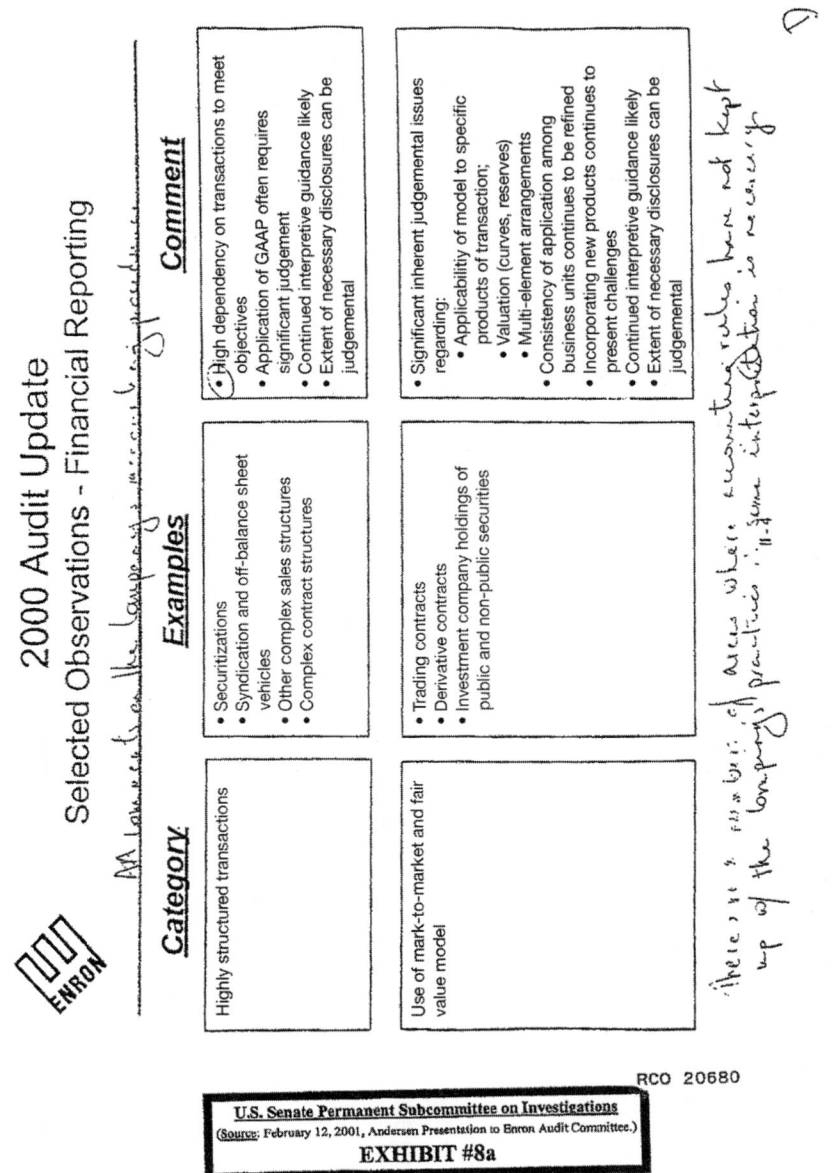

2000 Audit Update
Selected Observations – Financial Reporting

Category

Highly structured transactions

Use of mark-to-market and fair value model

Examples

- Securitizations
- Syndication and off-balance sheet vehicles
- Other complex sales structures
- Complex contract structures

- Trading contracts
- Derivative contracts
- Investment company holdings of public and non-public securities

Comment

- High dependency on transactions to meet objectives
- Application of GAAP often requires significant judgement
- Continued interpretive guidance likely
- Extent of necessary disclosures can be judgemental

- Significant inherent judgemental issues regarding:
  - Applicability of model to specific products of transaction;
    - Valuation (curves, reserves)
    - Multi-element arrangements
  - Consistency of application among business units continues to be refined
  - Incorporating new products continues to present challenges
  - Continued interpretive guidance likely
  - Extent of necessary disclosures can be judgemental

RCO 20680

Corporate Secretary notes on AA presentation:
There are a number of areas where accounting rules have not kept up with the Company's practices. [Therefore] some interpretation is necessary.

2000 Audit Update
Selected Observations – Financial Reporting

Category	Examples	Comment

Related party transactions	• LJM related activity
	• Syndication vehicles where company has an ownership interest
		• Relationship issues add scrutiny risk to:
		  • Judgemental structuring and valuation issues
		  • Understanding of transaction completeness
		• Required disclosures reviewed for adequacy

Other Material Judgemental Areas	• Azurix impairment • Impact of high volatility on mark-to-market valuations • Credit (California) • India Contingencies	• Company positions reviewed for reasonableness • Certain disclosures made as warranted
Classification issues	• Financial statements classification • Other public disclosures	• Categorization of activities between certain segments, operating vs. non-operating or recurring vs. non-recurring can be highly judgemental • Certain intersegment allocation practices need refinement

Project Raptor

Hedging Program for Enron Assets

EC 000025081

Purpose

Establish a risk management program in order to hedge the Profit & Loss volatility of Enron investments

Greg's Transaction last year LJM to hedge or increase the Company (?)

intended to use investment / raise financing?

Enron owns a member interest in Talon

o Talon also owns approx. $400 million of ENE stock which is subject to a 3 year stock restriction agreement - Talon cannot sell or hedge the stock.

[handwritten: Answer - AA has spent considerable time analyzing structure. Also looking to LJM disgorgement re 24 structure]

✓ ENE will help establish a non-affiliated vehicle ("Talon") as a hedge counterparty to selected investments.

✓ Excess stock from existing structured finance vehicles will be utilized to seed approximately $400 million of capital to Talon. *[handwritten: (is UBS forwarded position) As the stock increases/decreases value (currently held in SPV)]*

P Initially, vehicle can provide approximately $200 million of P & L protection to ENE. As ENE stock price increases, the vehicle's P & L protection capacity increases as well.

o LJM2 will provide non-ENE equity and will be entitled to a 30% annualized return plus fees.

o ENE will be entitled to 100% of the upside beyond LJM2's return hurdle.

[handwritten: Does not limit economic risk but transfers P & L volatility]

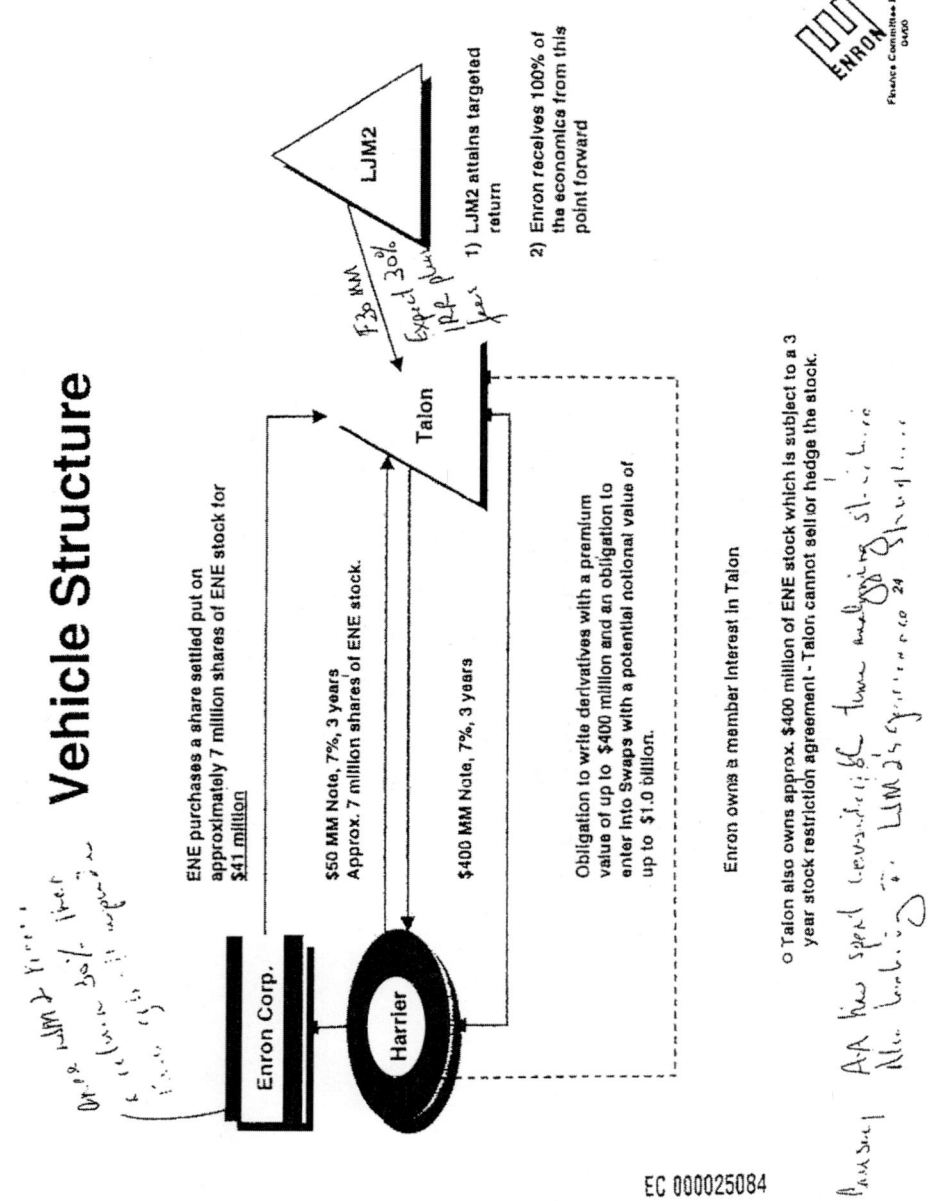

EC 000025084

Project Raptor

Risks

○ Accounting scrutiny

○ Substantial decline in the price of ENE stock
  – Program terminates early
  – Increases credit risk

○ Counterparty credit

Mitigants

○ Transaction reviewed by CAO and Arthur Anderson

○ Negotiation of early termination with LJM2

○ Assets of vehicle subject to a master netting agreement

Senator LEVIN. Well, these are not my terms. These are Arthur Andersen's terms and they are circled. The "H" is not my term. It stands for high. You can say that the "H" under rule changes means there is a high risk that the rule may change, and I fully agree with you, but by that same logic, the "H" under accounting judgments means there is a high risk involved in that judgment.

So, Dr. Jaedicke, these are not my terms. These are the documents presented to you with "H", high risk, circled by Arthur Andersen in 1999.

Next, Exhibit 3.[1] The handwriting on this document belongs to David Duncan.

Mr. JAEDICKE. Yes.

Senator LEVIN. It is his handwriting on it, and this is basically Andersen's version of the previous exhibit, with the same matrix, but now it is a document with their talking points for the presentation that was made to you at that London Audit Committee meeting.

I would like to direct your attention to the handwritten note in the lower right-hand corner. It is hard to read, so we put it up on the board here and made that Exhibit 4.[2] This is what that note says at the bottom. "Obviously, we are on board with all of these, but many push limits and have a high 'others could have a different view' risk profile." High-risk profile. This is Duncan's note on this document. Then it lists those various accounting practices which you also see on Exhibit 4.

So not only was the Audit Committee told by Andersen that although Andersen was on board, that many of Enron's accounting practices, in the words used there, his note, "push limits," and that others could view them as outside of compliance with Generally Accepted Accounting Principles. Now, do you remember David Duncan telling that to the Audit Committee on February 7, 1999?

Mr. JAEDICKE. I do not remember David Duncan telling us this particular note. David Duncan did tell us on several occasions that these were complex transactions, that they were complex structures, that Enron was a complex company. They were moving very fast, and very careful accounting judgments were required.

He also would, on occasion, try to indicate to us how much guidance was available on those. But in terms of—and I do not recall him saying, well, others could have a different view. But I think all of us understood that these were highly structured, new kinds of transactions, but please, sir, keep in mind, that was one

---

[1]   See Exhibit No. 3 which appears in the Appendix on page 208.
[2]   See Exhibit No. 4 which appears in the Appendix on page 209.

reason that Enron paid Arthur Andersen some pretty hefty fees, to try to be in on the beginning of these transactions so that those accounting judgments, they understood the transaction and that the accounting judgments would be properly made.

Mr. JAEDICKE. We knew that the company was engaged in high-risk and innovative transactions. . . .

If you go back and you look at the Audit Committee, the various meetings, Senator, you would find that on almost every agenda, there were listed—you would look at what were the audit emphases of the past quarter and what were the audit emphases of the quarter coming up, and they would almost always list related party transactions, structured transactions, securitizations, and mark-to-market and fair value. Those were almost always areas of emphasis.

Now, when we would ask them, even in executive session, about, OK, how do you feel about these, the usual expression was one of comfort. It was not, these are the highest risk transactions on our scale of one to 10 or whatever this is. If the information in this kind of a document had been conveyed to us in the terms that it showed here, the template that you showed me, the "H"s were almost always interpreted, at least by me, as saying if you want a template of those accounting areas that are important to Enron and deserve our emphasis, that is where you would look, and the "H"s were no surprise. Those were almost always on the agenda of the Committee.

Now, this kind of information, where you say pushing the limits or whatever—form over substance, I never, ever heard that term used.

Senator LEVIN. The reason that—

Mr. JAEDICKE. That I recall.

Senator LEVIN. The reason that is so important is because what was presented to you were the "H"s, not "I"s, not "M"s, not "L"s, "H"s, high-risk accounting judgments. You acknowledge that. Now the question is, well, wait a minute. Did that mean what it said? Then you have got a note contemporaneously from Duncan, as well as from the other witness who was there, saying you, in fact, were informed that these were pushing the limits at that meeting. You deny hearing that, but there is very strong evidence that, in fact, that occurred—the evidence: Contemporaneous notes, statement of another witness, and the internal documents of Arthur Andersen—show that was, indeed, their conclusion.

You put all that together, and the evidence is pretty strong that you were informed these were high-risk accounting practices but that you did not act on those notes and that information. That is what jumps out from these exhibits and from this testimony. So weigh that against "you do not remember"—it seems to leave me with one conclusion. You may not remember—

Mr. JAEDICKE. All I said was I do not remember the particular wording of the comment that you showed me on that particular— on that slide.

QUESTIONS ON ACCOUNTING RED FLAGS

This is the stuff of a classic "they saw red flags waving but proceeded ahead anyway" critique.

Do you conclude that the documents show "red flags"?

What should a director do when the outside auditor says that the accounting profile for the company includes some "high-risk" areas (326) or that "many" accounting issues "push limits and have a high 'others could have a different view' risk profile" (328)? Should a director simply demand that the business be restructured in a way that eliminates all "high" accounting risk and that never "push[es accounting] limits"? Even if the outside auditor says it is "on board" (*id.*)?

If the corporate secretary accurately captured what Arthur Andersen said to the Audit Committee about accounting rules not having " 'kept up' with Company practices" so that "some interpretation is necessary" (329), how do you think the directors should have reacted?

What should a director do when told, as Enron directors were (335) about the Raptor transaction, that a deal would create risk of "[a]ccounting scrutiny" but that it had been "reviewed by [the company's chief accounting officer] and [the outside auditor]"?

How about the idea that the shareholders want to make money, that directors sometimes have to approve taking risks to do that, and that directors are entitled to take calculated risks when nationally prominent advisers clear a deal? Is there a difference, in this regard, between a business risk and an accounting risk?

If the accountants are consistently—after stating the risks—expressing "comfort" (as Jaedicke testified at 337), why not go ahead?

After all, wasn't Enron paying the accountants those "hefty fees" (Jaedicke at 336–337) precisely so that they would make proper judgments on the close calls?

What is the relationship here between compliance with accounting rules, disclosure to the market, and making money for the shareholders?

B. COMPENSATION AND THE BOARD

Let's turn our attention now to compensation. Read below a description of Fastow's financial gains from the LJM partnerships, and the Enron Board's efforts to discover those gains, from pages 32–34 in The Role of the Board of Directors in Enron's Collapse: Report Prepared by the Permanent Subcommittee on Investigations of the Committee on Governmental Affairs, United States Senate, 107th Cong. (2002).

> **Inadequate Board Oversight of Fastow's LJM Compensation.** The Board's role in overseeing Mr. Fastow's LJM compensation was even more lax. For the first year, the Board apparently relied on Mr. Skilling to review Mr. Fastow's LJM-related income and asked no questions. In October 2000, after LJM1 had been operating for more than 1 year and the Finance Committee was told that LJM1 and LJM2 were engaging in multiple, high dollar transactions with Enron, the Finance Committee asked the Compensation Committee to conduct a one-time review of Mr. Fastow's compensation.
>
> Dr. LeMaistre, then Chairman of the Compensation Committee, was present at the Finance Committee meeting, and attempted to obtain the requested information on Mr. Fastow's LJM compensation. He indicated during his interview and at the hearing that, after the Finance Committee meeting, he asked Enron's senior compensation officer, Mary Joyce, to provide him with information on the outside income of all of Enron's "16(b) officers," a reference to top company officials identified according to an SEC regulation.[103] He said during his Subcommittee interview that he did not specifically name Mr. Fastow to Ms. Joyce because he did not want to start any office gossip. Ms. Joyce did not provide him with the information he requested. He said that he asked her a second time to obtain the information, but she again did not do so. He admitted that he never actually named Mr. Fastow to her or insisted that she obtain information about his LJM compensation. Instead, Dr. LeMaistre let the matter drop.
>
> At the hearing, Subcommittee Chairman Levin and Dr. LeMaistre had the following exchange.

---

[103]   Hearing Record at 68–69.

"Dr. LeMaistre: I asked Mary Joyce about it.

Sen. Levin: And what did she tell you?

Dr. LeMaistre: She said she did not have the information.

Sen. Levin: Did you say, well, I want it?

Dr. LeMaistre: She knew that I wanted it . . .

Sen. Levin: Did you get it?

Dr. LeMaistre: I did not.

Sen. Levin: This is the heart of the problem. You have got a Board that says, I want it. You have got a request for it. It does not come and you do nothing. That is an approach which is unacceptable for a Board."[104]

One year later, despite the Finance Committee's directive, Dr. LeMaistre had not obtained any information about Mr. Fastow's LJM compensation. Nor had any other Board member taken any steps to obtain this information. In October 2001, a *Wall Street Journal* article was published detailing Enron's transactions with LJM and alleging that Mr. Fastow had received compensation from LJM business transactions in excess of $7 million.[105]

In response, the Board directed two of its members, Dr. LeMaistre and John Duncan, to telephone Mr. Fastow and obtain information about his LJM investment and compensation. During his interview, Dr. LeMaistre told the Subcommittee staff that he asked the General Counsel of Enron, James Derrick, to draft specific questions for him to use in his conversation with Mr. Fastow. Mr. Derrick faxed a document with the questions to Dr. LeMaistre, who was then in Colorado.[106] After changing the order of the sentences to put the reference to "[w]e very much appreciate your willingness to visit with us" first, Dr. LeMaistre told the Subcommittee that he used the document as a script in his conversation with Mr. Fastow, as follows:

"We very much appreciate your willingness to visit with us. Andy, because of the current controversy surrounding LJM I and LJM II, we believe it would be helpful for the Board to have a general understanding of the amount of your investment and of your return on investment in the LJM

---

[104] *Id.* at 68.

[105] Hearing Exhibit 44b, "Enron CFO's Partnership Had Millions in Profit," *Wall Street Journal* (10/19/01).

[106] Hearing Exhibit 24b, script and handwritten notes of conversation between Dr. LeMaistre, John Duncan, and Mr. Fastow in October 2001. John Duncan was in Houston during the telephone call with Mr. Fastow and did not request or use the document faxed to Dr. LeMaistre.

entities. We understand that a detailed accounting of these matters will soon be done in connection with the response to the SEC inquiry. In responding to our questions with respect to your interest in the LJM entities, we would appreciate your including any interest . . . that the members of your family may have had in the entities."[107]

When Chairman Levin asked Dr. LeMaistre why his tone was so deferential to Mr. Fastow, Dr. LeMaistre said that the language had been drafted by legal counsel and he was concerned about seeking information from a special purpose entity that was supposed to be separate from Enron.

Dr. LeMaistre's handwritten notes on the document indicate that Mr. Fastow admitted receiving LJM compensation totalling $45 million, $23 million from LJM1 and $22 million from LJM2. A handwritten note in the margin of the document states "incredible," which Dr. LeMaistre said was his reaction to the compensation total, which was much greater than he had been expecting. Dr. LeMaistre also noted that Mr. Fastow declined to provide information related to his LJM investment return and promised to provide that information the next day. Mr. Duncan said during his interview that when Mr. Fastow failed to telephone with the information at the time promised, Mr. Duncan called him and was told by Mr. Fastow that he had not had the chance to obtain the requested information and would provide it later. Mr. Fastow apparently never provided that information to the Board.

Dr. LeMaistre and Mr. Duncan reported the October 23 conversation to the other Board members in a telephone Board meeting the next day. The other directors expressed surprise at the large amount of compensation, and the decision was made to place Mr. Fastow on leave immediately. Mr. Fastow was placed on leave on October 24, 2001.

During his interview, Dr. LeMaistre noted that he asked Mr. Fastow whether any Enron employee other than Mr. Fastow and Mr. Kopper had "any economic interest in or derive[d] any benefit from" the LJM partnerships.[108] He said that Mr. Fastow had replied "no," which the Board later discovered to be untrue. He and other Board members said that it was during the Powers investigation that they first learned of the Southampton partnership, which Mr. Fastow had established with five other

---

[107] Hearing Exhibit 24b.

[108] *Id.*

Enron employees to invest in LJM1 and enabled these additional Enron employees to benefit financially at Enron's expense.[7]

QUESTIONS ON COMPENSATION TO OFFICERS FROM RELATED-PARTY TRANSACTIONS

Do you see two different problems here?

Does the board need to know what a top officer is getting from a related-party transaction in part to determine whether the related-party transaction itself is fair to the company? Why?

Should the board also consider how much money the officer is receiving from such transactions when the board decides what salary, bonus, and equity compensation the company pays the officer? Why?

What about the shareholders? Should they know about the compensation in related-party transactions?

What about the amount of time the officer devotes to the related entity? Should a board be concerned that the officer will be diverted from his or her corporate duties?

How will the board get the information about the related party's payments to the officer? How can the board actually confirm that information?

Turning to more traditional compensation committee fare, consider "findings" on three more pages (49–51) from The Role of the Board of Directors in Enron's Collapse: Report Prepared by the Permanent Subcommittee on Investigations of the Committee on Governmental Affairs, United States Senate, 107th Cong. (2002).

> **Finding (5): The Enron Board of Directors approved excessive compensation for company executives, failed to monitor the cumulative cash drain caused by Enron's 2000 annual bonus and performance unit plans, and failed to monitor or halt abuse by Board Chairman and Chief Executive Officer Kenneth Lay of a company-financed, multi-million dollar, personal credit line.**

> Enron provided its executives with lavish compensation. On more than one occasion, it paid tens of millions of dollars to a single executive as a bonus for work on a single deal. Stock options were

---

[7] *The Role of the Board of Directors in Enron's Collapse: Report Prepared by the Permanent Subcomm. on Investigations of the Comm. on Governmental Affairs, U.S. Senate*, 107th Cong. 32–34 (2002) [Senate Comm. Report on Role of Enron Board].

distributed in large numbers to executives. One executive, Lou Pai, accumulated enough stock options that, when he exercised them and sold the underlying stock in 2000, he left the company with more than $265 million in cash. Mr. Lay, alone, accumulated more than 6.5 million options on Enron stock. [165] In 2000, Mr. Lay's total compensation exceeded $140 million, including $123 million from exercising a portion of his Enron stock options,[166] an amount which exceeded average CEO pay at U.S. publicly traded corporations by a factor of ten and made him one of the highest paid CEOs in the country.[167]

The Enron Board, through its Compensation Committee, was not only informed of the company's lavish executive compensation plans, it apparently approved them with little debate or restraint. One Board member said during his interview that Enron's philosophy was to provide "extraordinary rewards for extraordinary achievement"; others claimed that the company was forced to provide lavish compensation to attract the best and brightest employees. Dr. LeMaistre testified that he "did not worry" about high levels of compensation because he checked regularly with the Board's compensation consultant, Towers Perrin, and was informed that Enron was "right on target" in its compensation practices.[168] The evidence suggests that keeping up with competitor pay, rather than overseeing existing compensation plans, was the central objective of the Enron Compensation Committee.

One example of the Compensation Committee's lavish compensation philosophy, combined with its failure to conduct adequate compensation oversight, involves its May 1999 decision to permit Mr. Lay to repay company loans with company stock. The Compensation Committee had already given Mr. Lay a $4 million line of credit which, in August 2001, it increased to $7.5 million. During their interviews, the Committee members said that they knew of the line of credit, but had been unaware that, in 2000, Mr. Lay began using what one Board member called an "ATM approach" toward that credit line, repeatedly drawing down the entire amount available and then repaying the loan with

---

[165]   "Office of the Chair Compensation Summary" (10/31/01), Bates WP1797.

[166]   Hearing Exhibit 52, "Confidential for Enron Board of Directors, Public Relations, Investor Relations & HR Use Only; Potential Questions—Enron Proxy 2001" (4/13/01), Bates CL410-14, at 1.

[167]   See, for example, annual executive compensation survey by *Business Week* (4/16/01), which determined that average CEO pay in 2000 at 365 publicly traded companies in the United States was $13.1 million. In February 2001, Mr. Lay resigned his CEO post in favor of Mr. Skilling, but reclaimed it in August 2001, after Mr. Skilling left the company.

[168]   Hearing Record at 46.

Enron stock. Records show that Mr. Lay at first drew down the line of credit once per month, then every 2 weeks, and then, on some occasions, several days in a row.[169] In the 1-year period from October 2000 to October 2001, Mr. Lay used the credit line to obtain over $77 million in cash from the company and repaid the loans exclusively with Enron stock.[170] Several directors confirmed that Mr. Lay still owed the company about $7 million.

The interviewed Board members said they had been unaware of these transactions at the time and agreed that they could fairly be characterized as stock sales. They indicated that they had been unaware at the time that, by characterizing the stock transfers as loan payments rather than stock sales, Mr. Lay bypassed requirements for reporting insider stock sales on a quarterly basis and instead delayed reporting the transactions to the SEC and investing public until the end of the calendar year in which they took place.

At the hearing, when Dr. LeMaistre, former Compensation Committee Chairman, was asked whether his Committee should have been monitoring the credit line, he testified that, "We never had any responsibility to monitor this."[171] When asked whether he would agree that Mr. Lay had "abused" his credit line, Dr. LeMaistre testified that "it was not a term I care to use" and that he would stop short of characterizing Mr. Lay's actions as an abuse "because I do not know the circumstances."[172] Mr. Blake, another Compensation Committee member, stated, "I do not want to go close to the word 'abuse', but I would say that as a CEO, it is not what you say, it is what you do. Sale of a stock in the nature that took place was inappropriate. . . . I was absolutely shocked by this. . . . [I]f we had a chance to have known that occurred, we would have taken immediate and corrective action to ensure that behavior would not happen again."[173] Both Dr. LeMaistre and Mr. Blake seemed to deny responsibility for monitoring the CEO's credit line, even though the Board's Compensation Committee is charged with overseeing CEO compensation and no one other than the Board had the authority to monitor or restrict the Chief Executive Officer's actions. Mr. Lay used his credit line to withdraw $77 million in cash from the company in 1 year, replaced

---

[169]   Hearing Exhibit 36a, "Ken Lay's Repayment of Cash Loans by Transferring Enron Stock Back to Enron," prepared by the Subcommittee based upon subpoenaed documents provided by Mr. Lay, an example of which appears in Hearing Exhibit 36b.

[170]   An Enron filing in Federal bankruptcy court in June 2002, listing payments to Enron officers during 2001, states that, altogether in 2001, the company loaned Mr. Lay over $81 million.

[171]   Hearing Record at 90.

[172]   *Id.* at 89.

[173]   *Id.* at 90.

the cash with company stock, and never mentioned his borrowings or stock sales to the Board or the public. Despite learning of his conduct after the fact, the Board members at the hearing were reluctant to express strong criticism of Mr. Lay.

A second example of the Compensation Committee's poor compensation oversight involves the huge annual and special bonus plans it approved for Enron executives. During their interviews, the Compensation Committee and other Board members indicated that they had been unaware of the total amount of bonuses paid in early 2001 for work performed in 2000. That year, Enron executives received about $430 million in annual bonuses under Enron's normal bonus plan. In addition, in exchange for meeting certain stock performance targets, a special program called the Performance Unit Plan paid bonuses to about 65 Enron executives totaling another $320 million. Board members indicated that they had been unaware that the company had paid out almost $750 million in cash bonuses for a year in which the company's entire net income was $975 million. Apparently, no one on the Compensation Committee had ever added up the numbers.

The Compensation Committee appeared to have exercised little, if any, restraint over Enron's compensation plans, instead deferring to the compensation plans suggested by management and the company's compensation consultants. During their interviews, the Committee members said it had not occurred to them that, by giving Enron executives huge stock option awards, they might be creating incentives for Enron executives to improperly manipulate company earnings to increase the company stock price and cash in their options. One Board member admitted, however, that Enron was a culture driven by compensation. Another said, when asked why Enron executives misled the Board and cheated the company, that he "only can assume they did it for the money."[8]

QUESTIONS ON REVOLVING LOANS AND RULES OF THUMB FOR EXECUTIVE COMPENSATION

Think about Lay's loans.

The Enron Board (or at least the Compensation Committee) knew that the company had made a $7.5 million line of credit available to Lay. But the directors did not realize that Lay repeatedly drew down on the line, repaying

---

8   *Id.* at 49–51.

with Enron stock so that he was effectively using the credit line to convert his stock to cash.

What kind of monitoring would have kept the Committee adequately informed of Lay's actions?

One of the Committee members testified that he was "shocked" by what Lay had done. Are you? Why?

Assume that one rationale for equity compensation is to align the interests of management with those of the rest of the shareholders. If executives—by the means that Lay used or any other means—can quickly convert the shares to cash, does equity compensation serve that purpose?

Would you want to restrict the right of executives to dispose of stock that they receive as part of their compensation? Would such restrictions reduce the value of that compensation to the executives? Would that in turn require the company to transfer more shares to the executives in order to provide them with some target value?

Focus for a moment on the nearly $750 million that the company paid out in bonuses for the year in which Enron reported net income of $975 million (345). Should a board use a rule of thumb that the company should not pay out in cash bonuses an aggregate amount exceeding X% of its profits? Does that make sense? Always? Even if not always, should a company employ such a rule as a presumption from which it is prepared to deviate but only with a clearly articulated reason?

What other rules of thumb do you recommend?

Should a compensation committee reduce such rules to writing?

C. COMPOSITION OF THE BOARD

The Enron proxy statement for the company's May 2001 annual meeting described its directors in these words:

ROBERT A. BELFER, 65
Director since 1983
Mr. Belfer's principal occupation is Chairman and Chief Executive Officer of Belco Oil & Gas Corp., a company formed in 1992. Prior to his resignation in April 1986 from Belco Petroleum Corporation ("BPC"), a wholly owned subsidiary of Enron, Mr. Belfer served as President and then Chairman of BPC.

NORMAN P. BLAKE, JR., 59
Director since 1993
Mr. Blake is Chairman, President and Chief Executive Officer of Comdisco Inc., a diversified technical equipment leasing and

information technology services company. Previously, Mr. Blake served as Chief Executive Officer and Secretary General of the United States Olympic Committee. Mr. Blake served as Chairman, President and Chief Executive Officer of the Promus Hotel Corporation from December 1998 until November 1999 when it merged with the Hilton Hotels Corporation. From November 1990 until May 1998, he served as Chairman, President and Chief Executive Officer of USF & G Corporation until its merger with the St. Paul Companies. Mr. Blake is also a director of Owens-Corning Corporation.

RONNIE C. CHAN, 51
Director since 1996
For the past ten years, Mr. Chan has been Chairman of Hang Lung Group, comprising three publicly traded Hong Kong-based companies involved in property development, property investment and hotels. Mr. Chan also co-founded and is a director of various companies within Morningside/ Springfield Group, which invests in and manages private companies in the manufacturing and service businesses, and engages in financial investments. Mr. Chan is also a director of Standard Chartered PLC and Motorola, Inc.

JOHN H. DUNCAN, 73
Director since 1985
Mr. Duncan's principal occupation has been investments since 1990. Mr. Duncan is also a director of EOTT Energy Corp. (the general partner of EOTT Energy Partners, L.P.) and Group I Automotive Inc.

WENDY L. GRAMM, 56
Director since 1993
Dr. Gramm is an economist and Director of the Regulatory Studies Program of the Mercatus Center at George Mason University. From February 1988 until January 1993, Dr. Gramm served as Chairman of the Commodity Futures Trading Commission in Washington, D.C. Dr. Gramm is also a director of IBP, [I]nc., State Farm Insurance Co. and Invesco Funds. Dr. Gramm was also a director of the Chicago Mercantile Exchange until December 31, 1999.

ROBERT K. JAEDICKE, 72
Director since 1985
Dr. Jaedicke is Professor (Emeritus) of Accounting at the Stanford University Graduate School of Business in Stanford, California.

He has been on the Stanford University faculty since 1961 and served as Dean from 1983 until 1990. Dr. Jaedicke is a director of California Water Service Company and Boise Cascade Corporation and he plans to retire from the Boise Cascade Corporation board in April 2001. Dr. Jaedicke was also a director of GenCorp, Inc. until July 2000.

KENNETH L. LAY, 58
Director since 1985
Mr. Lay has been Chairman of the Board of Enron since 1986. From 1986 until February 2001, Mr. Lay was also the Chief Executive Officer of Enron. Mr. Lay is also a director of Eli Lilly and Company, Compaq Computer Corporation, EOTT Energy Corp. (the general partner of EOTT Energy Partners, L.P.), i2 Technologies, Inc. and NewPower Holdings, Inc.

CHARLES A. LEMAISTRE, 77
Director since 1985
For 18 years, Dr. LeMaistre served as President of the University of Texas M.D. Anderson Cancer Center in Houston, Texas and now holds the position of President Emeritus.

JOHN MENDELSOHN, 64
Director since 1999
Since July 1996, Dr. Mendelsohn has served as President of the University of Texas M.D. Anderson Cancer Center. Prior to 1996, Dr. Mendelsohn was Chairman of the Department of Medicine at Memorial Sloan-Kettering Cancer Center in New York. Dr. Mendelsohn is also a director of ImClone Systems, Inc.

PAULO V. FERRAZ PEREIRA, 46
Director since 1999
Mr. Pereira is Executive Vice President of Group Bozano. Mr. Pereira served for over five years as President and Chief Operating Officer of Meridional Financial Group and Managing Director of Group Bozano. Mr. Pereira is also the former President and Chief Executive Officer of the State Bank of Rio de Janeiro.

FRANK SAVAGE, 62
Director since 1999
Since 1995, Mr. Savage has served as Chairman of Alliance Capital Management International (a division of Alliance Capital Management L.P.). Mr. Savage is also a director of Lockheed Martin Corporation, Alliance Capital Management L. P. and Qualcomm Corp.

JEFFREY K. SKILLING, 47
Director since 1997
Since February 2001, Mr. Skilling has served as President and Chief Executive Officer of Enron. Mr. Skilling served as President and Chief Operating Officer of Enron from January 1997 through February 2001. From August 1990 until December 1996, he served as Chairman and Chief Executive Officer of Enron North America Corp. and its predecessor companies. Mr. Skilling is also a director of the Houston Branch of the Federal Reserve Bank of Dallas.

JOHN WAKEHAM, 68
Director since 1994
Lord Wakeham is a retired former U.K. Secretary of State for Energy and Leader of the Houses of Commons and Lords. He served as a Member of Parliament from 1974 until his retirement from the House of Commons in April 1992. Prior to his government service, Lord Wakeham managed a large private practice as a chartered accountant. He is currently Chairman of the Press Complaints Commission in the U.K. and chairman or director of a number of publicly traded U.K. companies.

HERBERT S. WINOKUR, JR., 57
Director since 1985
Mr. Winokur is Chairman and Chief Executive Officer of Capricorn Holdings, Inc. (a private investment company) and Managing General Partner of Capricorn Investors, L.P., Capricorn Investors II, L.P. and Capricorn Investors III, L.P., partnerships concentrating on investments in restructure situations, organized by Mr. Winokur in 1987, 1994 and 1999, respectively. From August 2000 until March 2001, Mr. Winokur served as Nonexecutive Chairman of Azurix Corp. Prior to his current appointment, Mr. Winokur was Senior Executive Vice President and a director of Penn Central Corporation. He is also a director of NATCO Group, Inc., Mrs. Fields' Holding Company, Inc., CCC Information Services Group, Inc. and DynCorp.[9]

FIRST SET OF QUESTIONS ON BOARD COMPOSITION

How do these folks look at first blush?

Any immediate concerns?

---

[9]   Enron Corp., Definitive Proxy Statement, Schedule 14A (filed Mar. 27, 2001) at 2–5.

They even had a Stanford emeritus accounting professor on the board. He chaired the Audit Committee. Good enough?

Finally, read from pages 8–11 and 51–55 of The Role of the Board of Directors in Enron's Collapse: Report Prepared by the Permanent Subcommittee on Investigations of the Committee on Governmental Affairs, United States Senate, 107th Cong. (2002).

> **Enron Board.** In 2001, Enron's Board of Directors had 15 members, several of whom had 20 years or more experience on the Board of Enron or its predecessor companies. Many of Enron's Directors served on the boards of other companies as well. At the hearing, John Duncan, former Chairman of the Executive Committee, described his fellow Board members as well educated, "experienced, successful businessmen and women," and "experts in areas of finance and accounting."[7] The Subcommittee interviews found the Directors to have a wealth of sophisticated business and investment experience and considerable expertise in accounting, derivatives, and structured finance.
>
> Enron Board members uniformly described internal Board relations as harmonious. They said that Board votes were generally unanimous and could recall only two instances over the course of many years involving dissenting votes. The Directors also described a good working relationship with Enron management. Several had close personal relationships with Board Chairman and Chief Executive Officer (CEO) Kenneth L. Lay. All indicated they had possessed great respect for senior Enron officers, trusting the integrity and competence of Mr. Lay; President and Chief Operating Officer (and later CEO) Jeffrey K. Skilling; Chief Financial Officer Andrew S. Fastow; Chief Accounting Officer Richard A. Causey; Chief Risk Officer Richard Buy; and the Treasurer Jeffrey McMahon and later Ben Glisan. Mr. Lay served as Chairman of the Board from 1986 until he resigned in 2002. Mr. Skilling was a Board member from 1997 until August 2001, when he resigned from Enron.
>
> The Enron Board was organized into five committees:
>
> > (1) The **Executive Committee** met on an as needed basis to handle urgent business matters between scheduled Board meetings. Its members in 2001 were Mr. Duncan, the Chairman; Mr. Lay, Mr. Skilling, Mr. Belfer, Dr. LeMaistre, and Mr. Winokur.

---

[7]   Hearing Record at 14.

(2) The **Finance Committee** was responsible for approving major transactions which, in 2001, met or exceeded $75 million in value. It also reviewed transactions valued between $25 million and $75 million; oversaw Enron's risk management efforts; and provided guidance on the company's financial decisions and policies. Its members in 2001 were Mr. Winokur, the Chairman; Mr. Belfer, Mr. Blake, Mr. Chan, Mr. Pereira, and Mr. Savage.

(3) The **Audit and Compliance Committee** reviewed Enron's accounting and compliance programs, approved Enron's financial statements and reports, and was the primary liaison with Andersen. Its members in 2001 were Dr. Jaedicke, the Chairman; Mr. Chan, Dr. Gramm, Dr. Mendelsohn, Mr. Pereira, and Lord Wakeham. Dr. Jaedicke and Lord Wakeham had formal accounting training and professional experience. Dr. Mendelsohn was the only Committee member who appeared to have limited familiarity with complex accounting principles.

(4) The **Compensation Committee** established and monitored Enron's compensation policies and plans for directors, officers and employees. Its members in 2001 were Dr. LeMaistre, the Chairman; Mr. Blake, Mr. Duncan, Dr. Jaedicke, and Mr. Savage.

(5) The **Nominating Committee** nominated individuals to serve as directors. Its members in 2001 were Lord Wakeham, the Chairman; Dr. Gramm, Dr. Mendelsohn, and Mr. Meyer.

The Board normally met five times during the year, with additional special meetings as needed. Board meetings usually lasted 2 days, with the first day devoted to Committee meetings and a Board dinner, and the second day devoted to a meeting of the full Board. Committee meetings generally lasted between 1 and 2 hours and were arranged to allow Board members, who typically sat on three Committees, to attend all assigned Committee meetings. Full Board meetings also generally lasted between 1 and 2 hours. Special Board meetings, as well as meetings of the Executive Committee, were typically conducted by telephone conference.

Committee chairmen typically spoke with Enron management by telephone prior to Committee meetings to develop the proposed Committee meeting agenda. Board members said that Enron management provided them with these agendas as well as extensive background and briefing materials prior to Board meetings including, in the case of Finance Committee members, numerous Deal Approval Sheets (DASHs) for approval of major transactions. Board members varied in how much time they spent reading the materials and preparing for Board meetings, with the reported preparation time for each meeting varying between 2 hours and 2 days. On some occasions, Enron provided a private plane to transport Board members from various locations to a Board meeting, and Board members discussed company issues during the flight. Enron also organized occasional trips abroad which some Board members attended to view company assets and operations.

During the Committee meetings, Enron management generally provided presentations on company performance, internal controls, new business ventures, specific transactions, or other topics of interest. The Finance Committee generally heard from Mr. Fastow, Mr. Causey, Mr. Buy, Mr. McMahon, and, occasionally, Mr. Glisan. The Audit Committee generally heard from Mr. Causey, Mr. Buy, and Andersen personnel. The Compensation Committee generally heard from the company's top compensation official, Mary Joyce, and from the company's compensation consultant, Towers Perrin. On occasion, the Committees heard from other senior Enron officers as well. At the full Board meetings, Board members typically received presentations from each Committee Chairman summarizing the Committee's work and recommendations, as well as from Enron management, and, occasionally, Andersen or the company's chief outside legal counsel, Vinson & Elkins. Mr. Lay and Mr. Skilling usually attended Executive, Finance, and Audit Committee meetings, as well as the full Board meetings. Mr. Lay attended many Compensation Committee meetings as well. The Subcommittee interviews indicated that, altogether, Board members appeared to have routine contact with less than a dozen senior officers at Enron. The Board did not have a practice of meeting without Enron management present.

Regular presentations on Enron's financial statements, accounting practices, and audit results were provided by Andersen to the Audit Committee. The Audit Committee Chairman would then report on the presentation to the full Board. On most occasions, three Andersen senior partners from Andersen's Houston office attended Audit Committee meetings. They were D. Stephen Goddard, head of the Houston office; David Duncan, head of the Andersen "engagement team" that provided auditing, consulting, and other services to Enron; and Thomas H. Bauer, another senior member of the Enron engagement team. Before becoming head of the Houston office, Mr. Goddard had led the Enron engagement team for Andersen. Mr. Duncan became the "worldwide engagement partner" for Enron in 1997, and from that point on typically made the Andersen presentations to the Audit Committee. The Audit Committee offered Andersen personnel an opportunity to present information to them without management present.

Minutes summarizing Committee and Board meetings were kept by the Corporate Secretary, who often took handwritten notes on Committee and Board presentations during the Board's deliberations and afterward developed and circulated draft minutes to Enron management, Board members, and legal counsel. The draft minutes were formally presented to and approved by Committee and Board members at subsequent meetings.

Outside of the formal Committee and Board meetings, the Enron Directors described very little interaction or communication either among Board members or between Board members and Enron or Andersen personnel, until the company began experiencing severe problems in October 2001. From October until the company's bankruptcy on December 2, 2001, the Board held numerous special meetings, at times on almost a daily basis.

Enron Board members were compensated with cash, restricted stock, phantom stock units, and stock options.[8] The total cash and equity compensation of Enron Board members in 2000 was valued by Enron at about $350,000 or more than twice the national average for Board compensation at a U.S. publicly traded corporation.[9] 10

> **Finding (6): The independence of the Enron Board of Directors was compromised by financial ties between the company and certain Board members. The Board also failed to ensure the independence of the company's auditor, allowing Andersen to provide internal audit and consulting services while serving as Enron's outside auditor.**

---

[8] See Hearing Exhibits 35a and 35b on Enron Board Member compensation, prepared by the Subcommittee based upon information in Enron filings with the Security and Exchange Commission (SEC). Phantom stock units at Enron were deferred cash payments whose amounts were linked to the value of Enron stock.

[9] See "Director Compensation; Purposes, Principles, and Best Practices," Report of the Blue Ribbon Commission of the National Association of Corporate Directors (2001) at page V (average total Board compensation at top 200 U.S. public corporations in 2000, was $138,747).

10 Senate Comm. Report on Role of Enron Board, *supra* note 7, at 8–11.

Board Independence. At the May 7 hearing, the expert witnesses testified that the independence and objectivity of the Enron Board had been weakened by financial ties between Enron and certain directors. These financial ties, which affected a majority of the outside Board members, included the following.[174]

— Since 1996, Enron paid a monthly retainer of $6,000 to Lord John Wakeham for consulting services, in addition to his Board compensation. In 2000, Enron paid him $72,000 for his consulting work alone.[175]

— Since 1991, Enron paid Board member John A. Urquhart for consulting services, in addition to his Board compensation. In 2000, Enron paid Mr. Urquhart $493,914 for his consulting work alone.[176]

— Enron Board member Herbert Winokur also served on the Board of the National Tank Company. In 1997, 1998, 1999, and 2000, the National Tank Company recorded revenues of $1,035,000, $643,793, $535,682 and $370,294 from sales to Enron subsidiaries of oilfield equipment and services.[177]

— In the past 5 years Enron and Kenneth Lay donated nearly $600,000 to the M.D. Anderson Cancer Center in Texas. In 1993, the Enron Foundation pledged $1.5 million to the Cancer Center. Two Enron Board members, Dr. LeMaistre and Dr. Mendelsohn, have served as president of the Cancer Center.[178]

— Since 1996, Enron and the Lay Foundation have donated more than $50,000 to the George Mason University and its Mercatus Center in Virgin[i]a.[179] Enron Board member Dr. Wendy Gramm is employed by the Mercatus Center.

— Since 1996, Enron and Belco Oil and Gas have engaged in hedging arrangements worth tens of millions of dollars. [180] In 1997, Belco bought Enron affiliate Coda Energy.[181] Enron

---

[174]   Hearing Exhibit 43, "Enron Board of Directors—Financial Ties to Enron," prepared by the Subcommittee.

[175]   Enron 2001 Proxy.

[176]   *Id.*

[177]   Enron 2000 and 2001 Proxy.

[178]   M.D. Anderson Cancer Center records.

[179]   *New York Times,* 11/30/01.

[180]   Enron 2001 Proxy.

[181]   Enron 1998 Proxy.

Board member Robert Belfer is former Chairman of the Board and CEO of Belco.

— Charl[e]s Walker, a noted tax lobbyist, was an Enron Board member from 1985 until 1999. In 1993–1994, Enron paid more than $70,000 to two firms, Walker/Free and Walker/Potter that were partly owned by Mr. Walker, for governmental relations and tax consulting services. This sum was in addition to Mr. Walker's Board compensation.[182] Enron was also, for more than 10 years ending in 2001, a major contributor of up to $50,000 annually to the American Council for Capital Formation, a non-profit corporation that lobbies on tax issues and is chaired by Mr. Walker.[183]

A number of corporate governance experts contacted by the Subcommittee staff identified these financial ties as contributing to the Enron Board's lack of independence and reluctance to challenge Enron management. At the May 7 hearing, Charles Elson, Director of the Center for Corporate Governance at the University of Delaware, testified that public company directors should have "no financial connection to the company whatsoever" other than their Board compensation, but the Enron Board was "problematic" because a number of directors "were service providers or recipients of corporate largess in some way, shape, or form."[184] He testified:

> "By taking those fees, you are effectively becoming part of the management team, and I think there is a real problem with exercising independent judgement vis-a-vis what the management has done if you feel part of that team, either through participating in the development of management plans and strategies or the fear that if one objects too strenuously, those consulting fees may disappear. . . . You may take what they are telling you at face value without being more probative because of the relationship. . . . [I]f a director's role is as a consultant, hire the director as a consultant. If the director's role is to be a director, hire them as a director. You cannot blend the two."[185]

Robert H. Campbell, retired Chairman and CEO of Sunoco, Inc., who presently sits on the Boards of several large corporations, testified that "consulting arrangements with directors is

---

[182] Enron 1994 and 1995 Proxy.
[183] Subcommittee staff interview of Mr. Walker.
[184] Hearing Record at 94–95.
[185] Hearing Record at 106–107.

absolutely incorrect, absolutely wrong" because directors are already paid a substantial fee to be available to management and provide their perspective on company issues.[186]

The three experts at the May 7 hearing also criticized the compensation paid to the Board members, noting that $350,000 per year[187] was significantly above the norm and that much of the compensation was in the form of stock options which enabled Board members to benefit from stock gains, without risking any investment loss.[188] Mr. Elson criticized stock options because "[t]here is no real downside. The worst you can lose is the expectancy of great riches."[189] All three experts urged companies to reconsider awarding excessive Board compensation and urged them to award compensation in the form of stock rather than stock options.

Auditor Independence. The hearing experts also criticized the Enron Board and its Audit Committee for inadequate oversight to ensure the independence and objectivity of Andersen in its role as the company's outside auditor. The Audit Committee formally reviewed Andersen's independence annually, and Committee members told the Subcommittee staff there had never been any sign of a problem. The evidence suggests, however, that the Audit Committee did not probe the independence issue, nor did it initiate the type of communications with Andersen personnel that would have led to its discovering Andersen concerns with Enron accounting practices.

The Audit Committee had very limited contact with Andersen, essentially communicating with Andersen personnel only at Board meetings. The Audit Committee Chairman for more than 10 years was Dr. Jaedicke. Despite his long tenure on the Audit Committee, the interviews disclosed that Dr. Jaedicke had "rarely" had any contact with Andersen outside of an official Audit Committee or Board meeting. None of the other interviewed Audit Committee members had ever contacted anyone from Andersen regarding Enron outside of an official Enron Committee or Board meeting. None had ever telephoned Andersen directly.

The Audit Committee members indicated that they had thought Andersen and Enron had a good working relationship, and taken great comfort in knowing that Andersen was more than Enron's

---

[186]   Hearing Record at 107.

[187]   See Hearing Exhibits 35a and 35b, on Enron Board Member compensation, prepared by the Subcommittee.

[188]   Hearing Record at 110–112.

[189]   Id. at 111.

outside auditor, but also provided Enron with extensive internal auditing and consulting services, combining its roles into what Enron called "an integrated audit." Dr. Jaedicke maintained that it was a significant benefit to Enron for Andersen to be involved with Enron's activities on a day-to-day basis and to help the company design its most complex transactions from the start. Although one Board member, Lord Wakeham, indicated that he had been concerned that this high level of involvement meant Andersen might be too close to Enron management, most Board members indicated that issue had not been a concern. No Board member expressed any concern that Andersen might be auditing its own work, or that Andersen auditors might be reluctant to criticize Andersen consultants for the LJM or Raptor structures that Andersen had been paid millions of dollars to help design.[190]

In contrast, the accounting and corporate governance experts at the May 7 hearing condemned the very concept of an integrated audit, not only for diluting the outside auditor's independence, but also for reducing the effectiveness of an outside audit by allowing the auditor to audit its own work at the company. Mr. Sutton called it a "terrible idea," while Mr. Campbell called it a "horrible practice and I do not think it should be permitted."[191]

Enron Board members told the Subcommittee staff that they had been unaware of any tensions between Andersen and Enron and unaware of the many concerns Andersen had with Enron's accounting practices. The interviewed Board members said that they had not been informed and were unaware of a February 2001 visit paid by the head of Andersen, Joseph Berardino, to Enron's headquarters and did not know why the meeting took place or what was discussed. They also said they were unaware that, shortly after the visit, in March 2001, a senior Andersen partner, Carl Bass, was removed from his Enron oversight role at Enron's request. The Board members observed that they had given Andersen regular opportunities outside the presence of Enron management to communicate any concerns about the company, including whether company officials were pressuring Andersen accountants who raised objections to company proposals. They expressed shock and dismay that Andersen had never conveyed

---

[190] See, for example, Powers Report at 5 ("Andersen billed Enron $5.7 million for advice in connection with the LJM and Chewco transactions alone, above and beyond its regular audit fees.") and 132 ("Andersen's total bill for Raptor-related work came to approximately $1.3 million. Indeed, there is abundant evidence that Andersen in fact offered Enron advice at every step, from inception through restructuring and ultimately to terminating the Raptors.").

[191] Hearing Record at 105 and 106.

its many concerns about Enron's accounting and transactions to the Enron Board.

The interviewed Board members indicated that they had not considered whether Andersen might be reluctant to express serious concerns about Enron accounting practices out of an unwillingness to upset Enron management or endanger its fees. A number of the interviewed directors discounted the importance of Andersen's fees, even though Enron was one of Andersen's largest clients and, during 2000, paid Andersen about $52 million or $1 million per week for its work. Andersen's consulting fees at Enron exceeded its auditing fees for the first time in 1999, and, in 2000, totaled about $27 million compared to auditing fees of about $25 million.[192]

When asked by Senator Collins at the hearing if he had "ever known an auditor to come in and say, we are not independent, we are too close to management," Dr. Jaedicke said no, "[t]hey would not last very long if they did that." Senator Collins responded:

> "Exactly my point. . . . When you are making over $40 million a year, the auditor is not likely to come to the Audit Committee and say anything other than that they are independent. Is it not the job of the Audit Committee to make sure that the auditor truly is giving full, accurate, and appropriate advice to the Board?"

The facts suggest that the Enron Audit Committee went through the motions of asking Andersen about its independence, relied on what it was told, and did little more to evaluate the relationship between the auditor and the company. Had it dug deeper, the Enron Audit Committee might have uncovered the ongoing tensions between the company and its auditor and the many misgivings Andersen expressed internally while going along with Enron's high risk accounting.[11]

QUESTIONS ON BOARD PROCESSES AND SECOND SET OF QUESTIONS ON BOARD COMPOSITION

The board met regularly five times a year, with the meetings two days in length—and had special meetings as well (351). Committee chairs actively participated in developing the agendas for the committee meetings (*id.*). Directors received extensive background and briefing materials before

---

[192] Hearing Exhibit 7b, "Summary of Fees—Activity Overview" (Audit Committee presentation, 5/1/00).

[11]   *Id.* at 51–55.

meetings (351–352). The Compensation Committee obtained the views of a respected compensation consultant (352). Three Andersen partners attended most Enron Audit Committee meetings, and that committee offered Andersen an opportunity to present information outside the presence of management (352–353). The Board was well compensated for its work (353). Doesn't it look like the Enron Board had a lot going for it, at least on paper?

What do you think of the independence issues raised by the Senate committee report? Does each of the several kinds of payments and business or charitable relationships raise independence questions that strike you as serious?

- The consulting fees paid to Wakeham and Urquhart (354)?

- The fees paid to the Walker enterprises for tax consulting and government relations services (355)?

- The business that Enron did with companies associated with Winokur and Belfer (354–355)?

- The charitable contributions to foundations with which LeMaistre, Mendelsohn, and Gramm were associated and to the non-profit lobbying outfit chaired by Walker (354–355)?

Are you concerned that the Board members were paid too much (356)? That stock options constituted a significant part of their compensation (*id.*)? Why? How would the amount of their compensation, or its composition, affect directors' ability to do their board work well?

Now think back to Andersen's role in structuring the complicated financial transactions. Did that role compromise their independence as an auditor?

Why do you think that Andersen failed to convey concerns to the Audit Committee even though Andersen had opportunities to meet with the Committee outside the presence of management (357–358)? Is it possible that Andersen feared it would not be reappointed to audit Enron after doing so? But wouldn't the professional norms of the accounting profession stress that any such fears must be put aside?

And how about the story of an Andersen partner being removed from his oversight role, perhaps at the request of Enron (357)? Can you think of instances in which a company could legitimately go to an auditor and ask that a member of the audit team be taken off the audit engagement?

CHAPTER 10

REFORMS I: FINANCIAL CERTIFICATIONS, INTERNAL CONTROLS, AND CODES OF CONDUCT

■ ■ ■

The last seven chapters looked at the two financial meltdowns that led directly to corporate governance reform early this century. We now begin our study of the reforms themselves. We will not cover them all. Many of those we will address stem from the Sarbanes-Oxley Act of 2002, which was signed into law on July 30, 2002.[1] The book refers to that act as "SOX." Other reforms derive from the Dodd-Frank Wall Street Reform and Consumer Protection Act, which became law in 2010.[2] The book refers to that act as "the Dodd-Frank Act" or simply "Dodd-Frank."

This Chapter Ten begins with two SOX reforms that focus directly on top management's personal responsibility for financial reports—personal officer certifications of reported financial results and clawbacks of pay to top officers after their companies restate financial numbers. The chapter next addresses internal financial controls, the SOX provisions that require management assessment of those controls, the resulting requirement for an annual audit of those controls by the outside auditor, and an additional set of controls called "disclosure" controls. The chapter ends with a discussion of corporate codes of conduct.

A. THE 302 CERTIFICATION

SOX section 302 ordered the SEC to issue rules requiring individual managers of each public company to certify among other things that "the financial statements, and other financial information included in the [periodic reports under the 34 Act], fairly present in all material respects the financial condition and results of operation of the issuer."[3] As we will see shortly, the certification covers more than just the financial numbers, but focus now on what the Commission regulation requires as to the financials.

---

[1]   116 Stat. 745 (2002).
[2]   124 Stat. 1376 (2010).
[3]   116 Stat. at 777; 15 U.S.C. § 7241(a)(3).

The SEC regulation mandates that each public company must include, as exhibits to each 10-Q and 10-K, certifications by the CEO and CFO stating:[4]

> I, [identify the certifying individual], certify that:
>
>> 1.   I have reviewed this [specify report] of [identify registrant];
>>
>> 2.   Based on my knowledge, this report does not contain any untrue statement of a material fact or omit to state a material fact necessary to make the statements made, in light of the circumstances under which such statements were made, not misleading with respect to the period covered by this report;
>>
>> 3.   Based on my knowledge, the financial statements, and other financial information included in this report, fairly present in all material respects the financial condition, results of operations and cash flows of the registrant as of, and for, the periods presented in this report. . . .[5]

Both the CEO and the CFO must separately sign such a certification for each 10-K and 10-Q.

The certification is not tied to formal accounting rules. To the contrary, the SEC has said that:

> [t]he certification statement regarding fair presentation of financial statements and other financial information is not limited to a representation that the financial statements and other financial information have been presented in accordance with "generally accepted accounting principles" and is not otherwise limited by reference to generally accepted accounting principles. We believe that Congress intended this statement to provide assurances that the financial information disclosed in a report, viewed in its entirety, meets a standard of overall material accuracy and completeness that is broader than financial reporting requirements under generally accepted accounting principles. In our view, a "fair presentation" of an issuer's financial condition, results of operations and cash flows encompasses the selection of appropriate accounting policies, proper application of appropriate accounting policies, disclosure of

---

[4]   Companies must file 10-Qs and 10-Ks if they (1) trade on a national exchange; (2) have both (a) total assets exceeding $10 million and (b) record security holders numbering at least 2000 (or, for companies other than banks and bank holding companies, record holders who are not accredited investors totaling at least 500); or (3) have filed a registration statement under the Securities Act that has become effective. Each such company will file a 10-Q for each of the first three fiscal quarters in a fiscal year and a 10-K after the fourth quarter, covering the entire year.

[5]   17 C.F.R. § 229.601(b)(31)(i) (setting out the exact words for the certifications, with the certifications required by 17 C.F.R. §§ 240.13a-14(a), 240.15d-14(a)).

financial information that is informative and reasonably reflects the underlying transactions and events and the inclusion of any additional disclosure necessary to provide investors with a materially accurate and complete picture of an issuer's financial condition, results of operations and cash flows.[6]

QUESTIONS ON THE 302 CERTIFICATION

Why do you think Congress and the SEC believe that this kind of certification—to fair presentation, not just compliance with accounting rules—is a good idea?

But what about the CEO who signs a certification? If the accountants tell the CEO that the numbers are OK under accounting rules, how is he or she to know that—despite that assurance—the numbers might not "fairly present" the company's financial condition and results of operations? Are there CEOs who lack the knowledge and experience to make that determination? And what about the CFOs? Are there even some CFOs who may not be able to certify to fair presentation every time? Are all the financial neonates out there saved by the "[b]ased on my knowledge" qualifier with which the critical paragraph begins?

Does the standard seem to invite after-the-fact quarrels, with the regulators or shareholders saying that the reported numbers—even though they met all the accounting tests—did not tell the full story?

What is the significance of the phrase "other financial information included in this report" in paragraph 3 of the certification? Does this phrase suggest that, if the numbers in the financial statements do not, for whatever reason, reflect economic reality, an executive's certification will still be truthful if the report has explained the economic reality in some part of the report outside the financial statements? If so, who on the executive team is going to be in charge of drafting that language? And what professionals are going to have primary responsibility for that language—the lawyers or the accountants?

Do you think that certifications like this are helpful? Do you think they bring home to the signing executives that they are truly and individually responsible for fair financial disclosure in periodic SEC filings?

Will such a sense of responsibility depend on recent events? In particular, will signing certifications be just another part of business routine after two or three years without pictures in the paper of executives in handcuffs?

---

[6]   Certification of Disclosure in Companies' Quarterly and Annual Reports, 67 Fed. Reg. 57,276, 57,279 (Sept. 9, 2002) (adopting release) (footnotes omitted).

Now turn to another certification.

B. THE 906 CERTIFICATION

SOX section 906 added a second certification requirement, again applicable to 10-Qs and 10-Ks.[7] This one too must be signed by the CEO and CFO and must state, in the words of the statute, that "the financial statements fully compl[y] with the requirements of section 13(a) or 15(d) of the [Exchange Act] and that information contained in the periodic report fairly presents, in all material respects, the financial condition and results of operations of the [company.]"[8] Congress added this section to the federal criminal code, providing that anyone certifying while "knowing" that the accompanying report did not meet the certification requirements could be fined up to $1,000,000 and imprisoned up to 10 years and that anyone who "willfully" certified while "knowing" the report did not meet requirements could be fined up to $5,000,000 and imprisoned up to 20 years.[9] So, the CEO and CFO now sign, for each 10-Q and 10-K, not only a certification under 302 but a certification under 906.

While the CEO and CFO must sign separate 302 certifications, there is no such requirement for the 906 certifications. Some companies file two such certifications, one signed by the CEO and one by the CFO. Some companies file only one 906 certification that is signed by both the CEO and CFO. While neither the SEC nor the Department of Justice has mandated any particular words for a 906 certification, here is one filed by General Electric with a 10-Q for the third quarter of 2015:

> In connection with the Quarterly Report of General Electric Company (the "registrant") on Form 10-Q for the period ended September 30, 2015, as filed with the Securities and Exchange Commission on the date hereof (the "report"), we, Jeffrey R. Immelt and Jeffrey S. Bornstein, Chief Executive Officer and Chief Financial Officer, respectively, of the registrant, certify, pursuant to 18 U.S.C. § 1350, that to our knowledge:
>
> (1) [t]he report fully complies with the requirements of section 13(a) or 15(d) of the Securities Exchange Act of 1934, as amended; and
>
> (2) [t]he information contained in the report fairly presents, in all material respects, the financial condition and results of operations of the registrant.[10]

---

[7]   116 Stat. at 806.

[8]   18 U.S.C. § 1350(b).

[9]   18 U.S.C. § 1350(c).

[10]   Gen. Elec. Co., Quarterly Report, Form 10-Q, Exh. 32 (filed Oct. 30, 2015), https://www. sec.gov/Archives/edgar/data/40545/000004054515000114/ge10q3q15ex32.htm.

The CEO and the CFO then signed this one document.

QUESTIONS ON THE 906 CERTIFICATION

Why did Congress put in this additional certification requirement? Do you think it is a good idea? Again, is it fair to the executives?

Is any unfairness mitigated by the knowledge qualifier to criminal liability? But does that qualifier then remove, or even diminish, the incentive for these top executives to find out whether the financial statements are accurate?

Does the effectiveness of this certification depend upon vigorous criminal enforcement that receives widespread publicity?

Note, as a technical matter, that 906 was self-executing. That is, the section did not say that the SEC had to issue regulations; it just said that the executives had to make the certifications. The requirement was effective without any SEC rulemaking. The SEC, however, has issued regulations requiring that the 906 certifications be included as exhibits to periodic reports.[11]

C. THE SECTION 304 CLAWBACK AND THE DODD-FRANK EXPANSION

SOX has one other particularly interesting "personal responsibility" section. SOX section 304 added this to title 15 of the U.S. Code:

Sec. 7243.   Forfeiture of certain bonuses and profits

(a) Additional compensation prior to noncompliance with Commission financial reporting requirements

If an issuer is required to prepare an accounting restatement due to the material noncompliance of the issuer, as a result of misconduct, with any financial reporting requirement under the securities laws, the chief executive officer and chief financial officer of the issuer shall reimburse the issuer for—

> (1) any bonus or other incentive-based or equity-based compensation received by that person from the issuer during the 12-month period following the first public issuance or filing with the Commission (whichever first occurs) of the

---

[11]   17 C.F.R. §§ 229.601(b)(32), 240.13a-14(b), 240.15d-14(b)—both providing that the "requirement may be satisfied by a single certification signed by an issuer's principal executive and principal financial officers."

financial document embodying such financial reporting requirement; and

(2) any profits realized from the sale of securities of the issuer during that 12-month period.

(b) Commission exemption authority

The Commission may exempt any person from the application of subsection (a) of this section, as it deems necessary and appropriate.[12]

You know what a restatement is already. It is a set of financial statements that a company publishes that corrects material errors in previously published financial statements.

QUESTIONS ON THE LANGUAGE OF THE SOX CLAWBACK

What does "misconduct" mean? Does it mean that restatements resulting from honest mistakes do not trigger the clawbacks and that only real efforts to cook the books will do so?[13]

Whose misconduct will be sufficient to trigger a clawback? In particular, must the CEO or CFO himself or herself commit misconduct in order that the executive's compensation and stock sale profits be subject to recapture?[14]

---

[12]   116 Stat. at 778; 15 U.S.C. § 7243.

[13]   *See* HAROLD S. BLOOMENTHAL, SARBANES-OXLEY ACT IN PERSPECTIVE § 11:6, 865–66 (2016 ed.) (suggesting that misconduct could cover negligence).

[14]   *Compare* Rachael E. Schwartz, *The Clawback Provision of Sarbanes-Oxley: An Underutilized Incentive to Keep the Corporate House Clean*, 64 BUS. LAW. 1 (2008) (arguing that no personal misconduct by the CEO or CFO is necessary) *with* John P. Kelsh, *Section 304 of the Sarbanes-Oxley Act of 2002: The Case for a Personal Culpability Requirement*, 59 BUS. LAW. 1005 (2004) (arguing that such personal misconduct is required).

Cases deciding the issue hold that 304 requires a CEO to disgorge even without proof that he or she personally participated in the misconduct leading to the misstatement. *SEC v. Jenkins*, 718 F. Supp. 2d 1070, 1074–79 (D. Ariz. 2010); *SEC v. Baker*, No. A-12-CA-285-SS, 2012 WL 5499497, at *5–6 (W.D. Tex. 2012):

> Although it might be surprising at first glance to require CEOs and CFOs to reimburse their employers when they have not done anything illegal, there are good policy reasons why Congress may have provided for the broad scope of § 304 suggested by the SEC.
>
> . . . .
>
> "Imagine if someone told you that they would take away half of everything you earned this year if you did not catch the misconduct of one of your employees. You would most likely be highly motivated to catch the misconduct." [Alison] List, *[The] Lax Enforcement [of Section 304 of Sarbanes-Oxley: Why is the SEC Ignoring Its Greatest Asset in the Fight Against Corporate Misconduct?*, 70 OHIO ST. L.J. 195 . . .], at 195 [(2009)]. "[Sarbanes-Oxley] . . . requires CEOs and CFOs to certify their companies' financial reports, outlaws fraud and deception by managers in the auditing process, prevents CEOs and CFOs from benefitting from profits they receive as a result of misstatements of their company's financials, and facilitates the imposition of judicial bars against officers and directors who have violated the securities laws." S. Rep. No. 107-205, 2002 WL 1443523, at *23 (2002) (emphasis added).

Notice that this is a very different type of statute. It reaches down into the corporation to the way in which modern compensation is structured. It says that if the company reports materially false numbers, the executives have to give back bonuses and stock profits *to the company* if the company restates the numbers due to misconduct. It is designed to reduce the incentive for fraud and to encourage the top executives to prevent fraud.

GENERAL QUESTIONS ON THE SOX CLAWBACK

Would a clawback in circumstances in which the CEO and CFO personally do nothing wrong to cause the publication of financial numbers that must later be restated provide an effective incentive for those officers to take steps to ensure that no one else in the company does so? Does that depend on whether the clawback is quickly and reliably enforced, and the knowledge of the executives that the clawback will in fact occur?

Is the statutory clawback effectively an addition to the CEO and CFO employment agreements? If so, is such an addition an appropriate role for federal legislation?

Why didn't companies that wanted to avoid restatements before the passage of the Sarbanes-Oxley law routinely structure employment contracts in this way? Why didn't they universally include clawbacks on the simple rationale that executives could not keep money awarded to them on the basis of financial numbers that, as it ultimately turned out, the company did not achieve? Can you think of other provisions that might be added today to executive employment contracts that would further decrease the incentive for fraud, and would be fair to the executives?

Who can sue to recover the clawback? The courts hold that only the SEC can bring such an action.[15]

QUESTIONS ON ENFORCEMENT OF THE SOX CLAWBACK

Doesn't restricting the 304 plaintiff to the SEC considerably weaken the section's deterrent power, given the resource constraints on that agency?[16]

Baker, 2012 WL 5499497, at *5.

[15]   *See In re Digimarc Corp. Derivative Litig.*, 549 F.3d 1223, 1229–33 (9th Cir. 2008); *accord Cohen v. Viray*, 622 F.3d 188, 193–94 (2d Cir. 2010).

[16]   In a few cases, the SEC obtained very large clawbacks. Famously, the CEO of UnitedHealth Group, Inc. agreed to settle an options backdating case, in part by, "pursuant to

Does leaving the decision to seek the clawback to the Commission ensure that this sanction will be reserved for only egregious cases?

———————

The Dodd-Frank Act requires the SEC to issue a rule requiring national exchanges to incorporate into their listing standards a requirement that listed companies "develop and *implement* a policy" that

> in the event . . . the issuer is required to prepare an accounting restatement due to the material noncompliance of the issuer with any financial reporting requirement under the securities laws, the issuer will recover from any current or former executive officer of the issuer who received incentive-based compensation (including stock options awarded as compensation) during the 3-year period preceding the date on which the issuer is required to prepare an accounting restatement, based on the erroneous data, in excess of what would have been paid to the executive officer under the accounting restatement.[17]

This new requirement would apply more broadly than § 304—with the new listing standards extending clawbacks to all "executive officers."[18] It does not require that a restatement triggering the recoupment result from "misconduct" but only from a failure to comply with financial reporting requirements. It recaptures only compensation that would not have been paid but for the false numbers. And it appears to be mandatory—with the policy being one by which the issuer "will recover" the clawback amount.[19]

———————

Section 304 of the Sarbanes-Oxley Act, reimburs[ing] UnitedHealth for all incentive- and equity-based compensation he received from 2003 through 2006, totaling approximately $448 million in cash bonuses, profits from the exercise and sale of UnitedHealth stock, and unexercised UnitedHealth options." SEC, Litig. Release No. 20387 (Dec. 6, 2007), http://www.sec.gov/litigation/litreleases/2007/lr20387.htm. More modestly but still in a large amount, the CEO of Beazer Homes, USA Inc. settled an accounting fraud case with the Commission by "agree[ing] to reimburse Beazer $6,479,281 in cash, 40,103 restricted stock units (or its equivalent), and 78,763 shares of restricted stock (or its equivalent). This reimbursement represent[ed] McCarthy's entire fiscal year 2006 incentive bonus ($5,706,949 in cash and 40,103 in restricted stock units), $772,232 in stock sale profits, and 78,763 shares of restricted stock granted in 2006." Press Release, SEC, *SEC Obtains Settlement With CEO to Recover Compensation and Stock Profits He Received During Company's Fraud* (Mar. 3, 2011), http://www.sec.gov/news/press/2011/2011-61.htm. *See also* Press Release, SEC, *SEC Announces Half-Million Dollar Clawback from CFOs of Silicon Valley Company That Committed Accounting Fraud* (Feb. 10, 2015), https://www.sec.gov/news/press release/2015-28.html.

   [17]   Pub. L. No. 111-203, § 954, 124 Stat. 1376, 1904 (2010) (codified at 15 U.S.C. § 78j-4(b)(2)) (emphasis added).

   [18]   Exchange Act regulations define "executive officers" to include "president, any vice president . . . in charge of a principal business unit, division or function (such as sales, administration or finance), any other officer who performs a policy making function or any other person who performs similar policy making functions." 17 C.F.R. § 240.3b-7.

   [19]   As of mid-July 2016, the Commission had proposed, but not adopted, clawback regulations.

We turn next to two sets of "controls" the SEC has required in the wake of Sarbanes-Oxley.

D. INTERNAL CONTROLS

Congress required that SOX 302 certifications cover not just the financial numbers but also "internal controls."[20] SOX section 404 also required the SEC to prescribe rules requiring each public company to (i) acknowledge management's responsibility for establishing and maintaining "an adequate internal control structure and procedures for financial reporting" and (ii) include in its annual report an "assessment" of the effectiveness of that structure and those procedures.[21]

Note, importantly, that federal law has required public companies to "devise and maintain" internal controls since the Foreign Corrupt Practices Act ("FCPA") was passed in the late 1970s.[22]

The final SOX regulations borrowed much of the FCPA language to define "internal control over financial reporting" as:

> a process designed by, or under the supervision of, the issuer's principal executive and principal financial officers, or persons performing similar functions, and effected by the issuer's board of directors, management and other personnel, to provide reasonable assurance regarding the reliability of financial reporting and the preparation of financial statements for external purposes in accordance with generally accepted accounting principles and includes those policies and procedures that:

---

[20]   116 Stat. at 777; 15 U.S.C. § 7241(a)(4).

[21]   116 Stat. at 789; 15 U.S.C. § 7262(a).

[22]   The FCPA prohibited U.S. public companies from paying bribes to foreign government officials in order to obtain or retain business. Since bribes had been paid by slush funds kept off the books, the FCPA included recordkeeping requirements to ensure, for example, that company records show how assets are used and to provide reasonable assurance against unauthorized payments from slush funds. The FCPA contained this provision:

> Every issuer which has a class of securities registered pursuant to section 12 of [the 34 Act] and every issuer which is required to file reports pursuant to section 15(d) of [that Act] shall . . . devise and maintain a system of internal accounting controls sufficient to provide reasonable assurances that
>
> (i)   transactions are executed in accordance with management's general or specific authorization;
>
> (ii)   transactions are recorded as necessary (I) to permit preparation of financial statements in conformity with generally accepted accounting principles or any other criteria applicable to such statements, and (II) to maintain accountability for assets;
>
> (iii)   access to assets is permitted only in accordance with management's general or specific authorization; and
>
> (iv)   the recorded accountability for assets is compared with the existing assets at reasonable intervals and appropriate action is taken with respect to any differences.

91 Stat. 1494 (1977). This language remains in the 34 Act today. 15 U.S.C. § 78m(b)(2)(B).

(1) [p]ertain to the maintenance of records that in reasonable detail accurately and fairly reflect the transactions and dispositions of the assets of the issuer;

(2) [p]rovide reasonable assurance that transactions are recorded as necessary to permit preparation of financial statements in accordance with generally accepted accounting principles, and that receipts and expenditures of the issuer are being made only in accordance with authorizations of management and directors of the issuer; and

(3) [p]rovide reasonable assurance regarding prevention or timely detection of unauthorized acquisition, use or disposition of the issuer's assets that could have a material effect on the financial statements.[23]

The regulations require that each SEC-reporting company "must maintain . . . internal control over financial reporting."[24] In addition, the management of each company filing 10-Qs and 10-Ks with the Commission must evaluate the effectiveness of the company's "internal control over financial reporting" as of the end of each fiscal year.[25] The principal executive and financial officers must participate in that evaluation, and it must be conducted using a "suitable, recognized control framework that is established by a body or group that has followed due-process procedures, including the broad distribution of the framework for public comment."[26] The Commission specifically referenced a "framework" developed by the Committee of Sponsoring Organizations of the Treadway Commission ("COSO").[27] COSO is a private sector initiative jointly sponsored and funded by the American Accounting Association, the American Institute of Certified Public Accountants, Financial Executives International, the Institute of Management Accountants, and The Institute of the Internal Auditors.[28] The SEC has issued interpretive guidance and provided in a regulation that "an evaluation that is conducted in accordance with the interpretive guidance issued by the Commission in Release No. 34-55929

---

[23]   17 C.F.R. §§ 240.13a-15(f), 240.15d-15(f). As you see, the language in this regulation is similar in significant respects to that in the FCPA, quoted in the preceding footnote.

[24]   17 C.F.R. §§ 240.13a-15(a), 240.15d-15(a).

[25]   17 C.F.R. §§ 240.13a-15(b) & (c), 240.15d-15(b) & (c).

[26]   17 C.F.R. §§ 240.13a-15(c), 240.15d-15(c).

[27]   Management's Report on Internal Control Over Financial Reporting and Certification of Disclosure in Exchange Act Periodic Reports, 68 Fed. Reg. 36,636, 36,639 n.42, 36,642 (June 18, 2003).

[28]   See the description at http://www.coso.org/. COSO's original framework was dated 1992. See http://www.coso.org/guidance.htm. In 2006, COSO published a framework for internal control over financial reporting at smaller public companies. Id. COSO published an updated framework in 2013. Id. The 2013 framework is meant to replace the 1992 one. COSO, Internal Control— Integrated Framework, Executive Summary, Foreword (2013) http://www.coso.org/documents/ 990025P_Executive_Summary_final_may20_e.pdf.

will satisfy the evaluation" requirement, with that release then specifically mentioning the COSO framework.[29]

Management must make an annual report on internal controls identifying the framework it used to evaluate the controls[30] and must state "whether or not internal control over financial reporting is effective."[31] This annual report must appear in the 10-K.[32] "Management is not permitted to conclude that the [company's] internal control . . . is effective if there are one or more material weaknesses" in the control system.[33] And, if such a weakness is found, management's assessment must disclose it in its report.[34]

The management must also report to the audit committee and the outside auditor any "significant deficiency" in internal control over financial reporting.[35]

A "significant deficiency" is a control weakness that is less serious than a "material weakness." Here are the SEC definitions of those terms:

> The term *significant deficiency* is a deficiency, or a combination of deficiencies, in internal control over financial reporting that is less severe than a material weakness, yet important enough to merit attention by those responsible for oversight of the registrant's financial reporting.[36]

> The term *material weakness* is a deficiency, or a combination of deficiencies, in internal control over financial reporting such that there is a reasonable possibility that a material misstatement of the registrant's annual or interim financial statements will not be prevented or detected on a timely basis.[37]

By a circuitous route, SOX ended up requiring not only that the public company's management annually evaluate the effectiveness of the company's internal control over financial reporting but that the company's outside auditor *audit* those controls and provide its own opinion on their

---

[29]   17 C.F.R. §§ 240.13a-15(c), 240.15d-15(c); *see* Commission Guidance Regarding Management's Report on Internal Control Over Financial Reporting Under Section 13(a) or 15(d) of the Securities Exchange Act of 1934, 72 Fed. Reg. 35,324, 35,326–27 and nn.23–25 (June 27, 2007).

[30]   17 C.F.R. § 229.308(a)(2).

[31]   17 C.F.R. § 229.308(a)(3).

[32]   Form 10-K, Item 9A, cross-referencing 17 C.F.R. § 229.308.

[33]   17 C.F.R. § 229.308(a)(3).

[34]   *Id.*

[35]   *See* paragraph 5 of the certification that the CEO and CFO must sign, set out below, at note 61.

[36]   17 C.F.R. § 240.12b-2 (emphasis in original).

[37]   *Id.* (emphasis in original).

effectiveness.[38] It is not clear that Congress intended this result,[39] which increased costs.

---

[38]   SOX § 404(a) required the SEC to issue regulations requiring management of each public company to include in the company's annual report "an assessment, as of the end of the most recent fiscal year of the issuer, of the effectiveness of the internal control structure and procedures of the issuer for financial reporting." 116 Stat. 789 (codified at 15 U.S.C. § 7262(a)(2)). Section 404(b) then required that the SEC regulations include a requirement that the public company's outside auditor "attest to, and report on, the assessment made by management," with that attestation "made in accordance with standards for attestation engagements issued or adopted by the" Public Company Accounting Oversight Board ("PCAOB") that SOX established as set out in Chapter Eleven. In its Standard No. 2, adopted in 2004, the PCAOB determined that the attestation to management's report on internal controls would require that the outside auditor conduct an audit of those controls.

> Reliable financial reporting is too important to relegate an auditor's attestation to a rubber-stamped endorsement of management's report on internal controls. As a result, the PCAOB is requiring that auditors perform an audit of internal control over financial reporting and to perform that audit in conjunction with the audit of a company's financial statements.

> The one audit cannot be separated from the other. The information the auditor learns as a result of auditing the company's financial statements has a direct and important bearing on the auditor's conclusion about the effectiveness of the company's internal control over financial reporting.

PCAOB Release No. 2004-001 at 3 (March 9, 2004).

> In preparing PCAOB Auditing Standard No. 2, the Board was guided by a number of broad considerations that have effect throughout the standard. Those broad considerations included: that "attestation" is insufficient to describe the process of assessing management's report on internal controls; that an audit of internal control over financial reporting must be integrated with an audit of the company's financial statements. . . .

Id. at 6. Standard No. 2 therefore required that the independent auditor's report on internal control include an opinion on whether management's assessment of the effectiveness of the company's internal controls was fairly stated, in all material respects, and an opinion on whether the company maintained, in all material respects, effective internal control over financial reporting as of the specified date. *Id.* at 23.

The PCAOB superseded its Standard No. 2 with Standard No. 5, which continued to require that the outside auditor conduct an audit of an issuer's internal control over financial reporting. Standard No. 5 also continued to require the auditor to provide its own evaluation of the public company's internal controls. PCAOB Release No. 2007-005A at A1-4 (June 12, 2007) [PCAOB Standard No. 5 Release] ("The auditor's objective in an audit of internal control over financial reporting is to express an opinion on the effectiveness of the company's internal control over financial reporting.") and A1-34 (auditor's report must include "[t]he auditor's opinion on whether the company maintained, in all material respects, effective internal control over financial reporting as of the specified date"). Standard No. 5 continued to provide that "[t]he audit of internal control over financial reporting should be integrated with the audit of the financial statements." *Id.* at A1-5.

The PCAOB reorganized its auditing standards in 2015. PCAOB Release No. 2015-002 (March 31, 2015). Standard No. 5 is now the reorganized auditing standard ("AS") 2201. *Id.* at A2-1. That current auditing standard applies when the auditor is engaged to "perform an audit of management's assessment of the effectiveness of internal control over financial reporting." AS 2201.01 & n.2. As before, the audit of internal controls should be integrated with the audit of the financial statements. AS 2201.06. The auditor's objective, as before, is "to express an opinion on the effectiveness of the company's internal control over financial reporting." AS 2201.03. And, as before, the auditor's report "must include . . . [t]he auditor's opinion on whether the company maintained, in all material respects, effective internal control over financial reporting. . . ." AS 2201.85(k).

[39]   BLOOMENTHAL, *supra* note 13, § 3:16, 122–23 (PCAOB decision to require audit of internal control over financial reporting "may or may not have been contemplated by [SOX]").

The result is that the outside auditor for a company provides, at the end of the audit cycle, not only an opinion on the company's financial statements, but also the *auditor's opinion* on the effectiveness of the company's internal control over financial reporting. The audit of internal control over financial reporting is integrated with the audit of the company financial statements. Like management, the outside auditor cannot opine that the public company's internal control over financial reporting is effective if the audit finds one or more material weaknesses.[40] The auditor must also identify, to management and the company's audit committee, all material weaknesses and significant deficiencies that the audit finds.[41]

In addition to the complete management evaluation each year and the annual outside audit, the SEC requires that management evaluate, at the end of each quarter, "any change in the . . . internal control over financial reporting, that occurred during [that quarter] . . . that has materially affected, or is reasonably likely to materially affect" the internal controls.[42] The company must disclose—in its 10-Q if the quarter ended is one of the first three and in its 10-K if the quarter ended is the fourth—each such change.[43]

The requirements (i) that management assess and report on internal financial controls and (ii) for an annual audit of internal controls generated heated debate over the cost those requirements imposed and whether the costs were excessive. The Foley & Lardner law firm commissioned a study of proxy statement data that found, for S&P 500 companies, the following average audit fees for the following fiscal years:

Fiscal Year 2001	Fiscal Year 2002	Fiscal Year 2003	Fiscal Year 2004
$2,934,000	$4,048,000	$4,809,000	$7,443,000

The firm attributed the increase for the audit of fiscal year 2004 financials "to the substantial costs associated with the financial control audits required under section 404 of the Sarbanes-Oxley Act, which phased in for most domestic public companies at the end of 2004."[44]

A later study based on a survey of auditors found that the costs of complying with section 404—both the costs that public companies incurred internally and the increased auditing costs—declined significantly in the second year of compliance.

---

[40] PCAOB AS 2201.90, *supra* note 38.

[41] AS 2201.78 (all material weaknesses to both management and the audit committee); 2201.80 (significant deficiencies to audit committee); 2201.81 (all deficiencies to management).

[42] 17 C.F.R. §§ 240.13a-15(d), 240.15d-15(d).

[43] 17 C.F.R. § 229.308(c); Form 10-K, Item 9A (cross-referencing 17 C.F.R. § 229.308); Form 10-Q, Item 4 (cross-referencing 17 C.F.R. § 229.308(c)).

[44] FOLEY & LARDNER LLP, THE COST OF BEING PUBLIC IN THE ERA OF SARBANES-OXLEY 5–6 (June 16, 2005).

Comparison of Year-One and Year-Two[45] Section 404 Implementation Cost Summary Average per Smaller Company (rounded)			
	Year Two in 000s ($)	Year One in 000s ($)	Percent Change
Section 404 Audit Fees	336	423	-20.6%
Internal Issuer and Third-Party 404 Costs	524	818	-36.0%
Total Section 404 Costs	860	1,241	-30.7%
Average Company Revenue	359,680	324,230	
Total Section 404 Costs as a Percentage of Revenue	0.24%	0.38%	
Section 404 Audit Fees as a Percentage of Revenue	0.09%	0.13%	

---

[45] CRA International, Sarbanes-Oxley Section 404 Costs and Implementation Issues: Spring 2006 Survey Update 7, 10 (Apr. 17, 2006). A study of small public companies (with a public float between $50 million and $100 million in 2004) found—after controlling for a number of factors (including use of one of the large auditing firms, company size [as measured by market capitalization, assets, and sales], company complexity [as measured by number of business segments], number of geographic segments, and audit risk [as measured by leverage and receivables scaled by assets])—that section 404 increased audit fees by 74.4% or "$528,000 for the mean firm." Peter Iliev, *The Effect of SOX Section 404: Costs, Earnings Quality, and Stock Prices*, 65 J. Finance 1163, 1175, 1177 (2010).

Comparison of Year-One and Year-Two Section 404 Implementation Cost Summary Average per Larger Company (rounded)			
	Year Two in 000s ($)	Year One in 000s ($)	Percent Change
Section 404 Audit Fees	1,570	2,020	-22.3%
Internal Issuer and Third-Party 404 Costs	3,200	6,490	-50.7%
Total Section 404 Costs	4,770	8,510	-43.9%
Average Company Revenue	8,820,000	7,920,000	
Total Section 404 Costs as a Percentage of Revenue	0.05%	0.11%	
Section 404 Audit Fees as a Percentage of Revenue	0.02%	0.03%	

The SEC issued interpretive guidance and the PCAOB revised its relevant auditing standard in 2007 in ways that could reduce costs.[46] The Commission also delayed the effective dates for full 404 compliance by smaller companies,[47] and eventually the Dodd-Frank Act included a provision that section 404 would not fully apply to smaller public companies at all.[48]

---

[46] Commission Guidance Regarding Managements Report on Internal Control Over Financial Reporting Under Section 13(a) or 15(d) of the Securities Exchange Act of 1934, 72 Fed. Reg. 35,324 (SEC June 27, 2007); PCAOB Standard No. 5 (now AU 2201), *supra* note 38. As the PCAOB put it, the benefits from internal control over financial reporting "have come at a significant cost. Costs have been greater than expected and, at times, the related effort has appeared greater than necessary to conduct an effective audit of internal control over financial reporting." PCAOB Standard No. 5 Release, *supra* note 38, at 2. The Board made its change both to "focus[ ] auditors on the most important matters in the audit of internal control over financial reporting and eliminate[ ] procedures that the Board believes are unnecessary to an effective audit of internal control." *Id.*, at 3. See similar statements in Press Release, SEC, *Commission Statement on Implementation of Internal Control Reporting Requirements* (May 16, 2005), https://www.sec. gov/news/press/2005-74.htm. Both the Board and the SEC sought to ease the burden at smaller public companies. PCAOB Standard No. 5 Release at 3 (Board "sought to make the internal control audit more clearly scalable for smaller and less complex public companies"); Commission Guidance, at 35,336 ("We believe the principles-based guidance permits flexible and scalable evaluation approaches that will enable management of smaller public companies to evaluate and assess the effectiveness of ICFR without undue cost burdens.").

[47] BLOOMENTHAL, *supra* note 13 at §§ 3:21, 3:31.

[48] Pub. L. No. 111-203, § 989G(a), 124 Stat. 1376, 1948 (2010) (codified at 15 USCA § 7262(c)), exempting non-accelerated filers, which are companies with less than $75 million in equity held by non-affiliates (*See* 17 C.F.R. 240.12b-2(1)) from 404(b), which is the attestation requirement that the PCAOB converted into a required annual audit of internal control over financial reporting. The smaller companies still remain subject to the remaining requirements—that they create and maintain internal control over financial reporting and that management conduct annual assessments of those controls, etc. But the smaller companies are not required to have their outside accounting firms conduct yearly audits of the controls. The JOBS Act provided

Against the costs, weigh the additional disclosures that 404 and the related internal control audits have produced. The Wall Street Journal reported in March 2005 that "[m]ore than 500 public companies [had] reported deficiencies with their internal accounting controls. . . ."[49] The paper's examination of 50 filings revealed "that the reported weaknesses range[d] from minor issues that are easily correctable to larger problems that may require restating past financial results."[50] Equipment manufacturer Terex Corp. concluded that it would restate financials after replacing a financial reporting system in order to comply with SOX, and truck manufacturer Navistar International Corporation decided to restate after "an evaluation of its internal controls found 'weaknesses in the disclosure controls and procedures within the company's finance subsidiary.' "[51]

The number of reported material weaknesses declined, by one count, from 629 in the first year that companies had to report to 141 in 2011.[52] Whether that is good news or not is hard to say. An SEC accountant opined in late 2013 that the decline might signal a failure to report all weaknesses.[53]

E. DISCLOSURE CONTROLS

Even before the passage of Sarbanes-Oxley, the SEC had proposed that companies should "[m]aintain sufficient procedures to provide reasonable assurance that the company is able to collect, process and disclose, within the time periods specified in [SEC] rules and forms, the information, including non-financial information, required to be disclosed in its periodic and current reports filed pursuant to the Exchange Act."[54] These became known as "disclosure controls."

---

similar relief for "emerging growth companies." Pub. L. No. 112-106 § 103, 126 Stat. 306 at 310 (codified at 15 U.S.C. § 7262(b)).

[49]   Deborah Solomon, *Accounting Rule Exposes Problems but Draws Complaints About Costs*, WALL ST. J., Mar. 2, 2005, http://www.wsj.com/articles/SB110971840422767575.

[50]   *Id.*

[51]   *Id.*

[52]   Emily Chasen, *SEC Official Sounds Alarm on Decline in 'Material Weaknesses,'* WALL ST. J. CFO J., Dec. 5, 2013, http://blogs.wsj.com/cfo/2013/12/05/sec-official-sounds-alarm-on-decline-in-material-weaknesses/.

[53]   *Id.* (referring to Brian T. Croteau, Deputy Chief Accountant, Office of the Chief Accountant, SEC, Remarks Before the 2013 AICPA National Conference on Current SEC and PCAOB Developments—Audit Policy and Current Auditing and Internal Control Matters (Dec. 9, 2013), https://www.sec.gov/News/Speech/Detail/Speech/1370540472057 ("I continue to question whether all material weaknesses are being properly identified. It is surprisingly rare to see management identify a material weakness in the absence of a material misstatement. This could be either because the deficiencies are not being identified in the first instance or otherwise because the severity of deficiencies is not being evaluated appropriately.")).

[54]   Certification of Disclosure in Companies' Quarterly and Annual Reports, 67 Fed. Reg. 41,877, 41,881 (June 20, 2002).

SEC regulations define "disclosure controls and procedures" to mean:

controls and other procedures of an issuer that are designed to ensure that information required to be disclosed by the issuer in the reports that it files or submits under the [Exchange] Act . . . is recorded, processed, summarized and reported, within the time periods specified in the Commission's rules and forms. Disclosure controls and procedures include, without limitation, controls and procedures designed to ensure that information required to be disclosed by an issuer in the reports that it files or submits under the Act is accumulated and communicated to the issuer's management, including its principal executive and principal financial officers, or persons performing similar functions, as appropriate to allow timely decisions regarding required disclosure.[55]

The SEC recommends that each company set up "a committee with responsibility for considering the materiality of information and determining disclosure obligations on a timely basis."[56] The Commission said that the committee "could include the principal accounting officer (or the controller), the general counsel or other senior legal official with responsibility for disclosure matters who reports to the general counsel, the principal risk management officer, the chief investor relations officer (or an officer with equivalent responsibilities) and such other officers or employees, including individuals associated with the [company's] business units, as the [company] deems appropriate."[57]

The regulations require that management "maintain disclosure controls and procedures"[58] and that management—with the participation of the principal executive and financial officers—evaluate those controls as of the end of each quarter.[59] Each quarter, the company must disclose "the conclusions of the . . . principal executive and principal financial officers . . . regarding the effectiveness of the [company's] disclosure controls and procedures" based upon their evaluation.[60]

The establishment and evaluation of internal controls over financial reporting and disclosure controls are tied into the 302 certification signed by the principal executive officer and principal financial officer. The certification reads in part:

---

[55]   17 C.F.R. §§ 240.13a-15(e), 240.15d-15(e).

[56]   Certification of Disclosure in Companies' Quarterly and Annual Reports, 67 Fed. Reg. 57,276, 57,280 (Sept. 9, 2002).

[57]   *Id.* at 57,280 n.60.

[58]   17 C.F.R. §§ 240.13a-15(a), 240.15d-15(a).

[59]   17 C.F.R. §§ 240.13a-15(b), 240.15d-15(b).

[60]   17 C.F.R. § 229.307; Form 10-K, Item 9A (referencing 17 C.F.R. § 229.307); Form 10-Q, Item 4 (referencing 17 C.F.R. § 229.307).

4.   The registrant's other certifying officer(s) and I are responsible for establishing and maintaining disclosure controls and procedures (as defined in Exchange Act Rules 13a-15(e) and 15d-15(e)) and internal control over financial reporting (as defined in Exchange Act Rules 13a-15(f) and 15d-15(f)) for the registrant and have:

> (a)   [d]esigned such disclosure controls and procedures, or caused such disclosure controls and procedures to be designed under our supervision, to ensure that material information relating to the registrant, including its consolidated subsidiaries, is made known to us by others within those entities, particularly during the period in which this report is being prepared;

> (b)   [d]esigned such internal control over financial reporting, or caused such internal control over financial reporting to be designed under our supervision, to provide reasonable assurance regarding the reliability of financial reporting and the preparation of financial statements for external purposes in accordance with generally accepted accounting principles;

> (c)   [e]valuated the effectiveness of the registrant's disclosure controls and procedures and presented in this report our conclusions about the effectiveness of the disclosure controls and procedures, as of the end of the period covered by this report based on such evaluation; and

> (d)   [d]isclosed in this report any change in the registrant's internal control over financial reporting that occurred during the registrant's most recent fiscal quarter (the registrant's fourth fiscal quarter in the case of an annual report) that has materially affected, or is reasonably likely to materially affect, the registrant's internal control over financial reporting; and

5.   The registrant's other certifying officer(s) and I have disclosed, based on our most recent evaluation of internal control over financial reporting, to the registrant's auditors and the audit committee of the registrant's board of directors (or persons performing the equivalent functions):

> (a)   [a]ll significant deficiencies and material weaknesses in the design or operation of internal control over financial reporting which are reasonably likely to adversely affect the registrant's ability to record, process, summarize and report financial information; and

(b) [a]ny fraud, whether or not material, that involves management or other employees who have a significant role in the registrant's internal control over financial reporting.[61]

The relationship between "disclosure controls" and "internal control over financial reporting" is ill defined.[62]

QUESTIONS ON INTERNAL AND DISCLOSURE CONTROLS

The requirement that companies maintain internal control systems, certify to facts concerning those systems, and obtain an audit of those systems each year is a long way from simply saying that companies must report accurately.[63] The internal control requirements reach far down inside companies. While the law and regulations do not mandate any particular set of controls, they do require that whatever controls a public company adopts be effective within the meaning of the regulations. Should the federal government affect internal company affairs at this level of detail? Right down to referencing a particular "framework" a company might use to evaluate its internal controls and suggesting who might sit on a disclosure committee? Why or why not?

If federal law had required internal financial controls since the 1970s (see note 22), why did SOX impose the costs that it did? Was it just that companies now had to pay money to check the controls? Or did companies discover that the controls they thought were adequate would not satisfy an independent audit, so that the companies needed to spend more money to bring the controls up to snuff?

Each company's auditor will audit the company's internal controls over financial reporting. This check by the auditor may encourage companies to maintain high-quality systems of internal controls. But what about its disclosure controls and procedures? Is it realistic to suppose that, without an audit, a company will vigorously evaluate whether its disclosure controls and procedures are ineffective, correcting any weaknesses it finds?

Top officers will have to make judgment calls when certifying compliance with financial and disclosure control evaluations. For example, they must annually assess the internal controls and provide their conclusions on the controls' effectiveness. They will have to certify that they have reported to the auditor and the audit committee "all significant deficiencies and material weaknesses in the design or operation of" internal controls that are even "reasonably likely to adversely affect the [company's] ability to record, process, summarize and report financial information." Officers must also evaluate the effectiveness of disclosure controls quarterly and report their conclusions in

---

[61]   17 C.F.R. § 229.601(b)(31)(i).

[62]   *See* ROBERT E. BUCKHOLZ, JR., ET AL., PUBLIC COMPANY DESKBOOK § 5I:3 (2016).

[63]   Remember, as you consider the questions, that federal law dating back to the Foreign Corrupt Practices Act required public companies to implement and maintain internal controls. See *supra* note 22. SOX added the assessment and, indirectly, the audit of such controls.

periodic filings. Who will advise the officers on all of this? What role will the lawyers play? Can attorneys appropriately advise on whether something is a "significant deficiency" or a "material weakness" in the internal controls?

What do you think of placing responsibilities relating to the controls personally on the CEO and the CFO? Will those responsibilities remind the CEO and CFO of their accountability so that they make sure the controls are in place and that the controls are strong? Will those responsibilities distract the top officers from making money for the shareholders? On balance, do you think that the personal responsibility is helpful?

F. CODES OF CONDUCT

We turn now to a reform aimed not just at compliance with federal disclosure law, but at both the broader target of corporate culture and the narrower target of related-party transactions.

SOX section 406 required the SEC to issue rules requiring each SEC-reporting company to disclose "whether or not, and if not, the reason therefor, such [company] has adopted a code of ethics for senior financial officers, applicable to its principal financial officer and comptroller or principal accounting officer, or persons performing similar functions."[64] It also required the Commission to revise its rules so that companies were required to file 8-Ks whenever they changed the code or granted any waiver from the code applying to senior financial officers.[65] To qualify as a code of ethics under section 406, a code had to include "such standards as are reasonably necessary to promote—(1) honest and ethical conduct, including the ethical handling of actual or apparent conflicts of interest between personal and professional relationships; (2) full, fair, accurate, timely, and understandable disclosure in the periodic reports required to be filed by the [company]; and (3) compliance with applicable governmental rules and regulations."[66] When the SEC issued the regulations, it required disclosure of whether the code also covered the CEO.

As with some of the other "disclosure" rules, we can look at this, in part, as an effort to encourage companies to create such codes (to the extent that they did not already exist) in order to avoid telling the investment community that they did not have them.

Here is the rule, in Item 406 of Regulation S-K, requiring each public company to:

(a) [d]isclose whether the [company] has adopted a code of ethics that applies to the [company's] principal executive officer,

---

[64]   116 Stat. 745, 789–90; 15 U.S.C. § 7264(a).

[65]   15 U.S.C. § 7264(b).

[66]   15 U.S.C. § 7264(c).

principal financial officer, principal accounting officer or controller, or persons performing similar functions. If the [company] has not adopted such a code of ethics, explain why it has not done so.

(b) For purposes of this Item 406, the term *code of ethics* means written standards that are reasonably designed to deter wrongdoing and to promote:

(1) [h]onest and ethical conduct, including the ethical handling of actual or apparent conflicts of interest between personal and professional relationships;

(2) [f]ull, fair, accurate, timely, and understandable disclosure in reports and documents that a registrant files with, or submits to, the Commission and in other public communications made by the registrant;

(3) [c]ompliance with applicable governmental laws, rules and regulations;

(4) [t]he prompt internal reporting of violations of the code to an appropriate person or persons identified in the code; and

(5) [a]ccountability for adherence to the code.

(c) The [company] must:

(1) [f]ile with the Commission a copy of its code of ethics that applies to the [company's] principal executive officer, principal financial officer, principal accounting officer or controller, or persons performing similar functions, as an exhibit to its annual report;

(2) [p]ost the text of such code of ethics on its Internet website and disclose, in its annual report, its Internet address and the fact that it has posted such code of ethics on its Internet Web site; or

(3) [u]ndertake in its annual report filed with the Commission to provide to any person without charge, upon request, a copy of such code of ethics and explain the manner in which such request may be made.

(d) If the [company] intends to satisfy the disclosure requirement under Item 10 of Form 8-K regarding an amendment to, or a waiver from, a provision of its code of ethics that applies to the registrant's principal executive officer, principal financial officer, principal accounting officer or controller, or persons performing similar functions and that relates to any element of the code of ethics definition enumerated in paragraph (b) of this Item by posting such information on its Internet website, disclose the [company's] Internet address and such intention.

Instructions to Item 406. 1. A [company] may have separate codes of ethics for different types of officers. Furthermore, a *code of ethics* within the meaning of paragraph (b) of this Item may be a portion of a broader document that addresses additional topics or that applies to more persons than those specified in paragraph (a). In satisfying the requirements of paragraph (c), a [company] need only file, post or provide the portions of a broader document that constitutes a *code of ethics* as defined in paragraph (b) and that apply to the persons specified in paragraph (a).

2.   If a [company] elects to satisfy paragraph (c) of this Item by posting its code of ethics on its website pursuant to paragraph (c)(2), the code of ethics must remain accessible on its Web site for as long as the [company] remains subject to the requirements of this Item and chooses to comply with this Item by posting its code on its Web site pursuant to paragraph (c)(2).[67]

An 8-K disclosure filing must be made "within four business days after occurrence of [a listed] event."[68] 8-K Item 5.05 describes in these words the required filings related to codes of ethics:

(a)   Briefly describe the date and nature of any amendment to a provision of the [company's] code of ethics that applies to the [company's] principal executive officer, principal financial officer, principal accounting officer or controller or persons performing similar functions and that relates to any element of the code of ethics definition enumerated in Item 406(b) of Regulations S-K (17 C.F.R. 228.406(b)).

(b)   If the [company] has granted a waiver, including an implicit waiver, from a provision of the code of ethics to an officer or person described in paragraph (a) of this Item 5.05, and the waiver relates to one or more of the elements of the code of ethics definition referred to in paragraph (a) of this Item 5.05, briefly describe the nature of the waiver, the name of the person to whom the waiver was granted, and the date of the waiver.

(c)   The [company] does not need to provide any information pursuant to this Item 5.05 if it discloses the required information on its Internet website within four business days following the date of the amendment or waiver and the [company] has disclosed in its most recently filed annual report its Internet address and intention to provide disclosure in this manner. If the [company]

---

[67]   17 C.F.R. § 229.406 (emphasis added).

[68]   Form 8-K, General Instruction B.1.

elects to disclose the information required by this Item 5.05 through its website, such information must remain available on the website for at least a 12-month period. Following the 12-month period, the registrant must retain the information for a period of not less than five years. Upon request, the [company] must furnish to the Commission or its staff a copy of any or all information retained pursuant to this requirement.

Instructions.

1.   The [company] does not need to disclose technical, administrative or other non-substantive amendments to its code of ethics.

2.   For purposes of this Item 5.05:

> (i)   [t]he term <u>waiver</u> means the approval by the [company] of a material departure from a provision of the code of ethics; and

> (ii)   [t]he term <u>implicit waiver</u> means the [company's] failure to take action within a reasonable period of time regarding a material departure from a provision of the code of ethics that has been made known to an executive officer, as defined in Rule 3b-7 (17 C.F.R. 240.3b-7) of the [company].

While a SOX section 406 code is optional, the NYSE *requires* listed companies to adopt "a code of business conduct and ethics for directors, officers and employees."[69] The commentary says that codes "must require that any waiver of the code for executive officers or directors may be made only by the board or a board committee."[70] Further, codes "must . . . contain compliance standards and procedures that will facilitate the effective operation of the code. These standards should ensure the prompt and consistent action against violations of the code."[71] The commentary adds that codes should address conflicts of interest; corporate opportunities; confidentiality (of information entrusted to officers, employees, and directors by their company and its customers); fair dealing (with

---

[69]   NYSE LISTED COMPANY MANUAL § 303A.10 [NYSE MANUAL]. The requirement dates back to the major revision in governance listing standards approved by the SEC on November 4, 2003. SEC, Self-Regulatory Organizations; New York Stock Exchange, Inc. and National Association of Securities Dealers, Inc.; Order Approving Proposed Rule Changes, 2003 WL 22509738 (SEC Nov. 4, 2003), at *7 ("NYSE Section 303A(10) would require each listed company to adopt and disclose a code of business conduct and ethics for directors, officers and employees, and to promptly disclose any waivers of the code for directors or executive officers.") [SEC Order Approving NYSE and NASDAQ Listing Standard Changes Nov. 2003]. The text cites to and quotes from the NYSE Listed Company Manual as amended and effective in April 2016. Quotations from the New York Stock Exchange Listed Company Manual reprinted with permission from the New York Stock Exchange.

[70]   NYSE MANUAL § 303A.10 cmt.

[71]   *Id.*

customers, suppliers, employees, and competitors); protection and proper use of company assets (with assets used only for legitimate business purposes); and compliance with laws, rules, and regulations (with specific reference to prohibitions on insider trading).[72] And the commentary advises that codes should encourage internal discussion when ethical choices seem difficult, should encourage reports of illegal or unethical behavior, and should ensure that company employees know that the company will not permit retaliation for such reports made in good faith.[73]

NASDAQ has a similar requirement. Its rule says that (i) companies must adopt codes of conduct applicable to all directors, officers, and employees; (ii) codes must comply with SOX section 406 and the implementing SEC regulations; (iii) codes must "provide for an enforcement mechanism"; and (iv) any waivers of codes for directors or executive officers must be approved by boards of directors and disclosed in an 8-K filing within four business days.[74] NASDAQ Stock Market Rule IM-5610 adds, among other things, that "illegal action must be dealt with swiftly and the violators reported to the appropriate authorities."

One purpose of the codes is to control conflicts of interest of the sort that plagued Enron. Among other things, the system set up by the federal securities laws is designed to alert investors to conflicts of interest by the disclosure of waivers from code prohibitions of conflict-producing transactions.[75]

Companies may be able, however, to draft codes in such a way that approval of a related-party transaction can be granted without any "waiver." A study by Professor Madoka Mori found, through a search of the SEC database of company filings, only "twenty-six waivers granted by eighteen companies in the period from March 1, 2004 to February 28,

---

[72] *Id.*

[73] *Id.*

[74] NASDAQ STOCK MARKET RULE 5610. The NASDAQ requirement also dates back to the 2003 overhaul of governance listing standards. SEC Order Approving NYSE and NASDAQ Listing Standard Changes Nov. 2003, *supra* note 69, at *16 ("Nasdaq proposes NASD Rule 4350(n) and related Interpretive Material [now renumbered and part of the NASDAQ Stock Market Rules], which would require each listed company to adopt a code of conduct applicable to all directors, officers and employees, and to make such code publicly available."). The text cites to and quotes from the NASDAQ Stock Market Rules as amended and effective in April 2016. Quotations from the NASDAQ Stock Market Rules reprinted with permission from Nasdaq, Inc. Copyright © 2016 by Nasdaq, Inc. All rights reserved.

[75] Of course, it is possible to use the codes for other purposes. *See* Gap, Inc. Code of Business Conduct, http://www.gapinc.com/content/dam/gapincsite/documents/COBC/COBC_english.pdf (last visited Apr. 29, 2016). The Gap code addresses, among other things, (i) discrimination, harassment, and retaliation (at 5–7); (ii) workplace violence, use of drugs and alcohol, and compliance with safety laws and regulations (at 7); and (iii) what an employee should do if he or she sees counterfeit merchandise (at 23). Gap has a separate code for vendor conduct, Gap, Inc. Code of Vendor Conduct, http://www.gapinc.com/content/dam/gapincsite/documents/Codeof VendorConduct_FINAL.pdf (last visited Sept. 5, 2016), which addresses such matters as use of child labor (at 14).

2006."[76] Professor Mori concluded that some companies had structured their codes so that they would not generate reportable "waivers" even when the relevant authority inside the company approved a transaction involving a conflict:

> [T]he SEC defines a "waiver" as "the approval by the registrant of a material *departure* from a provision of the code of ethics." This definition has enabled some companies to avoid "waivers" that are otherwise required to be reported by adopting codes that provide for approvals, permissions, or authorizations. (All three will be referred to as "approvals.") These are separate from "waivers" that must be disclosed publicly and in a timely manner pursuant to section 406 of SOX and Item 5.05 of Form 8-K. As long as such a company complies with its code by providing the requisite approval, there is, at least arguably and in a technical sense, no "departure" from the code and, accordingly, no "waiver." For example, a company might even state in its code that "complying with this code by obtaining approval where required will not be deemed to be a waiver of any provision of this code." Obviously, if a company can avoid creating a "waiver" in this way, it will file fewer 8-Ks to report waivers.[77]

QUESTIONS ON THE CODES OF CONDUCT

How specific should these codes be?

How will they affect private civil litigation? Is there any way to control that effect?

How will they affect negotiations with the government if the company commits, say, a securities violation and you as counsel are trying to talk the government into a settlement that (i) does not include the government saying publicly that the company committed fraud and (ii) does not include stiff monetary penalties?

Will codes actually encourage ethical behavior? Aside from enforcement, how could companies use the codes to do that? Is it likely to be worth the effort?

What about enforcement? Should companies establish some separate enforcement apparatus and set of procedures for the codes? Or does this fold into the general internal and disclosure control processes and the whistle-blower procedure for the audit committee?

---

[76] Madoka Mori, *A Proposal to Revise the SEC Instructions for Reporting Waivers of Corporate Codes of Ethics for Conflicts of Interest*, 24 YALE J. ON REG. 293, 304 (2007). "All of the twenty-six waivers were granted in conflict-of-interest situations, twenty of which were granted for related-party transactions, three for corporate opportunities, two for outside employment, and one for personal relationships." *Id.* at 305.

[77] *Id.* at 305–06 (citations omitted).

Should companies adopt codes of the sort that the Mori article describes—that employ non-reportable approvals for related-party transactions instead of waivers? Is there any harm in companies doing so, given that

- 17 C.F.R. § 229.404(a) requires a description of any transaction during the last fiscal year, or currently proposed transaction, in which a public company was or is to be involved, where the amount involved exceeds $120,000 and "a related person had or will have a direct or indirect material interest," with "related person" defined to include, among others, any director, director nominee, or executive officer;

- 229.404 (b) requires a description of the company's policies and procedures for approving or ratifying any such transaction; and

- Schedule 14A (17 C.F.R. § 240.14a-101) Item 7(b) requires that a company include the 229.404(a) and (b) disclosures in its proxy statement when the company solicits proxies for election of directors?

Was the Form 8-K provision designed to provide more rapid disclosure than that provided by 17 C.F.R. §§ 229.404(a) & (b); 240.14a-101 (Item 7(b))? Should Item 5.05 of Form 8-K be expanded to include not only waivers and amendments to a company's code of ethics, but also material approvals (defined by a dollar threshold) permitted by the terms of the code of ethics? Would this result in the disclosures SOX section 406 was meant to require?

Do you think that lawyers who draft codes designed to avoid reportable waivers are acting ethically? Appropriately? If you conclude that a reportable waiver, rather than a nonreportable approval, should precede any interested party transaction involving a company's top officers or directors, do you blame Congress or the SEC for creating a reporting requirement that was so easily avoided?

CHAPTER 11

REFORMS II: AUDITOR REFORM[1]

■ ■ ■

We saw in the last chapter that SOX required public companies' management to evaluate internal financial controls and that SOX resulted in a required annual audit of the controls by companies' outside auditors. Congress also focused directly on those auditors. This Chapter Eleven begins with a description of the obstacles that Congress thought might prevent outside auditors from performing their audits with sufficient skepticism and vigor, and what Congress saw as defects in the peer-review system the accounting profession had in place for firms auditing public companies. The chapter then describes the reforms that Congress enacted to remove those obstacles, and the new system that Congress created to register, inspect, and discipline auditors.

A. PROBLEMS THAT THE REFORMERS SAW WITH AUDITORS

A company's financial statements are put together by its own accountants under the supervision of management. Management—particularly top management—usually holds equity interests in the company. Management therefore hopes that reported financial numbers will increase the price of the company's stock, which will drive up the value of the stock and stock derivatives (such as options) that management holds. Management also benefits more directly from financial numbers when companies tie bonus payments to firm financial performance.

The auditor checks a company's financial statements through an audit in order to find errors that should be corrected, independent of the effect of the corrections on management's interests. If the auditor concludes, for example, that the revenue or profit numbers in the company-prepared financial statements are inaccurately high by a material amount or that liabilities are inaccurately low by a material amount, the auditor will require that the company lower the revenues or profits or increase the liabilities in order that the auditor provide an opinion that the financial statements fairly reflect the company's financial condition and results. The

---

[1]   I have used in this chapter material from my article, William O. Fisher, *Lawyers Keep Out: Why Attorneys Should Not Participate in Negotiating Critical Financial Numbers Reported by Public Company Clients*, 2010 BYU L. Rev. 1501 (2010), and drafts of that article. I have done so with permission from the Brigham Young University Law Review.

lower revenue or profit figures or the higher liabilities figure may decrease the company's stock price (or impede its rise), to the detriment of management's wealth. If the auditor finds that numbers to which management bonuses are tied are too high by a material amount, the change that lowers those numbers may reduce management bonuses.

If an auditor is beholden to management, it might not conduct the kind of thorough audit that would uncover the errors that, if corrected, could hurt management in these ways.

Conflict of interest created by the desire to obtain consulting work. By 2002, regulators and Congress perceived a structural bias in the relationship of auditors to their clients. Large accounting firms not only audited public companies but provided services such as management consulting, and those non-audit services formed a large part of the auditing firms' business overall. In some cases, the consulting business produced a large percentage of the revenue that the client paid and provided higher profit margins than the audit work itself.

The legislative history of the Sarbanes-Oxley Act of 2002 included a report by the Senate Banking Committee on S. 2673, which became the bill that a conference committee—without itself producing a report—changed into SOX.[2] That report highlighted the auditor independence issues raised by consulting services:

> There is arguably an inherent conflict in the fact that an auditor is paid by the company for which the audit is being performed. That conflict is implicit in the relationship between the auditor and the audit client. In the last 15 years, however, the rapid growth in management consulting services offered by the major accounting firms has created a second, more substantial conflict that has eroded the independence that the auditor must bring to the audit function.

> According to the SEC, 55 percent of the average revenue of the big five accounting firms came from accounting and auditing services in 1988. Twenty-two percent of the average revenue came from management consulting services. By 1999, those figures had fallen to 31 percent for accounting and auditing services, and risen to 50 percent for management consulting services. Recent data reported to the SEC showed on average public accounting firms' non-audit fees comprised 73 percent of their total fees, or $2.69 in non-audit fees for every $1.00 in audit fees. At the same time, the

---

[2]   *See* 3 JOHN T. BOSTELMAN, ET AL., THE PUBLIC COMPANY DESKBOOK, Appx. A (2d ed. 2014) for a brief summary of the lawmaking.

frequency of financial restatements by public companies has dramatically increased.[3]

The Deputy Chairman of the AICPA Commission on Auditors' Responsibilities testified during one of the many hearings leading to SOX that

> [t]he [Panel on Audit Effectiveness of the Public Oversight Board] reported that the ratio of auditing revenues to consulting revenues from SEC clients went from 6:1 in 1990 to 1.5:1 in 1999.[4]

It had "been reported that in the year 2000 Andersen was paid [by Enron] audit fees of approximately $25 million and non-audit fees of approximately $27 million."[5] And

> [c]omparisons of the amounts of audit fees to nonaudit fees for a range of companies and auditors have revealed ratios of nonaudit to audit fees ranging as high as nine to one. The expressed general concern is that an audit cannot be objective if the auditor is receiving substantial nonaudit fees.[6]

Walking this problem through step by step, the provision by an accounting firm of both audit and consulting services to the same client raised concern that, where management hired an accounting firm for the consulting work, the accounting firm might audit with less skepticism, and might otherwise seek to please management during the audit, so as not to lose lucrative consulting business or fail to win such business.

> The key reason why awarding consulting contracts and other non-audit work to the audit firm is troubling is because it results in conflicting loyalties. While the board's audit committee is formally responsible for hiring and firing the outside auditor, *management* controls virtually all the other types of non-audit work the audit firm may do for the company. Those contracts with *management* blur the reporting relationship—it is difficult to believe that auditors do not feel pressure for the overall success of their firm with the client.[7]

---

[3]   S. REP. NO. 107-205 at 14–15 (2002) [Senate Report on SOX].

[4]   *The Legislative History of the Sarbanes-Oxley Act of 2002: Accounting and Investor Protection Issues Raised by Enron and Other Public Companies: Hearings Before the S. Comm. on Banking, Hous., and Urban Affairs, Vol. II*, 107th Cong. 725, 733 (2002) (prepared statement of Lee J. Seidler, Deputy Chairman of the 1978 AICPA Commission on Auditors' Responsibilities) [Seidler Stmt. to Senate Comm.].

[5]   *The Legislative History of the Sarbanes-Oxley Act of 2002: Accounting and Investor Protection Issues Raised by Enron and Other Public Companies: Hearing Before the S. Comm. on Banking, Hous., and Urban Affairs, Vol. I*, 107th Cong. 69, 70 (prepared statement of David S. Ruder, Chairman, U.S. Securities and Exchange Commission, 1987 to 1989).

[6]   *Id.*

[7]   Senate Report on SOX, at 15–16 (quoting letter from John H. Biggs, Chairman, President and CEO, Teachers' Insurance and Annuity Association—College Retirement Equities Fund

The issue was personal as well as institutional, as auditing partners at accounting firms in at least some cases received extra compensation if their auditing clients also bought the firms' consulting services. One witness before the Senate Committee referred to the SEC's proceedings against Arthur Andersen for its audits of Waste Management, noting that

- Robert Allgyer was Arthur Andersen's engagement partner for the Waste Management Account;

- between 1991 and 1997, Andersen billed Waste Management about $7.5 million in audit fees and $11.8 million in other fees;

- Andersen Consulting billed Waste Management $6 million in additional non-audit fees; and

- "[i]n setting Allgyer's compensation, Andersen took into account, among other things, [Andersen's] billings to [Waste Management] for audit and nonaudit services."[8]

The witness commented that Allgyer was "cross-selling" non-audit services and that "if Allgyer were to take a strong stand against the client he would have risked losing not only future audit fees, but also the even larger consulting fees."[9] More generally, the Senate committee report on SOX quoted an institutional investor as stating that auditors' "own compensation packages may be tied to consulting and non-audit services being provided by their firm to [audit clients]."[10] SEC Chairman Levitt had foreshadowed this concern in 1999, commenting:

> I also wonder about compensation—especially among the line partners. What drives their compensation? Is it the audit function, or is the audit merely a conduit to the cross-selling of other, more lucrative firm services?[11]

Regulators and legislators feared that the lure of more money in their own pockets might consciously or subconsciously tempt audit partners to go easier during audits—and not insist on changes in financial numbers that might decrease the price of company stock that management held and decrease bonuses tied to financial results—in order to maintain a friendly relationship with management, so that management would be more inclined to award consulting work to the partners' firms, which would in turn pay the partners more.

(TIAA-CREF), to Chairman Paul S. Sarbanes, June 28, 2002) (emphasis added) [Biggs Letter to Senate].

[8]   Seidler Stmt. to Senate Comm., *supra* note 4, at 732–33.

[9]   *Id.* at 733.

[10]   Senate Report on SOX, at 16 (quoting Biggs Letter to Senate).

[11]   Arthur Levitt, U.S. Securities and Exchange Commission Chairman, Remarks to the Panel on Audit Effectiveness of the Public Oversight Board (Oct. 7, 1999), http://www.sec.gov/news/speech/speecharchive/1999/spch301.htm.

Conflict of interest created by movement of accountants from auditors to the companies they audited. There were, reformers thought, other structural biases inclining auditors to agree too readily with management during an audit. For example, in a number of instances in which a company filed false financial statements, the accounting and finance staff at the company included former partners or employees from its auditing firm, raising many questions, including (1) whether an auditor with a possible future at an audit client might dial down skepticism during an audit in order to further his or her future job prospects, and (2) whether an auditor would skeptically evaluate the numbers put together by a former colleague now at the client company.[12]

The Enron Examiner found that "[f]rom 1989 through 2000, at least eighty-six Andersen accountants left Andersen to become employed by Enron, some of whom became key executives in Enron's accounting and treasury functions."[13] When the SEC announced the settlement with Arthur Andersen in the Waste Management matter for mis-accounting during the years 1992 through 1996, the Commission pointed out that:

- Andersen has served as Waste Management's auditors since before Waste Management became a public company in 1971.

- Andersen regarded Waste Management as a "crown jewel" client.

- Until 1997, every chief financial officer ("CFO") and chief accounting officer ("CAO") in Waste Management's history as a public company had previously worked as an auditor at Andersen.

- During the 1990s, approximately 14 former Andersen employees worked for Waste Management, most often in key financial and accounting positions.[14]

---

[12]   *See* Seidler Stmt. to Senate Comm., *supra* note 4, at 735:

There are positive aspects to this flow. The company hires people already familiar with operations. If the auditor retains the professional sense of being a CPA, as well as being a corporate manager[,] such employment is likely to be a positive force for integrity of the company's financial reporting.

There are also negatives. In the worst case, the former auditor knows exactly how his or her former firm conducts the audit, and how to conceal information from them. In a less ominous sense, the former auditor knows how far former compatriots can be pushed to accept results preferred by management. In general, "we are all friends," is not exactly the appropriate relationship between independent auditor and client. Recall that Allgyer, the Andersen audit partner[,] had a "personal style that . . . fit well with the Waste Management officers."

[13]   Final Report of Neal Batson, Court-Appointed Examiner, dated November 4, 2003 and filed in the Enron bankruptcy, *In re Enron Corp.*, Case No. 01-16034 (AJG), U.S. Bankruptcy Court, Southern District of New York at 39.

[14]   Press Release, SEC, *Arthur Andersen LLP Agrees to Settlement Resulting in First Antifraud Injunction in More Than 20 Years and Largest-Ever Civil Penalty ($7 Million) in SEC*

Ineffective peer-review system. Leading up to the Enron and WorldCom debacles, the auditing profession was largely self-regulated. Accounting firms auditing public companies peer-reviewed each other, under the supervision of the Public Oversight Board ("POB"), with each firm reviewed once every three years, and the review focusing on the quality and control systems at the firm.[15] Each review concluded with an opinion. Reviewers overwhelmingly issued opinions finding no serious quality control problems with the peers they inspected.[16] As Congress conducted the hearings leading up to the Sarbanes-Oxley legislation, witnesses testified to the actual or perceived unwillingness of firms to criticize each other in peer reviews.[17]

B. REFORMS TO INCREASE AUDITOR INDEPENDENCE

Some reforms specifically regulate the interaction between auditing firms and their clients.

Reducing the conflict of interest created by non-audit work. Before Sarbanes-Oxley, the SEC adopted in 2000 regulations that forbade

---

Enforcement Actions Against a Big Five Accounting Firm (June 19, 2001), http://www.sec.gov/news/headlines/andersenfraud.htm.

[15]   2 LOUIS LOSS, ET AL., SECURITIES REGULATION 460–63 (5th ed. 2014).

[16]   Gilles Hilary & Clive Lennox, *The Credibility of Self-Regulation: Evidence from the Accounting Profession's Peer Review Program*, 40 J. ACCT. ECON. 211, 214–15, 216–18 (2005) (describing the review system, the four types of opinions with which reviews concluded, and what percentages of each type were issued; finding that almost 96% of the peer reviews in a sample of 1,001 opinions issued in the years 1997–2003 found no serious quality control weakness at the reviewed firm).

[17]   *See Accounting Reform and Investor Protection: Hearing on S. 2673 Before the Comm. On Banking, Hous., and Urban Affairs*, 107th Cong. 24 (2002) (statement of Harold M. Williams, Chairman, U.S. Securities and Exchange Commission, 1977 to 1981:

   Under the peer review system adopted in 1977, the firms periodically review each other. To my knowledge, there has never been a negative review of a major firm. . . . Peer review has proved itself insufficient. Particularly as the Big 8 has become only the Big 5, peer review in its present form becomes too incestuous.);

id. at 246–47 (statement of Lynn E. Turner, Chief Accountant, U.S. Securities and Exchange Commission, 1998 to 2001) (referring to "the current system of 'backslapping' peer reviews," and adding:

   [W]hen the SEC staff raised questions with the peer reviewers, meaningful and satisfactory responses were generally not forthcoming. The responses we did receive continually sounded like a rationalization of whatever had been done. Yet the public continued to be provided with the blue ribbon seal of approval by the very profession under scrutiny. Eventually this led to the SEC removing the "endorsement" of the peer review process from its Annual Report to Congress in 1999.);

id. at 747 (statement of Abraham J. Briloff, Emanuel Saxe Distinguished Professor Emeritus, Bernard M. Baruch College, CUNY) ("peer review became nought but mutual back scratching"); *id.* at 903 (statement of Aulana L. Peters, Member, Public Oversight Board, Former Commissioner, U.S. Securities and Exchange Commission, Retired Partner, Gibson, Dunn & Crutcher) (referring to the "perception . . . that the peer reviews are done in a clubby atmosphere where individual firms may be unwilling to criticize their competitors because they do not want to set themselves up to be criticized in the future themselves").

auditors of public companies from performing specified non-audit services for audit clients.[18] SOX section 201 put those prohibitions into the Exchange Act.[19] The Commission then issued a new regulation. Here it is:

An accountant is not independent if, at any point during the audit and professional engagement period, the accountant provides the following non-audit services to an audit client:

(i) *Bookkeeping or other services related to the accounting records or financial statements of the audit client.* Any service, unless it is reasonable to conclude that the results of these services will not be subject to audit procedures during an audit of the audit client's financial statements, including:

(A) [m]aintaining or preparing the audit client's accounting records;

(B) [p]reparing the audit client's financial statements that are filed with the Commission or that form the basis of financial statements filed with the Commission; or

(C) [p]reparing or originating source data underlying the audit client's financial statements.

(ii) *Financial information systems design and implementation.* Any service, unless it is reasonable to conclude that the results of these services will not be subject to audit procedures during an audit of the audit client's financial statements, including:

(A) [d]irectly or indirectly operating, or supervising the operation of, the audit client's information system or managing the audit client's local area network; or

(B) [d]esigning or implementing a hardware or software system that aggregates source data underlying the financial statements or generates information that is significant to the audit client's financial statements or other financial information systems taken as a whole.

(iii) *Appraisal or valuation services, fairness opinions, or contribution-in-kind reports.* Any appraisal service, valuation service, or any service involving a fairness opinion or contribution-in-kind report for an audit client, unless it is reasonable to conclude that the results of these services will not be subject to

---

[18]   Revision of the Commission's Auditor Independence Requirements, 65 Fed. Reg. 76,008, 76,084–85 (Dec. 5, 2000).

[19]   116 Stat. 745, 771–72 (2002) (adding 15 U.S.C. § 78j-1(g) ("unlawful" for auditors to provide identified non-audit services to audit clients); Strengthening the Commission's Requirements Regarding Auditor Independence, 68 Fed. Reg. 6006, 6045–46 (Feb. 5, 2003) (adopting revised regulation).

audit procedures during an audit of the audit client's financial statements.

(iv) *Actuarial services.* Any actuarially-oriented advisory service involving the determination of amounts recorded in the financial statements and related accounts for the audit client other than assisting a client in understanding the methods, models, assumptions, and inputs used in computing an amount, unless it is reasonable to conclude that the results of these services will not be subject to audit procedures during an audit of the audit client's financial statements.

(v) *Internal audit outsourcing services.* Any internal audit service that has been outsourced by the audit client that relates to the audit client's internal accounting controls, financial systems, or financial statements, for an audit client unless it is reasonable to conclude that the results of these services will not be subject to audit procedures during an audit of the audit client's financial statements.

(vi) *Management functions.* Acting, temporarily or permanently, as a director, officer, or employee of an audit client, or performing any decision-making, supervisory, or ongoing monitoring function for the audit client.

(vii) *Human resources.*

    (A) Searching for or seeking out prospective candidates for managerial, executive, or director positions;

    (B) Engaging in psychological testing, or other formal testing or evaluation programs;

    (C) Undertaking reference checks of prospective candidates for an executive or director position;

    (D) Acting as a negotiator on the audit client's behalf, such as determining position, status or title, compensation, fringe benefits, or other conditions of employment; or

    (E) Recommending, or advising the audit client to hire, a specific candidate for a specific job (except that an accounting firm may, upon request by the audit client, interview candidates and advise the audit client on the candidate's competence for financial accounting, administrative, or control positions).

(viii) *Broker-dealer, investment adviser, or investment banking services.* Acting as a broker-dealer (registered or unregistered), promoter, or underwriter, on behalf of an audit client, making investment decisions on behalf of the audit client or otherwise having discretionary authority over an audit client's investments, executing a transaction to buy or sell an audit client's investment, or having custody of assets of the audit client, such as taking temporary possession of securities purchased by the audit client.

(ix) *Legal services.* Providing any service to an audit client that, under circumstances in which the service is provided, could be provided only by someone licensed, admitted, or otherwise qualified to practice law in the jurisdiction in which the service is provided.

(x) *Expert services unrelated to the audit.* Providing an expert opinion or other expert service for an audit client, or an audit client's legal representative, for the purpose of advocating an audit client's interests in litigation or in a regulatory or administrative proceeding or investigation. In any litigation or regulatory or administrative proceeding or investigation, an accountant's independence shall not be deemed to be impaired if the accountant provides factual accounts, including in testimony, of work performed or explains the positions taken or conclusions reached during the performance of any service provided by the accountant for the audit client.[20]

A public company will decline to hire its auditor for such services because, if the auditor provides any of these services, the auditor is not "independent," and the auditor cannot provide the audit opinion that the company needs for its 10-K—an outcome that would defeat a major purpose of the audit.[21] An auditor will decline to offer such services to audit clients, both because doing so would defeat the purpose of the audit for the reason just set out and because it is "unlawful" for the auditor to provide them.[22]

The law still permits an accounting firm to provide, to audit clients, non-audit services other than those on the prohibited lists. But as to these, the law requires, with a *de minimus* exception, that the audit committee at each company pre-approve all such non-audit work provided by the audit firm (as well as all audit services) and requires that audit committee approval of the non-audit services be disclosed in periodic filings.[23] And the law requires that a public company disclose the amount that it paid its

---

[20]   17 C.F.R. § 210.2-01(c)(4) (emphasis added).

[21]   Public companies file their annual report on Form 10-K. 17 C.F.R. § 249.310. The Form 10-K must include financial statements that meet the requirements of Regulation S-X. Form 10-K, Part II, Item 8(a). Regulation S-X in turn requires that the financial statements in the annual report be audited. 17 C.F.R. § 210.3-01(a). And only an "independent" accounting firm can conduct an audit for that purpose. 17 C.F.R. § 210.1-02(d).

[22]   15 U.S.C. § 78j-1(g).

[23]   SOX §§ 201–02; 116 Stat. at 771–73 (adding 15 U.S.C. § 78j-1(h), (i)); *see also* 17 C.F.R. § 210.2-01(c)(7) (auditor not independent unless its work is pre-approved by audit committee or falls within pre-approval policies or is *de minimus*).

outside auditor for permitted non-audit work.[24] Thus, (i) the audit committee—not management—controls engagement of the auditor for non-audit work that the auditor performs for the company, and (ii) investors see the dollar amount paid for permissible non-audit work and can determine for themselves whether that amount might bias the audit.

By the time SOX became law in July 2002, industry changes had removed much of this issue. In 1998, there were five large accounting firms in the U.S.[25] Arthur Andersen went out of business as a result of its indictment for obstruction of justice in the Enron investigation.[26] By 2002, the remaining "Big 4" audited "over 97 percent of all public companies with sales over $250 million."[27] Three of the Big 4 sold or divested large portions of their consulting services,[28] so that the three selling firms received, in 2002, no revenue from management consulting.[29]

But SOX and resulting regulation do not prohibit an accounting firm from offering non-audit services to companies that are not employing that

---

[24]   Item 9(e) of the Schedule 14A requires that public companies' proxy statements for shareholder meetings at which directors will be elected:

  (e)(1) Disclose, under the caption Audit Fees, the aggregate fees billed for each of the last two fiscal years for professional services rendered by the principal accountant for the audit of the registrant's annual financial statements and review of financial statements included in the registrant's Form 10-Q (17 C.F.R. 249.308a) or services that are normally provided by the accountant in connection with statutory and regulatory filings or engagements for those fiscal years.

  (2) Disclose, under the caption Audit-Related Fees, the aggregate fees billed in each of the last two fiscal years for assurance and related services by the principal accountant that are reasonably related to the performance of the audit or review of the registrant's financial statements and are not reported under paragraph (e)(1) of this section. Registrants shall describe the nature of the services comprising the fees disclosed under this category.

  (3) Disclose, under the caption Tax Fees, the aggregate fees billed in each of the last two fiscal years for professional services rendered by the principal accountant for tax compliance, tax advice, and tax planning. Registrants shall describe the nature of the services comprising the fees disclosed under this category.

  (4) Disclose, under the caption All Other Fees, the aggregate fees billed in each of the last two fiscal years for products and services provided by the principal accountant, other than the services reported in paragraphs (e)(1) through (e)(3) of this section. Registrants shall describe the nature of the services comprising the fees disclosed under this category.

17 C.F.R. § 240.14a-101 (Item 9).

[25]   U.S. GENERAL ACCOUNTING OFFICE, PUBLIC ACCOUNTING FIRMS: MANDATED STUDY ON CONSOLIDATION AND COMPETITION 11 (2003).

[26]   *Id.* at 12.

[27]   *Id.* at 16.

[28]   *Id.* at 9.

[29]   *Id.* at 17. Both before and after SOX, accounting firms offered non-audit services that were not "management consulting," including work falling into some of the categories on the list of prohibited services—e.g., actuarial services. Therefore, the GAO study did not show that the three firms had no business other than their audit work, simply that they did not have a management consulting practice.

firm as an auditor.[30] Thus, an accounting firm could audit the financial statements of public company A and still provide consulting services to public company B, whose financial statements the accounting firm did not audit. By the end of 2012, Deloitte's consulting and advisory services accounted for nearly 40% of its business. As all of the four major outside accounting firms auditing public companies built or rebuilt such practices, the trend raised concerns that public confidence in audits might suffer and that accounting firms' focus on high-quality audits might decline as well.[31] This concern thus rested not on the notion that an accounting firm auditing a public company would conduct a less aggressive audit in order to win consulting business at *that* company, but on the notion that an accounting firm with a large and lucrative consulting business might (i) lose its cultural focus on audit precision, and (ii) allocate time and other resources to consulting work, to the detriment of its auditing practice.

By the close of 2013, the audit regulator that SOX established reportedly planned "to ask major accounting firms about their recent push into consulting and what they are doing to avoid any problems it could pose. . . ."[32] By the end of the following year, the head of the new regulator's Division of Registration and Inspection expressed concern about "audit firms buying consulting businesses" and said that the regulator was "paying particular attention to the services provided (both attest and consulting)—on a global level—in order to evaluate whether firms are maintaining their independence in both fact and appearance. We are particularly concerned with how this will affect the quality of the audit."[33]

---

[30]   15 U.S.C. § 78j-1(g) (unlawful for auditor to provide any of the listed services to an audit client "contemporaneously with the audit"); 17 C.F.R. § 210.2-01(c)(4) (auditor not independent if it provides any of the listed services "at any point during the audit and professional engagement period," with that period (per subsection (f)(5)) including both the period covered by the financial statements being audited and the period beginning at the earlier of the time the auditor signs an engagement letter for the audit or the date when it begins the audit work and ending when either "the audit client or the accountant notifies the Commission that the client is no longer that accountant's audit client").

[31]   Michael Rapoport, *Eyebrows Go Up as Auditors Branch Out*, WALL ST. J., Dec. 6, 2012, http://online.wsj.com/news/articles/SB10001424127887324705104578149222319470606.   The article reported former Federal Reserve Chair Volcker as saying, "If firms become too preoccupied with consulting, I think it hurts the authenticity of the audit," the SEC's chief accountant as expressing concern that this trend could "distract" accounting firms away from audits and that the trend "weakens the public trust" in audits, the chair of the auditor regulator created by SOX as worrying that a focus on consulting "threatens to weaken the strength of the audit practice in the [accounting firms] overall," and an academic pointing to the possibility that consulting practices could grow to the extent that the major accounting firms only "dabble" in auditing. *Id.* (internal quotation marks omitted).

[32]   Michael Rapoport, *Big Four Firms to Be Questioned on Push into Consulting*, WALL ST. J., Dec. 9, 2013, http://online.wsj.com/news/articles/SB10001424052702303560204579248480 271764214.

[33]   Helen A. Munter, Director, Division of Registration and Inspections, PCAOB, Remarks Before AICPA Conference on Current SEC and PCAOB Developments, Dec. 10, 2014, http:// pcaobus.org/News/Speech/Pages/12102014_Munter_AICPA.aspx.

QUESTIONS ON THE EFFORTS TO REDUCE AUDITOR CONFLICTS CREATED BY OFFERING NON-AUDIT SERVICES

What do you think of the flat prohibition against accounting firms offering whole categories of services to audit clients? Why not just leave to each audit committee the task of ensuring that the accounting firm its company hires for the audit does not provide so much consulting work that it loses its auditing independence?

How do you like the disclosure provisions, particularly the requirement to tell investors how much money the company paid the auditor for permitted non-audit services? But again, why not let the auditors provide any and all services to audit clients, require disclosure of amounts paid for each type of service, and leave it to investors to punish the stock prices of companies that pay their outside accounting firms so much that those payments may compromise audit quality?

Are you concerned about the post-SOX increase in consulting businesses at major accounting firms auditing publicly traded companies? Is that increase, in your view, without danger so long as an accounting firm does not provide consulting services to its audit clients?

Beyond the long list of non-audit services outside auditors could not offer audit clients at all, the SEC adopted a rule that an accounting firm is not independent "if, at any point during the audit and professional engagement period, any audit partner earns or receives compensation based on the audit partner procuring engagements with that audit client to provide any products or services other than audit, review or attest services."[34] This regulation reaches deep into the bowels of the auditing firm, prohibiting the firm from including in compensation packages incentive payments for a defined type of business development.

Otherwise reducing possible conflicts of interest created by relations between auditors and management, including the possible conflict created by movement of accountants from auditors to clients. SOX section 203 makes it unlawful for an accounting firm to provide audit services to an SEC-registered company "if the lead (or coordinating) audit partner (having primary responsibility for the audit), or the audit partner responsible for reviewing the audit, has performed audit services for that issuer in each of the 5 previous fiscal years. . . ."[35] This effectively requires audit partner rotation at least at the top of the team every five years,[36]

------

[34]   17 C.F.R. § 210.2-01(c)(8).

[35]   116 Stat. at 773; 15 U.S.C. § 78j-1(j).

[36]   *See* 17 C.F.R. § 210.2-01(c)(6)(i)(A)(1) (SEC regulation on partner rotation). The "lead partner" is the one with "primary responsibility for the audit," and the "concurring or reviewing partner" is the one "performing a second level of review to provide additional assurance that the

which in turn may (i) reduce the probability that the leader of the audit team develops a relationship with management that is so close as to reduce the healthy skepticism that an audit requires and (ii) provide periodically a "fresh look" at audit issues.[37]

SOX section 206 prohibits an accounting firm from auditing a public company "if a chief executive officer, controller, chief financial officer, chief accounting officer, or any person serving in an equivalent position for the issuer, was employed by that . . . accounting firm and participated in any capacity in the audit of that issuer during the 1-year period preceding the date of the initiation of the audit."[38] In implementing this statute, the Commission defined "financial reporting oversight role" as "a role in which a person is in a position to or does exercise influence over the contents of the financial statements or anyone who prepares them, such as when the person is a member of the board of directors or similar management or governing body, chief executive officer, president, chief financial officer, chief operating officer, general counsel, chief accounting officer, controller, director of internal audit, director of financial reporting, treasurer, or any equivalent position."[39] The SEC provided that an outside auditor could not be independent if anyone at the client in such a financial oversight role had been, within the year preceding the commencement of an audit, the lead partner, the concurring partner, or any other member of the audit team who devoted more than 10 hours to the audit, review, or attest services for that client.[40]

---

financial statements subject to the audit or review are in conformity with generally accepted accounting principles and the audit or review and any associated report are in accordance with generally accepted auditing standards and rules promulgated by the [SEC] or the [PCAOB]." 17 C.F.R. § 210.2-01(f)(7)(ii)(A) & (B).

Note that partner rotation was not new. The Legislative History of the Sarbanes-Oxley Act of 2002: Accounting and Investor Protection Issues Raised by Enron and Other Public Companies: Hearings Before the S. Comm. on Banking, Hous., and Urban Affairs, Vol. II, 107th Cong. 551, 559 (2002) (prepared statement of David M. Walker, Comptroller General of the United States) ("Currently, there are no time limits for rotation of audit firms, although the AICPA requirements for member firms that audit SEC registrants require partner rotation every 7 years. The concerns are that the auditor may become too close to management over a period of years and, therefore, threaten the auditor's objectivity."). SOX reduced the time to rotation from seven years to five.

[37]   *See* Senate Report on SOX, *supra* note 3, at 21 ("[T]he Committee recognizes the strong benefits that accrue for the issuer and its shareholders when a new accountant 'with fresh and skeptical eyes' evaluates the issuer periodically.").

[38]   116 Stat. at 774–75; 15 U.S.C. § 78j-1(*l*).

[39]   17 C.F.R. § 210.2-01(f)(3)(ii).

[40]   17 C.F.R. § 210.2-01(c)(2)(iii)(B).

QUESTIONS ON PARTNER ROTATION AND WHAT ARE EFFECTIVELY RESTRICTIONS ON THE MOVEMENT OF ACCOUNTANTS FROM AUDITORS TO AUDIT CLIENTS

What do you think of the required partner rotation? Pluses and minuses?

Should the federal government control deployment of labor resources at a private accounting firm that audits privately owned but publicly traded companies? Should the federal government restrict job mobility of individual accountants at accounting firms that serve as auditors for public companies, and restrict hiring decisions at those companies, by prohibiting the companies from hiring individual accountants from their auditors—at least for some time, and into certain positions—except at the cost of disqualifying the accounting firms from the audit work? Or do you see the intrusion here as a light one that still permits an audit client to hire from the accounting firm performing the audit—just not the particular accountants on the audit team, unless the client places those accountants in positions outside financial oversight for the one-year cooling-off period?

C. AN ENTIRELY NEW REGULATORY SCHEME FOR AUDITORS

To attack directly the weakness created by industry-administered peer review, Congress created, through Sarbanes-Oxley, an entirely new structure to supervise auditors of public companies. SOX established the Public Company Accounting Oversight Board ("PCAOB" or "Board") as a non-profit corporation[41] and required that auditors of public companies register with the Board.[42] The Board consists of five members who are selected by the SEC,[43] and is charged with establishing auditing standards, inspecting registered firms, and enforcing the Board's rules.[44]

The PCAOB inspects the registered accounting firms that can audit public companies in order, among other things, to "identify any act or practice or omission to act by the registered public accounting firm, or by any associated person thereof . . . that may be in violation of [SOX], the rules of the [PCAOB], the rules of the [SEC], the firm's own quality control

---

[41]   SOX § 101, 15 U.S.C. § 7211.

[42]   An audit of a public company must be performed by an accounting firm that is not only "independent" under the SEC's definition, and is also "a registered public accounting firm," SOX § 102(a), 15 U.S.C. § 7212(a), which means a firm that is registered with the PCAOB, SOX § 2(5) & (12), 15 U.S.C. § 7201(5) & (12).

[43]   SOX § 101 (e)(1) & (4), 15 U.S.C. § 7211(e)(1) & (4).

[44]   SOX § 103(a)(1), 15 U.S.C. § 7213(a)(1). The rules establishing those standards are not effective until approved by the SEC, and the SEC has the power to abrogate, delete, or add to Board rules. SOX § 107(b)(2) & (5), 15 U.S.C. § 7217(b)(2) & (5).

policies, or professional standards."[45] The Board inspects, *every year*, accounting firms that audit more than 100 public companies and inspects, at least *once every three years*, firms that audit 100 or fewer public companies.[46] Subject to certain significant limitations, the PCAOB shall "ma[k]e [a written report containing the PCAOB's findings for each inspection] available in appropriate detail to the public . . . , except that no portion[ ] of [an] inspection report that deal[s] with criticisms of or potential defects in the quality control systems of the firm under inspection shall be made public if those criticisms or defects are addressed by the firm, to the satisfaction of the Board, not later than 12 months after the date of the inspection report."[47]

The PCAOB is a large operation. Its 2016 budget set total outlays at over $257.7 million.[48]

> The Board currently has leased office space at its headquarters in Washington, D.C., and its technology center in Ashburn, Virginia, in addition to regional office space to support its inspections staff in Atlanta, Georgia; Charlotte, North Carolina; Chicago, Illinois; Irving, Texas; Denver, Colorado; Irvine, California; New York, New York; and San Mateo, California. The 2016 Budget also includes funds for satellite locations in Boston, Massachusetts; Houston, Texas; Los Angeles, California; Philadelphia, Pennsylvania; Fort Lauderdale, Florida and Tampa, Florida.[49]

In a given year, the Board may inspect more than 200 accounting firms auditing public companies and, in the process, look at their work on hundreds of audits.[50] The Board devotes a great deal of attention to the inspections of each of the largest auditing firms. For example, the PCAOB conducted its 2013 inspection of Deloitte & Touche LLP from April 2013

---

[45]   SOX § 104(c)(1), 15 U.S.C. § 7214(c)(1).

[46]   SOX § 104(b), 15 U.S.C. § 7214(b); PCAOB Rule 4003(a), (b).

[47]   SOX § 104(g)(2), 15 U.S.C. § 7214(g)(2). Because the Board must spend the time necessary to determine whether such a submission adequately addresses concerns about the registered firm's quality control systems and because the firm has a right to appeal an adverse determination to the SEC, the time between the Board's final report and the publication of the portion of the report criticizing quality control systems can exceed 12 months. *See* note 52 *infra*.

[48]   Public Company Accounting Oversight Board 201 Budget by Division/Office, http:// pcaobus.org/About/Ops/Documents/Fiscal%20Year%20Budgets/2016.pdf.

[49]   *Id*. at note 8.

[50]   *See* PCAOB, 2014 Annual Report at 5, http://pcaobus.org/About/Ops/Documents/Annual %20Reports/2014.pdf ("Registered firms that issue audit reports for more than 100 public companies and other issuers are required to be inspected annually. In 2014, the PCAOB inspected nine such firms. As part of these inspections, PCAOB inspectors examined portions of more than 310 audits performed by these firms. Registered firms that issue audit reports for 100 or fewer issuers are, in general, inspected at least once every three years. At any time, the PCAOB may also inspect any other registered firm that plays a role in the audit of an issuer. The PCAOB inspected 210 firms in these categories in 2014, including 57 non-U.S. firms located in 23 jurisdictions. In the course of those inspections, PCAOB staff examined portions of more than 470 audits.").

through January 2014 by performing fieldwork at Deloitte's "National Office and at 30 of its approximately 66 U.S. practice offices," with that fieldwork including "reviews of portions of 52 audits performed by the Firm and a review of the Firm's audit work on one other issuer audit engagement in which the Firm played a role but was not the principal auditor."[51]

The provision prohibiting publication of portions of inspection reports critical of audit firms' quality control systems if the firms promptly take remedial actions satisfying the Board seems to provide a powerful incentive for the firms to implement such remedial measures. The overwhelming majority of inspection reports—even 36 months following their date (which should allow time not only for an accounting firm to submit evidence of remediation within 12 months of the report's issuance, but also for the Board to determine whether the remediation is satisfactory)—contain no public portion discussing quality control deficiencies, thereby indicating that the inspected firms resolved any such deficiencies to the satisfaction of the Board.[52] But even where the public portions of PCAOB inspection

---

[51]   PCAOB, Report on 2013 Inspection of Deloitte & Touche LLP 2 (May 6, 2014), http://pcaobus.org/Inspections/Reports/Documents/2014_Deloitte_Touche.pdf [2013 D&T Report].

[52]   The Board's rules provide that its Director of Registration and Inspections will provide a draft report to an inspected firm, and the firm will have an opportunity to submit a written response. PCAOB Rule 4007. The Board transmits its final inspection report, in full, to the firm, to each "appropriate state regulatory authority," and to the SEC. PCAOB Rule 4008. When a final report "contains criticisms of, or potential defects in, the quality control systems of the firm," the firm may "submit evidence or otherwise demonstrate to the Director . . . that it has improved such systems, and remedied such defects no later than 12 months after the issuance of the . . . final inspection report." PCAOB Rule 4009(a). "If the Board determines that the firm has satisfactorily addressed the criticisms or defects in the quality control system," the Board notifies the accounting firm, the SEC, and the state regulatory agencies to which the PCAOB sent the inspection report. PCAOB Rule 4009(b) & (c). The Board makes public the portion of the inspection report containing those criticisms and defects only if either (i) the accounting firm fails to make any submission, within 12 months of issuance of the final report, to show that it has improved its quality control systems and remedied the defects the inspection found or (ii) the firm makes a timely submission but the Board finds that the submission does not satisfactorily address the criticisms or defects and the firm either does not exercise its right to appeal to the SEC or does appeal, but unsuccessfully. PCAOB Rule 4009(d). An accounting firm has the right to seek SEC review of a Board determination that the firm has failed to address the quality control issues the inspection identified in a manner sufficient to avoid publication of the portion of the inspection report describing those issues. SOX § 104(h)(1), 15 U.S.C. § 7214(h)(1). See PCAOB, The Process for Board Determinations Regarding Firms' Efforts to Address Quality Control Criticisms in Inspection Reports, PCAOB Release No. 104-2006-077 (Mar. 21, 2006), for a description of the manner in which the Board and inspected firms interact during the 12-month period and the standard that the Board employs to determine whether the firms have done enough to avoid the adverse publicity attending publication of the portion of the inspection report setting out quality control problems. As that release sets out, a firm that does nothing to resolve those issues with the Board may not only face publication of the previously embargoed portion of the inspection report, but perhaps another quick inspection and possibly a disciplinary proceeding. Id. at 3 n.8. As a practical matter, this process means that the delay—between issuance of a final report finding defects in or containing criticisms of an audit firm's quality control systems and publication of the portion of the report describing those defects or criticisms—can exceed 12 months following the date on which the Board issues the report. As an example, the Board released in June 2014 the quality control criticism in the inspection report of Ernst & Young dated November 30, 2011. In the Matter of Ernst & Young LLP's Quality Control Remediation Submission, PCAOB Release No.

reports do not contain quality control findings, they *do* include specific descriptions of what the Board concludes were audit errors.[53] Presumably,

---

104-2014-101 (June 11, 2014), https://pcaobus.org/Inspections/Documents/06112014_EY_Remediation.pdf.

The threat of publicity has, at least in part, prodded firms to address found quality control deficiencies. After the PCAOB conducted its first inspections of the Big Four firms in August 2004, it reported:

> Both the Act and the Board's rules . . . made plain that the Board would publicly disclose [quality control] criticisms if the firm failed to address them to the Board's satisfaction within 12 months.

> Aware of the prospect of such disclosure, each firm engaged in substantial dialogue with the Board's staff during the 12-month period concerning the firm's efforts to address the criticisms, and each firm made a timely submission, pursuant to PCAOB Rule 4009, concerning those efforts ("Rule 4009 submission"). With respect to each of those Rule 4009 submissions, the Board determined that the firm addressed the quality control criticisms to the Board's satisfaction for purposes of Section 104(g)(2) of the Act. As a result, under the Act, "no portions of the inspection report that deal with [the quality control criticisms] shall be made public."

PCAOB, Observations on the Initial Implementation of the Process for Addressing Quality Control Criticisms Within 12 Months After an Inspection Report, PCAOB Release No. 104-2006-078, at 1–2 (Mar. 21, 2006) (footnotes omitted); *see also* PCAOB 2006 Annual Report at 10 ("The PCAOB's findings [in the report just quoted] supported the legislative hypothesis that firms could be genuinely motivated by the prospect of keeping the Board's quality control criticisms confidential when firms took appropriate steps to remediate quality control deficiencies within 12 months of a Board report describing deficiencies.").

The Board experienced similar success with auditing firms overall. In August 2016, the PCAOB website listed 1958 inspection reports dated more than three years before that date. http://pcaobus.org/Inspections/Reports/Pages/default.aspx (last visited Aug. 21, 2016). Of those, the PCAOB identified 217 (a bit over 11%) as containing quality control criticisms that the Board had identified through inspection and that had not been addressed to the Board's satisfaction.

During its first several years, the Board did not release the quality control portion of any report for any of the Big Four accounting firms, thus suggesting that none of the major firms were operating with any significant unremediated quality control problems. But that streak did not last. *See* Michael Rapoport, *Regulators Unseal Past Criticisms of Ernst*, WALL ST. J. May 24, 2013, at C3 (Board released confidential quality control portions of the inspection report on Ernst & Young; "E&Y is the third of the Big Four accounting firms to receive such a rebuke in the past two years. The board unsealed parts of two PricewaterhouseCoopers LLP inspection reports in March, and part of a Deloitte & Touche LLP report in 2011.").

[53] Here is the Board's policy on publication of specific auditing gaffes that inspections find:

> [T]he public portions of the reports include descriptions of issues identified by the Board's staff in the course of reviewing the firms' performance on selected audit engagements. Specifically, the reports may describe apparent departures from auditing standards, related attestation standards, ethical standards, independence standards, and the firm's own quality control policies and procedures [though not the quality control *systems*, as noted above].

PCAOB, Statement Concerning Issuance of Inspection Reports, PCAOB Release No. 104-2004-001, at 6–7 (Aug. 26, 2004), http://pcaobus.org/Inspections/Documents/Statement_Concerning_Inspection_Reports.pdf.

The Board follows this policy unstintingly. For example, without identifying the particular audit clients, the Board, in the report on its 2013 inspection, specifically criticized Deloitte's audits at 15 different public companies. 2013 D&T Report, *supra* note 51, at 4–18. Here is one such criticism:

Issuer A

In this audit, the Firm failed in the following respects to obtain sufficient appropriate audit evidence to support its audit opinions on the financial statements and on the effectiveness of ICFR [internal control over financial reporting]—

- The Firm's procedures to test controls over revenue were insufficient. Specifically—

the publication of what the PCAOB considers an error that an auditor made during an audit embarrasses both the accounting firm and the

---

    o   For one category of revenue, the Firm's testing of the control it selected over the accuracy of billing rates consisted of observing evidence that the control occurred, without evaluating whether the control addressed whether these rates were consistent with customer orders and relevant regulatory requirements. (AS No. 5, paragraph 42)

    o   For this category of revenue, the Firm also failed to identify and test any controls over changes to billing rates that were made using the method the issuer most frequently used to effect billing rate changes. (AS No. 5, paragraph 39)

    o   The Firm failed to identify and test any controls over whether, for a significant sub-category of revenue, the customers had agreed to purchase services from the issuer. (AS No. 5, paragraph 39)

    o   For another category of revenue, the Firm limited its testing of two controls, involving the review and approval of billing rates and changes to billing rates, to inquiring of issuer personnel, inspecting an invoice, and obtaining evidence that certain rates or changes to certain rates had been approved. The Firm's procedures, however, failed to include evaluating the effectiveness of the review and approval process. (AS No. 5, paragraphs 42 and 44)

- The Firm's substantive procedures to test revenue were insufficient. Specifically—

    o   The Firm designed its substantive procedures—including sample sizes and, in the performance of substantive analytical procedures, thresholds for investigation of differences from expectations—to test certain revenue based on a level of control reliance that was not supported due to the deficiencies in the Firm's testing of controls that are discussed above. As a result, certain of the Firm's sample sizes were too small to provide sufficient evidence, and certain of the thresholds for further investigation were too high. (AS No. 13, paragraphs 16, 18, and 37; AU 329, paragraph .20; AU 350, paragraphs .19 and .23)

    o   For many of the items selected for testing revenue, the Firm's procedures were insufficient, as it failed to test whether the following criteria for recognizing revenue had been met: that there was persuasive evidence of an arrangement, that collectibility was reasonably assured, and/or that services had been rendered at the time revenue was recognized. In addition, for certain of the items selected for testing, the Firm failed to test the accuracy and completeness of data that it used in its testing. (AS No. 14, paragraph 30; AS No. 15, paragraph 10)

- The Firm's procedures to test controls over the valuation and existence of certain categories of long-lived assets were insufficient. Specifically—

    o   Regarding additions to one category of long-lived assets, the Firm's testing of two review controls over the capitalization of certain costs was limited to inquiry and procedures designed to verify that the reviews had occurred, without evaluating whether the reviews effectively assessed the appropriateness of recording these costs as additions to assets. The Firm also failed to test controls over the accuracy and completeness of reports used in the performance of a third control over the capitalization of these costs. (AS No. 5, paragraphs 39, 42, and 44)

    o   The Firm failed to identify and test any controls over the accounting for additions to another category of long-lived assets. (AS No. 5, paragraph 39)

- The Firm designed its substantive procedures—including sample sizes—to test the valuation and existence of certain categories of long-lived assets based on a level of control reliance that was not supported due to the deficiencies in the Firm's testing of controls that are discussed above. As a result, the sample sizes the Firm used to test these assets were too small to provide sufficient evidence. (AS No. 13, paragraphs 16, 18, and 37; AU 350, paragraphs .19 and .23)

2013 D&T Report, *supra* note 51, at 4–6. The point is that PCAOB inspection reports demonstrate that the Board looks at audit work in detail and makes detailed criticisms.

individuals within it who conducted the audit singled out for criticism. All of this may encourage other accountants—both in the criticized firm and in other firms—to avoid that error and thereby avoid public criticism, in a later PCAOB report, for committing it. Auditors may also be generally more careful, knowing that the regulator is examining audits and looking for mistakes that it will reprove if found. On the other hand, to whatever extent the PCAOB criticizes judgment calls in audits performed by auditors doing their best, the public embarrassment may not affect behavior and, from the viewpoint of the auditor community, may appear to constitute random and arbitrary punishment.

Congress empowered the PCAOB not only to inspect accounting firms that audit public companies but also to conduct investigations and institute disciplinary proceedings against those firms and the individual accountants in them.[54] The Board may investigate and impose sanctions for violations by a registered auditing firm of any provision of "this Act [SOX], the rules of the Board, the provisions of the securities laws relating to the preparation and issuance of audit reports and the obligations and liabilities of accountants with respect thereto, including the rules of the Commission issued under this Act, or professional standards"[55] and may impose any of an impressive array of sanctions at the conclusion of such proceedings.[56] The Board coordinates its investigations of federal securities violations with the SEC, and may refer an investigation to other federal

---

[54]   SOX § 105, 15 U.S.C. § 7215. Board rules permit both informal inquiries (Rule 5100) and formal investigations (Rule 5101(a)(1)). In formal investigations, the Board may "require the testimony of any registered public accounting firm or any person associated with [such a] firm" (Rule 5102(a)) and "may issue an accounting board demand for the production of audit work papers or any other document or information in the possession" of a registered firm (Rule 5103(a)). The Board may ask the SEC to issue subpoenas to "any person" to aid PCAOB investigations. PCAOB Rule 5111(a). The Board's rules include elaborate provisions for instituting and conducting disciplinary proceedings. PCAOB Rules 5200 *et seq.*, 5400 *et seq.*

[55]   SOX § 105(b)(1), (c)(4), 15 U.S.C. § 7215(b)(1), (c)(4); *see* PCAOB Rules 5100(a), 5101(a)(1), 5300(a).

[56]   SOX § 105(c)(4), 15 U.S.C. § 7215(c)(4). The sanctions include temporary or permanent revocation of registration (and consequent inability to audit public companies), temporary or permanent bars forbidding individual accountants from associating with registered auditors, limitation of firm activities (which can include a prohibition against accepting new clients for some period of time), civil monetary penalties (up to $131,185 per violation with a $983,888 cap per case for individuals and up to $2,623,700 per violation with a $19,677,750 per case cap for firms), required additional training or education, employment by a firm of an independent monitor to observe and report on future compliance, implementation of new firm procedures to effectuate future compliance, and a requirement that a firm "obtain an independent review and report on one or more engagements." PCAOB Rule 5300(a); Adjustments to Civil Monetary Penalty Amounts, 81 Fed. Reg 43,042, 43,044 (July 1, 2016). Any firm or individual accountant who is the subject of a disciplinary proceeding may make a written offer of settlement, and the sanctions included in an agreed-upon settlement are not constrained by the sanctions set out in the SOX or the Board's rules. PCAOB Rules 5205, Note 1 to Rule 5300.

Aside from disciplinary proceedings based on substantive violations, the Board has the authority to, and the rules in place to, bring such proceedings based on the failure of a registered firm or associated individual to cooperate in a PCAOB investigation. SOX § 105(b)(3), 15 U.S.C. § 7215(b)(3); PCAOB Rules 5110, 5300(b).

regulatory agencies, to the Department of Justice for possible criminal prosecution, to state regulatory authorities (such as those licensing accountants), and to state attorney generals.[57]

The Board generally publicizes disciplinary proceedings only when they are concluded and all time for review has passed.[58] The public record suggests a fairly extensive PCAOB enforcement program.[59] Proceedings culminating in sanctions include punishments meted out to accountants at firms of all sizes, including large and prestigious firms, often by orders entered after settlements in which the respondents did not admit or deny wrongdoing.[60]

---

[57]   SOX § 105(b)(4), 15 U.S.C. § 7215(b)(4); PCAOB Rule 5112.

[58]   SOX § 105(c)(2), (d)(1)(C), 15 U.S.C. § 7215(c)(2), (d)(1)(C); PCAOB Rules 5108, 5203.

[59]   Here is part of the enforcement summary from the Board's 2014 Annual Report:

As of Dec. 31, 2014, Board disciplinary proceedings involving formal allegations of misconduct involving 16 firms and individual auditors were pending but could not be publicly disclosed by the Board because of the statutory restriction.

The Board made public 24 settled disciplinary orders in 2014, imposing sanctions on auditors ranging from censures to monetary penalties to revocations of a firm's registration and bars on an individual's association with registered accounting firms. One of these proceedings involved alleged violations of the antifraud provisions of the Securities Exchange Act of 1934. Eleven of the settlements occurred after the PCAOB had initiated nonpublic disciplinary proceedings; the remaining 13 cases were initiated and settled concurrently.

In all of the settled proceedings, the firms and the associated persons neither admitted nor denied the Board's findings. The final outcome in one adjudicated disciplinary proceeding was also made public in 2014. This proceeding resulted in a permanent revocation of a firm's registration and the imposition of a $10,000 penalty.

At 15, http://pcaobus.org/About/Ops/Documents/Annual%20Reports/2014.pdf.

By late June 2016, the Board's website showed 155 settled disciplinary proceedings and 16 adjudicated proceedings in the approximately 13½ years during which the Board had operated. PCAOB, Disciplinary Proceedings, http://pcaobus.org/Enforcement/Decisions/Pages/default.aspx (last visited June 27, 2016) and http://pcaobus.org/Enforcement/Adjudicated/Pages/default.aspx (last visited June 27, 2016).

[60]   *See, e.g.*, Order Making Findings and Imposing Sanctions, *In re Randall A. Stone, CPA*, PCAOB Release No. 105-2014-007 (July 7, 2014), http://pcaobus.org/Enforcement/Decisions/ Documents/Stone.pdf (barring PricewaterhouseCoopers partner from association with any accounting firm registered with the Board, with permission to petition for reinstatement after three years and imposing $50,000 civil penalty, resolving charges of among other things ignoring or failing to investigate indicators that an audit client improperly recognized revenue on sales to one of its major distributors); Order Making Findings and Imposing Sanctions, *In re Thomas J. Linden, CPA*, PCAOB Release No. 105-2009-004 (Aug. 11, 2009), http://pcaobus.org/enforcement/ decisions/documents/08-11_linden.pdf (barring Deloitte & Touche partner from association with any accounting firm registered with the Board, with permission to petition for reinstatement after two years and imposing $75,000 civil penalty, resolving charges of actively assisting a client to avoid revising reported financial results after discovery that earnings were overstated, including by initiating a 50% increase in Deloitte's planned tolerance for misstatements); Order Instituting Disciplinary Proceedings, Making Findings, and Imposing Sanctions, *In re Christopher E. Anderson, CPA*, PCAOB Release No. 105-2008-003 (Oct. 31, 2008), http://pcaobus.org/ Enforcement/Decisions/Documents/10-31_Anderson.pdf (barring Deloitte & Touche partner from association with any registered firm for one year, restricting his participation in audits for an additional year, and imposing $25,000 civil money penalty, resolving charges of participating in the same wrongdoing as Thomas Linden); Order Instituting Disciplinary Proceedings, Making Findings, and Imposing Sanctions, *In re Stephen J. Nardi, CPA*, PCAOB Release No. 105-2007-008 (Dec. 14, 2007), http://pcaobus.org/Enforcement/Decisions/Documents/12-14_Nardi.pdf

The SEC retains its own right to sanction auditors for securities law violations[61] and to "censure [an auditor] or deny [to the auditor],

---

(barring a partner at BDO Seidman, LLP from associating with any registered auditing firm, with opportunity to petition for relief in one year, resolving charges of, among other things, ordering a manager at BDO Seidman to sign a document indicating that the manager had performed a timely and detailed review of audit papers when the manager had not done so); Order Instituting Disciplinary Proceedings, Making Findings, and Imposing Sanctions, *In re Ann Marie Fitzpatrick, CPA*, PCAOB Release No. 105-2007-007 (Dec. 14, 2007), http://pcaobus.org/Enforcement/ Decisions/Documents/12-14_Fitzpatrick.pdf (censuring the audit manager at BDO Seidman, LLP, who signed and initialed audit papers, and backdated her signature, in order to falsely attest to having performed a timely and detailed review); Order Instituting Disciplinary Proceedings, Making Findings, and Imposing Sanctions, *In re James L. Fazio, CPA*, PCAOB Release No. 105-2007-006 (Dec. 10, 2007), http://pcaobus.org/Enforcement/Decisions/Documents/12-10_Fazio.pdf (barring a partner at Deloitte & Touche LLP from associating with any registered auditing firm, with opportunity to petition for relief in two years, resolving charges of failure to adequately audit reserve for returned products); Order Instituting Disciplinary Proceedings, Making Findings, and Imposing Sanctions, *In re Deloitte & Touche LLP*, PCAOB Release No. 105-2007-005 (Dec. 10, 2007), http://pcaobus.org/Enforcement/Decisions/Documents/12-10_Deloitte.pdf (censuring the firm and imposing a $1,000,000 civil money penalty, resolving charges of assigning a partner to an audit despite serious questions that facts known to the firm raised about the partner's competence to perform the audit); Order Instituting Disciplinary Proceedings, Making Findings, and Imposing Sanctions, *In re Susan E. Birkert, CPA*, PCAOB Release No. 105-2007-003 (Nov. 14, 2007), http://pcaobus.org/Enforcement/Decisions/Documents/11-14_Birkert.pdf (barring a Lead Senior at KPMG LLP from associating with any registered auditing firm, with opportunity to petition for relief after one year, resolving charges of investing money in the stock of an audit and review client while she was working on a review for that client).

[61]   For example, the SEC can seek an injunction against anyone or any organization that violates the 34 Act or related rules, 15 U.S.C. § 78u(d)(1), and can request a court in such actions to impose civil monetary penalties, *id.* § 78u(d)(3), and to order "any equitable relief that may be appropriate or necessary for the benefit of investors," *id.* § 78u(d)(5), which can include disgorgement, *see SEC v. Cavanagh*, 445 F.3d 105, 116–21 (2d Cir. 2006). The SEC can pursue primary violators of those statutes and rules, including those who participate in a substantial way in the preparation of false financial statements. *See McConville v. SEC*, 465 F.3d 780, 786–88 (7th Cir. 2006), *cert. denied*, 128 S. Ct. 48 (2007). The SEC can also pursue "any person that knowingly or recklessly provides substantial assistance to another person in violation of [the Securities Exchange Act], or of any rule or regulation issued under [that Act]." 15 U.S.C. § 78t(e).

The Commission staff can bring administrative proceedings against violators before the SEC's administrative law judges ("ALJs"), asking the ALJs for cease-and-desist orders, 15 U.S.C. § 78u-3(a), to require disgorgement of gains that a respondent obtained from the violation, *id.* § 78u-3(e), and to impose civil monetary penalties, *id.* 78u-2. The relief in these administrative proceedings can reach not only primary violators but "any other person that is, was, or would be a cause of the violation, due to an act or omission the person knew or should have known would contribute to such violation." 15 U.S.C. § 78u-3(a).

SOX's creation of the PCAOB did not restrict the SEC's authority to bring enforcement actions against auditors in federal court or before ALJs. Indeed, the text of the statute suggests that the enforcement authority of the two bodies overlaps. SOX provides that a violation of "any rule of the [PCAOB] shall be treated for all purposes in the same manner as a violation of the Securities Exchange Act of 1934 . . . or the rules and regulations issued thereunder, . . . and any . . . person [violating those rules] shall be subject to the same penalties, and to the same extent, as for a violation of that Act or such rules or regulations," SOX § 3(b)(1), 15 U.S.C. § 7202(b)(1), and amends the statutes authorizing the SEC to bring enforcement actions in federal court and before ALJs so that the Commission can bring such actions on the basis of PCAOB violations, SOX § 3(b), amending 15 U.S.C. §§ 78u, 78u-3. Similarly, SOX empowers the PCAOB to sanction not only violations of the Board's rules and professional standards, but also violations of "the provisions of the securities laws relating to the preparation and issuance of audit reports and the obligations and liabilities of accountants with respect thereto." SOX § 105(c)(4), 15 U.S.C. § 7215(c)(4). The Board is required to "notify the [SEC] of any pending Board investigation involving a potential violation of the securities laws, and thereafter to coordinate its work with the work of the Commission's Division of Enforcement, as necessary to protect an ongoing Commission

temporarily or permanently, the privilege of appearing or practicing before [the Commission]."[62] The Commission has used its power to impose, on major accounting firms and the accountants practicing in them, significant sanctions for audit improprieties in the years since the passage of Sarbanes-Oxley, often by orders entered after settlements in which the respondents did not admit or deny wrongdoing.[63]

---

investigation," SOX § 105(b)(4)(A), 15 U.S.C. § 7215(b)(4)(A), and is authorized but not required to refer an investigation to the SEC, SOX § 105(b)(4)(B)(i), 15 U.S.C. § 7215(b)(4)(B)(i).

[62]   17 C.F.R. § 201.102(e).

[63]   *See* Order Instituting Public Administrative and Cease-and-Desist Proceedings Pursuant to Sections 4C and 21C of the Securities Exchange Act of 1934, and Rule 102(e) of the Commission's Rules of Practice, Making Findings, and Imposing Remedial Sanctions and a Cease-and-Desist Order, *In re BDO USA, LLP*, SEC Admin. Proceeding, File No. 3-16800 (Sept. 9, 2015), https://www.sec.gov/litigation/admin/2015/34-75862.pdf (firm agreed to pay over $2.1 million and to undertake a wide array of prophylactic measures, including a far-ranging review of its quality controls and retention of an independent consultant to determine whether BDO policies provide reasonable assurance of compliance with SEC regulations and PCAOB standards, resolving charges that BDO violated auditing standards by giving unqualified opinions to a client that provided incomplete and conflicting information about cash comprising approximately half of the client's assets, with the firm "acknowledg[ing] that its conduct violated the federal securities laws"); Order Instituting Public Administrative and Cease-and-Desist Proceedings Pursuant to Sections 4C and 21C of the Securities Exchange Act of 1934, and Rule 102(e) of the Commission's Rules of Practice, Making Findings, and Imposing Remedial Sanctions and a Cease-and-Desist Order, *In re Ernst & Young LLP*, SEC Admin. Proceeding, File No. 3-15970 (July 14, 2015), https://www.sec.gov/litigation/admin/2014/34-72602.pdf (firm agreed to pay $4,071,925.98 in disgorgement, interest, and a civil penalty, resolving charges that firm violated independence rules by providing legislative advisory services to audit clients); Order Instituting Public Administrative and Cease-And-Desist Proceedings Pursuant to Sections 4C and 21C of the Securities Exchange Act of 1934, Section 9(f) of the Investment Company Act of 1940, and Rule 102(e) of the Commission's Rules of Practice, Making Findings, and Imposing Remedial Sanctions and a Cease-and-Desist Order, *In re Deloitte & Touche LLP, et al.*, SEC Admin. Proceeding, File No. 3-16672 (July 1, 2015), https://www.sec.gov/litigation/admin/2015/34-75343.pdf (firm agreed to pay $1,113,916 in disgorgement, interest, and a civil penalty, resolving charges that firm violated independence rules through an affiliate that had a business relationship with an individual who was a member of the audit committees at three clients); Order Instituting Public Administrative and Cease-and-Desist Proceedings Pursuant to Sections 4C and 21C of the Securities Exchange Act of 1934, and Rule 102(e) of the Commission's Rules of Practice, Making Findings, and Imposing Remedial Sanctions and a Cease-and-Desist Order, *In re Ernst & Young LLP, et al.*, SEC Admin. Proceeding, File No. 3-13114 (Aug. 5, 2008), https://www.sec.gov/litigation/admin/2008/34-58309.pdf (firm agreed to pay $2,918,987.79 in disgorged fees and interest on fees, one individual partner agreed to cease-and-desist order, and a second partner agreed to be barred from SEC practice, with the opportunity to apply for reinstatement after one year, resolving charges that firm violated independence rules because it had a business arrangement with an individual who was a board member of two audit clients and on the audit committee of a third audit client, and that individual participated in the creation of promotional CDs for use in EY marketing); Order Instituting Public Administrative Proceedings Pursuant to Rule 102(e) of the Commission Rules of Practice, Making Findings, and Imposing Remedial Sanctions, *In re Ernst & Young Chartered Accountants, et al.*, SEC Admin. Proceeding, File No. 3-12703 (July 19, 2007), https://www.sec.gov/litigation/admin/2007/34-56104.pdf (Irish member firm of Ernst & Young Global agreed to pay $725,000 and undertake extensive remedial steps, including additional training, resolving charges growing out of audit during which accountants failed to detect a variety of GAAP violations, including improper recognition of revenue from software sales and improper accounting for reciprocal non-monetary transactions with customers); Order Instituting Public Administrative and Cease-and-Desist Proceedings Pursuant to Section 21C of the Securities Exchange Act of 1934 and Rule 102(e) of the Commission's Rules of Practice, Making Findings, and Imposing Remedial Sanctions, *In re Ernst & Young, LLP*, SEC Admin. Proceeding, File No. 3-12600 (Mar. 26, 2007), https://www.sec.gov/litigation/admin/2007/34-55523.pdf (firm agreed to pay a total of $1,587,170.42 to resolve alleged

violations of auditor independence standards by "assisting one client, American International Group, Inc . . . , in its development and marketing of an accounting-driven financial product and then advising an audit client, The PNC Financial Services Group, Inc . . . , on the accounting treatment for a version of that product in PNC's financial statements" (at 2)); Order Granting Motion for Expedited Entry of Final Order and Notice That Initial Decision Has Become Final, *In re Ernst & Young*, SEC Admin. Proceeding, File No. 3-10933 (Apr. 26, 2004), https://www.sec.gov/litigation/admin/33-8413.htm (firm ordered to pay $2,164,500 in disgorged fees and interest and to retain independent consultant, and to refrain from accepting audit engagements for new public company clients for a period of six months, after initial ALJ decision on Apr. 16, 2004, finding that EY violated auditor independence standards when auditing PeopleSoft while, among other things, the EY consulting practice had a business arrangement with PeopleSoft to sell services to third parties and that arrangement paid EY about $425 million); Order Instituting Public Administrative Proceedings Pursuant to Rule 102(e) of the Commission's Rules of Practice, Making Findings, and Imposing Remedial Sanctions, *In re Press C. Southworth*, SEC Admin. Proceeding, File No. 3-12811 (Sept. 19, 2007), https://www.sec.gov/litigation/admin/2007/34-56470.pdf (PwC partner agreed to bar from practicing before the SEC, with opportunity to apply for reinstatement after two years, resolving charges of highly unreasonable conduct in audit that, among other things, provided a clean opinion on financial statements failing to disclose that the issuer used proceeds from notes to make loans, not permitted by bond indentures, to borrowers that did not have the ability to repay); Order Instituting Public Administrative Proceedings Pursuant to Rule 102(e) of the Commission's Rules of Practice, Making Findings, and Imposing Remedial Sanctions, *In re Amber Schatz*, SEC Admin. Proceeding, File No. 3-12603 (Mar. 29, 2007), https://www.sec.gov/litigation/admin/2007/34-55554.pdf (PwC senior associate accountant agreed to bar from practicing before the SEC, with opportunity to apply for reinstatement after one year, resolving charges of violating auditor independence standards by accepting a personal loan from client's CFO during an audit); Order Instituting Public Administrative Proceedings Pursuant to Rule 102(e) of the Commission's Rules of Practice, Making Findings, and Imposing Remedial Sanctions, *In re Andrew J. McAdams*, SEC Admin. Proceeding, File No. 3-12227 (Mar. 3, 2006), https://www.sec.gov/litigation/admin/34-53404.pdf (PwC partner agreed to bar from practice before the SEC, with opportunity to apply for reinstatement after two years, to resolve charges of repeated instances of unreasonable conduct relating to discovery and correction of fictitious revenue, a variety of improper inventory entries, and failure to write down obsolete inventory); Order Instituting Public Administrative Proceedings Pursuant to Rule 102(e) of the Commission's Rules of Practice, Making Findings, and Imposing Remedial Sanctions, *In re Nicholas DiFazio*, SEC Admin. Proceeding, File No. 3-12971 (Feb. 26, 2008), https://www.sec.gov/litigation/admin/2008/34-57381.pdf (Deloitte & Touche partner agreed to bar from practice before SEC, with opportunity to apply for reinstatement after three years, resolving charges of repeated instances of unreasonable conduct in audit of financials that misreported increase in warranty reserves as a charge to shareholders' equity); Order Instituting Public Administrative Proceedings Pursuant to Rule 102(e) of the Commission's Rules of Practice, Making Findings, and Imposing Remedial Sanctions, *In re Duane Higgins*, SEC Admin. Proceeding, File No. 3-12970 (Feb. 26, 2008), https://www.sec.gov/litigation/admin/2008/34-57380.pdf (Deloitte & Touche partner agreed to bar from practice before SEC, with opportunity to apply for reinstatement after two years, resolving charges of repeated instances of unreasonable conduct in an audit of a client that treated as a sale and purchase, rather than a financing, a series of transactions in which the client sold its precious metals inventory to a bank, entered into a forward purchase agreement to buy the precious metals back, and never transferred the risks of ownership); Order Instituting Public Administrative Proceedings Pursuant to Rule 102(e) of the Commission's Rules of Practice, Making Findings, and Imposing Remedial Sanctions, *In re Deloitte & Touche LLP, et al.*, SEC Admin. Proceeding, File No. 3-11911 (Apr. 26, 2005), https://www.sec.gov/litigation/admin/34-51607.pdf (firm agreed to pay $375,000 and accepted censure, and partner and manager agreed to bar from practicing before the SEC, with rights to apply for reinstatement after respectively two and one years, to resolve charges of repeated instances of unreasonable conduct during an audit that failed to uncover, among other things, improper treatment of vendor allowances and inadequate allowance for obsolete inventory at a high-risk client); Order Instituting Public Administrative Proceedings Pursuant to Rule 102(e) of the Commission's Rules of Practice, Making Findings, and Imposing Remedial Sanctions, *In re Deloitte & Touche LLP*, SEC Admin. Proceeding, File No. 3-11910 (Apr. 26, 2005), https://www.sec.gov/litigation/admin/34-51606.pdf (firm agreed to pay $25 million, and to take remedial measures to be evaluated in 18 months by an independent consultant, resolving charges of repeated instances of unreasonable conduct in an audit that failed to detect misreporting of more than $1 billion in debt for which client was jointly and severally liable with entities controlled by the client's officers and directors).

QUESTIONS ON THE PCAOB

Was the PCAOB overkill?

Bearing in mind that accounting is a profession (as is lawyering), do auditors really need to have a national bureaucracy, albeit in the form of a non-profit corporation, inspecting them periodically?

Or are inspections just the thing to keep the auditors on their toes, since the audit clients—and investors in them—are unlikely to act as a reliable quality control?

Should a similar body regulate law firms that advise public companies on their securities filings? Should such a body review and comment on the advice that the law firms provide to companies about their filings with the SEC?

In *Free Enterprise Fund v. Public Company Accounting Oversight Board*,[64] the Supreme Court considered whether the creation of the PCAOB violated the U.S. Constitution. The majority concluded that, as written, the SOX provisions establishing the Board deprive the President of the constitutionally mandated ability to " 'take Care that the Laws be faithfully executed.' "[65] SOX states that the SEC, which appoints members of the PCAOB, can only remove a member "for good cause shown."[66] All parties conceded that the President can only remove SEC Commissioners for " 'inefficiency, neglect of duty, or malfeasance in office.' "[67] The majority reasoned that a President therefore could not simply remove a PCAOB member whom the President "determine[d] . . . [to be] neglecting his duties or discharging them improperly."[68] "That judgment is instead committed to [the SEC], [whose members] may or may not agree with the President's determination, and whom the President cannot remove simply because [they] disagree[ ] with him."[69] This double "for cause" insulation of PCAOB members from presidential removal—President cannot remove SEC Commissioners except for cause and SEC Commissioners cannot remove PCAOB members except for cause—"contravenes the President's 'constitutional obligation to ensure the faithful execution of the laws.' "[70] Despite this constitutional defect, the majority did not strike down the SOX

---

[64]   561 U.S. 477 (2010).

[65]   *Id.* at 484 (quoting U.S. Const. art. II, § 3).

[66]   SOX § 101(e)(6), 15 U.S.C. § 7211(e)(6).

[67]   *Free Enter. Fund*, 561 U.S. at 487 (quoting *Humphrey's Executor v. United States*, 295 U.S. 602, 620 (1935)).

[68]   *Id.* at 484.

[69]   *Id.*

[70]   *Id.* (quoting *Morrison v. Olson*, 487 U.S. 654, 693 (1988)).

sections creating the PCAOB in their entirety but opted instead to excise the "unconstitutional tenure provisions" so that PCAOB members are "removable by the [SEC] at will."[71] This leaves the SEC "fully responsible for the [PCAOB's] actions, which are no less subject than the [SEC's] own functions to Presidential oversight."[72]

The majority's opinion changed little in the securities world. The PCAOB continued to promulgate auditing standards, inspect accounting firms auditing public companies, publish inspection reports to the extent provided in the statute and PCAOB rules, and bring disciplinary actions against audit firms and individual auditors. The circumstance that the PCAOB members are now subject to at-will removal by the SEC should make those members no more disinclined to thwart the SEC's will than before this ruling, given the extensive control the SEC already had over PCAOB actions.[73]

---

[71]   *Id*. at 508–09.

[72]   *Id*. at 509.

[73]   Here is a summary, provided by the dissent:

- No Accounting Board rule takes effect unless and until the Commission approves it, § 7217(b)(2);

- The Commission may "abrogat[e], delet[e] or ad[d] to" any rule or any portion of a rule promulgated by the Accounting Board whenever, in the Commission's view, doing so "further[s] the purposes" of the securities and accounting-oversight laws, § 7217(b)(5);

- The Commission may review any sanction the Board imposes and "enhance, modify, cancel, reduce, or require the remission of" that sanction if it finds the Board's action not "appropriate," §§ 7215(e), 7217(c)(3);

- *The Commission may promulgate rules restricting or directing the Accounting Board's conduct of all inspections and investigations*, §§ 7211(c)(3), 7214(h), 7215(b)(1)–(4);

- *The Commission may itself initiate any investigation or promulgate any rule within the Accounting Board's purview, § 7202, and may also remove any Accounting Board member who has unreasonably "failed to enforce compliance with" the relevant "rule[s], or any professional standard,"* § 7217(d)(3)(C) (emphasis added);

- *The Commission may at any time "relieve the Board of any responsibility to enforce compliance with any provision" of the Act, the rules, or professional standards if, in the Commission's view, doing so is in "the public interest,"* § 7217(d)(1) (emphasis added).

... Moreover, the Commission has general supervisory powers over the Accounting Board itself: It controls the Board's budget, §§ 7219(b), (d)(1); it can assign to the Board any "duties or functions" that it "determines are necessary or appropriate," § 7211(c)(5); it has full "oversight and enforcement authority over the Board," § 7217(a), *including the authority to inspect the Board's activities whenever it believes it "appropriate" to do so*, § 7217(d)(2) (emphasis added). And it can censure the Board or its members, as well as remove the members from office, if the members, for example, fail to enforce the Act, violate any provisions of the Act, or abuse the authority granted to them under the Act, § 7217(d)(3).

Id. at 528–29 (Breyer, J, dissenting) (alterations in original).

D. SUMMARY OF AUDITOR REFORMS

The reforms hit the auditors from all sides. They reached down into the accounting firms to change their business model and their compensation schemes.

The reforms reached into the public companies and effectively restricted their hiring policies, thereby restricting the movement of individual accountants from auditors to audit clients.

The reforms imposed a far-reaching regulatory system on the auditors—vastly more intrusive and public than the peer-review system. Two agencies now pursue accounting firms, and individual accountants, for auditing errors that amount to securities law violations or failures to adhere to professional standards.

The regulatory avalanche resulted in significant part from the view that auditors are truly gatekeepers,[74] guarding the integrity of the financial numbers that public companies provide to the investment community, and that, as the auditing profession was organized before SOX, it failed to serve that gatekeeping purpose.

QUESTIONS ON THE AUDITOR REFORMS OVERALL

Is there any more real reforming to be done in the auditor arena? Or will future efforts simply try to influence what the PCAOB looks for in its inspections and as it and the SEC bring disciplinary and enforcement proceedings?

To this point in your study, do you conclude that the auditor reforms were useful? Note that we will return in Chapter Twenty to the question of how we might evaluate the reforms.

---

[74]   See Chapter One at pages 22–23.

CHAPTER 12

REFORMS III: THE AUDIT COMMITTEE[1]

■ ■ ■

Many of the reforms concentrate on board committees, particularly the audit committee. This Chapter Twelve begins with audit committee reform that preceded SOX, then turns to the SOX provisions and listing standards affecting audit committees. Regulation by these sources addresses the composition of audit committees, including the independence of the directors who serve on the committees and the financial sophistication of those directors. Regulation also focuses on audit committees' control over the hiring and evaluation of outside auditors and on the relationship between outside auditors and audit committees during audits. The NYSE prescribes a long list of tasks the committees must perform, including tasks far afield from the annual audit. After reviewing these requirements, the chapter concludes by summarizing some of the research showing how audit committee behavior has changed.

A. BACKGROUND OF AUDIT COMMITTEE REFORMS

As we saw in Chapter Two, regulation can be accomplished through listing standards. In order for its securities to trade on an exchange, a company must comply with the standards that the exchange sets. These are called "listing standards." Some of the standards are quantitative— providing, for example, that companies cannot trade on an exchange unless they are of a certain size. But listing standards also include qualitative requirements that, in recent years, have focused on such matters as audit committees. Because the exchanges are "self-regulatory organizations" under the 34 Act, they develop their own standards. But the exchanges must submit proposed standards to the SEC, which can approve or disapprove them.

The recent history of audit committee reform begins with the Blue Ribbon Panel on audit committees put together in 1998 by the National Association of Securities Dealers (NASD), the SEC, and the New York

---

[1]   I have used in this chapter material from my article, William O. Fisher, *Lawyers Keep Out: Why Attorneys Should Not Participate in Negotiating Critical Financial Numbers Reported by Public Company Clients,* 2010 BYU L. Rev. 1501 (2010), and drafts of that article. I have done so with permission from the Brigham Young University Law Review.

Stock Exchange (NYSE). The Blue Ribbon Panel made its report in 1999. The report contained many recommendations.

As a direct result, the NYSE and the NASD (for NASDAQ) adopted listing standards that required each listed company to have an audit committee comprised of at least three members, all of whom had to be "independent." The term was defined to exclude directors having certain specified relationships with their corporations.[2] Both sets of standards included a limited exception from the independence requirement for one committee member. In addition, both sets of standards required each audit committee to have a "charter." That charter had to say that (a) the outside auditor was responsible to the board and the audit committee and (b) the audit committee was responsible for getting from the auditor a statement of the various relationships the auditor had with the company and then discussing with the auditor whether those relationships impacted the auditor's independence.[3]

Both sets of listing standards also required the audit committee charter to provide that the entire board and the audit committee had the authority and responsibility to select, evaluate, and where appropriate replace, the outside auditor (or to nominate the outside auditor to be proposed in any proxy statement, in those companies whose shareholders voted on the auditor).[4]

QUESTIONS ON AUDIT COMMITTEE CONTROL OVER HIRING AND EVALUATING THE OUTSIDE AUDITOR

Do you see why this seems to be a good idea—giving the power to hire and fire the auditor to the audit committee instead of leaving that to management? On the other hand, how likely is it that an audit committee would hire an auditor that management really could not abide? Should an audit committee consult with management before hiring or firing an auditor? What form should any such consultation take?

Aren't we a long way from free-form corporate governance permitted by the Delaware corporations law, with the listing standards actually assigning a specific job to the board and one of its committees? A good idea?

---

[2]   This chapter does not discuss the definition of "independent" director. Chapter Fourteen does.

[3]   The NYSE listing standards (as of October 2003) set out these requirements in sections 303.01 and 303.02 of the New York Stock Exchange Listed Company Manual. The NASDAQ standards (as of October 2003) appeared in section 4350(d) of the NASD Manual, with "independent" director defined at section 4200(a)(14).

[4]   NYSE LISTED COMPANY MANUAL § 303.01(B)(1)(b) (2003) [NYSE MANUAL]; NASD MANUAL § 4350-1(d)(1)(C) (2003).

The audit committee standards also reflected a concern that the committee members have sufficient accounting savvy to do their job. The NYSE standards required that each committee member "shall be financially literate, as such qualification is interpreted by the company's Board of Directors in its business judgment, or must become financially literate within a reasonable period of time after his or her appointment to the audit committee."[5] Those standards also required that at least one committee member "have accounting or related financial management expertise, as the Board of Directors interprets such qualification in its business judgment."[6]

The NASDAQ standard said that each committee member must be "able to read and understand fundamental financial statements, including a company's balance sheet, income statement and cash flow statement" or "become able to do so within a reasonable time" after joining the committee.[7] The NASDAQ standard also said that at least one member of the committee must have "past employment experience in finance or accounting, requisite professional certification in accounting, or any other comparable experience or background which results in the individual's financial sophistication, including being or having been a chief executive officer, chief financial officer or other senior officer with financial oversight responsibilities."[8]

Again, we are a long way from Delaware corporate law. Now we are even prescribing the substantive qualifications that certain board members must have. Stop for a moment here and reflect on questions to which we will return.

QUESTIONS ON RULES IMPOSED FROM OUTSIDE THE CORPORATION THAT RESTRICT THE DIRECTORS THAT THE SHAREHOLDERS CAN ELECT

Don't the shareholders elect the directors? Why can't they have anyone on the board that they want? Why should they have to put up with these qualifications that limit whom they can elect?

Or were the qualifications phrased in such a general way as to give the shareholders plenty of leeway in choosing who would be on the board?

---

5   NYSE MANUAL § 303.01(B)(2)(b) (2003).

6   *Id.* § 303.01(B)(2)(c).

7   NASD MANUAL § 4350-1(d)(2)(A) (2003).

8   *Id.*

Why not simply require companies to state the financial education and experience of those board members who are nominated, and who then serve, on audit committees so that shareholders can express any displeasure (i) by voting against (or withholding votes from) committee members with inadequate experience and knowledge or (ii) by selling the stock of companies whose audit committee members lack adequate experience or knowledge?

———————

In addition to the new listing standards, the Blue Ribbon Panel recommended that the SEC adopt new audit committee rules, and the Commission did so. Those rules required each reporting company to disclose in its proxy statement whether its audit committee had a written charter approved by the full board; include a copy of the charter as an appendix to the proxy statement unless a copy had been appended sometime in the last three years; disclose whether its audit committee members met the independence tests in the applicable listing standards; and say whether the audit committee had (i) reviewed and discussed the audited financials with management, (ii) discussed certain matters with the outside auditor as required by auditing standards, (iii) obtained certain information from the auditor relevant to the auditor's independence, and (iv) discussed independence issues with the auditor. In addition, the rules required each public company to state in its proxy statement whether its audit committee had "recommended to the Board of Directors that the audited financial[s] . . . be included" in the company's 10-K.[9] These

---

[9]   Find the SEC adoption of the disclosure requirements at Audit Committee Disclosure, 64 Fed. Reg. 73,389 (Dec. 30, 1999), with the regulations at 73,401–03. More specifically as to the discussions between the outside auditor and the audit committee, these pre-SOX regulations required statements as to whether an audit committee had discussed with the auditor the matters required to be discussed by Statement on Auditing Standards No. 61 ("SAS 61"), as it existed at the time or as later modified or supplemented. *Id.* at 73,390, 73,402 (17 C.F.R. § 229.306(a)(2)). As amended effective for audits of financial statements for periods ending on or after December 15, 2000, SAS 61 required, among other things, that the auditor

- "should determine that the audit committee is informed about the initial selection of and changes in significant accounting policies or their application";
- "should also determine that the audit committee is informed about the methods used to account for significant unusual transactions and the effect of significant accounting policies in controversial or emerging areas for which there is a lack of authoritative guidance or consensus";
- "should determine that the audit committee is informed about the process used by management in formulating particularly sensitive accounting estimates and about the basis for the auditor's conclusions regarding the reasonableness of those estimates";
- "should inform the audit committee about adjustments arising from the audit that could, in [the auditor's] judgment, either individually or in the aggregate, have a significant effect on the [company's] financial reporting process";
- "should inform the audit committee about uncorrected misstatements aggregated by the auditor during the current engagement and pertaining to the latest period presented that were determined by management to be immaterial, both individually and in the aggregate, to the financial statements taken as a whole"; and

regulations survive today, although now a company may simply make the audit committee charter available on its website.[10]

Note that this SEC regulation does not require the audit committees to have a certain composition, to discuss the audited financials with management and the auditors, or to recommend the inclusion of the financials in the 10-K. It simply requires the committee to say whether or not the committee's composition meets relevant listing standards and whether the committee has performed identified tasks. The idea is that just this disclosure requirement places great pressure on committees to act in a certain way. For example, the market might punish stocks of companies whose audit committees said that they had not recommended that the financial statements go into the 10-K. We will see this technique again.

Note that the regulations through this pressure effectively give the audit committee fairly specific assignments. Again, consider whether this is a good idea. And reflect that, even before Sarbanes-Oxley, we were a long way from the old notion, dominating state corporation statutes, that government should leave to the corporations themselves just how they run their internal affairs.

Now let us look at Sarbanes-Oxley and audit committees.

- "should discuss with the audit committee the auditor's judgments about the quality, not just the acceptability, of the entity's accounting principles as applied in its financial reporting."

PCAOB AU Section 380.07–.11, https://pcaobus.org/Standards/Auditing/Pages/AU380.aspx, superseded by PCAOB Auditing Standard No. 16, which is now AU 1301. Pre-SOX rules also required that the auditor provide specified information to the audit committee regarding the auditor's independence. See the requirement that companies disclose whether its auditor provided that information to its audit committee. Audit Comm. Disclosure, 64 Fed. Reg., at 73,390, 73,402 (17 C.F.R. § 229.306(a)(3), referring to Independence Standards Board Standard No. 1, https://pcaobus.org/Standards/EI/Documents/ISB1.pdf, superseded now by PCAOB Rule 3526).

[10]   17 C.F.R. §§ 229.407(d)(1), (2) & (3)(i) & Instruction 2 to Item 407; 240.14a-101 (Item 7(d)). Note that 407(d)(2) does not require disclosure of whether the members of the audit committee are independent, but requires (as did the 1999 regulation) that, if the audit committee includes a director who is not independent under the relevant listing standard, the company describe the "nature of the relationship that makes that individual not independent and the reasons for the board of directors' determination" to appoint the director to the audit committee nonetheless. But 17 C.F.R. § 229.407(a) requires disclosure—in a proxy distributed in connection with election of directors—of which directors and which director candidates are independent within the meaning of the relevant listing standards, and 407(b)(3) requires identification of each audit committee member. As a result, the current scheme, like the one put in place in 1999, demands that the company disclose whether the audit committee members are independent.

NYSE-listed companies *must* post their audit committee charters on their websites. NYSE MANUAL § 303A.07(b) *Website Posting Requirement* ("A listed company must make its audit committee charter available on or through its website.").

In 2003, both the NYSE and NASDAQ made substantial changes in the governance provisions of their listing standards, including changes affecting audit committees. SEC, Self-Regulatory Organizations; New York Stock Exchange, Inc. and National Association of Securities Dealers, Inc.; Order Approving Proposed Rule Changes, 2003 WL 22509738 (SEC Nov. 4, 2003), at *6–7 (NYSE), *14–15 (NASDAQ). Here and elsewhere, the citations to the NYSE MANUAL are to the MANUAL as amended and effective in April 2016, unless specifically dated otherwise.

B. SARBANES-OXLEY AND AUDIT COMMITTEES

We have already seen that SOX requires the audit committee to pre-approve all auditing and non-auditing services performed by the company's auditor. The law, however, requires much more.

Requirement for specified auditor communications with audit committees. SOX section 204 requires auditors to timely report to audit committees "all critical accounting policies and practices."[11] It is difficult to intuit what "critical accounting policies" include, but the Commission has said that they are the accounting policies that "are both most important to the portrayal of the company's financial condition and results, and [that] require management's most difficult, subjective or complex judgments, often as a result of the need to make estimates about the effect of matters that are inherently uncertain."[12] Critical accounting policies could include, for example, the protocols by which a company estimates warranty cost claims or returns. They could also include the policies that govern the company's valuation of assets that do not trade in a deep and organized market—illiquid assets.

SOX section 204 also requires auditors to report to audit committees "all alternative treatments of financial information within generally accepted accounting principles that have been discussed with management officials of the [company], ramifications of the use of such alternative disclosures and treatments, and the treatment preferred by the [auditor]."[13]

Generally accepted accounting principles ("GAAP") are far from definitive on many issues. It happens not infrequently that GAAP permits a company to choose between different methods it might use to get to the accounting numbers generated by a transaction, a category of transactions, or some category of costs or revenues. Management and the auditors may argue over which accounting treatment to use in reporting economic events. SOX section 204 requires that the audit committee receive a meaningful report on such disagreements, including information on how

---

[11]   Sarbanes-Oxley Act of 2002, Pub. L. No. 107-204, § 204,116 Stat. 745, 773 (2002); 15 U.S.C. § 78j-1(k)(1), with the requirement repeated at 17 C.F.R. § 210.2-07(a)(1). Audit rules in effect before SOX addressed auditor communication with audit committees, as set out in note 9 above. As you read through the communications required by SOX, keep in mind that some of them were already required by audit standards, but were now written into federal law.

[12]   Accounting Policies; Cautionary Advice Regarding Disclosure, 66 Fed. Reg. 65,013, 65,013 (Dec. 17, 2001). When the SEC adopted the implementing rule for SOX section 204, it specifically suggested that companies and auditors refer to the 2001 statement in order to determine what should be communicated to the audit committee. Strengthening the Commission's Requirements Regarding Auditor Independence, 68 Fed. Reg. 6006, 6028 (Feb. 5, 2003).

[13]   116 Stat. at 773; 15 U.S.C. § 78j-1(k)(2); *see* the same requirement in 17 C.F.R. § 210.2-07(a)(2), but note that it is there limited to "material items" that the auditor has discussed with management.

different accounting approaches would affect company numbers and which accounting approach the outside auditor favors.

Here is some of the SEC commentary on the requirement for communications relating to alternative accounting treatments, noting that the requirement relates to both accounting policies and specific transactions:

> We recognize that the complexity of financial transactions results in accounting answers that are often the subject of significant debate between management and the [auditor].
>
> We believe that communications regarding [accounting treatment of] specific transactions should identify, at a minimum, the underlying facts, financial statement accounts impacted, and applicability of existing corporate accounting policies to the transaction. In addition, if the accounting treatment proposed does not comply with existing corporate accounting policies, or if an existing corporate accounting policy is not applicable, then an explanation of why the existing policy was not appropriate or applicable and the basis for the selection of the alternative policy should be discussed. Regardless of whether the accounting policy selected preexists or is new, the entire range of alternatives available under GAAP that were discussed by management and the [auditor] should be communicated along with the reasons for not selecting those alternatives. If the accounting treatment selected is not, in the [auditor's] view, the preferred method, we expect that the reasons why the [auditor's] preferred method was not selected by management also will be discussed.
>
> Communications regarding general accounting policies should focus on the initial selection of and changes in significant accounting policies, as required by [generally accepted auditing standards], and should include the impact of management's judgments and accounting estimates, as well as the [auditor's] judgments about the quality of the [company's] accounting principles. The discussion of general accounting policies should include the range of alternatives available under GAAP that were discussed by management and the [auditor] along with the reasons for selecting the chosen policy. If an existing accounting policy is being modified, then the reasons for the change also should be communicated. If the accounting policy selected is not the [auditor's] preferred policy, then we expect the discussions to include the reasons why the [auditor] considered one policy to be preferred but that policy was not selected by management.[14]

---

[14]   Strengthening the Commission's Requirements Regarding Auditor Independence, 68 Fed. Reg. 6006, 6028–29 (Feb. 5, 2003) (footnote omitted).

As you see, the tone suggests a presumption that the company should adopt the treatment that the auditor favors.

QUESTIONS ON THE EFFECT OF REQUIRING COMMUNICATION OF ALTERNATIVE TREATMENTS TO THE AUDIT COMMITTEE

To the extent that management and the auditor disagree on a "soft" number (one that depends on an estimate), does the requirement that all of this be disclosed to the audit committee—together with the auditor's preferred outcome—increase the probability that the auditor's position will prevail?

How likely is it that an audit committee will insist, in all cases of disagreement, that the company use the treatment that the auditor favors?

SOX section 204 further requires auditors to report to audit committees "other material written communications between the [auditor] and . . . management . . . , such as any management letter or schedule of unadjusted differences."[15] The schedule of unadjusted differences is the list of errors that the auditors identified and that management did not change.[16]

One effect of the required disclosure to the audit committees of the *unadjusted* differences[17] is to permit the committees to see the unadjusted differences and check for themselves whether those differences are immaterial. In part, this may permit an audit committee to determine how ready the auditor was to give way to the management.

By auditing standard, the auditor must also disclose to the audit committee the non-trivial *adjusted* differences, which show what errors management made that would have persisted in the financial statements except for the auditor's diligence.[18] This information permits the committee to see how egregious the management's errors were before the audit began.

---

[15]   116 Stat. at 773; 15 U.S.C. § 78j-1(k)(3); *see* the same requirement in 17 C.F.R. § 210.2-07(a)(3).

[16]   Today, this list is called the "schedule of uncorrected misstatements." PUB. CO. ACCOUNTING OVERSIGHT BD. AUDITING STANDARDS: Communications with Audit Committees, AS 1301.18.

[17]   Here is how AS 1301.18, *supra* note 16, puts it (footnotes omitted):

The auditor should provide the audit committee with the schedule of uncorrected misstatements related to accounts and disclosures that the auditor presented to management. The auditor should discuss with the audit committee, or determine that management has adequately discussed with the audit committee, the basis for the determination that the uncorrected misstatements were immaterial, including the qualitative factors considered.

[18]   *See* AS 1301.19:

QUESTIONS ON THE REQUIREMENT THAT WRITTEN COMMUNICATIONS BETWEEN AUDITORS AND MANAGEMENT GO TO THE AUDIT COMMITTEE

Does the fact that written communications between the auditor and management are reported to the audit committee affect the discussions between management and the auditors? If so, in what way?

Requirements that audit committees resolve disagreements between auditors and management and that financial statements include all material audit adjustments identified by the auditor. Beyond the required reports that bring accounting differences between management and the auditors to the audit committee's attention, SOX section 301 requires the committee to resolve any such disputes that management and the auditor do not resolve themselves. Thus, the section commanded the SEC to issue regulations requiring the exchanges to prohibit the listing of companies unless

> [t]he audit committee of each issuer, in its capacity as a committee of the board of directors, shall be directly responsible for the appointment, compensation, and oversight of the work of any registered public accounting firm employed by that issuer (*including resolution of disagreements between management and the auditor regarding financial reporting*) for the purpose of preparing or issuing an audit report or related work, and each such registered public accounting firm shall report directly to the audit committee.[19]

Here is another specific job for the audit committee, and this one puts the committee on the hot seat.

The auditor should communicate to the audit committee those corrected misstatements, other than those that are clearly trivial, related to accounts and disclosures that might not have been detected except through the auditing procedures performed, and discuss with the audit committee the implications that such corrected misstatements might have on the company's financial reporting process.

[19]   116 Stat. at 776 (emphasis added); 15 U.S.C. § 78j-1(m)(2) (emphasis added). Specifically, the law provided that the SEC "shall, by rule, direct the national securities exchanges and national securities associations to prohibit the listing of any security of an issuer that is not in compliance with the requirements of any portion of paragraphs (2) through (6)"—paragraph (2) of which is quoted in the text. The Commission issued a regulation requiring listing standards to include this mandate. 17 C.F.R. § 240.10A-3(b)(2). Note that, by auditing standard, the auditor is required to "communicate to the audit committee any disagreements with management about matters, whether or not satisfactorily resolved, that individually or in the aggregate could be significant to the company's financial statements or the auditor's report." AS 1301.22, *supra* note 16. So an unresolved disagreement should come to the committee's attention unless it is insignificant.

SOX section 301 also effectively writes into federal law the listing standards requirement that audit committees be responsible for hiring, evaluating, and firing the auditor. The section also requires that listing standards make the audit committee responsible for the auditor's "compensation," which raises a point to which we will return.

The regulatory path here is also interesting. Congress wants companies to do something. So it requires the SEC to adopt a regulation that, in turn, requires exchanges to adopt listing standards that, in turn, force companies to do what Congress desired in order that the companies continue to have their stocks traded in established markets.

As a last point on the relationship between audit committees and auditors, SOX section 401 adds a provision stating that financial statements that are filed with the Commission and required to be prepared in accordance with GAAP "shall reflect all material correcting adjustments that have been identified by [the auditor] in accordance with generally accepted accounting principles and the rules and regulations of the Commission."[20] Therefore, only unadjusted differences that are not material in the auditor's opinion should remain and, if an auditor simply will not budge on a dispute with management on an adjustment that the auditor believes is material, the audit committee, in deciding the disagreement between management and the auditor, will have to side with the auditor.

QUESTIONS ON HOW THE RESPONSIBILITIES PLACED ON AUDIT COMMITTEES AFFECT THE AUDITOR'S POWER TO FORCE AN AUDITED COMPANY TO MAKE THE CHANGES IN FINANCIAL STATEMENTS THE AUDITOR BELIEVES BEST

Given all the attention to audit committees and the possibility of being sued—will committees simply go along with whatever the outside auditor wants, even on immaterial matters? Or take management's position if the committee and the auditor agree that that position is more conservative?

Do these provisions effectively give more muscle to the auditors as they try to get a company to do the right thing, even in cases where the disagreement between management and the auditor is over an immaterial amount? Is that also the effect of the requirement that the auditor "report directly to the audit committee"?

How so?

---

[20]   116 Stat. at 785–86; 15 U.S.C. § 78m(i).

Requirement that audit committees establish whistleblower procedures. Turning from the relationship of the audit committee and auditors to the relationship between the committee and whistleblowers, several corporate scandals featured employees who warned their superiors of accounting problems before the storm broke. For example, an anonymous letter to Ken Lay at Enron (later determined to have been written by a vice president for corporate development) said that the author was "incredibly nervous that we will implode in a wave of accounting scandals."[21] To make sure that complaints like this can get to the audit committees, SOX section 301 provides that

> [e]ach audit committee shall establish procedures for—
>
>> (A) the receipt, retention, and treatment of complaints received by the issuer regarding accounting, internal accounting controls, or auditing matters; and
>>
>> (B) the confidential, anonymous submission by employees of the issuer of concerns regarding questionable accounting or auditing matters.[22]

Again, the law commanded the SEC to issue a regulation charging the exchanges with prohibiting the listing of any company whose audit committee did not have such procedures. The SEC promulgated that rule.[23] Implementing listing standards followed.[24]

Audit committee authority to hire advisers and to determine what those advisers, and the outside auditor, are paid. Now we turn to a particularly interesting aspect of the audit committee reforms. This, too, was accomplished by SOX 301's mandate that the SEC prescribe listing standards containing certain requirements for audit committees. The exchanges must prohibit the listing of securities issued by a company that does not provide its audit committee with:

---

[21]   *Text of Watkins' Letter to Lay After Departure of Chief Executive*, N.Y. TIMES, Jan. 16, 2002, http://www.nytimes.com/2002/01/16/business/16TEXT.html?pagewanted=all.

[22]   116 Stat. at 776; 15 U.S.C. § 78j-1(m)(4).

[23]   17 C.F.R. § 240.10A-3(b)(3).

[24]   NYSE MANUAL § 303A.06 ("Listed companies must have an audit committee that satisfies the requirements of Rule 10A-3 under the Exchange Act"); NASDAQ STOCK MARKET RULE 5605(c)(3) [NASDAQ RULE] ("The audit committee must have the specific audit committee responsibilities and authority necessary to comply with Rule 10A-3(b)(2), (3), (4) and (5) under the Act"). After NASDAQ became an exchange, listed companies were no longer governed by the NASD Manual. The rules are now in the NASDAQ Stock Market Rules. Here and elsewhere, the citations to the NASDAQ Stock Market Rules are to the Rules as of April 2016, unless specifically dated otherwise. Quotations from the New York Stock Exchange Listed Company Manual reprinted with permission from the New York Stock Exchange. Quotations from the NASDAQ Stock Market Rules reprinted with permission from Nasdaq, Inc. Copyright © 2016 by Nasdaq, Inc. All rights reserved.

(5)   Authority to engage advisers

Each audit committee shall have the authority to engage independent counsel and other advisers, as it determines necessary to carry out its duties.

(6)   Funding

Each issuer shall provide for appropriate funding, as determined by the audit committee, in its capacity as a committee of the board of directors, for payment of compensation—

(A) to the registered public accounting firm employed by the issuer for the purpose of rendering or issuing an audit report; and

(B) to any advisers employed by the audit committee under paragraph (5).[25]

This is a federal law defining the power of a board *committee* to hire advisers and requiring that a company pay for the advisers. And the "appropriate funding" level will be "determined by the audit committee."

QUESTIONS ON THE FEDERAL DEFINITION
OF THE AUDIT COMMITTEE'S POWERS

What does this law do to the relationship between the audit committee and the rest of the board? Does it mean that the committee can hire a large law firm to conduct an extensive and expensive investigation without the approval of the whole board?

Does the law mean that the committee can pay the auditor whatever amount the committee thinks is appropriate to buy the kind of audit the company needs—even if a majority of the board believes that the audit is costing too much? Might a committee rely on this law to buy a gold-plated audit simply to get the maximum protection for the committee itself in any future accounting-based securities lawsuit? If so, is this incentive helpful?

Can the audit committee even hire a second accounting firm under this provision—again even though a board majority might think it unnecessary—to help the committee resolve one of those differences between management and the auditor that now lands on the audit committee's agenda?

Is that good? Or bad? Or is all of this too hypothetical because the board as a whole can control the audit committee by the board's power over which directors sit on that committee?

---

[25]   116 Stat. at 776–77; 15 U.S.C. § 78j-1(m). *And see* the related SEC regulation at 17 C.F.R. § 240.10A-3(b)(4) & (5).

Composition of the audit committee—independence and expertise.
Finally, we turn to the composition of the audit committee. Again through
a law requiring a regulation that would in turn require listing standards,
Congress said this in SOX section 301 about who can serve on an audit
committee:

(A) In general

Each member of the audit committee of the issuer shall be a
member of the board of directors of the issuer, and shall otherwise
be independent.

(B) Criteria

In order to be considered to be independent for purposes of this
paragraph, a member of an audit committee of an issuer may not,
other than in his or her capacity as a member of the audit
committee, the board of directors, or any other board committee—

(i) accept any consulting, advisory, or other compensatory
fee from the issuer; or

(ii) be an affiliated person of the issuer or any subsidiary
thereof.[26]

The SEC regulation prohibits even "indirectly" accepting the
proscribed fees and adds this elaboration:

The term *indirect acceptance by a member of an audit committee
of any consulting, advisory or other compensatory fee* includes
acceptance of such a fee by a spouse, a minor child or stepchild or
a child or stepchild sharing a home with the member or by an
entity in which such member is a partner, member, an officer such
as a managing director occupying a comparable position or
executive officer, or occupies a similar position (except limited
partners, non-managing members and those occupying similar
positions who, in each case, have no active role in providing
services to the entity) and which provides accounting, consulting,
legal, investment banking or financial advisory services to the
issuer or any subsidiary of the issuer.[27]

---

[26]   116 Stat. at 776; 15 U.S.C. § 78j-1(m)(3); *and see* the SEC regulation at 17 C.F.R.
§ 240.10A-3(b)(1)(i) & (ii).

[27]   17 C.F.R. § 240.10A-3(e)(8) (emphasis added).

The stock exchanges have their own requirements that members of audit committees must be
independent. *See* NYSE MANUAL §§ 303A.02 (defining independent director); 303A.07(a)
(requiring all members of an audit committee to satisfy that definition); NASDAQ RULE 5605(a)(2)
(defining independent director); 5605(c)(2)(A)(i) & (2)(B) (requiring all members of audit committee
to satisfy that definition, but making an exception for one member of the committee under

Among other things, this regulation means that, if you are a partner in a law firm performing work for the company, you cannot serve on the company's audit committee. The same is true if you are a partner in an investment banking firm working for the company.

Since the law effectively prohibits an "affiliated person of the issuer or any subsidiary" from serving on an audit committee, consider the definition of "affiliate":

(1)(i)   The term *affiliate* of, or a person *affiliated* with, a specified person [which, critically for our purposes, can include a company], means a person that directly, or indirectly through one or more intermediaries, controls, or is controlled by, or is under common control with, the person specified.

(ii)(A)   A person will be deemed not to be in control of a specified person for purposes of this section if the person:

> (1) [i]s not the beneficial owner, directly or indirectly, of more than 10% of any class of voting equity securities of the specified person; and

> (2) [i]s not an executive officer[28] of the specified person.

(B) Paragraph (e)(1)(ii)(A) of this section only creates a safe harbor position that a person does not control a specified person. The existence of the safe harbor does not create a presumption in any way that a person exceeding the ownership requirement in paragraph (e)(1)(ii)(A)(1) of this section controls or is otherwise an affiliate of a specified person.

(iii) The following will be deemed to be affiliates:

> (A) [a]n executive officer of an affiliate;

> (B) [a] director who also is an employee of an affiliate;

> (C) [a] general partner of an affiliate; and

> (D) [a] managing member of an affiliate.

(4) The term *control* (including the terms *controlling, controlled by* and under *common control with*) means the possession, direct or indirect, of the power to direct or cause the direction of the

---

exceptional circumstances). The listing standards then provide that the audit committee members must also satisfy the independence standards in the SEC regulation implementing SOX 301. *See* NYSE MANUAL § 303A.07(a); NASDAQ RULE 5605(c)(2)(A)(ii).

[28]   Exchange Act regulations define "executive officers" to include "president, any vice president . . . in charge of a principal business unit, division or function (such as sales, administration or finance), any other officer who performs a policy making function or any other person who performs similar policy making functions." 17 C.F.R. § 240.3b-7.

management and policies of a person, whether through the ownership of voting securities, by contract, or otherwise.[29]

One interesting result is that a controlling shareholder cannot sit on the audit committee.

QUESTION ABOUT PROHIBITING A CONTROLLING SHAREHOLDER FROM SERVING ON AN AUDIT COMMITTEE

Is this prohibition a good idea or a bad one?

Congress did more with audit committee composition, adding a provision concerning audit committee expertise. SOX section 407 required the SEC to issue regulations requiring public companies to disclose "whether or not, and if not, the reasons therefor, the audit committee . . . is comprised of at least 1 member who is a financial expert, as such term is defined by the Commission."[30] The SEC has issued rules defining an "audit committee financial expert" as:

(ii)   . . . a person who has the following attributes:

(A) [a]n understanding of generally accepted accounting principles and financial statements;

(B) [t]he ability to assess the general application of such principles in connection with the accounting for estimates, accruals and reserves;

(C) [e]xperience preparing, auditing, analyzing or evaluating financial statements that present a breadth and level of complexity of accounting issues that are generally comparable to the breadth and complexity of issues that can reasonably be expected to be raised by the registrant's financial statements, or experience actively supervising one or more persons engaged in such activities;

(D) [a]n understanding of internal control over financial reporting; and

(E) [a]n understanding of audit committee functions.

(iii) [a] person shall have acquired such attributes through:

(A) [e]ducation and experience as a principal financial officer, principal accounting officer, controller, public

---

[29]   17 C.F.R. § 240.10A-3(e)(1) & (4) (emphasis added).

[30]   116 Stat. at 790; 15 U.S.C. § 7265. *And see* the SEC regulation at 17 C.F.R. § 229.407(d)(5)(i); Form 10-K (Item 10).

accountant or auditor or experience in one or more positions that involve the performance of similar functions;

(B) [e]xperience actively supervising a principal financial officer, principal accounting officer, controller, public accountant, auditor or person performing similar functions;

(C) [e]xperience overseeing or assessing the performance of companies or public accountants with respect to the preparation, auditing or evaluation of financial statements; or

(D) [o]ther relevant experience.[31]

If a company determines that it has one or more audit committee financial experts on its audit committee, then the company must disclose their names.[32] If the company does not include any such members, the company must explain why it does not.[33] Clearly, this puts pressure on companies to find a director who can qualify as an audit committee financial expert, and put him or her on the board. Companies have responded by doing just that. A 2015 analysis of proxy statements filed by companies in the S&P 100 index found that every company disclosed at least one such expert, 76% disclosed more than one, and nearly 60% "included disclosure relevant to the financial literacy of their audit committee members."[34]

Once again, we are miles from the old state corporation law scheme we reviewed in Chapter Two. Here the regulation not only defines the qualifications of desirable committee members but also gives examples of specific backgrounds they might have.

QUESTIONS ON THE AUDIT COMMITTEE FINANCIAL EXPERT

Is it an appropriate or useful function for the federal government to define a special kind of director who might sit on a committee of a publicly traded company's board?

----

[31]   17 C.F.R. § 229.407(d)(5)(ii) & (iii). The SEC rule requires that each company disclose whether its audit committee includes at least one "audit committee financial expert" and, if not, why not. *Id.* § 229.407(d)(5)(i). While this puts pressure on each company to include such an expert on its audit committee, the SEC rule does not require that a company have such an expert on the committee, and does not otherwise demand that audit committee members have any particular accounting or financial ability. Through their listing standards, however, the exchanges require that all committee members be financially literate and that one possess financial expertise or sophistication. NYSE MANUAL § 303A.07(a) Commentary; NASDAQ RULE 5605(c)(2)(A).

[32]   17 C.F.R. § 229.407(d)(5)(i)(B).

[33]   17 C.F.R. § 229.407(d)(5)(i)(A)(2) & (C).

[34]   DELOITTE LLP, CURRENT TRENDS IN AUDIT COMMITTEE REPORTING 1–2 (2015), https://www2.deloitte.com/content/dam/Deloitte/us/Documents/audit/us-audit-current-trends-audit-committee-reporting.pdf.

Note that, once more, while the regulation is phrased in terms of disclosure, the idea is that companies will prefer to put an expert on the committee rather than explain why they do not have one. Is it appropriate or useful for the federal government to pressure public companies in this way to appoint a special kind of director to sit on a particular board committee?

Does this unnecessarily interfere with shareholder sovereignty?

Some research finds that a company's announcement that its board has appointed a director to the audit committee with accounting expertise increases the company's stock price, albeit by a small amount.[35] Why not simply let the market—by favorable stock price effect—encourage companies to find such directors and appoint them to audit committees?

You might ask what director would want to be identified as an audit committee financial expert since being one might paint a large target on the director's back. In part to fight against such reticence to serve, the Commission explicitly said that the designation or identification of a director as an "audit committee financial expert" "does not impose . . . any duties, obligations or liability that are greater than [those] imposed on such person as a member of the audit committee and board of directors in the absence of such designation or identification."[36]

C. NEW LISTING STANDARDS AND AUDIT COMMITTEES

In the wake of Enron, WorldCom, and Sarbanes-Oxley, the NYSE and NASDAQ revised their listing standards, effective in November 2003 but subject to transition provisions. The NYSE and NASDAQ have since amended their new standards after the initial significant revision. Some of these cumulative changes simply conform the listing standards to the requirements of SEC regulations mandated by SOX. But in some respects the listing standards go even further.

As you will recall, the pre-SOX listing standards required that audit committees be staffed by directors who were all "independent." Many of the post-SOX changes to audit committee listing standards have to do with the

---

[35]   *See* Mark DeFond, *Does the Market Value Financial Expertise on Audit Committees of Boards of Directors?*, 43 J. ACCOUNT. RES. 153 (2005) (sample included announcements of 702 outside director appointments to the audit committees of 509 companies, at 162, where the directors were appointed to that committee during the period 1993–2002 and were still on the committee in 2002–2003, at 160; event study analysis showed 1.3% cumulative abnormal three-day returns around announcements, where the appointed director had accounting expertise, at 168; further analysis found that this effect occurred "only when the appointing firm ha[d] relatively strong corporate governance," at 179, as measured by such matters as whether the company's board size was smaller than the median size and whether the percentage of independent directors on the board exceeded 60%, at 171–72 tbl.4).

[36]   17 C.F.R. § 229.407(d)(5)(iv)(B).

definition of an "independent" director. We will take up that revised definition in Chapter Fourteen.

But the NYSE listing standards do much more than implement SOX provisions and require that directors on audit committees meet exchange standards for independence. In particular, they add tasks for the audit committees over and above those set out in SOX. The NYSE standards set out the following additional duties:

- obtaining from the auditor and reviewing each year a report describing: (1) the auditing firm's internal quality-control procedures; (2) any material issues respecting audits raised by (a) the most recent internal quality control review or peer review or (b) governmental or professional inquiries or investigations in the last five years; and (3) any steps that the auditor has taken to deal with such issues;[37]

- meeting to review and discuss not only the annual financial statements with the auditor and management, but also quarterly statements, and disclosures in the portion of SEC periodic filings denominated Management's Discussion and Analysis of Financial Condition and Results of Operations;[38]

- discussing earnings press releases, and financial information and earnings guidance provided to analysts and rating agencies;[39]

- discussing policies with respect to risk assessment and risk management;[40]

- meeting separately and periodically not only with management and the outside auditor but also with the internal auditors;[41]

- reviewing with the outside auditor any audit problems or difficulties (which would include not just a review of differences between management and the auditor but also

---

[37]   NYSE MANUAL § 303A.07(b)(iii)(A).

[38]   *Id.* § 303A.07(b)(iii)(B).

[39]   *Id.* § 303A.07(b)(iii)(C).

[40]   *Id.* § 303A.07(b)(iii)(D). This book discusses risk management, and the board's participation in risk management, in later chapters. The NYSE listing standards recognize that risk management responsibilities within the board may disperse beyond the audit committee:

The audit committee should discuss the listed company's major financial risk exposures and the steps management has taken to monitor and control such exposures. The audit committee is not required to be the sole body responsible for risk assessment and management, but . . . the committee must discuss guidelines and policies to govern the process by which risk assessment and management is undertaken.

Id. § 303A.07(b)(iii)(D) Commentary.

[41]   *Id.* § 303A.07(b)(iii)(E). The new NYSE listing standards also require companies to "have an internal audit function." *Id.* § 303A.07(c).

such matters as the auditor's access to company documents), and management's response;[42] and

- setting clear hiring policies for employees or former employees of outside auditors.[43]

In addition, the new NYSE rules require the audit committee charter to provide for "an annual performance evaluation of the audit committee."[44]

Just hitting every item on the list and then evaluating its own performance could take the audit committee significant time.

QUESTIONS ON THE TASKS ASSIGNED TO AUDIT COMMITTEES BY THE NYSE LISTING STANDARDS

When you add up all the very specific responsibilities of audit committees now, are you comfortable with all these assignments?

How do these specific tasks affect the application of the business judgment rule? Clearly, this list of specific tasks supplants the freedom that the business judgment rule gives directors to decide what tasks merit their attention. But can directors on the audit committee still depend on the business judgment rule to shield them from lawsuits that allege that they violated their duty of care based on their decisions about the amount of time they devoted to each of their audit committee assignments? Do directors still get the benefit of the business judgement rule to protect against attacks based on their substantive decisions in performing these assignments?

NASDAQ has also revised its audit committee listing standards, but the NASDAQ revision sticks pretty close to the SOX requirements.[45] NASDAQ has also adopted a rule that saddles each audit committee (unless a company designates some other independent body of the board) with the job of reviewing and approving related-party transactions.[46]

Both sets of standards continue to require that audit committee members possess some degree of expertise. The NYSE listing standards state:

---

[42]   *Id.* § 303A.07(b)(iii)(F).

[43]   *Id.* § 303A.07(b)(iii)(G). The standards require the audit committee of each listed company to have a written charter that "addresses" the "duties and responsibilities of the audit committee—which, at a minimum, must include" the matters listed in the text. *Id.* § 303A.07(b)(iii).

[44]   *Id.* § 303A.07(b)(ii).

[45]   NASDAQ Rule 5605(c).

[46]   *Id.* at Rule 5630(a).

Each member of the audit committee must be financially literate, as such qualification is interpreted by the listed company's board in its business judgment, or must become financially literate within a reasonable period of time after his or her appointment to the audit committee. In addition, at least one member of the audit committee must have accounting or related financial management expertise, as the listed company's board interprets such qualification in its business judgment. While the Exchange does not require that a listed company's audit committee include a person who satisfies the definition of audit committee financial expert set out in Item 407(d)(5)(ii) of Regulation S-K, a board may presume that such a person has accounting or related financial management expertise.[47]

The NASDAQ listing standards provide:

Each Company must have, and certify that it has and will continue to have, an audit committee of at least three members, each of whom must: . . . (iv) be able to read and understand fundamental financial statements, including a Company's balance sheet, income statement, and cash flow statement. Additionally, each Company must certify that it has, and will continue to have, at least one member of the audit committee who has past employment experience in finance or accounting, requisite professional certification in accounting, or any other comparable experience or background which results in the individual's financial sophistication, including being or having been a chief executive officer, chief financial officer or other senior officer with financial oversight responsibilities.[48]

D. CHANGE IN AUDIT COMMITTEE BEHAVIOR

Before the reforms, audit committees were not very active. An SEC chairman complained of hearing about "one audit committee that convenes only twice a year before the regular board meeting for 15 minutes and whose duties are limited to a perfunctory presentation."[49] That example was not far off from the typical level of audit committee activity at the time. Robert Jaedicke, the chair of the Audit Committee at Enron during the period in which it committed its wrongdoing, testified to his "understanding that audit committees of most corporations, like Enron,

---

[47]   NYSE MANUAL § 303A.07(a) Commentary.

[48]   NASDAQ RULE 5630(a).

[49]   Arthur Levitt, Chairman, U.S. Sec. and Exch. Comm'n, The "Numbers Game," Remarks at NYU Center for Law and Business (Sept. 28, 1998), http://www.sec.gov/news/speech/speech archive/1998/spch220.txt.

typically meet for a few hours several times a year."[50] As we have seen, the WorldCom Audit Committee similarly devoted little time to meetings. See page 135.

The low level of activity displayed by the committees at these two famously troubled companies was typical of the time. Audit committee activity increased after Sarbanes-Oxley.

One study reported that the average number of audit committee meetings per year at a random sample of 30 small companies (market value of less than $75 million) rose from 1.7 in 1998 to 5.1 in 2004, while the number at a sample of 30 medium-sized companies (market value from $75 million to $700 million) rose from 2.3 to 6.2, and the number at 30 large companies (market value over $700 million) increased from 3.2 to 8.2.[51] Another study of 164 companies found that "[f]rom 2002 to 2006, the average annual number of audit committee meetings doubled from about five to ten meetings," with 60% holding nine or more meetings in 2006, compared to 7% in 2002.[52]

Moreover, audit committees now have greater expertise and are more active in discussions between management and auditors. Cohen, Krishamoorthy, and Wright reported in a 2002 article the results of interviews with 36 practicing auditors at large firms.[53] This survey— conducted before SOX became law—found that (i) auditors met with the committees about two to three times a year, (ii) auditors believed that "members of the audit committee often lack[ed] the expertise to perform their job effectively," and (iii) the meetings with the committees were generally passive ones in which the auditors reported and the directors on the committee listened but did not actively discuss matters.[54] Some audit firm partners "indicated that, in general, audit committees [were]

---

[50]   *The Role of the Board of Directors in Enron's Collapse: Hearing Before the Permanent Subcomm. of Investigations of the S. Comm. on Governmental Affairs*, 107th Cong. 19, 20 (2002) (statement of Robert Jaedicke, Former Audit and Compliance Comm. Chair, Bd. of Directors, Enron Corp.). The Enron audit committee met four to five times a year. *Id.* at 20. Meetings were short. *Id.* at 458–61 (draft minutes of Audit and Compliance Committee meeting on Feb. 7, 2000, convened at 3:40 PM and adjourned at 4:50 PM), 500–05 (draft minutes of Audit and Compliance Committee meeting on Feb. 12, 2001, convened at 1:40 PM, recessed at 3:15 PM, then reconvened for 10 minutes on Feb. 13 at 7:50 AM and adjourned at 8:00 AM), 517–19 (draft minutes of Audit and Compliance Committee meeting on Nov. 2, 2001, convened at 9:00 PM and adjourned at 9:40 PM).

[51]   James S. Linck, et al., *The Effects and Unintended Consequences of the Sarbanes-Oxley Act on the Supply and Demand for Directors,* 22 REV. FIN. STUD. 3287, 3296, 3307 tbl.5 (2009).

[52]   HURON CONSULTING GROUP, 2007 AUDIT COMMITTEE RESEARCH REPORT (2007), http://www.financialexecutives.org/eweb/upload/FEI/Huron_Audit%20Comm%20Report_2007%2092007.pdf. On the other hand, 1,034 public company responses to a 2015 survey reported an average number of 5.6 audit committee meetings each year. NATIONAL ASSOCIATION OF CORPORATE DIRECTORS, 2015–2016 NACD PUBLIC COMPANY GOVERNANCE SURVEY 4, 24 (2015).

[53]   Jeffrey Cohen, et al., *Corporate Governance and the Audit Process*, 19 CONTEMP. ACCT. RES. 573, 581 (2002).

[54]   *Id.* at 586.

ineffective and [were] not powerful enough to resolve contentious matters with management."[55]

A similar survey by the same researchers in 2008 reported on interviews conducted in 2006 with 30 partners and managers at large accounting firms.[56] These auditors reported that, on average, they met with audit committees 6.4 times a year.[57] This time "93 percent of the auditors reported that the audit committee had sufficient expertise, and 96 percent note[d] that audit committee members have sufficient power to confront management with respect to the financial reporting process."[58] Respondents reported that directors on the committees actively participated in give-and-take discussion during the meetings,[59] with 37% of respondents saying that the committees asked many questions,[60] 52% that audit committees impacted "[r]esolution of contentious issues,"[61] and a number of respondents suggesting that managements were now disinclined to have a disagreement with auditors that went to audit committees.[62]

Perhaps even more important, two other studies found that audit committee members are more likely to support adjustments recommended by auditors after the reforms than before.[63] DeZoort, Hermanson, and

---

[55]   *Id.*

[56]   Jeffrey Cohen, et al., *Corporate Governance in the Post Sarbanes-Oxley Era: Auditors' Experiences*, 27 CONTEMP. ACCT. RES. 751, 754–55 (2010). This later article states that the interviews underlying the earlier article were conducted "prior to the passage of SOX." *Id.* at 751.

[57]   *Id.* at 760 tbl.3.

[58]   *Id.* at 768.

[59]   *Id.* at 769–70.

[60]   *Id.* at 760 tbl.3.

[61]   *Id.*

[62]   Auditors saw the committees as wanting management and the auditors to work out disagreements. *Id.* at 766–67. But one partner reported:

In the course of the discussions with the audit committee we were reporting on adjustments not recorded and the audit committee chairman said, I don't think so, I think we should record known errors [and] departures from GAAP. So we want you to go back and record that adjustment. . . .

Id. at 766. Another senior partner commented:

Audit committees challenge management . . . [T]hey ask questions of management whereas in the old days it was much more focused on the auditors. So it is very even. Audit committees are much more serious today than they used to be. . . . It's a completely different view than it was pre-Sarbanes. And that to me is the biggest benefit of the entire Sarbanes-Oxley Act.

Id. at 768.

One other comment by a senior partner at an auditing firm reflects the shift in power between auditors and management: "[CFOs] don't want to have unrecorded adjustments on their score sheet as it were, [i.e.,] on the summary of adjustments[,] because they know they are going to get picked at from the audit committee." *Id.* at 772.

[63]   F. Todd DeZoort, et al., *Audit Committee Member Support for Proposed Audit Adjustments: Pre-SOX versus Post-SOX Judgments*, 27 AUDITING: J. PRAC. THEORY, May 2008, at 85, 85 [DeZoort 2008], which includes the results of the post-SOX experiment and contrasts those results with the pre-SOX experiment reported in F. Todd DeZoort, et al., *Audit Committee Member*

Houston presented a hypothetical to 131 audit committee members before the passage of the Sarbanes-Oxley Act and to 241 audit committee members after that legislation became law. In the hypothetical, management had written down a portion of inventory and the auditor had recommended an additional write-down "equal to three percent of pre-tax income, making the materiality of the adjustment unclear."[64] The researchers measured the "audit committee member['s] judgment about the auditor's proposed adjustment . . . on a continuous scale from 0 = definitely do not adjust to 100 = definitely adjust."[65] A higher score indicated a greater likelihood the audit committee would support the auditor. DeZoort and his colleagues found that, without controlling for other variables, the mean post-SOX support score (65.85) was 11.6% higher than the mean pre-SOX score (58.99) and that this difference was statistically significant.[66] Even after controlling for other variables such as whether the additional adjustment would cause the earnings per share to fall below analysts' forecast and whether the adjustment was proposed for a quarterly report or an annual report, DeZoort and his fellows still found "that audit committee members are significantly more supportive of the auditor-proposed adjustment post-SOX than pre-SOX."[67] The researchers, in addition, determined that, after SOX as opposed to before SOX, audit committee members had more confidence that a typical committee member had the expertise to evaluate this issue and that audit committee members felt more responsibility for resolving the issue.[68]

All of this suggests that the reforms improved the process by which audit committees go about their work. The committees work harder. They are more skilled. They ask more questions. They resolve conflicts between management and the outside auditor. In doing so, they are more likely to support the auditor.

Of course, it is another question altogether whether any of this improves the outcome—the accuracy of public company published financial results.

Support for Proposed Audit Adjustments: A Source Credibility Perspective, 22 AUDITING: J. PRAC. THEORY, Sept. 2003, at 189.

[64] DeZoort 2008 at 87, 89–90.

[65] *Id.* at 93 tbl.2.

[66] *Id.* at 92, 93 tbl.2.

[67] *Id.* at 93–94.

[68] On a scale ranging from -5, for strongly disagreeing that a typical audit committee member had the expertise to evaluate the issue, to 5, for strongly agreeing that a typical member had such expertise, the post-SOX score (2.13) was considerably higher than the pre-SOX score (1.20). *Id.* at 92, 93 tbl.2. On a scale ranging from 0 (indicating that the audit committee member did not feel at all responsible for resolving the issue) to 100 (member felt very responsible), the mean score increased from 78.41 pre-SOX to 83.05 post-SOX. *Id.* at 92, 93 tbl.2.

QUESTIONS ON PROCESS AND OUTCOME

If a reform produces process benefits, is that enough? What if we can measure the process benefit (expertise and impact of the audit committee) and see that it is real but cannot measure the benefit of the reform to the ultimate outcome (quality of financial disclosure)?

What is the accounting "outcome" that we can use to test whether the auditor and audit committee reforms have succeeded? Even if we settle on a measure for such a test and find an improvement in that measure, how can we be confident that the improvement results from the auditor and audit committee reforms—as opposed to better shareholder monitoring or more determined criminal enforcement against corporate fraud?

We will return to these questions in Chapter Twenty.

———————

CHAPTER 13

REFORMS IV: OTHER COMMITTEES

■ ■ ■

The reforms reach not only audit committees, but compensation committees and nominating committees, as well. This Chapter Thirteen examines reforms for the compensation committee first and for the nominating committee (for NYSE-listed companies, the nominating/corporate governance committee) second.

A. COMPENSATION COMMITTEES

What rules require the compensation committees must do. The NYSE requires that companies listing securities on that exchange have compensation committees[1] and that those committees must each have a written charter that, at a minimum, imposes responsibility to

(A) review and approve corporate goals and objectives relevant to CEO compensation, evaluate the CEO's performance in light of those goals and objectives, and, either as a committee or together with the other independent directors (as directed by the board), determine and approve the CEO's compensation level based on this evaluation;

(B) make recommendations to the board with respect to non-CEO executive officer compensation, and incentive-compensation and equity-based plans that are subject to board approval; and

(C) prepare the disclosure required by Item 407(e)(5) of Regulation S-K [i.e., a compensation committee report, which must state whether the committee "has reviewed and discussed the Compensation Discussion and Analysis" which each public company must include in its 10-K or proxy statement, and

---

[1]   NYSE LISTED COMPANY MANUAL § 303A.05(a) [NYSE MANUAL]. The NYSE added the requirement that listed companies have compensation committees in a major revision of its corporate governance listing standards approved by the SEC on November 4, 2003. SEC, Self-Regulatory Organizations; New York Stock Exchange, Inc. and National Association of Securities Dealers, Inc.; Order Approving Proposed Rule Changes, 2003 WL 22509738 (SEC Nov. 4, 2003), at *6 ("NYSE proposes to require each listed company to have a compensation committee composed entirely of independent directors") [SEC Order Approving NYSE and NASDAQ Listing Standard Changes Nov. 2003]. The compensation committee provision was subsequently amended. The text quotes from the NYSE Listed Company Manual as of April 2016. Quotations from the New York Stock Exchange Listed Company Manual reprinted with permission from the New York Stock Exchange.

whether, based on the review and discussions, the committee "recommended to the board of directors that the Compensation Discussion and Analysis be included" in the relevant filing.].[2]

Commentary to this listing standard states that

[i]n determining the long-term incentive component of CEO compensation, the committee should consider the listed company's performance and relative shareholder return, the value of similar incentive awards to CEOs at comparable companies, and the awards given to the listed company's CEO in past years.[3]

NASDAQ rules provide that each listed company "must have, and certify that it has and will continue to have, a compensation committee of at least two members," and that the committee must have a charter.[4] But while NASDAQ—like the NYSE—requires that the committee have a charter, it leaves the responsibilities of the committee open, except for demanding that the charter "must specify . . . the compensation committee's responsibility for determining, or recommending to the board for determination, the compensation of the chief executive officer and all other Executive Officers of the Company."[5]

---

[2]   *Id*. § 303A.05(b)(i), with quotation from Item 407(e)(5) of Regulation S-K (17 C.F.R. § 229.407(e)(5)). Commentary to 303A.05 states that "[b]oards may allocate the responsibilities of the compensation committee to committees of their own denomination, provided that the committees are composed entirely of independent directors. Any such committee must have a committee charter."

[3]   *Id*. at Commentary.

[4]   NASDAQ STOCK MARKET RULE 5605(d)(1), (d)(2)(A) [NASDAQ RULE]. Like the NYSE, NASDAQ revised its corporate governance listing standards extensively by revisions approved by the SEC on November 4, 2003, in the same order approving the NYSE changes. SEC Order Approving NYSE and NASDAQ Listing Standard Changes Nov. 2003, *supra* note 1. That revision provided that "the compensation of the CEO of a [NASDAQ] listed company . . . be determined or recommended to the board for determination either by a majority of the independent directors, or by a compensation committee comprised solely of independent directors." *Id*. at *13. In addition, "if the compensation committee was comprised of at least three members, one director, who [was] not independent (as defined in [the listing standards]) and [was] not a current officer or employee or a Family Member of such person, would be permitted to be appointed to the committee if the board, under exceptional and limited circumstances, determine[d] that such individual's membership on the committee [was] required by the best interests of the company and its shareholders, and the board disclose[d], in the next annual meeting proxy statement subsequent to such determination (or, if the issuer [did] not file a proxy, in its Form 10-K . . .), the nature of the relationship and the reasons for the determination. A member appointed under such exception would not be permitted to serve longer than two years." *Id*. NASDAQ subsequently amended that standard, including by an amendment approved by the SEC on January 11, 2013, which required NASDAQ-listed companies to have compensation committees. SEC, Self-Regulatory Organizations; The NASDAQ Stock Market LLC; Notice of Filing of Amendment Nos. 1 and 2, and Order Granting Accelerated Approval of Proposed Rule Change as Modified by Amendment Nos. 1 and 2 to Amend the Listing Rules for Compensation Committees to Comply with Rule 10C-1 under the Act and Make Other Related Changes, Release No. 34-68640, 2013 WL 166323 (SEC Jan. 11, 2013), at *2 ("Nasdaq proposes that each listed company be required to have a compensation committee"). The text quotes from the NASDAQ Stock Market Rules as of April 2016. Quotations from the NASDAQ Stock Market Rules reprinted with permission from Nasdaq, Inc. Copyright © 2016 by Nasdaq, Inc. All rights reserved.

[5]   *Id*. § 5605(d)(1), with quotation from subpart (B).

Reform issues for compensation committees. One consistent issue is whether compensation committees set salaries, bonuses, and other elements of compensation without undue influence from the executives who will receive the pay—particularly CEOs. That concern prompted three types of reforms aimed at (i) the independence of the directors who serve on committees; (ii) the committees' ability to independently select and control any compensation consultants, or other advisers, who provide the information and ideas that help shape compensation packages; and (iii) the independence of such compensation consultants.

Independence of compensation committee members. Before the reforms, compensation committees were often not independent. In 2002, the New York Times reported that, of some 2,000 U.S. companies studied, the compensation committees of more than 20% included members having business or other relationships with the companies' CEOs that might bias the members in the CEOs' favor.[6]

In 2003, the NYSE and NASDAQ required that all members of a compensation committee be "independent directors," as each of those exchanges defined that term (with a limited exception provided by NASDAQ for one committee member).[7] Although this book defers elaboration of that term to Chapter Fourteen, the requirement that directors on a compensation committee be "independent" within the meaning of the applicable listing standards is important to note here.[8]

The Dodd-Frank Wall Street Reform Act added a mandate that the SEC direct the national stock exchanges to prohibit the listing of any equity security (with some exceptions, including for securities issued by controlled companies) unless "each member of the compensation committee of the board of directors" is "independent" and that, in determining independence for this purpose, "relevant factors" are considered, including:

> (A) the source of compensation of a member of the board of directors of an issuer, including any consulting, advisory, or other compensatory fee paid by the issuer to such member of the board of directors; and

---

[6]   Diana B. Henriques & Geraldine Fabrikant, *Deciding on Executive Pay: Lack of Independence Seen*, N.Y. TIMES, Dec. 18, 2002, at A1 (saying, for example, that at Clear Channel Communications, only one of five compensation committee members was conflict-free and that at the Great Atlantic and Pacific Tea Company, only one of three had no independence-compromising relationship).

[7]   *See supra* notes 1 and 4.

[8]   NYSE MANUAL § 303A.05(a); NASDAQ RULE 5605(d)(2)(A)(i), but note that 5605(d)(B) provides that, if the committee has at least three members, one member can fail the independence test in the rules if he or she "is not currently an Executive Officer or employee or a Family Member of an Executive Officer" and the board as a whole determines that "exceptional and limited circumstances" and "the best interests of the Company and its Shareholders" require that individual's membership on the committee.

(B) whether a member of the board of directors of an issuer is affiliated with the issuer, a subsidiary of the issuer, or an affiliate of a subsidiary of the issuer.[9]

Note that this regulation demands only that these factors be considered, not that they are determinative. Given that limited effect and given the elaborate definitions of "independence" that the NYSE and NASDAQ already employ, it is hard to know whether this new law affects the listing standards significantly, or the composition of compensation committees.[10]

QUESTIONS ON DIRECTOR INDEPENDENCE AND COMPENSATION COMMITTEES

What kinds of relationships could compromise the independence of directors sitting on a compensation committee and setting the pay for a company's CEO?

Are some kinds of relationships always compromising? Some so likely to be compromising that they should be banned even if in rare cases they would not bias compensation decisions? Some creating a small but still significant chance of bias so that the director should be permitted to sit on the compensation committee, but only after whole-board approval following review of the potentially compromising facts?

---

[9]   124 Stat. 1376, 1901, § 952, codified at 15 U.S.C. § 78j-3(a)(1), (2)(B), (3). The securities regulations define "[a]n 'affiliate' of, or a person 'affiliated' with, a specified person, [as] a person that directly, or indirectly through one or more intermediaries, controls, or is controlled by, or is under common control with, the person specified." 17 C.F.R. § 240.12b-2. The SEC issued the regulation. Listing Standards for Compensation Committees, 77 Fed. Reg. 38,422 (June 27, 2012) [2012 SEC Comp. Comm. Regs.] (codified, with respect to the independence requirements set out in the text, at 17 C.F.R. § 240.10C-1(a), (b)(1), with (b)(1)(iii)(4)(B) permitting exchanges to "exempt from the requirements of paragraph (b)(1) . . . a particular relationship with respect to members of the compensation committee, as each national securities exchange . . . determines is appropriate.").

[10]   Since the NYSE requires listed company boards to affirmatively determine that each independent director "has no material relationship with the listed company" (NYSE MANUAL § 303A.02(a)(i)) and categorically prohibits directors from being "independent" if they have any of a long list of relationships with the issuer (id. § 303A.02(a)(ii)), that exchange simply adds that, in making an independence determination with respect to a director who will serve on the compensation committee, each board "must consider all factors specifically relevant to determining whether a director has a relationship to the listed company which is material to that director's ability to be independent from management in connection with the duties of a compensation committee member, including, but not limited to" the two factors that the statute identified (id. at 303A.02(a)(ii)). NASDAQ similarly requires that all directors serving on a compensation committee meet that exchange's general definition of "independence," which includes a long list of relationships that preclude independence and, in addition, requires that the board must "affirmatively determin[e] the independence of any director who will serve on the compensation committee," taking into account "all factors specifically relevant to determining whether a director has a relationship to the Company which is material to that director's ability to be independent from management in connection with the duties of a compensation committee member, including, but not limited to" the two factors listed in the text. See NASDAQ RULE 5605(a), (d), (d)(2)(A).

Should major shareholders, who fall within the securities law definition of "affiliate," be precluded from membership on compensation committees—given that some research and anecdotal reports suggest that large shareholder presence on compensation committees helps to deter excessive executive pay and may have other benefits?

Compensation committee control over consultants and advisers. Compensation committees frequently obtain information from compensation consultants. Obviously, if the executives whose compensation a committee controls are selecting and evaluating a compensation consultant—or control the award of work to the compensation consultant on matters other than executive pay—the compensation consultant could be inclined to advise the committee in such a way as to increase the pay that the committee then awards to the executives.

To try to prevent the very executives whose pay a compensation committee sets from controlling the appointment of and fee paid to the consultant advising the committee, the Dodd-Frank law requires that "[t]he compensation committee of an issuer, in its capacity as a committee of the board of directors, may, in its sole discretion, retain or obtain the advice of a compensation consultant" and that "[t]he compensation committee of an issuer shall be directly responsible for the appointment, compensation, and oversight of the work of a compensation consultant."[11]

Dodd-Frank adds that "[t]he compensation committee of an issuer, in its capacity as a committee of the board of directors, may, in its sole discretion, retain and obtain the advice of independent legal counsel and other advisers," and that "[t]he compensation committee of an issuer shall be directly responsible for the appointment, compensation, and oversight of the work of independent legal counsel and other advisers."[12]

To ensure that the compensation committee can get whatever advice it needs, Dodd-Frank further mandates that "[e]ach issuer shall provide for appropriate funding, as determined by the compensation committee in its capacity as a committee of the board of directors, for payment of reasonable

---

[11]   124 Stat. 1376, 1902, § 952, codified at 15 U.S.C. § 78j-3(c)(1)(A) & (B), with implementing regulation at 17 C.F.R. § 240.10C-1(b)(2)(i) & (ii) and complementary listing standards at NYSE MANUAL § 303A.05(c)(i) & (ii) and NASDAQ RULE 5605(d)(3)(A) & (B).

[12]   124 Stat. 1376, 1902, § 952, codified at 15 U.S.C. § 78j-3(d)(1) & (2), with implementing regulation at 17 C.F.R. § 240.10C-1(b)(2)(i) & (ii) and complementary listing standards at NYSE MANUAL § 303A.05(c)(i) & (ii) and NASDAQ RULE 5605(d)(3)(A) & (B).

compensation . . . to a compensation consultant; and . . . to independent legal counsel or any other adviser to the compensation committee."[13]

All of the reforms set out above were accomplished by the Dodd-Frank law requiring the SEC to issue regulations mandating exchanges to incorporate the compensation committee requirements into listing standards.[14]

QUESTION ON LEGAL COUNSEL FOR THE COMPENSATION COMMITTEE

Why would a compensation committee need "independent legal counsel" in addition to a compensation consultant?

What compensation consultants do and how their work affects compensation amounts. A substantial majority of public companies employ compensation consultants to advise on executive pay packages.[15] Some argue that these consultants are in part to blame for the large increases in CEO pay at U.S. public companies.

A compensation consultant will often, for each client company's compensation committee, construct a group of "peer" companies, often companies in the same industry as the client company and about the same size. The consultant then collects information on CEO pay at those peer companies and ranks all the CEO pay, from top to bottom. The consultant advises the client company on where its CEO stands in this ranking. For example, the client company's CEO's pay might place him or her at the 75th percentile, meaning that 25% of the CEOs at companies of roughly similar size in the same industry are paid more and 75% are paid less. Or the client company's CEO's pay might place him or her at the 50th percentile, meaning that half of the CEOs at companies of roughly similar size in the same industry are paid more and half are paid less.

The compensation committee can then try to adjust the CEO's pay so that it is higher or lower, or remains the same, in comparison with the pay of CEOs at comparable companies. One criticism is that, if most compensation committees try to pay their CEOs at more than the 50th

---

[13]   124 Stat. 1376, 1902, § 952, codified at 15 U.S.C. § 78j-3(e), with implementing regulation at 17 C.F.R. § 240.10C-1(b)(3) and complementary listing standards at NYSE MANUAL § 303A.05(c)(iii) and NASDAQ RULE 5605(d)(3)(C).

[14]   124 Stat. 1376, 1903, § 952, codified at 15 U.S.C. § 78j-3(f).

[15]   A survey in March through May 2015, drawing 1,034 public company responses, reported that almost 76% of those companies had presentations from compensation consultants during the preceding year. NATIONAL ASSOCIATION OF CORPORATE DIRECTORS, 2015–2016 NACD PUBLIC COMPANY GOVERNANCE SURVEY 4, 38 (2015).

percentile (on the theory that most committees believe that their CEOs are in the upper half of CEOs in terms of talent and performance), the pay of all CEOs will necessarily keep marching upward. The reforms do not address this issue.

There are many components to executive pay. Chapter Sixteen identifies and explains those components. But note here that the compensation consultant can provide information from peer companies on different components of executive pay, as well as information about the total pay for each officer position (CEO, CFO, etc.) at other companies.

QUESTION ON CREEPING PEER COMPANY STATISTICS THAT CAN BE CREATED BY BOARDS' DECISIONS TO PAY THEIR CEOS ABOVE THE MEDIAN

How can compensation committees fight what may be the natural tendency to compensate their CEOs over the 50th percentile, thereby contributing to an upward "creep" driving all CEO pay higher?

Compensation consultants' independence. Compensation consultants faced the same type of conflict of interest that the pre-reform auditors faced. Some of the firms selling compensation advice also sold other services that generated more revenue than the compensation consulting services and were purchased for companies by the very executives on whose compensation the firms consulted.

A congressional report in late 2007 described the issue and provided some statistics:

> Large companies routinely retain compensation consultants to provide advice on executive pay, such as developing compensation peer groups. . . . These consultants can be retained by either the corporate board (typically, the compensation committee of the board) or management, and they may advise the board, management, or both on executive pay issues. Whether retained by the board or management, these consultants can have a major impact on executive pay decisions.

> According to experts on executive compensation, compensation consultants can have a conflict of interest if they provide other services to a company at the same time that they are providing executive compensation advice. The concern is that the ability of consultants to provide independent, unbiased advice to directors regarding the pay of senior executives can be compromised if the senior executives are at the same time paying the compensation

consultants to provide other services to the company. These other services can include a wide range of activities, including employee benefit administration, human resource management, and actuarial services.

To assess the extent of consultant conflicts of interest, Chairman Waxman wrote to request nonpublic information from six leading compensation consultants: Frederick W. Cook & Company, Hewitt Associates, Mercer Human Resources Consulting, Pearl Meyer & Partners, Towers Perrin, and Watson Wyatt. For each consultant, the Committee requested data on the value of the executive compensation consulting services and any other services that the consultant provided to Fortune 250 companies from January 1, 2002, through December 31, 2006. The compensation consultants were asked to report to the Committee as executive compensation consulting fees any revenues earned for work related to the compensation of the most senior executives of the companies, including such services as devising equity compensation plans, designing compensation peer groups, and providing pay survey data. The consultants were asked to report fees earned for services related to compensating employees other than senior executives or for other work unrelated to compensation as "other" revenue.[16]

* * *

Compensation consultant conflicts of interest are pervasive. In 2006, at least 113 of the Fortune 250 companies received executive pay advice from consultants that were providing other services to the company.

The fees earned by compensation consultants for providing other services often far exceed those earned for advising on executive compensation. In 2006, the consultants providing both executive compensation advice and other services to Fortune 250 companies were paid almost 11 times more for providing other services than they were paid for providing executive compensation advice. On average, the companies paid these consultants over $2.3 million for other services and less than $220,000 for executive compensation advice.

Some compensation consultants received over $10 million in 2006 to provide other services. One Fortune 250 company paid a compensation consultant over $11 million for other services in 2006, over 70 times more than the company paid the consultant for executive compensation services. Another Fortune 250

---

[16]   MAJORITY STAFF OF H. COMM. ON OVERSIGHT AND GOVERNMENT REFORM, EXECUTIVE PAY: CONFLICTS OF INTEREST AMONG COMPENSATION CONSULTANTS 1–2 (Dec. 2007).

company also paid a compensation consultant over $11 million for other services, over 50 times more than it paid the consultant for executive compensation advice.

There appears to be a correlation between the extent of a consultant's conflict of interest and the level of CEO pay. In 2006, the median CEO salary of the Fortune 250 companies that hired compensation consultants with the largest conflicts of interest was 67% higher than the median CEO salary of the companies that did not use conflicted consultants. Over the period between 2002 and 2006, the Fortune 250 companies that hired compensation consultants with the largest conflicts increased CEO pay over twice as fast as the companies that did not use conflicted consultants.[17]

Some academic research supports the conclusion that CEOs are paid more when the compensation committees are advised by consultants who provide other services to the CEOs' firms. One study reviewed data from 1,046 public companies during the 2006 fiscal year.[18] It found that, after controlling for such variables as firm size, book-to-market ratio, stock returns over the last three years, and industry,[19] "CEO pay is 18% higher in the US companies . . . where the consultants provide services in addition to compensation consulting."[20]

The researchers also found, counter-intuitively, that "CEO pay is 13% higher where the board retains its own compensation consultant."[21]

To disclose compensation consultants' possible conflicts to investors, SEC regulations require that public companies report

(iii) [a]ny role of compensation consultants in determining or recommending the amount or form of executive and director compensation (other than any role limited to consulting on any broad-based plan that does not discriminate in scope, terms, or operation, in favor of executive officers or directors of the [company], and that is available generally to all salaried employees; or providing information that either is not customized for a particular [company] or that is customized based on parameters that are not developed by the compensation consultant, and about which the compensation consultant does not provide advice) during the [company's] last completed fiscal

---

[17] *Id.* at i–ii (emphasis in original).

[18] Kevin J. Murphy & Tatiana Sandino, *Executive Pay and "Independent" Compensation Consultants*, 49 J. ACCT. ECON. 247, 248, 249–50 (2010).

[19] *Id.* at 254–55.

[20] *Id.* at 255. The study further concluded that the type of "other service" the consultant provided made a difference—in particular finding that there was "no evidence that CEO pay in the US is higher when the consultant also serves as the company's actuary." *Id.* at 260.

[21] *Id.*

year, identifying such consultants, stating whether such consultants were engaged directly by the compensation committee (or persons performing the equivalent functions) or any other person, describing the nature and scope of their assignment, and the material elements of the instructions or directions given to the consultants with respect to the performance of their duties under the engagement:

(A) [i]f such compensation consultant was engaged by the compensation committee (or persons performing the equivalent functions) to provide advice or recommendations on the amount or form of executive and director compensation (other than any role limited to consulting on any broad-based plan that does not discriminate in scope, terms, or operation, in favor of executive officers or directors of the [company], and that is available generally to all salaried employees; or providing information that either is not customized for a particular [company] or that is customized based on parameters that are not developed by the compensation consultant, and about which the compensation consultant does not provide advice) and the compensation consultant or its affiliates also provided additional services to the [company] or its affiliates in an amount in excess of $120,000 during the [company's] last completed fiscal year, then disclose the aggregate fees for determining or recommending the amount or form of executive and director compensation and the aggregate fees for such additional services. Disclose whether the decision to engage the compensation consultant or its affiliates for these other services was made, or recommended, by management, and whether the compensation committee or the board approved such other services of the compensation consultant or its affiliates.

(B) [i]f the compensation committee (or persons performing the equivalent functions) has not engaged a compensation consultant, but management has engaged a compensation consultant to provide advice or recommendations on the amount or form of executive and director compensation (other than any role limited to consulting on any broad-based plan that does not discriminate in scope, terms, or operation, in favor of executive officers or directors of the [company], and that is available generally to all salaried employees; or providing information that either is not customized for a particular [company] or that is customized based on parameters that are not developed by the compensation consultant, and about which the compensation consultant does not provide advice) and such compensation consultant or its affiliates has provided additional services to the [company] in an amount in excess of $120,000 during the [company's] last completed fiscal year, then disclose the aggregate fees for determining or recommending the amount or form of executive and director compensation and the aggregate fees for any additional services provided by the compensation consultant or its affiliates.[22]

The Dodd-Frank Wall Street Reform Act then went further, requiring the SEC to "identify factors that affect the independence of a compensation consultant, legal counsel, or other adviser to a compensation committee," which "shall include—

(A) the provision of other services to the issuer by the person that employs the compensation consultant, legal counsel, or other adviser;

(B) the amount of fees received from the issuer by the person that employs the compensation consultant, legal counsel, or other adviser, as a percentage of the total revenue of the person that employs the compensation consultant, legal counsel, or other adviser;

(C) the policies and procedures of the person that employs the compensation consultant, legal counsel, or other adviser that are designed to prevent conflicts of interest;

(D) any business or personal relationship of the compensation consultant, legal counsel, or other adviser with a member of the compensation committee; and

(E) any stock of the issuer owned by the compensation consultant, legal counsel, or other adviser."[23]

The law then required the SEC to issue a regulation prohibiting exchanges from listing securities unless the compensation committees at the issuers could "only select a compensation consultant, legal counsel, or other adviser . . . after taking into consideration the factors identified by the Commission."[24]

---

[22]   Proxy Disclosure Enhancements, 74 Fed. Reg. 68,334, 68,345–49, 68,364–65 (Dec. 23, 2009), with resulting regulations at 17 C.F.R. § 229.407(e)(3)(iii) & (iv); 17 C.F.R. § 240.14a-101 (Item 7(d)) (requiring disclosure in proxy statement).

[23]   124 Stat. 1376, 1901, § 952, codified at 15 U.S.C. § 78j-3(b)(2).

[24]   124 Stat. 1376, 1901, § 952, codified at 15 U.S.C. § 78j-3(b)(1). The resulting regulations require that listing standards state that "[t]he compensation committee of a listed issuer may select a compensation consultant, legal counsel or other adviser to the compensation committee only after taking into consideration the following factors, as well as any other factors identified by the relevant national securities exchange or national securities association in its listing standards," with the "following factors" being the five set out in the statute quoted in the text, and a sixth, which reads: "Any business or personal relationship of the compensation consultant, legal counsel, other adviser or the person employing the adviser with an executive officer of the issuer." 17 C.F.R. § 240.10C-1(b)(4). *See* the resulting listing standards at NYSE MANUAL § 303A.05(c)(iv) and NASDAQ RULE 5605(d)(3)(D).

But none of this precluded the compensation consultants from providing other services to the companies whose boards the consultants advised on executive pay or precluded compensation committees from actually retaining consultants that provided other services. The law and regulations required only disclosure.

QUESTIONS ON THE INDEPENDENCE OF COMPENSATION CONSULTANTS

Why do compensation committees need consultants at all?

Should the committees impose independence requirements on consultants, rather than simply "considering" factors that might affect independence? What would those requirements look like?

Will giving the compensation committee "sole authority to retain and terminate the consulting firm, including sole authority to approve the firm's fees and other retention terms" really ensure that the consultant is doing what the committee wants instead of what the CEO wants? Is it likely that a committee will employ a consultant that the CEO doesn't like?

Will market discipline work? That is, will investors punish companies that pay their compensation consultants more than $120,000 a year for work on other matters by discounting the price of those companies' stock?

Even if investors do not punish those companies, will potentially adverse publicity in the financial and mass-audience media lead compensation committees to hire only consultants that do not provide other services to the committees' companies? Will the disclosures about compensation consultants thereby influence their independence from management indirectly, by companies declining to use compensation consultants for other work in order to avoid having to reveal that they have done so?

If you believe that top executives are simply paid too much, will the reforms aiming to improve the independence of compensation consultants result in lower pay?

Annual evaluation of compensation committees. Each compensation committee for an NYSE-listed company must have a charter that not only sets out the committee's purpose and responsibilities but also addresses "an annual performance evaluation" of the committee itself.[25]

---

25   NYSE MANUAL § 303A.05(b)(ii).

B. NOMINATING COMMITTEES

What the nominating committees do. Nominating committees identify director candidates. These candidates, after the whole board approves them, appear on the company proxy card and in the company's proxy statement. These candidates therefore do not have to spend any money to run. The company foots the entire bill for preparation and distribution of the proxy statement and proxy card. These candidates usually run unopposed, and almost always win.

The NYSE has also placed miscellaneous governance responsibilities on the nominating committee. In fact, the NYSE calls this committee the nominating/corporate governance committee. Here is the NYSE's description of that committee's responsibilities, which must be embodied in a written charter:

> (b) The nominating/corporate governance committee must have a written charter that addresses:
>
> > (i) the committee's purpose and responsibilities—which, at minimum, must be to: identify individuals qualified to become board members, consistent with criteria approved by the board, and to select, or to recommend that the board select, the director nominees for the next annual meeting of shareholders; develop and recommend to the board a set of corporate governance guidelines applicable to the corporation; and oversee the evaluation of the board and management; and
> >
> > (ii) an annual performance evaluation of the committee.[26]

NASDAQ rules provide that director nominees be selected, or recommended to the board for selection, by either a majority of independent directors on the board or by a nominations committee.[27] A committee

---

[26] NYSE MANUAL § 303A.04(b). The 2003 changes in NYSE listing standards imposed the requirement that listed companies have this committee. SEC Order Approving NYSE and NASDAQ Listing Standard Changes Nov. 2003, *supra* note 1, at *6 ("NYSE proposes to require each listed company to have a nominating/corporate governance committee composed entirely of independent directors."). The text cites to and quotes from the listing standard, as later amended, and effective in April 2016.

[27] NASDAQ RULE 5605(e)(1). The 2003 changes in NASDAQ listing standards imposed this requirement. SEC Order Approving NYSE and NASDAQ Listing Standard Changes Nov. 2003, *supra* note 1, at *14 ("Nasdaq proposes to amend NASD Rule 4350(c) to require director nominees to either be selected or recommended for the board's selection either by a majority of independent directors, or by a nominations committee comprised solely of independent directors," with the new rule to include a limited exception possible for one of the committee members.). The text cites to and quotes from the listing standard, as later amended, and effective in April 2016.

SEC regulations demand that

[i]f the [public company] does not have a standing nominating committee or committee performing similar functions, state the basis for the view of the board of directors that it

charter, or a board resolution, must address "the nominations process and such related matters as may be required under the federal securities laws."[28]

Reform issues for nominating committees: overview. Boards are largely self-perpetuating. When a director retires or passes away, articles and bylaws usually permit the board to appoint the replacement as soon as the old director retires or dies. Then the board nominates the new director for election by the shareholders at the next annual meeting (or the next one at which the replaced director would have come up for election, if the board had staggered terms). The board usually also renominates those current directors who are alive and well and wish to continue their service.

Reforms directed to the nominating committee reflect two concerns. The first is that top management, and particularly the CEO, may in fact control director nominations, regardless of the formal role that the nominating committee plays. If so, then top management may effectively control the board, thereby undermining board oversight of top management performance. This concern has motivated reforms designed to (i) ensure the independence of nominating committees and (ii) ensure that the nominating committees (as opposed to top officers) select and control those who assist the committees (such as search firms) in selecting candidates for directorships. And one reform requires that companies disclose who recommended a candidate in the first place, which could force disclosure of a CEO's attempt to pack a board.

The second concern is that the self-perpetuating nature of board membership—which is effectuated through the nominating committee—creates a closed system. By law, the shareholders elect the board. But they do so overwhelmingly in uncontested elections. Therefore, the elections are effectively decided by nominations, which in turn are controlled by the nominating committees. Even assuming that a committee is independent of the executives at a company, the committee might rely overmuch on their own networking to consider only the small number of candidates that they know themselves. This could lead to selection of candidates based more on relationships than the benefit the company would derive from the candidates' service as directors. It could effectively exclude a whole raft of candidates with new ideas. Moreover, any system relying only on the directors for nominations could exclude shareholders from the nomination

---

is appropriate for the [company] not to have such a committee and identify each director who participates in the consideration of director nominees.

17 C.F.R. § 229.407(c)(1); 17 C.F.R. § 240.14a-101 (Item 7(d)) (requiring disclosure in proxy statement). This seems designed to pressure those public companies that do not have nominating committees into creating them.

[28]   NASDAQ RULE 5605(e)(2). SEC rules require each public company to state whether its nominating committees has a "charter" and, if so, to either post it on the company website or include it as an appendix to the proxy statement every three years. 17 C.F.R. § 229.407(c)(2)(i) & Instruction 2 to Item 407.

process, which—since most director elections are uncontested—is the most important part of director selection.

A potpourri of reforms attempts to address this second concern. Many of them simply require disclosures that cannot truthfully be made unless a company's search for director candidates is driven by rational concerns. And a few reforms require disclosures designed to press companies into considering candidates whom shareholders propose.

Finally, the NYSE requires that the nominating committee also serve as a listed company's "governance committee" and, among other things, create "corporate governance guidelines."

Independence of nominating committee members. The NYSE requires that each member of a nominating/corporate governance committee be a director who qualifies as "independent" under the definition of that term in the NYSE listing standards.[29] NASDAQ listing standards also require that director nominations originate from either a committee of directors who are independent under those standards, or, if no such committee exists, a majority of the independent directors.[30] No federal law or SEC regulation defines the factors relevant to the director independence for nominating committee members.

QUESTIONS ON NOMINATING COMMITTEE MEMBERSHIP AND QUESTIONS ON BOARD EVALUATIONS

Who should be on a nominating committee? Once we eliminate, through independence screens, those who will toady to management, what other criteria will identify a good nominating committee member?

Should potential nominating committee members take a "governance" course so that they can better recognize individuals whose service on the board will benefit the company? Should a company have on its nominating committee those lucky few who seem to know everybody worth knowing and who would therefore be a good source of director candidates?

As we have seen with the compensation committee and now with the nominating committee, the NYSE wants boards and committees to be evaluated. Directors may also participate in continuing-education programs. As a lawyer, do board evaluations at your clients give you any concerns? What will you recommend to address those concerns? Consider the same questions as to the continuing education for directors.

---

[29] NYSE MANUAL § 303A.04(a).

[30] NASDAQ RULE 5605(e)(1). But NASDAQ provides a limited exception to the independence rule for one member of a nomination committee, similar to the exception provided for one member of the compensation committee. *Id.* at 5605(e)(3).

Does the business judgment rule help here—by giving such wide leeway to director action that any statements made in board or director evaluations, and in any board governance education, will have little effect on liability for violation of the duty of care?

What do you think of having all these committee "charters"? How would they help or hurt in litigation down the line? How will they affect committee performance? Would you want them "bare bones" or sporting rococo detail?

What kind of an "annual performance evaluation" of a board or committee would be helpful to the board? To the committee?

Should the nominating committee be evaluated according to the performance—as directors—of the director candidates that the committee selects?

Should the compensation committee be evaluated according to the performance of the CEO whose pay package the committee designed in order to incentivize high performance?

The requirement that director nomination be controlled by independent directors has an important caveat, embodied in this commentary for the NYSE rule:

> If a listed company is legally required by contract or otherwise to provide third parties with the ability to nominate directors (for example, preferred stock rights to elect directors upon a dividend default, shareholder agreements, and management agreements), the selection and nomination of such directors need not be subject to the nominating committee process.[31]

NASDAQ provides a similar interpretive comment.[32] These exceptions raise a very good point. Sometimes, in exchange for putting money into a company, an investor insists on board representation.[33]

---

[31]   NYSE MANUAL § 303A.04 Commentary.

[32]   NASDAQ RULE 5605(e)(4), and IM-5605-7, which states: "This rule does not apply in cases where the right to nominate a director legally belongs to a third party. For example, investors may negotiate the right to nominate directors in connection with an investment in the Company, holders of preferred stock may be permitted to nominate or appoint directors upon certain defaults, or the Company may be a party to a shareholder's agreement that allocates the right to nominate some directors. Because the right to nominate directors in these cases does not reside with the Company, Independent Director approval would not be required."

[33]   Both the new NYSE standards (in the introductory commentary to section 303A.00) and the NASDAQ standards (in 5615(c)(2)) also exempt from the compensation and nomination committee requirements any "controlled company"—i.e., one in which more than 50% of the voting power is held by an individual, a group, or another company.

QUESTIONS ON HOW GOVERNANCE STANDARDS AND PRACTICES MAY AFFECT DEAL NEGOTIATIONS

Should a company be careful today not to let too many of its board seats become "dedicated" to investors? Can it now argue in negotiations with an investor that the investor should not get board seats because that would create a bad corporate governance odor?

Is that argument likely to work, if the company is seeking money from an investor that really wants a say on the board, and the knowledge of company operations and plans that accompanies board representation?

Nominating committee control over search firms and disclosure of search firm roles. Nominating committees, like compensation committees, may use outside consultants. A nominating committee might, for example, use a search firm to find possible director candidates.[34] The listing standards seek to ensure that the committee (presumably as opposed to company executives, particularly the CEO) hire and control any such search firm. Here is the relevant NYSE commentary on its nominating committee listing standard:

> The nominating/corporate governance committee charter . . . should give the nominating/corporate governance committee sole authority to retain and terminate any search firm to be used to identify director candidates, including sole authority to approve the search firm's fees and other retention terms.[35]

The NASDAQ rules do not include a similar requirement.

SEC regulations require public disclosure to reveal the input of search firms on the nomination of director candidates:

> If the [company] pays a fee to any third party or parties to identify or evaluate or assist in identifying or evaluating potential [director] nominees, disclose the function performed by each such third party[.][36]

---

[34]   DAVID LARCKER & BRIAN TAYAN, CORPORATE GOVERNANCE MATTERS 89 (2d ed. 2016) ("According to the [National Association of Corporate Directors], approximately 50 percent of companies use a search firm [to help find new directors]. However, this varies with firm size. Eighty-two percent of large companies (market capitalization greater than $10 billion) use a search firm, while smaller firms are considerably less likely to do so.") (footnote omitted).

[35]   NYSE MANUAL § 303A.04 Commentary.

[36]   17 C.F.R. § 229.407(c)(2)(viii); 17 C.F.R. § 240.14a-101 (Item 7(d)) (requiring disclosure in proxy statement).

QUESTIONS ON SEARCH FIRMS LOCATING DIRECTORS
AND NOMINATING COMMITTEE RELATIONS
WITH THE WHOLE BOARD

Does use of search firms to find directors bother you as somehow inconsistent with shareholder democracy? Will the search firms suggest "professional directors"—those who are making a living as directors of public companies and who provide their resumes to the search firms in the hope that the search firms will pass those resumes along to nominating committees? If so, is that helpful or harmful? Does use of search firms simply open the board to more possibilities, with the nominating committee still able to identify candidates through any other means?

If you ran a mutual fund with a large investment in a public company, what would you see as the advantages of that company finding a new director via a search firm? What disadvantages?

Should the nominating committee control the nominating process? Or is this a matter that does not require expertise and on which all board members (or all independent directors) should contribute on an equal basis? If the latter is the case, does that circumstance suggest that the relationship between the nominating committee and the whole board should differ from the relationship between the audit committee and the whole board, or the relationship between the compensation committee and the whole board?

Required disclosure of the sources of nominees. Search firms are only one potential source of potential director candidates. Other sources include the CEO or an important shareholder. Obviously, if the CEO suggests a candidate to the nominating committee, the committee and full board then nominate that candidate, and the candidate wins election (as is most probable), then the new director may understand that he or she "owes" his or her seat on the board to the CEO. That director might therefore be ill-inclined to criticize the CEO's performance or disagree with the CEO's proposals.

SEC regulations now provide:

> With regard to each nominee approved by the nominating committee for inclusion on the [company's] proxy card (other than nominees who are executive officers or who are directors standing for re-election), state which one or more of the following categories of persons or entities recommended that nominee: Security holder, non-management director, chief executive officer, other executive officer, third-party search firm, or other specified source.[37]

---

[37] 17 C.F.R. § 229.407(c)(2)(vii); 17 C.F.R. § 240.14a-101 (Item 7(d)) (requiring disclosure in proxy statement).

QUESTIONS ON THE EFFECT OF DISCLOSING WHO RECOMMENDED A DIRECTOR NOMINEE

Will the requirement that the recommender be disclosed deter CEOs from dominating the nomination process?

What legitimate and helpful role, if any, does the CEO play in the selection of new directors?

Disclosure of nominating committee's criteria for selecting director candidates, the processes for selecting candidates, and the particular strengths that each nominated candidate will bring to board deliberations. A number of required disclosures seem designed to encourage rationality (as opposed to, say, cronyism) in the nomination process. Put another way, companies can make the disclosures—without fear of drawing criticism— only if their nomination criteria and process are well thought out.

Thus, companies must

[d]escribe any specific minimum qualifications that the nominating committee believes must be met by a nominating committee-recommended nominee for a position on the [company's] board of directors, and describe any specific qualities or skills that the nominating committee believes are necessary for one or more of the [company's] directors to possess.[38]

And SEC regulations require that public companies "briefly discuss," for each director and each director nominee (who will likely be a sitting director), "the specific experience, qualifications, attributes or skills that led to the conclusion that the person should serve as a director for the [company] at the time that the disclosure is made, in light of the [company's] business and structure."[39]

Public companies must also "[d]escribe the nominating committee's process for identifying and evaluating nominees."[40]

---

[38] 17 C.F.R. § 229.407(c)(2)(v); 17 C.F.R. § 240.14a-101 (Item 7(d)) (requiring disclosure in proxy statement).

[39] 17 C.F.R. § 229.401(e)(1), Form 10-K, Item 10 (requiring disclosure in company 10-K), with companies regularly providing this information in proxy statements, which the companies incorporate by reference in their 10-Ks per the Form 10-K permission under the heading titled "Documents Incorporated by Reference."

[40] 17 C.F.R. § 229.407(c)(2)(vi).

QUESTIONS ON DISCLOSURE OF CRITERIA AND PROCESS FOR SELECTING NOMINEES AND DISCLOSURE OF THE STRENGTHS THAT NOMINEES BRING TO BOARD SERVICE

Do you think these disclosures are useful? Or are companies likely to describe criteria, processes, and candidate strengths in such general terms that the disclosures add very little?[41]

---

[41]   To think about these questions, consider disclosures from the 2015 proxy statement filed by Worthington Industries, Inc., a company engaged in steel processing and the manufacture of metal products such as pressure cylinders:

> When considering candidates for the Board, the Nominating and Governance Committee evaluates the entirety of each candidate's credentials but does not have specific eligibility requirements or minimum qualifications which must be met by a Nominating and Governance Committee-recommended nominee and has not adopted a formal policy with regard to the consideration of diversity in identifying director nominees. However, the Corporate Governance Guidelines provide that the retirement age for directors is 75, and a director is to submit his or her resignation to be effective at the conclusion of the three-year term immediately after attaining age 75. The Nominating and Governance Committee considers those factors it deems appropriate, including, but not limited to, independence, judgment, skill, diversity, strength of character, experience with businesses and organizations of comparable size or scope, experience as an executive of or adviser to public and private companies, experience and skill relative to other Board members, specialized knowledge or experience, and the desirability of the candidate's membership on the Board and any committees of the Board. Depending on the current needs of the Board, the Nominating and Governance Committee may weigh certain factors more or less heavily. The Nominating and Governance Committee does, however, believe that all members of the Board should have strong character and integrity, a reputation for working constructively with others, sufficient time to devote to Board matters, and no conflict of interest that would interfere with his or her performance as a director.

> While the Board and the Nominating and Governance Committee do not have specific eligibility requirements and do not, as a matter of course, weigh any of the factors they deem appropriate more heavily than others, both the Board and the Nominating and Governance Committee believe that, as a group, the directors should have diverse backgrounds and qualifications. The Company believes that the members of the Board, as a group, have such backgrounds and qualifications.

> The Nominating and Governance Committee considers candidates for the Board from any reasonable source, including shareholder recommendations, but does not evaluate candidates differently based on the source of the recommendation. The process for seeking and vetting additional director candidates is ongoing and is not dependent upon the existence of a vacancy on the Board. Accordingly, the Board believes that this ongoing identification of qualified candidates functions as an appropriate director succession plan. Pursuant to its charter, the Nominating and Governance Committee has the authority to retain consultants and search firms to assist with the process of identifying and evaluating director candidates and to approve the fees and other retention terms for any such consultant or search firm. The Nominating and Governance Committee has never used a consultant or search firm for such purpose, and, accordingly, the Company has paid no such fees.

Worthington Indus., Inc., Definitive Proxy Statement, Schedule 14A (filed Aug. 12, 2015) at 18.

Here are the descriptions, in this proxy statement, of the qualities and skills fitting nominees for directorship, with each such description following a short business biography: "Mr. Blystone's business acumen, his long service on our Board, and his collegial style and leadership resulted in his election as the Lead Independent Director of the Company and make him well qualified to continue to serve on the Board." *Id.* at 20. "Mr. Davis' financial knowledge and depth of experience in equity investing, strategic matters, acquisitions, financial analysis and investment banking make him well qualified to continue to serve on the Board, and qualify him as an 'audit committee financial expert,' as defined by applicable SEC Rules." *Id.* "Dr. Ribeau brings extensive experience

Even if you conclude that the disclosures are not generally useful, might they nevertheless serve a good purpose in specific cases? Which ones?

Will shareholders pressure companies to make the disclosures meaningful?

Shareholder participation in the nomination process at the company. Shareholders can, of course, run their own candidates for the board. But running candidates against those nominated by the company's board is expensive and confrontational. Typically, shareholders run opposition candidates as part of a larger effort to either take over a company or radically influence company strategy. The reforms discussed next—and a much more aggressive reform called "proxy access" that Chapter Fourteen will cover—are designed for the shareholder who wants to play a role in director selection through the company's own nomination process rather than through a contested director election.

Several disclosure requirements provide shareholders with information they can use to suggest nominees to the nominations committee. One requires a public company to state

> (ii) [i]f the nominating committee has a policy with regard to the consideration of any director candidates recommended by security holders, provide a description of the material elements of that policy, which shall include, but need not be limited to, a statement as to whether the committee will consider director candidates recommended by security holders;

> (iii) [i]f the nominating committee does not have a policy with regard to the consideration of any director candidates recommended by security holders, state that fact and state the basis for the view of the board of directors that it is appropriate for the [company] not to have such a policy;

> (iv) [i]f the nominating committee will consider candidates recommended by security holders, describe the procedures to be followed by security holders in submitting such recommendations;[42]

Faced with the alternative of either (i) stating that the nominating committee has *no* policy regarding suggestions by shareholders of director candidates and (ii) stating that it does (and establishing and disclosing a

---

in managing the issues that face large public institutions. His background as the leader of a billion-dollar public institution and as an educator and administrator enables him to provide insight relative to management, educational, financial, human resources and public policy matters and make him well qualified to continue to serve on the Board." *Id.* at 20–21.

[42]   17 C.F.R. § 229.407(c)(2)(ii)–(iv); 17 C.F.R. § 240.14a-101 (Item 7(d)) (requiring disclosure in proxy statement).

procedure by which the company will consider shareholder suggestions), most companies will select the second option. The first option suggests a disdain for shareholders that would likely draw both adverse financial press coverage and adverse shareholder reaction.

A second disclosure seems designed to level the playing field so that potential director candidates whom shareholders suggest do not have to clear higher hurdles than those the nominating committee discovers through other means:

> (vi) Describe the nominating committee's process for identifying and evaluating nominees for director, including nominees recommended by security holders, and any differences in the manner in which the nominating committee evaluates nominees for director based on whether the nominee is recommended by a security holder. . . .[43]

A third disclosure provides shareholders with the company's track record in nominating director candidates suggested by shareholders:

> If the [company's] nominating committee received, by a date not later than the 120th calendar day before the date of the [company's] proxy statement released to security holders in connection with the previous year's annual meeting, a recommended nominee from a security holder that beneficially owned more than 5% of the [company's] voting common stock for at least one year as of the date the recommendation was made, or from a group of security holders that beneficially owned, in the aggregate, more than 5% of the [company's] voting common stock, with each of the securities used to calculate that ownership held for at least one year as of the date the recommendation was made, identify the candidate and the security holder or security holder group that recommended the candidate and disclose whether the nominating committee chose to nominate the candidate, *provided, however*, that no such identification or disclosure is required without the written consent of both the security holder or security holder group and the candidate to be so identified.[44]

Remember that this disclosure is designed to affect whether the nominating committee *itself* will decide to nominate, and therefore include on the company proxy card and describe in the company proxy statement, a director candidate that a shareholder suggests. We will consider in Chapter Fourteen the different question of whether shareholders should be permitted to put a director candidate on the company's proxy card, and a

---

[43]   17 C.F.R. § 229.407(c)(2)(vi); 17 C.F.R. § 240.14a-101 (Item 7(d)) (requiring disclosure in proxy statement).

[44]   17 C.F.R. § 229.407(c)(2)(ix); 17 C.F.R. § 240.14a-101 (Item 7(d)) (requiring disclosure in proxy statement).

description of the candidate in the company proxy, *even if the nominating committee does not support the candidate.*

With that targeted consideration in mind, this third disclosure seems aimed at revealing whether the company's nominating committee is responsive to shareholders or not.

QUESTIONS ON SHAREHOLDER NOMINATION OF DIRECTOR CANDIDATES

We will come back to this question later, but now that you see it for the first time, do you think it is wise for shareholders to be involved in the selection of director candidates? Are there possible downsides? Which shareholders are likely to nominate candidates? Do those shareholders have any special interests that are not shared by the rest of the stockholders?

Why does the last-quoted regulation focus on nominees recommended by large shareholders (owning more than 5%) who have held company stock for one year or more? Are those shareholders somehow better than the rest? More likely to recommend worthy director candidates?

A push toward diversity. SEC regulations now demand that a public company disclose

> whether, and if so how, the nominating committee (or the board) considers diversity in identifying nominees for director. If the nominating committee (or the board) has a policy with regard to the consideration of diversity in identifying director nominees, describe how this policy is implemented, as well as how the nominating committee (or the board) assesses the effectiveness of its policy.[45]

QUESTIONS ON DIVERSITY IN DIRECTOR NOMINATIONS

Do you like this disclosure? Would your attitude be influenced by studies showing the effect of board diversity on company financial performance?

Does this disclosure—to the extent to which it is designed to encourage racial and gender diversity on boards—seem to derive too greatly from a social agenda that is not linked to traditional securities law concerns? Or are agendas

---

[45] 17 C.F.R. § 229.407(c)(2)(vi); 17 C.F.R. § 240.14a-101 (Item 7(d)) (requiring disclosure in proxy statement).

other than financial ones inevitably intertwined with government regulation of commerce?

More generally, should disclosure requirements encourage nominating committees to select particular types of candidates? If you like this concept, what other director characteristics might the government encourage? Would you support disclosure—by companies doing more than 50% of their business in a foreign land—of whether they have a policy for considering board candidates from that other country?

––––––––––

The governance committee concept. Return for a moment to the NYSE's nomination/governance committee listing standard. Note that it requires the committee to "develop and recommend to the board a set of corporate governance guidelines applicable to the corporation. . . ."[46] Public companies now formally embrace such "corporate governance guidelines" or "principles." Here is the link to those that General Electric has adopted: http://www.ge.com/sites/default/files/GE_governance_principles.pdf. Here is the link to those adopted by ConAgra Foods: http://www.conagrafoods. com/investor-relations/corporate-governance/principles.

The NYSE standard also requires the nominating/governance committee to "oversee the evaluation of the board and management."[47] It is difficult to know what this means.

––––––––––

QUESTIONS ON THE DUTIES BEYOND DIRECTOR NOMINATION THAT THE NYSE PLACES ON THE NOMINATING COMMITTEE

How does "a set of corporate governance principles" relate to a corporation's bylaws and articles of incorporation?

In what way should the nominating committee "oversee the evaluation of the board and management"? Does the nominating committee become an uber-committee that somehow "oversees" all other committees and "evaluates" the board? Isn't the compensation committee charged with evaluating at least the CEO?

––––––––––

---

[46]   NYSE MANUAL § 303A.04(b)(i).

[47]   *Id.*

CHAPTER 14

REFORMS V: INDEPENDENT DIRECTORS, GOVERNANCE SCORING, SHAREHOLDERS[1]

■ ■ ■

For some years now, a good deal of corporate governance discussion has focused on "independent directors," the notion being that if we staff boards with directors who are sufficiently independent of management, governance will improve. We have already seen that Sarbanes-Oxley requires audit committees to be staffed by directors who do not receive any consulting or, advisory fees from the company and who are not "affiliates" of the company.[2] Dodd-Frank requires that members of the compensation committees be independent and requires consideration of certain factors when making the independence determination.[3]

But it is in the listing standards that the idea of director "independence" has fermented to wine with a complex taste. This Chapter Fourteen therefore begins by considering both the definition of independent director in the listing standards and the degree to which those standards demand independence in the board as a whole and in committees. The chapter then turns to research on the relationship between an independent board and company financial performance, followed by a discussion of governance indices (with which academics and commercial providers have sought numerical ways to measure the quality of a company's governance), and the relationship of those indices to financial performance. The last part of the chapter considers reforms designed to increase the power of shareholders, the role of activist shareholders (particularly activist hedge funds), and the role of proxy advisers who advise institutional shareholders on how to vote.

A. NYSE DEFINITION OF "INDEPENDENT DIRECTOR"

Here is the current definition of "independence" in the NYSE Listed Company Manual, found in section 303A.02, and dating back (albeit with

---

[1]   I take some portions of this chapter from my article *When the Government Attempts to Change the Board, Shareholders Should Know*, 40 PEPP. L. REV. 533 (2013). I have done so with permission from the Pepperdine Law Review.

[2]   15 U.S.C. § 78j-1(m)(3)(B).

[3]   15 U.S.C. § 78j-3(a)(2)(B) & (3).

later amendment) to an overhaul of the listing standards approved by the SEC in 2003:

> In order to tighten the definition of "independent director" for purposes of these standards:

> (a)(i)   No director qualifies as "independent" unless the board of directors affirmatively determines that the director has no material relationship with the listed company (either directly or as a partner, shareholder or officer of an organization that has a relationship with the company).[4]

>> (ii) In addition, in affirmatively determining the independence of any director who will serve on the compensation committee of the listed company's board of directors, the board of directors must consider all factors specifically relevant to determining whether a director has a relationship to the listed company which is material to that director's ability to be independent from management in connection with the duties of a compensation committee member, including, but not limited to:

>>> (A) the source of compensation of such director, including any consulting, advisory or other compensatory fee paid by the listed company to such director; and

---

[4]   The commentary to this general requirement states:

It is not possible to anticipate, or explicitly to provide for, all circumstances that might signal potential conflicts of interest, or that might bear on the materiality of a director's relationship to a listed company (references to "listed company" would include any parent or subsidiary in a consolidated group with the listed company). Accordingly, it is best that boards making "independence" determinations broadly consider all relevant facts and circumstances. In particular, when assessing the materiality of a director's relationship with the listed company, the board should consider the issue not merely from the standpoint of the director, but also from that of persons or organizations with which the director has an affiliation. Material relationships can include commercial, industrial, banking, consulting, legal, accounting, charitable and familial relationships, among others. However, as the concern is independence from management, the Exchange does not view ownership of even a significant amount of stock, by itself, as a bar to an independence finding.

NYSE LISTED COMPANY MANUAL § 303A.02 Commentary [NYSE MANUAL]. The NYSE added the detailed description of independence in a major revision of its corporate governance listing standards approved by the SEC on November 4, 2003. SEC, Self-Regulatory Organizations; New York Stock Exchange, Inc. and National Association of Securities Dealers, Inc.; Order Approving Proposed Rule Changes, 2003 WL 22509738 (SEC Nov. 4, 2003), at *4–5 [SEC Order Approving NYSE and NASDAQ Listing Standard Changes Nov. 2003]. The text cites to and quotes from the NYSE Listed Company Manual as amended and effective in April 2016. Quotations from the New York Stock Exchange Listed Company Manual reprinted with permission from the New York Stock Exchange.

(B) whether such director is affiliated with the listed company, a subsidiary of the listed company or an affiliate of a subsidiary of the listed company.

(b) In addition, a director is not independent if:

(i) [t]he director is, or has been within the last three years, an employee of the listed company, or an immediate family member[5] is, or has been within the last three years, an executive officer,[6] of the listed company.

(ii) The director has received, or has an immediate family member who has received, during any twelve-month period within the last three years, more than $120,000 in direct compensation from the listed company, other than director and committee fees and pension or other forms of deferred compensation for prior service (provided such compensation is not contingent in any way on continued service).

(iii)(A) The director is a current partner or employee of a firm that is the company's internal or external auditor; (B) the director has an immediate family member who is a current partner of such a firm; (C) the director has an immediate family member who is a current employee of such a firm and personally works on the listed company's audit; or (D) the director or an immediate family member was within the last three years a partner or employee of such a firm and personally worked on the listed company's audit within that time.

---

[5]   The related commentary defines an "immediate family member" to include:

a person's spouse, parents, children, siblings, mothers and fathers-in-law, sons and daughters-in-law, brothers and sisters-in-law, and anyone (other than domestic employees) who shares such person's home. When applying the look-back provisions in [subsection] (b), listed companies need not consider individuals who are no longer immediate family members as a result of legal separation or divorce, or those who have died or become incapacitated.

NYSE MANUAL § 303A.02 General Commentary to Section 303A.02(b).

[6]   Footnote 1 of § 303A.02(b)(i) defines "executive officer" by referring to SEC rule 16a-1(f), which provides:

The term "officer" shall mean an issuer's president, principal financial officer, principal accounting officer (or, if there is no such accounting officer, the controller), any vice-president of the issuer in charge of a principal business unit, division or function (such as sales, administration or finance), any other officer who performs a policy-making function, or any other person who performs similar policy-making functions for the issuer. Officers of the issuer's parent(s) or subsidiaries shall be deemed officers of the issuer if they perform such policy-making functions for the issuer. . . .

NOTE: "Policy-making function" is not intended to include policy-making functions that are not significant.

17 C.F.R. § 240.16a-1(f).

(iv) The director or an immediate family member is, or has been with[in] the last three years, employed as an executive officer of another company where any of the listed company's present executive officers at the same time serves or served on that company's compensation committee.

(v) The director is a current employee, or an immediate family member is a current executive officer, of a company that has made payments to, or received payments from, the listed company for property or services in an amount which, in any of the last three fiscal years, exceeds the greater of $1 million, or 2% of such other company's consolidated gross revenues.[7]

The commentary addresses relationships created by charitable donations that a company makes:

Contributions to tax exempt organizations shall not be considered payments for purposes of Section 303A.02(b)(v), provided however that a listed company shall disclose either on or through its website or in its annual proxy statement, or if the listed company does not file an annual proxy statement, in the company's annual report on Form 10-K filed with the SEC, any such contributions made by the listed company to any tax exempt organization in which any independent director serves as an executive officer if, within the preceding three years, contributions in any single fiscal year from the listed company to the organization exceeded the greater of $1 million, or 2% of such tax exempt organization's consolidated gross revenues. If this disclosure is made on or through the listed company's website, the listed company must disclose that fact in its annual proxy statement or annual report, as applicable, and provide the website address. Listed company boards are reminded of their obligations to consider the materiality of any such relationship in accordance with Section 303A.02(a) above.

QUESTIONS ON NYSE DEFINITION OF DIRECTOR INDEPENDENCE

Is the first provision—that the board must make an affirmative determination of independence—useful, given the later specific provisions? Why?

Look hard at the last specific exclusion. Is it a good one, particularly as a flat rule instead of a presumption? Should we consider a director not

---

7   NYSE MANUAL § 303A.02.

"independent" just because his or her daughter-in-law is the president of a company that derives a shade over the greater of $1 million or 2% of its gross revenues from the listed company?

The listing standards stamp the board with "independence." The NYSE requires that a majority of the entire board be independent directors.[8] It requires that all members of the compensation, nominating/corporate governance, and audit committees be "independent."[9]

B. NYSE-REQUIRED MEETINGS OF NON-MANAGEMENT OR INDEPENDENT DIRECTORS

NYSE Listed Company Manual section 303A.03 requires the "non-management directors" to "meet at regularly scheduled executive sessions without management."

The "non-management" directors are

all those who are not executive officers, and includes such directors who are not independent by virtue of a material relationship, former status or family membership, or for any other reason.[10]

As an alternative, however, "listed companies may instead choose to hold regular executive sessions of independent directors only."[11] The requirement for separate meetings seeks to "empower non-management directors to serve as a more effective check on management."[12]

"In order that all interested parties (not just shareholders) may be able to make their concerns known to the non-management or independent directors," an NYSE listed company must disclose a way in which such parties may "communicate directly with the presiding director [at the executive sessions of the non-management or independent directors] or with those directors as a group," and the exchange suggests that that method might mimic the procedures that audit committees are required to establish in order to receive, retain, and address complaints about accounting and auditing, including complaints submitted anonymously.[13]

---

8   NYSE MANUAL § 303A.01.

9   *Id.* §§ 303A.04(a), 303A.05(a), 303A.07(b).

10   *Id.* § 303A.03 Commentary.

11   *Id.*

12   *Id.* § 303A.03.

13   *Id.* § 303A.03 Disclosure Requirements.

QUESTIONS ON EXECUTIVE SESSIONS

Is it better for the non-management directors to meet "at regularly scheduled executive sessions" or to meet only as needed?

Should there be a standard agenda for executive sessions?

How should the agenda be set?

C. ENFORCEMENT OF NYSE LISTING STANDARDS

Section 303A.12, in subparts (a) and (b), requires each listed company's CEO to annually certify that he or she is not aware of any violation of the exchange's corporate governance listing standards (but allows the CEO to "qualify[ ] the certification to the extent necessary") and to promptly notify the exchange of any material non-compliance with the governance standards after any executive officer of the company becomes aware of the same. Subpart (c) of 303A.12 then requires the listed company to submit "an executed Written Affirmation annually to the NYSE. In addition, each listed company must submit an interim Written Affirmation as and when required by the interim Written Affirmation form specified by the NYSE," which requires the submission of an Interim Written Affirmation within five business days of any of a number of events, including the departure of any director, the addition of any director, or a change in the composition of the audit committee, the compensation committee, or the nominating/corporate governance committee. The Written Affirmations must be in the form specified by the NYSE and address details of compliance with 303A. Section 303A.13 permits the exchange to "issue a public reprimand letter to any listed company that violates a NYSE listing standard."[14]

If a company advises the exchange that it is in material violation of a listing requirement—such as the one demanding independence of a majority of the board—or if it receives a letter of reprimand or similar communication, it must disclose the substance of the advice, letter, or similar communication through a Form 8-K filing within four business days.[15]

---

[14] You can find the certification and affirmations at 2 ROBERT E. BUCKHOLZ, JR., ET AL., PUBLIC COMPANY DESKBOOK §§ 5B:2.4, 5D:2.4 (3d ed. 2016). Find the instructions for submitting affirmations at pages 5B-25 and following, which include at -25 to -27 the events triggering the need to submit an interim affirmation and the requirement that an interim affirmation must be submitted within five business days of a triggering event.

[15] Form 8-K, Item 3.01 and General Instruction B1.

D. NASDAQ DEFINITION OF "INDEPENDENT DIRECTOR" AND REQUIRED EXECUTIVE SESSIONS

Here is the current NASDAQ definition of an "independent director":

(2) "Independent Director" means a person other than an Executive Officer or employee of the Company or any other individual having a relationship which, in the opinion of the Company's board of directors, would interfere with the exercise of independent judgment in carrying out the responsibilities of a director. For purposes of this rule, "Family Member" means a person's spouse, parents, children and siblings, whether by blood, marriage or adoption, or anyone residing in such person's home. The following persons shall not be considered independent:

(A) a director who is, or at any time during the past three years was, employed by the Company;

(B) a director who accepted or who has a Family Member who accepted any compensation from the Company in excess of $120,000 during any period of twelve consecutive months within the three years preceding the determination of independence, other than the following:

(i) compensation for board or board committee service;

(ii) compensation paid to a Family Member who is an employee (other than an Executive Officer) of the Company; or

(iii) benefits under a tax-qualified retirement plan, or non-discretionary compensation.

Provided, however, that in addition to the requirements contained in this paragraph (B), audit committee members are also subject to additional, more stringent requirements under Rule 5605(c)(2).

(C) a director who is a Family Member of an individual who is, or at any time during the past three years was, employed by the company as an Executive Officer;

(D) a director who is, or has a Family Member who is, a partner in, or a controlling Shareholder or an Executive Officer of, any organization to which the Company made, or from which the Company received, payments for property or services in the current or any of the past three fiscal years that exceed 5% of the recipient's consolidated gross revenues for that year, or $200,000, whichever is more, other than the following:

> (i) payments arising solely from investments in the Company's securities; or

> (ii) payments under non-discretionary charitable contribution matching programs.

(E) a director of the Company who is, or has a Family Member who is, employed as an Executive Officer of another entity where at any time during the past three years any of the Executive Officers of the Company serve[d] on the compensation committee of such other entity; or

(F) a director who is, or has a Family Member who is, a current partner of the Company's outside auditor, or was a partner or employee of the Company's outside auditor who worked on the Company's audit at any time during any of the past three years.[16]

NASDAQ Stock Market Rules section IM-5605 says that "[u]nder paragraph (D), a director who is, or who has a Family Member who is, an executive officer of a charitable organization may not be considered independent if the company makes payments to the charity in excess of the greater of 5% of the charity's revenues or $200,000. However, NASDAQ encourages companies to consider other situations where a director or their Family Member and the company each have a relationship with the same charity when assessing director independence."

As do the new NYSE standards, the NASDAQ "independent" director standards spread their impact throughout the board. A majority of all directors must meet the independence requirements, as must all members of the nominations, compensation, and audit committees (with a limited exception for one director on each of those committees).[17]

NASDAQ adds for the audit committee that each member (i) must meet the SOX independence requirement for that committee and (ii) must "not have participated in the preparation of the financial statements of the company or any current subsidiary of the company at any time during the past three years," but also adds a limited exception from the listing

---

[16]   NASDAQ STOCK MARKET RULE 5605(a)(2) [NASDAQ RULE]. The same SEC order in late 2003 approving changes in the NYSE listing standards approved a major revision of the NASDAQ standards, which included the elaborate definition of independence. SEC Order Approving NYSE and NASDAQ Listing Standard Changes Nov. 2003, *supra* note 4, at *11–13. The text cites to and quotes from the NASDAQ Stock Market Rules as amended and effective in April 2016. Quotations from the NASDAQ Stock Market Rules reprinted with permission from Nasdaq, Inc. Copyright © 2016 by Nasdaq, Inc. All rights reserved.

[17]   NASDAQ RULE 5605 (b)(1), (c)(2)(A), (d)(1)(B), (e)(1)(B).

standard's independence (though, obviously, not from the federal law independence requirement) for one member of the committee.[18]

NASDAQ requires that independent directors have "regularly scheduled meetings at which only independent directors are present ('executive sessions')."[19]

QUESTION ON *NASDAQ* DEFINITION OF *DIRECTOR INDEPENDENCE*

Again, do we really need to categorically determine that a director is not independent because his son-in-law is the president of a charity to which the company made payments of the greater of $200,000 or 5% of the charity's revenues?

E. ENFORCEMENT OF NASDAQ LISTING STANDARDS

NASDAQ has no elaborate, ongoing certification and affirmation requirements similar to those imposed by the NYSE. But it does require that an issuer "must provide NASDAQ with prompt notification after an Executive Officer of the Company becomes aware of any non-compliance by the Company with the requirements of this Rule 5600 Series,"[20] which includes the principal governance listing standards in 5605. NASDAQ may issue a public reprimand to a company that violates the governance listing standards, and NASDAQ delisting provisions specifically reference those standards.[21]

---

[18]   *Id.* 5605(c)(2)(A) & (B). Under both the NYSE and the NASDAQ listing standards, members of the audit committee must meet not only the "independence" test that the exchange imposes, but also the independence test imposed by federal law. NYSE MANUAL § 303A.07(a); NASDAQ RULE 5605(c)(2)(A)(ii). Similarly, both exchanges require that compensation committee members be independent under the exchange definition of that term and that the statutorily prescribed considerations for independence of compensation committee members be taken into account in determining independence. 15 U.S.C. § 78j-3(a)(3); NYSE MANUAL § 303A.02(a)(ii); NASDAQ RULE 5605(d)(2)(A).

[19]   *Id.* 5605(b)(2).

[20]   NASDAQ RULE 5625.

[21]   NASDAQ RULE 5810(c)(4) (staff may issue "a Public Reprimand Letter in cases where the Company has violated a Nasdaq corporate governance or notification listing standard (other than one required by Rule 10A-3 of the Act) and Staff determines that delisting is an inappropriate sanction"). Specific references to corporate governance listing standards in the delisting section of the rules include Rules 5810(c)(2)(A)(ii) (company may submit a plan of compliance where deficiency consists of failure to meet Rule 5605 requirements for boards and board committees), 5810(c)(3)(E) (specific time periods to cure deficiency consisting of failure to meet majority board requirement or audit committee composition requirement); and 5820(d)(2) (Listing Council, to which a company may appeal a Hearings Panel decision that reviewed a staff determination,

F. THE RADICAL NATURE OF
THE DIRECTOR RULES

We are miles from the state corporate law scheme that permits anyone to serve on the board. We are now talking about detailed "independence" qualifications for a majority of the board and for all the members of the key committees. And if a member of an NYSE-listed company's audit committee also serves on the audit committee of more than two other public companies, the board must affirmatively determine that such extensive service does not impair the committee member's ability to perform effectively.[22]

QUESTIONS ON COMPLIANCE WITH THE
"INDEPENDENT DIRECTORS" RULES

How should companies satisfy themselves that possible candidates for board positions meet the independence qualifications? What would you advise as a lawyer? Should the candidates fill out questionnaires? Should they sign under penalty of perjury? Would you recommend an investigation as well? How would the company find that daughter-in-law who is the CEO of a company doing 2% of its business with your client? Is this a role that director search companies might perform?

G. INDEPENDENT DIRECTORS AND
FINANCIAL PERFORMANCE

The shareholder has not purchased stock in order to periodically marvel at the independence of the board. The shareholder wants a return.

There is a significant question as to whether increasing the percentage of independent board members improves corporate financial or stock price performance. Two researchers reported in 1999 the result of their study of

---

may"consider any action taken by a Company during the review process that would have constituted a violation of Nasdaq's corporate governance requirements had the Company's securities been trading on Nasdaq at the time.").

[22]   A "Disclosure Requirement" attached to NYSE MANUAL § 303A.07(a) says:

If an audit committee member simultaneously serves on the audit committees of more than three public companies, the board must determine that such simultaneous service would not impair the ability of such member to effectively serve on the listed company's audit committee and must disclose such determination either on or through the listed company's website or in its annual proxy statement or, if the listed company does not file an annual proxy statement, in its annual report on Form 10-K filed with the SEC. If this disclosure is made on or through the listed company's website, the listed company must disclose that fact in its annual proxy statement or annual report, as applicable, and provide the website address.

the relationship—at 928 large U.S. companies during the period 1985–95—between the percentage of independent directors on a board and various financial metrics, including Tobin's q,[23] return on assets,[24] turnover ratio,[25] operating margin,[26] and sales-per-employee. After controlling for board size, CEO stock ownership, outside director ownership, number of outside 5% owners, firm size, and industry, the researchers' multiple regression analysis found a *negative* correlation between board independence and these financial metrics.[27]

One of those researchers, and another colleague, performed a later study, using data from 1996 to 2003.[28] After controlling for a variety of factors, they found that the ratio of unaffiliated independent directors to total board membership "is *negatively* correlated with contemporaneous and subsequent operating performance"[29] and that "[c]ontrary to claims in the literature, none of the governance measures are correlated with future stock market performance."[30]

While they are certainly not the last word on the matter, these studies give pause when considering whether greater director independence will spur better corporate operating and financial performance.[31]

---

[23]   Tobin's q is a measure of the relationship between a company's market value and its book value and can be measured in somewhat different ways, one of which computes the ratio as equal to *(total assets + market value of equity – book value of equity – deferred taxes) / (total assets)*. Sanjai Bhagat & Brian Bolton, *Corporate Governance and Firm Performance*, 14 J. CORP. FIN. 257, 262 (2008) [Bhagat, *Governance and Firm Performance*].

[24]   Return on assets can be computed as equal to *(operating income) / end-of-year total assets*. *Id.* at 261 tbl.1.

[25]   Turnover ratio is equal to *sales / assets*. Sanjai Bhagat & Bernard Black, *The Uncertain Relationship Between Board Composition and Firm Performance*, 54 BUS. LAW. 921, 946 tbl.3 (1999).

[26]   Operating margin is equal to *(operating income) / sales. Id.*

[27]   *Id.* at 945, 946 tbl.3. The researchers used the logarithm of 1990 sales as the control variable for firm size. *Id.* at 946 tbl.3.

[28]   Bhagat, *Governance and Firm Performance, supra* note 23, at 261 tbl.1 (2008). The study investigated the effects of a variety of corporate governance variables on company financial performance, not just director independence. Table 1 shows the years for which the data for the different variables were available. Data for the percentage of all directors who were unaffiliated and independent came from the years 1996–2003. *Id.* I therefore assume that the computations of the relationship between that variable and company performance were made for those years.

[29]   This study used return on assets and Tobin's q to measure operating results. *Id.* at 266 tbl.4 (Panel D), 267 tbl.5.

[30]   *Id.* at 271.

[31]   On the other hand, more targeted studies suggest that independent directors do improve results under certain circumstances. One study concluded that outside directors improved firm performance when the cost of acquiring information about the firm was low but damaged performance when the cost of information was high. Ran Duchin, et al., *When Are Outside Directors Effective?*, 96 J. FIN. ECON. 195 (2010). The sample covered 1996–2005 and included 15,820 firm-years for 2,897 firms. *Id.* at 201. The researchers measured the cost to the outside director of acquiring information about the firm by (i) the number of analysts covering the firm (the more analysts, the more information about the firm was publicly available, hence the lower the cost to the director of acquiring information); (ii) the dispersion of analyst forecasts (the greater the dispersion, the more opaque the firm, hence the higher the cost of acquiring information); and (iii)

H. GOVERNANCE SCORES AND CORPORATE PERFORMANCE

The emphasis on corporate governance has spawned a new industry, comprised of academics and organizations that rate company governance.

---

analyst forecast error (the larger the error, the more opaque the firm, hence the higher the cost of acquiring information). *Id.* at 201–02. After controlling for such factors as board size, firm age, leverage ratio, and firm size, the researchers found that "[f]or firms in the lowest information cost quartile . . . , a 10% increase in the percentage of outside directors . . . [was] associated with 1.3% higher [return on assets, defined as "operating income before depreciation divided by book assets"], 8.1% higher [Tobin's q, defined as "the market value of assets divided by the book value of assets"], and 3.8% higher annual stock returns over the sample period." *Id.* at 200 (listing some of the control variables), 201 tbl.2 (definition of terms), 204 (quotation). On the other hand, "[f]or firms in the highest information cost quartile . . . , a 10% increase in the percentage of outside directors [was] associated with 1.7% lower [return on assets], 15.8% lower [Tobin's q], and 2.4% lower annual stock returns. . . ." *Id.* at 204.

A second study concluded that independent outside directors at target firms increased shareholder wealth in successful tender offers. James F. Cotter, et al., *Do Independent Directors Enhance Target Shareholder Wealth During Tender Offers?*, 43 J. FIN. ECON. 195 (1996). The researchers studied 169 tender offers during 1989–92. *Id.* at 197. They defined independent outside directors as those who did not work and had not worked for the target company and did not have "substantial business or family ties with management (as indicated by the proxy statement) nor have potential business ties with the firm"; and they defined an independent board as one with at least 50% independent outside directors. *Id.* at 198–99. The authors controlled for the market value of the targets, whether they had poison pills, whether they had golden parachutes, managerial stock ownership, affiliated and unaffiliated blockholders, and industry-adjusted operating return on assets in the three years before the tender offer. *Id.* at 199–200. They defined target shareholder gains as "the percentage price change from 30 days before the first tender offer rumor to the final tender offer bid price if the bid [was] successful, or to the stock price 90 days after the resolution of the tender offer if the bid [was] not successful." *Id.* at 206 tbl.2. The researchers found that, while the target shareholder gains in unsuccessful offers were not statistically different between firms with independent boards and those without, *id.* at 212, "the shareholder gains in successful tender offers [were] . . . 22 percentage points higher" at targets with independent boards. *Id.* at 205.

A third study found that independent directors improved market reaction to bidding firms' announcements of tender offers. John W. Byrd & Kent A. Hickman, *Do Outside Directors Monitor Managers?*, 32 J. FIN. ECON. 195 (1992). The study covered 128 tender offers by 111 firms over the period 1980–87. *Id.* at 199. The researchers defined independent outside directors as those who were neither (i) corporate officers, retirees from the corporation, or family members, nor (ii) affiliated with the corporation in some way such as by providing investment banking, commercial banking, legal, or consulting services or as by holding an officer or director position at a firm supplier or customer. *Id.* at 199. They defined "independent board" to mean a board with at least half independent outside directors. *Id.* at 200. The researchers found that the average abnormal return on the bidder's stock price (return in excess of estimated return) over the two-day period commencing one day before announcement of the tender offer and ending on the day of the announcement was -1.23% for the total sample, only -0.07% for the bidders with independent boards, and -1.86% for the bidders with non-independent boards. *Id.* at 207. The researchers concluded that "less-negative returns to shareholders are associated with boards of directors in which at least half the members are independent of firm managers." *Id.* at 219.

An article that among other things collects citations to the literature reaches this conclusion:

> Undoubtedly, increased board independence may be of some value in controlling some of the agency costs and behavioral biases in acquisition transactions. Several studies have [also] shown that independent directors are more likely to function effectively in specific situations, such as with respect to CEO turnover or some executive compensation decisions. Empirical studies are thus far inconclusive on whether independent directors do much to improve firm performance.

Afra Afsharipour, *A Shareholder['s] Put Option: Counteracting the Acquirer Overpayment Problem*, 96 MINN. L. REV. 1018, 1066–67 (2012) (footnotes omitted).

For example, Institutional Shareholder Services ("ISS")—which, among other things, provides proxy voting recommendations—developed what it called the "Corporate Governance Quotient," or "CGQ."

The indices used to measure the quality of governance frequently included scores not only for the matters this and previous chapters discuss—such as independent directors—but also for corporate rules that affect the ability of hostile bidders to buy the corporation. The notion was that rules serving to protect inefficient management from such bidders (who wish to take over a company, throw out the poor-performing managers, replace them with more competent executives, and thereby raise the value of the company) constitute poor governance because they interfere with the market for corporate control.

Here is a description of various indices, circa 2008. As you read, note the different sets of variables the indices use, reflecting very determined attempts to find some formula that would usefully summarize governance quality at any company in one number or a few numbers.

> *Gompers, Ishii, and Metrick's G-Index.*—The creation of firm-level corporate governance indices began with GIM's research, which was published in 2003 but widely circulated in 2001. GIM constructed their index from data on the governance characteristics of over 1,000 firms, including most large public corporations (the Fortune 500 and Standard & Poor's 500), compiled by the Investor Responsibility Research Center (IRRC), a nonprofit research group that served institutional investors. . . .
>
> GIM constructed a governance index that they considered to reflect the "balance of power between shareholders and managers." Relying on the IRRC's judgment as to which corporate governance mechanisms investors considered to be important, GIM added up the number of provisions that each firm had of the twenty-four items, assigning one point for each provision that they viewed as restricting shareholder rights, and one point for the absence of either of two provisions that they viewed as constraining manager power and thereby enhancing shareholder rights.[32]

* * *

> The groupings of the governance provisions in the [GIM] index are as follows:
>
> > (1) "Delay": Four provisions for delaying hostile takeover bidders (the presence of blank check preferred stock, a

---

[32]   Sanjai Bhagat, et al., *The Promise and Peril of Corporate Governance Indices*, 108 COLUM. L. REV. 1803, 1819–20 (2008) (footnotes omitted) [Bhagat, *Promise and Peril*]. Quotations from this article reprinted with permission from the Columbia Law Review.

classified board, restrictions on shareholders' ability to call special meetings, and restrictions on shareholders' ability to act by written consent);

(2) "Voting": Six provisions involving shareholder voting rights (the presence of cumulative voting, confidential voting, supermajority voting for business combinations, dual class stock, and limitations to shareholders' ability to amend the bylaws or certificate of incorporation);

(3) "Protection": Six provisions protecting directors and officers from legal liability or compensating them for termination (limited liability provisions, indemnification provisions in charters or bylaws, indemnification contracts, golden parachutes, severance contracts not conditioned on control changes, and compensation plans with changes-in-control provisions);

(4) "Other": Six other takeover defenses (the presence of antigreenmail charter provisions, fair price provisions, other constituent provisions, poison pills, silver parachutes, and pension parachutes);

(5) "State": Incorporation in a state with one of six state takeover laws (antigreenmail, business combination freeze, control share acquisition, fair price, other constituencies, and redemption rights statutes).

Because of overlap between some of the tracked firm-level provisions and state takeover laws, the twenty-eight tracked provisions are collapsed into twenty-four unique provisions.[33]

* * *

Bebchuk, Cohen, and Ferrell's E-Index.—Lucian Bebchuk, Alma Cohen, and Allen Ferrell (BCF) advanced a competing governance index to the G-Index, one composed of a subset of G-Index factors. Accepting as the most probable explanation of GIM's results that corporate governance positively affects performance, BCF sought to construct what they regarded to be a better-motivated index in relation to theory and intuition regarding the efficacy of particular defenses. They selected the six IRRC takeover-defense provisions that they considered to contribute the most to managerial entrenchment. These provisions included poison pills and staggered boards—the combination of which Bebchuk had previously emphasized was the most potent of takeover defenses—as well as golden parachutes. BCF's inclusion of golden parachutes as one of the more formidable defenses is, however,

---

[33]   *Id.* at 1870.

problematic because there is a theoretical and empirical literature that, at odds with BCF's contention, suggests that golden parachutes in fact facilitate takeovers.

In constructing their index, BCF followed GIM's approach, according equal weight (one point) to the presence of any of the six provisions. The index is called the "Entrenchment Index" or "E-Index." BCF expected their index to outperform GIM's as a predictor of corporate performance because the E-Index contained the provisions that, in BCF's view, were most likely to thwart a hostile takeover.[34]

* * *

Brown and Caylor's Gov-Score Index.—Lawrence Brown and Marcus Caylor created a more extensive governance index than the G and E indices, using firm-level governance information obtained from ISS. Brown and Caylor's index, which they call "Gov-Score," is a sum of fifty-one factors (a subset of the sixty-one factors and three combination measures collected by ISS)—nine are in the G-Index, and a tenth, incorporation in a state with a takeover statute, is a composite of the four state-takeover-statute components of the G-Index. Following BCF's refinement of the G-Index, Brown and Caylor also constructed "Gov-7," a subindex consisting of seven of the components in Gov-Score.[35]

---

[34]   *Id.* at 1821–22 (footnotes omitted).

[35]   *Id.* at 1823 (footnotes omitted). Here is a description of the variables in the Brown and Caylor index:

> The groupings of ISS minimally acceptable corporate governance standards comprising Gov-Score (factors also in the G-Index are in italics) are as follows:
>
> (1) "Audit" (four factors): Audit committee consists solely of independent outside directors; auditors ratified by shareholders at most recent annual meeting; consulting fees paid to auditors less than audit fees paid; company has formal policy on auditor rotation;
>
> (2) "Board of directors" (seventeen factors): Managers respond to shareholder proposals within twelve months of meeting; CEO serves on no more than two other public corporation boards; all directors attended at least 75% of board meetings or had valid excuse for non-attendance; size of board between six and fifteen; no former CEO is a director; no CEO related-party transactions listed in proxy; board has more than 50% independent outside directors; compensation committee comprised solely of independent outside directors; CEO and chair positions are separated or lead director is specified; shareholders vote on directors selected to fill vacancies; *annual director elections*; shareholder approval to change board size; nominating committee comprised solely of independent outside directors; governance committee meets at least once a year; *cumulative voting rights*; board guidelines in proxy statement; policy requiring outside directors to serve on no more than five additional boards;
>
> (3) "Charter/bylaws" (seven factors): *Majority vote for merger; no poison pill or shareholder approved pill; shareholders can call special meetings; majority vote to amend charter or bylaws; shareholders may act by nonunanimous written consent; no blank check preferred stock; board cannot amend bylaws without shareholder approval or can do so only under limited circumstances;*

* * *

Proprietary Governance Indices.—The commercial indices ranking public corporations' governance quality, which are provided by proxy research and advisory services, differ distinctively from the academic indices on several important dimensions. First, firms' scores on the proprietary indices do not consist of summations of equally weighted factors. Rather, commercial index providers vary the weights accorded different governance factors, using either their discretion regarding the importance of the factor or quantitative analyses to determine the appropriate weights. Second, commercial indices deemphasize takeover defenses, in contrast to the indices constructed by GIM and BCF; for example, some do not even include defenses as a

---

(4) "Director education" (one factor): At least one director has participated in [an] ISS-accredited director education program;

(5) "Executive and director compensation" (ten factors): No interlocking directors on compensation committee; nonemployees do not participate in pension plans; no option repricing in past three years; shareholder approval of stock incentive plans; directors receive all or part of fees in stock; no corporate loans to executives to exercise options; last time shareholders voted on pay plan ISS did not deem the cost to be excessive; average options granted in past three years as percentage of basic shares outstanding no more than 3% ("option burn rate"); prohibition on option repricing; stock options are expensed;

(6) "Ownership" (four factors): All directors with more than one year of service own stock; officers' and directors' stock ownership at least 1% and not over 30%; executives subject to stock ownership guidelines; directors subject to stock ownership guidelines;

(7) "Progressive practices" (seven factors): Mandatory retirement age for directors; board performance regularly reviewed; board-approved CEO succession plan in place; board has outside advisors; directors must submit resignation upon change in job status; outside directors meet without CEO and disclose number of times they meet; director term limits;

(8) "State of incorporation" (one factor): Incorporation in state with no takeover statutes.

All of the factors in ISS's "charter/bylaw" grouping are also in the G-Index; the remaining G-Index components included in Gov-Score are in the "board of directors" category. In addition, although Brown and Caylor do not identify the state of incorporation factor as in the G-Index, it is essentially a composite of the four components in that index's "State" grouping.

The subset of factors in Gov-7 (ISS grouping in parentheses; factors also in the E-Index in italics) are as follows:

(1)   *Annual director elections* (Board of directors);

(2)   *No poison pill or shareholder approved pill* (Charter/bylaws);

(3)   No option repricing in past three years (Executive and director compensation);

(4)   Directors subject to stock ownership guidelines (Ownership);

(5)   All directors attended at least 75% of board meetings or had valid excuse for non-attendance (Board of directors);

(6)   Average options granted in past three years as percentage of basic shares outstanding no more than 3% (Executive and director compensation);

(7)   Board guidelines are in each proxy statement (Board of directors).

Id. at 1870–72.

governance factor, while others place greater weights on the non-takeover-related factors (internal governance measures such as board and executive compensation attributes). Third, some commercial indices are relative rankings of firms in relation to other firms in their industry, market, or geographic region, whereas the academic indices are absolute rankings of governance quality independent of the practices of comparable firms. Finally, the leading provider by far of this type of service, ISS, updates the factors in its index to capture trends in corporate governance. For example, it recently incorporated two items that have become the focus of activist institutional investor attention—majority voting for directors and option backdating—while eliminating option expensing (since expensing is now required).[36]

---

[36]   *Id.* at 1824–25 (footnotes omitted). Here is a more elaborate description of the various commercial indices:

1.   *The Corporate Library's Board Effectiveness Rating.*—The Corporate Library (TCL), an investor research firm established by investor activist Neil Minow, produces research reports and commentary on corporate governance and does not provide consulting or other services to firms that it evaluates. It has developed a proprietary measure of the quality of firms' governance, which measures a "Board's Effectiveness," and is a letter grade from A to F, representing an assessment of the effectiveness of four governance components of the company's governance quality. The components of the rating are as follows:

    (1)   Board Composition and Succession Planning;

    (2)   CEO Compensation;

    (3)   Takeover Defenses;

    (4)   Board Level Accounting Concerns.

TCL notes that its rating focuses on "board actions [rather than] board policies and structures," with the exception of the specific board composition component (number (1) above). The component analysis is not based on compliance with a best practices "checklist" but on quantitative screens related to board behavior and decision making and on what it considers to be poor governance practices, containing "more than 1,100 individual data points." The quantitative screening is supplemented by the more subjective analysis of its staff to compute the final rating.

    TCL has also calculated a Best Practices Compliance score or benchmark, developed from other organizations' guidelines, that ranged from 0 to 100, and included such factors as whether the firm has a classified board, majority outside directors, independent chair or lead director, audit committee of only independent directors, formal governance policy, and the characteristics of directors (number who are over seventy years old, serve on more than four other boards, and have more than fifteen years of service). However, it considered the effectiveness rating and not the compliance score as the preferable metric of a company's governance quality, and it no longer refers to the compliance benchmark in the publicly available material on its website.

2.   *GovernanceMetrics   International's   Market   and   Industry   Indices.*— GovernanceMetrics International is an international governance rating organization, founded by individuals experienced in the investor relations and advising industry, that markets research and analyses principally to institutional investors. It provides advisory services to a variety of nonprofit organizations, such as stock exchanges, as well as to investors, but it does not provide proxy voting advisory services. Its "overall rating" governance score, which ranges from one to ten and is derived from a statistical algorithm assigning numerical values to individual metrics falling within six general governance areas, is computed as a comparative score based on the governance practices and policies of other firms in the rated company's home state or region (the "home market" rating) or

all firms in GMI's universe (the "global" rating). The governance areas ("Research Categories") are as follows:

(1)   Board Accountability;

(2)   Financial Disclosure and Internal Controls;

(3)   Shareholder Rights;

(4)   Executive Compensation;

(5)   Market for Control and Ownership Base;

(6)   Corporate Behavior and Corporate Social Responsibility Issues.

3.   *Institutional Shareholder Services' Corporate Governance Quotient.*—ISS is the market leader in the provision of proxy advisory and corporate governance services to institutional investors. It also provides governance and proxy consulting services to issuers. It has been in the advisory business for over two decades, during which it acquired competitors and expanded its services (acquiring most recently the proxy research firm IRRC in 2005, before it was itself acquired in 2006). ISS rates companies according to a "Corporate Governance Quotient," which is derived from sixty-three governance factors (also referred to as governance criteria) that are grouped into four key governance areas, combining eight governance categories on which companies are evaluated. The weights assigned to the individual components are a function of their correlations with performance measures. The ratings are calculated as percentages indicating where a firm stands in relation to other firms in its industry or market. For example, a value of 97.5 means that the company outperformed 97.5% of firms in its industry or stock market index, according to ISS's statistical algorithm combining governance factors. The governance areas and weights are as follows:

(1)   Board of directors—40%;

(2)   Compensation—30%;

(3)   Takeover defenses—20%;

(4)   Audit—10%.

The eight most important governance variables that enter into the rating, in order of their weighting are

(1)   Audit committee with all independent outside directors;

(2)   Average options granted in past three years are no more than 2% of basic shares outstanding, or within one standard deviation of industry mean ("option burn rate");

(3)   All audit committee members are financial experts;

(4)   Board controlled by supermajority (over 90%) of independent outside directors;

(5)   Board has only one nonindependent director;

(6)   Directors subject to stock ownership requirements;

(7)   Board controlled by supermajority (between 75% and 90%) of independent outsiders;

(8)   Incorporation in state with no takeover statutes.

The sixteen performance measures ISS used to test its governance rating factors, which are divided into four categories of performance, are as follows:

(1)   Risk (two measures): Volatility; Altman's Z-score (probability of bankruptcy);

(2)   Market (two measures): Total Shareholder Return; Tobin's Q;

(3)   Valuation (three ratio measures): Price to Book; Price to Cash Flow; Price to Earnings;

(4)   Profitability (nine measures): Dividend; Return on Invested Capital; Return on Equity; Return on Investment; Cash Flow Return on Investment; Net Profit Margin; EBITDA Margin; Sales Growth; Free Cash Flow to Sales.

The factors that ISS uses change over time, reflecting changing trends in corporate governance. For example, it no longer includes a factor for whether firms expense options, because that accounting treatment is now required and no longer voluntary. In addition, it now includes a factor for whether the company has majority-vote director elections—a governance issue that first appeared on activist institutional investors' agendas in any serious form in 2005—and a factor for whether the company has backdated options, an accounting issue—some would call it a scandal—that first came to light in 2006.

As you can see, the indices were many in number and complex in construction. But are they of any use? In particular, are they useful tools for investors who seek a return?

Looking at numbers for the 1,500 largest U.S. corporations during the period 1998–2002, Sanjai Bhagat and two co-authors found no positive correlations between such indices and return on assets.[37] They also found largely *negative* correlations between the indices and stock return.[38] In contrast, the researchers found a positive correlation between the median dollar value of director stockholding—a much simpler measure than the indices—and return on assets and stock return.[39]

---

4. *Egan-Jones Proxy Services' Corporate Governance Ratings.*—Egan-Jones Proxy Services provides assistance in proxy voting, offering research, recommendations, and voting services (such as automated vote execution, recordkeeping, and vote disclosure reporting). Although its affiliated business has provided credit rating analysis for many years, it began to offer proxy recommendations commercially in 2003 (in conjunction with the increased emphasis on corporate governance and particularly the new SEC regulations regarding disclosure of mutual funds' voting). In addition to offering general voting services evaluating the impact on shareholder value, it provides voting guidelines tailored to certain labor union funds' needs, which ensure that "the rights and interests of labor are respected." Egan-Jones provides an "overall" rating and specific ratings on the following five factors:

> (1) Voting process;
>
> (2) Board independence;
>
> (3) Board skills;
>
> (4) Financial performance;
>
> (5) Disclosure/controls.

How, if at all, it combines the five factors into an overall rating is not publicly disclosed. All six ratings are in the form of letter grades (with pluses and minuses).

5. *Glass, Lewis & Company's Board Accountability Index.*—Glass, Lewis & Company, which provides research and advisory services to institutional investors, was established in 2003 by Lynn Turner, Chief Accountant of the Securities and Exchange Commission during Arthur Levitt's chairmanship. It markets a governance ranking, termed the "Board Accountability Index," that is derived from BCF's research, and which it considers a "governance-enhanced" S&P 500 index. It uses a "modified market-cap weighting algorithm" that adjusts an S&P 500 index company's weight by the presence or absence of five of the six components of BCF's entrenchment index. The component that Glass Lewis excludes is the supermajority requirement for charter amendments.

Id. at 1872–76 (footnotes omitted).

[37]   *Id.* at 1844–45 & tbl.1. They also found a *negative* correlation between return on assets and the percentage of independent directors on the board. *Id.* The researchers used simultaneous equations which controlled for a variety of factors, including leverage and industry performance. *Id.* at 1841, 1844.

[38]   *Id.* at 1847–48 tbl.2.

[39]   *Id.* at 1844–45 & tbl.1, 1847–48 tbl.2. *And see* Anup Agrawal and Tareque Nasser, Blockholders on Boards and CEO Compensation, Turnover and Firm Valuation 7–8 (defining an "IDB" as "an independent director who is (or represents) a blockholder" who either controls at least 1% of the equity voting power or owns at least 1% of the equity cash flow rights), 25 and tbl.2 on unnumbered page (using a sample of 11,547 firm-years over 1998–2006), (Sept. 2012) (unpublished draft) (on file with author and available at http://bama.ua.edu/~aagrawal/IDB-CEO.pdf). The researchers found, after controlling for other variables, that an individual or hedge fund IDB on a board is associated with lower CEO compensation but a private equity IDB is associated with higher CEO compensation, *id.* at 16–17, that (after adding more controls) an IDB is associated with a much higher probability of CEO turnover in the face of poor market-adjusted stock return,

The researchers concluded

that there is no consistent relation between governance indices and measures of corporate performance. Namely, there is no one "best" measure of corporate governance: The most effective governance system depends on context and on firms' specific circumstances. It would therefore be difficult for an index, or any one variable, to capture nuances critical for making informed decisions. As a consequence, we conclude that governance indices are highly imperfect instruments for determining how to vote corporate proxies, let alone for making portfolio investment decisions, and that investors and policymakers should exercise caution in attempting to draw inferences regarding a firm's quality or future stock market performance from its ranking on any particular corporate governance measure.[40]

A second set of researchers found that three of the commercial scoring systems—the Corporate Governance Quotient (CGQ) developed by ISS, the GovernanceMetrics International (GMI) measure, and The Corporate Library (TCL) rating—awarded scores that, at the end of 2005, were not correlated (except for a moderate correlation between the CGQ and the GMI scores); meaning, roughly, that any one company might receive a high score from one of the systems and a low score from another.[41] Thus, whatever else they measured, they did not test for some consensus view of good governance.

The researchers also tested the extent to which scores from these indices at the end of 2005 predicted events that occurred in following years. They found that (i) the GMI score improved the prediction of which firms would restate financials—over an estimating model built around other financial factors associated with restatements—but only by raising the percent correctly predicted from 63.19% to 65.24%, while "[t]here [was] no

---

id. at 21–22, and that an IDB is associated with a higher industry-adjusted Tobin's q, *id.* at 22–23, a measure that the authors used for firm valuation, *id.* at 22. The researchers concluded that "these effects are substantial and are generally larger when an IDB serves on the board's compensation committee," and, further, that "individual investors" who are IDBs "drive most of our results." *Id.* at 26.

[40]   Bhagat, *Promise and Peril, supra* note 32, at 1803 (abstract).

On the other hand, two academics concluded that corporate performance correlated well to ISS's CGQ on September 26, 2003. Lawrence D. Brown & Marcus L. Caylor, Corporate Governance Study: The Correlation between Corporate Governance and Company Performance 6 n.1 (2004). They found, for example, "firms in the bottom decile of industry-adjusted CGQ® . . . have 5-year returns that are 3.95% below the industry average, while firms in the top decile of industry-adjusted CGQ have 5-year returns that are 7.91 over the industry-adjusted average." *Id.* at 1. Similarly, firms with industry-adjusted CGQs in the bottom 10% showed -0.85 return on assets, -4.86 return on equity, and -0.75 return on investment, compared with 9.78, 18.98, and 17.93 for firms in the top 10%. *Id.* at tbl.2 (Panel A).

[41]   Robert M. Daines, et al., *Rating the Ratings: How Good Are Commercial Governance Ratings?*, 98 J. FIN. ECON. 439, 443 (2010) (describing data set), 444 (reporting on correlation test).

evidence that other ratings could predict restatements in a meaningful way";[42] (ii) none of the three significantly predicted industry-adjusted return on assets (ROA) once contemporaneous ROA was taken into account;[43] (iii) none significantly predicted Tobin's q when contemporaneous Tobin's q was included in the model;[44] and (iv) there was some statistical relationship between the CGQ and TCL scores at the end of 2005 and excess stock returns three years later, but not clearly of a size that would direct successful stock trading once transaction costs were taken into account.[45] All in all, the researchers concluded "that these governance ratings have either limited or no success in predicting firm performance or other outcomes of interest to shareholders . . . [and that] even when there is a statistical association with future outcomes, the substantive economic effect is small."[46]

In 2010, ISS substituted, for its CGQ, a new measurement for corporate governance called "Governance Risk Indicators." Interestingly, ISS stated expressly that the Governance Risk Indicators were not intended to predict future company performance or returns.[47] In February 2013, ISS replaced the Governance Risk Indicators with Governance QuickScore.[48]

In early 2014, ISS updated its scoring system to QuickScore 2.0.[49] The new system provided scores for a company on each of four factors (which ISS called "pillars"): Board Structure, Shareholder Rights, Compensation/Remuneration, and Audit.[50] The scoring took into account some 200 variables.[51] The score for any given company on any given factor (or "pillar") was an integer between 1 and 10, indicating the decile ranking

---

[42]   *Id.* at 447.

[43]   *Id.* at 450.

[44]   *Id.* at 451.

[45]   *Id.* at 454.

[46]   *Id.* at 460.

[47]   RiskMetrics Group, *FAQ Transition Plan for Institutional Investors*, question 16 and answer, http://www.issgovernance.com/files/FAQ-GRId-institutional.pdf (last visited May 6, 2016). *See* a sample Governance Risk Indicator report at http://www.issgovernance.com/files/SampleGRIdForProxy.pdf (last visited May 6, 2015) and a lengthy explanation of the scoring system at http://www.issgovernance.com/files/GRId_Tech_Doc_Final_20100915.pdf (last visited May 6, 2016).

[48]   Broc Romanek, *Governance Ratings: ISS Changes "GRId" to "QuickScore,"* THECORPORATECOUNSEL.NET. (Jan. 23, 2013) http://www.thecorporatecounsel.net/Blog/2013/01/webcast-pat-mcgurns-forecast-for-1.html. ISS said that the score was constructed by using "a quantitatively-driven methodology that looks for correlations between governance factors and key financial metrics, with a secondary policy-based overlay that aligns the qualitative aspect of governance with ISS policy." *New Scoring and Screening Solution Designed to Help Institutional Investors Identify Governance Risk in Portfolio Companies*, ISSGOVERNANCE.COM (Feb. 25, 2013) http://www.issgovernance.com/iss-launches-governance-quickscore/.

[49]   *ISS Governance QuickScore 2.0: Overview and Updates* (Jan. 2014), http://www.iss governance.com/file/files/ISSGovernanceQuickScore2.0.pdf (last visited May 6, 2016).

[50]   *Id.* at 3.

[51]   *Id.*

into which the company fell for that factor, relative to other companies in the same "index" (apparently, for the U.S., either the Russell 3000 or the S&P 500) and the same region (e.g., U.S.)—with a score of 1 meaning that the company was in the top 10% for the pillar.[52] ISS then also provided an overall score.[53]

In late 2014, ISS introduced QuickScore 3.0.[54] This system continued to use four pillars: Board Structure, Shareholder Rights & Takeover Defenses, Compensation/Remuneration, and Audit & Risk Oversight.[55] ISS expanded coverage with this new system to companies in emerging markets and to more companies in Europe.[56] It also added a factor that considers board response to controversies,[57] and incorporated into audit and risk analysis "an in-depth review of investigations and enforcement actions including reviewing the type of regulatory investigation and the materiality of penalties or resolutions to such cases."[58]

You can find the ISS scores on Yahoo Finance. Thus, a check of Yahoo Finance on June 28, 2016, showed General Electric Company's ISS Governance QuickScore as 2. The pillar scores were Audit: 2; Board: 7; Shareholder Rights: 1; Compensation: 4.[59]

ISS has itself changed over the years. MSCI, Inc. bought ISS in 2010, then sold it to a private equity firm in 2014.[60]

Other major commercial governance rating companies also experienced organizational change and also changed their rating systems. GovernanceMetrics International and The Corporate Library combined in 2010 (into a company called GMI Ratings, which also included the formerly independent Audit Integrity).[61] In 2014, MSCI acquired GMI Ratings.[62] MSCI produces what it calls "ESG ratings."[63] These ratings address

---

[52]   *Id.* at 3, 9.

[53]   *Id.* at 3.

[54]   *ISS Governance QuickScore 3.0: Overview and Updates* (Oct. 2014, revised May 2015), http://www.issgovernance.com/file/products/quickscore_techdoc.pdf (last visited May 6, 2016).

[55]   *Id.* at 3.

[56]   *Id.* at 4.

[57]   *Id.* at 4, 27.

[58]   *Id.* at 4.

[59]   http://finance.yahoo.com/q/pr?s=GE+Profile (last visited June 28, 2016). For a law firm summary of the new QuickScore, *see* Venable LLP, *ISS Introduces QuickScore 3.0* (Nov. 6, 2014), https://www.venable.com/files/Publication/193ce5f8-f10c-442c-a27d-145cfd16137a/Presentation/PublicationAttachment/4b40c851-daa3-4091-888b-1961eb744795/Venable_Maryland_Law_Memo-ISS_Introduces_QuickScore_3.0.pdf.

[60]   Reuters, *Update 3: MSCI to sell proxy advisory firm ISS for $364 million* (Mar. 18, 2014), http://www.reuters.com/article/2014/03/18/msci-sale-idUSL3N0MF35M20140318.

[61]   *See* the description of Governance Metrics International at http://www.csrhub.com/data source/governance-metrics-international/.

[62]   MSCI, *Our Story*, https://www.msci.com/our-story (last visited May 6, 2016).

[63]   MSCI, *MSCI ESG Ratings*, https://www.msci.com/esg-integration (last visited May 6, 2016).

environmental, social, and governance issues, particularized by industry, and weight the scores on those issues, producing an industry-adjusted rating from AAA to CCC.[64] GMI also computes an Accounting and Governance Risk (AGR®) rating for over 29,000 companies, which is designed to identify companies with a higher risk of publishing misleading financial numbers.[65] The model focuses on "extreme values in accounting and non-accounting metrics that may be indicators of opaque and potentially misleading financial reporting," and ranks companies in percentiles by region, with lower scores indicating higher risk and companies categorized as "very aggressive" (lowest 10%), "aggressive" (next 25%), "average" (next 50%), or "conservative" (next 15%).[66]

As you can see, the commercial ratings have deconstructed over time so that the providers offer ratings on specific subjects, including, in MSCI's case, scores on environmental and social matters.

———————————

QUESTIONS ON GOVERNANCE SCORING SYSTEMS

Do you think that governance scoring systems are likely to help shareholders when the shareholders vote in director elections? Are the scoring systems likely to help investors who are considering whether to purchase the stock of different companies with different ratings? If you were buying stock, would you try to get one or more of these ratings for a company that you were considering? Would you pay for that information? Would you pay as much for that information as the information you could obtain from a traditional investor service such as Value Line?

If you were advising a company, would you tell the directors that they should pay attention to the company's governance rating? Would you counsel the company to pay money to a consultant to find out how to raise the rating?

If you were an enforcement official at the SEC, would you use the GMI AGR ratings to help you allocate investigative resources? Would you target for possible investigation companies that the rating system puts into the "very aggressive" category?

———————————

---

[64] MSCI, *ESG Ratings Methodology Executive Summary*, 2–5 (May 2015), https://www. msci.com/documents/10199/123a2b2b-1395-4aa2-a121-ea14de6d708a (last visited May 6, 2016). *See* two pages from a sample report at MSCI, *MSCI ESG Ratings*, https://www.msci.com/ documents/1296102/1636401/MSCI_ESG_Ratings.pdf/9f0a999b-4419-4a0a-b6ef-0248f40ca2c9 (last visited May 6, 2016).

[65] MSCI, MSCI ESG AGR FACTSHEET (Oct. 2014), https://www.msci.com/documents/ 1296102/1636401/MSCI_ESG_AGR_factsheet_July2015.pdf/1276b028-aee5-40e5-b1ad-85a2ac664841 (last visited May 6, 2016).

[66] *Id.* (showing pages from sample report).

I. SHAREHOLDER INFLUENCE IN CORPORATE GOVERNANCE

Shareholders participate in corporate governance by voting—voting for directors and voting on other matters submitted to shareholders.[67] Governance rules affect that voting.

Different types of investors. Different shareholders have different appetites for opposing the issuer on a matter submitted for a stockholder vote. Retail shareholders seldom have an incentive to initiate opposition voting campaigns. If they are well advised, they own a diversified portfolio, with only a small percentage of their total holdings in any one stock. The time and effort that it would take to initiate a voting campaign—for example, to unseat all members of a compensation committee that the investor believed awarded too much compensation to a CEO—might not justify the marginal gain in the value of the stock that the investor owned in the relevant company, even if the investor's campaign proved successful and that success produced some incremental increase in stock return.

Mutual funds may concentrate on buying and selling stocks, rather than trying to change the direction of companies by voting stock.

Union pension funds and the organizations that manage the money in public employee retirement systems, however, are more active. So are some hedge funds.

The general structure of director elections. In the typical corporate election, the nominations committee of the board of directors renominates the sitting directors. The company sends out a proxy statement asking shareholders to sign a proxy form effectively voting their shares for the renominated directors. Federal law requires that the proxy form provide shareholders with the means to express their displeasure with the nominees by either "withholding" their votes from the nominated candidates or voting against all of them (if state law allows), or withholding as to, or voting against (if state law allows), any one of them.[68] Of course,

---

[67] For example, in 2003, the SEC approved NYSE and NASDAQ rules requiring shareholder approval for most equity compensation plans and material revisions to those plans. Self-Regulatory Organizations; New York Stock Exchange, Inc. and National Association of Securities Dealers, Inc.; Order Approving NYSE and Nasdaq Proposed Rule Changes and Nasdaq Amendment No. 1 and Notice of Filing and Order Granting Accelerated Approval to NYSE Amendments No. 1 and 2 and Nasdaq Amendments No. 2 and 3 Thereto Relating to Equity Compensation Plans, 2003 WL 21488831 (SEC June 30, 2003). The current rules are at NYSE MANUAL § 303A.08 and NASDAQ RULE 5635(c).

[68] Federal regulations require that a proxy form to vote shares in a director election "shall clearly provide . . . [one of several defined] means for security holders to withhold authority to vote for each nominee," or, "[i]f applicable state law gives legal effect to votes cast against a nominee," the proxy form may "provide a similar means for security holders to vote against each nominee" either instead of, or in addition to, the opportunity to withhold votes for the nominee. 17 C.F.R. § 240.14a-4(b)(2) & Instruction 2.

anyone other than the sitting board can run a slate of directors and seek proxies for their election. But that seldom happens.

Instead, in the great majority of corporate elections, the directors nominated by the sitting board run unopposed. One study of 2,488 director elections at public companies during 1996 to 2005 found only 4 at which the number of nominees did not exactly match the number of directors to be elected.[69] And, in the great majority of cases, each director receives an overwhelming number of affirmative votes out of all the votes cast for his or her seat—i.e., very few shares are withheld or voted against. Thus, in the same sample, 94.27% of shares voting were cast for director nominees on average.[70]

Nevertheless, shareholder votes even in an uncontested election can make a difference. Suppose, for example, that shareholders believe that the CEO is overpaid. The shareholders might withhold their votes from members of the company's compensation committee, particularly from the chair of that committee.[71] The study just referenced found that

> a 1% decrease in the average vote for a compensation committee member reduces unexplained CEO compensation [compensation not explained by size of company, prior-year stock return, industry, and year] by $143,000 in the next year . . . [and] a 1% decrease in the compensation committee chair votes is associated with a reduction in unexplained CEO compensation by approximately $220,000 in the following year.[72]

Recent reforms that increase shareholder voting clout, including majority voting. Many individuals hold indirect interests in stock, through mutual funds. The individuals buy shares in a fund. The fund, in turn, buys stock in publicly traded companies (and sometimes private companies), called the fund's "portfolio companies." The fund holds the right to vote the stock in director elections at portfolio companies and on other matters requiring shareholder votes at the portfolio companies. For many years, mutual funds overwhelmingly—and seemingly without much analysis— voted the stock in whatever way the board and management of the portfolio companies recommended.

---

[69]   Jie Cai, et al., *Electing Directors*, 64 J. FINANCE 2389, 2390 (2009) [Cai, *Electing Directors*].

[70]   *Id*. at 2397 tbl.1.

[71]   While the mean percentage of "for" votes is quite high,

the range of votes is very large; some boards, as well as some individual directors, receive less than 40% of the votes. In addition, the within firm range is interesting. The average range within a firm is 7.4%, but the maximum is 57%. A dispersion within a firm implies more dissatisfaction with a particular director.

Id. at 2396.

[72]   *Id*. at 2410, with "abnormal CEO compensation" explained at 2398.

In 2003, the SEC issued two sets of rules designed to require that mutual funds vote the shares in a more thoughtful manner and to permit the shareholders in the funds to monitor those votes. First, the SEC promulgated a rule requiring the managers running the funds to adopt and implement "written policies and procedures that are reasonably designed to ensure that the [managers] vote[ ]" portfolio company shares "in the best interest of" the funds.[73] Second, the SEC adopted a rule requiring the mutual funds to disclose their voting in corporate elections at portfolio companies.[74] While not giving shareholders in the mutual funds more power, this second reform permits the owners of shares in the mutual funds to know how the funds are voting their stock in portfolio companies, thereby giving those beneficial holders at least some ability to hold the funds accountable for such votes.

But probably the most important shareholder voting reform in recent years has been the adoption of majority voting rules at a large number of public corporations. Here is a description of the background and scale of that reform, with the following passage taken from a note published in 2007:

> Director elections in the United States have traditionally been conducted by plurality voting. Under a plurality voting regime, a candidate for director must receive a greater number of the votes cast in an election than any other candidate in order to obtain a board seat, even if he or she does not receive an outright majority.[75]

> * * *

> [T]he vast majority of U.S. board elections are uncontested, with the number of candidates equaling the number of seats up for election. Since plurality voting is the norm in director elections, the unopposed candidates—who have invariably been selected by

---

[73]   Proxy Voting by Investment Advisers, 68 Fed. Reg. 6585, 6586, 6593 (Feb. 7, 2003) [Proxy Voting by Investment Advisers] (now providing, at 17 C.F.R. § 275.206(4)-6(a), that it is a "fraudulent, deceptive, or manipulative act, practice or course of business" under the Investment Advisers Act to exercise voting authority for a fund without adopting and implementing such policies and procedures).

[74]   Disclosure of Proxy Voting Policies and Proxy Voting Records by Registered Management Investment Companies, 68 Fed. Reg. 6564, 6581–85 (Feb. 7, 2003) (requiring funds to disclose their votes in an SEC filing available to the public via the Commission's database and revising various forms to mandate that mutual funds advise their shareholders that they can obtain fund voting records by accessing the SEC database or by requesting information from the fund or, if the fund posts its voting record on its website, by visiting the fund website); *see also* 17 C.F.R. § 270.30b1-4; SEC, Form N-1A, at Item 17(f) (2016), https://www.sec.gov/about/forms/formn-1a.pdf; SEC, Annual Report of Proxy Voting Record of Registered Management Investment Company, Form N-PX, http://www.sec.gov/about/forms/formn-px.pdf.

[75]   Vincent Falcone, Note, *Majority Voting in Director Elections: A Simple, Direct, and Swift Solution?* 2007 COLUM. BUS. L. REV. 844, 847 (2007). Quotations from this article reprinted with permission from the Columbia Business Law Review, this article in its Vol. 2007, Issue 3.

the corporation—are guaranteed board seats even if more votes are withheld than are cast in their favor. Thus, the plurality standard and the limits of the American proxy voting system have combined to ensure that incumbent directors will be reelected even if only a single vote is cast in their favor and every other shareholder stands opposed.[76]

* * *

Since its inception, the majority voting movement has grown with remarkable speed and met with considerable success. In 2004, twelve shareholder majority voting proposals were voted on, garnering an average vote of 12%. In 2005, shareholders voted on sixty-seven proposals, receiving an average vote of 44.3%. In 2006, eighty-four shareholder proposals came to a vote, with average approval of 47.7%. As of August 21, 2007, forty-six proposals have been voted on, averaging 49.4% shareholder approval. In response to actual or anticipated shareholder proposals, more than 180 companies have adopted some form of majority voting, including over 52% of the S&P 500 and 45% of Fortune 500 companies. Furthermore, the Delaware, Washington, and California legislatures have adopted statutes facilitating the adoption of a majority voting standard, and the American Bar Association ("ABA") has amended the MBCA to the same end.[77]

* * *

Most corporations adopting a majority voting standard have chosen to follow the "director resignation policy" approach, pioneered by Pfizer in June 2005. Under Pfizer's corporate governance policy, "[i]n an uncontested election, any nominee for Director who receives a greater number of votes 'withheld' from his or her election than votes 'for' such election . . . shall promptly tender his or her resignation following certification of the shareholder vote." Following the tender, "[t]he Corporate Governance Committee shall consider the resignation offer . . . and recommend to the Board whether to accept it." Based on that recommendation, the entire board, excluding the tendering director, must then decide whether to accept or reject the resignation "within 90 days following certification of the shareholder vote."[78]

* * *

---

[76]   *Id.* at 849 (footnotes omitted).

[77]   *Id.* at 854–55 (footnotes omitted).

[78]   *Id.* at 861–62 (footnotes omitted).

[T]he board of Intel decided to adopt a hybrid resignation policy/majority voting bylaw. The basic procedure for ousting directors is the same under the Intel approach as under the Pfizer approach. If more votes are cast "against" than "for" a candidate in an uncontested election, he or she "shall offer to tender his or her resignation to the Board." The independent Corporate Governance and Nominating Committee must then make a recommendation to the full board as to whether to accept or reject the resignation, with the tendering director being excluded from the deliberations. The major difference between the Intel and Pfizer approaches is that Intel's board took the additional step of amending the bylaws to affirmatively provide that "each director shall be elected by the vote of a majority of the votes cast. . . ."

Virtually every corporation that has implemented majority voting has done so by adopting a Pfizer-style director resignation policy or an Intel-style modified majority voting bylaw, sometimes with minor variations. As of June 2006, at least 140 companies have adopted Pfizer-style director resignation policies, and at least forty have enacted Intel-style modified majority voting bylaws.[79]

By early 2014, some 90% of S&P 500 companies employed some form of majority voting for directors.[80] While these voting protocols may not result in many directors actually losing their position, the adoption of these schemes emphasizes to the directors that their positions are at least at risk. Directors appreciating that risk may be more sensitive to any significant drop in affirmative votes, which in turn could prompt directors to respond substantively to such a drop. As an example, members of compensation committees may become increasingly sensitive to the number of shares that are withheld from their election or voted against them, and respond by greater reductions in CEO pay than in the past.[81]

Such sensitivity creates opportunities for some institutional shareholders, particularly the activist shareholders that this chapter will describe shortly. On the other hand, one of the conundrums facing mutual funds, now that they must disclose their votes and now that their votes may really "count" with more election-sensitive directors, is to decide how to vote in corporate elections when the money they manage is invested in

---

[79] *Id.* at 864–65 (footnotes omitted).

[80] Skadden, Arps, Slate, Meagher & Flom LLP & Affiliates, *US Corporate Governance: Boards of Directors Face Increased Scrutiny* (Jan. 16, 2014), http://www.skadden.com/sites/default/files/publications/US_Corporate_Governance_Boards_of_Directors_Face_Increased_Scrutiny.pdf. ("Approximately 90 percent of S&P 500 companies (and approximately 46 percent of Russell 3000 companies) have a majority voting standard in director elections and/or a policy requiring resignation if a director fails to get majority support. . . .").

[81] *See* the text at *supra* notes 71–74.

dozens or hundreds of publicly traded companies. Some turn to proxy advisers, described in more detail in the last section of this chapter.

QUESTIONS ON MAJORITY VOTING

Which directors should shareholders target for withhold votes?

- Those on audit committees of companies that are under SEC investigation for accounting wrongdoing? Those on audit committees of companies that have issued restatements?

- Those on compensation committees where the CEO has been paid too much in light of the company's performance?

- All directors at companies that have for some period of time underperformed peer companies?

- All directors at companies that have taken on "excessive" risk?

How much influence is it healthy for proxy advisers to have on shareholder votes? Are they shadow shareholders now? And who are the folks inside the advisers who are deciding on the recommendations? Answer now, and answer again after reading the last portion of this chapter.

SEC proposal to permit shareholders to nominate board candidates under certain limited conditions and to require that companies include shareholders' nominees in the company proxy statement. In October 2003, the SEC proposed rules that would have (i) given stockholders some limited right to nominate director candidates and (ii) forced companies to include those candidates in the companies' proxy statements and on the companies' proxies.[82] That latter right was key. Shareholders today can nominate their own candidates and wage a "proxy fight." But such a fight requires preparation and distribution of proxy statements. It is simply too expensive in most cases, unless the forces behind the fight are trying to take over the company or very substantially change its strategy.

The SEC proposal was aimed at a different case, where shareholders are not seeking to seize control of a company, but simply want to make a change in the board and are dissatisfied with the candidates whom the company keeps nominating. The SEC proposal was referred to as the "proxy access" proposal—giving such shareholders access to a public company's proxy and proxy statement.

---

[82] Security Holder Director Nominations, 68 Fed. Reg. 60,784 (Oct. 23, 2003) (SEC's proposal).

The 2003 SEC proxy access proposal drew heavy criticism from parts of the business community and divided the Commission. The SEC did not adopt it.

The SEC proposed another version of such a rule in 2009,[83] and adopted that rule, after further revisions, in 2010.[84] While the new rule was complicated, here were some basics:

1.   Only a shareholder or group of shareholders owning at least 3% of the securities entitled to vote for directors could nominate directors.[85] The nominating shareholder or each member of a nominating group had to have held the threshold percentage for at least three years and had to hold those shares through the election of the directors for which the shareholder or group nominated a candidate.[86]

2.   The total number of shareholder nominees could not exceed the greater of one or 25% of the entire board.[87]

3.   No person could be nominated by shareholders if that nominee's service on the board would violate controlling state or federal law or the rules of a national securities exchange on which the issuer's stock was listed, and each nominee had to meet the objective criteria for independence imposed by a national securities exchange on which the issuer's stock was listed.[88]

4.   The nominating shareholder or group could include in the company's proxy statement up to 500 words in support of each nominee.[89]

As the rationale for the rule, the SEC stated:

The right to nominate is inextricably linked to, and essential to the vitality of, a right to vote for a nominee. The failure of the proxy process to adequately facilitate shareholder nomination rights has a direct and practical effect on the right to elect directors.[90]

---

[83]   Facilitating Shareholder Director Nominations, 74 Fed. Reg. 29,024 (June 18, 2009) (proposing release).

[84]   Facilitating Shareholder Director Nominations, 75 Fed. Reg. 56,668 (Sept. 16, 2010) (codified at, among other places, 17 C.F.R. §§ 200, 232, 240.14a-11, 249). This and succeeding footnotes cite to the rules as codified. As explained in the text, a judicial decision invalidated the rules. They no longer appear in the C.F.R.

[85]   *Id*. at 56,782–83 (Rule 14a-11(b)(1)).

[86]   *Id*. at 56,783 (Rule 14a-11(b)(2)).

[87]   *Id*. at 56,785 (Rule 14a-11(d)).

[88]   *Id*. at 56,784 (Rule 14a-11(b)(8) & (9)).

[89]   *Id*. at 56,785, 88, 91 (Rule 14a-11(c); Schedule 14A, Item 7(e); Schedule 14N, Item 5(i)).

[90]   Facilitating Shareholder Director Nominations (proposing release), *supra* note 83, at 29,027 (footnotes omitted).

The Business Roundtable sued to prevent implementation of this rule and won, in part because the court found that the SEC had acted arbitrarily and capriciously in failing to consider the costs and benefits of the rule.[91] The SEC issued a press release after the court decision, stating that an amendment to its Rule 14a-8 would take effect, permitting shareholders at each public company to place on the company's proxy a proposal to give shareholders the right to nominate board candidates whom the company must then include on its proxy and identify in its proxy statement. Thus, whether to permit shareholders access to the company's proxy is now a decision for each company to make for itself.

Here is part of the SEC Chair's statement in the release:

I firmly believe that providing a meaningful opportunity for shareholders to exercise their right to nominate directors at their companies is in the best interest of investors and our markets. It is a process that helps make boards more accountable for the risks undertaken by the companies they manage. I remain committed to finding a way to make it easier for shareholders to nominate candidates to corporate boards.

Last year, when the Commission adopted Rule 14a-11 [the proxy access rule], it also adopted amendments to Rule 14a-8, the shareholder proposal rule. Under those amendments, eligible shareholders are permitted to require companies to include shareholder proposals regarding proxy access procedures in company proxy materials. Through this procedure, shareholders and companies have the opportunity to establish proxy access standards on a company-by-company basis—rather than a specified standard like that contained in Rule 14a-11.

Although the amendments to Rule 14a-8 were not challenged in the litigation, the Commission voluntarily stayed the effective date of those amendments at the time it stayed the effective date of Rule 14a-11. The Commission's stay order provides that the stay of the effective date of the amendments to Rule 14a-8 and related rules will expire without further Commission action when the court's decision is finalized, which is expected to be September 13. Accordingly, absent further Commission action, Rule 14a-8 will go into effect and a notice of the effective date of the amendments will be published.[92]

---

[91]   *Bus. Roundtable v. SEC*, 647 F.3d 1144 (D.C. Cir. 2011).

[92]   Press Release, SEC, *Statement by SEC Chairman Mary L. Schapiro on Proxy Access Litigation* (Sept. 6, 2011), http://www.sec.gov/news/press/2011/2011-179.htm.

QUESTIONS ON THE SEC PROPOSAL TO PERMIT CERTAIN SHAREHOLDERS TO PUT CANDIDATES ON THE BALLOT FOR DIRECTOR POSITIONS AND INCLUDE THOSE CANDIDATES IN THE COMPANY'S PROXY STATEMENT

What do you think of the regulation that the SEC adopted (later struck down in litigation)? Was the ownership threshold fair? Did the threshold effectively limit use of the rule, at most companies, to institutional investors? Is that good?

What about the holding period? Should the nominating shareholder or group have had to intend to hold through the term that the nominee(s) would serve, if elected?

If the rule had gone into effect, do you think that shareholders would have taken advantage of it?

Note how the shareholders, like the company's nominating committee, were constrained by independence requirements in selecting the men and women that the shareholders want to populate the board. If you liked the independence criteria when you thought about their limiting the nominating committees, do you still like them when you think about them limiting the shareholders?

How would the election of a shareholder nominee affect the ability of the board to work as a group? How would such an election affect the relationship between management and the board?

When would it be a good idea for shareholders to nominate candidates (e.g., after several years during which the issuer's performance fell below the industry mean)?

Does the rationale of the SEC's proposal depend on shareholder primacy? If so, how does that affect your view of the proposal's worth?

Do you like where the rulemaking and related litigation came out—with shareholders at each company able to decide whether to adopt proxy access— but no mandate from the government to all companies?

Whether shareholder voting is the answer. Think again about shareholder suffrage in these days of dispersed stock holdings and liquid markets. Put that together with the notion that the investor wants to make money on the stock that he or she buys.

QUESTIONS ON THE RELATIONSHIP BETWEEN SHAREHOLDER INFLUENCE AND CORPORATE SCANDALS

Isn't it easier to sell the stock you own in a company with which you are dissatisfied than to find a director candidate, go through the nominating routine at a company that has adopted a proxy access procedure (assuming that you meet any share percentage threshold), and wait to see how the director election turns out? What role does shareholder voting really play today?

If ownership is realistically divorced from control—and the board and management are disconnected from the shareholders—is that itself a circumstance that has contributed to accounting scandals and unduly risky operations at financial institutions?

Is there a sense in which shareholders themselves are largely unconcerned with a scandal at a particular company? If an investor's investments are diversified—perhaps because the investments are in a diversified fund—is there a chance that the spread of investments and the buying and selling of large numbers of stocks will unwittingly diversify the investor over fraud as well as over other risks?

Assume, for this thought, that Enron and WorldCom were out-and-out frauds. Perhaps a fund in which a hypothetical investor put his or her money bought Enron stock when that stock was low but sold Enron stock while it was flying high. The fund thereby benefited from the Enron fraud. But perhaps the fund bought WorldCom stock when its price was high and sold that stock following the price decline after WorldCom announced accounting irregularities. The fund thereby lost from the WorldCom fraud. Overall the fund may have been unharmed from the two frauds, when they are considered together.

Maybe the diversified investor only cares about the scandals because, when they seem to come in legions, the market suffers as a whole. If that is so, perhaps we should rely on regulation instead of shareholder votes to keep companies in line. What do you think?[93]

Increased large shareholder activism. Recent years have seen something of a surge in shareholder activism, expressed in many forms.

In some cases, shareholders publicly announced that they were withholding votes from directors and encouraged others to do so—with real results. The Disney shareholders provide an example. Roy Disney, Walt's nephew, urged shareholders to withhold votes from Michael Eisner, who was the company's chief executive but also a member of the board, the

---

[93]   One scholar argues that even large numbers of diversified institutional investors can suffer net loss from securities fraud. Alicia Davis Evans, *Are Investors' Gains and Losses from Securities Fraud Equal Over Time? Theory and Evidence* 4 (Univ. Mich. Law & Econ., Olin Working Paper No. 09-002, 2015), http://papers.ssrn.com/sol3/papers.cfm?abstract_id=1121198.

board chair, and up for election as a director. About 45% of the votes were "withheld" from Eisner at the March 3, 2004 shareholder meeting, with both Fidelity Investments and T. Rowe Price Group withholding their votes. Eisner was re-elected to the board and remained CEO, but the board took away his chairmanship. A number of state pension funds (from California, Connecticut, New York, North Carolina, and Ohio) then asked George Mitchell (the new board chair) if the funds could meet with directors in order to discuss Disney's long-term performance and its governance. By the end of September 2004, Eisner announced that he would not seek to renew his contract as chief executive, which was set to expire in September 2006, Disney announced that it would immediately hire an executive search firm and name a successor to Eisner by June 2005, and Roy Disney proclaimed victory.[94] In fact, by mid-March 2005, Disney named its president Robert Iger as the successor to Eisner, who would be leaving his CEO position one year before his contract ended.[95]

Shareholders flexed their muscles outside annual meetings as well. Tweedy, Browne, a money management firm owning 17.7% of Hollinger International, asked the Hollinger Board to investigate payments to Conrad M. Black (the chairman and chief executive) and other executives—thereby setting in train a complicated series of events which, among other things, saw Black leave his executive position and lawsuits flourish between Black and the company.[96] Black was criminally prosecuted.[97] He was convicted.[98]

Institutional shareholders acting as lead plaintiffs in federal securities cases have insisted in some instances on governance reforms as part of

---

[94]   *See* Laura M. Holson, *MediaTalk; For Disney's Embattled Chief, a Double Rebuke From Fidelity*, N.Y. TIMES, Mar. 15, 2004, http://www.nytimes.com/2004/03/15/business/mediatalk-for-disney-s-embattled-chief-a-double-rebuke-from-fidelity.html?_r=0; Laura M. Holson, *Pension Funds of 5 States Seek to Meet Disney Directors*, N.Y. TIMES, Mar. 23, 2004, http://www.nytimes.com/2004/03/23/business/pension-funds-of-5-states-seek-to-meet-disney-directors.html; Laura M. Holson & Geraldine Fabrikant, *Disney Chief to Leave, Setting Off Race for Job*, N.Y. TIMES, Sept. 11, 2004, http://www.nytimes.com/2004/09/11/business/media/disney-chief-to-leave-setting-off-race-for-job.html; Laura M. Holson, *Disney to Hire Search Firm To Find New Chief by June*, N.Y. TIMES, Sept. 22, 2004, http://www.nytimes.com/2004/09/22/business/media/disney-to-hire-search-firm-to-find-new-chief-by-june.html; Bloomberg News, *Dissidents at Disney Say They've Won*, Sept. 29, 2004, http://www.nytimes.com/2004/09/29/business/media/dissidents-at-disney-say-theyve-won.html.

[95]   *See* Laura M. Holson, *No. 2 at Disney to Take Charge, One Year Early*, N.Y. TIMES, Mar. 14, 2005, http://query.nytimes.com/gst/fullpage.html?res=9C0CEED7153CF937A25750C0A 9639C8B63.

[96]   *See* Patrick McGeehan, *Shareholders Ask Hollinger to Investigate Executive Pay*, N.Y. TIMES, May 21, 2003, http://www.nytimes.com/2003/05/21/business/shareholders-ask-hollinger-to-investigate-executive-pay.html; Geraldine Fabrikant & Floyd Norris, *Hollinger Files Stinging Report On Ex-Officials*, N.Y. TIMES, Sept. 1, 2004, http://www.nytimes.com/2004/09/01/business/media/hollinger-files-stinging-report-on-exofficials.html.

[97]   Geraldine Fabrikant, *News Tycoon Stole Millions, U.S. Charges*, N.Y. TIMES, Nov. 18, 2005, http://www.nytimes.com/2005/11/18/business/news-tycoon-stole-millions-us-charges.html.

[98]   *U.S. v. Black*, No. 12 C 4306, 2013 WL 608300, at *1–2 (N.D. Ill. Feb. 19, 2013).

class action settlements. In May 2003, Hanover Compressor Co. settled a securities class action for $80 million plus a number of governance reforms requiring, among other things, two-thirds of the board to be independent directors, institution of a "lead" independent director, and shareholder nomination of one or two directors. In December 2003, Sprint settled a case for $50 million plus requirements that two-thirds of the board be independent and that the board have a "lead" independent director.[99]

Activist hedge funds have, however, created the biggest stir in the world of shareholder power. Such funds purchase modest percentages of publicly traded companies' stock, then wage campaigns to pressure the boards and managements of the companies to change their businesses. The funds do this in order to increase the value of the companies in which they have invested. Unlike Roy Disney, who was concerned with one company with which his family had long-standing ties, the activist hedge funds invest and wage campaigns for change again and again. It is their business.

Here is a description of how activist hedge funds operate and some statistics on their success.

> What, based on the record so far, have the hedge funds actually done to their targets? To address the question, [this study] collects information on 130 domestic firms identified in the business press since 2002 as investment targets of "activist" hedge funds, surveying the funds' demands, their tactics, and the results of their interventions for the targets' governance and finance.[100]

> * * *

> Engagements between activists and targets start with a letter and a follow-up call, usually occurring just prior to the filing of a Schedule 13D that makes public the fund's ownership of 5% or more of the target's stock. The letter (and the call, if taken) tells the target that it is undervalued and outlines steps that the fund recommends to realize value for the shareholders in the near future. The fund then asks for a meeting.

> Target management has two choices at this point. It can take the call and convene a meeting, looking toward a back-and-forth in which it defends its business plan and attempts to persuade the fund to take a passive, patient view of its investment. Alternatively, it can refuse to engage; many targets have made this choice. The immediate result of refusal is often a public rebuke in the fund's first 13D filing. The rebuke will be addressed

---

[99]   Bruce D. Angiolillo, *Settlement Issues in Securities Class Actions: The Defense Perspective in 2004*, PLI Program Materials for Securities Litigation & Enforcement Institute 2004, at 297, 330–32.

[100]   William W. Bratton, *Hedge Funds and Governance Targets*, 95 GEO. L.J. 1375, 1380 (2007). Quotations from this article reprinted with permission from Professor Bratton.

to the target shareholders, telling them that the fund has made constructive suggestions that the managers have ignored. Subsequent correspondence with the target likewise goes into the SEC file, which serves as the de facto press room in the fund's campaign. Where, as with the cases in the sample here, the business press takes an interest in the matter, a new filing can prompt a new round of reports.

Consultants who market themselves as defensive advisors to managers coping with activist interveners stress the initial stage's importance. They recommend engagement with the goal of inducing more moderate responses. They also recommend advance planning—managers should be ready with a persuasive analysis that defends the business plan and, if possible, counters value claims made by the fund. The more effectively a target has communicated the case for its business plan to the investment community prior to the engagement, the stronger the target's position in the negotiation. Even better, say the consultants, the firm should avoid being a target in the first place, anticipating the activists by remitting excess cash to the shareholders and actively monitoring and managing its mix of businesses. The consultants offer good advice. Even so, there is no case in the sample where an early meeting leads a hedge fund to abandon a publicized value maximization plan and accept the target's existing approach.

By contrast, in 18% of the hostile cases, the engagement never gets past the initial stage, with the fund's public presence alone inducing target management to make concessions. The wolf pack effect contributes to such decisions. The 13D filing sends a signal to other funds who take positions in the target stock. The target sees little chance of victory in a contest fought to the finish and so either comes to the table and settles or preemptively takes an action recommended by the activist. These initial stage concessions encompass a wide range of outcomes. On the minimal end, the concession implies no commitment—for example, the target engages an investment banker to look into value-creating alternatives or it appoints an additional independent director from the financial sector. More concrete initial stage concessions come in the form of asset sales and cash payouts. Even the ultimate concession—the sale of the company—occurred at the early stage when Knight-Ridder sold itself in 2006. In still other cases, the target makes a process commitment to the activist's agenda by conceding to it one or more seats on the board of directors. Thus did Jerome York join the General Motors board as Kirk Kerkorian's designee.[101]

* * *

In the more usual case, the target rejects the fund's proposals, sometimes with a peremptory announcement and sometimes after a formal meeting. The activist typically responds by threatening a proxy fight. The threat moves the engagement to the next stage. The activist has the choice of making good on the threat and incurring the expense of proxy solicitation, or of sitting back, keeping up the pressure, and waiting for concessions. The latter route appears to be preferred. Although a proxy contest at a small firm can cost as little as $100,000, the average cost ranges between $250,000 and $1 million.

Meanwhile, the line separating a proxy threat from a proxy contest is not very clear under today's liberalized SEC proxy rules. An activist that has "threatened" a proxy contest to no effect often follows up by announcing its "intent to solicit" proxies.[102]

The activist's statement of intent to solicit, while manifestly made in the hope of never getting to the point of filing and distributing a definitive proxy statement, nonetheless is credible. The activists, faced with a recalcitrant target, do make good on their threats and solicit. . . .

Activist tenacity is particularly evident in thirteen campaigns extending for more than one year. Typically, the fund accepts a minor concession, say, as in the case of Topps, agreeing to hire an investment banker to look into value alternatives. When this process leads to nothing, the fund proceeds with a proxy fight in a subsequent year. In the case of RedEnvelope, the campaign has been going on for three years, involving a proxy loss in 2004, a win along with management concessions in 2005, and another pending contest in 2006. . . .

Once a proxy contest ripens into a bona fide solicitation, many target managers settle after running a preliminary vote count and getting bad news. A small number of contests have gone to the count. The activists have garnered board seats in nineteen of these. Management has won a solicitation in seven cases, two of them issue-based and five involving dissident board slates. Just looking at the contests for board seats, this outcome means a 79% success rate. This figure compares with a 52% success rate derived

---

[101]   *Id.* at 1402–03 (footnotes omitted).

[102]   *Id.* at 1403–04 (footnotes omitted).

by Ikenberry and Lakonishok for a sample of ninety-seven board contests between 1968 and 1987. By historical standards, then, the hedge funds are doing well.[103]

* * *

Table V sets out results respecting the targets in the hostile sample, as of December 31, 2006. Each case is assigned one outcome; for cases involving ongoing campaigns with multiple results over time, the figures reflect the most recent event in the case. Table V arranges the outcomes to highlight the cases' process characteristics, breaking out three categories—settlement, pressure, and full-dress proxy contest. A "settlement" implies an arrangement concluded as the result of negotiations between the activist and the target. These tend to accompany the initiation of a proxy fight. Concessions resulting from "pressure," in contrast, do not stem from face-to-face agreements and often occur as the target's unilateral action, at least when viewed from outside. Together these cases make up 67% of the sample and 80% of the group of successes. The class of proxy contest victories makes up 17% of the sample and 20% of the successful group.

"Success" is defined capaciously to include any cognizable target concession. Cash payouts bring the target into the success category in 29% of the hostile cases. Other indicia of success include board membership (40% of the hostile targets), sale or liquidation of the target (28%), and the sale or spin off of a division (21%). "Success" also includes minor concessions like investment banker engagement and governance overhauls.[104]

Here is Table V, from page 1406 of the article, reformatted for presentation in this book:

---

[103]   *Id.* at 1404–05 (footnotes omitted).
[104]   *Id.* at 1405–06 (footnote omitted).

Table V: Outcomes (percent of the hostile sample)				
Successful Outcomes: 84%				
Settlement: Board Seat	Settlement: No Board Seat	Pressure: Major Concession	Pressure: Minor Concession	Proxy Contest: Board Seat
23	7	24	13	17
Other Outcomes: 16%				
Proxy Contest Pending	Pressure Fails: Withdrawal	Proxy Fails: Withdrawal	Other Failure	Outcome Open
2	2	1	2	9

The remarkable point is that a single hedge fund, with a low percentage of total ownership, can get this whole process started.

The degree to which activist hedge funds affect corporate governance depends on the funds' ability to convince investors to put their money into the funds. That, in turn, depends in significant part on whether the funds' activism yields returns. One study of activist hedge funds found that, from 2003 through 2006, they "outperformed the equity-oriented hedge funds in addition to the market indices."[105]

Hedge funds generally took a beating during the market downturn in 2008:

[Hedge funds] are in the throes of an unprecedented shakeout. . . .

No one knows how much more hedge funds might have to sell to meet a rush of redemptions.[106]

. . . Wall Street is buzzing about how much money could be pulled out of hedge funds—and which funds might bear the brunt of the redemptions.

Funds have set aside billions of dollars in cash to prepare for withdrawals. . . .[107]

---

[105] Alon Brav, et al., *The Returns to Hedge Fund Activism*, 64 FIN. ANAL. J. 45, 59 (2008).

[106] Hedge funds may permit their investors to redeem their interests—i.e., get their money out of the fund.

[107] Louise Story, *Investors Flee as Hedge Fund Woes Deepen*, N.Y. TIMES, Oct. 23, 2008, http://www.nytimes.com/2008/10/23/business/23hedge.html. But even during periods of low stock prices, the activists retained sufficient influence to sometimes affect events. *See* Reuters, *After Criticism, Wyndham Drops Plan to Issue Stock*, N.Y. TIMES, Feb. 17, 2009, http://www.nytimes.com/2009/02/17/business/worldbusiness/17bizbriefs-BMWTHEGERMAN_BRF.html ("The hotel

But the market turned in 2009, and the funds expanded.[108] Warnings to corporations of possible hedge fund attacks also continued. In June 2013, the well-known corporate lawyer Martin Lipton posted this comment:

> The 2013 proxy season saw a continuance of the high and increasing level of activist campaigns experienced during the last ten years. There have been more than 300 activist attacks on major companies during this period. No company is too big to become the target of an activist, and even companies with sterling corporate governance practices and positive share price performance, including outperformance of peers, may be targeted. Among the major companies that have been attacked are Apple, Sony, Hess, P&G, McDonald's, ITW, DuPont, Target, Pepsi and Kraft. There are more than 100 hedge funds that have engaged in activism and they frequently gain the backing of ISS and major institutional investors, some of which have investments in activist funds. Major investment banks, law firms, proxy solicitors, and public relations advisors are now representing activists.[109]

In the first half of 2014, activist hedge funds showed 6.5% gains, quite good, but behind the 7.1% increase in the S&P 500.[110] By the middle of 2015, the funds were beating the market again.[111] In early 2016, however, the activists' losses exceeded the decline in the market overall.[112]

QUESTIONS ON ACTIVIST HEDGE FUNDS

Do the activist hedge funds serve the useful purpose of mobilizing shareholders against inefficient management and boards? Or are the funds likely to be short-term players who will harm corporations?

---

owner Wyndham Worldwide dropped plans on Monday to issue up to $200 million in stock after a prominent hedge fund manager criticized the idea and its shares sank nearly 30 percent.").

[108] *See* David Ellis, *Hedge funds: They're back!*, CNN Money, Mar. 12, 2010, http://money.cnn.com/2010/03/11/news/companies/hedge_fund/.

[109] Martin Lipton, *Dealing with Activist Hedge Funds*, The CLS Blue Sky Blog (June 21, 2013), http://clsbluesky.law.columbia.edu/2013/06/21/dealing-with-activist-hedge-funds/.

[110] Rob Copeland, *Returns from Activist Hedge Funds Are Causing a Stir*, WALL ST. J., July 7, 2014, http://www.wsj.com/articles/returns-from-activist-hedge-funds-are-causing-a-stir-1404773120.

[111] Stephen Gandel, *Activist Hedge Funds Are Beating the Market: What Are They Doing Right?*, FORTUNE, Aug. 11, 2015, http://fortune.com/2015/08/11/activist-hedge-funds-are-beating-the-market-what-are-they-doing-right/ ("In 2015 so far, hedge funds of activist shareholders are up three times as much as the market.").

[112] Stephan Gandel, *Activist Hedge Funds Have Their Worst Month in Years*, FORTUNE, Feb. 5, 2016, http://fortune.com/2016/02/05/activist-hedge-funds-have-their-worst-month-in-years/ ("Activist hedge funds lost just over 6.1% in January, according to Hedge Fund Research, which released its monthly numbers on Friday," while the S&P 500 was down 5%).

The considerable influence wielded by activist hedge funds raised concern among board members and management. They worried that the funds would be short-term investors, forcing companies to take steps that would produce immediate gains but cause lasting harm. This concern has generated research. This book does not purport to collect all such research. But here is an excerpt from one provocative study:

> In this paper, we [examine] the most extensive and thoroughly documented set of observations of hedge fund activism to date, extending from the beginning of 2001 through the end of 2006.
>
> We find that hedge funds increasingly engage in a new form of shareholder activism and monitoring that differs fundamentally from previous activist efforts by other institutional investors. . . . Unlike mutual funds and pension funds, hedge funds are able to influence corporate boards and managements due to key differences arising from their different organizational form and the incentives that they face. Hedge funds employ highly incentivized managers who manage large unregulated pools of capital. Because they are not subject to regulation that governs mutual funds and pension funds, they can hold highly concentrated positions in small numbers of companies, and use leverage and derivatives to extend their reach. Hedge fund managers also suffer few conflicts of interest because they are not beholden to the management of the firms whose shares they hold. In sum, hedge funds are better positioned to act as informed monitors than other institutional investors.
>
> Hedge fund activists tend to target companies that are typically "value" firms, with low market value relative to book value, although they are profitable with sound operating cash flows and return on assets. Payout at these companies before intervention is lower than that of matched firms. Target companies also have more takeover defenses and pay their CEOs considerably more than comparable companies. Relatively few targeted companies are large-cap firms, which is not surprising given the comparatively high cost of amassing a meaningful stake in such a target. Targets exhibit significantly higher institutional ownership and trading liquidity. These characteristics make it easier for activists to acquire a significant stake quickly.
>
> Our first piece of evidence regarding the impact of hedge fund activism is based on the market's reaction to intervention announcements. We find that the market reacts favorably to activism, consistent with the view that it creates value. The filing of a Schedule 13D revealing an activist fund's investment in a target firm results in large positive average abnormal returns, in

the range of 7% to 8%, during the (−20,+20) announcement window. The increase in both price and abnormal trading volume of target shares begins 1 to 10 days prior to the Schedule 13D's filing. We find that the positive returns at announcement are not reversed over time, as there is no evidence of a negative abnormal drift during the 1-year period subsequent to the announcement. We also document that the positive abnormal returns are only marginally lower for hedge funds that disclosed substantial ownership positions (through quarterly Form 13F filings) before they filed a Schedule 13D, which is consistent with the view that the abnormal returns are due to new information about activism, not merely that about stock picking. Moreover, target prices decline upon the exit of a hedge fund only after it has been unsuccessful, which indicates that the information reflected in the positive announcement returns conveys the market's expectation for the success of activism.

We next examine the cross-section of these abnormal returns. Activism that targets the sale of the company or changes in business strategy, such as refocusing and spinning-off noncore assets, is associated with the largest positive abnormal partial effects, at 8.54% and 5.95%, respectively (the latter figure is lower than the overall sample average because most events target multiple issues). This evidence suggests that hedge funds are able to create value when they see large allocative inefficiencies. In contrast, we find that the market response to capital structure-related activism—including debt restructuring, recapitalization, dividends, and share repurchases—is positive yet insignificant. We find a similar lack of statistically meaningful reaction for governance-related activism—including attempts to rescind takeover defenses, to oust CEOs, to enhance board independence, and to curtail CEO compensation. Hedge funds with a track record of successful activism generate higher returns, as do hedge funds that initiate activism with hostile tactics.

The positive market reaction is also consistent with ex post evidence of overall improved performance at target firms. On average, from the year before to the year after an announcement, total payout increases by 0.3 to 0.5 percentage points (as a percentage of the market value of equity, relative to an all-sample mean of 2.2 percentage points), and book value leverage increases by 1.3 to 1.4 percentage points (relative to an all-sample mean of 33.5 percentage points). Both changes are consistent with a reduction of agency problems associated with free cash flow and subject managers to increased market discipline. We also find improvement in return on assets and operating profit margins, but this takes longer to manifest. The postevent year sees little change compared to the year prior to intervention. However, EBITDA/Assets (EBITDA/Sales) at target firms increases by 0.9 to 1.5 (4.7 to 5.8) percentage points 2 years after intervention. Analyst expectations also suggest improved prospects at target firms after hedge fund intervention. During the months before Schedule 13D filings, analysts downgrade (future) targets more than they upgrade them, whereas after an intervention is announced, analysts maintain neutral ratings. Given that successful activism often leads to attrition through the sale of the target company, any ex post performance analysis based on surviving firms may underestimate the positive effect of activism.

Hedge fund activists are not short-term in focus, as some critics have claimed. The median holding period for completed deals is about 1 year, calculated as from the date a hedge fund files a Schedule 13D to the date when the fund no longer holds a significant stake in a target company. The calculation substantially understates the actual median holding period, because it necessarily excludes a significant number of events for which no exit information was available by March 2007. Analysis of portfolio turnover rates of the funds in our sample suggests holding periods of closer to 20 months.[113]

FINAL QUESTION ON ACTIVIST INVESTORS

Does this additional information change your view on the social and economic value of activist investors?

---

[113] Alon Brav, et al., *Hedge Fund Activism, Corporate Governance, and Firm Performance*, 63 J. FINANCE 1729, 1730–32 (2008). Quotation republished with permission of American Finance Association from Hedge Fund Activism, Corporate Governance, and Firm Performance, Alon Brav, et al, Vol. 63, No. 4, The Journal of Finance, copyright 2008; permission conveyed through Copyright Clearance Center, Inc. *See also* Lucian A. Bebchuk, et al., *The Long-Term Effects of Hedge Fund Activism*, 115 COLUM. L. REV. 1085 (2015) (examining about 2,000 activist investor interventions during the period 1994 to 2007 (at 1090, 1100 & tbl.1); finding improved average and median industry-adjusted Tobin's q and return on investment during the five years following interventions (at 1105–06 & tbl.3); and, after performing additional analyses, finding "no evidence" that the interventions "are followed in the long term by declines in operating performance" but, to the contrary "evidence that such interventions are followed by long-term improvements, rather than declines, in performance" (at 1155).

J. PROXY ADVISERS

While the activist shareholders pick their targets and wage war, what of the other institutional shareholders? In particular, what of the diversified mutual funds?

These institutional investors each purchase stock in many different companies so that each mutual fund has the opportunity to vote shares each year at annual meetings for a vast number of public companies in its portfolio. Each fund hires a manager that buys and sells shares with fund money and votes the shares that the fund owns. In late 2011 and early 2012, managers of $15.4 trillion of assets in aggregate said that they each "cast votes at anywhere from several hundred meetings to over 15,000. For approximately half the participants [in the study], annual meeting volume [was] between 4,500 and 10,000."[114] At every such shareholder meeting, a manager may cast votes (i) on each director nominee, (ii) for or against the company's overall executive pay system (called the "say-on-pay" vote, by which shareholders express non-binding approval or disapproval of company pay to top officers, as explained more fully in later chapters), and (iii) for or against any other matters subject to shareholder votes.[115]

As a practical matter, it would not be cost effective for every manager of diversified funds—in preparation for the annual meeting of each public company in which the funds it manages are invested—to independently analyze whether to vote for each director candidate, how to vote on the say-

---

[114]   ROBYN BEW & RICHARD FIELDS, VOTING DECISIONS AT US MUTUAL FUNDS: HOW INVESTORS REALLY USE PROXY ADVISERS 1, 14 (2012) [BEW, HOW FUNDS USE PROXY ADVISERS].

[115]   For example, listing standards require that shareholders vote on equity compensation plans. NYSE MANUAL § 303A.08; NASDAQ RULE 5635(c). The Internal Revenue Code also requires that shareholders approve incentive plans in order that the compensation to any executive under those plans not count towards the $1 million limit on a company's deduction of the compensation to that executive. 26 U.S.C. § 162(m)(1), (m)(4)(C)(ii). Shareholders have the right not only to propose resolutions at shareholder meetings, but—subject to certain important limitations—the right to require that a shareholder-proposed resolution appear on the proxy card that the company distributes to shareholders and to require that the company's proxy statement include the shareholders' brief statement supporting a resolution. 17 C.F.R. § 240.14a-8. One count through June 30, tallied 536 shareholder proposals voted on at the 2015 annual meetings of U.S. companies in the Russell 3000 index. SULLIVAN & CROMWELL LLP, 2015 PROXY SEASON REVIEW 1 (July 20, 2015). For example, Chevron shareholders voted on 10 different shareholder proposals at the company's 2015 meeting. Those proposals recommended all kinds of actions, including that the company (i) disclose its charitable contributions of $5,000 or more; (ii) report annually on "the results of company policies and practices, above and beyond regulatory requirements, to minimize the adverse water resource and community impacts from the company's hydraulic fracturing operations associated with shale formations"; (iii) propose a bylaw to permit shareholders to nominate director candidates who would then have to be included on the company's proxy card, with a supporting statement by the nominating shareholders included in the company's proxy statement; (iv) nominate, as a board seat becomes available, an independent director who "has a high level of expertise and experience in environmental matters relevant to hydrocarbon exploration and production and is widely recognized in the business and environmental communities as an authority in such field, as reasonably determined by the company's board"; and (v) amend the company bylaws to permit holders of 10% of the outstanding common stock to call a special shareholders meeting. Chevron Corp., Definitive Proxy Statement, Schedule 14A (filed Apr. 9, 2015) at 61–81.

on-pay resolution, and how to vote on each other proposal presented for a shareholder vote.[116] Many managers of institutional investors therefore turn to proxy advisers.[117] The two largest proxy advisers are Institutional Shareholder Services ("ISS") and Glass Lewis and Co. ("Glass Lewis")

---

[116] *See* Daniel M. Gallagher, SEC Commissioner, *Outsized Power & Influence: The Role of Proxy Advisers*, Harvard Law School Forum on Corporate Governance and Financial Regulation, (Sept. 5, 2014), http://corpgov.law.harvard.edu/2014/09/05/outsized-power-influence-the-role-of-proxy-advisers/ ("one study found that 'most institutional investor holdings are relatively small portions of each firm's total securities. For example, in our sample . . . the mean (median) holding of an individual stock by institutional investors is 0.3% (0.03 %).' Given that institutional investors hold stock in hundreds or thousands of companies (for example, TIAA CREF holds stock in 7,000 companies), institutional investors—particularly the smaller ones—may not be able to invest in the costly research needed to ensure that they cast each vote in the best interest of their clients. The logical answer is to outsource the research function to a third party, who could do the needed research and sell voting recommendations back to investment advisers for a fee: a proxy advisory firm.") [Gallagher on Proxy Advisers].

[117] *See* STANFORD GRADUATE SCHOOL OF BUSINESS, RR DONNELLY, EQUILAR, ROCK CENTER FOR CORPORATE GOVERNANCE, 2015 INVESTOR SURVEY: DECONSTRUCTING PROXY STATEMENTS— WHAT MATTERS TO INVESTORS (2015). The researchers surveyed "64 asset managers and owners with a combined $17 trillion in assets" in the fall of 2014. *Id.* at 1. The authors reported that 63% of the owners and asset managers stated that a third-party proxy adviser was one information source on which their organizations relied in making proxy voting decisions. *Id.* at 6. *See also* Stephen J. Choi & Jill E. Fisch, *On Beyond CalPers: Survey Evidence on the Developing Role of Public Pension Funds in Corporate Governance*, 61 VAND. L. REV. 315, (2008) at 321 (survey conducted in 2006), at 321–22 ("sample consisted of all the public pension funds whose attorney representatives were members of the National Association of Public Pension Fund Attorneys"; "Of the 124 surveys we sent, we received responses from forty public pension funds, giving us a response rate of approximately 32%. Responding funds ranged in size from less than $1 billion in assets under management to approximately $150 billion in assets. Our funds came from twenty-five states plus the U.S. Virgin Islands."), at 324 (results showed that 8 funds, or 20% of those responding, delegated voting authority to proxy advisers to vote according to the proxy advisers' recommendations, while 15 funds, or 37.5%, delegated voting to proxy advisers to vote shares according to the funds' own guidelines).

A series of legal requirements and SEC interpretations of those requirements encouraged mutual fund managers to seek the assistance of proxy advisers in voting portfolio shares. *See* Gallagher on Proxy Advisers, *supra* note 116. Briefly, the SEC in 2003 required that mutual fund managers—called "investment advisers" in federal securities law—vote the shares of portfolio companies in the best interests of the investors in the mutual funds. *See supra* note 73 and accompanying text. The SEC also required that mutual funds disclose how their managers voted the shares, as well as the policies determining how the shares were voted. *See supra* note 74 and accompanying text. At the same time, the SEC warned that fund managers must not vote the shares to promote their own interests, such as getting or retaining contracts to manage pension assets at portfolio companies. Proxy Voting by Investment Advisers, *supra* note 73, at 6586. The Commission said that a fund manager could cleanse votes of portfolio company stock of any manager conflict by voting on the basis of a recommendation by an independent third party. *Id.* at 6588; SEC, No-Action Letter to Egan-Jones Proxy Services, May 27, 2004, 2004 WL 1201240, at *2. Although the SEC cautioned fund managers that they must screen such third parties for the third parties' own conflicts in making the recommendations, SEC Egan-Jones No Action Letter at *2, the staff also indicated that the managers could perform that screening by review of a third party's conflict procedures and implementation of those procedures. SEC, No-Action Letter to ISS, Sept. 15, 2004, 2004 WL 2093360, at *2. A legal bulletin suggests that a mutual fund and its investment adviser could decide not to vote portfolio company shares at all. SEC, Staff Legal Bulletin No. 20, Proxy Voting: Proxy Voting Responsibilities of Investment Advisers and Availability of Exemptions from the Proxy Rules for Proxy Advisory Firms, June 30, 2014, question 2 and answer, http://www.sec.gov/interps/legal/cfslb20.htm. But such a decision could create quorum difficulties at portfolio company meetings.

whose clients manage, respectively, $25 trillion and $15 trillion in assets.[118]

The proxy advisers offer administrative services, such as executing and submitting proxies on behalf of clients, and preparing required reports on proxy voting.[119] More importantly for this chapter, the proxy advisers recommend how institutional investors should vote their shares.[120]

The advisers publish extensive voting guidelines.[121] They then use these guidelines to make specific recommendations for voting on individual director candidates and other matters submitted to shareholders, including say-on-pay resolutions.[122] The proxy advisers influence institutional

---

[118]   LARCKER, GOVERNANCE MATTERS 364 (2d ed. 2016). For a history of proxy advisory services, see Stephen J. Choi, et al., *Director Elections and the Role of Proxy Advisors*, 82 S. CAL. L. REV. 649, 651–60 (2009); U.S. GOVERNMENT ACCOUNTABILITY OFFICE, CORPORATE SHAREHOLDER MEETINGS: ISSUES RELATING TO FIRMS THAT ADVISE INSTITUTIONAL INVESTORS ON PROXY VOTING 6–9 (2007).

[119]   INDEPENDENT DIRECTORS COUNCIL & INVESTMENT COMPANY INSTITUTE, REPORT ON FUNDS' USE OF PROXY ADVISORY FIRMS (2015) [IDC, FUNDS' USE OF PROXY ADVISERS] at 3, identifying as one of the services that proxy advisory firms provide:

> [a]ssisting with the administrative tasks associated with proxy voting, including keeping track of meeting dates and voting instructions, executing proxies in accordance with clients' instructions (which may include voting in accordance with a fund's proxy voting guidelines that the proxy advisory firm inputs into its system as part of the fund's account setup), generating voting reports, providing coverage and translation services with respect to foreign issuers, and compiling information for funds' annual proxy voting filings with the SEC on Form N-PX.

See 17 C.F.R. § 270.30b1-4 (requiring mutual funds to "file an annual report on Form N-PX . . . not later than August 31 of each year, containing the [fund's] proxy voting record for the most recent twelve-month period ended June 30.").

[120]   IDC, FUNDS' USE OF PROXY ADVISERS, *supra* note 119, at 3, characterizing an additional service offered by proxy advisers as "[a]nalyzing, providing research, and making voting recommendations on the matters presented for shareholder vote, which fund [managers] may take into account to varying degrees in deciding how to vote." A proxy adviser may also offer yet more services. As set out earlier in this chapter, ISS publishes corporate governance ratings on public companies. And it sells consulting services to public companies on governance matters. *See* ISS brochure, last updated on April 13, 2015, http://www.issgovernance.com/file/duediligence/1_iss-adv-part-2a-4-13-2015.pdf, at 7 (reporting that an "ISS wholly-owned subsidiary, ISS Corporate Services, Inc. ('ICS'), serves the corporate issuer community by providing products and services that enable issuers to understand and implement corporate governance best practices"). ICS specifically offers consulting services for the development of compensation programs. The services include use of a "proprietary Pay-for-Performance Modeler" with an "online tool [companies can use to] build custom CEO pay analyses to assess pay and performance alignment using the . . . tests employed by ISS in assessing quantitative concern." ISS, Compensation Solutions, Test Pay-for-Performance Alignment, https://www.isscorporatesolutions.com/test-pay-for-performance-alignment/ (last visited May 6, 2016).

[121]   *See* the 2015 guidelines at ISS, UNITED STATES SUMMARY PROXY VOTING GUIDELINES (Updated Mar. 4, 2015) [ISS 2015 GUIDELINES], which ran to 69 numbered pages, and GLASS LEWIS & CO., PROXY PAPER™ GUIDELINES: 2015 PROXY SEASON, AN OVERVIEW OF THE GLASS LEWIS APPROACH TO PROXY ADVICE—UNITED STATES (2015) [GLASS LEWIS 2015 GUIDELINES], which ran to 45 numbered pages.

[122]   For example, both the major proxy advisers recommended voting against the JPMorgan Chase & Co. ("JPMorgan") say-on-pay resolution in 2015. *See* Emily Glazer, *ISS, Glass Lewis Recommend Vote Against J.P. Morgan CEO Dimon's Pay Package*, WALL ST. J., May 6, 2015, http://www.wsj.com/articles/iss-recommends-vote-against-j-p-morgan-ceo-dimons-pay-package-1430926690.

investor voting both directly and indirectly. Some managers that use a proxy adviser to vote stock appear to simply instruct the adviser to vote according to the proxy adviser's recommendations, and others, while voting the shares themselves, cast their votes in lockstep with an adviser's recommendations.[123] Still other fund managers formulate their own voting guidelines but take proxy advisers' guidelines into account in doing so,[124] and indeed may create their own guidelines simply by customizing a proxy adviser's set to a greater or lesser extent.[125] Even managers that do not follow a proxy adviser's recommendations may take a closer look at a particular director candidate or say-on-pay resolution if proxy advisers recommend negative votes.[126]

---

[123]   BEW, HOW FUNDS USE PROXY ADVISERS, *supra* note 114, at 18 ("Of the asset managers with whom we spoke, a few said they have adopted the voting policies developed by one or another of the proxy firms. One participant in this group said, '*We used to have custom guidelines. But over time, we realized they were very close to [those of the proxy adviser we use], so much so that our guidelines resulted in very few different votes, so we converged. We consider it a cleaner baseline than the accumulation of custom guidelines. We still retain the right and the responsibility to go in a different direction when we need to.*' ") (emphasis in original). Stephen Choi, et al., *Who Calls the Shots? How Mutual Funds Vote on Director Elections*, 3 HARV. BUS. L. REV. 35 (2013) [Choi, *Who Calls the Shots?*] ("[W]e treat the funds comprising a cluster as a single fund, reflecting our determination that the lockstep vote by a cluster represents a single voting decision." (at 50); "Of the 127 clusters in our sample, we find that 10 virtually always follow ISS, voting in accordance with the ISS recommendation in 99.5% or more of their votes, and that another 26 appear to follow ISS to a lesser degree," i.e., "either follow ISS 'for' recommendations in at least 99.95% of the votes . . . , follow ISS 'withhold' recommendations in at least 99.95% of the votes . . . , or vote in accordance with ISS recommendations more than 99% of the time." (at 51–52 & n.92)).

Some funds are "passive" in the sense that their managers make investments automatically, without fund manager analysis of individual companies. For example, index funds simply buy the stocks in the index they mimic. BEW, HOW FUNDS USE PROXY ADVISERS, *supra* note 114, at 15 ("Many observers believe that 'index funds vote with ISS because they can't justify to shareholders why they invest in their own analysis.' One participant said, '*[T]he passive side is probably more reliant on proxy firms because they don't have the resources to look at every indexed stock to the same degree. That would be [my] biggest area of concern regarding undue influence of the proxy firms.*' ") (emphasis in original; footnote omitted) (first quotation from *Audit Committee Leadership Summit, Shareholder Engagement: The Influence of Proxy Advisory Firms and the Role of the Board* 5).

[124]   BEW, HOW FUNDS USE PROXY ADVISERS, *supra* note 114, at 16–17 ("[V]oting decision-making is '*a dynamic, ongoing process, not a snapshot,*' which requires substantial work in advance of the end vote. Proxy ballot outcomes are influenced by decisions made months earlier, beginning with those related to voting policy. According to participants in our research, proxy advisers play an important role at this stage, though for most, they are not the sole source of policy input.") (emphasis in original), at 17 ("Most research participants reported that they use custom voting guidelines. However, even those in this camp said they make active use of proxy firms' policy statements to help flag issues and trends of importance.").

[125]   *Id.* at 17 ("[I]n a December 2011 webcast on 2012 benchmark voting policy changes, ISS said it implements '400+ client-specific custom [voting] policies,' which in aggregate account for more than '50 percent of ballots that flow through ISS' voting system.' It has also acknowledged that 'many of our clients can have voting guidelines that closely follow our recommendations.' ") (quoting Patrick McGurn, Martha Carter, Carol Bowie & Debra Sisti, *Twelve for 2012: Notable Changes to the ISS Benchmark Voting Policy for the Upcoming Proxy Season*, 3 (December 7, 2011); Audit Committee Leadership Summit, *Shareholder Engagement: The Influence of Proxy Advisory Firms and the Role of the Board*, 6.)

[126]   *Id.* at 23 (reporting that some funds "[u]se proxy adviser recommendations to flag a company for further review," with one participant in the interviews saying: "We used Glass Lewis's

The proxy advisers are powerful. Some studies find an astounding correlation between negative proxy adviser recommendations and negative votes by shareholders. One as yet unpublished study of shareholder votes in the period 2003–2010 found that a negative ISS recommendation against a director candidate was associated with 20% more shareholder votes withheld from that candidate, even after controlling for other variables such as abnormally high CEO pay and abnormally low stock return.[127] A study of 2011 votes on say-on-pay resolutions found a negative ISS recommendation associated with an almost 25% increase in "no" votes (i.e., votes *dis*approving the company's executive pay scheme) and a negative recommendation by both ISS and Glass Lewis was associated with a more than 38% increase in "no" votes.[128]

---

pay-for-performance methodology last year as a guideline. If they give a company an F three years in a row, we'll take a closer look [at the say-on-pay resolution].") (emphasis omitted).

[127] Yonca Ertimur, et al., *Understanding Uncontested Director Elections: Determinants and Consequences* (Mar. 2016) (draft provided by Professor Ertimur on June 4, 2016) [Ertimur, *Understanding Director Elections*]. The researchers examined "all uncontested director elections held at S&P 500 firms between 2003 and 2010, resulting in a sample of 23,844 director-firm-year-level observations." *Id.* at 10. They found that

> when ISS issues a withhold recommendation (1,673 cases, 7.0% of the sample), the mean votes withheld is 24.70%, versus 3.6% when ISS issues a favorable recommendation; an increase of 21.1%.
>
> Notably, 69.4% of the directors targeted by ISS receive votes withheld of more than 20%—a level typically viewed by boards as evidence of significant dissent and there is no case of votes withheld greater than 50% without a negative ISS recommendation. In other words, there is not only a strong statistical association between high shareholder dissent and ISS recommendations, but also an almost one-to-one mapping: most negative ISS recommendations result in relatively high votes withheld, and rarely do high votes withheld occur absent a negative ISS recommendation. . . .
>
> . . . [N]egative recommendations from the second most influential proxy advisor, Glass Lewis & Co (GL), are associated with an increase in votes withheld of only 8.0% (from 3.7% to 11.7%), likely due to GL's smaller client base. . . . [O]nly 17% of the directors targeted by GL receive votes withheld of more than 20%.

Id. at 10–11 (citations and footnote omitted).

Even after controlling for a variety of factors—including abnormal CEO compensation, abnormal stock market returns, industry-adjusted return on assets, percentage of outside directors, whether a director was over 65 years of age, and percentage of institutional holdings—the researchers found that "[a] withhold recommendation from ISS is associated with 20.6% more votes withheld," although the percentage increase from a Glass Lewis recommendation fell to 4.6. *Id.* at 11, 53 tbl.2.

[128] Yonca Ertimur, et al., *Shareholder Votes and Proxy Advisors: Evidence from Say on Pay*, 51 J. ACCT. RES. 951, 953 (2013) [Ertimur, *Shareholder Votes and Proxy Advisors*] ("Negative ISS (GL) recommendations are associated with 24.7% (12.9%) more votes against the compensation plan. When both recommend Against, voting dissent is higher by 38.3%."). The study analyzed votes at 1,275 firms in the S&P 1500, *id.* at 953, and controlled for the percentage of shares held by blockholders (in this study, owners with more than 5% of outstanding shares) as well as abnormal returns, CEO total pay, growth in CEO pay, and total percentage of institutional shareholding, *id.* at 975–77.

> This study also found
>
> that an ISS *Against* recommendation, on average, is associated with a vote against by 34.4% (= 19.8%/57.5%) of the nonblockholders and 24.5% (= 5.0%/20.4%) of the blockholders (the corresponding figures for GL are 17.6% and 13.7%). Hence, as conjectured, [proxy advisers'] influence is stronger among institutional investors with

Not surprisingly, results vary from study to study. One set of scholars studying director elections in 2005 and 2006 argues that the effect of the proxy advisers dropped after controlling for the factors that might otherwise incline shareholders to vote against individual director nominees, such as "whether the company was in the top or bottom 5% of the companies ranked based on the abnormal holding period return for the three-year period prior to the meeting date for the year of the recommendation," and whether the company's CEO ranked in the top 5% for excess compensation.[129] After controlling for these other factors, the researchers concluded that "the impact of an ISS recommendation range[d] from 6% to 13% for the median company."[130] But this is still a substantial influence. Moreover, the control variables suggest that the causal connection is hard to trace. Thus, it is possible that shareholders rely on

---

lower incentives to do their own independent research. This result is consistent with recent research showing that mutual funds' votes tend to deviate from [proxy advisers'] recommendations more often when the funds hold a large stake in the portfolio firm and have greater incentives to perform their own research.

Id. at 979–80 (citation omitted).

[129]   Stephen Choi, et al., *The Power of Proxy Advisors: Myth or Reality?*, 59 EMORY L.J. 869, 889 (2010) [Choi, *Proxy Advisor Myth or Reality*] (also listing as other factors for which the researchers controlled: whether the company had cumulative voting, a classified board, a poison pill, or golden parachutes). The sample for this study comprised director elections in 2005 and 2006 at companies that were in the S&P 1500 as of June 30 of the prior year. *Id.* at 885. The study defined excess compensation "as the difference between the total CEO compensation for the year prior to the meeting date (as provided by the Compustat Executive Compensation database) minus the expected total CEO compensation," which the researchers calculated with a complicated formula. *Id.* at 899 n.103.

It is also possible that the decisions of certain influential mutual funds magnify the effect of the proxy advisers. Choi, *Who Calls the Shots?*, *supra* note 123 (studying votes of 719 mutual funds in 56 fund families in uncontested director elections in 2005 and 2006 at S&P 1500 companies (at 45–46) and finding that the probability that 30% or more of the shares voted would be withheld from a director nominee was 79% if ISS made a negative recommendation *and* Fidelity voted against the director (at 63–64)).

[130]   Choi, *Proxy Advisor Myth or Reality*, *supra* note 129, at 906 (adding that "we consider it likely that an ISS recommendation shifts 6% to 10% of shareholder votes—a material percentage but far less than commonly attributed to ISS."). This result is consistent with Cai, *Electing Directors, supra* note 69, at 2395–96 (using "a sample of 13,384 director elections at 2,488 different shareholder meetings" in 2003–2005), at 2403 tbl.III (Panels B & C) (summary statistics showing that the difference in the mean percentage of votes cast for a director nominee in an uncontested election declined by 18.68% where ISS recommended voting against the director, but that the difference dropped to 8.8% after controlling for firm-level effects by comparing the vote for the director against whom ISS had made a negative recommendation to the votes for directors at the same firm against whom ISS had not made such a recommendation), at 2405–06 tbl.IV (showing that regressions controlled for such variables as whether the director was over 65, CEO compensation (whether high or low), industry-adjusted EBITA and excess return—also showing that a negative ISS recommendation was associated with 8.43% to 8.74% fewer votes for the director ISS opposed versus the votes at the same company for directors that ISS did not oppose), at 2417 ("Abnormal CEO compensation is the residual from a compensation regression where the dependent variable is the total CEO compensation and the independent variable[s] include log assets, prior-year stock return, industry and year dummies, estimated with all ExecuComp firms during our sample period. The high CEO compensation dummy equals 1 if the director is the CEO and his abnormal compensation is positive, and 0 otherwise. The low CEO compensation dummy equals 1 if the director is the CEO and his abnormal compensation is negative, and 0 otherwise.") (emphasis removed).

the proxy advisers to bring facts or factors—which the shareholders would consider important, such as low comparative stock returns and high comparative CEO pay—to their attention, either through recommendations[131] or through the guidelines that the proxy advisers

---

[131]   Choi, *Proxy Advisor Myth or Reality, supra* note 129, at 881–82:

> Of course, proxy advisors may be the source of the information underlying shareholder voting decisions. . . . The relevant underlying information is generally available to the public, but as long as the shareholder is not willing to conduct the requisite research, the proxy advisor's report is likely to become the exclusive source of information relevant to shareholder voting decisions. Under this circumstance, had the shareholder not subscribed to the services of the advisor, the shareholder would not have learned of the information.

In such a case, the proxy adviser may well be the "but for" cause of the shareholder vote.

See also BEW, HOW FUNDS USE PROXY ADVISERS, *supra* note 114, at 13–14 (footnote omitted) (emphasis removed):

> Virtually unanimously, research participants highlighted the value they derive from the role proxy advisers play in "digest[ing] and normaliz[ing] the vast quantities of data present in proxy statements in a short period of time." One asset manager said, "Proxy firms play a critical role in presenting the data: it's concise, consistent, and you always know where things are." . . . Indeed, according to some participants, the value of proxy firm voting recommendations is distinctly secondary: "We don't necessarily agree with everything they say, but they do a tremendous amount of work pulling information together and packaging it, so we can take what we want."

Further complicating causality, the ISS voting guidelines—which produce the ISS voting recommendations—are influenced by the institutional shareholders, since ISS consults with shareholders in developing the guidelines. *See* ISS, Policy Outreach, http://www.issgovernance.com/policy-gateway/policy-outreach/ (last visited May 6, 2015) ("ISS kicked off its annual global policy formulation process in July 2015 by inviting institutional investors, corporate issuers, corporate directors and various other governance market constituents to participate in its 2016 proxy voting policy survey. . . . After analysis and consideration of the survey responses, ISS will later open a comment period for all interested market participants on the final proposed changes to our policies for 2016. The open comment period is designed to elicit objective, specific feedback from investors, corporations and other industry constituents on the practical implementation of proposed policy updates as well as new policies."). Specifically, as to say-on-pay recommendations, ISS states that it takes into account three factors, one of which is the alignment of CEO pay and performance. ISS 2015 GUIDELINES, *supra* note 121, at 37–40. ISS uses its own complicated formula to evaluate the alignment of CEO pay and company performance. ISS, EVALUATING PAY FOR PERFORMANCE ALIGNMENT 6–11 (Nov. 2014) [ISS PAY/PERFORMANCE ALIGNMENT]. ISS created that formula after taking into account investor input. *Id.* at 3 (saying that "[i]nvestor feedback on the issue of pay-for-performance has indicated a preference for putting the focus on long-term alignment, board decision-making, and pay relative both to market peers and to absolute shareholder returns," then explaining that the formula uses "rankings of CEO pay and performance relative to peers over three years" and "CEO pay trends relative to shareholder return trends over five years"). ISS says that it has "validated" the formula by back-testing it against shareholder voting on say-on-pay resolutions. *Id.* at 3 ("Extensive back-testing has also validated that this approach generally aligns with shareholder opinions as expressed through say-on-pay vote."), 12 ("Another assessment of the effectiveness of these measures to determine pay-for-performance alignment is the relationship they have with the outcomes of management say-on-pay (MSOP) votes at companies' annual meetings in 2011. Using a panel of 1,967 companies where vote results and all three measures [used in the ISS analysis] were available, we regressed vote results against the three measures. The results indicate that all three measures are statistically significant (p<.02) predictors of vote results, with the strongest effect coming from the RDA measure."), 7 (explaining RDA as the relative degree of alignment, which "compares the percentile ranks of a company's CEO pay and TSR [total shareholder return, accounting for both stock price appreciation and dividends] performance, relative to an industry-and-size derived comparison group, over one- and three-year periods"). To the extent that institutional investors influence ISS, the ISS guidelines and recommendations simply mirror the same priorities back to the investors.

publish before the proxy season begins.[132] In short, the evidence shows that proxy advisers significantly influence shareholder votes.

Moreover, public company boards view the proxy advisers as influential, with the boards magnifying that influence by taking proxy adviser guidelines or recommendations into account in formulating compensation programs.[133] A survey of 110 companies in late 2011 found that 70% "reported that their compensation programs were influenced by the guidance received from proxy advisory firms or by the policies of those firms."[134] An unpublished study of votes on directors during the period 2003–2010 concluded that an ISS negative recommendation related to executive compensation was, after controlling for other factors, associated with a next-year change in CEO pay that "translate[d] into a $1.68 million reduction in total CEO pay, corresponding to 12.4% (17.1%) of the mean (median) CEO pay at these firms prior to the [negative] recommendation."[135] A study of 2011 votes on say-on-pay found that 55% of the companies whose resolutions garnered an ISS negative

---

[132]   *See supra* note 121 and accompanying text.

[133]   The influence that proxy advisers have on boards as the boards compose compensation packages has spawned a market for compensation consultant advice on whether the package a company is considering will draw a negative proxy adviser recommendation. Thus, Equilar, Inc. offers its clients tools with which to predict whether the clients' compensation scheme will score well or ill under the Glass Lewis and ISS pay-or-performance analysis. *See* Equilar, Shareholder Engagement, http://www.equilar.com/shareholder-engagement.html (last visited May 6, 2016) ("Equilar is the exclusive license holder of the Glass Lewis Pay-for-Performance (P4P) model. Obtain your actual Glass Lewis pay-for-performance grade using the most recent compensation and performance information available. . . . To ensure the greatest coverage of pay-for-performance analytics, Equilar provides a simulator for the Institutional Shareholder Services (ISS) P4P model. Our ISS P4P simulator is based on the company's publicly disclosed methodology model and includes in-depth forecasting and editing capabilities."). *And see* the description of services offered by ICS, an ISS subsidiary, in *supra* note 120. One commercial study found that "[i]n 2013, the majority of respondents (73%) replicated ISS's quantitative Pay-for-Performance tests in order to prepare for ISS's evaluation," with 56% using an outside consultant to perform that task and 25% paying ISS a fee for preliminary test results. MERIDIAN COMPENSATION PARTNERS, LLC, 2013 TRENDS AND DEVELOPMENTS IN EXECUTIVE COMPENSATION 9 (May 2013). The survey garnered responses from 136 companies. *Id* at 4.

[134]   David F. Larcker, et al., *The Influence of Proxy Advisory Firm Voting Recommendations on Say-on-Pay Votes and Executive Compensation Decisions, Director Notes from The Conference Board,* at 4 (Mar. 2012). The survey results, in more detail showed:

> During the 2011 proxy season, 72.0 percent of companies reviewed the policies of a proxy advisory firm or engaged with a proxy advisory firm to receive feedback and guidance on their proposed executive compensation plan.
>
> A large majority of companies (70.4 percent) reported that their compensation programs were influenced by the guidance received from proxy advisory firms or by the policies of these firms.
>
> Companies reported making a broad range of changes to their compensation program in response to proxy advisory firm policies. Roughly a third (31.7 percent) enhanced disclosure in the annual proxy, and 23.8 percent reduced or eliminated certain severance benefits. In addition, 15.8 percent reduced other benefits and perquisites, 12.9 percent adopted stock ownership guidelines or retention guidelines, and 8.9 percent introduced performance-based equity awards.

Id. at 4–5.

[135]   Ertimur, *Understanding Director Elections, supra* note 127, at 28–29.

recommendation that year made changes in their compensation plans the next year in response to the vote, with the responsiveness well correlated to whether the percentage of shares voted against the resolution exceeded the 30% level identified by ISS as the threshold that should trigger particular concern.[136]

The proxy advisers employ elaborate analyses to evaluate the compensation that companies pay. ISS determined whether to recommend a vote for or against a say-on-pay resolution in the 2015 proxy season using three factors: (1) the degree to which executive pay at a company aligned with the company's performance, (2) the extent to which the company engaged in problematic pay practices, and (3) board communication and responsiveness.[137] ISS analyzed the first factor—pay-performance alignment—through a quantitative model that took into account (i) the pay and performance of the company being evaluated, versus the pay and performance of comparable companies over a three-year period; (ii) a comparison of the executive pay at the company being evaluated as compared with the median pay at comparable companies; and (iii) the absolute pay at the company being evaluated, over a five-year period, compared against the change in the value of an investment in that company over that same time.[138] The variables in the analysis included total shareholder return, which is the return to shareholders through both dividends and stock price appreciation.[139] ISS also employed what it called a "qualitative" analysis of pay for performance, but this too involved some

---

[136]   Ertimur, *Shareholder Votes and Proxy Advisors, supra* note 128, at 954 (citation omitted):

> [W]e expand the sample to firms in the Russell 3000 that received ISS *Against* recommendations in 2011. For each of the 269 resulting firms, we examine the 2012 proxy statement to identify whether the firm discloses changes to the compensation plan explicitly made in response to the 2011 SOP [say-on-pay] vote. . . . We find that 55% of the sample firms report compensation changes in response to the SOP vote, a remarkable figure given firms' reluctance to respond to nonbinding votes unless supported by a majority of the votes cast. Firms' responsiveness increases with the extent of SOP voting dissent and exhibits a striking discontinuity: the frequency of compensation changes increases from 32% to 72% around a 30% SOP voting dissent. The discontinuity is evidence of the significant influence of ISS, which after the 2011 proxy season had indicated that firms failing to "adequately" respond to SOP voting dissent above 30% would receive a negative recommendation in 2012 on the SOP proposal and the election of compensation committee members.

See also id. at 984–86.

[137]   ISS, 2015 U.S. COMPENSATION POLICIES, FREQUENTLY ASKED QUESTIONS 13 (Feb. 9, 2015) [ISS 2015 COMPENSATION PRACTICES].

[138]   The model used three screens: (i) "[r]elative [d]egree of [a]lignment," which "measure[d] . . . the percentile ranks of a company's CEO pay and TSR performance, relative to an industry-and-size derived comparison group, annualized for the prior three fiscal year periods"; (ii) "[m]ultiple of [m]edian," which "expresse[d] the prior year's CEO pay as a multiple of the median pay of its comparison group for the same period"; and (iii) "[p]ay-TSR [a]lignment," which was an "absolute measure compar[ing] the trends of the CEO's annual pay and the value of an investment in the company over the prior five-year period." *Id.* at 15.

[139]   *Id.*

quantitative measures, such as the "ratio of performance-to time-based equity awards"; the "overall ratio of performance-based compensation"; and "results of financial/operational metrics, such as growth in revenue, profit, cash flow, etc., both absolute and relative to peers"—as well as some non-quantitative factors such as "completeness of disclosure."[140] Turning to the second factor, ISS addressed problematic pay practices by looking for a laundry list of specific questionable pay arrangements, such as "[c]ontracts containing multi-year guarantees for salary increases, non-performance based bonuses, or equity compensation"; "[i]nclusion of performance-based equity or other long-term awards in the pension calculation"; "[c]hange in control cash payments exceeding 3 times base salary plus target/average/last paid bonus"; and "[d]ividends or dividend equivalents paid on unvested performance shares or units."[141] ISS evaluated the third factor—board communication and responsiveness—largely on whether the board adequately responded to a previous year's say-on-pay vote in cases where the shareholders' approval fell below 70%.[142]

The Glass Lewis compensation analysis was similarly complex.[143]

---

[140]   *Id.* at 15–16. *See* ISS PAY/PERFORMANCE ALIGNMENT, *supra* note 131, for more elaboration.

[141]   ISS 2015 COMPENSATION PRACTICES, *supra* note 137, at 29–30.

[142]   ISS stated that one factor it takes into account in determining whether to recommend voting against sitting directors who serve on the compensation committee (and possibly the entire slate of company-nominated directors) and in determining whether to recommend voting "no" on the say-on-pay resolution is whether

> The company's previous say-on-pay received the support of less than 70 percent of votes cast, taking into account:
>
> >   [t]he company's response, including:
>
> >   [d]isclosure of engagement efforts with major institutional investors regarding the issues that contributed to the low level of support;
>
> >   [s]pecific actions taken to address the issues that contributed to the low level of support
>
>   . . . .

ISS 2015 GUIDELINES, *supra* note 121, at 13.

[143]   Like ISS, Glass Lewis employed an analysis that was both quantitative and qualitative. As to its quantitative test:

> Our model benchmarks . . . executives' pay and company performance against peers selected using Equilar's market-based peer groups and across five performance metrics. By measuring the magnitude of the gap between two weighted-average percentile rankings (executive compensation and performance), we grade companies based on a school letter system: "A", "B", "F" etc.

GLASS LEWIS 2015 GUIDELINES, *supra* note 121 at 28. It examined such other quantitative data as the "quantum paid to executives." *Id.* at 27. Like ISS, Glass Lewis looked for "[p]roblematic contractual payments, such as guaranteed bonuses." *Id.* It also checked for company responsiveness where the favorable vote on say-on-pay fell to 75% or below. *Id.* at 28. And it articulated specific design features that it favored, including "a mix of corporate and individual performance measures" to determine short-term incentive compensation, "[p]erformance periods of at least three years," and "[t]wo or more performance metrics" for long-term incentive pay. *Id.* at 28–29.

QUESTIONS ON PROXY ADVISERS

Do the proxy advisers empower institutional shareholders, effectively permitting them to pool resources by paying the proxy advisers for careful consideration of the many matters on which shareholders vote—matters so numerous that any given fund manager cannot, without excessive cost, study each one in detail?

Or do the proxy advisers simply provide a convenient way for the managers of the institutional shareholders to dodge their responsibilities, by effectively leaving the hard questions to be answered by others?

Do you view the proxy advisers as an independent force in corporate governance? Or do you think that, since they ultimately depend on fees paid by institutional investors, the proxy advisers will *reflect* the views of those shareholders instead of *controlling* those views?

Do you want to know more about the people who run the proxy advisers? For example, do you want to know whether they have their own corporate governance agendas?

As this book is being prepared for publication, ISS is owned by Vestar Capital Partners, a private equity company.[144] Glass Lewis is owned by the Ontario Teachers' Pension Plan Board and Alberta Investment Management Corp.[145] The Ontario Teachers' Pension Plan is itself an institutional investor "[w]ith $171.4 billion in assets as of December 31, 2015."[146] The Alberta Investment Management Corp. is, as its name states, an investment management firm.[147] How does this ownership affect your view of these proxy advisers?

Is it ultimately good or bad for public companies to change their executive compensation systems based upon "guidelines" and sophisticated quantitative models developed by the proxy advisers? Is there a danger that the proxy advisers will be unable to adjust their criteria adequately to account for the particular circumstances of different companies, with public companies pushed by the proxy advisers toward cookie-cutter solutions? Or does the very uniformity of the analysis used by the proxy advisers impose some useful discipline on a system that would otherwise permit easy capture of boards by the executives whom the boards are supposed to oversee?

---

[144] ISS, History, http://www.issgovernance.com/about/iss-history/ (last visited Sept. 14, 2016).

[145] Glass Lewis, Company Overview, http://www.glasslewis.com/company-overview/ (last visited Sept. 14, 2016).

[146] Ontario Teachers' Pension Plan, Home Page, http://www.otpp.com/ (last visited Sept. 14, 2016).

[147] Alberta Investment Management Corporation, Home Page, https://www.aimco.alberta.ca/ (last visited Sept. 14, 2016).

CHAPTER 15

NEW SHAREHOLDERS: GOVERNMENTS[1]

∎ ∎ ∎

Governments, as well as private investors, have taken equity interests in public companies. This Chapter Fifteen considers two categories of government shareholders: sovereign wealth funds and the United States government. In discussing the U.S. government as a shareholder, the chapter focuses on corporate governance at AIG during the credit crisis.

A. SOVEREIGN WEALTH FUNDS

Twenty-six countries with sovereign wealth funds ("SWFs") organized the International Working Group of Sovereign Wealth Funds (the "IWG") in late April and early May 2008.[2] The members negotiated among

---

[1]   I have used in this chapter material from my article, William O. Fisher, *When the Government Attempts to Change the Board, Investors Should Know*, 40 PEPP. L. REV. 533 (2013). I have done so with the permission of the Pepperdine Law Review.

[2]   The IWG included the United States, which identified the Alaska Permanent Fund Corporation as an SWF. Sovereign Wealth Funds Generally Accepted Principles and Practices 49 (Oct. 2008) [2008 Sovereign P&P]. Here is the description of that fund:

> The Alaska Permanent Fund was created by the people of Alaska in 1976 to save a portion of the state's oil revenue for the future. The Fund is currently [2008] worth about US $37 billion.

> In 1980, the Alaska State Legislature created the Alaska Permanent Fund Corporation to manage the investments of the Permanent Fund outside of the State Treasury. The investments are guided by a six-member board of trustees, appointed by the Governor.

> The Trustees have maintained a conservative asset mix over the years. The current asset allocation includes 53 percent in U.S., non-U.S., and global equities, 22 percent in U.S. and non-U.S. fixed income, and 10 percent in real estate. The Fund also has allocations of 6 percent to private equity, 6 percent to absolute return strategy investments, and 3 percent to infrastructure investments.

> The Permanent Fund is made up of two parts: reserved (principal) and unreserved assets. The Constitution does not allow the reserved portion of the Fund to be spent. The Alaska State Legislature may spend the unreserved part of the Fund as it chooses.

> Prior to 2005, the Legislature had only used the earnings of the Fund for one purpose: the Permanent Fund Dividend program (administered by the Department of Revenue). This program annually distributes a portion of the unreserved assets to every eligible Alaskan. These dividends have ranged from US$331 in 1984 to US$1,964 in 2000. In the fall of 2008, dividends of approximately US$2,000 will be paid to more than 600,000 Alaskans.

Id. Quotations from the Sovereign Wealth Funds Generally Accepted Principles and Practices reprinted with permission from the International Forum of Sovereign Wealth Funds. In 2015, the Alaska Permanent Fund dividend equaled $2,072 per recipient. Alaska Department of Revenue, Permanent Fund Dividend Division, Overview of the 2015 Dividend Calculation, https://pfd.alaska.gov/LinkClick.aspx?fileticket=m6LKKFK70ug%3d&tabid=504&portalid=6 (last visited

themselves a set of principles, called the Santiago Principles.[3] They are also known as Sovereign Wealth Funds Generally Accepted Principles and Practices ("GAPP"). In the 2008 document setting out these principles, the IWG provided this definition:

> SWFs are defined as special purpose investment funds or arrangements, owned by the general government. Created by the general government for macroeconomic purposes, SWFs hold, manage, or administer assets to achieve financial objectives, and employ a set of investment strategies which include investing in foreign financial assets. The SWFs are commonly established out of balance of payments surpluses, official foreign currency operations, the proceeds of privatizations, fiscal surpluses, and/or receipts resulting from commodity exports.[4]

The funds self-described their various purposes:

> SWFs are created by governments for a variety of policy purposes such as (i) stabilization funds (e.g., Russia, Chile, and Mexico), where the primary objective is to insulate the budget and the economy against commodity price swings; (ii) savings funds for future generations (e.g., Libya and Kuwait), which aim to convert non-renewable assets into a more diversified portfolio of assets to meet public sector superannuation liabilities in the future and mitigate the possible Dutch disease[5] effects of spending resource revenue; and (iii) reserve investment corporations (e.g., Korea, and Singapore's GIC), whose assets or assets under management, to some extent, are still counted as reserve assets, and are established to increase the return on reserves. These purposes or objectives may be multiple, overlapping, or changing over time.

> The SWF's policy purpose guides its investment policy and asset management strategy. For instance, stabilization funds, which serve short- to medium-term objectives, usually have shorter investment horizons. By contrast, savings funds, which have longer-term objectives, typically aim at generating higher returns over a long time horizon. SWFs whose objective is to hedge against country-specific risks may hold assets with negative correlation to the country's major exports to offset terms-of-trade shocks. Many

---

Apr. 29, 2016). As of September 30, 2016, the fund was worth $54,722,800,000. Alaska Permanent Fund Corporation, http://www.apfc.org/home/Content/home/index. cfm (last visited Oct. 5, 2016).

  [3]   The IWG spawned a more permanent organization called the International Forum of Sovereign Wealth Funds. Its home page is http://www.ifswf.org/.

  [4]   2008 Sovereign P&P, *supra* note 2, at 27 (emphasis removed).

  [5]   "Dutch disease refers to the situation where a boom in a commodity sector of the economy could lead to a loss of competitiveness for other sectors in this economy." *Id*. at 13 n.15.

> SWFs only invest abroad, thus illustrating how the SWF's purpose can affect its investment policy.[6]

SWFs control a vast amount of money.

> The numbers, size and prominence of SWFs in global capital markets have expanded exponentially in the past few years. Today [article published in 2008 but using 2007 figures], the estimated assets under management for the top twenty SWFs amount to over $2 trillion, and the total value of assets managed by SWFs equals almost half the market capitalization of the Tokyo Stock Exchange. Collectively, SWF-managed assets roughly equal those in hedge funds and private equity funds combined. The current $2.2 trillion in SWFs compares with about $1–1.5 trillion in hedge fund assets and about $0.7–1.1 trillion in private equity. The five largest SWFs are ADIA [the Abu Dhabi Investment Authority] from the United Arab Emirates, Norway's Government Pension Fund, Singapore's Government Investment Corporation (another Singapore fund, Temasek, is in the top ten), the Kuwait Investment Authority, and the China Investment Corporation. Each of these funds, as well as Temasek and Russia's Stabilization Fund, has assets in excess of $100 billion.[7]

It is hard to find comparable year-to-year numbers for the total investments by SWFs, but one count shows an increase in assets under management by SWFs to have grown from $3.07 trillion in December 2008 to $6.31 trillion in March 2015.[8] Norway, United Arab Emirates, Saudi Arabia, China, Kuwait, Singapore, and Qatar have the largest funds.[9]

> SWFs have made large but not controlling equity investments in major U.S. companies.

> [R]eserve-rich countries have begun to change their investment strategy. Until recently [writing in 2008], these surpluses were conservatively invested, heavily in U.S. treasury securities and other national government bonds. Capital was recycled without economic or political disruption. That pattern has changed, but for

---

[6]   *Id.* at 12–13 (footnotes omitted).

[7]   Ronald J. Gilson & Curtis J. Milhaupt, *Sovereign Wealth Funds and Corporate Governance: A Minimalist Response to the New Mercantilism*, 60 STAN. L. REV. 1345, 1356 (2008) (citing in relevant notes 47 and 48 to GERARD LYONS, STANDARD CHARTERED BANK, STATE CAPITALISM: THE RISE OF SOVEREIGN WEALTH FUNDS (2007), first cited at 1354 n.44) [Gilson, *Sovereign Wealth Funds*]. Quotations from this article republished with permission of the Board of Trustees of the Leland Stanford Junior University, from Ronald J. Gilson & Curtis J. Milhaupt, Sovereign Wealth Funds and Corporate Governance: A Minimalist Response to the New Mercantilism, Vol. 60, Issue 5, copyright 2008; permission conveyed through Copyright Clearance Center, Inc.

[8]   Preqin Ltd., *2015 Preqin Sovereign Wealth Fund Review: Exclusive Extract* 5 fig.1 (June 2015).

[9]   SWF Institute, http://www.swfinstitute.org/sovereign-wealth-fund-rankings/ (last visited Apr. 29, 2016).

economic reasons rather than because of changes in international relations or foreign policy. Many governments have recently announced plans to shift investment strategies for sovereign assets from conservative holdings of government bonds to higher-risk/higher-return investments in equities or corporate acquisitions. Even the Norwegian Government Pension Fund, the most conservative of the sovereign wealth funds, has increased its allocation to equity by half—from 40% to 60% of its portfolio. China has also signaled its intent to increase its equity investments, both in its sovereign wealth funds and in the portfolio of the government pension fund. The announced reason for these changes in portfolio strategy is straightforward. Like the Bush administration's plan to shift social security investments into the capital markets, reserve-rich countries say they are seeking the higher returns and greater diversification associated with investing in a broader range of asset classes.

The result has been a boom in high-profile, and highly controversial investments. The Abu Dhabi Investment Authority (ADIA) recently acquired Citibank debt convertible into 4.9% of its common stock, which would make ADIA one of the bank's largest shareholders. A Chinese fund purchased just under 10% of Blackstone's equity in 2007. Chinese and Singaporean entities are discussing the purchase of a significant stake in Barclays. Another Abu Dhabi entity purchased 8.1% of the common stock of Advanced Micro Devices [AMD], a U.S. chipmaker with Defense Department contracts. Somewhat less controversially but no less significantly, SWFs have recently made multi-billion dollar investments in U.S. investment banks such as Citigroup, Morgan Stanley and Merrill Lynch, whose capital was depleted by the meltdown in the subprime mortgage market. Collectively, sovereign wealth funds have invested approximately $60 billion in Western banks since May 2007.[10]

One concern, which stretches outward from corporate governance to national security interests, is that SWFs might use their shareholdings for purposes other than to achieve a return on investment. Such other purposes could be dictated by the governments controlling the funds.

Viewed from this side, national security concerns anchor one end of a continuum of issues concerning when the interests of a foreign government may differ from those of an ordinary shareholder. To illustrate the point, consider that critics of the Abu Dhabi SWF investment in AMD expressed concern about industrial espionage, not just national security. Similarly, consider SWFs'

---

[10]   Gilson, *Sovereign Wealth Funds, supra* note 7, at 1347–49 (footnotes omitted).

rapid infusion of capital into U.S. commercial and investment banks in the wake of the subprime writedowns. Few domestic financial institutions provided capital. If the investment opportunity was attractive in purely economic terms, why were the SWFs the principal investors? Perhaps the investments were attractive to SWFs because they got something more than a purely financial investment. Or perhaps SWF investments were particularly attractive to the current managers of the investment banks struggling with subprime writedowns because they could act quickly and were thought unlikely either to agitate for change or to seek control, an unusual combination of characteristics for investors in companies whose operating strategies created the need for massive capital investments in the first place. The European Commission raises concerns that SWF investment policy "may reflect a desire to obtain technology and expertise to benefit national strategic interests, rather than being driven by normal commercial interests in expansion to new products and markets."[11]

Two scholars—Professors Gilson and Milhaupt—proposed in 2008 to address this issue so (although this proposal has not been adopted):

> [T]he equity of a U.S. firm acquired by a foreign government-controlled entity would lose its voting rights, but would regain them when transferred to non-state ownership. The result is to separate control from investment value; the expected returns to a foreign-sovereign equity investor remain identical to those of other shareholders, yet the foreign government entities lose direct influence over management through voting. Sovereign investors with purely financial motives will still invest; the proposal does not raise the cost of their investments. Sovereigns seeking strategic benefits from equity investments, however, will find SWFs to be a less attractive vehicle by which to achieve their ends. This adjustment mitigates the potential conflict of interest that animates the SWF debate without affecting the benefits that SWFs bring to the capital market.[12]

On the other side, the Santiago principles—which are "a voluntary set of principles and practices that the members of the IWG support and either have implemented or aspire to implement"[13]—seek to reassure primarily Western governments that the SWFs are investing for investment return, not to advance other national objectives. Here are some of the principles:

---

[11]   *Id*. at 1351–52 (footnotes omitted).

[12]   *Id*. at 1352–53.

[13]   2008 Sovereign P&P, *supra* note 2, at 5.

GAPP 9. Principle

The operational management of the SWF should implement the SWF's strategies in an independent manner and in accordance with clearly defined responsibilities.

. . .

GAPP 18. Principle

The SWF's investment policy should be clear and consistent with its defined objectives, risk tolerance, and investment strategy, as set by the owner or the governing bod(ies), and be based on sound portfolio management principles.

. . .

GAPP 19. Principle

The SWF's investment decisions should aim to maximize risk-adjusted financial returns in a manner consistent with its investment policy, and based on economic and financial grounds.

GAPP 19.1. Subprinciple

If investment decisions are subject to *other than* economic and financial considerations, these should be clearly set out in the investment policy and be publicly disclosed.

GAPP 19.2. Subprinciple

The management of an SWF's assets should be consistent with what is generally accepted as sound asset management principles.

. . .

GAPP 21. Principle

SWFs view shareholder ownership rights as a fundamental element of their equity investments' value. If an SWF chooses to exercise its ownership rights, it should do so in a manner that is consistent with its investment policy and protects the financial value of its investments. The SWF should publicly disclose its general approach to voting securities of listed entities, including the key factors guiding its exercise of ownership rights.[14]

An "online self-assessment tool developed by [the International Forum of Sovereign Wealth Funds] to observe Members' implementation" of the Santiago Principles found that

---

[14]   *Id.* at 7–9 (some emphasis removed). In addition, the principles address the fear that—because SWFs are owned by governments that can influence the value of stocks and may have special information affecting stock values—an SWF might have and use an advantage over private investors. GAPP 20 provides that "[t]he SWF should not seek or take advantage of privileged information or inappropriate influence by the broader government in competing with private entities." *Id.* at 8.

- 21 of the 25 members (84 percent) of IFSWF responded to the 2013 Survey . . . ;

- 13 of the 21 respondents have fully implemented all 24 GAPPs of the Santiago Principles . . . ; [and]

- On average, 86 percent of the 24 GAPPs have been fully implemented. . . .[15]

FIRST QUESTIONS ON SWFS

Do SWFs pose a national security threat to the United States? If so, is that a corporate governance matter? Or is this issue best left to laws or regulations that provide the U.S. government with tools to block foreign investments on a case-by-case basis?

Even if SWF ownership does not by itself implicate corporate governance, wouldn't the Gilson, Milhaupt proposal do so, by stripping shares of voting rights while held by SWFs?

Does stated adherence by an SWF to some internationally endorsed set of principles comfort you to the extent that you have concerns?

Although they raise potential concerns of strategic influence, the perception of the SWFs as welcome or unwelcome investors in U.S. companies varies over time. During the credit crisis, large SWF investments in troubled U.S. financial institutions garnered applause. And whatever threat SWFs pose seems smaller at times when the price of oil has fallen and the investment power of SWFs decreases, since the sale of oil provides the wealth that many of the most powerful SWFs invest.[16]

To illustrate changing attitudes, in 2007 the Bush administration reportedly worried that SWFs were acquiring assets in the United States.[17] Among other things, concern reportedly surfaced that SWFs might use investments to influence changes in government policies; for example, by

---

[15]   International Forum of Sovereign Wealth Funds, *2013 Report on the International Forum of Sovereign Wealth Funds (IFSWF) Members' Experiences in the Application of the Santiago Principles* 3 (2013).

[16]   As one article summarizes:

Most sovereign wealth funds are financed by the sale of commodities, especially oil. Prominent examples include the Norway Government Pension Fund and the various Middle Eastern SWFs. Non-commodity funds are typically established through transfers of assets from foreign-exchange reserves generated by trade surpluses. The China Investment Corporation is the most prominent example.

Gilson, *Sovereign Wealth Funds, supra* note 7, at 1354–55.

[17]   Steven R. Weisman, *A Fear of Foreign Investments*, N.Y. TIMES, Aug. 21, 2007, http://www.nytimes.com/2007/08/21/business/worldbusiness/21wealth.html.

lobbying for change in U.S. prescription drug programs after investing in a U.S. pharmaceutical company or by bargaining for U.S. government economic support of a company in which an SWF had invested in exchange for the SWF's sponsoring government's support of an American foreign policy objective.[18] In 2008, however, Lawrence Summers, at the time a former U.S. Treasury Secretary and later the head of the National Economic Council in the Obama administration,[19] and Ben Bernanke, the chair of the Federal Reserve,[20] lauded investments made by SWFs in U.S. financial institutions experiencing distress as the credit crisis unfolded.

Then the SWFs were hit in two ways in 2008 and 2009, with the price of oil plunging and the value of their U.S. investments (including those infusions of cash into endangered American banks) dropping precipitously. This combination reportedly reduced SWFs' inclination to make new investments in American companies, which in turn put them further from the U.S. public's (and Washington's) mind and therefore decreased the fear that those investments might be used to serve some state-sponsored purpose far from investment return.[21] In 2009, however, SWF investments in U.S. firms picked up.[22]

---

[18]   *Id.*

[19]   Stanley Reed, *Sovereign Wealth Funds Top Davos Talk*, BUSINESSWEEK, Jan. 24, 2008, http://www.bloomberg.com/bw/stories/2008-01-23/sovereign-wealth-funds-top-davos-talk   (with Summers reportedly "express[ing] serious concerns about the [SWFs]" but "acknowledge[ing that] the world was a better place for [the SWFs] having poured money into damaged banks in recent months"). To illustrate the range of thought on SWFs, the CEO of a large private equity company said that (i) he had been dealing with SWFs for decades, (ii) they did not operate differently than state pension funds in the U.S., and (iii) the SWF that was the largest shareholder in his firm did not have a seat on the board or "try to influence activities." In counterpoint, Summers expressed concern that SWFs might be *too passive* as investors—inclined to let unproductive management stay in place rather than sell their investments and face unpleasant publicity as a result. *Id.*

[20]   *Bloomberg News, Bernanke Says Banks Need More Capital,* N.Y. TIMES, May 16, 2008, http://www.nytimes.com/2008/05/16/business/16fed.html (with Bernanke reported as saying that the SWFs' investment in American banking had been "very positive" and "very constructive").

[21]   Landon Thomas Jr., *Sovereign Funds Now Prefer Hoarding Cash to Rescuing U.S. Financial Firms,* N.Y. TIMES, Oct. 13, 2008, http://www.nytimes.com/2008/10/14/business/worldbusiness/14wealth.html (quoting an international finance analyst at the Council on Foreign Relations as noting "a complete unwillingness on the part of sovereigns to hold anything else but super safe Treasury bills" and observing that the drop in oil prices and world-wide economic decline had changed the expectation that SWFs would look to the long term and ride out market volatility); Stanley Reed, *Sovereign Wealth Funds Taste Bitter Losses,* BUSINESSWEEK, Dec. 11, 2008, http://www.bloomberg.com/news/articles/2008-12-11/sovereign-wealth-funds-taste-bitter-lossesbusiness week-business-news-stock-market-and-financial-advice (including an estimate from a Morgan Stanley economist that SWF portfolios had suffered an 18% to 25% decline in 2008 and quoting the economist as saying, "You don't lose 25% of your assets without consequences"); Keith Bradsher, *China Shuns Investments in West's Finance Sector,* N.Y. TIMES, Dec. 3, 2008, http://www.nytimes.com/2008/12/04/business/worldbusiness/04yuan.html (reporting a Chinese official as saying that his country did not plan to invest more money in Western financial institutions and recounting Chinese SWF fund losses on investments in the Blackstone Group, Morgan Stanley, and Barclays).

[22]   David Barboza & Keith Bradsher, *China Lists $9.6 Billion in Shares of U.S. Companies,* N.Y. TIMES, Feb. 8, 2010, http://www.nytimes.com/2010/02/09/business/global/09invest.html?_r=0

Unsurprisingly, SWF assets can be directed not only into U.S. investments but also to investments in the sponsoring country's own economy. This, too, might reduce concern over their participation in U.S. companies. In 2011, China used its SWF resources to support the stock prices of its own banks, which had declined over worry about losses on domestic loans and requirements to raise additional capital to meet regulatory requirements.[23]

The actual involvement of SWFs in the U.S. economy—as opposed to speculation about what they might do—connects the funds to mainstream investment activity. In 2012, Qatar's SWF increased its stake in Xstrata— an Anglo-Swiss mining company—as part of an effort to force Glencore International to pay a higher price in Glencore's bid to acquire Xstrata.[24] In 2013, the Kuwaiti SWF participated in a group of investors trying to buy a British water company called Severn Trent.[25] U.S. companies, outside the financial sector, occasionally solicit investments from SWFs. In 2013, the private equity owners of Neiman Marcus contacted SWFs to determine their interest in buying that upscale retailer.[26]

SECOND QUESTIONS ON SWFS

Should U.S. government leaders contact the leaders of other countries to encourage them to prompt SWFs in their countries to make investments in American companies during an economic crisis such as the financial meltdown in 2008?

If that happens, how should U.S. investors in those American companies react? How should the boards of those companies react?

(saying that China's SWF had purchased more than $9 billion in U.S. equities in 2009, through investments in such companies as Bank of America and Citigroup).

[23] Keith Bradsher, *China's Sovereign Wealth Fund Tries to Bolster Stocks of Major Banks*, N.Y. TIMES, Oct. 10, 2011, http://www.nytimes.com/2011/10/11/business/global/china-takes-bigger-stake-in-4-of-its-banks.html.

[24] William Alden, *Qatar Fund Raises Stake in Xstrata*, N.Y. TIMES DEALBOOK, Aug. 23, 2012, http://dealbook.nytimes.com/2012/08/23/qatar-fund-raises-stake-in-xstrata/?ref=sovereign wealthfunds.

[25] William Alden, *Investor Group Ends Bid for British Water Utility*, N.Y. TIMES DEALBOOK, June 11, 2013, http://dealbook.nytimes.com/2013/06/11/investor-group-ends-bid-for-british-water-utility/.

[26] Mike Spector, et al., *Neiman to Approach Sovereign Wealth Funds as Buyers*, WALL ST. J., May 10, 2013, http://www.wsj.com/articles/SB1000142412788732424304578475021424343 51726 (reporting that sources "familiar with the deliberations" said that "Dallas-based Neiman plans to contact funds including the Government of Singapore Investment Corp., the Kuwait Investment Authority and the Qatar Investment Authority to gauge interest in buying the century-old department-store chain").

Would such events make the American companies beholden to the U.S. or foreign governments in a way that would damage the ability of the management, board, and shareholders to control the affairs of the companies?

If you had concerns about SWF investments in U.S. companies when you earlier considered those investments, are you still concerned now, given that those investments seem to increase or decrease with economic ups and downs and sometimes draw praise from American policy makers?

B. THE U.S. GOVERNMENT

Between October 28, 2008 and September 16, 2009, the United States government purchased various securities, including frequently preferred stock (and in most cases warrants as well), in more than 100 financial institutions and other companies (including General Motors).[27] We will study the credit crisis that prompted these investments in Chapter Eighteen. For now, we will take a deep dive into government ownership in one case in which the U.S. intervened in an extreme way in the governance of a publicly traded company by, among other things, obtaining majority stock voting control.

Although not typical, the government aid to American International Group, Inc. ("AIG") rewards study. The aid arrived in several packages. We will study only two, and will not follow the full cycle of government stock ownership, which has now come to an end.[28]

---

[27]   U.S. Treasury Department *Troubled Asset Relief Program Transactions Report For Period Ending September 16, 2009*, http://www.treasury.gov/initiatives/financial-stability/reports/Documents/transactions-report_09162009.pdf.

[28]   For a summary of the assistance, and restructuring of the government aid, *see* William K. Sjostrom, Jr., *The AIG Bailout*, 66 WASH. & LEE L. REV. 943, 963–75 (2009). The government and AIG recast their relationship in January 2011. AIG completely paid all amounts owing on the September 22, 2008 Credit Agreement. Am. Int'l Grp., Inc., Current Report, Form 8-K (filed Jan. 14, 2011). AIG preferred stock then held by the Trust described in the text converted to AIG common stock, and AIG preferred stock owned directly by the U.S. Department of the Treasury ("Treasury") converted partly to AIG common stock, partly to a new class of preferred, and partly to interests in other special investment vehicles. *Id.* The Trust transferred all of its AIG common stock to the Treasury. *Id.* After this recapitalization, the Treasury held approximately 92% of all outstanding AIG common stock. *Id.* In May 2011, AIG sold 100 million shares of AIG common stock to the public, and the government sold 200 million of its common shares to the public. Am. Int'l Grp., Inc., Current Report, Form 8-K (filed May 27, 2011). In 2012, the government sold more than 206 million shares in March, more than 188 million in May, more than 188 million in August, almost 637 million in September, and more than 234 million in December. Am. Int'l Grp., Inc., Current Report, Form 8-K (filed Mar. 13, 2012); Am. Int'l Grp., Inc., Current Report, Form 8-K (filed May 10, 2012); Am. Int'l Grp., Inc., Current Report, Form 8-K (filed Aug. 8, 2012); Am. Int'l Grp., Inc., Current Report, Form 8-K (filed Sept. 14, 2012); Am. Int'l Grp., Inc., Current Report, Form 8-K (filed Dec. 14, 2012). The last of these sales brought the government's common stock holding in AIG to an end. Am. Int'l Grp., Inc., Prospectus Supplement, Rule 424(b)(3) (dated Dec. 10, 2012, filed Dec. 12, 2012) at S-3.

The first aid package transferred control of the company to the federal government. The second imposed a raft of governance restrictions.

The first round of aid to AIG and the transfer of control. The first round of relief consisted of an $85 billion revolving credit facility provided to AIG by the Federal Reserve Bank of New York ("NY Fed").[29] The Credit Agreement for that facility was dated September 22, 2008, and included a covenant that AIG

> shall issue to the Trust[30] Equity Interests in the Borrower[31] having the principal terms and conditions specified in Exhibit D (the "Trust Equity"), evidenced by documentation in form and substance satisfactory to the Lender[32] and accompanied by such officers' certificates, opinions of counsel and other customary closing documentation as the Lender may require. In furtherance of the foregoing, the Borrower shall (A) enter into such agreements and take such other actions as shall in the judgment of the Lender be necessary to effect the issuance of the Trust Equity, (B) use its best efforts to obtain all material approvals from Governmental Authorities required for the issuance of the Trust Equity, (C) comply with any instructions or directions provided to the Borrower by the Lender in connection with obtaining the approvals referred to in clause (B) above and (D) not take any actions that are inconsistent with obtaining the approvals referred to in clause (B) above. The Borrower shall use all reasonable efforts to cause the composition of the board of directors of the Borrower to be, on or prior to the date that is ten days after the formation of the Trust, satisfactory to the Trust in its sole discretion.[33]

Keep the last sentence in mind as you read on.

Exhibit D to the Credit Agreement was a "Summary of Terms of Preferred Stock and Related Issues," which provided that AIG would issue 100,000 shares of Convertible Participating Serial Preferred Stock to "a new trust established for the benefit of the United States Treasury." It further provided that

> [t]he Preferred Stock will vote with the common stock on all matters submitted to AIG's stockholders, and will be entitled to an aggregate number of votes equal to (i) the Initial Number of

---

[29]   Am. Int'l Grp., Inc., Current Report, Form 8-K, Exh. 99.1 (Credit Agreement) (filed Sept. 26, 2008) [Credit Agreement].

[30]   The Credit Agreement was between AIG and the NY Fed. The "Trust" was "the trust or other entity formed for the purpose of holding the Trust Equity." *Id.* § 1.01.

[31]   The "Borrower" was AIG.

[32]   The NY Fed was the Lender.

[33]   Credit Agreement, *supra* note 29, § 5.11.

Shares (as defined below), as adjusted pursuant to the anti-dilution provisions, minus (ii) the votes, if any, attributable to shares of common stock previously issued on any partial conversion of the Preferred Stock; provided that the number of votes attributable to the Preferred Stock shall not exceed 79.9% of the aggregate number of votes of the Preferred Stock and the shares of common stock then outstanding.

The Preferred Stock will be entitled to participate in any dividends paid on the common stock, and shall receive (i) the dividends attributable to the Initial Number of Shares, as adjusted pursuant to the anti-dilution provisions, minus (ii) the dividends, if any, paid with respect to shares of common stock previously issued on any partial conversion of the Preferred Stock; provided that the dividends attributable to the Preferred Stock shall not exceed 79.9% of the aggregate amount of dividends paid on the Preferred Stock and the shares of common stock then outstanding.

Immediately after the stockholder vote,[34] the Preferred Stock will be convertible into a number of shares of common stock (the "Initial Number of Shares") equal to 79.9% of that number plus the sum of the common stock then outstanding and the maximum number of shares then reserved for issuance with respect to AIG's Equity Units.

. . . .

AIG and its board will work in good faith with the trustees of the Trust to ensure corporate governance arrangements satisfactory to the trustees.[35]

Again, keep this last sentence in mind as you read on.

Since the preferred stock would vote on an "as converted" basis, the government was acquiring almost 80% of the voting power in AIG.[36]

Beginning even before the execution of the September 22, 2008 Credit Agreement and continuing thereafter, the government entered into the management of AIG in a very determined way:

Beginning on September 16, 2008, "the government in the form of the Federal Reserve, working with the Treasury, became very deeply involved in the overall strategy" of AIG. [quoting trial exhibit] When Mr. Geithner appointed Ms. Dahlgren [who worked

---

[34]   The Summary of Terms required AIG to call a shareholder meeting to vote on measures necessary to permit the conversion of the preferred to common. Credit Agreement, *supra* note 29, Exh. D.

[35]   *Id.*

[36]   Am. Int'l Grp., Inc., Current Report, Form 8-K (filed Sept. 26, 2008).

for the NY Fed] to head the AIG monitoring team, he told her "[y]ou're going to take on AIG, we are going to make them a loan, and you are going to run it." According to . . . Mr. Baxter [the NY Fed General Counsel], "we had a team that we sent to AIG to monitor AIG on a continuous basis." This team spent "an enormous amount of time over at AIG," including "people who spent much of their time at AIG [Financial Products] up in Connecticut." Ms. Dahlgren "spent at least part of every day at AIG" during the early stages of the Federal Reserve's monitoring of AIG. By October 2008, Ms. Dahlgren was leading an effort to replace current AIG board members with new members of the Government's choice. PTX 310 (Oct. 19, 2008 email, Dahlgren to Geithner, recommending new board members, and stating "Morris Offit is prepared to hand his resignation to Ed [Liddy] when he asks."). Even at earlier stages, [the NY Fed's] plan was to replace all of AIG's Board members. PTX 3248 at 2 (Sept. 20, 2008 Davis Polk email: "We plan to take out the board and insert our own people. . . ."); PTX 3290 (Sept. 16, 2008 Davis Polk email: "The Fed wants the entire board to resign and be replaced.").

The AIG monitoring team consisted of hundreds of government officials and outside advisers. The monitoring team included professionals "from Ernst & Young, from Morgan Stanley, and from Davis Polk." Dahlgren, Tr. 2603–04; PTX 524 (containing a "working group list" of team members from [the NY Fed], Morgan Stanley, Davis Polk, Blackstone, and Ernst & Young). Morgan Stanley had approximately "[one] hundred individuals throughout the firm in different disciplines" who worked on the AIG engagement "on behalf of" [the NY Fed]. Morgan Stanley's scope of work was very broad, and encompassed virtually every important decision and activity. Ernst & Young also had "upwards of [one] hundred people" assisting on the monitoring team. Blackrock worked to value AIG's assets and to devise, structure, and manage Maiden Lane II and Maiden Lane III [which purchased assets that were causing AIG's liquidity problems]. Approximately ten to twenty Davis Polk lawyers were working with Ms. Dahlgren on AIG.[37]

---

[37]   *Starr Int'l Co. v. United States*, 121 Fed. Cl. 428, 448 (2015) (most record references omitted). This passage comes from the Court of Claims decision in an action against the government by AIG shareholders. The court found that the government did not have the power to extract the ownership interest from AIG. *Id. at* 121 Fed. Cl. 428, 434–35, 466 (2015) ("Upon a full consideration of the record and the arguments of counsel, the Court finds that [the NY Fed's] taking of 79.9 percent equity ownership and voting control of AIG constituted an illegal exaction under the Fifth Amendment. The Board of Governors and the Federal Reserve Banks possessed the authority in a time of crisis to make emergency loans to distressed entities such as AIG, but

The government formed the trust (the "Trust") to hold the preferred AIG stock by an AIG Credit Facility Trust Agreement (the "Trust Agreement") dated January 16, 2009. That Trust Agreement provided that

> the Trustees shall possess all right, title, and interest in all Trust Stock held from time to time in the Securities Account for the sole benefit of the Treasury. The Securities Account shall be under the sole dominion and control of the Trustees for the sole benefit of the Treasury.[38]

> At all times prior to the termination of the Trust, the Trustees shall (subject to Section 2.05 hereof and the other provisions of this Section 2.04) exercise all rights, titles, powers, and privileges of a stockholder of [AIG], including, to the extent permitted by law, the right to convert [AIG] Preferred Stock to [AIG] Common Stock and the exclusive right to exercise any and all voting and other rights and benefits attached to, derived from, or otherwise attributable to the Trust Stock, including without limitation the right to vote to amend or cause the amendment of the certificate of incorporation or the by-laws of [AIG], and the right to vote to elect and remove, or cause the election or removal of, the directors of [AIG], all to the extent permitted by their ownership (as trustees hereunder) of the Trust Stock.[39]

The NY Fed, "in consultation with the Treasury Department," appointed the trustees[40] and held the power to appoint a successor if a trustee left.[41] An introductory "whereas" clause to the Trust Agreement, however, stated that the NY Fed "wishes the Trustees to have absolute discretion and control over the Trust Stock, subject to the terms of this Trust Agreement."[42] An "independence" section stated that

> A Trustee may not be an officer or employee of the [NY Fed], the Treasury Department or [AIG] and may not have any material financial interest in the [NY Fed] (other than a Federal Reserve pension) or [AIG] (other than an insurance policy or annuity), shall not have a parent, spouse or child employed by or serving as

---

they did not have the legal right to become the owner of AIG."). The decision was on appeal when this book went to print.

[38]   Am. Int'l Grp., Inc., Current Report, Form 8-K, Exh. 10.1 (AIG Credit Facility Trust Agreement) § 2.01(a) (filed Jan. 23, 2009).

[39]   *Id.* § 2.04(a). The trustees were forbidden to nominate for election or vote to elect as a director anyone who was—at the time of the nomination or vote, or during the year previous to his or her nomination—an officer, director, or senior employee of the NY Fed or the Treasury. *Id.* § 2.04(e). The trustees were also forbidden from "becom[ing] directors of [AIG] or otherwise becom[ing] responsible for directing or managing the day-to-day operations of [AIG] or any of its subsidiaries." *Id.* § 2.04(f).

[40]   *Id.* § 1.02; preamble at pg. 2.

[41]   *Id.* § 3.02(a).

[42]   *Id.* § 1.02; preamble at pg. 2.

an officer or director of the [NY Fed], the Treasury Department, or [AIG] and shall be compensated for services rendered in connection with the administration of the Trust only as provided in Section 3.04 hereof.[43]

The trustees were charged with developing a "divestiture plan" to sell or otherwise dispose of the preferred stock "in a value maximizing manner . . . no later than a reasonably practicable time after . . . the Credit Agreement is no longer in effect and . . . the Treasury Department no longer owns any [of the preferred stock it bought in the second round of aid to AIG, discussed below]."[44] In developing the plan, the trustees were to take into consideration, among other things, the impact of a sale or other disposition of the AIG preferred stock on general financial market conditions and the best interest of the Treasury.[45] The Trust Agreement states that the trustees could sell the AIG preferred stock "only with the prior approval of the [NY Fed], after its consultation with the Treasury Department."[46] Moreover, the Board of Governors of the Federal Reserve System held the power to terminate the Trust.[47]

The three trustees were Jill M. Considine, Chester B. Feldberg, and Douglas L. Foshee. Considine was a past CEO of The Depository Trust & Clearing Corporation, which provides clearing and settlement services for securities trades. Feldberg had been chair of Barclays Americas. Foshee had been the CEO of El Paso Corporation, an energy company. Each had long affiliations with the Federal Reserve System[48] and exercised their duties as trustees in coordination with the NY Fed.[49] Indeed, the

---

[43]   *Id.* § 3.01. Section 3.04 provided that each trustee would be paid $100,000 a year.

[44]   *Id.* § 2.05(a). The Credit Agreement to provide the first-round aid was dated September 22, 2008. As set out below, the government bought preferred stock in the second-round aid in November 2008. As a result of this chronology, the government already owned the second-round AIG preferred stock by the date of the Trust Agreement in January 2009.

[45]   *Id.* § 2.05(a).

[46]   *Id.* § 2.05(a)(iii).

[47]   *Id.* § 1.03.

[48]   The court deciding the shareholder case against the government said this about the trustees:

> To administer the trust, [the NY Fed], in consultation with the Treasury, selected three trustees who had close ties to the Federal Reserve System. Chester Feldberg worked at [the NY Fed] for 36 years and "had a close relationship with many Federal Reserve employees and officials." Jill Considine "had chaired the audit and risk committee of the board of directors of the Federal Reserve Bank" and had previously served a six-year term as a member of the board of the [NY Fed]. Douglas Foshee was the chair of the Board of Directors of the Federal Reserve Bank of Dallas, Houston Branch, and Central Houston, Inc. during the time he served as trustee.

Starr Int'l Co. v. United States, 121 Fed. Cl. 428, 450 (2015) (citations to the record omitted).

[49]   As the court put it:

> In their capacity as trustees, Mr. Feldberg, Ms. Considine, and Mr. Foshee understood they had fiduciary duties to the Treasury, and not to AIG's common stock shareholders. The trustees also knew they could not sell or dispose of the trust stock unless [the NY Fed] approved, and they questioned their level of independence. On October 30, 2008, the

government used the Trust to hold the stock in order to avoid potential legal problems that might arise if the stock were held by the NY Fed or the Treasury.[50]

AIG's corporate governance had to be "satisfactory" to the three trustees,[51] and AIG had to "use all reasonable efforts to cause the composition of [its] board . . . to be, on or prior to the date that [was] ten days after the formation of the Trust, satisfactory to the Trust in its sole discretion."[52]

The Trust bought the preferred stock, with the controlling voting rights, on March 4, 2009.[53] And, holding nearly 80% of the voting rights at AIG, the three trustees had the power to elect the board going forward.

The trustees, together with the NY Fed, then exercised their power to change the AIG Board to their liking. In its proxy statement for the 2009 shareholder meeting, AIG disclosed that "members of the U.S. government in connection with the transactions entered into between AIG and the NY Fed and the Department of the Treasury" had identified 2 of that year's 11 nominees—including the new CEO.[54] The trustees of the Trust identified

---

trustees sent a memorandum to Mr. Baxter seeking to clarify their level of independence. The trustees were concerned with Section 2.04(d) of the Trust Agreement which set forth two potentially conflicting goals for the trustees to consider when exercising their discretion. First, the trustees were to maximize AIG's ability to repay advances under the Credit Agreement. Second, the trustees were to manage AIG so as not to disrupt financial market conditions as it was in the "best interests of the stockholders of the Company [AIG]." *Id.* The Government never removed Section 2.04(d) from the Trust Agreement, but did specify the two goals were "non-binding" on the trustees' discretionary power to vote the trust stock. This position satisfied the trustees that they would be independent in performing their fiduciary duties as trustees.

During their time as trustees, Mr. Feldberg, Ms. Considine, and Mr. Foshee received information about AIG through [NY Fed] representatives, because the trustees did not attend AIG's board or committee meetings. The trustees engaged Spencer Stuart, an executive recruitment firm, to assist in identifying potential new candidates for AIG's board of directors. In June 2009, at the annual shareholder meeting, the trustees proposed the candidates for election. Before voting on matters and selecting the board of directors for AIG, however, the trustees consulted with [the NY Fed]. The trustees also did not participate in matters affecting the Trust's ownership rights, including the reverse stock split.

Id. at 450–51 (citations to the record omitted).

[50]   More from the court opinion:

During the period September 16–20, 2008, Mr. Baxter conceived of the idea of putting the Series C Preferred stock in a trust as a way to circumvent [the NY Fed's] and the Treasury's lack of authority to own AIG shares directly.

Id. at 449.

[51]   Credit Agreement, *supra* note 29, Exh. D.

[52]   Credit Agreement, *supra* note 29, § 5.11.

[53]   Am. Int'l Grp., Inc., Current Report, Form 8-K (filed Mar, 5, 2009); *see also* the Am. Int'l Grp., Inc., Current Report Amendment No. 1, Form 8-K/A (filed Mar. 13, 2009), which includes the Series C Perpetual, Convertible, Participating Preferred Stock Purchase Agreement as an exhibit.

[54]   Am. Int'l Grp., Inc., Definitive Proxy Statement, Schedule 14A (filed June 5, 2009) at 13, 18.

five others.[55] Putting it simply, the federal government chose 7 out of the 11 nominees—a majority of AIG's Board.

QUESTIONS ON TRANSFER TO THREE INDIVIDUALS OF CONTROL OVER AIG

The U.S. government recast its relationship with AIG a number of times. As part of a restructuring in January 2011, the Trust transferred its stock to the Treasury.[56] Was it better for the Treasury, rather than trustees, to control the voting power of the stock? If so, why? If not, why not?

Should public ownership of a company's stock be insulated from political pressure? Or is political pressure simply the expression of the will of the taxpayers who provided the money that the government committed to acquire the stock?

The second round of aid and prescriptive intervention in AIG governance. As just shown, the U.S. government controlled AIG after the first round of aid because it had majority voting control and could and did determine who was on the AIG board. A second round of investment, however, went beyond this overall control and required AIG to adhere to very specific rules reaching matters that the company's board would otherwise determine.

The U.S. government put $40 billion into AIG through the purchase of preferred stock in late November 2008, together with a warrant to buy almost 53.8 million shares of AIG common stock.[57] The Securities Purchase Agreement (the "SPA") for this transaction, among other things, imposed restrictions on AIG's executive compensation. Note that the restrictions set out below were supplemented by even more startling restrictions that we will examine in Chapter Seventeen. It is helpful now, however, to examine the compensation restrictions in the form in which they existed at the time of the second package of government assistance to AIG. They give us our first look at how deep federal control can penetrate into companies in which the U.S. government invests.

First, the SPA provided that:

---

[55]   *Id.*

[56]   Am. Int'l Grp., Inc., Current Report, Form 8-K (filed Jan. 14, 2011) (at the closing, the preferred stock held by the Trust was exchanged for AIG common stock, which was then transferred by the Trust to the Treasury).

[57]   Am. Int'l Grp., Inc., Current Report, Form 8-K (filed Nov. 26, 2008).

(a)   [u]ntil such time as the Investor[58] ceases to own any debt or equity securities of [AIG] acquired pursuant to this Agreement or the Warrant, [AIG] shall take all necessary action to ensure that its Benefit Plans[59] with respect to the Senior Executive Officers comply in all respects with Section 111(b) of the EESA, including the provisions for Systemically Significant Failing Institutions, as implemented by any guidance or regulation thereunder, including Notice 2008-PSSFI [the "Notice"], that has been issued and is in effect as of the Closing Date [November 25, 2008], including but not limited to provisions prohibiting severance payments to Senior Executive Officers, and shall not adopt any new Benefit Plan with respect to its Senior Executive Officers that does not comply therewith. "Senior Executive Officers" means the Company's "senior executive officers" as defined in subsection 111(b)(3) of the EESA and regulations issued thereunder, including the rules set forth in 31 C.F.R. Part 30, that have been issued and are in effect as of the Closing Date.[60]

Stop here. We now have a number of cross-references to laws and regulations. Senior executive compensation had to comply with section 111(b) of the Emergency Economic Stabilization Act of 2008 ("EESA"), Public Law 110-343. That section, before significant amendments postdating the November 25, 2008 closing date, included the following criteria for senior executive compensation:

(2)   . . . The standards required under this subsection shall include—

(A)   limits on compensation that exclude incentives for senior executive officers of a financial institution to take unnecessary and excessive risks that threaten the value of the financial institution during the period that the Secretary

---

[58]   The "Investor" was the U.S. Treasury Department.

[59]   "Benefit Plans" were defined to include "compensation, bonus, incentive and other benefit plans, arrangements and agreements (including golden parachute, severance and employment agreements)." Am. Int'l Grp., Inc., Current Report, Form 8-K, Exh. 10.1, Securities Purchase Agreement § 1.2(d)(iv)(A) (filed Nov. 26, 2008) [SPA].

[60]   *Id.* § 4.10(a) (emphasis omitted). The Emergency Economic Stabilization Act of 2008 ("EESA"), Pub. L. No. 110-343 provided in 111(b)(3) that "the term 'senior executive officer' means an individual who is one of the top 5 highly paid executives of a public company, whose compensation is required to be disclosed pursuant to the Securities Exchange Act of 1934, and any regulations issued thereunder, and non-public company counterparts." A notice issued under that act defined senior executive officer to include the principal executive officer, the principal financial officer, and "the three most highly compensated executive officers . . . other than" those two. Notice 2008-PSSFI at 2–3. The same definition appeared in 31 C.F.R. § 30.1, by reference to the SEC regulation that requires disclosure of compensation paid to those executives (2008). The C.F.R. rules referenced in this chapter were changed in 2009. We will look at the superseding rules in Chapter Seventeen. The rules cited here are those in effect on the November 25, 2008 closing date for the second round of U.S. government aid.

[of the Treasury] holds an equity or debt position in the financial institution;

(B) a provision for the recovery by the financial institution of any bonus or incentive compensation paid to a senior executive officer based on statements of earnings, gains, or other criteria that are later proven to be materially inaccurate; and

(C) a prohibition on the financial institution making any golden parachute payment to its senior executive officer during the period that the Secretary holds an equity or debt position in the financial institution.[61]

Second-round requirement that the compensation committee consider whether incentives encourage unnecessary and excessive risk. The government committed money to AIG because that company nearly failed during the credit crisis. At the time and later, there was considerable concern that compensation schemes at financial companies had encouraged companies to take the risks that matured into that crisis. The SPA referred to the Notice, which provided in part:

In order to comply with section 111(b)(2)(A) of EESA for purposes of participation in the program, a financial institution must comply with the following rules: (1) promptly, and in no case more than 90 days, after the purchase under the program, the financial institution's compensation committee, or a committee acting in a similar capacity, must review the [Senior Executive Officer] SEO incentive compensation arrangements with such financial institution's senior risk officers, or other personnel acting in a similar capacity, to ensure that the SEO incentive compensation arrangements do not encourage SEOs to take unnecessary and excessive risks that threaten the value of the financial institution; (2) thereafter, the compensation committee, or a committee acting in a similar capacity, must meet at least annually with senior risk officers, or individuals acting in a similar capacity, to discuss and review the relationship between the financial institution's risk management policies and practices and the SEO incentive compensation arrangements; and (3) the compensation committee, or a committee acting in a similar capacity, must certify that it has completed the reviews of the SEO incentive compensation arrangements required under (1) and (2) above. These rules apply while the Treasury holds an equity or debt position acquired under the program.

. . .

---

[61]   122 Stat. 3765, 3776–77 (2008).

Because each financial institution faces different material risks given the unique nature of its business and the markets in which it operates, the compensation committee, or a committee acting in a similar capacity, should discuss with the financial institution's senior risk officers, or other personnel acting in a similar capacity, the risks (including long-term as well as short-term risks) that such financial institution faces that could threaten the value of the financial institution. The compensation committee, or a committee acting in a similar capacity, should identify the features in the financial institution's SEO incentive compensation arrangements that could lead SEOs to take such risks. Any such features should be limited in order to ensure that the SEOs are not encouraged to take risks that are unnecessary or excessive.[62]

The Notice stated that the compensation committee could comply with the certification requirement by saying that " 'it has reviewed with senior risk officers the SEO incentive compensation arrangements and has made reasonable efforts to ensure that such arrangements do not encourage SEOs to take unnecessary and excessive risks that threaten the value of the financial institution.' "[63]

This was a direct intervention in corporate governance—identifying a criterion for compensation, and requiring the compensation committee of the board of directors to consider and act to implement this criterion, then certify that it had done so. The government also specifically required that, in integrating the criterion into its deliberations, the compensation committee "must meet at least annually with senior risk officers, or individuals acting in a similar capacity."

QUESTIONS ON THE RISK ANALYSIS REQUIRED OF THE COMPENSATION COMMITTEE

Would this risk analysis be helpful? How would the compensation committee identify incentive compensation arrangements that encouraged senior executive officers to take risks that were "unnecessary and excessive" and that "threaten[ed] the value" of AIG?

Did the requirement that the compensation committee had to consult with risk officers in the company increase the probability that the analysis would be helpful?

---

[62]   Notice 2008-PSSFI at 3–4. The wording of the Notice was incorporated into the Treasury regulations that the SPA references. *See* 31 C.F.R. § 30.3 (2008) (compensation committee to review senior executive compensation for incentive effect on risk-taking and certify that it has done so); 30.4 (compensation committee to consult with institution's senior risk officers).

[63]   Notice 2008-PSSFI at 4; 31 C.F.R. § 30.5(a) (2008).

What are the implications, for intra-corporate politics, of the risk officer commenting on the compensation of the CEO and other senior executives?

———————

Second-round requirement for clawback of compensation paid for performance based on materially inaccurate financial statements or other metrics. The Notice stated that

> [i]n order to comply with section 111(b)(2)(B) of EESA for purposes of participation in the program, a financial institution must require that SEO bonus and incentive compensation paid during the period that the Treasury holds an equity or debt position acquired under the program are subject to recovery or "clawback" by the financial institution if the payments were based on materially inaccurate financial statements or any other materially inaccurate performance metric criteria.[64]

The Notice went on to state that this clawback differed from that in SOX 304:

> Section 304 of Sarbanes-Oxley requires the forfeiture by a public company's chief executive officer and the chief financial officer of any bonus, incentive-based compensation, or equity-based compensation received and any profits from sales of the company's securities during the twelve-month period following a materially noncompliant financial report. Section 111(b)(2)(B) of EESA differs from section 304 of Sarbanes-Oxley in several ways. The standard under section 111(b)(2)(B) of EESA: applies to the three most highly compensated executive officers in addition to the [principal executive officer] and the [principal financial officer]; applies to both public and private financial institutions; is not exclusively triggered by an accounting restatement; does not limit the recovery period; and covers not only material inaccuracies relating to financial reporting but also material inaccuracies relating to other performance metrics used to award bonuses and incentive compensation.[65]

———————

QUESTIONS ON FINANCIAL CRISIS CLAWBACK

Do you think that this clawback was better than the one in SOX section 304? If so, why? Ask yourself now, although we will address this more fully later, whether the Treasury's rules, built on the bailout statute, might successfully define new "good governance" standards.

---

[64]   Notice 2008-PSSFI at 5; 31 C.F.R. § 30.6 (2008).
[65]   Notice 2008-PSSFI at 5; 31 C.F.R. § 30.7 (2008).

Second-round prohibition against golden parachute payments. The EESA and the Notice[66] prohibited "golden parachute" payments to senior executive officers while the government held a debt or equity position in a company by the bailout. At the time the U.S. government provided the second round of aid to AIG, "golden parachute" payment was defined to mean "any payment in the nature of compensation to (or for the benefit of) a[n] SEO made on account of an applicable severance from employment."[67] The limitation only applied where the senior executive officer was terminated involuntarily or in connection with the bankruptcy of the company,[68] and limited only (i) payments made as a result of such a termination that would not otherwise have been paid and (ii) "amounts that are accelerated on account" of such a severance.[69]

QUESTION ON SEVERANCE PAYMENT LIMITATION

How might such a severance payment limit the choice of candidates that a company could reasonably expect to hire into a senior executive position?

Second-round limitation on tax deductions for executive compensation. The amount of compensation deductible per senior executive officer dropped to $500,000, without an exception for performance-based compensation.[70]

Second-round limitation on bonus pools, prohibition on using bailout money to pay bonuses, and prohibition on using money for deferred compensation. Companies may establish bonus pools that limit the total amount that will be paid to executives in a given year for bonuses. Executives are sometimes permitted to defer receipt of some portion of their compensation in the year in which they are entitled to it. The SPA for the second-round purchase of the preferred stock from AIG included the following promises by AIG:

---

[66]   Notice 2008-PSSFI at 5; 31 C.F.R. § 30.8 (2008).

[67]   Notice 2008-PSSFI at 5.

[68]   Notice 2008-PSSFI at 5–6 (defining an "applicable severance" as one "(i) by reason of involuntary termination of employment with the financial institution . . . ; or (ii) in connection with any bankruptcy filing, insolvency, or receivership of the financial institution . . . .").

[69]   *Id.* at 6.

[70]   Notice 2008-PSSFI at 6; 31 C.F.R. § 30.10 (2008) (cross-referencing 26 U.S.C. § 162(m)(5) (2008), which included the $500,000 figure and, in (m)(5)(E), defined "executive remuneration" by reference to (m)(4) "without regard to" (m)(4)(C), which excluded certain performance-based compensation).

Unless the Investor ceases to own any debt or equity securities of [AIG] acquired pursuant to this Agreement or the Warrant, [AIG] shall take all necessary action to ensure that the annual bonus pools payable to the Senior Executive Officers and the Senior Partners in respect of each of 2008 and 2009 shall not exceed the average of the annual bonus pools paid to the Senior Executive Officers and the Senior Partners for 2006 and 2007 (in each case exclusive of [AIG's] historic quarterly bonus program including but not limited to supplemental bonus and quarterly cash payments, the amount of which will not increase for any participant) and subject to appropriate adjustment for new hires and departures.[71]

[AIG] confirms that none of (i) the proceeds of the Purchase Price nor (ii) the funds provided to the Company under the Credit Agreement (collectively "the Funds"), shall be used to pay annual bonuses, or other future cash performance awards to executives of the Company. . . .[72]

[AIG] confirms that none of the Funds shall be used to pay any electively deferred compensation in respect of or otherwise resulting from the termination of the deferred compensation plans by the Company. . . .[73]

QUESTIONS ON BONUS POOLS

Why did the U.S. government freeze the bonus pool number?

Was that wise?

Second-round limitations on lobbying and certain expenses. The SPA required AIG "to maintain and implement its comprehensive written policy on lobbying, governmental ethics and political activity and distribute such policy to all [AIG] employees and lobbying firms involved in any such activity."[74] The agreement also included this passage:

Until such time as the Investor ceases to own any Preferred Stock, [AIG] shall continue to maintain and implement its comprehensive written policy on corporate expenses and distribute such policy to all [AIG] employees. Any material

---

[71]   SPA, *supra* note 59, § 4.10(c). The Senior Partners were AIG employees who participated in AIG's Senior Partners Plan but who did not fall within the definition of an SEO. *Id.* § 4.10(b)(1).

[72]   *Id.* § 4.10(e).

[73]   *Id.* § 4.10(f).

[74]   *Id.* § 4.11.

amendments to such policy shall require the prior written consent of the Investor until such time as the Investor no longer owns any Preferred Stock, and any material deviations from such policy, whether in contravention thereof or pursuant to waivers provided for thereunder, shall promptly be reported to the Investor. Such policy shall, at a minimum: (i) require compliance with all applicable law; (ii) apply to [AIG] and [AIG] Subsidiaries; (iii) govern (a) the hosting, sponsorship or other payment for conferences and events, (b) the use of corporate aircraft, (c) travel accommodations and expenditures, (d) consulting arrangements with outside service providers, (e) any new lease or acquisition of real estate, (f) expenses relating to office or facility renovations or relocations and (g) expenses relating to entertainment or holiday parties; and (iv) provide for (a) internal reporting and oversight and (b) mechanisms for addressing non-compliance with the policy.[75]

QUESTIONS ON EXPENSES

Should the board of directors of all public companies adopt a policy on expenses for the corporation? What are the pros and cons?

Were entertainment and office renovation expenses at companies receiving government financial assistance during the credit crisis—as AIG was—nickel-and-dime matters? Or, in the context of a company controlled by the government on behalf of the people, did such expenses hold a greater importance and therefore require policing?

Second-round requirement for a new board committee. The second-round SPA required that

> [w]ithin 30 days of the Closing Date, and until such time as the Investor ceases to own any Preferred Stock, the Warrant or any other equity or debt securities of [AIG], [AIG] shall establish and maintain a risk management committee of the Board of Directors that will oversee the major risks involved in [AIG's] business operations and review [AIG's] actions to mitigate and manage those risks.[76]

---

[75]   *Id.* § 4.12.

[76]   *Id.* § 4.13.

QUESTIONS ON NEW BOARD COMMITTEE

Should all companies have a risk management committee?

What is the appropriate relationship between a board's risk management committee and the board's audit committee? *See* NYSE, Listed Company Manual section 303A.07(b)(iii)(D) (requiring the audit committee to have a written charter "that addresses . . . the duties and responsibilities of the audit committee—which, at a minimum, must include . . . [the duty to] . . . discuss policies with respect to risk assessment and risk management.").[77]

Other restrictions imposed in the second round. The SPA also included prohibitions against payments of dividends on the common stock and against repurchase of common stock.[78] While we do not tend to think of such restrictions as matters of corporate governance, they do restrict what a board can do in exercising its discretion. See pages 83–85.

---

[77]   The commentary to this subpart of the Manual states:

While it is the job of the CEO and senior management to assess and manage the listed company's exposure to risk, the audit committee must discuss guidelines and policies to govern the process by which this is handled. The audit committee should discuss the listed company's major financial risk exposures and the steps management has taken to monitor and control such exposures. The audit committee is not required to be the sole body responsible for risk assessment and management, but, as stated above, the committee must discuss guidelines and policies to govern the process by which risk assessment and management is undertaken. Many companies, particularly financial companies, manage and assess their risk through mechanisms other than the audit committee. The processes these companies have in place should be reviewed in a general manner by the audit committee, but they need not be replaced by the audit committee.

Quotations from the New York Stock Exchange Listed Company Manual reprinted with permission from the New York Stock Exchange.

[78]   *See* SPA, *supra* note 59, § 4.8(a), corrected to remove an extraneous closing parenthesis:

(a)   Prior to the earlier of (x) the fifth anniversary of the Closing Date and (y) the date on which the Preferred Stock has been redeemed in whole or the Investor has transferred all of the Preferred Stock to third parties which are not Affiliates of the Investor, neither [AIG] nor any [AIG] Subsidiary shall, without the consent of the Investor:

(i)   declare or pay any dividend or make any distribution on the Common Stock (other than (A) regular quarterly cash dividends of not more than the amount of the last quarterly cash dividend per share declared or, if lower, publicly announced an intention to declare, on the Common Stock prior to November 25, 2008, as adjusted for any stock split, stock dividend, reverse stock split, reclassification or similar transaction, (B) dividends payable solely in shares of Common Stock and (C) dividends or distributions of rights or Junior Stock in connection with a stockholders' rights plan); or

(ii)   redeem, purchase or acquire any shares of Common Stock or other capital stock or other equity securities of any kind of [AIG], or any trust preferred securities issued by [AIG] or any Affiliate of [AIG], other than [listing certain exceptions]. . . .

GENERAL QUESTIONS ABOUT GOVERNMENT CONTROL AT AIG

Are you untroubled by the prescriptive restrictions and requirements that the government imposed on AIG? Doesn't any investor that buys voting control have a right to negotiate hard to obtain the terms that it wants—including terms that affect corporate governance? Can't we expect that the terms will include some pretty intrusive ones when the investor puts the money in at a time when the company is on the brink of collapse?

Would you feel the same about such restrictions and requirements if the government imposed them on companies in which the government did not own a controlling stock position? What about on companies in which the government owned no stock at all? Putting it differently, are there some government-imposed changes affecting corporate governance you can swallow where the government gets them through a negotiated investment (even in negotiations conducted with a company in extremis), but that would stick in your craw if the government mandated them through law or regulation? Or do you conclude that any restriction or requirement that you believe improves corporate governance should be imposed on publicly traded companies regardless of government ownership?[79]

---

[79] I ask this question without implying that the restrictions and requirements at AIG were helpful or that they were harmful. The question is to prompt you to think about the role of government in corporate governance.

CHAPTER 16[1]

SELECTED COMPENSATION TOPICS

▪ ▪ ▪

This Chapter Sixteen begins by noting the limited substantive effect of reforms on executive compensation. It then describes the components of current executive compensation in greater detail, with special attention to equity compensation—one of the most important means by which companies seek to align the financial interests of officers with the financial interests of shareholders. The chapter proceeds next to devices that companies employ to prevent officers from severing that alignment by selling the equity with which companies pay them. Turning to a broader topic, the chapter discusses whether CEO pay is too high and, relatedly, whether CEO compensation is set by market forces. The chapter ends with summaries of some of the many studies investigating whether the manner in which firms pay their executives encourages behavior that is harmful to companies and their shareholders. In addressing whether CEO pay is excessive and whether it encourages misbehavior, the chapter does not attempt to give you answers to these questions, but to help you think about them.

A. LIMITED SUBSTANTIVE COMPENSATION REFORM TO DATE

Except at financial institutions, the reforms of recent years have reached only modestly into the substance of executive compensation.

The section 304 clawback (see pages 365–368) operates in the limited circumstance where a company has restated financial numbers due to misconduct. Its reach is restricted by court decisions that only the SEC can sue to enforce the giveback. See page 367 and note 15 there. As we saw (see page 368), the Dodd-Frank Wall Street Reform and Consumer Protection Act requires what is certainly a broader, and potentially a more effective, clawback.

In one other substantive provision, SOX section 402 prohibits, with some exceptions, personal loans by SEC-reporting companies to or for any

---

[1]   The Watson Wyatt Worldwide office in San Francisco and the Los Angeles office of Analysis Group, Inc. performed some of the research that this chapter includes. Analysis Group, Inc. also provided research and analytical assistance. Equilar, Inc. provided valuable compensation data that the chapter contains.

director or executive officer.[2] This provision may have been a reaction to the loans that WorldCom made to Ebbers and the revolving loans that Enron made to Lay, which Lay repaid with Enron stock.

Thus, the substance of compensation (with the important exception of pay in the financial sector) remains very largely in the hands of compensation committees, which are charged (among other things) with approving the compensation package for the CEO and a handful of other top executives at the corporation, or recommending those packages to the full board for approval. True, the reforms have required changes in the composition of compensation committees to strengthen their independence and have given shareholders an advisory vote on senior executive compensation (the "say on pay" vote). But these reforms go to the *process* of setting compensation, not its amount, form, and terms.

The continuing ability of companies to control compensation of senior executives has special importance for us. If the pay is too high or paid in a way that provides incentives to misstate financial numbers or to take improper risks, we can blame the companies, for they remain in control of this aspect of their governance. Moreover, the limited target at which that control is aimed makes compensation a special test. Even if we might conclude that a board's audit committee has a job too large for a part-time panel to discharge adequately, a standing compensation committee should be able to grapple with the pay for a few individuals. Indeed, if that is not so, perhaps boards cannot successfully govern anything at all.

B. COMPONENTS OF CEO PAY AND HOW IT IS MEASURED

CEO pay is the focus of compensation discussion. We turn now to the components of that pay. Then we will look more closely at equity pay, arguably the most important of those components.

Forms of compensation. We considered compensation in a very simple way in Chapter Five. See page 189. In fact, there are many different ways in which an executive—particularly a top executive—can be paid. Here is a more sophisticated, though still by no means exhaustive, list:

Base salary;

Annual incentives for performance during a single year (typically but not always payable in cash);

---

[2]   116 Stat. at 787–88; 15 U.S.C. § 78m(k).

Long-term incentives in the form of service-based stock awards (including unrestricted and restricted stock[3]) and/or option awards;

Long-term incentives in the form of performance-based cash payments or stock awards, which reward the executive for achieving or exceeding, over some period of time exceeding one year, pre-established target levels for financial measures—such as total shareholder return ("TSR," including both stock appreciation and dividends), return on assets, or return on equity—or operational measures, or strategic objectives;[4]

Pension or other actuarially defined retirement benefits (the value of which can change from year to year, often increasing as the executive remains employed at his or her company over time);

Perquisites (which may include personal travel on a company airplane or in company-owned vehicles, financial and tax planning paid for by the company, club memberships, a housing allowance, a security system at a personal residence, and "gross ups" (i.e., payments by the company to reimburse an executive for tax that he or she must pay on, for example, the value of other perquisites)); and

Post-employment payments and benefits—which may, depending on the arrangements with the executive, be paid on resignation, termination (including constructive termination by demotion or change of duties), or in connection with a change of control of the company (by, for example, a takeover).[5]

While not "compensation" in the traditional sense, the executive may also make money from his or her company by engaging in business transactions with it—related-party transactions.

Not all top executives receive compensation in all of these forms. A particular executive will often receive some subset of them. The SEC revised the disclosure of executive compensation in 2006 in an effort to

---

[3] Note that, even while stock is restricted, the form of the restricted stock grant may provide that the executive receives any dividends paid on the stock. Or the grant may not do so.

[4] The threshold for an incentive payment might be stated in absolute terms or defined by performance in relation to peer companies.

[5] To appreciate the complexity of executive compensation (i) read the SEC compensation disclosure provisions at 17 C.F.R. § 229.402 and (ii) review the description of compensation in a few proxy statements, where companies apply the SEC disclosure rules to describe what they have paid to their top officers. For a summary of compensation components that is a bit more detailed than that in the text, *see* DAVID LARCKER & BRIAN TAYAN, CORPORATE GOVERNANCE MATTERS 213–17 (2d ed. 2016) [LARCKER & TAYAN, GOVERNANCE MATTERS].

provide investors with a clearer picture of what companies are paying to top officers in these and other forms.[6]

QUESTIONS ON COMPLEXITY OF EXECUTIVE COMPENSATION

Presumably, CEO compensation is designed to accomplish at least two goals: (i) pay the executive enough so that he or she will not leave the company to work for another company and (ii) motivate the executive to make decisions that will further the welfare of the company, as the board interprets that welfare.

Do the variety and complexity of CEO compensation—which may differ from company to company—make it difficult for the CEO, or the board, to judge whether the compensation packages at other corporations offer such better remuneration that the CEO might be tempted to leave? How can the board overcome such difficulties?

Do the variety and complexity of CEO compensation make it difficult for the executive to know how any particular business decision will affect his or her overall financial well-being? If so, does the compensation then lose its ability to motivate choices that will further the company's welfare?

Do the variety and complexity increase the difficulty that shareholders experience as they attempt to determine whether compensation packages at different companies enhance shareholder value?

Measuring the value of equity compensation. The list of compensation components above shows that some are paid in cash and some in equity. We will delve into equity compensation in detail soon. But one initial question is how to measure equity compensation. There are two basic methods. The first is to measure the value of an equity award at the time it is granted. This is a straightforward exercise when the award takes the form of unrestricted (that is, freely tradable) stock in a company whose stock trades on an exchange. In that event, the value is simply the number of shares awarded multiplied by the market price of the shares on the date that the executive receives the stock. The second way to value equity compensation is to compute the net proceeds to the executive when he or she sells the stock. Assuming that the executive paid no cash for a grant of

---

[6]   The resulting rule is the one referenced in the preceding footnote. Find the SEC's proposing release for the new rule at Executive Compensation and Related Party Disclosure; Proposed Rule, 71 Fed. Reg. 6542 (Feb. 8, 2006), and the adopting release at Executive Compensation and Related Person Disclosure; Final Rule, 71 Fed. Reg. 53,158 (Sept. 8, 2006). The SEC added additional disclosure requirements, and changed one reporting figure, in late 2009. Proxy Disclosure Enhancements, 74 Fed. Reg. 68,334 (Dec. 23, 2009). The Dodd-Frank Wall Street Reform Act added two additional compensation reporting requirements. 124 Stat. 1376, 1903–04 (§ 953, codified in part at 15 U.S.C. § 78n(i), with the remainder to be codified at 17 C.F.R. § 229.402).

unrestricted stock, the total compensation measured in this way consists of the proceeds on sale.

Valuing restricted stock and stock options is more difficult. Measuring the value of an option or restricted stock award on the date that it is granted—which may be years before the executive can exercise the option or sell the stock after restrictions expire—involves both (i) projections of future events (such as whether the executive will remain employed at the company long enough for the option to vest or for restrictions on the stock to lapse) and (ii) choice of perspective—i.e., whether the value will be measured as the cost of the award to the company or as the value of the award to the executive. As to the choice of perspective, we will see shortly how difficult it is to determine the value, to the individual executive, of an option or restricted stock award. Partly for this reason, the common choice of perspective—for reporting the value of an option or restricted stock award as of the date of the grant—is to use the cost to the company, as determined by accounting rules. Even computing that cost is difficult. The methods that companies employ to compute the cost of option and restricted stock awards require assumptions that are a matter of judgment and that affect the recorded cost in a significant way.

A second way of measuring the value of option or restricted stock awards focuses not on the value of the equity when granted but on the profit that the executive makes when he or she sells it. For example, if an executive has an option to buy stock at $10/share, exercises that option, and immediately sells the stock for $12/share, the executive is said, by this approach, to have been compensated $2/share in the year of exercise and sale. As another example, if an executive has restricted stock that vests in a given year, and the executive sells the stock in that year at $12/share, then the executive is said, by this approach, to have been compensated in that year at $12/share.[7] One problem with this approach is that it defers determination of the value of the equity compensation, measuring it at the time that the executive disposes of the stock rather than when he or she receives the option or restricted stock grant—which is the time at which the company is making its compensation decision.[8]

No regulation currently requires that companies report the value of option and restricted stock awards based on the amounts executives receive when they sell the underlying stock. In fact, current accounting standards and SEC regulations require reporting grant date values for equity

---

[7]   This assumes, as would be usual in the public company case, that the executive did not pay for the restricted stock.

[8]   The two methods are not cumulative. For a given computation, we would not both say that (i) the executive was compensated, in the year of the stock option or restricted stock grant, at the computed grant date fair value and (ii) the executive was compensated again, in the year in which he or she sold the underlying stock, by the net amount realized on that sale.

compensation.[9] But some companies supplement the SEC-required disclosure with an alternate measure,[10] using terms such as realizable pay and realized pay.[11] The exact definitions of these terms may continue to evolve, and whether the SEC will eventually require disclosure of equity compensation using such a measure is unclear.

Measures of pay can drive conclusions. Our evaluation of executive compensation can depend on how we measure it. For example, the Business Roundtable, an association of chief executive officers, released in July 2006 a study prepared by Frederic W. Cook & Co., Inc., a compensation consulting firm.[12] Looking at CEO pay at 350 large companies over the period 1995 through 2005 and using grant date values for stock options and restricted stock, that study concluded that total CEO pay had increased at a compound annual growth rate of 9.6%, while total shareholder return at those same companies had increased at a compound annual growth rate of 9.9%.[13] This, of course, suggested that CEO pay was reasonable.

But a well-known financial commentator criticized the study on a variety of grounds, including that—(i) the study omitted (a) dividends paid to executives on their restricted stock, (b) pension benefits, and (c) severance packages; and (ii) the study used grant date values for stock options instead of the amounts that executives realized when they exercised options and sold the underlying stock.[14] Changing the computation—in particular by replacing amounts realized on equity sales instead of grant date values of equity awards—would have increased the compensation, and thereby disturbed the correlation with companies' growth that suggested that the compensation was appropriate.

---

[9]   17 C.F.R. § 229.402(c)(2)(v) & (vi).

[10]   The compensation consulting firm Frederic W. Cook looked at 250 large U.S. companies and found that 15 of those companies "provided supplemental realized compensation tables or charts in their 2012 proxy statements for some or all of their NEOs ['Named Executive Officers,' who are the CEO, CFO, and the three highest-paid executive officers other than the CEO and CFO; 17 C.F.R. § 229.402(a)(3)] (four for all NEOs and eleven for only the CEO)." Frederic W. Cook & Co., Inc., *Realized Pay—New Approach for Measuring Pay* (Nov. 6, 2012), at 2, http://www.fwcook. com/content/Documents/Publications/11-06-12_Realized_Pay--New_Approach_For_Measuring_ Pay.pdf.

[11]   *See* Cook, *Realized Pay*; EQUILAR, INC., INTRODUCTION TO REALIZABLE PAY (2012).

[12]   FREDERIC W. COOK, MERCER HUMAN RESOURCE CONSULTING RESEARCH ON CEO COMPENSATION FOR BUSINESS ROUNDTABLE, Chart A (showing the 9.6% and 9.9% calculations), Chart C (stating that "[t]otal compensation includes salary, earned annual bonus, *grant value* of restricted shares and stock options, and target value of earnout of any other new performance-based cash or equity awards") (June 29, 2006) (emphasis added), on file with author.

[13]   *Id.* at Chart A.

[14]   Gretchen Morgenson, *Is 'Total Pay' That Tough to Grasp?* N.Y. TIMES, July 9, 2006, http://www.nytimes.com/2006/07/09/business/yourmoney/09gret.html?pagewanted=all (saying with respect to options and restricted stock: "because the study covers 1995 through 2005, it's a fair guess that executives at these companies exercised boatloads of options and banked huge gains. Ditto for restricted shares.").

QUESTION ON MEASURING THE VALUE OF EQUITY COMPENSATION

Do you think it is more useful to measure equity compensation (i) on the date that it is granted, even when (for options with a vesting period or restricted stock with a vesting period) the executive cannot at that time convert the equity into cash or (ii) on the date that the executive sells the underlying shares, even though the sale date is years after the grant date and the value of the underlying shares may have been affected by all kinds of factors in the interim, including a general market increase or decrease?

C.   IMPORTANCE OF EQUITY COMPENSATION

Equity pay—that is, pay by vehicles that will ultimately give the executive common stock in his or her company—constitutes a majority of CEO pay in the United States today. One commercial study of 2014 CEO pay at companies in the S&P 1500 reported that top executives received on average 53% of their total compensation in equity.[15] At the S&P 500 companies, the average was 60%.[16]

Over time, a CEO paid in substantial part with equity may come to own a fortune in company stock. Recent figures show the median CEO equity holding at the 4,000 largest U.S. public companies is worth $14.9 million—with the median CEO holding at the 100 largest such companies worth $104.9 million.[17] When a CEO owns that much stock, even small changes in the stock price can make such large dollar changes in the CEO's wealth that "the incentives provided by the equity holdings are at least as important and often dominate the incentives provided by annual compensation."[18]

---

[15]   EQUILAR, INC. 2015 CEO PAY STRATEGIES 9 fig.3 (providing figures for 2014) (2015). "The S&P Composite 1500® combines three leading indices, the S&P 500®, the S&P MidCap 400®, and the S&P SmallCap 600® to cover approximately 90% of the U.S. market capitalization." S&P Dow Jones Indices, *S&P Composite 1500®*, http://us.spindices.com/indices/equity/sp-composite-1500 (last visited Apr, 29, 2016). The S&P 500 "includes 500 leading companies and captures approximately 80% coverage of available market capitalization." S&P Dow Jones Indices, *S&P 500®*, https://us.spindices.com/indices/equity/sp-500 (last visited Apr, 29, 2016). The S&P MidCap 400.

[16]   EQUILAR, INC. 2015 CEO PAY STRATEGIES 9 fig.3.

[17]   LARCKER & TAYAN, GOVERNANCE MATTERS, *supra* note 5, at 247–48.

[18]   *Id.* at 248.

D. DIFFERENT FORMS OF
EQUITY COMPENSATION

Companies can pay executives in equity in many ways, including by

Awarding fully vested (or "unrestricted") stock to executives, so that the executives own the stock outright as soon as the award is made;

Awarding executives options, permitting the executives to buy company stock at some time in the future and setting—by stated price or by a formula to compute a price—the amount of money that the executives will have to pay if and when they exercise the option to buy the company stock;

Awarding executives service-based restricted stock, which the executives will not own outright until the restrictions expire, with the restrictions ending after continued employment at the company for a specified time; or

Awarding stock that that is earned, at the end of a designated performance period, provided that the company achieves one or more pre-established performance goals over that period.

1. FULLY VESTED OR UNRESTRICTED STOCK

An unrestricted stock award, and the reason for making it, is easily understood. A company makes such an award by simply issuing stock to the executive. A company might make such an award as a signing bonus for a new CEO. After the company transfers the stock, and as long as the executive continues to own it, he or she is motivated to make decisions that will increase the value of that stock. If the value of the stock increases, the benefit accrues not only to the executive who received the unrestricted stock award but to all other shareholders as well. The executive is also motivated to avoid decisions that could decrease the value of the stock, as the executive will suffer a real wealth loss as the stock price declines. Avoiding declines in stock value benefits not only the executive but other shareholders too.

Options, restricted stock, and performance shares are a bit more complicated.

2. STOCK OPTIONS

A description of the traditional option. A stock option is a contract. By that contract, the company gives the executive the right (but not the obligation) to buy a fixed number of shares of company stock at a fixed price (the "exercise price"), usually the market price on the date of the option grant. Assume that price is $10 per share and that the company grants an option to buy three shares. Typically, the executive cannot exercise an option until the option "vests," which only occurs if the executive continues to work for the company for some specified period of time following the option grant (the "vesting period"). The company might stagger the vesting so that the option to buy one share vests one year after the grant date, the option to buy another vests two years after the grant, and the option to purchase the third share vests at the end of three years. In that case, the "vesting period" for the option on the first share is one year. The vesting period for the option on the second share is two years, and the vesting period for the option on the third share is three years.[19]

After any of these options vests, the executive has a certain period of time within which to exercise the option ("the exercise period"). Options exercise periods often continue for some considerable time; for example, 7 or 10 years. At any time during the exercise period, the executive can purchase, at the exercise price, the shares covered by the vested option. Options granted as part of compensation are typically non-transferable, meaning that the executive cannot sell or otherwise transfer the options to someone else or use them as collateral for a loan.

If an executive leaves the company before an option vests, the executive often loses all rights under the option. If the executive fails to exercise the option after it has vested and after the exercise period has expired, then the option expires and the executive loses all rights to buy the share at the exercise price. If an executive leaves the company after an option vests but before the exercise period has run, the executive will typically have the right to exercise the option within a defined period of 60 to 90 days.

Returning to our example, at the end of the first year after the option grant, the first option vests and the executive has the right to buy one share at $10. If the stock price at that time is below $10/share, the option is "out of the money," because the executive would have to pay more money to exercise the option and buy the share than the executive would receive on immediate sale of that share. The executive will not exercise the option.[20] Let's say in our case that the executive can exercise the option at any time (subject to insider trading limitations) during the seven years after the option vests. If the option is out of the money when it vests, the executive

---

[19]   On the other hand, a company might award an option grant by which *all* of the options vest at one time at the end of the vesting period. In our example, the grant might vest all the options at the end of the three years. In that case, the vesting period for all the options in the grant would be three years. Such vesting of *all* options in a given grant at the end of the vesting period is sometimes called "cliff vesting."

[20]   After all, the executive could simply buy a share of the company stock in the market for less than $10. Thus, if the executive wanted another share of stock, he or she would make that market purchase at less than $10/share rather than pay the company $10/share to exercise the option.

can simply let the option sit. He or she can exercise it later in the seven-year exercise period if the stock price rises above $10.

If the stock price when the first option vests is more than $10/share, the option is "in the money" as soon as it vests because the executive could buy the share underlying the option for $10 and immediately sell it for more. The executive then has a decision to make. He or she can exercise the option and buy the stock right away or let the option sit and exercise it at any time until it expires in seven years. If the executive does not exercise the option, he or she runs the risk that the price of the stock will decline to below the exercise price and fall "out of the money."

Assume, however, that the price is now $12/share and the executive wants to make some money right now. The executive might (i) borrow the $10 dollars to pay the company for the share (remember that the executive has an option to *buy* at $10 and so must *pay* the company $10 to exercise the option), (ii) buy the share, (iii) immediately sell it at $12 (unless some contractual or legal restriction prohibits a sale at this time), and (iv) repay the $10 loan. Assuming minimal transaction fees and interest, he or she has made about $2 after repaying the loan.[21]

The arguments in favor of options. First, proponents of options say that options align management's interests with those of the shareholders. That is, an executive makes money on an option if the price of the company's stock rises above the exercise price after the option vests and before the exercise period expires, and makes more money the more that share price increases. Options thereby give the executive a financial motivation to take those actions that will increase the price of the company's shares. And, of

---

[21]   There are a number of different specific steps that an executive might take to exercise an option, and the option award or the plan under which it is made typically will set out the methods that the executive can employ. Here is one example:

The vested and exercisable portion(s) of a Stock Option may be exercised, in whole or in part, by giving written notice of exercise to Worthington specifying the number of Common Shares to be purchased, which, if required by the Committee, shall be in a form specified by the Committee. Such notice shall be accompanied by payment in full of the Exercise Price. Unless otherwise specified by the Committee and reflected in the Award Agreement, the Exercise Price may be paid: (a) in cash or its equivalent; (b) by tendering Common Shares already owned by the Participant prior to the exercise date; (c) by a cashless exercise (including by delivering or surrendering outstanding vested and exercisable Awards, by withholding Common Shares which would otherwise be issued in connection with the exercise of a vested and exercisable Stock Option, or through a broker-assisted arrangement to the extent permitted by applicable laws, rules or regulations); or (d) through any combination of the methods described in subparagraphs (a), (b) and (c) (in each case, valuing Common Shares at Fair Market Value on the date of exercise). The Committee shall determine acceptable methods for tendering Common Shares (including by attestation if permitted by applicable laws, rules or regulations) and delivering or surrendering outstanding vested and exercisable Awards and may impose such conditions on the use of Common Shares or outstanding Awards to exercise Stock Options as it deems appropriate.

Worthington Indus. 2010 Stock Option Plan ¶ 9, Worthington Indus., Inc., Current Report, Form 8-K, Exh. 10.1 (filed Oct. 5, 2010).

course, the other shareholders benefit if the share price goes up. So, options can motivate executives to run the company in a way that sends the stock price up, and everybody—executives and other shareholders alike—benefits when that happens. Second, options may provide an executive with an incentive to stay with the company, in our example for the full three years, until all of the options vest. Remember that the executive often will lose all rights to an unvested option if he or she leaves the company.

Third, some companies—particularly startups—do not have much cash. They can sometimes convince key officers to join the company for a very modest cash salary plus options that will be quite valuable if the company succeeds, goes public, and enjoys a stock price surge.[22]

Problems with options. Critics of option compensation identify many problems. Here are five.

First, options can reward or punish in a capricious way. If the overall stock market rises, by definition many stock prices go up. Assume that an executive has vested options that she could exercise at $10/share and that the price of her company's stock increases in one year from $10 to $12/share. Suppose also that, on average, stocks of similar companies rise 40% in that year. The executive in our example can exercise her option, pay the company $10/share, and sell each share for $12, making a nice $2/share gain on her company's 20% stock price increase. Yet, she and her fellow executives at the company have produced an *inferior* result in the sense that their company's stock price has risen by a smaller percentage (+20%) than the industry average (+40%). She still, however, makes money on her options.

The reverse can also be true. Suppose that the stock price at our executive's company falls by $1 during the year—from $10/share to $9/share, a 10% drop. Now, her vested options are out of the money. She cannot make *any* profit by exercising the options to buy the shares and immediately selling them. But suppose that on average, stocks of similar companies fell by 20% during the year. Our executive and her company colleagues have produced a *superior* result in the sense that they have held the decline in the company's stock price to a lower percentage (-10%) than the average (-20%). Yet she is unable to make any money on her options.

One way to address this first problem is to index the option exercise price by, for example, the average increase or decrease in the prices of stocks issued by companies in the same industry. That way, the price at which the executive can exercise a vested option is determined not only by the price of the stock on the date the option was granted but by how stocks

---

[22] Since our study focuses on public companies, this factor is of less importance to us—except to note that many companies that are now public were earlier private companies. Some were startups. They might have needed cash then and, at that time, option compensation might have facilitated the use of scarce cash for product development, marketing, or some other company-growing purpose.

move in the industry after that date. For example, if the stock prices of similar companies on average increase 20% in the first year, the indexed exercise price for the option that vests at the end of that year in our example would be $12/share. The executive then makes no money if the price of a share of the stock in her company rises only to the same extent as the industry average; the executive would have to pay $12/share to exercise the option and could only sell the share in the market for that same amount. The option would only be in the money if the price of stock in the executive's company rose at a higher rate than the average rate of increase in the industry.[23]

The second problem with options is that they can create an incentive for wrongdoing. This is particularly true where top executives receive options on very large numbers of shares. Return to our example but assume that our executive has been granted an option on 500,000 shares that will vest in full at the end of the current quarter. Assume that the price of her company's stock is today $10/share and that that is the exercise price for her options. Suppose that the market has been very sensitive to whether or not companies in our executive's industry report earnings that are lower than, equal to, or higher than analysts have estimated. Investment analysts writing reports on her company have estimated that the company will make 6¢/share in this quarter. Our executive believes that the stock price will rise to $12 by the day when she can first exercise the options *if the company reports 7¢/share for the current quarter*. If that happens, she will be able to exercise her options for $5,000,000 and immediately sell them for $6,000,000, thereby making a cool million. The quarter is now coming to an end. But there is trouble. It looks like the earnings may only be 5¢/share. Our executive believes that if the company reports only 5¢/share, the stock price will fall to $9 per share. Her options would then be out of the money.

To make a million dollars, might our executive be tempted to fudge the reported numbers a bit—or just lean on the sales and financial staff to use some sales and accounting tricks that are within technical rules but not ordinarily used by the company—in order to report the extra 2¢ per share in earnings? Can't mega-grants of stock options create, in this way, an incentive for accounting chicanery? We will look at some empirical evidence testing this hypothesis later in this chapter.

A third problem with options is that the same option award can have a different value to different individual executives at the same company at the same time. The difference in value to different executives depends on

---

[23]   There are a variety of ways to tie options to company performance, but few large U.S. companies use any of them. *See* DAVID LARCKER & BRIAN TAYAN, CORPORATE GOVERNANCE MATTERS: A CLOSER LOOK AT ORGANIZATIONAL CHOICES AND THEIR CONSEQUENCES 242–43 (2011).

individual characteristics and circumstances that the company granting the options may not fully understand. Just as examples:

- Different executives may assign different probabilities to remaining with their company long enough for options to vest.

- Different executives may assign different probabilities to the company's stock price rising significantly above the exercise price during the exercise period.

- Even where executives assign the same probabilities to the two contingencies just set out, those executives who are more "risk averse" will discount the value of the options to a greater extent than those who are "risk tolerant." And the discount can be sensitive not only to risk appetite but to other factors—such as the executive's total wealth and the degree to which that wealth is concentrated in company stock.

As to the last point, Watson Wyatt, a national compensation consulting firm, published in 2004 the results of an online survey of high-income employees that, among other things, asked the employees to identify trade-offs between stock options at their companies and cash. Watson Wyatt then compared the difference between the cash equivalent, as identified by the survey respondents, and the value of the options as computed by the Black-Scholes method, which is often used to calculate—for purposes of financial reporting—the cost of options to the companies granting them.[24] The employees generally valued options at a cash equivalent below the value of the options as computed by Black-Scholes. Even more significantly for the discussion here, *the survey found that employees who were "conservative" investors*[25] *on average discounted the options to a cash equivalent 53% below the Black-Scholes value and that employees who were "aggressive" investors discounted the options by only 41%.*[26]

Academic modeling produces similar results, with calculations showing that the value of an option to an executive depends on the executive's risk aversion and his or her diversification:

---

[24]   Note 32 *infra* cites to a description of the Black-Scholes method for valuing options. As that description points out, there are reasons to question the value that the Black-Scholes method assigns to options, when the options are the sort that companies grant as part of compensation. But the point of the Watson Wyatt study is not that the Black-Scholes value is correct, but that it is the same for all respondents. Accordingly, the discount off that set value by different respondents provides a useful comparison among respondents.

[25]   Presumably, the respondents self-categorized their investment style.

[26]   WATSON WYATT WORLDWIDE, HOW DO EMPLOYEES VALUE STOCK OPTIONS? 6 (explaining methodology), 8 tbl.2 (results) [WATSON WYATT, HOW DO EMPLOYEES VALUE STOCK OPTIONS?].

For example, the table [omitted here] shows that a FMV[27] 10-year option on a $30 non-dividend-paying stock has a Black-Scholes value of $17.60. Assuming that the executive holds 50% of his wealth in company securities (equally divided between stock and options), he would be willing to pay the full Black-Scholes value if his risk aversion was low (RPA = 1.0), but would only pay $7.80 and $4.28 for relative risk aversion of 2.0 and 3.0, respectively. Similarly, assuming relative risk aversion of 2.0, the value of a FMV option falls from $7.80 to $3.57 as his stock holdings [in his company] (as a fraction of his wealth) increase from 50% to 75%, and falls to $1.62 when his stock holdings account for 90% of his wealth.[28]

The likelihood that different executives will value differently options granted on the same terms and conditions means that, when a company awards options to an executive, the company may not know what value that executive attributes to those options. This, in turn, makes it difficult for the company to fit the options into a total compensation package that attempts to convey a certain total value to the executive.

A fourth problem is that providing compensation in the form of options can be expensive. As the Watson Wyatt study suggests, the value of an option grant from the company's point of view (as measured, for example, by the Black-Scholes method) is quite a bit higher than the value to the employee. In that survey, the average discount by the employee off the Black-Scholes value was 40% for 100 options and 49% for 500 options.[29] As the study summarized, "Our best estimate is that employees are getting only $.50 to $.60 in value for every $1 worth of options they are receiving from employers."[30]

The fifth problem is that the cost of options to the issuing company is difficult to calculate. In a sense, that cost is the amount that an outside investor would pay for the option. But there may be no market price by which to assess that cost because, although options for a company's stock may trade, the options granted to executives come with restrictions that the options trading among outside investors do not have. For example, the options awarded to executives are non-transferable, whereas options traded in the options market by outside investors can be sold by those investors at any time. As another example, an outside investor holding an option bought on the open market can hedge against the risk inherent in

---

[27]   An "FMV" option is one with an exercise price equal to the market price of the company's stock on the date that the option is granted.

[28]   3B KEVIN J. MURPHY, HANDBOOK OF LABOR ECONOMICS, *Chapter 38: Executive Compensation,* 2513 (Orley Ashenfelter & David Card, eds., 1999).

[29]   WATSON WYATT WORLDWIDE, HOW DO EMPLOYEES VALUE STOCK OPTIONS? 11 tbls.3 & 4.

[30]   *Id.* at 7.

that option by such actions as short-selling the company's stock. But executive officers at public corporations cannot short their company's stock.[31]

Since there is no market equivalent for options granted to executives, the cost of the options to the issuing companies is calculated by using complicated mathematical models. The Black-Scholes method provides one model. So-called binomial, or lattice, methods provide another model.

We will not study the two options valuation techniques. You can find a good description of both techniques by David Harper on Investopedia.com.[32] Even though those descriptions are both complete and accessible, they demonstrate the complexity of the two techniques and that the value they compute for a given option award depends upon assumptions used as inputs to the models.

QUESTIONS ON OPTIONS

How do you come out on the debate over whether awarding managers plain vanilla options (with a fixed exercise price set at the market price of the stock on the date options are granted) is a good idea or a bad idea?

How would a compensation committee determine, in even a rough way, the value of an option package to a CEO? For example, how could the committee get a handle on the degree to which the CEO is risk averse in his or her personal financial matters? If the committee asked the CEO, would the CEO have an incentive to bias his or her answer toward greater risk aversion in order to increase the number of options in a grant? To avoid this problem, would a compensation committee need to study—or hire a consultant to study—the personal financial decisions of the executive over time, as by an examination of several years of his or her brokerage statements? Would this be too intrusive?

Is your view of whether a company should use options as compensation affected by the complicated methodologies that are used to calculate the cost, to the company, of option awards and the fact that the methodologies require the company to provide assumptions that affect the cost numbers that the methodologies produce? If so, how is your view affected by that consideration?

If you do not like option compensation generally, how do you feel about its use by startup companies that do not have sufficient cash to pay competitive salaries in that form?

---

[31]   15 U.S.C. § 78p(c).

[32]   David Harper, *ESOs: Using the Black-Scholes Model* http://www.investopedia.com/features/eso/eso2.asp (last visited Apr. 29, 2016.); David Harper, *ESOs: Using the Binomial Model* http://www.investopedia.com/features/eso/eso3.asp (last visited Apr. 29, 2016).

Note that companies' reliance on options has dramatically decreased in recent years, in part because of the new accounting rule that requires companies to expense options on their income statements and in part because stock prices have not always risen in recent years.[33] A 2005 news story said:

> [T]he proliferation of stock options ... has abated. A new regulatory requirement to expense options, combined with a sluggish stock market that made many of them valueless in 2000 through 2003, has caused a stampede away from options. Several compensation consultants say they expect that options will soon represent less than 30 percent of total [CEO] compensation. . . .[34]

A study by Towers Perrin found that, for Fortune 500 companies, stock options constituted 77% of CEO long-term incentive compensation in 2003, 62% in 2004, and 55% in 2005.[35]

This trend has continued. The following median figures for CEO compensation at the companies in the Standard and Poor's 500 Index[36] substantiate the shift away from options to stock awards—including service-based restricted stock and performance share awards, discussed below, and unrestricted stock:

---

[33]   Since an executive only realizes money on an option if the stock price of the executive's company rises over the option exercise price during the option exercise period, generally rising stock prices greatly increase the desirability of options. As explained in the next section, however, a typical service-based restricted stock award provides value to an executive when the award "vests," in the sense that the restrictions on the stock expire—regardless of whether the stock price of the executive's company has increased since the date of the grant. Thus, restricted stock awards provide value to an executive even if stock prices look like they might fall.

[34]   Claudia H. Deutsch, *My Big Fat C.E.O. Paycheck*, N.Y. TIMES, April 2, 2005, http://www.nytimes.com/2005/04/03/business/yourmoney/my-big-fat-ceo-paycheck.html.

[35]   TOWERS PERRIN, U.S. ECR PROXY PAY LEVEL DATABASE FORTUNE 500 TOP 5 PAY LEVELS 2 (2005).

[36]   The Standard & Poor's 500 Index is a broadly based, capitalization-weighted index of 500 stocks of large U.S. companies.

Fiscal Year[37]	Stock Awards	Option Awards
2006	$2,227,738	$1,940,748
2007	$2,482,892	$1,909,500
2008	$2,383,547	$1,784,672
2009	$2,237,590	$1,493,250
2010	$3,000,001	$1,600,000
2011	$3,291,626	$1,704,211
2012	$3,794,055	$1,349,981
2013	$4,257,244	$1,478,790
2014	$4,500,052	$1,279,390
2015	$5,096,000	$1,116,499

3. SERVICE-BASED RESTRICTED STOCK

Restricted stock in this context[38] is stock that vests over time, without any payment from the executive, and with the only vesting condition being the executive's continued employment at the company. We will call this stock "service-based restricted stock" although many simply call this instrument "restricted stock," with the principal restriction being that the executive cannot sell the stock or use it as collateral for a loan until the executive has completed the required service period.[39] Thus a company might grant five shares of service-based restricted stock to an executive, with the award providing for annual vesting of one share in each of the next five years. If the executive remained employed by the company for one full year following the date of grant, the restrictions on one share would expire, and the executive would own that share outright and be able (subject to insider trading law) to sell it. It is common to refer to the expiration of the resale restriction as "vesting." If the executive remained employed by the company for another year, a second share would vest, and the executive would come into unrestricted ownership of that second share. And so forth through the remaining three years. Unlike options, by which

---

[37]   Equilar, Inc., an executive compensation data firm, provided these figures to the author on June 1, 2016. You can find its home page at http://www.equilar.com. The table shows median figures for each category of compensation for CEOs in the S&P 500 companies in each of the listed years, counting only CEOs who served for the entire fiscal year.

[38]   The term "restricted" stock has a very different meaning in SEC Rule 144, which is not relevant to the discussion here.

[39]   As set out later in this chapter, it is possible to put additional conditions on lifting the restrictions—including conditions that can be satisfied only by specified company financial performance. But, in current compensation parlance, "restricted stock" is service-based restricted stock, with only continued employment needed for vesting. Restricted stock that vests only on both (i) continued employment and (ii) specified company financial performance is called "performance stock."

the executive can only obtain unrestricted shares by paying the option exercise price, the executive typically obtains unrestricted stock—without paying the company anything—when restricted stock vests.

Instead of granting service-based "restricted stock," some companies grant "restricted stock units" ("RSUs"). The typical difference between a restricted stock award and an RSU award is that, in the case of a restricted stock award, the shares are issued to the executive at the time of grant. Thereafter, the executive may vote the shares and, depending on the terms of the award, be eligible to receive any dividends declared on the shares (with the ultimate receipt of such dividends often being contingent upon the vesting of the award). On the other hand, an RSU grant is a promise to issue shares if and when the award vests. Since the company does not issue the shares on the date of the grant, the executive usually enjoys no ownership rights during the award's vesting period.

In our example, the company might award five RSUs, with annual vesting of one unit at the end of each of the next five years. At the end of the first year after the award, the company would "settle" the first unit by issuing to the executive one share of unrestricted stock. At the end of two years following the award, the company would settle the second unit by issuing to the executive another share of unrestricted stock.[40] And so on at the end of the third, fourth, and fifth years. Or, depending on the manner in which the RSU award is designed, the company might "settle" the RSUs in cash as they vest, with the amount of cash equaling the number of RSUs times the market price of a share of company stock at the time of each settlement.

Service-based restricted stock, like options, aligns the interests of the executive with those of the shareholders. The executive who has received a service-based restricted stock grant will be motivated to take actions that will increase the price of the stock so that, when he or she obtains control of the stock after it vests, the stock will be worth more to the executive. Of course, if the price of the company's stock goes up, the rest of the shareholders will benefit too. Moreover, service-based restricted stock retains its incentive properties even if a company's stock price falls. No matter what the stock price is at any time during the vesting period, the executive who is going to get the stock on vesting should work to increase the price above that level, as any increase from any level will provide a real benefit to the executive when the stock vests. By contrast, when a company's stock price has fallen dramatically below the exercise price after an option grant, the executive holding the option may see no action that he or she could take to bring the stock price up to a point where the option is

---

[40]   As with options, the company might "cliff" settle the RSUs, settling the entire award five years after grant by transferring five unrestricted shares to the executive at that time, with none of the shares transferred on any earlier date.

in the money. If the stock price falls to that extent, the option loses its power as an incentive.

Like options, service-based restricted stock grants provide an executive with an incentive to remain employed at the company until the stock vests.

Service-based restricted stock is "cheaper" for a company than stock options because employees, in subjectively valuing the award, apply a smaller discount to restricted stock than to options. The Watson Wyatt online survey found that the average employee discount off the Black-Scholes value for options on 100 shares of stock (a possible measure of the cost of the options to the company) was 40%, while the average discount for 100 shares of restricted stock off the grant date price of that stock was only 18%.[41]

Service-based restricted stock has been criticized for many of the same reasons as options. Here are four.

First, service-based restricted stock—when it vests—provides value to the executive immediately in the amount of the market price of the stock at the vesting date. Restricted stock accordingly provides economic benefit even to a poor manager. Thus, an executive whose company's stock price has underperformed the stock prices of peer companies (indeed, even a manager whose company's stock price has declined while the prices of peer companies' stocks have increased) will receive a benefit in the amount of the market value of the shares when they vest. Moreover, the executive receives that benefit without paying *any* money to the company, in contrast to the executive who exercises an option by paying the exercise price.

Second, any given award of service-based restricted stock—like any given options award—can deliver different values to different executives. The Watson Wyatt study found that employees with a "conservative" investment style discounted 100 shares of restricted stock by 22% off the price of the stock on the grant date, while employees with an "aggressive" investment style discounted the shares by only 10%.[42]

Third, as suggested by the preceding paragraph, service-based restricted stock may be, at least relative to cash, an expensive form of compensation because the value of a restricted stock award to an executive is likely to be lower than the cost of the award to the company.

---

[41]   WATSON WYATT, HOW DO EMPLOYEES VALUE STOCK OPTIONS?, *supra* note 26, at 7. Watson Wyatt conceded that computing the discount off the full grant date price of unrestricted shares "tends to overstate the discount, since the hypothesized three-year restriction on selling is likely to reduce [the restricted shares'] actual value relative to similar unencumbered shares." *Id.* at 6.

[42]   *Id.* at 12 tbl.5. Watson Wyatt acknowledged that using the full grant date value of an unrestricted share as the reference point, "tends to overstate the discount, since the hypothesized three-year restriction on selling the shares is likely to reduce their actual value relative to similar, unencumbered shares." *Id.* at 6.

Fourth, like options, service-based restricted stock can provide an incentive for wrongdoing. Suppose that the CEO in our options example holds 1,000,000 shares of restricted stock for which the restrictions are about to expire, so that she can (after the restrictions end) sell all 1,000,000 shares for cash. Analysts estimate that the company will report 6¢/share in earnings. The financial staff tells the CEO that it looks as though the company has only earned 5¢/share. The stock price is currently at $10/share. The CEO believes that, if the company reports 5¢/share earnings (below the analysts' estimate), the stock price will fall to $9/share; if the company reports 6¢/share, the stock price will remain at $10/share; and if the company reports 7¢/share, the price will rise to $12/share. Would the CEO be tempted to encourage the accounting staff to bend or break the rules so the company would report 7¢, seeing as that would make a $3,000,000 difference in the value of the shares she will soon own without restrictions and therefore be able to sell? As with the similar question about options, we will look later in this chapter at studies that test this possibility.

QUESTION ON RESTRICTED STOCK

Is your view of using service-based restricted stock for compensation different from your view of using options for compensation? If so, why?

---

4.   PERFORMANCE SHARES

The criticism that service-based restricted stock rewards an executive with *some* value, even if his or her company performs worse than peer companies over the vesting period (as measured by stock price in our examples, or by other financial metrics such as return on assets), can be overcome by conditioning the transfer of unrestricted stock to the executive on the company's achievement of one or more performance objectives. Typically, these objectives consist of one or more financial, operational, or strategic goals. Shares with such conditions are called "performance shares."

For example, a company might award three performance shares to its CEO on February 4, 2013, with all three shares to be earned, or "vest," on February 4, 2016, provided that (i) the CEO is still employed at the company on February 4, 2016; *and* (ii) the company's total shareholder return ("TSR," equal to share price increase plus dividends[43]) over the three-year period February 4, 2013 through February 4, 2016 exceeds the

---

[43]   TSR calculations often assume the reinvestment of any dividends into the stock over the period during which the TSR is measured.

TSR during that period at 80% of the companies included in the Standard and Poor's 500 Index. The executive could not sell the shares—or use them as collateral—until and unless both conditions were satisfied.[44]

Instead of awarding performance shares, a company might award "performance share units" ("PSUs"). In our example, the company might award three PSUs to the CEO. If, on February 4, 2016, the CEO is still employed at the corporation and if—during the three-year period from February 4, 2013 through February 4, 2016—the TSR at the executive's corporation exceeded the TSR at 80% of the companies in the Standard & Poor's 500, then the company would settle the PSUs by transferring three shares of the company's unrestricted common stock to the CEO.

Performance shares can be customized in elaborate ways. For example, the performance objective for all the shares in an award might be a weighted average of several different financial metrics, or the shares in a single award could be divided into different groups, with the settlement of each group dependent on a different metric. As another example, the number of performance shares ultimately transferred to the executive could fluctuate depending on the *degree* of financial success the company enjoyed during the measurement period (or "performance period," as it is called). In our case, the company might structure a performance share award to transfer to the executive all three shares if—by the end of the performance period—the TSR at the executive's company exceeded that of the TSR at 80% of the S&P 500 companies, transfer only two of the three shares if the TSR at the executive's company exceeded the TSR of only 60% to 79% of the S&P 500 companies, transfer only one share if the TSR at the executive's company exceeded the TSR at only 51% to 59% of the S&P 500 companies, and otherwise transfer none of the shares.

Although a relatively recent development, performance shares are now widely used. The Equilar compensation data company, reporting on 2012 compensation, provided these numbers:

> The trends in this year's CEO Pay Strategies study [published in 2013 and reporting on 2012 compensation at the S&P 500 companies] are a continuation of findings from past years' reports, reinforcing the idea that companies are still moving toward equity with the use of more performance shares and [fewer] options.[45]

---

[44] Thus, "performance shares" are simply a form of restricted stock—with the restrictions on transfer (by sale or use as collateral) lifted only if *two* conditions are satisfied: (i) the executive continues to work for the company for some period of time (the only condition that must be satisfied with service-based restricted stock) and (ii) the company has, by the end of the performance period, achieved pre-specified performance objectives. But, as set out in note 39 *supra*, in current compensation parlance, "restricted stock" is what this book calls "service-based restricted stock," and stock that is further restricted by a performance condition is called "performance stock."

[45] EQUILAR, INC., CEO PAY STRATEGIES 2013, COMPENSATION AT S&P 500 COMPANIES 4 (2013), http://www.shrm.org/templatetools/toolkits/documents/equilar-2013-ceo-pay-stategies-

Following the trends of the last few years, performance share grants continued to grow in 2012. Three-quarters of executives received at least one grant of performance shares, up from 68.2 percent in the previous year.[46]

In both of the last two fiscal years, the combination of granting options and performance shares has remained the most popular equity design. The most significant growth in equity mix was seen in granting both restricted and performance-based shares, a method used by twice as many companies as last year. Following the general trend of a reduction in option awards, all equity mixes involving options declined from last year, with the exception of the combination of options and performance shares.

With performance shares increasing in popularity, more companies have switched to granting performance shares as their only method of equity compensation[;] this mix accounts for 44 companies this year as opposed to 33 in 2011. Overall, equity is an important factor in compensation, with approximately 3 percent of companies not granting any form of equity to their executives.

The following graph shows the number of S&P 500 CEOs who received the specified equity mixes.[47]

---

report.pdf. Quotations and graphics from all Equilar reports reprinted with permission from Equilar, Inc., an executive compensation data firm.

[46]   *Id.* at 11.

[47]   *Id.* at 13, with the bar graph below from the same page.

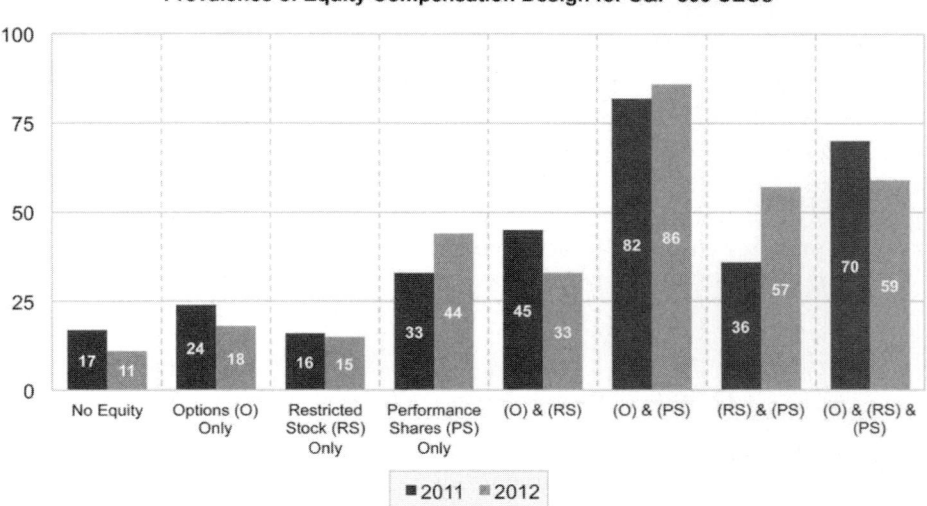

Prevalence of Equity Compensation Design for S&P 500 CEOs

In 2013, equity compensation overall and performance-based equity continued to increase, while options decreased:

> The share of total compensation deriving from equity has never been higher, reaching median values of 62.9% in the S&P 500 and 56.3% in the S&P 1500. Likewise, the share of CEOs receiving some form of performance-based equity in 2013 stood at 75.7% in the S&P 500 and 63.8% in the S&P 1500. Median S&P 500 performance stock compensation grew to $3,407,781 in 2013, up 7.3% from 2012 and 52.0% since 2009. This evolution of CEO pay mix represents a continued convergence toward the vehicles most favored by investors as companies lacking clear alignment between pay and performance face increasing difficulty garnering shareholder support for Say on Pay votes. Options in particular have declined in terms of the average value delivered to a CEO as many investors question whether they are the most preferable compensation vehicle for large, mature companies not expected to experience meteoric growth.[48]

By 2015, more than 80% of S&P 500 companies awarded performance-based equity to their CEOs.[49] At those S&P 500 companies using multiple equity vehicles, the most popular combinations were (nearly tied in frequency): (i) options, performance shares, and service-based restricted

---

48   EQUILAR, INC., 2014 CEO PAY STRATEGIES 4 (2014).
49   EQUILAR, INC., 2016 CEO PAY TRENDS 15 (2016).

stock; (ii) service-based restricted stock and performance shares; and (iii) options and performance shares.[50]

Obviously, performance shares can suffer from some of the same problems that plague service-based restricted shares. Different executives at the same company might subjectively value the same performance share award differently, so that the company may be unable to determine the value that its CEO attributes to the grant. And the performance objectives conceivably could provide an executive with an incentive to cheat or engage in sharp practice in order to achieve the condition necessary to receive the maximum possible number of shares at the end of the performance period.

QUESTIONS ON PERFORMANCE SHARES

To what extent do performance shares serve different purposes than service-based restricted stock and options?

If a company grants performance shares, should it also grant service-based restricted stock? Should it also grant options? Why have a mix of equity vehicles instead of just one?

If a company uses a full suite of compensation incentive devices—cash bonuses dependent on financial and operational measures, service-based restricted stock, options, and performance shares—do the problems raised by complexity (e.g., whether the CEO can determine which of two alternative business decisions will most advance his or her overall personal financial fortunes) increase, or do the complexities created by each of the different incentive devices somehow cancel each other out?

Will the executive simply avoid certain choices because he or she can see that such choices will hurt him or her with respect to one form of the several forms of compensation? Or will "good" decisions almost always increase the value that the executive receives from each type of incentive compensation and "bad" decisions almost always decrease the value that the executive receives from each type?

E. EQUITY OWNERSHIP AND RETENTION REQUIREMENTS

All of the forms of equity compensation align the financial incentives of top executives with the interests of the shareholders and, at least in theory, promote decisions that will sustain and grow the value of a company's stock. But once the executives sell the equity, it no longer provides that incentive. Thus, a CEO who receives a stock option award in

---

[50]   *Id.* at 17.

2013 that fully vests in 2016 has an incentive during the vesting period to take action that will increase the price of his or her company's stock. That incentive continues during the exercise period, unless the executive exercises the option and sells the stock. But if the CEO does exercise the option and sells the shares acquired by the exercise, the incentive provided by those shares ends with that sale. The same is true of equity that the CEO acquires through unrestricted stock awards, the vesting of service-based restricted stock (or settlement of RSUs), and the vesting of performance shares (or settlement of PSUs). Once the executive has obtained full rights to the equity *and sold it*, that equity no longer incentivizes the executive to take actions that will increase his or her company's stock price.

Aside from continually granting new options, new service-based restricted shares, and new performance shares, companies often employ two devices to stop (or slow down) executive equity sales that effectively "unwind" the incentives that equity compensation creates. The two devices are (i) stock ownership guidelines and (ii) stock retention requirements.

Stock ownership guidelines typically require top executives to hold equity in their company equal in value to some multiple of their base salaries. For example, a CEO might be required to hold equity valued at five times his or her base salary, with the next tier of executives (those reporting directly to the CEO) each required to hold equity equal in value to three times his or her base salary. The guidelines usually provide some period of time—such as five years from the adoption of the guidelines or from the date on which an individual is named to a position subject to the guidelines—for an executive to acquire the requisite equity value.

Stock retention (or "holding") requirements largely fall into two categories. First, some companies that have stock ownership guidelines require an executive who is either subject to such a guideline for the first time or whose stock ownership guideline increases (e.g., as a result of a promotion) to hold all new equity that he or she acquires until the executive satisfies the newly applicable ownership minimum. Second, some companies forbid executives from selling shares that they acquire through new equity awards for some period of time after acquisition—regardless of how much stock the executive owns. For example, a company might require an executive who exercises an option to buy 1,000 shares of stock to retain those 1,000 shares for one year after the option exercise—regardless of what other company stock the executive owns.

Companies need not have either ownership guidelines or retention requirements. Some have neither. Some have both. Some have only ownership guidelines, and some have only retention requirements. Moreover, ownership guidelines and retention requirements—where they are used—differ from company to company.

Here are findings by the Equilar compensation data firm, from its review of 2012 disclosures by 94 public companies in the Fortune 100:[51]

The prevalence of Fortune 100 companies with publicly-disclosed stock ownership policies for executives increased . . . to 89.4% in 2012. This [percentage] includes companies that disclosed ownership guidelines, holding requirements, or both. In 2012, 38.1% of these companies [i.e., 38.1% the 89.4%] maintained ownership guidelines without formal holding requirements, while 6.0% of companies with ownership policies disclosed only holding requirements. The remaining 55.9% of companies had both ownership guidelines and holding requirements.[52]

As to ownership guidelines:

The design of ownership guidelines varies between companies. Some companies choose to define guidelines as a multiple of base salary, others choose to designate a target number of shares that executives must acquire, and a small number of companies choose to use both of these in a hybrid design.

The most common guideline structure, used by 82.3% of companies with ownership guidelines in 2012, defines target ownership levels as a multiple of base salary.[53]

* * *

Ownership guidelines are not limited to the CEO level, and many apply to executives several tiers below the C-Suite. Since 82.3% of ownership guidelines at Fortune 100 companies are structured as a multiple of base salary, examining how ownership requirements vary across executive positions can provide insight into the relationship between position responsibility and required equity ownership levels.

In general, ownership requirements increase with job responsibility. The median ownership multiple for CEOs was 6.0 times base salary, while the median multiple at the vice president level was 1.0 times base salary.

---

[51]   EQUILAR, INC., 2013 EXECUTIVE STOCK OWNERSHIP GUIDELINES REPORT 4–5 (2013), http://www.fwcook.com/alert_letters/Equilar-Cook_2013_Executive_Stock_Ownership_ Guidelines_Report.pdf ("Equilar's 2013 Executive Stock Ownership Guidelines study is primarily derived from data disclosed in fiscal 2012 proxy filings of Fortune 100 companies. Additional information, if available, was collected from the corporate governance section of company websites. For fiscal 2012, this study includes information from 94 public companies."). The Fortune 100 is a list of companies compiled annually by FORTUNE magazine. It is a list of the 100 largest publicly and privately held companies in the United States, with size measured by gross revenues.

[52]   *Id.* at 6–7.

[53]   *Id.* at 8.

The following graph displays the median base salary multiple for key executive positions at Fortune 100 companies in 2012.[54]

Median Salary Multiple by Position

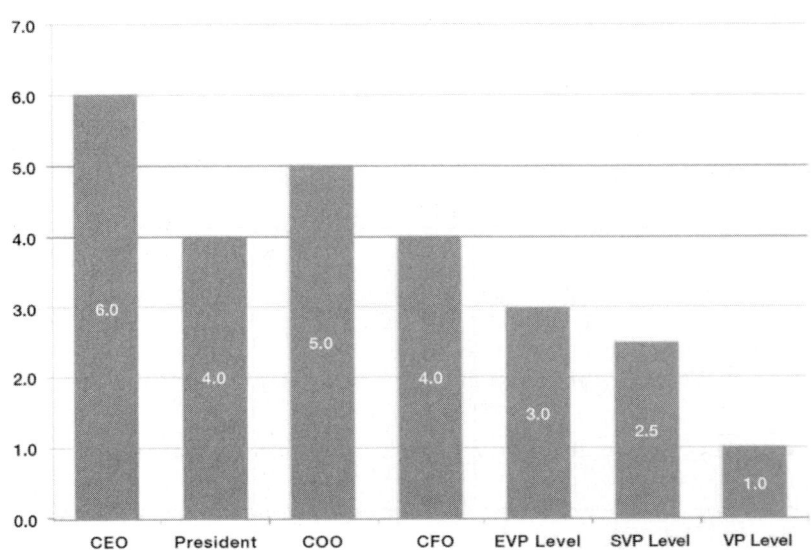

As to retention (or "holding") requirements:

There are several different models for holding requirements. The most common are guidelines that apply until ownership guidelines are met, also known as pre-ownership guideline holding requirements. . . .

Some companies prefer to institute general holding requirements, which specify that shares acquired upon the vesting of stock or exercise of options must be held for a specific time frame. In 2012, these time frames ranged from as little as a year to as long as when the executive retires. Companies without ownership guidelines can still institute a general holding requirement. . . .

Lastly, companies may choose to institute a combination of pre-guideline holding requirements and general holding requirements. . . .

---

[54]   *Id.* at 15.

In 2012, having only a pre-guideline holding requirement was the most common model, with 63.5% of companies that use holding requirements choosing this method. . . . The second most common model is employing only general requirements, which 26.9% of companies use. Lastly, 9.6% of companies have a combination of holding requirements.[55]

QUESTIONS ON OWNERSHIP GUIDELINES AND RETENTION REQUIREMENTS

Do you favor these devices?

How do they affect the value of equity compensation granted to executives? Is the effect on that value uniform among executives? Is it uniform, year over year, for a given executive?

If these devices are intended to prevent an executive from unwinding the alignment of his or her financial fortunes with those of his or her companies' shareholders, does the effect of these devices depend on the percentage of the executive's total wealth comprised of the stock that these devices force the executive to own? If so, should each company adjust the minimums according to that percentage?

F. GROWTH IN CEO PAY AND WHETHER IT IS TOO HIGH

It is difficult to obtain comparable statistics on CEO pay going back over many years. Statistics from long ago—based on reports filed by companies under SEC disclosure regulations that differ from those in place today—may not provide figures that can usefully be compared with current compensation.

It does seem clear that pay has gone up since the 1970s and that equity compensation has played a large role in that increase.

Here is one summary:

There has been a large increase in the use of stock options to provide CEO compensation and incentives. In 1980, CEO annual flow compensation was mainly in the form of cash salary and bonus (Hall and Liebman 1998), with only 30 percent of CEOs receiving new option grants. Mean salary and bonus was $655,000, compared with $155,000 from new option grants. By 1994, options had become a major component of CEO flow

---

[55]   *Id.* at 12.

compensation, with 70 percent of CEOs receiving new option grants, and mean option grants amounting to $1.2 million (valued by the Black and Scholes [1973] model), compared with $1.3 million in cash pay. In addition to being an important component of chief executive compensation, stock options are an important component of CEO equity incentives. Hall and Liebman (1998) report that in 1980, 57 percent of CEOs held some amount of options, and by 1994, this figure had reached nearly 90 percent. In Core and Guay's (1999) sample of CEOs from the 1992–1996 period, options contributed approximately one-third to the value of the median CEO's equity portfolio and contributed roughly one-half of the median CEO's total equity incentives (that is, the sensitivity of portfolio value to stock price).[56]

Another study found that, over the period 1970–2002, the

pay for chief executive officers (CEOs) in large US firms increased dramatically ..., driven by an explosion in grants of share options.... [A]verage total remuneration for CEOs in S&P 500 firms (adjusted for inflation using 2002-constant dollars) increased from about $850,000 in 1970 to over $14 million in 2000, falling to $9.4 million in 2002.

Over this time period, the average grant-date Black-Scholes value of options soared from near zero in 1970 to over $7.0 million in 2000, falling to $4.4 million in 2002. The difference between the $7.0 million option grant value in 2000 and the $14 million total compensation is made up of cash compensation, restricted stock, retirement benefits, and payouts from a variety of long-term incentive plans.[57]

At page 25, this second study provides the following graph:

---

[56]   John E. Core, et al., *Executive Equity Compensation and Incentives: A Survey*, FRBNY ECON. POL. REV. 27, 29 (April 2003). Quotation reprinted with permission from Professors Core and Guay.

[57]   Michael C. Jensen & Kevin J. Murphy, *Remuneration: Where we've been, how we got to here, what are the problems, and how to fix them* 24–25 (European Corporate Governance Institute, Finance Working Paper No. 44/2004, July 2004). Quotation and graphic reprinted with permission from Professors Jensen and Murphy.

Figure 1   Average Cash and Total Remuneration for CEOs in S&P 500 Firms, 1970-2002

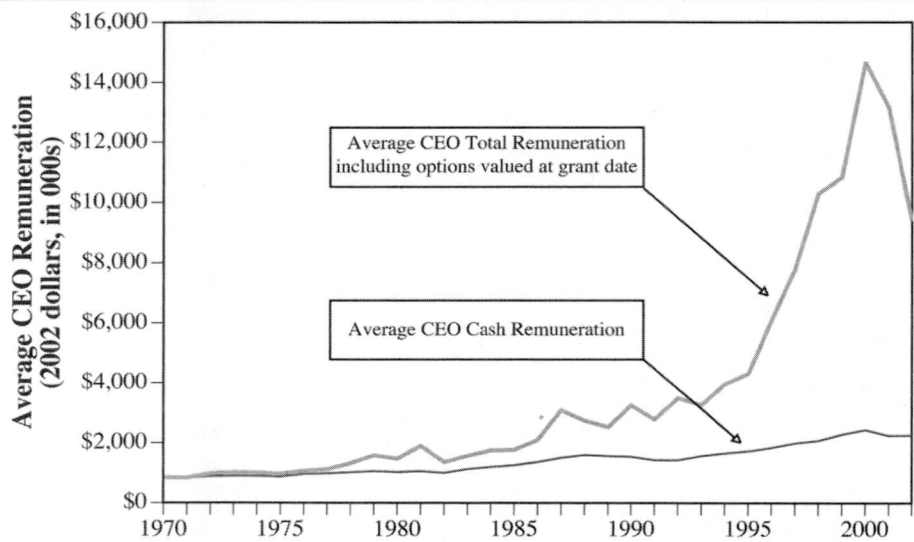

Note: Sample is based on all CEOs included in the S&P 500, using data from Forbes and ExecuComp. CEO total pay includes cash pay, restricted stock, payouts from long-term pay programs and the value of stock options granted using ExecuComp's modified Black-Scholes approach. (Total pay prior to 1978 excludes option grants, while total pay between 1978 and 1991 is computed using the amounts *realized* from exercising stock options during the year, rather than grant-date values.)

The following table includes more recent median figures, compiled by the Equilar compensation data company, showing compensation paid to CEOs at the S&P 500 companies for the years 2006 through 2015:[58]

---

[58]   Equilar, Inc. is an executive compensation data firm. You can find its home page at http://www.equilar.com. Note that the number in each category is the median for that category for CEOs in the S&P 500 companies in each of the listed years, counting only CEOs who served for the entire fiscal year. Because each category is a median for that category itself, the columns for the different components of compensation do not sum in a given year to the Total Compensation for that year. Equilar compiled this data from SEC filings that the companies made, which valued the non-cash compensation in the manner that the SEC prescribed.

Compensation data derive from proxy statements, each one of which reports the compensation paid for the preceding year. Thus, the 2015 numbers were reported in 2016 proxy statements.

Fiscal Year	Base Salary ($)	Bonus + Non-Equity Incentive Plan Compensation ($)	Stock Awards ($)	Option Awards ($)	All Other Compensation ($)	Total Compensation ($)
2006	1,000,000	1,924,288	2,227,738	1,940,748	191,414	9,831,841
2007	1,000,000	1,788,930	2,482,892	1,909,500	167,709	8,970,981
2008	1,001,538	1,325,650	2,383,547	1,784,672	169,177	8,214,996
2009	1,000,000	1,478,348	2,237,590	1,493,250	132,275	7,984,162
2010	1,000,000	2,020,000	3,000,001	1,600,000	140,586	9,606,351
2011	1,026,346	2,000,000	3,291,626	1,704,211	148,188	10,092,893
2012	1,048,303	1,800,402	3,794,055	1,349,981	161,159	10,549,893
2013	1,099,500	1,989,488	4,257,244	1,478,790	161,734	10,492,426
2014	1,103,277	2,057,000	4,500,052	1,279,390	172,045	11,548,620
2015	1,124,228	1,952,645	5,096,000	1,116,499	151,184	10,967,246

From the graph and the table, we can see that (i) CEO pay exploded during the 1990s, (ii) the numbers are still high, but (iii) the pay dropped in 2007 through 2009, before (iv) climbing again and reaching in 2011 and after levels exceeding that in 2006. Consider, now, whether the pay today is too high.

There is no one way to evaluate CEO pay to determine whether it is reasonable. The methods described below are illustrative, not exhaustive. This book does not promote any particular method of determining whether CEO pay is excessive and takes no position on whether CEO compensation is too high today. This discussion aims only to stimulate your thinking.

We could use absolute numbers. Such an approach might conclude that $9 million or $10 million, or some other figure, is the most that should be paid to any CEO for work in one year.[59] But sports stars sometimes make more than $10 million in a single year.

We could compare executive pay to the profits that companies make and argue that top executives should be paid no more than some certain percentage of profits. The compensation paid to the top-five executives as a percentage of their companies' earnings—with the data taken from a large set of public companies other than real estate investment trusts and investment funds—was 5.2% during the period 1993–1997 and 8.1% during

---

[59] See Scott Thurm, *What's a CEO Worth? More Firms Answer $10 Million*, WALL ST. J., May 15, 2013, http://www.wsj.com/articles/SB10001424127887324031404578483683405105480.

the period 1999–2003.[60] But what is the appropriate percentage, or the appropriate maximum percentage? And what if company profits decline in a given year without the executives being at fault?

We could compare CEO pay with the minimum wage, or with average pay for workers in the U.S. Or we could look at the multiple at any given company of the CEO's pay to the average (or median) pay of workers at that company or the average (or median) pay of workers in that industry. Here are some figures, using a metric of this sort:

> Across the Standard & Poor's 500 Index of companies, the average multiple of CEO compensation to that of rank-and-file workers is 204, up 20 percent since 2009. . . .

> These multiples are based on CEO pay for either the fiscal year ending in 2011 or 2012, as disclosed in the companies' most recent filings before noon on March 26. Because most companies don't disclose their average workers' pay, Bloomberg used U.S. government data on worker compensation by industry. The average ratio for the S&P 500 companies is up from 170 in 2009, when the financial crisis reduced many compensation packages. Estimates by academics and trade-union groups put the number at 20-to-1 in the 1950s, rising to 42-to-1 in 1980 and 120-to-1 by 2000.[61]

---

[60]   Lucian Bebchuk & Yaniv Grinstein, *The Growth of Executive Pay*, 21 OXF. REV. ECON. POL. 283, 297 & tbl.8 (2005) [Bebchuk, *Growth of Pay*].

[61]   Elliot Blair Smith & Phil Kuntz, *CEO Pay 1,795-to-1 Multiple of Wages Skirts U.S. Law*, BLOOMBERG, Apr. 30, 2013, http://www.bloomberg.com/news/2013-04-30/ceo-pay-1-795-to-1-multiple-of-workers-skirts-law-as-sec-delays.html (noting that the CEO of J.C. Penney Co. "got a compensation package worth 1,795 times the average wage and benefits of a U.S. department store worker when he was hired in November 2011, according to data compiled by Bloomberg.").

Of course, CEO equity pay, as we have seen, can be measured in different ways. One count includes the value of stock options exercised in a given year (what might be called realized pay on the options), and concludes:

> The CEO-to-worker compensation ratio was 20-to-1 in 1965 and 29.9-to-1 in 1978, grew to 122.6-to-1 in 1995, peaked at 383.4-to-1 in 2000, and was 295.9-to-1 in 2013, far higher than it was in the 1960s, 1970s, 1980s, or 1990s.

> If Facebook, which we exclude from our data due to its outlier high compensation numbers, were included in the sample, average CEO pay was $24.8 million in 2013, and the CEO-to-worker compensation ratio was 510.7-to-1.

Lawrence Mishel & Alyssa Davis, *CEO Pay Continues to Rise as Typical Workers Are Paid Less*, ECONOMIC POLICY INSTITUTE, Issue Brief, June 12, 2014, http://www.epi.org/publication/ceo-pay-continues-to-rise. These figures compare "the average compensation of the CEOs in the 350 publicly owned U.S. firms (i.e., firms that sell stock on the open market) with the largest revenue each year" to "the annual compensation (wages and benefits of a full-time, full year worker) of a private-sector production/nonsupervisory worker (a group covering more than 80 percent of payroll employment)," with the post-1996 figures "the average annual compensation of the production/nonsupervisory workers in the key industries of the firms included in the sample." *Id.* The "options-realized measure reflects what CEOs report as their Form W-2 wages for tax reporting purposes" and also includes "salary, bonuses, restricted stock grants, and long-term incentive payouts." *Id.*

The Dodd-Frank law and resulting SEC regulation require companies to publish a ratio of "the median of the annual total compensation of all employees" to "the annual total compensation of the chief executive officer."[62] But what should the average multiple, or maximum multiple, be of CEO pay over that of rank-and-file employees?

We could consider changes over time, to see whether the increase in CEO pay can be explained by changes in other variables that might be logically related to pay. One study purported to demonstrate that, if the pay in 2003 had borne the same statistical relationship to industry, firm size (measured by sales), return on assets, and stock return as the pay did to those variables in 1993, the 2003 pay would have been less than half what it was.[63] But another study concluded that "[t]he sixfold increase in CEO pay between 1980 and 2003 can be attributed to the sixfold increase in market capitalization of large U.S. companies during that period. When stock market valuations increase by 500%, under constant returns to scale, CEO 'productivity' increases by 500%, and equilibrium CEO pay increases by 500%."[64] But should pay for a top executive increase simply because the company that he or she runs gets bigger?

We could examine whether changes in CEO pay at a company correlate well with company performance over time, particularly as compared with the performance of similar companies. This approach appeals because (i) most CEO pay is delivered in forms designed to encourage top executives to make decisions that will improve the performance of their companies and (ii) investors want the stocks in which they put their money to outperform alternative investments. As we saw in Chapter Fourteen, proxy

---

[62]   124 Stat. 1376, 1904, § 953(b)(1); Pay Ratio Disclosure, 80 Fed. Reg. 50,104 (Aug. 18, 2015) (adding 17 C.F.R. § 229.402(u)). Instruction 8 to Item 402(u) states that "emerging growth companies" do not need to disclose this ratio.

[63]   Bebchuk, *Growth of Pay, supra* note 60, at 289.

[64]   Xavier Gabaix & Augustin Landier, *Why Has CEO Pay Increased So Much?*, 123 QUARTERLY J. ECON. 49, 50 (2008). But these authors concede that

> other interpretations . . . are reasonable. In particular, the model highlights contagion as another potential source of increased compensation. If a small fraction of firms decides to pay more than the other firms (perhaps because of bad corporate governance), the pay of all CEOs can rise by a large amount in general equilibrium.

Id. at 50–51. The two authors of this study and a third researcher produced a follow-up study, which reported:

> [O]ver the recent period 2004–11, movements in CEO compensation closely follow movements in firm size. In particular, CEO pay and firm size have both decreased during the crisis (2007–9): average total firm values decreased by 17.4%, equity values by 37.9% and compensation indices by 27.7%. During 2009–11, we observe a rebound of firm values by 19%, equity values by 27% and compensation indices by 22%. We see these fairly proportional changes over successive episodes of market drops and market rebound as a strong validity test for the size of stakes view.

Xavier Gabaix, et al., *CEO Pay and Firm Size: An Update After the Crisis*, 124 ECON. J. F40, F49 (2014) (with firm value equal to market capitalization at end of fiscal year plus book value of debt (F43), and the two compensation indices described at F44).

advisers recommend voting for or against say-on-pay resolutions in part based on quantitative models comparing pay and performance.

Following this line of thought, the Dodd-Frank law requires the SEC to issue a rule requiring public companies to disclose in proxy solicitations for annual shareholder meetings "information that shows the relationship between executive compensation actually paid and the financial performance of the issuer, taking into account any change in the value of the shares of stock and dividends of the issuer and any distributions."[65] To implement this mandate, the SEC has proposed a rule that would require a public company to disclose not only a special measure of "actual pay" to its CEO over the last five years but also the total shareholder return ("TSR") for the company over that time and the TSR on the stocks of similar companies.[66] But is shareholder return through stock price change and dividends the best measure of company performance?

We could examine the difference between CEO pay and the pay to other executives in the same firm. One study defined the pay "gap" between the CEO and the next highest paid executive as the difference between the total compensation paid to the CEO and the total compensation paid to the next highest paid executive, divided by the total paid to the CEO.[67]

The study concluded that—after controlling for factors such as the firm size, interest expense, earnings before extraordinary items, and return on assets—the performance of a company, as measured by Tobin's q,[68] declined as the pay gap increased.[69] A second study reached similar conclusions:

---

[65]   124 Stat. 1376, 1903–04, § 953(a); 15 U.S.C. § 78n(i). The JOBS Act exempts emerging growth companies from this disclosure requirement. Pub. L. No. 112-106 § 102, 126 Stat. 306 at 309 (codified at 15 U.S.C. § 78n(i)).

[66]   The Commission's proposal would, among other things, define "compensation actually paid" as the amount in the "Total Compensation" column of a company's Summary Compensation Table per 17 C.F.R. § 229.402(c)(2)(x), modified to (i) exclude changes in the present value of defined benefit and actuarial pension plans that are not attributable to the applicable year of service, and (ii) include the value of equity awards at vesting rather than at grant. Pay Versus Performance, 80 Fed. Reg. 26,330, 26,332, 26,363 (proposed 17 C.F.R. 229.402(v)(2)(iii)) (May 7, 2015). The company would have to provide that compensation "actually paid" over the last five years, together with the cumulative total shareholder return for the company during each of those years and the cumulative total shareholder return from holding the stocks of peer companies, with the peer group defined as the same index or peer group used for the performance graph per 17 C.F.R. § 229.201(e)(1)(ii) or the companies disclosed in the Compensation Discussion and Analysis as those used to benchmark compensation. Id. at 26,363–64 (proposed 17 C.F.R. 229.402(v)(5) & Instruction 7). The proposed regulation would also require disclosure of the average compensation actually paid to the executives, other than the CEO, whose compensation must be disclosed in the Summary Compensation Table.

[67]   Zhichuan (Frank) Li, *Performance Mutual Monitoring and Corporate Governance*, 45 J. BANK. FIN. 255, 258 (in description of tbl.1) (2014).

[68]   The author characterizes Tobin's q as "the ratio of the market value of the firm to its replacement value." Id. at 258.

[69]   Id. at 258–60 ("a simple [regression] reports a negative relation between the *GAP* in period t and Tobin's q in period t + 1" (at 260)), 262 tbl.3 Panel A. The study found that "[f]or an

Our new measure is CEO Pay Slice (CPS), which is defined as the fraction of the aggregate compensation of the firm's top-five executive team captured by the CEO.[70]

First, CPS is negatively correlated with accounting profitability. Firms with high CPS tend to have a lower industry-adjusted operating income to assets ratio.

Second, high-CPS firms tend to make worse acquisition decisions as judged by the market's reaction to their acquisition announcements. . . . If the acquiring firm has higher CPS, the stock return accompanying the acquisition announcement is lower and more likely to be negative.

Third, firms with higher CPS are more likely to provide their CEO with opportunistically timed option grants. High CPS is associated with an increased likelihood of the CEO's receiving a lucky option grant with an exercise price equal to the lowest price of the grant month.

Fourth, CPS is associated with CEO turnover. The probability of a CEO turnover after bad performance is lower if CPS is higher controlling for the CEO's length of service.

Fifth, stock market returns accompanying the filing of proxy statements tend to be lower for periods where CPS increases.[71]

This suggests that CEO pay is too high if the CEO's portion of compensation paid to the top five executives exceeds some certain percentage. But what is the optimal relationship between the CEO's pay and the pay of other top executives? Where is the line—as measured by that relationship—separating too much pay from pay that is not too much?[72]

---

increase in the *GAP* of one standard deviation, Tobin's q one period forward is lower by the equivalent of $20 million." *Id.* at 256. The author related this result to the notion that the pay differential reflected the degree to which the second-highest paid executive can monitor the CEO, with that monitoring leading to "better executive decisions." *Id.* at 256. But the author also found a positive relationship between firm value and instances in which the second-highest paid executive either held the title of president or served on the board of directors or was independent in the sense of having joined the company before the CEO—with these factors presumably increasing the power of that executive to monitor the CEO. *Id.* at 260, 262 tbl.3 Panel A.

[70] Lucian Bebchuk, et al., *The CEO Pay Slice*, 102 J. FIN. ECON. 199, 200 (2011). The study uses pay figures from the period 1993–2004, *id.* at 202. Quotations from this article republished with permission of Elsevier B.V. from The CEO pay slice, Lucian Bebchuk, et al., Vol. 102, Issue 1, Journal of Financial Economics copyright 2011; permission conveyed through Copyright Clearance Center, Inc.

[71] *Id.* at 200.

[72] There are other comparisons that may be helpful when considering the compensation of top officers at publicly traded companies. We might compare their pay with the pay at privately held companies. *See, e.g.,* N. Gregory Mankiw, *Defending the One Percent*, 27 J. ECON. PERSPECT. 21, 31 (Summer 2013) (characterizing one study as "report[ing] that over the past three decades, executive pay in the closely-held firms has outpaced that in public companies" and another study

QUESTIONS ON THE LEVEL OF EXECUTIVE PAY

Do you think that CEOs are paid too much? About the right amount? Too little?

What criteria do you use to make your determination?

Should a compensation committee pay attention to such matters as

- the relationship of the CEO's pay to the pay of an average American worker (or the median pay of employees at the company),

- the relationship of CEO pay to the company's earnings,

- the difference between the CEO's pay and the compensation of the next highest paid executive in the company, or

- the relationship between changes in the CEO's pay and changes in the company's TSR relative to the TSR of other companies?

G. WHETHER CEO PAY REFLECTS COMPETITION

One answer to the complaint that CEO pay is too high is that the pay is set by competition and therefore reflects the market's rational allocation of resources. Some, however, argue that no such effective competition exists. Here are passages from pages 20–41 in *Searching for a Corporate Savior: The Irrational Quest for Charismatic CEOs*, by Rakesh Khurana. Mr. Khurana was an Assistant Professor of Business Administration at the Harvard Business School when he published this book. He is now a full professor at that school. I have left out the first chapter in which he described in detail the process by which Bank One came to hire Jamie Dimon as its CEO in March 2000.

CHAPTER 2: A Different Kind of Market

The succession process that resulted in Jamie Dimon's hiring as the CEO of Bank One followed an increasingly familiar script. A company's performance declines, and the board responds by forcing out the incumbent CEO, who is blamed for its troubles. An

---

as "find[ing] that when public companies go private, the CEOs tend to get paid more rather than less in both base salaries and bonuses"). We might compare the growth in CEO pay to the increase in pay to other top earners. *See, e.g.*, Steven N. Kaplan & Joshua Rauh, *It's the Market: The Broad-Based Rise in the Return to Top Talent*, 27 J. ECON. PERSPECT. 35, 36–43 (Summer 2013) (showing increase in income to S&P 500 CEOs, top 25 hedge fund managers, partners at top 50 law firms, and top 25 salaries in, respectively, professional baseball, basketball, and football).

external search is initiated with an extraordinary emphasis on hiring a candidate with demonstrable "leadership" and "charismatic" qualities. Much less emphasis is placed on the company's strategic situation and how appropriate the background of the candidate is in light of this. The entire search process is orchestrated to produce a corporate "savior," to find a new CEO whom investors and the business media regard as a star. The standard profile of this savior is of an individual who has served as a CEO or president at a high-performing and well-regarded company. Only a few candidates make it through this filtering process. Using the elusive concepts of leadership to distinguish among the candidates, directors come to focus their attention on a single individual. Next comes the effort of convincing this person to accept the position. To rationalize the organizational and monetary resources that go into recruiting the favored candidate, boards convince themselves that the person they have identified through the search process is, in fact, worth the effort and expense—that he (or, more rarely, she) really is a better candidate than any available inside the firm. Not only is the new executive now expected to be the solution to the company's problems, but his very presence is interpreted by the financial markets and the business media as a vote of confidence by the directors that these problems can and will be quickly solved. Everyone's expectations run high.

This storyline, however, often has a dubious ending from the point of view of those whose long-term interests directors are supposedly representing (i.e., shareholders). In the effort to convince the candidate to join the firm, directors yield control of the process to the demands of the recruit, who is in an unusually strong position to bargain with the board about subsequent power and compensation arrangements. If the new CEO is unable to deliver results relatively quickly, the wisdom of the selection is questioned. In some instances, boards find themselves trapped in an infinite loop of dashed expectations and CEO churn.

The extraordinary focus on the CEO as the source of a company's problems, and the blind faith that directors show in the charismatic CEO's powers to heal what ails the firm, introduce the first strain of irrationality into what—considering what companies believe to be at stake in the choice of a new CEO—one might expect to be a rational, carefully considered process. The widespread, firmly held belief in the overriding importance of the CEO is all the more noteworthy considering that there is no conclusive evidence linking leadership to organizational performance. In fact, most academic research that has sought to measure the impact of the CEO on firm performance confirms Warren Buffett's observation that when good management is brought into a bad business, it is the reputation of the business that remains intact.

Small Numbers of Buyers and Sellers

Rather than being what economists call a "perfect" market, with large numbers of buyers and sellers engaged in relatively anonymous exchange, the external CEO labor market is one in which buyers and sellers—or at least those considered *qualified* sellers—are relatively few. The number of buyers is a function of how many (or rather how few) companies are looking for a new CEO at any given time. Indeed, most potential candidates are aware of which companies are conducting a CEO search, particularly when poor performance has led to the decision to change CEOs. (Recall that, in the case of Bank One, Dimon himself felt that he would likely be considered for the CEO position, and therefore had expected a call from the search firm.) The small number of "sellers" in the external CEO market (for reasons that will become apparent momentarily, "sellers" has to be used in a very restricted sense in this context) can be illustrated by the lists of candidates that the Bank One search committee considered at various points in its CEO search. Drawing on both the directors' and the search consultants' knowledge of the banking industry, the Bank One search committee and its consultants produced an initial list of the leading lights of finance, one that contained thirty names. After a week of fact checking, the search consultants reduced this first list but also added some women and minorities whose names had not originally appeared. They then gave the search committee a booklet with profiles of each of the remaining candidates. The names of almost all of these candidates were familiar to the directors since the pared-down list was a virtual dream team for banking and finance. Some of the directors even knew several of the candidates personally.

A situation such as that in which the Bank One directors were aware of the candidates, and the candidates of the vacant CEO position at Bank One, is not unusual in CEO searches by large, publicly held firms. Relatively few CEO positions open up each year in comparison to other positions. Table 2.1 presents the number of outsider CEO searches undertaken by the firms in the sample in comparison to searches for vice presidents of marketing by these same firms. Firms conduct only one-sixth as many CEO searches as they do VP-marketing searches. Moreover, search firms receive no unsolicited resumes from individuals looking for CEO jobs. One search consultant cogently summarizes both consultants' and directors' common perception by stating that "unlike [with] other positions, the CEO market is not simply a problem of a person looking for a job, but a job looking for a person."

Table 2.1 also quantitatively represents the most commonly held perception of directors, executive search firms, and CEO candidates about this market—that the supply of qualified candidates for the CEO position in large corporations is thin. When contrasting the search for a CEO with that for other executives, one search consultant whom I interviewed commented that "the number of people who can run a 50,000-person organization is small, and most of us know them off the top of our head." Directors, too, lament the presumed shortage of CEO talent.

TABLE 2.1

Search Firm Statistics Contrasting CEO Search with VP Marketing Search

	CEO		VP Marketing	
	Firm A	Firm B	Firm A	Firm B
Number of Outside Searches	31	45	190	221
Initial Set of Candidates Collected	30	36	310	380
Candidates Contacted by ESF	18	19	92	80
Candidates Interviewed by ESF	5	7	17	14
Candidates Interviewed by Client	3	3	6	6
Average Days Search is Open	187	173	36	29
Number of Unsolicited Resumes	0	0	2500	~3000*

Data reported are rounded averages for CEO searches conducted between 1990 and 1998.

*Firm B did not differentiate in its database between Senior VP and VP positions, thus an approximation was made using the 1998 proportion of senior VP to VP of marketing searches.

Ideally, of course, one would want lots of organizations and lots of executives looking at one another to ensure a good match over the long run between executives and open CEO positions. Most firms, however, rarely realize these conditions in their external CEO searches. Yet while describing the condition of small numbers of buyers and sellers in the external CEO market, it is important to note that this scarcity is exacerbated, if not actually created, by the participants themselves.

The shortage of qualified sellers is at its core a misperception largely driven by the fact that boards employ extremely limiting criteria to define the pool of eligible candidates. These criteria, which are loosely (if at all) coupled to the specific strategic challenges facing the firm, are adopted largely with the intention of producing a candidate who will be seen as legitimate by external constituents, namely, financial analysts and the business media. The application of these criteria focuses the board's attention on a small number of candidates. As a result, the perceived shortage of qualified CEO candidates is exactly that— more social fiction than empirical reality. Bank One's directors, for example, insisted on a candidate who would restore the credibility of the company with Wall Street and financial analysts. This translated into a candidate pool in which the final external candidates were either CEOs or presidents of major financial institutions that had performed relatively well and were recognized as being of high quality and status. (Additional support for this interpretation is found in Table 2.1, which shows that the number of candidates perceived to be qualified for the position in the initial stages of a CEO search averages only thirty. On average, only five of these candidates are formally interviewed by the directors.) For their part, most of these candidates shared Dimon's view that there were "likely only one or two other firms I would ever be happy at."

How does the "thinness" of the external CEO market affect its functioning? The number of buyers and sellers in a market is both an indication of the number of alternative relationships available to actors and a critical element in their definition of the market itself. For competitive markets to exist, economists have argued, the number of buyers and sellers must be so large that the ordinary transactions of any single one of them do not appreciably affect the conditions under which other transactions are made. Conversely, the smaller the number of sellers in a given market, the greater the effect of the transactions of any one seller on the fortunes of the others. In the external CEO market, the initial, totally artificial reduction of the size of the candidate pool is generally followed by a similar market-distorting maneuver during the negotiation of compensation. Both Derek Bok and

Graef Crystal have argued that the reason CEO pay continues to ratchet upward—even during periods of declining firm performance—is that it is usually anchored to a median calculated from a ranking of a small number of other CEOs. Because the comparison group is small and most boards have adopted a convention to pay their CEOs above the median of their comparison group, an increase in pay for one CEO will result in raising the pay of others. The ratcheting is further exacerbated by CEOs' exertion of influence on the comparison group, via their chosen compensation consultants, by "eliminating certain companies and adding others."

Small or thin markets also reduce competition by limiting the set of other actors with whom a focal actor may contract in efforts to conduct transactions, and by making the search for these trading partners more problematic. For example, buyers and sellers in disconnected or sparse networks may not be aware of the full range of trading partners or opportunities for exchange. Even actors in the same social networks may not be aware of each other's complementary interests if the actors constituting that network are differentiated with regard to activities or interests or beliefs about what is discussable, so that direct interchange between such actors is muted. For example, two members of a golf club or university club may not be aware of how they could benefit each other if talking business at the club is discouraged. This suggests that two actors will be accessible to each other for exchange only if their interests become known and are tolerably consistent. This creates a problem in CEO search because both candidates and boards of directors lack the information necessary to make informed decisions. Aside from the small number of companies known to be searching for a new CEO, a potential CEO candidate will not know what opportunities exist in the market. Similarly, directors will not know if there are qualified people who would be willing to take on the position for less pay than the small number they have already identified as candidates presumably would.

Another analysis of the significance of small numbers of buyers and sellers in a market has been proposed by the sociologist Wayne Baker, who studied the Chicago commodities markets to demonstrate the implications of the numbers of buyers and sellers for a market. Baker found that in contrast to the competitive markets typically described by economists, in which no set of buyers or sellers can dominate the market, many commodities markets were specialized and esoteric, and only a handful of dealers in the world knew how to buy and sell the goods in them.

Baker found that to work, these markets needed extensive coordination between buyers and sellers to create the market in the first place. That is, the formal market structure of thinly traded commodities was supplemented and occasionally subverted by an informal social structure of roles, relationships, and collective action. People would often repeatedly trade with the same people. At other times, traders would avoid taking opportunistic advantage of another trader whose financial exposure was too great. One consequence of this small number of participants is that these markets did not display the processes of equilibrium so often assumed in standard economic analysis. Instead, there were large price discrepancies and evidence that the participants' behavior resembled that in a village store, with concerns about interpersonal relationships, reciprocity, and trust—rather than the relentless pursuit of profit—undergirding the behavior of the traders.

Elements such as reciprocity and trust, in turn, become important in the external CEO labor market owing to a second fundamental condition of this market: the risks faced by both buyers and sellers.

High Risk

Previous researchers have not explicitly considered the problem of identifying the potential pool of candidates in the external CEO market. Since most candidates in the CEO labor market are already employed, those seeking to employ them do not have a clear view of whether any of these individuals would be willing to leave their current positions or whether they would be interested in a particular firm that has an opening. The basic condition of a passive CEO labor market creates a high-risk situation for both firms and potential candidates.

The risks to both the candidates (sellers) and the firm (buyer) in this market is reflected in much of the behavior that we observed in considering Bank One's CEO search. In the Bank One case, once the search committee had whittled its list of thirty candidates down to five finalists, the Russell Reynolds consultants arranged the interviews to ensure the utmost confidentiality and even secrecy. One reason for the secrecy was that, with the exception of Dimon, the external final candidates were actively employed as CEOs or presidents at other firms. The *Chicago Tribune* and the *Chicago Sun-Times* published rumors about the identity of the candidates almost daily, and if it could be confirmed that any of the finalists other than Istock and Dimon had interviewed for the position, it would not bode well for these executives at their current firms. Since all of the finalists except for Istock were from outside Chicago, the consultants were careful to schedule interviews in Chicago for days when board meetings were also being held, so as not to arouse suspicion among Bank One executives should any of them run into an out-of-town director. They also took pains to schedule the candidates' flights to eliminate any possibility of their seeing one another at the airport. The interviews were held in Russell Reynolds' downtown Chicago offices, where Redmond and Tribbett carefully choreographed arrivals, departures, and the use of rooms to ensure, again, that there would be no possibility of the candidates' catching so much as a glimpse of one another.

Meanwhile, even though Jamie Dimon was not actively employed at the time of the Bank One search—and therefore not at risk himself—even his name had to be kept under wraps for the sake of Bank One. Tribbett points out that if it had become public that Dimon was being considered, and then that he was not interested in the position or had actually refused it, any CEO who was eventually appointed, no matter how good he might be, would find it difficult to succeed. "If employees and analysts think the selected CEO is the 'second-best' person to run the firm, he has no shot," says Tribbett. (As confirmation of this, consider the example of AT&T's 1997 CEO search, which will be discussed in greater detail in chapter 4. John Walter was clearly the second choice of the AT&T board when C. Michael Armstrong refused the position, and AT&T's image was dealt a severe blow.) Moreover, not wanting to be regarded as the second choice, the remaining strong candidates often withdraw themselves from consideration in circumstances where this danger exists, thereby often forcing the search to start all over again.

Confidentiality also becomes an issue when obtaining information about a candidate's skills or capabilities, since such information cannot be obtained directly from his or her current employer. As one consultant comments, "You can't exactly go to the guy's boss and let him know you are thinking of hiring his CEO." Although general information about a candidate's educational background can be collected easily from public sources, the firm searching for a CEO must rely on other, more private sources to gain particular knowledge about a candidate's capabilities, temperament, character, and skills. Economists describe this need for detailed information as linked to the problem of adverse selection, a process by which the least desirable objects from any observationally similar group enter a market in which information is poorly distributed between buyers and sellers.

Although on the surface they may appear alike, outside candidates cannot be presumed equal. Some outsiders have deceptive career patterns and are available in the market because they continue to fail upward. Legal requirements and privacy protections make it hard to find detailed information about a candidate's history. In other words, if a board relied simply on the information produced by the conventional market process, it would know little other than what the résumé and the candidate offered. In an example of the pitfalls of such an approach, consider the CEO search at Sunbeam that resulted in the hiring of Al Dunlap, a case in which the search firm was unaware that the candidate it had placed had been dismissed from a previous job for overseeing an accounting fraud that had culminated in the firm's bankruptcy. While I will return to this point in chapters 4, 5, and 6, for now keep in mind that much of the particular information required to minimize risks to the hiring firm is gathered not by the search firm but by the directors. To obtain such information, directors rely on their prominence and strong ties to individuals who have had direct experience with the persons under consideration.

While some degree of adverse selection is always inherent in transactions in which information about an individual's past behavior is incomplete, the problem is aggravated by a second type of risk specific to information about present and future behavior. This second type is now commonly described as an agency problem. Whenever one individual depends on the action of another, an agency relationship arises; for example, a lawyer is an agent for his or her client, and a CEO is an agent for the shareholders. An agency problem arises when participants in an exchange have divergent objectives, and information about how they are behaving and will behave in the future is imperfect or unavailable.

In the relationships that exist between CEOs and their companies, agency costs can be quite high. Michael Jensen and others have offered examples of cases in which self-interested decisions by CEOs at the expense of shareholders have led to multibillion-dollar losses. Moreover, even when information comes to light about irresponsible actions on the part of a CEO, it is often difficult to remove him. A CEO cannot be dismissed as easily as other members of the organization. CEOs, in fact—despite the increase in CEO dismissals over the last decade—have several tools at their disposal to make themselves both difficult and costly to replace, including controlling the agenda of board meetings and the ability to appoint board members. Under such risky conditions, directors would not likely participate in the exchange that external CEO search represents without a means for reducing the information uncertainty associated with adverse selection and agency relationships.

Returning again to the case of Bank One, neither Bank One's directors nor Dimon had the information required to engage in fully informed decision-making. Let us consider the situation from Dimon's point of view first. While the Bank One directors were somewhat forthcoming with their leading candidate regarding the problems facing the bank, they also wanted him to take the job and so tried not to make these problems look insurmountable. In any event, most had only limited understanding of the firm's situation by virtue of being directors rather than full-time executives. (Most of the information that Bank One's external directors relied on for assessing the firm's condition came from the external environment and from former First Chicago executives— agents whose motivations potentially diverged from those of the directors themselves.) While Dimon, in the meantime, contacted financial analysts to better understand Bank One's problems, he recognized that analysts rely primarily on financial indicators to analyze the company. One ironic consequence of this particular information asymmetry was that Dimon was able to negotiate a relatively high salary and guaranteed bonus as a type of insurance in the event that the problems at Bank One proved to be more severe than he understood. Thus the apparent risk to Dimon turned out to increase the risk to the directors.

For their part, in an effort to gain specific and detailed information about Dimon, Bank One's directors relied on trusted social connections, particularly with other directors who had known or worked with Dimon in the past. Yet even after gathering as much information of this kind as possible, the directors found it impossible to know ex ante whether they had made an intrinsically sound choice. By picking a candidate who was highly regarded (given Dimon's performance as president of one of the most highly regarding financial institutions in the world, Citigroup), they hoped at least to be able to justify their decision to others. In its manifest concern for the opinions of others, their strategy for dealing with risk points to the third key feature of the external CEO market.

Concerns about Legitimacy

The third important feature of the external CEO labor market is the way in which it is driven by concerns about legitimacy. According the sociologist Richard Scott, the legitimacy of an action "is determined by the amount of consensus within the relevant sector or field regarding the appropriateness of the means selected to achieve the desired ends." Because the directors and candidates involved in external CEO search are embedded in a community of overlapping business and social relationships, they are particularly sensitive to maintaining the appearance of propriety in the conduct of the search among their peers. Moreover, because the opinions of external actors such as analysts and the business media are so important to ensuring the eventual acceptance of the candidate, that the process be perceived by these outsiders as both objective and proper is critical.

In the Bank One search, the directors faced enormous pressure from shareholders, analysts, and the business press first to fire McCoy and then to act quickly to find a successor. This successor was also going to have to be someone whose appointment would signal to this external audience that Bank One was serious about solving its problems, and that is still enjoyed sufficient prestige to achieve outside director John Hall's stated goal of finding "the best person in the United States to lead us back to the top"—which would require mounting what outsiders would accept as a wide-ranging, objective search. (The very real link between the external CEO search process and the maintenance of a firm's standing in the eyes of external constituents is reflected in the stock market's response first to the news of McCoy's departure, then to Dimon's appointment, and eventually to the doubts that were quickly raised about the latter's ability to perform as expected. The idea that the CEO's performance determines a company's fortunes may be a myth, but that does not make it any less powerful.) Finally, the search had to be pursued in the midst of more-or-less open strife between two opposing factions on the board. The highly politicized context that this conflict created made it all the more imperative that the Bank One directors and their candidates appear to have conducted themselves appropriately.

The importance of concerns about legitimacy in the external CEO search process is highlighted by one aspect of the role of the executive search firm: the part that search consultants play in overcoming the reservations both parties may feel about their own participation in the market. Although a key part of the search firm's role, this function is easily obscured by other issues that arise between firms in the market for a CEO and CEO candidates.

The high stakes and high risks for both directors and candidates in external CEO searches greatly increase the possibility of heightened emotions among the actors: for example, the hiring firm can easily become frustrated with a candidate who seems to take too long to make a decision, or who is perceived as making extraordinary demands regarding compensation, perquisites, or employment contracts. Much as in international diplomacy, such complex, emotionally fraught negotiations usually require the participation of a third party to resolve not only substantive issues such as compensation but also human issues such as frustration or anger—factors that can easily poison a working relationship between a board and its desired candidate. One consultant, describing his job as "part recruiter, part messenger, and mostly marriage counselor," recounts a particularly intense negotiation in which the firm had become frustrated with the "seemingly endless demands the candidate was making on compensation-related issues":

> [Steve] kept making a longer and longer list of what he thought should be covered in order to "make him whole" as a consequence of the move. Meanwhile, the board was getting pretty annoyed at looking at the detailed requests about unexercised options, initiation fees at new country clubs, and deferred compensation, etc. I saw what was happening with respect to the frustration level. . . . I stepped in and said, "Why don't we just put all of this into a one-time signing bonus? In that way, [Steve] doesn't have to go through accounting for every little cost he was going to incur and the board didn't have to review and approve every one of these . . . expenses." . . . [T]hey [quickly] came to an agreement on an amount that was perceived fair by both sides. I think it was twenty percent of the first year's cash compensation.

When search consultants are asked to explain why candidates and directors—often portrayed as the kinds of people who are rational, cool, and in control of their emotions—become so sensitive and easily frustrated during negotiations, they almost always seem irritated by a question about what to them is an obvious point. In two-person interactions, they point out, directly negotiating a salary or other sensitive matters can provoke intense emotions. The use of an intermediary, however, dampens the feelings that normally arise in such negotiations and represents one party's demands or responses to the other in a more conciliatory, objective manner.

This explanation of the search consultant's role in facilitating negotiations between boards and CEO candidates is a plausible one, and in several other settings, such as divorces and labor-management negotiations, seems to be a principal reason why third parties are brought into tense negotiations. However, we can look at the intermediary in an external CEO search in another way by considering the hesitancy that both firms and candidates express about actively participating in this market at all. We have just seen how the involvement of an executive search firm in an external CEO search helps protect participants from risk. Yet the executive search firm's role also helps allay concerns about how the appropriateness of their actions will be perceived both by their peers and by outsiders. For example, both directors and candidates feel constrained by norms concerning the propriety of contacts, in the course of an external CEO search, between board members and CEO candidates who belong to competing firms. In the face of such constraints, the search firm protects both parties from appearances of impropriety by eliminating the need for direct contact between the two in the early phases of a search. That directors and candidates, in turn, are generally linked to one another by personal connections creates another legitimacy issue that the executive search firm helps to resolve. In this case, the mere presence of a third party mediator lends an appearance of distance and objectivity to what otherwise might be suspected by outsiders to be an essentially social exchange.

In view of these realities, a more far-reaching interpretation of the search consultant's role than the "marriage counselor" one would start with the supposition that the gap between buyers and sellers in a market is, in part, institutional, and is linked to the degree to which participation in a market is normatively legitimate. In legitimate markets, buyers and sellers can engage openly (and presumably with less heightened emotions) in exchanges without fear of repercussions. By contrast, in markets of questionable legitimacy, actors may be unwilling or hesitant to engage or participate, even if their interests suggest that an exchange would be mutually beneficial. The role of the executive search firm thus is to help both searching firms and candidates to overcome their ambivalence about participating in a market of this particular kind.

The concern with market legitimacy on the parts of buyers and sellers, in turn, highlights an important fact about interaction, even in markets: it is shaped by a collective, communal structure. Some interactions that could take place in a market do not, in fact, do so because all interaction occurs in a context of institutional constraints, including rules and roles. Rules impose some of these constraints: for example, the rule that organizations cannot exchange cost information with competitors. Role expectations impose constraints as well: directors, for instance, are asked to resign or recuse themselves from decisions when their memberships on other boards present the potential for a conflict of interest. Under conditions in which a market is perceived as illegitimate, actors may be unwilling to make even initial contact or to engage in ephemeral transactions with others unless there is a means of keeping appropriate distance until a transaction can be consummated. Indeed, in the external CEO market, the role of legitimacy concerns is underscored by the numerous informal restrictions and rules that influence the manner in which interactions must take place. The enforcement of restrictions on, for example, the ways that candidates can be approached is part of this market's distinctive character. In the external CEO market, legitimacy concerns are particularly acute because market decisions occur not only at the level of the individual organization but also at the organizational field level, in which other actors evaluate the outcome.

Under these circumstances, the best searches serve to legitimate both the search process itself and the final choice of the search committee and board so that a new CEO can have a smooth transition into the position. Missteps during the search process can leave organizational observers and constituents alike seething about the search and hostile to its outcome. The search ends up an abysmal failure, not because the wrong candidate was selected, but because someone who may have been right for the organization is handicapped by the mishandling of the process. The outcome of a search that, from a strategically sound perspective, may be seen as appropriate may be rejected by both internal and external constituents because of the manner in which the process was executed.

Much of the board's concern with legitimacy in external CEO search stems, in part, from a weakening of the boundaries and secrecy that once surrounded CEO succession. Naming a new CEO is no longer considered a divine right of the CEO or even of the board. Whereas in the past CEOs or boards of directors could be allowed to choose the successor because of the perceived validity of peer review—the thinking being that people who have been in positions of leadership are best positioned to decide who can run the corporation—the internal succession process now has the aroma of a smoke-filled room. CEO succession is increasingly treated as an event in which external constituencies have both a strong interest in the outcome and a right to influence it.

These external constituencies, namely Wall Street analysts and the business media, now constitute a legitimating authority for most organizations. Ezra Zuckerman, a sociologist of markets, has documented the increased power of Wall Street analysts in the determination of an organization's stock performance. He argues that investors, especially institutional investors, increasingly rely on the judgments of these analysts when making investment decisions. Board members, as result, must now pay more attention to them, too. "If you go back a few years ago," notes George Kennedy, a director of several public firms, "I don't recall reading the analyst reports on the boards that you served on, everybody else's view as to how things were going. You might read the articles in the *Wall Street Journal* if you are on the board, obviously, but I don't remember reading all those reports." Other directors observe that, through clipping services, they now receive almost every newspaper or magazine article that mentions companies on whose boards they serve. The cumulative result of these changes is to focus directors' attention away from the immediate situation of the firm and toward the externally relevant actors. Directors who control organizations now try to interpret their external environment and then make succession decisions based on their reading of those external actors whose opinions they most value—and with good reason. (Again, the example of AT&T's 1997 CEO search—and the subsequent search the firm had to undertake nine months later—provides a vivid illustration of this point, one that I provide in chapter 4.)

A market characterized by small numbers of buyers and sellers, high risk to both, and such concerns about legitimacy as those outlined above, does indeed bear little resemblance to what is most often meant by a "market," even though previous observers have generally described it as such. The reason for the current lack of understanding of the true nature of the external CEO labor market is that none of the lenses that have been used for observing and analyzing it are adequate for perceiving, much less comprehending, its complexity.[73]

QUESTIONS ON COMPENSATION COMMITTEE ACTION IN THE ABSENCE OF A WELL-DEVELOPED MARKET FOR CEO TALENT

If a single director on a compensation committee believes that the absence of a true market for CEOs has driven CEO pay too high, what can he or she do?

Suppose that an entire compensation committee agrees with that view? What can one compensation committee do?

---

[73]   RAKESH KHURANA, SEARCHING FOR A CORPORATE SAVIOR: THE IRRATIONAL QUEST FOR CHARISMATIC CEOS 20–41 (2002) (footnotes omitted). Copyright © 2002 by Princeton University Press. Reprinted by permission.

Even if the process and outcomes are irrational, should the committee and the board as a whole at any given company accept them anyway, because the rest of the business community accepts them? Would it take a broad-based shareholder revolt, or some other transformative event, to bring CEO pay down or significantly reduce the rate at which it increases? Is some kind of government intervention advisable?

How could a company retain credibility with Wall Street if it became the lone ranger on CEO compensation, paying significantly below the current median for similarly sized companies in the same industry? How could such a company persuade talented executives to work for it?

To what extent, more generally, should directors take compensation actions (such as using multiple equity vehicles to deliver CEO compensation or setting the length of the measurement period for performance shares at three years instead of five years) that they believe are less than optimal for the company because Wall Street expects those actions and the price of the company's shares might fall if the company's compensation practices differed significantly from those prevalent in the corporate community and in the company's industry?

Does the duty of care, qualified by the business judgment rule, prohibit a compensation committee from "going along with the crowd" and itself engaging in behavior that, when committees at other companies do likewise, helps to frustrate a true market for CEO talent?

Is there anything in the reforms we have studied to this point that prevents a compensation committee from "going along with the crowd"?

H. WHETHER COMPENSATION ENCOURAGES BAD BEHAVIOR

In recent years, many academics have expressed concern that some forms of compensation—particularly equity compensation and even more particularly stock option compensation—can encourage executives to make decisions that harm their companies. Two types of poor decisions figure into the debate—decisions leading to misreported financial numbers, and decisions taking too much risk. Here are some of the studies.

Compensation as an incentive to misstate financial numbers. The discussion earlier in this chapter suggested that large equity holdings in options and restricted stock might influence a top executive at a company to manipulate financial results in a manner that would increase the price of his or her company's stock or prevent a stock price decline. Large amounts of equity owned outright—in unrestricted shares—could provide a similar incentive for wrongdoing.

A number of finance studies address this issue, and what follows is a summary of a few of them.[74] Several of the studies relate equity compensation to accounting restatements. As you know, if a company discovers that any of the numbers in a set of previously published financial statements was materially wrong, the company will issue a corrected set of financial numbers called a "restatement."

One study examined 215 companies (i) with data in ExecuComp[75] and (ii) that announced restatements during the period 1995 to 2002 because the originally published financials did not accord with generally accepted accounting principles.[76] The study compared these companies that announced restatements with all other companies in the S&P 1500 that did not.[77]

The researchers found that the probability of a restatement increased with "option sensitivity" (defined as the change in the value of the CEO's stock options per 1% change in company stock price) and that the magnitude of the restatement (measured by its effect on company net income) also increased with option sensitivity.[78] The researchers also tested for, but did *not* find, a positive effect on misreporting from any of the

---

[74]   It is vital that you bear two points in mind. First, this book does not attempt to provide anything like a comprehensive survey of the studies considering whether equity compensation and equity holdings acquired by purchase or by founding a company create a significant incentive for wrongdoing. This chapter summarizes only a few studies to (hopefully) get you interested in this topic.

Second, it is hard to know how much importance to place on any financial study unless we review it closely. The stock market as a whole has acted very differently during some multi-year periods than during others, so the time period of a study might influence its results. A study might have so few events in a sample that it sheds little light on a question. In the same vein, a close read of a study must try to determine whether the study has yielded statistically significant results, which requires some knowledge of the manner in which statisticians evaluate the reliability of results in light of sample size and distribution of values in a sample. Most studies "control" for variables other than the one examined in an attempt to find the independent statistical significance of the variable studied—e.g., in determining the effect of option compensation on the probability that a company will report false financial numbers, a study might control for other forms of compensation, the size of different companies, differences in the degree to which existing debt is placing a strain on the companies in the study, and the variations in recent price performance of the different companies' stock. Obviously, if a study fails to control for a factor that might influence the result in a significant way, the study's conclusion may be wrong. In only a few cases will this chapter point to problems of these sorts in the studies the text reviews.

[75]   ExecuComp is a database that contains information on the compensation paid to top executives at companies in the S&P 1500 Index.

[76]   Natasha Burns & Simi Kedia, *The Impact of Performance-based Compensation on Misreporting*, 79 J. FIN. ECON. 35 (2006) [Burns, *Impact of Performance-based Compensation*]. Quotations from this article republished with permission of Elsevier B.V., from The impact of performance-based compensation on misreporting, Natasha Burns & Simi Kedia, Vol. 79, Issue 1, Journal of Financial Economics copyright 2005; permission conveyed through Copyright Clearance Center, Inc.

[77]   *Id.* at 36. The S&P Composite 1500 combines three Standard and Poor's indices—the S&P 500, the S&P MidCap 400, and the S&P SmallCap 600. *See* S&P Dow Jones Indices, *S&P Composite 1500®*, http://us.spindices.com/indices/equity/sp-composite-1500 (last visited May 6, 2016).

[78]   Burns, *Impact of Performance-based Compensation*, *supra* note 76, at 36–37.

following: (i) CEO equity (presumably shares owned outright), (ii) restricted stock awards, (iii) long-term incentive payouts,[79] or (iv) cash salary plus cash bonus.[80]

The authors explained the special power of options to motivate misreporting in these words:

> Option compensation makes CEO wealth a convex function of stock price. Consequently, the CEO benefits from an increase in the stock price associated with aggressive accounting. However, the loss to CEO wealth in the event of a decline in stock price is limited. . . .
>
> Like stock options, equity and restricted stock also tie CEO wealth to stock price. Equity and restricted stock might also generate incentives to misreport. However, in contrast to options, the payoff from equity and restricted stock has a symmetric relation to stock price, thereby exposing the CEO to price declines associated with the announcement of a restatement unless the CEO unwinds his equity and restricted stock holdings prior to the restatement.[81]

Here is one of the principal findings:

> We begin by reporting summary statistics of the sensitivity of components of CEO compensation for restating and nonrestating firm-years. . . . The mean (median) value of option sensitivity for misreported firm-years is $567,802 ($132,367). On average, the value of the stock options held by the CEO changes by $567,802 for a 1% change in stock price. This is significantly higher, at the 1% level [meaning that there is at least a 99% probability that the difference does not occur by chance], than the mean (median) value of $263,595 ($79,998) for nonrestating firm-years. There appears to be significant evidence, in univariate tests, that CEOs have larger incentives from stock options in misreported years.[82]

---

[79]   The authors defined long-term incentive payouts as those paid to executives "usually based on a three-to-five-year moving average of firm performance." *Id.* at 50. They commented that "ExecuComp does not provide information on the details of the payout, but reports only its value." *Id.*

[80]   *Id.* at 37.

[81]   *Id.* at 36–37. A convex wealth function of stock price means that wealth increases (decreases) at an accelerated (decelerated) rate the more the stock price increases (declines). The value of call options is convex because the change in the value of an option is much smaller when the share price is below the exercise price than when it is above the exercise price. The convexity of call options hinges on the fact that options will not be exercised when the stock price is below the exercise price, so the negative value of an option that is already out of the money does not increase much as the price of the stock falls further below the exercise price.

[82]   *Id.* at 51. The unit of observation in this study was a "firm-year." A "misreported firm-year" was a year for which an S&P 1500 firm restated its financial figures, and a "nonrestating firm-year" was a year for which an S&P 1500 firm did not restate. Years that were not restated by

After (i) running regressions to control for different industries, different sizes of companies, and different market-to-book valuations and (ii) computing the independent statistical relationship of the different types of compensation to restatements, the researchers still found that option sensitivity was related to restatements, while (a) equity-owned-outright sensitivity, (b) restricted stock sensitivity,[83] (c) salary and bonus sensitivity,[84] and (d) long-term incentive payments were not.[85]

A second study examined 358 companies (i) with data in ExecuComp and (ii) that were sued in class actions by shareholders alleging violations of the securities laws from and including 1993 to and including 2002.[86]

---

a firm that issued a restatement in some other year were included in "nonrestating firm-years." *Id.* at 46.

[83]   "Consistent with the measure of option sensitivity, sensitivity of restricted stock and equity holdings is defined as the change in the value of these holdings for a 1% change in firm value." *Id.* at 50.

[84]   The researchers used a proxy for this sensitivity. The proxy was the estimated coefficient of change in net income from a regression of changes in salary plus bonus on changes in net income within the industry in which a firm operated. *Id.* at 51.

[85]   *Id.* at 53–56. A study of 87 firms that the SEC accused of accounting wrongdoing during the period 1991 through 2005 (each one matched against an industry-and size-matched control firm) reached a different conclusion:

> Our sample consists of firms that are subjects of Securities and Exchange Commission's (SEC) Accounting and Auditing Enforcement Releases (AAERs) from 1991–2005. We focus on AAERs in which the SEC believes that there is sufficient evidence of accounting fraud to bring a case against a firm or its executives. For ease of exposition, hereafter we refer to these firms as fraud firms. For the executives at each fraud firm, we compare the financial incentives from stock and option holdings to similar metrics for executives at industry-and size-matched control firms that are not subjects of AAERs.
>
> . . . .
>
> . . . . [W]e find that incentives from unrestricted stock for the median fraud executive are 54% greater than those of the median control executive; at the 75th percentile, they are 84% greater. . . . Unrestricted stock is also the largest incentive source at fraud firms, whereas vested options are the largest source at control firms. Controlling for corporate governance, firm, and CEO characteristics, the likelihood of fraud is positively related to incentives from unrestricted stock, and is unrelated to incentives from vested options, unvested options, and restricted stock.
>
> . . . . We find that fraud firms have significantly greater pre-fraud sales growth, which suggests that more of their value stems from growth opportunities.
>
> . . . .
>
> . . . . Operating and stock return results imply that executives at fraud firms likely anticipate large stock price declines if they do not fraudulently prop up earnings. Executives with large stockholdings suffer greater financial losses from stock price declines than executives with large option holdings because of the linearity (convexity) of stock (option) payoffs.

Shane A. Johnson, et al., *Managerial Incentives and Corporate Fraud: The Sources of Incentives Matter*, 13 REV. FIN. 115, 116–17 (2009). Johnson and his fellow researchers also found—after running regressions designed to control for such other variables as the percentage of insiders on the board, the percentage of insiders on the audit committee, and leverage—that "only incentives from unrestricted stock are positively related to the likelihood of fraud after controlling for other potential determinants of fraud." *Id.* at 137; *see also id.* at 136–37 tbl.V. Quotations from this article reprinted with permission from Professors Johnson, Ryan, and Tian.

[86]   David J. Denis, et al., *Is There a Dark Side to Incentive Compensation?*, 12 J. CORP. FIN. 467 (2006). Quotations from this article republished with permission of Elsevier B.V., from Is there

These researchers matched each of the firms in the sample with another firm of about the same size and in the same industry.[87] They measured "option intensity" as "the change in the value of the executive's option portfolio from a $1000 change in the value of the firm's equity."[88]

This study team found a positive relationship between (i) CEO option intensity and (ii) the likelihood that a firm would be sued for securities fraud[89]:

> [T]here is a significant difference between the incentives from options of the sample firms and those of the control firms. The average option intensity is $3.59 per $1000 change in shareholder wealth for the sample firms and $3.04 per $1000 change in shareholder wealth for the control firms. The difference is significant at the 0.04 level using a pairwise *t*-test [meaning that there is at least a 96% probability that the difference is not the result of chance]. Median option intensity is also larger in the sample firms ($1.84 vs. $1.70). However, this difference is not statistically significant [meaning that the difference could be due to chance].

> Importantly, the difference in option intensity appears to be economically relevant. To gauge economic significance, we first compute the difference in stock price from its highest value during the class period to its value following the class period. We then compute an industry-adjusted change as the difference between the firm's change in stock price and that of the median firm in the same industry. Finally, we multiply this industry-adjusted change in stock price times the firm's number of shares to arrive at an industry-adjusted change in equity value. Under the admittedly simplistic assumption that the stock price high during the class period is a consequence of fraud, whereas the post-class price is a measure of the "true" stock price, the industry-adjusted difference represents a measure of the change in equity value due to the alleged fraud. The average industry-adjusted drop in equity value is $8.37 billion. The average difference in option intensity between the sample and control firms is 0.56. Thus, on average, the CEO of the sample firm stands to gain an extra $4.65 million

---

a dark side to incentive compensation?, David J. Denis, et al., Vol. 12, Issue 3, Journal of Corporate Finance copyright 2005; permission conveyed through Copyright Clearance Center, Inc.

[87] *Id*. at 472.

[88] *Id*. at 476. The "value of the firm's equity" was market capitalization—the number of outstanding shares times the share price.

[89] "Over 90% of the complaints allege either a material misrepresentation (65.7% of the sample) or misstated financial results (25.7% of the sample). Misstated financial results are a special case of material misrepresentation that involve errors in the financial statements (i.e., an inappropriate booking of earnings)." *Id*. at 472.

(8.37 billion × 0.56 / 1000) from the alleged fraud. In other words, the differences in option intensity appear to be large enough to have a meaningful influence on the incentive to commit fraud.[90]

These researchers found no statistically positive significant relationship between (i) long-term incentive payments; (ii) cash compensation; or (iii) restricted shares, on the one hand, and being sued for securities fraud, on the other hand.[91] When they ran regressions to compute the independent statistical significance of the different methods of compensation to the probability of being sued for securities violations, the authors of this study again found that option intensity was a significant positive predictor of being sued, while salary, bonus, restricted shares, and long-term incentive payments were not.[92]

A third study examined 95 companies (i) that announced financial restatements during 2001 or 2002, (ii) that were not financial services firms, and (iii) for which ExecuComp and Compustat[93] had data.[94] The researchers paired each company that restated with another company that did not, with the "control" firm paired to the restating firm by industry, size, and time.[95] The study attempted to test the relationship between the value of in-the-money options (both vested and unvested) and the likelihood that a company would restate.

Again, the researchers found that large option holdings were associated with restatements:

> Over time CEOs accumulate in-the-money options of substantial value. With the maximum set at $150 million, the average value of in-the-money options held by CEOs at restating firms is $22,085,280 (median of $3,928,670), greatly exceeding the average amount at matched firms of $5,167,250 (median of $386,250), and these differences are significant at the 0.001 level.[96]

---

[90]   *Id*. at 477–78 & tbl.4.

[91]   *Id*. at 479, 478 tbl.4.

[92]   *Id*. at 479–82. The regressions included variables to control for book-to-market ratio, return on assets, firm size, leverage, risk of financial distress, and the need for external financing.

[93]   Compustat is a database that contains historical financial and market data for publicly traded companies.

[94]   Jap Efendi, et al., *Why Do Corporate Managers Misstate Financial Statements? The Role of Option Compensation and Other Factors*, 85 J. FIN. ECON. 667, 677–79 (2007). Quotations from this article republished with permission of Elsevier B.V., from Why do corporate managers misstate financial statements? The role of option compensation and other factors, Vol. 85, Issue 3, Journal of Financial Economics copyright 2007; permission conveyed through Copyright Clearance Center, Inc.

[95]   *Id*. at 668.

[96]   *Id*. at 682. The "0.001 level" means that there was a less than one-tenth of 1% probability that the difference between the values resulted from chance.

To analyze the significance of option holdings while taking into account multiple other factors, the researchers ran regressions.[97] Here they tested the relationship between the probability of a restatement, on the one hand, and on the other hand, the multiple of salary representing the value of in-the-money options.[98] That examination yielded these results:

> The likelihood of a restatement increases by 43.3% when the CEO holds in-the-money options at the 90th percentile compared to a CEO with option holdings at the 10th percentile. . . . Compared to a CEO with no stock options, we find that the probability of a restatement increases by only 3% if the CEO has in-the-money options that approximate the median value in our sample of 3.28 times salary (median salary is roughly $500,000). If the CEO has in-the-money options at the 70th percentile (about nine times salary), the increase in restatement probability is still only 9%, but after this point the probability increases rapidly. The increase is 21% at the 80th percentile [at which the CEO has options worth 21.66 times annual salary], 43% at the 90th percentile [options worth 53.55 times salary], and 56% at the 95th percentile [options worth 136.36 times salary].[99]

By contrast, the researchers found statistically insignificant the differences between the restating firms' and control firms' (i) restricted stock grants, (ii) restricted stock holdings, and (iii) the Black-Scholes value of option grants.[100]

This book does not advocate that companies should forego equity compensation. Nor does it purport to compare the benefits of such compensation (by aligning the interests of executives with those of non-management shareholders) against the cost of any increase in the probability of misreported financial numbers.

---

[97] Efendi, et al. included in the regressions variables to control for differences in total assets; differences in debt-to-assets ratios; whether the CEO was also the board chair; the relationship between the change in CEO salary and change in firm net income, earnings per share, and revenue; and the amount of capital raised in the restated year. *Id.* at 685–88.

[98] If the value of the in-the-money options for a CEO was three times the value of his or her annual salary, then the value of the option variable in the regression was 3.0.

[99] *Id.* at 689, 690 fig.2.

[100] *Id.* at 688. The researchers defined "restricted stock grant" to mean the "value of restricted stock granted to the CEO during the year determined at the date of grant" and "restricted stock holdings" as the "value of the CEO's restricted stock holdings at the end of the year." *Id.* at 684 tbl.2.

As we have seen, the proportion of equity compensation comprised of stock options and the proportion comprised of restricted stock have changed over time. Evaluation of studies investigating whether one type of equity compensation is related to misreporting but another is not might have to take this into account.

The point is simply that there is some empirical evidence[101] supporting the commonsense intuition that an officer who has a large equity stake in a company, especially through options (on which the executive has large as yet unrealized gains), might be tempted to (i) cause the company to publish false and favorable information so (ii) the executive can realize a gain through stock sales while the price of the company's shares is inflated by the market's reaction to the false and favorable information.

QUESTIONS ON EQUITY COMPENSATION AND FINANCIAL MISREPORTING

After reviewing these studies, do you conclude that option compensation encourages financial misreporting?

Do you conclude that unrestricted stock grants or restricted stock grants do not?

To the extent that you conclude that equity compensation of any sort creates some incentive for financial misstatements, does that incentive outweigh the value such compensation provides by encouraging executives to make decisions that will increase the price of company stock and hence benefit all shareholders?

If a compensation committee decides to grant equity compensation to a CEO, should the audit committee at that same company take special care to avoid fraud? If so, does this suggest that the division of duties between the audit and compensation committees may not be wise? Or that the board as a whole should address matters in which one committee's work affects another committee's work?

---

[101]   A study based on a large sample of companies, covering the years 2001–2005, generated matched pairs of companies by using a sophisticated algorithm designed to fold multiple control variables into the matching process. Christopher S. Armstrong, et al., *Chief Executive Officer Equity Incentives and Accounting Irregularities*, 48 J. ACCT. RES. 225 (2010) (including at 228–31 a table of previous studies and their conflicting findings on the relationship between equity incentives and accounting improprieties; describing the sample at 231–32 to include more than double the size of samples using ExecuComp data; stating at 239 that the researchers used "a matched-pair research design that matches a treatment firm with a control firm that is similar across all observable relevant variables. Our matching algorithm uses the common partial-match variables plus all other variables that would typically be included as control variables."). The results did "not support the notion that higher equity-incentive levels are associated with a greater incidence of accounting-related restatements," produced "no evidence that higher equity incentives are associated with a higher frequency of accounting-related lawsuits," and provided "no evidence of a positive association between equity incentives and the incidence of" periods of accounting fraud identified in Accounting and Auditing Enforcement Releases issued by the SEC. *Id.* at 251, 226 (defining AAERs), 232 & 236 (defining the negative outcomes: accounting-related restatements, accounting-related lawsuits, and accounting manipulation alleged in AAERs).

Compensation as an incentive to take unreasonable risks. If a CEO holds unvested options, the CEO might take large risks, hoping to strike it rich with a stock price that explodes by the time he or she can exercise the options. If, on the other hand, the risky steps lead to stock price decline, the CEO might not be too disturbed, as the CEO would simply not exercise the options and hence never pay for the stock.

To start testing this idea against data and more sophisticated theory, consider one unpublished study and one article. The unpublished study used data from 1992–1999.[102] It found a positive relationship between stock option risk-taking incentive[103] and one-year ahead stock price volatility (which was the measure of risk).[104] However, the study also found that

> an increase of one standard deviation in ESO [executive stock option] risk incentives is likely to increase the variance of future stock returns by 1.56%. This 1.56% increase in future stock return volatility translates into an increase in the mean (median) CEO ESO portfolio value of $46,000 × 1.56 = $72,000 ($16,000 × 1.56 = $25,000). Further the 1.56% change is approximately 7.2% of the standard deviation of one-year ahead stock return volatility of 21.8%. Some might consider these effects relatively small.[105]

Turning from the analysis of empirical data to modeling, one published article sought to prove, through equations, that options compensation can actually make management too risk averse.[106] The textual explanation ran so:

> Issued at-the-money, ESOs can provide incentives for managers to take risks. However, if traditional calendar vesting options move deep in-the-money, perhaps years prior to vesting, they lose their convexity in payoffs and may generate counterproductive incentives that cause risk-averse managers to *reject* profitable risky projects.[107]

---

[102] Michelle Hanlon, et al., *Large Sample Evidence on the Relation Between Stock Option Compensation and Risk Taking* 1, 14 (Apr. 21, 2004) (unpublished study), http://papers.ssrn.com/sol3/papers.cfm?abstract_id=427260.

[103] The researchers defined option risk-taking incentive as the "sensitivity of [executive stock option] values to stock return volatility." *Id.* at 1. So, if a given increase in the future volatility of a company's stock increased the value of a first CEO's option holdings by a greater dollar amount than the same increase in volatility increased the value of a second CEO's option holdings, then the options held by the first CEO would, by this study, provide a greater incentive for risk than the options held by the second CEO.

[104] *Id.* at 2.

[105] *Id.* at 23. *See also id.* at 34 ("the *ex post* risk taking arising from [executive stock option] risk incentives is not large").

[106] Neil Brisley, *Executive Stock Options: Early Exercise Provisions and Risk-taking Incentives*, 61 J. FINANCE 2487 (2006).

[107] *Id.* at 2488.

The significance of this published article is not that options *never* incentivize risk-taking. The significance is that (i) it is possible to find studies and thinking that challenge a conclusion that options *always* lead to excessive risk-taking and (ii) whether or not options provide an incentive to increase risk depends on the circumstances.

We will return to the relationship between compensation and risk-taking when we study the credit crisis.

———————

QUESTIONS ON EQUITY COMPENSATION AND RISK

Do either of the pieces summarized in the text affect your views on the relationship between equity compensation and risk-taking? If so, how?

Does the time period covered by the one empirical study (1992–1999) affect your view as to the study's relevance to the meltdown at financial institutions in 2008?

How would you counsel a compensation committee so that it might obtain the benefits of equity compensation, but still fight any tendency of such compensation to encourage company executives to take risks that are too great for the best interests of the company?

How could *holding* stock (owned outright, with no restrictions) affect risk-taking? Wouldn't an executive avoid excessive risk to protect his or her wealth? Is the key to preventing excessive risk-taking therefore to require that executives hold their equity stake in the company—i.e., to restrict sale of equity? Widening the focus, is there some combination of equity held outright, unvested stock options, and unvested restricted stock that will strike the right balance between encouraging a CEO to take risks that will benefit the company yet avoid risks that run too great a chance of seriously hurting the company? If such a balanced set of equity holdings exists, does it vary from one individual executive to another? What are the chances that a compensation committee can find the balance for the particular CEO at that committee's company?

———————

CHAPTER 17

GOVERNMENT CONTROL OF COMPENSATION DURING THE FINANCIAL CRISIS

■ ■ ■

This Chapter Seventeen describes extensive intervention by the federal government in executive compensation at corporations receiving federal money during the credit crisis. We have already seen some of the intervention, at AIG, in Chapter Fifteen. As this chapter further examines the government's actions, it asks you to consider, particularly: (1) whether the government intervention was excessive, taking into account the relationship of the government to the affected companies; and (2) whether the government control of executive compensation at companies taking money from the government during the credit crisis provides ideas that might be usefully employed at other companies after that crisis?[1]

A. STATUTE

Section 111(b) of the Emergency Economic Stabilization Act ("EESA") of 2008 (as significantly amended and expanded by the American Recovery and Reinvestment Act of 2009) provided:

(a) DEFINITIONS. For purposes of this section, the following definitions shall apply:

(1) SENIOR EXECUTIVE OFFICER. The term "senior executive officer" means an individual who is 1 of the top 5 most highly paid executives of a public company, whose compensation is required to be disclosed pursuant to the Securities Exchange Act of 1934, and any regulations issued thereunder, and non-public company counterparts.

(2) GOLDEN PARACHUTE PAYMENT. The term "golden parachute payment" means any payment to a senior executive officer for departure from a company for any reason, except for payments for services performed or benefits accrued.

---

[1]   I ask these questions to stimulate thought and discussion. I do not intend, by asking the questions, to suggest that I support government regulation of executive compensation at publicly traded companies.

(3) TARP RECIPIENT. The term "TARP recipient" means any entity that has received or will receive financial assistance under the financial assistance provided under the TARP.[2]

(4) COMMISSION. The term "Commission" means the Securities and Exchange Commission.

(5) PERIOD IN WHICH OBLIGATION IS OUTSTANDING; RULE OF CONSTRUCTION. For purposes of this section, the period in which any obligation arising from financial assistance provided under the TARP remains outstanding does not include any period during which the Federal Government only holds warrants to purchase common stock of the TARP recipient.

(b) EXECUTIVE COMPENSATION AND CORPORATE GOVERNANCE.

(1) ESTABLISHMENT OF STANDARDS. During the period in which any obligation arising from financial assistance provided under the TARP remains outstanding, each TARP recipient shall be subject to

(A) the standards established by the Secretary under this section; and

(B) the provisions of section 162(m)(5) of the Internal Revenue Code of 1986, as applicable.

(2) STANDARDS REQUIRED. The Secretary shall require each TARP recipient to meet appropriate standards for executive compensation and corporate governance.

(3) SPECIFIC REQUIREMENTS. The standards established under paragraph (2) shall include the following:

(A) Limits on compensation that exclude incentives for senior executive officers of the TARP recipient to take unnecessary and excessive risks that threaten the value of such recipient during the period in which any obligation arising from financial assistance provided under the TARP remains outstanding.

(B) A provision for the recovery by such TARP recipient of any bonus, retention award, or incentive compensation paid to a senior executive officer and any of the next 20 most highly-compensated employees of the TARP recipient based on statements of earnings, revenues,

---

[2]   TARP stood for "Troubled Asset Relief Program."

gains, or other criteria that are later found to be materially inaccurate.

(C) A prohibition on such TARP recipient making any golden parachute payment to a senior executive officer or any of the next 5 most highly-compensated employees of the TARP recipient during the period in which any obligation arising from financial assistance provided under the TARP remains outstanding.

(D)(i)   A prohibition on such TARP recipient paying or accruing any bonus, retention award, or incentive compensation during the period in which any obligation arising from financial assistance provided under the TARP remains outstanding, except that any prohibition developed under this paragraph shall not apply to the payment of long-term restricted stock by such TARP recipient, provided that such long-term restricted stock—

(I) does not fully vest during the period in which any obligation arising from financial assistance provided to that TARP recipient remains outstanding;

(II) has a value in an amount that is not greater than 1/3 of the total amount of annual compensation of the employee receiving the stock; and

(III) is subject to such other terms and conditions as the Secretary may determine is in the public interest.

(ii) The prohibition required under clause (i) shall apply as follows:

(I) For any financial institution that received financial assistance provided under the TARP equal to less than $25,000,000, the prohibition shall apply only to the most highly compensated employee of the financial institution.

(II) For any financial institution that received financial assistance provided under the TARP equal to at least $25,000,000, but less than $250,000,000, the prohibition shall apply to at least the 5 most highly-compensated employees of the financial institution, or such higher number as the Secretary may determine is in the public interest with respect to any TARP recipient.

(III) For any financial institution that received financial assistance provided under the TARP equal to at least $250,000,000, but less than $500,000,000, the prohibition shall apply to the senior executive officers and at least the 10 next most highly-compensated employees, or such higher number as the Secretary may determine is in the public interest with respect to any TARP recipient.

(IV) For any financial institution that received financial assistance provided under the TARP equal to $500,000,000 or more, the prohibition shall apply to the senior executive officers and at least the 20 next most highly-compensated employees, or such higher number as the Secretary may determine is in the public interest with respect to any TARP recipient.

(iii) The prohibition required under clause (i) shall not be construed to prohibit any bonus payment required to be paid pursuant to a written employment contract executed on or before February 11, 2009, as such valid employment contracts are determined by the Secretary or the designee of the Secretary.

(E) A prohibition on any compensation plan that would encourage manipulation of the reported earnings of such TARP recipient to enhance the compensation of any of its employees.

(F) A requirement for the establishment of a Board Compensation Committee that meets the requirements of subsection (c).

(4) CERTIFICATION OF COMPLIANCE. The chief executive officer and chief financial officer (or the equivalents thereof) of each TARP recipient shall provide a written certification of compliance by the TARP recipient with the requirements of this section—

(A) in the case of a TARP recipient, the securities of which are publicly traded, to the Securities and Exchange Commission, together with annual filings required under the securities laws; and

(B) in the case of a TARP recipient that is not a publicly traded company, to the Secretary.

(c) BOARD COMPENSATION COMMITTEE.

(1) ESTABLISHMENT OF BOARD REQUIRED. Each TARP recipient shall establish a Board Compensation Committee, comprised entirely of independent directors, for the purpose of reviewing employee compensation plans.

(2) MEETINGS. The Board Compensation Committee of each TARP recipient shall meet at least semiannually to discuss and evaluate employee compensation plans in light of an assessment of any risk posed to the TARP recipient from such plans.

(3) COMPLIANCE BY NON-SEC REGISTRANTS. In the case of any TARP recipient, the common or preferred stock of which is not registered pursuant to the Securities Exchange Act of 1934, and that has received $25,000,000 or less of TARP assistance, the duties of the Board Compensation Committee under this subsection shall be carried out by the board of directors of such TARP recipient.

(d) LIMITATION ON LUXURY EXPENDITURES. The board of directors of any TARP recipient shall have in place a company-wide policy regarding excessive or luxury expenditures, as identified by the Secretary, which may include excessive expenditures on

(1) entertainment or events;

(2) office and facility renovations;

(3) aviation or other transportation services; or

(4) other activities or events that are not reasonable expenditures for staff development, reasonable performance incentives, or other similar measures conducted in the normal course of the business operations of the TARP recipient.

(e) SHAREHOLDER APPROVAL OF EXECUTIVE COMPENSATION.

(1) ANNUAL SHAREHOLDER APPROVAL OF EXECUTIVE COMPENSATION. Any proxy or consent or authorization for an annual or other meeting of the shareholders of any TARP recipient during the period in which any obligation arising from financial assistance provided under the TARP remains outstanding shall permit a separate shareholder vote to approve the compensation of

executives, as disclosed pursuant to the compensation disclosure rules of the Commission (which disclosure shall include the compensation discussion and analysis, the compensation tables, and any related material).

(2) NONBINDING VOTE. A shareholder vote described in paragraph (1) shall not be binding on the board of directors of a TARP recipient, and may not be construed as overruling a decision by such board, nor to create or imply any additional fiduciary duty by such board, nor shall such vote be construed to restrict or limit the ability of shareholders to make proposals for inclusion in proxy materials related to executive compensation.

. . .

(f) REVIEW OF PRIOR PAYMENTS TO EXECUTIVES.

(1) IN GENERAL. The Secretary shall review bonuses, retention awards, and other compensation paid to the senior executive officers and the next 20 most highly-compensated employees of each entity receiving TARP assistance before the date of enactment of the American Recovery and Reinvestment Act of 2009 [February 17, 2009], to determine whether any such payments were inconsistent with the purposes of this section or the TARP or were otherwise contrary to the public interest.

(2) NEGOTIATIONS FOR REIMBURSEMENT. If the Secretary makes a determination described in paragraph (1), the Secretary shall seek to negotiate with the TARP recipient and the subject employee for appropriate reimbursements to the Federal Government with respect to compensation or bonuses.

(g) NO IMPEDIMENT TO WITHDRAWAL BY TARP RECIPIENTS. Subject to consultation with the appropriate Federal banking agency (as that term is defined in section 3 of the Federal Deposit Insurance Act [12 U.S.C. § 1813]), if any, the Secretary shall permit a TARP recipient to repay any assistance previously provided under the TARP to such financial institution, without regard to whether the financial institution has replaced such funds from any other source or to any waiting period, and when such assistance is repaid, the Secretary shall liquidate warrants associated with such assistance at the current market price.

(h) REGULATIONS. The Secretary shall promulgate regulations to implement this section.[3]

B. RELATED REGULATIONS AND THE POWER OF THE TREASURY SPECIAL MASTER

The companies to which the compensation regulations applied. The Treasury issued elaborate regulations[4] to implement the law just quoted for companies that received government assistance under TARP.[5] Hundreds of companies received such money, most frequently by government purchase of preferred stock in the companies (often accompanied by purchase of warrants for the purchase of common stock).[6] The Treasury regulations applied to a company so long as any TARP "obligation" owing from the company to the government remained "outstanding,"[7] with "obligation" defined as

> a requirement for, or an ability of, a TARP recipient to repay financial assistance received from Treasury, as provided in the terms of the applicable financial instrument and related agreements, through the repayment of a debt obligation or the redemption or repurchase of an equity security, but not including warrants to purchase common stock of the TARP recipient.[8]

The regulations defined "senior executive officer[s]" ("SEOs") of a company to be any "named executive officer" under SEC definitions,[9] which in turn defined such officers to include the principal executive officer ("PEO"), the principal financial officer ("PFO"), and the three most highly paid individuals in the company other than the PEO and PFO who were also

---

[3]   12 U.S.C. § 5221. Find the initial version of this section in the Emergency Economic Stabilization Act of 2008 at 122 Stat. 3765, 3776–77 (2008), and the heavily amended version in the American Recovery and Reinvestment Act of 2009 at 123 Stat. 115, 516–20 (2009). Following the amendment, the Treasury issued regulations that superseded the regulations cited in Chapter Fifteen. *See* the June 2009 rules at TARP Standards for Compensation and Corporate Governance, 74 Fed. Reg. 28,394 (June 15, 2009) and TARP Standards for Compensation and Corporate Governance; Correction, 74 Fed. Reg. 63,991 (Dec. 7, 2009). This chapter cites to those superseding regulations.

[4]   31 C.F.R. § 30.0 *et seq.*

[5]   EESA, Pub. L. No. 110-343, § 101 *et seq.*

[6]   By going to http://www.treasury.gov/initiatives/financial-stability/reports/Pages/TARP-Investment-Program-Transaction-Reports.aspx, you can find a list of the companies (in documents titled "TARP Transactions Reports") into which the government had invested TARP money, as of a given date.

[7]   31 C.F.R. § 30.2; EESA § 111(a)(5), (b)(1), as amended by the American Economic Recovery and Reinvestment Act, Pub. L. No. 111-5, § 7001, 123 Stat. 115, 517 (2009), codified at 12 U.S.C. § 5221(a)(5), (b)(1).

[8]   31 C.F.R. § 30.1.

[9]   31 C.F.R. § 30.1 (cross-referencing 17 C.F.R. § 229.402(a)(3)).

"executive officers" under SEC rules.[10] Those rules defined an "executive officer" as

> [the] president, any vice president of the registrant in charge of a principal business unit, division or function (such as sales, administration or finance), any other officer who performs a policy making function or any other person who performs similar policy making functions for the registrant.[11]

Regulatory tasks for the compensation committee. The regulations required that a TARP recipient's compensation committee must:

> (1) [d]iscuss, evaluate, and review at least every six months *with the TARP recipient's senior risk officers* the SEO compensation plans to ensure that the SEO compensation plans do not encourage SEOs to take unnecessary and excessive risks that threaten the value of the TARP recipient;

> (2) [d]iscuss, evaluate, and review *with senior risk officers* at least every six months employee compensation plans in light of the risks posed to the TARP recipient by such plans and how to limit such risks;

> (3) [d]iscuss, evaluate, and review at least every six months the employee compensation plans of the TARP recipient to ensure that these plans do not encourage the manipulation of reported earnings of the TARP recipient to enhance the compensation of any of the TARP recipient's employees;

> (4) [a]t least once per TARP recipient fiscal year, provide a narrative description of how the SEO compensation plans do not encourage the SEOs to take unnecessary and excessive risks that threaten the value of the TARP recipient, including how these SEO compensation plans do not encourage behavior focused on short-term results rather than long-term value creation, the risks posed by employee compensation plans and how these risks were limited, including how these employee compensation plans do not encourage behavior focused on short-term results rather than long-term value creation, and how the TARP recipient has ensured that the employee compensation plans do not encourage the manipulation of reported earnings of the TARP recipient to

---

[10]   17 C.F.R. § 229.402(a)(3). This SEC regulation covers all individuals who served as (i) PEO or (ii) PFO during the last fiscal year and (iii) the three most highly compensated other executive officers at the end of the fiscal year. In addition, the regulation covers disclosure of compensation paid to "[u]p to two additional individuals for whom disclosure would have been provided [in category (iii)] but for the fact that the individual was not serving as an executive officer . . . at the end of the last completed fiscal year." *Id.* § 229.402(a)(3)(iv). This made a total of five to seven SEOs at a given company at any given time.

[11]   17 C.F.R. § 240.3b-7.

enhance the compensation of any of the TARP recipient's employees; and

(5) [c]ertify the completion of the reviews of the SEO compensation plans and employee compensation plans required under paragraphs (a)(1), (2), and (3) of this section.[12]

The Treasury specified how the compensation committee must perform the reviews in subparts (1) and (2) above *and what the committee should do as a result of each review*:

At least every six months, the compensation committee must discuss, evaluate, and review *with the TARP recipient's senior risk officers* any risks (including long-term as well as short-term risks) that the TARP recipient faces that could threaten the value of the TARP recipient. The compensation committee *must identify the features in the TARP recipient's SEO compensation plans that could lead SEOs to take these risks and the features in the employee compensation plans that pose risks to the TARP recipient*, including any features in the SEO compensation plans and the employee compensation plans that would encourage behavior focused on short-term results and not on long-term value creation. The compensation committe[e] is *required to limit these features to ensure that the SEOs are not encouraged to take risks that are unnecessary or excessive and that the TARP recipient is not unnecessarily exposed to risks.*[13]

The compensation committee must discuss, evaluate, and review at least every six months the terms of each employee compensation plan and *identify and eliminate the features in these plans that could encourage the manipulation of reported earnings of the TARP recipient to enhance the compensation of any employee.*[14]

Note that these regulations by law interjected a new participant into compensation deliberations, "senior risk officers."

The regulations set out what Treasury would consider an adequate certification that the compensation committee had performed these tasks,[15] and required that at least once each year, each TARP recipient's compensation committee

provide a narrative description identifying each SEO compensation plan and explaining how the SEO compensation plan does not encourage the SEOs to take unnecessary and

---

[12]   31 C.F.R. § 30.4(a) (emphasis added).

[13]   31 C.F.R. § 30.5 (emphasis added).

[14]   31 C.F.R. § 30.6 (emphasis added).

[15]   31 C.F.R. § 30.7(a).

excessive risks that threaten the value of the TARP recipient. The compensation committee must also identify each employee compensation plan, explain how any unnecessary risks posed by the employee compensation plan have been limited, and further explain how the employee compensation plan does not encourage the manipulation of reported earnings to enhance the compensation of any employee.[16]

TARP recipients who filed reports under the Securities Exchange Act had to make these disclosures in the Compensation Committee Report, which generally appeared in the company's proxy statement for its annual meeting.[17]

QUESTIONS ON THE TARP ASSIGNMENTS TO COMPENSATION COMMITTEES

Were the various risk-related limitations on executive compensation and the assignments to the compensation committees of TARP recipients justified on the theory that the government only put TARP in place because participants in the financial industry took risks that matured and threatened the country's financial system? Did that rationale depend on a connection between compensation structures and risk-taking? Did these assignments increase the probability that a TARP recipient would repay the government?

Do you think that TARP recipients changed their compensation structures as a result of these new assignments to their compensation committees? If so, why? If not, why not?

Should risk officers be included in board discussions on compensation *by law*? Even in companies in which the government has not invested? That is, do the TARP regulations, in this respect, provide a model for companies not subject to TARP?

Forced adoption of perquisite and entertainment policy. TARP regulations required recipients to "adopt an excessive or luxury expenditures policy."[18] The regulations defined such expenditures in a way that included certain perquisites such as travel in a company airplane and also included expenditures on events and entertainment:

---

[16]   31 C.F.R. § 30.7(b).

[17]   31 C.F.R. § 30.7(c) (cross-referencing 17 C.F.R. § 229.407(e)). Item 11 of Form 10-K's Part III requires the compensation disclosure set out in Item 402 of Regulation S-K. By General Instruction G(3) in Form 10-K, companies may satisfy that disclosure obligation in Form 10-K by incorporating future disclosures from their later-filed annual meeting proxy statements.

[18]   31 C.F.R. § 30.12.

The term "excessive or luxury expenditures" means excessive expenditures on any of the following to the extent such expenditures are not reasonable expenditures for staff development, reasonable performance incentives, or other similar reasonable measures conducted in the normal course of the TARP recipient's business operations:

(1) [e]ntertainment or events;

(2) [o]ffice and facility renovations;

(3) [a]viation or other transportation services; and

(4) [o]ther similar items, activities, or events for which the TARP recipient may reasonably anticipate incurring expenses, or reimbursing an employee for incurring expenses.[19]

Companies had to post their policies on their websites.[20]

---

[19] 31 C.F.R. § 30.1.

[20] 31 C.F.R. § 30.12. The Citigroup policy included little substance but did show that the company had some controls in place. Two sections provided:

3.2 CLIENT ENTERTAINMENT AND TICKETS

Client Entertainment is governed by the Citi Code of Conduct and Citi's expense policies. Client entertainment must support a legitimate business purpose. The amount that may be reimbursed to employees for client entertainment must be subject to a daily maximum per individual. This daily maximum may be adjusted as necessary by the Citi CFO to accommodate business needs, geographic and economic conditions, the competitive environment and other industry or market considerations. A Citi employee must be present at client entertainment events. Details regarding the expenditure and the nature of the business discussed must be provided as a condition to reimbursement.

Tickets for sporting or other events used for client entertainment must be managed to minimize costs through bulk purchasing and effective inventory control. Only a limited number of individuals have specific delegated authority to approve ticket purchases. The list of authorized approvers and their respective delegations of authority may be adjusted as necessary by the Citi CFO to accommodate business needs, geographic and economic conditions, the competitive environment and other industry or market considerations.

. . . .

3.4 AVIATION

The use of Citi's corporate aircraft for business travel requires written approval by a member of Citi's Operating Committee and the Director of Citi Aviation.

Chartered aircraft may only be used for business travel if commercial flights are not reasonably available or if required for security, confidentiality or other reasons. The use of chartered aircraft requires written approval by a member of Citi's Operating Committee, the Citi CFO and the Director of Citi Aviation.

Personal use of Citi's corporate aircraft by the Citi CEO must be subject to a written reimbursement agreement. Personal use by any other Citi executive is not permitted except in an emergency situation and only upon written approval by the Citi CEO.

Purchases and sales of corporate aircraft require approval of the Board of Directors.

Citi Luxury Expenditure Policy 4, 5 (Sept. 14, 2009, with some amendments in 2011), http://www.citigroup.com/citi/corporategovernance/data/lux_exp_policy.pdf.

Citi's statement that the policy "supports Citi's existing expense policies and governance framework for managing the company's business operations in a prudent, cost-effective manner" (*id.* at 3)—suggested that few of the words in the mandated document worked change. Citi

Required "Say on Pay" vote by shareholders. EESA section 111(e), as amended by the American Economic Recovery and Reinvestment Act, required that each TARP recipient conduct a non-binding vote of shareholders annually "to approve the compensation of executives."[21] The accompanying Treasury regulation provided that the vote, known as a "Say on Pay" vote, must be "a separate shareholder vote to approve the compensation of executives, as required to be disclosed pursuant to the Federal securities laws (including the compensation discussion and analysis, the compensation tables, and any related material)" and that, in conducting the vote, the "TARP recipient must comply with any [applicable] rules, regulations, or guidance promulgated by the SEC."[22] The applicable SEC regulation simply repeated this requirement.[23]

QUESTIONS ON SAY ON PAY VOTES

Do you think that the Say on Pay Votes (which we will see again, when they were required at all public companies) influenced boards, given that the votes were non-binding?

Would shareholders vote against approval?

If you were running an institutional shareholder, what criteria would you employ to determine whether you would vote "no" on a resolution to approve executive compensation? Would you, for example, presumptively vote "no" where a company had not reduced CEO pay after its total shareholder return was in the bottom half of its industry over the previous one-and three-year periods?

Substantive regulation of compensation for all TARP recipients. The Treasury regulations included substantive requirements that applied to all TARP recipients.

One regulation required that companies receiving TARP money have a right to claw back bonuses that the companies paid to executives but later determined were not earned, and that the companies exercise those rights:

> To comply with the standards established under section 111(b)(3)(B) of EESA, a TARP recipient must ensure that any bonus payment made to a[n] SEO or the next twenty most highly compensated employees during the TARP period is subject to a

---

maintains the policy today, with some changes, even though Citi has repaid the government's TARP investment. *See* http://www.citigroup.com/citi/investor/data/lux_exp_policy.pdf.

[21]   12 U.S.C. § 5221(e).

[22]   31 C.F.R. § 30.13.

[23]   17 C.F.R. § 240.14a-20.

provision for recovery or "clawback" by the TARP recipient if the bonus payment was based on materially inaccurate financial statements (which includes, but is not limited to, statements of earnings, revenues, or gains) or any other materially inaccurate performance metric criteria. Whether a financial statement or performance metric criteria is materially inaccurate depends on all the facts and circumstances. However, for this purpose, a financial statement or performance metric criteria shall be treated as materially inaccurate with respect to any employee who knowingly engaged in providing inaccurate information (including knowingly failing to timely correct inaccurate information) relating to those financial statements or performance metrics. Otherwise, with respect to a performance criteria, whether the inaccurate measurement of the performance or inaccurate application of the performance to the performance criteria is material depends on whether the actual performance or accurate application of the actual performance to the performance criteria is materially different from the performance required under the performance criteria or the inaccurate application of the actual performance to the performance criteria. *The TARP recipient must exercise its clawback rights* except to the extent it demonstrates that it is unreasonable to do so, such as, for example, if the expense of enforcing the rights would exceed the amount recovered. For the purpose of this section, a bonus payment is deemed to be made to an individual when the individual obtains a legally binding right to that payment.[24]

Note that this clawback differed from that in SOX 304 (see pages 365–368). The TARP regulation put the burden on the company to ensure that the company had the clawback right and put the burden on the company to either exercise that right or "demonstrate[ ] that it is unreasonable to do so." Moreover, the clawback extended to payments made to all SEOs and all of the next 20 most highly paid employees. No restatement was needed in order to trigger the clawback, only a material mistake in any "performance metric" or a deliberate false statement by the bonus recipient with respect to the metric. On the other hand, the amount clawed back was limited by the bonus payment that the company made that was based on the inaccurate metric. This TARP clawback informed the more widely applicable Dodd-Frank clawback that we saw earlier (page 368). That is, the chronological progression was SOX 304 clawback → TARP clawback → Dodd-Frank clawback.

---

[24]   31 C.F.R. § 30.8 (emphasis added).

A second substantive regulation limited payments to executives when they left:

> A TARP recipient must prohibit any golden parachute payment to a[n] SEO and any of the next five most highly compensated employees during the TARP period. A golden parachute payment is treated as paid at the time of departure and is equal to the aggregate present value of all payments made for a departure. Thus, a golden parachute payment during the TARP period may include a right to amounts actually payable after the TARP period.[25]

Treasury defined "golden parachute" as

> any payment for the departure from a TARP recipient for any reason, or any payment due to a change in control of the TARP recipient or any entity that is included in a group of entities treated as one TARP recipient, except for payments for services performed or benefits accrued.[26]

Permitted payments for "services performed or benefits accrued" generally consisted of "payment[s that] would be made regardless of whether the employee departs or the change in control event occurs, or if the payment is due upon the departure of the employee, regardless of whether the departure is voluntary or involuntary."[27] The regulation excepted from the definition of "golden parachute" any payment that the corporation made when the executive left the company due to death or disability.[28]

A third substantive regulation, applicable to all TARP recipients, limited bonuses. Generally, and in accord with EESA section 111(b)(3)(D)(ii), as amended by the American Economic Recovery and Reinvestment Act, "a TARP recipient [had to] prohibit the payment or accrual of any bonus payment"[29] to any of the following:

> (i)   [t]he [one] most highly compensated employee of any TARP recipient receiving less than $25,000,000 in financial assistance;

> (ii)   [a]t least the five most highly compensated employees of any TARP recipient receiving $25,000,000 but less than $250,000,000 in financial assistance;

---

[25]   31 C.F.R. § 30.9(a).

[26]   31 C.F.R. § 30.1.

[27]   *Id.*

[28]   *Id.*

[29]   Treasury defined a "bonus payment" as "a payment that is, or is in the nature of, a bonus, incentive compensation, or retention award." 31 C.F.R. § 30.1.

(iii) [t]he SEOs and at least the ten next most highly compensated employees of any TARP recipient receiving $250,000,000 but less than $500,000,000 in financial assistance; and

(iv) [t]he SEOs and at least the twenty next most highly compensated employees of any TARP recipient receiving $500,000,000 or more in financial assistance.[30]

Treasury rules, like EESA section 111(b)(3)(D)(i), permitted one important exception—a TARP recipient might award to covered executives "long-term restricted stock . . . provided that the value of this grant may not exceed one third of the employee's annual compensation as determined for that fiscal year."[31] This "long-term restricted stock," or restricted stock units, had to be payable in (or have a value based on) the corporation's common stock,[32] and could "not become transferable . . . or payable as applied to a restricted stock unit, at any time earlier than permitted under the following schedule . . . :

(i)   25% of the shares or units granted at the time of repayment of 25% of the aggregate financial assistance received.

(ii) An additional 25% of the shares or units granted (for an aggregate total of 50% of the shares or units granted) at the time of repayment of 50% of the aggregate financial assistance received.

(iii) An additional 25% of the shares or units granted (for an aggregate total of 75% of the shares or units granted) at the time of repayment of 75% of the aggregate financial assistance received.

(iv) The remainder of the shares or units granted at the time of repayment of 100% of the aggregate financial assistance received."[33]

A fourth substantive regulation prohibited a TARP recipient from paying—to its senior executive officers and to the next 20 most highly compensated employees—any "gross-up,"[34] defined as "any reimbursement of taxes owed with respect to any compensation, provided that a gross-up does not include a payment under a tax equalization agreement" (which is an agreement to

---

[30]   31 C.F.R. § 30.10(a) & (b).

[31]   31 C.F.R. § 30.10(e)(1).

[32]   31 C.F.R. § 30.1 (providing that " 'long-term restricted stock' means restricted stock or restricted stock units that include the following features: . . . The restricted stock or restricted stock units are issued with respect to common stock of the TARP recipient. For this purpose, a restricted stock unit includes a unit that is payable, or may be payable, in cash or stock, provided that the value of the payment is equal to the value of the underlying stock.").

[33]   31 C.F.R. § 30.1.

[34]   31 C.F.R. § 30.11(d).

reimburse an employee for extra taxes that the employee pays to a foreign government when working overseas).[35]

QUESTIONS ON THE SUBSTANTIVE REGULATION OF EXECUTIVE COMPENSATION AT TARP RECIPIENTS

Were the substantive compensation regulations justified by the circumstance that the government put money into the TARP recipients when they were experiencing financial distress? Consider each restriction separately—clawbacks, limitations on the amount and form of bonuses, severance payments, and gross-ups—when you address this question. Did these restrictions increase the probability that a TARP recipient would pay the TARP funding back to the government? Or were they compensation reforms that the politicians thought "right" and were in a position to impose on a certain group of companies? Did these restrictions on employee compensation run the risk that highly qualified executives, who might have had the ability to bring the companies back to profitability faster, might choose to work for companies that were not subject to such restrictions, leading to a slower recovery by TARP-funded companies from their financial distress?

Do you believe that these restrictions provide a model that corporate America should follow? Again, consider each of the substantive regulations separately when you address this question.

If you consider these restrictions to be a model, should we *force* all public companies to adopt them (or similar compensation restrictions) by a law, by a regulation, or by listing standards?

Additional substantive control of compensation at companies receiving especially large amounts of federal money. The regulations defined companies receiving "exceptional financial assistance" as those receiving "financial assistance provided under the Programs for Systemically Significant Failing Institutions, the Targeted Investment Program, the Automotive Industry Financing Program, and any new program designated by the Secretary as providing exceptional financial assistance."[36] These companies included General Motors, GMAC, AIG, and Citigroup.[37]

---

[35]   31 C.F.R. § 30.1.

[36]   *Id.*

[37]   *See* U.S. Dept. of the Treasury, Office of Financial Stability, Troubled Asset Relief Program, Transactions Report for Period Ending September 30, 2010, at 18, 20, 21 [Sept. 30, 2010 TARP List], https://www.treasury.gov/initiatives/financial-stability/reports/Documents/10-1-10%20Transactions%20Report%20as%20of%209-29-10.pdf.

Each of the companies receiving "exceptional financial assistance" had to submit the pay packages that it proposed—for its SEOs and the next 20 most highly paid employees[38]—to the Special Master for TARP Executive Compensation.[39] That Special Master, originally Kenneth Feinberg and later Patricia Geoghegan, served at the pleasure of the Secretary of the Treasury,[40] and exercised extraordinary power.

Regulations provided the Special Master with

> responsibility for interpreting section 111 of EESA, these regulations, and any other applicable guidance, to determine how the requirements under section 111 of EESA, these regulations, and any other applicable guidance, apply to particular facts and circumstances. Accordingly, the Special Master shall make all determinations, as required, as to the meaning of such guidance and whether such requirements have been met in any particular circumstances.[41]

In that connection, the regulations specified that the Special Master

> shall determine whether *the compensation structure* for each SEO or most highly compensated employee of a TARP recipient receiving exceptional assistance, *including the amounts payable or potentially payable under such compensation structure*, will or may result in payments that are inconsistent with the purposes of section 111 of EESA or TARP, or are otherwise contrary to the public interest.[42]

When making the determinations on the proposed compensation for the SEOs and the other 20 executives, the Special Master was to apply "principles" that the Treasury regulations laid out so:

> (1) Principles. . . . . The principles are intended to be consistent with sound compensation practices appropriate for TARP recipients, and to advance the purposes and considerations described in EESA sections 2 and 103, including the maximization

---

[38]   The number of executives subject to this requirement varied in the same way as the number of executives subject to the bonus restriction, with 31 C.F.R. § 30.16(a)(3) cross-referencing 31 C.F.R. § 30.10. Since all of the companies that received "exceptional financial assistance" received more than $500 million in such assistance (*see* 24 Sept. 30, 2010 TARP List at 18, 20, 21), the special substantive individual review went down, in each, to the 20 most highly paid employees other than the SEOs. 31 C.F.R. § 30.16(a)(3)(i) (with this review encompassing "the compensation structure . . . , including the amounts payable or potentially payable under such compensation structure."). In addition to individualized determinations for these top officers and most highly paid employees, the Special Master also reviewed the "compensation structure" for the next 75 most highly compensated employees, but without making individual payment determinations. 31 C.F.R. § 30.16(a)(3)(ii)). This chapter does not discuss the Special Master's determinations for that second tier of employees.

[39]   31 C.F.R. §§ 30.16(a)(3), 30.10(b)(1).

[40]   31 C.F.R. § 30.16(a).

[41]   *Id.*

[42]   31 C.F.R. § 30.16(a)(3) (emphasis added).

of overall returns to the taxpayers of the United States and providing stability and preventing disruptions to financial markets. The Special Master has discretion to determine the appropriate weight or relevance of a particular principle depending on the facts and circumstances surrounding the compensation structure or payment under consideration, such as whether a payment occurred in the past or is proposed for the future, the role of the employee within the TARP recipient, the situation of the TARP recipient within the marketplace and the amount and type of financial assistance provided. To the extent that two or more principles may appear inconsistent in a particular situation, the Special Master will determine the relative weight to be accorded each principle. In the case of any review of payments already made under paragraph (c)(2) of this section, or of any rights to bonuses, awards, or other compensation already granted, the Special Master shall apply these principles by considering the facts and circumstances at the time the compensation was granted, earned, or paid, as appropriate.

(1) . . . (i)   Risk. The compensation structure should avoid incentives to take unnecessary or excessive risks that could threaten the value of the TARP recipient, including incentives that reward employees for short-term or temporary increases in value, performance, or similar measure that may not ultimately be reflected by an increase in the long-term value of the TARP recipient. Accordingly, incentive payments or similar rewards should be structured to be paid over a time horizon that takes into account the risk horizon so that the payment or reward reflects whether the employee's performance over the particular service period has actually contributed to the long-term value of the TARP recipient.

(ii) Taxpayer return. The compensation structure, and amount payable where applicable, should reflect the need for the TARP recipient to remain a competitive enterprise, to retain and recruit talented employees who will contribute to the TARP recipient's future success, and ultimately to be able to repay TARP obligations.

(iii) Appropriate allocation. The compensation structure should appropriately allocate the components of compensation such as salary, short-term and long-term incentives, as well as the extent to which compensation is provided in cash, equity or other types of compensation such as executive pensions, other benefits, or perquisites, based on the specific role of the employee and other relevant circumstances, including the nature and amount of current compensation, deferred compensation, or other compensation and benefits previously paid or awarded. The appropriate allocation may be different for different positions and for different employees, but generally, in the case of an executive or other senior level position a significant portion of the overall compensation should be long-term compensation that aligns the interest of the employee with the interests of shareholders and taxpayers.

(iv) Performance-based compensation. An appropriate portion of the compensation should be performance-based over a relevant performance period. Performance-based compensation should be determined through tailored metrics that encompass individual performance and/or the performance of the TARP recipient or a relevant business unit taking into consideration specific business objectives. Performance metrics may relate to employee compliance with relevant corporate policies. In addition, the likelihood of meeting the performance metrics should not be so great that the arrangement fails to provide an adequate incentive for the employee to perform, and performance metrics should be measurable, enforceable, and actually enforced if not met. The appropriate allocation and the appropriate performance metrics may be different for different positions and for different employees, but generally a significant portion of total compensation should be performance-based compensation, and generally that portion should be greater for positions that exercise higher levels of responsibility.

(v) Comparable structures and payments. The compensation structure, and amount payable where applicable, should be consistent with, and not excessive, taking into account compensation structures and amounts for persons in similar positions or roles at similar entities that are similarly situated, including, as applicable, entities competing in the same markets and similarly situated entities that are financially distressed or that are contemplating or undergoing reorganization.

(vi) Employee contribution to TARP recipient value. The compensation structure, and amount payable where applicable, should reflect the current or prospective contributions of an employee to the value of the TARP recipient, taking into account multiple factors such as revenue production, specific expertise, compliance with company policy and regulation (including risk management), and corporate leadership, as well as the role the employee may have had with respect to any change in the financial health or competitive position of the TARP recipient.

(2) Further guidance. The Secretary reserves the discretion to modify or amend the foregoing principles through notice, announcement or other generally applicable guidance, provided that such guidance shall apply only prospectively from its date of publication and shall not provide a basis for reconsideration of a determination of the Special Master, except as the Special Master deems appropriate in light of such modification or amendment.[43]

After the Special Master employed these principles to review a company's proposed compensation for the executives subject to this extraordinary review, the Special Master issued a determination that, following a short period in which the company could seek reconsideration on limited grounds, became final.[44]

QUESTIONS ON THE SPECIAL MASTER'S POWER

Before we look at how Special Master Feinberg exercised his powers, what do you think of those powers? Did the Special Master have too much power? Was he an uber compensation committee? By law, he determined the dollar pay and the pay structure for the top executive cadre. He was told to employ some criteria that might be particularly appropriate from a creditor's point of view, such as whether compensation packages incentivized risk-taking that jeopardized the TARP recipients' value that, in turn, contributed to its ability to pay back the government.

But he was also charged with employing other factors, at least a bit more distant from the companies' ability to repay the government (although, to the extent that any criterion affected ability to hire and retain talent, that criterion at least indirectly affected the company's ability to repay) and much closer to the factors that any compensation committee would use:

a. tailored metrics that encompass individual performance and/or the performance of the TARP recipient or a relevant business unit, taking into consideration specific business objectives;

b. compensation structures and amounts for persons in similar positions or roles at similar entities that are similarly situated; including, as applicable, entities competing in the same markets and

---

[43] 31 C.F.R. § 30.16(b).

[44] 31 C.F.R. § 30.16(c). "The request for reconsideration must specify a factual error or relevant new information not previously considered, and must demonstrate that such error or lack of information resulted in a material error in the initial determination." 31 C.F.R. § 30.16(c)(1).

similarly situated entities that were financially distressed or that were contemplating or undergoing reorganization; and

c.   the current or prospective contributions of an employee to the value of the TARP recipient, taking into account multiple factors such as revenue production, specific expertise, compliance with company policy and regulation (including risk management), and corporate leadership, as well as the role the employee may have had with respect to any change in the financial health or competitive position of the TARP recipient.

And remember that the regulations provided that

[t]he Special Master has discretion to determine the appropriate weight or relevance of a particular principle depending on the facts and circumstances surrounding the compensation structure or payment under consideration, such as whether a payment occurred in the past or is proposed for the future, the role of the employee within the TARP recipient, the situation of the TARP recipient within the marketplace and the amount and type of financial assistance provided. To the extent that two or more principles may appear inconsistent in a particular situation, the Special Master will determine the relative weight to be accorded each principle.

Are you comfortable with the idea that the TARP Special Master—a government official—used these criteria to set or adjust the details of the pay packages of top executives? If so, does your comfort depend on the government's having had a financial interest in the companies because it provided enormous amounts of money to each of them during a national financial crisis?

Do you think that a special master employed by the federal government would do a better job of setting compensation than compensation committees, the directors on which must comply with fiduciary duties under state law? If so, why? If not, why not?

Should we have a pay czar from the government, or multiple czars if needed, set the pay for the top executives at all publicly traded companies today?

C. THE PAY CZAR IN ACTION

The pressures the Pay Czar felt and the methodology the Pay Czar employed. Special Master Feinberg found that the pay criteria handed to him were difficult to apply and that (not surprisingly) the companies balked at those criteria and (somewhat surprisingly) so did the Treasury.

Special Master Feinberg told [the Special Inspector General for the Troubled Asset Relief Program] SIGTARP that these criteria are inherently inconsistent because of conflicting goals and company-specific circumstances. He explained that the criteria intended for institutions to remain competitive and to promote employee retention . . . do not allow for compensation structures similar to those of some market participants because they are deemed to be excessive and not performance based over the long term. On October 21, 2010, Feinberg testified before the Congressional Oversight Panel ("COP") that the clear direction given to him was that the most important goal was to get these seven companies to repay TARP. He also testified, "Congress felt that the single most important thing I could do is get those seven companies to repay the taxpayer . . . Secretary Geithner made that clear. Congress made that clear. The Administration made that clear. And we succeeded, with three of those companies already repaying."

Feinberg told SIGTARP that political perception "very much" played a role in his decisions. He said he was mindful of Congress' intent, the oversight that Congress would conduct, and that U.S. House of Representatives Committee on Financial Services Chairman Barney Frank and U.S. Senate Banking, Housing, and Urban Affairs Committee Chairman Christopher Dodd had spoken frequently on the Congressional goals and intent.

Feinberg said he was pressured by TARP companies and Treasury officials. He told SIGTARP that TARP companies placed pressure on him to let the companies pay executives enough to keep them from quitting, and that Treasury officials placed pressure on him to let the companies pay executives enough to ensure companies would remain competitive and be able to repay TARP funds. Feinberg testified to the House Committee on Financial Services, "The tension between reining in excessive compensation and allowing necessary compensation is, of course, a very real difficulty that I have faced and continue to face in making individual compensation determinations." Feinberg told SIGTARP that every day he was pressured to soften his stance and that Government officials reminded him that the companies had large obligations to repay the taxpayers. On October 21, 2010, Feinberg told COP, ". . . we heard over and over again that if we didn't provide competitive pay packages, those top officials would leave and go elsewhere . . . they might even go to China. Everybody was going to go to China to work if these companies lost these officials. They're still there. Eighty-five percent of these specific individuals whose pay by statute we regulated are still there."

For one company (AIG), Feinberg told SIGTARP that he was pressured by other Treasury officials, specifically the Office of

Financial Stability ("OFS"), which administers TARP, that he needed to be careful, that AIG owed Treasury a fortune and Treasury did not want it to go belly up. Despite this pressure, Feinberg told SIGTARP that no one trumped his decisions.[45]

To apply the possibly conflicting pay principles (and perhaps also in reaction to the conflicting pressures upon him), Special Master Feinberg

established a three-step methodology to set pay, which included cash salary, stock salary, and long-term restricted stock, for the Top 25 employees at each of the seven TARP exceptional assistance recipients.

First, OSM [Office of the Special Master for TARP Executive Compensation] sets total compensation on the OSM prescription that it should generally not exceed the 50th percentile of total compensation for similarly situated employees. The first step in the formula was to determine each employee's total compensation by basing it on the 50th percentile compensation level for the employee's position, scope, and responsibilities relative to what their peers in comparable positions are earning. To determine the 50th percentile, OSM uses the U.S. Mercer Benchmark Database and Equilar's Total Compensation Report to determine whether the market data submitted by the seven TARP companies were reasonable.

Second, OSM sets cash salaries using an OSM prescription that generally salaries should not exceed $500,000 per year, except for good cause shown. OSM determines cash salary by assessing the market data, the prior years' compensation, the importance of the position and individual, the risk that an employee would leave, and any unique circumstances. While OSM staff told SIGTARP that the $500,000 cash salary limit was based partially on President Obama's statement that salaries should be limited to $500,000, the Special Master said that he was not influenced by the President's statements on salary. The decision to limit cash salaries to $500,000 and to increase the proportion of compensation in the form of stock, Feinberg said, was his decision to strike a balance between reducing excessive risk and providing enough compensation to keep employees' "skin in the game." In testimony before COP, Feinberg stated that OSM came up with the $500,000 figure based on the packages submitted by companies, empirical evidence, and

---

45   Office of the Special Inspector General for the Troubled Asset Relief Program, *The Special Master's Determinations for Executive Compensation of Companies Receiving Exceptional Assistance Under TARP* 6–7 (Jan. 23, 2012) (footnote omitted) [SIGTARP 2012 Report], https://www.sigtarp.gov/Audit% 20Reports/SIGTARP_ExecComp_Audit.pdf.

a sense of what Congress and Treasury intended in the statute and regulations. In testimony before the House Committee on Financial Services, Feinberg said that he made exceptions to that limit for "good cause," and he told SIGTARP that those exceptions varied by company.

. . . .

Third, OSM determines how much of the remaining compensation would be paid in stock salary with a value dependent on the company's future success and long-term restricted stock. OSM determined the amount of stock salary and long-term restricted stock by deducting the cash salary (generally up to $500,000) from total compensation. The Recovery Act limited long-term restricted stock to one-third of the employee's total pay. Accordingly, OSM calculated the amount of long-term restricted stock, and the remainder of the compensation package was stock salary.

In testimony to the House Committee on Oversight and Government Reform, the Special Master said that he used stock salary to encourage senior executives to remain at the companies to maximize their benefit from the profitability of the company. Although the stock vests each pay cycle, it is generally redeemable only in three equal annual installments, beginning on the second anniversary of the grant date.

To tie individual compensation to long-term company success, OSM used long-term restricted stock contingent on the employee achieving specific performance criteria. Long-term restricted stock does not fully vest until the repayment of TARP financial assistance. OSM officials told SIGTARP that companies were very hesitant to pay long-term restricted stock because there was no certainty that some of the companies would ever be free of TARP.[46]

---

[46]   *Id.* at 9–11 (footnotes omitted) (emphasis in original).

QUESTIONS ON THE COLLISION BETWEEN THE REGULATORY CRITERIA, POLITICS, AND THE NEED TO KEEP COMPANIES AFLOAT IN ORDER THAT THEY REPAY THE GOVERNMENT MONEY

Can a government-administered executive compensation scheme ever be free of politics?

Does reduction of executive compensation necessarily threaten the viability of companies at which the reduction takes place?

If so, could the government avoid that effect by restricting executive compensation at all companies so that executives could never move to other companies that would pay them vastly more than the regulated compensation?

Would such a scheme give the government too much power? Would such a scheme cause the most talented executives to move out of the country and work for companies overseas that compete with U.S. businesses?

Was the Pay Czar truly revolutionary in practice, given that he started with 50th percentile numbers?

How does the conflict between the Pay Czar and the Treasury affect your thinking? If there is no single U.S. government view on appropriate compensation at a particular company, how can we be sure that the "correct" view (whatever we conclude that to be) prevails when government regulates executive pay packages in detail?

———————

The decisions that the Pay Czar reached. To get a feel for the Special Master's actions based on his three-step reconciliation of the criteria in the statute and the practical realities he faced, consider his 2009 "determination" for Citigroup, Inc. ("Citi"). Citi submitted proposed 2009 pay packages for covered top executives on August 14, 2009, and, after the company provided additional information, the Special Master deemed the submission substantially complete on August 31.[47] The Special Master responded with a determination on October 22.[48]

Some of Citi's proposals and the Special Master's responses show the vast power that the Special Master had and was willing to exercise. He made changes to the cash components of salaries, the stock components of salaries, and long-term incentive awards.

———————

[47] Letter from Kenneth R. Feinberg to Michael S. Helfer, Oct. 22, 2009, and accompanying Annex A and Exhibits I & II at A2 [Citi 2009 Determination]. This letter, and the other letters in this section, can be found at http://www.treasury.gov/initiatives/financial-stability/TARP-Programs/executive-comp/Pages/Special_Master-Determination_Letters_Fact_Sheets_and_Reports.aspx.

[48] Citi 2009 Determination.

The Pay Czar's 2009 decision on Citi cash salaries.

With the exception of the [CEO], who has agreed to continue receiving an annual base salary of $1 during 2009, [Citi] generally proposed to increase cash salaries . . . [to] as high as $800,000 per year. [Citi's] submission . . . asserted that base salaries at this level could be justified by reference to the compensation of comparable employees at comparable financial institutions.[49]

. . . .

The Special Master has concluded generally that, for Covered Employees at Exceptional Assistance Recipients, cash salaries should generally target the 50th percentile [as compared to persons in similar positions or roles at similar entities] because such levels of cash salaries balance the need to attract and retain talented [employees] with the need for compensation structures that reflect the circumstances of Exceptional Assistance Recipients. . . . The Special Master has concluded that the proposed cash salaries are inconsistent with the Public Interest Standard [in 31 C.F.R. 30.16(a)(3)[50]] because the amounts potentially payable to certain Covered Employees cannot be supported by comparison to cash salaries provided to persons in similar positions or roles at similar entities.[51]

Therefore, the Pay Czar approved cash salaries, for the executives subject to this extraordinary scrutiny, of either $475,000 or $500,000 (with the exceptions of the CEO at $1 and another employee to be paid $0 in cash)[52]— a substantial reduction on the high end from the $800,000 that Citi had proposed.

The Pay Czar's 2009 decision on Citi stock salaries. Citi proposed that part of executive salaries be paid in stock.

[T]he Special Master reviewed the amounts of compensation to be granted in the form of stock salary . . . [and] concluded that the proposed amounts . . . cannot be supported by comparison to the compensation payable to persons in similar positions or roles at similar entitles. The Special Master has concluded that lesser amounts payable in the form of stock salary are consistent with the Public Interest Standard.[53]

---

49   *Id.* at A5.
50   *Id.* at A3.
51   *Id.* at A7–A8.
52   *Id.* at E1.
53   *Id.* at A8.

While Citi had suggested that "one-third of the stock [salary] be transferable upon grant; one-third be transferable on the first anniversary of the grant date; and one-third be transferable on the second anniversary of the grant date,"[54] the Special Master

> concluded that [this] proposal, which contemplates that one[-]third of stock salary will be transferable *immediately* by the employee, does not provide sufficient alignment with long-term value creation.
>
> . . . Stock that is immediately transferable permits an employee to liquidate his or her investment in the stock immediately rather than over the period designed to reflect performance. Accordingly, . . . [it] is inconsistent with the Public Interest Standard.
>
> . . . [Therefore,] stock salary may only be redeemable in three equal, annual installments beginning on the second anniversary of grant, with each installment redeemable one year early if [Citi] repays its TARP obligations.[55]

Accordingly, the Special Master set out in a table incorporated into his determination the amount of stock salary for each of the covered executives he reviewed and set the terms of those stock grants to be "stock vests at grant and is redeemable in three equal, annual installments beginning on the 2nd anniversary of grant."[56]

The Pay Czar's 2009 decision on Citi long-term incentive awards. Citi proposed long-term incentive awards, but the Special Master did not like them.

> [Citi] proposed that employees . . . be eligible, in the discretion of [Citi], for grants of substantial incentive awards. . . . [Citi] proposed that the awards be payable in the form of restricted [Citi] stock that vested if the employee remained employed by [Citi] on the second anniversary of the grant date.[57]
>
> * * *
>
> [T]he Special Master has concluded that the proposed incentive awards are inconsistent with the Public Interest Standard because they could be granted without respect to the achievement of objective, measurable performance metrics.
>
> . . . [T]he Special Master has concluded that the proposed incentive awards are inconsistent with the Public Interest

---

[54]   *Id.* at A5–A6.

[55]   *Id.* at A8 (emphasis in original).

[56]   *Id.* at E1.

[57]   *Id.* at A6.

> Standard because they would have vested over a period too short to be relevant to the long-term performance of [Citi].
>
> Accordingly, . . . [the incentive awards] will not vest unless the employee remains employed until the third anniversary of grant. In addition, as required by the Rule [31 C.F.R. § 30.1], these awards may only be redeemed in 25% installments for each 25% of [Citi's] TARP obligations that are repaid.[58]

The Special Master therefore changed the restricted stock grants, including in his table not only the amounts of each grant but also this about their terms:

> Long-term restricted stock may be granted upon the achievement of specified, objective performance criteria that have been developed and reviewed in consultation with the Office of the Special Master and certified by the Personnel and Compensation Committee of [Citi's] Board of Directors. Any such stock may vest only if the employee remains employed by [Citi] on the third anniversary of grant (or, if earlier, upon death or disability). The stock shall be transferable only in 25% increments for each 25% of TARP obligations repaid by [Citi].[59]

The Pay Czar's 2010 AIG decisions. Recall from Chapter Fifteen that the U.S. government obtained voting control at AIG in connection with the first-round government bailout. Through the Trust that held the stock, the government had such control in 2009 and 2010.[60] Nevertheless, the Special Master changed even AIG's compensation proposals. Thus, in 2010, the Special Master

- "determined that the proposed cash salaries would not be consistent with the Public Interest Standard because they generally exceeded $500,000 and do not appropriately consider the amounts payable in 2010 to Covered Employees under previously existing cash 'retention awards' ";[61]

---

[58]   *Id.* at A9.

[59]   *Id.* at E2.

[60]   Am. Int'l Grp., Inc., Definitive Proxy Statement, Schedule 14A (filed June 5, 2009) at 12; Am. Int'l Grp., Inc., Definitive Proxy Statement, Schedule 14A (filed Apr. 12, 2010) at 11–12.

[61]   Letter from Kenneth R. Feinberg to Robert Benmosche, Mar. 23, 2010, and accompanying Annex A and Exhibits I & II at A7 [AIG 2010 Determination]. The $500,000 may have come from President Obama, who said on Feb. 4, 2009:

> We are going to be demanding some restraint in exchange for federal aid so that when firms seek new federal dollars, we won't find them up to the same old tricks. As part of the reforms we're announcing today, top executives at firms receiving extraordinary help from U.S. taxpayers will have their compensation capped at $500,000, a fraction of the salaries that have been reported recently. And if these executives receive any additional compensation, it will come in the form of stock that can't be paid up until taxpayers are paid back for their assistance.

- "found that the amounts of stock salary proposed by AIG were excessive in comparison to payments provided to persons in similar positions or roles at similar entities, and that such payments would be inconsistent with the Public Interest Standard";[62] and

- found that the structure of long-term incentive awards failed to satisfy the principles that an appropriate portion of compensation be performance based and determined by measurable metrics "because [the awards] generally allocated no more than 10% of a Covered Employee's compensation to long-term restricted stock based on the achievement of performance measures."[63]

Therefore, the Special Master reduced some of the proposed cash salaries and stock salaries and increased the proportion of total compensation consisting of long-term incentive awards.[64] His determination further provided that the long-term incentive awards would be "payable only upon the achievement of specified, objective performance criteria to be developed and reviewed in consultation with the Office of the Special Master."[65]

QUESTIONS ON THE SPECIAL MASTER'S POWERS AS EMPLOYED

What do you think of the Special Master's powers now?

Should a Special Master employed by the Treasury be intervening in this way to very particularly affect the number of dollars paid to an executive in cash as part of salary, the amount paid to the executive in stock as part of salary, the terms of stock awards that are part of salary, and the percentage of total compensation consisting of incentive stock awards?

Whether the Pay Czar provides a model. One press account stated that Special Master Feinberg "came up with his own blueprint for compensation boundaries" and "noted that its strictures could be applied not only to

---

Office of the Special Inspector General for the Troubled Asset Relief Program, *Treasury Significantly Loosened Executive Pay Limits Resulting in Excessive Pay for Top 25 Employees at GM and Ally (GMAC) When the Companies Were Not Repaying TARP in Full and Taxpayers Were Suffering Billions of Dollars in Losses* 1 (Sept. 24, 2014) (quoting remarks during a press conference), https://www.sigtarp.gov/Audit%20Reports/SIGTARP_Special_Master_Report.pdf.

[62]   AIG 2010 Determination, *supra* note 61, at A7.

[63]   *Id.* at A9.

[64]   *Id.* at A7, A9, and E1 (showing the amounts the Special Master approved).

[65]   *Id.* at A9.

corporate wards of the state under the Troubled Asset Relief Program but also in myriad other boardrooms."[66]

QUESTIONS ON THE GOVERNMENT AS AN AGENT OF COMPENSATION REFORM

Did the government—through the EESA, Treasury regulations, and Special Master determinations—provide model rules for compensation committees of all companies (e.g., no cash salary in excess of $500,000, with a significant amount of salary in some kind of stock grant, and incentives in stock that the executive can reduce to cash only over a number of years)? Should these constitute at least default rules from which compensation committees of all companies should only depart if they have good reason? Or are companies too diverse for such rules of thumb to be useful for all of them?

Is some catalyst needed—whether it be government or not—to shake compensation paradigms and, in particular, to reduce CEO compensation? Or do you conclude that compensation is already well controlled—at least in some gross sense—by stock price changes in response to compensation decisions, shareholder voting at annual meetings in response to those decisions, and fiduciary duties imposed on corporate directors?

In fact, the Special Master experience appeared to have limited continuing effect even at the companies that left the Special Master's jurisdiction:

> Chrysler, Citigroup, and Ally executives said they would not fully follow the Special Master's determination framework after they exited TARP. Chrysler executives told SIGTARP that the company executives' mentality was, "Let's get through this." The executives also said that the firm's cash compensation was not competitive and the company would be unable to retain employees at its current compensation levels.
>
> Citigroup's then-Vice Chairman Edward J. Kelly, III, told SIGTARP that there were important principles that emerged from OSM's determinations, and that the company would maintain items such as clawbacks, deferred compensation, and performance tests. But the executive also said that company executives were less certain whether the company would use stock salary as a form of deferred compensation. Ally CEO Carpenter

---

[66] Devon Leonard, *EXECUTIVE PAY: A SPECIAL REPORT; Bargains in the Boardroom?*, N.Y. TIMES, Apr. 4, 2010, http://query.nytimes.com/gst/fullpage.html?res=9E05E6D71F38F937A3 5757C0A9669D8B63.

said he agreed with paying for long-term performance, but that certain clawbacks are not realistic.

Bank of America CEO Brian T. Moynihan told SIGTARP that the company enhanced compensation in early 2010 and assessed best practices of the industry. He said the company did not necessarily follow the Special Master's practices after it exited TARP, but that some of OSM's components were involved. He said the company already had a robust compensation structure with clawbacks. He also told SIGTARP the company did away with the Special Master's $500,000 cash salary limit because it limited the company's ability to attract and retain qualified executives.

GM and AIG executives were much less nuanced in their dissents with OSM's framework: GM CEO Whitacre said that GM would not maintain any of the Special Master's practices once the company exits TARP. AIG CEO Benmosche said the Special Master's practices would have no lasting impact. He also said, however, that pay and performance must be linked, and if the majority of income is fixed, or guaranteed, then pay is not linked to performance.[67]

---

[67]   SIGTARP 2012 Report, *supra* note 45, at 42–43.

CHAPTER 18[1]

THE CREDIT CRISIS

■ ■ ■

This Chapter Eighteen first compares the credit crisis with the scandals at WorldCom and Enron, positing that the credit crisis reflected maturation of unexpected risk more than fraudulent accounting leading to restatements. The chapter then describes the mortgage-backed securities that in large part created the risk that matured. It concludes by discussing crisis events at three companies—Bear Stearns, Lehman Brothers, and AIG—and some of the governance issues those events raise.

A. THE CREDIT CRISIS AND ACCOUNTING MANIPULATION

The Sarbanes-Oxley reforms aimed significantly at improving accounting in order to reduce restatements. A private company called Audit Analytics assembled the data in the following table. The researchers searched SEC filings for restatements and counted those filed by companies, funds, and trusts—including foreign filers.

---

[1]   Analysis Group, Inc. provided analytical and research assistance for this chapter.

Year	Number of Restatements
2001[2]	625
2002	700
2003	788
2004	937
2005	1,574
2006	1,851
2007	1,271
2008	951
2009	834
2010	851
2011	844
2012	853
2013	871
2014	855
2015	737

Some of the SOX regulations did not go into effect until a few years after Congress passed the statute in 2002. For example, it was only for fiscal years ending after November 14, 2004 that the first wave of companies was subject to audits of their internal controls over financial reporting. The numbers of restatements then increased.

Conceivably, if the reforms were working, they made auditors more aggressive. This might explain the increase in restatements in 2005 and 2006. Perhaps the decreases in each year from and including 2007 to and including 2009, and the modest increase thereafter until a downturn in 2015, reflect better financial reporting as a cumulative effect of the SOX reforms. In any event, the total numbers of restatements decreased following 2007, with that decrease persisting through the credit crisis in 2008 and 2009 and not significantly increasing in the two following years.

Some companies did restate during the credit crisis. New Century Financial Corporation, the second largest originator of subprime residential mortgage loans, announced on February 7, 2007, that it was restating financial numbers, and then filed for bankruptcy on April 2,

---

[2]   AUDIT ANALYTICS, 2015 FINANCIAL RESTATEMENTS: A FIFTEEN YEAR COMPARISON 5 (2016) (numbers in table above taken from Audit Analytics graph). Data on restatements used with permission from Audit Analytics.

2007.[3] Citigroup reduced its reported net income for the third quarter of 2007 by $116 million (to $2.21 billion) between the press release containing the initial numbers and the company's filing of its 10-Q for the quarter— attributing the reduction to a write-down of collateralized debt obligations,[4] one of the several kinds of financial instruments at the center of the credit crisis. But the company said that the reduction was not technically a "restatement."[5] The reduction in income amounted to less than 1%. JPMorgan Chase & Co. ("JPMorgan") announced a restatement in August 2006 affecting cash flows in 2003–2005 that "related to certain residential mortgages and other loans that had been originated or purchased with the intent to sell," but the restatement did not affect revenues, net income, earnings per share, or total assets.[6]

Other companies prominently involved in credit crisis news restated financial numbers, but not because of the problems related to the mortgage-backed securities at the center of the crisis events. Bank of America restated earnings in early 2006, actually increasing earnings by $345 million over a several year period—with the change related to derivatives used to hedge against interest rate and foreign currency volatility.[7] AIG announced multiple restatements in 2005, before the credit crisis ripened.[8]

The following table provides restatement figures for firms with SIC codes 6000–6999, which focus on financial institutions and real estate.

---

[3]   Final Report of Michael J. Missal, Bankruptcy Court Examiner, dated February 29, 2008 and filed in the New Century Bankruptcy, *In re New Century TRS Holdings, Inc.*, No. 07-10416 (KJC), U.S. Bankruptcy Court, District of Delaware at 1, http://s3.documentcloud.org/documents/ 30572/missal-final-report-on-the-bankruptcy-of-new-century.pdf.

[4]   Andrew Ross Sorkin, *Citi Rewrites Recent History on Earnings*, N.Y. TIMES, Nov. 5, 2007, http://dealbook.blogs.nytimes.com/2007/11/05/citi-rewrites-recent-history-on-earnings/.

[5]   *Id.*

[6]   JPMorgan Chase & Co., Current Report, Form 8-K, (filed Aug. 3, 2006).

[7]   *Bank to Restate Earnings*, N.Y. TIMES, Feb. 23, 2006, http://query.nytimes.com/gst/full page.html?res=9D02E2DA1E3EF930A15751C0A9609C8B63.

[8]   *See* Gretchen Morgenson, *A.I.G. to Restate Its Earnings for 3rd Time This Year*, N.Y. TIMES, Nov. 10, 2005, http://query.nytimes.com/gst/fullpage.html?res=9D0CE6DE123EF933A257 52C1A9639C8B63.

In February 2007, Merrill Lynch (i) changed its business segment reporting and restated prior financials to reflect the new segmentation; (ii) restated cash flows from loans held for sale as cash from operating activities instead of from investing activities; and (iii) recategorized "its master note program borrowings as secured short-term borrowings, whereas in prior periods, these borrowings were classified as payables under repurchase agreements," and restated prior period cash flows to conform to this recategorization. Merrill Lynch & Co., Form 10-K (filed Feb. 26, 2007) at 22, 31, 78. The following year, Merrill Lynch reported restating financial numbers for 2005 and 2006 due to "an error resulting from the reclassification of certain cash flows from trading liabilities into derivative financing transactions" that "resulted in an overstatement of cash used for operating activities and a corresponding overstatement of cash provided by financing activities" but did not affect earnings. Merrill Lynch & Co., Form 10-K (filed Feb. 25, 2008) at 155.

Year	Number of Restatements
2001[9]	78
2002	109
2003	126
2004	130
2005	210
2006	227
2007	195
2008	143
2009	128
2010	123
2011	126
2012	153
2013	153
2014	141
2015	115

These numbers for the financial sector generally correlate with the overall restatement numbers, with an increase in 2005 and 2006, followed by decreases after 2007 that continue through the credit crisis and persist through 2011.

The credit crisis, therefore, did not center on financial statements that included materially false numbers in violation of accounting rules.[10] It differed in that important way from the events that motivated SOX.

---

[9] Audit Analytics provided disaggregated restatement data, and Analysis Group created the table from that data.

[10] That does not necessarily mean that the financial reporting of companies at the epicenter of the crisis did not mislead in an illegal way. *See, e.g., U.S. v. Rigas*, 490 F.3d 208, 220–21 (2d Cir. 2007) (affirming convictions on Rule 10b-5 counts, for actions unrelated to the credit crisis, against a challenge that government failed to prove violation of generally accepted accounting principles ("GAAP"); "Even if Defendants complied with GAAP, a jury could have found, as the jury did here, that Defendants intentionally misled investors"). One view of the credit crisis is that, whether they restated or not, financial firms were engaged in fraud that included publication of false financial figures. *See Public Policy Issues Raised by the Report of the Lehman Bankruptcy Examiner: Hearing Before the H. Comm. on Fin. Servs.*, 111th Cong. 122, 126–27 (2010) (statement of William K. Black, Associate Professor of Economics & Law, University of Missouri–Kansas City).

B. CREDIT CRISIS AS REALIZATION OF UNANTICIPATED RISK

The financial system, and the economy as a whole, suffered during the credit crisis. But we focus on the governance of individual public companies. Stock prices of those companies provide one perspective. The companies hardest hit were those in the financial sector—banks (commercial and investment) and other financial companies such as AIG, an insurance company. Here are graphs that reflect the decline in stock value of the financial sector overall and then for Bear Stearns, Lehman Brothers, and AIG:

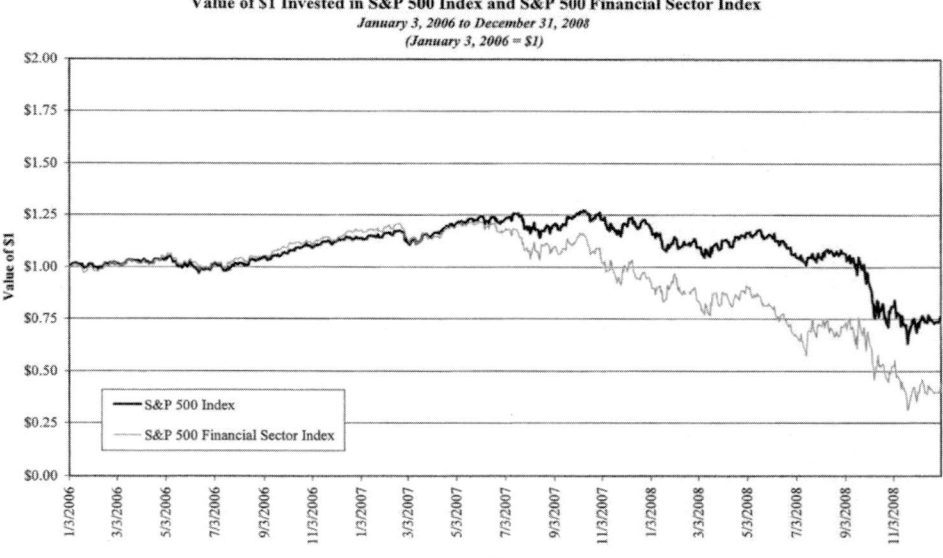

Value of $1 Invested in S&P 500 Index and S&P 500 Financial Sector Index
January 3, 2006 to December 31, 2008
(January 3, 2006 = $1)

Notes: All values have been indexed to $1 on January 3, 2006. The S&P 500 Financial Sector Index includes banks, diversified financial, insurance, and real estate companies in the S&P 500.
Sources: CRSP and Bloomberg.

Value of $1 Invested in Bear Stearns Co., Inc., S&P 500 Index and S&P 500 Financial Sector Index
January 3, 2006 to December 31, 2008
(January 3, 2006 = $1)

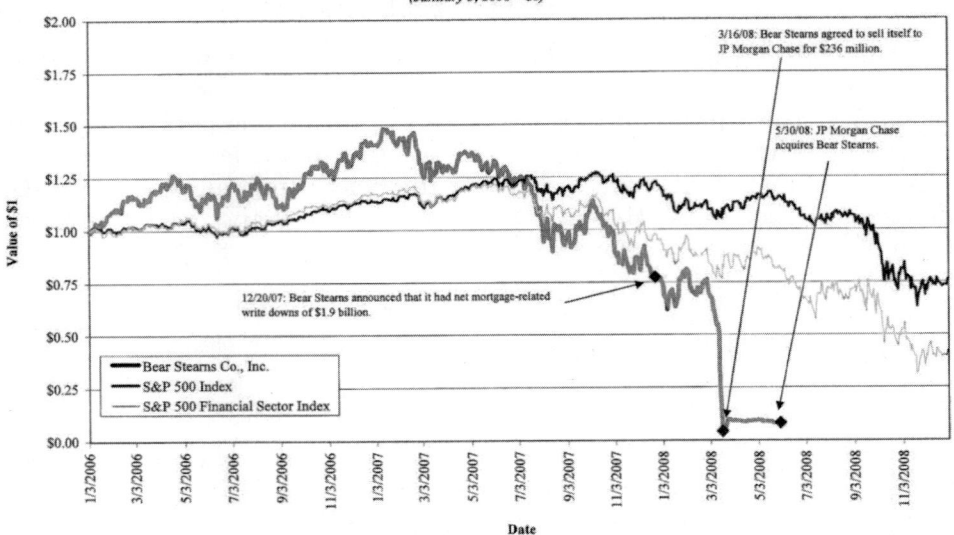

Notes: All values have been indexed to $1 on January 3, 2006. The S&P 500 Financial Sector Index includes banks, diversified financial, insurance, and real estate companies in the S&P 500.
Sources: CRSP, Bloomberg, Bear Stearns 8K, and The New York Times.

Value of $1 Invested in Lehman Brothers Holding, Inc., S&P 500 Index and S&P 500 Financial Sector Index
January 3, 2006 to December 31, 2008
(January 3, 2006 = $1)

Notes: All values have been indexed to $1 on January 3, 2006. The S&P 500 Financial Sector Index includes banks, diversified financial, insurance, and real estate companies in the S&P 500.
Sources: CRSP, Bloomberg, Lehman Brothers 8Ks, and The New York Times.

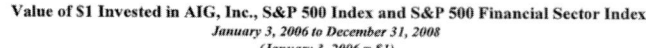

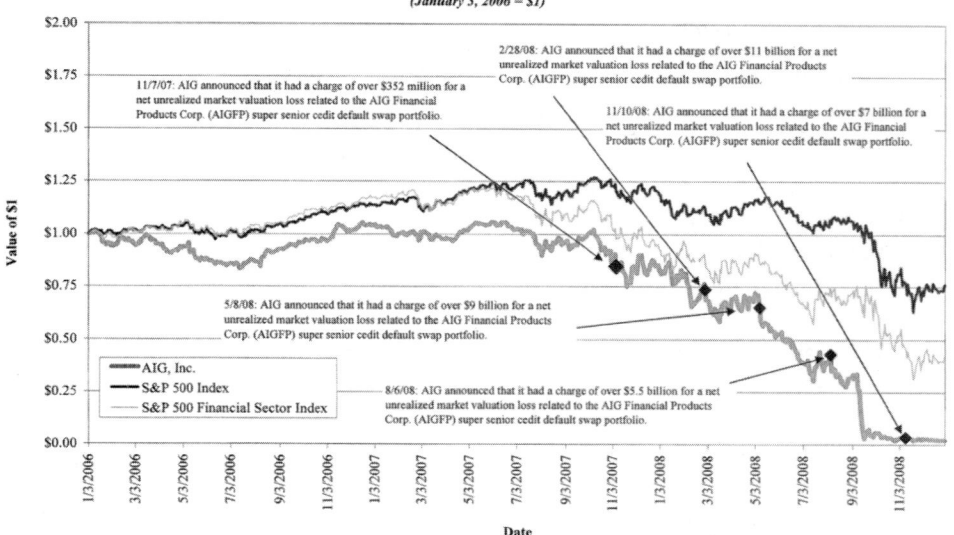

Value of $1 Invested in AIG, Inc., S&P 500 Index and S&P 500 Financial Sector Index
January 3, 2006 to December 31, 2008
(January 3, 2006 = $1)

Notes: All values have been indexed to $1 on January 3, 2006. The S&P 500 Financial Sector Index includes banks, diversified financial, insurance, and real estate companies in the S&P 500.
Sources: CRSP, Bloomberg, and AIG 8Ks.

Stock value decline resulting from maturation of unexpectedly high risk. The precipitous decline in stock values in 2008—with the drop to near zero at Lehman, Bear, and AIG—suggests that the market responded to *unexpected* negative information about the financial companies. And the graphs suggest that the unexpected information consisted at least in part of asset value write-downs. A company writes down the value of an asset when its value declines and accounting rules require the company to recognize that decline in the company's reported financial numbers. A write-down is different from a restatement. A restatement acknowledges that earlier published numbers were materially false when published. A write-down acknowledges that the value of an asset—even though reported accurately in past financial statements—has now declined. For our purposes now, a charge for an unrealized market valuation loss is similar.

In a very simplified sense, the write-downs reflected the maturation of risk. The market did not understand, before the write-downs, that the value of the assets held by financial companies might deteriorate or that the risk of deterioration was as high as it was. The market also did not understand the liquidity problems that this deterioration would create. The market accordingly was surprised by the write-downs (or at least by their size) and the resulting liquidity emergencies.

The next sections describe some of the critical assets and how they lost their value.[11]

The economics and chain of sales underlying the underappreciated risk. Most home purchasers in the U.S. fund house acquisition with debt. Some of the resulting debt is "subprime" debt. One definition identifies subprime debt

> by borrower characteristics: The Board of Governors of the Federal Reserve System, the Office of the Comptroller of the Currency, the Federal Deposit Insurance Corporation, and the Office of Thrift Supervision list a previous record of delinquency, foreclosure, or bankruptcy; a credit score of 580 or below on the Fair, Isaac and Company (FICO) scale; and a debt service-to-income ratio of 50 percent or greater. . . .[12]

The percentage of new mortgages[13] that constituted subprime debt grew rapidly from 1990 onward:

> The market for subprime mortgages grew very fast. Jaffee (2008) documents two periods of exceptional subprime mortgage growth. The first expansion occurred during the late 1990s, when the volume of subprime lending rose to $150 billion, totaling some 13 percent of total annual mortgage originations. This expansion came to a halt with the dotcom crisis of 2001. A second expansion phase was from 2002 until 2006 . . . , when the subprime component of mortgage originations rose from $160 billion in 2001 to $600 billion by 2006 (see Calomiris, 2008), representing more than 20 percent of total annual mortgage originations.[14]

Banks making mortgage loans often do not hold the loans until they are paid off. Instead, mortgage loans are "securitized," which loosely means that many different mortgage loans are packaged together, with interests in the packages then sold to investors. Here is a more nuanced explanation:

> The process starts with the mortgagor or borrower, who applies for a mortgage in order to purchase a property or to refinance [an] existing mortgage. The originator, possibly through a broker (yet another intermediary in this process), underwrites and initially

---

[11]   The credit crisis is more complicated than a tidy explanation focusing on residential mortgages suggests, in part because problems that began with those mortgages radiated out to other assets.

[12]   Paul Mizen, *The Credit Crunch of 2007–2008: A Discussion of the Background, Market Reactions, and Policy Responses*, FED. RES. BANK OF ST. LOUIS REV. 531, 536 (Sept./Oct. 2008) [Mizen, *Credit Crunch*].

[13]   During the run-up to the credit crisis, many home loans—subprime and others—were taken out not to buy houses but as second mortgages by which the owners of houses that had appreciated as housing prices increased monetized that increased home value. For ease of exposition, the text deals with mortgages to purchase homes, rather than second mortgages.

[14]   Mizen, *Credit Crunch, supra* note 12, at 536.

funds and services the mortgage loans.[15] Table 2 [omitted here] documents the top 10 subprime originators in 2006, which are a healthy mix of commercial banks and non-depository specialized mono-line lenders [including New Century Financial, Countrywide, and Citigroup]. The originator is compensated through fees paid by the borrower (points and closing costs), and by the proceeds of the sale of the mortgage loans. For example, the originator might sell a portfolio of loans with an initial principal balance of $100 million for $102 million, corresponding to a gain on sale of $2 million. The buyer is willing to pay this premium because of anticipated interest payments on the principal.

The pool of mortgage loans is typically purchased from the originator by an institution known as the arranger or issuer. The first responsibility of the arranger is to conduct due diligence on the originator. This review includes but is not limited to financial statements, underwriting guidelines, discussions with senior management, and background checks. The arranger is responsible for bringing together all the elements for the deal to close. In particular, the arranger creates a bankruptcy-remote trust that will purchase the mortgage loans, consults with the credit rating agencies in order to finalize the details about deal structure, makes necessary filings with the SEC, and underwrites the issuance of securities by the trust to investors. Table 3 [omitted here] documents the list of the top 10 subprime MBS issuers in 2006. In addition to institutions which both originate and issue on their own [such as Countrywide and New Century], the list of issuers also includes investment banks [such as Lehman Brothers] that purchase mortgages from originators and issue their own securities. The arranger is typically compensated through fees charged to investors and through any premium that investors pay on the issued securities over their par value.

[One] friction in the process of securitization involves an information problem between the originator and arranger. In particular, the originator has an information advantage over the arranger with regard to the quality of the borrower. Without adequate safeguards in place, an originator can have the incentive to collaborate with a borrower in order to make significant misrepresentations on the loan application, which, depending on the situation, could be either construed as predatory lending (the lender convinces the borrower to borrow "too much) or predatory borrowing (the borrower convinces the lender to lend "too much"). . . .

---

[15]   To service a mortgage means to perform such duties as collecting loan payments and performing the accounting to record the interest and principal that the payments cover.

There are several important checks designed to prevent mortgage fraud, the first being the due diligence of the arranger. In addition, the originator typically makes a number of representations and warranties (R&W) about the borrower and the underwriting process. When these are violated, the originator generally must repurchase the problem loans. However, in order for these promises to have a meaningful impact on the friction, the originator must have adequate capital to buy back those problem loans. Moreover, when an arranger does not conduct or routinely ignores its own due diligence, . . . there is little to stop the originator from committing widespread mortgage fraud.[16]

So far, we have the mortgagor (home buyer) and the originator—who funds the loan by providing the money to buy the house and then packages multiple loans into pools. The originator then sells a pool to an arranger (also called the issuer in the excerpt above) that then sells the pool to a trust that the arranger creates. The trust funds the purchase of the pool by selling its own debt—backed by the loans in the pool—to investors,[17] after rating agencies rate the debt that the trust sells. The trust debt is a "mortgage-backed security." Where the mortgage loans in the pool are home loans, the debt sold by the trust is called a "residential mortgage-backed security"—"RMBS."

> The pool of mortgage loans is sold by the arranger to a bankruptcy-remote trust, . . . that issues debt to investors. This trust is an essential component of credit risk transfer, as it protects investors from bankruptcy of the originator or arranger. Moreover, the sale of loans to the trust protects both the originator and arranger from losses on the mortgage loans, provided that there have been no breaches of representations and warranties made by the originator.

> The rating agencies assign credit ratings on mortgage-backed securities issued by the trust. These opinions about credit quality are determined using publicly available rating criteria which map the characteristics of the pool of mortgage loans into an estimated loss distribution.[18]

We need to stop here and note that RMBSs the trusts sold were typically divided into tranches. In its simplest form (and RMBSs could be much more complicated than this example), the idea behind tranching is that all the

---

[16]   ADAM B. ASHCRAFT & TIL SCHUERMANN, FED. RES. BANK OF N.Y. STAFF REP., UNDERSTANDING THE SECURITIZATION OF SUBPRIME MORTGAGE CREDIT, STAFF REP. NO. 318, at 5–6 (Mar. 2008), https://www.newyorkfed.org/medialibrary/media/research/staff_reports/sr318.pdf [ASHCRAFT, UNDERSTANDING SECURITIZATION].

[17]   The initial purchaser of the debt issued by the trust may itself be a fund, which sells its own securities to its own investors. Some portion of those securities may be debt.

[18]   ASHCRAFT, UNDERSTANDING SECURITIZATION, *supra* note 16, at 6–7.

payments by the home owners on the mortgage loans held by a trust would themselves be pooled. The pool of payments would then be paid out—to make the interest and principal payments to the buyers of the RMBSs—so that the buyers of RMBSs in the highest tranches would be paid first, with the buyers of RMBSs in the next highest tranches paid second, and so on, with the buyers of RMBSs in the lowest tranche paid last. This meant that, as mortgagors failed to make payments on their mortgages, the buyers of the lowest RMBS tranche would be hurt first, and only after all the RMBS payments to them were unpaid would the buyers of the next higher tranche lose RMBS payments. The purchasers of the highest RMBS tranche would not lose payments until the number of mortgagors who failed to make payments grew to such an extent that total payments from all mortgagors failed to total the amounts owed on the top tier RMBS tranche. Putting it another way, the top-tier tranche would be the last to suffer and so was the safest. In some cases, the originator or arranger would buy a significant part of the lowest, most risky tranche (sometimes called "equity" tranche, even though the RMBS securities were debt).

The report of the National Commission on the Causes of the Financial and Economic Crisis in the United States provided this example:

> To demonstrate how this process worked, we'll describe a typical deal, named CMLTI 2006-NC2, involving $947 million in mortgage-backed bonds. In 2006, New Century Financial, a California-based lender, originated and sold 4,499 subprime mortgages to Citigroup, which sold them to a separate legal entity that Citigroup sponsored that would own the mortgages and issue the tranches. The entity purchased the loans with cash it had raised by selling the securities these loans would back. The entity had been created as a separate legal structure so that the assets would sit off Citigroup's balance sheet, an arrangement with tax and regulatory benefits.

> The 4,499 mortgages carried the rights to the borrowers' monthly payments, which the Citigroup entity divided into 19 tranches of mortgage-backed securities; each tranche gave investors a different priority claim on the flow of payments from the borrowers, and a different interest rate and repayment schedule. The credit rating agencies assigned ratings to most of these tranches for investors, who—as securitization became increasingly complicated—came to rely more heavily on these ratings. Tranches were assigned letter ratings by the rating agencies based on their riskiness. In this report, ratings are generally presented in S&P's classification system, which assigns ratings such as "AAA" (the highest rating for the safest investments, referred to here as triple-A), "AA" (less safe than AAA), "A," "BBB," and "BB," and further distinguishes ratings

with "+" and "–." Anything rated below "BBB-" is considered "junk." Moody's uses a similar system in which "Aaa" is highest, followed by "Aa," "A," "Baa," "Ba," and so forth. For example, an S&P rating of BBB would correspond to a Moody's rating of Baa. In this Citigroup deal, the four senior tranches—the safest—were rated triple-A by the agencies.

Below the senior tranches and next in line for payments were eleven "mezzanine" tranches—so named because they sat between the riskiest and the safest tranches. These were riskier than the senior tranches and, because they paid off more slowly, carried a higher risk that an increase in interest rates would make the locked-in interest payments less valuable. As a result, they paid a correspondingly higher interest rate. Three of these tranches in the Citigroup deal were rated AA, three were A, three were BBB (the lowest investment-grade rating), and two were BB, or junk.

The last to be paid was the most junior tranche, called the "equity," "residual," or "first-loss" tranche, set up to receive whatever cash flow was left over after all the other investors had been paid. This tranche would suffer the first losses from any defaults of the mortgages in the pool. Commensurate with this high risk, it provided the highest yields (see figure 5.3). In the Citigroup deal, as was common, this piece of the deal was not rated at all. Citigroup and a hedge fund each held half the equity tranche.[19]

The purchasers of the low-tranche RMBSs might repackage those tranches into a collateralized debt obligation (CDO), which itself issued tranched debt securities. The national commission on the credit crisis described that process so:

> In the first decade of the 21st century, a previously obscure financial product called the collateralized debt obligation, or CDO, transformed the mortgage market by creating a new source of demand for the lower-rated tranches of mortgage-backed securities.
>
> Despite their relatively high returns, tranches rated other than triple-A could be hard to sell. If borrowers were delinquent or defaulted, investors in these tranches were out of luck because of where they sat in the payments waterfall.
>
> Wall Street came up with a solution. . . . That is, they built new securities that would buy the tranches that had become harder to sell. Bankers would take those low investment-grade tranches,

---

[19] THE FINANCIAL CRISIS INQUIRY COMMISSION, FINAL REPORT OF NATIONAL COMMISSION ON THE CAUSES OF THE FINANCIAL AND ECONOMIC CRISIS IN THE UNITED STATES, THE FINANCIAL CRISIS INQUIRY REPORT at 71–72 (2011) [FINANCIAL CRISIS INQUIRY REPORT] (footnote omitted).

largely rated BBB or A, from many mortgage-backed securities and repackage them into the new securities—CDOs. Approximately 80% of these CDO tranches would be rated triple-A despite the fact that they generally comprised the lower-rated tranches of mortgage-backed securities. CDO securities would be sold with their own waterfalls, with the risk-averse investors, again, paid first and the risk-seeking investors paid last. As they did in the case of mortgage-backed securities, the rating agencies gave their highest, triple-A ratings to the securities at the top (see figure 8.1).

Still, it was not obvious that a pool of mortgage-backed securities rated BBB could be transformed into a new security that is mostly rated triple-A. But math made it so. The securities firms argued—and the rating agencies agreed—that if they pooled many BBB-rated mortgage-backed securities, they would create additional diversification benefits. The rating agencies believed that those diversification benefits were significant—that if one security went bad, the second had only a very small chance of going bad at the same time. And as long as losses were limited, only those investors at the bottom would lose money. They would absorb the blow, and the other investors would continue to get paid.[20]

* * *

To see in more detail how the CDO pipeline worked, we revisit our illustrative Citigroup mortgage-backed security, CMLTI 2006-NC2. Earlier, we described how most of the below-triple-A bonds issued in this deal went into CDOs. One such CDO was Kleros Real Estate Funding III, which was underwritten by UBS, a Swiss bank. The CDO manager was Strategos Capital Management, a subsidiary of Cohen & Company; that investment company was headed by Chris Ricciardi, who had earlier built Merrill's CDO business. Kleros III, launched in 2006, purchased and held $9.6 million in securities from the A-rated M5 tranche of Citigroup's security, along with 187 junior tranches of other mortgage-backed securities. In total, it owned $975 million of mortgage-related securities, of which 45% were rated BBB or lower, 16% A, and the rest higher than A. To fund those purchases, Kleros III issued $1 billion of bonds to investors. As was typical for this type of CDO at the time, roughly 88% of the Kleros III bonds were triple-A-rated. At least half of the below-triple-A tranches issued by Kleros III went into other CDOs.[21]

---

[20]   *Id*. at 127–28 (footnote omitted).

[21]   *Id*. at 132–33 (footnotes omitted).

The tranches at the top of the RMBS and CDO debt ladders were the safest. They were referred to sometimes as the "super-senior" tranches. But note too that their safety would decline as lower tranches suffered non-payment as a result of mortgagor default. As the lower tranches of an RMBS or CDO debt suffered losses, the probability of the higher tranches suffering loss increased. As a result, the price of the higher tranches would decline in the secondary market for that debt security.[22]

Here are two graphics.[23] The first shows how pools of mortgages became RMBSs. The second shows how the lower tranches of RMBSs became CDOs.[24]

---

[22]   When a trust sold the tranches to investors, that sale occurred in the "primary" market. When one of the purchasers of a portion of a tranche sold that debt to another investor, that sale occurred in the "secondary" market.

[23]   The first comes from page 73 of the Financial Crisis Inquiry Report and the second from page 128 of that report.

[24]   The figures refer to both subprime and "Alt-A" mortgages. Alt-A mortgages included interest-only mortgages and payment-option ARMs. Option ARMs let borrowers pick their payment each month, including payments that actually increased the principal—any shortfall on the interest payment was added to the principal, something called negative amortization. If the balance got large enough, the loan would convert to a fixed-rate mortgage, increasing the monthly payment—perhaps dramatically. *Id.* at 105.

Residential Mortgage-Backed Securities

Financial institutions packaged subprime, Alt-A and other mortgages into securities. As long as the housing market continued to boom, these securities would perform. But when the economy faltered and the mortgages defaulted, lower-rated tranches were left worthless.

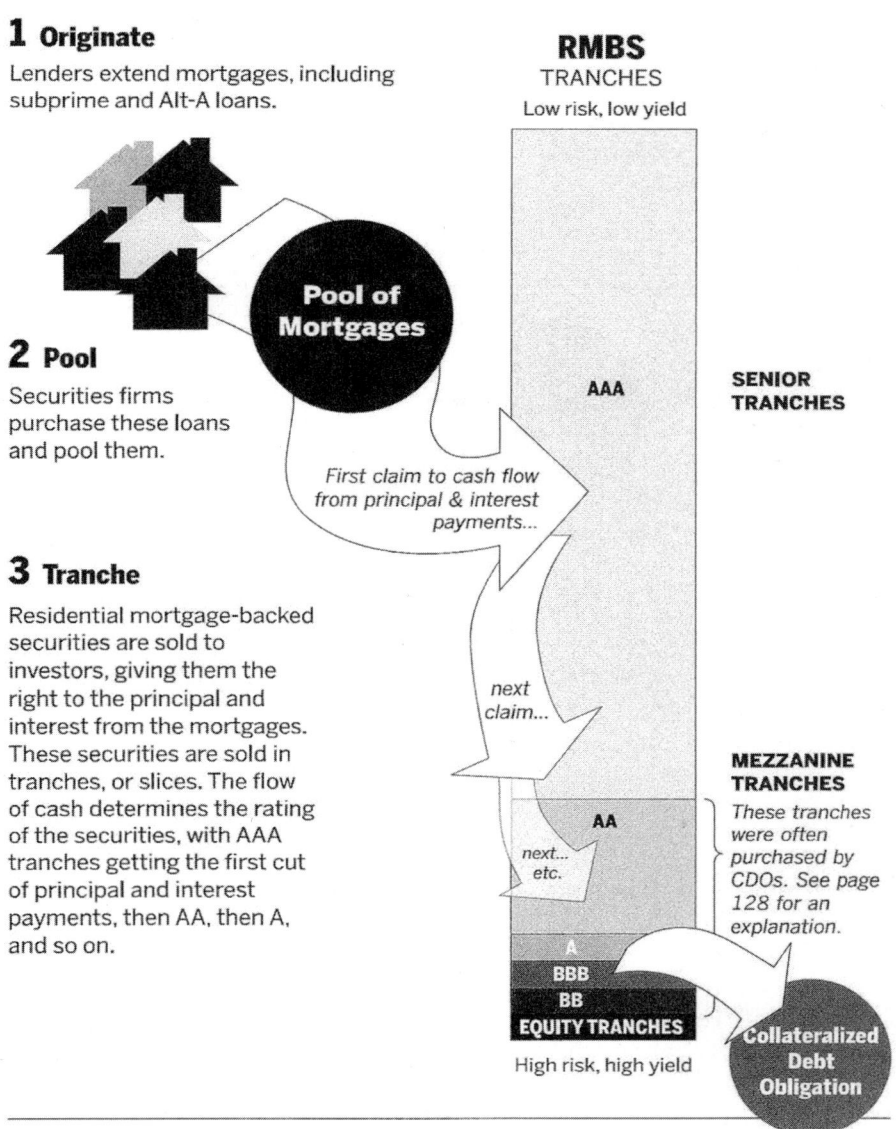

1 Originate

Lenders extend mortgages, including subprime and Alt-A loans.

2 Pool

Securities firms purchase these loans and pool them.

3 Tranche

Residential mortgage-backed securities are sold to investors, giving them the right to the principal and interest from the mortgages. These securities are sold in tranches, or slices. The flow of cash determines the rating of the securities, with AAA tranches getting the first cut of principal and interest payments, then AA, then A, and so on.

RMBS
TRANCHES
Low risk, low yield

Pool of Mortgages

First claim to cash flow from principal & interest payments...

next claim...

next...
etc.

AAA

AA

A
BBB
BB
EQUITY TRANCHES

High risk, high yield

SENIOR TRANCHES

MEZZANINE TRANCHES

These tranches were often purchased by CDOs. See page 128 for an explanation.

Collateralized Debt Obligation

Figure 5.3

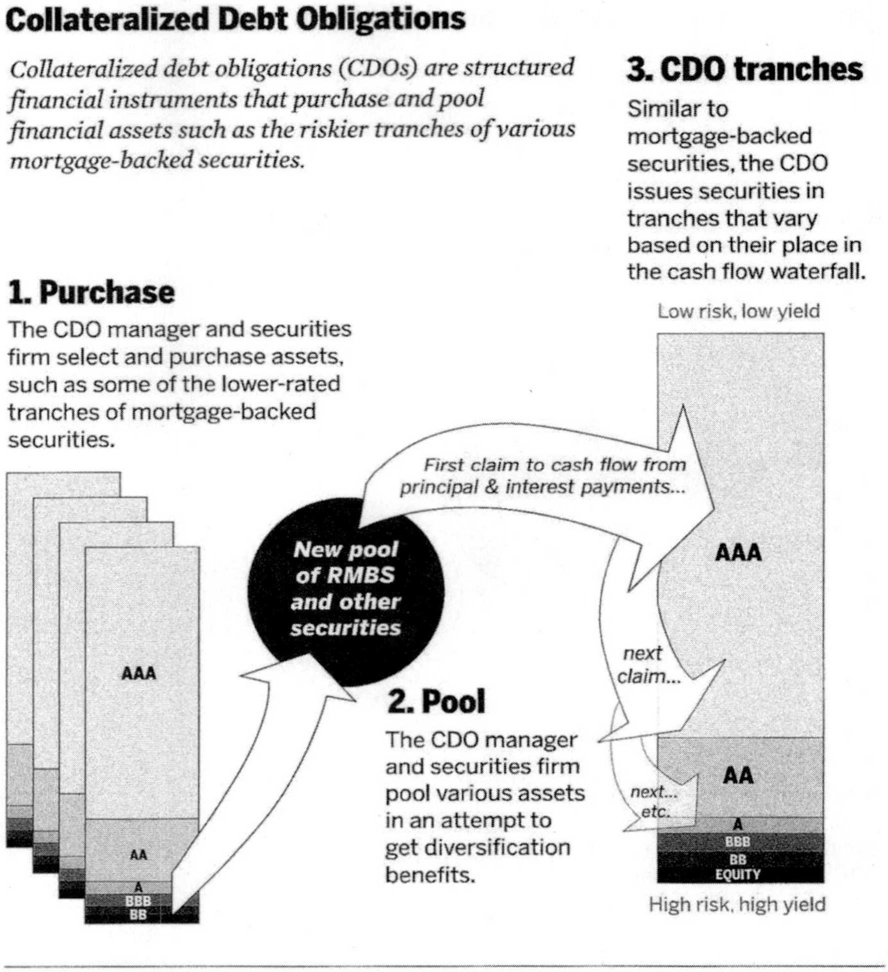

Collateralized Debt Obligations

Collateralized debt obligations (CDOs) are structured financial instruments that purchase and pool financial assets such as the riskier tranches of various mortgage-backed securities.

3. CDO tranches

Similar to mortgage-backed securities, the CDO issues securities in tranches that vary based on their place in the cash flow waterfall.

1. Purchase

The CDO manager and securities firm select and purchase assets, such as some of the lower-rated tranches of mortgage-backed securities.

Low risk, low yield

First claim to cash flow from principal & interest payments...

New pool of RMBS and other securities

AAA

next claim...

2. Pool

The CDO manager and securities firm pool various assets in an attempt to get diversification benefits.

AAA

next... etc.

AA

AA

A

BBB

BB

A
BBB
BB
EQUITY

High risk, high yield

Figure 8.1

Even more exotic investments included CDO² (CDO squared) debt, issued by vehicles that bought CDOs. Exotics also included synthetic CDOs. Synthetic CDOs did not include mortgage-backed securities put provided a return to different sets of investors dependent on the performance of "reference securities"—such as RMBS and CDO debt that the synthetic CDO vehicle did not own. They were very complex.[25]

The rating agencies played a key role. They rated the various tranches of the RMBSs and CDOs, giving higher ratings to the higher tranches (see the AAA ratings in the diagrams above), and these ratings gave the purchasers of those tranches confidence that they were purchasing safe

---

[25]   *Id.* at 142–46.

investments.[26] Some investors, such as pension funds, could not buy the RBMS or CDO debt if it was rated below specified levels.[27] Moreover, "[m]any investors, such as some pension funds and university endowments, relied on credit ratings because they had neither access to the same data as the rating agencies nor the capacity or analytical ability to assess the securities they were purchasing."[28]

But the rating agencies were arguably conflicted because they were paid by the RMBS or CDO issuers to provide ratings for the debt that those issuers were selling.[29] Moreover, the RMBS and CDO risk was hard to evaluate. The RMBSs and CDOs were ultimately backed by mortgages and "once the loans had been pooled, repackaged, and sold without much effort to define ownership of the underlying asset, it was difficult to determine who owned the property. [In addition], differences in the various state laws meant that the rules permitting the lender to pursue the assets of the borrower were not uniform across the country."[30]

Perhaps most importantly, the ratings agencies used models to rate tranches. Like all models, the models that the rating agencies used to rate RMBS debt and CDO debt employed assumptions. The national commission on the credit crisis provided the following description of the methodology:

> Since the mid-1990s, Moody's has rated tranches of mortgage-backed securities using three models. The first, developed in 1996, rated residential mortgage-backed securities. In 2003, Moody's created a new model, M3 Prime, to rate prime, jumbo, and Alt-A deals. Only in the fall of 2006, when the housing market had already peaked, did it develop its model for rating subprime deals, called M3 Subprime.

> The models incorporated firm- and security-specific factors, market factors, regulatory and legal factors, and macroeconomic trends. The M3 Prime model let Moody's automate more of the process. Although Moody's did not sample or review individual loans, the company used loan-level information from the issuer. Relying on loan-to-value ratios, borrower credit scores, originator quality, and loan terms and other information, the model simulated the performance of each loan in 1,250 scenarios, including variations in interest rates and state-level unemployment as well as home price changes. On average, across the scenarios, home prices trended upward at approximately 4%

---

[26]   *See* Mizen, *Credit Crunch*, *supra* note 12, at 554.

[27]   FINANCIAL CRISIS INQUIRY REPORT, *supra* note 19, at 119.

[28]   *Id.*

[29]   *See* Mizen, *Credit Crunch*, *supra* note 12, at 551.

[30]   *Id.* at 540–41.

per year. The model put little weight on the possibility prices would fall sharply nationwide. Jay Siegel, a former Moody's team managing director involved in developing the model, told the FCIC [the Financial Crisis Inquiry Commission], "There may have been [state level] components of this real estate drop that the statistics would have covered, but the 38% national drop, staying down over this short but multiple-year period, is more stressful than the statistics call for." Even as housing prices rose to unprecedented levels, Moody's never adjusted the scenarios to put greater weight on the possibility of a decline. According to Siegel, in 2005, "Moody's position was that there was not a . . . national housing bubble."

When the initial quantitative analysis was complete, the lead analyst on the deal convened a rating committee of other analysts and managers to assess it and determine the overall ratings for the securities. Siegel told the FCIC that qualitative analysis was also integral: "One common misperception is that Moody's credit ratings are derived solely from the application of a mathematical process or model. This is not the case. . . . The credit rating process involves much more—most importantly, the exercise of independent judgment by members of the rating committee. Ultimately, ratings are subjective opinions that reflect the majority view of the committee's members." As Roger Stein, a Moody's managing director, noted, "Overall, the model has to contemplate events for which there is no data."

After rating subprime deals with the 1996 model for years, in 2006 Moody's introduced a parallel model for rating subprime mortgage-backed securities. Like M3 Prime, the subprime model ran the mortgages through 1,250 scenarios. Moody's officials told the FCIC they recognized that stress scenarios were not sufficiently severe, so they applied additional weight to the most stressful scenario, which reduced the portion of each deal rated triple-A. Stein, who helped develop the subprime model, said the output was manually "calibrated" to be more conservative to ensure predicted losses were consistent with analysts' "expert views." Stein also noted Moody's concern about a suitably negative stress scenario; for example, as one step, analysts took the "single worst case" from the M3 Subprime model simulations and multiplied it by a factor in order to add deterioration.

To rate CMLTI 2006-NC2, our sample deal, Moody's first used its model to simulate losses in the mortgage pool. Those estimates, in turn, determined how big the junior tranches of the deal would have to be in order to protect the senior tranches from losses. In analyzing the deal, the lead analyst noted it was similar to another Citigroup deal of New Century loans that Moody's had rated earlier and recommended the same amount. Then the deal [rating] was tweaked to account for certain riskier types of loans, including interest-only mortgages. For its efforts, Moody's was paid an estimated $208,000 (S&P also rated this deal and received $135,000.)[31]

The investors in an RMBS or CDO could protect themselves against non-payment by the issuer of the RMBS or CDO by purchasing a hedge in the form of a credit default swap (CDS), which obligated the issuer of the CDS to pay the purchaser of the RMBS or CDO if the issuer of the RMBS or CDO defaulted.[32] But the CDSs—which could be customized—were often more complicated than that. They were not really insurance policies because a claim would not be paid out of a pool of premium payments of many different policyholders, but by the single entity—such as AIG—that sold the CDS protection to the buyer. Accordingly, the likelihood that the CDS buyer would be paid depended critically on the CDS seller's ability to pay whatever came due as a result of a RMBS or CDO default. To protect against the resulting risk that the CDS seller would not be able to pay—called the "counterparty risk"—CDS buyers often negotiated a requirement that the seller post collateral with the buyer if either (i) the price of the RMBS tranche or CDO tranche held by the CDS purchaser fell in the secondary market by a specified amount or percentage (which would reflect increased risk that the RMBS or CDO tranche would ultimately default) or (ii) the creditworthiness of the CDS seller fell (as indicated by a decline in the rating of debt that the seller issued).[33] These arrangements had the following effect:

> [M]ost of AIG's credit default swap contracts required that collateral be posted to the purchasers, should the market value of the referenced securities decline by a certain amount, or should rating agencies downgrade AIG's long-term debt. That is, collateral calls could be triggered even if there were no actual cash losses in, for example, the super-senior tranches of CDOs upon which the protection had been written.[34]

As a result of all these interrelated transactions, the purchasers of the RMBS and CDO debt may have considered themselves protected from risk in several ways.

Diversification. The RMBSs and CDOs were backed by *pools* of mortgages and related loans. Intuition tells us that the risk

---

[31]   FINANCIAL CRISIS INQUIRY REPORT, *supra* note 19, at 120–21 (footnotes omitted).

[32]   *See* Mizen, *Credit Crunch, supra* note 12, at 543.

[33]   The CDSs were sold in the over-the-counter market. That is, they were customized products, without standard terms.

[34]   FINANCIAL CRISIS INQUIRY REPORT, *supra* note 19, at 243.

inherent in a pool of loans is lower than the risk inherent in any single loan. An individual home owner might lose his or her job and default on a particular loan, bringing the value of that loan down to the value of the house that is mortgaged for it, less foreclosure costs. But that particular default would have little effect on the value of a large pool of loans, of which the defaulting loan was only one. Indeed, the value of that pool would have been, at the time the tranches in it were sold, discounted for the risk that some borrowers would default.

Debt ratings. Many of the RMBS and CDO tranches had high debt ratings.

Hedge. A purchaser of RMBS or CDO debt could buy protection in the form of a CDS.

QUESTIONS ON *RMBS* AND *CDO DEBT*

Would a board at company X have violated the duty of care in authorizing purchases of the top tranches of RMBSs and CDOs, assuming that those tranches received high ratings from the rating agencies and assuming that the board conditioned the purchases on the purchase, by X, of CDSs to protect X against the possibility that the RMBS and CDO debt X bought would not pay out?

Would such a board have been guilty of bad governance, or of making a bad business decision, in authorizing such purchases? Would your answer depend on the percentage of X's total assets invested in RMBS and CDO debt? If so, how should a board have decided what percentage was appropriate?

The problem was that some events increased the probability of default by whole categories of borrowers. For example, all home buyers who hoped to refinance at a lower rate when their houses appreciated in value might not be able to do so if housing prices started to fall, or failed to rise, in many different parts of the country at the same time. Since the benefit of diversification depended on a low correlation between mortgage defaults, the higher the correlation (roughly, the more likely that a default by one mortgagor would occur at the same time as the default by another mortgagor), the smaller the advantage of diversification by owning an interest in RMBSs backed by large pools of mortgages. Moreover, debt ratings might not reflect this risk because, for example, the models that the rating agencies used did not include an assumption that housing prices could fall dramatically in many parts of the country at once and remain depressed for a prolonged period of time. And, if a large number of RMBS or CDO tranches began to default (or their prices in the secondary market declined simply because the perceived probability of default increased), then any issuer of CDSs, such as AIG, might be unable to pay on all of them, or post the collateral that the CDSs required. Moreover, the value of the CDSs to those who sold them (like AIG) would decline, as that value depended on the amount by which the time-discounted payments for the hedges exceeded the time- and probability-discounted costs of paying on the hedges and posting collateral.

Now read one description of how things came apart:

Policymakers, regulators, markets, and the public began to realize that subprime mortgages were very high-risk instruments when [mortgage] default rates mounted in 2006. It soon became apparent that the risks were not necessarily reduced by pooling the products into securitized assets because the defaults were positively correlated. This position worsened because subprime mortgage investors concentrated the risks by leveraging their positions with borrowed funds, which themselves were funded with short-term loans. Leverage of 20:1 transforms a 5 percent realized loss into a 100 percent loss of initial capital; thus, an investor holding a highly leveraged asset could lose all its capital even when default rates were low.

Figure 4 shows the effects of the housing [price] downturn from 2005—when borrowers seeking to refinance to avoid the higher rates found they were unable to do so. [With the graph in Figure 4 showing that the rate of default in subprime mortgages rose from about 11% in 2005 to about 19% in 2008.][35]

An increase in subprime mortgage defaults in February 2007 had caused some excitement in the markets, but this had settled by March. However, in April New Century Financial, a subprime specialist, had filed for Chapter 11 bankruptcy and laid off half its employees; and in early May 2007, the Swiss-owned investment bank UBS had closed the Dillon Reed hedge fund after incurring $125 million in subprime mortgage-related losses. This also might have seemed an isolated incident, but that month Moody's announced it was reviewing the ratings of 62 asset groups (known as tranches) based on 21 U.S. subprime mortgage securitizations. This pattern of downgrades and losses was to repeat itself many times over the next few months. In June 2007 Bear Stearns supported two failing hedge funds, and in June and July 2007 three ratings agencies—Fitch Ratings, Standard & Poor's, and Moody's—all downgraded subprime-related mortgage products from their "safe" AAA status. Shortly thereafter Countrywide, a U.S. mortgage bank, experienced large losses, and in August two

---

[35]   *See* Mizen, *Credit Crunch, supra* note 12, at 539–40 & fig.4 (footnotes omitted).

European banks, IKB (German) and BNP Paribas (French), closed hedge funds in troubled circumstances.[36]

The ratings downgrades were unexpected.[37] And they eventually reached tranches that originally had received very high credit ratings, as this more detailed account explains:

In early 2007, a Moody's special report ... about the sharp increases in early [mortgagor] payment defaults stated that the foreclosures were concentrated in subprime mortgage pools. In addition, more than 2.75% of the subprime mortgages securitized in the second quarter of 2006 were 60 days delinquent within six months, more than double the rate a year earlier (1.25%). The exact cause of the trouble was still unclear to the ratings agency, though. "Moody's is currently assessing whether this represents an overall worsening of collateral credit quality or merely a shifting forward of eventual defaults which may not significantly impact a pool's overall expected loss."

For the next few months, the company published regular updates about the subprime mortgage market. Over the next three months, Moody's took negative rating actions on 4.5% of the outstanding subprime mortgage securities rated Baa. Then, on July 10, 2007, in an unprecedented move, Moody's downgraded 399 subprime mortgage-backed securities that had been issued in 2006 and put an additional 32 securities on watch. The $5.2 billion of securities that were affected, all rated Baa and lower, made up 19% of the subprime securities that Moody's rated Baa in 2006. For the time being, there were no downgrades on higher-rated tranches.

. . . .

Then, on October 11, Moody's downgraded another 2,506 tranches ($33.4 billion) of subprime mortgage-backed securities and placed 577 tranches ($23.8 billion) on watch for potential downgrade. Now the total of securities downgraded and put on watch represented 13.4% of the original dollar volume of all 2006 subprime mortgage-backed securities that Moody's had rated. Of the securities placed on watch in October, 48 tranches ($6.9 billion) were originally Aaa-rated and 529 ($16.9 billion) were Aa-rated. All told, in the first 10 months of 2007, 92% of the mortgage backed security deals issued in 2006 had at least one tranche downgraded or put on watch.

---

[36]   *Id.* at 533 (footnote omitted)
[37]   *Id.* at 542.

By this point in October, 13% of the loans in our case study deal CMLTI 2006-NC2 were seriously delinquent and some homes had already been repossessed. The M4 through M8 tranches were downgraded as part of the second wave of mass downgrades. Five additional tranches would eventually be downgraded in April 2008.

Before it was over, Moody's would downgrade 83% of all the 2006 Aaa mortgage backed securities tranches and all of the Baa tranches. For those securities issued in the second half of 2007, nearly all Aaa and Baa tranches were downgraded. Of all tranches initially rated investment grade—that is, rated Baa3 or higher— 76% of those issued in 2006 were downgraded to junk, as were 89% of those from 2007.[38]

As the ratings on the tranches declined, so did the prices for the tranches in the secondary market, and the depth of that market, so that some of the RMBSs and CDOs became difficult to sell quickly in large amounts at more than fire-sale prices. As the prices of the RMBSs and CDOs declined, financial firms owning them marked these assets to market, with the resulting write-downs hurting financial results. As their financial results deteriorated, the firms found it harder to continue to obtain financing, particularly financing on the mortgage-backed securities that were losing value. Where the financing was extremely short term, this produced a liquidity crunch—with the firms unable to pay financing costs that came due and unable to sell the RMBSs and CDOs at prices sufficient to pay off the financing.

Through 2007 and into 2008, as the rating agencies downgraded mortgage-backed securities and CDOs, and investors began to panic, market prices for these securities plunged. Both the direct losses as well as the marketwide contagion and panic that ensued would lead to the failure or near failure of many large financial firms across the system. The drop in market prices for mortgage-related securities reflected the higher probability that the underlying mortgages would actually default (meaning that less cash would flow to the investors) as well as the more generalized fear among investors that this market had become illiquid. Investors valued liquidity because they wanted the assurance that they could sell securities quickly to raise cash if necessary. Potential investors worried they might get stuck holding these securities as market participants looked to limit their exposure to the collapsing mortgage market.

As market prices dropped, "mark-to-market" accounting rules required firms to write down their holdings to reflect the lower

---

38   FINANCIAL CRISIS INQUIRY REPORT, *supra* note 19, at 221–23 (footnotes omitted).

market prices. In the first quarter of 2007, the largest banks and investment banks began complying with a new accounting rule and for the first time reported their assets in one of three valuation categories: "Level 1 assets," which had observable market prices, like stocks on the stock exchange; "Level 2 assets," which were not as easily priced because they were not actively traded; and "Level 3 assets," which were illiquid and had no discernible market prices or other inputs. To determine the value of Level 3 and in some cases Level 2 assets where market prices were unavailable, firms used models that relied on assumptions. Many financial institutions reported Level 3 assets that substantially exceeded their capital. For example, for the first quarter of 2007, Bear Stearns reported about $19 billion in Level 3 assets, compared to $13 billion in capital . . .

Mark-to-market write-downs were required on many securities even if there were no actual realized losses and in some cases even if the firms did not intend to sell the securities. The charges reflecting unrealized losses were based, in part, on credit rating agencies' and investors' expectations that the mortgages would default.[39]

We turn now to how these problems affected three different firms. In each case, we will examine only a portion of the firm's problems.

C. BEAR STEARNS: SHORT-TERM FINANCING AND LIQUIDITY

As the graph earlier in this chapter shows, Bear Stearns' value dropped disastrously, with the firm eventually falling into the arms of JPMorgan in a deal originally priced at $2/Bear Stearns share and then repriced to about $10.40/share.[40] When it suffered this near total collapse, Bear possessed the capital that the SEC prescribed by its Consolidated Supervised Entities ("CSE") program but could not borrow the money that it needed to roll over the very short-term borrowing that constituted a significant percentage of its capital structure.[41]

---

[39]   *Id.* at 226–27.

[40]   For a history of the merger negotiations and the explanation of Bear's last days as an independent company—as provided to the Bear shareholders when they were asked to vote in favor of the JPMorgan deal—*see* The Bear Stearns Companies, Inc., Definitive Proxy Statement, Schedule 14A (filed Apr. 28, 2008) at 27–39.

[41]   SEC OFFICE OF THE INSPECTOR GENERAL, SEC'S OVERSIGHT OF BEAR STEARNS AND RELATED ENTITIES: THE CONSOLIDATED ENTITY PROGRAM, REP. NO. 446-A, 5 (2008) [SEC'S OVERSIGHT OF BEAR STEARNS] ("Due to Bear Stearns' lenders not rolling over secured financing, Bear Stearns faced severe liquidity problems on March 14, 2008."); 6 ("For the first time, a major investment bank that was well-capitalized and apparently fully liquid experienced a crisis of confidence that denied it not only unsecured financing, but short-term secured financing. . . .")

Bear was a large player in the subprime mortgage business:

> In mortgage securitization, Bear followed a vertically integrated model that made money at every step, from loan origination through securitization and sale. It both acquired and created its own captive originators to generate mortgages that Bear bundled, turned into securities, and sold to investors. The smallest of the five large investment banks, it was still a top-three underwriter of private-label mortgage-backed securities from 2000 to 2007. In 2006, it underwrote $36 billion in collateralized debt obligations of all kinds, more than double its 2005 figure of $14.5 billion. The total included $6.3 billion in CDOs that included mortgage-backed securities, putting it in the top 12 in that business. As was typical on Wall Street, the company's view was that Bear was in the moving business, not the storage business—that is, it sought to provide services to clients rather than take on long-term exposures of its own.

> Bear expanded its mortgage business despite evidence that the market was beginning to falter, as did other firms such as Citigroup and Merrill. As early as May 2006, Bear had lost $3 million relating to defaults on mortgages which occurred within 90 days of origination, which had been rare in the decade. But Bear persisted, assuming the setback would be temporary. In February 2007, Bear even acquired Encore Credit, its third captive mortgage originator in the United States, doubling its capacity. The purchase was consistent with Bear's contrarian business model—buying into distressed markets and waiting for them to turn around.[42]

Consistent with the strategy that it would sell rather than hold mortgage-backed securities, Bear was reducing its portfolio of mortgage-related assets, bringing them down by about $10 billion from November 2007 to February 2008 so that, by that time, Bear owned only about $36.7 billion in mortgages and mortgage-backed securities.[43] But, of course, $36.7 billion was still a large amount.

Bear relied heavily on very short-term financing called "repos," which essentially amounted to very short, sometimes overnight, loans by third parties to Bear, with Bear effectively posting security for those loans.[44] By

---

(quoting statement by the SEC Chair in the wake of the Bear Stearns collapse), https://www.sec.gov/about/oig/audit/2008/446-a.pdf.

[42] FINANCIAL CRISIS INQUIRY REPORT, *supra* note 19, at 280–81 (footnotes omitted).

[43] *Id.* at 286.

[44] In a repo, Bear technically sold securities to counterparties, promising to repurchase them at the end of the repo for an amount slightly in excess of the price that Bear received on the sale—with the difference effectively interest on what was economically similar to a short-term secured loan. The section of this chapter on Lehman describes repos in greater detail.

the end of 2007, Bear was borrowing some $102 billion in the secured repo market.[45] Some of the securities that Bear posted as collateral for the loans consisted of mortgage-backed securities that Bear owned.[46]

This meant that Bear might buy an RMBS with borrowed money, then pay off that borrowing by repoing—i.e., selling the RMBS for a very short time (perhaps even just overnight) with the obligation to buy the RMBS back, which Bear would do with a further borrowing, which it would in turn pay off by repoing that RMBS again—and so on in a continuing cycle. All this worked well, until the counterparties on the repos refused to enter into new transactions. At that point, Bear would have to pay its then-current borrowing off, which Bear would not be able to do by selling the RMBS if the price of that security in the secondary market had declined below the amount of the related borrowing.

Bear also had a very large prime brokerage business, which included holding large amounts of cash and securities for hedge funds. Indeed, Bear was the second biggest player in that market. Under the terms of prime brokerage agreements, Bear had the ability—while the accounts were with Bear—to loan out the money in the accounts to other Bear customers, and to use some of the securities in the accounts as security for loans from lenders to Bear.[47] However, if a hedge fund wanted its money back from a

---

[45]   FINANCIAL CRISIS INQUIRY REPORT, *supra* note 19, at 283.

[46]   *Id.* at 284 ("Often, backing Bear's borrowing were mortgage-related securities. . . .").

[47]   Here is more detailed description of prime banking:

"Prime brokerage" is the package of services that securities broker-dealers offer to large active investors, especially hedge funds. These services typically include trade execution, settlement, accounting and other record keeping, financing, and, critically, holding customers' cash and securities.

The relationship between a prime broker and its clients has the two features necessary for a run. First, even though securities entrusted to a prime broker belong to the client, it can be difficult or impossible for the client to extract its securities once the prime broker fails. As a result, customers are likely to withdraw their assets at the first sign that their prime broker is in difficulty. Second, . . . prime brokers often use their clients' assets as an important access to funding, or "liquidity." When a substantial number of clients leave, the broker must either quickly find new financing or sell assets to raise capital. As a result, concern that a prime broker is in trouble can be self-fulfilling.

. . . .

Broker-dealers depend on the assets of their prime brokerage customers for liquidity in two important ways. First, the dealer can offer cash loans to one client, funded by cash held on deposit by another client. Second, the dealer can pledge a customer's securities as collateral to obtain a loan from another bank or dealer. Such loans can finance the broker's own trading as well as loans to its customers.

Suppose Bank X has two prime-brokerage clients, Hedge Fund A and Hedge Fund B. It holds $250 million in cash belonging to A. If B requests a cash loan of $150 million, the broker can fund that loan from the $250 million deposited by A. If Hedge Fund A moves its prime brokerage account to another bank, however, then Bank X must immediately find $150 million in new cash from other sources.

Securities deposited with a prime brokerage are also a source of liquidity. Though these securities belong to the client and are not assets of the broker-dealer, the broker-dealer can use part of these securities as collateral for its own borrowing. If the client withdraws its assets, the broker must replace the collateral with uncommitted assets,

prime brokerage account, Bear had to send it back—in cash. Similarly, if a hedge fund wanted its securities back, Bear had to provide those too.

Bear reported fiscal year 2007 earnings of only $233 million, in comparison with $2.1 billion in fiscal 2006,[48] largely as a result of a $1.9 billion write-down of mortgage-related assets in the fourth quarter of FY 2007, which produced a loss for that quarter.[49] As Bear's financial condition declined, prime brokerage clients demanded their cash and securities and the repo lenders refused to roll over the very significant short-term debt that formed an essential part of Bear's capital structure. Bear simply did not have the cash with which to pay off that debt.

> During the fall [2007], Federated Investors, which had taken Bear Stearns off its list of approved commercial paper counterparties, continued to provide secured repo loans. Fidelity Investments, another major lender, limited its overall exposure to Bear, and shortened the maturities. In October, State Street Global Advisors refused any repo lending to Bear other than overnight.

> Often, backing Bear's borrowing were mortgage-related securities and of these, $17.2 billion—more than Bear's equity—were Level 3 assets.

> In the fourth quarter of 2007, Bear Stearns reported its first quarterly loss, $379 million.[50]

* * *

The hedge funds that were clients of Bear's prime brokerage services were particularly concerned that Bear would be unable to return their cash and securities. Lou Lebedin, the head of Bear's prime brokerage, told the FCIC that hedge fund clients occasionally inquired about the bank's financial condition in the latter half of 2007, but that such inquiries picked up at the

---

which it may not have, sell assets on the market and repay the loan, or raise new capital by selling debt or equity. Because loans collateralized by securities typically come due at the start of the next business day, the broker needs to act quickly, even desperately. If, as is typically the case in a financial crisis, the market for the broker's securities is illiquid, or the opportunity motivating its trades has gotten worse, the broker must close out its position at a loss, weakening it further.

. . . .

There is nothing inherently nefarious or unethical about a prime broker using a client's assets to fund its own or other clients' activities. . . . The problem with using a client's assets in this way is that it makes the bank susceptible to a run. . . .

COUNCIL ON FOREIGN RELATIONS, SQUAM LAKE WORKING GROUP ON FINANCIAL REGULATION, PRIME BROKERS AND DERIVATIVES DEALERS 2–4 (2010) (footnotes omitted). Quotation reprinted with permission from the Council on Foreign Relations.

[48]   The Bear Stearns Companies, Inc., Current Report, Form 8-K, Exh. 99.2 (press release) (filed Dec. 21, 2007).

[49]   *Id.*

[50]   FINANCIAL CRISIS INQUIRY REPORT, *supra* note 19, at 284 (footnotes omitted).

beginning of 2008, particularly as the cost increased of purchasing credit default swap protection on Bear. The inquiries became withdrawals—hedge funds started taking their business elsewhere. "They felt there were too many concerns about us and felt that this was a short-term move," Lebedin said. "Often they would tell us they'd be happy to bring the business back, but that they had the duty to protect their investors." Renaissance Technologies, one of Bear's biggest prime brokerage clients, pulled out all of its business. By April, Lebedin's prime brokerage operation would be holding $90 billion in assets under management, down more than 40% from $160 billion in January.[51]

* * *

Bear opened for business on Monday, March 10, [2008,] with approximately $18 billion in cash reserves. . . . While "everything rolled" during the day—that is, Bear's repo lenders renewed their commitments—SEC officials worried that this would "probably not continue."[52]

* * *

Repo lenders who had already tightened the terms for their contracts over the preceding four or five months shortened the leash again, demanding more collateral from Bear Stearns. Worries about a default quickly mounted.

By that evening, Bear's ability to borrow in the repo market was drying up. The SEC noted that some large and important money funds, including Fidelity and Mellon, had told Bear after the close of business Wednesday they "might be hesitant to roll some funding tomorrow." The SEC said that though they believed the amounts were "very manageable (between $1 and $2 billion)," the withdrawals would not send a helpful signal to the market. . . .

Upton, the [Bear Stearns] treasurer, said that before that week, he had never worried about the disappearance of repo lending. By Thursday, he believed the end was near. Bear executives informed the board that . . . $14 billion in repo was not going to roll over, and that "there was a reasonable chance that there would not be enough cash to meet [Bear's] needs." Some repo lenders were already so averse to Bear that they stopped lending to the company at all, not even against Treasury collateral, Upton told

---

[51]   *Id.* at 286.

[52]   *Id.*

the FCIC. . . . By that night, liquidity had dwindled to a mere $2 billion. . . .

Bear had run out of cash in one week.[53]

Like other financial institutions, Bear used, as one risk management tool, stress test scenarios that assumed various negative developments and then projected how Bear would fare in each. At Bear, "[m]ost of these proposed scenarios related to the market for residential mortgages."[54] While the stress tests results did not suggest looming disaster, that was because the scenarios did not include "a complete meltdown of mortgage market liquidity accompanied by fundamental deterioration in the mortgages themselves, resulting from falling housing prices."[55] The SEC's Division of Trading and Markets nevertheless viewed Bear's stress test scenarios as "consistent with industry practices" noting that "the entire banking sector failed to anticipate the magnitude and scope of the housing decline. . . ."[56] On the other hand, an outside study of Bear's risk management, commissioned by the board, concluded in January 2008

> risk assessment was "infrequent and ad hoc" and "hampered by insufficient and poorly aligned resources," "risk managers [were] not effectively positioned to challenge front office decisions," and risk management was "understaffed" and considered a "low priority."[57]

QUESTIONS ON BEAR STEARNS

Do you fault Bear's Board for permitting Bear to become reliant on overnight repo financing that could, by definition, evaporate overnight?

What if that financing was integral to the company's business strategy?

Should the board have become involved in selecting the scenarios for stress testing?

Does it make sense to stress test for Armageddon?

---

[53]   *Id.* at 288 (footnotes omitted).

[54]   SEC's OVERSIGHT OF BEAR STEARNS, *supra* note 41, at 24.

[55]   *Id.* at 25.

[56]   *Id.* at 27.

[57]   FINANCIAL CRISIS INQUIRY REPORT, *supra* note 19, at 284.

D. LEHMAN: RISK MANAGEMENT

Lehman Brothers Holdings Inc. filed for bankruptcy at 1:45 AM on September 15, 2008.

Risk management system. Before we get to the reasons for Lehman's failure, we need to understand Lehman's risk management. Lehman "maintained an extensive risk management system, which was operated by its Global Risk Management Group ('GRMG'), [with] risk managers embedded in the various business lines, and its Finance Department."[58] "By 2008, Lehman's GRMG had grown to include roughly 450 professionals, with staff in each of the firm's trading centers."[59]

The firm evaluated its risk by a suite of elaborate measures. These included Value-at-Risk ("VaR"), which "was an expression of the firm's maximum potential one day loss on its trading positions under normal market conditions in any one of 19 trading days over a 20 trading day period."[60] Lehman set VaR limits for the firm as a whole and for divisions, business lines, and regions.[61]

Lehman used "risk appetite" as a second risk measurement. Lehman defined "risk appetite"

> as "the amount of money that the Firm [was] 'prepared to lose' over one year due to market, event and counterparty credit risk." The metric was designed "to maintain a minimally acceptable [return to its investors] and compensation adequacy including maintaining sufficient headcount to protect the franchise for the long term." Thus, risk appetite was a numerical expression of "the largest reduction in revenue [that] Lehman [could] tolerate without suffering larger adverse consequences . . . such as compensation inadequacy, ratings downgrades, or loss of confidence in the Firm."[62]

Again, Lehman selected the acceptable number for this metric for the firm overall, and then for divisions, regions, and business lines.[63]

---

[58]   8 Report of Anton R. Valukas, Examiner, dated March 11, 2010 and filed in the Lehman Brothers bankruptcy, *In re Lehman Brothers Holdings, Inc.*, Chapter 11 Case No. 08-13555 (JMP), U.S. Bankruptcy Court, Southern District of New York, Appx. 8 at 1 [Lehman Bankruptcy Examiner Rpt.]. You can find all volumes of the Lehman Examiner's Report at http://web.stanford.edu/~jbulow/Lehmandocs/origIndex.html.

[59]   *Id.*

[60]   *Id.* at 7.

[61]   *Id.* at 8.

[62]   *Id.* at 9–10 (quoting Lehman documents) (footnotes omitted).

[63]   *Id.* at 13–18.

Lehman employed stress tests as a risk management tool, as it was required to do under the SEC's CSE program, in which Lehman participated.[64]

Lehman's stress testing did not include the application of limits. Thus, the stress loss amounts that Lehman generated were not measured against any predetermined standard.

Lehman employed a variety of market stress tests to measure risk. Lehman's stress tests were designed to measure the firm's vulnerability to macro economic events which could affect the firm's entire portfolio as well as localized stress scenarios that were "designed to explore the specific vulnerabilities of each line of business and region." For example, Lehman conducted stress tests based on historical market events such as the October 1987 market crash and the 1998 Russian financial crisis. In addition, Lehman's risk managers developed and conducted other stress tests that were based on hypothetical market scenarios such as the impact of a potential "[l]iquidity [c]runch due to central banks globally raising rates," jumps in oil prices caused by supply disruptions and "[m]ajor shifts in yield and spread curves such as steepening or flattening, or parallel shifts up or down." Lehman ran stress tests based on 13 or 14 different scenarios.[65]

Lehman incorporated into its risk management measures of its equity, liquidity, and funding adequacy.[66] And Lehman had single transactional

---

[64]   *Id*. at 28.

[65]   *Id*. at 30 (quoting Lehman documents) (footnotes omitted).

[66]   Here is a description:

The firm employed various metrics to gauge its equity sufficiency, including: (1) the CSE Total Capital Ratio; (2) risk equity; and (3) the Equity Adequacy Framework ("EAF"). The CSE Framework was a regulatory requirement imposed by the SEC. Risk equity and EAF were internal measures that the firm employed to determine its equity needs. In addition, the firm used the Cash Capital Model to measure its liquidity and long term ability to fund illiquid positions.

Under the CSE Program, Lehman was required to maintain minimum capital. Specifically, the SEC required Lehman to maintain a total capital ratio of 10%. The Tier 1 capital ratio was a measure that was similar to the total capital ratio, except that certain types of debt and hybrid securities were excluded from the calculation.

In addition, Lehman used the "Risk Equity Model to determine the equity to be allocated to each of [its] businesses." Risk Equity was a numerical expression of each business' market risk, event risk, counterparty credit risk, operating risk, and legal risk, plus certain other equity that the firm needed to allocate to the businesses, such as buildings and other tangible operating assets.

In mid 2007, Lehman developed EAF as a shadow risk equity tool and supplement to Risk Equity. EAF "calculate[d] the equity required to enable restructuring in a crisis" outside of bankruptcy without access to unsecured debt. The metric was designed to ensure that Lehman had "sufficient time . . . to arrange for the disposition of assets or restructuring of liabilities" and "assess[ ] [the firm's] equity adequacy in a potential Lehman specific crisis to ensure that the Firm would have sufficient equity capital to absorb any potential losses and funding impairments caused by the . . . crisis." Lehman viewed the EAF as the best measure of equity sufficiency because, unlike Lehman's other limits, as well as balance sheet limits (to restrict the amount of assets a division or business line could originate in a quarter).[67]

At every regular board meeting, management reported on the firm's risk appetite and usage limits.[68] The Lehman Bankruptcy Examiner found it unclear whether an increase in the firm's risk appetite required board approval.[69] But the firm resolved, within management, breaches of limits and requests for increases in limits or exceptions to limits.[70]

The overall point is that Lehman was trying to manage risk, and its effort to do so was organized and staffed with hundreds of professionals.

Lehman's decision to accept risk. Lehman decided in 2006 to adopt an aggressive business strategy by which it would commit its own capital to investments in real estate, loans for leveraged acquisitions, and private equity-like investments.[71] In addition, since Lehman (like Bear) originated subprime loans through subsidiaries and since the market for mortgage-backed securities dried up as the subprime crisis progressed, Lehman ended up with mortgages that it could not move into securities—adding to the investments that Lehman had to fund with its own capital.[72]

Importantly, Lehman saw the credit crisis, at least at the beginning, as an opportunity to make money from a countercyclical strategy,[73] even though, in the end, the illiquid assets that Lehman acquired as it implemented this strategy contributed to the company's collapse.[74] Along the way, the management, with the board's knowledge (at least to a significant extent), exceeded limits set in the company's risk measurements. At least in the bankruptcy Examiner's view, however, neither the officers nor the board violated the duty of care:

> Lehman had sophisticated policies, procedures, and metrics in place to estimate the risk that the firm could assume without

---

models, it "fully [met] the needs of effective capital management, e.g., transparency, practicality, and timeliness." According to various presentation materials that Lehman distributed to its external constituents, EAF was one of "the Firm's primary economic capital model[s]."

In addition, Lehman employed the Cash Capital Model ("Cash Capital") to measure its[ ] liquidity and long term ability to fund illiquid positions. In a liquidity event, the firm assumed that it would not be able to access the unsecured debt market and secured funding would be limited. Thus, all illiquid assets had to be funded with cash capital. Sources of cash capital included equity, long term debt and evergreen facilities with a term of twelve months or longer.

Id. at 31–34 (footnotes omitted).

[67] *Id.* at 34–42.
[68] *Id.* at 10, 21.
[69] *Id.* at 16.
[70] *Id.* at 14–16 (risk appetite), 37 (single transaction limit), 40–41 (balance sheet limits).
[71] 1 Lehman Bankruptcy Examiner Rpt., *supra* note 58, at 43.
[72] *Id.* at 44.
[73] *Id.* at 45.
[74] *Id.* at 45.

jeopardizing its ability to achieve a target rate of return, and to apprise management and the Board whether Lehman was within various risk limits. Lehman also used an array of stress tests to determine the potential financial consequences of an economic shock to its portfolio of assets and investments. Lehman had an extensive staff that was devoted solely to risk management.

These risk limits and stress tests, however, did not impose legal requirements on management or prevent management and the Board from exceeding those limits if they chose to do so. The role of the risk limits and stress tests was to cause management to consider whether a particular investment or a broad business strategy was worth the risk it carried. In addition, Lehman used its risk management system to promote its capabilities to investors, rating agencies, and regulators. Lehman's management always retained the discretion to use its judgment to decide whether to pursue particular strategies or transactions.

The Examiner did find that in pursuing its aggressive growth strategy, Lehman's management chose to disregard or overrule the firm's risk controls on a regular basis. The question whether there is a colorable claim that Lehman's senior officers breached their fiduciary duty of care focuses on facts relating to Lehman's acquisition of potentially illiquid investments in 2007 and the manner in which management used Lehman's risk management system as part of its process of making investment decisions:

- Lehman's management decided to exceed risk limits with respect to Lehman's principal investments, namely, the "concentration limits" on Lehman's leveraged loan and commercial real estate businesses, including the "single transaction limits" on the leveraged loans. These limits were designed to ensure that Lehman's investments were properly limited and diversified by business line and by counterparty. Lehman took highly concentrated risks in these two business lines, and, partly as a result of market conditions, ultimately exceeded its risk limits by margins of 70% as to commercial real estate and by 100% as to leveraged loans.

- Lehman's management excluded certain risky principal investments from its stress tests. Although Lehman conducted stress tests on a monthly basis and reported the results of these stress tests periodically to regulators and to its Board of Directors, the stress tests excluded Lehman's commercial real estate investments, its private equity investments, and, for a time, its leveraged loan commitments. Thus, Lehman's management did not have a regular and systematic means of analyzing the amount of catastrophic loss that the firm could suffer from these increasingly large and illiquid investments.

- Lehman did not strictly apply its balance sheet limits, which were designed to contain the overall risk of the firm and maintain the firm's leverage ratio within the range required by the credit rating agencies, but instead decided to exceed those limits. . . .

- Lehman's management decided to treat [the] primary firm wide risk limit—the risk appetite limit—as a "soft" guideline, notwithstanding Lehman's representations to the Securities Exchange Commission ("SEC") and the Board that the risk appetite limit was a meaningful constraint on Lehman's risk taking. Lehman management's decision not to enforce the risk appetite limit was apparent in several ways:

    o Between December 2006 and December 2007, Lehman raised its firm-wide risk appetite limit three times, going from $2.3 to $4.0 billion.

    o Between May and August 2007, Lehman omitted some of its largest risks from its risk usage calculation. The primary omitted risk was a $2.3 billion bridge equity position in the Archstone Smith Real Estate Investment Trust ("Archstone" or "Archstone REIT") real estate transaction, an extraordinarily large and risky commitment. Had Lehman's management promptly included that risk in its usage calculation, it would have been immediately apparent that Lehman was over its risk limits.

    o After Lehman did include the Archstone risk in the firm's risk appetite usage, Lehman continued to exceed the limit for several more months. Rather than aggressively reduce Lehman's balance sheet in response to these indicators of excessive risk taking, Lehman raised its firm wide risk limit again.

Although these decisions by Lehman's management ultimately proved to be unwise, the Examiner finds insufficient evidence to support a determination that Lehman's senior officers' conduct with respect to risk management was outside the business judgment rule or reckless or irrational.[75]

The Examiner finds insufficient evidence to support a determination that Lehman's senior managers breached their

---

[75]   *Id.* at 48–51 (footnotes omitted).

fiduciary duty of candor, which required them to provide the Board with material reports concerning Lehman's risk and liquidity.

The factual issues relevant to the duty of candor are the same risk management issues relevant to the duty of care. Lehman's officers did not disclose certain information concerning the amount or duration of the firm wide risk limit overages, their decisions to exceed certain concentration limits, or the limitations in the firm's stress testing. Nor did Lehman's officers disclose that Lehman's originations of Alt A mortgages—mortgages that were considered riskier than typical prime mortgages but not so risky as to be categorized as "subprime"—were exposing the firm to subprime mortgage risk, even as Lehman was curtailing originations of loans actually denominated as "subprime." Lehman's directors generally said that if such risk management issues were significant and long lasting, they would have liked to have received more information about them, but would not necessarily have taken action as a result.

However, the Examiner found that Lehman's management did inform the Board, clearly and on more than one occasion, that it was taking increased business risk in order to grow the firm aggressively; that the increased business risk resulted in higher risk usage metrics and ultimately firm wide risk limit overages; and that market conditions after July 2007 were hampering the firm's liquidity. Lehman's management also informed the Board, accurately, that the subprime mortgage crisis was constricting profitability and that management was tightening origination standards and taking other steps to address that crisis.

These disclosures were not so incomplete as to lead to the conclusion that Lehman's management misled the Board of Directors. Nor did Lehman's officers have a legal duty to disclose additional details to the Board. Lehman's risk limits and controls were designed primarily for management's internal use in making business decisions concerning the core issue faced by any financial institution: what business risks to take and what business risks to decline. While the overall risk management of the firm is an appropriate topic for board consideration, the day to day decisions are primarily the responsibility of officers, not directors.[76]

* * *

[A] claim that the directors failed to satisfy their duty to monitor the extent of risk assumed by management and its compliance

---

[76]   *Id.* at 52–54 (footnotes omitted).

with corporate risk policies would require proof that the directors failed to monitor managers' judgment as to internal procedures that were not legally binding. The business judgment rule applies with particular force to such a claim because the question of how much risk an investment bank can reasonably assume goes to the core of its business.

The Examiner finds insufficient evidence of a breach of fiduciary duty by any Lehman director. The directors received reports concerning Lehman's business and the level and nature of its risk taking at every Board meeting. Although these reports noted the elevated levels of risk to Lehman's business beginning in late 2006, management informed the directors that the increased risk taking was part of a deliberate strategy to grow the firm. The directors continued to receive such reports throughout 2007, and were repeatedly informed about developments in the subprime markets and the credit markets generally. Management assured the directors that it was taking prudent steps to address these risks but that management saw the unfolding crisis as an opportunity to pursue a countercyclical growth strategy. Management's reports to the directors did not contain "red flags" imposing on the directors a duty to inquire further.[77]

Why Lehman failed. Although a full analysis of Lehman's failure would require a long exposition, the short story is that Lehman had large amounts of assets, including not only mortgage-backed securities but also commercial real estate, which were illiquid—i.e., that Lehman could not quickly sell to raise money. Lehman used many of those illiquid assets as collateral to secure very short-term lending, in the same repo market on which Bear had depended. When the lenders in that market (and its clearing bank) refused to do business with Lehman at all, or only if Lehman posted additional collateral (because the counterparties viewed the collateral that Lehman was posting as having deteriorated in value and Lehman's financial condition had declined due significantly to write-downs of those assets),[78] Lehman found itself without sufficient cash to keep going.

---

[77]   *Id.* at 55–56 (footnote omitted).

[78]   Here is a brief chronology:

- On March 18, 2008, Lehman announced that in the first quarter of fiscal 2008, it had earned $489 million and taken a $1.8 billion asset write-down, $800 million of which derived from residential mortgage holdings. Lehman Bros. Holdings, Inc., Current Report, Form 8-K, Exh. 99.1 (press release) 1, 2, 13 (filed Mar. 18, 2008).

- In June, Lehman announced a $2.8 billion loss for the second quarter, including a $3.7 billion asset write-down, $2 billion of which derived from residential mortgage-related positions. Lehman Bros. Holdings, Inc., Current Report, Form 8-K, Exh. 99.1 (press release) 1, 9 (filed June 9, 2008); Lehman Bros. Holdings, Inc., Current

Before getting into the chronology, we need to expand our understanding of repos. In a two-party repo transaction, a broker-dealer might sell a security to a money market fund at the close of business on day one and promise to repurchase the security on the morning of day two at a price slightly above the price that the money market paid to the broker-dealer on day one. Although the transaction involved a sale and repurchase (hence the name "repo"), it was economically much like a secured loan— with the money market as the lender (sometimes called an "investor"), the broker-dealer as the borrower, the securities as the collateral, and slight difference between the price the investor paid in buying the securities and the price that the broker-dealer paid to repurchase them as the interest. The discussion below adopts the terminology of loans, even though the transactions were sales and repurchases.

Lehman engaged in "tri-party repos."

As implied by its name, triparty repo involves three parties: an investor (typically a pension fund, money market mutual fund or bank), a borrower (such as a broker-dealer) and a clearing bank. In a triparty repo, a triparty clearing bank such as JPMorgan acts as an agent, facilitating cash transactions from investors to broker-dealers, which, in turn, post securities as collateral. The broker dealers and investors negotiate their own terms; JPMorgan acts only as an agent. Triparty repos typically mature overnight, although investors and broker dealers can also enter into "term repos" (repos that mature at a later time) or "open repos" (repos without a set maturity date that permit the agreement to be terminated on any day).

Each night collateral is allocated to investors (into designations called "triparty shells"), either manually by the broker dealer or, more typically, through an automated process in JPMorgan's Broker Dealer Automation System ("BDAS"). The investors, in turn, provide overnight or longer term funding to the broker dealer. The following morning, JPMorgan "unwinds" the triparty repos, returning cash to the triparty investors [to pay off the overnight funding] and retrieving the securities posted the night before by the broker dealer. These securities then serve as collateral against the risk created by JPMorgan's cash advance [on behalf of the broker-dealer] to [pay off the overnight] investors. During the business day, broker dealers arrange the funding that

---

Report, Form 8-K, Exh. 99.1 (press release) 1, and Exh. 99.2 Attachment I (filed June 16, 2008).

- On September 10, Lehman provided preliminary third quarter financial results, projecting a $3.9 billion loss, with a $5.6 billion write-down, $4.9 billion of which derived from residential mortgage-related positions. Lehman Bros. Holdings, Inc., Current Report, Form 8-K, Exh. 99.1 (press release) 1, Exh. 99.2 Attachment I (filed Sept. 10, 2008).

they will need at the close of business through new triparty repo agreements. This new funding must repay the cash that JPMorgan advanced during the business day, as well as any other non JPMorgan cash needs. Thus, throughout the day, broker dealers send instructions into JPMorgan's system to indicate the details of new triparty repos (e.g., collateral amount and type) that will close at the end of the day. The process then repeats itself.[79]

Effectively, this meant that JPMorgan substituted itself as lender to Lehman during the day. Thus, the collateral that Lehman posted to secure an overnight repo loan from a money market mutual fund—that would be paid off by an intra-day loan from JPMorgan the next morning—would have to be acceptable both to that fund (which would take the risk of a Lehman default overnight) and JPMorgan (which would take the risk of a Lehman default during the day). JPMorgan grew wary of the value of the collateral that Lehman was posting, and JPMorgan's ability to sell that collateral to cover any Lehman default, and therefore demanded that extra collateral be posted, in cash, directly with JPMorgan. As set below, that demand contributed to Lehman's liquidity failure, as did the rather sudden unwillingness of the counterparties like money market funds to continue to continue to enter into overnight repos.

With that further briefing under our belt, here is how Lehman crashed:

> After the demise of Bear Stearns in March 2008, most observers . . . viewed Lehman Brothers as the next big worry among the four remaining large investment banks. . . .
>
> . . . .
>
> The chief concerns were Lehman's real estate-related investments and its reliance on short-term funding sources, including . . . $197 billion of repos at the end of the first quarter of 2008. . . .
>
> . . . . If money market funds, hedge funds, and investment banks believed Lehman's assets were worth less than Lehman's valuations, they would withdraw funds, demand more collateral, and curtail lending. That could force Lehman to sell its assets at fire-sale prices, wiping out capital and liquidity virtually overnight.[80]
>
> * * *
>
> . . . . [Lehman] was reliant on repo funding, particularly the portions that matured overnight and were collateralized by illiquid assets. As of mid-June, [2008,] 62% of Lehman's liquidity

---

[79]   4 Lehman Bankruptcy Examiner Rpt., *supra* note 58, at 1085–87; *see also* FINANCIAL CRISIS INQUIRY REPORT, *supra* note 19, at 283–84.

[80]   FINANCIAL CRISIS INQUIRY REPORT, *supra* note 19, at 325–26.

was dependent on borrowing against nontraditional securities, such as illiquid mortgage-related securities—. . . of which investors were becoming increasingly wary.

On July 10, Federated Investors—a large money market fund and one of Lehman's largest tri-party repo lenders—notified JP Morgan, Lehman's clearing bank, that Federated would "no longer pursue additional business with Lehman,". . . . Dreyfus, another large money market fund and a Lehman tri-party repo lender, also pulled its repo line from the firm.[81]

* * *

On September 4, executives from Lehman Brothers apprised executives at JP Morgan, Lehman's tri-party repo clearing bank, of the third-quarter results that it would announce two weeks later. A $3.9 billion loss would reflect "significant asset write-downs." The firm was also considering several steps to bolster capital, including an investment by Korea Development Bank. . . . The executives also discussed JP Morgan's concerns about Lehman's repo collateral.

On Monday, September 8, more than 20 New York Fed officials were notified of . . . Lehman's tri-party repo exposure at roughly $200 billion. . . . The documentation further noted that 10 counterparties provided 80% of Lehman's repo financing, and that intraday liquidity provided by Lehman's clearing banks could become a problem. Indeed, JP Morgan, Citigroup, and Bank of America had all demanded more collateral from Lehman, with the threat they might "cut off Lehman if they don't receive it."

On Tuesday morning, September 9, news there would be no investment [in Lehman] from Korea Development Bank shook the market. . . .

That same day, [Lehman's CEO] agreed to post an additional $3.6 billion of collateral to JP Morgan [which, as clearing broker for the repos, provided vital intra-day loans to Lehman].

. . . .

Before the market opened on Wednesday, Lehman announced its $3.9 billion third-quarter loss, including a $5.6 billion write-down. Four hours later, Matthew Rutherford, an adviser to Treasury, emailed colleagues that several large money funds had reduced their exposure to Lehman, although there was not yet "a wholesale pull back of [repo] lines."

---

[81]   *Id.* at 328 (footnotes omitted).

"Importantly, Fidelity, the largest fund complex, stressed that while they hadn't made any significant shifts yet today, they were still in the process of making decisions and wanted to update me later in the day," Rutherford wrote. By Friday, Fidelity would have reduced its tri-party repo lending to Lehman to less than $2 billion from over $12 billion the previous Friday; according to Fidelity's response to an FCIC survey of market participants, in the week prior to Bear's demise in March, Fidelity had pulled its entire $9.6 billion repo line to that company.[82]

* * *

[On Thursday,] JP Morgan demanded that Lehman post another $5 billion in cash "by the opening of business tomorrow in New York"; if it didn't, JP Morgan would "exercise our right to decline to extend credit to you [for the intraday loans]." JP Morgan CEO Dimon, President Black, and [Chief Risk Officer] Zubrow had first made the demand in a phone call earlier that evening to Lehman CEO Fuld, CFO Ian Lowitt, and Treasurer Paolo Tonucci. Tonucci told the JP Morgan executives on the call that Lehman could not meet the demand. Dimon said Lehman's difficulties in coming up with the money were not JP Morgan's problem, Tonucci told the FCIC. "They just wanted the cash. We made the point that it's too much cash to mobilize. There was no give on that. Again, they said 'that's not our problem, we just want the cash.'" When Tonucci asked what would keep JP Morgan from asking for $10 billion tomorrow, Dimon replied, "Nothing, maybe we will."

Under normal circumstances, Tonucci would not have tolerated this treatment, but circumstances were far from normal. "JPM as 'clearing bank' continues to ask for more cash collateral. If we don't provide the cash, they refuse to clear, we fail," was the message circulated in an email to Lehman executives on Friday, September 12. So Lehman "delivered the $5 billion in cash only by pulling virtually every unencumbered asset it could deliver."[83]

In the face of the possibility that JPMorgan on Monday, September 15, might still refuse to extend intra-day credit to Lehman to repay the overnight repo financing[84] and after efforts to arrange a sale of Lehman—or some other privately financed solution to its problems—failed over the weekend, Lehman filed for bankruptcy.[85]

---

[82]   *Id*. at 330–31 (footnote omitted).
[83]   *Id*. at 333 (footnotes omitted).
[84]   *Id*. at 334–35.
[85]   *Id*. at 333–39.

QUESTIONS ON LEHMAN BROTHERS

The Examiner looks at the interaction between the officers and the board, and the actions of the board itself, through the lens of the duty of care (or, as Delaware now characterizes the board's oversight duty, as part of the duty of loyalty). So the Examiner is looking for violation of a minimum standard. But think about the following questions not from that legal standpoint but from the standpoint of good governance.

What role does risk management properly play? Is it simply to maintain, in a structured way, some balance between risk and return?

Should risk management be structured, with measurements along various metrics, as Lehman structured it?

What are the conditions under which additional risk should be consciously assumed, as by raising numerical risk limits?

Who should make that decision? What role should a board play? For example, should board approval at Lehman have been required for a change in the risk appetite for a particular business line even if that change did not alter the risk appetite figure for Lehman as a whole?

Echoing a question considered after studying the Bear failure, is the Lehman Board at fault for letting Lehman become so dependent on overnight financing?

E. AIG: DISCRETE OPERATIONS AND LIQUIDITY

As we saw in Chapter Fifteen, AIG's problems culminated in a massive bailout by the United States government, beginning in September 2008. Two parts of AIG's operations were hardest hit.

First, AIG Financial Products ("AIGFP") sold credit default swaps protecting the owners of debt securities against decline in the value of those securities, which included CDOs backed at least in part by residential mortgages. The CDSs required AIGFP to post collateral if certain events occurred, such as downgrades in the credit ratings for the CDOs that the CDSs effectively insured, or a severe decline in the market prices of the CDOs. When the credit rating agencies downgraded CDO ratings in the 2008, AIGFP was required to post massive amounts of collateral. The amount that AIG needed to post also increased when AIG's own credit rating fell in 2008. AIG's credit rating fell, in part due to its declining financial results, which in turn resulted in part from charges reflecting a decline in the value, to AIG, of the CDSs it had sold.[86]

Second, AIG was in the business of lending securities. If an investor sells short—i.e., without owning the security that he or she or it is selling— that short seller must borrow the security from a security lender in order to deliver the security to the buyer from the short seller. The short seller deposits cash collateral with the securities lender. The short seller can return the borrowed security and, when it does, the securities lender must return the cash collateral.

> As the subprime crisis deepened, and investors grew worried about AIG's solvency (initially owing to its CDS portfolio), counterparties to securities lending transactions sought to ring-fence their duration exposure to AIG. They did this initially by shortening the length of their exposure to AIG—for example, from 90-day or 30-day liabilities to 3-day or overnight ones—before ultimately opting to close out their exposure, demanding the return of their cash collateral in exchange for the securities they had borrowed. Between September 12 and September 30, 2008 securities lending counterparties demanded that AIG return approximately $24 billion in cash.[87]

Unfortunately, AIG had invested that cash collateral in residential mortgage-backed securities. AIG could not find a market to sell those

---

[86]   As the graph on page (639) reflects, AIG repeatedly announced charges of billions of dollars to reflect the unrealized loss in the value of its CDS portfolio. In brief,

- On November 7, 2007, AIG announced it had earned $3.09 billion in net income for the third quarter of 2007, down from $4.22 billion in the third quarter of 2006, and that the Q3 2007 results included a $352 million pre-tax ($229 million after tax) charge for "unrealized market valuation loss related to AIG[FP]'s super senior [CDS] portfolio." Am. Int'l Grp., Inc., Current Report, Form 8-K, Exh. 99.1 (press release) (filed Nov. 7, 2007).

- On February 28, 2008, AIG announced it had suffered a $5.29 billion net loss for the fourth quarter of 2007, which included an $11.47 billion pre-tax ($7.46 billion after tax) charge for unrealized market valuation loss on the AIGFP CDS portfolio. Am. Int'l Grp., Inc., Current Report, Form 8-K, Exh. 99.1 (press release) (filed Feb. 28, 2008).

- On May 8, 2008, the company announced a $7.81 billion loss in the first quarter of 2008, including a $9.11 billion pre-tax ($5.92 billion after tax) charge for unrealized market valuation loss on the AIGFP CDS portfolio. Am. Int'l Grp., Inc., Current Report, Form 8-K, Exh. 99.1 (press release) (filed May 8, 2008).

- On August 6, 2008, AIG announced a $5.36 billion loss for the second quarter of 2008, including a $5.56 billion pre-tax ($3.62 billion after tax) charge for unrealized market valuation loss on the AIGFP CDS portfolio. Am. Int'l Grp., Inc., Current Report, Form 8-K, Exh. 99.1 (press release) (filed Aug. 6, 2008).

- On November 10, 2008, the company announced a $24.47 billion loss for the third quarter of 2008, including a $7.05 billion pre-tax ($4.59 billion after tax) charge for unrealized market valuation loss on the AIGFP CDS portfolio. Am. Int'l Grp., Inc., Current Report, Form 8-K, Exh. 99.1 (press release) (filed Nov. 11, 2008).

[87]   CONGRESSIONAL OVERSIGHT PANEL, JUNE OVERSIGHT REPORT, THE AIG RESCUE, ITS IMPACT ON MARKETS, AND THE GOVERNMENT'S EXIT STRATEGY 35 (June 10, 2010) (footnote omitted).

securities in quantities sufficient, and at prices sufficient, to generate the cash that it needed to return to the securities borrowers.

The need for cash in these two parts of AIG's business created a liquidity crisis:

> In the second half of 2008, AIG experienced an unprecedented strain on liquidity. This strain led to a series of transactions with the NY Fed and the United States Department of the Treasury. The two principal causes of the liquidity strain were demands for the return of cash collateral under the U.S. securities lending program and collateral calls on AIGFP's super senior multi-sector CDO credit default swap portfolio.
>
> Under AIG's securities lending program, cash collateral was received from borrowers in exchange for loans of securities owned by AIG's insurance company subsidiaries. The cash was invested by AIG in fixed income securities, primarily residential mortgage-backed securities (RMBS), to earn a spread. During September 2008, borrowers began in increasing numbers to request a return of their cash collateral. Because of the illiquidity in the market for RMBS, AIG was unable to sell RMBS at acceptable prices and was forced to find alternative sources of cash to meet these requests. As of the end of August, AIG's U.S. securities lending program had approximately $69 billion of borrowings outstanding. . . .
>
> Additionally, throughout the second half of 2008, declines in the fair values of the super senior multi-sector CDO securities protected by AIGFP's credit default swap portfolio, together with ratings downgrades of the CDO securities, resulted in AIGFP being required to post significant additional collateral. As of the end of August 2008, AIG had posted approximately $19.7 billion of collateral under its super senior credit default swap portfolio.[88]

And one additional note:

> On Monday morning—after Lehman had declared bankruptcy, and with no private-sector solution on the horizon—the Fed initiated an effort to have JP Morgan and Goldman Sachs assemble a syndicate of banks to lend about $75 billion to keep AIG afloat. In the afternoon, the rating agencies announced their assessments, which were even worse than expected. All three

---

[88] Am. Int'l Grp., Inc., Annual Report, Form 10-K (filed Mar. 2, 2009) at 40. The CDSs were "super senior" because AIGFP was assuming a "layer of credit risk senior to a risk layer that has been rated AAA by the credit rating agencies, or if the transaction is not rated, equivalent thereto." Am. Int'l Grp., Inc., Annual Report, Form 10-K (filed Feb. 28, 2008) at 122. While the CDOs causing the greatest trouble were "multi-sector," as of December 31, 2007, the notional amount of AIGFP's CDS portfolio hedging "multi-sector" CDOs totaled $78 billion, with "[a]pproximately $61.4 billion in notional amount of the multi-sector CDO pools includ[ing] some exposure to U.S. subprime mortgages." *Id.*

rating agencies announced downgrades of AIG: S&P by three notches to A-, and Moody's and Fitch by two notches to A2 and A, respectively. The downgrades triggered an additional $13 billion in cash collateral calls on AIG Financial Products' credit default swaps. Goldman Sachs alone requested $2.1 billion. Demands hit $32 billion, and AIG's payouts increased to $19.5 billion. The company's stock plummeted 61% to $4.76 from the closing price of $12.14 the previous Friday—a fraction of its all-time high of $145.84.

The syndicate of banks did not agree on a deal, despite the expectations of Fed officials.[89]

This led to the $85 billion credit facility provided by the government—and the government's voting control over AIG—that Chapter Fifteen described.

QUESTIONS ON AIG

Here is an excerpt from page 108 of AIG's Form 10-K for the year ended 2007 (filed Feb. 28, 2008), with the table reformatted slightly to improve readability:

---

[89]   FINANCIAL CRISIS INQUIRY REPORT, *supra* note 19, at 349 (footnotes omitted).

AIG's securities lending program is a centrally managed program facilitated by AIG Investments primarily for the benefit of certain of AIG's Insurance companies. Securities are loaned to various financial institutions, primarily major banks and brokerage firms. Cash collateral equal to 102 percent of the fair value of the loaned securities is received. The cash collateral is invested in highly-rated fixed income securities to earn a net spread.

AIG's liability to the borrower for collateral received was $82.0 billion and the fair value of the collateral reinvested was $75.7 billion as of December 31, 2007. In addition to the invested collateral, the securities on loan as well as all of the assets of the participating companies are generally available to satisfy the liability for collateral received.

The composition of the securities lending invested collateral by credit rating at December 31, 2007 was as follows:

(in millions)	AAA	AA	A	BBB/ Not Rated	Short-Term	Total
Corporate debt	$1,191	$9,341	$3,448	$160	$ —	$14,140
Mortgage-backed, asset-backed and collateralized	47,180	2,226	22	82		49,510
Cash and short-term investments	—	—	—	—	12,012	12,012
Total	$48,371	$11,567	$3,470	$242	$12,012	$75,662

How was the AIG Board supposed to see this risk? First, don't the investments look safe—with the huge majority of the mortgage-related investments given the highest possible credit rating? Second, how was the board—overseeing a gigantic insurance company—even going to focus on the risk that might lie in these investments?

Turning to Financial Products, not even the senior AIG executives realized that the CDSs could require collateral posting, until the first collateral calls arrived. And AIGFP thought that the super-senior CDO tranches against which it wrote the CDSs were completely safe:

[M]ost of AIG's credit default swap contracts required that collateral be posted to the purchasers, should the market value of the referenced securities decline by a certain amount, or should rating agencies downgrade AIG's long-term debt. That is, collateral calls could be triggered even if there were no actual cash losses in, for example, the super-senior tranches of CDOs upon which the protection had been written. Remarkably, top AIG executives— including CEO Martin Sullivan, CFO Steven Bensinger, Chief Risk Officer Robert Lewis, Chief Credit Officer Kevin McGinn, and Financial Services Division CFO Elias Habayeb—told FCIC investigators that they did not even know about these terms of the swaps until the collateral calls started rolling in during July [2007].

. . . .

. . . . [Even when the collateral calls arrived,] AIG's models showed there would be no defaults on any of the bond payments that AIG's swaps insured.[90]

If the top executives at the parent company, who interacted with the board, did not know of the collateral provisions of the CDSs written on the super-senior tranches of the CDOs, how was the board ever going to find out—particularly if the folks in AIGFP were sure, on the basis of quantitative modeling, that the super-senior tranches would not default?

AIGFP was a small part of AIG—with 377 employees out of AIG's 116,000. As one observer later put it: "It is beyond shocking that this small operation could blow up the holding company."[91] How was the board supposed to spot the problem in this relatively small operation operating principally in London? On the other hand, AIGFP had generated in 2005 about 17.5% of AIG's total operating income.[92] Shouldn't that have triggered some board-level attention?

As you consider these questions, do so not only in light of the minimum standards imposed by corporate fiduciary duties but also in light of what you consider good governance practices (which, of course, must still take into account the size and complexity of the company that the officers are managing and that the board is overseeing).

---

[90]   *Id.* at 243–44.

[91]   Gretchen Morgenson, *Behind Insurer's Crisis, Blind Eye to a Web of Risk*, N.Y. TIMES, Sept. 27, 2008 (quoting Robert Arvanitis, chief executive of Risk Finance Advisors), http://www.ny times.com/2008/09/28/business/28melt.html?_r=0.

[92]   *Id.*

CHAPTER 19

COMPENSATION, RISK, AND REFORMS TO CHANGE COMPENSATION IN FINANCIAL COMPANIES

■ ■ ■

Chapter Eighteen posits that the credit crisis featured the maturation of unexpected risk. In the aftermath, there was considerable concern that compensation systems in major financial institutions encouraged officers and employees to engage in transactions that increased their personal pay but that endangered their companies because the transactions were too risky. Reforms coming out of the crisis focused on risk management and, in particular in the financial industry, on the relationship between compensation and company risk. This Chapter Nineteen first considers compensation as a contributing factor to the crisis, then turns to resulting reforms. While the chapter devotes some attention to reforms designed to link compensation to risk at all public companies, it concentrates on reforms in the financial industry, where the government is substantively changing compensation in a significant way. Although Chapters Fifteen and Seventeen already showed us substantive government control over compensation during the credit crisis, the reforms described in this chapter are not intended as temporary steps affecting companies while they receive crisis-motivated government funding, but as permanent changes.

A. COMPENSATION AND THE CREDIT CRISIS

Consider first conclusions from the report by the Financial Crisis Inquiry Commission (the "FCIC"). In these passages, the commission relates compensation to the meltdown:

> Compensation systems—designed in an environment of cheap money, intense competition, and light regulation—too often rewarded the quick deal, the short-term gain—without proper consideration of long-term consequences. Often, those systems encouraged the big bet—where the payoff on the upside could be huge and the downside limited.[1]

---

[1] THE FINANCIAL CRISIS INQUIRY COMMISSION, FINAL REPORT OF NATIONAL COMMISSION ON THE CAUSES OF THE FINANCIAL AND ECONOMIC CRISIS IN THE UNITED STATES, THE FINANCIAL CRISIS INQUIRY REPORT xix (2011).

* * *

When the investment banks went public in the 1980s and 1990s, the close relationship between bankers' decisions and their compensation broke down. They were now trading with shareholders' money. Talented traders and managers once tethered to their firms were now free agents who could play companies against each other for more money. To keep them from leaving, firms began providing aggressive incentives, often tied to the price of their shares and often with accelerated payouts. To keep up, commercial banks did the same. Some included "clawback" provisions that would require the return of compensation under narrow circumstances, but those proved too limited to restrain the behavior of traders and managers.[2]

* * *

Studies have found that the real value of executive pay, adjusted for inflation, grew only 0.8% a year during the 30 years after World War II, lagging companies' increasing size. But the rate picked up during the 1970s and rose faster each decade, reaching 10% a year from 1995 to 1999. Much of the change reflected higher earnings in the financial sector, where by 2005 executives' pay averaged $3.4 million annually, the highest of any industry. Though base salaries differed relatively little across sectors, banking and finance paid much higher bonuses and awarded more stock. And brokers and dealers did by far the best, averaging more than $7 million in compensation.

Both before and after going public, investment banks typically paid out half their revenues in compensation. For example, Goldman Sachs spent between 44% and 49% a year between 2005 and 2008, when Morgan Stanley allotted between 46% and 59%. Merrill paid out similar percentages in 2005 and 2006, but gave 141% in 2007—a year it suffered dramatic losses.

As the scale, revenue, and profitability of the firms grew, compensation packages soared for senior executives and other key employees. John Gutfreund, reported to be the highest-paid executive on Wall Street in the late 1980s, received $3.2 million in 1986 as CEO of Salomon Brothers. Stanley O'Neal's package was worth more than $91 million in 2006, the last full year he was CEO of Merrill Lynch. In 2007, Lloyd Blankfein, CEO at Goldman Sachs, received $68.5 million; Richard Fuld, CEO of Lehman Brothers, and Jamie Dimon, CEO of JPMorgan Chase, received about $34 million and $28 million, respectively. That year Wall

---

[2]   *Id.* at 62.

Street paid workers in New York roughly $33 billion in year-end bonuses alone. Total compensation for the major U.S. banks and securities firms was estimated at $137 billion.

Stock options became a popular form of compensation, allowing employees to buy the company's stock in the future at some predetermined price, and thus to reap rewards when the stock price was higher than that predetermined price. In fact, the option would have no value if the stock price was below that price. Encouraging the awarding of stock options was 1993 legislation making [annual] compensation in excess of $1 million taxable to the corporation unless performance-based. Stock options had potentially unlimited upside, while the downside was simply to receive nothing if the stock didn't rise to the predetermined price. The same applied to plans that tied pay to return on equity: they meant that executives could win more than they could lose. These pay structures had the unintended consequence of creating incentives to increase both risk and leverage, which could lead to larger jumps in a company's stock price.[3]

* * *

SEC Chairman Mary Schapiro told the FCIC, "Many major financial institutions created asymmetric compensation packages that paid employees enormous sums for short-term success, even if these same decisions result[ed] in significant long-term losses or failure for investors and taxpayers."[4]

* * *

Options Group, which compiles compensation figures for investment banks, examined the mortgage-backed securities sales and trading desks at 11 commercial and investment banks from 2005 to 2007. It found that associates had average annual base salaries of $65,000 to $90,000 from 2005 through 2007, but received bonuses that could well exceed their salaries. On the next rung, vice presidents averaged base salaries and bonuses from $200,000 to $1,150,000. Directors averaged $625,000 to $1,625,000. At the top was the head of the unit. For example, in 2006, Dow Kim, the head of Merrill's Global Markets and Investment Banking segment, received a base salary of $350,000 plus a $35 million bonus, a package second only to Merrill Lynch's CEO.[5]

---

[3]   *Id.* at 62–63 (footnotes omitted).

[4]   *Id.* at 64 (footnote omitted).

[5]   *Id.* at 118 (footnotes omitted).

As the last sentence suggests, fingers pointed to those who were well paid and at the center of the crises at particular firms. Two of those firms were Bear Stearns and AIG.

Here is information about compensation at Bear:

In January 2008, before the report was completed, [James] Cayne resigned as CEO, after receiving $93.6 million in compensation from 2004 through 2007. He remained as non-executive chairman of the board. Some senior executives sharply criticized him and the board. Thomas Marano [head of Global Mortgages and Asset Backed Securities] told the FCIC that Cayne played a lot of golf and bridge. Speaking of the board, Paul Friedman, a former senior managing director at Bear Stearns, said, "I guess because I'd never worked at a firm with a real board, it never dawned on me that at some point somebody would have or should have gotten the board involved in all of this," although he told the FCIC that he made these comments in anger and frustration in the wake of Bear's failure. In its final report on Bear, the Corporate Library, which researches and rates firms for corporate governance, gave the company a "D," reflecting "a high degree of governance risk" resulting from "high levels of concern related to the board and compensation." . . .

At Bear, compensation was based largely on the return on equity in a given year. For senior executives, about half of each bonus was paid in cash, and about half in restricted stock that vested over three years and had to be held for five. The formula for the size of each year's compensation pool was determined by a subcommittee of the board. Stockholders approved the performance compensation plan and capital accumulation plan for senior managing directors. Cayne told the FCIC he set his own compensation and the compensation for all five members of the Executive Committee. According to Cayne, no one, including the board, questioned his decisions.

For 2007, even with its losses, Bear Stearns paid out 58% of revenues in compensation. [Michael] Alix, who sat on the Compensation Committee, told FCIC staff the firm typically paid 50% but that the percentage increased in 2007 because revenues fell—if management had lowered compensation proportionately, he said, many employees might have quit. Base salaries for senior managers were capped at $250,000, with the remainder of compensation a discretionary mix of cash, restricted stock, and options.

From 2000 through 2008, the top five executives at Bear Stearns took home over $326.5 million in cash and over $1.1 billion from stock sales, for more than a total of $1.4 billion. This exceeded the annual budget for the SEC. Alan Schwartz, who took over as CEO after Cayne and had been a leading proponent of investing in the mortgage sector, earned more than $87 million from 2004 to 2007. Warren Spector, the co-president responsible for overseeing the two hedge funds that had failed, received more than $98 million during the same period. Although Spector was asked to resign, Bear never asked him to return any money. In 2006, Cayne, Schwartz, and Spector each earned more than 10 times as much as Alix, the chief risk officer.[6]

Recall that AIG suffered in part from the CDSs written by its Financial Products business based in London. Mr. Cassano ran that operation. He, too, received large-dollar compensation:

> In the case of the London subsidiary that ran the operation, the bonus pool was 30% of new earnings. Financial Products CEO Joseph J. Cassano made the allocations at the end of the year. Between 2002 and 2007, the least amount Cassano paid himself in a year was $38 million. In the later years, his compensation was sometimes double that of the parent company's CEO.[7]

QUESTIONS AFTER YOUR FIRST VIEW OF FINANCIAL FIRM COMPENSATION

As you can see, one overall theme is that compensation should not have been structured so that individuals at the center of the crisis could make and keep large amounts of money even though their actions ultimately contributed to the death or near-death of their companies. Do you agree with that view? If so, what is the relevant time span? That is, suppose that someone started to work at Bear Stearns in 1980 and worked there continuously until the firm suffered its crisis in 2008. Would you be concerned about the money that he or she earned in 1980, or 2000, and never had to return to the company or its shareholders? Or is your concern limited to the compensation earned during the period of time during which the firm made the particular business moves that led to disaster? What if the individual worked in a part of the firm doing business that did not lead to Bear's demise?

What if Bear had not failed at all, but had sold its risky mortgage-related business before the dam broke? In other words, would you still be concerned over large dollars earned by the folks at Bear who worked on the mortgage-related business if Bear had had the good sense or good luck to pass that risk along to others in time to avoid problems for Bear?

---

[6]   *Id.* at 285 (footnotes omitted).

[7]   *Id.* at 141 (footnotes omitted).

Do you save your concern for only those dollars the Bear folks earned after the risks of the mortgage-related business became clear? In other words, are you distressed only because they deliberately took large risks and then pocketed and did not return large compensation amounts when those risks matured? If so, how would you determine when they began taking risks that they should not have taken? And what if they deliberately took risks—as did Lehman—while making a bet (informed by the firm's prior experience) that it could make money by pursuing a countercyclical strategy?

How can you avoid "hindsight bias" as you attempt to determine whether Bear or Lehman took "excessive risk"—given that Bear collapsed into a low-dollar merger with JPMorgan and Lehman went bankrupt?

One difficulty in determining whether compensation contributed to unhealthy risk-taking is that the analysis quoted above does not show the entire pay packages that executives (or traders, for that matter) received. Read now a more complete picture provided by the Lehman Bankruptcy Examiner at pages 1–35 of Appendix 11 in volume 8 of his report:

> Lehman allocated compensation based primarily on net revenue.[8] Revenue not yet recognized but recorded based on mark-to-market valuations was included in net revenue and, therefore, impacted compensation decisions. This inclusion naturally created incentives to value investments highly, avoid writedowns and otherwise seek to maximize short-term profits so as to generate higher net revenue leading to higher compensation. The Examiner has not found evidence that Lehman personnel deliberately engaged in misconduct designed to exploit these incentives.

> Although risk-based metrics and similar criteria did play some role in compensation decisions, it was a minor, not central, role. Compensation decisions were driven largely by net revenue, market comparisons and employee attrition concerns. Lehman's compensation practices were similar to those of its Wall Street peers. While Lehman's vesting and delivery periods for its stock awards were notably longer than its peer firms, Lehman's compensation practices were similar to those used by the other major investment banks.

---

[8]   From Lehman's SEC filings, I gather that "net revenue" equaled "total revenues" minus "interest expense." *See* Lehman Bros. Holdings Inc., Annual Report, Form 10-K (filed Jan. 29, 2008) at 29.

II. THE COMPENSATION AND BENEFITS COMMITTEE OF THE BOARD

The first step of Lehman's annual compensation process began with meetings of the Compensation and Benefits Committee ("Compensation Committee") of the Board of Directors, which in 2007 and 2008 consisted of John F. Akers, Marsha "Marty" Johnson Evans, Sir Christopher Gent and John D. Macomber. Tracy Binkley, Lehman's Head of Human Resources, served as Secretary for meetings, while Richard S. Fuld, Jr., Lehman's Chief Executive Officer and Chairman of the Board, and others (Joseph M. Gregory, President and Chief Operating Officer ("COO"), Anthony J. Collerton, COO of Human Relations, and Thomas A. Russo, Chief Legal Officer, among others) regularly attended Compensation Committee meetings by invitation. These meetings generally took place on a monthly or near-monthly basis.

The Compensation Committee's primary role was to set the firm's compensation ratio (defined below) and to supervise the allocation of available compensation derived from the ratio into compensation pools for each division. In addition, the Compensation Committee determined the mix of cash compensation and equity compensation (awarded as restricted stock units ("RSUs") or options), as well as set the deferred component of total compensation.

A. Determining Lehman's Compensation Ratio

Each year, the Compensation Committee determined Lehman's aggregate compensation expense (consisting of both fixed compensation expenses and discretionary, performance-based bonus expenses) by calculating a ratio of total compensation and benefits expense to net revenue (the "compensation ratio"). In addition to net revenue, the Compensation Committee considered factors such as: the need to maximize returns to shareholders; investments of the firm in strategic hiring; and rewarding performance in a competitive manner in light of current market conditions. Throughout the year, the Compensation Committee consulted quarterly revenue projections and real-time results provided by the Finance Department to estimate and forecast the firm's compensation ratio.

The quarterly revenue projections included analysis of the impact of slightly different compensation ratio levels on pre-tax margin, return on equity ("ROE"), earnings per share ("EPS"), discretionary bonuses and total compensation for non-guaranteed non-new hire ("NGNNH") employees.

The "compensation pool" was finalized in the fourth quarter of each Lehman fiscal year (September through November), when Lehman was able to accurately predict its annual net revenues based on Finance Department accruals and to compare its compensation estimates to the estimates of its competitors. As Lehman's fiscal year-end approached, the compensation ratio fluctuated based on what Lehman learned from outside consultants regarding the compensation ratios used by competitors such as Goldman Sachs, Bear Stearns, Morgan Stanley and Merrill Lynch.

Lehman's compensation ratio typically ranged between 48% and 50% of net revenue, and was 49.3% of net revenue in each of fiscal years 2005, 2006 and 2007. . . .

Excluding Merrill Lynch, the 2007 average of competitors' compensation ratios was 53.5%; the 2006 average of competitors' compensation ratios was 46.9%. Lehman attempted to maintain or reduce its compensation ratio on a year-to-year basis as a signal to the market that it was committed to controlling compensation expenses—while salaries of individual employees and executives might increase, Lehman was maintaining and/or decreasing its compensation expenses as an overall percentage of firm expenses.

Early in 2008, Lehman projected declining revenue due to market conditions. To maintain total compensation at a dollar level comparable to past levels despite declining revenues, and thus avoid potential employee exodus to competitors, Lehman projected an increase in the firm's compensation ratio during the first quarter of 2008. . . .

Beginning second quarter 2008, the compensation ratio method of determining total compensation was no longer viable, as firm-wide net revenue was negative $668 million. Despite having firm-wide negative net revenue for second quarter 2008, certain Lehman divisions, i.e., Investment Management and Investment Banking, had performed well during that period. Consequently, Lehman management determined that employees in those better performing divisions should be paid compensation commensurate with compensation paid to employees in similar divisions at Lehman's peer firms, in order to protect the Lehman franchise. Preliminary market indications following second quarter 2008 suggested that pay for the lead investment banks was likely to be down approximately 25% to 30% overall from 2007. Consistent with these indications, the Compensation Committee also planned to target a 30% reduction in pay for NGNNH employees for 2008; the Compensation Committee determined it would be difficult to both maintain the franchise and initiate any pay cuts of over 30%. In addition, beginning in January 2008, the Compensation Committee began exploring alternative long-term compensation models, including changes to its equity award plan, which would lower overall compensation costs.

B.   Cash-Equity Mix of Compensation and Vesting

In addition to setting the firm's compensation ratio, the Compensation Committee also determined the cash-equity mix (the percentage of compensation paid in cash versus that portion paid in equity) and the deferred component of total compensation for all Lehman employees. As an individual's total compensation increased, the deferred component increased correspondingly. In Lehman's view, individuals with significant portions of their total compensation in the form of deferred compensation had an incentive to promote the firm's long-term success. . . .

. . . [In 2008,] employees receiving compensation greater than $750,000 received a significant portion of their total compensation (65%) in equity.

The firm's cash-equity mix of compensation in 2007 was 32% cash to 68% equity. Lehman's mix was consistent with that of its peer group, which ranged from a low of 11% cash compensation at Goldman Sachs to a high of 39% cash compensation at Bear Stearns. . . .

Since 2005, Lehman's equity compensation component consisted exclusively of RSUs, and each RSU grant entitled an employee to one share of Lehman stock after a period of years. The following [table] depicts Lehman's equity vesting and delivery schedule. The vesting schedule refers to the time period before an employee received his or her RSUs. The delivery schedule refers to the time period before the RSUs converted into unrestricted stock.

Firm	Discount	Vesting Schedule						Delivery Schedule					
		at grant	year 1	year 2	year 3	year 4	year 5	at grant	year 1	year 2	year 3	year 4	year 5
Citigroup[1]	25.00%		25.00%	25.00%	25.00%	25.00%			25.00%	25.00%	25.00%	25.00%	
Credit Suisse[2]	n/a		33.00%	33.00%	33.00%				33.00%	33.00%	33.00%		
ISUs (in lieu of discount)					100.00%						100.00%		
Deutsche Bank	9.00%			50.00%	25.00%	25.00%				50.00%	25.00%	25.00%	
Goldman Sachs	0.00%	40.00%			60.00%						100.00%		
JP Morgan	0.00%			50.00%	50.00%					50.00%	50.00%		
Merrill Lynch	0.00%		25.00%	25.00%	25.00%	25.00%			25.00%	25.00%	25.00%	25.00%	
Morgan Stanley	0.00%			50.00%	50.00%					50.00%	50.00%		
UBS	0.00%		33.00%	33.00%	33.00%				33.00%	33.00%	33.00%		
Lehman Brothers													
2007 MD — Principal					50.00%		50.00%						100.00%
2007 MD — Discount	30.00%						100.00%						100.00%
2007 SVP and below — Principal				100.00%									100.00%
2007 SVP and below — Discount	25.00%						100.00%						100.00%
2008 Proposed	0.00%		33.00%	33.00%	33.00%						100.00%		

[1] Discount provided on deferral levels up to $500k in bonus only. Discretionary supplemental awards in 2007.

[2] Equity discounts replaced in 2006 by a new performance-based Incentive Stock Unit ("ISU") program; ISUs were communicated as equivalent to RSUs with a 20% discount. Deferral % of 100% above $4 million in bonus.

In 2007, as in all prior years, RSUs were issued to employees at a discount to market price. Therefore, the total value of the RSUs an employee received consisted of two components: a portion of the value was attributable to his or her actual RSU award (principal portion), and a portion was attributable to the discount to market price (discount portion). Managing directors received RSUs at a discount of 30% to market price, and Senior Vice Presidents and other lower-ranking employees received RSUs at a discount of 25% to market price. In 2007, 50% of a Managing director's principal portion RSUs vested after three years, and the remaining 50% vested after five years. The discount portion of RSUs granted to a Managing director also vested after five years. Similarly, the principal portion of the RSUs granted to Senior Vice Presidents and lower-ranking employees vested after two years, and the discount portion of the RSUs vested after five years.

Lehman's RSU vesting and delivery schedules were longer than those of its peer firms. Lehman Managing directors experienced equity vesting after as long as five years (50% of the principal portion, and 100% of the discount portion), and Lehman postponed share delivery until after five years, whereas the vesting and delivery periods of Lehman's peer firms concluded after three or four years.

Annual limits were imposed on Executive Committee members, limiting the amount of equity they were permitted to liquidate based on the market value of their equity holdings at the beginning of each year. For 2008, the annual liquidation limit was 20%, which was calculated using a pre-tax equity value that included RSUs, option gains and the pre-tax equivalent of shares owned.

According to Lehman witnesses, longer vesting and delivery, as well as restrictions on the amount of equity Executive Committee members could liquidate annually, helped to align executive interests with the long-term goals of the firm and its shareholders. A forthcoming article in the *Yale Journal on Regulation* by Harvard Law School Professors Lucian A. Bebchuk, Alma Cohen and Holger [Spamann, subsequently published and cited later in this chapter] calls that assumption into question, noting that the top five executives at Lehman received cash bonuses and proceeds from stock sales totaling $1 billion between 2000 and 2008 and that Lehman top executives had regular short-term incentives to attempt to increase the stock price on the shares that they were selling as they became vested and delivered. Indeed, although Lehman's vesting and delivery schedules were longer than peers' vesting and delivery schedules, Lehman's schedules were still focused on short-term firm performance (five years or less).

C. Dividing Compensation Between Lehman Divisions

After determining the firm's compensation ratio and the cash-equity mix, the Compensation Committee turned to the next step in the annual compensation process—dividing the compensation pool among Lehman's divisions. Once the Compensation Committee finalized the total firm-wide compensation pool in the fourth quarter of each fiscal year and Lehman could accurately predict annual revenues based on Finance Department estimates, and after Lehman compared its predicted compensation to the compensation estimates of its Wall Street competitors, the Compensation Committee divided the compensation pool among Lehman divisions.

A portion of the firm's total compensation pool was fixed, representing compensation or benefit obligations that the firm had committed to honor, such as compensation agreements or contracted-for salaries for current and former employees, health care costs, retirement benefits, contractual severance packages and amortization of equity awards that had been given to employees in past years (normally amortized over five years). These fixed obligations were satisfied first, with all remaining funds in the compensation pool then allocated to divisions for employee bonuses.

Rather than applying the firm's compensation ratio to determine divisional compensation allocations, the Committee employed a discretionary process that analyzed a number of factors. The compensation ratio for Investment Banking was greater than the firm-wide compensation ratio of 49.3%, while the compensation ratio for Capital Markets was lower than the firm-wide compensation ratio. The compensation ratio for Investment Management fluctuated above and below the firm-wide compensation ratio. . . .

The Compensation Committee apportioned draft pools of compensation to each division based primarily on each division's net revenue and the prevailing practices in the market. This process had a stated rationale "to provide a level of transparency in the determination of compensation at the divisional level in order to more clearly demonstrate the tie between financial performance and compensation, providing strong incentives for divisional performance," and "to encourage revenue maximization" and "aggressive management of non-personnel expenses."

The Compensation Committee used performance-based metrics as well as more subjective criteria to allocate pools of compensation to each division. From the revenue projections provided by the Finance Department, Lehman would calculate pre-compensation profits before taxes ("PCPBT"), and then input that figure into the compensation model. Beginning in 2003, Lehman supplemented its PCPBT-based compensation model by also considering an Economic Value Added ("EVA") metric, which included a risk component based on a "use of equity" charge. Lehman viewed its PCPBT-based compensation model as a competitive advantage because it aligned pay with performance, provided more accountability and allowed management to take steps to optimize performance.

The Compensation Control Group within the Finance Department provided the Compensation Committee, Chief Financial Officer and Chief Accounting Officer with a presentation of data on six or seven performance statistics for each division in any given year versus the division's previous year's performance. These included: net revenues, changes in headcount, PCPBT, EVA and ROE. The Compensation Committee also received a presentation during the fourth quarter detailing compensation expenses (expressed in terms of NGNNH compensation), and the Compensation Committee was presented with alternatives for distributing compensation to divisions. The Compensation Committee used outside consultants (including Johnson & Associates, Inc. and MGMC, Inc.), to analyze competitive gaps and market indicators.

The Compensation Committee used these performance results as a baseline for allocating compensation to each Lehman division, followed by a review of subjective criteria to determine divisional compensation allocations. These criteria and considerations included:

- [n]ew businesses that were in early stages of their growth that had not yet generated sufficient compensation to pay employees competitively;

- [s]ignificant market pressures in business sectors, reflecting market premiums paid by new entrants into that sector;

- Lehman's decision to grow a business sector in accordance with the firm's long term strategic plan;

- [f]ranchise preservation issues driven by the market cycle, where Lehman paid a division/business at higher levels in order to protect its investment in key employees; and

- [r]eward for "One Firm" behaviors such as cross selling or client management activities where the revenue benefit accrued to another business unit.

No formal or written guidelines existed as to the weight assigned to either the divisional performance results or the subjective criteria. The compensation pool for a division did not increase or decrease in a directly proportional manner to that division's net revenue performance. Divisions that Lehman wanted to grow, for example, were generally allocated compensation pools larger than their net revenue performance might have dictated. Similarly, a higher share of compensation was paid out to divisions such as Investment Banking, which did not pose a significant risk to Lehman's balance sheet assets, than to riskier businesses such as

Real Estate, which exposed Lehman's balance sheet to potential losses.

In fiscal year 2007, for example, Lehman's Fixed Income Division ("FID")[9] generated $3.4 billion less PCPBT as compared to fiscal year 2006, but nevertheless, FID employees received similar compensation to what they had received in 2006. Specifically, while the compensation model indicated that for 2007 FID compensation should be reduced by $888 million from 2006 compensation, senior management and the Compensation Committee reduced FID compensation by only $80 million. Similarly, in 2007, model results indicated that the Equities Division should have received a $477 million increase in compensation from 2006, based on an approximately $1.8 billion increase in PCPBT and improved profitability. However, following senior management and Compensation Committee adjustments, the division received an increase of only $229 million.

The Compensation Committee applied a similar process to determine compensation allocations to individual business lines within divisions. For example, within FID's Rates and Products subdivision, the Commodities segment's 2006 net revenues and compensation ratio were $27.8 million and 195%, respectively. The segment's 2007 net revenue and compensation ratio were $231 million and 48.9%, respectively. These ratios are consistent with witness interviews stating that the segment was a start-up in 2006 from which Lehman did not expect high net revenues, yet determined that it was appropriate to compensate employees commensurate with their market peers in order to attract and retain them to further grow the business. The segment saw substantial growth by 2007, and therefore, the 2007 segment ratio was more consistent with the firm's overall compensation ratio. Finally, compensation decisions made by Lehman's competitors in regard to their comparative divisions played a role in Lehman's allocations, as Lehman attempted to prevent attrition by matching the compensation of its competitors. There is also some indication that the Compensation Committee retained a "holdback" pool of compensation that could be paid to certain divisions for adjustment purposes.

III. DETERMINING INDIVIDUAL EMPLOYEE COMPENSATION

After divisional and business line compensation was allocated, each division head would allocate the pool of compensation to be received by its executives and employees. Division heads had

---

9   FID included Lehman's mortgage-related securities businesses.

autonomy regarding individual compensation decisions, and the specific performance metrics they relied upon to apportion compensation to their executives and employees varied based on market practices in each division's business line. Compensation decisions for individual employees depended on that specific employee's functions, but all performance indicators were net-revenue-based. Lehman's Compensation and Control Group met monthly with each division's Chief Administrative Officer ("CAO") to review the division's compensation models.

While each division and business unit had autonomy and discretion over its own compensation process, each division reported its compensation allocation results (including its list of top compensated employees) to the Executive Committee. An illustrative example of how FID carried out the compensation process in 2007 was described as follows:

Once FID received the bonus pool package from the Finance Department in early November 2007, a "round one" meeting followed involving a large, representative group of FID Managing Directors, including Mary Pat Archer, Roger Nagioff, Thomas Humphrey, Alex Kirk, Andrew J. Morton, Kentaro Umezaki and Ravi Mattu. Nagioff, with assistance from Archer, outlined for the group the firm-wide approach for that year's compensation. Nagioff explained the process and made recommendations on how round one would work in terms of dividing compensation between business units and employees. Additionally, he would set targets for FID in terms of fitting the division's total compensation decisions within Lehman's overall annual targets (expressed as a percentage change from the previous year in terms of NGNNH compensation). The group reviewed relative performance, historic compensation, efficiencies with regard to headcount, [and] headcount and performance of the business on a year-over-year basis. The group then made a preliminary allocation of divisional compensation pool funds among its business units following a bottom-up review (ensuring everyone in the division received the bonus they deserved to retain key employees) and a top-down review (ensuring guarantees for new hires were paid). Nagioff was the final decision-maker if conflicts within the group could not be resolved.

Following round one, the heads of each business unit had another week to allocate compensation to employees using an online bonus system. Individual employee compensation allocation was a discretionary process and decisions appear to have been made primarily by a series of performance criteria that varied by class of professional rather than by division. FID business unit heads ranked their employees in quartiles, designating the top 25% of performers as "1"s on down to the bottom 25% of employees (who performed below expectations) as "4"s; while the 1–4 ranking was not strictly determinative of compensation, the expectation was that employees at higher levels (1–2) would receive higher bonus compensation than those at lower levels (3–4). After making preliminary allocations to employees, the business heads reported to Nagioff, Archer and the larger group on how they had allocated bonuses within their business unit, and they prepared rosters listing each employee's compensation from high to low that year, as well as, a history of each employee's compensation from previous years. Some adjustments would be made at this time to conform compensation within the division amongst employee groups (so that, for example, administrative assistants in one business unit were not disproportionately compensated compared to administrative assistants in another business unit). These adjustments concluded round one.

Nagioff then met with Gregory so that compensation decisions could be reviewed by the Compensation Committee. The Compensation Committee reviewed the details of the top 200 to 250 earners in each division as well as of any employees whose compensation had drastically increased or decreased from the previous year. Once the Compensation Committee had finalized the firm-wide net revenues at the end of November, round two would begin whereby FID would reallocate compensation as necessary based on any increase or decrease in its final compensation pool from the Compensation Committee. FID occasionally would retain a small pool of compensation in a reserve for adjustments or to fix any misallocations from the previous rounds.

Once round two was over, the direct managers of each business line would communicate the bonuses to their employees as part of the employees' performance reviews, normally finishing that part of the process by late December.

Final approval of all compensation decisions was vested in the Compensation Committee. Indeed, on one occasion, management was reprimanded for awarding a compensation package without prior Board approval. While the Board ultimately approved the package, it informed Fuld and management that all such decisions were required to be approved by the Board.

IV. CONSIDERATION OF RISK IN LEHMAN'S COMPENSATION PRACTICES

While Lehman's compensation practices were predominately driven by net revenue-based metrics, risk did play some role in compensation decisions. For example, at the firm-wide level, although the EVA compensation metric was net revenue-based, the metric also considered balance sheet risk necessary to achieve net revenues. Additionally, Lehman divisions with fee-based net revenues (such as Investment Banking) generally received higher compensation allocations on a percentage-of-net-revenue basis than divisions that undertook significant balance sheet risk, such as real estate.

Risk also played a role in compensation through balance sheet limits. Businesses that exceeded balance sheet limits theoretically faced penalties that could include the diminution of their compensation pool. As Umezaki noted, balance sheet usage and limit breaches triggered penalties in the net-revenue metrics used by Lehman, thereby affecting divisional compensation in a negative manner.

As recently as 2004, FID used a "Compensation Scorecard" that included risk-weighted metrics such as "return on risk equity" and "return on net balance sheet" to determine business unit compensation pool allocations. Similarly, divisional compensation metrics, year-over-year divisional performance data and internal divisional performance tracking documents submitted to the Compensation Committee by the Compensation Control Group assessed divisional performance relative to Value at Risk ("VaR"), balance sheet usage and risk appetite. The Compensation Committee's review of these documents indicates at least some consideration of risk in making compensation decisions.

Beginning in the first quarter of 2008, Lehman adopted a new competency measure for the Equities Sales force that addressed risk appreciation. This competency measure consisted of four criteria: (1) awareness (the employee's understanding of the risks inherent in the market and transactions); (2) communication (the employee's ability to share and highlight key risks to partners in trading and control areas); (3) client skills (negotiating transaction terms for optimum risk-reward profile); and (4) shareholder/manager behavior (deploying capital efficiently and in consideration of clients' historical trading impact with awareness of ownership of the risks and rewards of transactions).

Witnesses offered differing opinions concerning the weight given to risk factors in making compensation decisions. Archer, FID

Chief Accounting Officer, did not recall any discussion of VaR during FID's 2007 bonus pool meetings. Archer noted that while business heads were responsible for the risk component of FID, if a risky trade had been made successfully, then the trade would have been completed and the risk aspect would not have been discussed as part of the group's assessment of an employee for compensation purposes.

Umezaki, Global Head of FID—Business Strategy in 2007, expressed concern regarding the weight (or lack thereof) that risk factors were given in regard to compensation decision-making. Specifically, in an April 19, 2007 email, Umezaki offered feedback on balance sheet issues, and noted:

> Incentives and motivation: the majority of the trading businesses focus is on revenues, with balance sheet, risk limit, capital or cost implications being a secondary concern. The fact that [traders] haven't heard that those items matter [in] public forums from senior management recently reinforces this revenue oriented behavior implicitly. In my opinion, this group is not behaving "badly": they are just getting conflicting messages that go unreconciled ("grow revenues" from FID; "manage balance sheet" from Finance, if you will). We also don't have a strong enough mechanism to reinforce "better" behavior around these nonrevenue metrics, as comp is tied to revenues at the divisional level. Tough problem to solve given the way we incent today. We've been debating this for a good decade now. . . .

Gelband, former head of FID, indicated that he made an effort to adjust compensation decisions to reflect the amount of risk that the business unit or that the individual had taken. Nagioff similarly stated that risk-based metrics were considered in dividing FID's compensation pool to FID's business lines, but not in any specific mathematical way.

According to Gregory, the focus of the Executive Committee in making adjustments to divisional compensation was less on the amount of risk a division had taken, and more on general fairness and equity, with the Executive Committee considering the full interests of the firm when considering how much balance sheet certain divisions used as compared to others. Gregory disagreed with other witnesses in this regard, stating that employees in risk-taking businesses could be paid compensation based on a similar or even larger share of their revenues than employees in fee-based businesses. Gregory provided the example of Investment Banking, where he stated that the business and employees received a larger share of compensation than their revenues would otherwise indicate because Investment Banking created substantial ancillary profits through other revenue streams.

Finally, Lehman witnesses noted that product controllers'[10] compensation was not tied to the division or to the performance of the product, and therefore, there was no compensation-based incentive for these employees to miss-mark positions or avoid write-downs.

V. COMPENSATION BASED ON UNREALIZED MARK-TO-MARKET PROFITS

In calculating net revenue, Lehman included revenue not yet recognized but recorded based on mark-to-market positions, and such revenue was considered in determining divisional and employee net revenue contributions for compensation purposes. The compensation pool would, therefore, have increased or decreased (and a division's and/or individual's compensation would have been affected) by the amount of unrealized mark-to-market gain or loss. With the exception of the compensation process for proprietary traders, no mechanism existed by which Lehman could "claw-back" compensation paid to employees based on mark-to-market revenues that were recorded but never realized.

In discussing the proper approach for paying compensation on the KSK Energy transaction, for which the firm booked a large mark-to-market profit, Henry Klein, Chris O'Meara, and David Goldfarb engaged in an e-mail exchange and noted that booking the transaction as an unrealized gain and paying compensation based on that methodology "is not different" from how Lehman's Global Trading Strategies ("GTS") group was compensated on other deals:

> GTS is paid on the basis of the market value of its portfolio at year end as reflected on Lehman's books. The Firm is always at risk that we have a very profitable year, it pays out a lot of compensation, and then we lose money and never make profits again. Any compensation paid by Lehman to GTS employees is based on the assumption that GTS continues to exist and continues to be profitable over time (there is no clawback). . . . KSK is mark to fair market value defined as the value that we believe we could sell the position for. Last year, the mark was included in GTS P&L for compensation

---

[10]   Product controllers checked the prices at which business desks marked their holdings.

purposes, last year and this year it is included in the P&L of
the Firm and is also included in the P&L for the leveraged
partnership. Choosing to exclude the mark for compensation
purposes when it is included for every other purpose seems
arbitrary to me.

This e-mail suggests that for Lehman's GTS group, Lehman's
practice was to include unrealized mark-to-market profits in net
revenue and compensation decisions and that there was concern,
given the size of the KSK transaction, that the policy should
possibly be reconsidered with respect to the particular
transaction.

Given that compensation was impacted by mark-to-market
valuations, incentives existed for traders and business units to
value investments highly so as to generate higher net revenues
and thus higher compensation. Similarly, given that the net
revenue-based compensation model was employed firm-wide,
write-downs on positions also had a negative effect on
compensation, creating incentive for employees and divisions to
avoid such write[-]downs, and/or retain unprofitable investments
solely to avoid revenue decreasing (and thus compensation-
decreasing) write-downs.

The Examiner reviewed thousands of electronic and hard copy
materials authored by Lehman employees which related to
compensation decisions, and also conducted dozens of interviews
of personnel involved in the compensation process. The Examiner
found no evidence that Lehman personnel deliberately engaged in
misconduct designed to exploit Lehman's compensation system.
However, Lehman's net revenue-driven compensation structure—
a structure used by most of Lehman's peers, and which structure
is the subject of an ongoing national debate—naturally created
incentives for the maximization of short-term profits.[11]

QUESTIONS AFTER YOUR SECOND VIEW OF FINANCIAL FIRM COMPENSATION SYSTEM

Does the Lehman system seem wild, crazy, risk-inducing, and nutty? Or
does it seem carefully crafted and carefully administered?

---

[11]   8 Report of Anton R. Valukas, Examiner, dated March 11, 2010 and filed in the Lehman
Brothers bankruptcy, *In re Lehman Brothers Holdings, Inc.*, Chapter 11 Case No. 08-13555 (JMP),
U.S. Bankruptcy Court, Southern District of New York, Appx. 11 at 1–35 (footnotes omitted).

Do you like the system of providing the majority of compensation (almost 70%) in restricted stock units that did not provide officers or employees with stock they could actually sell until five years after the award?[12] Do you agree with the Examiner's judgment that "Lehman's schedules were still focused on short-term performance (five years or less)"? What would constitute long term? And why would anyone work for an employer if 70% of the compensation was deferred for more than five years?

What about the notion that net revenues could be increased by a mark-to-market profit in year one, even though the investment might decline and be sold by Lehman in a later year for a smaller profit or even for a loss? How would you adjust the compensation system to prevent that result? What if the value of the investment simply decreased in year two but the firm did not sell the asset? Is the system fair and appropriate if the year one mark-to-market increase is included in compensation computations in year one and the year two mark-to-market decrease is included in compensation computations in year two or the ultimate loss is included in the compensation computations in the year in which the investment loss is realized?

What is the relationship between compensation and risk management? That is, suppose that the Lehman compensation system did encourage risk-taking. If the firm had religiously enforced its several risk metrics and if it had not consciously increased the amount of risk that it was willing to take as measured by those metrics, would that have sufficiently controlled risk? That is, if one aspect of corporate governance induces risk in order to make profit, is it sufficient that another aspect of corporate governance reduces or controls risk in order to avert loss? Or does every aspect of governance have to depress risk?

One final set of facts needs mention. Many of the leaders of the companies that failed or nearly failed owned stock in those companies that was, before the crisis hit, worth millions and millions of dollars. In some part, those holdings reflected company-imposed limitations on sale of equity. For example, as set out above, Lehman prohibited each member of its Executive Committee from selling in 2008 more than 20% of the equity in the firm that the executive held, as measured by the value of all the executive's holdings (including not only shares owned outright but also

---

[12]   Here is a description of the Lehman restricted stock units:

For 2007, the equity award is in the form of restricted stock units ("RSUs") for all employees and will be granted in early December. Each RSU represents the conditional right to receive one share of Lehman Brothers Holdings Inc. common stock five years after the grant date, on or about November 30, 2012. You can consider the RSUs as shares of Lehman Brothers common stock which you will be entitled to receive at that time, provided you meet certain terms and conditions. The 2007 RSUs cannot be sold, traded, or pledged for that five-year period.

Lehman Bros., 2007 Equity Award Program 1 (2007), https://www.jenner.com/lehman/docs/debtors/LBEX-AM%205641408-5641416.pdf.

RSUs). But some leaders of companies that ran into trouble did not sell all of the stock they *could* sell. When the price of their companies' stock declined, they suffered huge losses.

The New York Times reported that Bear Stearns chairman James Cayne kept the "vast bulk of his 5.6 million shares" through that company's decline and, while his holdings had been worth over $1 billion in early 2007, he sold them in 2008—after Bear's troubles—for $61 million.[13] The Times similarly reported that Richard Fuld, the Lehman CEO, held stock in his company worth $827.1 million in January 2007 that was worth only $2.3 million on September 19, 2008.[14]

One possibility is that the compensation systems could not have contributed to the credit crisis at these firms because the executive at the top of each had so much to lose by long-term risk—the destruction of his enormous wealth—that he would never have deliberately sanctioned excessive risk.

As suggested in the Lehman Examiner's report, an article co-authored by Lucian Bebchuk, Alma Cohen, and Holger Spamann argues against this theory.[15] Bebchuk and his co-authors conclude that both Fuld and Cayne came out ahead, during the period 2000–2008 when you compare (a) the value of each CEO's equity in his company at the beginning of 2000 against (b) the sum of (i) the value of the equity when the firm collapsed, plus (ii) the cash bonuses that each received over that time, plus (iii) the net cash[16] that each received from selling shares over that period.

As to Cayne at Bear, Bebchuk and his colleagues estimate that the CEO's equity holdings at the beginning of 2000 were worth $360,277,489.[17] Against that amount, Cayne had by the time his firm was sold a total of $388,254,070—in the value remaining in the Bear stock that he held at that time, plus the cash bonuses that he received over the 2000–2008 period, plus the net cash from his sales of Bear stock over those years.[18] Similarly, as Bebchuk and his co-authors calculate it, Fuld at Lehman started 2000 with equity in his company worth $300,768,127.[19] While his stock was worth virtually nothing when Lehman filed for bankruptcy in

---

[13]   Landon Thomas, Jr., *Down $900 Million or More, the Chairman of Bear Sells*, N.Y. TIMES, Mar. 28, 2008, http://www.nytimes.com/2008/03/28/business/28bear.html?_r=0.

[14]   *The Shareholders at the Top*, N.Y. TIMES, Sept. 21, 2008, http://query.nytimes.com/gst/fullpage.html?res=9C0DE4DD143BF932A1575AC0A96E9C8B63.

[15]   Lucian Bebchuk, et al., *The Wages of Failure: Executive Compensation at Bear Stearns and Lehman 2000–2008*, 27 YALE J. REG. 257 (2010).

[16]   Bebchuk and his colleagues defined net cash as the difference between the gross proceeds on sales in each year minus the amount in that year that the CEO paid for stock, either by exercising options or by purchasing shares in the open market. *Id.* at 268.

[17]   *Id.* at 272, 282 tbl.5.

[18]   *Id.* at 281 tbl.4.

[19]   *Id.* at 282 tbl.5.

2008, Fuld had, over the 2000–2008 time frame, received cash bonuses and net cash from his sales of Lehman stock equal to $522,730,780.[20]

The Bebchuk article's point is simply that even though the two CEOs lost a great deal of wealth when their companies failed, the compensation systems at their companies still might have provided them incentives to seek short-term gains through transactions that would not benefit long-term shareholders:

> [O]ur analysis indicates that the cases of Bear Stearns and Lehman provide (if anything) a basis for concerns about the incentives executives had. The analysis indicates that the design of the firms' performance-based compensation did not produce a tight alignment of executives' interests with long-term shareholder value. Rather, the design provided executives with substantial opportunities (of which they made considerable use) to take large amounts of compensation based on short-term gains off the table and retain it even after the drastic reversal of the two companies' fortunes.[21]

Nevertheless, Bebchuk and his fellow researchers concede that "the executives would have made much more had the firms not collapsed,"[22] and that "the executives holding so many shares at the time of the collapse indicates that they had not foreseen in 2007 (or early 2008) that such a collapse was around the corner."[23] At another point, they say that "the fact that the executives did not sell in 2007 all the shares they were free to sell indicates that they did not anticipate that a collapse of their firms was around the corner."[24] And the researchers acknowledge that, given their equity holdings, "[t]here can be little doubt that the . . . executives had strong reasons to prefer that their companies survive."[25]

Ultimately, Bebchuk and his colleagues appear to argue that if the Bear and Lehman compensation systems had been set up differently, Cayne and Fuld would have suffered more and that, as it was, they could take large risks with asymmetric outcomes—if the risks paid off for their companies, they would increase their wealth even more, but if the risks brought disaster to their companies, they would still have the plentiful money that they extracted—through cash bonuses and stock sales—over the time that the risks were run.

---

[20]   *Id.* at 281 tbl.4. Bebchuk and his colleagues make similar findings with aggregate figures for the other four named executive officers at Bear, and at Lehman. *Id.* at 281 tbl.4, 282 tbl.5.

[21]   *Id.* at 274.

[22]   *Id.* at 261.

[23]   *Id.* at 264.

[24]   *Id.* at 274.

[25]   *Id.* at 264.

QUESTIONS ON THE BEBCHUK ANALYSIS

When it is all said and done, what do you make of the Bebchuk piece? Does it change your mind about equity holdings as a means of incentivizing executives to avoid undue risk (however you define that term)?

Bebchuk and his co-authors criticize the Lehman and Bear schemes, which permitted sales of equity five years after a compensation equity award, as permitting "all long-serving executives . . . to unload the equity incentives awarded to them five years earlier," thereby giving the executives "ample reason to pay close attention to and place considerable weight on their companies' short-term stock prices."[26] But if the Bear or Lehman CEO caused his company to take an unduly risky action to increase short-term stock price in order to sell equity that he had been awarded five years earlier, wouldn't he have endangered the value of the equity that he could sell the next year, and the year after that?

Are Bebchuk et al. simply observing, in the end, that anyone who is very, very wealthy may be less risk averse simply for that reason? Does that, in turn, mean that a company should design its compensation system so that no executive gets wealthy while he or she is still working there? Would you work for a company that deliberately designed its compensation system so that you would not become wealthy?

If five years is not long term for Bebchuk, what is? Should we define long term as the average or median length of time shareholders of NYSE companies hold a stock position (perhaps excluding from the computations holding periods for high-frequency traders)? Should we define it as the 75th or 80th or 90th percentile of such holding periods? Is it until retirement? Until death?

B. REQUIRED DISCLOSURES AT ALL PUBLIC COMPANIES ABOUT RISK AND COMPENSATION

The credit crisis spawned two sets of reforms—both related to risk management. The first set mandated increased disclosure about risk management. The second set of reforms—restricted to the financial industry—required companies to expressly connect compensation to risk management. This section looks at the disclosure reforms.

In December 2009, the SEC adopted what it called proxy disclosure enhancements.[27] Among other things, the new disclosure rules required

---

[26]   *Id*. at 270.

[27]   Proxy Disclosure Enhancements; Final Rule, 74 Fed. Reg. 68,334 (Dec. 23, 2009) [Proxy Risk Management Disclosures].

each public company to include, in its Compensation Discussion and Analysis,[28] a "Narrative Disclosure of the Company's Compensation Policies and Practices as They Relate to the Company's Risk Management."[29] The SEC described this new disclosure so:

> To the extent that risks arising from the [company's] compensation policies and practices for its employees are reasonably likely to have a material adverse effect on the [company], discuss the [company's] policies and practices of compensating its employees, including non-executive officers, as they relate to risk management practices and risk-taking incentives. While the situations requiring disclosure will vary depending on the particular [company] and compensation policies and practices, situations that may trigger disclosure include, among others, compensation policies and practices: at a business unit of the company that carries a significant portion of the [company's] risk profile; at a business unit with compensation structured significantly differently than other units within the [company]; at a business unit that is significantly more profitable than others within the [company]; at a business unit where compensation expense is a significant percentage of the unit's revenues; and that vary significantly from the overall risk and reward structure of the [company], such as when bonuses are awarded upon accomplishment of a task, while the income and risk to the [company] from the task extend over a significantly longer period of time. The purpose of this paragraph(s) is to provide investors material information concerning how the [company] compensates and incentivizes its employees that may create risks that are reasonably likely to have a material adverse effect on the [company]. While the information to be disclosed pursuant to this paragraph(s) will vary depending upon the nature of the [company's] business and the compensation approach, the following are examples of the issues that the [company] may need to address for the business units or employees discussed:
>
>> (1) [t]he general design philosophy of the [company's] compensation policies and practices for employees whose behavior would be most affected by the incentives established by the policies and practices, as such policies and practices relate to or affect risk taking by employees on behalf of the [company], and the manner of their implementation;

---

[28]   SEC regulations require proxy statements to include an elaborate disclosure of executive compensation, called the Compensation Discussion and Analysis.

[29]   Proxy Risk Management Disclosures, *supra* note 27, at 68,335–38.

(2) [t]he [company's] risk assessment or incentive considerations, if any, in structuring its compensation policies and practices or in awarding and paying compensation;

(3) [h]ow the [company's] compensation policies and practices relate to the realization of risks resulting from the actions of employees in both the short term and the long term, such as through policies requiring claw backs or imposing holding periods;

(4) [t]he [company's] policies regarding adjustments to its compensation policies and practices to address changes in its risk profile;

(5) [m]aterial adjustments the [company] has made to its compensation policies and practices as a result of changes in its risk profile; and

(6) [t]he extent to which the [company] monitors its compensation policies and practices to determine whether its risk management objectives are being met with respect to incentivizing its employees.[30]

This requirement was strangely limited, as it only applied if the company admitted to "risks arising from the [company's] compensation policies and practices for its employees [that] are reasonably likely to have a material adverse effect on the [company]." The adopting release specifically stated that

disclosure under the amendments is only required if the compensation policies and practices create risks that are reasonably likely to have a material adverse effect on the company.[31]

Moreover, the rule did "not require a company to make an affirmative statement that it has determined that the risks arising from its compensation policies and practices are not reasonably likely to have a material adverse effect on the company."[32] But the rule did focus on one concern that we will see again: that compensation schemes could reward short-term behavior (such as "bonuses . . . awarded upon the accomplishment of a task") that produces risks that might mature over a long period of time ("while the income and risk to the [company] extend over a significantly longer period of time").

---

30   *Id.* at 68,363–64 (codified at 17 C.F.R. § 229.402(s)).

31   *Id.* at 68,337.

32   *Id.* at 68,338.

The 2009 proxy changes also required companies to "disclose the extent of the board's role in the risk oversight of the [company], such as how the board administers its oversight function, and the effect that this has on the board's leadership structure."[33] The SEC envisioned that such disclosure

> might address questions such as whether the persons who oversee risk management report directly to the board as whole, to a committee, such as the audit committee, or to one of the other standing committees of the board; and whether and how the board, or board committee, monitors risk.[34]

The SEC had more ideas about this disclosure:

> We were persuaded by commenters who noted that risk oversight is a key competence of the board, and that additional disclosures would improve investor and shareholder understanding of the role of the board in the organization's risk management practices.[1] Companies face a variety of risks, including credit risk, liquidity risk, and operational risk. . . . [D]isclosure about the board's involvement in the oversight of the risk management process should provide important information to investors about how a company perceives the role of its board and the relationship between the board and senior management in managing the material risks facing the company. This disclosure requirement gives companies the flexibility to describe how the board administers its risk oversight function, such as through the whole board, or through a separate risk committee or the audit committee, for example. Where relevant, companies *may want to address whether the individuals who supervise the day-to-day risk management responsibilities report directly to the board as a whole or to a board committee or how the board or committee otherwise receives information from such individuals.*[35]

The italicized portion of this passage suggests another theme: that a company's risk management cadre should have greater influence, as it would if it periodically addressed the board or submitted reports to the board.

All public companies must make the disclosures that these regulations set out when they seek proxies to vote in director elections.[36]

———————————

---

[33]   *Id.* at 68,365 (codified at 17 C.F.R. § 229.407(h)).

[34]   *Id.* at 68,344.

[35]   *Id.* at 68,345 (emphasis added).

[36]   17 C.F.R. § 240.14a-101, Item 7(b) & (c); Item 8(a).

QUESTIONS ON THE RISK MANAGEMENT DISCLOSURES

Do you think that conditioning the requirement to discuss the relationship of compensation to risk-taking on a company's acknowledgment that "risks arising from the [company's] compensation policies and practices ... are reasonably likely to have a material adverse effect on the [company]" took the bite out of the regulation, especially since a company would not, in order to avoid any disclosure, have to affirmatively state that its policies and practices were *not* reasonably likely to have that effect? Is such a regulation nevertheless useful because it at least gets each company thinking about the relationship between compensation and risk-taking and, even if not reporting it, determining that its compensation policies and practices are not likely to hurt the company in a material way?

Does the requirement that each company disclose the board's role in risk management serve a useful purpose? Will it lead only to general statements of no help to either investors or regulators?[37] Will that requirement, again however, perhaps prompt boards to think about their appropriate risk management role and to engage in substantive discussions with management about risk that otherwise would not have occurred?

Is it appropriate (and, if so, helpful) for the SEC to suggest that risk management personnel within a public company have direct access to the board? As a matter of psychology, if the board has to listen to, or read papers prepared by the risk management personnel (whose job it is, after all, to caution against at least some risks), is that enforced attention to risk likely to temper the board's enthusiasm for risky strategies, projects, and transactions that top management recommends? Do you think it would have made a difference at Lehman, where the board understood that company was increasing its risk appetite limit?

C. REFORMS AIMED AT COMPENSATION IN FINANCIAL COMPANIES

Overview. The government is forcing complex and far-reaching compensation change in the financial industry. We will look, in order, at (i) statutory provisions in the Dodd-Frank Wall Street Reform and Consumer Protection Act, signed into law on July 21, 2010 ("Dodd-Frank"), governing financial institution compensation; (ii) the 2010 "guidance" provided by financial regulators; (iii) the rules that the regulators proposed in 2011, but did not adopt, to implement the Dodd-Frank provisions; (iv) the effect of this regulatory thinking on large bank compensation, as disclosed in 2012

---

[37]   For an example of such a disclosure see Intel Corp., Definitive Proxy Statement, Schedule 14A (filed Apr. 4, 2016) at 20-21.

and 2013 proxy statements; and (v) the 2016 revision to the proposed rules, approval of which was pending when this book went to print.

Statute. Section 956 of Dodd-Frank reads:

(a) ENHANCED DISCLOSURE AND REPORTING OF COMPENSATION ARRANGEMENTS.

> (1) IN GENERAL. Not later than 9 months after the date of enactment of this title, the appropriate Federal regulators jointly shall prescribe regulations or guidelines to require each covered financial institution to disclose to the appropriate Federal regulator the structures of all incentive-based compensation arrangements offered by such covered financial institutions sufficient to determine whether the compensation structure—
>
> > (A) provides an executive officer, employee, director, or principal shareholder of the covered financial institution with excessive compensation, fees, or benefits; or
> >
> > (B) could lead to material financial loss to the covered financial institution.
>
> (2) RULES OF CONSTRUCTION. Nothing in this section shall be construed as requiring the reporting of the actual compensation of particular individuals. Nothing in this section shall be construed to require a covered financial institution that does not have an incentive-based payment arrangement to make the disclosures required under this subsection.

(b) PROHIBITION ON CERTAIN COMPENSATION ARRANGEMENTS. Not later than 9 months after the date of enactment of this title, the appropriate Federal regulators shall jointly prescribe regulations or guidelines that prohibit any types of incentive-based payment arrangement, or any feature of any such arrangement, that the regulators determine encourages inappropriate risks by covered financial institutions—

> (1) by providing an executive officer, employee, director, or principal shareholder of the covered financial institution with excessive compensation, fees, or benefits; or
>
> (2) that could lead to material financial loss to the covered financial institution.

(c) STANDARDS. The appropriate Federal regulators shall—

> (1) ensure that any standards for compensation established under subsections (a) or (b) are comparable to the standards established under section of the Federal Deposit Insurance

Act (12 U.S.C. 2 1831p-1) for insured depository institutions; and

(2) in establishing such standards under such subsections, take into consideration the compensation standards described in section 39(c) of the Federal Deposit Insurance Act (12 U.S.C. 1831p-9 1(c)).

(d) ENFORCEMENT. The provisions of this section and the regulations issued under this section shall be enforced under section 505 of the Gramm-Leach-Bliley Act and, for purposes of such section, a violation of this section or such regulations shall be treated as a violation of subtitle A of title V of such Act.

(e) DEFINITIONS. As used in this section—

(1) the term "appropriate Federal regulator" means the Board of Governors of the Federal Reserve System, the Office of the Comptroller of the Currency, the Board of Directors of the Federal Deposit Insurance Corporation, the Director of the Office of Thrift Supervision, the National Credit Union Administration Board, the Securities and Exchange Commission, the Federal Housing Finance Agency; and

(2) the term "covered financial institution" means—

(A) a depository institution or depository institution holding company, as such terms are defined in section 3 of the Federal Deposit Insurance Act (12 U.S.C. 1813);

(B) a broker-dealer registered under section 15 of the Securities Exchange Act of 1934 (15 U.S.C. 78o);

(C) a credit union, as described in section 19(b)(1)(A)(iv) of the Federal Reserve Act;

(D) an investment advisor, as such term is defined in section 202(a)(11) of the Investment Advisers Act of 1940 (15 U.S.C. 80b-2(a)(11));

(E) the Federal National Mortgage Association;

(F) the Federal Home Loan Mortgage Corporation; and

(G) any other financial institution that the appropriate Federal regulators, jointly, by rule, determine should be treated as a covered financial institution for purposes of this section.

(f) EXEMPTION FOR CERTAIN FINANCIAL INSTITUTIONS. The requirements of this section shall not apply

to covered financial institutions with assets of less than
$1,000,000,000.[38]

Note, first, that this section applies only to "covered financial institutions"
but that this term includes banks, bank holding companies, and broker-
dealers with assets of $1 billion or more. Since all of the traditional
investment banks converted to bank holding companies during the credit
crisis, the section covers all the major investment houses like Goldman
Sachs, as well as Bank of America, JPMorgan, and Citigroup. Note, second,
that subpart (a) simply requires reporting. Note, third, however, that
subpart (b) mandates prohibitions by the banking authorities (and, for
broker-dealers, by the SEC) against both (i) "any types of incentive-based
payment arrangement, or any feature of any such arrangement that the
regulators determine encourages inappropriate risks . . . by providing an
executive officer, employee, director, or principal shareholder . . . with
excessive compensation, fees, or benefits" and (ii) "any types of incentive-
based payment arrangement, or any feature of any such arrangement, that
the regulators determine encourages inappropriate risks . . . that could
lead to material financial loss to the covered financial institution." This is
direct substantive federal regulation of compensation.

*The banking authorities' 2010 guidance on sound incentive
compensation policies.* Shortly before Dodd-Frank became law in July 2010,
the federal banking authorities (which included the Office of the
Comptroller of the Currency [the "OCC"], the Board of Governors of the
Federal Reserve System [the "Fed"], the Federal Deposit Insurance
Corporation [the "FDIC"], and the Office of Thrift Supervision [the "OTS";
and together with the OCC, the Fed, and the FDIC, the "Agencies"]) issued
Guidance on Sound Incentive Compensation Policies in June 2010, after
reviewing comments on proposed guidance they had published in October
2009.[39] While the Agencies styled the publication "guidance," the
regulators said that they would be "actively monitor[ing] the actions taken
by banking organizations in this area" and "[w]here appropriate, the
Agencies will take supervisory or enforcement action to ensure that
material deficiencies that pose a threat to the safety and soundness of the
organization are promptly addressed."[40] As a result, financial firms subject
to the "guidance" would be foolish to ignore it and, effectively, will have to
at least bend in its direction.

The guidance attributed the credit crisis in part to compensation
practices that encouraged individuals within financial institutions to
engage in excessively risky transactions and to receive compensation for

---

[38]   124 Stat. 1376, 1905–06 (codified at 12 U.S.C. § 5641).

[39]   Guidance on Sound Incentive Compensation Policies, 75 Fed. Reg. 36,395, 36,396 (June
25, 2010) [Banking Guidance]. The guidance applied to, among others, bank holding companies
like Bank of America. *Id.* at 36,398.

[40]   *Id.* at 36,413.

doing so—compensation that was based on short-term gains on transactions, without regard to the risks that the transactions posed for the banks' long-term health.

> Compensation practices were not the sole cause of the financial crisis, but they certainly were a contributing cause—a fact recognized by 98 percent of the respondents to a survey of banking organizations engaged in wholesale banking activities conducted in 2009 by the Institute of International Finance and publicly by a number of individual financial institutions.[41]

* * *

> [O]ffering large payments to managers or employees to produce sizable increases in short-term revenue or profit—without regard for the potentially substantial short or long-term risks associated with that revenue or profit—can encourage managers or employees to take risks that are beyond the capability of the financial institution to manage and control.[42]

The regulators concluded that simply designing compensation to align the interests of executives with the interests of shareholders is not sufficient to control risks:

> Aligning the interests of shareholders and employees . . . is not always sufficient to protect the safety and soundness of a banking organization. Because banking organizations benefit directly or indirectly from the protections offered by the Federal safety net (including the ability of insured depository institutions to raise insured deposits and access the Federal Reserve's discount window and payment services), shareholders of a banking organization in some cases may be willing to tolerate a degree of risk that is inconsistent with the organization's safety and soundness. Thus, a review of incentive compensation arrangements and related corporate governance practices to ensure that they are effective from the standpoint of shareholders is not sufficient to ensure they adequately protect the safety and soundness of the organization.[43]

The regulators also asserted that banks cannot adequately control risk through risk management techniques that do not address compensation:

> A number of commenters expressed the view that increased controls could mitigate a lack of balance in incentive compensation arrangements. Under this view, unbalanced incentive compensation arrangements could be addressed either

---

[41]   *Id.* at 36,398.

[42]   *Id.* at 36,396.

[43]   *Id.*

through the modification of the incentive compensation arrangements or through the application of additional or more effective risk controls to the business. The final guidance recognizes that strong and effective risk-management and internal control functions are critical to the safety and soundness of banking organizations. However, the Agencies believe that poorly designed or managed incentive compensation arrangements can themselves be a source of risk to banking organizations and undermine the controls in place. Unbalanced incentive compensation arrangements can place substantial strain on the risk-management and internal control functions of even well-managed organizations. Furthermore, poorly balanced incentive compensation arrangements can encourage employees to take affirmative actions to weaken the organization's risk-management or internal control functions.[44]

In other words, it is not sufficient to have hundreds of risk management professionals working throughout a bank (as Lehman had); multiple measures of risk with limits on each (as Lehman had); and processes in place to review exceptions to the limits (as Lehman had). Banks must adjust their compensation to reflect risk too.

The guidance organizes itself around three principles. The first principle requires "balanced risk-taking incentives." Here is part of the regulators' discussion of that principle:

Incentive compensation arrangements should balance risk and financial results in a manner that does not encourage employees to expose their organizations to imprudent risks.

Incentive compensation arrangements typically attempt to encourage actions that result in greater revenue or profit for the organization. However, short-run revenue or profit can often diverge sharply from actual long-run profit because risk outcomes may become clear only over time. Activities that carry higher risk typically yield higher short-term revenue, and an employee who is given incentives to increase short-term revenue or profit, without regard to risk, will naturally be attracted to opportunities to expose the organization to more risk.

An incentive compensation arrangement is balanced when the amounts paid to an employee appropriately take into account the risks (including compliance risks), as well as the financial benefits, from the employee's activities and the impact of those activities on the organization's safety and soundness. As an example, under a balanced incentive compensation arrangement,

---

[44]   *Id.* at 36,400.

two employees who generate the same amount of short-term revenue or profit for an organization should not receive the same amount of incentive compensation if the risks taken by the employees in generating that revenue or profit differ materially. The employee whose activities create materially larger risks for the organization should receive less than the other employee, all else being equal.

The performance measures used in an incentive compensation arrangement have an important effect on the incentives provided employees and, thus, the potential for the arrangement to encourage imprudent risk-taking. For example, if an employee's incentive compensation payments are closely tied to short-term revenue or profit of business generated by the employee, without any adjustments for the risks associated with the business generated, the potential for the arrangement to encourage imprudent risk-taking may be quite strong. Similarly, traders who work with positions that close at year-end could have an incentive to take large risks toward the end of a year if there is no mechanism for factoring how such positions perform over a longer period of time. The same result could ensue if the performance measures themselves lack integrity or can be manipulated inappropriately by the employees receiving incentive compensation.

On the other hand, if an employee's incentive compensation payments are determined based on performance measures that are only distantly linked to the employee's activities (e.g., for most employees, organization-wide profit), the potential for the arrangement to encourage the employee to take imprudent risks on behalf of the organization may be weak. For this reason, plans that provide for awards based solely on overall organization-wide performance are unlikely to provide employees, other than senior executives and individuals who have the ability to materially affect the organization's overall risk profile, with unbalanced risk-taking incentives.

Incentive compensation arrangements should not only be balanced in design, they also should be implemented so that actual payments vary based on risks or risk outcomes. If, for example, employees are paid substantially all of their potential incentive compensation even when risk or risk outcomes are materially worse than expected, employees have less incentive to avoid activities with substantial risk.[45]

---

[45]   *Id.* at 36,407–08.

* * *

[F]uture revenues that are booked as current income may not materialize, and short-term profit-and-loss measures may not appropriately reflect differences in the risks associated with the revenue derived from different activities (e.g., the higher credit or compliance risk associated with subprime loans versus prime loans).[12] In addition, some risks (or combinations of risky strategies and positions) may have a low probability of being realized, but would have highly adverse effects on the organization if they were to be realized ("bad tail risks"). While shareholders may have less incentive to guard against bad tail risks because of the infrequency of their realization and the existence of the Federal safety net, these risks warrant special attention for safety-and-soundness reasons given the threat they pose to the organization's solvency and the Federal safety net.

. . . Reliable quantitative measures of risk and risk outcomes ("quantitative measures"), where available, may be particularly useful in developing balanced compensation arrangements and in assessing the extent to which arrangements are properly balanced. However, reliable quantitative measures may not be available for all types of risk or for all activities, and their utility for use in compensation arrangements varies across business lines and employees. The absence of reliable quantitative measures for certain types of risks or outcomes does not mean that banking organizations should ignore such risks or outcomes for purposes of assessing whether an incentive compensation arrangement achieves balance. For example, while reliable quantitative measures may not exist for many bad-tail risks, it is important that such risks be considered given their potential effect on safety and soundness. As in other risk-management areas, banking organizations should rely on informed judgments, supported by available data, to estimate risks and risk outcomes in the absence of reliable quantitative risk measures.

. . . [At large banking organizations (LBOs[46]),] [s]imulation analysis of incentive compensation arrangements is one way of

---

[12] Importantly, the time horizon over which a risk outcome may be realized is not necessarily the same as the stated maturity of an exposure. For example, the ongoing reinvestment of funds by a cash management unit in commercial paper with a one-day maturity not only exposes the organization to one-day credit risk, but also exposes the organization to liquidity risk that may be realized only infrequently.

46   The guidance defined large banking organizations to "include, in the case of banking organizations supervised by (i) the Federal Reserve, large, complex banking organizations as identified by the Federal Reserve for supervisory purposes; (ii) the OCC, the largest and most complex national banks as defined in the Large Bank Supervision booklet of the Comptroller's Handbook; (iii) the FDIC, large complex insured depository institutions (IDIs); and (iv) the OTS,

[assessing in advance of implementation whether such arrangements are likely to provide balanced risk-taking incentives]. Such analysis uses forward-looking projections of incentive compensation awards and payments based on a range of performance levels, risk outcomes, and levels of risks taken. This type of analysis, or other analysis that results in assessments of likely effectiveness, can help an LBO assess whether incentive compensation awards and payments to an employee are likely to be reduced appropriately as the risks to the organization from the employee's activities increase.

. . . .

. . . Four methods are often used to make compensation more sensitive to risk. These methods are:

[1] *Risk Adjustment of Awards:* The amount of an incentive compensation award for an employee is adjusted based on measures that take into account the risk the employee's activities may pose to the organization. Such measures may be quantitative, or the size of a risk adjustment may be set judgmentally, subject to appropriate oversight.

[2] *Deferral of Payment:* The actual payout of an award to an employee is delayed significantly beyond the end of the performance period, and the amounts paid are adjusted for actual losses or other aspects of performance that are realized or become better known only during the deferral period.[13] Deferred payouts may be altered according to risk outcomes either formulaically or judgmentally, subject to appropriate oversight. To be most effective, the deferral period should be sufficiently long to allow for the realization of a substantial portion of the risks from employee activities, and the measures of loss should be clearly explained to employees and closely tied to their activities during the relevant performance period.

[3] *Longer Performance Periods:* The time period covered by the performance measures used in determining an employee's award is extended (for example, from one year to two or more years). Longer performance periods and deferral of payment

---

the largest and most complex savings associations and savings and loan holding companies." *Id.* at 36,400 n.9.

[13] The deferral-of-payment method is sometimes referred to in the industry as a "clawback." The term "clawback" also may refer specifically to an arrangement under which an employee must return incentive compensation payments previously received by the employee (and not just deferred) if certain risk outcomes occur. Section 304 of the Sarbanes-Oxley Act of 2002 (15 U.S.C. § 7243), which applies to chief executive officers and chief financial officers of public banking organizations, is an example of this more specific type of "clawback" requirement.

are related in that both methods allow awards or payments to be made after some or all risk outcomes are realized or better known.

[4] *Reduced Sensitivity to Short-Term Performance:* The banking organization reduces the rate at which awards increase as an employee achieves higher levels of the relevant performance measure(s). Rather than offsetting risk-taking incentives associated with the use of short-term performance measures, this method reduces the magnitude of such incentives. This method also can include improving the quality and reliability of performance measures in taking into account both short-term and long-term risks, for example improving the reliability and accuracy of estimates of revenues and long-term profits upon which performance measures depend.[14] [47]

The regulators further stressed that where the evaluation of risk depended on the judgment of managers, such evaluation should be controlled by "policies and procedures that describe how managers are expected to exercise that judgment."[48] They also recognized that equity compensation might be "helpful in restraining the risk-taking incentives of senior executives and other . . . employees whose activities may have a material effect on the overall financial performance of the organization," but would not be as likely to restrain risk by "lower-level . . . employees . . . because [they] are unlikely to believe that their actions will materially affect the organization's stock price."[49]

For the top officers at LBOs,

[i]ncentive compensation arrangements . . . are likely to be better balanced if they involve deferral of a substantial portion of the executives' incentive compensation over a multi-year period in a way that reduces the amount received in the event of poor performance, substantial use of multi-year performance periods, or both. Similarly, the compensation arrangements for senior executives at LBOs are likely to be better balanced if a significant portion of the incentive compensation of these executives is paid in the form of equity-based instruments that vest over multiple years, with the number of instruments ultimately received

---

[14]   Performance targets may have a material effect on risk-taking incentives. Such targets may offer employees greater rewards for increments of performance that are above the target or may provide that awards will be granted only if a target is met or exceeded. Employees may be particularly motivated to take imprudent risk in order to reach performance targets that are aggressive, but potentially achievable.

[47]   *Id.* at 36,408–09.

[48]   *Id.* at 36,409.

[49]   *Id.* at 36,409–10.

dependent on the performance of the organization during the deferral period.[50]

The regulators came out against "golden parachutes" and "golden handshakes":

> Arrangements that provide for an employee (typically a senior executive), upon departure from the organization or a change in control of the organization, to receive large additional payments or the accelerated payment of deferred amounts without regard to risk or risk outcomes can provide the employee significant incentives to expose the organization to undue risk. For example, an arrangement that provides an employee with a guaranteed payout upon departure from an organization, regardless of performance, may neutralize the effect of any balancing features included in the arrangement to help prevent imprudent risk-taking.

> Banking organizations should carefully review any such existing or proposed arrangements (sometimes called "golden parachutes") and the potential impact of such arrangements on the organization's safety and soundness. In appropriate circumstances an organization should consider including balancing features—such as risk adjustment or deferral requirements that extend past the employee's departure—in the arrangements to mitigate the potential for the arrangements to encourage imprudent risk-taking. . . .

> [At LBOs:] Provisions that require a departing employee to forfeit deferred incentive compensation payments may weaken the effectiveness of the deferral arrangement if the departing employee is able to negotiate a "golden handshake" arrangement with the new employer.[16] This weakening effect can be particularly significant for senior executives or other skilled employees at LBOs whose services are in high demand within the market.

> Golden handshake arrangements present special issues for LBOs and supervisors. For example, while a banking organization could adjust its deferral arrangements so that departing employees will continue to receive any accrued deferred compensation after departure (subject to any clawback or malus[17]), these changes

---

[50]   *Id.* at 36,410.

[16]   Golden handshakes are arrangements that compensate an employee for some or all of the estimated, non-adjusted value of deferred incentive compensation that would have been forfeited upon departure from the employee's previous employment.

[17]   A malus arrangement permits the employer to prevent vesting of all or part of the amount of a deferred remuneration award. Malus provisions are invoked when risk outcomes are

could reduce the employee's incentive to remain at the organization and, thus, weaken an organization's ability to retain qualified talent, which is an important goal of compensation, and create conflicts of interest. Moreover, actions of the hiring organization (which may or may not be a supervised banking organization) ultimately may defeat these or other risk-balancing aspects of a banking organization's deferral arrangements. LBOs should monitor whether golden handshake arrangements are materially weakening the organization's efforts to constrain the risk-taking incentives of employees. The Agencies will continue to work with banking organizations and others to develop appropriate methods for addressing any effect that such arrangements may have on the safety and soundness of banking organizations.[51]

The regulators recognized that none of the guidance policies would do any good unless officers and employees realized how risk-taking actions affected their compensation:

> In order for the risk-sensitive provisions of incentive compensation arrangements to affect employee risk-taking behavior, the organization's employees need to understand that the amount of incentive compensation that they may receive will vary based on the risk associated with their activities. . . . Where feasible, an organization's communications with employees should include examples of how incentive compensation payments may be adjusted to reflect projected or actual risk outcomes.[52]

FIRST QUESTIONS ON THE GUIDANCE

A lot of this seems to make sense, doesn't it? But are you comfortable with the federal government getting involved in this degree of detail in compensation matters at individual companies?

Does your answer to the last question depend on whether maturation of risk at financial institutions might trigger payments of federal money to deposit holders or other parties (for example through the FDIC)?

In a company like Bank of America, does this guidance—enforced through bank examinations and possible sanctions—make the federal regulators larger players in compensation decisions than shareholders? Than outside

---

worse than expected or when the information upon which the award was based turns out to have been incorrect. Loss of unvested compensation due to the employee voluntarily leaving the firm is not an example of malus as the term is used in this guidance.

[51]   *Id.*

[52]   *Id.*

compensation consultants? Than compensation committees? Are you comfortable with that development?[53]

Why didn't shareholders and compensation committees insist, before the credit crisis, that compensation arrangements be designed to control risk to the same extent as suggested by guidance? Does their failure to do so call into question the entire traditional scheme of corporate governance?

Is it the place of the federal government to make the overall judgment that risk management controls apart from compensation are insufficient to control high-risk activities and that instead, risk adjustments must be an inherent part of compensation arrangements too?

Does any of this address the level of risk that a bank can or should take? If not, does it make sense?

The guidance identifies, as the second of its three principles, "compatibility [of incentive compensation policies and practices] with effective controls and risk-management."[54] Among other things, this principle suggests a role for risk management personnel in setting incentive compensation and evaluating its effectiveness in controlling risk:

> [B]anking organizations should have policies and procedures that ensure that risk-management personnel have an appropriate role in the organization's processes for designing incentive compensation arrangements and for assessing their effectiveness

---

[53]   The Federal Reserve Board undertook a review of incentive compensation practices at 25 large and complex banking organizations in late 2009. BOARD OF GOVERNORS OF THE FEDERAL RESERVE SYSTEM, INCENTIVE COMPENSATION PRACTICES: A REPORT ON THE HORIZONTAL REVIEW OF PRACTICES AT LARGE BANKING ORGANIZATIONS 1 (2011). The resulting report observed that many of the firms had already taken steps to adjust incentive awards for risk:

> For example, senior executives now have more than 60 percent of their incentive compensation deferred on average, higher than illustrative international guidelines agreed by the Financial Stability Board, and some of the most senior executives have more than 80 percent deferred with additional stock retention requirements after deferred stock vests.
>
> . . . .
>
> An example of a leading-edge practice that is now used by a few firms is including in internal profit measures used in incentive compensation awards a charge for liquidity risk that takes into account stressed conditions.
>
> . . . .
>
> Almost all firms now use vehicles for some employees that adjust downward the amount of deferred incentive compensation that is paid if losses are large.

Id. at 1–2. But the report stated that "every firm needs to do more," *id.* at 1, and that "[t]he Federal Reserve will continue to work with these firms through the supervisory process to ensure improvement and progress are sustained." *id.* at 3. This suggested that the Fed would act as an uber-consultant, with the power to enforce its recommendations through banking sanctions.

[54]   Banking Guidance, *supra* note 39, at 36,410.

in restraining imprudent risk-taking.[18] Ways that risk managers might assist in achieving balanced compensation arrangements include, but are not limited to, (i) reviewing the types of risks associated with the activities of covered employees; (ii) approving the risk measures used in risk adjustments and performance measures, as well as measures of risk outcomes used in deferred-payout arrangements; and (iii) analyzing risk-taking and risk outcomes relative to incentive compensation payments.[55]

As the regulators saw it, because of their critical role, the "risk-management personnel involved in the design, oversight, and operation of incentive compensation arrangements should have appropriate skills and experience needed to effectively fulfill their [duties]," and their compensation "should be sufficient to attract and retain" risk-management personnel with those skills and experience.[56] Moreover, "to help preserve the independence of their perspectives, the incentive compensation received by risk-management and control personnel staff should not be based substantially on the financial performance of the business units that they review. Rather, the performance measures used in the incentive compensation arrangements for these personnel should be based primarily on the achievement of the objectives of their functions (e.g., adherence to internal controls)."[57]

As its third principle, the guidance posits that financial firms "should have strong and effective corporate governance to help ensure sound compensation practices."[58] Specifically,

[g]iven the key role of senior executives in managing the overall risk-taking activities of an organization, the board of directors of a banking organization should directly approve the incentive compensation arrangements for senior executives. The board also should approve and document any material exceptions or adjustments to the incentive compensation arrangements established for senior executives and should carefully consider and monitor the effects of any approved exceptions or adjustments on the balance of the arrangement, the risk-taking incentives of the senior executive, and the safety and soundness of the organization.[59]

---

[18] Involvement of risk-management personnel in the design and monitoring of these arrangements also should help ensure that the organization's risk-management functions can properly understand and address the full range of risks facing the organization.

55   *Id.* at 36,411.

56   *Id.*

57   *Id.*

58   *Id.* at 36,412.

59   *Id.* (footnote omitted).

The board of directors of a banking organization should closely monitor incentive compensation payments to senior executives and the sensitivity of those payments to risk outcomes. In addition, if the compensation arrangement for a senior executive includes a clawback provision, then the review should include sufficient information to determine if the provision has been triggered and executed as planned.

The board of directors of a banking organization should seek to stay abreast of significant emerging changes in compensation plan mechanisms and incentives in the marketplace as well as developments in academic research and regulatory advice regarding incentive compensation policies. . . .

The board of an LBO or other organization that uses incentive compensation to a significant extent should receive and review, on an annual or more frequent basis, an assessment by management, *with appropriate input from risk-management personnel*, of the effectiveness of the design and operation of the organization's incentive compensation system in providing risk-taking incentives that are consistent with the organization's safety and soundness. These reports should include an evaluation of whether or how incentive compensation practices may increase the potential for imprudent risk-taking.

The board of such an organization also should receive periodic reports that review incentive compensation awards and payments relative to risk outcomes on a backward-looking basis to determine whether the organization's incentive compensation arrangements may be promoting imprudent risk-taking. Boards of directors of these organizations also should consider periodically obtaining and reviewing simulation analysis of compensation on a forward-looking basis based on a range of performance levels, risk outcomes, and the amount of risks taken.

. . . .

The board of directors of a banking organization should have, or have access to, a level of expertise and experience in risk-management and compensation practices in the financial services industry that is appropriate for the nature, scope, and complexity of the organization's activities. This level of expertise may be present collectively among the members of the board, may come from formal training or from experience in addressing these issues, including as a director, or may be obtained through advice received from outside counsel, consultants, or other experts with expertise in incentive compensation and risk-management. The board of directors of an organization with less complex and extensive incentive compensation arrangements may not find it necessary or appropriate to require special board expertise or to retain and use outside experts in this area.

In selecting and using outside parties, the board of directors should give due attention to potential conflicts of interest arising from other dealings of the parties with the organization or for other reasons. The board also should exercise caution to avoid allowing outside parties to obtain undue levels of influence. While the retention and use of outside parties may be helpful, the board retains ultimate responsibility for ensuring that the organization's incentive compensation arrangements are consistent with safety and soundness.[60]

SECOND QUESTIONS ON THE GUIDANCE

Once again, the federal government prescribes for the board of directors. Some of the prescriptions simply repeat current protocols or "best practices"—e.g., that the board should approve the compensation packages for top executives. But other prescriptions and suggestions may require significant changes—e.g., that the risk management personnel should have direct access to the board to address the relationship between risk and compensation, and that the board should consider reviewing (i) backward-looking analyses of how compensation affected risk at the company and (ii) forward-looking simulations of how compensation would reward risk-taking in the future. Are you comfortable with this level of direction, or suggestion?

What about the guidance that the board should have, or have access to, risk management expertise? At first blush, that seems to make sense. And the guidance says that the board might find the expertise in its own members or outside consultants. But does this mean that bank regulators should criticize a board because the members of the compensation committee do not understand—even with the help of an expert—a complicated "simulation" of how compensation would reward risk-taking? What if the directors at a financial institution take the view that forward-looking simulations are baloney? Should the banking regulators be able to effectively override this judgment (which for most companies would be inconsistent with the business judgement rule and the general deference to the board in fulfilling its fiduciary duties)?

Compensation rules proposed in 2011 by financial industry regulators collectively. Dodd-Frank's section 956 contemplates *mandatory* rules for "covered financial institutions" ("CFIs")—including banks, bank holding

---

[60]   *Id.* at 36,412–13 (emphasis added).

companies, and broker-dealers with assets of $1 billion or more. So, after providing the 2010 guidance, the bank regulators and the SEC jointly issued proposed rules in 2011.[61] This section discusses that proposal. Instead of adopting those rules, the regulators issued revised proposed rules in 2016. The last section of this chapter discusses that revised proposal.

Under the 2011 proposed rules, a CFI would have submitted to its primary regulator (the SEC for broker-dealers and, for example, the Fed for a bank holding company) an annual report on incentive-based compensation sufficient to permit the regulator to assess "whether the structure or features of those arrangements provide or are likely to provide covered persons with excessive compensation, fees, or benefits . . . or could lead to material financial loss to the [CFI]."[62] If the CFI had total consolidated assets of $50 billion or more, the report would also have had to describe the incentive-based compensation policies and procedures applied to the company's executive officers and any other employees that the board had identified as "hav[ing] the ability to expose the [CFI] to possible losses that are substantial in relation to the [CFI's] size, capital, or overall risk tolerance."[63] The reports by all CFIs would also have had to include "specific reasons why the [CFI] believes the structure of its incentive-based compensation plan does not encourage inappropriate risks by the [CFI] by providing covered persons with: (i) [e]xcessive compensation; or (ii) [i]ncentive-based compensation that could lead to a material financial loss to the [CFI]."[64]

The regulations would have *prohibited* "any type of incentive-based compensation arrangement, or any feature of any such arrangement, that encourages inappropriate risks by the [CFI] by providing a covered person with excessive compensation."[65] Thus, the proposed rules linked

---

[61]   Incentive-Based Compensation Arrangements, 76 Fed. Reg. 21,170 (Apr. 14, 2011).

[62]   *Id*. at 21,215 (SEC proposed 17 C.F.R. § 248.204(a)). The joint proposing release included regulations for each of the regulators, each set of which mirrored the others. This chapter cites only to the proposed SEC regulations (which would have added part 248 to Title 17 of the Code of Federal Regulations), but note that the proposed rules included the following definitions:

(c)   *Covered financial institution* meant, in the Office of the Comptroller of the Currency version of the proposed regulations, a national bank or a Federal branch or agency of a foreign bank that has total consolidated assets of $1 billion or more (21 C.F.R. § 42.3(c)), includes, in the Federal Reserve Board version of the proposed regulations, any bank holding company with total consolidated assets of $1 billion or more (12 C.F.R. § 236.3(c)), and, in the SEC version of the proposed regulations, means any broker or dealer or investment adviser registered with the SEC (17 C.F.R. § 248.203(c)).

(d)   *Covered person* meant any executive officer, employee, director, or principal shareholder of a covered financial institution in all three versions (21 C.F.R. § 42.3(d), 12 C.F.R. § 236.3(d), 17 C.F.R. § 248.203(c)).

Id. at 21,204, 21,206, 21,215.

[63]   *Id*. at 21,215–16 (SEC proposed 248.204(c)(3)). All parenthetical citations to the proposed regulations omit "17 C.F.R. § " so that proposed 17 C.F.R. § 248.204(c)(3) appears as 248.204(c)(3).

[64]   *Id*. at 21,216 (SEC proposed 248.204(c)(5)).

[65]   *Id*. (SEC proposed 248.205(a)(1)).

"excessive" compensation to risk. The rules would have defined "excessive compensation" generally and included a list of factors to apply that definition:

> (a) . . . . (2) *Standards.* An incentive-based compensation arrangement provides excessive compensation when amounts paid are unreasonable or disproportionate to the services performed by a covered person, taking into consideration:
>
> > (i) [t]he combined value of all cash and non-cash benefits provided to the covered person;
> >
> > (ii) [t]he compensation history of the covered person and other individuals with comparable expertise at the [CFI];
> >
> > (iii) [t]he financial condition of the [CFI];
> >
> > (iv) [c]omparable compensation practices at comparable [CFIs], based upon such factors as asset size, geographic location, and the complexity of the [CFI's] operations and assets;
> >
> > (v) [f]or postemployment benefits, the projected total cost and benefit to the [CFI];
> >
> > (vi) [a]ny connection between the individual and any fraudulent act or omission, breach of trust or fiduciary duty, or insider abuse with regard to the [CFI]; and
> >
> > (vii) [a]ny other factors the Commission determines to be relevant.[66]

The proposed rules also would have *prohibited* incentive-based compensation "that encourages inappropriate risks by the [CFI]," providing that "[a]n incentive-based compensation arrangement . . . does not comply with [this prohibition] unless it"

> (i) [b]alances risk and financial rewards, for example by using deferral of payments, risk adjustment of awards, reduced sensitivity to short-term performance, or longer performance periods;
>
> (ii) [i]s compatible with effective controls and risk management; and
>
> (iii) [i]s supported by strong corporate governance, including active and effective oversight by the [CFI's] board of directors or a committee thereof.[67]

---

[66]   *Id.* (SEC proposed 248.205(a)(2)).

[67]   *Id.* (SEC proposed 248.205(b)(1) & (2)).

So here it is. The "guidance" would have been turned into formal requirements. And presumably, the SEC would—for broker-dealers (as would the Fed for bank holding companies)—have assessed companies' compliance with the prohibitions against both excessive compensation and compensation schemes that encouraged inappropriate risk. This carried at least the potential for regulators to second-guess compensation committees or, through written interpretation or iterative decisions relating to one company after another, to effectively establish substantive standards for compensation.

But the 2011 proposal also included specific prescriptions. At CFIs with consolidated assets of $50 billion or more, the incentive compensation would have had to provide for

(A) [a]t least 50 percent of the annual incentive-based compensation of [each] executive officer to be deferred over a period of no less than three years, with the release of deferred amounts to occur no faster than on a pro rata basis; and

(B) [t]he adjustment of the amount required to be deferred under [subpart (A) immediately above] to reflect actual losses or other measures or aspects of performance that are realized or become better known during the deferral period.[68]

The proposed regulations also had assignments for the boards of CFIs with consolidated assets of $50 billion or more, with the language echoing, again, the earlier bank regulator "guidance":

(A) The board of directors, or a committee thereof, of the [CFI] shall identify those covered persons (other than executive officers) who individually have the ability to expose the [CFI] to possible losses that are substantial in relation to the [CFI's] size, capital, or overall risk tolerance. These covered persons may include, for example, traders with large position limits relative to the [CFI's]overall risk tolerance and other individuals who have the authority to place at risk a substantial part of the capital of the [CFI];

(B) The incentive-based compensation arrangement for any covered person identified pursuant to [subpart (A) immediately above] must be approved by the board of directors, or a committee thereof, of the [CFI] and such approval must be documented;

(C) The board of directors, or committee thereof, may not approve the incentive-based compensation arrangement for any covered person identified pursuant to [subpart (A) above] unless the board or committee determines that the arrangement, including the method of paying compensation under the arrangement,

---

[68]   *Id.* (SEC proposed 248.205(b)(3)(i)).

effectively balances the financial rewards to the covered person and the range and time horizon of risks associated with the covered person's activities, employing appropriate methods for ensuring risk sensitivity such as deferral of payments, risk adjustment of awards, reduced sensitivity to short-term performance, or longer performance periods; and

(D) In fulfilling its duties under [subpart (C) immediately above], the board of directors or committee thereof must evaluate the overall effectiveness of the balancing methods used in the identified covered person's incentive-based compensation arrangements in reducing incentives for inappropriate risk taking by the identified covered person considering the methods' suitability for balancing the full range of risks presented by that covered person's activities, and the methods' ability to make payments sensitive to all the risks arising from the covered person's activities, including those that may be difficult to predict, measure or model.[69]

Beyond this, the proposed regulations would have "prohibit[ed]" incentive-based compensation for officers or employees covered by the regulations at any CFI unless the compensation arrangements included "policies and procedures" to "monitor compliance" with these rules.[70] The "policies and procedures [would have been required], at a minimum" to

(1) [b]e consistent with the reporting requirements . . . of this part and prohibitions [against excessive compensation and compensation that could lead to material loss at a CFI];

(2) [e]nsure that risk-management, risk-oversight, and internal control personnel have an appropriate role in the [CFI's] processes for designing incentive-based compensation arrangements and for assessing their effectiveness in restraining inappropriate risk-taking;

(3) [p]rovide for the monitoring by a group or person independent of the covered person, where practicable in light of the [CFI's] size and complexity, of incentive-based compensation awards and payments, risks taken, and actual risk outcomes to determine whether incentive-based compensation payments for covered persons, or groups of covered persons, are reduced to reflect adverse risk outcomes or high levels of risk taken;

(4) [p]rovide for the [CFI's] board of directors, or committee thereof, to receive data and analysis from management and other sources sufficient to allow the board, or committee thereof, to

---

[69]   *Id.* (SEC proposed 248.205(b)(3)(ii)).

[70]   *Id.* at 21,216–17 (SEC proposed 248.206(a)).

assess whether the overall design and performance of the [CFI's] incentive-based compensation arrangements are consistent with [Dodd-Frank § 956];

(5) [e]nsure that documentation of the [CFI's] processes for establishing, implementing, modifying, and monitoring incentive-based compensation arrangements is maintained that is sufficient to enable the Commission to determine the [CFI's] compliance with [Dodd-Frank § 956 and the prohibitions in the regulations against excessive compensation and compensation that could lead to material financial loss by the CFI];

(6) [c]onsistent with [the special 50% deferral for a minimum of three years, applicable to incentive compensation for executive officers at CFIs with $50 billion or more in assets], where deferral is used in connection with an incentive-based compensation arrangement, provide for deferral of incentive-based compensation awards in amounts and for periods of time appropriate to the duties and responsibilities of the [CFI's] covered persons, the risks associated with those duties and responsibilities, and the size and complexity of the [CFI] and provide that the deferral amounts paid are adjusted to reflect actual losses or other measures or aspects of performance that are realized or become better known during the deferral period; and

(7) [s]ubject any incentive-based compensation arrangement to a corporate governance framework that provides for ongoing oversight by the board of directors or a committee thereof, including the approval by the board of directors or a committee thereof of incentive-based compensation to executive officers.[71]

QUESTIONS ON THE 2011 PROPOSED REGULATIONS

Wouldn't these regulations have constituted direct federal regulation of compensation? While they purported to be limited by relating risk to amounts and structure of compensation, couldn't virtually any aspect of compensation be related to risk? Do you see any principled boundary?

Which would have been more intrusive—the general prohibitions against excessive compensation and compensation that could lead to material loss, each with standards or principles, or the express requirement for a minimum three-year deferral of at least 50% of the compensation for executive officers at large CFIs, with mandatory adjustment of payouts depending on losses during the deferral period?

----

[71]   *Id.* at 21,217 (SEC proposed 248.206(b)).

Even if risk management personnel should have some role in designing compensation, how large a role should that be? Should they also have a role in monitoring payments to ensure they are reduced to reflect adverse risk outcomes? Won't risk management professionals always be cautious? Might they be too cautious? Had these regulations been adopted, could a board have safely overruled a risk management recommendation on compensation?

If you like the idea of these proposed regulations for financial institutions, why not have them in place for all other public companies?

Even if such proposed regulations are not formally extended to companies outside the financial sector, should other companies' boards look to the regulations as some kind of norm or set of best practices?

Do the authors of the proposed regulations appear to trust the shareholders or the boards? Or do they largely see the boards as means to implement compensation principles and standards that right-thinking people or "experts" (i.e., the regulators) decide are best?

Large bank compensation after the 2010 guidance and the 2011 proposed regulations. The 2010 guidance—and likely the thinking reflected in the 2011 proposed rules—had a real effect on the industry. A review of 2012 and 2013 proxy statements filed by 23 publicly traded financial companies provides provocative information.[72] As suggested by the comment set out in note 53 above,

> [t]he initial guidance provided by the Federal Reserve in 2010 . . . was principles-based. However, as the Federal Reserve has gone through multiple rounds of reviews with the LCBO (Large Complex Banking Organization) group and its first rounds of reviews with the next tier of banks with assets >$50 billion, the Federal Reserve appears to be more prescriptive in its interactions with financial institutions.

> [O]ver the past three years, as risk management processes have vastly improved, the Federal Reserve has become progressively more detailed in the compensation-related input they provide to regulated institutions. The Federal Reserve has provided guidance to companies on specific areas of executive compensation. . . .[73]

Probably the most interesting findings reveal a conflict between the regulators and shareholders, with the regulators pressuring banks to

---

[72] COMPENSATION ADVISORY PARTNERS, INFLUENCE OF FEDERAL RESERVE ON COMPENSATION DESIGN IN FINANCIAL SERVICES: AN ANALYSIS OF COMPENSATION DISCLOSURES OF 23 LARGE BANKING ORGANIZATIONS (2013). Quotations from this report reprinted with permission from Compensation Advisory Partners, LLC.

[73] *Id.* at 2.

reduce the sensitivity of compensation to bank performance, as measured by investors through such metrics as a comparison of the total shareholder return ("TSR," which includes dividends plus stock price appreciation) from holding one bank's stock as opposed to the TSR from holding another bank's stock.

Compensation that simply increases with stock price may reward poor management at company A, when the stock prices of all companies in A's industry increase but the increase in A's stock price is below the average or median increase of the stock prices of other industry participants. For that reason, recent compensation design often links at least some significant portion of top executive compensation to the *relative* performance of his or her company against the industry's performance.

The federal bank regulators have urged the banks to avoid such comparative measures because they might encourage executives to take undue risks:

> The Federal Reserve is concerned that relative measures may reward companies for underperformance and could lead companies to take on excessive risk to "chase after" leading performers. They prefer absolute performance objectives. . . .[74]

This has put the regulators at odds with shareholders, and the big banks have pushed back against this regulator pressure, by combining absolute and relative measures:

> Historically, shareholders and other external constituents have pushed for more companies to use relative performance measures as they are viewed as a "truer" measure of company performance that is less subject to "sandbagging" by management or the influence of market or other external factors (all boats rise . . .). In addition, shareholder advisors rely heavily on relative performance comparisons in making Say on Pay vote recommendations.

> Based on our analysis, this is an area where companies have been reluctant to make a shift. About 60% of the companies that we analyzed continue to use relative performance measures as part of their long-term incentive design. It is a fairly even mix between relative TSR and relative Return on Equity, with a few companies

---

[74] *Id.* at 2. The regulators have two other reasons for opposing relative measures:

Relative performance measures do not communicate a clear goal to management teams, as the performance objective is a moving target, based not only on the firm's performance, but also on the performance of its peers[.]

Performance can be strong on a relative basis, but be poor on an absolute basis (for example, the best performing banks in 2008 and 2009 were still poor performers on an absolute basis)[.]

Id. at 5.

using other financial metrics. The majority of companies now combine the relative measures with an absolute financial performance measure [i.e., one measured only by the financial number generated at the executive's bank], most typically Return on Equity to provide the appropriate risk-balancing the Federal Reserve has been seeking.[75]

In a similar vein, the bank regulators oppose long-term incentives ("LTIs") that include very high upside rewards. Thus, many LTIs set a target award to be paid if the company achieves a target number for a financial measure, then also provide that the award increases if the company exceeds that target. The amount of the maximum award is often expressed as a percentage of the target award. The federal regulators oppose very large maximum awards because of concern that executives may take undue risks to reach the financial results that will yield the very large maximum payouts. The regulators instead favor discretionary determination of LTI awards, at least to some extent.

All of this puts the regulators again at odds with shareholders, who like incentives encouraging executives to reach "stretch" goals and who dislike discretionary LTI awards because shareholders believe boards may hand them out regardless of performance, and because discretionary awards fail to convey to executives what they should do in order to get extra pay and therefore do not provide a clear incentive. The financial firms have responded to regulator pressure by reducing the multiple by which maximum LTI awards can exceed targets.

An area where the Federal Reserve appears to be surprisingly prescriptive is in encouraging companies to reduce incentive plan upside opportunities. From a compensation perspective, this runs counter to designs that are preferred by shareholders who expect a strong pay-for-performance program. The Federal Reserve is opposed to formulaic plans that can lead to substantial payouts when performance is strong, but does not necessarily understand that discretionary plans can lead to comparable payouts. A potentially unintended consequence of this point of view is to encourage companies to reduce the transparency of incentive plan design leading to reduced line-of-sight for executives. An important tenet of compensation theory is that executives have a clear understanding of the process and approach that will be used to determine their incentive. Given the Federal Reserve's preference for discretion, the relationship between performance results and incentive payouts may be weakened, particularly at higher performance levels. Again, regulatory guidance may lead to a major misalignment with shareholders.

---

[75] *Id.*

Shareholders also prefer incentive plans with direct linkage between payouts and pre-established performance objectives. They are concerned that discretion is frequently used to the advantage of executives and at the expense of shareholders. However, recognizing the concerns of the Federal Reserve, *firms have reduced the maximum opportunity from 200% of target (a broad industry company standard) to 150% or 125% of target* so they can continue to address shareholder desires for a more formulaic structure while mitigating Federal Reserve concerns about leverage.[76]

The regulators also have pressured banks to reduce or eliminate stock options as a form of compensation, on the theory that options provide upside reward without downside cost and so encourage risky business decisions. Option compensation has declined at large banks:

> To state it plainly, the Federal Reserve does not like stock options as an incentive vehicle. Its concerns are similar to those raised by other critics of stock options in the past. Stock options may encourage executives to take on additional risk to increase the stock price, but do not focus management on avoiding decreases in the stock price. From a shareholder perspective, stock options have historically been an attractive vehicle because executives only receive value when the stock price appreciates. Many Compensation Committee members also like that stock options do not require the negotiation of goal setting associated with long-term performance plans. When used in combination with ownership guidelines and post-exercise holding requirements, many of the concerns with options can be addressed.

> Most companies in the financial services industry have recently reduced or eliminated the use of stock options (eliminated by Bank of America, BNY Mellon, Citigroup, Discover Financial, Goldman Sachs, PNC, Regions, and Wells Fargo; reduced by BB&T, Comerica, Fifth Third, Huntington Bancshares, KeyCorp, Northern Trust, and US Bancorp). We expect this trend to continue. Stock options have largely been replaced by

---

[76]   *Id.* at 4 (emphasis added). The survey showed other changes in large bank compensation practices—changes that shareholders may not oppose, such as (1) "includ[ing] corporate and individual risk assessments in the process for determining the size of annual incentive pools and individual awards" (*id.* at 4); (2) "add[ing] a risk-based vesting measure to what would otherwise be a time-vested award of stock options or restricted stock" (*id.* at 6); (3) "add[ing] a discretionary assessment of whether or not executives took inappropriate risks that could potentially lead to a material loss for the company and subject[ing] deferred compensation to a potential reduction or elimination based on this assessment" (*id.*); (4) employing "a quantitative threshold (e.g., a loss, or a return below a threshold level) that triggers a qualitative review that could lead to a reduction or elimination of outstanding deferred awards" (*id.*); and (5) imposing super-long holding periods for stock obtained as equity compensation, with "nearly 50% of LCBOs hav[ing] a requirement that executives hold a portion (typically 50%) of net after-tax shares to retirement" (*id.* at 7).

performance shares. While the Federal Reserve tends to like time-vested restricted stock, shareholders are not enamored by the vehicle as it is often viewed as a form of semi-guaranteed (i.e., non-performance-based) compensation.[77]

QUESTIONS ON THE BANK REGULATORS VERSUS SHAREHOLDERS

Should the federal bank regulators seek, by application of the guidance, to reduce the sensitivity of top executive compensation at publicly traded companies to financial performance measures that shareholders believe important?

Will investors be hurt by such actions or will they simply adjust the bank holding companies'[78] stock prices to account for the circumstance that executives at those companies may not try as hard as executives at other companies to take the actions that will improve stock performance?

Does all of this suggest that our traditional model of corporate governance should be expanded so that the participants include—at least in highly regulated industries—the regulators as well as boards, managements, and shareholders?

If so, what is the proper relationship between the regulators and the shareholders? Should the shareholders have some well-defined mechanism to make their views on compensation, even compensation at particular companies, known to the regulators? For example, should the currently non-binding say-on-pay votes be changed so that they have some *binding* effect on financial institutions, *and their regulators*?

Should the regulators, without any legal requirement to bend to stockholders' wishes, attempt to balance the interests of the shareholders against the responsibility to protect the financial system?

The revised 2016 proposed regulations. The regulators never adopted the rules that they proposed, in 2011, to implement the Dodd-Frank compensation provisions. Instead, in the spring of 2016, the regulators

---

[77]   *Id.* at 5. *See also*, for an analysis of options and banking risk, David F. Larcker, et al., *Follow the Money: Compensation, Risk, and the Financial Crisis*, Stanford Closer Look Series (Sept. 8, 2014), https://www.gsb.stanford.edu/sites/default/files/43_FinancialCrisis.pdf. And note that, as set out in Chapter 16, public companies overall have reduced the proportion of CEO compensation comprised of options.

[78]   Banks, like many large companies, operate largely through subsidiaries. The bank companies whose stock we can buy on the stock exchanges are bank holding companies, which then operate through banking and brokerage subsidiaries. Bank holding companies are regulated by the Federal Reserve.

proposed a revised set.[79] The new proposal is even more elaborate than the one the Agencies advanced in 2011.

It divides CFIs[80] into three categories, defined by average consolidated assets: Level 1 institutions, with assets of $250 billion or more; Level 2 institutions, with assets of $50 billion or more but less than $250 billion; and Level 3 institutions, with assets of $1 billion or more but less than $50 billion.[81] Similar to the 2011 proposal, the 2016 proposal defines "covered person" to include "any executive officer, employee, director, or principal shareholder who receives incentive-based compensation at a [CFI]."[82] But the new proposal breaks out two sets of officers and employees. It defines "senior executive officer" ("SEO") to include "a covered person who holds the title or, without regard to title, salary, or compensation, performs the function of one or more of the following positions at a [CFI]": the "[p]resident, chief executive officer, executive chairman, chief operating officer, chief financial officer, chief investment officer, chief legal officer, chief lending officer, chief risk officer, chief compliance officer, chief audit executive, chief credit officer, chief accounting officer, or head of a major business line or control function."[83] And the 2016 proposed rules include a new definition for "significant risk taker" ("SRT"), applicable to Level 1 and Level 2 CFIs only and summarized by the following table.

---

[79]   Incentive-Based Compensation Arrangements, 81 Fed. Reg. 37,670 (June 10, 2016) [2016 Compensation Proposal]. The proposed rules are largely identical for the different agencies, which include the Department of the Treasury, the Federal Reserve System, the FDIC, the National Credit Union Administration, and the SEC. As with the 2011 proposal, the regulated financial institutions to which the 2016 proposal would apply include banks, bank holding companies, registered broker-dealers, and investment advisers. *Id.* at 37,673, 37,684–85. This chapter cites only to the SEC rules, which would be added as a Part 303 to Title 17 of the Code of Federal Regulations.

[80]   The 2016 proposal refers to "covered institutions." *Id.* at 37,832 (SEC proposed 303.2(i)), while the 2011 proposal referred to "covered financial institutions," *see* note 62 *supra*. For consistency with the description of the 2011 proposal, this chapter continues to refer to these entities as "CFIs."

[81]   *Id.* at 37,832–33 (SEC proposed 303.2(b), (v)–(x)). All parenthetical citations to the proposed regulations omit "17 C.F.R. § " so that proposed 17 C.F.R. § 303.2(b), (v)–(x) appears as 303.2(b), (v)–(x).

[82]   *Id.* at 37,832 (SEC proposed 303.2(j)). A principal shareholder is "a natural person who, directly or indirectly, or acting through or in concert with one or more persons, owns, controls, or has the power to vote 10 percent or more of any class of voting securities of a [CFI]." *Id.* at 37,833 (SEC proposed 303.2(bb)).

[83]   *Id.* at 37,833 (SEC proposed 303.2(gg)). Note that this definition of senior executive officer is different from the definition of that same term in the TARP program discussed in Chapters Fifteen and Seventeen. As used in the description of the regulations proposed in 2016, the acronym "SEO" refers to senior executive officer as defined in the text to which this footnote attaches.

Definition of Significant Risk Taker[84]	
Level 1 CFI	Level 2 CFI
Covered person, other than an SEO, for whom incentive compensation comprised at least one-third of annual base salary plus incentive compensation for the last calendar year ended at least 180 days before the beginning of the relevant performance period	Covered person, other than an SEO, for whom incentive compensation comprised at least one-third of annual base salary plus incentive compensation for the last calendar year ended at least 180 days before the beginning of the relevant performance period
and who meets any of the following three criteria	
Is among the 5% highest paid individuals receiving incentive compensation last year (excluding SEOs), with pay measured as base salary plus incentive compensation	Is among the 2% highest paid individuals receiving incentive compensation last year (excluding SEOs), with pay measured as base salary plus incentive compensation
Or	Or
May commit or expose 0.5% or more of common equity tier 1 capital or (for a broker-dealer) 0.5% or more of tentative net capital	May commit or expose 0.5% or more of common equity tier 1 capital or (for a broker-dealer) 0.5% or more of tentative net capital
Or	Or
Is designated an SRT by the CFI, or by the regulating agency because of the individual's ability to expose the CFI to risks that could lead to material financial loss in relation to the CFI's size, capital, or overall risk tolerance	Is designated an SRT by the CFI, or the regulating agency because of the individual's ability to expose the CFI to risks that could lead to material financial loss in relation to the CFI' s size, capital, or overall risk tolerance

The new proposal would require all CFIs to "create annually and maintain" for at least seven years records that document the structure of all its incentive-based compensation arrangements and that, at a minimum, include (i) "copies of all incentive-based compensation plans

[and] a record of who is subject to each plan,"[85] with an "incentive-based compensation plan" defined as "a document setting forth terms and conditions governing the opportunity for and the payment of incentive-based compensation payments to one or more covered persons";[86] and (ii) "a description of how the incentive-based compensation program is compatible with effective risk management and controls."[87] In addition, each Level 1 and Level 2 CFI would have to create yearly and maintain for at least seven years records of (iii) SEOs and STRs "listed by legal entity, job function, organizational hierarchy, and line of business";[88] (iv) "incentive-based compensation arrangements" for SEOs and STRs, "including . . . [the] percentage of incentive-based compensation deferred and form of award,"[89] with an "incentive-based compensation arrangement" defined as "an agreement between a [CFI] and a covered person, under which the [CFI] provides incentive-based compensation to the covered person, including incentive-based compensation delivered through one or more incentive-based compensation plans";[90] (v) "any forfeiture and downward adjustments or clawback reviews and decisions" for SEOs and SRTs (discussed more below);[91] and (vi) "material changes to the [CFI's] incentive-based compensation arrangements and policies."[92] Level 1 and Level 2 CFIs would also have to "create and maintain records in a manner that allows for an independent audit of incentive-based compensation arrangements, policies, and procedures," and they would have to provide the records described in the immediately preceding sentence with the frequency, and in the form, requested by the regulator.[93]

The new proposal, like the older one, contains substantive regulation. As would the 2011 proposal, the 2016 proposal would forbid all CFIs from

---

[84]   *Id.* (SEC proposed 303.2(hh)). If the regulating agency determines that a Level 1 CFI's "activities, complexity of operations, risk profile, and compensation practices are similar to those of a Level 2 covered institution," the Level 1 CFI may vary the first of the three criteria by restricting it to the highest paid 2%. *Id.* at 37,834 (SEC proposed 303.2(hh)(4)). Common equity tier 1 capital is a technical banking term, and tentative net capital is a technical broker-dealer term. But the idea behind linking the definition of an SRT to these measures is, stated somewhat less technically, to include those who have "authority to commit or expose 0.5 percent or more of the [CFI's] capital." *Id.* at 37,692. This elaborate definition supplants the 2011 proposal's requirement that the board of directors identify those, other than executive officers, "hav[ing] the ability to expose the [CFI] to possible losses that are substantial in relation to the [CFI's] size, capital, or overall risk tolerance." *See* text accompanying note 63 *supra*. Here and elsewhere, the summary omits any description of the intricacies in the rules that deal with affiliated companies.

[85]   *Id.* at 37,835 (SEC proposed 303.4(f)).

[86]   *Id.* at 37,833 (SEC proposed 303.2(t)).

[87]   *Id.* at 37,835 (SEC proposed 303.4(f)).

[88]   *Id.* (SEC proposed 303.5(a)(1)).

[89]   *Id.* (SEC proposed 303.5(a)(2)).

[90]   *Id.* at 37,832–33 (SEC proposed 303.2(s)).

[91]   *Id.* at 37,835 (SEC proposed 303.5(a)(3)).

[92]   *Id.* at 37,835 (SEC proposed 303.5(a)(4)).

[93]   *Id.* (SEC proposed 303.5(b) & (c)).

using incentive pay that "encourages inappropriate risks" by either (i) providing "a covered person with excessive compensation, fees, or benefits" or (ii) employing any type of compensation arrangement or any feature that "could lead to material loss to the [CFI]."[94] Similar to the 2011 proposal, the 2016 proposal defines "excessive compensation" generally as "amounts paid [that] are unreasonable or disproportionate to the value of the services performed by a covered person" after taking into account "all relevant factors, including, but not limited to" the laundry list from 2011.[95] Similar to the one in 2011, the 2016 proposal provides that a compensation arrangement "encourages inappropriate risks that could lead to material loss to the [CFI]" unless it "[a]ppropriately balances risk and reward," "[i]s compatible with effective risk management and controls," and "[i]s supported by effective governance."[96] But under the 2016 proposal, balancing risk and reward would require that an incentive-based compensation "arrangement include[ ] financial and non-financial measures of performance, including considerations of risk-taking, that are relevant to a covered person's role within a [CFI] and to the type of business in which the covered person is engaged and that are appropriately weighted to reflect risk-taking," "allow non-financial measures of performance to override financial measures of performance when appropriate in determining incentive-based compensation," and provide that "[a]ny amounts to be awarded under the arrangement are subject to adjustment to reflect actual losses, inappropriate risks taken, compliance deficiencies, or other measures or aspects of financial and non-financial performance."[97] This substantive requirement, which did not appear in the 2011 proposal, applies to all CFIs.

While the Agencies' 2011 proposal would have required deferral of annual incentive compensation at CFIs with assets of $50 billion or more, their 2016 proposal is much more elaborate. It would establish deferral prescriptions for both SEOs and STRs at Level 1 and Level 2 CFIs. In doing so, the proposal would split incentive compensation into two categories: "qualifying incentive-based compensation," for which the performance period is less than three years, and "long-term incentive plan" compensation, for which the performance period is three years or more.[98] The following table sets out the scheme:

---

[94]   *Id.* at 37,834 (SEC proposed 303.4(a)).

[95]   *Id.* (SEC proposed 303.4(b)). While the list no longer includes the catchall referring to "[a]ny other factors that the [regulator] determines to be relevant," the list is non-exclusive.

[96]   *Id.* at 37,834–85(SEC proposed 303.4(c)).

[97]   *Id.* at 37,835 (SEC proposed 303.4(d)).

[98]   *Id.* at 37,833 (SEC proposed 303.2(y) & (cc)).

Required Minimum Deferral for Incentive-Based Compensation[99]			
Level of CFI/ Position of Individual	Type of Incentive Compensation	Minimum Percent That Must Be Deferred	Minimum Number of Years of Deferral
Level 1/SEO	Qualifying	60	4
Level 1/STR	Qualifying	50	4
Level 1/SEO	Long-Term Incentive	60	2
Level 1/STR	Long-Term Incentive	50	2
Level 2/SEO	Qualifying	50	3
Level 2/STR	Qualifying	40	3
Level 2/SEO	Long-Term Incentive	50	1
Level 2/STR	Long-Term Incentive	40	1

Since the proposal defines "deferral period" as the "period of time between the date a performance period ends and the last date on which the incentive-based compensation awarded for the performance period vests,"[100] a Level 1 CFI that computed it owed 100,000 performance shares to its CEO (who by definition is an SEO) at the end of a one-year performance period (an annual incentive award) would be able to transfer only 40,000 of those shares to the CEO immediately at the end of that period. The remaining 60,000 shares would then have to vest over the next four years.

Moreover, the proposed rules would control both the vesting schedule for deferred compensation at Level 1 and Level 2 CFIs and the composition of the pay that is deferred. Specifically, the 2016 proposal provides that vesting "may not" occur "faster than on a pro rata annual basis beginning no earlier than the first anniversary of the end of the performance period for which the amounts were awarded," and further provides that this schedule cannot be accelerated except in the case of death or disability.[101] Moreover, the deferred amount cannot consist of only equity but "must include substantial portions of both deferred cash and equity-like

---

[99]   *Id.* at 37,835–36 (SEC proposed 303.7(a)).
[100] *Id.* at 37,832 (SEC proposed 303.2(*l*)).
[101] *Id.* at 37,835–36 (SEC proposed 303.7(a)(1)(iii)(A) & (B), (a)(2)(iii)(A) & (B)).

instruments throughout the deferral period."[102] And the proposal would limit the extent to which options could count towards the required percentage deferred. In particular, "the total amount of . . . options [that are received for a performance period and] that may be used to meet the minimum deferral amount requirements . . . is limited to no more than 15 percent of the amount of total incentive-based compensation awarded to the [SEO or SRT] for that performance period."[103] The 2011 proposal did not contain either the requirement that both cash and equity be deferred or the limitation on counting options towards the required percentage of compensation deferred.

While the 2011 proposal included a general requirement to adjust deferred compensation to reflect actual losses, the 2016 proposal is much more elaborate. It would require that a Level 1 or Level 2 CFI have multiple opportunities to reduce incentive compensation in light of maturing risks. The CFI would have to structure incentive compensation so that it could reduce the amount at any time between the commencement of a performance period and the end of the deferral period. And the CFI would have to retain the ability to claw back incentive compensation under LTIs even after the deferral ended.

In particular, the Level 1 and Level 2 institutions would have to "place at risk of downward adjustment all of [an SEO's or SRT's] incentive-based compensation amounts not yet awarded for the current performance period, including amounts payable under long-term incentive plans" and "place at risk of forfeiture all unvested deferred incentive-based compensation of any [SEO or SRT], including unvested deferred amounts awarded under long-term incentive plans."[104] The Level 1 or Level 2 CFI would have to, at a minimum,

> consider forfeiture and downward adjustment . . . due to any of the following adverse outcomes at the [CFI]:
>
> (i) [p]oor financial performance attributable to a significant deviation from the risk parameters set forth in the [CFI's] policies and procedures;
>
> (ii) [i]nappropriate risk taking, regardless of the impact on financial performance;
>
> (iii) [m]aterial risk management or control failures;
>
> (iv) [n]on-compliance with statutory, regulatory, or supervisory standards that results in:

---

[102]   *Id.* at 37,836 (SEC proposed 303.7(a)(4)(i)). This assumes that the CFI issues equity.

[103]   *Id.* (SEC proposed 303.7(a)(4)(ii)).

[104]   *Id.* (SEC proposed 303.7(b)(1)).

(A) [e]nforcement or legal action against the [CFI] brought by a federal or state regulator or agency; or

(B) [a] requirement that the [CFI] report a restatement of a financial statement to correct a material error; and

(v) [o]ther aspects of conduct or poor performance as defined by the [CFI].[105]

The downward adjustment and forfeiture review would have to consider reducing compensation not only of an SEO or SRT "with direct responsibility" for the adverse outcome but also for an SEO or SRT who had "responsibility due to [his or her] role or position in the [CFI's] organizational structure . . . for the events related to the forfeiture and downward adjustment."[106] The 2016 proposal lays out six factors that the Level 1 or Level 2 CFI would have to consider in determining the amount of a downward adjustment or forfeiture: (i) "intent of the [SEO or SRT] to operate outside the risk governance framework approved by the [CFI's] board of directors or to depart from the [CFI's] policies and procedures"; (ii) the SEO's or SRT's "level of participation in, awareness of, or responsibility for the events triggering the . . . review"; (iii) "actions the [SEO or SRT] took or could have taken to prevent [those] events"; (iv) the "financial and reputational impact of [those] events . . . to the [CFI], the line or sub-line of business, and individuals involved, as applicable, including the magnitude of any financial loss and the cost of known or potential subsequent fines, settlements, and litigation"; (v) "causes of [those] events . . . including any decision-making by other individuals"; and (vi) "[a]ny other relevant information, including past behavior and past risk outcomes attributable to the [SEO] or [SRT]."[107]

The 2016 proposal also provides that Level 1 and Level 2 CFIs must include clawback provisions in incentive compensation arrangements permitting the institutions, at a minimum, to claw back incentive compensation "from a current or former" SEO or SRT for a period of "seven years following the date on which such compensation vests" if the CFI "determines that the [SEO or SRT] engaged in [(i) m]isconduct that resulted in significant financial or reputational harm to the [CFI]; [(ii) f]raud; or [(iii) i]ntentional misrepresentation of information used to determine the [SEO's or SRT's] incentive-based compensation."[108]

The 2016 proposal would regulate compensation substantively in three other ways not found in the 2011 proposal. First, we saw in the last section that regulators have applied supervisory pressure to institutions to reduce the percentage by which maximum incentive payments may exceed

---

[105]   *Id.* (SEC proposed 303.7(b)(2)).
[106]   *Id.* (SEC proposed 303.7(b)(3)).
[107]   *Id.* at 37,836–37 (SEC proposed 303.7(b)(4)).
[108]   *Id.* at 37,837 (SEC proposed 303.7(c)).

payments for target performance. The new proposal would prohibit a Level 1 or Level 2 CFI from paying an SEO—regardless of how high the performance—more than 125% of the target amount for the applicable incentive-based compensation and prohibits such a CFI from paying an SRT—regardless of how high the performance—more than 150% of the target amount for the applicable incentive-based compensation.[109] Second, the proposal would forbid a Level 1 or Level 2 CFI from "us[ing] incentive-based compensation measures that are based solely on industry peer performance comparisons."[110] The proposal would, however, permit the CFI to combine a relative performance measure with a measure unique to the CFI, such as that CFI's return on tangible common equity.[111] Third, the proposal would prohibit a Level 1 or Level 2 CFI from "provid[ing] incentive-based compensation to a covered person that is based solely on transaction revenue or volume without regard to transaction quality or compliance of the covered person with sound risk management."[112] Note that these last two prohibitions would apply to any officer, employee, or director at a Level 1 or Level 2 CFI who receives incentive compensation, not just SEOs and SRTs.[113]

Level 1 and Level 2 CFIs would also, under the 2016 proposal, have to meet more elaborate governance requirements. The compensation committees of such CFIs' boards would have to obtain input—"on the effectiveness of risk measures and adjustments used to balance risk and reward in incentive-based compensation arrangements"—from the audit and risk committees of the board "and [the] risk management function," which presumably means risk management professionals in the CFI.[114] Moreover, the compensation committee would have to receive, at least annually, both a written assessment from management and an "independent" written assessment from "the internal audit or risk management function of the [CFI], developed independently of the [CFI's] management"—with each assessment addressing "the effectiveness of the [CFI's] incentive-based compensation program and related compliance and control processes in providing risk-taking incentives that are consistent with the risk profile of the [CFI]."[115]

---

[109]   *Id.* (SEC proposed 303.8(b)).

[110]   *Id.* (SEC proposed 303.8(c)).

[111]   *Id.* at 37,735.

[112]   *Id.* at 37,837 (SEC proposed 303.8(d)).

[113]   *Id.* at 37,735.

[114]   *Id.* at 37,837 (SEC proposed 303.10(b)(1)).

[115]   *Id.* (SEC proposed 303.10(b)(2) & (3)).

The 2016 proposal contains other details, including, as examples, the requirement for Level 1 and Level 2 CFIs to "develop and implement policies and procedures . . . that . . . [s]pecify the substantive and procedural criteria for application of forfeiture and clawback . . . and . . . [e]nsure appropriate roles for risk management, risk oversight, and other control function personnel in the [CFI's] processes for [(i) d]esigning incentive-based compensation arrangements, and determining

QUESTIONS ON THE 2016 PROPOSED REGULATIONS

The regulators seem to have become more prescriptive over time. Certainly, they proposed much more elaborate rules in 2016 than in 2011. Do you like the detail of the 2016 proposal—including the differing minimum percentages and minimum years of deferrals for compensation paid to SEOs and SRTs at Level 1 and Level 2 CFIs?

Do you think the regulators, in the future, will delve ever more deeply into compensation inside financial institutions? Can you see any principled way for them to determine when they have done enough or to determine whether a particular detail should be left to the board of directors or compensation committee?

Should the proposed regulations have permitted adjustment of the deferral requirements (or other highly prescriptive provisions) based on the particular financial businesses in which a CFI participates?[116] Should they have permitted adjustment based on the strength of a CFI's board or based on the strength of a CFI's risk management personnel? If so, how would the strength of the board or risk management cadre be measured? Would any such adjustments likely produce disparate treatment for CFIs without easily explained or applied criteria—that is, without apparent justice? If such adjustments are not practical, does that illustrate a fundamental difficulty with centralized control of private companies by a government bureaucracy that is not responsible for managing a business?

Will all the deferrals of compensation and possible downward adjustments, forfeitures, and clawbacks reduce the value that individuals working at CFIs place on their compensation packages? Is that good because they will take fewer risks for such uncertain and chronologically distant pay? Is it bad because it will discourage talented men and women from working in this industry at all?

Should the government participate, in a similar detailed way, in the compensation decisions at companies in other important industries? If so, which ones? Should the government exercise this degree of detailed control in all publicly traded companies, regardless of industry?

---

awards, deferral amounts, deferral periods, forfeiture, downward adjustment, clawback, and vesting; and [(ii) a]ssessing the effectiveness of incentive-based compensation arrangements in restraining inappropriate risk-taking." *Id*. at 37,837–38 (SEC proposed 303.11(b) & (j)). The proposal also would require at Level 1 and Level 2 CFIs that the "individuals engaged in control functions [have] the authority to influence the risk-taking of the business areas they monitor" and "are compensated in accordance with the achievement of performance objectives linked to their control functions and independent of the performance of those business areas." *Id*. at 37,837 (SEC proposed 303.9(b)).

[116]   Note that the regulators can adjust the definition of SRT to some extent based on such factors. *See* note 84 *supra*.

To an extent, the 2016 proposed regulations would codify current practices.[117] If you have qualms about the detail into which the regulations reach, do your concerns diminish to the extent they require financial firms to continue doing what they are already doing? Or do you remain concerned because the guidance may have pushed the firms into current practice? Or are you nevertheless concerned that converting current practices into regulations could stifle innovation? How do you balance your concerns against the possibility that the proposed regulations might decrease the probability of another financial crisis?

---

[117] *See* 2016 Compensation Proposal, *supra* note 79, at 37,766–76 (analysis provided by the SEC of "Current Incentive-Based Compensation Practices," including many tables.

CHAPTER 20

EVALUATING THE REFORMS

■ ■ ■

It is vital to ask whether the reforms worked.

This Chapter Twenty considers that question in two stages. First, it asks whether reforms aimed at improving financial reporting have objectively improved that reporting and whether reforms aimed at improving executive compensation have objectively improved that compensation. Second, it asks whether the process by which the reforms were constructed was likely to yield useful law. The chapter does not attempt to provide definitive answers. It aims to stimulate your thinking.

A. DETERMINING OBJECTIVELY WHETHER THE REFORMS HAVE IMPROVED MATTERS

Whether the reforms aimed at better financial reporting have produced more reliable numbers. Both Enron and WorldCom restated their financial numbers. We already have the definition of a restatement under our belts. A company "restates" its financial numbers when, for example, the company publicly discloses in November of a year that the financial numbers it published in April for the first quarter of the year were materially wrong, and the company provides, in November, corrected (or as they say in the accounting world, "restated") financial numbers for the first quarter.

One way to determine whether the reforms aimed at improving financial reporting have worked is to examine restatements both before the reforms and after. Here is a table that we saw in Chapter Eighteen, showing the number of restatements by public companies (domestic and foreign), counted on a consistent basis over years that begin before Sarbanes-Oxley and extend through 2015:

2001[1]	625
2002	700
2003	788
2004	937
2005	1,574
2006	1,851
2007	1,271
2008	951
2009	834
2010	851
2011	844
2012	853
2013	871
2014	855
2015	737

It is hard to interpret these numbers. On the one hand, the number of restatements in recent years is *above* the pre-reform number in 2001. But that could result from better internal controls and better auditing *after* the reforms were put in place, with those better controls and that better auditing finding more material errors in financial statements.

We also see the number of restatements increasing in the first few years *after* the passage of Sarbanes-Oxley in 2002. But this may reflect the circumstance that the adoption of implementing regulations—and the dates to comply with those regulations—stretched out over several years.[2] The increase could result from companies finding and dealing with problems after more robust internal controls and more vigorous outside auditing took hold. If so, then perhaps the 2005 through 2007 figures should constitute our baseline because they reflect the true state of financial reporting before the reforms worked their effect. In that case, the

---

[1]   AUDIT ANALYTICS, 2015 FINANCIAL RESTATEMENTS: A FIFTEEN YEAR COMPARISON 5 (2016) (numbers in table above taken from Audit Analytics graph) [2016 RESTATEMENT STUDY]. Data on restatements in this report, set out in the text above and elsewhere, are used with permission from Audit Analytics.

[2]   Accelerated filers—public companies (1) with $75 million or more in equity held by non-affiliates, and that (2) had been a public company for at least 12 months, and (3) had filed at least one 10-K—were required to include management assessments of internal control over financial reporting ("ICFR") and an auditor's opinion on ICFR in annual reports on fiscal years ending after November 15, 2004. HAROLD S. BLOOMENTHAL, SARBANES-OXLEY ACT IN PERSPECTIVE § 3.21 (2016 ed.). Most of these companies would have first filed those reports in 2005.

decline in restatements after the 2005–2007 peak suggests that the reforms improved financial reporting.

In analyzing the restatement figures, we may have to consider the number of public companies over the time the figures cover. That number has declined over the post-reform years. Here is a table showing the decline[3]:

Number of Companies Listed on NASDAQ and NYSE				
	January 2003	January 2006	January 2010	January 2016
Domestic	5,138	4,638	4,394	4,343
Foreign	847	780	777	903
Total	5,985	5,418	5,171	5,246

We might decide to look not at the total number of restatements but the number of restatements per 100 public companies, or some similar figure. We might exclude foreign companies on the ground that the reforms did not fully apply to them.[4]

Even if we conclude, after making an adjustment for the numbers of public companies in different years, that there has been a meaningful reduction in the number of restatements from 2005–2007 to today (as we likely would since the percentage decline in restatements exceeds the percentage decline in public companies), we then must ask whether the reforms we have considered *caused* the reduction. For example, while we have not discussed it, Arthur Andersen, which audited both Enron and WorldCom and was before 2002 one of the largest accounting firms in the United States, was destroyed by a federal criminal indictment based on Arthur Andersen's work for Enron.[5] Perhaps the complete destruction of

---

[3]   World Federation of Exchanges, Monthly Reports, Number of Listed Companies, Equity 1.2 Tables, http://www.world-exchanges.org/home/index.php/statistics/monthly-reports.

[4]   SOX reforms applied to foreign issuers registered under section 12 of the Securities Exchange Act, although there were some exceptions. *See* Roberta S. Karmel, *The Securities and Exchange Commission Goes Abroad to Regulate Corporate Governance*, 33 STETSON L. REV. 849, 861–85 (2004); Ethiopis Tafara, U.S. Securities and Exchange Commission, Acting Director, Office of International Affairs, *Addressing International Concerns under the Sarbanes-Oxley Act* (June 10, 2003), https://www.sec.gov/news/speech/spch061003et.htm. Other country-specific factors could have affected the frequency of restatements by overseas issuers.

[5]   A report on consolidation in the auditing industry stated:

In 2001, Arthur Andersen LLP (Andersen) was the fourth-largest public accounting firm in the United States, with global net revenues of over $9 billion. On March 7, 2002, Andersen was indicted by a federal grand jury and charged with obstructing justice for destroying evidence relevant to investigations into the 2001 financial collapse of Enron. At the time of its indictment, Andersen performed audit and attest services for about 2,400 public companies in the United States, including many of the largest public companies in the world.

. . . .

that firm—rather than any or all of the reforms—has caused the remaining outside auditors to be more careful. And, if they have been more careful as a result, that additional care may be significantly responsible for the decline in restatements.

But perhaps our focus solely on the number of restatements is wrong to begin with. Perhaps we should focus on the severity of the restatements. For example, we might consider whether the average amount of income restated has been going up or down. For this analysis, I do not have figures stretching back to 2001, but only to 2007:

Average Income Adjustment Per Restatement by Companies on Amex, NASDAQ, or NYSE[6]	
Year	Average Income Adjustment
2007	-$3,640,142[7]
2008	-$6,125,967
2009	-$4,624,605
2010	-$5,934,222
2011	-$12,941,142
2012	-$5,831,183
2013	-$3,210,297
2014	-$3,113,747
2015	-$5,200,144

These figures do not permit us to compare pre-reform financial reporting with post-reform reporting because they do not cover the pre-reform years. So perhaps they are not helpful at all. Or maybe they reveal that, whatever else may be said about the reforms, they are not *constantly* pushing the severity of restatements down. The average amount of income restated has bounced around considerably, with the ending figure above the beginning figure. On the other hand, perhaps averages are always susceptible to wide variation from outlier data points. Perhaps median numbers would be more informative.

Between October 2001 and December 2002, 1,085 public companies audited by Andersen switched to a new auditor of record.

U.S. GENERAL ACCOUNTING OFFICE, GAO-03-864, REPORT TO THE SENATE COMMITTEE ON BANKING, HOUSING, AND URBAN AFFAIRS AND THE HOUSE COMMITTEE ON FINANCIAL SERVICES: PUBLIC ACCOUNTING FIRMS MANDATED STUDY ON CONSOLIDATION AND COMPETITION 101 (2003).

Arthur Andersen dissolved in 2002. *Id.* at 12.

[6]   2016 RESTATEMENT STUDY, *supra* note 1, at 6 (table above reprinting Audit Analytics table with minor formatting changes).

[7]   A negative number means that the companies, on average, reported income that was too high and that the restatements, on average, reduced the companies' income by the amount the table includes.

Other numbers might be revealing, such as the average number of days covered by a restatement or the average number of days between the announcement that previous numbers were materially false and the filing of corrected, restated numbers. Here are tables reporting those numbers, with the first set of figures stretching back before Sarbanes-Oxley's enactment in 2002.

Average Number of Days Covered by Restatement[8]	
2001	472
2002	564
2003	592
2004	639
2005	743
2006	718
2007	638
2008	513
2009	493
2010	515
2011	514
2012	546
2013	570
2014	533
2015	498

We see a decline after 2005–2006. But the 2015 number is above the 2001 number.

---

[8]   2016 RESTATEMENT STUDY, *supra* note 1, at 7 (numbers in table above taken from Audit Analytics graph). For example, if the restatement covered the second quarter only of one year, the number for the particular company making the restatement would be the number of days in that quarter.

Average Number of Days to File a Restatement Following Announcement That Numbers Were Wrong[9]	
2007	30.11
2008	16.40
2009	19.97
2010	4.14
2011	13.93
2012	10.62
2013	5.45
2014	4.54
2015	3.22

This last table shows a pronounced drop-off after 2007. While the figures vary a good deal after that year, they are all significantly below the 2007 figure. Moreover, the figures for 2013–2015 are quite low.

QUESTIONS ON RESTATEMENT NUMBERS

What do you think? Are any of these numbers revealing? Do they permit you to reach a conclusion as to the efficacy of the SOX reforms?

Can you think of some other way to slice restatement numbers that would be more helpful?

Assume, for the moment, that the numbers set out above show the reforms have helped. Assume also that factors other than the reforms— such as the demise of a huge accounting firm as a result of its involvement with Enron—did not cause the changes in restatements that we applaud.

How would we then decide *which* reforms caused this improvement? For example, would we give all the credit to the requirement for internal control over financial reporting ("ICFR") and the related requirements for management assessment of ICFR and the outside audit (at least for the larger companies) of ICFR? Or would we attribute the success to the creation and operation of the PCAOB? Or maybe to reform of the outside accounting firms that conduct the audits (i.e., the elimination of whole categories of services that they can provide to audit clients, the requirement to rotate the lead and review auditors every five years, and

---

[9]   *Id.* at 9 (numbers in table above taken from Audit Analytics graph).

the prohibition against compensating audit partners for cross-selling non-audit services to audit clients)?

_____

QUESTIONS ON PINPOINTING THE REFORMS
THAT MADE A DIFFERENCE

If you conclude that the reforms helped, is it worth the effort to find out which ones drove the improvement?

Do you want to find out whether the ICFR and, in particular, the management assessment, and even more particularly, the required outside audit of ICFR were responsible? Is that important because those reforms added significant cost?

Do you want to try to fine-tune the reforms, to obtain the best combination of cost and benefit? Or is that just too much to ask, or too picky?

_____

Another way to test the success of financial reporting reforms is to determine the cost to investors from restatements before the reforms and the cost to investors from restatements after the reforms. One way to measure that cost is by the decrease in market capitalization resulting from the announcement of restatements. Thus, suppose that public company A has 10 million shares of common stock outstanding. Suppose that A's stock is selling at $9/share on the day before A announces a restatement and drops to $8/share on the day after A announces a restatement. We might initially conclude that investors lost a total of $10 million as a result of the restatement—i.e., a loss of $1 on each of the 10 million shares.

But wait. How do we know that the $1 drop per share was caused entirely by the announcement of the restatement? What if the market as a whole went down on the day that A disclosed its intention to restate? Or what if the stocks of all companies in A's industry declined on that day? How will we separate out the decline caused by the restatement announcement from a decline caused by other factors that were depressing the market or the industry?[10]

Experts often use an "event study" to sort out whether company-specific news—such as the announcement of a restatement—caused a stock price change, as opposed to factors affecting the market or industry

_____

[10]   Of course, if the market or industry stock prices actually *increased* on the day that A announced the restatement, then the actual loss that the restatement disclosure caused might *exceed* the loss computed on the basis of the $1 price drop.

overall.[11] What is now called the Government Accountability Office conducted two studies of restatements, using event study methodology (albeit in a rather crude way). Here is a table showing results:

Market-Adjusted Loss from Restatements[12]			
Year	Total Market-Adjusted Loss in Market Capitalization (in millions)	Number of Restatements Analyzed	Average Market-Adjusted Loss in Market Capitalization (in millions)
1997	3,200	80	40
1998	21,300	87	245
1999	18,400	145	127
2000	26,300	152	173
2001	20,400	181	113
2002 (through March 26)	6,000	44	136
2003	20,100	242	83
2004	16,600	297	56
2005 (through September)	1,900	401	4.7

---

[11]   Here is a description of an event study:

"An event-study is an empirical analysis that assesses the effect of the announcement on the stock's price by comparing the actual return (the percentage change in the stock price) during the period of disclosure with the predicted return if the information had not been disclosed. By comparing the stock under consideration to a benchmark index of comparable stocks (which may be a market index, an industry index, or another comparable set of stocks such as companies that went public contemporaneously with the defendant firm) during a control period, one can, using regression analysis, eliminate the effects of non-firm-specific events and calculate the stock's predicted return during the period under investigation if there had been no new, material firm-specific information. The difference between the actual return and the predicted return is the amount that is attributed to the disclosure."

The event study also determines whether this difference, called the abnormal return, is statistically significant—that is, whether there is a high probability that the abnormal return did not simply occur by chance.

William O. Fisher, *Does the Efficient Market Theory Help Us Do Justice in a Time of Madness?*, 54 EMORY L.J. 843, 872–73 (2005) (footnotes omitted) (quotation marks added) (quoting Janet C. Alexander, *The Value of Bad News in Securities Class Actions*, 41 UCLA L. REV. 1421, 1433 (1994)).

[12]   From U.S. GOVERNMENT ACCOUNTING OFFICE, GAO-03-138, FINANCIAL STATEMENT RESTATEMENTS: TRENDS, MARKET IMPACTS, REGULATORY RESPONSES, AND REMAINING CHALLENGES (2002) and U.S. GOVERNMENT ACCOUNTABILITY OFFICE, GAO-06-678, FINANCIAL RESTATEMENTS: UPDATE OF PUBLIC COMPANY TRENDS, MARKET IMPACTS, AND REGULATORY

The numbers look encouraging (particularly the decline in the average loss), what with the drop in 2004 and part of 2005. But the 2005 figure is not for a full year, and the table only includes a small number of post-reform years.[13]

QUESTIONS ON EVENT STUDY COMPUTATIONS OF MARKET CAPITALIZATION DROP

Do you think that the aggregate market-adjusted capitalization decline is a better measure of financial misstatement harm than any of the restatement counts that appear earlier in this chapter?

Would you compare a decline in market capitalization loss to the cost of financial reporting reforms in order to decide whether the reforms were, on balance, beneficial?

Should the government conduct a more recent study computing investor loss caused by restatements so that we could get a better look at whether the reforms have had a lasting positive effect by this measure?

Whether the reforms aimed at better financial reporting have improved the audit process. We could measure progress in terms of process. For example, in the financial reporting sphere, we might measure progress by such statistics as those at the end of Chapter Twelve. Audit committees meet more frequently. Outside auditors evaluate the audit committee members as being more knowledgeable. Audit committee members ask better questions during meetings with auditors, and committee members contribute more frequently to the resolution of accounting issues. Moreover, we know that, with some exceptions (including the smaller companies), outside auditors now audit companies' internal control over financial reporting.

ENFORCEMENT ACTIVITIES (2006). To compute these numbers, the GAO ran an event study for each company that had announced a restatement and for which the GAO could obtain reliable market prices. The GAO ran a regression to find the abnormal return on each stock during the period from the trading day before the announcement through the trading day after the announcement, with the abnormal return defined as the difference between the actual return and the return predicted by a model relating the price movement of the studied stock to the price movement of the Wilshire Total Market Index during the 120 trading days before the restatement. GAO 2002 Restatement Study, at 77–81 (describing methodology); GAO 2006 Restatement Update 55–59 (same). The numbers in all columns of the table, except the last column, are found at page 26 of the GAO 2002 Restatement Study and page 24 of the GAO 2006 Restatement Update. The numbers in the last column result from dividing the total market-adjusted loss in a year by the number of restatements analyzed.

[13]   *See supra* note 2.

QUESTIONS ON PROCESS MEASURES

Are process measures important? Would you be satisfied that the reforms were useful if the process measures showed improvement but the outcome measures did not (e.g., if there were significantly more restatements today than before the reforms and if the restatements were unquestionably more serious)?

Are the process measures helpful if we find the outcome measures ambiguous?

Do we need more process reforms—e.g., a requirement that audit committee members have even more accounting expertise, as measured by education and experience?

Whether the reforms aimed at improving top executive compensation have improved CEO pay. When we turn from financial reporting to executive compensation, we immediately encounter a basic problem: we do not have an easy measure of "good" or "bad" compensation. That is, when a company has to restate its published figures, we know that the company's financial reporting failed in a material way to meet the accepted technical test of compliance with carefully crafted, generally accepted accounting principles. Therefore, numbers and severity of restatements measure financial reporting accuracy, at least within the limits of those rules.

But compensation is different, particularly when looked at overall. That is, we might decide that certain compensation instruments or structures fail to properly incentivize executives. For example, we might conclude that companies should not use plain vanilla options because they reward executives for a general rise in stock prices or an increase in stock prices throughout an industry—and therefore reward executives for stock price increases to which their decisions did not contribute. As another example, we might decide that a company should not pay a top executive who is leaving a company a large sum if the executive is departing because he or she has done a poor job. A large severance or retirement package in such a case arguably rewards poor performance.

But there is no universal agreement, even on these small matters. Many companies still believe that stock options—when mixed with other forms of compensation—remain an effective way by which businesses can encourage CEOs to take actions to improve share price, without the companies paying out cash to the executives. And "parachute" payments can be an essential part of a deal to lure an executive to company X who is well ensconced at company Y. After all, that executive may be well on his or her way to earning very significant contingent compensation at Y (e.g., restricted stock that vests over time). That executive may realize that, if he or she moves to company X, he or she runs the risk that the move will not work out and that he or she may be forced out at X. In that event, the executive will have lost the contingent compensation at Y (which the executive had a high probability of realizing) and not yet earned time-dependent compensation at X. The executive may demand, as a condition on the move to X, that X agree to hedge the executive against such a downside risk by promising to pay the executive—if he or she is forced out at X—some amount commensurate with the amount that the executive would likely have realized if he or she had simply stayed with Y.

The absence of a universal measure of "good" or "bad" compensation is even more pronounced when we ask whether the *total value* of a pay package (salary, annual bonus, long-term bonus, equity, pension) is appropriate. As discussed in Chapter Sixteen, we could measure the propriety of total CEO compensation by some ratio of CEO compensation to compensation of an average worker, or as some multiple of the total pay provided to the second highest paid executive (or a multiple of the average total pay to the four highest paid officers who are below the CEO in the corporate hierarchy). We could measure the propriety of pay by relating it to the size of a company (determined by annual revenue, for example) or by relating it to the amount of the company's profits. But there is no universally accepted system—such as GAAP comprises for financial statements—that gives us the right ratio or relationship for any of these measures.

So what are we to do?

Evaluation of CEO compensation by shareholder approval. One possible answer is to effectively conduct a company-by-company survey in which shareholders vote on whether they agree with the compensation for the top executives or not. We have such surveys available.

Recall that Congress imposed a non-binding "say on pay" vote at companies that took federal money during the credit crisis.[14] The Dodd-Frank law later imposed this requirement on all public companies.[15]

> [(a)] (1) IN GENERAL. Not less frequently than once every 3 years, a proxy or consent or authorization for an annual or other meeting of the shareholders for which the proxy solicitation rules of the Commission require compensation disclosure shall include a separate resolution subject to shareholder vote to approve the compensation of executives, as disclosed pursuant to [the SEC regulations mandating extensive executive pay disclosures at 17 C.F.R. § 229.402], or any successor thereto.

---

[14]   *See* Chapter Seventeen.

[15]   Congress exempted "emerging growth companies" from this requirement in the JOBS Act, Pub. L. No. 112-106 § 102, 126 Stat. 306 at 308–09 (codified at 15 U.S.C. § 78n-1(e)(2)).

(2) FREQUENCY OF VOTE. Not less frequently than once every 6 years, a proxy or consent or authorization for an annual or other meeting of the shareholders for which the proxy solicitation rules of the Commission require compensation disclosure shall include a separate resolution subject to shareholder vote to determine whether votes on the resolutions required under paragraph (1) will occur every 1, 2, or 3 years.

. . . .

(c) RULE OF CONSTRUCTION. The shareholder vote referred to in subsection[ ] (a) . . . shall not be binding on the issuer or the board of directors of an issuer, and may not be construed—

(1) as overruling a decision by such issuer or board of directors;

(2) to create or imply any change to the fiduciary duties of such issuer or board of directors;

(3) to create or imply any additional fiduciary duties for such issuer or board of directors; or

(4) to restrict or limit the ability of shareholders to make proposals for inclusion in proxy materials related to executive compensation.[16]

Thus, public companies today include some variation of the following resolution, on which Worthington shareholders voted at their 2014 annual meeting:

RESOLVED, that the shareholders of Worthington Industries, Inc. (the "Company") approve, on an advisory basis, the compensation of the Company's NEOs[17] as disclosed in the

---

[16]   Pub. L. No. 111-203, § 951, 124 Stat. 1376, 1899 (2010), codified at 15 U.S.C. § 78n-1(a). The SEC adopted implementing regulations. Shareholder Approval of Executive Compensation and Golden Parachute Compensation, 76 Fed. Reg. 6010 (Feb. 2, 2011) (with these regulations codified at 17 C.F.R. § 240.14a-4(b)(3), 240.14a-21).

[17]   "NEO" stands for named executive officer. Item 402 of Regulation S-K, which is the key regulation defining required disclosure of executive compensation at public companies, defines "named executive officers" so:

(i)   All individuals serving as the registrant's principal executive officer or acting in a similar capacity during the last completed fiscal year ("PEO"), regardless of compensation level;

(ii)   All individuals serving as the registrant's principal financial officer or acting in a similar capacity during the last completed fiscal year ("PFO"), regardless of compensation level;

(iii)   The registrant's three most highly compensated executive officers other than the PEO and PFO who were serving as executive officers at the end of the last completed fiscal year; and

(iv)   Up to two additional individuals for whom disclosure would have been provided pursuant to paragraph (a)(3)(iii) of this Item but for the fact that the individual was not

Company's proxy statement for its 2015 Annual Meeting of Shareholders pursuant to the executive compensation disclosure rules in Item 402 of SEC Regulation S-K (including the Compensation Discussion and Analysis, the Fiscal 2015 Summary Compensation Table and the related executive compensation tables, notes and narratives).[18]

The individuals identified in that summary compensation table were the Chairman of the Board and Chief Executive Officer; the Executive Vice President and Chief Financial Officer; the President and Chief Operating Officer; the President, Worthington Cylinder Corporation; and President, The Worthington Steel Company.[19] Hence, the vote on the resolution was a referendum on the pay to the public company's top officers and the top officers of two subsidiaries. In Worthington's case, the shareholders overwhelmingly approved the resolution with 48,386,967 shares voted in favor and 1,696,955 shares voted against.[20] While the results of such "say on pay" votes are not binding on the board, the votes do disclose whether the shareholders are satisfied with top executive compensation.

If shareholder satisfaction is the test for compensation and if we use the say on pay shareholder advisory votes to measure satisfaction, a large majority of shareholders in the great majority of public companies are satisfied with top officer pay. Equilar provides the following graph, with the 2015 figure showing results up to November of that year:[21]

---

serving as an executive officer of the registrant at the end of the last completed fiscal year.

17 C.F.R. § 229.402(a)(3).

[18] Worthington Indus., Inc., Definitive Proxy Statement, Schedule 14A (filed Aug. 12, 2015) at 71.

[19] *Id.* at 44.

[20] Worthington Indus., Inc., Current Report, Form 8-K (filed Sept. 29, 2015).

[21] http://sayonpay.equilar.com/sayonpay/home;jsessionid=E640FF7AF54A72508CB65 68D8FB1B39A.sayonpay_jvm (chart from Nov. 1, 2015). Equilar, Inc. Say on Pay Tracker, sayonpay.equilar.com, November 1, 2015. Graphic reprinted with permission from Equilar Inc., an executive compensation data firm.

Passing Percentage of U.S. Companies

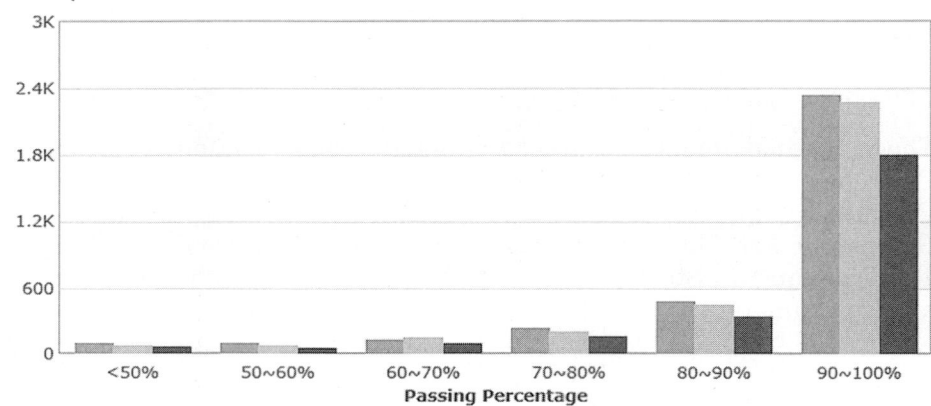

# of Companies

2013 (3,334 Companies)   2014 (3,181 Companies)   2015 (2,472 Companies)

QUESTIONS ON SHAREHOLDER APPROVALS IN SAY ON PAY VOTES

Does the overwhelming approval of shareholders for the current pay structures and amounts at their companies satisfy you that top executive compensation is as it should be?

If not, who are law students or law professors to judge that the compensation is somehow "wrong" if a company's owners approve of it?

Do you believe that the shareholders are uninformed? Do you believe that they simply vote to approve compensation so long as a company is doing well?[22]

Whether the reforms have helped stakeholders. You may view the evaluations to this point as too shareholder-centric, with reforms designed to improve financial reporting evaluated by a reduction in restatement-caused losses to shareholders and executive compensation evaluated by shareholder votes. If you favor the stakeholder view of corporate purpose, you probably would want other measures.

---

[22]   Remember that stock prices generally went up during 2012–2015, which covers the period encompassed by the Equilar graph. Perhaps shareholders are more inclined to approve top officer pay when stock prices increase.

S&P 500 Index (Adjusted Close)							
1/3/12	7/2/12	1/2/13	7/1/13	1/2/14	7/1/14	1/2/15	11/2/15
1,277.06	1,365.51	1,462.42.	1,614.96	1,831.98	1,973.32	2,058.20	2,104.05

*QUESTIONS ON EVALUATING REFORMS BY
BENEFITS TO STAKEHOLDERS*

What measure would you use to determine whether a given reform, a given set of reforms, or the reforms overall, have yielded net benefits to stakeholders?

Would you measure net benefits or net costs to each set of stakeholders, then employ an algorithm to weigh them against each other?

Would you compute the net benefits or net costs in dollars? In some other units?

However you computed them, how would you disentangle the benefits or costs from the reforms with all the other factors that affect the well-being of different stakeholders?

B. EVALUATING THE REFORMS BY THE MANNER IN WHICH THEY CAME INTO BEING

A second way to evaluate the reforms is by examining how they were created. Were they the product of considered dissection of the ills to which they were addressed? Or were they cobbled together during crises in order that politicians could claim—before microphones and cameras—that they were getting something done?

The view that the process was deeply flawed. This question has produced a remarkable, and at least in this small corner of academia, famous piece of writing: Roberta Romano's article calling the Sarbanes-Oxley Act "quack corporate governance."[23] What follows are excerpts setting out Professor Romano's thesis and then discussing some of the reforms that we have studied:

> SOX was enacted in a flurry of congressional activity in the runup to the midterm 2002 congressional elections after the spectacular failures of the once highly regarded firms Enron and WorldCom. Those firms entered bankruptcy proceedings in the wake of revelations of fraudulent accounting practices and executives' self-dealing transactions. But many of the substantive corporate governance provisions in SOX are not in fact regulatory innovations devised by Congress to cope with deficiencies in the business environment in which Enron and WorldCom failed.

---

[23]   Roberta Romano, *The Sarbanes-Oxley Act and the Making of Quack Corporate Governance*, 114 YALE L.J. 1521 (2005) [Romano, *Quack Governance*]. Quotations from this article reprinted with permission from the Yale Law Journal.

Rather, they may more accurately be characterized as recycled ideas advocated for quite some time by corporate governance entrepreneurs. In particular, the independent-director requirement and the prohibition of accounting firms' provision of consulting services to auditing clients had been advanced as needed corporate law reforms long before Enron appeared on any politician's agenda.[24]

* * *

. . . . [I]t was widely perceived in the media that members of Congress were motivated by reelection concerns when a statute was hurriedly enacted in the summer prior to the midterm elections, after months of languishing in committee, following heightened attention on corporate malfeasance as the WorldCom scandal erupted post-Enron. The suggestion from the media was that the priority of members of Congress was to enact something, with the specific content of less concern and importance.[25]

* * *

The substantive corporate governance mandates in SOX that are the focus of this Article consist of the provisions that require independent audit committees, restrict corporations' purchases of nonauditing services from their auditors . . . , and require executive certification of financial statements. . . . [N]one of the fifty states nor the District of Columbia, whose corporate laws governed the matters covered by the new SOX provisions, mandated the practices that Congress did in SOX. It is instructive that the SOX initiatives are not to be found in any state corporation codes. The message of the empirical finance and accounting literature is that this absence is not fortuitous, because the literature suggests that the mandates will not provide much in the way of benefit to investors.

The fact that the literature indicates that the corporate governance provisions in SOX are ill conceived raises the puzzling question of why Congress would enact legislation that in all likelihood will not fulfill its objectives. Simply put, the corporate governance provisions were not a focus of careful deliberation by Congress. SOX was emergency legislation, enacted under conditions of limited legislative debate, during a media frenzy involving several high-profile corporate fraud and insolvency cases. These occurred in conjunction with an economic downturn, what appeared to be a free-falling stock market, and a looming election campaign in which corporate scandals would be an issue.

---

[24]   Romano, *Quack Governance*, at 1523–24 (footnote omitted).

[25]   *Id*. at 1525–26 (footnotes omitted).

The healthy ventilation of issues that occurs in the usual give-and-take negotiations over competing policy positions, which works to improve the quality of decisionmaking, did not occur in the case of SOX. That is because the collapse of Enron and its auditor, Arthur Andersen, politically weakened key groups affected by the legislation, the business community and the accounting profession. Democratic legislators who crafted the legislation relied for policy guidance on the expertise of trusted policy entrepreneurs, most of whom were closely aligned with their political party. Insofar as those individuals were aware of a literature at odds with their policy recommendations, they did not attempt to square their views with it. Nor did legislators of either party follow up on the handful of comments that hinted at the existence of studies inconsistent with those recommendations. Republican legislators, who tended to be more sympathetic to the regulatory concerns of accountants and the business community, dropped their bill for the Democrats, determining that it would be politically perilous to be perceived as obstructing the legislative process and portrayed as being on the wrong side of the issue.[26]

* * *

Section 301 of SOX requires all listed companies to have audit committees composed entirely of independent directors, as defined by Congress. The rationale for the rule is that such directors can be expected to be effective monitors of management and thereby reduce the possibility of audit failure, because their financial dependence on the firm is limited to directors' fees (misstating earnings will not, for example, increase their income as could be the case for insiders with bonus compensation related to earnings). Congress also mandated disclosure of whether any of those directors are "financial expert[s]," along with an explanation—for firms with no expert on the audit committee—of why no committee members are experts.

A large literature has developed on whether independent boards of directors improve corporate performance. Across a variety of analytical approaches, the learning of that literature is that independent boards do not improve performance and that boards with too many outsiders may, in fact, have a negative impact on performance. There are fewer studies of the relation between audit committee composition and firm performance (four in total). None of these studies have found any relation between audit committee independence and performance, using a variety of performance measures including both accounting and market

---

[26]   *Id.* at 1527–29 (footnote omitted) (with minor alteration to correct typographical error).

measures as well as measures of investment strategies and productivity of long-term assets.

While not as extensive as the literature on board composition and performance, many more studies have examined the impact of the independence of audit committees on the probability of financial statement misconduct than on performance. Table 4 (in the Appendix [and not reprinted here]) compiles the findings of studies on audit committee independence. The definition of independence used by researchers is the same as that adopted by Congress in SOX, which excludes individuals employed by or otherwise affiliated with the issuer or a subsidiary or those receiving consulting or other compensatory fees from the issuer (other than for director service). The measures of financial statement misstatements are abnormal accruals,[27] financial statement restatements and fraud, SEC actions, third-party or contract fraud allegations, and stock market responses to unexpected earnings ("earnings informativeness"). The question raised by this research, from the perspective of the SOX mandate on audit committee composition, is whether Congress has accurately matched a problem with a solution.

Of the sixteen studies collected in Table 4 [not reprinted here], ten (including the four studies of explicit performance measures already noted) do not find that complete independence of the audit committee improves performance—a finding equally consistent whether performance is measured conventionally or by the existence of accounting improprieties—and one study reports inconsistent results (under one model formulation, independence improves performance, but not under all other models tested). The data are mixed on whether even a committee with a majority of independent directors improves performance, but the issue for SOX is whether complete independence improves on the effect of a majority-independent committee, not the efficacy of a majority of independent directors.

A few studies find that having a director with financial expertise improves performance and, more specifically, that complete

---

[27]   Researchers measure "abnormal accruals" or "discretionary accruals" by "(i) creat[ing] a model to predict the accruals . . . that an audit client would have if accruals were determined purely by the relationship between certain financial values (such as change in revenues minus change in receivables), (ii) us[ing] the model to predict accruals for each firm in a sample, [and] (iii) subtract[ing] the predicted accruals from actual accruals. . . ." William O. Fisher, *Lawyers Keep Out: Why Attorneys Should Not Participate in Negotiating Critical Financial Numbers Reported by Public Company Clients*, 2010 BYU L. REV. 1501, 1519 n.59 (2010). Researchers surmise that abnormal or discretionary accruals can be used to manipulate reported financial numbers. *Id.* at 1516 n.50, 1519 n.59. For purposes of studying this phenomenon, "[a]ccruals are components of earnings that are not reflected in current cash flows." Daniel Bergstresser & Thomas Philippon, *CEO Incentives and Earnings Management*, 80 J. FIN. ECON. 511, 512 (2006).

independence is less significant than expertise with respect to the relation between audit committee composition and accounting statement quality. These results are notable in that SOX does not mandate the presence of a financial expert on the audit committee (it has only a disclosure requirement regarding financial expertise on the committee), while it does mandate completely independent audit committees.

It should be noted that these studies, as with all regression analyses, cannot demonstrate causality. For example, the finding of statistical significance for director expertise in relation to financial statement restatements can be considered evidence that directors with expertise are effective monitors of accounting controls and audit quality—the rationale for reforming corporate governance in this regard. But it is also possible that firms that are better managed, and hence less likely to restate their financial statements, choose to have independent directors with expertise. That is, a finding of significance may be a function of self-selection and not of the efficacy of the corporate governance mechanism. Accordingly, if selection effects explain the study results, then that would strengthen the case against the mandate.

The compelling thrust of the literature on the composition of audit committees, in short, does not support the proposition that requiring audit committees to consist solely of independent directors will reduce the probability of financial statement wrongdoing or otherwise improve corporate performance. Not only is that the case for the overwhelming majority of studies, but also, and more importantly, that is so for the studies using the more sophisticated techniques. It should further be noted that, using conventional confidence standards with properly specified statistical tests, false positives—statistically significant results—can be expected five percent of the time, even though there is no significant relation between variables. Indeed, a commonly expressed concern regarding literature reviews that is not applicable to these data is that significant results are overstated because papers finding insignificant relations between the variables of interest typically do not get published in academic journals (the " 'file drawer' problem"). In the audit committee literature, by contrast, the finding of insignificance was considered important enough by journal editors to merit publication, and it is easy enough to grasp that significant results in a small number of papers could well be false positives, the product of random error.[28]

---

[28]   Romano, *Quack Governance, supra* note 23, at 1529–33 (footnotes omitted).

* * *

Section 201 of SOX prohibits accounting firms from providing specified nonaudit services to firms that they audit. . . . Although this provision is included in SOX's cluster of provisions directed at the accounting profession, it is, in fact, a substantive corporate governance mandate. Congress is substituting its judgment regarding what services a company can purchase from its auditor for that of corporate boards or shareholders. The rationale for the ban was that the receipt of high fees for nonaudit services compromises auditor independence by providing auditors with a financial incentive to permit managers to engage in questionable transactions or accounting practices in the audit.

Because the provision of nonaudit services by auditors had been subject to persistent efforts at elimination by the SEC prior to SOX's prohibition, numerous studies have sought to gauge whether the provision of such services by the external auditor compromises audit quality (the rationale advanced for banning the practice). The variables most frequently used to measure the importance of nonaudit services to the auditing firm are the fee ratio (the ratio of nonaudit to total fees or to audit fees paid to the external auditor) and total fees (the sum of nonaudit and audit fees paid to the external auditor); others include fee measures that adjust the amounts by client to construct a proxy for the client's importance to the auditor and percentile ranks, by auditor, of a firm's nonaudit and audit fees. Higher values of the various fee variables are considered to represent a nonindependent auditor (that is, the potential for auditor compromise is expected to depend directly on the fees received for nonaudit services). Several variables are used to measure audit quality, including abnormal accruals, measures of earnings conservatism, earnings surprises, financial statement restatements, and issuance of qualified audit opinions.

The findings of the studies on nonaudit services are collected in Table 5 (in the Appendix [not reprinted here]). The overwhelming majority of the studies (nineteen of twenty-five) suggest that SOX's prohibition of the purchase of nonaudit services from an auditor is an exercise in legislating away a nonproblem. The majority (fifteen) find no connection between the provision of nonaudit services and audit quality. One finds no connection when the auditors are the Big Five (including Arthur Andersen) accounting firms (the firms of concern to Congress in enacting SOX, because they audit nearly all large public companies). And three find that nonaudit services improve audit quality (and two of the fifteen that find no relation also find that audit quality improves in at least one model specification), which directly contradicts the rationale for the SOX prohibition.

Of the remaining six studies, five find that audit quality is compromised, while one finds that audit quality is compromised in only one of several model specifications. However, the results of the initial and leading study by Frankel et al., which found that audit quality (measured by abnormal accruals) is compromised by the purchase of nonaudit services, are not robust. Numerous studies, summarized in Table 5, have redone the analysis of Frankel et al., refining the model in a variety of ways. These include, among others, controlling for factors known to affect the audit performance measure used in the original study and using auditor independence measures that take account of the importance of the client to the auditor. When the model is refined by any of those methods, the original results do not hold up. As a consequence, valid policy inferences cannot be drawn from the Frankel et al. study. This could also be true for the other studies finding a significant inverse relation between nonaudit fees and audit quality. Less prominent than the Frankel et al. study but using the same methodology, those studies have not been the objects of further research.

The conclusion that audit quality—and hence auditor independence—is not jeopardized by the provision of nonaudit services is compelling not only because it is the finding of the vast majority of studies but also because it is the result of the studies using the most sophisticated techniques, as well as those whose findings are most robust to alternative model specifications. The absence of a systematic inverse relation between nonaudit fees and audit quality (across all measures of audit quality) in the scholarly literature is consistent with the Panel on Audit Effectiveness's failure to identify a single instance of a compromised audit by auditors providing nonaudit services in its field study of auditor independence. That finding no doubt contributed to the Panel's decision, as well as to that of the Independence Standards Board, not to recommend banning the provision of nonaudit services and to opt instead for bolstering the audit committee function by proposing that audit committees be composed of independent and financially literate directors.[29]

* * *

Section 302 of SOX requires the CEO and CFO to certify that the company's periodic reports do not contain material misstatements or omissions and "fairly present" the firm's financial condition and

---

[29]   *Id.* at 1533–37 (footnotes omitted).

the results of operations. The certification requirement contains substantive corporate governance mandates. It imposes on the signing officers the responsibility for establishing and maintaining internal controls and for evaluating the effectiveness of those controls, along with the duty to disclose to the audit committee any deficiencies in the internal control design or any fraud involving any officer or employee with a significant role in the company's internal controls. The officers' signature certifies both the undertaking of those tasks and the veracity of the financial information. Section 404 contains a related filing requirement, a management report attested to by the external auditor assessing the internal controls.[30]

* * *

As indicated in Table 7 (in the Appendix [not reprinted here]), two studies have sought to measure the efficacy of the SEC's rule requiring executive certification of the financials of the largest firms, as a means of evaluating SOX's expansion of the requirement to all firms, by examining stock price reactions to timely and untimely certifications. The research question is whether the SEC requirement of certification provided new information to investors about firms' financial conditions—as the literature puts it, was the requirement "value relevant"?—and more specifically, did a failure to comply, or early compliance, provide information to investors?

The informational effect of the requirement is ambiguous because the results of the two studies are inconsistent. As Table 7 indicates, one study finds that the certification requirement had no impact, suggesting that investors did not obtain new information about firms from their failure to certify—that is, that the earnings certification required by the SEC was a "nonevent." But the other study finds that for a subset of firms considered to be informationally opaque (bank holding companies), early certification provided new, and positive, information to the market.

Two points should be made that caution against generalization from the study finding no effect. First, the small number of firms that failed to certify in time limits the power of the test. Second, by the time the SEC issued the earnings certification order, the market had, in all likelihood, adjusted stock prices for an "Enron effect," reducing the value of firms with opaque financial statements and numerous off-balance-sheet transactions, and many firms had reacted by voluntarily increasing their disclosure

---

[30]   *Id.* at 1540 (footnotes omitted).

to provide more transparent reports. It is therefore possible that in the future, under different market circumstances (for example, in a time of less investor scrutiny of firms), a failure to certify earnings might provide new information about the firm. But a similar caution applies against generalizing from the study finding a price impact. It is an open question whether the positive reaction was a one-time effect or whether in the future certification will continue to provide new information to investors about financial firms.

The contrary findings of the two event studies of the certification requirement render it difficult to draw any definitive conclusion regarding the efficacy of the provision for improving the ability of investors to distinguish between high- and low-quality firms. There is a need for considerably more research in order to draw strong inferences.[31]

Romano then argues that, although these reforms had no clear research supporting them, they were shoehorned into SOX, at the behest of advocates who had been unsuccessful (or only partially successful) in promoting the reforms in the past. A "we must pass some law now" mood gripped Congress and motivated legislators to latch on to these ready-made regulatory steps. Here is part of her interpretation of the legislative history:

> The corporate governance mandates were neither a principal nor a subsidiary focus of legislative consideration. With the exception of the restriction on the provision of nonaudit services by auditors, for all practical purposes they were not even discussed. The legislation in both houses was considered within a narrow time frame: Only one day, for instance, was allocated for the House's consideration of the Financial Services Committee's bill. The Senate debate, which lasted a week, was conducted under a Republican press for a cloture motion that succeeded, restricting the time for legislative consideration as well as permissible amendments. Hence, the usually key role of committees in the formulation of legislation was virtually absolute, and in the committees, the Democrats' drafting was heavily informed by the views of former SEC Chairman Levitt and his former SEC chief accountant Lynn Turner.

> In a remarkable turn of events, [former SEC Chairman] Levitt was able to revive his agenda for accounting regulation (particularly the prohibition on nonaudit services), which had failed less than two years earlier when confronted with bipartisan congressional support for the accounting profession's position

---

[31]   *Id.* at 1541–42 (footnotes omitted).

against Levitt's proposals. Levitt had ready-made solutions for perceived problems with the accounting profession. In conjunction with his longtime support of and affiliation with the Democratic Party, his background in the securities industry and as a regulator who took on the accounting profession made him a natural and trusted source for advice and guidance among Democrats.[32]

QUESTIONS ON ROMANO'S VIEW OF THE MANNER IN WHICH SOX WAS CREATED

Are you convinced by Romano? Even if not totally convinced, does she shake whatever conviction you had that the reforms were well founded?

But isn't reform often driven by crisis? And, as a political reality, doesn't that inevitably mean that some—perhaps even a majority of reforms at a given time—will be pulled together in a hurry without a review of all the studies that academics have performed?

Do you trust academic studies anyway? If you do not, to what empirical sources would you have legislators and regulators turn?

The rejoinder that the process worked just fine. As you might expect, Romano has not gone unchallenged. Perhaps the best response is by Robert Prentice and David Spence.[33] Professors Prentice and Spence argue that Romano's interpretation is a partisan attack:

> Professor Romano's is a highly stylized recounting of these undisputed facts. To Professor Romano, the story of SOX is a three-act play. In Act One, right-thinking Republicans fend off attempts by wrong-thinking Democrats to amend the securities laws in ways that (we are told) are bad, because they are inconsistent with "the empirical literature." In Act Two, high-profile accounting and fraud scandals combine with the bursting of the stock market bubble. These events have little or nothing to do with the problems to which Democrats' proposed amendments were aimed, but the public wrongly suspects that the two are connected. In Act Three, the legislative battle is rejoined, but this

---

[32]   *Id.* at 1549–50 (footnotes omitted). Professor Bainbridge at UCLA has followed Romano by providing a similar view of certain provisions in the Dodd-Frank law and a similar interpretation of their history. Stephen Bainbridge, *Dodd-Frank: Quack Corporate Governance Round II*, 95 MINN. L. REV. 1779 (2011).

[33]   Robert A. Prentice & David B. Spence, *Sarbanes-Oxley as Quack Corporate Governance: How Wise Is the Received Wisdom?*, 95 GEORGETOWN L.J. 1843 (2007). Quotations from this article reprinted with permission from Professors Prentice and Spence.

time misguided public pressure leads right-thinking Republicans to a hasty surrender to wrong-thinking Democrats (against their better judgment), and SOX is born. So while one might easily see in the passage of SOX a competition of ideas over time, with one set of ideas emerging victorious because public events lent more credence to them, Professor Romano sees instead only the triumph of wrongheadedness, which she implicitly defines as the set of proposals Democrats favored.[34]

Prentice and Spence contend that the empirical evidence does, in fact, support the view that greater audit committee independence fosters better financial reporting:

> Numerous studies support the notion that more independence on audit committees improves financial reporting, just as does more independence on the board as a whole. For example, Krishnan finds that increasing the independence of audit committees reduces internal control problems. At least six other studies conclude that more independent audit committees tend to reduce earnings management. Other studies find that more independence on an audit committee tends to translate into fewer earnings restatements, less fraud, fewer SEC enforcement actions, and less illicit opinion shopping. Bryan and colleagues find that firms with active and independent audit committees tend to have greater earnings transparency and informativeness, consistent with the theory and requirements of SOX. Overall, more independent audit committees tend to translate into better auditing, more informative and credible earnings disclosure, and other benefits.

> As with boards in general, the studies regarding the independence of audit committees are not unanimous; neither, however, are they closely divided. The large majority supports the positions of the corporate governance entrepreneurs whom Romano disparages. As Turley and Zaman recently observed, "the independence of [audit committee] members [has] consistently been found to be associated with a lower likelihood of problems in financial reporting quality."

> SOX critics might well point out that up to this point, we are just wandering around in the neighborhood but have still not addressed SOX's specific requirement that *all* members of the audit committee be independent. This would be a fair objection, but many experts and committees in America and around the world have suggested that audit committees should indeed be comprised totally of independent directors. Furthermore,

---

[34] *Id.* at 1851.

substantial empirical evidence supports the conclusion that it is beneficial to require all members (and not just a majority) of the audit committee to be independent.

Four studies of how auditors interact with audit committees, undertaken in the United States, Canada, Singapore, and Australia and New Zealand, all find better performance when audit committees are composed solely of independent directors. Several studies indicate that audit committees composed entirely of independent directors are more likely to take their financial reporting responsibilities more seriously and to be more active. This greater activity translates into better performance. Abbott and colleagues find fewer restatements when audit committees are completely independent. Bédard and colleagues determine that "a majority of outside members [of the audit committee] is not sufficient to decrease the likelihood of aggressive earnings management and that 100 percent is the critical threshold." Chtourou and colleagues also find reduced earnings management with audit committees composed only of outside directors. McMullen and Raghunandan find that firms subject to SEC enforcement actions or restating their earnings are less likely to have *all* independent directors on their audit committees than firms not engaged in similar misconduct. Carcello and colleagues find that firms with more active and independent audit committees are associated with higher audit fees—presumably reflecting higher audit quality. In another study they conclude that these firms reduce purchases of nonaudit services from their auditors in order to improve the appearance and reality of auditor independence and thereby increase the credibility of their financial statements. The benefits of an entirely independent audit committee are clear enough to creditors that firms with such entirely independent committees enjoy lower debt financing costs.

Although not all studies find advantages from raising the requirement from a majority independent audit committee to a fully independent audit committee, the empirical evidence supporting SOX's requirement that audit committees be entirely independent is plentiful. Whether accidentally or not, Congress seems to have made the right call regarding audit committees.

Post-SOX impact studies should be particularly persuasive, and their results tend to support SOX's audit committee requirements. In 2006, Aggarwal and Williamson studied six corporate governance requirements imposed by SOX and by the stock exchanges as a response to the Enron scandal, including the requirement that the board consist of a majority of independent directors and the audit committee consist of only independent directors. They concluded that firms that had voluntarily adopted those requirements between 2001 and 2005 were rewarded by the marketplace in an economically and statistically significant manner and that these corporate governance provisions "did target relevant governance attributes."

Institutional Shareholder Services found that throughout most of the world, corporate governance reforms were viewed as important priorities by most institutional investors who thought about needed reforms in the capital markets. Because SOX's governance reforms had already instituted the needed changes, corporate governance reform was not found to be an important priority in the United States. A study by GovernanceMetrics International found SOX reform had led to a 10% improvement in the corporate governance performance of large U.S. companies and to a 40% rebound in the stock market, concluding that SOX's benefits outweigh its costs, even if those costs are substantial.

Chhaochharia and Grinstein's recent study found that several of SOX's provisions, including those relating to independence of boards and board committees, created abnormal positive returns for large and medium-sized firms that had not been in compliance with the requirements but would benefit when forced to comply by SOX. Their results suggested "that the corporate governance rules had an economically significant impact on firm value, and that firms that [were] less compliant with the rules realize[d] a greater value improvement compared to firms that are more compliant with the rules."

The accumulated empirical evidence establishes that there is no credible basis to claim that SOX's audit committee provisions amount to "quack corporate governance."[35]

Prentice and Spence argue that research supports the notion that reducing non-audit services provided by auditors at least leads to the *perception* of better financial reporting and that *perceived independence* is important by itself:

> An agency problem arises when one group (officers) manage assets belonging to another group (investors). Both economic reasoning (which suggests that a rational manager will try to advance his self-interest when handling others' money) and behavioral psychology (which indicates that even managers consciously trying to act in their principals' best interests will unconsciously tend to act in their own best interests) indicate that effective monitoring of those agents will generally be a good idea.

---

[35]   *Id.* at 1872–79 (footnotes omitted).

Overall, the empirical evidence supporting accountant self-serving bias is substantial and has been documented in numerous areas of endeavor—for example, tax, auditing, and consulting. The common sense story regarding excessive provision of nonaudit services (NAS) goes like this: During the 1990s, audit firms became intensely interested in selling NAS beyond the tax services they had traditionally provided. These large accounting firms may have used audit services as a loss leader. Whether or not they did, "Big Accounting" saw consulting fees skyrocket. In order to keep audit clients happy and purchasing consulting services, auditors often looked the other way when clients wished to be too aggressive in their accounting.[36]

* * *

Before we examine the evidence in detail, note that Romano focuses solely on independence in fact (also known as in-dependence in mind), which refers to whether actual decisions of audit firms and audit partners are affected by their desire to sell auditing services. Courts, standard-setting bodies, the SEC, and the accounting profession itself all agree that *independence in appearance* is just as important for the capital markets as independence in fact. And a large body of empirical evidence shows that audit firm provision of consulting services to audit clients tends to substantially undermine the appearance of independence in the eyes of financial statement consumers such as banks, stock analysts, and lay and institutional investors.

. . . .

. . . [W]ith measures of investor sentiment reaching all-time lows, a Congress concerned with restoring investor faith in the capital markets sensibly paid attention to investor perceptions. In post-Enron studies in the United States, Krishnan and colleagues, Mishra et al., Higgs and Skantz, and Krishnamurthy et al. all found that investors believe that provision of nonaudit services impairs auditor independence.

These perceptions have real impacts. Gul and colleagues found that investors perceive more auditor bias when higher levels of NAS are provided, thereby reducing their perception of the quality of a firm's reported earnings. Francis and Ke recently found that investors perceive that high levels of NAS fees compromise auditor independence and that this conclusion affects their investment decisions. Davis and Hollie discovered that when investors perceive that auditor independence is impaired because

---

[36]   *Id.* at 1879–80 (footnotes omitted).

of a high level of NAS, they invest less confidently and pricing becomes less efficient. Brandon and colleagues learned that bond analysts punish firms that pay too much in the way of consulting fees to their auditors. Amir and colleagues also found that "when non-audit services outweigh the auditing service at the client level, auditor's independence is questioned and bond ratings are negatively affected."

A Congress acting with the primary goal of restoring the market's faith in public companies' financial disclosures could not afford to ignore appearances. There is substantial evidence that Sarbanes-Oxley as a whole did effectively restore investors' confidence in the capital markets, and it is quite likely that the provision relating to consulting services played an important role. Because the capital markets are deeply and concretely affected by appearances, and because "even placebos can really alleviate illness," it was not quackery for Congress to legislate with independence in appearance in mind.[37]

Prentice and Spence then go on to contend that at least some empirical research shows that reducing non-audit services provided by auditors *in fact* improves financial reporting, although they concede that there is no research consensus on this issue:

> Turning to independence in fact, it is true that a large number of studies have failed to find convincing evidence that provision of nonaudit services (NAS) significantly impairs independence. However, many studies have found at least some evidence that [the] NAS provision may impair independence in fact.
>
> Looking at restatements, Kinney and colleagues recently found mixed results. They found a significant positive association between unspecified non-audit services and restatements, but they found no significant association between either financial information systems design and implementation or internal audit services and restatements, providing some evidence that provision of "NAS may create an economic dependence that leads to more restatements and that there are insufficient compensating financial reporting quality enhancements to offset the dependence." On the other hand, the authors found that provision of tax services (which SOX does not outlaw) specifically was correlated to *fewer* restatements. Admittedly, most studies have failed to find a solid link between NAS provision and earnings restatements.

---

[37]   *Id*. at 1882–86 (footnotes omitted).

Other academics have studied the impact of NAS provision on auditors' willingness to issue qualified opinions for clients. Wines found evidence indicating that Australian auditors are less likely to issue qualified opinions for clients to whom they provide higher levels of NAS. Sharma and Sidhu found in Australia that auditors providing more NAS were less likely to issue a going concern opinion, indicating an impairment of independence. Firth did a similar study in Great Britain and uncovered evidence that "the higher the consultancy fees paid to the auditor, the more likely the audit report will be clean." However, more studies have not found such an impact.

Focusing on the relationship between NAS provision and accrual quality, Srinidhi and Gul found a significant *negative* relationship between the magnitude of NAS and accrual quality, concluding that their results suggest that "non-audit fees result in economic bonding and consequent loss of audit quality."

Looking at audit failure as measured by litigation, Bajaj and colleagues found that "nonaudit fees are indeed higher than normal in cases for which there was a severe audit failure . . ."; however, because of various limitations in their study they refused to interpret higher compensation for consulting activities as evidence of lack of auditor independence. On the other hand, a different study failed to find that increased NAS is associated with less conservative financial reporting.

The largest number of studies on the effect of NAS provision on independence has examined the impact on earnings management. Logically, if NAS provision causes independence problems, then one should see more earnings management by firms purchasing substantial amounts of NAS from their auditors. Frankel and colleagues did find more earnings management where audit firms provided more NAS. Gore and colleagues found similar results in a U.K. study, especially where non-Big 5 firms were involved. Dee and colleagues also reported significant associations between measures of earnings management and provision of NAS, concluding that their findings "suggest that auditors that earn a higher proportion of their fees from the provision of non-audit services to their clients allow more income increasing accruals." Ferguson and colleagues, in another U.K. study, found positive and significant associations between three measures of NAS provision and three distinct indicators of earnings management, concluding that "[o]verall, these results are consistent with the proposition that higher levels of economic bonding between auditor and client resulting from the joint provision of NAS may reduce auditors' willingness to restrain clients' opportunistic accounting practices and may, in turn, reduce the quality of financial reporting." This substantial body of work provides a reasonable empirical basis for Congress's ban on many types of NAS, even though many other studies have not concluded that auditor provision of NAS tends to increase earnings management and several of them rejected the conclusions of Frankel and colleagues.

One reason these studies conflict may be that academics have yet to figure out how to tease out the real causal factors. . . .

Another complication is that most studies look at overall [outside accounting] firm revenues. This approach is problematic because key decisions are more often made at local offices by an audit partner whose career, like that of David Duncan of Arthur Andersen (the engagement partner on the Enron account), may depend upon keeping just one or two clients happy.

The debate over whether NAS provision impairs independence in fact remains unresolved, although the majority of academic studies fail to find direct evidence of impairment. Nonetheless, respected academics, experienced regulators, and various boards and commissions have believed that NAS provision impairs auditor independence. The evidence has been sufficiently persuasive that Japan, France, Belgium, and Italy have prohibited auditors from supplying NAS to audit clients, and other E.U. nations severely restrict or discourage the joint provision of audit and nonaudit services. Before heavy lobbying by the Anglo-American accounting profession successfully intervened, the European Commission's proposed Eighth Directive on Company Law would have prohibited auditors from rendering any additional services to their audit clients. Perhaps these agencies were willing to ban NAS because it is also true that few empirical studies demonstrate any meaningful benefit from joint provision of auditing and NAS, so even an unjustified separation "should generate no great concern."[38]

Prentice and Spence offer this passage to support the reform requiring top executive officers to certify that periodic reports fairly present, in all material respects, the financial condition and results of their companies:

[A]t the time Romano wrote, only two studies had been done. Bhattacharya et al. found that the market had already separated firms with good earnings transparency from those with bad transparency so that the SEC's initial required certification by selected firms in August of 2002 was a "non-event," concluding

---

[38]   *Id.* at 1886–91 (footnotes omitted).

that "[t]he SEC order did not help, but neither did it hinder, the market's ability to differentiate further between these two types of firms." Hirtle, on the other hand, looked only at bank holding companies and found that "BHCs subject to the SEC's order experienced positive and statistically significant abnormal returns from certification," which would indicate that the certification provided valuable information to investors.

Most newer studies have found positive results flowing from the certification, consistent with Hirtle's findings, and contradicting the "neither helped nor hindered" conclusion of Bhattacharya et al. These newer studies have tended to find that the disclosures have provided useful information to investors, restored investors' confidence in the market, and rewarded firms with better internal controls, as intended by Congress.

For example, Vermeer studied firms that voluntarily certified financial statements and found that such firms were less likely to engage in earnings management, concluding that "[s]ection 302 may provide value by enhancing the credibility of those companies that did not provide certification under a voluntary system." Chang et al. examined the impact on share prices of firms that certified; they found evidence that the provision advanced SOX's goal of decreasing investor mistrust of corporate disclosures, concluding that "[t]aken together, our results suggest that the SEC order requiring filing of sworn statements by CEOs and CFOs had a positive effect on the market value of certifying firms, consistent with the notion that certification improved investors' confidence in corporate disclosures." Hammersley and colleagues studied cases where section 302 certifications revealed material weaknesses and concluded that the market reaction in terms of volume and direction suggested that the disclosures provide investors "with much more timely information about the quality of a company's internal control system than was previously available." Beneish et al. looked at stock returns and cost of capital effects in the wake of section 302 disclosures of internal control weaknesses and found significantly negative abnormal returns as well as positive abnormal increases in implied cost of capital, indicating that "these disclosures inform investors about the financial reporting quality of disclosing firms." Ashbaugh-Skaife et al. studied Section 302 (and 404) reports and found that firms disclosing an internal control problem experienced large increases in costs of capital, indicating "that internal control risk matters to investors and that firms reporting strong internal controls or firms that correct prior internal control problems benefit from lower costs of equity capital beyond that predicted by other internal control risk factors."

Clearly, today a strong empirical case indicates that section 302 certifications not only warn CEOs and CFOs to take their responsibilities seriously, but also provide valuable information to the capital markets.[39]

QUESTIONS ON THE RESPONSE TO ROMANO

Is your head spinning now? How are we to judge between the Romano summary of empirical literature and the Prentice/Spence summary? Should we, for example, exclude all studies based on data sets from other countries until and unless we can satisfy ourselves that confounding factors, which might affect the results, are not present in those other countries?

What do you think of the Prentice/Spence reliance in part on studies that report investor perceptions? On the one hand, should we trust those perceptions because the investors are actually putting their money into the market and therefore have a keen incentive to reach judgments that are fundamentally sound? On the other hand, should we discount those perceptions given that investors did not tumble to the frauds at either Enron or WorldCom and failed to appreciate, until too late, the risks that matured into the credit crisis? Or are investor perceptions independently important simply because, whether well founded or not, they affect securities prices?

Do we need to judge the research summaries? Or is it sufficient that at least *some* research supports a given reform? Alternatively, should we impose a reform only when a research *consensus* supports it?

---

[39] *Id.* at 1900–01.

CHAPTER 21

CORPORATE SOCIAL RESPONSIBILITY[1]

■ ■ ■

This Chapter Twenty-One begins with the definition of corporate social responsibility ("CSR"). It turns next to what I will call the three different kinds of CSR. The chapter then discusses whether boards are the proper bodies to make social decisions and whether director elections should focus on CSR. A final section raises duty of loyalty and director independence issues that corporate giving can create. As is true throughout this book, this chapter focuses only on publicly traded corporations and turns to Delaware for state corporate law.

I do not mean, by the discussion in this chapter or by the phrasing of any question, to promote any particular definition of corporate social responsibility, to promote any particular corporate action, or to argue that any given level of socially motivated corporate action is right or wrong. I aim to get you thinking, not to proselytize.

A. DEFINING CORPORATE SOCIAL RESPONSIBILITY

Compliance with the law. We could define CSR as simply compliance with applicable law. Surely CSR includes such compliance or, at least, precludes conscious efforts to break the law. Board action to deliberately cause a corporation to violate the law constitutes bad faith or a breach of the duty of loyalty.[2] And directors have an affirmative duty to oversee

---

[1]   I have used in this chapter material from my article, William O. Fisher, *When the Government Attempts to Change the Board, Investors Should Know*, 40 PEPP. L. REV. 533 (2013). I have done so with permission from the Pepperdine Law Review.

[2]   *See Desimone v. Barrows*, 924 A.2d 908, 934–35 (Del. Ch. 2007) (footnote omitted):

[B]y consciously causing the corporation to violate the law, a director would be disloyal to the corporation and could be forced to answer for the harm he has caused. Although directors have wide authority to take lawful action on behalf of the corporation, they have no authority knowingly to cause the corporation to become a rogue, exposing the corporation to penalties from criminal and civil regulators. Delaware corporate law has long been clear on this rather obvious notion; namely, that it is utterly inconsistent with one's duty of fidelity to the corporation to consciously cause the corporation to act unlawfully. The knowing use of illegal means to pursue profit for the corporation is director misconduct.

management's efforts to establish systems to monitor compliance with the law.[3]

Even though this first try at a definition seems to limit the term, it still gives CSR some of its traditional bite, which derives essentially from the notion that CSR demands that a corporation, to some extent, sacrifice the interests of the shareholders to the interests of other constituencies (such as customers, suppliers, employees, and residents in the communities in which the corporation does business). Thus, even if we limit CSR to compliance with law, we can still argue over how *much* money a socially responsible corporation should spend to promote compliance. For example, we could argue in a particular case that CSR demands that a company should spend more money on legal compliance than the amount that would minimize the sum of compliance costs plus the expected costs (in fines, lawsuits, legal costs, and loss of good will) of the residual non-compliance. We could argue that CSR requires spending more than that sum, even though doing so arguably hurts the shareholders by reducing their return.

Trading off the interests of shareholders to benefit others by doing more than the law requires. Limiting the definition of CSR to simply complying with the law is, for most, unsatisfying.

A more encompassing definition, which fits better with the manner in which the term is commonly used, embraces an obligation for a corporation to do more than it must. In particular, CSR might be said to require that a corporation (a) take action *that it is not legally required to take or refrain from action that it is legally permitted to take,* (b) without regard to whether taking the action, or refraining from acting, will harm shareholders, (c) in order to benefit non-shareholders. What distinguishes this definition of CSR from the earlier one is that this definition requires a corporation to go *beyond its legal obligations* in helping non-shareholders and, at times, to do so even though the action helping non-shareholders will hurt

---

[3]   *See In re Citigroup Inc. Shareholder Derivative Litig.*, 964 A.2d 106, 122–23 (Del. Ch. 2009) (observing that the Delaware Supreme Court "approved the *Caremark* standard for director oversight liability" in *Stone v. Ritter*, 911 A.2d 362 (Del. 2006); saying, in addition, that "[i]n a typical *Caremark* case, plaintiffs argue that the defendants are liable for damages that arise from a failure to properly monitor or oversee employee misconduct or violations of law"); *Stone v. Ritter*, 911 A.2d 362, 368 (stating that "[t]he *Caremark* Court opined it would be a 'mistake' to interpret this Court's decision in *Graham* [*v. Allis-Chalmers Mfg. Co.*, 188 A.2d 125 (Del. 1963)] to mean that: 'corporate boards may satisfy their obligation to be reasonably informed concerning the corporation, without assuring themselves that information and reporting systems exist in the organization that are reasonably designed to provide to senior management and to the board itself timely, accurate information sufficient to allow management and the board, each within its scope, to reach informed judgments concerning both the corporation's compliance with law and its business performance' " (quoting *In re Caremark Int'l Inc. Derivative Litig.*, 698 A.2d 959, 970 (Del. Ch. 1996)); 369 (quoting *Caremark* again for the proposition that " 'a sustained or systematic failure of the board to exercise oversight—such as an utter failure to attempt to assure a reasonable information and reporting system exists—will establish the lack of good faith that is a necessary condition to liability' " (from 698 A.2d at 971)).

shareholders in the sense of reducing the economic return on their shares that they would otherwise enjoy.

CSR in this sense posits that the corporation should decide its actions after taking into account the effects on all of those it touches—each one of which has a moral claim on the corporation that goes beyond contract terms and beyond regulatory requirements—and that sometimes consideration of one or more other affected groups must trump consideration of shareholders.[4] This broader normative focus derives, to some extent, from the notion that a corporation affecting multiple "constituencies" has the duty to treat each of them well and sometimes help one, even if doing so will harm another.[5]

We will take this broader definition of CSR as our own for purposes of this chapter. We will also broadly define the non-shareholder constituencies whose interests a board of directors of a public company should take into account when making its decisions.

B. SOFT, MEDIUM, AND HARD CSR

Since the essence of CSR lies in the potential (and in some cases actual) conflict between the interests of shareholders and the interests of other constituencies, we may usefully divide CSR actions into three categories—soft, medium, and hard—depending on the degree to which the CSR might harm shareholders.

Soft CSR. Soft CSR actions are those that a corporation performs for the purpose of benefiting non-shareholders but that do not, in fact, appreciably hurt shareholders. These actions do not appreciably hurt the shareholders in the short term. They do not appreciably hurt the

---

[4]   *See, e.g.,* Michael R. Siebecker, *A New Discourse Theory of the Firm After Citizens United,* 79 GEO. WASH. L. REV. 161, 174–75 (2010) ("With the identity of the corporation organically shifting to accommodate its enhanced role in shaping markets and communities, '[c]orporate internal governance issues, once considered strictly economic and confined to internal corporate stakeholders, have been broadened to include . . . the concerns of outside stakeholders beyond the regulatory authority of the chartering state.' ") (quoting Larry Catá Backer, *The Private Law of Public Law: Public Authorities as Shareholders, Golden Shares, Sovereign Wealth Funds, and the Public Law Element in Private Choice of Law,* 82 TUL. L. REV. 1801, 1807 (2008)); Julian Velasco, *The Fundamental Rights of the Shareholder,* 40 U.C. DAVIS L. REV. 407, 454 (2006) ("To be a meaningful concept, [corporate] social responsibility [to stakeholders other than shareholders] must extend beyond legal requirements—and thus, by definition, cannot be legally enforceable.").

[5]   *See, e.g.,* Reuven S. Avi-Yonah, *The Cyclical Transformations of the Corporate Form: A Historical Perspective on Corporate Social Responsibility,* 30 DEL. J. CORP. L. 767, 814 (2005) (referring to one school of thought that "emphasizes the benefits of corporate existence derived from the state" that create "an implicit contract . . . that the corporation will help the state in mitigating harms that [the corporation] causes even in the absence of legal responsibility"). Other scholars rest broad corporate moral obligations on the notion that parties affected by a business rely upon it. *See* David Millon, *Communitarianism in Corporate Law: Foundations and Law Reform Strategies,* in PROGRESSIVE CORPORATE LAW 1, 9, 10 (Lawrence E. Mitchell ed., 1995).

shareholders in the long term. They never hurt the shareholders in a significant way. In fact, they may help the shareholders.

We can all think of such actions. A corporation operating in the Southwest might install solar panels because its board of directors wants to reduce carbon emissions and thereby help slow global warming.[6] If, following the installation, the reduction in money paid to power companies from which the corporation would otherwise purchase electricity exceeds the cost of installing and maintaining the solar panels (including the return that the corporation could otherwise earn on the capital that it devotes to the solar panel installation), then the shareholders actually *gain* from the installation, even though we assume in this hypothetical that the board of directors was *motivated* to install the solar panels by a desire to reduce global warming rather than a desire to increase shareholder return.[7]

Very few oppose such "soft" CSR. No one gets hurt. Everyone benefits. Without question, public company boards can—without violating any duty—vote to commit their corporations to soft CSR actions.

On the other hand, precisely because soft CSR is non-controversial, it is not particularly interesting at a theoretical level.

Medium CSR. Medium CSR encompasses actions that hurt shareholders in the short term but benefit them in the long term. Since the shareholder base in publicly traded companies is constantly changing, medium CSR hurts those shareholders who (a) hold stock at the time the corporation's action either reduces shareholder return or slows its rise and (b) sell the stock before the action produces the long-term benefit that improves shareholder return.[8] Of course, the shareholders who hold the corporation's stock when the benefits from the CSR action ultimately accrue will gain. But the circumstance that the shareholders suffer now and that the "now" encompasses the time during which some shareholders

---

[6]   Assume for this example that the earth is warming at a rate that will produce terrible consequences and that carbon emissions from human activity contribute significantly to that warming.

[7]   This is an important point. If a corporation takes socially beneficial action simply *because* that action is economically sound and will therefore improve shareholder return, then—even though we might applaud such action—we will not call it CSR of any sort. For our analysis, a corporation takes action that constitutes CSR when the corporation acts *for the purpose of helping a non-shareholder constituency*. In the case of global warming, all humans on the earth constitute the non-shareholder constituency. And again, remember that we are making for purposes of this hypothetical the assumptions in note 6 *supra*.

Note that, in calculating the cost of a CSR action—as with other expenditures—the corporation will take account of any tax benefits the action produces.

[8]   On first analysis, we might conclude that *no* shareholders will be hurt because the market will immediately impound the long-term benefits into the short-term price. But the long-term benefits will inevitably be uncertain, and the market may discount for that uncertainty, with that discount perhaps too high because the market underestimates the probability that the action will produce benefits for the company or underestimates the amount of those benefits.

will sell, differentiates this CSR from the "soft" CSR discussed above, which describes only actions in which everybody wins all the time.

We can construct any number of examples of medium CSR. A corporation doing business overseas might, for example, begin funding schools in the communities in which it operates. The corporation might start with funding elementary schools, on the theory that the funding will make a difference only if it begins to impact the education of a student at an early stage in that child's learning. The corporation might then increase the funding to encompass middle schools and high schools as the students from the elementary schools initially receiving funding pass into those upper grades. If one effect of the funding is to improve the potential high-school graduate workforce from which the corporation can hire, then the benefits to the company will not begin to accrue until the graduation from high school of the first class that was favorably affected by the first funding of the elementary schools.

The corporation's stock price and its dividends may suffer when the company begins funding schools because, initially, the funding will cost money but produce no benefits.[9] But if the effort succeeds in developing a more educated population, the corporation may benefit by access to that more talented pool of potential employees later. Assuming this is so, this medium CSR action harms shareholders in the short run (because dividends decline or fail to rise as they otherwise would) and harms those shareholders who sell during the short term (as they receive a lower price on sale than they otherwise would). But assuming a large enough benefit from the better-educated workforce, it helps shareholders who hold through to the long term.

As with soft CSR, boards can—without violating any duty—commit their corporations to medium CSR in the exercise of their reasonable business judgment. The short-term/long-term dichotomy has been resolved in favor of this conclusion.[10]

---

[9]   And, as set out in note 8 *supra*, the ultimate benefits may be so uncertain that investors may sharply discount those benefits in valuing the company's stock.

[10]   Thus, the American Law Institute's *Principles of Corporate Governance* (1994) states in section 2.01:

(a)   Subject to the provisions of Subsection (b) and § 6.02 (Action of Directors That Has the Foreseeable Effect of Blocking Unsolicited Tender Offers), a corporation . . . should have as its objective the conduct of business activities with a view to enhancing corporate profit and shareholder gain.

(b)   Even if corporate profit and shareholder gain are not thereby enhanced, the corporation, in the conduct of its business:

(1)   [i]s obliged, to the same extent as a natural person, to act within the boundaries set by law;

(2)   [m]ay take into account ethical considerations that are reasonably regarded as appropriate to the responsible conduct of business; and

There is another—academic—justification for medium CSR. It differs from the short-term/long-term justification we just reviewed. Professors Margaret Blair and Lynn Stout developed this alternative justification. It argues that business output is a "team production," with the team including participants other than shareholders and with the corporation able to flourish economically only if it honors obligations to other team members by taking actions beyond those to which the company is legally bound.

> In this scenario, a number of individuals come together to undertake a team production project that requires all to make some form of enterprise-specific investment. Perhaps one individual brings critical technical skills to the table, while another has a talent for management, and a third provides marketing insights. They may lack financial capital, however, so they seek out wealthy friends or family members to put up initial funding. Thus, a team is born. Undertaking team production, however, requires each of the members to make irrevocable investments that leave them vulnerable to opportunistic exploitation by other team members. The marketing specialist, for example, must develop specialized knowledge and personal contacts (firm-specific human capital) whose value is vulnerable to actions and decisions of the team as a whole—likewise for the technical specialist. And while the cash contributions of financial investors may initially be generic and fungible, once those funds have been used to purchase specialized assets or to pay wages, they effectively become sunk in the firm.[11]

---

(3)   [m]ay devote a reasonable amount of resources to public welfare, humanitarian, educational, and philanthropic purposes.

Comment f to this section (reprinted extensively in note 6 to Chapter One) states expressly: "Activity that entails a short-run cost to achieve an appropriately greater long-run profit is . . . not a departure from the economic objective." Copyright in the Principles of Corporate Governance is held by the American Law Institute, which has granted permission through agreement with West Academic for reprinting in this book.

While the *Principles* section 2.01 seems concentrated on charity and philanthropy, the principle that short-run corporate profit may be sacrificed for actions contributing to the public good—provided that those actions will produce long-run profit—translates easily into an endorsement of medium CSR. *See also Revlon, Inc. v. MacAndrews & Forbes Holdings, Inc.,* 506 A.2d 173, 182 (Del. 1986) ("A board may have regard for various constituencies in discharging its responsibilities, provided there are rationally related benefits accruing to the stockholders."); *Paramount Communications, Inc. v. Time, Inc.,* 571 A.2d 1140, 1150 (Del. 1989) ("[A]bsent a limited set of circumstances as defined under *Revlon* [as when a board has put a company up for immediate sale], a board of directors, while always required to act in an informed manner, is not under any per se duty to maximize shareholder value in the short term. . . .").

[11]   Margaret M. Blair & Lynn A. Stout, *A Team Production Theory of Corporate Law,* 85 VA. L. REV. 247, 275–76 (1999) (footnote omitted). Quotations from this article republished with permission of the Virginia Law Review Association, from Margaret M. Blair & Lynn A. Stout, A Team Production Theory of Corporate Law, Vol. 85, No. 2, Virginia Law Review, copyright 1999; permission conveyed through Copyright Clearance Center, Inc.

While each of the team participants can leave the firm at any time, a participant will "lose the value of [his or her or its] firm-specific investments" by doing so.[12] In this way of looking at a corporation, each of the team members cedes control to a "mediating hierarchy" topped by the board of directors that is supposed to take actions—including actions not compelled by contract or law—to keep the team functioning well:

> [A] public corporation is a team of people who enter into a complex agreement to work together for their mutual gain. Participants— including shareholders, employees, and perhaps other stakeholders such as creditors or the local community—enter into a *"pactum subjectionis"* under which they yield control over outputs and key inputs (time, intellectual skills, or financial capital) to the hierarchy. They enter into this mutual agreement in an effort to reduce wasteful shirking and rent-seeking by relegating to the internal hierarchy the right to determine the division of duties and resources in the joint enterprise. They thus agree not to specific terms or outcomes (as in a traditional "contract"), but to participation in a process of internal goal setting and dispute resolution. Hence the mediating hierarchy of a corporation [ultimately the board] can be viewed as a substitute for explicit contracting that is especially useful in situations where team production requires several different team members to make various kinds of enterprise-specific investments in projects that are complex, ongoing, and unpredictable.[13]

* * *

> Thus, the primary job of the board of directors of a public corporation is not to act as agents who ruthlessly pursue shareholders' interests at the expense of employees, creditors, or other team members. Rather, the directors are trustees *for the corporation itself*—mediating hierarchs whose job is to balance team members' competing interests in a fashion that keeps everyone happy enough that the productive coalition stays together.[14]

This theory justifies actions—beyond those legally required—to benefit any member of the "team," even if that action harms the shareholders on the team, so long as the actions benefit the team overall. And this theory justifies such actions not on the basis of ultimate return to shareholders alone but on the reasoning that the actions it motivates are supported by directors' commitment to the entire "productive coalition." Of course, application of the theory would redound to shareholder advantage in the

---

[12]   *Id.* at 279.

[13]   *Id.* at 278 (footnotes omitted).

[14]   *Id.* at 280–81.

sense that the actions the theory motivates would "keep[ ] everyone happy enough that the productive coalition stays together."

QUESTIONS ON MEDIUM CSR

Do you find medium CSR, justified by the short-term/long-term reasoning attractive? Why? Is it because, even if you believe that a corporation should help other constituencies, you feel uneasy in favoring action helping those other constituencies at the expense of the shareholders?

If a board wants to analyze whether a long-term/short-term analysis justifies a CSR action, what does a board have to do in order to satisfy the duty of care?

Do you think that a board, as a matter of good governance, should do more? Specifically, do you think that a board should make a numerical calculation of the short-term harm to shareholders and the long-term benefit to shareholders—then weigh one against the other? Should the board attempt to determine how many of the company's current shareholders are likely to sell within the "short term" in order to calculate the likely harm from the action? Do the degree of precision and depth of analysis depend on the amount of money that the company will devote to the CSR action being contemplated or to the ratio of that money to some company-wide financial figure such as annual net income? Or do you believe that, since CSR is inherently good, no sophisticated calculation is needed even for good governance?

How does the "team production" theory strike you? True enough, all participants in a corporation make "firm-specific" investments that may be hard to recover on an exit. For example, an employee learns the specific manner in which his or her employer's computer system works, and that knowledge may be of no use in another job. Similarly, the investor who puts money into a company may not be able to exit easily, at least at some points, because, as an example, the company has not yet completed a product development. But shouldn't the pay to the employee—and the return demanded by those contributing capital—be priced to take these risks into account? If the market has priced in the risk that exit may not recover full labor or capital investment, why is some extra-contractual and extra-legal obligation owed to the employee or the capital contributor? And how is that obligation affected by such government programs like unemployment payments?

If you like the team production theory, how do you think a board should use it? Could a board satisfy its duty of care in voting against layoffs in response to falling demand for the company's products by saying that the workers who manufacture those products have an unrecoverable "investment" in their jobs at the company, constitute an important part of the "team," and need the money from their jobs—all of which creates an implied obligation for the corporation to keep them employed even if this will harm the shareholders (and perhaps other stakeholders, such as suppliers who have extended credit to the company on the assumption that the corporation will act in a manner that maximizes efficient operation)?

Even if the board could satisfy its duty of care by such reasoning, should it do more in order to practice good governance? In particular, should the board try to rigorously analyze the size of the unrecoverable firm-specific investment the workers have in the company and then weigh that against the harm to shareholder return?

In short, if you liked the rigor that the reforms imposed in the financial reporting area, how would you like similar rigor in medium CSR?

Without rigor, does CSR have any real limits, other than those created by the visceral reactions of the directors?

Hard CSR. Hard CSR is where the rubber meets the road. These are actions that cannot under any theory be considered to help shareholder return. The corporation simply decides to sacrifice shareholder return in order to take an action not legally required, or refrain from an action that the corporation can legally take, in order to help a non-shareholder constituency at the expense of the shareholders.

Many shy away from hard CSR, often by arguing that whatever action they are proposing, it must benefit the shareholders in some way, at some time, and therefore is actually medium CSR. Lack of rigorous analysis in considering medium CSR actions facilitates this argument. And loose analysis might permit a board to take what is really a hard CSR action while describing it to themselves and the investment community as one that will help the shareholders eventually.

QUESTIONS ON HARD CSR

Remember that we are *not* considering actions from which a corporation refrains because they are illegal, or actions that a corporation takes because they are legally compelled. We are considering a corporation acting within its legally permitted discretion.

Is it ever appropriate for a corporation to take an action not legally mandated, or refrain from taking an action not legally prohibited, when (a) the board elects to do so for the purpose of helping a non-shareholder constituency and (b) the board knows that doing so will significantly hurt shareholder return, in both the short and the long term?

If so, what analytical construct would we use to determine when a board should do so and when it should not? If we have no analytical construct, how can hard CSR ever be limited? Do we simply wait for the shareholders to impose a limit by voting out directors at an annual meeting?

If the directors are untethered from an overriding obligation to the one constituency that elects them, will they feel free to direct the resources and energies of the corporations they lead to the implementation of their own social and political agendas? Overall, will society gain or lose? Consider this question under two assumptions: (i) your social and political agenda matches that of most corporate directors and (ii) your social agenda differs from that of most directors.

A final question on soft, medium, and hard CSR: Is this entire construct too focused on the shareholders, resting on a presumption that their return should dominate corporate purpose?

C. SUITABILITY OF BOARDS TO DECIDE SOCIAL ISSUES

Corporate boards arguably labor under at least three handicaps when making CSR decisions.

Boards lack social science expertise. The first is that the boards, as currently constituted, feature members with executive backgrounds. And the boards have no staff. As we have seen, boards have trouble even ensuring that they receive adequate information from management on operational and financial matters. To ask boards to seriously investigate a social issue and determine how the company's resources can best be deployed to advance a particular social goal may ask from boards more than their abilities can deliver. For example, suppose a board is considering laying off 1,000 people in a manufacturing plant in Cincinnati but wants to consider a hard CSR alternative of simply keeping the plant open, with low production, and not discharging any employees, even though doing so will hurt shareholder return.

Suppose that the board is considering this move because its members fear that laying off the workers will increase poverty in Cincinnati. How could a corporate board evaluate this possibility? Estimating the effect on poverty would require projecting how many of the employees who lose their jobs with the company will be rehired and when, particularly how many will be rehired before their unemployment benefits expire. The estimate could also depend on the availability of other government antipoverty programs, the eligibility of the workers for those programs, and on the mobility of the laid-off workers (because, if a laid-off employee leaves Cincinnati, the fact that he or she has been laid off would not impact poverty *in Cincinnati*).

QUESTIONS ON BOARD EXPERTISE AS TO SOCIAL ISSUES

Are you troubled by the lack of expertise? Could a board fill this gap easily by hiring outside experts as needed to summarize current research on any particular social issue that the board wants to address and to make any estimates that the board wants of the impact company choices are likely to have on the social variables that interest the board? Could a board fill this gap by causing the company to hire a permanent staff of experts in subjects relevant to the impact of company actions on non-shareholder constituencies?

If we want boards to make hard CSR choices intelligently, will the directors need the ability not only to read expert reports on non-financial matters but also to critically evaluate them? Are directors likely to have the training and skills to determine the reliability of a report on a social issue or a projection of social effects from company action?

If boards currently do not have the desirable expertise, is it possible to change the mechanics by which boards are chosen so that they do?

Or does the absence on particular boards of social science expertise simply mean that hard CSR decisions should be limited to matters on which there can be no serious question about the effect of corporate action, so that no such expertise is needed? If we unleash boards on social issues, however, how can we be sure that they restrict themselves to consensus issues?

――――――――――

Boards are not elected in a way that ensures that the directors reflect widely held sentiments on social issues. The ability of boards to make "good" CSR decisions is hindered, in a second way, by the circumstance that it is the shareholders who elect directors. Hence, it is to the shareholders that directors will be accountable for CSR choices.

These shareholder voters—who hold the whip-hand over the directors—are not the same set of voters who elect legislators. Instead, many of the share votes are cast by institutional investors, such as the managers of mutual funds. Even the retail investors who cast their votes are unlikely to represent the lower-income deciles of the population overall. Accordingly, the voting does not assure that—even if shareholders know the social positions of the candidates—the shareholders will elect boards whose social agendas and priorities reflect those of the population at large. It is therefore unclear that corporate directors have electoral legitimacy to make medium or hard CSR decisions.

――――――――――

QUESTIONS ON THE LEGITIMACY OF DIRECTORS
TO ADDRESS SOCIAL ISSUES

Why should we trust directors of large corporations to make important social decisions? How can we be sure that their views will accord with those of society at large when the directors answer only to shareholders?

Isn't the current set of corporate directors unrepresentative of the American people? Don't the directors come from the most privileged segment of society?[15]

What if the directors, following their own possibly misguided views, pursue some social policy with which the majority of Americans disagree? Again, are we counting on directors to discipline themselves to take CSR decisions solely to advance consensus social goals?

If we encourage boards to use corporate resources for social purposes, will directors grandstand, helping non-shareholder constituencies not to advance their deeply held beliefs but to garner the psychic rewards of newspaper mentions, television interviews, and awards at lavish banquets?

Each board controls only its own company and therefore has a limited reach. A third stumbling block to "good" CSR decision making is that each company's board deals only with that company. Hence, each board cannot make and implement actions that depend on the comparative advantage—in reaching a social goal—of different companies acting or refraining from acting in a particular way. For example, assume that an industry producing an unquestionably useful product consists entirely of three companies. Assume that production of the three companies, in the aggregate, creates large amounts of greenhouse gases.[16] Assume that one company uses an advanced production technology that limits greenhouse gases but the other two employ an old technology that produces a considerably larger amount of such gases per unit of product made.

Suppose that (taking all the costs and benefits into account) society would be best off if the two companies with the old technology would change

---

[15]   On the other hand, perhaps legislators suffer from the same limitation. *See* Center for Responsive Politics, *Millionaires' Club: For First Time, Most Lawmakers are Worth $1 Million-Plus*, Jan. 9, 2014, http://www.opensecrets.org/news/2014/01/millionaires-club-for-first-time-most-lawmakers-are-worth-1-million-plus/ ("For the first time in history, most members of Congress are millionaires, according to a new analysis of personal financial disclosure data by the Center for Responsive Politics. [¶] Of 534 current members of Congress, at least 268 had an average net worth of $1million or more in 2012, according to disclosures filed last year by all members of Congress and candidates. The median net worth for the 530 current lawmakers who were in Congress as of the May filing deadline was $1,008,767—an increase from the previous year when it was $966,000. . . . Breaking the numbers down further, congressional Democrats had a median net worth of $1.04 million, while congressional Republicans had a median net worth of almost exactly $1 million. In both cases, the figures are up from last year, when the numbers were $990,000 and $907,000, respectively.").

[16]   For purposes of this hypothetical, make again the assumptions in note 6 *supra*.

to more environmentally friendly production techniques. But suppose they will not do so voluntarily because—for each of them—the immediate cost to that company exceeds any short-term return to that company, and neither of their boards wants to make a medium or hard CSR decision to make the change. If the board of the third company makes a medium or hard CSR decision to switch to an even more advanced, but extremely expensive process, in order to reduce its emissions further, but by a small amount, the effect will only modestly reduce emissions, may drive up the prices that this efficient company must charge for its products, or may drive that company out of business altogether. Society suffers.

The best solution may be to force the two companies using the environmentally inefficient technology to convert to more gas-limiting technologies, or incentivize them to do so. The government—having the ability to regulate the industry overall—could impose this solution. But the board at the efficient company, governing only that company, cannot.

QUESTIONS ON REACH OF ANY PARTICULAR BOARD AND QUESTION ON CSR OVERALL

Does this example trouble you? Or are boards so unlikely to take steps that will seriously disturb allocative efficiency in this way that we should just live with the low incidence of such decisions?

Overall, do you believe that public companies today take so few medium and hard CSR steps, and that most of such steps are so meager, that the upside from moving companies along the continuum to more such steps will swamp the downside that these problems create?

D. POSSIBLE IMPLICATIONS OF CSR FOR BOARD ELECTIONS

The preceding discussion raised the question of whether the existing cadre of corporate directors is a good group to make social decisions, as they will if they use corporate resources to solve social problems and see that as a corporate goal even in instances in which return to shareholders will suffer. This raises two questions. The first is whether the voter base for director elections should be expanded. Should the voters in such elections include employees, customers, suppliers, and members of the communities in which the corporations operate? Or should some entity that might represent a composite of all affected groups (such as the federal government) participate in the corporate director voting?

QUESTIONS ON VOTING BY NON-SHAREHOLDERS IN DIRECTOR ELECTIONS

If non-shareholders vote in director elections, what number or proportion of the total votes should non-shareholders cast? Should the number or proportion be the same for each company?

How should the votes that the non-shareholders cast be divided among different non-shareholder groups (e.g., how many for employees and how many for the communities in which a corporation does business)?

If non-shareholders vote, how will the elections be conducted? In particular, how will the candidates reach the voters—e.g., through direct mail, radio or television advertisements, some sort of Internet site?

Should we have two elections at each company each year—one exactly as we have now in which only shareholders vote for some number of directors or some proportion of the total board, and one in which non-shareholders vote for the rest of the board?

If some directors are elected by shareholders and other directors by non-shareholders, should the directors elected by non-shareholders vote only on matters that seriously implicate CSR? If so, how will a board decide which matters fall into and outside that category?

Would voting by other constituencies impose social costs, by reducing the focus of corporations on profit and thereby reducing the efficiency of their operation and their drive for innovation? Would a switch to voting by both shareholders *and* other constituencies impose legal costs, such as required compensation to those shareholders who owned the exclusive voting rights at the time the voting scheme was changed to give votes to others as well?

Perhaps we are not ready for the radical approach just described. Perhaps we are willing to leave the election of directors as it is—with only shareholders voting. Perhaps we thereby accept whatever disjunction exists between the social priorities of shareholders and the social priorities of the broader American public.[17]

---

[17] Of course, many individual Americans invest in the stock market, although the percentage doing so varies over time. *See* http://www.gallup.com/poll/182816/little-change-percentage-americans-invested-market.aspx (lasted visited Feb. 18, 2016) (showing the percentage ranging from 52% to 65% in the period 2000–2015, with 55% of respondents in April 2015 answering that they, personally or with a spouse, are invested in the stock market directly, or indirectly through a mutual fund, IRA, or 401(k)).

Whether mutual fund votes in corporate elections reflect the CSR judgments of the investors in the funds is hard to know, except in those cases in which the mutual fund itself advertises as investing in companies that take aggressive CSR action or companies that score well on some social/environmental measure. The shares of the public companies that are owned by mutual funds are voted by the investment advisory firms running the funds. Disclosure of Proxy Voting Practices and Proxy Voting Records by Registered Management Investment Companies, 68 Fed. Reg. 6564, 6564–65 (Feb. 7, 2003) [Mutual Fund Proxy Voting Disclosure]. Mutual funds must disclose how

But even if we do not change the voter base for director elections, we might still consider changing the required disclosure about director nominees. At present, when a company seeks proxies to vote for director candidates nominated by the sitting board, the company must disclose, for each candidate:[18] (1) the nominee's name and age;[19] (2) any family relationship between the nominee and other nominees or directors or executive officers;[20] (3) the business experience of the nominee during the past five years;[21] (4) "the specific experience, qualifications, attributes or skills that led to the conclusion that the [nominee] should serve as a director for the [company] at the time that the disclosure is made, in light of the [company's] business and structure," including, "[i]f material, . . . information about the person's particular areas of expertise or other relevant qualifications";[22] (5) directorships held by the nominee in other public companies;[23] (6) involvement, during the last 10 years, of the nominee in any of a number of legal proceedings if the involvement is "material to an evaluation of the [nominee's] ability or integrity";[24] (7) a description of each transaction with the company in which the amount involved exceeded $120,000 and in which the nominee had a material financial interest;[25] (8) any late filing of legally required reports describing transactions by the nominee in the company's stock during the company's most recent fiscal year;[26] (9) whether the nominee will be an "independent"

---

those votes are cast. 17 C.F.R. § 270.30b1-4; SEC, Form N-1A, at Item 27(d)(6); SEC, Annual Report of Proxy Voting Record of Registered Management Investment Company (Form N-PX). These rules at least provide the opportunity for mutual fund investors to know how the mutual funds are voting shares of portfolio stocks. But it may be a stretch to assume that any large percentage of mutual fund investors will study such voting and take effective action to affect it in order that funds, other than those that state they invest according to social criteria, vote for directors holding a particular view of CSR. On the other hand, perhaps diversified mutual funds that do not currently emphasize social priorities when making investment decisions may determine that their marketing benefits from taking some step like incorporating ESG ratings into their analysis. See the discussion of such a rating system in Chapter Fourteen.

[18]   *See* Schedule 14A, 17 C.F.R. § 240.14a-101, Items 7, 8 [Proxy Schedule].

[19]   Proxy Schedule Item 7(b) and 17 C.F.R. § 229.401(a).

[20]   Proxy Schedule Item 7(b) and 17 C.F.R. § 229.401(d).

[21]   Proxy Schedule Item 7(b) and 17 C.F.R. § 229.401(e)(1).

[22]   *Id.*

[23]   Proxy Schedule Item 7(b) and 17 C.F.R. § 229.401(e)(2).

[24]   Proxy Schedule Item 7(b) and 17 C.F.R. § 229.401(f). These proceedings include bankruptcies (personal or of businesses in which the nominee was a general partner or an executive officer, with a two-year lookback for the entities), criminal cases other than those arising out of minor traffic violations, actions ending in court injunctions against engaging in any type of business practice or against acting as a broker, and actions in which a court found the nominee to have violated state or federal securities law.

[25]   Proxy Schedule Item 7(b) and 17 C.F.R. § 229.404(a).

[26]   Proxy Schedule Item 7(b) and 17 C.F.R. § 229.405. The nominee would have been required to submit such reports if he or she had been a director in that last fiscal year and was being nominated for re-election at the shareholder meeting for which the company was seeking proxies, or if the nominee had been an executive officer or a holder of 10% or more of the company's outstanding capital stock.

director under the exchange listing standards applicable to the company;[27] (10) if the nominee is running for election by shareholders for the first time, "which one or more of the following categories of persons or entities recommended that nominee: [s]ecurity holder, non-management director, chief executive officer, other executive officer, third-party search firm, or other specified source";[28] and (11) if the nominee is a sitting director, information about the compensation the nominee received from the company.[29]

While this disclosure is extensive, none of it provides shareholders with information about the nominee's social or political views or attitude towards CSR, particularly medium or hard CSR—except, for example, if the corporation identifies a director nominee as selected due to his or her "experience, qualifications, attributes or skills" related to CSR. Yet, if boards are to address social issues through CSR actions, shareholders arguably must have such expanded disclosure. Without this information, shareholders have no chance to vote their shares for nominees who will use corporate resources to advance the social agendas that the shareholders support and against nominees who will use corporate resources to advance social agendas that the shareholders oppose.

QUESTIONS ON CSR DISCLOSURES
BY DIRECTOR NOMINEES

Should the SEC require that director nominees state their position on CSR, in particular their position on medium and hard CSR? Should that be done not only so that shareholders can cast informed votes in director elections but also so that investors—who are considering whether to buy or sell a stock— have some idea of the board's inclination to sacrifice shareholder return for the benefit of other constituencies?

If such disclosure is required, of what should it consist? Should a director nominee be required to state his or her political party affiliation? Should he or she be required to list recent political contributions? Should he or she be required to disclose membership in advocacy organizations (e.g., pro-life or pro-choice groups if the candidate is nominated for the board of a drug or medical device manufacturer)?

---

[27] Proxy Schedule Item 7(c) and 17 C.F.R. § 229.407(a).

[28] Proxy Schedule Item 7(d) and 17 C.F.R. § 229.407(c)(2)(vii).

[29] Proxy Schedule Item 8. In addition, Nasdaq-listed corporations must also disclose—in advance of shareholder meetings at which directors will be elected—all agreements or arrangements between (i) any director or nominee, on the one hand, and (ii) any person or entity other than the company, on the other hand, where the agreements or arrangements relate to compensation or other payment (including a non-cash payment) in connection with that person's candidacy or service as a director. NASDAQ Stock Market Rule 5250(b)(3).

Would such disclosure deter worthy director prospects from accepting nominations?

Would all of this threaten to turn director elections into raucous affairs that resemble our political elections? If so, would that be a good development or a bad one?

E. PHILANTHROPY, BOARD INDEPENDENCE, AND THE DUTY OF LOYALTY

Corporations have the power to give money to charitable causes, educational institutions, and cultural projects.[30] Such gifts are often justified as medium CSR, with the notion being that the gifts redound to the advantage of the corporation and its shareholders by reason of the favorable publicity that the gifts generate.

We have already seen that such gifts can call into question the independence of directors. As set out in Chapter Nine, Kenneth Lay (at critical times the Enron Board chair and CEO), and the Enron Foundation gave an aggregate of more than $2 million to the M.D. Anderson Cancer Center. Two of the Enron directors had served as president of the Center. A Senate subcommittee suggested that these circumstances raised questions about the independence and objectivity of those two directors.

Both the NYSE and NASDAQ require that corporate gifts to charitable organizations in which a director serves be taken into account in determining whether the director is "independent" for purposes of each stock exchange's respective listing standards.[31]

Gifts, either by the company or by directors personally, can also impact the independence of any particular director for state corporate law

---

[30] *See, e.g.,* Del. Gen. Corp. Law § 122 (9) ("[e]very corporation created under this chapter shall have the power to . . . [m]ake donations for the public welfare or for charitable, scientific, or educational purposes. . . .").

[31] The NYSE, by commentary, (i) reminds boards that they should consider contributions to tax exempt organizations when determining whether a director is independent per NYSE Inc., Listed Company Manual § 303A.02(a)(i); (ii) requires disclosure of corporate contributions "made by the listed company to any tax exempt organization in which any independent director serves as an executive officer if, within the preceding three years, contributions in any single fiscal year from the listed company to the organization exceeded the greater of $1 million, or 2% of such tax exempt organization's consolidated gross revenues"; but (iii) does not categorically deny a director "independent" status per § 303A.02(b)(v) simply because he or she (or an immediate family member) is an executive officer of such an organization. Commentary to § 303A.02(b). NASDAQ interprets its categorical prohibition against a director being "independent" due to payments by the listed company to an "organization" in which the director or a family member is an executive officer to mean that "a director who is, or who has a Family Member who is, an Executive Officer of a charitable organization may not be considered independent if the Company makes payments to the charity in excess of the greater of 5% of the charity's revenues or $200,000." NASDAQ Stock Market Rule 5605(a)(2)(D), IM 5605. And the interpretation further "encourages Companies to consider other situations where a director or their Family Member and the Company each have a relationship with the same charity when assessing director independence."

purposes. For example, the board can appoint a special litigation committee of independent directors to examine allegations brought in a derivative suit and that committee can ask the court in which the derivative suit is filed to dismiss those allegations. Famously, charitable contributions, and other connections between directors, frustrated such an effort in a case involving Stanford professors. *In re Oracle Derivative Litigation*, 824 A.2d 917 (Del. Ch. 2003). While the facts were complicated, here is the court's summary:

> In this opinion, I address the motion of the special litigation committee ("SLC") of Oracle Corporation to terminate this action, "the Delaware Derivative Action," and other such actions pending in the name of Oracle against certain Oracle directors and officers. These actions allege that these Oracle directors engaged in insider trading while in possession of material, non-public information showing that Oracle would not meet the earnings guidance it gave to the market for the third quarter of Oracle's fiscal year 2001. The SLC bears the burden of persuasion on this motion and must convince me that there is no material issue of fact calling into doubt its independence. This requirement is set forth in *Zapata Corp. v. Maldonado*[, 430 A.2d 779 (Del. 1981)] and its progeny.

> The question of independence "turns on whether a director is, *for any substantial reason*, incapable of making a decision with only the best interests of the corporation in mind." That is, the independence test ultimately "focus[es] on impartiality and objectivity." In this case, the SLC has failed to demonstrate that no material factual question exists regarding its independence.

> During discovery, it emerged that the two SLC members—both of whom are professors at Stanford University—are being asked to investigate fellow Oracle directors who have important ties to Stanford, too. Among the directors who are accused by the derivative plaintiffs of insider trading are: (1) another Stanford professor, who taught one of the SLC members when the SLC member was a Ph.D. candidate and who serves as a senior fellow and a steering committee member alongside that SLC member at the Stanford Institute for Economic Policy Research or "SIEPR"; (2) a Stanford alumnus who has directed millions of dollars of contributions to Stanford during recent years, serves as Chair of SIEPR's Advisory Board and has a conference center named for him at SIEPR's facility, and has contributed nearly $600,000 to SIEPR and the Stanford Law School, both parts of Stanford with which one of the SLC members is closely affiliated; and (3) Oracle's CEO, who has made millions of dollars in donations to Stanford through a personal foundation and large donations indirectly through Oracle, and who was considering making

donations of his $100 million house and $170 million for a scholarship program as late as August 2001, at around the same time period the SLC members were added to the Oracle board. Taken together, these and other facts cause me to harbor a reasonable doubt about the impartiality of the SLC.

It is no easy task to decide whether to accuse a fellow director of insider trading. For Oracle to compound that difficulty by requiring SLC members to consider accusing a fellow professor and two large benefactors of their university of conduct that is rightly considered a violation of criminal law was unnecessary and inconsistent with the concept of independence recognized by our law. The possibility that these extraneous considerations biased the inquiry of the SLC is too substantial for this court to ignore. I therefore deny the SLC's motion to terminate.[32]

Aside from independence issues, corporate generosity may raise duty of loyalty questions, particularly where a company makes gifts at the behest of the CEO or other top officer or at the behest of a director.[33] In such a case, the officer or director may effectively use the company's money as a substitute for, or to augment, a gift from personal resources. And the officer or director may reap reputational advantages, as when he or she arranges for the gift to be made and is then honored at a high-society dinner, or in print, or by the recipient's attaching the officer's or director's name to a building, program, or scholarship. For example, Tyco International gave

---

[32]   824 A.2d at 920–21 (footnotes omitted). A later Delaware decision summarized two similar cases:

In *The Limited,* the court concluded that a director, the university president of the alma mater of the corporation's largest stockholder, and the corporation's founder, President, Chairman, and CEO, was not independent [of the founder/President/Chair/CEO for purposes of determining demand futility] in part because of a successful solicitation [by the director] of [a] $25 million donation to the university [from the founder/President/Chair/CEO]. *The Limited, Inc. S'holders Litig.* [No. CIV.A. 17148-NC], 2002 WL 537692 at *6–7 [(Del. Ch. Mar. 27, 2002)]. In *Fuqua*, the court found that the sole member of the special litigation committee was not independent [of the CEO] because he was President of Duke University, which had recently received a $10 million pledge from the company [and the CEO], and the CEO was a trustee of Duke. [*Lewis v.*] *Fuqua*, 502 A.2d [962] at 966–67 [(Del. Ch. 1985)]. Indeed, the CEO was J.B. Fuqua of the eponymous Fuqua School of Business at Duke University.

In re J.P. Morgan Chase & Co. Shareholder Litig., 906 A.2d 808, 822 n.48 (Del. Ch. 2005).

[33]   *See* Barnali Choudhury, *Serving Two Masters: Incorporating Social Responsibility into the Corporate Paradigm*, 11 U. PA. J. BUS. L. 631, 658–59 (2009) (concluding that "the duty of loyalty does not generally prohibit corporate managers from engaging in strategic business decisions that result in non-monetary benefits to themselves, so long as the acts are not solely motivated out of self[-]interest"; also that "whereas a donation to a corporate manager's 'pet' charity would be prohibited, charitable donations made indiscriminately would not.") (footnotes omitted).

$2.5 million to Middlebury College in the 1990s. The school used the money to create The Kozlowski Fund, named after the Tyco CEO.[34]

A corporation might employ any of a number of techniques to avoid such results. To prevent improper credit to individual officers or directors for corporate philanthropy, a company might adopt a policy that forbids recipients of corporate contributions from attaching the name of any officer or director to anything funded by the contributions—building, scholarship, program, center, faculty chair, or anything else. Or the board could delegate gift-giving recommendations to an advisory committee to which no officer or director belongs. It could adopt a policy that requires the company to report each year, in its annual report to shareholders, all gifts that the company made over some *de minimis* amount, together with—for each gift—a description of how the giving opportunity came to the company's attention, with the description to include the role played by any officer or director. It could adopt a policy that gifts over a certain amount must be approved by the board of directors or a committee of the board and that any director who brought such a giving opportunity to the company's attention could not vote on the gift. A corporation might adopt a rule that no officer or director could appear at a banquet or other event celebrating a gift.

A company could create and fund a foundation to make gifts. The governing body of the foundation might be constituted in a way so as to minimize the chance that top officers or directors of the company could control how the foundation gives away its money.

QUESTIONS ON GIVING AND GOVERNANCE

Will concentration on the relationship between corporate philanthropy and director independence chill company giving, with worthwhile contributions foregone simply because a director has some connection with the possible recipient, or because checking for connections raises the transaction costs of giving?

The independence issues at Enron and Oracle resulted in significant part from gifts or possible gifts that individual officers and directors made—out of their personal wealth—to research or educational institutions. Should each public corporation insist that each director and each top officer annually provide to the company a list of charitable gifts so that the company's lawyers can check for possible effects of gifts by director B and officer C on the

---

[34] Pierce Graham-Jones, *Trustee Resigns Kozlowski Credited for Tyco Donation to Middlebury*, THE MIDDLEBURY CAMPUS, Sept. 25, 2002, http://middleburycampus.com/article/trustee-resigns-kozlowski-credited-for-tyco-donation-to-middlebury/; for other examples, *see* Stephanie Strom, *In Charity, Where Does a C.E.O. End and a Company Start?*, N.Y. TIMES, Sept. 22, 2002, http://www.nytimes.com/2002/09/22/business/yourmoney/22CHAR.html?pagewanted=all.

independence of director A in making decisions affecting B or C? Or is this too great an intrusion into personal privacy?

Can a step such as disclosing the name of any director who brought a giving opportunity to the company, be effective absent some monitoring? Who will perform that work? The internal auditors? Is this a good use of their time?

Is concern about public recognition for executives or directors who facilitate some piece of corporate giving a tempest in a teapot? After all, are we all better off if corporations give away more money? If so, why be too picky about how it is done?

Is our view affected by our own social and political theories? For example, if we favor loose control over director and officer influence on company contributions, does our indulgence extend to the case in which the board makes a $500,000 gift to an exclusive middle school in Manhattan that educates the children of the city's wealthy?

Does separating directors from corporate giving weaken the link between the gifts and some benefit to the company, a link on which a medium CSR justification depends?

———————————

CHAPTER 22

THE LAWYERS AT LAST

■ ■ ■

In the days after Enron, the accountants took a terrific shellacking. But the reformers did not forget the lawyers. This Chapter Twenty-Two begins with the statute requiring the SEC to issue rules of professional conduct for attorneys. It then includes the complete set of rules that the SEC adopted, followed by an analysis of those rules that I prepared for a practice treatise. The chapter ends with questions about the rules and questions about your moral life as a lawyer.

A. STATUTE REQUIRING NEW ATTORNEY RULES

SOX section 307 instructed the SEC to:

issue rules, in the public interest and for the protection of investors, setting forth minimum standards of professional conduct for attorneys appearing and practicing before the Commission in any way in the representation of issuers, including a rule—

(1) requiring an attorney to report evidence of a material violation of securities law or breach of fiduciary duty or similar violation by the company or any agent thereof, to the chief legal counsel or the chief executive officer of the company (or the equivalent thereof); and

(2) if the counsel or officer does not appropriately respond to the evidence (adopting, as necessary, appropriate remedial measures or sanctions with respect to the violation), requiring the attorney to report the evidence to the audit committee of the board of directors of the issuer or to another committee of the board of directors comprised solely of directors not employed directly or indirectly by the issuer, or to the board of directors.[1]

B. ATTORNEY RULES ADOPTED BY THE SEC

The SEC proposed rules that would have required attorneys finding evidence of wrongdoing at a public company both to report "up the ladder"

---

[1]   116 Stat. at 784; 15 U.S.C. § 7245.

in a public company and, under certain circumstances, to "report out" to the SEC. The SEC adopted only the "up the ladder" rules.

Here are the SEC rules, which appear in 17 C.F.R. 205.

§ 205.1 Purpose and scope.

This part sets forth minimum standards of professional conduct for attorneys appearing and practicing before the Commission in the representation of an issuer. These standards supplement applicable standards of any jurisdiction where an attorney is admitted or practices and are not intended to limit the ability of any jurisdiction to impose additional obligations on an attorney not inconsistent with the application of this part. Where the standards of a state or other United States jurisdiction where an attorney is admitted or practices conflict with this part, this part shall govern.

§ 205.2 Definitions.

For purposes of this part, the following definitions apply:

(a) *Appearing and practicing* before the Commission:

(1) [m]eans:

(i) [t]ransacting any business with the Commission, including communications in any form;

(ii) [r]epresenting an issuer in a Commission administrative proceeding or in connection with any Commission investigation, inquiry, information request, or subpoena;

(iii) [p]roviding advice in respect of the United States securities laws or the Commission's rules or regulations thereunder regarding any document that the attorney has notice will be filed with or submitted to, or incorporated into any document that will be filed with or submitted to, the Commission, including the provision of such advice in the context of preparing, or participating in the preparation of, any such document; or

(iv) [a]dvising an issuer as to whether information or a statement, opinion, or other writing is required under the United States securities laws or the Commission's rules or regulations thereunder to be filed with or submitted to, or incorporated into any document that will be filed with or submitted to, the Commission; but

(2) [d]oes not include an attorney who:

(i) [c]onducts the activities in paragraphs (a)(1)(i) through (a)(1)(iv) of this section other than in the context of providing legal services to an issuer with whom the attorney has an attorney-client relationship; or

(ii) [i]s a non-appearing foreign attorney.

(b) *Appropriate response* means a response to an attorney regarding reported evidence of a material violation as a result of which the attorney reasonably believes:

(1) [t]hat no material violation, as defined in paragraph (i) of this section, has occurred, is ongoing, or is about to occur;

(2) [t]hat the issuer has, as necessary, adopted appropriate remedial measures, including appropriate steps or sanctions to stop any material violations that are ongoing, to prevent any material violation that has yet to occur, and to remedy or otherwise appropriately address any material violation that has already occurred and to minimize the likelihood of its recurrence; or

(3) [t]hat the issuer, with the consent of the issuer's board of directors, a committee thereof to whom a report could be made pursuant to § 205.3(b)(3), or a qualified legal compliance committee, has retained or directed an attorney to review the reported evidence of a material violation and either:

(i) [h]as substantially implemented any remedial recommendations made by such attorney after a reasonable investigation and evaluation of the reported evidence; or

(ii) [h]as been advised that such attorney may, consistent with his or her professional obligations, assert a colorable defense on behalf of the issuer (or the issuer's officer, director, employee, or agent, as the case may be) in any investigation or judicial or administrative proceeding relating to the reported evidence of a material violation.

(c) *Attorney* means any person who is admitted, licensed, or otherwise qualified to practice law in any jurisdiction, domestic or foreign, or who holds himself or herself out as admitted, licensed, or otherwise qualified to practice law.

(d) *Breach of fiduciary duty* refers to any breach of fiduciary or similar duty to the issuer recognized under an applicable federal or state statute or at common law, including but not limited to misfeasance, nonfeasance, abdication of duty, abuse of trust, and approval of unlawful transactions.

(e) *Evidence of a material violation* means credible evidence, based upon which it would be unreasonable, under the circumstances, for a prudent and competent attorney not to conclude that it is reasonably likely that a material violation has occurred, is ongoing, or is about to occur.

(f) *Foreign government issuer* means a foreign issuer as defined in 17 CFR 230.405 eligible to register securities on Schedule B of the Securities Act of 1933 (15 U.S.C. 77a *et seq.*, Schedule B).

(g) *In the representation of an issuer* means providing legal services as an attorney for an issuer, regardless of whether the attorney is employed or retained by the issuer.

(h) *Issuer* means an issuer (as defined in section 3 of the Securities Exchange Act of 1934 (15 U.S.C. 78c)), the securities of which are registered under section 12 of that Act (15 U.S.C. 78l), or that is required to file reports under section 15(d) of that Act (15 U.S.C. 78o(d)), or that files or has filed a registration statement that has not yet become effective under the Securities Act of 1933 (15 U.S.C. 77a *et seq.*), and that it has not withdrawn, but does not include a foreign government issuer. For purposes of paragraphs (a) and (g) of this section, the term "issuer" includes any person controlled by an issuer, where an attorney provides legal services to such person on behalf of, or at the behest, or for the benefit of the issuer, regardless of whether the attorney is employed or retained by the issuer.

(i) *Material violation* means a material violation of an applicable United States federal or state securities law, a material breach of fiduciary duty arising under United States federal or state law, or a similar material violation of any United States federal or state law.

(j) *Non-appearing foreign attorney* means an attorney:

(1) [w]ho is admitted to practice law in a jurisdiction outside the United States;

(2) [w]ho does not hold himself or herself out as practicing, and does not give legal advice regarding, United States federal or state securities or other laws (except as provided in paragraph (j)(3)(ii) of this section); and

(3) [w]ho:

(i)   [c]onducts activities that would constitute appearing and practicing before the Commission only incidentally to, and in the ordinary course of, the practice of law in a jurisdiction outside the United States; or

(ii)   [i]s appearing and practicing before the Commission only in consultation with counsel, other than a non-appearing foreign attorney, admitted or licensed to practice in a state or other United States jurisdiction.

(k)   *Qualified legal compliance committee* means a committee of an issuer (which also may be an audit or other committee of the issuer) that:

(1)   [c]onsists of at least one member of the issuer's audit committee (or, if the issuer has no audit committee, one member from an equivalent committee of independent directors) and two or more members of the issuer's board of directors who are not employed, directly or indirectly, by the issuer and who are not, in the case of a registered investment company, "interested persons" as defined in section 2(a)(19) of the Investment Company Act of 1940 (15 U.S.C. 80a-2(a)(19));

(2)   [h]as adopted written procedures for the confidential receipt, retention, and consideration of any report of evidence of a material violation under § 205.3;

(3)   [h]as been duly established by the issuer's board of directors, with the authority and responsibility:

(i)   [t]o inform the issuer's chief legal officer and chief executive officer (or the equivalents thereof) of any report of evidence of a material violation (except in the circumstances described in § 205.3(b)(4));

(ii)   [t]o determine whether an investigation is necessary regarding any report of evidence of a material violation by the issuer, its officers, directors, employees or agents and, if it determines an investigation is necessary or appropriate, to:

(A)   [n]otify the audit committee or the full board of directors;

(B)   [i]nitiate an investigation, which may be conducted either by the chief legal officer (or the equivalent thereof) or by outside attorneys; and

(C)   [r]etain such additional expert personnel as the committee deems necessary; and

(iii) [a]t the conclusion of any such investigation, to:

(A) [r]ecommend, by majority vote, that the issuer implement an appropriate response to evidence of a material violation; and

(B) [i]nform the chief legal officer and the chief executive officer (or the equivalents thereof) and the board of directors of the results of any such investigation under this section and the appropriate remedial measures to be adopted; and

(4) [h]as the authority and responsibility, acting by majority vote, to take all other appropriate action, including the authority to notify the Commission in the event that the issuer fails in any material respect to implement an appropriate response that the qualified legal compliance committee has recommended the issuer to take.

(l) *Reasonable* or *reasonably* denotes, with respect to the actions of an attorney, conduct that would not be unreasonable for a prudent and competent attorney.

(m) *Reasonably believes* means that an attorney believes the matter in question and that the circumstances are such that the belief is not unreasonable.

(n) *Report* means to make known to directly, either in person, by telephone, by e-mail, electronically, or in writing.

§ 205.3 Issuer as client.

(a) *Representing an issuer.* An attorney appearing and practicing before the Commission in the representation of an issuer owes his or her professional and ethical duties to the issuer as an organization. That the attorney may work with and advise the issuer's officers, directors, or employees in the course of representing the issuer does not make such individuals the attorney's clients.

(b) *Duty to report evidence of a material violation.*

(1) If an attorney, appearing and practicing before the Commission in the representation of an issuer, becomes aware of evidence of a material violation by the issuer or by any officer, director, employee, or agent of the issuer, the attorney shall report such evidence to the issuer's chief legal officer (or the equivalent thereof) or to both the issuer's chief legal officer and its chief executive officer (or the equivalents thereof) forthwith. By communicating such information to the issuer's officers or directors, an attorney does not reveal client

confidences or secrets or privileged or otherwise protected information related to the attorney's representation of an issuer.

(2) The chief legal officer (or the equivalent thereof) shall cause such inquiry into the evidence of a material violation as he or she reasonably believes is appropriate to determine whether the material violation described in the report has occurred, is ongoing, or is about to occur. If the chief legal officer (or the equivalent thereof) determines no material violation has occurred, is ongoing, or is about to occur, he or she shall notify the reporting attorney and advise the reporting attorney of the basis for such determination. Unless the chief legal officer (or the equivalent thereof) reasonably believes that no material violation has occurred, is ongoing, or is about to occur, he or she shall take all reasonable steps to cause the issuer to adopt an appropriate response, and shall advise the reporting attorney thereof. In lieu of causing an inquiry under this paragraph (b), a chief legal officer (or the equivalent thereof) may refer a report of evidence of a material violation to a qualified legal compliance committee under paragraph (c)(2) of this section if the issuer has duly established a qualified legal compliance committee prior to the report of evidence of a material violation.

(3) Unless an attorney who has made a report under paragraph (b)(1) of this section reasonably believes that the chief legal officer or the chief executive officer of the issuer (or the equivalent thereof) has provided an appropriate response within a reasonable time, the attorney shall report the evidence of a material violation to:

(i) [t]he audit committee of the issuer's board of directors;

(ii) [a]nother committee of the issuer's board of directors consisting solely of directors who are not employed, directly or indirectly, by the issuer and are not, in the case of a registered investment company, "interested persons" as defined in section 2(a)(19) of the Investment Company Act of 1940 (15 U.S.C. 80a-2(a)(19)) (if the issuer's board of directors has no audit committee); or

(iii) [t]he issuer's board of directors (if the issuer's board of directors has no committee consisting solely of directors who are not employed, directly or indirectly, by the issuer and are not, in the case of a registered investment company, "interested persons" as defined in section 2(a)(19) of the Investment Company Act of 1940 (15 U.S.C. 80a-2(a)(19))).

(4) If an attorney reasonably believes that it would be futile to report evidence of a material violation to the issuer's chief legal officer and chief executive officer (or the equivalents thereof) under paragraph (b)(1) of this section, the attorney may report such evidence as provided under paragraph (b)(3) of this section.

(5) An attorney retained or directed by an issuer to investigate evidence of a material violation reported under paragraph (b)(1), (b)(3), or (b)(4) of this section shall be deemed to be appearing and practicing before the Commission. Directing or retaining an attorney to investigate reported evidence of a material violation does not relieve an officer or director of the issuer to whom such evidence has been reported under paragraph (b)(1), (b)(3), or (b)(4) of this section from a duty to respond to the reporting attorney.

(6) An attorney shall not have any obligation to report evidence of a material violation under this paragraph (b) if:

(i) [t]he attorney was retained or directed by the issuer's chief legal officer (or the equivalent thereof) to investigate such evidence of a material violation and:

(A) [t]he attorney reports the results of such investigation to the chief legal officer (or the equivalent thereof); and

(B) [e]xcept where the attorney and the chief legal officer (or the equivalent thereof) each reasonably believes that no material violation has occurred, is ongoing, or is about to occur, the chief legal officer (or the equivalent thereof) reports the results of the investigation to the issuer's board of directors, a committee thereof to whom a report could be made pursuant to paragraph (b)(3) of this section, or a qualified legal compliance committee; or

(ii) [t]he attorney was retained or directed by the chief legal officer (or the equivalent thereof) to assert, consistent with his or her professional obligations, a colorable defense on behalf of the issuer (or the issuer's officer, director, employee, or agent, as the case may be) in any investigation or judicial or administrative proceeding relating to such evidence of a material violation, and the chief legal officer (or the equivalent thereof) provides reasonable and timely reports on the progress and outcome of such proceeding to the issuer's board of directors, a committee thereof to whom a report could be made pursuant to paragraph (b)(3) of this section, or a qualified legal compliance committee.

(7) An attorney shall not have any obligation to report evidence of a material violation under this paragraph (b) if such attorney was retained or directed by a qualified legal compliance committee:

    (i)   [t]o investigate such evidence of a material violation; or

    (ii)   [t]o assert, consistent with his or her professional obligations, a colorable defense on behalf of the issuer (or the issuer's officer, director, employee, or agent, as the case may be) in any investigation or judicial or administrative proceeding relating to such evidence of a material violation.

(8) An attorney who receives what he or she reasonably believes is an appropriate and timely response to a report he or she has made pursuant to paragraph (b)(1), (b)(3), or (b)(4) of this section need do nothing more under this section with respect to his or her report.

(9) An attorney who does not reasonably believe that the issuer has made an appropriate response within a reasonable time to the report or reports made pursuant to paragraph (b)(1), (b)(3), or (b)(4) of this section shall explain his or her reasons therefor to the chief legal officer (or the equivalent thereof), the chief executive officer (or the equivalent thereof), and directors to whom the attorney reported the evidence of a material violation pursuant to paragraph (b)(1), (b)(3), or (b)(4) of this section.

(10) An attorney formerly employed or retained by an issuer who has reported evidence of a material violation under this part and reasonably believes that he or she has been discharged for so doing may notify the issuer's board of directors or any committee thereof that he or she believes that he or she has been discharged for reporting evidence of a material violation under this section.

(c) *Alternative reporting procedures for attorneys retained or employed by an issuer that has established a qualified legal compliance committee.*

(1) If an attorney, appearing and practicing before the Commission in the representation of an issuer, becomes aware of evidence of a material violation by the issuer or by any officer, director, employee, or agent of the issuer, the attorney may, as an alternative to the reporting requirements of paragraph (b) of this section, report such evidence to a qualified legal compliance committee, if the issuer has previously formed such a committee. An attorney who reports evidence of a material violation to such a qualified legal compliance committee has satisfied his or her obligation to report such evidence and is not required to assess the issuer's response to the reported evidence of a material violation.

(2) A chief legal officer (or the equivalent thereof) may refer a report of evidence of a material violation to a previously established qualified legal compliance committee in lieu of causing an inquiry to be conducted under paragraph (b)(2) of this section. The chief legal officer (or the equivalent thereof) shall inform the reporting attorney that the report has been referred to a qualified legal compliance committee. Thereafter, pursuant to the requirements under § 205.2(k), the qualified legal compliance committee shall be responsible for responding to the evidence of a material violation reported to it under this paragraph (c).

(d) *Issuer confidences.*

(1) Any report under this section (or the contemporaneous record thereof) or any response thereto (or the contemporaneous record thereof) may be used by an attorney in connection with any investigation, proceeding, or litigation in which the attorney's compliance with this part is in issue.

(2) An attorney appearing and practicing before the Commission in the representation of an issuer may reveal to the Commission, without the issuer's consent, confidential information related to the representation to the extent the attorney reasonably believes necessary:

    (i) [t]o prevent the issuer from committing a material violation that is likely to cause substantial injury to the financial interest or property of the issuer or investors;

    (ii) [t]o prevent the issuer, in a Commission investigation or administrative proceeding from committing perjury, proscribed in 18 U.S.C. 1621; suborning perjury, proscribed in 18 U.S.C. 1622; or committing any act proscribed in 18 U.S.C. 1001 that is likely to perpetrate a fraud upon the Commission; or

(iii) [t]o rectify the consequences of a material violation by the issuer that caused, or may cause, substantial injury to the financial interest or property of the issuer or investors in the furtherance of which the attorney's services were used.

§ 205.4 Responsibilities of supervisory attorneys.

(a) An attorney supervising or directing another attorney who is appearing and practicing before the Commission in the representation of an issuer is a supervisory attorney. An issuer's chief legal officer (or the equivalent thereof) is a supervisory attorney under this section.

(b) A supervisory attorney shall make reasonable efforts to ensure that a subordinate attorney, as defined in § 205.5(a), that he or she supervises or directs conforms to this part. To the extent a subordinate attorney appears and practices before the Commission in the representation of an issuer, that subordinate attorney's supervisory attorneys also appear and practice before the Commission.

(c) A supervisory attorney is responsible for complying with the reporting requirements in § 205.3 when a subordinate attorney has reported to the supervisory attorney evidence of a material violation.

(d) A supervisory attorney who has received a report of evidence of a material violation from a subordinate attorney under § 205.3 may report such evidence to the issuer's qualified legal compliance committee if the issuer has duly formed such a committee.

§ 205.5 Responsibilities of a subordinate attorney.

(a) An attorney who appears and practices before the Commission in the representation of an issuer on a matter under the supervision or direction of another attorney (other than under the direct supervision or direction of the issuer's chief legal officer (or the equivalent thereof)) is a subordinate attorney.

(b) A subordinate attorney shall comply with this part notwithstanding that the subordinate attorney acted at the direction of or under the supervision of another person.

(c) A subordinate attorney complies with § 205.3 if the subordinate attorney reports to his or her supervising attorney under § 205.3(b) evidence of a material violation of which the subordinate attorney has become aware in appearing and practicing before the Commission.

(d) A subordinate attorney may take the steps permitted or required by § 205.3(b) or (c) if the subordinate attorney reasonably believes that a supervisory attorney to whom he or she has reported evidence of a material violation under § 205.3(b) has failed to comply with § 205.3.

§ 205.6 Sanctions and discipline.

(a) A violation of this part by any attorney appearing and practicing before the Commission in the representation of an issuer shall subject such attorney to the civil penalties and remedies for a violation of the federal securities laws available to the Commission in an action brought by the Commission thereunder.

(b) An attorney appearing and practicing before the Commission who violates any provision of this part is subject to the disciplinary authority of the Commission, regardless of whether the attorney may also be subject to discipline for the same conduct in a jurisdiction where the attorney is admitted or practices. An administrative disciplinary proceeding initiated by the Commission for violation of this part may result in an attorney being censured, or being temporarily or permanently denied the privilege of appearing or practicing before the Commission.

(c) An attorney who complies in good faith with the provisions of this part shall not be subject to discipline or otherwise liable under inconsistent standards imposed by any state or other United States jurisdiction where the attorney is admitted or practices.

(d) An attorney practicing outside the United States shall not be required to comply with the requirements of this part to the extent that such compliance is prohibited by applicable foreign law.

§ 205.7 No private right of action.

(a) Nothing in this part is intended to, or does, create a private right of action against any attorney, law firm, or issuer based upon compliance or noncompliance with its provisions.

(b) Authority to enforce compliance with this part is vested exclusively in the Commission.

C. ANALYSIS OF THE ATTORNEY RULES

Here is my analysis of the SEC rules:[2]

The "up the ladder" rules apply to any attorney who is "[a]ppearing and practicing before the Commission." That includes any attorney who (1) "[t]ransact[s] any business with the Commission, including communications in any form;" (2) "[p]rovid[es] advice in respect of the [federal] securities laws or [SEC rules or regulations] regarding any document that the attorney has notice will be filed with or submitted to, or incorporated into any document that will be filed with or submitted to, the Commission, including the provision of such advice in the context of preparing, or participating in the preparation of, any such document;" or (3) "[a]dvis[es] an issuer as to whether information or a statement, opinion, or other writing is required under the [federal] securities laws or [SEC rules or regulations] to be filed with or submitted to, or incorporated into any document that will be filed with or submitted to, the Commission[.]" 17 C.F.R. § 205.2(a)(1)(i), (iii) and (iv).

The definition clearly covers attorneys who are working on SEC filings—including registration statements, periodic filings, and 8-Ks. The more difficult question is whether the second part of the definition, as set out above, reaches lawyers who prepare commercial documents that end up as exhibits to SEC filings. As that portion of the definition reads, it will reach such attorneys only if they (1) advised "in respect of" the federal securities laws "regarding [the] document," and (2) had notice the document would be included as an exhibit to an SEC filing. 17 C.F.R. § 205.2(a)(1)(iii). Assuming that the commercial lawyer preparing a contract provides no securities advice with respect to the document, the circumstance that the document later becomes an exhibit to a 10-K, 10-Q, or 8-K should not bring the lawyer within the 205 rules.[122]

---

[2]   This excerpt was originally published as Section 7B, "SEC Rules Requiring Counsel to Report Evidence of Material Violations 'Up the Ladder' " of Chapter 36, "Obligations and Potential Liabilities of Attorneys in Public and Private Offerings" by William O. Fisher, from the treatise, VENTURE CAPITAL & PUBLIC OFFERING NEGOTIATION, Michael J. Halloran, et al., Editors, © CCH Incorporated, 1994 and Supplemented 2015. Reprinted with the permission of CCH Incorporated. To order a complete copy of this work, please contact the publishers at https://lrus.wolterskluwer.com/.

[122]   The third part, as set out in the text, of the definition of "appearing and practicing before the Commission" raises the question of whether it covers an attorney who advises a client that it need not file a registration statement because a 33 Act exemption applies. The answer to this question turns on the circumstance that an attorney has reporting obligations under the 205 rules only if that attorney is "appearing and practicing before the Commission in the representation of

The rules impose a reporting obligation when an attorney, "appearing and practicing before the Commission in the representation of an issuer, becomes aware of evidence of a material violation." 17 C.F.R. § 205.3(b)(1).[123] A "material

---

an issuer." 17 C.F.R. § 205.3(b)(1). An "issuer" for the purpose of the new attorney rules includes any company filing reports under Section 15(d) of the 34 Act, any company that has registered securities under Section 12 of the 34 Act, and any company that files or has filed a registration statement under the 33 Act that has not yet become effective but that has not been withdrawn. 17 C.F.R. § 205.2(h). It therefore includes companies in IPO registration. An "issuer" also includes "any person controlled by an issuer, where an attorney provides legal services to such person on behalf of, or at the behest, or for the benefit of the issuer, regardless of whether the attorney is employed or retained by the issuer." *Id.* The rules therefore reach an attorney retained by a public company to counsel a wholly owned subsidiary, provided that the attorney is "appearing and practicing before" the SEC. 68 Fed. Reg. at 6303 (adopting release). This definition of an "issuer" coupled with the language of 205.2(a)(1)(iv) appears to mean that the new rules by their terms cover attorneys who advise that an exemption to registration applies when the company making the private offering is a 34 Act reporting company or has filed a registration statement, or is a wholly owned subsidiary of such a company. In that event, the attorney appears to be "advis[ing] an issuer as to whether information or a statement . . . or other writing" (in this case a registration statement) "is required under the United States securities laws or the Commission's rules or regulations thereunder to be filed with . . . the Commission." 17 C.F.R. § 205.2(a)(1)(iv). But the rules do not seem to reach an attorney who advises a company on registration exemptions when that company (i) has not filed any registration statement, (ii) is not an SEC-reporting company, and (iii) is not a subsidiary of a company falling into either of those categories. [Note, however, that the SEC's more general rule governing practice of professionals before it (in 17 C.F.R. § 201.102), may reach attorneys who provide opinions, on registration exemptions, to non-reporting companies. *See* Thomas Lee Hazen, *Administrative Law Controls on Attorney Practice—A Look at the Securities and Exchange Commission's Lawyer Conduct Rules*, 55 ADMIN. L. REV. 323 (2003).

> Section 307 of Sarbanes-Oxley mandates the adoption of rules relating to the representation of issuers. Section 307 of Sarbanes-Oxley defines "issuer" to cover only those companies that are or are about to become traded publicly. In contrast, the SEC rules of practice are not expressly limited to representation of public companies. For example, Rule 102(f) explicitly applies to "[t]ransacting any business with the Commission." Thus, the terms of the SEC's rules of practice appear to extend the SEC's authority over lawyers to the representation of non-public companies that issue securities. Any time a company issues securities, registration under the 1933 Act is required unless there is an available exemption. The wording of the 1933 Act presumes that registration is required and then places the burden on the person offering or selling securities to establish an exemption from registration.

> Therefore, legal representation of non-public companies is covered by Rule 102 because, in order to avoid the registration provisions of the Securities Act of 1933, an exemption from registration must be established. In framing a securities transaction that does not require SEC registration, it would appear that the lawyer is necessarily practicing before the Commission insofar as he or she is striving to achieve an exemption from registration. Thus, this type of representation would subject an attorney to the terms of SEC Rule 102 even though the Sarbanes-Oxley Act is limited only to representation of public companies.

Id. at 343–44 (footnotes omitted).]

The new SEC rules not only address the conduct of attorneys performing corporate work but also cover attorneys who represent issuers in administrative proceedings and investigations. 17 C.F.R. § 205.2(a)(1)(ii). This kind of representation is typically viewed as litigation and is therefore outside the scope of this chapter.

[123]   The rules recognize that law firms and legal departments are often hierarchies. The rules define a "subordinate attorney" as one who "appears and practices before the Commission in the representation of an issuer on a matter under the supervision or direction of another attorney (other than under the direct supervision or direction of the issuer's chief legal officer ["CLO"] (or the equivalent thereof))." 17 C.F.R. § 205.5(a). A "supervisory attorney" is one "supervising or directing" another attorney in such a representation. 17 C.F.R. § 205.4(a). Supervisory attorneys

violation" is "a material violation of an applicable United States federal or state securities law, a material breach of fiduciary duty arising under United States federal or state law, or a similar material violation of any United States federal or state law." 17 C.F.R. § 205.2(i).[124] "Evidence" of such a violation "means credible evidence, based upon which it would be unreasonable, under the circumstances, for a prudent and competent attorney not to conclude that it is reasonably likely that a material violation has occurred, is ongoing, or is about to occur." 17 C.F.R. § 205.2(e). The attorney discovering the evidence must determine, perhaps with the help of others in his or her firm who are designated to supervise compliance with the new rules, whether the violation is (or was or will be) "material," which in the securities law context can require a determination as to whether a misstatement or omission is (or was) material. If the violation is not (or was not or will not be) material, then no reporting obligation arises.

Eight points bear emphasis. First, the rules are not limited to the circumstance in which the attorney comes across evidence of a serious securities violation; they also cover instances in which the attorneys come across evidence of a material violation of any fiduciary duty owed to the issuer. Quite broadly, they also extend to [attorneys who obtain evidence of] "a similar material violation of any United States federal or state law." 17 C.F.R. § 205.2(i). Second, the rules apply both when the attorney finds evidence of a past violation (although in that case the appropriate response may be that the violation was cured) and when the attorney finds evidence of a violation that has not yet occurred but is about to occur. The rules also apply if the violation is ongoing.

Third, in order to reach the triggering threshold, the evidence does not have to convince the particular attorney that the violation has

---

must make "reasonable efforts to ensure that" subordinate attorneys comply with the rules. 17 C.F.R. § 205.4(b). A subordinate attorney who becomes aware of evidence of a material violation complies with his or her obligations under the rules by reporting that evidence to his or her supervisory attorney (17 C.F.R. § 205.5(c)), who then bears the responsibility for making the report to the CLO that the rules require (17 C.F.R. § 205.4(c)). If the subordinate attorney believes that the supervising attorney has failed to make the required report, the subordinate attorney "may" do so himself or herself. 17 C.F.R. § 205.5(d).

Some in-house legal departments and law firms have designated which attorneys are "supervising" and which are "subordinate" to clarify responsibilities. In addition, many law firms with public company practices, and legal departments of public companies, have adopted 205 policies to educate their lawyers and their clients. Some firms have established 205 committees to which their lawyers submit material violation issues.

[124] The rules define "[b]reach of fiduciary duty" as "any breach of fiduciary or similar duty to the issuer recognized under an applicable Federal or State statute or at common law, including but not limited to misfeasance, nonfeasance, abdication of duty, abuse of trust, and approval of unlawful transactions." 17 C.F.R. § 205.2(d).

occurred, is occurring, or will occur. The standard is whether it would have been *objectively* unreasonable for an attorney—with the experience that the lawyer under consideration had and under the circumstances that he or she faced[125]—not to have concluded that it was reasonably likely that a violation had occurred, was occurring, or would occur. If it was objectively unreasonable, then the circumstance that the attorney was trying hard—and *subjectively* believed that there had not been, was not, and would not be a violation—will be no defense to a charge that the attorney broke the rule. Fourth, as the adopting release put it, the

> rule's definition of "evidence of a material violation" makes clear that the initial duty to report up-the-ladder is not triggered only when the attorney "knows" that a material violation has occurred or when the attorney "conclude[s] there has been a violation, and no reasonable fact finder could conclude otherwise." That threshold for initial reporting within the issuer is too high. Under the Commission's rule, evidence of a material violation must be reported in all circumstances in which it would be unreasonable for a prudent and competent attorney not to conclude that it is "reasonably likely" that a material violation has occurred, is ongoing, or is about to occur. To be "reasonably likely" a material violation *must be more than a mere possibility, but it need not be "more likely than not."* . . . The term "reasonably likely" qualifies each of the three instances when a report must be made. Thus, a report is required when it is reasonably likely a violation has occurred, when it is reasonably likely a violation is ongoing or when it is reasonably likely a violation is about to occur.

68 Fed. Reg. at 6302 (emphasis added).

Fifth, the "evidence" of the violation must be "credible" so that unsubstantiated rumor and innuendo are not enough. Sixth, the standard is phrased as a double negative—that the evidence makes it "unreasonable" for an attorney "not to conclude" that a violation is "reasonably likely." The standard thereby "recognizes that there is a range of conduct in which an attorney may engage without being unreasonable." 68 Fed. Reg. 6302 (adopting release). The rules do not intend to trigger the reporting obligation

---

[125] The standard is objective, not subjective. The measure is what a prudent and competent attorney would conclude. This standard, however, will take into account such factors as "the attorney's professional skills, background and experience, the time constraints under which the attorney is acting, the attorney's previous experience and familiarity with the client, and the availability of other lawyers with whom the lawyer may consult." 68 Fed. Reg. at 6302 (adopting release).

"by 'a combination of circumstances from which the attorney, in retrospect, should have drawn an inference.'" *Id.* The double negative accordingly seems intended to avoid after-the-fact "gotcha" discipline on close calls and to aim the rule at conduct towards the more extreme end of the spectrum.[126]

Seventh, the rules do not limit the reporting obligation to instances in which the material violation relates to the particular matter on which the attorney is working. The rules require only that the evidence come to the lawyer while "appearing and practicing before the Commission in the representation of [the] issuer." 17 C.F.R. § 205.3(b)(1). This seems to extend, therefore, to the instance in which the attorney working on a securities filing discovers in his or her work a violation that is not a securities violation.

Eighth, the SEC rules say expressly that they "supplement applicable standards of any jurisdiction where an attorney is admitted or practices and are not intended to limit the ability of any jurisdiction to impose additional obligations on an attorney not inconsistent with the application of [the rules]" and also state that *"[w]here the standards of a state or other United States jurisdiction where an attorney is admitted or practices conflict with [these Commission rules], [these Commission rules] shall govern."* 17 C.F.R. § 205.1 (emphasis added). Thus, the SEC unequivocally will take the position that "up the ladder"

---

[126] The proposing release did not contain the double negative and defined evidence of a material violation as simply evidence "that would lead an attorney reasonably to believe" that a violation had occurred, was occurring, or would occur. 67 Fed. Reg. at 71678. The final rule—with the double negative—seems to have narrowed the definition. Yet, even with the broader definition in the proposing release, the SEC said:

> In proposing this rule, the Commission does not intend to inhibit the consultative process between an issuer and its attorney. The duty to report "up the ladder" under section 205.3(b)(2) does not arise from a consultation in which an attorney advises an officer or employee of an issuer that the law regarding a proposed course of action is unsettled and there is some possibility that a court might hold in the future that the action violated the securities laws. Nor does it arise where an officer actually pursues a course of action despite being advised by the attorney that the course of action has been held illegal by courts in three states, in none of which the issuer does business, even if the attorney thinks there is a reasonable argument that other courts would also be likely to find it illegal. The course of action is not clearly illegal, because its legality has not been addressed by courts in any state where the issuer does business. The duty to report does not even arise where the officer tells the attorney that he or she intends to pursue a course of action that the attorney thinks is clearly illegal where the issuer does business, because the officer might reconsider and not do what he or she said he or she would do. The attorney's reporting obligation is not triggered until the attorney can be sure that the officer or employee will actually pursue an illegal course of action.

67 Fed. Reg. at 71683. While this passage is out of tune with the final rule stating, in 205.2(e), that an attorney may have "evidence of a material violation" even if the violation is only "reasonably likely" to occur, the passage does suggest that the rule is aimed at the more extreme cases and also suggests that the duty to report arises only after timely efforts have failed to dissuade a prospective violator from going forward with the violation.

disclosure under its rule is required even where local ethics rules make such disclosure permissive. As the SEC put it in its adopting release: "The language which we adopt today clarifies that [these rules do] not preempt ethical rules ... that establish more rigorous obligations.... At the same time, the Commission reaffirms that its rules shall prevail over any conflicting or inconsistent laws of a state or other United States jurisdiction in which an attorney is admitted or practices." 68 Fed. Reg. at 6297.

When a covered attorney becomes aware of "evidence of a material violation," that attorney must "forthwith" report the evidence to the client's "chief legal officer [CLO] (or the equivalent thereof) or to both the ... chief legal officer and [the] chief executive officer [CEO]." 17 C.F.R. § 205.3(b)(1).[127] The SEC did not define "forthwith," but the clear implication is that the report[ ] must be made quickly. Law firms will therefore want to be sure that, if they are referring 205 reporting issues to a committee or reviewing them in some other way, they complete such internal reviews very expeditiously. Note that the Commission placed the reporting obligation on the "attorney," so it appears to be a personal obligation rather than one that the attorney can pass on to his or her firm.

A 205 report of "evidence of a material violation" triggers an obligation by the CLO (or equivalent) to conduct an inquiry to determine whether the violation "has occurred, is ongoing, or is about to occur." 17 C.F.R. § 205.3(b)(2).[128] The CLO must

---

[127] Many companies without an in-house legal staff would probably consider their chief financial officer to be the closest equivalent of a "chief legal officer." However, the proposing release said that "[w]here an issuer has no general counsel or chief legal officer, the 'equivalent' would be the chief executive officer." 67 Fed. Reg. at 71685.

If the reporting attorney "reasonably believes that it would be futile" to report to the CLO or CEO—as might be the case if those two officers were themselves involved in the violation—the attorney may report directly to the issuer's audit committee or other committee of outside directors (if the issuer has no audit committee) or to the whole board (if the issuer has no such other committee). 17 C.F.R. § 205.3(b)(4).

[128] If the company has a "qualified legal compliance committee" ("QLCC") that the company established before receiving the report, the CLO can simply send the evidence on to that committee to investigate. 17 C.F.R. § 205.3(b)(2). Indeed, if the company has a QLCC, the attorney coming across evidence of [a] material violation can report that evidence directly to that committee. 17 C.F.R. § 205.3(c)(1).

If the evidence goes to a QLCC by either route, then the QLCC has full responsibility for evaluating the evidence and recommending the response to it. 17 C.F.R. §§ 205.2(k)(3), 205.3(c). Once the CLO advises the reporting attorney that the matter has gone to the QLCC or the reporting attorney provides the evidence to the QLCC, the reporting attorney has no further obligation to assess the issuer's response. 17 C.F.R. § 205.3(c).

The rules include an elaborate set of requirements for a QLCC, which may be an issuer's audit committee or another committee that includes at least one member of the issuer's audit committee and two or more other directors who are not employed by the issuer, either directly or indirectly. 17 C.F.R. § 205.2(k).

communicate the results of the inquiry to the reporting attorney. If the CLO has determined that no violation has occurred, is occurring, or is about to occur, then the CLO notifies the reporting attorney of that conclusion and "advise[s] the reporting attorney of the basis for such determination." 17 C.F.R. § 205.3(b)(2). Otherwise, the CLO "shall take all reasonable steps to cause the issuer to adopt an appropriate response, and shall advise the reporting attorney thereof." *Id.*

Whether the CLO provides a "no violation" report or a report that the company is taking steps to address a violation, the reporting attorney must evaluate the CLO's response. Specifically, the reporting attorney must decide whether he or she "reasonably believes" that the CLO has provided an "appropriate response" within a "reasonable time." 17 C.F.R. § 205.3(b)(3). The SEC recognized in its adopting release that this decision will be a judgment call:

It is unclear how many companies will establish QLCCs. Institutional investors may see a company's decision to establish such a committee as a commitment to good corporate governance. If a company has a QLCC, the CLO and other reporting attorneys can hand off responsibility to that committee and thereby save themselves the time of formulating or evaluating responses. And, if a company receives a substantial number of 205 reports, a formal committee might be more likely than a harried CLO to develop a routine and apply consistent standards when responding. On the other hand, a QLCC puts the burden generated by 205 reports on a committee of directors. The committee must determine whether an investigation is necessary and, if so, involve the CLO or outside counsel to conduct it. *See* 17 C.F.R. § 205.2(k)(ii)(B) (QLCC must have authority to "[i]nitiate an investigation, which may be conducted either by the chief legal officer . . . or by outside attorneys"). More importantly, after an investigation, the QLCC has the job of recommending an "appropriate response" and informing the CLO, CEO, and the full board about the investigation "and the appropriate remedial measures to be adopted." 17 C.F.R. § 205.2(k)(3)(iii)(A) & (B). All of that is quite a lot to put on the directors sitting on the committee, and directors might be reluctant to serve on a QLCC because of all the work and because membership on the committee might increase the probability that they would be pursued in lawsuits even though "the Commission does not intend service on a QLCC to increase the liability of any member of a board of directors under state law and, indeed, expressly finds that it would be inconsistent with the public interest for a court to so conclude." 68 Fed. Reg. at 6305 (adopting release). Moreover, the QLCC must have "the authority and responsibility, acting by majority vote, to take all other appropriate action, including the authority to notify the Commission in the event that the issuer fails in any material respect to implement an appropriate response that the [QLCC] has recommended the issuer to take." 17 C.F.R. § 205.2(k)(4). Boards may be reluctant to cede to the majority of a small committee the authority to turn the company in to the regulators. And there is always the possibility that some court might conclude that the QLCC's authority to report to the SEC carries with it some sort of obligation to do so under certain circumstances—which would also increase both the burden and the exposure for those directors taking a seat on the committee.

One academic, searching EDGAR filings, found only 231 operating companies that reported having formed a QLCC between October 2002 and September 30, 2005. Robert Eli Rosen, *Resistances to Reforming Corporate Governance: The Diffusion of QLCCs*, 74 FORDHAM L. REV. 1251, 1258–59 (2005). *See also* Linda Chatman Thomsen, et al., *General Counsel Under Scrutiny*, Corporate Counsel Institute 2010 101, 106 (2010) ("Few companies have established a standalone QLCC; it is more common for companies to designate an existing board committee as a QLCC, but even this approach is rare among public companies. During the 2009 proxy season, approximately 125 public companies discussed a QLCC in their proxies.").

The Commission's intent is to permit attorneys to exercise their judgment as to whether a response to a report is appropriate, so long as their determination of what is an "appropriate response" is reasonable.

68 Fed. Reg. at 6298. Effectively, the new rules convert attorneys into minders for their clients.

An "appropriate response" can take any of three forms.

1.   The CLO or CEO may tell the reporting attorney that, after an inquiry, the company has determined that no material violation has occurred, is occurring, or is about to occur. This constitutes an "appropriate response"—*provided* that the CLO or CEO sets out "the basis for such determination" and the reporting attorney then "reasonably believes" that there is no such violation. 17 C.F.R. §§ 205.2(b)(1), 205.3(b)(2). "The circumstances a reporting attorney might weigh in assessing whether he or she could reasonably believe that [this is an appropriate response] would include the amount and weight of the evidence of a material violation, the severity of the apparent . . . violation and the scope of the investigation into the report." 68 Fed. Reg. at 6300 (adopting release). It would not be enough that the CLO baldly asserted there was no violation. "On the other hand, . . . [the reporting attorney] . . . may rely on reasonable and appropriate factual representations and legal determinations of persons on whom a reasonable attorney would rely." *Id.*

2.   The CLO or CEO may advise the reporting attorney that, after an inquiry, there was or is a material violation but that the issuer "has, as necessary, adopted appropriate remedial measures, including appropriate steps or sanctions to stop any material violations that are ongoing, to prevent any material violation that has yet to occur, and to remedy or otherwise appropriately address any material violation that has already occurred and to minimize the likelihood of its recurrence." 17 C.F.R. § 205.2(b)(2). This is an "appropriate response" if, after those steps are described, the outside counsel "reasonably believes" that the company has really done all that. 17 C.F.R. § 205.2(b).

Two points deserve special comment. First, the SEC's adopting release says: "The Commission believes that the [final rule] make[s] clear that the issuer must adopt appropriate remedial measures or sanctions to prevent future violations, redress past violations, and stop ongoing violations and consider the feasibility of restitution. The concern that . . . [a report of remedial measures that] are ongoing but not completed must be deemed to be inappropriate . . . appears to be overstated. Many remedial measures, such as disclosures and the cessation of ongoing material violations, will occur in short order once the decision has been made to pursue them. Beyond this, the reasonable time period after which a reporting attorney is obligated to report further up the ladder would include a reasonable period of time for the issuer to complete its ongoing remediation." 68 Fed. Reg. at 6300. This suggests that, where the company's actions in response to a violation will take time, the reporting attorney needs to monitor those actions in order to determine that the company, in the words of 205.2(b)(2), "has, as necessary, adopted appropriate remedial measures." It also suggests that, if the company does not implement its proposed actions within a reasonable time, the reporting attorney should conclude that the company has not "adopted" those measures within the meaning of 205.2(b)(2) and that the company response was accordingly not "appropriate."

What constitutes a "reasonable period of time" for a company to implement its response presumably will vary with the circumstances. For example, if the company is hiring a new staffer to monitor a particular type of activity that caused the reported violation, the supply of individuals with the capabilities to undertake the monitoring could affect how quickly the company could effect a hire. If the violation was linked to a recurring event, the amount of time that would be reasonable could also depend on when the event recurs. Many other factors could affect the calculation of a "reasonable period of time" in which to complete remedial efforts.

Second, the reference in the adopting release to "consider[ing] the feasibility of restitution" (68 Fed. Reg. at 6300) raises the thorny point of whether an "appropriate response" to a past securities violation includes some payment to third parties, like injured shareholders. Presumably, all kinds of questions would enter into deciding whether a payment should be made—including the certainty that the violation caused damage, the financial condition of the issuer, and the practicalities of finding and paying injured shareholders. These will be especially tough calls. Neither the rules nor the proposing or adopting releases provide much help.

3.   The CLO or CEO may tell the reporting attorney that the company, "with the consent of [its] board of directors" or its audit committee (or, if it does not have an audit committee, another committee comprised solely of independent directors), has retained or directed an attorney to review the reported evidence.[129]   17 C.F.R.   § 205.2(b)(3). But this response is adequate only if the reporting attorney "reasonably believes" that the company either (a) "[h]as substantially implemented any remedial recommendations made by such attorney after a reasonable investigation and evaluation of the reported evidence"[130] or (b) has been advised by that attorney that he or she can, "consistent with . . . professional obligations, assert a colorable defense on behalf of the [company] (or the issuer's officer, director, employee, or agent, as the case may be) in any investigation or judicial or administrative proceeding relating to the reported evidence." 17 C.F.R. § 205.2(b)(3)(i) & (ii). The Commission's adopting release states that "requiring the Commission staff to bear the burden of proving its case" can be a "colorable defense," provided that the attorney can do so consistent with such professional obligations as requirements that pleadings be filed in good faith and after reasonable investigation. 68 Fed. Reg. at 6301 & 6300 n. 36. It is important to this third possible response that the investigation and defense be undertaken with the knowledge and consent of the board or appropriate committee, and the reporting attorney relying on this response will want to satisfy himself or herself that this is the case.[131]

---

[129]   The rules do not say whether the attorney to whom the matter is referred must be an outside attorney, or can be an inside attorney, and it therefore appears that either will do. But companies would be well advised to consider here the same factors that ordinarily play into the selection of counsel for other internal investigations. For example, it probably would be unreasonable or unwise to refer a potentially serious matter involving the CEO to the most junior attorney who works on a large in-house staff and who has no experience in investigations.

[130]   This requirement in 205.2(b)(3)(i)—that the reporting attorney reasonably believe that the issuer "has" substantially implemented these remedial recommendations by the counsel retained to review a matter—should be interpreted in the same way as the requirement in 205.2(b)(2) that the reporting attorney reasonably believe that the issuer "has, as necessary, adopted appropriate remedial measures" in a remedial plan that the CLO describes after determining that a violation has occurred, is ongoing, or is about to occur. As set out in the text, the SEC indicated in its adopting release that the issuer does not have to complete all remedial measures immediately. Some may take time. If so, the reporting attorney seems required to monitor developments to see whether the company is proceeding at a reasonable pace.

[131]   Although the attorney who is retained or directed to investigate the evidence is also governed by the 205 rules, he or she need not make a 205 report if (a) the attorney reports the result of his or her investigation to the CLO and both of them reasonably believe that there is no violation; (b) the attorney reports the results of the investigation to the CLO and the CLO reports to the board or a committee of independent directors or a QLCC; or (c) the attorney is retained or directed to assert a colorable defense in a proceeding and the CLO provides reasonable and timely

If the attorney who reported the evidence of a material violation does not receive one of these "appropriate response[s] within a reasonable time," then that attorney must report the "evidence of a material violation" to the client's audit committee, to another committee consisting of outside directors (if the company does not have an audit committee) or to the board as a whole (if there is no such other committee). 17 C.F.R. § 205.3(b)(3). If the outside attorney does not thereafter receive an "appropriate response," the attorney must explain—to the CLO, CEO, and directors to whom the attorney reported—the reasons that the attorney believes the response is inadequate. 17 C.F.R. § 205.3(b)(9).[132]

---

reports on the progress and outcome of the proceeding to the board, a committee of independent directors, or a QLCC. 17 C.F.R. § 205.3(b)(6). Similarly, an attorney who is retained or directed by a QLCC to investigate or assert a colorable defense does not have a 205 reporting obligation (17 C.F.R. § 205.3(b)(7)), although that attorney would of course report developments to the QLCC.

[132] The new rules contain one other, very controversial, provision that deserves special attention. The rules say that an "attorney appearing and practicing before the Commission in the representation of an issuer may reveal to the Commission, without the issuer's consent, confidential information related to the representation to the extent the attorney reasonably believes necessary: (i) [t]o prevent the issuer from committing a material violation that is likely to cause substantial injury to the financial interest or property of the issuer or investors; . . . or (iii) [t]o rectify the consequences of a material violation by the issuer that caused, or may cause, substantial injury to the financial interest or property of the issuer or investors in the furtherance of which the attorney's services were used." 17 C.F.R. § 205.3(d)(2). These conditions for this permissive disclosure are similar to, but not identical to, the ABA Model Rule 1.6(b)(2) & (3) exceptions to confidentiality. But the ABA rule requires that, even in the case of a current or prospective fraud, the client "has used or is using the lawyer's services" "in furtherance of" the crime or fraud. And the additional disclosure provision in ABA Model Rule 1.13(c) is limited to "clear[ ] . . . violation[s] of law" that are "reasonably certain to result in substantial injury to the [corporation.]"

The SEC's permissive disclosure provision raises the question of whether an attorney practicing before the Commission could reveal client confidences to the SEC for the purposes set out in 205.3(d)(2)(i) or (iii) if the applicable state ethics rule, or a statute, prohibited such disclosure. The SEC rules state that they "supplement applicable standards of any jurisdiction where an attorney is admitted or practices" but that the SEC rules "govern" to the extent that state standards conflict with the Commission rules. 17 C.F.R. § 205.1. The SEC rules also provide that "[a]n attorney who complies in good faith with the [Commission rules] shall not be subject to discipline or otherwise liable under inconsistent standards imposed by any state or other United States jurisdiction where the attorney is admitted or practices." 17 C.F.R. § 205.6(c).

The Washington State Bar Association issued in 2003 an opinion stating that "[t]o the extent [205.3(d)] authorize[s] but do[es] not require revelation of client confidences and secrets under certain circumstances, a Washington lawyer should not reveal such confidences and secrets unless authorized to do so under the [Washington Rule of Professional Conduct 1.6, as it was then written]." *Interim Formal Ethics Opinion: The Effect of the SEC's Sarbanes-Oxley Regulations On Washington Attorneys' Obligations Under the RPCs,* as adopted and approved by the Washington State Bar Association Board of Governors on July 26, 2003, at 1. The opinion relied heavily on the point that 205(d) simply permitted, but did not require, the disclosures that it described. *Id.* at 7. The SEC responded to a proposed version of the Washington State opinion with a letter from its General Counsel arguing that a federal agency can "implement rules of conduct that diverge from and supersede state laws that address the same conduct" and that any state bar disciplinary proceeding against an attorney acting in good faith under 205.3(d)(2) would thwart the Commission rules. Public Statement by SEC Official: Letter Regarding Washington State Bar Association's Proposed Opinion on the Effect of the SEC's Attorney Conduct Rules (July 23, 2003), http://www.sec.gov/news/speech/spch072303gpp.htm. The Washington State July 2003 ethics opinion was titled an "interim" opinion because that state was, at the time its bar issued the opinion, considering changes to its confidentiality rules. Washington adopted those changes in 2006, bringing its state rules closer to the ABA Model Rules 1.6 and 1.13. . . . By adding permissive disclosure of "information relating to the representation . . . to prevent, mitigate, or rectify substantial injury to the financial interests or property of another that is reasonably certain to result or has resulted from the client's commission of a crime or fraud in furtherance of which the client has used the lawyer's services," new Washington Rule 1.6(b)(3) appears to allow Washington lawyers to report to the SEC under at least some circumstances, thereby at least easing the federalism conflict between the Washington State Bar rules and 205.3(d)(2).

The California Bar has also expressed concern over the relationship between the SEC rule's permissive disclosure provision and state law governing lawyer confidentiality. The Corporations Committee of the Business Law Section of The State Bar of California wrote a letter dated August 13, 2003 to the Commission's General Counsel questioning the SEC's authority to issue 205.3(d), saying that any attorney who violated Business and Professions Code 6068(e) would be subject to discipline and that the state bar had no power to refuse to enforce that state statute mandating confidentiality unless an appellate court ruled that the SEC rule preempted the state law. Letter from Keith P. Bishop & Bruce Davis to Giovanni P. Prezioso (Aug. 13, 2003), http://www. dwalliance.com/sbar/SEC.PDF. In 2004, the California State Bar, through the Corporations Committee of the Business Law Section and the Committee on Professional Responsibility and Conduct, issued an Ethics Alert stating that 205.3(d)(2)'s permission to disclose client confidences appears to conflict with the duty of California's client confidentiality law (Bus. & Prof. Code § 6068(e)) and warning that, despite the provision in 205.6(c), good faith disclosure to the SEC under 205.3(d)(2) may not save a California attorney from bar discipline or liability to a client. The Alert said:

> Notwithstanding the "good faith" defense of Rule 205.6(c), if the Part 205 Rules are held *not* to preempt state law, California attorneys disclosing client confidences to the SEC could potentially be subject to State Bar discipline and/or breach of fiduciary duty claims. Even if the SEC's claim of preemption is upheld, an attorney must take into account the risk that a court could conclude he or she did not satisfy the "good faith" defense. Thus, California attorneys cannot presume there is a safe harbor if they disclose client confidences to the SEC.
>
> . . . Given the apparent conflict between the provisions of the Part 205 Rules permitting disclosure of client confidences to the SEC and the fiduciary duty of California attorneys to maintain client secrets and confidences, it may be safer for California attorneys not to accept the SEC's invitation to disclose client confidences to the SEC, at least until such time as the preemption and good faith issues have been decided by a court of competent jurisdiction.

Ethics Alert: The New SEC Attorney Conduct Rules v. California's Duty of Confidentiality, at 4–5, [http://ethics.calbar.ca.gov/Portals/9/documents/Publications/EthicsHotliner/Ethics_Hotliner-SEC_Ethics_Alert-Spring_04.pdf (last visited May 11, 2016)] (emphasis added). The California Corporations Committee has published an article arguing that (i) "a court could reasonably conclude" that the portion of the SEC rules permitting lawyers to break client confidence in order to report to the SEC exceeds the authority granted to the Commission to issue attorney rules and (ii) "a court should conclude that neither Section 307 of the Sarbanes-Oxley Act nor the Part 205 Rules preempt state regulation of the attorney-client relationship and the prohibition of an attorney disclosing confidential information of a client without its consent." Corp. Comm. of the Bus. L. Section of the Cal. St. Bar, *Conflicting Currents: The Obligation to Maintain Inviolate Client Confidences and the New SEC Attorney Conduct Rules*, 32 PEPP. L. REV. 89, 148 (2004). [*See also* N.Y. County Law. Assn. Comm. on Prof'l Ethics Formal Op. 746 (Oct. 7, 2013), https://www. nycla.org/siteFiles/Publications/Publications1647_0.pdf (stating that the SEC's 205 reporting out rule "is broader than, and inconsistent with, the New York RPC exceptions to the confidentiality requirement" (at 7) and concluding that, despite the SEC rule, "New York lawyers, in matters governed by the New York RPC, may not disclose confidential information under the Dodd-Frank whistleblower regulations, except to the extent permissible under the Rules of Professional Conduct." (at 15).)]

Without itself deciding whether the SEC validly promulgated its permissive reporting out provision, the North Carolina State Bar has ruled:

> [U]nless and until the Fourth Circuit Court of Appeals or the US Supreme Court determines that Rule 205 was not validly promulgated, (a) there will be a presumption that Rule 205 was promulgated by the Commission pursuant to a valid exercise of

Of course, all of this could be frustrated if executives at the issuer simply fired an attorney who tried to make a 205 report. To address that possibility, the rules provide that, if the reporting attorney is discharged and reasonably believes that the reason is a report required by the rule, then the attorney "may" notify the client's board, or a committee of the board, of that belief. 17 C.F.R. § 205.3(b)(10).

QUESTIONS ON THE "UP THE LADDER" RULES AND BIG PICTURE QUESTIONS ON YOUR MORAL LIFE AS A CORPORATE ATTORNEY

Were these rules necessary? Did they simply codify what would have been good practice anyway?

Look at the definition of "evidence of a material violation" in 205.2(e). Why did the Commission use the odd formulation "unreasonable . . . not to conclude"?

Why did SOX and the SEC rules say that a "material violation" extends beyond securities laws to breaches of fiduciary duty? *See* 205.2(i). Why did the Commission extend the definition to also include a "similar violation of any United States federal or state law"? *Id.* What does that encompass?

Is the SEC using its coercive power to override state rules of ethics? *See* 205.3(d)(2)(i) and (iii). If so, is that good or bad?

Do you think it unfair, or unreasonable, or damaging to the attorney-client relationship to put the reporting attorney in the position of judging whether the client has made an "appropriate response" to the attorney's report that he or she has become aware of evidence of a material violation? *See* 205.3(b)(1), (3) and (9). But if you feel that way, who else should determine whether the client's response to the attorney's report is "appropriate"?

If the lawyer comes across evidence of a past violation, can the lawyer simply conclude that it is immaterial because all the statutes of limitation have run? Could the lawyer conclude that the company has delivered an

---

authority and (b) a North Carolina attorney may, without violating the North Carolina Rules of Professional Conduct, disclose confidential information as permitted by Rule 205 although such disclosure would not otherwise be permitted by the NC Rule.

Lawyer for Publicly Traded Company May "Report Out" Pursuant to SEC Regulations, 2005 Formal Op. 9, 2006 WL 980308, at *3 (N.C. St. Bar Jan. 20, 2006).

North Carolina's Rule permits an attorney to reveal information from a representation to the extent the lawyer reasonably believes necessary in order to "prevent the commission of a crime by the client" or "to prevent, mitigate, or rectify the consequences of a client's criminal or fraudulent act in the commission of which the lawyer's services were used." N.C. Rule of Prof'l Conduct 1.6(b)(2) & (4). Hence, the absolution in the SEC rule would be necessary—in order to avoid an ethics violation—only when the lawyer discovered a past fraud in which the attorney's services had not been used.

"appropriate response" if the general counsel provides facts showing that the statutes have run? *See* 205.2(b).

What do the SEC rules require in the case where the attorney believes that the client might be about to publish misleading financial numbers? Does the attorney effectively become a consulting accountant? What if the company's inside accountants approve the numbers and the company's outside auditor gives a clean opinion on financial statements including the numbers, but the attorney still believes that the numbers do not adequately reflect economic truth? Do the new rules require the attorney to pit his or her accounting "expertise" against that of accounting professionals?

Making this personal, when you interview with a law firm that represents public companies, will you ask the lawyers there how they are handling 205 reports? Whether they have set up a committee to address 205 issues? Whether they have written guidelines for, and training on, 205? Maybe you want to give them a hypothetical to see how they do on the rules. Is this one good way to investigate a firm's commitment to ethical practice? Or just a good way to ensure that you do not receive an offer?

Much more generally, what do you want out of your practice? Assume that you want to make a good living and participate in significant corporate deals of your time. Still, what role in your professional aspirations do the kinds of things we have covered in this book play? Are you going to be simply a facilitator for your corporate clients? Less pejoratively, do you understand your role to be that of a non-judgmental adviser whose self-image is largely divorced from what your clients do?

Or do you view your role to include keeping your clients on the straight and narrow? And, if so, how will you be able to play that role without becoming a smug naysayer? How will you be able to play that role in Enron and WorldCom situations when you are not an accountant? What does the "straight and narrow" mean anyway? If a client wants to do something that is legal and will help its shareholders, are you really the one to say "stop" because you think the client has not reached its decision through good governance or even because you think that some additional disclosure about the decision would be fair to investors, though not required by law? Should you say "stop" just because it makes you feel better about yourself? [I do not mean this last question to rhetorically guide you to an answer. The question is a serious one.]

Will your moral satisfaction depend upon the firm with which you practice and the small group of attorneys in that firm with whom you work each day? Before you join up, how can you investigate the firm's commitment to a moral practice? How can you investigate the commitment of the group within the firm to which you will be assigned? If you discover after several months of work that you are not morally compatible with your colleagues, will you have the courage to move to a different firm or to a different group within the same firm?

––––––––––

INDEX

References are to Pages